World Wide Web

J O U R N A L

Fourth International World Wide Web Conference

The Web Revolution

December 11-14, 1995
Boston, Massachusetts, USA

Conference Proceedings

http://www.w3.org/WWW4/

O'Reilly & Associates, Inc.

WORLD WIDE WEB JOURNAL

ISSUE ONE: CONFERENCE PROCEEDINGS, FOURTH INTERNATIONAL WORLD WIDE WEB CONFERENCE

Printing History:

November 1995: First Edition

ISSN: 1085-2301

ISBN: 1-56592-169-0

WELCOME

On behalf of the Conference Organizing Committee, the Massachusetts Institute of Technology's Laboratory for Computer Science, its World Wide Web Consortium team, and the Open Software Foundation Research Institute, we are pleased to welcome you to the Fourth International World Wide Web Conference: "The Web Revolution." In this fifth year of the Web's existence, we are on the threshold of a veritable revolution in the manner in which we conduct our affairs. This revolution is truly worldwide. The efforts of individuals on six continents have produced thousands of Web servers spanning the globe, and yet to the user it appears that the information on them can be accessed effortlessly. One need only "point and click" the mouse to obtain information from almost any part of the globe. This globalization and simplicity of access have been achieved by the efforts of thousands of individuals around the world. We publicly acknowledge the contributions of those individuals by dedicating this conference to them, for they are the true creators of the "Web Revolution."

As always, the success of a conference is dependent both on the dedication of the chairs of the various aspects of the conference and of their volunteers. Therefore, we give special thanks to the Program Committee who refereed almost 200 papers. Our immense gratitude also goes to Tim Berners-Lee, Chair of the Program Committee, for organizing the refereeing process used for paper selection. We would also like to thank those who organized other aspects of the conference, in particular the Chairs of: Tutorials and Workshops, Stavros Macrakis and Barbara Kucera; Developers' Day, Jim Gettys; Posters, David Kranz; Panels, Dale Dougherty; and Birds-of-a-Feather, Roy Fielding. Furthermore, we acknowledge the efforts of a multitude of volunteers, most of whom are identified on the credits page. We also thank those individuals who worked to make this conference a success but volunteered their efforts too late to be included on that page.

Spanning four days, the conference offers a host of Web-related tutorials, workshops, paper sessions, speeches and exhibits. We thank these contributors for their endeavors and the wealth of information they will provide. We extend a special thanks to the authors who submitted papers to our experimental refereeing process for their prompt response to the call for papers and for the timeliness with which they responded to the referees' comments, allowing us to meet the publication deadlines.

Of course, no conference would be successful without the attendees. At the most recent count, six weeks before the conference begins, there are over 1200 registrants from 37 countries. We anticipate that between 1500 and 2000 individuals will attend the conference. We sincerely hope that at the close of the "Web Revolution" our efforts will have met or exceeded your expectations for the conference.

Last, it is a testament to the efforts of the International World Wide Web Conference Committee (IW3C2) that each of the previous three conferences left a very favorable impression on its attendees, gaining in both stature and popularity with each succeeding year. We, along with the IW3C2, aspire to continue that tradition. Thus, our collective aspiration is to maintain the conference's quality, increase its scope and hold it at a venue that will allow a modest increase in the number of attendees. With the assent of the IW3C2, we have received the torch from Detlef Krömker and his team in Darmstadt, who hosted an exemplary conference last April; we benefitted from their guidance and insight. At this conference's conclusion we will pass the same torch on to Jean-François Abramatic and INRIA, who will host the next conference in Paris in the spring of 1996.

—Albert Vezza & Dr. Ira Goldstein
Co-chairs

CREDITS

CONFERENCE ORGANIZING COMMITTEE

Conference Co-chairs

Albert Vezza, MIT-Laboratory for Computer Science
Ira Goldstein, OSF-Research Institute

Program Committee

Tim Berners-Lee, Chair, MIT-Laboratory for Computer Science

Jean-François Abramatic, INRIA
Robert Cailliau, CERN
Dave Clark, MIT-LCS
Dan Connolly, MIT-LCS
Jim Gettys, DEC
Thomas Greene, MIT-LCS
Joseph Hardin, NCSA
Russell Jones, DEC
Dan Kalikow, DEC
Tim Krauskopf, Spyglass Inc.
Barbara Kucera, NCSA
Stavros Macrakis, OSF-RI
Larry Masinter, XEROX
Jim Miller, MIT-LCS
Corinne Moore, CommerceNet
Dave Raggett, HP
R.P.C. Rodgers, NLM
Michael Schwartz, University of Colorado, Boulder
Karen Sollins, MIT-LCS
Win Treese, Openmarket
Albert Vezza, MIT-LCS
Stuart Weibel, OCLC
Mary Ellen Zurko, OSF-RI

Awards Co-chairs

Robert Cailliau, Yuri Rubinsky

Panels Chair

Dale Dougherty

Birds-of-a-Feather Chair

Roy Fielding

Developers Day Chair

Jim Gettys

Posters Chair

David Kranz

IW3C2 Conference Coordinator

Barbara Kucera

Tutorial/Workshop Co-chairs

Stavros Macrakis, Barbara Kucera

Cover art by Michael Vezza

Michael Vezza currently teaches at Montserrat College of Art in Beverly, Massachusetts, and exhibits at "Gallery on 2nd" in New York City. He has a BA from Kenyon College and an MFA from The New York Academy of Art.

Local Arrangement Chair

Thomas Greene

Managers

Venue Liaison: Beth Curran
Registration Database: Jacqueline Dulmaine
Network: Kevin Garceau
Volunteers: Sylvia Fry and Susan Hardy
Webmaster: Karen MacArthur
Paper Submission Database: Jason Matthews
Conference Graphics Designer: Anne McCarthy
Registration: Julianne Orsino
M-Bone: George Rabatin and Jaromir Likavec
Conference Server: Jay Sekora
Television: Prof. Carol O'Neill and Paul Beck
Emerson College TV Crew: Patricia Aaron, Paul Beck, Julie Caldwell, Sean Callahan, Sharra Calloway-Owens, Catherine Cappas, Niki Caputo, Joseph Dhosi, Colin Eby, Julie Esguerra, Nancy Esslinger, Ines Hofmann, Nadine Iskandar, Jacqueline Jones, Ilyas Kirmani, Jonathan Landay, Elizabeth Lautieri, Patrick McGonigle, Caroline Mudge, Christopher Nye, Robert Pearson

INTERNATIONAL WWW CONFERENCE COMMITTEE

Detlef Krömker, Chair, Fraunhofer Institute for Computer Graphics (Germany)

Jean-François Abramatic, INRIA (France)
Tim Berners-Lee, MIT-LCS
Robert Cailliau, CERN (Switzerland)
Dale Dougherty, Songline Studios
Ira Goldstein, OSF-RI
Joseph Hardin, National Center for Supercomputing Applications (NCSA)
Tim Krauskopf, Spyglass, Inc.
Barbara Kucera, NCSA
Corinne Moore, CommerceNet
R. P. C. Rodgers, U.S. National Library of Medicine
Yuri Rubinsky, SoftQuad Inc. (Canada)
Tony Rutkowski, Internet Society
Philip Tsang, Charles Sturt Univ. (Australia)
Albert Vezza, MIT-LCS
Stuart Weibel, OCLC Office of Research

OTHER CONTRIBUTORS

MIT Audio Visual: David Broderick and David Scannell
Program Design: Marcia Ciro, Paper Trace Studio
Cover Design: Hanna Dyer, O'Reilly & Associates
Production: Jane Ellin, O'Reilly & Associates
Exhibition: Barbara Gavin, DCI
Production: Nicole Gipson, O'Reilly & Associates
Network: Joan McCardle, EMI
Text Design: Nancy Priest, O'Reilly & Associates
Prodution Tools: Mike Sierra, O'Reilly & Associates
Project Management: Donna Woonteiler, O'Reilly & Associates

E D I T O R I A L

Welcome to the World Wide Web Journal.

The World Wide Web Consortium (W3C) is forging a global partnership between a newly emerging Internet industry and a vitally important network of academic researchers. We recognize that we need to work together to help the Web realize its full potential for the widest possible audience around the world.

Working together well demands high levels of communication, allowing researchers aware of tomorrow's problems to collaborate with companies anxious to make today's powerful products. Fortunately, we have the Web itself to help us communicate and work with colleagues in all time zones.

Yet all forms of communication are important, not just what can be accomplished using the Web, if we are to achieve our goals. The International World Wide Web Conference gives researchers and commercial developers a chance to meet in-person and discuss important ideas. Attendees will come away with a greater understanding of how varied the Web is, and how much we value what we have in common on the Web. This is one reason why the W3C wanted to host this and the next International World Wide Web Conference. It is also the reason why the W3C is initiating a new journal, to be published by O'Reilly & Associates.

The proceedings of the Fourth International World Wide Web Conference form the first issue of the *World Wide Web Journal* (W3J). The proceedings were a special and easy way to fill—indeed overfill—the first issue with good content, including 57 refereed technical papers (indicated by the "W3J" logo), as well as the two best papers from regional conferences. Like these proceedings, the Journal will appear in print, providing yet another context to communicate about important developments on the Web.

There are two major forms of development on the Web: those that investigate new ideas given the existing clients and protocols, and those that introduce a new protocol feature. Because the interoperability of the Web depends on common protocol standards, and because new features are defined and constrained by those protocols, the W3C's interest tends to be in those developments that influence protocol design. However, most of these changes start as needs felt by users, and they first show up as limit-pushing applications of the existing protocols. The Journal, then, must report both needs and experience, and document proposed changes to protocols.

The Journal will also provide a forum for the consortium team to offer its editorial comment on issues that impact the quality or integrity of the Web. For instance, architectural principles on which certain features of the Web hang can be needlessly undermined in pursuit of new features.

The World Wide Web Journal will have an independent Editorial Advisory Board that will help set the editorial direction of the Journal. The Board will ensure that paper selection is fair, based on an evaluation of academic quality, engineering soundness, and relevance to the needs of the present or future.

The Journal will also be published on the Web, and provide the basis for hypertext discussion and annotation. It will be archived so that future research can build upon it. This is in keeping with the goal that the Web should encompass all levels of activity, from the casual to the formal.

From time to time I receive email messages of thanks "for the Web," and I take the launching of the Journal as an opportunity to pass these thanks on to all you webmasters, researchers, product developers, writers, designers, surfers, script-writers, and philosophers who have joined together and are making it all happen. Let the Journal, like the rest of the Web, be a place where we can meet, and share our hopes and dreams.

—Tim Berners-Lee
Cambridge, Massachusetts, October 1995

C O N T E N T S

MEDIA

MOBILE CODE

SECURITY

CLIENT-SIDE TECHNIQUES

BEST PAPERS FROM REGIONAL CONFERENCES

RESULTS FROM THE THIRD WWW USER SURVEY

James E. Pitkow, Colleen M. Kehoe

Abstract

*The tremendous success of the World Wide Web has led to an ever-increasing user base. Intuitively, one would expect this base to change over time as more people from different segments of the population become Web users and advocates. What exactly have these changes been? How do the original Web users differ from the new users from major online service providers like Prodigy? What trends exist and what picture do they paint for the future of the Web user population? This paper, drawing on results from three User Surveys spanning over a year and a half, attempts to answer these and other questions about who is using the Web and why. Additionally, a review of the methodology, questionnaires, and new architectural enhancements is presented. Although the surveys lack the scientific rigor of controlled and accepted methods of surveying, we discuss analyses that help us understand the limitations and process of this new type of surveying. Finally, new quantitative analysis techniques are presented based upon post-hoc log file analysis, yielding guidelines for Web-based survey design. **Keywords:** World Wide Web, surveys, demographics, log file analysis, design guidelines.*

Introduction

Even with its limited but expanding degree of interactivity, the Web poses unique opportunities for distributed surveying across loosely-coupled heterogenous environments like the Internet. Yet, these same opportunities to pioneer a new terrain require conservative interpretation of collected data due to the absence of time-tested validation and correction metrics which exist for other surveying techniques.

Part of the initial impetus behind the surveys was to experiment with the Web to determine its viability as a powerful surveying medium. This hypothesis was based upon the easy-to-use, point-and-click interface Web browsers provide. Supporting evidence that the Web is indeed an effective medium is twofold. First, the response rates for the surveys (1,300 respondents for the First Survey, 3,500 for the Second, and 13,000 for the Third) are orders of magnitude above those

reported for Usenet news-based surveys and non-specialized emailings. Second, a Usenet news pilot study conducted during the fall of 1994 found a two to one preference for responding to survey announcements via the Web versus email [1]. The User Surveys continue to provide fertile testing ground for this hypothesis.

Yet, the advantages of Web-based surveying are not limited to response rates. Foremost, the use of adaptive surveying decreases the number and complexity of questions asked of each user, as only pertinent questions and choices are presented. Because each questionnaire dynamically *adapts* based on the user's input, the database of potential questions can be large while the number of questions given to a particular user remains relatively small. Additionally, the submission, storage, collation, and analysis processes all occur in an electronic medium, limiting human effort to developing processing programs and ensuring the integrity of the collected data.[*] This removes any

---

[*] Theoretically, since users are presented with a fixed set of choices, the data received by the server ought to be free of errors. In practice however, we typically observe that several browsers mangle the returned values due to internal programming errors. For this reason, we highly encourage activities that establish test suites for WWW browsers to identify and correct FORM submission-based problems before the browsers are publicly released.

errors that typically occur in surveying techniques that rely upon human encoding of the collected data. Despite these advantages, we observe that the Web's degree of interaction does not produce the ideal surveying environment—one where adaptation occurs instantly on the client.

GVU's First WWW User Survey was conducted during January 1994 and was the first publicly accessible Web-based survey. The initial idea behind the survey was to begin to characterize WWW users as well as demonstrate the Web as a powerful surveying tool. The survey was perceived successful as over 1,500 users world wide participated. The response rate was limited, however, due to the lack of non-UNIX clients that correctly processed FORMs.

The Second Survey was advertised and made available to the Web user population for 38 days during October and November 1994. During this period, over 18,000 total responses to the questionnaires from over 4,000 users were received. This survey provided the first cross-platform analysis of Web users as FORMs capable browsers were readily available. New to the surveys was the addition of adaptive questioning to the survey software and the incorporation of the Consumer Sections as pre-tests developed by the University of Michigan's Hermes Project.

Walk-Through of the Survey Interaction

In order to convey the sense of interaction present while completing the surveys, a quick walk-through follows (see [3] for more details on survey execution and architecture). Essentially, the respondents are led through a series of *"question-answer-adapt/re-ask"* cycles. Upon selection of a questionnaire from the Main Launching Page that provides access to all the questionnaires, the surveying software generates the default set of questions from the question database. No adaptation occurs during this stage. The user then responds to the questions displayed by their WWW browser by selecting options pre-

sented via radio buttons, pulldown menus, scrolling lists, and check boxes. The surveys intentionally avoid the use of open-ended text entry, as this increases the complexity of response processing.

Once the user completes the set of questions, they click on the "Submit Responses" button of the page. This returns the responses to the survey server. Upon receipt, the survey software inspects each response which results in the one of the following three scenarios:

- The response triggers an adaptive question based upon the value of the returned response. The corresponding follow-up question is extracted from the database and added to the list of questions returned to the user for the next iteration.

- The software determines that a question has been asked but not yet answered. In this case, the question is added to the list of questions returned for completion.

- The response is an acceptable reply to a non-adaptive question. The response is noted and no follow-up action occurs.

After all the responses have been inspected, the list of adapted and unanswered questions is returned to user, and another iteration occurs. This cycle continues until all questions have been asked and have been responded to completely. When this happens, the software records that the user has completed the questionnaire and writes the results to disk. The user is returned to the Main Launching Page that lists all the questionnaires that have yet to be completed.

Since the software keeps track of who has filled out which questionnaires, multiple submissions are easily detected. When this occurs, the user is presented with the option to overwrite their previous responses or to preserve them. No method currently exists for a user to inspect the submitted responses above those facilities offered by the browser, e.g. use of the "Back" button.

The integration of adaptive questions into the surveys serves several purposes. Most importantly, it reduces the number and complexity of questions presented to each user. For example, an interesting marketing question is "Where are you located?" Clearly, the space required to list all countries would easily fill several screens; this is undesirable and inefficient. However, staging the question in two parts, one that asks for the primary geographical region of the user and the other that provides a list of countries in that region, reduces the amount of space required to pose the question as well as the cognitive load necessary for the user to correctly answer the question. This method also enables the acquisition of detailed responses, which facilitates a more in-depth understanding of the user population.

Architectural Enhancements

The Third Survey included a trial implementation of *longitudinal tracking* for survey participants. Longitudinal tracking is a method for studying a specific group of users over several surveys. This allows us to investigate how these users' answers change over time and to ask more questions than a one-time survey allows. Since the questionnaires are designed for new as well as returning survey participants, many questions are duplicated from previous surveys. However, when a former survey participant returns to take the current survey, duplicated questions are already filled in with their previous answers. These answers can then be reviewed and changed if necessary. We expect that this implementation of longitudinal tracking will encourage users to participate in more than one survey and will enable us to collect an enriched set of data.

Before answering any of the questionnaires, each user is asked to enter an ID to be used for tracking. Users are cautioned against using an existing password as their ID to avoid potential security hazards. Users are then assigned an internal, unique identifier which is a combination of their ID and a part of their IP address, supplied by

their browser. (In the released datasets, these identifiers are replaced by generic identifiers of the form "idxx" to preserve the participants' anonymity.) Finally, users are asked to "Hotlist" the page whose URL contains their identifier and to use this entry whenever accessing the surveys.

When a user returns to take the next survey, the survey software tries to determine the user's unique identifier. During this process, the option to "Choose a New ID" is always present, so that users can choose not to participate in longitudinal tracking if they prefer. If the user returns through their Hotlist entry, their identifier can be immediately extracted from the URL. If not, the user can enter their ID by hand. If the user cannot remember their ID (or has changed to an IP addresses outside their previous domain and class), they can enter the machine name from which they answered the last survey. They are then presented with a list of valid IDs for that machine from which to choose. If the user still cannot find their old ID, they are asked to simply enter a new ID.

Once a user's identifier has been found, to confirm their identity, they are asked for their age and geographic location during the last survey. Note that this is not an attempt at true, reliable authentication; it is designed to minimize errors in identification and to discourage blatant misidentification attempts. If the user's answers match those given for the last survey, the user is marked in the survey database as "verified" for the remainder of the current survey. If the answers do not match, the user may enter a different ID and try again, or simply choose a new ID and continue with the survey.

This implementation of longitudinal tracking will be fully deployed in the Fourth Survey.

Survey Questions

As with the Second Survey, the questionnaires were separated into four main categories: General Demographics, Web and Internet Usage, Authoring & Information Providers, and the Consumer Section. Since very little is known about the new and expanding market segment of Web Service Providers (companies that offer Web-based services like page design, server space, etc.), we included a pre-test questionnaire for this category. The use of high level categories enabled users to quickly finish sections and select only those areas that are applicable. We note that one long survey containing all questions may discourage potential respondents.

The number of questions in the General Demographics category was doubled since the last survey to 21. Presuming that most people would fill in this portion of the survey, but maybe not others, we included some of the top-level questions from other categories. Thus, users were asked the usual demographic questions regarding age, gender, geographical location, occupation, income, race, level of education, marital status, impairments, etc., as well as questions regarding frequency of Web browser use, primary computing platform, the nature of their primary Internet access provider, etc. For sensitive questions, we provided a "Rather Not Say!" option. Standard to all questionnaires was the inclusion of a text-entry comment box at bottom of the page soliciting users' free-form input.

Of interest is not only who is using the Web, but how they are using it. The second category addressed this topic by posing 28 questions directed toward user's behavior and motivations. Respondents were queried about their frequency and periodicity of Web use, preferences for different types of Web sites and pages, regularity of accesses to different information sources, etc. Questions directed toward users' primary reasons for using the Web were also asked.

Another area of interest surrounds the creation and publishing of HTML documents and their maintenance. The Authoring and Providers section (13 questions) initially identified users who have published information and those that also have maintained HTTPd servers. For authors, questions that determine the learnability of HTML, the sources consulted during learning, as well as understanding some of the advanced features like CGI were posed. Additional questions were asked regarding the number of documents they have authored and converted and the types of pages they create. For Webmasters, information is gathered about which server they operate, which port it listens to, whether proxy and mirroring services are provided, and policies for advertising.

In cooperation with the Hermes Project at the University of Michigan, (and in line with our open policy of incorporating other research agendas into the surveys), the Consumer Section that was pre-tested during the Second Survey was fully deployed. These questions were directed towards understanding consumer purchasing behaviors, attitudes towards online commerce and security as well as plans for future purchases. The questions were specifically designed to allow for comparisons of Web commerce to more traditional practices, such as catalogue shopping and ordering via telephone.

Limitations of the Results and Methodology

Highly distributed, heterogeneous, electronic surveying is a new field, especially with respect to the Web. Our adaptive WWW-based surveying techniques are pioneering and as such, require conservative interpretation of collected data due to the absence of tested validation metrics. These metrics depend upon data collected via accepted methods. To date, we know of no such study that has been published nor of any datasets made available to perform these analyses, though several such studies are underway.

Basically, the survey suffers two problems: self-selection and sampling. When people decide to participate in a survey, they select themselves. This decision may reflect some systematic selecting principle (or judgment) that affects the collected data. Just about all surveys suffer from self-selection problems. For example, when a potential respondent hangs up on a telephone-based surveyor, self-selection has occurred. Likewise, when a potential respondent does not send back a direct mail survey, self-selection has occurred.

The other issue is sampling. There are essentially two types of sampling: random and non-probabilistic. Random selection is intended to minimize bias and make the sample as typical of the population as possible. To accomplish this, steps need to be taken to get respondents in a random manner, e.g., drawing numbers out of a hat. Our survey uses a form of non-probabilistic sampling which relies on users who see announcements of the survey to participate. Since respondents are gathered in this manner, segments of the entire Web users population may not be aware of the surveys and therefore may not participate. As a result, all segments of the user population may not be represented in our sample. This reduces the ability of the gathered data to generalize to the entire user population.

Since the Web does not have a broadcast mechanism (yet), we used the following diverse mediums to attract respondents:

- A special link on the Prodigy Web access page

- Links on high exposure WWW pages, e.g., links for the duration of the survey on NCSA's "What's New," Hotwired, Lycos, etc.

- Announcements on WWW and Internet related Usenet newsgroups, e.g., *comp.infosystems.www.**, *comp.internet.net-happenings*, etc.—two postings at equal intervals

- Unsolicited write-ups in numerous computer and Internet related trade magazines, and daily newspapers

- *www-surveying* mailing list announcement

One could argue that this diversified exposure minimizes any systematic effect introduced via the sampling method. We tend to agree, but have taken steps to further explore this issue.

Specifically, we designed the Third Survey to enable us to determine how the respondents found out about the survey. This allows us to group respondents accordingly and look for significant differences between these user populations. For all users, 50% found out about the survey via other WWW pages, with 20.3% finding out via "Other" sources, and 17.9% finding out via Usenet newsgroup announcements. WWW-based listserver/mailing lists, e.g., *www-announce*, etc. accounted for only 6% of all respondents finding out about the survey and thus are not tremendously lucrative means of attracting attention.

"Remembered from last survey" was the least effective method cited (0.4%). This indicates that reliance on former survey participant's memories is not a very robust means of accomplishing longitudinal user tracking. While very few users found out about the Third Surveys via the *www-surveying* mailing announcement (1.1%) compared to other methods, we note that the 142 users who did respond accounted for one fourth of the survey mailing list at the time. Thus, specialized mailing lists seem to be a fairly effective way to announce the beginning of a survey.

In order to determine if the way people found out about the survey systematically biases the sample, we stratified users into groups based upon how they enter the survey. Statistical analysis was performed to determine if these subsamples differed. There were no significant differences between the ways women and men found out about the surveys for the following categories: remembering to take the survey, other Web pages, the newspaper, other sources, and listserver announcements. There were differences found for finding out via friends, magazines, Usenet newsgroups, and the www-surveying mailing list. Given the low effectiveness of all but other Web pages and Usenet news announcements, we conclude that these differences lead to nominal effects.

Thus, the surveys do not appear to suffer critically from sampling biases with respect to gender.[*] If a segment of the Web user population were excluded, statistically we'd expect to find similar response distribution for women and men. Still, the data we're about to present is only a snapshot of users who chose to respond—we do not make the claim that the data is representative of the entire Web population.

Execution Environment

The survey ran from April 10*th* through May 10*th*, 1995. The server used for the survey operates NCSA's HTTP version 1.3 and ran on a dedicated Sun OS 4.1.3 Sparc 2 installed with a four 75 MHz co-processor HyperSparc. The machine had three gigabytes of disk and 128 megabytes of RAM. The server resided on the College of Computing's internal CDDI ring via a CDDI jumper. This internal ring connects to Georgia Tech's internal and subsequently external FDDI rings, which has a T3 connection to SuraNET. The Survey Modules are written in Perl 4.36 and were not compiled. No notable disruptions or denial of service occurred during the sampling period.

Results

Overall, there were a total of 26,468 responses to all questionnaires combined (38,602 including the Consumer Sections). These responses were submitted from 13,982 unique users.[†] This represents the largest response rate to any Web-based survey known to date. It also represents the most comprehensive online survey of Web users, asking over 138 questions across all questionnaires. Below we present some of the more interesting findings and trends, since presentation of all the results is not possible. Interested readers should consult the online version at the site <URL:*http://www.cc.gatech.edu/gvu/user_surveys*> in order to access all results, including over 200 graphs and

detailed interpretations for each question. For the Consumer Surveys, please see the pages maintained by the Hermes Team at <URL:.*http://www.umich.edu/~sgupta/hermes/survey3*>.

Statistical Inferences

All analyses were performed using Splus version 3.1 for UNIX. Tests for significant interactions amongst variables were performed using the classical chi-squared for independence of categorical data, with significance being determined at $p <= 0.01$ level. Tests for differences between stratified samples were performed using a two-sided alternative for the Wilcox rank sum statistic. Since all tests included N > 49, the normal approximation was used, which was replaced by the Lehmann approximation in the event of ties. Significance was determined at the $p <= 0.01$ and confirmed by checking that Z was either < -2.58 or > 2.85.

General Demographics

Analysis of the data for the Third Survey resulted in many interesting findings. Overall, we observed substantial shifts between the demographics of the users who filled out the first two surveys and the third. The users in the Third Survey represent less and less the "technology developers/pioneers" of the First Survey (primarily young, computer-savvy users) and more of what we refer to as the "early adopters/seekers of new technology." These adopters are not typically provided access to the Web through work or school, and as a result, actively seek out local or major Internet access providers, like Prodigy.

Why All This Mentioning of Prodigy?

Due to an arrangement with Prodigy (the first major online service to enable Web access), a

---

[*] Despite this, we remain unconvinced that the survey's sampling methodology is optimal and welcome suggestions and comments on this subject.
[†] All collected datasets are publicly available online via URL *http://www.cc-gatech.edu/gvy/user_surveys/* and URL *ftp://ftp.cc.gatech.edu/gvu/www/survey/survey-04-1995/datasets.*

link to the surveys was placed on Prodigy's Web entry page for ten days during the surveying period. This provided us with the ability to compare Prodigy's users to users in general—the first comparison of these two populations that we know of. Additionally, we stratified the respondents by location (Europe and US) and gender (Women and Men) and performed statistical tests on all questions for differences between groups. All analyses showed differences between groups except where noted, which is not surprising given the large number of data points.

What Is the Average Age?

One category that has changed considerably over time is age. The mean age for the Third Survey is 35.0 (median 35.0), up almost four years from the Second Survey. Also, only 30.4% were between the ages of 21 and 30, compared to 56% of the respondents for the First Survey. We observe no statistically significant differences across gender for age (average age for women is 35.2 years old vs. 35.2 for men).

What Is the Gender Ratio and How Has It Changed Over Time?

As for gender, 15.5% of the users are female, 82.0% male and 2.5% chose to "Rather not say!" Compared to the Second Survey, women represent a 6% increase and men an 8% decrease. Compared to the First Survey in January of 1994, this represents a 10% increase for women and a 12% decrease for men. This trend is quite linear ($R2 = 0.98$) and suggests an even male/female ratio could be achieved during the first quarter of 1997. In summary, there exists a trend for the Web towards older users and towards more balanced gender ratios. This progression is clearly away from the young technically savvy male population of a year and half ago.

Also, we observe higher female ratios in the US, with 17.1% of the users being female, 80.3% male and 2.6% chose to "Rather not say!" For Prodigy, the ratios were even more in favor of women, with 19.1% female and 78.8% male. This 1 to 4

female to male ratio more accurately reflects the proportions outside the Web and suggests that as more major online services join the Web and Internet, more balanced female/male ratios are likely to occur. The US and Prodigy ratios also indicate that the US is integrating women more quickly into the user population than other parts of the world.

What Is the Average and Median Income?

The overall median income is between US$50,000 and US$60,000, with an estimated average household income of US$69,000. European respondents continue to lag in income, with an average income of US$53,500. Prodigy users' income is the highest of all sampled groups, with a median income in the range of US$60,000 and US$75,000 and an estimated average income of US$80,000.

What About Location,Marital Status, Race, and Occupation?

For classification by major geographical location, 80.6% of the respondents are from the US, 9.8% from Europe, and 5.8% from Canada and Mexico, with all other major geographical locations represented to a lesser degree. Steps toward replicating the survey on other continents and providing some multilingual support might alter these differences. Overall, 50.3% of the users are married, and 40.0% are single. The percentage of users who report being divorced is 5.7%. Occupationwise, computer-related fields (31.4%) and education-related fields (including students) (23.7%) still represent the majority of respondents, though their dominance over other occupations has been declining. Professional (21.9%), management (12.2%), and "other" occupations (10.8%) fill out the other categories. 82.3% of the respondents are white, with none of the other groups reporting over 5% of the responses. To characterize the sampled population, we find that the respondents are typically white, married, and

North American, with computer or educational occupations.

How Willing Are Users to Pay for Access to Web Sites?

Overall, 22.6% of the respondents stated outright that they would not pay fees to access material from WWW sites. This is the same ratio observed in the Second and First Surveys. Additionally, there were no statistically significant differences found between the Prodigy and non-Prodigy response distributions for this question (despite the fact Prodigy users already pay in a direct sense for accessing Web sites). This implies that as the Web continues to increase its user base, we expect to find a 20% negative response to paying for access to Web sites.

What Is the Primary Computing Platform?

The distribution of primary computing platforms across all sampled populations more closely resembles computer marketing reports than previous surveys: 52.0% Windows, 26.2% Macintosh, and 8.8% Unix. These platforms account for 87% of all platforms reported.

WWW Usage and Preferences

While our survey does not answer the question, "How many Web users are there?" it does provide insight into potentially more interesting areas such as why people use Web and in what manner. Thus, regardless of overall size, we can gain an understanding of users behind the explosive revolution of the Web.

How Often Do People Use their Web Browser?

In general, people spend a considerable amount of time on the Web, with 41% of the users reporting that they use their browser between 6 and 10 hours/week and 21% between 11 and 20 hours/ week, an increase of 5% and 6%, respectively, since last October. Over 72% responded that they

use their Web browser at least once a day. These findings are very encouraging for services like electronic news that attempt to provide daily content—the audience is tuned-in and present.

Why Do People Use Their Web Browser?

The most common use of browsers is simply for browsing (82.6%) followed by entertainment (56. 6%) and work (50.9%). The category with the least number of responses is shopping (10.5%) (respondents were allowed to choose more than one answer). More users from Europe primarily use their browsers for academic research than do users in the US (45.1% vs. 32.6%). Thus while "surfing" still constitutes the primary reason for using the Web, more serious endeavors like work and research are emerging. These findings support the claim that the Web is not just for fun and games.

What Do People Do with Their Web Browser and with What Regularity?

The following questions are scored on a 1 (never) to 9 (regularly) scale. The most popular activity for using Web browsers is to replace other interfaces for accessing information (6.7) such as those for FTP, and Gopher. Other categories include accessing reference information (6. 2), electronic news (5.7) and product information (5.1). Thus, we find support for the notion that Web browsers are becoming the default interface to the Internet. The least-frequently cited activity for using Web browser is shopping (2.9), which may very well be due to the lack of merchandise on the Web and ubiquitous, secure payment schemes. Interestingly, the response distributions are quite similar to those from the Second Survey, indicating a stable characteristic.

How Likely Are People to Archive Web Documents?

In general, users print and save documents with approximately the same regularity (3.9 for print and 4.5 for save). These numbers are right around the "Sometimes" option (4.5), which indicates that not many documents are pulled off the Web. Interestingly, this finding is supported by the research done by Catledge and Pitkow on Web browsing strategies, which also observed low archiving rates based upon monitoring actual user's browsing behavior [2].

How Fast Are People's Connections to the Internet?

The most common connection speed is 14 Kb/sec (43.8%) followed by 10 Mb/sec (13.1%). This uneven distribution is a result of the Prodigy users, 73.2% of whom have 14.4 connections, and those users who have high speed connections provided via work or school.

Authoring and Providers

How Easy Was It for People to Learn HTML?

Good news—HTML, the markup language used for writing Web documents, is easy to learn. Most users (82.0%) spent between 1 and 6 hours learning HTML. Many users learned HTML in only 1 to 3 hours (55.2%). CGI was rated the most difficult (5.0) to learn followed by FORMs (4.0), ISMAP (3.9), and HTML overall (2.5). Interestingly, none of these averages are near the maximum difficulty rating of 9.0. Nearly 25% of the users sampled have authored HTML.

How Do Users Learn About HTML?

Online documentation was consulted by 88.4% of users in learning HTML. The next two most popular sources, books and friends, were consulted by only 29.2% and 25.2% of users, respectively (respondents were allowed to choose more than one answer). Hence, use of the Web as a learning medium or to disseminate reference materials corresponds to the behavior of many Web users and is thus recommended for such purposes.

How Much Does Advertising on the Web Typically Cost?

When queried about charging for advertising on their site, the vast majority of Webmasters replied that the question was "Not Applicable" (70.6%) or that they "Don't Allow Ads" (24.0%) for a total of 94.6%. For those that do allow ads, the largest percentage (3.3%) charge under $50 per week. Only 0.4% charge over $501 per week. Thus, the Web provides an inexpensive advertising medium for most sites.

What About HTTPd Servers?

As far as HTTPd servers, the most popular server is NCSA's (38.6%) followed by MacHTTP (20.8%) and CERN's (18.5%). In Europe, however, the most popular server is CERN's (34.9%). Only a small percentage of sites operate a proxy server (12.6%) and most HTTP servers do not mirror other sites (91.5%). The most common server connection speed is 10 Mb/sec (32.3%). The next most common are 1 Mb/sec with 18.0% and 56 Kb/sec with 14.1%, indicating ample throughput to the Internet for over half of the HTTPd servers. This suggests that the lag often experienced by users is primarily a result of their connection speed or the load experienced by the server. Roughly 11% of the users population sampled is composed of Webmasters.

Web Service Providers

What Types of Services Are Being Offered?

Over half of all Web Service Provider companies sampled (633 total) provide page design (79.0%). Other services are also offered, in the following proportions: Internet/Web consulting (72.8%), other types of services (67.8%), disk space (59.4%), Internet/Web marketing advice (56.2%), CGI scripting (54.7%), and traffic analysis of page accesses (52.1%). Additionally, the providers were equally likely to provide Domain Name Service (DNS) Registration (46.1%) as to not provide DNS services (46.9%).

How Many Customers and Employees do They Have?

Nearly half the providers report having between 1 and 10 customers (42.6%), with 9.3% reporting having no customers and 23.2% reporting having over 100 customers. US providers are more likely to have a larger customer base (23.7% US vs. 15.8% European with over 100 customers). The majority of providers have under 10 employees (67.3%), with 16.9% having between 11 and 50, 3.3% having between 51 and 100, and 12.5% having over 100 employees.

How Long Have They Been in Business?

Over half of the providers have been in business over 10 months (53.7%). Between January and March 1995, 17.5% of the providers surveyed went online. The startup rate for Web Service Provider companies is fairly consistent (around 10% per month). Thus, most of the Web Services Providers sampled appear to be smaller, recently established companies, with moderate client-bases.

Population Analysis

The response rate to the three surveys has risen dramatically from 1,300 to 3,500 to 13,000 users. The growth is linear under log transform, with the regression equation ($R2 = 0.987$) being:

f(response rate) = $5.96 + e1.51X$

Given this limited model, it becomes possible to predict the response rate for future surveys. The log transform model predicts 38,000 users for the Fourth Survey. This estimate represents an upper bound, with the lower and middle bounds predicted as 18,000 users based upon a linear model and 30,000 users based upon a 2*nd* degree polynomial curve fitting the equation:

f(response rate) = $3650 X2 - 8750X + 6400$

Log File and Path Analysis

Web-based surveying is a new and exciting medium for collecting data. However, very little is known about how users take Web-based surveys and what parameters affect survey completion. Towards this end, we employed several existing log file analysis techniques and defined new ones to begin to determine and quantify the parameters at play. The next section presents our findings and one of the new techniques.

During the surveying period, 279,770 files totalling over 1.3 gigabytes were transmitted (average 6,824 files/day and 3.3 megabytes/day). Of these requests, slightly over 0.1% resulted in errors, with the most frequent error being "Code 404 Not Found Requests". This indicates that nearly all users who attempted to participate in the surveys were able to successfully access the pages. This round of surveys was the smoothest to date, with accesses to the Help and FAQ (Frequently Asked Questions) pages each accounting for under one percent of the total file requests. Over 71% of the browsers had image loading turned on, as measured by the ratio of the number of accesses to the Entry pages versus the number of accesses to the image (13 KB interlaced GIF) embedded within these pages.

These descriptive statistics are not very informative. Additionally, exploration into previous hypertext research into the analysis of event driven log files did not reveal many useful techniques. The research typically takes a users path and converts this into a state matrix for subsequent clustering analysis. These analyses usually involve a small number of paths and lose the important sequential nature of hypertext traversals. Given that we wish to explore the paths of over 13,000 users and not have to individually inspect each instance, we developed several new methods of analysis.

One method introduces the notion of *attrition* and *attrition curves*. Attrition can best be thought of in terms of the paths taken by users through an information space. These paths are determined by the underlying structure of hyperlinks, that is, which pages are connected to what. We know that certain users will visit a page and not continue traversing the hyperlinks contained in that page. Others, however, will proceed to traverse the presented links, thus continuing down a path. *Attrition* can be understood as a measure of users who stop traversing verses the users who continue to traverse the hyperlinks from a given page. Attrition is calculated across a group of users. *Attrition curves* are defined as the plot of attrition ratios for all pages along a certain path.

In order to compute attrition, we gathered the paths taken by all users and applied software that tabulates the occurrences of *k-substrings* in an *n-string* for all *k* between 1 and 50. The actual paths taken by users are collated and compose the n-string. Our software exploits the fact the set of k-substrings within the n-string may be a subset of the information space if not all possible paths were traversed. In practice, we observe this property to be true, which greatly reduces the complexity of the computation.

Figure 1 represents the paths taken by respondents for each questionnaire. Access to each questionnaire was provided via the "Main Launching Page." The loop-backs result from users who did not complete all questions on the questionnaire. The adaptive questionnaires are displayed as two consecutive nodes. Attrition for each traversal is shown as the percent of users who did not proceed along that path. For a more complete discussion of the diagram see the below explanation.

For example, suppose a user takes the path {*a, b, c, a, b*}, where *a, b* represents the user traversing the hyperlink link contained in *a* to *b*. The tabulation of the 2-substring of the 6-string would be {*ab*, 2} {*bc*, 1}{*ca*, 1}. Stated in terms of paths, we note that the user traversed the subpath from *a* to *b* twice and the subpaths from *b* to *c* and *c* to *a* once. The calculation of k-substrings was computed for all paths taken by all users (48,243 total paths) for the entire survey information space.

This set of k-substrings provides the input for calculating attrition, which we define next.

Let G = (V, E) be the directed graph with vertices V and edges E. Let P = {N} be the set of all paths taken by all users through G with N being a subset of V and $p(u, v)$ defining the path from vertex *u* to *v*. Attrition for $p(u, v)$ is thus the sum of accesses to *u* minus the sum of $p(u, v)$ traversals divided by sum of accesses to *u*. That is:

$$\text{Attrition } (u, v) - \frac{\Sigma(u) \qquad \Sigma(u, v)}{\Sigma(u)}$$

Now, let T be defined as the n-string composed of all vertices along $p(u, z)$ where n equals the length of $p(u, z)$ and I equal the set of vertices from *u* to *z*. The attrition curve for a given vertex *u* to vertex *z* is defined as the attrition plots for all pairs (u, i) where *i* is an element of I.

Figure 1 shows the results of the attrition analysis for the main body of the survey. Given the sensitive nature of some of the questions on the General Demographics questionnaire, it is not surprising to see such a high attrition rate. Losing 8 out of every 100 users may indeed be enough of a loss to warrant the removal of these questions in future surveys. Plus we see that over a quarter of the users went to the information providers page and did not continue. This is most likely due to the fact that they were neither HTML authors nor Webmasters.

Loop-backs occur when a user fails to complete the entire set of questions, which results from our software enforcing question completion. The attrition rates for loop-backs range from 0.60% (Gathering and Purchasing) to 5.43% (Security Issues). Interestingly, the Security Issues questionnaire managed to cause problems with some Web browsers, which were unable to successfully submit the results even though all questions had been completed. The Gathering & Purchasing questionnaire did not enforce question completion as all answers were optional check boxes. Thus, the results of these analyses make sense and help quantify the effects of attrition on user behavior.

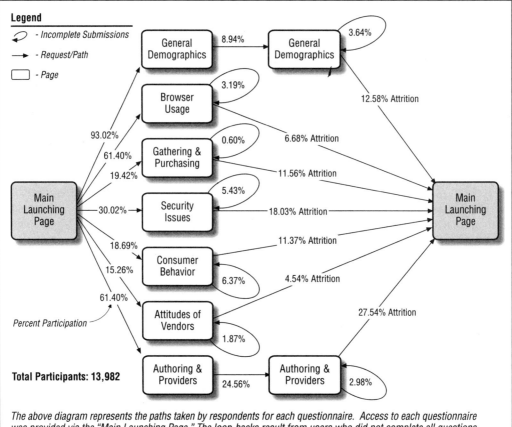

Figure 1: Paths of respondents to questionnaires

Other, more conventional analyses were also performed to gain a better understanding the effects of questionnaire ordering on the Main Launching Page. That is, what effect does the ordering of possible questionnaires have on which questionnaire users participate? For starters, we determined each user's reading time per page. This was then averaged across all users for all pages. Table One displays the results of this analysis along with the relationship between position, participation, attrition, and the number of questions each questionnaire contained. Correlation analysis of these factors reveals that there is a significant relation between position and reading time (Spearman's r = -0.89) which is modeled as a linear fit ($R2$ = 0.73) of the form:

f(reading time) = -2.88 * position + 4.78

This means that questionnaires placed first on the Main Launching Page were read for longer periods of time. Intuitively this makes sense as users get tired during the surveys presented later. Also, we observe correlation between position and participation (r = -0.83), which is modeled as a power fit ($R2$ = 0.94) of the form:

f(participation) = 9.63 * position-0.95

Table 1:   Summary of Exploration into the Effect of Questionnaire Ordering on Other Attributes

Questionnaires (in order of position)	Questions	Participation (%)	Attrition (%)	Net Loss (People)	Avg. Reading Time (sec)
General Demographics	21	93.02	12.58	1636	44.15
Browser Usage	28	61.40	6.68	130	37.03
Author & Providers	13	24.00	27.54	924	46.13
Security Issues	21	30.02	10.03	421	36.43
Consumer Behavior	16	18.69	11.37	297	35.91
Attitudes of Vendors	28	15.26	4.54	97	28.41
Gathering & Purchasing	41	19.42	11.56	314	26.44

Thus, the positioning of questionnaires has a significant effect on how many people take the surveys. The extent of this relationship can been seen from Table 1 as nearly 60% of the users who took the General Demographics section did not take any of the last five questionnaires.

As one would then expect, reading time and participation are also correlated ($r = 0.78$), yielding an interpretation that the higher the chance of users taking a survey, the greater the chance they are to spend time reading it. In addition, the number of questions and the time spent reading each questionnaire are correlated ($r = -0.67$). There are no significant interactions between all the other variables as tested by pairwise analysis. Important to note is that attrition is not correlated to participation. This further confirms that the effects of self-selection on the collected data are nominal.

Empirically Supported Guidelines

- Place the most important questionnaires at the top of the page.

- Place the questionnaires with the most questions near the top of the page.

- Understand the trade-off between gathering sensitive information and attrition.

- Enforcing question completion does not drastically increase attrition.

Conclusion

Clearly, today's Web is not the same Web of January 1994. The infusion of National and Global Information Infrastructure focus combined with easily acquired interfaces to the Web has left its trail across the surveys. The surveyed Web user populations have rapidly flowed from the originators of the technology to the initial users in the educational and research settings to the users provided connectivity at work and school to those who actively seek out Web connectivity. The WWW User Surveys are able to keep pace with the fluidity by identifying and quantifying real changes in the adaptation of what may very well be the most important revolution since Gutenberg.

The use of the Web as a surveying tool has also provided the means for research into a number of areas beyond the collected demographic data. Part of our research efforts are currently being spent creating a surveying environment in Java that is closer to the ideal surveying environment. It will allow instantaneous survey adaptation as opposed to the *"question-answer-adapt/re-ask"* cycle currently used. We are also exploring the relationship between user characteristics and navigational behavior. New log file analysis techniques as well as the development of our log file analysis software will also continue. As always, we welcome and encourage the participation of other research agendas and thank the Web community for their participation and for providing us with this opportunity. ∎

References

1. Alao, F. Pilot Study of Network Surveying Techniques, 1994 ((manuscript not published).

2. Catledge, L. and Pitkow, J. "Characterizing Browsing Strategies in the World-Wide Web," *Journal of Computer Networks and ISDN systems*, Vol. 27, no. 6, 1995.

3. Pitkow, J. and Recker, M. "Results from the First World-Wide Web Survey," *Journal of Computer Networks and ISDN systems*, Vol. 27, no. 2, 1994.

4. Pitkow, J. and Recker, M., "Using the Web as a Survey Tool: Results from the Second World-Wide Web User Survey." *Journal of Computer Networks and ISDN systems*, Vol. 27, no. 6, 1995.

Acknowledgments

Georgia Tech's Graphics, Visualization, and Usability (GVU) Center operates the surveys as a pubic service as part of its commitment to the Web and Internet communities.

This material is based upon work supported under a National Science Foundation Graduate Research Fellowship. Thanks to all members of the GVU, its director Dr. Jim Foley, and staff for their support and help. Special thanks extend to Kipp Jones, Dan Forsyth, Dave Leonard, and Randy Captenter and the entire Computer Network Services staff for their technical support and generous donation of equipment. Additional thanks go to Laurie Hodges for guidance. Finally, James would like to thank Dr. Jorge Vanegas for implicit funding throughout the surveys.

About the Authors

James Pitkow
Georgia Institute of Technology
Atlanta, GA 03002-0280
pitkow@cc.gatech.edu

James Pitkow received his B.A. in Computer Science Applications in Psychology from the University of Colorado Boulder in 1993. He is a Graphics, Visualization, and Usability (GVU) Center graduate student in the College of Computing at Georgia Institute of Technology. His research interests include event analysis, user modeling, adaptive interfaces, and usability.

Colleen Kohoe
Georgia Institute of Technology
Atlanta, GA 03002-0280
colleen@cc.gatech.edu

Colleen Kehoe received her B.S. in Computer Science from Stevens Institute of Technology in Hoboken, NJ in 1994. She is currently a Ph.D. student in the Graphics, Visualization, and Usability Center of the College of Computing at the Georgia Institute of Technology. Her current interests include educational technology, visualization, cognitive science and Web-related technologies.

THE OPEN MEETING
A WEB-BASED SYSTEM FOR CONFERENCING AND COLLABORATION

Roger Hurwitz, John C. Mallery

Abstract

*An asynchronous collaboration system was developed for Vice President AL Gore's Open Meeting on the National Performance Review. The system supported a large online meeting with over 4000 participants and successfully achieved all its design goals. A theory for managing wide-area collaboration guided the implementation as it extended an earlier system developed to publish electronic documents. It provided users access over SMTP and HTTP to hypertext synthesized from an object database and structured with knowledge representation techniques, including a light-weight semantics based on argument connectives. The users participated in policy planning as they discussed, evaluated, and critiqued recommendations by linking their comments to points in the evolving policy hypertext. These policy conversations were structured according to a link grammar that constrained the types of comments which could be attached in specific discourse contexts. Persistent actions enforced constraints on man-machine tasks, such as moderation workflow. Timely delivery of newly moderated comments kept the conversation gain at a level comparable to tightly-focused mailing lists threading out from specific points in the hypertext. After reviewing the architecture and performance of the system in this Open Meeting, the paper closes with discussion of lessons learned and suggestions for future research. **Keywords:** Collaboration, form processing, HTTP, information access, link grammar, National Performance Review, organization theory, persistent actions, semantic network, SMTP, surveys, typed links, URN, White House, World Wide Web*

Introduction

A recent Open Meeting of several thousand Federal workers under the auspices of Vice President Al Gore demonstrated that the World Wide Web can support productive, wide-area collaboration for policy planning and problem solving. The collaboration system implemented for this meeting enabled the participants to find and discuss proposals for bureaucratic reforms, which had been prepared by the National Performance Review (NPR). The resulting policy conversations, which crossed traditional agency boundaries, mobilized support for the proposals, helped refine them and gave NPR feedback on their recommendations. The collaboration architecture was effective because it built upon a theory that identified the interactions needed for productive discussion and problem solving, and

also provided ways to reduce the obstacles to such interactions that arise with a large, dispersed group of participants.

After first describing the Open Meeting event, we examine the general theory it embodies as a guide for other wide-area collaboration applications. Next, we review the architecture of the system, and then, evaluate its performance during the Open Meeting. The conclusion offers some suggestions for refining the system and managing wide-area collaboration over the Web.

The Open Meeting Concept

The Open Meeting application implemented the idea that messages posted to an online discussion can be linked by a light-weight semantics into structured discourse and that the discourse can be modeled as extensible hypertext. The idea for the event itself originated with National Performance Review staffers, who sought an online meeting to disseminate and discuss NPR proposals for reinventing government operations. In their view, a successful meeting would involve several thousand workers, from a wide range of government organizations, who easily access texts relevant to their interests and link their comments in coherent, virtual conversations. The meeting would itself demonstrate a key element of these proposals—the use of computer networks to coordinate policy planning and actions across traditional organizational boundaries. NPR recognized that the conventional technologies for online asynchronous discussion—*viz.*, listserve, newsgroups, and electronic bulletin boards—were not well-suited for such a meeting.

Our research group at the M.I.T. Artificial Intelligence Laboratory considered the meeting an opportunity to implement and test our ideas for managing public access and participation via the Internet in government inquiry and regulatory processes. In such processes, a government agency typically has its experts prepare proposals, and then, invites comments from its relevant public. This public, in turn, hires consultants to prepare briefs and speak at hearings. Because Internet use will broaden and cheapen access to these processes, it will dramatically increase the number of responses to the proposals, and consequently, subject agency officials to information overload. This undesirable result can be attenuated by intelligent routing that decomposes the comment stream by policy proposal and directs comments to the responsible officials.

In an initial public comment system, people would attach their views to documents under review according to the type of their comment. Officials would retrieve these comments by target and type from a database of review documents. Alternatively, the submitted comments could be matched against profiles that indicated the relevance of these categories for the individual officials. For officials reviewing public comments on a proposal the system functions as an annotation

server, which enables them to retrieve specified types of comments on individual proposals. When users both receive and reply to one another's comments, it supports discussions that are composed of the typed and threaded comments.

The Open Meeting application was designed to deliver the necessary support for the meeting organized by the NPR staff. It would build on the Communications Linker System (COMLINK), which was developed as a publication system during 1992-1993 for handling subscription and distribution of documents, based on combinations of categories from a domain taxonomy [7]. The Open Meeting would extend COMLINK mainly by adding typed links between documents in the database.

Given the anticipated character of the meeting's textual environment, the web was a self-evident choice for data entry and display in the system, but the distribution of computer resources among the prospective users made email access as equally self-evident. In December 1994, the time of the event, fewer than half the registrants had a web client and fewer still had clients which supported interactive forms through which comments could be sent to the server. Since all registrants had email, we provided both Web and email access, and as a result, we were later able to compare their respective effects on users' experience of and satisfaction with the meeting.

Textbase

Together with NPR, we made several non-technological choices that affected the organization and interactions in the meeting. These choices concerned the proposals and background material to be included in the initial textbase, how their texts would be presented and the types of comments participants could make on these texts. To provide common grounds for discussions across organizational boundaries, we selected reports which NPR had recently completed about reinventing Federal operating systems, like procurement or information manage-

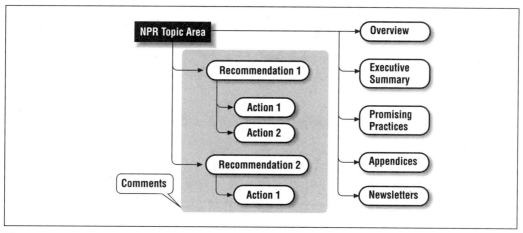

Figure 1:   The standard node

ment, that are found in all federal government departments and agencies. Because the reports had the same generic parts, namely an *Executive Summary*, a set of *Recommendations* and attached enabling *Actions*, and *Appendices* on the implementations of the recommendations, the set was easily reconfigured into a hypertext. A standard node architecture maintained structural analogies across the main branches of the hypertext to simplify implementation and provide a consistent user interface. A root document, which presented the plan of the meeting, branched to eleven nodes, one for each operating system. The standard node included hyperlinks to the various parts of the reports and to additional relevant documents: an *Overview* of several paragraphs and reports of *Promising Practices*, that fulfilled recommendations for the system. During the meeting, *Newsletters*, which summarized the ongoing discussions, would be attached to their respective nodes (Figure 1).

Interestingly, the textual components of the standard node correspond to the generic parts of a strategic model or plan for reforming the operating system: The *Executive Summary* states the problem, the *Recommendations* propose solutions and means of obtaining them, the *Actions* describe tactics and the *Promising Practices* are

example solutions. On this view, the conversations about these texts during the meeting are part of a problem solving process that generates refinements and evaluations as well as support for the proposed solutions (Figure 2).

A recommendation in the Open Meeting environment is consequently an evolving document—its own hypertext—that can be represented by a page with hyperlinks to pages for its original text, the associated enabling actions and the comments in the discussion about it. (Figure 3). The header for each page includes the title, time of submission, author and a location-independent document identifier. To facilitate navigation, each page showed its context with anchors to the immediate parent and to pages summarizing related material. For email users, a text arrived embedded in a form with which one could order one or more the texts subsumed by the present text. A topic node form, for example, included the *Overview* text and an order form for the various parts of the report including the individual recommendations, listed by their titles.

Link Grammars

Comments in discussions are instances of conversational moves which appropriately reply to preceding comments. In ordinary conversation,

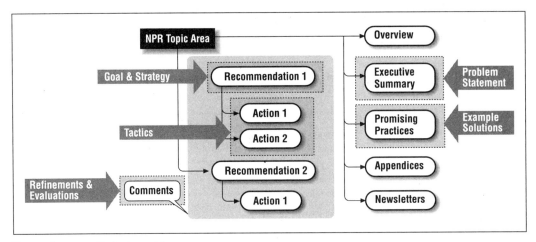

Figure 2:   Strategic model

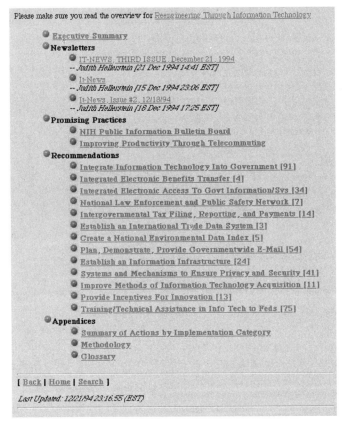

Figure 3:   One of ten NPR topic areas

speakers implicitly recognize these moves, their intentions, and their expectations of reply. In more stylized discussions, speakers often announce the type of statements they make, **e.g.**, "I have a question," to clarify their relation to a previous statement and to cue the expected type of reply. When comments are threaded through their targets, the identification of a conversational move indicates the relationships between otherwise opaque texts, and the sequence of typed conversational connectives indicates a flow of intentions and expectations.

What link-type grammar is appropriate for an online meeting? By grammar, we mean a set of rules that specify the admissible ways in which comments can be linked to an evolving hypertext based on their type and the context. These rules formalize the quasi-normative order of a conversation and prevent incoherent or inappropriate sequences. Such rules can be enforced at a dynamically reconfigurable interface which limits the choice of link type to those links that can be legally attached to the target comment.

The selection of link types and a composition grammar govern the character and development of knowledge in an online discussion. Conversations that permit only agreement or disagreement [1, 9] are more conflictual or stunted than those

also permitting alternatives, examples given and questions and answers. Since the Open Meeting was convened to discuss policy and rule making, we wanted a set of link types that were familiar in policy debates, and that could express differences of opinion without polarizing participants. After careful consideration, we excluded simple endorsements of a proposal and motions that would call a vote, and narrowed the choices to *Agreement, Disagreement, Question, Answer,* (propose an) *Alternative, Qualification* ("yes, but"), or (report a) *Promising Practice* (Table 1). The *Root* document explained these types and asked Open Meeting participants to use this link semantics to frame their comments.

Certain institutional and logical conditions dictated the attachment rules in this grammar. Some NPR assertions has been vetted and were officially beyond debate; consequently, no comments could be attached to the *Overviews, Executive Summaries, Appendices* and *Promising Practices*. Second, it did not seem reasonable to comment on the *Newsletter* summaries of discussions. Third, other kinds of attachments, namely an alternative or qualification to a question, and an alternative to an alternative, answer or promising practice, were excluded for illogic.

Table 1: Open Meeting Comment Link Types

Icon	Link Type	Description
	Agree	A reason to support the recommendation or action
	Qualify	A qualification that explains exceptions or extensions for a recommendation or action
	Alternative	An alternative way to implement a recommendation or action
	Disagree	A reason to challenge why or how a recommendation or action can work
	Example	A report of a promising practice that illustrates one good way to realize a recommendation
	Question	A question about a recommendation or action
	Answer	An answer to someone else's question

Conversation Displays

An Open Meeting participant submits a comment on a commentable text (*Recommendations, Actions*, other comments) by editing the form attached to that text. The form captures the target's document identifier, lists the comment types that can be attached to the target, and provides queries for the comment title and text. The database creates a document object for the comment and uses the link information in generating a virtual page that displays the current state of the discussion.

The page includes a hyperlink to the recommendation and hyperlinks to the the comments, each listing the comment title, author, time of submission and link type, with the last indicated by a distinctive icon, as well as type name. These hyperlinks are displayed as a recursively indented outline, so hyperlinks that directly attach to the same target are below it, with the same offset. Hyperlinks to all comments in sequences and subsequences attached to one target are listed before the hyperlink to the next target. The layout (Figure 4) provides a synoptic view of the discussion.

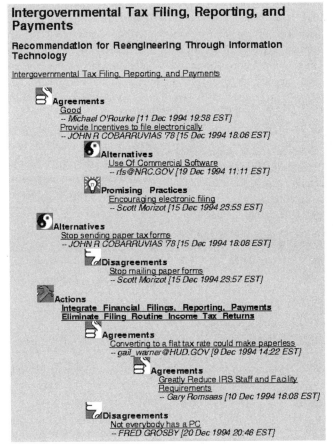

Figure 4:   A NPR recommendation, implementing actions, and linked comments

Moderation

To minimize the posting of low quality, redundant and inappropriate comments, the Open Meeting was moderated. Moderators were assisted by administrative tools, which include moderation forms, canned response letters, virtual queues to allocate work, and a constraint-based view system. A moderator can use these tools to overview all submissions to the meeting, access unreviewed and otherwise pending submissions for a topic, rate a submission, accept it to make it visible, reject it, return it for revision, or defer a decision to another moderator (Figure 5). Moderation exploits the database support of views, since accepting a comment merely changes status of its visibility to the public (Figure 8). Views then are displays generated by constraints that determine what gets shown to whom. Although this interface generation idea can be used to apportion the textbase according to arbitrary criteria the Open Meeting employed only user and moderator views. Working with their view, moderators could see all submitted documents with their review status and could retrieve comments based on the quality ratings (Figure 6).

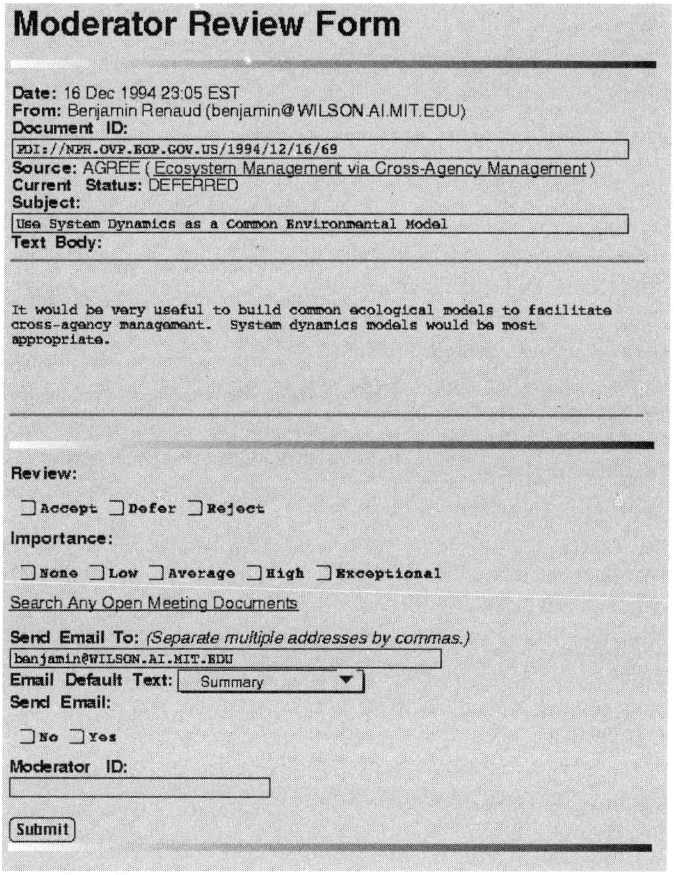

Moderator Review Form

Date: 16 Dec 1994 23:05 EST
From: Benjamin Renaud (benjamin@WILSON.AI.MIT.EDU)
Document ID:

`PDI://NPR.OVP.EOP.GOV.US/1994/12/16/69`

Source: AGREE (Ecosystem Management via Cross-Agency Management)
Current Status: DEFERRED
Subject:

`Use System Dynamics as a Common Environmental Model`

Text Body:

`It would be very useful to build common ecological models to facilitate`
`cross-agency management.  System dynamics models would be most`
`appropriate.`

Review:

☐ Accept ☐ Defer ☐ Reject

Importance:

☐ None ☐ Low ☐ Average ☐ High ☐ Exceptional

Search Any Open Meeting Documents

Send Email To: *(Separate multiple addresses by commas.)*
`benjamin@WILSON.AI.MIT.EDU`
Email Default Text: | Summary ▼ |
Send Email:

☐ No ☐ Yes

Moderator ID:

[Submit]

Figure 5:   Moderator Review Form

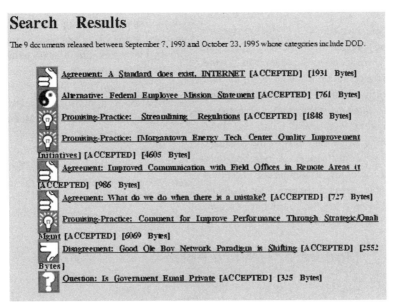

Search Results

The 9 documents released between September 7, 1993 and October 23, 1995 whose categories include DOD.

Agreement: A Standard does exist, INTERNET [ACCEPTED] [1931 Bytes]

Alternative: Federal Employee Mission Statement [ACCEPTED] [761 Bytes]

Promising-Practice: Streamlining Regulations [ACCEPTED] [1848 Bytes]

Promising-Practice: [Morgantown Energy Tech Center Quality Improvement Initiatives] [ACCEPTED] [4605 Bytes]

Agreement: Improved Communication with Field Offices in Remote Areas (t [ACCEPTED] [986 Bytes]

Agreement: What do we do when there is a mistake? [ACCEPTED] [727 Bytes]

Promising-Practice: Comment for Improve Performance Through Strategic/Qnali Mgmt [ACCEPTED] [6069 Bytes]

Disagreement: Good Ole Boy Network Paradigm is Shifting [ACCEPTED] [2552 Bytes]

Question: Is Government Email Private [ACCEPTED] [325 Bytes]

Figure 6: Moderator Search Results for exceptional comments concerning the Department of Defense

Ancillary Pages

The Open Meeting environment included friendly interfaces for retrieval of particular text types and online help. A search interface supported retrieval of documents satisfying near boolean combinations of reinvention topic (node), link type and government organizations mentioned in the document text. *Promising Practices* and *News* interfaces enabled retrieval of hyperlinks to all the promising practices or newsletters by their reinvention topic. These were implemented by standing search URLs, which pointed to the search specifications for the required documents rather than the documents themselves and hence avoided the problem of updating hotlinks. A general help page listed hyperlinks to Vice President Gore's welcoming letter to the Open Meeting, to his memo authorizing federal workers to participate during work hours, and to various FAQs.

Wide-Area Collaboration

Wide-area collaboration refers to communication and coordinated action among groups that are large, geographically dispersed, and generally, do not know each other. These kinds of systems are distinguished from *groupware* oriented toward small groups precisely because the system must take over many tasks previously performed by people in small groups.

- *Large-scale communication.* When large numbers of people are involved it is no longer possible for individuals to see all of the communications traffic.

- *Decomposition.* Communications must be broken up into smaller packets that are narrowly focused. The decomposition can occur along several dimensions:
  - Time: *Asynchronous* communications becomes the norm. Relaxation of synchronous constraints on participation is essential because large groups are difficult or impossible to schedule, especially across multiple time zones.

- Space: *Geographic* decomposition provides a way to focus collaboration whenever the domain has spatial extent.
- Content: Specialization by interest, role or function provide the most general way to hierarchically decompose a task domain.

In general, task decomposition allows group size and task elements to be scaled down to a manageable size. The key idea is to reduce the volume of communications and increase the locality of communications in order to match information processing levels with people's ability to cope with complexity and with their commitment to the collaboration.

- *Structuring information fragments.* The decomposition of communications creates a later need to reintegrate information for coherent reconfiguration and presentation to people. The reintegration and delivery options depend critically on the structuring techniques used to organize information fragments.
  - Minimize redundancy by recognizing equalities: In wide-area collaborations with large communication flows, it is essential to reduce information that could otherwise obscure new information. Because people are still needed to recognize similarities and equalities in the various pieces of information, the organizing strategy and the user interface must help them discover whether information they intend to link has already been linked.
  - Danger of self-amplifying redundancy: As the quantity of redundant information increases, it is increasingly difficult to recognize prior similarities, and a wide-area collaboration system risks descent into an unmanageable morass at an accelerating rate.
  - Atomic propositions: It is easier to spot redundancies when comments are short and addressed to one point. Several statements of this type are better than a single

large statement, interweaving multiple themes.
  - Knowledge-level annotations: A set of statements that are largely opaque to a computer system can be organized into traversable hypertext or a semantic network by making assertions or annotations about them. The more explicit the semantics of these assertions, the more useful computer manipulations becomes possible.

- *Focus activities and interactions.* Communications decomposition should cluster information and actions into meaningful and coherent chunks that match cognitive capacity and motivational level of participants.

- *Locate interest, expertise, resources, responsibility.* Wide-area collaboration involves the coordination of actions and human resources in addition to information assembly. Coordinating action provides a criterion for decomposing information about agents according to several dimensions:
  - Interest in participating
  - Expertise or special knowledge
  - Ability to provide or deploy resources
  - Responsibility for making decisions

Knowledge-Level Techniques

If effective wide-area collaboration depends on a fine-grained decomposition of information structures and communications processes, it also requires a repertoire of *knowledge-level techniques* for structuring information fragments. Knowledge-level techniques refer to a continuum of approaches for organizing information packets based on their semantic or knowledge content.

Systems of categories organized from general to specific, or taxonomies, provide one of the most powerful ways to organize hypermedia nodes. Taxonomies allow inferences about similarity. Typed links are another extremely powerful way to make statements about how hypermedia nodes relate. These important concepts from the field of Artificial Intelligence comprise the basic building blocks for knowledge-level techniques. In an application, these ideas need to be combined with a *domain theory*

Various knowledge level techniques were applied in the Open Meeting.

- *Information access*
  - Boolean combinations of features: Once features are associated with information fragments, they can be retrieved in sets by combining boolean operators (*e.g.*, AND, OR, and NOT).
  - Taxonomic subsumption: By organizing categories into hierarchies, it becomes possible to make inferences about similarity based on the set of categories spanning a hypermedia node. Additionally, a node inherits certain capabilities based on the set of categories that span it.
  - Typed links: When the links between hypermedia nodes are typed, they can be used to retrieve other nodes with specific relationships to a given node. Additionally, when the links are first-class objects, information about the link instance can be associated with it.
  - Attachments: Nodes can be filtered according to special special-purpose attachments like *Generic Reviews* that provide a characterization along a dimension or *Discourse Contexts* that provide location in organizational processes.
  - Role-based views: Nodes and links may be differentially accessible depending on application-specific roles, for example, moderators vs. users in the Open Meeting.

- *Structure the information base*
  - Fully categorizing the evolving hypertext: Categorization is a key mechanism for hypertext reassembly that allows regions to be found by boolean combinations of categories, and sometimes can uniquely locate hypertext nodes.

- *Category coherence.* If commentary and other hypertext nodes are thematically atomic and adequately covered by their categories, they can be manipulated reasonably by means of those categories. If the content spans additional categories, the value of categorization declines.
  - Linking commentary recursively: Linked conversations focus the evolution of debate to the extent that comments remain on topic, *i.e.,* with the range of their categories.

- *Link grammar.* A link semantics adds an important source of coherence when it expresses which conversation moves are possible by particular people in situations. Here, a grammar explicitly the moves (links) and their composition rules. The representation of the discourse context (*e.g.*, Time, Speaker, Affiliation) reflects and guides organizational processes.

Architecture: The COMLINK Substrate

The Communications Linker System (COMLINK) provides a foundation for research into intelligent network services through a general-purpose substrate that is configured by a small amount of application-specific code. The core of COMLINK is a transaction-controlled, persistent-object database. Users interact with the database via email servers and Web servers. These servers present messages or Web pages whose content is generated on the fly from the database. Dynamic Form Processing module [6, 7, 8, 10] manages all interactions with users over *both* email or World Wide Web using a single, unified paradigm that, *inter alia*, validates all user input. Figure 7 summarizes the COMLINK architecture.

The database defines persistent objects related to the domain of network services. These persistent objects are defined with the Common Lisp Object System [4, 11]. They support multiple inheritance, a mix of persistent and dynamic instance vari-

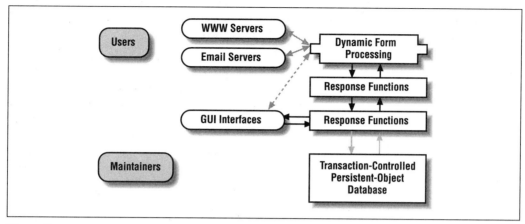

Figure 7:   Communications Linker System

ables, as well as multimethods, which allow method invocations to dispatch on possibly multiple arguments.

Basic Database Entities

The database represents the entire range of entities relevant to structuring a hypertext, operating on it, and providing interactive access to it over SMTP and HTTP.

- *Documents.* Document objects can be created from a variety of different mixins depending on the kind of document. The same document can exist in multiple formats, for example, ASCII versus HTML. Although document properties (*e.g.*, categories, dates, authors) are indexed in the database, the body text is stored in a file system but accessed via a transaction on the document. Small documents like comments use all the same machinery as large documents.

- *Persistent Document Identifiers (PDI).* These PDIs are a kind of prototypical URNs which have the form *pdi://logical.authority.dns.name/yearmonth/day/unique-id.document-format*. Because every document stored in the database has a PDI, external references to documents over email or WWW are easy, uniform, and indepen-

dent of physical location. PDIs provide the critical reference resolution capability necessary to link documents with comments and to attach generic reviews.

- *Persistent categories.* All documents have associated categories that characterize their content. Various taxonomic inferences such as subsumption and exclusivity are available. The database actually contains flat features with a one-to-one mapping to categories that are taxonomically structured in dynamic memory. This allows the taxonomy to be reorganized without the need to perform hazardous surgery on a running database.

- *Taxonomic email routing.* Two types of message routing need database support:
  - Static mailing lists: Mailing lists, subscriptions, and subscribers are represented as database objects. Mailing lists are organized in a generalization hierarchy such that messages to a superior are sent to all inferiors. Mailing lists can be active or inactive. User subscriptions connect subscribers to mailing lists and can be active or inactive. Periodically, all active mailing lists are written out to a mailbox table that drives an associated SMTP mailer.

- Virtual mailing lists: Document universes associate collections of documents, categories, and document selectors. A document selector is a pattern of categories that selects documents for transmission to a recipient. When documents are transmitted through a document universe, the categories attached to the document are matched against all active document selectors, and when matches succeed, the document is sent to the subscriber associated with the selector. Currently, document selectors first match against a document intersection of attractor categories, and second, filter documents by a union of repulsor categories. Document distribution occurs within a transaction in order to assure reliable and atomic delivery to all recipients.

- *Ontology of network entities.* Beyond these major database entities, there are comprehensive variety of objects defined for users, contexts, hosts and domains.

Link Representation

The basic ontology provides the database support needed to access or route documents according to taxonomic categories, but it made no provision for representing links between document or making assertions about them. For the Open Meeting, relations were added to the COMLINK substrate. Borrowing from our research in natural language understanding [5], the approach added bidirectional ternary relations as first-class database objects. This small addition turned the document database into a semantic network with typed nodes.

Ternary relations have three components: a subject, an object, and a relation type. In this case, relations are used to link document objects. The PDIs used a document identifiers make it easy to link documents or comments together, regardless of their physical location. In the Open Meeting application, the relation types were the argument connectives and several internal links. Addition-

ally, relations are explicitly represented as first-class objects so that assertions can be made about the relations as well.

In our natural-language research, we use ternary relation knowledge representations to represent English sentences because they are arbitrarily expressive, they can encode higher order logics, and yet, they support efficient computations. Thus, this approach to light-weight semantics for linking documents together evolves smoothly to heavy-weight semantics as ever more intensive knowledge-level techniques are combined with hypertext.

Generic Reviews

There are many applications that need to attach rankings, reviews, or discrete values to database objects. A generic review system was implemented that uses a single set of entity definitions to implement any range of reviews schemes, provided review values can be encoded in a numeric scale. While database objects in persistent memory are attached appropriately and hold a number representing the application meaning, these numbers are translated for use in dynamic memory as necessary and relevant for the application.

- *Appraisal.* These are the generic reviews about an entity that are provided by users or programs. These can be active or inactive.

- *Reviewable Object.* A mixin allows any database entity to be reviewed by attaching an appraisal value.

- *Reviews.* Reviews name a specific scheme for generic reviews and associate a function for asserting, interpreting, and comparing appraisal values. Whenever there are multiple appraisals for objects, reviews maintain appraisal aggregates.

Moderation Workflow

In the Open Meeting, generic reviews implemented the following capabilities:

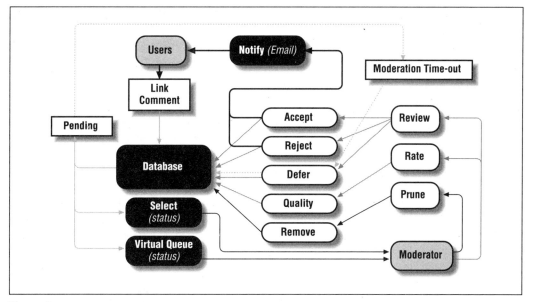

Figure 8:   Moderation Work Flow

- *Quality ratings.* Moderators rated the quality of comments as *low, average, high,* or *exceptional.*

- *Moderation status.* Comments submitted by users could have any status of the following at a specific time: *unseen, pending, accepted, rejected, deferred,* or *removed.*

- *Virtual moderation queues.* Moderation workflow is managed by virtual queues (Figure 8) that allocate moderation tasks. When a moderator pops a review task, the task is locked so other moderators to receive tasks without two receiving the same task. Virtual queues are defined by retrieval criteria:
  - Availability: Document whose moderation status is *unseen* or *deferred* but not *pending* are available for moderation.
  - Ordering: Documents available for moderation are ordered according to the time when they were submitted, thus implementing a FIFO queue.
  - Domain: A boolean combination of categories circumscribe the documents avail-

able for moderation by moderators to a specific region of the hypertext.

This approach allows applications to reconfigure moderator queues in dynamic memory by merely changing the combination of categories that define a virtual task queue for moderation. The flexibility inherent in the approach makes implementation of distributed moderation easy and dynamic load balancing of work over a moderator pool possible.

Persistent Actions

Email servers in COMLINK implement reliable tasking by maintaining a queue of pending requests in a task directory. Although this approach works for tasks invoked by users via email form processing, it does not provide a very general or flexible model that could help with access via the Web. The stateless nature of HTTP means that all information regarding a web transaction exists only within the transaction and disappears afterwards. Persistent actions stored in a transaction-controlled database provide a general, fine-grained, and flexible way to ensure the reliable execution of tasks in networked environments—which are notoriously prone to availability problems and a range of other exceptional conditions.

Persistent actions represent tasks (computations) as database objects. They transfer the reliability of transaction-controlled database operations to the task domain. Reliable tasking works by posting a persistent action to be executed at a specific time, which may be immediate or in the future. Some actions are cyclic and are repeated at specific intervals. When the execution time is reached, the task runs the operation with all associated parameters in its own thread. If the operation succeeds, the persistent action is removed from the database. If the operation fails, the persistent action is rescheduled for execution after an application-defined delay. Transaction control assures that the task is reliably posted in the first place, and deleted only after successful completion.

In the Open Meeting, persistent actions were used for:

- *Moderation time-out.* A problem with the moderation lock system (discussed above) is that a moderator may lock a document for review, but may fail to complete the review. In this case, nobody else could review the document because it would remain in a *pending* state. This problem is solved in allocation transaction by posting a persistent action to revert the status of a document to *deferred* unless the moderator submits a review within a application-specific interval (1 hour in the Open Meeting). (Figure 8)

- *Document transmission.* When documents are distributed automatically, there are opportunities for failure between the time a system accepts a document from a reliable email server to the time it hands the message off to a reliable SMTP mailer. For example, the system crashes. Since accepting a document involves storing it in the database with a transaction, we reliably accept documents and assist the reliability regime of the email server. When the document is marked for transmission, a persistent action is posted to transmit the document. The persistent action is deleted from the database only after the document is successfully transmitted.

- *Link transmission.* Transmission of document alone is not enough to reassemble a mirror of the hypertext database. In the Open Meeting, the same mechanism as document transmission was used to transmit a *link View.* This link stream contains the link types and attachment PDIs allows mirroring sites to maintain an exact copy of the textbase.

Persistent actions provide a means to enforce constraints on processes in the face of error and uncertainty. The moderation workflow example illustrates how a human process can be coupled with computer support to reliably achieve a task with a number of unreliable parts.

Context Information

Representing the context of communications is a key element in understanding organizational interactions that may occur in wide-area collaborations. Since one purpose of the Open Meeting was to create a framework for conversations accross traditional organizational boundaries, the system needed to track the interactions of participants as representatives of their organizations.

- *Discourse context.* The discourse context, which is known as deixis by linguists and provenance by librarians, is available as an object class that can be mixined into major document classes. The representation builds from a conceptualization of agents, actions, and roles:
  - Communicative act: This is the act of communication by a specific communicator over a specific time interval and originating from a specific location. Possible communicators include: people, organizations, and computational agents.

– Communicative role: Any communicative act can occupy the following roles with regard to a specific document: (1) **source**—the agent who is producing the text; (2) **recipient**: the agent to whom the text is directed; and (3) **audience**: the agent(s) who may also receive the text but who are not the intended direct recipients.

- *Network topology.* Email addresses are associated with representations of human and computer agents. The topology of host addresses is represented for Internet Hosts and X.400 Addresses. Although this representation of hosts and domains was originally intended to support maintenance activities (e.g., failed mail processing), it is helpful for understanding of organizational context to the extent that this is correlated with network topology, which is quite high X.400 addresses.

The discourse context provides a means to ground link grammars organizationally; situations and roles constrain the possible links. (Of course, discourse context also supplies information for natural language systems to resolve intersentential pronouns and indexicals).

Architecture: The Open Meeting Application

Hypertext Synthesis

The primary datastructure of the Open Meeting is the database representation of the hypertext. There were two logical views of the structure:

- *User view.* Users could see only nodes, documents, and links that moderators had accepted. This applied to both browsing the hypertext and searching via categories and link types.

- *Moderator view.* Moderators could see all nodes, documents, and links as well as the moderation status and any internal quality ratings.

In principle, all views of this structure are synthesized on the fly, whether a user is viewing the structure via email or via the Web. Although the overall views presented over email and the Web are the same, differences in the character of these transport media imposed some asymmetries in the user interface, even though both views accessed the same functionality on the same structure. One invariant across all views and user interfaces was the need to provide context-sensitive navigation. Every presentation to users had a variety of links for stepping around the structure and returning to known reference points.

Email Hypertext

Many Federal workers who participated in the Open Meeting had only email access, and consequently, email hypertext browsing was the key technology that made possible their participation. Email hypertext pages always use ASCII forms that rely on the dynamic form processing facility. Hyperlinks are replaced by analogous queries preceding or following any text body. Because email transport is not realtime, there is no need for special caching to improve performance. Users step through pages at the rate of email roundtrips between themselves and the Open Meeting server. For this reason, it was very important to minimize the number of transactions required to traverse structures or accomplish some task, which is usually the number of form submissions by email. The constraint on minimizing email roundtrips introduced some divergence in the interface models between the Web and email views. For example, a single page might offer more options than the corresponding Web page. Context-sensitive navigation was especially important for email users. Despite these efforts, email access remained substantially more clumsy than Web access due to clients which are limited to linear, text-based interfaces and delay times which are often present in transport and processing.

Despite these drawbacks, the email interface served some very important functions in the Open Meeting:

- *Authentication.* Because wide-spread authentication of users was unavailable in the Web browsers at the time, we used a technique of email authentication pioneered in a precursor Community Forum System that deployed at the MIT Artificial Intelligence Laboratory during the Presidential campaign in October 1992. Namely, if a user can receive and respond to an email form sent to their email address, then there is a high probably that the user actually controls that address and their identity is authentic. This assumption is even stronger at government sites where many of our Federal workers were located because these computers are usually tightly controlled. The trick in the scheme is that the form arrives with query values defaulted to request the desired service, and so, the service is not performed unless the user decides to return the form. This kind of email authentication was applied to:
  - Participation surveys: All participants in the Open Meeting had to complete a participation survey [3] running during several months before the event.
  - Linking comments: Both email and Web users needed to request a comment form while visiting the target node, and then, reply to the email forms they received. This email form contained the document identifier (PDI) for the target node and would accept a range of link types according to the link grammar.
  - Subscription: While visiting a hypertext node, both email and Web users could subscribe or unsubscribe to any comments attached to the node or topically-related nodes. Either choice on both the email and Web interfaces caused the system to send them an email form requesting confirmation. Because the hypertext

was fully categorized, the system knew the exact category combination required to subscribe to any node, and consequently, the users were freed from the need to specify the category combination themselves or for that matter to learn how to specify these in the first place. Similarly, a user could unsubscribe by visiting the hypertext node from which the subscription was originally requested.

- *Notification.* When user subscribed to a node in the hypertext structure, they would receive all comments and newsletters attached within the scope of the categories spanning the node. Of course, new attachments were not transmitted until a moderator accepted the comment. Unlike other comment contexts, here the comment stream arrived in a form that allowed immediate response because the system already had confidence in the subscribed users' identities. Although transaction costs were relatively higher for a Web user to submit their first comment, these costs were neutral for email users, and substantially lower for subscribed users because this notification capability relieved people from a need to constantly check to see if new comments were available. Thus, timely delivery of newly moderated comments kept the conversation gain at a level comparable to custom mailing lists tightly focused on specific regions of the hypertext structure.

Email Caching Strategy

During the Open Meeting, a simple governor limited the rate at which COMLINK accepted messages over SMTP and sufficed to keep computational load within hardware capabilities. The message traffic (*e.g.*, submissions of surveys and comment) was heavily biased towards form processing that invoked relatively expensive database transactions. Fortunately, the SMTP protocol allows an email server to use unaffiliated store-and-forward mailers (Figure 9) out in the net-

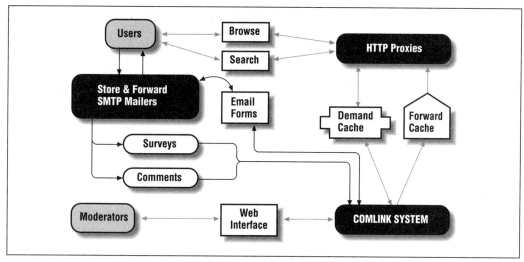

Figure 9:   HTTP and SMTP Traffic Flow

work to buffer the message traffic. This network buffering allows an overloaded email server to spread out message receipt and processing to periods of lower activity. This email strategy works as long as a server clears the backlog within 24 hours,

Web Caching Strategy

The realtime interactive properties of Web access threatened to put undue load on the main server (Symbolics XL1200 Lisp Machine) that had more than enough work managing the database as it handled all email communications and served web pages to moderators. In anticipation of this bottleneck, we deployed a caching proxy (CERN server) between the main database server and the Web users. (Figure 9) The only traffic at issue was Web-based browsing and searchesTwo caching strategies were employed:

- *Forward caching* was combined with incremental page synthesis to maintain updated user and moderator views for browsing. As users submitted comments, the transaction that linked them into the moderator view would also invoke an incremental update of

all pages affected by the change in the moderator view.

- Moderator view: When, and if, a moderator accepted a user's comment, the transaction which changed its status to *accepted* also invoked an incremental update but this time not just to all the effected moderator pages but also to the relevant user pages. The moderator structure involved updating all superior pages to the root (one more page) because information about the review status of comments appeared all the way up.

- User view: For the user structure, moderator acceptance of a new comment required an update to the page summarizing the recommendation to show the new attachment and a incrementing of a number on the main topic node that indicated the number of comments below on a recommendation page.

An important computational property of this update strategy was that these updates only propagated changes upwards in the hypertext structure. Since the HTML structure was a shallow tree with rapid fan-in, this was quite efficient and imposed no debilitating load on the backend server.

- *On-demand caching* with timeout was used for searches because we did not want to cache all possible searches. By caching searches with a fifteen minute timeout, we were assured of maintaining a relatively fresh cache while removing load from the backend server for high frequency searches. The same strategy was applied for both user and moderator views.

Although the Web caching strategy was designed to allow replication of the caching proxy, loading never became high enough to require additional hardware.

Use Patterns

The Open Meeting achieved its initial goal of attracting the attention of a large number of government workers from a wide range of organizations and geographic locations. Of the 4200 people who returned an online registration survey:

- 85% were government workers, and another 4% were state or local government workers.

- Respondents were drawn from all fifty states, twenty foreign countries, and even US Navy ships at sea. Fewer than 40% were from "inside the Beltway" (DC, Maryland, and Virginia).

- Their profile was similar to government workers in general for age (early 40s) and experience (54% were more than 10 years in government), but they were considerably more senior, technically oriented, educated and male than government workers generally. (60% vs. 25% in supervisory capacities; 47% vs. 15% with MA or more; 66% vs. 11% in information systems or engineering; 30% vs. 42% female.)

- In comparison to the estimates of Internet users at the time (December, 1994), this population was older, more educated and had a lower percent of males.

The differences between the registrants and all government workers highlight the importance of commitment and access for wide-area collaboration. Supervisors and other managers have a greater interest in proposals for bureaucratic reform than those they supervise, and engineering and information system workers have greater access to email and World Wide Web. Access also explains some anomalies in the distribution of the registrants. Generally, the larger and more technology-involved organizations, like the Defense, NASA and Interior, had the largest numbers of registrants, but the under-representation of similar organizations, notably Treasury and NSA was due to their massive use of firewalls to restrict network access and penetration.

Hypertext Access

During the two week meeting itself, there were 35,000 Web accesses from nearly 1500 different hosts, exclusive of those by moderators and maintainers. While low by current standards for prominent government sites, **e.g.**, the White House, this volume compares favorably with traffic at specialized and professional online forums. It is also large enough for the distribution of accesses over the pages to suggest how people navigate a complex information and conversation environment.

Table 2 shows a nearly consistent pattern of attrition of hosts with number of transactions from the root page, with the one exception being the smaller number who accessed the *Newsletters* than the *Comments*, although access to *Newsletters* was closer to the root. However, data for the second week alone would show a consistent pattern of attrition, since the *Newsletters* were not posted during the first week of the event. The newsletters in fact received considerable attention, either as a means by which users caught up on discussions or a substitute for reading the discussions themselves. Relatively few users moved

Table 2: Open Meeting WWW Accesses

Content Area	Hosts	Accesses	Root %
Root	1467	4000	100
Node Structure	1072	10600	73
Overviews	745	2900	51
Newsletters	318	2182	22
Recommendations, Actions	620	3700	42
Comments	514	8000	35
Search Interface	283	605	19
Full Taxonomy	37	78	3

outside the fixed-topology hypertext environment to accessing documents directly through the search interface.

These usage patterns suggest that most Web users explored several topics broadly but shallowly by looking at Overviews, some Recommendations and available Newsletters. They "felt" their way through the information, not sure of what they were seeking and more inclined to quit the search than go beneath the top level information. About one third of total users also explored one or two topics deeply by traversing the hypertext at the comments level and using the search interface. Because the surveys show the registrants as a whole were highly motivated, the main difference between the two groups of seekers was likely information literacy, with the in-depth seekers the more literate. The distribution of the nearly 1000 subscriptions to conversations, for which the in-depth seekers were necessarily responsible tells us members of this group remained tightly focused. The subscriptions clustered around those conversations which attracted the most comments, rather than being used as a means to branch out. The pattern is consistent with our earlier remarks that localizing communication is the means to handle large and complex information flows. It also underscores that both the computer literate and the less experienced need low transaction-cost navigation tools that sketch the whole domain and lead to specific topics of interest.

Linking Commentary

Out of 1300 comments submitted, moderators accepted 1013, which were contributed by 290 different individuals. Some conversations included ten or more speakers and had several branches. Although the moderators did not correct identifications of link types, we observed no mistaken identifications among submitted comments, except for one or two cases where a contributor may have deliberately mislabelled the type. The comments were generally positive and serious, with few flames. Half the comments were *Agreement* and 15% were *Disagreements*. *Questions* (167), *Alternatives* (106), and *Promising Practices* (72) accounted for nearly all of the rest, suggesting the contributors' willingness to use the meeting as a sounding board for ideas. Relatively few of the questions were answered (37), and almost no one used the more cognitively complex *Qualification* link (3).

While the ratio of contributors to accessors compares to the low ratios for newsgroups, the participation rate at the Open Meeting was higher for those reaching the comment level in this more complex environment. That result agrees with our theory regarding the effects of localizing communication. Low contribution levels are predictable in wide-area collaboration or problem solving, especially when participants have only general rather than specific functional roles. But, participants are likely to participate when conversations and work are localized and closer to their experiences and knowledge. Because the Open Meeting structure localizes communication, we might expect typically higher participation in collaborations that run several months and are free of external distractions, like approaching holidays.

Participant Satisfaction

Web users were generally satisfied with the meeting and they complained only about an overwhelming amount of text to read and being forced to submit their comments and survey responses via email rather than the Web. The email users complained about the clumsiness of email to traverse hypertext, poor instructions and network delays. These differences reflect, on one hand, the greater interactivity of Web GUIs for hypertext, and, on the other, the fact that the least technically experienced people, who needed the most instruction, had the less sophisticated equipment. They also indicate the need for caution in planning to use email as transport in advanced information environments. Contemporary email does not easily support complex processes, like concurrent multilateral discussions of issues or wide-area collaboration. Instead of simplifying to accommodate the email limitations, the demand for broad participation which email satisfies should motivate upgrading the resources of the less technologically experienced and more basically equipped. But the SMTP transport need not be discarded; as we have seen, use of email subscriptions to track conversations spares the user the transaction costs involved in periodically revisiting the hypertext. Indeed recent trends toward closer integration of clients for reading email and browsing the Web may make SMTP a more useful transport media for wide-area collaboration systems.

Conclusion

The success of the Open Meeting demonstrates the importance of taxonomic decomposition and meaningful link types in the organization of wide-area collaboration. The meeting showed

that people can use typed links which they understand to create argument-structured discourse in a policy planning situation.

A desirable next step is to develop links grammar for decision processes. To generate the kind of knowledge process they seek, convenors of wide-area collaborations may select an appropriate set of link types and composition grammar. In the Open Meeting, the link grammar used did not provide for termination of a conversation. Other planning or action grammars can provide termination—like cloture in parliamentary debate. Interestingly, if we vary decision grammars according to different agent capabilities and functional roles, we start modeling reconfigurable organizations. The views into these processes can similarly be generated for different agents according to their capabilities and roles. Thus, power and social relations within the organization come to be defined by what an agent can do based on information accessible to the agent. This functional division of labor and knowledge, in turn, defines the organization as a process. Thus, experiments in wide-area collaboration promises contributions to new organization theories.

Another step devises link grammars for knowledge formation in scientific communities, and building research in scientific paradigms. Churchman [2] outlines methods of inquiring that can be constructed on the basis of several famous epistemologies. We should try to correlate each of these with a link semantics and explore their productivity in wide-area scientific collaboration. Finally, since wide-area collaborations will include the coordination of work as well as integration of information and opinions, we need to develop systems that can recognize collaborative situations, infer possible options, and recommend strategies or identify resources. These kinds of wide-area collaboration systems promise to help scientists conduct research more effectively as disciplines grow in complexity and knowledge advances more rapidly.

The World Wide Web offers *unprecedented* opportunities for wide-area collaboration at a time when nothing less seems likely to cope with endemic and emergent global problems. We have argued that collaboration systems can begin to manage the complexity by supporting the specialization and localization of knowledge, planning and evaluation. Successful systems will then face the challenge of reintegrating all their partial results. ■

Acknowledgments

Benjamin Renaud contributed significantly to operation of the Open Meeting as well as the implementation and design of a number of the application components, including the moderator interface, generation and caching of virtual pages, and some email interfaces. Mark Nahabedian helped us recover from some disk drive failures. The Vice President's 1994 Open Meeting on the National Performance Review was a collaborative effort between The M.I.T. Artificial Intelligence Laboratory, The White House, National Performance Review, Lawrence Livermore National Laboratory, and Mitre Corporation. Randy Katz that made this project happen by bringing together the players, who included Larry Koskinen and Andy Campbell from NPR. Jonathan P. Gill and Thomas Kalil provided inspiration and critical support for the effort. Howard E. Shrobe helped with earlier versions of the Communication Linker System and provided endless moral support. This paper describes research done at the Artificial Intelligence Laboratory of the Massachusetts Institute of Technology. Support for the M.I.T. Artificial Intelligence Laboratory's artificial intelligence research is provided in part by the Advanced Research Projects Agency of the Department of Defense under contract number MDA972-93-1-003N7.

References

1. T. Berners-Lee and A. Luotonen, "Web Interactive Talk," Dialectical collaboration system deployed on the net in June, 1994. Geneva: World Wide Web Group, CERN, 1994.

2. C. W. Churchman, *The Design of Inquiring Systems: Basic Concepts of Systems and Organization*, New York, Basic Books, 1971.

3. R. Hurwitz and J. C. Mallery, "Survey of Participants in the Vice President's Open Meeting on the National Performance Review," Cambridge: M.I.T. Artificial Intelligence Laboratory, December, 1994. *http://www.ai.mit.edu/projects/iiip/doc/open-meeting/participation-survey.html*

4. S. E. Keene, *Object-Oriented Programming in Common LISP: A Programmer's Guide to CLOS*, Reading: Addison-Wesley, 1989.

5. J. C. Mallery, "Semantic Content Analysis: A New Methodology for the RELATUS Natural Language System," in V. M. Hudson, *Artificial Intelligence and International Politics* Boulder: Westview, 1991. *http://www.ai.mit.edu/people/jcma/papers/1991-aiip/raiip3.html*

6. J. C. Mallery, "A Common Lisp Hypermedia Server," *Proceedings of the First International Conference on the World Wide Web*, Geneva, May 1994. *http://www.ai.mit.edu/projects/iiip/doc/cl-http/server-abstract.html*

7. J. C. Mallery, "The Communications Linker System: An Overview," paper presented at *The 1994 Meeting of the American Political Science Association*, New York City, September 1994. *http://www.ai.mit.edu/projects/iiip/doc/comlink/overview.html*

8. J. C. Mallery, "Dynamic Form Processing: A General Framework for Interactivity," paper presented at *The Second International Conference on The World-Wide Web*, Chicago, October 1994. *http://www.ai.mit.edu/projects/iiip/talks/www94b-dynamic-forms-abstract.html*

9. N. Rescher, *Dialectics: A Controversy-Oriented Theory of Truth*, Albany: SUNY, 1977.

10. R. Rao, W. M. York, and D. Doughty, "A Guided Tour of the Common LISP Interface Manager," *LISP Pointers*, 4 (1991).

11. G. L. Steele, *Common LISP: The Language*, Bedford: Digital Press, 1990. *http://www.cs.cmu.edu:8001/afs/cs.cmu.edu/project/ai-repository/ai/html/cltl/clm/clm.html*

About the Authors

Roger Hurwitz is a research scientist at the M.I.T. Artificial Intelligence Laboratory, an architect of the Open Meeting System, and a contributor to COMLINK Development. His work focuses on the modeling, measurement, and management of collective actions, public communications flows, and organizational intelligence. It draws on knowledge representation, discourse analysis, organization theory, and social science models and survey techniques. Hurwitz holds a Ph.D. from M.I.T., has taught at M.I.T. and the Hebrew University (Jerusalem), and has consulted for major communication companies and UN agencies. A member of several professional committees on the globilization of scientific communications, his publications concern paradigm development in the social sciences, patterns of media diffusion in late industrial societies, and process models of collective actions and knowledge formation. Current projects include the use of the Open Meeting System for interorganizational planning, collaboration, and knowledge formation, and the creation of an analytic environment for tracking aggregate national and international media flows.

John C. Mallery is technical director of the Intelligent Informaton Infrastructure Project at the Artificial Intelligence Laboratory of the Massachusetts Institute of Technology. His research interests center around new ways to model international interactions and new ways to incorporate advanced computational methods into interactive political communication. He has developed computer systems that construct natural language models from narrative text, learn if-then rules from complexly structured event data, and conduct automatic opinion surveys over global computer networks. An electronic publications system that he developed for use during the 1992 presidential campaign currently serves as the primary distribution hub for press releases by the U. S. White House. His current research explores intelligent information access, wide-area collaboration, knowledge-based organizations, and global knowledge webs.

USING VERSIONING TO PROVIDE
COLLABORATION ON THE WWW

Fabio Vitali, David G. Durand

Abstract

This paper proposes a new content type for communicating version information between Web browsers and clients. This is an enabling technology for a variety of possible WWW applications, including very flexible annotation and collaboration facilities. The relation of version management to consistency in hypertext systems is discussed in terms of how it meets some basic requirements for collaborative systems. **Keywords:** *Version control, collaboration support, collaborative editing, link consistency*

Introduction

This paper describes *VTML* (Versioned Text Markup Language), a markup language for storing document version information. VTML can easily be implemented within a text editor, and provides a notation and semantics for tracking successive revisions to a document. The main purpose of VTML is to allow asynchronous collaboration in the creation and editing of text documents. This is based on our previous work [9, 6] in systems and models for version control for hypertext.

Version control allows different instances of the same document to coexist, enabling individual and comparative display as well as automated or assisted merging and differencing. Version control systems are routinely used in many fields of computer science such as distributed DBMS [2], Software Engineering [12], hypertext [5], and CSCW. VTML is a general versioning language allowing for a large number of different applications in all these fields, and particularly in the joint editing of hypertext documents such as those available on WWW.

Naturally, most authors are not going to give away disk space so that others can revise their work, but with VTML it is possible, in principle, to enable universal write access on the Web. With VTML's ability to store changes externally to a document, someone with access to the Web

can publish *correction* or *update* documents that create a new version of another author's work stored separately. Access control for derived works becomes a matter of who has access to the relatively small server resources needed to make changes available. The author and the author's server do retain an imprimatur to mark revisions as "official." Such free access raises two fundamental requirements: consistency and accountability.

Consistency is a problem since the meaning of a link depends on the state of the document to which it refers. When documents are edited or revised, locations change, potentially destroying a record of what text was linked. Even if the link is translated to the corresponding part of the new document, the meaning may have changed significantly enough to make the original link and comment meaningless or incorrect. The use of symbolic identifiers avoids the problem of shifting text locations, but is, practically, only available to an author, since the original document must be changed to create the link destinations.

Accountability addresses who is responsible for a document, and while always important is even more critical in the case of documents with multiple authors or successive versions. A reader needs to know who has authored a document, whether the document was modified, and, if so, by whom.

In a versioned context, both consistency and accountability can be managed much more easily. The most important characteristic of versions is that they are immutable: rather than overwriting old data as simple file systems do, new versions are simply added to the repository, superseding, but not replacing their previous versions. This guarantees that links to old versions are always accessible, and that they are always in context (temporally as well as spatially). Since links frequently remain relevant in later versions of a document, it is also desirable that data locations are tracked through successive versions of a document, so that current location of externally-stored links can be determined.

Accountability is enhanced because each server is responsible for the versions or updates it stores, and can retain any author or group identification information desired. VTML provides specific ways to record this information so that every change made to a document can be tracked to the person who made it.

Versioning also provides a solution to the problem of addressability, identified by Engelbart. Because one needs to be able to refer to any point in a document from outside that document, there must be a way to deal with change, or at least mitigate its effects. Because versions are immutable, they are addressable across time, even as the document they relate to evolves. Additionally, any convenient structural addressing scheme can be used to reference within a versioned document, whether the scheme is a character offset in a file or a path specification through a structured tree. All methods are safe to use, as the navigational procedure for *that version* is fixed forever. This concept is the key that allows document information to be stored outside the document itself, allowing you to externally create and manage resources such as external modifications, annotations, external links (like HyTime's ilink[4], chunk inclusions, private links, and documents of links (e.g., paths and guided tours). These facilities incur no update cost: no explicit update of external references is

required when changing the referenced document, since the external references are all grounded by the persistent addressing schema provided by the versioning system.

Bear in mind that this solution handles the problem of references to document-internal objects. Fully persistent references depend on a location-independent naming scheme. VTML does not address this latter problem, though it is compatible with, and indeed, depends on, such a scheme. For the World Wide Web, the URN (Universal Resource Name) protocols under development within the IETF will provide such an infrastructure.

VTML associates every editing operation on the document with a specific version and each version with its author and the date on which it was created. The division of labor between client and server is simple. Document creation and editing happens *locally* (users work on their own computers), *asynchronously* (there is no requirement for immediate notification of the users' actions), and *in parallel* (all users can work on the same document independently, creating their own separate revised versions). These features make both simultaneous (as in GINA [1]) and non-simultaneous collaborations possible. The delta-based nature of VTML also helps keep storage size reasonable, as constant data is generally not duplicated between versions. The deltas recorded are, however, expected to reflect the actual editing operations performed by users, rather than solving the expensive problem of the minimum space to store differences between versions. We believe the changes stored should reflect what actions were actually performed on the document, in order to be truly meaningful to users of the system.

VTML data is stored in markup tags alongside the affected data, or externally in separate documents. The simplest VTML implementation is as a preprocessor that interprets VTML tags, producing a stream of characters for some other processor or protocol. For instance, to display a requested version, the document and its external resources can be read and parsed, and the content of the requested version created on the fly. VTML can store versioning information on anything represented as a linear document, but is particularly suited for distributed hypertext documents such as those created by collaboration on the WWW. VTML makes it possible to display selected versions (both subsequent and alternative ones), compare them, and merge them.

The purpose of this paper is to describe the uses of a versioning system in a cooperative environment for joint editing of written texts—particularly HTML and SGML documents. In the next section, a number of issues regarding collaboration in a versioned environment are described, and in the section after, the versioning language VTML is introduced, with a brief description of its syntax and features and a discussion of version numbers and VTML applications.

Issues in Versioning for Collaboration

Version management has a number of effects on collaborative editing and linking of documents. We are concentrating on asynchronous collaboration, that occurs over a long-enough time (days to years) that collaborators will need to work in isolation as well as cooperatively. In particular, we assume that the machines being used by collaborators cannot count on constant availability of a link to other collaborators' machines. This *parallel asynchronous collaboration* leaves the greatest freedom of interaction to the collaborating team.

We also consider and define our view of the fundamental nature of a versioning system. Versioning systems, besides providing useful tools for the management of the complex and dynamic evolution of documents, also gracefully allow asynchronous parallel collaboration, thus becoming a fundamental tool for joint editing.

But, even more importantly, versioning creates a persistent addressing scheme on versioned documents, which is fundamental for sophisticated uses of references. We will examine the ways in which these immutable addresses can be fully exploited in the context of a hypertext system like the WWW.

Parallel Asynchronous Collaboration

A number of collaboration models are possible, for group and distributed editing:

- *Synchronous collaboration* on a document requires simultaneous interaction of all interested parties. There are situations where the document serves as a communicative prop for meeting support, even though the end result might have some value after the end of the editing session. From the point of view of geographically separated authors working on a document, there are several problems with synchronous interfaces. For example, some problems with synchronous collaboration are the need for object locking, bandwidth to provide awareness of other users' actions, possible maximum limits on the allowable number of collaborating partners, and the cognitive load of tracking multiple insertion points and action focuses. If synchronous communication is not a primary need, the only advantage of synchronous editing is the provision of a single, consistent state of the document at the end of the editing session.

- *Serialized asynchronous collaboration* accords write access to only one author at a time, thus locking the document to other authors until the first one is finished. This policy overcomes most of the problems that arise in synchronous collaboration, and still has the advantage of having one consistent state of the document after each editing session. However, it prevents simultaneous, independent editing of the same document, and subjects document availability to unpredictable delays from network partitions, system crashes and the coffee breaks of the author who has write access. Furthermore, it does not allow offline editing, since it strongly invites the author with the write token to return it immediately after he/she has finished the editing session, and does not allow, for instance, modifying a document while keeping the token for a whole weekend.

- *Parallel asynchronous collaboration*, on the other hand, allows all authors to modify the document independently and in parallel, creating several independent and simultaneous states of the document (called *variants*), which may need to be merged into one final state. By removing or postponing the convergence of the document to a single state, it overcomes most of the practical obstacles to the editing process imposed by other collaboration schemes.

Versioning Systems

A *versioning system* is a software module that maintains identity relationships between different instances of a single data object. Each instance is a *version* of the object, and is connected to the other versions in a possibly complex structure of ancestors, descendants, and siblings. Documents are thus shaped as a sequence, or a tree, or a directed acyclic graph of versions, so that the content of any desired version is determined by the operations performed on the sequence of nodes connecting it to the root of the derivation.

A versioning system allows parallel asynchronous collaboration, since it facilitates the display of differences between several subsequent versions of a document (*time-based versioning*), or the tracking of modifications between several different variants of the same version (*author-based versioning*). Furthermore, by allowing automatic merging, a versioning system makes it possible to build a single final state of the document as the result of several parallel contributions, making the collaboration converge to a single state as it would with the other kinds of collaboration.

Since version editing never impacts other users' activities, the check-in operation of a private version can happen at any time after several versions have been produced. Thus, it is possible for a user to download a working draft locally, work on it several times, produce several successive versions, and then send the final one or the whole set of them back to a server where the official copy of the document is stored. Furthermore, *emergent collaborations* become possible. Any user having read access to a document can create a modified version of it and submit it to the original authors, who may decide to put it in the set of official versions. Becoming part of the group of authors of a document is thus possible at any time, even for someone unknown to the author.

A versioning system allows distribution of a team over a large-scale network without inherent scale problems in the number of authors, available documents, or involved servers. The system can avoid many standard techniques such as locking and replication of objects or synchronization and serialization of operations. It would pose minimal constraints on the distributed system in terms of network load, maximum allowable number of collaborating partners, client-server interaction patterns, and other factors.

Reliable Persistent Addresses

Another important advantage for hypertext versioning systems is the management of the persistent relationships of a versioned object. This feature is particularly important for hypertext: links are the explicit mark of an existing relationship between two given data objects. When either of the two objects is modified, the relationship needs to change as well. HTML has both ends of the link stored along with the data to which they refer (the <A HREF> and <A NAME> tags), so that the update of the links is automatically performed when the documents are changed.

However, requiring internal storage of this kind of relationship has several drawbacks: basically, one must have write permission on a document to insert new relationships. Thus, it is impossible for us to add an internal HTML link, a comment, or new content to a document, unless we own it.

Even if a browser allows us to add new data to a document by storing it locally (i.e., externally to the document), there still would be a key consistency problem: if the original copy of the document is changed, the references stored locally are no longer valid, because the positions to which they refer have moved.

VTML offers a solution based on a simple consideration on versions: the addresses of the chunks of every version of a document are unique, global, stable, and independent of the addresses of chunks inserted in alternative versions. Furthermore, they may be derived from the addresses of previous versions, by recording successive edits performed in the meantime (such as insertions, deletions, and modifications), or, when this is not possible, through a sufficiently effective *diff* mechanism on the two versions [10].

This means that, by storing the successive operations that were done on ·the document, we are able to build persistent addresses of chunks in any version we are interested in. Furthermore, operations that do not belong to the chain of versions we are interested in may be stored as well: as long as it is possible to determine that they are irrelevant to the desired versions, they and their associated data can be completely ignored.

Being able to compute the position of any chunk in any version of a document means that references need not be modified when the document is changed and a new version is created. Instead, the current values can be computed when they are needed. References can be stored externally and independently of the document: it is possible to make local references to remote documents or to readable documents on which we have no write permission.

In hypertext, external references allow point-to-point (or span-to-span) links to be stored separately from the document to which they refer. Point-to-point links are extremely useful in sev-

eral situations where the length of the document cannot be decided arbitrarily (for instance, when using electronic instances of long linear texts such as traditional books).

External links are also ideal for implementing private links: users will be able to create personal point-to-point links on public documents, and store them on their computers. Links are always consistent, do not use public disk space, and do not clog public documents. We believe that all other solutions for private links have greater drawbacks than external links on versioned documents.

Finally, external references provide the basis for a truly useful inclusion facility: users are not limited to including whole documents, but can specify parts of them, being confident that the correct part will be retrieved again no matter what has happened to the document since the inclusion was specified. This form of inclusion is more like copy and paste, where the source of the data is still available, the source can be displayed, the data is not actually duplicated, and the data can be requested to modify and update according to what has happened in the source document in the meantime. The form of inclusion provided by versioning subsumes the functions of intelligent copy & paste and hot and warm links.

VTML

VTML is a markup language designed to attach version information to the chunks of a document. Because every chunk is the result of a modification operation performed to one version, VTML tags identify the modifications themselves.

VTML information is supposed to be read by a parser before the visualization of the document. The parser will filter the content of the tags depending on the version. VTML data is printable, human-readable, and easily recognizable. In particular, VTML tags are put into SGML comments, so that they can be ignored by unaware tools.

VTML stores information on two editing operations: INSertions and DELetions. Support for other operations (particularly MOVe and SUBstitute) is possible and could be easily added to the grammar and the current implementation when needed.

Description of VTML

VTML encloses all tags with the strings `<!--{` and `}-->`. `<!--` and `-->` enclose SGML comments, and are ignored by HTML browsers and SGML tools. They make it possible to store versioning information and yet have it ignored by unaware tools.

VTML documents

```
<!--{VTML    attributes }-->
VTML document    <!--{/VTML}-->
```

A VTML document is contained within a VTML tag. Many different documents can be contained in a single file, each enclosed in a VTML tag. The attributes of this tag define general characteristics of the document:

- NAME

  A string containing the name of the document. This string can be its URL, or any other identifying string. It is used to select which, of many submitted documents, is the one to be displayed. With external modifications, it is used to identify the document to which the modifications need to be applied. **Required**

- GROUP

  A comma-separated list of names of the authors of all the versions of a document. A format has yet to be defined for this field.

- NUMBERING

  The type of version numbering used in the document. The possible values are "LSHAPED" (default), "OUTLINE," and "REVERSE." There are several ways to number versions, as specified later.

- CVERS

  The version number of the current version. This is the version that is automatically displayed if no version number is selected by the user. It should be automatically updated whenever new versions are checked in. **Required**

VTML defines four kinds of data tags: internal modifications, external modifications, attribute lists, and merge instructions.

Internal modifications

```
<!--{INS   attributes }--> text   <!--{/
INS}-->,  <!--{DEL    attributes }-->
text   <!--{/DEL}-->
```

INS and DEL tags are stored within the document to which they refer, and attach version information to the text contained within the tag.

Inserting data means adding new data at a given position of the document. The new data is added at the point of insertion and is a successor of the version that inserted its immediate context. Deleted data is simply located and labeled. No modifications are possible to deleted data in any version that is a descendent of that version. Any alternate versions whose deletions overlap with each other are required to break up the deleted ranges to create a properly nested tree of insertions and deletions. A picture of such a tree is shown in Figure 1. Each consistent selection of tags creates a complete document when displayed.

Deleted chunks are not removed from the document, but are flagged as deleted and ignored during display. Thus, the internal tags of a VTML document typically contain all the data necessary to compute the content of any version of the document, and not merely the ones making up the most recent one.

Since persistent addresses of independent variants are independent, one can store side by side information about incompatible versions regardless of their order. It is thus possible to maintain

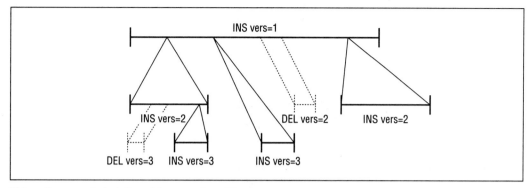

Figure 1:   A depiction of the tree of modification tags

a complete set of tags of all existing versions of a document, even when they belong to separate branches of the version tree.

The attributes are:

- ATTR
  The numeric identifier of an attribute list containing attributes for this tag. Attribute lists are used to store attributes common to several tags. An attribute explicitly recorded on a tag takes precedence over any value specified for it in a separate attribute list.

- AUTHOR
  The name of the author of the modification. The format is as yet undefined (any string can do), but in principle it should be shaped according to a given grammar and be relevant to the names contained in the GROUP attribute of the whole VTML document. **Required**

- VERSION
  The version number of the version in which the modification was performed. During editing, it should be the value "CURRENT." The check-in operation substitutes all CUR-RENT values with the correct version number, determined at check-in. The value needs to be consistent with the version numbering selected in the NUMBERING attribute. **Required**

- DATE
  The date and time in which the version was checked in. During editing, it should be the value "NOW." The check-in operation substitutes all NOW values with the correct date and time of check in. **Required**

- STATUS
  A value specifying the relative importance of the modification. The possible values are, orderly: "MANDATORY," "LIKELY" (default), "SUGGESTED," and "HINTED." They can be used to implement role-based collaborative software, or as a hint for deciding which of several incompatible variants to choose during a merge.

- COMMENT
  A quoted free text string containing a comment on the modification.

Merge tags

```
<!--{MERGE   attributes }-->
```

Merging is the act of creating a new version containing the modifications performed in several parallel variants of the same document. Merging is intended to make different variants of the same document converge to a single new version.

Merging is performed by approving or refusing each single modification performed in the affected variants. A whole subtree can be made

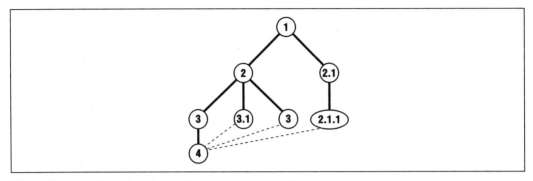

Figure 2:   A tree of versions with a branch converging to one node

to converge to a single version: there is no limit to the number of different versions involved. The only requirement is that all versions involved need to be stored as internal tags; that is, they must be physically present within the VTML document (see the discussion of external tags).

Merge tags are used to bypass the effects of an operation performed in a version that has been merged.

In VTML, merging does not disrupt the shape of the tree. Rather, one of the variants is selected as the main ancestor of the merge version, and the others share with it a special merge relationship. This enables VTML to use and exploit tree numbering for versions. In Figure 2, 4 is the version number of the merge session of versions 3, 3.1, 3. 2, and 2.1.1. According to the schema, however, the merge session is a direct descendant of version 3 and has a different relationship with the other versions.

According to the VTML versioning model, all modifications performed in any direct ancestor of a version are automatically accepted in the current version, while all modifications belonging to versions outside of the chain of direct ancestors are ignored. The MERGE tag overrides this rule:

- All data that has been inserted in a version of a different chain and that needs to be included in the merged version is enclosed in a MERGE tag.

- All data that has been deleted in a version of the same chain and that needs to be included in the merged version is also enclosed in a MERGE tag.

Thus, in the example depicted in Figure 2, all data that are present in version 3 are included; all data that are deleted in version 3 are ignored unless they have been enclosed in a MERGE tag; and all data that are present in version 3.1, 3.2, or 2.1.1 are ignored unless they have been enclosed in a MERGE tag.

External modifications

```
<!--{EXTINS  attributes }--> text  <!-
-{/EXTINS}-->        ,        <!--{EXTDEL
attributes }-->
```

EXTINS and EXTDEL tags refer to modifications that are stored outside the document to which they refer.

The purpose of EXTINS and EXTDEL, on the other hand, is to represent operations affecting another document. They are useful when parsing a base document that needs to be displayed, and several other documents containing externally-stored modifications to the base document. Our current implementation requires that the external modifications be parsed before the data to which they refer.

Versions can be freely externalized or internalized as needed. It is possible at any moment to

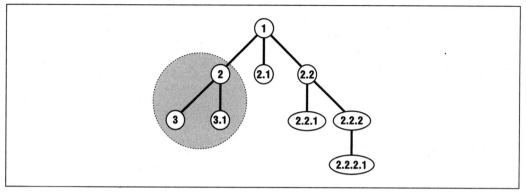

Figure 3: A tree of versions with a branch of nodes selected out

externalize some internal modifications tags, and to insert as internal tags the external modifications of one or more versions. There are only two constraints on the relationship between internal and external tags:

- If a version is external, all versions deriving from it need to be external as well. For instance, in Figure 3, if version 2 is external, then versions 3 and 3.1 need to be external, too, while versions 2.1, 2.2, and the others can be either internal or external as desired.

- All versions taking part in a merge session need to be internal. Merge tags identify, among several conflicting modifications, which one belongs to the merge version. Thus all tags of the versions being merged must be internal to the document.

The attributes for external modifications are the same as those for internal modifications, plus some others that are specific for external information:

- SRC
  The name of the source document, i.e., the one to which the modification should be applied. When displaying the document, this value is checked against the value of the NAME attribute of the document to be displayed. **Required**

- SRCVERS
  The version number of the document to which the modification should be applied. The pair SRC, SRCVERS identifies the context on which the modification occurred. **Required**

- TGT
  The name of the target document; i.e., the one that is created when performing the external modification. If absent, it is considered to be equal to the value of the SRC tag.

- TGTVERS
  The version number that will be created when applying the modification to the source document and source version. It needs to be consistent with the source version number (i.e., it needs to be a first-level descendant). **Required**

- POS
  An integer specifying the position of the source version where the modification needs to be applied. It relies on the consistent addressing mechanism enabled by VTML versioning. **Required**

- LENGTH
  An integer specifying the length of the string that needs to be deleted. It is only significant within an EXTDEL tag. **Required in EXTDEL tags**, ignored in EXTINS.

One should note that insertions and deletions are particular cases of a more general operation: substitution. Substitution needs three parameters: the starting position (the POS attribute), the length of the string to be replaced (the LENGTH attribute), and the string that will replace the original string (the content of the tag). Insertion is the same as substituting the inserted text for a null string at a certain position, while deleting means replacing a string starting in position POS and LENGTH characters long with the null string.

Attribute list

```
<!--{ATTR ID=  n   attributes }-->
```

This tag introduces a list of attributes that are shared by many different tags in the document. Usually all modifications of a version will share author, date, and version number; and all external modifications also will share source version and document, and target version and document.

An attribute list thus associates a list of attributes with a numeric identifier that can be referred to within the other tags. The attributes contained in the referenced attribute list are applied to the tag content as if they were put within the tag itself.

Thus, for instance, the following fragment:

```
<!--{INS vers=1 author="fabio"
    date="Jul 16, 1995"}--> This is <!--
    {DEL vers=CURRENT author="david"
    date=NOW}--> your<!--{/DEL}--> <!--
    {INS vers=CURRENT author="david"
    date=NOW}--> my <!--{/DEL}-->
    document.
```

could be written more compactly as:

```
<!--{ATTR ID=1 vers=1 author="fabio"
    date="Jul 16, 1995"}--> <!--{ATTR
    ID=2 vers=CURRENT author="david"
    date=NOW}--> <!--{INS ATT=1}-->
    This is <!--{DEL ATT=2}--> your<!--
    {/DEL}--> <!--{INS ATT=2}--> my <!--
    {/DEL}--> document.
```

An attribute list can appear anywhere in the VTML document, provided that it appears before any reference to it has been made. Only one attribute list can be referenced within a VTML tag. ATTR attributes are ignored: an attribute list cannot refer recursively to another attribute list. Attribute lists can contain any of the aforementioned attributes, in any order. The only required attribute is:

- ID
  The identifier of the attribute list. A unique number within the VTML document.

How VTML Works

In this section we will briefly examine the basic algorithm employed by the VTML parser.

Determining the content of a given version means examining each tag and deciding whether it still exists or if it exists already in the selected version. During parsing, a stack of versions is created. Whenever a new tag is encountered, it is pushed onto the stack and the text content is examined.

The function `doPrint()` controls the display of a text:

```
doPrint(content)
char *content ;
/* SIMPLIFIED */
{
 if ((type == INS) || (type == MERGE))
  if (in_chain(version,verstbd))
   printf("%s",content) ;
 else
  if ((!in_chain(version,verstbd)) &&
   ( in_chain(lastins,verstbd)))
    printf("%s",content) ;
}
```

The type of the tag is examined. If the type is INS or MERGE, then it is necessary to check whether the version of the tag is an ancestor of the version that is to be displayed (verstbd). If so, the string is displayed. On the other hand, if the type is DEL, then we should check that the version of the tag is not an ancestor (and thus also deleted in this version), and that the version in which the text was inserted is an ancestor of the version to be displayed. If so, the text is displayed. The big simplification in the code above is the elimination of the recursive calls required to handle any nested tags that might be present in `content`.

Determining whether a version is an ancestor of the version to be displayed can be done using the version number associated with the text.

Version Numbering

The numbering of versions is very important for VTML because all computations on tag content depend on the version number associated with it. We have sought a schema for version numbering that is printable, easy to understand, and easy to compute.

Versions of a document rigidly adhere to a tree structure. Even merging, as we implement it, does not disrupt the tree structure. Thus, version numbering will be a kind of tree nodes numbering. Easy computation implies that the chosen numbering schema must allow simple and fast algorithms to determine basic facts about nodes, such as who is the direct ancestor, who is the n-th sibling, etc.

We have distinguished three such numbering schema, which we call *outline numbering, reverse outline numbering*, and *L-shaped numbering:*

- *Outline numbering.* 1 is the number of the root. If x is the number of a node, the first son will have number x.1. The n-th brother of x.1 will have number x.n. This means that any new level of the tree will add a new item to the dotted sequence of numbers, while any new item at the same level will modify the last item of the sequence.

- *Reverse outline numbering.* 1 is the number of the root. If x is the number of a node, the first son will have number x+1. The first brother of x+1 will have number (x+1).1. Any further brother will add a new ".1" to the sequence. This means that any new level of the tree will grow the last item of the dotted sequence of numbers, while any new

item at the same level will add a new item to the sequence.

- *L-shaped numbering.* 1 is the number of the root. The number is obtained by counting the sequence of downward steps and of rightward steps (L-shaped paths) necessary to get from the root to the selected node. Each pair of numbers is an L-shaped path. L-shaped numbering, it can be proved, is shorter than both previous methods for sufficiently broad or deep trees, though in some unlikeiy special cases it can actually produce longer version numbesr. L-shaped numbering is the default value for version numbering.

These systems are all very similar, building strings of numbers separated by dots. VTML, with its declaration of versioning schemes, can work with any kind of versioning schema (the current implementation accepts only L-shaped), provided that the numbering of version is consistent.

VTML Usage

VTML is not an end-user tool. In our opinion, it should be hidden to the user and only examined by software modules. We envision two software modules using it:

- *A WWW authoring environment.* A WWW browser with editing capabilities will make heavy use of VTML. VTML will help create a friendly editing environment, with versioning capabilities, collaboration support, external markup for private annotations, and links on remote documents. The VTML parser will be called when displaying selected versions of the document, and even (with a small modification in the `doPrint()` function) to display color coded comparisons of different versions and variants. Furthermore, VTML tags shall be inserted by the editor routines devoted to handle insertions and deletions of data.

- *A server script.* In order to exploit VTML completely, one needs to interface VTML-aware tools with the rest of the Web. Particularly, VTML documents must be capable of being passed transparently to HTML browsers. The optimal solution is to define VTML as a new content type and use HTTP content-type negotiation.

When receiving a GET request from an unaware browser for the document *http://my.host/dir/file.vtml*, the parser will generate a single version (the current version as determined by the CVERS attribute). To ask for a specific version, an unaware browser will specify the version number as a further path specification, such as in *http://my.host/dir/file.vtml/3.1.1*. The VTML script will then create and deliver the correct requested version.

The VTML parser will also handle PUT requests for new documents, or for new versions of existing ones. It will receive either external modifications or complete VTML documents, and store them as needed. Depending on the server, it can internalize external modifications, or merge two complete submissions to form a single document containing two parallel variants.

Currently, a minimal parser of the complete VTML language is available. It can be tried out at the address *http://radames.cs.unibo.it:8088/fabio/vtml.html*. The server accepts any valid VTML file and generates the requested version. Error messages and value checking are minimal to non-existent (for instance, any string is accepted in the DATE attribute).

Previous Work

This paper builds on a long, if narrow, tradition of attention to versioning issues in hypertext systems. Delisle [3] created the notion of "contexts." which nest in the same way that VTML tags do, and for similar reasons. Greif and Sarin [7] identified the problems with collaborating over real networks, and thus provided a part of the motivation for this work. Prakash and Knister [13], in the context of synchronous editing, reported interesting work on reconciliation of histories. We avoid some of the complication of their algorithms by not ordering any operations in time unless the version tree forces us to.

Osterbye [11] has analyzed user issues in versioning and hypertext. Our work is at the level of a substrate for the sorts of facilities and issues he discusses. Haake [8] has explored implementation and user-interface issues in several papers. Some notion of the range of interest in the field can be found in the proceedings of the Workshop on Versioning Systems [5].

The prior work on Palimpsest [6] has formed a background to this work. Palimpsest provides a coherent semantics for an even more flexible versioning scheme, suitable for implementing a variety of data structures. The VTML proposal is simpler, easier to understand, and tailored to the Web's existing technology, in keeping with the WWW philosophy of creating easy to implement and understand methods and protocols. It also takes advantage of the fact that all structural and linking information currently stored in the web is in the form of byte streams containing HTML tags, so it need not structurally represent documents to version them effectively.

Conclusion

We have presented a description of how version management can help solve some thorny collaboration issues in distributed editing environments, and presented a language, VTML for the recording and transmission of editing histories to support such versioning. The design and implementation of the language have been specified in some detail.

This kind of version description is a start at defining a new collaboration protocol that can work with the sort of distributed hypertext embodied by the WWW. Its status as an overlay on other data (particularly SGML data), means that it could fit on top of a variety of applications. One problem that is not well addressed by HTTP at the moment is the issue of transformations and encapsulated data formats. A proper solution to this problem would really be the idea solution to the problem of integrating VTML into the Web.

We intend to continue the implementation work we have started with a custom client that will create and use VTML files to track its activities. Hopefully these basic ideas will serve as a foundation for further development to advance us to the day when the WWW is as much of a writing and collaboration medium as it is a reading and publication one today.

The authors would like to thank Jerry Fowler of Rice University for a helpful reading of a draft of this paper.

Portions of this work were completed under the auspices of the open LTR project #20179 "Pagespace." ∎

References

1. Berlage, T. and Genau, A. "A framework for shared applications with replicated architecture. In *Proceedings of the Conference on User Interface Systems and Technology.* November 1993.

2. Coulouris, G. F. and J. Dollimore, *Distributed Systems: Concepts and Design.* Addison-Wesley. 1988.

3. Delisle, N. M. and M. D. Schwartz. "Contexts — A Partitioning Concept for Hypertext" *TOIS.* 5(3): 168-186, 1987.

4. DeRose, Steven J. and David G. Durand, *Making Hypermedia Work: A User's Guide to HyTime.* Kluwer Academic. 1994.

5. Durand, D. G., A. Haake, D. Hicks and F. Vitali, *Proceedings of the Workshop on Versioning in Hypertext systems.* Held at the European Conference on Hypertext. 1994. Available at *http://cs-www.bu.edu/students/grads/dgd/workshop/Home.html*

6. Durand, David G., "Palimpsest, a Data Model for Revision Control." *Proceedings of the CSCW '94 Workshop on Collaborative Hypermedia Systems,* Chapel Hill, North Carolina, USA. GMD Studien Nr. 239. Gesellschaft für Mathematik und Datenverarbeitung MBH 1994. Available via anonymous FTP at *ftp.darmstadt.gmd.de* within the file */pub/wibas/CSCW94/workshop-proc.ps.Z*

7. Greif, I. and S. Sarin, "Data sharing in group work" ACM *Transactions on Office Information Systems.* 5(2): 187-211, 1987.

8. "Under CoVer: The Implementation of a Contextual Version Server for Hypertext Applications" *Proceedings of the ACM Conference on Hypertext,* Edinburgh, 1994.

9. C. Maioli, S. Sola, F. Vitali, "Versioning for Distributed Hypertext Systems," *Proceedings of the Hypermedia '94 Conference,* Pretoria, South Africa, March 1994. Available via anonymous FTP at *ftp.cs.unibo.it* as */pub/UBLCS/Versioning.ps.gz*

10. Neuwirth, C. M., R. Chandhok, D. S. Kaufer, P. Erion, J. Morris and D. Miller, "Flexible Diff-ing in a Collaborative Writing System" *CSCW '92: Proceedings of the ACM Conference on Computer Supported Cooperative Work.* 51-58, 1992.

11. Osterbye, K, "Structural and Cognitive Problems in Providing Version Control for Hypertext" in *Proceedings of the ACM Conference on Hypertext,* Milano, Italy, 1992.

12. Tichy, W. F. "RCS—A System for Version Control" *Software—Practice and Experience.* 15(7): 637-654, 1985.

13. Prakash, A. and M. J. Knister. "Undoing Actions in Collaborative Work" *CSCW '92: Proceedings of the ACM Conference on Computer Supported Cooperative Work.* 273-280, 1992.

About the Authors

Fabio Vitali

University of Bologna, Italy

Fabio Vitali holds a doctorate in Computers and Law from the University of Bologna, and is currently doing research under a Post-Doctoral grant at the Department of Mathematics of the same University. He was the main architect of the RHYTHM hypertext system, and is currently working on the PageSpace project for applying coordination languages to the World Wide Web, and the TextTiles project for adding versioning capabilities (and hence collaboration and external anchoring) to the World Wide Web. Among his interests are versioning systems, externalization of data attributes, and distributed, collaborative hypertext systems.

David G. Durand

[*http://cs-www.bu.edu:80/students/grads/dgd/*]

Computer Science Department, Boston University

David Durand is a doctoral candidate at Boston University, working on version control and collaborative editing in hypertext systems. His thesis is on the Palimpsest model for change-oriented version control of data structures. He served on the TEI committees on Metalanguage and Syntax and Committee on Hypertext. He is also a Senior Analyst at *Dynamic Diagrams* working on automated analysis of Web documents for visualization and navigation, and the integration of the Web with SGML-based publication processes.

GROUP ASYNCHRONOUS BROWSING ON THE WORLD WIDE WEB

Kent Wittenburg, Duco Das, Will Hill, Larry Stead

Abstract

The goal of our Group Asynchronous Browsing (GAB) research is to provide tools for people to leverage the information hunting and gathering activities of other people or groups of people on the World Wide Web. To date we have focused on taking advantage of the personal subject indices that are being constructed today with bookmarks or hotlists of widely available browsers. We have also concentrated on monitoring URLs that may themselves serve as living resources on particular subject areas. In support of the former, we have created a server that collects and merges bookmark/hotlist files of participating users. The server can serve subsets of these merged bookmark files to either standard HTML client browsers or to a client built with the multiscale visualization tool Pad++. For the latter, we have built a tool called WebWatch that can monitor URLs of interest and alert users when significant updates appear.
Keywords: *Information retrieval, resource discovery, tools and browsers, information visualization, community-based navigation*

Introduction

Multitudes of intelligent agents are creating browsable information structures on today's World Wide Web. These intelligent agents are not semi-autonomous computer processes, but rather, people. One of the most effective ways to find information is to find the right person or people who are likely to know about what we are looking for and ask them. In fact, word of mouth and email may currently be the most effective resource discovery tools on today's World Wide Web. The goal of Bellcore's research in Group Asynchronous Browsing (GAB) is to provide tools for better utilization of people's knowledge of the World Wide Web by leveraging the efforts that individuals and groups are already putting forth as they browse. Today's World Wide Web browsers all have some sort of bookmark or hotlist facility with which users can take note of resources that are relevant to their interests and to which they expect to return. Some, such as Netscape's bookmark facility, offer the ability to structure relevant URLs into subject hierarchies. Furthermore, many individuals, groups, and institutions are making significant

efforts in providing hand-built subject-oriented guides to the World Wide Web in the form of HTML files directly. For examples, see the Clearinghouse for Subject-Oriented Internet Resource Guides [2] or Yahoo [18]. These subject-oriented guides range from general purpose, for instance, Yahoo [18], to quite specific, for instance, a resource on visual languages and visual programming [16]. Among the issues we see with the utilization of such subject guides are (1) how to find them (the URLs themselves as well as the relevant subject heading(s) within the more general purpose guides), (2) how to combine information from different guides for effective and efficient browsing, and (3) how to keep abreast of changes to them in order to discover additional resources that the keepers of these guides might add. We tend to see the more formal general purpose guides and the more informal personal bookmark files as part and parcel of the same sort of activity.

Our main effort so far has revolved around the creation of a server that collects and merges personal bookmark files of participating users. Besides personal bookmark files, we have included one general purpose subject guide in our initial experiments as well, namely, Yahoo [18], whose role we will subsequently explain. Such a database combined with a World Wide Web server, which we call a Group Asynchronous Browsing (GAB) server, can then provide access to a merged subject tree structure in various ways. This collection of tools is intended to address the issue of how to utilize the browsing activities of others to discover resources, some of which themselves may be guides to further World Wide Web resources. Secondly, we have created a tool that can monitor resources of interest and alert users when significant updates appear. This tool, which we call WebWatch, serves the purpose of resource discovery by drawing users' attention to changes to a known document which itself may be a subject guide to other World Wide Web resources. These tools go part way towards meeting requirements for providing asynchronous, community-based browsing on the World Wide Web.

In the remainder of this paper we will first discuss a vision and the current status of our GAB server. Next, we will describe a client application we have created to visualize and browse over merged subject trees in the GAB database that is built on Pad++ [1, 13], a substrate for creating zoomable human computer interfaces. Then we will briefly discuss WebWatch and conclude with comments on limitations and future research.

The GAB Server

The obvious move for providing access to personal or general subject-oriented indices is to manually or automatically collect them into a database and then provide query or browse capabilities over this database. Yahoo, for instance, includes many entries that themselves are subject-oriented indices and one may search this index of indices. A few research projects have also investigated collecting personal hotlists [8] or history lists [10] into centralized servers. Following Furnas and Zacks [4], we have noted the potential benefits to resource discovery of a data structure called a multitree. For personal

bookmark files, which we have so far focused on, a multitree structure can be created in which resources that appear across different subject-oriented bookmark files are shared in an internal graph structure. Browsers over this merged subject tree structure can then provide "backlinks" from shared resources to any and all subject headings which include them. The essential point to note with respect to information discovery is that, starting from some particular resource, new resources that have a good chance of being similar to it may be discovered by navigating "up" to any of the subject headings that include this starting resource and then navigating "down" from those subject headings to other, potentially unknown, resources. Assuming that participating users will construct bookmark files of general utility, we hypothesize that multitree browsing over merged bookmark files might be a cost-effective method for resource discovery since it so thoroughly leverages human judgment, the best arbiter of information quality and relevance.

Figure 1 is an abstract example of such a merged subject multitree, where each subject tree is indicated with a different color and the categorized URLs are indicated as capital letters at the trees' leaves. Subject headings would be attached to each of the nonterminal nodes of the trees. This example only shares tree structure at the terminal nodes of the trees, which is consistent with the sharing of links that occur across personal bookmark or hotlist files, but it should be noted that multitrees can share nonterminal nodes as well.

One of our goals then is to explore World Wide Web services that might be based on such merged subject trees. Assuming that a server is involved, there are several issues that must be addressed. First, there is the data gathering problem, i.e., the server must acquire access to useful subject trees. To date, we have assumed that, with one exception, these are in the form of individual bookmark files that can be created with widely available browsers. For each service that a server then might offer, there is the issue of how to define a client request as well how to define a

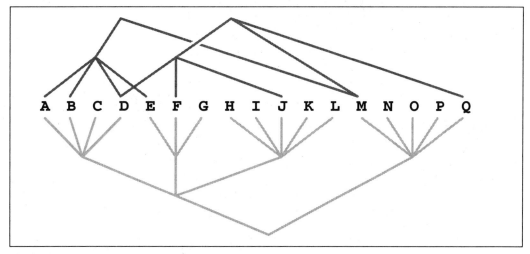

Figure 1:   A multitree composed of three different subject hierarchies

server response. We have considered both browsing and querying services that make use of structural relationships in the merged subject trees. Various user interfaces are of course possible, some of which are afforded by existing World Wide Web clients and some of which would require customized browsers.

To date our implementation has focused on the server response side for standard World Wide Web browsers as well as for a customized client. The data gathering problem we have finessed so far by experimenting only with World Wide Web users within our own organization whose personal bookmark files are accessible within our local file structure. However, note that this local scenario may well be useful for intra-organizational information sharing that is deliberately kept proprietary. For wider public access, a forms interface such as can be seen in Webhound [17] could be used for users to submit their bookmark files to a GAB server. We started with bookmark files associated with the widely available Netscape Navigator. Our choice of Netscape is not to be taken as an endorsement of this product, however. Any tool for hierarchical organization of World Wide Web resources would do. Specialized clients that incorporate

more sophisticated personal indexing facilities such as Paint [12] or Simon [8] would make our proposal easier to realize in one sense; however, choosing a commercial client that is in widespread use brings with it obvious advantages.

We have so far explored three services:

- In response to a request that specifies a subset of trees from the multitree database, generate an HTML document, usable by any standard World Wide Web client browser, that merges the specified trees and includes internal cross-referencing links for browsing.

- In response to a request as in (1), generate a script, useable by a Pad++ client that we have designed, that affords browsing over a zoomable treemaps visualization of the merged tree set.

- In reponse to a query-by-example in the form of one or more URLs, provide HTML text (that can be appended to any standard HTML document or offered as a dynamically generated page) that will provide links to resources in the GAB database that are related in a structural way to the one or more URLs submitted.

The first two services involve a "top-down" request on the client side that specifies which subject trees to include by simply choosing them from a list. Once this data is received on the client side, it may be browsed there. We envision that this sort of request, refined to include searches on other features of the participating user community and augmented to include the choice of specifying individual subject headings, might be useful for browsing over a relatively unconnected GAB subject tree. The hypothesis is that if one can choose a promising set of subject trees, perhaps by identifying a suitable group of people, it may be fruitful to simply browse over the merger of the trees looking for new resources. A possible indicator of quality of URLs in this scenario is the number of occurrences of a particular resource across the collected group. In other words, if a resource is indexed by many people, it may indicate that the resource is likely to be a better one compared to ones that are not so widely included.

Figure 2 shows a screen dump of an HTML document, being viewed through a commercial World Wide Web browser, that is the result of a query to the GAB server to include a set of participating users' bookmark files (along with Yahoo). The subject headings are indicated as paths from the root of the bookmark tree files. URLs that appear in other GAB subject trees are evidenced as "See Also" crosslinks that appear indented below the URLs in question. The user can then browse to potentially related URLs by clicking on a cross reference link that will jump to that portion of the document that includes other subject listings that also included that same URL. So, for example, note that the URL titled "The Mother-of-all BBS", categorized under Kent Wittenburg's bookmarks with the subject path "WWW Resources: Navigation" also appears under Will Hill's bookmarks under the category "Search Engines." A click on the latter link will jump to that category of Will Hill's, where related resources may then appear.

One of the weaknesses of this browsing method is that users can easily become disoriented about where they are in the information space—an intra-document instance of the well-known "lost in hyperspace" problem. Our informal observation is that this phenomenon invariably occurs when one makes an abrupt jump to another location in the document that is off screen initially. While there are various ways to address this navigation issue in the context of dynamic generation of sets of HTML documents, the Pad++ multitree browser, discussed in the next section, is motivated in part as a visually-oriented solution to this problem.

An alternative to the top-down query method for a GAB server is for the server itself to do the navigating and return just those resources which are presumed to be the best for the client's purposes. Here the client's request comes in the form of one or more URLs, and the GAB server responds with the "close relatives" of those URLs. This is a query-by-example scenario where the measure of relevance is defined structurally. Our starting point for the relevant relation over nodes in a multitree is the sibling relation, defined as follows:

> With respect to some node X and some multitree MT, the siblings of X in MT = { Z | Z is an immediate child of some immediate parent node of X in MT, and Z does not equal X}.

The siblings of some information resource are those resources that have been been placed in at least one common subject category as the original. A procedure for collecting siblings would make the navigation moves mentioned earlier: from a starting URL, move up the subject multitree to all subject headings that contain this URL; then move down and collect any new URLs that are contained within these subject headings. For example, in Figure 1, the siblings of A are {B, C, D, E}. The siblings of D are {A, B, C, E, F, J}. Augmentations to this basic procedure might, for instance, filter out any siblings already known to the client if the user's history list is accessible.

Figure 2: An HTML document generated by the GAB server representing a subject tree merger

A slightly more distant relation over nodes in a multitree is the cousin relation. It is essentially the transitive closure of the sibling relation, but we find it convenient to distinguish siblings from cousins and so define it as follows:

> With respect to some node X and some multitree MT, the cousins of X in MT = { Z | Z is a sibling of Y, Y is a sibling of X, and Z is not a sibling of X.} The cousins of an information resource are those resources that have at least one subject

category in common with a sibling of the original resource. For example, the cousins of A in the multitree of Figure 1 are {F, G, J}.

The cousins {F, J} are related through A's sibling D. The cousins {F, G} are related through A's sibling E.

An issue we encountered early on in our experiments was the problem of sparse connectivity in a merged subject-tree database. If the original subject trees share no common resources, it is difficult to leverage the collective subject trees with structural relations in the ways we have been describing. We conducted some informal experiments to determine how much sharing of URLs there was across actual user bookmark files in our organization. It turned out that the amount of sharing was surprisingly low. Even within our local computer graphics and interactive media group at Bellcore, a group who all use the World Wide Web regularly and who would presumably have common interests, we found a very low incidence of shared resources.

As a reponse to this problem, we came up with the idea of using the cousin relation in conjunction with one or more general purpose subject indices to provide the glue that connected a group of personal bookmark files. The general idea here is to increase connectivity across a relatively sparsely connected GAB database by taking advantage of the presumably larger coverage of one or more general purpose subject trees (which can be merged into a single multitree). The tree colored green in Figure 1 is meant to suggest the role of the general purpose subject multitree. It will tend to cover more of the World Wide Web than any relatively small collection of personal bookmark files, which are suggested by the red and blue trees. Thus, even though one may find no common linkages across the personal bookmark file collection directly, there is still a means of indirectly finding related resources by going through the green tree. Our initial experiments used Yahoo [18] in the role of general subject multitree.

Figure 3 is a screen dump of a page automatically generated by our GAB server in response to a query containing the URL whose title is "Bellcore Information and Sciences Technologies Home Page." There were siblings found in only one user's bookmarks, but there were a greater number of cousins from three of the participating users. The implication is that a subject category of Yahoo contained a link to the resource "Bellcore Information and Sciences Technologies Home Page" and that other resources that

appeared under this category were shared in the subject trees of the three other users. We include a link to the mediating Yahoo subject category as well, since users may be interested in jumping there directly for futher browsing.

Our hypothesis is that the more general "cousins" relation will afford more connectivity in a GAB server, and this hypothesis has been borne out by our initial observations. Ultimately, the right choice of which relation to use may have to be fine-tuned and could well differ across specific instances of GAB databases. Combining other evaluations of the usefulness of some potentially new resource with these purely structural relations is also possible, e.g., community-based recommendations [6, 17].

Visualization with a Pad++ Client

As we have noted earlier and has been remarked elsewhere [11, 3], there is a reason to suppose that effective visualizations of complex hypermedia structures may attenuate the "lost in hyperspace" syndrome. In our GAB work we have so far focused on visualizing the GAB database itself, which we suppose may be useful for resource discovery under conditions of sparse connectivity and perhaps for other tasks as well. Furnas and Zacks [4] describe several interfaces for browsing of multitrees, and these may indeed be of interest for GAB. Here we offer a new multitree browser that leverages the infinite zooming and navigational features of Pad++. It uses treemaps [7] as a starting point for the layout.

Pad++ [1, 13] and its forebears [14] provide a substrate for creating interactive graphics on an infinitely scalable surface with smooth zooming and panning. One hypothesis is that hierarchical relations can be naturally captured with scale: information that is deeper in the hierarchy can be represented as being smaller on the Pad++ surface. Treemaps [7], a method for visualization of hierarchical information based on spatial containment, seemed to us to be the most promising lay-

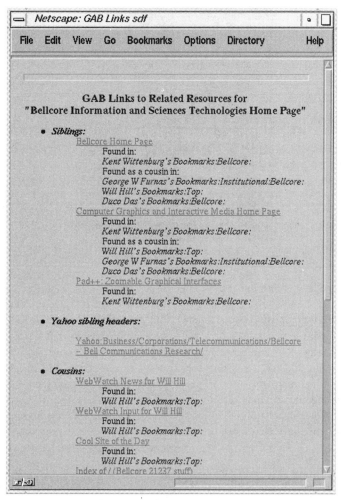

Figure 3: GAB server response for related resource query

out strategy for zoomable multitree data. Most other alternatives that occurred to us required some form of dynamic changes to object positions during user interactions. Smooth animation for arbitrary object movement or generalized warping was not yet well-supported in Pad++ at the time we did this research. Also, dynamically shifting layout brings with it a host of other issues involving cognitive continuity that we supposed might be handled by general panning and zooming features alone if reasonable static layouts could be found.

Figure 4 shows a screen capture of our Pad++ multitree browser together with a standard HTML client that may be controlled through Pad++. The Pad++ client is automatically invoked as a helper application from the file returned by the GAB server, which it tags with a Pad++ MIME type.

Each user subject tree in the Pad++ visualization is assigned a unique color hue. The coloring algorithm chooses points of equal distance from the continuum of hues proportional to the number of users. Color saturation is bound to hierarchical depth; it is reduced at each lower level of

Figure 4:   The Pad++ multitree browser as helper app

the tree. Both intermediate and terminal nodes of the multitree are represented as rectangles. Their names are displayed in the translucent status bar. A double click with the left mouse button will cause the system to smoothly zoom/pan to the rectangle of interest. In addition to system-controlled zooming and panning, the user is also able to control panning and zooming directly. As the user zooms in, nodes higher up in the hierarchy slowly dissolve while revealing more of their descendants.

Figure 5 is suggestive of the system behavior during a zoom in to a subject category of one of the users. The actual application simply narrows the frame as the view is smoothly zoomed towards its destination. If a user wants to look at the contents of a resource itself, she double-clicks on its name and a message to open that resource is conveyed to the standard World Wide Web browser.

Multitrees are of course not just trees, which treemaps are designed to support, and so a solution for adapting treemaps to the more general graph structure of multitrees was required for this visualization. For purposes of layout, we created a tree out of our original multitree by (1) adding a root node whose immediate children were the

root nodes of each of the subject trees in the GAB database and (2) for each shared node, adding an additional level in the tree consisting of cross references to the subject headings containing those shared nodes. This is a graphical rendition of a structure that is also evident in the HTML nested lists of Figure 2. The cross references are then color-coded to the subject trees which contain them. Besides the participating users subject trees, we also include cross-references into Yahoo, which are colored red.

Consider the visualization encoding exemplified in Figure 5. "Navigation" is a subject heading. It is assigned a rectangle colored by its host subject tree. This green rectangle contains several other green rectangles that represent the URLs categorized as navigation resources. Those URLs that appear elsewhere in the multitree structure under different subject categories enclose additional rectangles of different colors, one for each cross-referenced subject heading.

As for navigating, clicking on a cross-reference rectangle invokes a system-generated pan/zoom that smoothly zooms out until both the point of origin (i.e., the cross reference) as well as the destination are in the view and then zooms in on the destination, after which the shared node

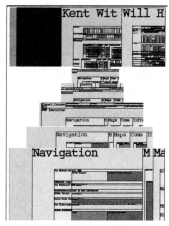

Figure 5:   Zooming in to see more detail in a subject tree

blinks. We believe such automatically computed pan/zoom trajectories [5] are a very significant feature of Pad++ navigation and uniquely characterize this browsing and visualization approach. The hypothesis is that one can overcome the "lost in hyperspace" feeling garnered from abrupt transitions in hyperspace by always getting an automatically generated bird's eye view as a transition when making large jumps from one part of the space to another. Note that this hypothesis is only sustainable if the user is in fact able to acquire some familiarity with the global layout— thus the importance of maintaining continuity through relatively static spatial positioning.

Our Pad++ client has other features as well. With a slider the user is able to rescale the treemap, which has the following sigificance. A value of 100% yields the classic no-offset treemap (where only terminal nodes are afforded real estate), whereas a value of, for example, 40% yields a layout where adjacent tree levels differ in size by orders of magnitude. Imagine being able to stretch and compress a tree arbitrarily as one is looking down from the top. As the tree stretches, the levels that are lower in the hierarchy get smaller and further away. This leaves more screen real estate that might be used to display information about the local levels one can see clearly. It also diminishes the load on the percep-

tual system by making the overall display less cluttered. There is a need for further research in exploring these layout options through "semantic zooming," a concept in the Pad community that signifies that the system might choose to display information differently depending on how much screen real estate is afforded a particular object.

Monitoring Through WebWatch

Requirements for group asynchronous browsing include not only the need to find and browse subject-oriented indices in a community of interest but also the need to stay abreast of changes to those indices. The task of keeping informed of new, relevant, and significant developments in their areas of responsibilities is becoming an important part of the job responsibilities of today's knowledge workers.

We developed WebWatch as a portable service to help users keep abreast of new developments in their favorite World Wide Web pages. WebWatch makes it easy to monitor any Web page in HTML format. On a daily basis, WebWatch alerts its users to new Web resources as they appear at monitored locations. WebWatch outputs an HTML formatted page which reports added and/ or deleted resources at any monitored location in the Web. For example, Figure 6 shows the result

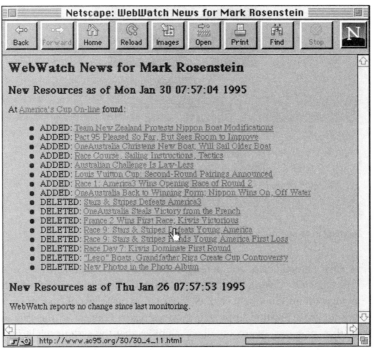

Figure 6:   An example page generated by WebWatch

of a WebWatch report for the resource "America's Cup On-line."

Reported are anchors that are "new for me here since the last time I checked." This type of service is most useful in a large, rapidly changing, and unpredictable information environment.

How does it work? Users of WebWatch use Xcut&paste to copy and paste in anchors into their WebWatch subscription page. This is an HTML page whose anchors point at resources to be monitored for the user. Entry of an anchor into a WebWatch subscription file activates the monitoring of the selected Web location. WebWatch fetches the last modified date (if available) of the resource and compares that date with its own page records. If the resource has been modifed more recently than WebWatch records, or if WebWatch has no record, WebWatch fetches the document to *diff* against the last copy it fetched.

Nightly, a chron file, which is an Emacs batch-mode program, wakes up WebWatch. WebWatch relies upon Emacs W3 functionality. It fetches and stores new copies of all monitored HTML World Wide Web resources. Old and new versions are *diff*d to identify additions and deletions. These are analyzed for anchors pointing at resources. New anchors added to monitored documents will contain URLs pointing at new resources. Deleted anchors will contain old URLs that no longer appear as resources in the monitored resource. Having collected these newly added resources and newly deleted resources, WebWatch generates an HTML page which encodes a tree whose leaves are added and deleted resources and whose upward paths are HTML heading levels from monitored resources. Only changes show up in each tree.

When is a new anchor really new? What constitutes a real change is a semantic question. Currently, WebWatch reports new links if the anchor in question has both a new reference location and name. If an anchor has only a new reference location and not a new label, we consider the change merely a house-keeping change. If an anchor has only a new label in the document but points to exactly the same reference location as last time, we consider the change only a cosmetic name change and do not report it as a new resource.

WebWatch appears to work well for the simple task for which it was designed. Monitoring locations for changes has been useful to the small group of current users. One user was able to purchase Van Halen tickets in a timely manner by monitoring the Van Halen concert schedule page and then ordering as soon as a nearby concert was announced. Two other users monitored news from the America's Cup races. It seems evident that there is a demand for some monitoring functionality on the World Wide Web, and we expect future browsers and/or servers to contain resource monitoring features that take into account personal interests, responsibilities, and history of interaction. As is discussed by LaLiberte and Braverman [9], there are still issues involving scalability that must be addressed when "what's new" services become commonplace on the World Wide Web.

Conclusion

We believe that our research on Group Asynchronous Browsing shows promise for attacking the resource discovery problem on the World Wide Web. As far as we know, this research brings a unique three-pronged approach to the problem: a GAB server for merged bookmarks and general subject indices, a Pad++ client for visualizing the GAB database, and a tool for monitoring resources of interest. Others have looked at pooling hotlists or annotations (e.g., [9, 15]), but we believe our approaches to browsing over merged subject trees involving the sibling and cousin relations to be novel. On the visualization side, Mukherjea and Foley [11] have also built a prototype that uses treemaps for visualizing Web structures. Our major contribution here

is to add zooming to treemaps that incorporates scaling options as well as navigation through crosslinking and automatic pan/zoom trajectories formulated in [5]. Immediate future work includes improving the client-side interface to the GAB server as well as fielding the GAB server more widely. We also expect to be doing some empirical experiments to test the validity of the visualization work, and there are many extensions that we would like to see including visualizations of web structures more generally.

Acknowledgments

This work has been supported by ARPA grant N66001-94-C-6039 under the ARPA Human Computer Interaction initiative. The Beyond Imitation Project, which has participation from University of New Mexico, New York University, and Bellcore is directed by Jim Hollan of the University of New Mexico. We are grateful for this support. The Pad++ team, Ben Bederson in particular, has been instrumental in this effort through the creation and support of the substrate for our visualization work. Thanks to Mark Rosenstein for his contributions to the GAB server and also to George Furnas for his many insightful criticisms and suggestions as well as for his inspiring research. Finally, thanks to David Filo and Jerry Yang for making a dump of the Yahoo database available for our research purposes. ∎

References

1. Benjamin B. Bederson and James D. Hollan, *Pad++: A Zooming Graphical Interface for Exploring Alternate Interface Physics*, Proceedings of ACM UIST '94 (Marina Del Rey, CA), ACM Press, 1994, pp. 17-26.

2. Clearinghouse for Subject-Oriented Internet Resource Guides, *http://www.lib.umich.edu/chhome.html*

3. Peter Doemel, *WebMap—A Graphical Hypertext Navigation Tool*, Second International conference on the World Wide Web (Chicago, IL), 1994, pp. 785-789, *http://www.ncsa.uiuc.edu/SDG/IT94/Proceedings/Searching/doemel/www-fall94.html*

4. George W. Furnas and Jeff Zacks, *Multitrees: Enriching and Reusing Hierarchical Structure*, Proceedings of CHI '94 Human Factors in Computing Systems (Boston, MA), ACM Press, 1994, pp. 330-336.

5. George W. Furnas and Benjamin B. Bederson, *Space-Scale Diagrams: Understanding Multiscale Interfaces*, Proceedings of CHI '95 Human Factors in Computing Systems (Denver, CO), ACM Press, 1995, pp. 234-241.

6. Will Hill, Larry Stead, Mark Rosenstein, and George Furnas, *Recommending and Evaluating Choices in a Virtual Community of Use*, Proceedings of CHI '95 Human Factors in Computing Systems (Denver, CO), ACM Press, 1995, pp. 194-201.

7. Brian Johnson and Ben Shneiderman, *Tree-maps: A Space-Filling Approach to the Visualization of Hierarchical Information Structures*, IEEE Visualization '91, 1991, pp. 284-291.

8. Mark J. Johnson, SIMON HOMEPAGE, *http://www.elec.qmw.ac.uk/simon/*

9. Daniel LaLiberte and Alan Braverman, *A Protocol for Scalable Group and Public Annotations*, Computer Networks and ISDN Systems 27: 911-919, 1995, *http://www.igd.fhg.de/www/www95/proceedings/papers/100/scalable-annotations.html*

10. Jong-Gyun Lim, *Using Coollists to Index HTML Documents in the Web*, Second International conference on the World Wide Web (Chicago, IL), 1994, pp. 831-838, *http://www.ncsa.uiuc.edu/SDG/IT94/Proceedings/Searching/lim/coollist.html*

11. Sougata Mukherjea and James D. Foley, *Visualizing the World-Wide Web with the Navigational View Builder*, Computer Networks and ISDN Systems 27:1075-1087, 1995, *http://www.igd.fhg.de/www/www95/proceedings/papers/44/mukh/mukh.html*

12. K.A. Oostendorp, W.F. Punch, and R.W. Wiggings, *A Tool for Individualizing the Web*, Second International conference on the World Wide Web (Chicago, IL), 1994, pp. 49-57, *http://www.ncsa.uiuc.edu/SDG/IT94/Proceedings/Agents/oostendorp/oostendorp.html*

13. Pad++: Zoomable Graphical Interfaces, home page created by Jonathan Meyer, *http://www.cs.unm.edu/pad++/begin.html*

14. Ken Perlin and David Fox, *Pad—An Alternative Approach to the Computer Interface*, Proceedings of ACM SIGGRAPH 1993 (Anaheim, CA), ACM Press, 1993, pp. 57-64.

15. Martin Roescheisen, Christian Mogensen, and Terry Winograd, *Beyond Browsing: shared comments, SOAPs, trails, and on-line communities*, Computer Networks and ISDN Systems 27: 739-749, 1995, *http://www.igd.fhg.de/www/www95/proceedings/papers/88/TR/WWW95.html*

16. The World Wide Web Virtual Library: Visual Languages and Visual Programming, *http://cuiwww.unige.ch/eao/www/Visual/Visual.Programming.biblio.html*

17. The Webhound WWW Interface, *http://rg.media.mit.edu:80/projects/webhound/www-face/*

18. Yahoo, *http://www.yahoo.com*

About the Authors

Kent Wittenburg
[*http://community.bellcore.com/kentw/home-page.html*]
Bellcore, Room MCC 1A-332R
445 South St.
Morristown, NJ 07962-1910
kentw@bellcore.com

Duco Das
[*http://community.bellcore.com/duco/home-page.html*]
Stevens Institute of Technology & Delft University of Technology
Julianalaan 132
2628 BL Delft, The Netherlands
duco@bellcore.com or
afstc029@IS.TWI.TUDelft.NL

Will Hill
Bellcore, AT&T Bell Labs, Room 2B-402
600 Mountain Ave.
Murray Hill, NJ 07974
willhill@research.att.com

Larry Stead
Bellcore, Room MCC-1A348R
445 South St.
Morristown, NJ 07962-1910
lstead@bellcore.com

Supporting Collaborative Information Sharing with the World Wide Web

The BSCW Shared Workspace System

Richard Bentley, Thilo Horstmann, Klaas Sikkel, Jonathan Trevor

Abstract

The emergence and widespread adoption of the World Wide Web (W3) offers a great deal of potential for the developers of collaborative technologies, both as an enabling infrastructure and a platform for integration with existing end-user environments. This paper describes a system which attempts to exploit that potential by extending the W3 to provide a set of basic facilities for collaborative information sharing. The BSCW Shared Workspace system was conceived as an alternative to tools which currently support collaborative working for widely dispersed working groups such as electronic mail and ftp. We report on the design and implementation of our system, the problems we encountered, and the benefits accruing from our choice of the W3 as an enabling platform. Our experiences suggest how recent developments in the W3 point the way to more suitable and powerful mechanisms to support the development of collaborative systems. **Keywords:** *BSCW, information sharing, applications*

Introduction

In its current form, the World Wide Web (W3) provides a simple and effective means for users to search, browse, and retrieve information, as well as to make information of their own available for others. The utility of this approach, whereby providers design and retain control over the form and content of their information, is evident from the growth of the W3 to become the primary means of accessing information over the Internet. This approach, however, does not provide support for more *collaborative* information sharing, where widely dispersed working groups can jointly author, comment, and annotate documents, negotiating and developing the form and content of the information as part of a group, rather than an individual, activity.

The Basic Support for Cooperative Work project (BSCW) at GMD is investigating the feasibility of extending the W3 to support such collaborative working. In this paper we report on the design and implementation of the BSCW Shared Work-

space system, an extended W3 server which provides basic facilities for (primarily asynchronous) collaborative information sharing, activity awareness and integration of external applications across Macintosh, PC, and UNIX platforms. The system integrates the simple facilities found in ftp—namely storage and retrieval of documents—with more sophisticated features such as group and member administration, check-in-/-out facilities, and access to meta-information regarding documents and members. In addition, the system provides a simple, event-based awareness service to inform users, at a glance, of the current status and past changes to information held in the workspace.

By discussing the development of this system, we hope to contribute to the ongoing debate regarding the extension of W3 protocols, architecture, and so on to support more collaborative work—an area which the W3 Consortium has signalled as an important aspect of future W3 innovation [1]. In the next section we outline the motivation for our system and a more general focus on collaborative information sharing, and discuss the potential of the W3 as a basis for developing collaboration technologies. We then describe the design of the system in detail, and consider the implications of our experiences for possible extension of W3. We conclude that recent innovations, particularly in the area of client-computation, hold great potential and are a more suitable means of extension than radical change to either W3 protocols or architecture.

Supporting Collaboration Within Widely Distributed Workgroups

The BSCW Shared Workspace system was conceived as a means of supporting the work of widely dispersed workgroups, particularly those involved in large research and development projects. Members of such projects may come from a number of organizations, in different countries, yet have a need to share and exchange information and often collaborate over its production. The geographical distribution prohibits frequent face-to-face meetings, and would clearly benefit from computer support for the collaborative aspects of the work. Unfortunately, the lack of common computing infrastructure within the group often prohibits deployment of such technology and causes serious problems for system developers who must pay close attention to issues of heterogeneous machines, networks, and application software.

As a consequence of these problems, despite over 10 years of research in the field of CSCW (Computer Supported Cooperative Work), email and ftp remain the state of the art in supporting collaboration within widely distributed workgroups. Although such tools facilitate information *exchange*, they provide little support for information *sharing*, whereby details of users' changes, annotations, and so on are made visible and available to all other participants. A conclusion drawn by many is that for more powerful CSCW technologies to flourish, a common infrastructure

that addresses problems of integration is required, allowing developers to focus on application details rather than complexities of different system configurations (e.g. [2, 3]). The W3 is the first real example of such a common infrastructure, offering huge potential to CSCW system developers through:

- Platform, network, and operating system transparency

- Integration with end-user environments and application programs

- A simple and consistent user interface across platforms

- An application programmer interface for "bolt-on" functionality

- Ease of deployment, facilitating rapid system prototyping

Given this potential, it is unsurprising that a number of W3-based collaboration systems have been developed. We can classify these systems in four broad categories, based on the extent to which they depart from existing W3 standards:

Purely W3-based

Such systems use standard W3 clients, comply with HTML and HTTP standards, and only extend server functionality using the CGI interface. Any additional client functionality is provided by helper applications (we do not include client APIs here, such as CCI, as they are not standardized across clients and platforms). An example of such a purely W3-based system is reported in [4].

Customized servers

As 1, but require special-purpose servers, to provide behavior beyond the possibilities offered by CGI. Such systems still support standard W3 clients and protocols, but the enhancements may reduce the portability of the server itself. InterNotes [5] is an example of such a customized server.

As 1 (and sometimes 2), but require particular or modified clients (often to support nonstandard HTML tags), or nonstandard client APIs, and could not necessarily be used with different platforms or different clients. These systems do, however, support the HTTP protocol. The Sesame client for Ubique's Virtual Places system [6] is an example.

Web-related

Such systems may provide a W3 interface, but support only limited interaction using the HTTP protocol. The Worlds system [7] is an example of this category.

In this classification, the degree of W3 compliance decreases from 1 to 4; one might say that a system in Category 1 inherits all the benefits of the W3 listed above, while a system in Category 4 gives the developer a free hand in choice of protocols, interface toolkits, and so on but few of the benefits. A major goal of our work was to produce a useful and *usable* system—one which could be deployed in our target domain and refined on the basis of actual usage feedback. We therefore set out the following design goals:

- No modification to the HTTP protocol

- No modifications to HTML, or client customization other than through Helper applications

- All server customization to be performed through the CGI interface

The following section describes the current version of the system we developed, and we then return to these three design goals to discuss the system's implementation.

The BSCW Shared Workspace System

The BSCW Shared Workspace system is a document storage and retrieval system extended with features to support collaborative information sharing. The system consists of a server which maintains a number of workspaces, accessible from different platforms using standard, unmodified W3 clients. Each workspace contains a number of shared information objects, and workspace members can perform actions to retrieve, modify, and request more details on these objects. The objects we currently support are documents, links (to normal W3 pages and other workspaces), folders, groups, and members. Figure 1 shows the user interface to a typical shared workspace, which is in fact the workspace we used in coauthoring this paper.

Each BSCW server maintains an index of all the workspaces it manages. Users access the index using a standard user-name and password scheme, and the server responds with a list of the workspaces the user can enter. Alternatively, workspace members can access the workspace directly if they know the URL. New users are added to the server by completing (or having an existing member complete) a simple registration form which asks for a user-name and the new user's email address. This information is then used to check if the user is already known to the server, and if not, an initial password is generated and mailed to the user at the given address. This simple registration scheme requires users to give a valid email address in order to log on to the system. Once logged on, users can change their password to something more suitable.

In the current version of the system, to access a workspace a user must be a member of the group "members," and can be added to this group by any existing group member. The member then sees a view of the root-folder of the workspace, similar to that in Figure 1. The form of this view is the same for each member, with a navigation bar at the top (and bottom) of the page, a (user-definable) workspace banner, a row of action buttons, and a listing of the contents of the current folder. The contents themselves are listed differently dependent on the *view-type* the user has currently selected.

In Figure 1, the member "trevor" has selected the *event-view* of the root-folder of the "Boston paper" workspace. He sees the workspace objects in this folder—in this case, a FrameMaker and a Microsoft Word document, two links to related W3 pages, a subfolder, the "members" group and the workspace Wastebasket. To the right of each object, one or more icons may be displayed which signal that events have occurred concerning that object. So in Figure 1, the document "Boston draft" has been written, while the "Screendumps" folder has been added to the workspace since "trevor" last logged in. Other events signalled in this way include "read," "renamed," "moved," "versioned," while a "deleted" event is signalled by the Wastebasket object becoming "full," as in Figure 1. Members can click on the event icon to get more information (such as who caused it and when it occurred), and can "catchup" events, similar to catching up read articles in a Usenet newsgroup, by clicking the "Catchup events" button above the workspace listing.

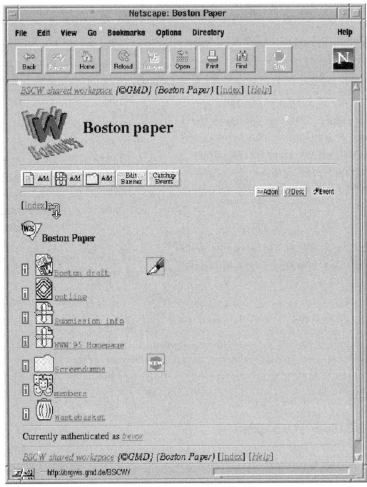

Figure 1:   The user interface to a BSCW Shared Workspace

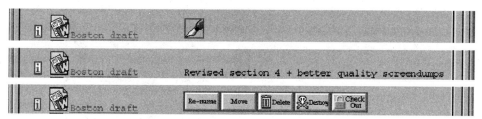

Figure 2: "Boston draft" in the event, description, and action views

The event-view is one of three possibilities for interacting with a workspace. The three toggle buttons under and to the right of the action buttons allow members to switch between the event-view, the description-view, and the action-view (Figure 2). The description view shows a one-line description of each workspace object, if one has been provided, while the action-view displays a list of buttons which allow members to manipulate each object. These action buttons are generated based on the member's access rights; for example, only the creator of an object can "destroy" that object (irrevocably remove it from the workspace), while all members may be able to "check out" a copy of a document object for editing. It is clear that these *policies* surrounding access to system functions have a great impact on how the system is used, and we have therefore deliberately isolated such policy decisions so that they can easily be tailored. To this end, we are currently working on an interface to allow members to specify the access policy associated with workspace objects.

Documents can be added to a workspace using a simple, platform-specific "helper application." An appropriate helper must be installed on each member's machine, and is executed when the member clicks the "Add Document" button (Figure 1). This helper allows members to select documents on their local file-store, specify a (possibly different) name for the document on the remote workspace, and transmit the document to the BSCW server. If the document is a new version of an existing document, the old version is moved to the workspace Wastebasket and a "versioned" event is generated. The old version is

therefore preserved and can be accessed unless explicitly "destroyed" (Figure 2).

The system provides a simple check-in/check-out facility to assist with version management, using a form of "soft-locks" to ensure members are aware of the current document status. If a member tries to retrieve a document which is currently checked out, a notification message is returned showing who has the document, but provides the option for the member to retrieve the document anyway. We are currently working on a more powerful version and locking management system, but believe this basic approach provides at least an awareness of the current activities of group members. In addition to this facility, the system also provides more standard operations associated with document management, such as renaming, moving, and deleting. Following the Macintosh metaphor, deleted workspace objects are stored in the workspace Wastebasket, allowing them to be restored if necessary.

Finally, it is possible to request a page of information about each object in the workspace by clicking the "info" button to the left of an object's icon (Figure 1). For document objects, this page includes details of the document creator, date added, MIME-type, etc. (Figure 3), and for members this provides contact details, home page URL, and so on. These pages allow members to access object actions (dependent on their access rights), such as "edit description," and are integrated, so that in Figure 3 members can click on the "document creator" and receive the info page on member "trevor."

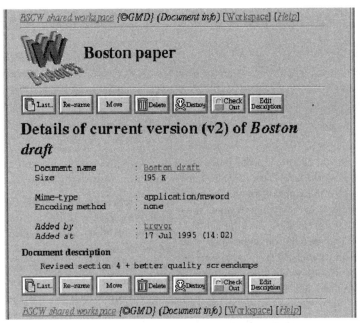

Figure 3: Information on the "Boston draft" document

This version of the BSCW Shared Workspace system is currently being evaluated with the aid of a number of researchers across Europe. Based on feedback from these trials, we hope to refine and extend the system to provide more flexible mechanisms which can be customized to the requirements of different workgroups; for example, we are currently investigating alternative methods of remote user administration, whereby users can "subscribe" to workspaces or, conversely, where member administration might be performed by one or more "privileged" users. Other topics for further work include multiple-group support, group mailing, and mail archiving. Readers interested in trying out the system for themselves are invited to do so. Directions are provided at the end of the paper.

Implementation of the BSCW System

The key components of the BSCW system are an extended W3 server, a simple gdbm database to store data about workspace objects such as documents and members, and several platform-specific helper applications for transferring documents to the server (Figure 4). The documents themselves are stored on the UNIX filesystem, while the database contains information such as document creator and version number, member contact details, and event information. The server makes extensive use of information in the database to generate the user interface to a workspace (Figure 1).

The current version of the server itself is an extended NCSA HTTP 1.4.2 daemon. While the majority of the extra functionality was provided through the CGI interface with Python scripts, it was necessary to add extra code and modify approximately 30 lines of the original server source. While a previous version of the system, built using the CERN server, was constructed entirely using the CGI interface [8], the restrictions this placed on the interface, and the need to duplicate much of the existing server functionality in the CGI scripts, led us to relax the third of

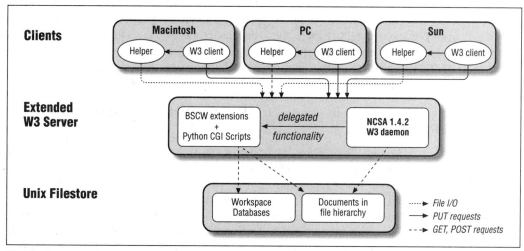

Figure 4: BSCW system architecture

our design goals as set out previously; as a consequence, our system falls into Category 2 of our classification of W3-based applications. To show why such server modification was necessary, we now focus on several key requirements which had to be supported by our system.

Implementation of the PUT Method

A lack of client support for selecting and sending documents to a HTTP daemon has required development of platform-specific helper applications. These helpers are started by a correctly configured client when a special MIME-type is received, sent by the server when the "Add Document" button is pressed (Figure 1). The helpers provide a file-browsing interface to the local filesystem, with versions for Macintosh, PC (Windows '95, NT, 3.1), and most UNIX platforms currently implemented. The implementation of the PUT protocol is, however, not trivial; for example, the server must ensure that files cannot be added which would be interpreted as scripts or configuration files. Our solution to this problem is a "double-handshaking" between the server and the helpers to verify files can be added, resulting in an overly complex protocol and introducing many points of possible failure. Fur-

thermore, an implementation based on external helpers applications has implications for security and access control, as adding files to protected file-systems requires helpers to ask users for user-name and password details they may have already supplied to their W3 client.

Full Support for MIME-types

The current server support for MIME-types relies on guessing the document type by examining its filename suffix. This is clearly unsuitable when documents must be shared between Macintosh (often no suffix, but a resource fork), PC (max. 3 character, case-insensitive suffix), and UNIX (variable length, case-sensitive suffix) platforms. Thus our server does not use filenames to select MIME-types, but rather retrieves the document type from the object database, in some ways simulating the resource fork properties of a Macintosh document. When a document is added, the helper uses a local configuration file to guess a suitable MIME-type. As there is no guarantee this is correct, users can override the helper's selection, as well as edit and extend the configuration file to suit their own requirements. It is worth noting, however, that although this method ensures that the correct application program is started, independently of a document's filename, many applications insist on a filename extension. This is particularly true on the PC, where the problem is compounded as it is not possible to configure most PC W3 clients to add an extension to received documents (as it is on the Sun, for example).

More Sophisticated Access Methods

The current access models supported by W3 servers allow user- and group-based access control limiting ability to send GET, POST, PUT, and other, as yet unimplemented, requests. Although the CERN server does implement per-file access control lists (ACLs), this still provides no way of expressing which *actions* (or scripts) can be requested in a particular context (per-document and user), what files are *visible* to different users, and whether users can modify the access permissions of others. We have therefore extended these models by storing more complex ACLs as part of each object in the object database. These ACLs take the form of rules, which describe the visibility of objects (for example, users can only see workspaces that they are members of) and the actions that users and groups can perform on them. These action rules are used by the server to suppress output of buttons which access action scripts denied to the current user, and by the scripts themselves to ensure the current user is authorized to perform the corresponding action.

An Enhanced User Interface to the File-store

The system requires a much richer, context-sensitive user interface to a workspace than is provided by standard server directory listings. In particular, the server must generate a different HTML page dependent on *who* the request is from, as users may have different actions they can perform (see above), different view-types selected, different event icons (dependent on when they last "caught up") and so on. This requires interac-

tion with the database to retrieve member details and also to check document types and whether documents are currently checked out in order to display appropriate icons. We were therefore forced to replace the existing directory listing routines for our BSCW server.

More Sophisticated Logging

The provision of awareness information regarding past activities of group members is essential for collaborative information sharing, as groups must coordinate their activities and maintain a shared understanding of the status of their work [9]. The event icons generated by the BSCW server are an attempt to support this awareness, but the logging facilities supported by existing servers only record request details and not the *results* of those requests. To capture this information and log it in a form suitable for the server to generate the event listing required generating and storing *event objects* in the workspace database.

Many of these innovations required modification of the core behavior of the HTTP server. However, rather than simply replacing server code with our own, we have extended the source so that our code is called only if the server is used to access a workspace; otherwise the server functions as a normal HTTP daemon. All the software required to install the system is public domain and commonly available, and, more importantly, we have made no modifications to clients, HTML, or HTTP. We therefore believe our system retains the advantages of W3 as an enabling platform, and provides a basic, though useful, set of facilities to support a more collaborative model of information sharing.

Recommendations and Discussion

Our experiences with the implementation of the BSCW system lead us to the following recommendations for extending the W3 for more collaborative work, yet preserving the benefits as a cross-platform enabling technology:

Client support for the PUT method

This is an obvious consequence of a more collaborative view of information sharing. The current state of the art requires developers to build their own, platform-specific helper applications if they wish to avoid modifying clients or using nonstandard APIs and client features (such as the <ENCTYPE> attribute supported by recent versions of the Netscape clients). Reliance on external helpers potentially can create problems with authentication, proxy servers, and so on.

Better support for MIME-types

This is required to enable true cross-platform information sharing. The current focus on filename suffix creates problems for the Macintosh, which uses resource forks, and requires general consistency in document naming. These problems seem to be symptomatic of a more general problem with file naming, as many PC applications insist on a suffix being present when passed a document from a W3 client.

A richer model of access control

The current methods provide little support for limiting information visibility, restricting access to certain functionality, and remote member administration. Differences in methods across servers inhibit the formulation of a richer and more general model.

Improved user interface facilities

Although HTML was never claimed to be a user interface description language, this is a function to which it is often put. Although features such as the <FRAME> tag supported by recent versions of Netscape increase the possibilities, such features are not supported by all clients and there is clearly a limit to interface techniques, such as multiple selections and semantic feedback, that can be described with such extensions. Perhaps a more specific user interface description language is required.

Better support for server customization

The CGI interface does not allow customization of core server functionality such as access logging, MIME-type mapping, etc. Although some servers such as Apache and Netsite provide more extensive APIs, it is often the case that much server functionality is unused or needs to be replaced for custom applications. A cleaner method of removing, replacing, and extending core components is required, perhaps in a similar manner to the module-based approach of the Spinner server [10].

These recommendations have arisen through an attempt to extend the W3 to support more collaborative information sharing, but many are more generally applicable; for example, client support for the PUT protocol is necessary for remote editing applications such as Grif [11], and the current support for MIME-types frustrates cross-platform document exchange. However, besides these general problems, in its current form the W3 suffers from a more serious limitation when considering support for collaborative sharing. This limitation concerns the fundamental architecture on which W3 is based, and becomes more apparent when we consider more synchronous sharing than that currently supported by the BSCW system. This architecture is based on a model of information provision which assumes information is relatively static, and no notification is required when information is changed.

This is a well-known argument in BSCW, concerning the distinction between *multiuser* and *collaborative* systems. Briefly (see [12] for more details), while a multiuser system seeks to hide the activities of other users to give each the impression they are interacting with a dedicated system, a collaborative system must often propagate and explicitly represent other users' activities to provide a common context for the collaborative work taking place. For the W3, all interaction is handled by the central server which gives no

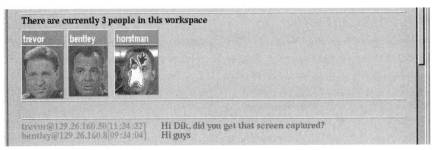

Figure 5:   The Java "talk" facility

indication of who else is, or has been, viewing the same page. Although the current, "consumer-provider" model of information exchange does not require such awareness support, this is not the case for more collaborative information sharing [9]. The problem is highlighted by a number of previous system developments, e.g., [4], and is manifest in many current debates including the provision of shared virtual worlds in VRML.

It is tempting to suggest that this model of sharing requires a radical extension to the basic W3 architecture. Indeed, this is one approach being taken in the Stanford Digital Library Project, where the use of CORBA protocols to support meta-information objects such as annotations is being investigated [13]. Although the integration of more powerful mechanisms like CORBA might address many of the current problems, it is clear that much work needs to take place before applications can be developed and deployed which make use of such advanced features. Instead, we suggest that the key to a more collaborative W3 in the short term lies in extending the basic mechanisms, preserving the simplicity and utility of the current approach. Ubique's Virtual Places system [6] offers one method through addition of a second server responsible for event propagation, but currently relies on the use of particular W3 clients. Perhaps a more flexible and extensible solution, however, is the integration of safe interpreter environments with W3 clients, allowing arbitrary code to be retrieved and executed at the client site. This approach—perhaps best developed in Sun's HotJava support for their Java

language [14]—has the additional advantages of reducing network traffic and the load on servers.

To demonstrate the potential of this approach, we have extended the BSCW system with a simple "talk facility" implemented using Java Applets (Figure 5). As with Virtual Places, end-users interacting with the same workspace see each other's icons and can type simple messages, click on the icon to "alert" a user, and establish a simple audio connection. We are currently experimenting with more advanced features such as shared pointers and simple shared editors, and we believe that this approach allows support for more synchronous collaborative information sharing, without compromising the existing W3 architecture. The recent decision of Netscape to license the Java interpreter for their own W3 clients makes this approach more realistic, and the benefits will become more apparent as richer interface toolkits and class libraries become available.

Conclusion

We have presented the BSCW Shared Workspace system and discussed our experiences with W3 as a platform for supporting collaborative work. The system is realized as an extended HTTP daemon, accessible from standard, unmodified W3 clients on a number of platforms. We are currently evaluating the system with the aid of researchers in several European countries, and we invite interested readers to install and try the system for themselves. (For details, see the BSCW home page *http://bscw.gmd.de/*).

The W3 offers an excellent opportunity to support collaboration within widely dispersed workgroups. As an enabling platform, integrated with different hardware and software, it has the potential to overcome many of the problems with current collaborative systems. We feel that for this potential to be realized, it is important that enhancements should not compromise the current availability and usability of W3, and to this end, we argue for extension of current mechanisms rather than radical change in the short term. In this paper we have highlighted several areas for extension, and suggested that the current innovations in client-side computation hold promise for future development. ■

References

1. *http://www.w3.org/hypertext/WWW/Collaboration/ Overview.html*

2. Patterson, J., Comparing the programming demands of single- and multi-user applications, in *Proceedings of UIST'91*, Hilton Head, SC, ACM Press, Nov. 11-13, 1991, pp 87-95.

3. Trevor, J., Rodden, T., and Mariani, J., The use of adapters to support cooperative sharing, in *Proceedings of CSCW'94*, Chapel Hill, NC, ACM Press, Oct. 22-26, 1994, pp 219-230.

4. Frivold, R., Lang, R., and Fong, M., Extending WWW for synchronous collaboration, in *Electronic Proceedings of Second WWW Conference: Mosaic and the Web, http://www.ncsa.uiuc.edu/ SDG/IT94/Proceedings/CSCW/frivold/frivold.html*

5. *http://www.lotus.com/inotes*

6. *http://www.ubique.com/*

7. *http://acsl.cs.uiuc.edu/kaplan/worlds.html*

8. Pollak, B., *Spezifikation und Implementierung von geographisch weit verteilten Arbeitsbereichen*, Master's Thesis, University of Kaiserslautern, Germany, March 1995.

9. Fuchs, L., Pankoke-Babatz, U., and Prinz, W., Supporting cooperative awareness with local event mechanisms: The GroupDesk system, in *Proceedings of ECSCW'95*, Stockholm, Kluwer Aca-demic Publishers, Sept. 11-15, 1995, pp 247-262.

10. *http://spinner.infovav.se/*

11. Quint, V., Roisin, C., and Vatton, I., A structured authoring environment for the World-Wide Web, in *Computer Networks and ISDN Systems: Proceedings of the Third International W3 Conference*, Darmstadt, Apr. 10-14, 1995, pp 831-839, *http:// www.igd.fhg.de/www/www95/papers/84/Edit-HTML.html*

12. Rodden, T., Mariani, J., and Blair, G., Supporting cooperative applications, in *Computer Supported Cooperative Work*, 1 (1), Stockholm, Kluwer Academic Publishers, 1992, pp 41-67

13. Röscheisen, M., Mogensen, C., and Winograd, T., Beyond browsing: Shared comments, SOAPs, Trails, and online communities, in *Computer Networks and ISDN Systems: Proceedings of the Third International W3 Conference*, Darmstadt, Apr. 10-14, 1995, pp 739-749, *http://www.igd.fhg.de/www/ www95/papers/88/TR/WWW95.html*

14. *http://java.sun.com*

About the Authors

Richard Bentley, Thilo Horstmann, Klaas Sikkel, and **Jonathan Trevor**
German National Research Centre for Information Technology (GMD FIT.CSCW)
Schloß Birlinghoven
D-53754 Sankt Augustin, Germany
Phone: +49 2241 14 2699
Fax: +49 2241 14 2084
{bentley, horstmann, sikkel, trevor} @gmd.de

A WEB OF DISTRIBUTED OBJECTS

Owen Rees, Nigel Edwards, Mark Madsen, Mike Beasley,
Ashley McClenaghan

Abstract

This paper describes work on interoperability between the World Wide Web and Distributed Object systems being carried out under the ANSA workprogramme, using the Object Management Group's CORBA architecture. The approach described offers the opportunity to bring the benefits of distributed object technology to the Web by using the CORBA infrastructure. This also offers a way to solve the current engineering problems by using available industry standard technology. ***Keywords:*** *Objects, CORBA, evolution, protocols, IDL, HTTP, interoperability*

Introduction

This paper describes work on interoperability between the World Wide Web and Distributed Object systems being carried out under the ANSA workprogramme. The primary objective of this work is to bring the added benefits of distributed object technology to the Web, without losing any of the features of the Web that have made it so successful.

We have been motivated in our work by the following observations:

- Current Web infrastructure is suffering from a number of early engineering decisions that have not scaled to cope with the demand..

- Web clients and servers are tending to become larger monolithic applications; a conventional library does not provide the necessary flexibility for change, optimization for performance, and scaling down for small devices (e.g., consumer appliances).

- The Web is document-centric, and provides little support for connecting interactive services, or for interacting with "intelligent content."

These observations have to be balanced against the success of the Web to date. Our ambition is to develop an evolutionary strategy which overcomes these limitations without imposing new restrictions.

The strategy for achieving this objective is to enable seamless interoperability between the World Wide Web and Distributed Object systems based on the Object Management Group's Common Object Request Broker Architecture (CORBA) [1]. Interoperability will make CORBA-based systems accessible to Web browsers, and make the information resources on the Web accessible to CORBA-based systems. Since CORBA is the leading industry standard for systems integration, it provides a pathway for linking the Web to a wide range of electronic information and business services.

Some of the benefits of using distributed objects are:

- *Ease of programming.* The underlying object model, the Interface Definition Language (IDL), and the supporting tools combine to simplify the task of writing distributed applications.

- *Extensibility and manageability.* Systems built from interacting objects are inherently extensible because objects can be easily added or replaced. Extensibility allows customised management interfaces to be added to the system.

- *Encapsulation and systems integration.* Distributed object technology has proved very effective in encapsulating "legacy systems" as objects. These objects offer interfaces that can then be used to implement an integrated system.

The work described here not only makes systems built with this technology accessible, but also uses this technology to build the gateways that provide the required interoperability. This approach demonstrates both the tools and the migration path that make moving the Web onto a CORBA infrastructure possible. Following this path will allow the Web to exploit the work on protocol engineering that has been done for CORBA platforms, as well as the results of the work now in progress on real-time and multi-media protocols for future CORBA systems [2].

The principles that are guiding the work are:

- *Evolution not revolution*. The results of this work must fit with what already exists, and offer an opportunity to exploit new facilities without demanding an irrevocable commitment in advance.

- *A usable version of the technology* must be made freely available.

- *Use existing work*, and especially freely available technology in order to promote compatibility with other initiatives, and widespread uptake.

Comparing CORBA and WWW

Object Request Brokers (ORBs), as defined by the OMG CORBA [1] specification, provide the mechanisms by which objects transparently make requests and receive responses. HTTP is, according to the Internet-Draft of March 1995 [3], a generic stateless object-oriented protocol, and based on a request/response paradigm. The similarities offer an opportunity to interoperate between CORBA-based systems and the World Wide Web, and the challenge is to combine their strengths, rather than to compound their weaknesses.

Methods

In CORBA, the methods a service supports are defined in an Interface Definition Language (IDL). Objects communicate with each other using ORBs which provide a transport protocol for passing invocation requests and replies between objects.

Many WWW services use HTTP. This defines both a transport protocol and a set of standard methods; two of the standard methods are mandatory for all "general purpose" HTTP servers (GET and HEAD), and these, together with POST, are supported and actively used on most of the currently deployed servers.

CORBA defines no standard methods which all application services are required to support. However, it does define an environment for building clients and servers which hides most of the complexity of the underlying platform from the programmer. From the IDL description of a service, client IDL stubs and server IDL skeletons are generated which hide the Application Programmer's Interface (API) of the underlying ORB from the application programmer. Hence remote invocation looks very similar to local invocation. This makes the process of writing new clients and servers relatively easy, and makes extending existing implementations easy as well. These features are important in integrating new information services into systems.

The use of IDL and tools has proved very effective in the development of distributed systems, and in particular, in interfacing to so-called "legacy systems." The ability to define interface types, with tools to help build clients and servers for those types, is one of the main strengths of the CORBA approach.

Transport

ORBs can support multiple transport protocols and hide from the programmer, many aspects of distribution (e.g., object location). In the future, all CORBA compliant ORBs will be required to include support for the General Inter-ORB Protocol (GIOP) [4] which specifies the message formats, and the Internet Inter-ORB Protocol (IIOP) which specifies how GIOP messages are exchanged using TCP/IP.

HTTP, as generally implemented, defines both message formats and mapping to TCP/IP. The draft specification for HTTP [3] attempts to separate these issues, but is constrained by the need to capture the existing practice.

One well known problem with HTTP is that a new TCP connection is opened for each request, and closed after the response has been delivered. This is an inefficient use of system and network resources and a source of delay. By contrast, GIOP is designed to allow a connection to be used for multiple requests, and also to allow overlapping requests; thus setup costs are amortized over many requests/replies. Several requests may be sent over the same connection without waiting for a reply, and the replies may be delivered in any order. The replies are matched to requests by the use of identifiers.

In a CORBA system, the ORB provides connection and session management to make best use of the available resources. The application need not be concerned with these matters, and does not need to be changed or reconfigured to adapt to different communication resources.

HTTP via CORBA

There are a number of possible approaches to carrying HTTP requests and responses over a CORBA-based system. The simplest one is to carry the whole request or response as a sequence of octets without attempting to resolve its structure in any way. This would allow the connection to be re-used, but would do little to provide interoperability.

A more useful approach is to define an IDL mapping of HTTP that promotes interoperability. The objective is to allow CORBA technology to be used to develop clients that can use resources from the Web, and servers that can provide resources to the Web. This means looking at HTTP as a set of methods with various arguments and results, and constructing gateways that convert between the HTTP representations and CORBA representations.

The IDL and stub compiler technology associated with CORBA means that it is possible to experiment with various mappings of HTTP, with a reasonable level of effort.

Strategy for Interoperability

A strategy for full interoperability must enable the benefits of the new technology, without losing the use of the old resources. Interoperability is achieved through gateways: an important test of the completeness of the interoperability is to be able to put together a pair of gateways that together behave like an HTTP proxy, but interact via a different protocol—IIOP. This is demonstrated in Figure 1.

Existing clients can connect to the gateway by using their proxy mechanism. Although most browsers have such a mechanism, any other clients that can use a proxy can also use the gateways.

After the gateways are available, one can provide clients and servers that use IIOP as their native protocol, and that can interact with the existing Web through the gateways, interact amongst themselves, and interact with other CORBA objects.

First Stage: Gateways Exploit the Proxy Mechanism

The first stage of the evolution path is to implement basic versions of the gateways that convert HTTP interactions into the corresponding interactions described by the IDL. The two gateways are I2H which forwards IIOP requests to HTTP, and H2I which forwards HTTP requests to IIOP.

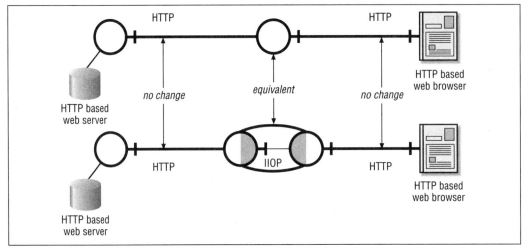

Figure 1:   A pair of complementary HTTP-IIOP and IIOP-HTTP gateways appear to act like a proxy from the point of view of the client and server

Where Should the Gateways be Located?

By locating the I2H gateway near to the server, and the H2I gateway near to the client, the IIOP protocol can be used over much of the route. While this part of the route accounts for a significant part of the round trip time, being able to re-use an existing connection should show an improvement. Figure 2 shows this arrangement.

An important part of the work will be detailed performance testing, both to measure where the time is being spent, and to identify how much difference the various kinds of connections make in going via the gateways.

Choosing the Route

Most current Web clients have a mechanism that allows them to connect to a proxy, and this can be used to route requests to the H2I gateway. To retrieve resources from servers that do not have an I2H gateway, H2I has to be a full HTTP proxy as well as a gateway to IIOP. This presents H2I with the problem of knowing when to use IIOP, and where to route the requests.

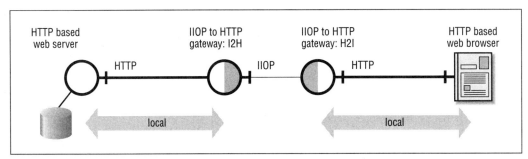

Figure 2:   The collocation of the basic IIOP-HTTP and HTTP-IIOP gateways with the server and client respectively

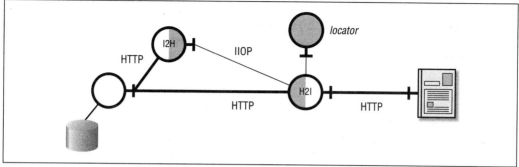

Figure 3:   The locator service interface is used by the client-side gateway to obtain an interface reference for the appropriate server-side gateway, and the client-side gateway then makes an IIOP connection to the server-side gateway. If the locator cannot provide an interface reference to a server-side gateway, the client-side gateway passes the request straight through to the server via HTTP.

This problem is handled in our scheme by a locator. The locator is defined as a separate service so that various strategies for deciding when to use IIOP can be explored. Figure 3 shows the locator service interface being used by the client-side gateway.

Defining the interface between H2I and the locator in IDL means that distributed object technology can be used to defer the decision about how the locator and H2I interact. H2I is written as if it is invoking the locator operations directly, and the locator is written as if it is being invoked directly. They can then either be linked into a single program, or linked to the generated stubs and skeletons so that they interact via the ORB. The ORB allows them to be located as close together or as far apart as you like.

Defining the locator as a distributed system object also means that H2I does not need to know whether it is a single object, or a collection of objects. The locator may consist of a number of objects located in various places, and interacting in order to ensure that the required data is available quickly whenever and wherever it is needed.

How Does the Locator Get Its Data?

There are various options for gathering the data that the locator needs.

- HTTP servers with an IIOP gateway send an extra header in HTTP responses. This is ignored by existing clients, but passed to the locator by the H2I proxy/gateway. The locator is responsible for understanding this header and updating its database. The problem with this approach is that the HTTP server must be modified to send the extra header, which conflicts with the original objective of requiring no change to existing clients and servers.

- Attempt IIOP, fall back to HTTP if it fails. In this case, H2I must report the result to the locator, and in the event of failure, be told what to do next. The advantage is that there is no need to change the existing clients or servers, but at the expense of a failed attempt that will introduce delay. In this case, the locator must have a way to guess a likely IIOP route for the resource which will have been identified by a URL.

- Use a *trader*. The locator calls another service to find out if there is a suitable IIOP service. The ISO ODP concept of a *trading service* [5] can be applied here, once again exploiting the results of existing work. A trading service allows a client to find service offers that match a set of constraints on the values of properties. A service provider exports its offer to a trader by listing the properties of the service and their values. A client can then import a service from a trader by specifying constraints on the properties. In general, the trading service is provided by a number of traders that interact in order to make the offers available throughout the trading space.

These options are not exclusive. There must be some strategy for dealing with failed IIOP attempts however the IIOP route may have been chosen. The locator can take account of information passed back in responses, whatever strategy it chooses in the absence of data. The locator may keep the data itself, or it may pass it on to a trading service where other locators can benefit from its experience.

By defining the locator interface, the various strategies can be explored without having to change H2I. A variety of locators offering the same interface but implementing different strategies to suit different circumstances is also a possibility.

Second Stage: Native IIOP Web Server and Client

After the gateways are available, clients and servers that use IIOP as their native protocol can be implemented. An IIOP client would not need to use the H2I gateway; an IIOP server would not need to use the I2H gateway.

The IDL mapping of HTTP provides an opportunity to replace the textual headers with a more compact, and easier to process representation. The best way to represent the header information in IDL is being studied. This is another case where it is very useful to be able to experiment with various IDL mappings. Although a more compact representation will be beneficial where there is a bandwidth limit, the advantage of reduced processing time will not be realised until the HTTP stages of the transmission are eliminated.

IIOP Native Browser

The simplest way to implement a native IIOP browser will be to add an IIOP protocol module to the W3C Reference Library (libwww - previously known as the Common Code Library) in a browser that is built over that library. This will reuse much of the code already written for H2I, including the locator, because the browser will have the same protocol selection requirement as H2I.

A disadvantage of this approach is that it contributes to the trend of browsers becoming larger and more complicated as more and more features are added to them. However, one of the advantages of distributed object technology is that it becomes easy to write "thin clients" that can run on small machines and interact with a server that implements what would normally be part of the application. An application composed of interacting objects can have those objects located on various machines so as to match the available processing, storage and communication resources. The idea of "thin clients" will become increasingly important due to the use of the Web by non-technical users, and the convergence of the Internet and consumer electronics.

One of the objectives of this work is to simplify the process of designing a modular browser that can take advantage of new resource discovery schemes, data formats, and anything else that may become available, simply by interacting with a new object. An example of this has been cited already: the locator is designed as a separate object. Whether to include the locator (locally) in the same address space as the browser, or to use the ORB to interact with it (remotely), can be decided at link time.

This technique of defining new services in IDL can be used to add additional features to the browser, deferring the decision of whether those features are implemented locally or remotely until link time. Using IDL also makes it easier to upgrade these "helper" services: a smarter locator using metadata could be used with no change to the client as the interface would remain unchanged (or perhaps inherit from the earlier version). This would make the deployment of URN/URC schemes [6] easier.

IIOP Native Server

One of the fundamental objectives of this work is backwards compatibility. A native IIOP server should be able to serve exactly the same file system as a current generation HTTP server using the *http://* scheme name. Thus, exactly the same URLs can be used to access resources using HTTP or IIOP. Our architecture supports this by introducing a level of indirection in a browser or gateway attempting to use IIOP: given a URL of the form *http://...* the locator is consulted to see if the resource can be retrieved using IIOP. The native IIOP server will also provide support for CGI [7].

The simplest way of building a native IIOP server would be to adapt an existing HTTP server by reusing the code written for I2H. This would make it easy to provide the same resources through both protocols. Indeed, the server could deal with HTTP and IIOP requests on the same TCP port: the first four bytes in an IIOP request are the four characters "GIOP" [4], enabling the server to distinguish requests using IIOP. This would make the task of the locator easier.

The immediate consequence of building such a server is that the need to use a gateway is removed. Thus we benefit from IIOP's connection management (discussed earlier) which should improve performance. However, the main advantages of distributed object technology are extensibility and modularity.

This extensibility and modularity can be exploited to add a management interface to the server. Putting management operations into an interface that is separate from the normal service interface has been a valuable technique in distributed systems. Having a separate management interface avoids the problem of having to find a safe way to perform management through the interface seen by normal users, and also avoids the need to perform management operations through the file system of the host that is running the server, and other local and system specific facilities. As you'll see later in the paper, the ability to define extra methods for a server can also be used as an alternative to CGI to build gateways to other applications (see later).

As an alternative to running both IIOP and HTTP servers, or constructing a server that supports both, the H2I gateway can be used to provide HTTP access to an IIOP-only server.

Implementation Experience

Prototypes of the gateways have been written, and work is continuing to implement improved gateways as well as the other components.

A Simple IDL Mapping of HTTP

The simple IDL mapping of HTTP which is used by the initial prototypes is shown below.

```
interface http {
/*
HTTP headers are represented as name
    value pairs and encoded as strings,
    e.g. "accept text/html"
*/
struct header {
string name;
string value;
};
/*
A request consists of a URL (encoded as
    a string) and a
sequence of headers. This is sufficient
    for all methods
except PUT and POST.
*/
struct request {string URL;
```

```
sequence< header > headers;
};
/*
PUT and POST require a body. So the
    request has an extra field: a
    sequence of octet. An octet is an 8
    bit quantity which will not undergo
    any conversion when transmitted by
    the communication system.
*/
struct request_body {
string URL;
sequence< header > headers;
sequence< octet > body;
};
/*
Responses to all requests consist of
    the status code and its
    correpsponding reason string, a
    sequence of headers, and the body
    as a sequence of octets. For
    responses with no body, a sequence
    of length zero is sent.
*/
struct response {
short respcode; /*The HTTP status code
    e.g. "200"; OK*/
string resptext; /*The HTTP Reason
    phrase*/
sequence< header > headers;
sequence< octet > body;
};
/* The standard HTTP methods*/
response GET (in request request);
response HEAD (in request request);
response POST (in request_body request);
response PUT (in request_body request);
response DELETE(in request request);
response LINK  (in request request);
response UNLINK(in request request);
};
```

This IDL is passed through a stub compiler to generate the header files, client stubs and server skeletons for the gateways. The stub compiler uses the IDL compiler frontend made available by SunSoft Inc., through OMG, with a back end written for this project.

The simple mapping above has a number of deficiencies, including:

- It does not attempt to match applicable headers to methods

- It bundles everything up into one argument and one result

After we have completed the implementation of the infrastructure described in this paper we plan to experiment with different, possibly more efficient mappings of HTTP. One obvious possibility is a binary encoding of the common standard HTTP headers, using strings only for unusual and extension headers. Another possibility is to deliver bodies through stream objects that support incremental and concurrent processing of the incoming data.

The I2H gateway provides the interface specified in the IDL. The first working prototype of I2H used the W3C Reference Library (libwww) version 3.1pre1, the Inter-ORB Engine written by SunSoft and published via OMG, and the headers and server skeletons generated from the IDL by the stub compiler. Figure 4 shows the architectural arrangement of these components in I2H.

Much of the work of processing the IIOP requests and responses is done by the generated skeletons, and the library functions called from the skeletons. Since the W3C Reference Library performs most of the work of accessing resources via HTTP (and other protocols), only a small amount of code is needed to connect these together.

The H2I gateway

The H2I gateway acts as a proxy to which existing Web clients, usually browsers, can connect. The first working prototype was a modified version of CERN HTTPD version 3.0, because most of the required mechanisms were already available. The first prototype had a fixed policy for using IIOP—all requests for HTTP URLs were sent via IIOP to an I2H gateway specified through an environment variable. This was sufficient to exercise the data paths, but was quickly replaced by a second prototype with a dynamic selection mechanism. Figure 5 shows the architecture of this second prototype for H2I.

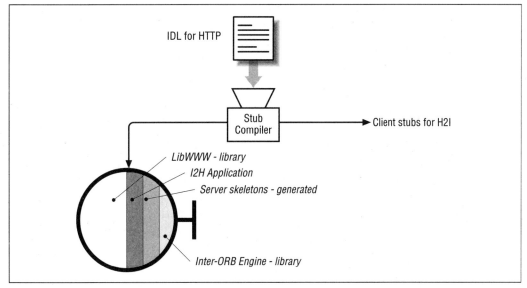

Figure 4: The architecture of the I2H gateway, showing how I2H binds the WWW Reference Library (LibWWW) components to the Inter-ORB Engine via the automatically generated server skeletons and a bespoke application layer.

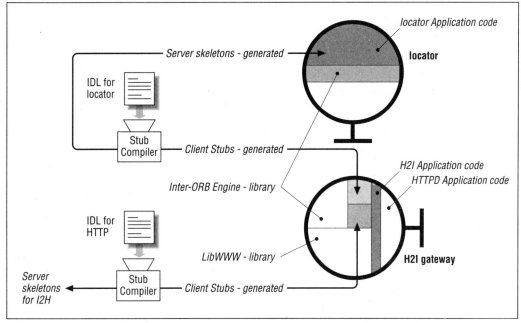

Figure 5: The architecture of the H2I gateway and the locator with which it interoperates. In addition to the component set used by I2H, H2I contains the client stubs derived from the IDL for the locator, and HTTPD-based application code. The locator has a simple layered server structure.

The H2I prototype is being used to explore the options for providing data to the locator. The first experiments use data delivered in extension HTTP headers that indicate the availability of an IIOP gateway. A modified CERN HTTPD is being used to send the extra HTTP header.

Stub Compiler for CGI

The initial approach of the project was to make the integration of distributed technology into the Web at the server side an easy process. The aim was to make distributed object systems rapidly available via the Web through HTML Forms.

One of the limitations of integrating legacy systems into the Web is the amount of time taken in creating the CGI [7] access programs and in generating the control forms. This problem is dealt with by using an IDL to describe the service being integrated.

A stub compiler for CORBA IDL was developed which generates the necessary template forms for the frontend, as well as the server skeletons for the CGI program which unmarshall the parameters. The advantages of this approach include:

- The entire process of stub generation is automatic, and in particular, the unmarshalling of CGI parameters is automatically correct.

- The template HTML forms are syntactically correct HTML.

- The template HTML forms that are created require only a few minutes of editing to be made fully suitable for the required task (generally this requires only sizing of input fields and addition of explanatory text).

The functioning of the IDL stub compiler for CGI is shown in Figure 6.

The principal limitation of the current implementation is that template forms do not take full advantage of HTML form functionality. Further work is needed to expand the range of types that can be mapped to form facilities, especially where there are choices of how to map a type to form facilities (e.g., an enumeration to radio buttons or a menu).

Another way of integrating existing systems into the Web is to define extension methods for a Web server which access other services. For an ORB or IIOP based server, much of the work of adding the new methods to the server would be done by the stub compiler, which would generate server skeletons for the new methods. HTML forms could be used to invoke the new methods. This approach may make the Web server stateful,

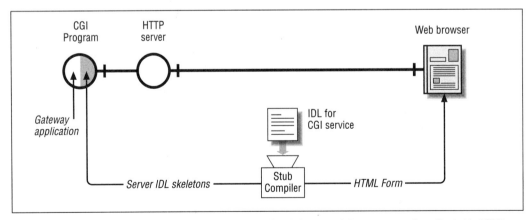

Figure 6: The generation of both the server-side IDL skeleton and the corresponding client-side HTML form, from the IDL for the CGI program, by the stub compiler.

since new methods cannot be guaranteed to support stateless interaction. Some may regard this as a disadvantage. In contrast, the CGI approach keeps the Web server stateless. However, since a new CGI process is forked to deal with each request, any state required by the gateway must be stored externally (e.g., on the local file system).

The ANSAweb stub compiler for CGI is available by anonymous FTP from the ANSA FTP server *ftp://ftp.ansa.co.uk/*. It is known to run on HP-UX and Solaris platforms. The package includes complete documentation and examples. A more detailed overview is given in reference [8].

Related Work

There are presently a number of projects aimed at putting objects into the WWW. Of these, the most closely related are the DCE-Web project, built around DCE, and the Web* project. These are described in further detail below.

DCE-Web and Wand

The OSF Research Institute has a number of projects which are applying the Distributed Computing Environment (DCE) to the Web. The most closely related to our work are the DCE-Web project [9] and its native DCE-Web server Wand [10].

In DCE-Web, HTTP protocol messages are packaged as DCE RPC data by the DCE-Web layer, a technique known as protocol tunnelling. Thus the HTTP protocol messages are communicated unchanged, minimizing the changes required to the core protocol processing functions of existing browsers and servers.

Our approach is to provide a mapping of HTTP to CORBA IDL. Complete backwards compatibility is maintained by use of gateways and dynamic protocol switching. (We intend to explore a number of mappings with a view to improving efficiency e.g. removing the need to parse ASCII headers.)

The main benefits of the DCE approach are security and naming. The DCE security services are used to provide fine-grained security and the DCE naming service can be used to name Web objects. This approach is complementary to our work, which emphasizes the benefits of extensibility and modularity inherent in distributed objects. Thus, we are able to create browsers which consist of collaborating objects (e.g., the use of the locator) are able to define new user methods for our Web servers, and can define separate management interfaces.

Web*

The Web* project [11] has developed a Tcl library which uses CORBA's Dynamic Invocation Interface to access Orbix services [12]. (Orbix is a commercial implementation of CORBA.) The Tcl Orbix clients are executed as CGI programs by either the NCSA or CERN Web servers. Using this technology, Web* has successfully used Orbix to provide a WWW interface to Oracle databases—another demonstration that CORBA technology is good at integrating existing information systems.

Our work focuses on applying CORBA technology to Web servers and browsers—the frontend of the Web. A native IIOP Web server could communicate with an Orbix service directly using IIOP, or it could use CGI to launch a Web* Tcl client.

The CGI stub compiler we have built is complementary to the Web* project. It uses CORBA IDL to describe the interface offered by the CGI program and from this generates template HTML forms and IDL server skeletons for the CGI program. This technique could be used by Web* to generate HTML forms to access its Tcl Orbix clients. Similarly, its Tcl Orbix clients could benefit from skeletons which automatically unmarshalled parameters sent by the Web server.

Summary

This paper has described work being carried out as part of the ANSA workprogramme to provide interoperability between the World Wide Web and CORBA-based distributed object systems. The key elements of the design are the representation of HTTP in IDL, and gateways that translate between HTTP and the IIOP encoding of the interfaces.

The gateways allow HTTP to be carried over IIOP and provide full interoperability between Web and CORBA clients and servers, as shown in Figure 7.

Prototypes of these gateways have been implemented. We are continuing to explore the opportunities offered by distributed object technology in the Web, and by Web technology in distributed object systems.

This work has already shown that object technology can be used to provide interoperability between the Web and distributed objects. The necessary protocol support for interoperability is provided by IIOP. We have also shown that IIOP can be seamlessly integrated into the Web via servers and proxies. In this way, the Web can already reap the benefits of distributed object technology such as:

- Ease of programming

- Extensibility and manageability

- Encapsulation and systems integration

Distributed object technology will help the Web to evolve into an information environment of the kind demanded by its users and by commercial interest. At the same time, distributed object technology now has the potential to be used and tested in the biggest distributed system ever built.

Ultimately, the Web will be used as an integrator for distributed object systems, and those object technologies will benefit from having the Web client architectures providing them with a globally uniform front-end.

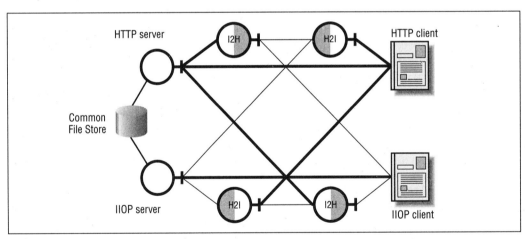

Figure 7: The architecture for interoperability between clients and servers with native IIOP and HTTP modes respectively. For clarity, the locator is not shown. This architecture is an automatic consequence of the manner in which the I2H and H2I gateways have been designed.

Acknowledgments

The authors would like to acknowledge the contributions of all members of the ANSA team, past and present; in particular, Andrew Herbert, towards the ideas discussed in this paper. We would also like to thank the sponsors of the ANSA workprogramme for providing the resources used in this work. ■

References

1. Object Management Group Inc, *The Common Object Request Broker: Architecture and Specification, Revision 1.2*, December 1993. OMG Document Number 93.12.43; *ftp://ftp.omg.org/pub/docs/93-12-43.ps*

2. Guangxing Li, *An Overview of Real-Time ANSAware 1.0, Distributed Systems Engineering* 2(1), 1995, pp28-38.

3. Tim Berners-Lee, Roy Fielding and Henryk Frystyk Nielsen, *Hypertext Transfer Protocol—HTTP/1.0*, work in progress within the HTTP Working Group of the IETF.

4. Object Management Group Inc, *Universal Networked Objects*. March 1995. OMG Document Number 95.3.10; *ftp://ftp.omg.org/pub/docs/95-3-10.ps*

5. Douglas Kosovic, *Trader Information Service. http://www.dstc.edu.au/AU/research_news/odp/trader/trader.html*

6. Karen Sollins and Larry Masinter, *Functional Requirements for Uniform Resource Names, Internet RFC 1737*, 20 December 1994. *ftp://ds.internic.net/rfc/rfc1737.txt*

7. Rob McCool, *The Common Gateway Interface. http://booboo.ncsa.uiuc.edu/cgi/overview.html*

8. Nigel Edwards, *Object Wrapping (for WWW)—The Key to Integrated Services?*, Document Identifier APM.1464, 1995. Architecture Projects Management Ltd, Cambridge. *http://www.ansa.co.uk/ANSA/ISF/1464/1464prt1.html*

9. *DCE-Web Home Page http://www.osf.org/www/dceweb/DCE-Web-Home-Page.html*

10. *Wand—Web and DCE Server. http://www.osf.org/www/wand/index.html*

11. *WEB* Home Page. http://webstar.cerc.wvu.edu/*

12. *The Orbix Home Page at IONA Technologies. http://www.iona.ie:8000/www/Orbix/index.html*

About the Authors

Owen Rees
[*http://www.ansa.co.uk/Staff/rtor.html*]
The ANSA Project, Architecture Projects Management Ltd, Poseidon House, Castle Park, Cambridge CB3 0RD, UK.
Tel +44-1223-568926; Fax +44-1223-359779.
rtor@ansa.co.uk

Nigel Edwards
Hewlett-Packard Laboratories, Filton Road, Stoke Gifford, Bristol, BS12 6QZ.
Tel +44-117-9228490; Fax +44-117-9229285.
nje@hplb.hpl.hp.com

Mark Madsen
[*http://www.ansa.co.uk/Staff/msm.html*]
The ANSA Project, Architecture Projects Management Ltd, Poseidon House, Castle Park, Cambridge CB3 0RD, UK.
Tel +44-1223-568934; Fax +44-1223-359779.
msm@ansa.co.uk

Mike Beasley
[*http://www.ansa.co.uk/Staff/mdrb.html*]
Architecture Projects Management Ltd, Poseidon House, Castle Park, Cambridge CB3 0RD, UK.
mdrb@ansa.co.uk

Ashley McClenaghan
[*http://www.ansa.co.uk/Staff/am.html*]
The ANSA Project, Architecture Projects Management Ltd, Poseidon House, Castle Park, Cambridge CB3 0RD, UK.
Tel +44-1223-568924; Fax +44-1223-359779.
am@ansa.co.uk

W3OBJECTS
BRINGING OBJECT-ORIENTED TECHNOLOGY TO THE WEB

David Ingham, Mark Little, Steve Caughey, Santosh Shrivastava

Abstract

In this paper we discuss some of the problems of the current Web and show how the introduction of object-orientation provides flexible and extensible solutions. Web resources become encapsulated as objects, with well-defined interfaces through which all interactions occur. The interfaces and their implementations can be inherited by builders of objects, and methods (operations) can be redefined to better suit the object. New characteristics, such as concurrency control and persistence, can be obtained by inheriting from suitable base classes, without necessarily requiring any changes to users of these resources. We describe the W3Object model which we have developed based upon these ideas, and show, through a prototype implementation, how we have used the model to address the problems of referential integrity and transparent object (resource) migration. We also give indications of future work.
Keywords: *World Wide Web, object-oriented, referential integrity, mobility, distributed systems*

Introduction

Electronic publishing in the large has grown massively since the advent of the World Wide Web. Many factors have contributed to its success, in particular, the simplicity of the system has played a significant role in its acceptance. Accessing information via the hypertext interface is relatively easy to learn and use. Becoming a publisher on the Web is also straightforward; users from all professions have been able to participate, resulting in the huge diversity of the information currently available. These factors coupled with free Web software with cross-platform support have helped the Web gain critical mass.

Within the current Web environment, hypertext links are used to glue together resources which are primarily static, read-only, and file-based (henceforth referred to as *standard resources*). Although, the Web has been very successful in serving such resources, it suffers from a number of shortcomings and it is questionable whether the current system will be able to scale indefinitely given the massive growth rates currently being witnessed. In particular, one highly visible problem is that of broken links between documents, caused by the lack of referential integrity

within the current hypertext implementation. With the predicted growth in the number of resources, this problem will increase in significance, and the Web will become more difficult to use and manage.

The future is also likely to bring new demands on the Web in terms of the types of resources that it will be required to serve. The Web has proved its usefulness in the organization of distributed documentation, and users will wish to access other kinds of resource, with richer interfaces, within the same environment. Furthermore, service providers will wish to take advantage of the Web in order to tap the potentially huge customer base.

In this paper, we will show how the current Web implementation is object-based, with a single interface, comprising the set of HTTP [1] operations. Although extensions have been implemented to allow the incorporation of *nonstandard resources*, it is the opinion of the authors that the system does not exhibit the necessary extensibility characteristics that are required if the Web is to cope with the introduction of more advanced resources and services. We will show how making the change to an object-oriented system can yield an extensible infrastructure that is capable of supporting existing functionality and allows the seamless integration of more complex resources and services. We aim to use proven technical solutions from the distributed object-oriented community to show how many of the current problems with the Web can be addressed within the proposed model.

In the next section, a critique of the current Web is presented, highlighting existing problems in serving standard resources and the current approach for incorporating nonstandard resources. The section entitled "W3Objects" describes the W3Object design, its aims, object model, and system architecture. The "Illustrations" section gives an example, describing how particular Web shortcomings can be addressed within the proposed architecture. The remaining sections describe our implementation progress, plans for further work and concluding remarks.

Critique of the Current Web

This section explores some of the problems with the current World Wide Web, which we have classified into three categories. Firstly, we consider the problems associated with the primary function of the Web, that is, in serving standard resources. The current techniques for incorporating nonstandard resources are then discussed. Finally, the recent proposals for extending the existing Web model are analyzed and reviewed.

Serving Standard Resources

Currently the Web is primarily populated with standard resources including Hypertext Markup Language (HTML) [2] documents, GIF images, postscript files, audio files, etc., with the common characteristics of being passive, read-only, and static. All resources are currently named using Uniform Resource Locators (URLs) [3], a locational naming scheme which describes the protocol used to access the resource, the Internet address of the server containing the resource, and the location of the resource within that

server. HTML documents contain hypertext links which are either intraresource, for providing multiple navigational paths through a document, or interresource, providing the *webglue*, allowing related resources to be connected.

One of the major advantages of the Web is the speed and ease by which information can be made available. In this environment Web resources are frequently created, moved, and destroyed in an ad-hoc manner, suiting the owner of the information or publishing site. These changes are usually made autonomously, with little regard for users of the information. There are three distinct problems tied together here, namely, referential integrity, migration transparency, and resource management. Quality of service, which is also affected by these issues, is also discussed.

Referential integrity

A system supports referential integrity if it guarantees that resources will continue to exist as long as there are outstanding references to the resources. The Web does not support this property and cannot do so since the system is unaware of the number of references that exist to a particular resource.

It is impractical to maintain every resource that has ever been published on a particular server forever, this simply does not scale. Resources that are no longer of value, for whatever reason, become garbage and need to be collected. This may involve moving the resources to backing storage, or in some cases, deleting the resources entirely. Access pattern information, which is currently available through examination of server logs, is not a sufficient basis to decide whether an object is safe to garbage collect as important though rarely used references to a resource may exist. Safe garbage collection can only be performed if referencing information is available.

The consequences of deleting resources that are still referenced affects both the user and the information provider. In the Web environment deleting a resource that is referenced by another resource results in a broken hypertext link. Such broken links are the single most annoying problem faced by browsing users in the current Web. Broken links result in a tarnished reputation for the provider of the document containing the link, annoyance for the document user, and possible lost opportunity for the owner of the resource pointed to by the link.

Migration transparency

In addition to the problems associated with deleting Web resources, migrating resources (either intra- or interserver) also has the potential to break hypertext links. Using the URL naming scheme, when a resource moves its identity also changes. Therefore, hypertext links to the old name will now break, with the same consequences as stated previously.

A partial solution to this problem is provided by the use of the HTTP redirect directive, which provides a forwarding pointer to the new location, allowing clients to rebind to the resource (automatically in the case of redirection-aware browsers). However, this is only a partial solution for the following reasons: firstly, documents containing references to the old location of the resource are not automatically updated, and so future requests will continue to access the old location first. Secondly, even if there were an automatic update mechanism, the lack of referential integrity means that the redirector can never

be safely removed since it is impossible to determine whether all of the links have been updated. There is also the possibility that the URL may be reallocated following the migration.

The IETF Uniform Resource Identifiers (URI) Working Group's [4] work on Uniform Resource Names (URNs) [5], an alternative naming scheme, based upon logical rather than locational naming attempts to address the problem of migration transparency. The mapping from logical name (URN) to locational name (URL) is stored within a name-server which is updated with the new URL when the resource moves [6]. The disadvantage of this approach is the performance penalty associated with name-server lookups, updates, and access bottlenecks. Furthermore, this scheme does not address the issue of referential integrity.

Resource and service management

As previously mentioned, most resource accesses through the Web are read-only operations. Updates to the resources by the information provider are performed using mechanisms orthogonal to the Web; that is, using the native commands and editing tools of the server machine. In effect Web resources reside in two distinct domains in parallel: the traditional structure of the filesystem and the complex interlinking Web of hypertext. Within these two environments, the interfaces to the resources as well as the relationships between the resources are fundamentally different, as illustrated in Figure 1.

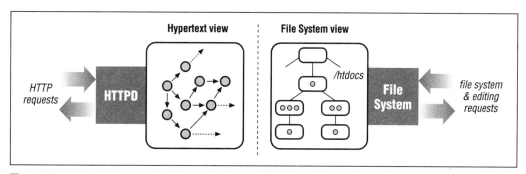

Figure 1:   Disjoint interfaces to Web resources

Maintenance operations carried out by the information provider or site maintainer typically require manipulation of the resources within both domains. As described earlier in the section entitled "Migration Transparency," moving a resource within the file system has the side effect of changing its name in the Web domain. To reflect such changes, other Web resources must also be modified. Further, the internal state of the moved resource may also require modification, due to the use of relative naming [7]. At present such changes are performed manually and are prone to mistakes and inconsistencies (although tools, for example, *MOMSpider* [8] exist to help eventually detect some of these). This can be seen as a result of having two parallel interfaces without any support for maintaining consistency.

Quality of service

The perceived quality of service (QoS) of the Web is influenced by many factors, including the broken link problems already mentioned. Even if a user holds a correct reference to an existing Web resource, it may still be unavailable due to a number of reasons, including unavailability of the machine serving the resource, and partitions in the network between the client and server. Partitions may either be real, caused by breaks in the physical network, or virtual, due to excessive network or server load making communications between the client and server impossible. Even if communication is possible, very poor response characteristics may effectively make the resource unusable. QoS will become more of an issue as the Web continues its transformation into a commercially oriented system

Technical solutions for improving QoS are fairly well understood, including caching for responsiveness, replication for availability, and migration for load balancing. Caching in the Web is reasonably common, both through the use of browser memory and disc caches, and also through the use of caching servers [9]. Effective caching is not a trivial task since there are many subtle problems that need to be addressed,

including cache consistency, accounting, etc. Current caching servers use a heuristic approach for consistency management, where resources can only apply coarse-grained tuning based on expiry dates. The IETF URI working group is implementing a framework for resource replication, but appear to only be addressing the problem within the realm of read-only, static resources, where a read-from-any policy is appropriate [6]. Replicating more complex read/write resources is much more difficult due to the problems associated with maintaining consistency between concurrent users and in the presence of failures.

Incorporating Nonstandard Resources

Those Web resources which possess a richer interface than standard resources are manipulated through the Common Gateway Interface (CGI) protocol [10], which sits above HTTP. Through this protocol it is possible to perform arbitrary operations, not supported directly by HTTP, on these resources. Such resources are still identified by URLs, but the HTTP daemon is able to distinguish CGI URLs from standard resources. Upon receiving a request containing a CGI URL, rather than dealing with the request itself the daemon invokes a CGI *script* identified in the URL. Additional parameters can be included in the URL, which the daemon passes directly to the script, to be used in an application specific manner in the servicing of the request. When the script finishes the request it returns a reply message to the client and terminates.

Unlike publishing standard resources, writing CGI scripts is not simple; the resources manipulated need no longer be read-only and the issues involved in interacting with them are much more complex. There is no support for controlled sharing of resources, and because HTTP is still the underlying communication protocol, connections between client and resource last only for each request. This forces users to adopt ad-hoc solutions to problems such as persistence, concurrency control, and sharing of resources between requests.

Extending the Model

The HTTP protocol specifies the operations a client can attempt to perform on a Web resource; for example GET, POST, etc. There is also support for an *extension method*, which allows user-specific operations to be added to the protocol. Resource providers who wish to use this feature, must liaise with the Internet Assigned Numbers Authority (IANA) to register these operations. The IETF have also proposed new standard methods to be incorporated into HTTP in response to user requests [11]. Irrespective of the approach used to add new methods to the protocol, changes will be required to both the daemon and browsers. Further, the new methods may be inappropriate for the majority of Web resources and there will still be requirements which they do not address. This will result in a further round of protocol negotiations and changes to Web software. There is a long lead time involved between initial method proposals and final implementations.

The result of this model and the constraints it imposes are that people may change the daemons in an ad-hoc manner. This makes migration of Web resources from modified daemons difficult because modifications need to be made to every daemon which services them. There is also no easy route for code reuse, leading to individuals implementing similar methods in different ways.

Conclusion

From an object perspective, the HTTP daemon provides a single interface through which all objects it manages are accessed. In effect, the current Web may be viewed as an object-based system with a single class of object. What is desired is the ability to modify this interface on a per-resource basis. Within the object-oriented paradigm such specializations are achieved through the use of inheritance, and it is the

absence of this which distinguishes an object-based from an object-oriented system [12].

We believe that the model and implementation we shall present in this paper represent a cleaner way of addressing the issues of flexibility and extensibility in a uniform manner, and can be used to provide solutions to the problems highlighted earlier. They can also be applied to the current Web with little or no modifications to users of these resources, and minor requirements from their providers. In the following sections we will describe our model and illustrate it with an implementation which supports referential integrity and transparent object migration.

W3Objects

The primary objective of our research is to develop an extensible Web infrastructure which is able to support a wide range of resources and services. Our model makes extensive use of the concepts of object-orientation to achieve the necessary extensibility characteristics. Within this object-oriented framework, proven concepts from the distributed object-oriented community will be applied to the problems currently facing the Web.

The next section introduces our object model, describing how the principles of object-orientation are applied to the Web domain. The interactions between the system components are described in the section entitled "System Architecture," which is followed by a section entitled "W3Object Properties" which classifies and describes a collection of properties applicable to different classes of W3Object.

Object Model

In the proposed model, Web resources are transformed from file-based resources into objects, *W3Objects*. W3Objects are *encapsulated* resources possessing internal state and a well-defined behavior. The objects themselves are responsible for managing their own state transitions and properties, in response to method invocations. This model supports *abstraction* since clients only interact with W3Objects through the published interfaces; the implementation of a particular operation is not externally visible.

Different classes of W3Object support different operational interfaces, which are obtained through the use of *interface inheritance*. Abstract classes are used to define an interface to a particular object abstraction, without specifying any particular implementation of the operations. Different classes of W3Object may share conformance to a particular abstract interface, but may implement the operations differently, in a manner appropriate to the particular class. For example, consider a `Manageable` interface, including a `migrate` operation, for moving objects from one location to another. While the same interface is appropriate for many classes of W3Object, the implementations may differ; for example, migration of a hypertext object may require some internal link manipulation operations in addition to the operations required by, say, a text file.

The use of interface inheritance provides *polymorphism*; that is, all derived classes that conform to an interface provided by some base class may be treated as instances of that base class, without regard for any other aspects of that class' behavior. Continuing with the previous example, consider a dedicated GUI-based Website management tool, providing a graphical interface for performing management-style operations on the objects; one such operation may be object migration. The management tool is able to abstract away from other features of the different objects (supported through various other interfaces) and simply address all of the different objects as instances of the `Manageable` interface. In addition to inheritance of interface, the model also supports *behavioral inheritance*, thereby supporting code reuse. For example, object properties such as persistence and concurrency control may be provided by *mixin* base classes to be inherited as required. Mix-in classes are not designed to be instantiated themselves. They are used to augment the functionality of the derived class, by providing some particular behavior, usually orthogonal to the primary function of the class.

The diagram in Figure 2 illustrates the key points of our object model by showing how two example W3Object classes, `Spreadsheet` and Play, are composed using both interface and behavioral inheritance. The abstract class, `Manageable` provides the interface description for management-style operations (only a single operation, `migrate`, is shown). Both of the derived classes inherit this interface, providing their own implementations. In addition, both of the derived classes provide other interfaces, describing the primary operations of the classes. The `Play` class, representing a theatrical performance, provides a `bookSeat` operation, and `Spreadsheet` provides `get` and `set` operations for manipulating the contents of the spreadsheet cells. Further, the `Spreadsheet` class is concurrency controlled, having derived this property from the mixin class, `ConcControllable`. The operations `setLock` and `releaseLock` are used in the implementation of the `get` and `set` operations to ensure the integrity of the spreadsheet in the event of concurrent access.

Also shown in the diagram are three different clients which manipulate instances of `Play` and `Spreadsheet`. A Website management tool, previously mentioned, is solely concerned with the operations provided through the `Manageable` interface. The tool is able to invoke the `migrate` operation on instances of either derived class without knowledge of the nature of the class. Two further clients are shown, a theatre booking application and a spreadsheet tool, which manipulate instances of `Play` and `Spreadsheet` respectively. The fact that these classes also conform to the Manageable interface is of no consequence to the clients who only interact with the objects via the interfaces supporting the classes' primary function.

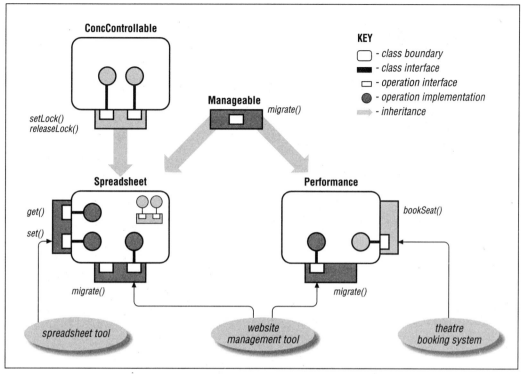

Figure 2:   Illustration of using the object model

System Architecture

In common with the current Web, the proposed W3Object architecture consists of three basic entity types, namely, clients, servers, and published objects. In the current Web environment, these three types correspond to Web browsers (e.g., mosaic), Web daemons (e.g., CERN HTTPD), and documentation resources (e.g., HTML documents) respectively. Our architecture supports both client-object (client-server), and interobject (peer-to-peer) communication.

Client-object interactions

Figure 3 illustrates the logical view of client-object interactions within the W3Object architecture. A single server process is shown, managing a single W3Object (although servers are capable of managing multiple objects of different types),

which is being accessed via two different clients, a standard Web browser, and a dedicated bespoke application. This diagram highlights *interoperability* as one of the key concepts of the architecture, that is, the support for object accessibility via different applications using multiple protocols.

As stated earlier, W3Objects are encapsulated, meaning that they are responsible for managing their own properties (e.g., security, persistence, concurrency control etc.) rather than the application accessing the object. For example, in the case of concurrency, the object manages its own access control, based upon its internal policy, irrespective of which application method invocations originate from.

The local representation of an object, together with the available operations, may vary depending upon the particular type of client accessing it.

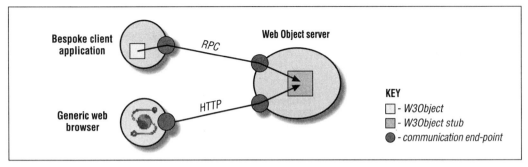

Figure 3:   Client-object interactions

The Web browser uses a URL to bind to the particular object in the server. The operations that are permitted on the object, via the URL, are defined by the HTTP protocol. The HTTP communication end-point of the server may perform name mapping between URL and the internal name for the object and may also map HTTP requests to appropriate method invocations on the object. Within the bespoke application, a client-stub object acts as the local representation of the remote object. From the point of view of the application, this stub object presents the illusion that the remote object is actually within the address space of the client. Like any other object, the stub presents a well-defined interface describing the supported operations. This interface has the potential to be much richer than that provided through HTTP, including application specific operations. Operation invocations on the stub are passed to the object using the remote procedure call (RPC) protocol. Client-stub objects may be automatically generated from a description of an object interface. Our implementation uses C++ as the definition language and we provide stub-generation support for creating client and server side stubs which handle operation invocation and parameter marshalling [13]. Other possible interface definition languages are possible, including CORBA IDL [14] and ILU ISL [15].

Continuing with the previous example of a Web-based theatre booking application; to support access via conventional browsers using HTTP,

the theatre object would conform to an HTTP interface, supporting an operation, say, `htmlGet`. An HTTP GET request from the browser would be mapped to an invocation of the `htmlGet` method of the object. Through this limited interface, the programme of events and availability information may be available. A client-stub object for the theatre may support more advanced operations such as seat booking using *atomic actions* (*transactions*).

Although not illustrated, a number of other client implementations are possible. The common gateway interface (CGI) could be used to provide a richer client-side interface than is readily available through HTTP. Although, it has been already stated that we believe CGI to be too low-level for direct programming, CGI interfaces to remote objects can be automatically created using stub-generation tools. We have implemented a basic stub-generator, which uses an abstract definition of the remote object, and ANSA have recently released a more complete tool [16] based on CORBA IDL. Recent developments using interpreted languages within the Web, including Java [17] and SafeTcl [18] are potentially very useful for developing client-side interfaces to W3Objects. Using such languages, complex, architecture-neutral, front-ends dedicated to a particular W3Object class can be developed, supporting rich sets of operations.

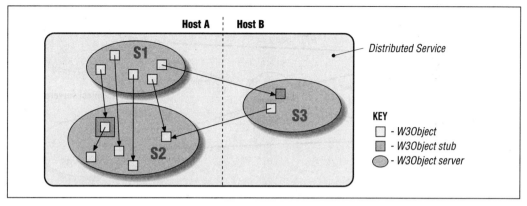

Figure 4:   Inter-object interactions

Inter-object interactions

In addition to client-object communication, our architecture also supports inter-object communication, regardless of the objects' location. In effect, the architecture may be viewed as a single distributed service, partitioned over different hosts as illustrated in Figure 4. Inter-object communication is used for a variety of purposes, including referencing, migration, caching, and replication.

In addition to W3Objects, servers may contain W3Object stubs, or aliases, which are named objects that simply forward operation invocations to another object, transparently to clients. One particular use of aliases is in implementation of name-servers, since a name-server may be viewed simply as a collection of named objects which alias other objects with alternative names (server S1 in diagram). Objects may also contain stubs to other objects (shown in S2 in diagram). This feature is used in our implementation of referencing, which is described further in the "Illustrations" section.

Implementation considerations

As previously mentioned, a particular W3Object server is capable of holding W3Objects belonging to a set of specific types. At the time it is created, it is unlikely that one can predict all of the object types that a particular server will be required to serve over its lifetime. This raises the question of how new types are introduced to the system. The usual approach is to bring down a server, rebuild it with the code which supports the new object types, and then restart it. This approach is less than ideal for an application such as the Web where there is a requirement for keeping downtime to a minimum. An alternative technique relies on *dynamic loading*, which allows an active process to load new code as necessary. Although this approach is clearly more elegant and we do not preclude its use, dynamic loaders currently suffer from lack of standardization and therefore portability. A third, more pragmatic, approach is to create another server to support the new object types. This approach may be desirable even if suitable dynamic loading support is available due to requirements for fault tolerance and security because, as a single server for all object types is a single point of failure, multiple servers can be used to protect users against such failures.

One method of interfacing with multiple servers is to make use of an HTTP Gateway, which uses stub objects to forward object invocations through to the appropriate server. The gateway is transparent to clients accessing the objects; incoming requests are simply forwarded to the destination object, which parses the request and

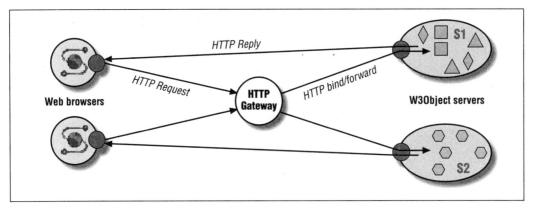

Figure 5: Client-object communication through gateway

replies accordingly. This is illustrated in Figure 5, in which server S1 manages a number of different types of object (illustrated by different shapes) and server S2 manages objects of a single type. As the processing of operations is entirely the responsibility of the individual object, the introduction of new object types is transparent to the gateway.

W3Object Properties

Based on critiques of the current Web by ourselves and others [19], and also our experience with distributed systems in general, we have attempted to identify the set of properties that are required by W3Objects. We have classified these properties into three categories: core properties, common properties, and class-specific properties. In this section we shall present what we believe to be the core properties required by all W3Objects and give examples of some common properties.

Core properties

Four properties have been identified as being the core requirements for W3Objects: Naming, Sharing, Mobility, and Referencing. The implementation of these properties is divided between the objects themselves and the supporting infrastruc-

ture which manages the objects. Each property will be considered in turn.

Naming. One of the fundamental concepts of the object-oriented paradigm is identity. The ability to name an object is required in order to unambiguously communicate with and about it. Context-relative naming is an essential feature of our environment so as to support interoperability and scalability. As mentioned previously, different clients may use different local representations of a remote object (URLs, client-stub objects, etc.). Since it is impractical to impose new naming conventions on existing systems, we require the ability to translate names between system-boundaries. Furthermore, for extensibility, we need to be able to incorporate new naming systems. Within our design, naming is provided via the object infrastructure. Context-relative naming is supported via the use of name-servers, implemented as collections of object aliases, as described previously.

Sharing. Implicit within the Web domain is the requirement that objects can be shared. Although the basic function of allowing multiple users to interact with objects is simple to achieve, there are a number of other associated mechanisms that require interaction with the base sharing functionality. Access control, either user and group based, or access restriction based on the location of the client, are both likely requirements. Additionally, with objects supporting a rich set of interfaces, the granularity of the control must be configurable.

Mobility. One of the lessons learned from the current Web is that support for object mobility is a necessary requirement for W3Objects. At object creation time, migration of the object may not be envisaged, but it is virtually impossible to predict the future requirements of a particular object. Mobility may be required for many reasons, including load balancing, caching, and improved performance through locality etc., with different forms of migration, including intra- or inter-host.

Referencing. In order to address what may be viewed as the primary problem with the current Web, namely referential integrity, we believe that low-level referencing support is required by all objects. A range of schemes is possible, including forward referencing [20], call-backs, and redirection through a location server (as in the URN approach). Referencing is closely related to mobility, since referencing schemes may be used to locate objects even in the event of object migration. Our approach to referencing is described in detail in the "Illustrations" section.

Common properties

There are a potentially large number of common properties for W3Objects which can be encapsulated within appropriate base classes. In the rest of this section we shall highlight four of these properties which we have selected based upon our experience of building reliable distributed systems [21].

Replication. There is a range of replication protocols from active to passive, and strong consistency to weak consistency. There is no single replication protocol which is suitable for every object which may need to be replicated and at the same time can satisfy a user's required quality of service [22]. As such, it is our intention to implement a suitable base class for object providers, which will enable them to select the appropriate replication protocol on a per object basis.

In addition object providers will also be able to select the optimum number and location of these replicas, and modify this as required [23].

Concurrency control. By enabling users to share arbitrary objects it may be necessary for these object state transitions to be managed through an appropriate concurrency control mechanism. Consider the theatre booking example earlier: if user A wishes to examine the seats which are available while user B is in the process of booking a seat, it would be desirable for B to lock the seat in order to prevent conflicting updates. There are a number of concurrency control mechanisms available, but our initial implementation will be based upon the familiar multiple reader, single writer policy.

Caching. The caching of object states, either at or close to users, can help alleviate problems of network congestion and latency. However, as with replication, there is a need for a range of caching policies based upon user requirements and object properties.

Fault tolerance. In a large-scale distributed system, fault tolerance is an important property. One way of addressing the issues of fault tolerance is by using atomic actions to control method invocations. Objects inherit necessary persistence and concurrency control characteristics, and application programmers then manipulate these objects within atomic actions which guarantee the usual ACID properties.

Illustrations

Having described our model in the previous sections, we shall now illustrate how two of the core properties, referencing and mobility, are implemented within the model. Our aim is to address the current problem of broken links and provide transparent object migration.

Referential Integrity

In our model Web resources are represented as W3Objects and may be referenced from some

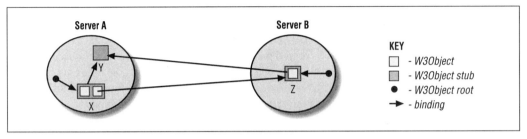

Figure 6:   Object referencing

root, either directly, via W3Object stubs, or by being contained within another W3Object (note that W3Object stubs are themselves W3Objects). This is illustrated in Figure 6, which shows a number of objects, all of which are reachable from some roots.

Our service maintains the distributed referencing graph and uses reference counting to detect unreferenced objects. Stubs, when created, perform an explicit *bind* operation on the object they refer to (thereby incrementing the object's reference count) and perform an *unbind* operation whenever the stub is deleted (thereby decrementing the count).

Reference from a root represents the service[[Otilde]]s continued interest in the object while stubs represent hypertext links from one object to another. Therefore an object is not available for deletion until (1) the service has expressed its lack of further interest in the object (by no longer referencing it from a root) and (2) there are no hypertext links from other objects. Once these conditions are met the object is marked as unreferenced and is available for deletion.

Migration Transparency

An object may be moved from one location to another (potentially to some remote site). Our service guarantees that object moves are transparent to all other objects i.e., references to the moved object continue to be valid. Whenever an object is moved a stub representing the object is left behind at the old location and this automati-

cally forwards invocations (without involving the invoker) to the new location. Further moves of the object may cause a chain of such stubs to be created (in a similar manner to that used by SSP chains [20]), leading ultimately to the real object. For example, in Figure 7, object Y has been moved, first to server B, and then subsequently to server C, leaving behind the forwarding chain shown. Whenever an invocation follows such a chain these indirections are short-cut i.e., the invoker[[Otilde]]s stub communicates directly with the W3Object at the new location. Following a short cut intermediate stubs which are no longer referenced are automatically garbage collected.

Using the short-cutting mechanism stubs will in general point directly at their W3Object; however, there may be circumstances where the chain becomes longer than is desirable, i.e., the Object moves a number of times between invocations from a particular stub. Long chains have more points of failure and a performance cost in the necessary indirections at invocation time, and consequently there may be situations in which long chains are to be avoided. Therefore as an extension to our basic forwarding location mechanism we allow stubs to register callbacks with objects such that, whenever an object moves, the registered stubs are automatically informed of the move. These stubs may either represent hypertext links from other resources and/or belong to a location service which offers the current position of the object to any of its users. More details are given in [24].

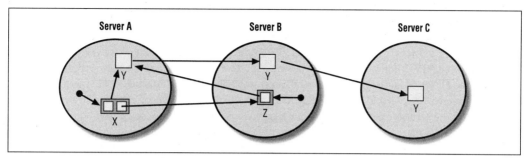

Figure 7:   Referencing chains

Our use of forward references is an entirely distributed solution which scales well by not relying on centralized location services or broadcasts of moves, as is proposed by Hyper-G [25]. Hyper-G ensures that all references to all resources are (eventually) updated to reflect any movement, but this requires additional network traffic that may be appropriate for individual enterprises but does not scale to a worldwide solution. Our system also guarantees that any object movement is transparent to any reference holder and does not require the handling of object faults and subsequent rebinding. Our policy is to provide inexpensive forward referencing (which introduces no extra network traffic when an object is moved) as the default location service but to offer alternative, potentially more expensive solutions such as callback and the use of location servers for resources with specific performance or fault-tolerance requirements. Our model allows the choice of appropriate location mechanisms for an application and the ability to vary that choice at run-time as required.

The mechanisms described above offer a consistent view of referencing within the system so long as (1) neither the referenced objects or their stubs can be lost through failures and (2) the bind and unbind operations are totally reliable. We guarantee that W3Objects and stubs recover from failures by saving them on stable store i.e., a file system. The bind and unbind operations use an RPC to access the W3Object, which may be held within a remote server (optimized to a

local procedure call whenever the object is held in the same server). Our remote object-invocation layer guarantees "at-most-once" semantics for the RPC; i.e., despite failures operations will eventually be performed.

Implementation Progress

Using Shadows, a lightweight object support system [26], we have begun the implementation of the core W3Object properties, concentrating initially on referential integrity and object mobility. During this prototyping stage, we have developed a system which operates in parallel with conventional HTTP daemons. Therefore, object states are stored in their native formats, (e.g., HTML files, etc.) and are available for direct manipulation through the standard file system and Web interfaces. The advantage of this approach is that we are able to develop and test our design without requiring site maintainers to alter any aspect of their existing Web configurations. The disadvantage is the inherent loose coupling between the two systems, requiring users to register entities with our service and be sufficiently disciplined so as not to delete entities directly through the file system without consulting the service. Following this prototyping stage we will introduce the HTTP Gateway and provide user-level tools to replace the direct manipulation of the object through the file system, without restricting the use of any existing resource manipulation tools, e.g., text editors.

In the prototype system, an additional daemon per host is used to provide the referencing service, which is administered using a GUI-based tool. This tool allows the site maintainer to browse through the entities currently being served by the HTTP daemon and to *include* them within the service. On being instructed to include a Web entity, the service creates a corresponding W3Object which is *registered*, causing it to be referenced from a root and thereby ensuring it is not immediately marked as unreferenced. The administration tool then parses the resource to identify any hypertext links it contains. If the links point to resources already included in the service, then references to their corresponding objects are created and stored within the newly created object, thereby extending the referencing graph. Links to resources not already within the service are reported back to the user who then has the option to explicitly include them if they are under his control. A *deregister* operation is used to express the site maintainer's lack of further interest in a resource which causes the reference count for the resource to be decremented. If the reference count reaches zero the site maintainer is informed that it is available for deletion. If the site maintainer confirms it is to be deleted then the W3Object is removed from the service and the corresponding resource removed from the file system. Deleting an object may result in the reference counts of other objects being decremented, i.e., those referenced from the deleted object.

The site maintainer may *move* a resource from one location to another (potentially to some remote site where the resource may come under new ownership). In addition to moving the object through the process described in the previous section, the service performs the following operations: (1) the resource is removed from the file system, (2) an HTTP redirector is inserted, (3) all relative URLs contained within the moving resource are transformed, and (4) the resource is placed in the file system at the new location.

The next stage of our development is to implement the full W3Object model as described in this paper, integrating the referencing work with other software subsystems developed locally as part of the Arjuna Project [27]. To provide the flexibility and extensibility we have described, we shall make use of the Gandiva system [28]] which supports the separation of object interfaces from implementation, and enables reconfiguration of this relationship without requiring the rebuilding of objects or applications. For the common W3Object properties we will make use of the work developed for the Arjuna system [21], which provides the necessary fault-tolerance and replication support.

Conclusion

As a way of serving standard resources, the Web has proven extremely successful but still suffers from a number of shortcomings. Furthermore, in order to cope with new resource types the Web needs improved flexibility and extensibility characteristics. We have illustrated how the application of the concepts of object-orientation can achieve these extensibility requirements and how problems, such as the lack of referential integrity, can be addressed through the application of techniques developed by the distributed object research community.

The W3Object model, presented in this paper, is intended to provide a flexible and extensible way of building Web applications, where Web resources are encapsulated as objects with well-defined interfaces. Objects inherit desirable characteristics, redefining operations as is appropriate; users interact with these objects in a uniform manner. We have identified three categories of object properties: core, common, and specific, and have described an implementation using the core properties which addresses what we believe to be one of the most significant problems facing the current Web—that of referential integrity. A key feature of our design is support for interoperability; for example, in addition to sophisticated clients which may use the rich object interfaces that our model provides, our implementation will also allow W3Objects to continue to be accessed using existing Web browsers. ■

Acknowledgments

The work reported here has been partially funded by grants from the Engineering and Physical Sciences Research Council (EPSRC) and the UK Ministry of Defense (Grant Numbers GR/H81078 and GR/K34863) and GEC-Plessey Telecommunications.

References

1. Berners-Lee, T., et al., *Hypertext Transfer Protocol—HTTP/1.0*, March 1995.
   URL:*http://www.ics.uci.edu/pub/ietf/http/draft-ietf-http-v10-spec-00.psZ*

2. Berners-Lee, T., and Connolly, D. W., *Hypertext Markup Language: A Representation of Textual Information and Metainformation for Retrieval and Interchange*, 1993.
   URL:*http://www.w3.org/hypertext/WWW/MarkUp/HTML.html*

3. Berners-Lee, T., et al., *Uniform Resource Locators (URL) (RFC1738)*, December 1994.
   URL:*http://www.cis.ohio-state.edu/htbin/rfc/rfc1738.html*

4. IETF Uniform Resource Identifiers (URI) Working Group
   URL:*http://www.ics.uci.edu/pub/ietf/uri/*

5. Mitra, et al., *Uniform Resource Names*, Internet Draft, November 1994.
   URL:*http://www.ics.uci.edu/pub/ietf/uri/draft-ietf-uri-resource-names-0.txt*

6. Hoffman, P. E., and Daniel, R. Jr., *URN Resolution Overview*, Internet Draft, April 1995.
   URL:*http://www.ics.uci.edu/pub/ietf/uri/draft-ietf-uri-urn-res-descript-0.txt*

7. Fielding, R., *Relative Uniform Resource Locators (RFC1808)*, June 1995.
   URL:*http://www.ics.uci.edu/pub/ietf/uri/rfc1808.txt*

8. Fielding, R., "**Maintaining Distributed Hypertext Infostructures: Welcome to MOMspider's Web**," *First International Conference on the World Wide Web*, 1994.
   URL:*http://www.ics.uci.edu/WebSoft/MOMspider/WWW94/paper.html*

9. Luotonen, A., *World Wide Web Proxies*, Computer Networks and ISDN Systems. Vol. 27, No.2, 1994.
   URL:*http://www1.cern.ch/PapersWWW94/luotonen.ps*

10. *The Common Gateway Interface*
    URL:*http://hoohoo.ncsa.uiuc.edu/cgi/*

11. *IETF Hypertext Transfer Protocol (HTTP) Working Group*, 1995
    URL:*http://www.ics.uci.edu/pub/ietf/http/*

12. Cardelli, L., and Wegner, P. *On Understanding Types, Data Abstraction, and Polymorphism*, ACM Computing Surveys Vol. 17, No. 4, p. 481, December 1985.

13. Parrington, G. D., *A Stub Generation System for C++*, USENIX Computing Systems Journal, Vol. 8, No. 2, Spring 1995, pp. 135-169
    URL:*http://arjuna.ncl.ac.uk/arjuna/papers/stub-gen-c++.ps*

14. OMG, *Common Object Request Broker Architecture and Specification*, OMG Document Number 91.12.1

15. Inter-Language Unification (ILU), Xerox Parc, 1991
    URL:*ftp://parcftp.par.xeroc.com/pub/ilu/ilu.html*

16. Edwards, N., *The ANSAweb stub-compiler*, 1995.
    URL:*http://www.ansa.co.uk/phase3-activities/ANSAweb.html*

17. Gosling, J., and McGilton, H., *The Java Language Environment: A White Paper*, Sun Microsystems, 1995.
    URL:*http://java.sun.com/whitePaper/javawhite-paper_1.html*

18. Borenstein, N.S., *EMail With A Mind of Its Own: The Safe-Tcl Language for Enabled Mail*, ULPAA '94, Barcelona, 1994.
    URL:*http://minsky.med.virginia.edu/sdm7g/Projects/Python/safe-tcl/ulpaa94.txt*

19. Edwards, N., and Rees, O., *Distributed Objects and The World Wide Web*, ANSA Technical Report APM.1283.00.08, 1994.
    URL:*http://www.ansa.co.uk/phase3-doc-root/sponsors/APM.1283.00.08.html*

20. Shapiro, M., Dickman, P., and Plainfosse, D., *Robust, Distributed References and Acyclic Garbage Collection*, Symposium on Principles of Distributed Computing, Vancouver, August 1992.
    URL:*ftp://ftp.inria.fr/INRIA/Projects/SOR/RDRAGC:podc92.ps.gz*

21. Parrington, G. D. et al., *The Design and Implementation of Arjuna*, USENIX Computing Systems Journal, Vol. 8, No. 3, Summer 1995, pp. 253-306

URL:*http://arjuna.ncl.ac.uk/arjuna/papers/design-implearjuna.ps*

22. Little, M. C., *Object Replication in a Distributed System*, PhD Thesis (Newcastle University Computing Science Laboratory Technical Report 376), September 1991.
URL:*ftp://arjuna.ncl.ac.uk/pub/Arjuna/Docs/Theses/TR-376-9-91_USLetter.ar.Z*

23. Little, M. C., and McCue, D., *The Replica Management System: A Scheme for Flexible and Dynamic Replication*, in *The Proceedings of the 2nd International Workshop on Configuration, Pittsburgh*, March 1994.
URL:*http://arjuna.ncl.ac.uk/arjuna/papers/replica_management_system.ps*

24. Caughey, S. J., and Shrivastava, S. K., *Architectural Support for Mobile Objects in Large Scale Distributed Systems*, In *The Proceedings of the 4th IEEE International Workshop on Object Orientation in Operating Systems (IWOOOS)*, Lund, Sweden, August 1995.

25. Kappe, F., *Hyper-G: A Distributed Hypermedia System*, in *The Proceedings of INET '93*.
URL:*http://info.iicm.tu-graz.ac.at/*

26. Caughey, S. J., et al., *SHADOWS: A Flexible Support System for Objects in a Distributed System*, *Proceedings of the 3rd IEEE International Workshop on Object Orientation in Operating Systems (IWOOOS)*, Ashville, North Carolina, USA, December 1993.

27. The Arjuna Project Information Web Page.
URL:*http://arjuna.ncl.ac.uk/*

28. Wheater, S. M. and Little, M. C. *The Design and Implementation of a Framework for Extensible Software*, Broadcast Project Technical Report, University of Newcastle upon Tyne, 1995.
URL:*http://arjuna.ncl.ac.uk/arjuna/papers/framework-extensible-software.ps*

About the Title

Since 1994, W3Objects has been known as WebObjects. We have been forced to change this owing to a recent trademark application by NeXT Computer Inc.

About the Authors

All of the authors share the common address:

Department of Computing Science,
University of Newcastle upon Tyne
Newcastle upon Tyne,
NE1 7RU, United Kingdom
Tel: +44 191 222 7972
Fax: +44 191 222 8232

David Ingham
[*http://www.cs.ncl.ac.uk/~dave.ingham*]
dave.ingham@ncl.ac.uk

David Ingham received his B.Eng. in Electrical and Electronic Engineering from Northumbria University in 1991 and an M.Sc. in Computing Software and Systems Design from Newcastle University in 1992. He is currently a Research Associate in the Department of Computing Science at Newcastle, where he is a member of the team developing the Arjuna reliable distributed programming system. His research interests include distributed computing, reliable systems, object-oriented computing and distributed-debugging tools.

Mark Little
[*http://www.cs.ncl.ac.uk/~m.c.little*]
m.c.little@ncl.ac.uk

Mark C. Little received his B.Sc. in Physics and Computing Science from Newcastle University in 1987 and a Ph.D. in Computing Science in 1991. Since 1990 he has been on the research staff of the Department of Computing Science at Newcastle where he is currently a Research Associate. He is one of the principal designers and implementors of the Arjuna reliable distributed programming system. His research interests include reliable distributed computing, object-oriented programming languages, object replication, and operating systems.

Steve Caughey
[*http://www.cs.ncl.ac.uk/~s.j.caughey*]
s.j.caughey@ncl.ac.uk

Steve Caughey obtained his B.Sc. in Physics from Queen's University, Belfast, in 1979 and was employed by a number of telecommunications companies working primarily in the areas of Operating System design, integration, and testing. In 1989 he obtained an M.Sc. in Computing Systems and Software Design from Newcastle University, and has since been employed by the University as a Research Associate. His research interests include large scale distribution, object migration, fault tolerance, and naming.

Santosh Shrivastava

[*http://www.cs.ncl.ac.uk/~santosh.shrivastava*]
santosh.shrivastava@ncl.ac.uk

Santosh Shrivastava obtained his PhD in Computing Science from Cambridge in 1975. After several years in industry, he joined the Computing Science Department of the University of Newcastle in 1975 where his present position is Professor of Computing Science. His main area of research is in fault-tolerant distributed computing. He is currently leading Arjuna and Voltan research groups. The Arjuna group has developed the Arjuna object-oriented fault-tolerant distributed system. Arjuna is forming the basis for research on new network services in large scale distributed systems. The Voltan group is undertaking research into high integrity real-time systems, which involves investigation of agreement protocols, failure detection and reconfiguration, communication primitives, clock synchronization and real-time scheduling. He has over 70 publications in the areas of fault-tolerance and distributed computing.

MAKING WORLD WIDE WEB
CACHING SERVERS COOPERATE

Radhika Malpani, Jacob Lorch, David Berger*

Abstract

Due to its exponential growth, the World Wide Web is increasingly experiencing several problems, such as hot spots, increased network bandwidth usage, and excessive document retrieval latency. The standard solution to these problems is to use a caching proxy. However, a single caching proxy is a bottleneck; there is a limit to the number of clients that can use the same cache, and thereby the effectiveness of the cache is limited. Also, a caching proxy is a single point of failure. We address these problems by creating a protocol that allows multiple caching proxies to cooperate and share their caches, thus increasing robustness and scalability. This scalability, in turn, gives each client an effectively larger cache with a higher hit rate. This paper describes a prototype implementation of this protocol that uses IP multicast to communicate between the servers. **Keywords:** *World Wide Web, WWW, proxy, cache, multicast, HTTP*

Introduction

The World Wide Web is a document distribution system based on a client/server model. Currently, the World Wide Web is experiencing exponential growth. According to [14], for example, in the first ten months of 1994 the amount of WWW traffic on the Internet doubled roughly every 11 weeks. This increasing use of the Web results in increased network bandwidth usage, straining the capacity of the networks on which it runs. It also leads to more and more servers becoming "hotspots," sites where the high frequency of requests makes servicing these requests difficult. This combination of increased network bandwidth usage and overloaded servers eventually results in increased document retrieval latency.

Caching documents throughout the Web helps alleviate the above problems. Due to the exponential growth of the WWW, considerable effort has been spent investigating caching of WWW objects. At first, caching meant that each client maintained its own cache. However, the benefits of caching grow with the number of clients shar-

ing the same cache, so the *caching proxy* was developed and used. Such a proxy services client requests from its cache whenever possible, getting the objects from their home servers if required. Unfortunately, a single caching proxy introduces a new set of problems, namely those of scalability and robustness, since a single server is both a bottleneck and a single point of failure. Scalability to large numbers of clients is important because the more clients sharing a cache, the larger the probability of getting a cache hit. Keeping these considerations in mind, we have designed and implemented a protocol to allow multiple independent caching servers to cooperate and jointly service a set of clients.

The rest of the paper is structured as follows. First, we describe related work, indicating the state of the art in caching on the WWW. Then, we describe the problems with current caching techniques, and our solution to these problems. Next, we describe our prototype implementation and describe and discuss measurements of this implementation. Finally, we discuss future work and state our conclusions.

---

* This material is based upon work supported under a National Science Foundation Graduate Research Fellowship.

Related Work

As discussed before, the WWW suffers from problems of high latency, network congestion, and server overload. Hence, considerable effort has been spent investigating one solution to this problem: caching WWW objects. The fundamental issues that have been considered include cache topology, cache replacement policy, cache consistency, whether caching is server- or client-initiated, and cachability of different objects. In addition, work has been done on optimizing caching server implementations.

There are two basic approaches to caching that have been explored: client side and server side solutions. In the server side solutions, servers shed load by duplicating their documents at *caching servers* spread throughout the WWW [4, 11]. Client side solutions usually use some sort of caching proxy that fields requests from one or more clients and caches objects on the clients' behalf. Our work only involves client side solutions and is orthogonal to any server side solutions.

Many client side caching servers have been developed recently. The most prominent of these is probably CERN's httpd 3.0 [13]. All clients using it can have the benefits of a shared cache. Also, its caching policies are configurable; in the server configuration file one can indicate, for any string pattern, the caching policy to be applied to URLs fitting this pattern.

Other caching servers similar to CERN's have appeared recently. The Lagoon caching server [7], developed at the Eindhoven University of Technology, is quite similar to CERN's server. Guenther Fischer modified a patch, designed to convert a server into a proxy, into a patch that converts a server into a caching proxy [10]. Also, Gertjan van Oosten wrote a perl script that can be installed in the *cgi-bin* directory of a server to convert it into a caching proxy [15].

Another caching server system, developed concurrently with the work done for this paper, is the Harvest cache [6]. Developed at the University of Colorado and the University of Southern California, the Harvest cache is a proxy designed to operate in concert with other instances of itself. These servers are typically configured as a tree, with each server considering certain other servers to be parents and certain other servers to be siblings. When a server receives a request for data that it does not have cached, it can call upon its siblings and parents in the tree to find if any of them have the data cached. One disadvantage of the Harvest cache approach is that it uses unicast to communicate with these siblings and parents; more efficient communication may be possible using multicasting.

A group at Boston University developed a cache that could be configured to work at either the client, the host, or the LAN level [5]. Clients either have their own caches, share with other clients on the same host, or share a cache with clients on the same LAN. Surprisingly, according to their results, the number of cache hits did not vary from configuration to configuration. However, as one might expect, a LAN level cache made more efficient use of resources than a host level cache, which in turn made more efficient use of resources than a client level cache. Finally, they observed that while they were able to get a significant number of hits from the cache, hit documents tended to be small and thus the number of bytes served out of the cache was lower than one might expect.

System Design

In this section, we discuss certain problems that current caching solutions have, and how we chose to solve them.

Problems Statement

Most of the work in client side solutions has concerned clients sharing a single caching proxy. But, as explained before, this approach has several problems. First, it lacks robustness, since the proxy serving a set of clients becomes a single point of failure. Second, it is a bottleneck, creating a limit on the number of clients that can share a cache. This, in turn, limits the effective cache size and hit rate that each client obtains.

For instance, here at the University of California at Berkeley, many different research groups use their own separate caching proxies. This is because there is no good way to share caching resources among different groups. Unfortunately, this means that the caching resources available to one group are limited to that group. If each client at U.C. Berkeley were able to access objects cached at *any* caching proxy on campus, they would make better use of the caching resources available. In other words, if all the existing individual caches could be combined to form a *global, distributed cache*, then we could improve the system without increasing the amount of resources used.

Solution

Our goal was to address the above-mentioned problems faced by single caching proxies. To obtain a system that was robust in the face of failures and that scaled well to a large population of clients, we needed to make multiple servers cooperate in such a way that they shared their individual caches to effectively create one large distributed cache. For robustness, all servers needed to be functionally equivalent so that any server could handle the request of any client. For scalability, we needed some means of distributing and balancing the load among the servers. At the same time, we needed to ensure that our protocol for making the servers cooperate did not significantly increase the network bandwidth usage. Therefore, we decided to use multicasting [8] wherever possible to make efficient use of network bandwidth.

Given the above considerations, we developed the following protocol. For each request, a client randomly picks a caching proxy server from a list of cooperating servers and sends its request to it. Let us refer to this proxy as the *master* for this request. If the master has the requested object in its local cache, it returns it to the client. Otherwise, it multicasts a query to the other cooperating servers asking if any of them has the object cached. If it receives no reply within a certain time, it acts as it normally would as a caching proxy, i.e., it contacts the host specified in the URL, requests the object, passes it on to the client, and caches it for future use. If any of the other proxies has the object cached, this caching proxy informs the master, so the master can *redirect* the client to this caching proxy. The client then makes a new request for the object to this caching proxy, and obtains the object from it. Note that in our protocol all servers are functionally equivalent in that any server can act as a master for any request. This protocol is presented graphically in Figure 1.

Most of the overhead of our technique comes from having the client make two requests in the case that it chooses the "wrong" proxy first: one to the master and another to the proxy to which it is redirected. The way we reduce this overhead is to have clients use the same proxy for retrieving inline images of a document that they use for retrieving the document to which these images belong. In this way, documents and their images tend to get cached at the same place. Furthermore, once the document is cached, a client requesting it will get redirected at most once during its requests for the document and its inline images.

Alternative Approaches

There are several other approaches and variants to our protocol that we considered but ultimately rejected. Here we discuss these variants and the reasons we rejected them.

In our protocol, the client makes a request to a single server and that server multicasts the request to other servers. An alternative approach is to have the client itself multicast its request to all the servers. The servers can then execute some distributed protocol to decide who should service the request, taking into account the contents of their caches and their loads. The advan-

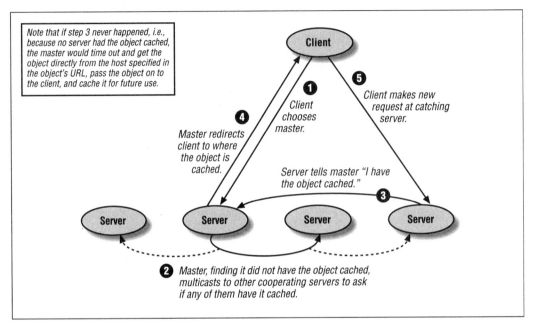

Figure 1:   Illustration of the protocol used

tage of this method is that the client need not know all the servers—it just needs to know the multicast address. Hence, servers can be added and dropped dynamically. However, this method has some serious disadvantages. First, it requires major modifications to the client software. Given the multiplicity of browser implementations, it seems unlikely that the implementors of all the different browsers would be willing to make the appropriate modifications to their software. To maximize the likelihood of widespread acceptance of our techniques, we wanted to modify the client as little as possible. Another disadvantage is that it requires all client machines to support IP multicast, which is not a reasonable assumption. Hence, we felt it would be best to restrict the requirement of multicast capability to the machines on which the servers run.

Given the server multicast approach, there are still a few different approaches we could have taken. One variant on our protocol is to have the server with the cached object send the data directly to the master, and for the master to pass

it on to the client. This approach was initially attractive as it requires no changes to the client. However, on further consideration, we decided against this approach as it loads two servers for a single request, and, depending on the relative positions of the client and the two servers, it can result in inefficient usage of network bandwidth. Furthermore, this makes the location of cached objects transparent to the client, making optimizations, such as always looking in the same place for inline images as for the document that contains them, impossible.

Another variant is to have the server with the cached object directly contact the client rather than having the master redirect the client. This is undesirable, since it requires the client to provide a mechanism for being contacted by a server other than the one to which it connects. This, in turn, requires major modifications to the way the client communicates with its proxies.

In our protocol, the server contacts the home server only after timing out on receiving no responses to its multicast request. Another approach is to have the server contact the home server while waiting for responses from the other servers, so that if no proxy has the data cached the master already has a head start in getting the data. However, the reduction in latency that this yields is at the cost of eliminating some of the benefits of caching in the first place: reducing network bandwidth use and reducing load on the host specified in the URL, in the case that the object is cached locally. Thus, we do not contact the host specified in the URL until it becomes clear that the object is not locally cached.

Implementation

To build on existing work, we decided to implement our new client and server as modifications of widely available products. We selected NCSA's Mosaic [1] as the basis for our client because of the availability and simplicity of its source code. We selected CERN's httpd 3.0 [13] as the basis for our server because its source code was available and already implemented proxy caching.

Client Modifications

The basic modification we made to the client was to implement the redirection mechanism. This was done by extending HTTP to include a special proxy redirect result code, 317, and by modifying the client to interpret this code. Upon receipt of this code, the client changes the proxy it uses to the one specified by this message, and then sends its request to this new proxy. The other modification we made to the client was to have it select a random proxy from a list of proxies for each new document requested. It then uses the same proxy for all related objects, such as inline images.

Note that we had to slightly modify HTTP to accommodate our protocol, adding a code for proxy redirect messages. This change seems justified, because the proxy redirect message is a natural extension to HTTP.

Server Modifications

Modifications to the server were more extensive. First, we had to make it select and join a multicast group, and listen to this multicast group at the same time as it was listening for client requests. Second, we had to change the way it treats client requests, to satisfy the protocol. Thus, when it fails to find an object in its cache, it sends a multicast message asking if the object is cached elsewhere. If there is no response within a certain time, it proceeds, as usual, by getting the object from the host specified in the URL, caching it, and returning it to the client. However, if there is a response, it instead sends a proxy redirect message to the client. Third, we had to modify the server to process queries it receives from other servers asking whether certain objects are cached. We did not have the server fork a separate process to handle each such query, as the servicing of each query was not expected to take a great deal of time.

Analysis

Although the primary purpose of our research was to show that our scheme for cooperation among multiple proxies could be implemented, we were also curious about the performance of our system and the system on which it was based. For this purpose, we obtained and analyzed measurements of the time it took to service requests under various conditions.

Testing Methodology

We will use the following terminology to refer to the four types of latency we measured. *Direct latency* is the time it takes to receive a document and its associated images directly from the hosts specified in the URLs for those objects. For instance, the time it takes to get both *http://Wall-Street-News.com/forecasts/* and *http://Wall-Street-News.com/forecasts/images/wall-street-news.gif* from *Wall-Street-News.com* is considered direct latency. *Proxy latency* is the time it takes to retrieve a document and all its associated images from a proxy when none of those objects have been previously cached locally. *Caching latency* is the time it takes to receive a document and all its associated images from a proxy that already has those objects cached. Finally, *redirection latency* is the time it takes to receive a document and all its associated images when they are all cached at the same proxy, but this is not the first proxy the client queries. Thus, it is the time it takes to receive a proxy redirect message from the "wrong" proxy, plus the caching latency at the "right" proxy. Note that, since our optimization attempts to cache the document and its images at the same proxy, we only incur the latency of receiving and processing a proxy redirect message once for each document, no matter how many images are associated with that document.

For our tests, we obtained a random set of URLs by invoking the "random link" feature of Yahoo [9] repeatedly. We eliminated from consideration any URLs that did not use the *http* scheme. We then wrote a simple program to fetch these documents, extract the URLs for their associated images, and determine the size of each document object and image object. For ease of analysis, we then threw out any documents that referenced the same image more than once, leaving us with 46 documents on which to perform the remainder of our measurements. Two of these turned out to be unreachable during our later experiments, so the results to follow concern 44 documents.

We wrote another program to determine the direct, caching, proxy, and redirect latencies for each document with associated images. We ran this program at night, when there would be less interference from other users of network bandwidth. The measurement program and two instantiations of our caching proxy ran on three different machines in our laboratory, all on the same subnet. We determined that in this configuration a 15 ms timeout on the multicast request was sufficiently long for the correct running of our protocol, but to be conservative we used a 40 ms timeout instead. In all our presentations of results, we have not made any effort to eliminate values that might be considered statistical outliers. This is because seemingly abnormal results are typically due to bursts of uncontrollable external network activity, which are an important aspect of the environment and should be taken into consideration.

Measurements

Each type of latency was measured fifty times for each document, and the average was taken of those fifty trials. All trials for a single document and its images were done consecutively, so that all data for any such document was taken under as similar network conditions as possible. Figure 2 shows the means of each type of latency for each of the documents studied. Note that the documents are numbered in order of increasing direct latency. So, for instance, the y-values plotted above the number 5 on the x-axis represent the average direct, proxy, caching, and redirection latencies for the document with associated images whose direct latency was the fifth smallest among all documents with associated images. Note that we have only plotted values for 43 of the 44 documents, as plotting the values for the document with the highest latency would render the scale too small. Figure 3 shows the mean of each type of latency across all documents with associated images, along with error lines proportional to the standard deviations.

Discussion

Note first that these latency values are only meaningful to average if one considers the workload to be one in which only the 44 documents studied are accessed, each of them is accessed with equal probability, and all of them are accessed at night from U. C. Berkeley. Any more general interpretation of one of our average values is not accurate unless one expects the distribution of latency values for our workload to be similar to that found in a realistic client workload. In the case of proxy and direct latencies, it is

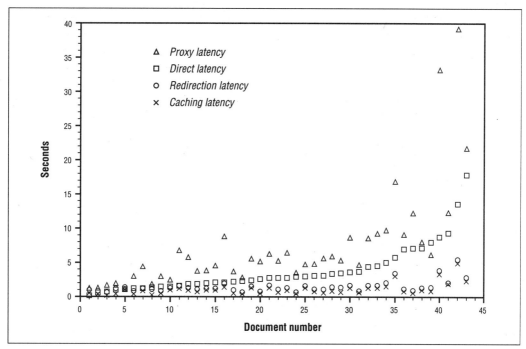

Figure 2: Latencies for various documents and their associated images

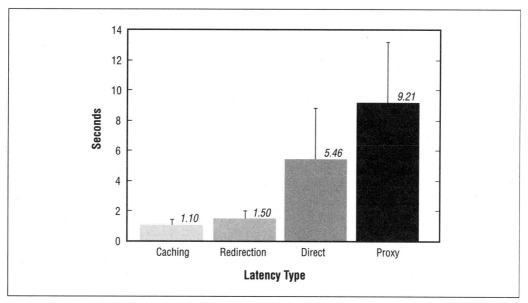

Figure 3: Means of different types of latency across all documents with associated images, with lines indicating the relative size of standard deviations

likely we have not achieved this goal, as these latencies are very dependent on the distance to the hosts and the time of access, and we have made no attempt to make the distribution of distances to hosts match that of any sort of typical client. On the other hand, since caching and redirection latency do not involve any communication with the host specified in the URLs, there should be no correlation between host distance and either type of latency. Also, there is little correlation between either type of latency and document size: both correlation coefficients have magnitudes under 0.05. Therefore, it seems likely that our caching and redirection latency values are appropriate to general workloads. However, one thing to be careful about is that the impact of redirection on latency is proportionally greater the fewer inline images a document has. If the distribution of number of inline images in documents in our workload is atypical of another workload, our redirection latency numbers may not be applicable to it.

The difference between the caching and redirection latency for a document and its images is equal to the amount of time it takes to receive a proxy redirect message. As expected, there was essentially no correlation between this value and the direct latency (correlation coefficient -0.01) or the size of the document (correlation coefficient -0.04). Therefore, we feel comfortable in averaging this number across all documents to determine an average latency for proxy redirect messages, obtaining the figure of 0.398 sec. The 95% confidence interval for this value is plus or minus 0.015 sec. Now, the average caching latency among all the documents with associated images we considered was 1.102 sec. Thus, in our workload, choosing the wrong proxy to service a request makes the request take on average 36% longer than choosing the right proxy. In a system of n cooperating servers, we can expect to incur this latency on cache hits (n-1)/n of the time. Note that the figure of 36% is specific to the document composition of our workload, but the figure of 0.398 sec is applicable to the retrieval of any document.

Most of the difference between proxy latency and direct latency is due to overhead of the original CERN server that we instrumented. Our figures show that, for our workload, the average proxy latency is 69% higher than average direct latency. However, the only part of this that is due to our technique is the 40 ms spent waiting for the multicast request to time out; thus, overhead from our protocol only accounts for 1.1% of the increase from direct latency to proxy latency. In other words, the CERN server alone takes 68% more time to service a cache miss than it would take without a caching proxy; with our modifications, this becomes 69%. Note, again, that these percentages are specific to our workload, but the figure of 40 ms overhead per cache miss is generally applicable.

Although proxy latency is significantly greater than direct latency, we believe that caching is still worthwhile. First, one must consider that although one pays a greater cost when a document misses in the cache, this is made up for when a document hits in the cache and the client experiences less latency. For our workload, average caching latency is 20% of average direct latency, and even average redirection latency is only 27% of average direct latency. Second, the benefits of caching go beyond reduction of document retrieval latency for cached objects. Caching also ensures reduced use of network bandwidth and reduced server load. These may, in turn, provide savings in document retrieval latency for all objects.

Thus, we can make the following comparison between our multiple proxy caching system and a single caching proxy. Our protocol permits sharing of multiple caches among many clients, hence we expect a higher cache hit rate. Since documents that hit in the cache take less time to retrieve than ones that miss, this will decrease our relative latency. The increased cache hit ratio will also translate into less use of network bandwidth and less load imposed on remote servers. The only overhead of our system over a single caching proxy is the 398 ms redirection delay if the **wrong** proxy is contacted first, and the additional 40 ms timeout delay if the requested object is not cached at any proxy.

Future Work

There are several areas open for future work. One of these is the evaluation of protocols other than the one we implemented. We have presented arguments for why we chose our approach; however, to empirically evaluate how justified our decisions were, it is necessary to implement the alternative protocols we have eschewed and to compare their performance to that of our approach. Especially interesting to consider would be implementations of a protocol involving multicast messages by the client. In an environment where multicasting was more prevalent, and the problem of reliable multicast was solved, this could well be a better protocol than ours.

Furthermore, evaluation of our approach could be better done with extensive traces of document retrieval patterns, which we do not have. Such traces would provide a more realistic workload from which to get more meaningful averages of latency values.

Another avenue of investigation is the extent to which our server selection method provides satisfactory load balancing. Although it is clear that in the long run, the expected number of requests processed by each server is the same as that of all other servers with which it cooperates, it might turn out that the variance of the randomness in our system is high enough that it is likely some server will nevertheless wind up with the bulk of the processing load or disk space requirement.

Finally, we feel it would be useful to evaluate alternative caching policies to the ones currently in use. The CERN approach described essentially embodies the pinnacle of current work in this area, and in our opinion it is still not the best that could be achieved. One reason for this is that it requires manual intervention to decide upon and

later tune such parameters as default expiry times for objects whose URLs conform to various patterns. More research is needed to determine how these parameters might be automatically set and modified by the server itself based on its ongoing experience. Improvement may also be possible in the estimation of expiry times for documents not containing "Expires" headers. We feel that there may be other information in a URL, besides the last-modified time, which is useful for this estimation.

Conclusion

The increasing popularity of the World Wide Web presents many challenges. A good solution to many of these challenges is caching, which reduces server load, document service time, and network load. However, the complexity of caching brings with it its own problems, some of which we have attempted to solve with our protocol for sharing caches among servers. The problems of robustness and scalability with number of clients can be solved by using multiple servers for a set of clients. Load balancing and sharing among such multiple servers can be achieved by ensuring that any server is equally likely to be chosen to satisfy any given client request. Finally, to solve the problem of communication overhead scaling poorly with communication among many servers, we propose the use of IP multicast to make this communication proceed efficiently.

We implemented the protocol that best met our needs to demonstrate the feasibility of such a protocol. We also performed measurements of this implementation to illustrate that the overhead involved in using multiple caching proxies instead of one is small, while the advantages obtained are several. We expect the sharing of caches will lead to higher hit ratios, with a corresponding decrease in network bandwidth usage, server load, and document retrieval latency.

Our system of using multiple servers to perform the work of one is generally applicable to most current caching architectures. In a hierarchical cache structure in which clients share proxies, which in turn share proxies, etc., it would be straightforward to replace each cache server by a cooperating set of servers that use our protocol.

∎

References

1. Andreesen, M., NCSA Mosaic home page, May, 1995.

2. Berners-Lee, T., Masinter, L., and McCahill, M., RFC 1738: uniform resource locators (URL), December, 1994.

3. Berners-Lee, T., Fielding, R., and Nielsen, H. F., Hypertext Transfer Protocol—HTTP/1.0, March, 1995.

4. Bestavros, A., Demand-based document dissemination for the World Wide Web, Technical Report BU-CS-95-003, Boston University Computer Science Department, Boston, MA, February, 1995.

5. Bestavros, A., Carver, R., Crovella, M., Cunha, C., Heddaya, A., and Mirdad, S., Application-level document caching in the Internet, Technical Report BU-CS-95-002, Boston University Computer Science Department, Boston, MA, March, 1995.

6. Chankhunthod, A., Danzig, P., Neerdales, C., Schwartz, M., and Worrell, K., A hierarchical Internet object cache, April, 1995.

7. De Bra, P. and Post, R., Information retrieval in the World Wide Web: making client-based searching feasible, *Proceedings of the First International Conference on the World Wide Web*, Geneva, Switzerland, May, 1994.

8. Deering, S., RFC 1054: host extensions for IP multicasting, May, 1988.

9. Filo, D., and Yang, J., Yahoo home page, July, 1995.

10. Fischer, G., *http://www.tu-chemnitz.de/~ftpadm/httpd/src/cache.html*

11. Gwertzman, J., and Seltzer, M., The case for geographical push-caching, Technical Report HU TR-34-94, Harvard University, DAS, Cambridge, MA, 1994.

12. Jain, R., *The Art of Computer System Performance Analysis: Techniques for Experimental Design, Measurement, Simulation, and Modeling*, John Wiley & Sons, New York, NY, 1991.

13. Luotonen, A., and Berners-Lee, T., CERN httpd Reference Manual, July, 1995.

14. O'Callaghan, D., A central caching proxy server for WWW users at the University of Melbourne, *Proceedings of AusWeb95, the First Australian World Wide Web Conference*, March, 1995.

15. van Oosten, G., Article posted to *comp.infosystems.www*, February, 1994.

About the Authors

Radhika Malpani
[*http://http.cs.berkeley.edu/~radhika/*]
University of California at Berkeley
radhika@cs.berkeley.edu

Radhika Malpani is a Ph.D. student in the computer science department of the University of California at Berkeley. She is a National Science Foundation Fellowship recipient. She holds a B.E. in electrical engineering from the Victoria Jubilee Technical Institute in Bombay, India. Her current research interests include continuous media applications for the Internet and the Mbone.

Jacob Lorch
[*http://http.cs.berkeley.edu/~lorch/*]
University of California at Berkeley
lorch@cs.berkeley.edu

Jacob Lorch is a Ph.D. student in the computer science department of the University of California at Berkeley. He is a National Science Foundation Fellowship recipient, as well as a member of ACM and IEEE. He holds a B.S. in computer science and a B.S. in mathematics from Michigan State University. His current research interests include operating systems techniques for reducing the power consumption of laptop computers, and caching strategies for the World Wide Web.

David Berger
[*http://www.eit.com/~dvberger/*]
Enterprise Integration Technologies
dvberger@eit.com

David Berger is a software engineer at Enterprise Integration Technologies (a subsidiary of Verifone). He is conceiving and developing products for the global Internet and the World Wide Web. A former graduate student in computer science at the University of California at Berkeley, he received an M.S. in 1995 while working on the Berkeley Video on Demand System. David also holds a B.A. in computer science from Rutgers University and is a member of the Phi Beta Kappa and Phi Eta Sigma national honor societies.

Caching Proxies
Limitations and Potentials

Marc Abrams, Charles R. Standridge, Ghaleb Abdulla,
Stephen Williams, Edward A. Fox

Abstract

As the number of World Wide Web users grows, so does the number of connections made to servers. This increases both network load and server load. Caching can reduce both loads by migrating copies of server files closer to the clients that use those files. Caching can either be done at a client or in the network (by a proxy server or gateway). We assess the potential of proxy servers to cache documents retrieved with the HTTP, GOPHER, FTP, and WAIS protocols using World Wide Web browsers. We monitored traffic corresponding to three types of educational workloads over a one-semester period, and used this as input to a cache simulation. Our main findings are (1) that with our workloads a proxy has a 30-50% maximum possible hit rate no matter how it is designed; (2) that when the cache is full and a document is replaced, classic least recently used (LRU) is a poor policy, but simple variations can dramatically improve hit rate and reduce cache size; (3) that a proxy server really functions as a second-level cache, and its hit rate may tend to decline with time after initial loading, given a more or less constant set of users; and (4) that certain modifications to proxy-server configuration parameters for a cache may have little benefit. **Keywords:** *Proxy server, caching, workload characterization*

Introduction

Without caching, the WWW would become a victim of its own success. As Web popularity grows, so does the number of clients accessing popular Web servers, and so does the network bandwidth required to connect clients to servers. Trying to scale network and server bandwidth to keep up with client demand is an expensive strategy.

An alternative is caching. Caching effectively migrates copies of popular documents from servers closer to clients. Web client users see shorter delays when requesting a URL. Network managers see less traffic. Web servers see lower request rates.

A cache may be used on any of the following: a per-client basis, within networks used by the Web, or on Web servers [5]. We study the second alternative, known as a "proxy server" or "proxy gateway" with the ability to cache documents. We use the term "caching proxy" for short.

A caching proxy has a difficult job. First, its arrival traffic is the union of the URL requests of many clients. For a caching proxy to have a cache hit, the same document must either be requested by the same user two or more times, or two different users must request the same document. Second, a caching proxy often functions as a second (or higher) level cache, getting only the misses left over from Web clients that use a per-client cache (e.g., Mosaic and Netscape). The misses passed to the proxy server from the client usually do not contain a document requested twice by the same user. The caching proxy is therefore, left to cache documents requested by two or more users. This reduces the fraction of requests that the proxy can satisfy from its cache, known as the *hit rate*.

How effective could a caching proxy ever be? To answer this, we first examine how much inherent duplication there is in the URLs arriving at a caching proxy. We simulate a proxy server with an infinite disk area, so that the proxy contains, forever, every document ever accessed. This gives an upper bound on the hit rate that a real caching proxy could ever achieve. The input to the simulation is traces of all URL accesses during one semester of three different workloads from a university community. Overall we observe a 30%-50% hit rate. We also examine the maximum disk area required for there to be no document replacement. We then consider the case of finite disk areas, in which replacement must occur, and compare the hit rate and cache size resulting from three replacement policies: least recently used (LRU) and two variations of LRU. LRU is shown to have an inherent defect that becomes more pronounced as the frequency of replacements rises. Finally, we use the best replacement policy and examine the effect on hit rate and cache size of restricting what document sizes to cache and whether to cache only certain document sizes, document types, or URL domains.

Caching in the World Wide Web

Caching is used in two forms in the Web. The first is a *client cache*, which is built into a Web browser. A Web browser with caching stores not only the documents currently displayed in browser windows, but also documents requested in the past. There are two forms of client caches: persistent and nonpersistent. A persistent client cache retains its documents between invocations of the Web browser; Netscape uses a persistent cache. A nonpersistent client cache (used in Mosaic) deallocates any memory or disk used for caching when the user quits the browser. Per-client caches may maintain consistency of cached files with server copies by issuing an optional conditional-GET to the http server or proxy server.

The second form of caching explored here is in the network used by the Web (i.e., the caching proxy mentioned earlier). The cache is located on a machine on the path from multiple clients to multiple servers. Examples of caching proxies are the CERN proxy server [7], the DEC SRC gateway [4], the UNIX HENSA Archive [11], and in local Hyper-G servers [2]. Normally a caching proxy is not on a machine that runs a WWW client or an HTTP server. The caching proxy caches URLs generated by multiple clients. It is possible to use caching proxies hierarchically, so that caching proxies cache URLs from other caching proxies. In this case the caches can be identified as first level caches, second level caches, and so on. A hierarchical arrangement is only one possible configuration; Smith [11, Figure 1] gives a nonhierarchical arrangement of large national and international caching proxies.

Why a Simulation Study?

One way to study cache performance is simply to configure a caching proxy and to collect the desired statistics. In fact, the workloads used in this paper were collected using a caching proxy for a previous study [1]. However, this has some problems. First, the WWW at present has no mechanism to tell if a cached document is not the latest version from the original server. (See [4, 11] for a discussion of the problem.) So studies that use real user workloads can never cache all documents to measure the maximum possible hit rate, because the users cannot live with outdated Web pages. Thus [1] and [4] only cache "nonlocal" documents (which are documents outside the Computer Science department in [1] and outside DEC SRC in [4]). Also [11] requires the user to prefix URLs with an explicit caching proxy name to request a cache search. Our simulation study here "replays" the URL requests recorded from our workload, and hence we can cache all URLs. A second reason for simulation is to compare different policies for cache management. A policy might restrict caching to documents of certain sizes or media types. A policy is also required for replacing documents in a full cache on identical URL traces. Finally a simulation can be used in a classic experiment design with analysis of variance to identify what effect a number of factors (e.g., cache size, replacement policy, domain, and document size and types cached, workload) have on hit rate. Such an experiment and analysis is performed here.

Workload Used in This Study

A critical issue in any performance study is the workload selected for the study. For this paper, we recorded all URL requests using HTTP, FTP, GOPHER, and WAIS protocols through WWW browsers that were made to proxy servers during one semester (Spring 1995) from three groups of users on the Virginia Tech campus. (Some days are missing from each workload due to problems in data collection, such as proxy-server crashes.) The workload tracing procedure is discussed in the Appendix. The three workloads are:

"Undergrad (U)"

> Workstations in an undergraduate computer science lab representing about 150 different user ids (however two of the ids were "guest" and "root," which means that more than 150 students used a Web browser), containing 79,718 accesses to the caching proxy (mostly with Netscape and sometimes with Mosaic)

"Graduate (G)"

> A popular host used by graduate computer science students, of whom at least 25 students used a Web browser, containing 55,186 accesses (almost exclusively Mosaic browsers)

"Classroom (C)"

> 26 workstations in a classroom on which students run a Web browser during sessions of a class on multimedia, containing 31,812 accesses (all Netscape browsers)

Workloads U and G represent a mixture of Web usage for classes; for general or recreational Web browsing; and, in workload G, for research. One distinction between workloads U and G is that material for many courses that the undergrads take is provided through the Web; in fact four courses are "paperless," and in one, even exams are taken through the Web. Workload C differs from the others in that the instructor often directs students to look at certain URLs or search for certain topics, and hence there should be a definite

correlation between the URLs that different clients request. We previously used these traces in a study to characterize the workload (e.g., distribution of document sizes and types accessed, distribution of Web server sites accessed) and evaluate cache hit rates using the CERN proxy server [1].

The three workloads represent what university campus Web clients do. This is useful to complement other workloads studied in the literature (e. g., in the section entitled "Comparison to Other Cache Studies"). In our campus workload students are free to access any URL in the World Wide Web for instructional, research, or recreational purposes, while a caching proxy in an industrial setting often restricts employee access of off-site material [4].

Caching Algorithms Studied

What document should be replaced when the cache is full and a request arrives for a URL not in the cache? To answer this question, we examine three replacement policies based on a least recently used (LRU) scheme. LRU was chosen as the basic replacement policy for two reasons: LRU is the most effective replacement policy in other caching enviroments—memory and disk— and a previous study [1] shows that rate of subsequent accesses to a particular page drops off significantly more than 28 hours after the last time that page was accessed. Strict LRU was chosen as one replacement policy with two LRU derivatives as the alternative policies. However, this question is more complex than the equivalent question for virtual memory and computer cache memory, because the documents cached typically have *different* sizes. Should many small documents be removed for a large document? If cache size is limited, is it better to hold many small documents or a few large documents?

We compare three cache replacement policies in this paper, described below. Suppose the proxy receives a request for a URL that is not in the cache. Let S denote the size of the document corresponding to the URL.

LRU

Classic least recently used [12]: When the free space in the cache is smaller than S, repeat the following until the free cache space is at least S: replace the LRU document. (LRU may discard many small documents to make room for one large document.)

LRU-MIN

A variant of LRU that tries to minimize the number of documents replaced. Let L and T denote, respectively, a list and an integer. (1) Set T to S. (2) Set L to all documents equal to or larger than T. (L may be empty.) (3) Remove the LRU of list L until the list is empty or the free cache space is at least T. (4) If the free cache space is not at least S, set T to $T/2$ and goto step (2).

LRU-THOLD

A variant of LRU that avoids the situation in which a document that is large compared to the cache size causes replacement of a large number of smaller documents. This policy is identical to LRU, except that no document larger than a threshold size is cached. (Even if the cache has room, a document whose size is larger than the threshold is never cached.)

Experiment Objectives and Design

Objectives

We want to assess:

1. What is the maximum cache hit rate that user access patterns allow, given an infinite cache size?

2. What is the cache size that various workloads require, if the cache is to have no replacement?

3. What is the mean *lifetime* of documents replaced in the cache (e.g., the time from when a document enters the cache until it is replaced, averaged over all replaced documents)?

4. How much effect do each of the following factors have on hit rate and cache size: disk area allocated for the cache, minimum document size cached, Internet domains cached, document types cached, workload characteristics, and cache replacement policy.

5. What cache parameter settings are best?

Experiment Design

We perform four experiments, whose factors and levels are summarized in Table 1. We use the following notation to refer to the factor levels. The term "MaxNeeded" in the table refers to the disk area needed for no replacements to occur from Experiment 1 (listed later in Table 2). A "text" document, in factor "Document type cached," is one with either no file name extension or the extension .txt or .html. The workload mnemonic (i.e., U,G,C) is suffixed by /A or /S (e.g., U/A, C/S) to denote use of the all versus some of the eight-day intervals into which the workload is partitioned, as discussed in the section "Experiment 1." Finally the workload mnemonic is suffixed by /MIN and /MAX (e.g., U/MIN) to denote the single eight-day interval of the workload that produced, respectively, the minimum or maximum disk area needed for no replacements in Experiment 1.

The response variables referred to in Table 1 are the mean hit rate averaged over all cache accesses, the cache size needed for no replacements to occur, and the mean lifetime of replaced documents.

Table 1: Factor-level Combinations for All Experiments

		Levels	
Factors:	Experiment 1	Experiment 2	Experiment 3
Disk area for cache	infinite	10, 50% of MaxNeeded	10, 50% 90% of MaxNeeded
Min. doc. size cached	0	0	0
Domain cached	all	all	all
Document type cached	all	all	all
Workload	U/A,G/A,C/A	U/S,C/S	U/S,C/S
Replacement policy	N/A	LRU-THOLD	LRU, LRU-MIN, LRU-THOLD
LRU-THOLD threshold	N/A	1, 4, 16, 32, 64K; 1M	best in exp. 2
Output measures:	Hit rate	Hit rate	Hit rate
	Max cache size	Max cache size	Max cache size
		Lifetime	Lifetime

	Experiment 4	
Factors:	Level -1	Level +1
Disk area for cache	50% MaxNeeded	50% MaxNeeded
Min. doc. size cached	1 kbyte	0 kbytes
Domain cached	off campus only	all
Document type cached	non-text only	all
Workload	U/S	C/S
Replacement policy	best in exp. 3	best in exp. 3
LRU-THOLD threshold	N/A	N/A
Output measures:	Hit rate	
	Max cache size	

Each of the four experiments is described below.

Experiment 1. Maximum Possible Hit Rate for a Caching Proxy

The purpose of Experiment 1 is to identify the maximum possible hit rate for our three different workloads, assuming an infinite-size cache. This represents the inherent "cachability" of client URL requests, regardless of the cache design. We used a one-factor experiment design. The single factor varied is "Workload."

It will be seen in the next section that workloads U and G are somewhat similar; of these workload U exhibits the largest dynamic range of cache sizes. To reduce the number of trials required for Experiments 2 to 4, we only consider workloads U and C.

Experiment 2. Optimal Threshold for the LRU-THOLD Replacement Policy

In the next experiment, we try to answer which replacement policy (LRU, LRU-MIN, or LRU-THOLD) is best under which circumstances. But one of the three policies—LRU-THOLD—requires a parameter (i.e., the threshold). To do this, we must know what threshold value to use. This is the object of Experiment 2. We used a full factorial experiment with three factors (Disk area,

Workload, and Threshold) and two replicas (with workloads U/MIN and U/MAX if factor "Workload" is U, or C/MIN and C/MAX if factor Workload is C). This led to 40 simulation runs.

Experiment 3. Comparison of Cache Replacement Algorithms

The purpose of Experiment 3 is to compare three cache replacement algorithms. We used a three-factor (Disk area, Workload, Replacement policy) full factorial experiment design, with two replications (just as in Experiment 2), requiring 36 simulation runs.

Experiment 4. Performance Impact of Caching

The purpose of Experiment 4 is to assess the effect of factors *other than* the replacement policy on hit rate and cache size. The factors varied are listed in Table 1. We used a (2**4)(2) experiment design, requiring 32 simulation runs. The experiment includes two replications as described in Experiment 2, and four factors with two levels (Disk area, Minimum document size cached, Domain cached, and Document type cached).

Experiment Results

Experiment 1

Due to a limitation in the language used for the simulation tool (SLAM II [8]), the simulation could not cache more than 8600 documents, which lim-

ited us to simulating eight days of traffic in the busiest case. Therefore we broke the observation period into eight-day intervals, and within each eight-day interval the maximum number of unique documents accessed is 8600.

Recall that the purpose of Experiment 1 is to determine the maximum possible hit rate, given an infinite disk area for caching. Figures 1 and 2 report, respectively, the hit rate and the cache size for no replacements for each interval and workload. It is evident from Figures 1 and 2 that workload C contains fewer days of trace data than the other workloads. This is because the class met four days a week, while the other workloads were collected seven days a week. Also workload C is not a multiple of eight days long, so when we divided it into eight-day periods, we ignored the first few days to achieve a multiple of eight days. Finally Figures 1 and 2 show that we did not start collecting workload U until after the semester began.

Table 2 contains summary statistics of the data. The data in Table 2 suggest that if a separate caching proxy had been used for each of the three workloads, and the proxy was restarted with an empty cache every eight days, then over the course of the spring semester one would see the following: The cache hit rate for the two laboratory workloads—U and G—would be statistically indistinguishable, with a similar mean (30% and 29%, respectively), variance, and minimum and maximum hit rates. The ratio of the best to the worst hit rate observed in any eight-day interval in the semester is roughly 2 to 1 for both

Table 2: Statistics of hit rate and cache size for no replacement for Experiment 1 with an eight-day interval

	Undergrad		Graduate		Classroom	
	Hit Rate (%)	Cache Size (Mbytes)	Hit Rate (%)	Cache Size (Mbytes)	Hit Rate (%)	Cache Size (Mbytes)
Sample Mean	30.0	86.497	29.2	80.780	46.0	75.249
Std. Dev.	6.6	41.465	5.9	24.631	2.7	44.123
Minimum	15.4	27.525	18.8	58.680	43.1	44.902
Maximum	38.6	159.930	36.1	129.969	48.4	125.865

Table 3: Statistics of hit rate and cache size for no replacement for Experiment 1 with a 12-day interval

| | Graduate | | Classroom | |
	Hit Rate (%)	Cache Size (Mbytes)	Hit Rate (%)	Cache Size (Mbytes)
Sample Mean	35.5	99.037	50.0	105.779
Std. Dev.	5.7	8.841	1.1	50.263
Minimum	27.4	91.906	49.2	70.238
Maximum	40.8	110.459	50.8	141.321

workloads. Furthermore, workload C has a 50% higher hit rate because the behavior of Web users in a classroom are correlated.

As for cache size required for no replacements, it is surprising that the sample mean size was similar for all three workloads, ranging from 75 Mbytes to 86 Mbytes (from Table 2). However the standard deviation for workload G was considerably smaller than the other two workloads. The largest difference in cache size exhibited by a workload was the ratio of about 6 to 1 for the maximum to the minimum cache size required for no replacement for all eight-day periods of workload U.

The results above correspond to a situation where a caching proxy is restarted with an empty initial cache every eight days. To explore the effect of interval length (eight days) on the results, we resimulated two of the workloads with longer intervals. Based on the statistical similarity in hit rate between the workloads Undergraduate and Graduate, we were able to drop the busiest (Undergraduate) and increase the cache interval to 12 days without violating the simulation's 8600 document limit. Table 3 reports the statistics.

Recall that whenever a client uses a private cache, our logs will contain only those URLs that are a private cache miss. So how effective is a per-client cache in learning a user's behavior? Figure 1 provides some insight. In each of the three hit rate curves in Figure 1, most line segments have a negative slope; in other words, most of the time the hit rate is more likely on any day to go *down* rather than *up* compared to the

previous day. While this might be a purely random phenomenon, we speculate that there is an explanation. As stated earlier, a proxy cache is really a second level cache, if clients have their own cache. The proxy cache is only sent misses on the (first level) client caches. If the client cache is persistent between invocation of clients (i.e., the client cache uses disk), then the proxy cache hit rate should decline over time as the per-client cache fills (or, in some sense, adapts to user behavior). In Figure 1 the classroom curve has a smaller slope than the negative slope portions of the two other curves. This may be due to our resetting the client disk and memory cache size to zero before many classes. (We found that 10-20% of the workstation users turned the cache on between our resetting them to zero.) In contrast, no attempt was made to defeat client caching in workloads U and G. Finally the only one of the three curves that contains more than one sharp increase in hit rate (i.e., the curve for workload U) does not start until about 1/3 the way into the spring semester; by this point the client caches had several weeks to fill, so that the data skips the period when the proxy cache hit rate declines rapidly due to the client cache filling.

Experiment 2

Recall that the purpose of Experiment 2 is to determine the optimal value of the threshold to use for the LRU-THOLD document replacement policy. "Optimal" means the value that maximizes hit rate. Figure 3 contains the experiment results.

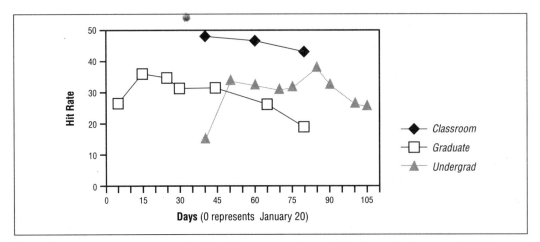

Figure 1: Cache hit rate as a function of measurement interval. The data collection period started on January 20, 1995, which is denoted by x-axis coordinate value zero. Each point plotted represents eight days of collected data.

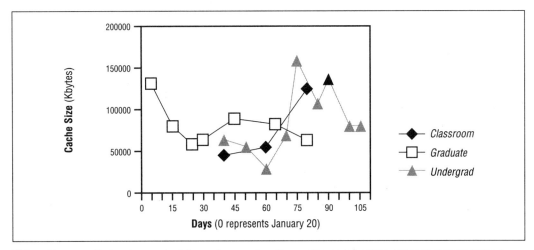

Figure 2: Cache size required for no document replacements, as a function of measurement interval

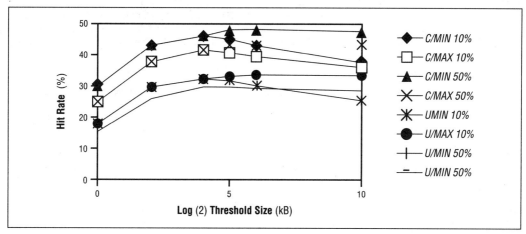

Figure 3: Cache hit rate with LRU-THOLD replacement policy as a function of threshold values. Percentages (e.g., 10%) refer to sizes of disk area used for caching, as a fraction of MaxNeeded from Experiment 1..

Analysis of variance (ANOVA) applied separately to data from each workload reveals that at alpha = 5% only the threshold level has a statistically significant effect on hit rate, explaining 90% and 77% of the variation in hit rates for workloads U and C, respectively

Three of the four curves for each workload in Figure 3 reach a maximum value and then decline. The optimal threshold for all workloads is 2**4 Kbytes when the disk area is 10% of the cache size required for no replacements. When the disk size available for caching is 50% of the cache size required for no replacements, the optimal threshold is 2**6 Kbytes for workloads C/MIN and U/MIN, and 2**10 Kbytes for workload C/MAX and U/MAX.

Experiment 3

Recall that Experiment 3 compares document replacement policies LRU, LRU-MIN, and LRU-THOLD, to identify which maximizes hit rate and minimizes disk size required for the cache. For LRU-THOLD, we used the thresholds listed in

Experiment 2. The experiment results are tabulated in Table 4.

In no case did LRU outperform the other replacement policies in Table 4. LRU-MIN achieved a higher hit rate than LRU-THOLD in five cases, and LRU-THOLD achieved a higher hit rate than LRU-MIN in four cases. Given that the optimal threshold for LRU-THOLD is a function of the workload and the ratio of the disk size available for the cache compared to the cache size needed for no replacement, LRU-MIN is the best policy: it requires no parameters and achieves the best performance most of the time. On the other hand, LRU-THOLD achieves dramatically smaller cache sizes with a small penalty in hit rate compared to LRU-MIN; thus LRU-THOLD is recommmended when disk size is limited compared to the cache size required for no replacement. Finally, the lifetimes reported in the table show that a document stays in the cache for greatly varying times—as much as ten times longer for LRU-THOLD compared to LRU. The short lifetimes for LRU might explain why its hit rates are never higher than the other policies: documents are replaced too frequently.

Table 4 : Comparison of document replacement policies LRU, LRU-MIN, and LRU-THOLD with three different sizes of disk areas for caching (i.e., 10%, 50%, and 90% of MaxNeeded) using three performance measures. Zero entries for lifetime indicate that no document was ever replaced during simulation. Asterisks denote optimal values, unless all three policies yielded the same value.

	Hit Rate (%)		Cache Size (Mbytes)		Lifetime (Hours)	
	U/MIN	U/MAX	U/MIN	U/MAX	U/MIN	U/MAX
10% MaxNeeded						
LRU	23.8	26.4	3.0	13.8*	1.3	15.0
LRU-MIN	31.0	28.1	3.0	13.8*	2.8	47.3
LRU-THOLD	31.5*	29.5	3.0	16.0	7.2	151.6
50% MaxNeeded						
LRU	31.2	30.3	13.8	80.0	4.3	104.1
LRU-MIN	32.9*	31.0	14.0	76.5*	7.7	119.2
LRU-THOLD	32.9*	32.1*	10.0*	80.0	0.0	178.9
90% MaxNeeded						
LRU	32.9	32.1	24.8	144.0	8.7	170.3
LRU-MIN	33.0*	32.1	25.0	144.0	10.0	45.3
LRU-THOLD	32.9	32.1	10.0*	85.9*	0.0	0.0
	C/MIN	C/MAX	C/MIN	C/MAX	C/MIN	C/MAX
10% MaxNeeded						
LRU	35.4	30.6	5.0	13.0	80.9	32.2
LRU-MIN	46.3*	41.1	5.0	13.0	291.0	42.0
LRU-THOLD	46.0	41.2*	5.0	13.0	629.8	324.4
50% MaxNeeded						
LRU	46.0	38.7	22.9	61.4	498.6	76.3
LRU-MIN	48.1*	43.1*	23.0	62.8	647.1	225.7
LRU-THOLD	48.1*	42.7	14.8*	26.2*	0.0	0.0
90% MaxNeeded						
LRU	48.4*	42.6	40.9	114.0	838.2	278.6
LRU-MIN	48.4*	43.1*	41.0	111.5	840.1	297.9
LRU-THOLD	48.1	42.7	14.8*	26.2*	0.0	0.0

ANOVA on each workload's hit rate reveals the following: For workload U, the disk size and replacement policy were statistically significant (p=0.001 and 0.018), with the disk size explaining most of the variation in hit rate (58%), and the policy explaining 18%. The interactions of disk size and hit rate were not significant. Error (variances among the two eight day intervals simulated) accounted for 12% of the variation. Thus the disk size for caching has a much larger influence on hit rate than the replacement policy, but replacement policy is more important than variation due to differences in observation period. In contrast, in workload C no factor was statistically significant, with the variances among the two eight-day intervals simulated explaining the most variation in hit rate (about 1/3).

Table 5: Ranking of Factor Levels Producing Top Four Hit Rates for Each Workload, with Corresponding Cache Sizes

Document type cached	Domain cached	Minimum document size cached	Hit Rate		Cache Size	
			U/S	C/S	U/S	C/S
All types (+1)	All (+1)	0 kbytes (+1)	32.0%	45.0%	45.2Mb	42.9Mb
Non Text (-1)	All (+1)	0 kbytes (+1)	30.0%	34.8%	40.0Mb	42.6Mb
All types (+1)	All (+1)	1 kbytes (-1)	18.5%	34.2%	45.2Mb	43.0Mb
Non Text (-1)	All (+1)	1 kbytes (-1)	16.8%	25.7%	40.0Mb	42.6Mb

Experiment 4

Recall that Experiment 4 investigates how various cache configuration parameters impact the hit rate and cache size. Table 5 lists the combination of factors that lead to the highest four hit rates. Interestingly, the workload did not matter in that the same factor-level combinations lead to the same position in the ranking table. The table also lists the resultant cache sizes, which varied no more than 10% from the maximum to the minimum observed. The conclusion from this data suggests that it is best to cache everything—regardless of document type, document size, or domain. The penalty for not caching all domains and all document sizes is a dramatic drop in hit rate—at least 10% for workload C, and almost 50% for workload U.

Applying the analysis of variance technique to our data shows that all factors and factor interactions are statistically significant at alpha = 5%. Factors "Domain cached" and "Minimum document size cached" explain most of the variation in hit rate (72% and 18% for workload U and 75% and 9% for workload C, respectively). Factor "Document type cached" accounted for almost no variation in hit rate in workload U, but 7% in workload C. All factor interactions and the error accounted for smaller percentages. Based on this, the decision of caching all documents, not just off-campus documents, is the most important. In fact, the hit rate is 16.8% and 20.0% higher in workloads U and C, respectively, when on-campus documents are also cached compared to not caching them. This illustrates how critical it is to

find a solution to the problem of identifying when cached documents are out of date with the HTTP proctocol to permit caching of all domains. On the other hand, caching text files provided little benefit to workload U (increasing hit rate only 1.3%), but was more critical in the workload C (increasing hit rate 6%).

Comparison to Other Cache Studies

We are aware of three studies in the literature that report cache performance: for the HENSA archive [11], for the DEC gateway [4], and for a proposed cache algorithm [8].

The cache size simulated in Experiment 1 is comparable to the data reported by Smith for the HENSA archive in March 1994 [11], which contained 7554 documents occupying 184 Mbytes of disk space (versus up to 8660 documents and a maximum of 159 Mbytes of disk space in Experiment 1). Given this, how do the hit rates compare? Smith reports that "on a typical working day we [the UNIX HENSA ARCHIVE] expect to serve at least 60% of requested documents out of the cache" [11]. Smith's 60% hit rate is above the mean, around 29-30%, that we found for workloads U and G and the 46% we found for workload C. However some differences exist. In the HENSA case, a user had to prefix a URL with the proxy name for caching to be activated. Therefore the HENSA server saw a subset of all user traffic. In contrast, our simulation study includes *all* URLs that clients send. Also, as noted in the

Introduction, some clients in workloads U and G used a client cache, which reduces the hit rate in the caching proxy. Smith does not state if clients accessing the HENSA archive used caching; if they did not, this would be one reason that the HENSA hit rate is higher.

Glassman reports a 30%-50% hit rate for the DEC SRC gateway [4], which looks similar to the 29%-50% range in Table 5. However the DEC gateway caches only nonlocal pages, whereas we cache all pages. Also, the number of users accessing the DEC gateway is much larger than in our study. Glassman asks in his paper, "Would a much larger or much smaller user population give different results?" As far as hit rate is concerned, the answer from our study is "no." Interestingly, the 75-86 Mbyte cache sizes we observed in eight-day intervals are about the same as the cache size in the first eight day period of [4, Figure 1].

Recker and Pitkow [10] also report hit rates. Unlike the workloads in this study or those of Smith and of Glassman, which represent all traffic originating from a set of clients, Recker/Pitkow's workload is all traffic to a single HTTP server (i.e. , www.gatech.edu), not to a proxy. Recker/Pitkow report a 67% hit rate for accesses from off-campus for a three-month period. The server they studied had fewer documents (2000) than were involved in the study here, or by Smith or by Glassman, but had a higher access rate than this study. We would expect the Recker/Pitkow hit rate to be higher than that observed here and by Smith and by Glassman because a URL names two fields (a server and a document), and accesses to a server cache are guaranteed to hit on one of the two fields (the server). In contrast accesses to a caching proxy has no such guarantee—the accesses go to any Web server worldwide.

One other study concerns caching proxy performance. Braun and Claffy [3] investigate the possibility of caching popular NCSA files at several sites around the country. Their study varies from this one in several ways. First, the recorded logs are only for two days of access. Second, the log-

ging was done on a file server, not a proxy server. Third, the server in the study is unique, in that Mosaic clients use NCSA as the default home page. The study does show, however, that by caching a very small subset of client access, a substantial savings in network load can be achieved. The evaluation of NCSA file retrievals showed that the top 25 files requested represented only 0.065% of the different files accessed, but accounted for 59% of the number of requests and 45% of the bytes transferred.

Conclusion and Future Work

Our simulation study of three workloads (from an undergrad lab, graduate users, and a classroom with workstations for all students) reveals the following insights into caching proxy design:

1. We confirmed previous data in the literature that a caching proxy has an upper bound of 30-50% in its hit rate, given an infinite-size cache and an eight-day cache purge interval.

2. With our workloads, a caching proxy's hit rate tends to *decline* with time. We hypothesize that the reason is that when Web browsers use their own caches, the proxy acts as a second-level cache. The caching proxy hit rate declines as the Web browsers' caches fill over time. The effect is more pronounced if most Web browsers used have persistent caches, such as the Netscape browser provides.

3. When the cache is full and documents must be discarded to make room for a new document, LRU could never outperform the other policies that we studied. LRU ignores the sizes of documents. Thus to make room for, say, a large video for one user, it might replace many small documents resulting in misses for many users. A more effective policy is LRU-MIN, which applies LRU only to the largest documents, and then to groups of successively smaller documents. If the disk size becomes small compared to the cache

size needed for no replacement to occur, then LRU-THOLD, which does not cache documents larger than a certain threshold, keeps the cache size moderate but yields performance comparable to LRU-MIN. The disadvantage of LRU-THOLD is that our study shows the optimal threshold to be primarily dependent on the workload and the disk size available for the cache. Finally, one could use an adaptive policy: use LRU-MIN until the cache size approached 100% of the available disk size, and then switch to LRU-THOLD with a threshold that is gradually reduced until the cache size reaches a low-water mark.

4. Our study reiterates the observation of Luotonen and Altis: "Caching is more effective on the proxy than on each client. This saves disk space since only a single copy is cached, and also allows for more efficient caching of documents that are often referenced by multiple clients as the cache manager can predict which documents are worth caching for a long time and which are not ... because it has many clients and therefore a larger sample size to base its statistics on" [6]. This is particularly true for machines that are used in a laboratory, in which case a single disk shared among users may have many copies of the same documents! A more effective solution may be to use a *nonpersistent* per-client cache when a caching proxy is available. (At the end of the semester in which we collected data, we deleted 0.5 Gbyte of per-client caches amassed by 150 user ids.)

5. Caching all documents—not just ones in a particular domain, such as those outside one's organization—dramatically increases hit rate. In our study, hit rate increases 16.8% to 20% when all document domains are cached.

6. A caching proxy is likely to have a variety of configuration parameters. We examined

three: Should all document types, or just nontext be cached? Should all document sizes be cached, or only ones above some minimum size? Should all domains be cached, or just off-campus? Our results are independent of workload. Naturally, caching more files maximizes hit rate. However, caching just nontext files produces the smallest drop in hit rate, but it is small for one workload and large for another. Not caching small (less than 1 Kbyte) documents makes the next drop, and not caching documents that are text or small makes the next drop in hit rate. Interestingly, the cache size varies no more than 10% for all these alternatives, suggesting that such "tuning" of a caching proxy is ineffective.

One caveat is in order for our study: to some degree we overestimate hit rate because we cannot distinguish which URLs represent CGI-script-generated documents, and hence should not be cached.

Our recommendation for someone configuring a cache for a situation similar in nature to our educational workloads (e.g., a department with workloads of up to 150 users) is that a modest disk size for caching per workload is required — 160 Mbytes was adequate for all cases in our study. One should expect about 1/3 of the requests outside the classroom will be cache hits and about 1/2 of the requests in the classroom will be hits. The best strategy is to make the disk area for the cache sufficiently large to avoid replacement. When the cache becomes full and replacements must occur, use—if available—a replacement policy that tries to replace documents of comparable size to the incoming document.

Listed below are some open problems that need exploration:

- How effective are *multi-level* caching proxies?

- Caches require some mechanism of insuring that cached documents are up-to-date, such as issuing a CONDITIONAL GET from the proxy to the source HTTP server to verify up-to-date cached documents. But these methods increase proxy and network loads, and can increase the delay that a user experiences in retrieving a cached document. A study of the performance impact of various proposed cache consistency policies is needed.

- Luotonen and Altis [7] suggest that the HTTP protocol be enhanced to allow multiple URL gets and responses over a single connection, rather than establishing one connection per GET. What impact would this have on the document transfer rate that a Web client user sees?

The full traces of the workloads used in this study; the tool used to analyze and transform the traces into simulation input files, called Chitra95 (described in [1]); and the Windows-based SLAM II [9] simulation used in this paper, called Web-Sim, are available from WWW location *http://www.cs.vt.edu/~chitra/www.html.* ∎

Acknowledgments

We thank Leo Bicknell and Carl Harris for providing the workload U trace logs. This work was supported in part by the National Science Foundation through CISE Institutional Infrastucture (Education) grant CDA-9312611, CISE RIA grant NCR-9211342, and SUCCEED (Cooperative Agreement No. EID-9109853). SUCCEED is an NSF-funded coalition of eight schools and colleges working to enhance engineering education for the twenty-first century. We also thank the Fall 1995 CS-5014 class at Virginia Tech for their informative critique of this paper.

References

1. M. Abrams, S. Williams, G. Abdulla, S. Patel, R. Ribler, E. A. Fox, "Multimedia Traffic Analysis Using Chitra95," to appear in *ACM Multimedia 95*, San Francisco, Nov. 1995; URL *http://www.cs.vt.edu/~chitra/docs/95multimediaAWAFPR/95multimediaAWAFPR.html.*

2. K. Andrews, F. Kappe, H. Maurer, K. Schmaranz, "On Second Generation Network Hypermedia Systems," *Proc. ED-MEDIA 95, World Conference on Educational Multimedia and Hypermedia,* Graz, Austria, June 17-21, 1995.

3. H. Braun and K. Claffy, "Web Traffic Characterization: An Assessment of the Impact of Caching Documents from NCSA's Web Server," *Proc. 2nd Int. WWW Conference,* Chicago, Oct. 1994; URL *http://www.ncsa.uiuc.edu/SDG/IT94/Proceedings/DDay/claffy/main.html*

4. S. Glassman, "A Caching Relay for the World Wide Web," In First International World Wide Web Conference, pages 69-76, May 1994; also appeared in *Computer Networks and ISDN Systems 27,* No. 2, 1994; URL *http://www1.cern.ch/PapersWWW94/steveg.ps/*

5. T.T. Kwan, R.E.McGrath, and D.A. Reed, "User Access Patterns to NCSA's World Wide Web Server," NCSA and University of Illinois Computer Science Technical Report, 1994.

6. A. Luotonen, *Configuration File of CERN httpd,* 1994; URL *http://www.w3.org/hypertext/WWW/Daemon/User/Config/Overview.html*

7. A. Luotonen and K. Altis, "World Wide Web Proxies", *1st Inter. Conf. on the WWW,* Geneva, May 1994; also appeared in *Computer Networks and ISDN Systems 27,* No. 2, 1994; URL *http://www1.cern.ch/PapersWWW94/luotonen.ps*

8. J. E. Pitkow and M. M. Recker, "A Simple Yet Robust Caching Algorithm Based on Dynamic Access Patterns," in *Proc. 2nd Int. WWW Conf.,* 1994; URL *ftp://ftp.gvu.gatech.edu/pub/gvu/tech-reports/94-39.ps.Z*

9. Pritsker, A. A. B., *Introduction to Simulation and SLAM II,* 3rd ed., Halsted, New York, 1987.

10. M. M. Recker and J. Pitkow, *Predicting Document Access in Large, Multimedia Repositories,* Graphics, Visualization, and Usability Center Tech. Rep. VU-GIT-94-39, Georgia Tech, August, 1994; URL *ftp://ftp.gvu.gatech.edu/pub/gvu/tech-reports/94-35a.ps.Z* and *94-35b.ps.Z*

11. N. Smith, *What Can Archives Offer the World-Wide Web,* University of Kent at Canterbury, 22 March 1994.

12. A. S. Tanenbaum, *Modern Operating Systems,* Prentice-Hall, 1992, pp. 111-112.

Appendix: Data Tracing Procedure

CERN HTTP servers were run as proxy servers during the spring semester of 1995 at Virginia Tech to collect data on client usage. This data was collected using the proxy-server log files.

Our users run either Mosaic or Netscape. To log Mosaic client requests, we modified the "Mosaic" command on our systems to invisibly invoke our proxy server. To log Netscape client requests, we asked users in workload G to set their client preferences to use the proxy. In workload U, the hosts were all on an isolated network that was forced to use the proxy server as a gateway to the Internet, thus guaranteeing all client requests were logged. In the classroom the authors manually set the preferences of clients to use the proxy before class.

The CERN HTTP server permits logging of all server activity in either a default or verbose mode; we used the default mode. The log file generated contains one record for each request sent by client to the proxy. A record contains the client machine name, the date and time the proxy received the request, the command (e.g., GET), the source URL, the document size returned, and the command return code. We ran our proxy server with caching turned on, to collect actual data on cache effectiveness for another study ([1]), but the proxy still logged *all* requests generated by clients in two files (for documents returned by the proxy versus documents returned by the source HTTP server).

7 October 1995

About the Authors

Marc Abrams
[*http://www.cs.vt.edu/vitae/Abrams.html*]
Computer Science Department
Virginia Tech
Blacksburg, VA 24061-0106 USA
abrams@vt.edu

Charles R. Standridge
Department of Industrial Engineering
FAMU-FSU College of Engineering
Tallahassee, FL 32310, USA
stand@evax11.eng.fsu.edu

Ghaleb Abdulla
[*http://csgrad.cs.vt.edu/~abdulla/*]
Computer Science Department
Virginia Tech
Blacksburg, VA 24061-0106 USA
abdulla@csgrad.cs.vt.edu

Stephen Williams
[*http://csgrad.cs.vt.edu/~williams/*]
Computer Science Department
Virginia Tech
Blacksburg, VA 24061-0106 USA
williams@csgrad.cs.vt.edu

Edward A. Fox
[*http://fox.cs.vt.edu/*]
Computer Science Department
Virginia Tech
Blacksburg, VA 24061-0106 USA
fox@vt.edu

IAFA TEMPLATES IN USE AS INTERNET METADATA

David Beckett

Abstract

Recently, there has been a growing need for a metadata standard for the Internet. The files that are available on ftp and WWW sites can be difficult to search if they are enclosed in a container format (e. g., tar), and bibliographical data can be deeply embedded in documentation. This paper describes how IAFA Templates[1] have been used in a real archive to store the metadata of lots of different types of documents and software and to derive WWW, gopher, and text indices from them. ***Keywords:*** *Metadata, IAFA templates, ALIWEB, SOIF, Harvest*

Introduction

Despite the popularity of the HTTP/HTML part of the Web, the most standard form for transmitting and sharing documents and software on the Internet is still via ftp and gopher sites. These have grown to be large resources of material, but unfortunately have been traditionally very badly indexed and organized.

If a gopher interface to an archive is available it can provide a menu-based interface in which the archive administrator can describe the resource, albeit in around a maximum of 70 characters for common terminal sizes, which is what most common gopher clients run on.

More commonly, only the anonymous ftp form was available, providing just the UNIX shell-like interface to the archive.

Usually, the donated files were lucky to have a single line of text describing the contents; more likely, the filename was the best hint to the package (*foobar-1.3.tar.gz* for version 1.3 of package foobar). Sometimes, there would be a *README* or index file in the same directory as the files with a description of each of the files in natural language. This would be fine for people prepared to look at every single *README* file in the

archive to find something, but natural language is not a good way to describe the files since the information is not structured and hence not machine readable/writable. There are also additional problems:

Difficult indexing locally
   The text in the *README* files could be fully indexed (inverted), but there would be no way of picking out the descriptions for individual files from the text.

Cannot do resource discovery well
   For similar reasons, remote indexers would have difficulty picking out files and would have to index the content of the files without really knowing what is there.

Index sharing is not possible
   There is no way to share indices without having a standard index/metadata format.

Hence the need for structured metadata standards for Internet archives.

Metadata Standards for the Internet

In May of 1993 I started to build the *Internet Parallel Computing Archive** at the *HENSA Unix*

---

* Internet Parallel Computing Archive at *http://www.hensa.ac.uk/parallel/.*

*Archive.** The materials gathered consist of software, papers, reports, bibliographies, documents, and many other types of file about Parallel and High Performance Computing, taken from several sources:

- Locally written

- Donated from external contributors

- From off-line sources

- *mirrored* [2] from other Internet sites

- Automatically archived such as USENET newsgroups

In the first three cases, it would be easy to only allow materials with correctly formatted metadata to be allowed on the archive, but the the latter cases are more difficult. *mirroring* is a process which makes an identical copy (a clone or mirror image) of the files on a remote site on the local site. Thus, these files cannot be modified locally, and any metadata must be external, in other files. For the newsgroups, there are a lot of articles being archived daily; so generating appropriate metadata by hand would be very tedious. Thus to handle all of the above sources, a metadata standard was needed with the following requirements:

- Easy for people to read and write

- Machine readable and writable for automatic creation, modification, and indexing and sorting

- Can describe the *form, contents,* and *location* of the information

- Structured to allow nesting

- Can be used for building multiple derived indices (WWW, text, gopher...)

Investigations were done into the metadata forms that were available at the time:

Linux Software Map (LSM) Templates

The Linux software archives at the SunSITEs† addressed their need for a metadata standard with structured *templates* [3] which contain the following 12 attributes appropriate to the archive needs: Title, Version, Entered-date, Description, Keywords, Author, Maintained-by, Primary-site, Alternate-site, Original-site, Platforms, Copying-policy

The form of the entries is similar to *Internet Mail headers* [4] with colon-separated attribute-value pairs that can wrap over several lines. There is a short description of the valid values for each field but little concrete data form; most of it is free-form text.

Later on, tools were built to process these templates, index them, and create such things as the *Linux Software Map* [5]. At present, when people are submitting something to the archive, they may be rejected by the maintainers if they do not have LSM templates written.

Unfortunately, the LSM templates are very much intended for software packages that are replicated at different sites and hence are not particularly appropriate for indexing a much richer set of files.

IAFA Templates

The *Internet Engineering Task Force* (IETF) Working Group on *Internet Anonymous FTP Archives* (IAFA), later called IIIR, have produced the IAFA Templates Internet Draft [1]. This defines a range of indexing information that can be used to describe the contents and services provided by anonymous FTP archives.

The draft has a rich range of templates, attributes, and values that can be used to describe common and useful elements. The goal is that these are to be used to index archives, made available pub-

---

* HENSA Unix Archive at *http://www.hensa.ac.uk/*.
† Linux archive, SunSITE USA at *ftp://sunsite.unc.edu/pub/Linux/welcome.html*.

licly in them to allow searching, indexing, and sharing of information on the archive contents, services, and administrative data.

This template scheme is based on the same RFC822 form as the LSM templates, with colon-separated attributes-values known as data elements. One or more data elements are collected into templates which have a single `Template-Type` field to describe the type of the basic template. Multiple templates can be collected in index files by separating with blank lines. The attributes can be structured in several ways:

- *Variant information* is used to support multiple languages, formats, of a document. For example, two variants of language available for an individual resource are: `Language-v0: English` and `Language-v1: Deutsch`.

- *Clusters* are classes of data elements that occur every time an individual or group is mentioned such as name, addresses, email addresses, telephone numbers, etc. Handles can be used to refer to clusters inside templates.

- *Handles* allow short unique strings to abbreviate a group of data elements for individuals or organizations. For example, `Author-Handle: Kim Jones` instead of all the individual elements of the USER cluster for Kim Jones.

There are 14 currently defined template types: SITEINFO, LARCHIVE, MIRROR, USER, ORGANIZATION, SERVICE, DOCUMENT, IMAGE, SOFTWARE, MAILARCHIVE, USENET, SOUND, VIDEO, FAQ and each has appropriate attributes defined for them. Most of the types are self-explanatory apart from SITEINFO which is a description of the FTP site and LARCHIVE which is a description of a logical (sub)archive. More types can be defined if necessary having the same basic attributes as DOCUMENT.

It also turns out that LSM Templates were based on an early draft of the IAFA Templates (June 1992) but modified to have more consistent elements. The later versions were modified to be more similar, but some differences remain.

IAFA Templates were the solution chosen to base my metadata on. They were rich and extensible and a standard, or albeit a draft one.

Using IAFA Templates

The first stage was to convert all the old *Index* files that had been written by hand into IAFA Template form. This was achieved by just mapping path, description pairs for each file into a simple form:

```
Template-Type: DOCUMENT
URI: path
Description: description
```

Of course, not everything is a document, and more intelligence was needed to determine the metadata.

Extensions to IAFA Templates

IAFA Templates were not sufficient to fully handle all my uses so new template types and elements were added, as the draft allows.

The information is structured hierarchically; hence there is a need to list the subdirectories for any given directory. There is no way to do that cleanly in the draft; the only way would be to rely on a convention that a DOCUMENT with a URI ending in a '/' is a directory. It is better to add a `Template-Type DIRECTORY` since a directory is *not* a document. Another template type that was added was EVENT, which was used to describe conferences, workshops, etc. which have a date range.

In addition, there was no way to describe symbolic links. These are used in my archive to point from one area to another so the directories */parallel/transputer/compilers/occam* and */parallel/occam/compilers* have the same content, but the names of the final directories are different. If the alternative, a site-relative URI, was used that would make the directory names the same and hence confusing for the browser. A simple extension to the format of the URI field allowed symbolic links to be added.

Another extension was the definition of the separation of templates. The draft uses a *blank line* defined as an empty line or a line consisting of only white space. I use just the former, an empty line, since that means paragraph breaks can be put in descriptive or other text (see example later).

Extra elements that were added include:

`X-Abstract`
> The abstract from a paper or report. This is more specific than a general `Description` field.

`X-Acronym`
> Rather than put the (say, conference) acronym in `Title`, it goes here.

`X-Gopher-Description(-v*)` and `X-HTML-Description(-v*)`
> Descriptions that are specifically written for gopher or HTML index output. Gopher descriptions need to be short to fit on the screen; HTML ones can have markup added.

`X-Start-Date` and `X-End-Date`
> For documents that describe a range, e.g., conferences

`X-Expires-Date`
> Documents that can be deleted at a certain point, for example, job offers and conference calls.

Implementation of IAFA Templates

This was written in Perl 5 as two programs. The first one, `update-afa-indices`, updates the IAFA indices by deleting templates for files that have gone, updating them for files that have changed in size and/or date, and adding new templates for new files. The second program, `afa-to-others` reads the IAFA indices and outputs several derived indices: text, gopher, and HTML.

Automatically Updating IAFA Templates (update-afa-indices)

This program implements three forms of automatic extraction of metadata:

- *From the URI (filename)*. This is a very cheap operation since it requires no access to the file system or reading of the file contents. This is what is commonly done with HTTP servers to define the MIME types of the files being delivered. Things that can be interpreted from this include the `Template-Type` and the `Format` of the the file. For example, files ending in *.ps* are assumed to be format `postscript`, template DOCUMENT, files ending in *.tar*, *.tgz*, *.taz*, *.tar.gz*, and *.tar.Z* were interpreted as the various forms of (compressed gzipped) tar SOFTWARE templates. For multiple levels of nesting, such things as `uuencoded compressed tar file` formats are possible. In later versions of the draft, this was changed to be the MIME [6] type of the document, but this would not be sufficient to describe the tar files above so the earlier version of the definition was kept. MIME types could be added easily.

- *From the file system information*. This information is usually kept in one place in the file system and can be found in a quick access. Things that can be interpreted from this include the `Size` of the file in bytes and the `Last-Revision-Date.`

- *From the contents of the file*. This is expensive to create and update since it requires expanding the presentation nesting. Essence [7] does sophisticated work on the contents but this software limited itself to extracting author information (`Author-Name` and `Author-Email`) from USENET and mail files. Because all of the above are generated by software, when they change, the software can update the metadata.

`update-afa-indices` operates on a directory tree (or subtree of it). In each directory, there is a single index file *AFA-INDEX* containing the templates for each of the files and directories in there. There is also a configuration file *.ixconfig* that allows specific files or directories to be excluded from the index. This allows mirrored areas to be kept the same as the remote site, but not all the files need to be shown. For example, if the entire contents of a text index file are represented in the index, there is no need to include a reference to that file.

The program walks the tree, reading the IAFA indices, and looks for differences between the templates and the entries in the file system for items 1 and 2 from the bulleted list above. Only if there is a difference is item 3 calculated, since it is an expensive operation. If the entry is new, it is appended to the end of the index. Files or directories that have been deleted are automatically removed from the index. After all the processing is done, the index file is sorted by fields that are configurable by the *.ixconfig* file.

Adding Hand-written Metadata to the IAFA Indices

In addition to the above automatically added metadata, there is scope for the administrator to add lots more fields which are difficult for automatic software to pick out, such as `Title` and `Description`, the main one which describes the contents. These are not checked or altered by the software when it does updates.

Building Derived Indices from IAFA Indices (afa-to-others)

This program reads the IAFA indices files and generates derived indices, specific to particular access methods. For example, given the following template:

```
Template-Type: EVENT
```

Description: Call for papers for the
    Fifth International Conference on
Parallel Computing (ParCo'95) being
    held from 19th-22nd September
1995 at International Conference
    Center, Gent, Belgium.

Topics:
Applications and Algorithms; Systems
    Software and Hardware.

Deadlines: Abstracts: 31st January
    1995; Notification: 15th April
1995; Posters: 30th June 1995.

See also <URL:http://www.elis.rug.ac.be/
    announce/parco95/cfp.html>
Author-Email: a.n.author@host.site.
    country
Author-Name: A. N. Author
Title: Fifth International Conference
    on Parallel Computing
X-Acronym: ParCo'95
X-End-Date: 1995-09-22
X-Expires-Date: 1995-09-22
X-Start-Date: 1995-09-19
Format-v0: ASCII document
Format-v1: PostScript document
Last-Revision-Date-v0: Wed, Jan 11
    11:24:39 1995 GMT
Last-Revision-Date-v1: Wed, Sep 21
    10:41:01 1994 GMT
Size-v0: 4516
Size-v1: 71330
URI-v0: parco95.ascii
URI-v1: parco95.ps
X-Gopher-Description-v0: 5th Int.
    Conference on Parallel Computing
(ParCo'95) CFP (ASCII)
X-Gopher-Description-v1: 5th Int.
    Conference on Parallel Computing
(ParCo'95) CFP (PS)

which describes a pair of files for a conference call, the derived text index output would be:

parco95.ascii
"Fifth International Conference on
    Parallel Computing"
Call for papers for the Fifth
    International Conference on Parallel
Computing (ParCo'95) being held from
    19th-22nd September 1995 at
International Conference Center, Gent,
    Belgium.

```
Topics: Applications and Algorithms;
    Systems Software and Hardware.
Deadlines: Abstracts: 31st January
    1995; Notification: 15th April
1995; Posters: 30th June 1995.
See also <URL:http://www.elis.rug.ac.be/
    announce/parco95/cfp.html>
Author: A. N. Author <a.n.author@host.
    site.country>. [ASCII document]


parco95.ps
"Fifth International Conference on
    Parallel Computing"
Call for papers for the Fifth
    International Conference on Parallel
Computing (ParCo'95) being held from
    19th-22nd September 1995 at
International Conference Center, Gent,
    Belgium.
Topics: Applications and Algorithms;
    Systems Software and Hardware.
Deadlines: Abstracts: 31st January
    1995; Notification: 15th April
1995; Posters: 30th June 1995.
See also <URL:http://www.elis.rug.ac.be/
    announce/parco95/cfp.html>
Author: A. N. Author <a.n.author@host.
    site.country>. [PostScript document]
```

and the derived gopher elements would be these entries in the gopher tree:

```
5th Int. Conference on Parallel
    Computing (ParCo'95) CFP (ASCII)
5th Int. Conference on Parallel
    Computing (ParCo'95) CFP (PS)
```

and the HTML element would be (as part of a conformant HTML 2.0 index file):

```
<DL>
<DT><A NAME="parco95.ascii"
    HREF="parco95.ascii"><B>Fifth
    Internation'
cument] (4516 bytes)<BR>
<DT><A NAME="parco95.ps" HREF="parco95.
    ps"><B>Fifth International Con'
ument] (71330 bytes)<BR>
<DD>Call for papers for the Fifth
    International Conference on Parallel
Computing (ParCo'95) being held from
    19th-22nd September 1995 at
International Conference Center, Gent,
    Belgium. <P>

<I>Topics:</I>
```

```
Applications and Algorithms; Systems
    Software and Hardware.<P>

<I>Deadlines:</I> Abstracts: 31st
    January 1995; Notification: 15th
    April
1995; Posters: 30th June 1995.<P>

See also <A HREF="http://www.elis.rug.
    ac.be/announce/parco95/cfp.html">'

Author: A. N. Author (<I>a.n.
    author@host.site.country</I>).
</DL>
```

which looks like this when displayed formatted:

Fifth International Conference on Parallel Computing (*ParCo'95*) [ASCII document] (4516 bytes)

Fifth International Conference on Parallel Computing (*ParCo'95*) [PostScript document] (71330 bytes)

Call for papers for the Fifth International Conference on Parallel Computing (ParCo'95) being held from 19th-22nd September 1995 at International Conference Center, Gent, Belgium.

Topics: Applications and Algorithms; Systems Software and Hardware.

Deadlines: Abstracts: 31st January 1995; Notification: 15th April 1995; Posters: 30th June 1995.

See also *http://www.elis.rug.ac.be/announce/parco95/cfp.html*

Author: A. N. Author (*a.n.author@host.site.country*).

Extra template types that were added for the derived indices were: X-AFA-HEADER and X-AFA-FOOTER, which were some text to be placed at the start or end of a derived index.

This software is also configurable by the *.ixconfig* file and it allows handwritten indices, e.g., the top *index.html,* which is the *home page,* to be left untouched. In addition, some areas can be left without indices, for example, directories containing icons used in the HTML pages.

Problems With IAFA Templates

There are some problems with the IAFA templates as they currently stand. As described above, some extra elements were needed for my application, and indeed they could be added. More fundamentally, there is a problem with the structuring of the nesting of data using variants. There is no way to describe a collection that, for example, contains multiple languages and multiple document types or authors with two affiliations.

There are also the problems of encoding; there is no way to use binary data, non-ASCII characters, or indeed, blanks in descriptions as paragraphs (without the extension I used). Some of these problems have been addressed in other formats, and other metadata standards for different purposes are being designed which may provide a rich enough structure to cope with these difficulties.

New Metadata Formats

Several new metadata formats have appeared more recently, albeit some still in unfinished or draft form.

Harvest Summary Object Interchange Format (SOIF) and Harvest

The *SOIF* Data format as described in [8] used by Harvest [9] is based on IAFA Templates and Bib-TeX but has some extra features. Unlike the templates, it was designed to support streams of (possibly compressed) SOIF data between systems allowing additions, deletions, and updates of the metadata. This is used by the Harvest system programs to communicate. SOIF also allows binary content in the values, by adding a length element to each value. There are not yet any *required* attributes defined by the standard although some are proposed. IAFA templates can be easily converted into SOIF format according to Koster in his *Future of ALIWEB* discussion [10].

Universal Resource Citations (URCs)

The latest Internet Draft [11] describes that one of the main uses of a URC is to map from a URN to a possibly empty list of URLs for a browser. The user may, however, want to take the URC for the resource and find out the metadata of the URLs—cost, bibliographical data, etc. in a form that is understandable by people. The requirements for URC also include that it must be parsable by a computer, be simple and structured for nesting. Two URC services have been proposed in Internet Drafts, a simple text one [12] and one using SGML [13].

Dublin Metadata Core Element Set

In March 1995, the *OCLC/NCSA Metadata Workshop* was held in Dublin, Ohio, USA, with selected invited attendees with specialities in library science, computer science, text encoding, and related areas. One of its goals was to define a simple set of elements suitable for naive users to describe networked electronic resources. This was restricted to those needed for resource discovery of what were called *Document-Like Objects* (DLOs). In the proceedings [14], the format of a set of 13 metadata elements, named the *Dublin Metadata Core Element Set*, were defined by the participants:

Subject, Title, Author, Publisher, OtherAgent, Date, ObjectType, Form, Identifier, Relation, Source, Language, Coverage

The elements are syntax-independent; no single encoding was defined, and it was intended that they could be mapped into more complex systems such as SGML or USMARC [15] and can use any appropriate cataloging code such as AACR2, LCSH, or Dewey Decimal.

Future Work and Wishes

A prototype customizable interface to the archive is under development. Users will be able to use an HTML FORM with buttons in it to describe how they want the presentation of the metadata, how rich, and in what form. This would generate indices customized to the user and the browser, depending on what level of conformance it had to standards (unknown HTML, HTML 2, HTML 3, ...).

In addition to the collated indexers like ALIWEB and Harvest, there are Web crawlers that try to "*index the web.*" These could benefit from rich metadata provided by the document authors or site administrators that would be difficult to extract automatically. In the best of all worlds, each WWW site would create the metadata for each of the files it wants to make available to the world, and the results would be distributed automatically using a hierarchy of caches (for efficiency). ALIWEB and Harvest allow forms of these kinds of systems to be built using IAFA templates and SOIF respectively. Then the Web-crawlers could get just the new metadata, rather than crawl the Web continually, and smartly index it with their own software.

Conclusion

A system has been designed for the Internet using IAFA templates as a basis. This has been very successful in organizing a large archive (> 440 Mbytes with > 750 IAFA indices) of varied materials and providing good, detailed information about them. The indices for each of the access methods for the archive are created automatically and give a consistent look to the users.

The use of gopher as an Internet service is declining, and the use of HTTP (the WWW) is rapidly increasing. This system shows that the metadata can remain independent and richer than the presentation format and can survive evolutionary changes in the technology. Similarly, when a new (or de facto) standard for Metadata appears, it should be easy to derive the metadata from the IAFA Templates.

The software can be found at the *HENSA UNIX Archive* at *ftp://unix.hensa.ac.uk/pub/tools/www/ iafatools/* and *http://www.hensa.ac.uk/tools/www/ iafatools/.* ∎

References

1. P. Deutsch, A. Emtage, M. Koster, and M. Stumpf, *Publishing Information on the Internet with Anonymous FTP (IAFA Templates),* IETF IAFA WG Internet Draft, January 1995, *ftp://nic.merit.edu/ documents/internet-drafts/draft-ietf-iiir-publishing-03.txt.*

2. L. McLoughlin, `mirror`, Imperial College, University of London, UK, *ftp://src.doc.ic.ac.uk/packages/ mirror/.*

3. J. Kopmanis and L. Wirzenius, *Linux Software Map Entry Template,* August 1994, *ftp://sunsite.unc. edu/pub/Linux/docs/lsm-template.*

4. D. Crocker, *Standard for the format of ARPA Internet Mail Messages, RFC822,* University of Delaware, August 1992, *ftp://nic.merit.edu/documents/ rfc/rfc0822.txt.*

5. T. Boutell and L. Wirzenius, *Linux Software Map,* June 1995, *http://siva.cshl.org/lsm/lsm.html.*

6. N. Borenstein and N. Freed, *MIME (Multipurpose Internet Mail Extensions),* September 1993, *ftp:// nic.merit.edu/documents/rfc/rfc1521.txt* and *ftp:// nic.merit.edu/documents/rfc/rfc1522.txt.*

7. Darren R. Hardy and Michael F. Schwartz, *Customized Information Extraction as a Basis for Resource Discovery,* Technical Report CU-CS-707-94, Department of Computer Science, University of Colorado, Boulder, March 1994 (revised February 1995). To appear, *ACM Transactions on Computer Systems.*

8. D. Hardy, M. Schwartz, and D. Wessels, *Harvest User's Manual,* University of Colorado, Boulder, USA, April 1995, *http://harvest.cs.colorado.edu/ harvest/user-manual/.*

9. C. Mic Bowman, P. B. Danzig, D. R. Hardy, U. Manber, and M. F. Schwartz, *The Harvest Information Discovery and Access System, Proceedings of the Second International World Wide Web Conference,* pp. 763-771, Chicago, Illinois, October 1994.

10. M. Koster, *ALIWEB, Proceedings of First International WWW Conference,* 25-27 May 1994, CERN, Geneva, Switzerland. ALIWEB is at *http://web. nexor.co.uk/public/aliweb/aliweb.html.*

11. R. Daniel Jr., and M. Mealling, *URC Scenarios and Requirements,* Internet Draft, March 1995, *ftp:// nic.merit.edu/documents/internet-drafts/draft-ietf-uri-urc-req-01.txt.*

12. P. E. Hoffman, and R. Daniel Jr., *Trivial URC Syntax: urc0*, Internet Draft, May 1995, *ftp://nic.merit. edu/documents/internet-drafts/draft-ietf-uri-urc-trivial-00.txt.*

13. R. Daniel Jr. and T. Allen, *An SGML-based URC Service*, Internet Draft, June 1995, *ftp://nic.merit. edu/documents/internet-drafts/draft-ietf-uri-urc-sgml-00.txt.*

14. Stuart Weibel, Jean Godby, Eric Miller, *OCLC/ NCSA Metadata Workshop Report*, Dublin, Ohio, USA, March 1995 *http://www.oclc.org:5046/conferences/metadata/dublin_core_report.html.*

15. USMARC Advisory Group, *Mapping the Dublin Core Metadata Elements to USMARC*, 1995, *gopher://marvel.loc.gov/00/.listarch/usmarc/dp86. doc.*

About the Author

David Beckett

[*http://www.hensa.ac.uk/parallel/www/djb1.html*] Computing Laboratory, University of Kent, Canterbury, CT2 7NF, England
D.J.Beckett@ukc.ac.uk

A WORLD WIDE WEB RESOURCE DISCOVERY SYSTEM

Budi Yuwono, Savio L. Y. Lam, Jerry H. Ying, Dik L. Lee

Abstract

As the WWW grows at an increasing rate, efforts to make the technology more manageable are in great demand. Applying advanced information retrieval techniques is one approach to such efforts. Despite the potential benefit of these techniques in reducing users information overload and improving the effectiveness of access to online information, little research has been done on applying them to the WWW environment. In this paper, we present our attempt to apply the vector space retrieval model, relevance feedback mechanisms and a hypertext mapping technique as an integrated resource discovery system to the WWW. This paper discusses some design issues involved, as well as practical issues such as retrieval effectiveness, usability, and scalability. **Keywords:** *Resource discovery, information retrieval, World Wide Web indexing, user interface*

Introduction

The explosive growth of the World Wide Web (WWW [4]) is making it difficult for a user to locate information that is relevant to his/her interest. There are just too many servers to access and pages to browse through; even keeping track of new information as it becomes available online is a very time consuming task. Many methods have been proposed to alleviate this so called internet resource discovery problem. In general, most methods employ keyword searching strategy which allows a user to locate WWW page addresses or URLs (Uniform Resource Locator [1]) by specifying a keyword or keywords. Given the keywords, such a system searches its index and, upon finding hits, shows a list of URLs with their respective titles, possibly ranked by their relevance scores. This search strategy complements browsing or hypertext navigation, which is the dominant access method of the WWW, by providing users with potentially relevant starting points for browsing.

As with other applications on the Internet that are distributed in nature, the WWW is highly diversified and is ever changing in a non-coordinated way. An ideal search tool should be able to keep track of such changes, detect any inconsis-

tencies caused by independent local modifications, and organize information into a structured index which enables efficient search. Such an index can substantially reduce network load since users need to access only the index data in order to locate resources. In this paper we present a WWW resource discovery system which employs a so-called Web robot to build and maintain an index database for keyword searching. This approach, as opposed to manual indexing, is suitable for the size and the dynamical nature of the WWW environment.

The issue in the design of a keyword-based search tool is how effective the tool can meet the user's information needs. This involves the choice of the search algorithm and the user-system interaction component. In our previous work, we have studied a number of document search and ranking algorithms for the WWW environment. From our empirical evaluation, we concluded that TFxIDF algorithm which is based on word distribution, outperforms other algorithms which rely on WWW hyperlink information [15].

No matter how good the search and ranking algorithm is, however, it does not guarantee that the documents or WWW pages with high relevance scores are actually relevant to the user's information need. Such discrepancies may be due to ill-defined queries, such as too few or too many keywords resulting in too general or too specific queries, problems related with synonyms and homonyms, or the user's unfamiliarity with the subject he/she is interested in. One of the approaches to alleviating this problem is by means of a relevance feedback mechanism, i.e., an interaction between the user and the system to iteratively refine a query until a desired set of retrieved documents is obtained. In this paper, we present a relevance feedback mechanism which is supported by the user interface component of our system. The mechanism expands the previous version of a query by adding certain keywords extracted from WWW pages marked as relevant by the user.

There is, however, a problem with the above scheme, namely judging which WWW pages retrieved by the search engine are relevant requires the user to access and read through the actual pages, which can be time consuming. Even if the user has the time and patience to do so, it may not be easy to fully make sense of the contents of the individual pages without examining the context at the neighboring pages. The reason is that in hypertext environments such as WWW's, a document or page is often only a small chunk of a larger discourse formed by a network of interlinked pages. Our system's user interface component alleviates this problem by presenting the search result in a hierarchical page map which shows the links among the hit pages and the links with the neighboring pages.

While different users may have different information needs, it is often desirable to share one user's discovery with other users who may find it interesting. To facilitate such information sharing, our index server allows any user to save his/her query statement on the server's side so that other user or the user him/herself can reuse it later. This mechanism can also save other users time to perform query refinement themselves.

The remainder of the paper is organized as follows. In the "System Decription" section, we provide a detailed description of the components of our WWW resource discovery system, namely the indexer robot, the search engine and the user interface. In the "Lessons Learned" section, we discuss lessons learned from the trial run of the system, particularly regarding its retrieval effectiveness, hypertext mapping capability and usability, and the issue of system scalability. In the "Other Work" section, we close this paper with brief comparisons with other work and conclusions.

System Description

The system's main components are the *indexer robot*, the *search engine*, and the *user interface*. Figure 1 shows the architecture of our WWW resource-discovery system (this service currently covers sites in Hong Kong, and is publicly accessible at *http://www.cs.ust.hk/cgi-bin/IndexServer/*).

Indexer Robot

The indexer robot is an autonomous WWW browser which communicates with WWW servers using HTTP (Hypertext Transfer Protocol [2]). It visits a given WWW site, traverses hyperlinks in a breadth-first manner, retrieves WWW pages, extracts keywords and hyperlink data from the pages, and inserts the keywords and hyperlink data into an index. A list of target sites is given to the indexer robot for creating the index initially. In order to accommodate the constantly growing number of WWW servers online, the system allows any user to register new sites or URLs with the system.

The index consists of a page-ID table, a keyword-ID table, a page-title table, a page modification-date table, a hyperlink table, and two index tables, namely, an inverted index and a forward index. The page-ID table maps each URL to a unique page-ID. The keyword-ID table maps each keyword to a unique keyword-ID. The page-title table maps every page-ID to the page's

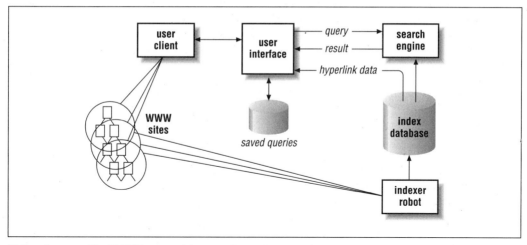

Figure 1:   The WWW Resource Discovery System's architecture

title. The page modification-date table maps every page-ID to the date when the page was last visited by the indexer robot. The hyperlink table maps each page-ID with two arrays of page-ID's, one array representing a list of pages referencing the page (incoming hyperlinks) and the other array representing a list of pages referenced by the page (outgoing hyperlinks). The inverted index table maps each keyword-ID to an array of <page-ID, word-position> pairs, each of which represents a page containing the keyword and the position of the word (order number) in the page. This word-position information is used in query by phrase, or keyword-order specific search, and the relevance feedback mechanism. The forward-index table maps a page-ID to an array of keyword-ID's representing keywords contained in the page. This forward index is used in the search algorithm, i.e., for computing the occurrence frequency of a word in a document, in the relevance feedback mechanism, and in various index maintenance functions. To obtain a fast access speed, hashing method is used to index each of these tables on the page-ID or key-word-ID attribute.

In extracting the keywords, we exclude high-frequency function words (stop-words), numbers, computer specific identifiers such as file-names,

directory paths, email addresses, network host names, and HTML (Hypertext Markup Language [3]) tags. To reduce storage overhead, the indexer robot only indexes words enclosed by HTML tags indicating tokens such as page titles, headings, hyperlink anchor names, words in bold-face, words in italic, and words in the first sentence of every list item. We assume that a WWW author will use these tags only on important sentences or words in his/her WWW pages. Thus, these words make good page identifiers. This is one of the advantages of adopting SGML (Standard General Markup Language), of which HTML is a subset. Words chosen as keywords are then stemmed by removing their suffices.

Resources using protocols other than HTTP (FTP, Gopher, Telnet, etc.) or in formats other than HTML text file (non-inline image, sound, video, binary, and other text files), click-able image maps, and CGI scripts are indexed by the anchor texts referencing them.

Periodic maintenance of the index files is performed bi-weekly by the indexer robot. First, the indexer robot checks the validity of every URL entry in the database by sending a special request to the WWW server containing the page to check whether the page has been modified since the time it was last accessed by the indexer robot. This special request, known as HEAD request, is a feature supported by HTTP. Non-routine index maintenance is also supported. This is performed at night in response to user requests received during the day to index new pages (URLs) or re-index updated pages. Such user requests are facilitated by an HTML form provided by the user interface component (to be discussed later).

The indexer robot has the capability of detecting looping paths, e.g., those caused by UNIX symbolic links, and does not visit the same page more than once unless the page has been modified since the time it was last visited by the robot. The latter is made possible by supplying the last access date and time into the HTTP request (using the `If-Modified-Since` request header field). As specified in the HTTP specification [2], the remote WWW server will not send the page content in response to the request if the page has not been modified since the specified time. Furthermore, the indexer robot will not even send an HTTP request if the page was last accessed by the robot within the last 24 hours. This is to prevent the robot from sending more than one HTTP requests for the same page during a maintenance batch. To prevent itself from roaming around uncontrollably from one server to the next, the indexer robot accesses one site at a time and only references within the same site domain as that of the referencing page are traversed. Finally, the indexer robot supports the proposed standard for robot exclusion[*] which prevents robots from accessing places where, for various reasons, they are not welcome.

The indexer robot is written in the C language. All index files are implemented using the GNU GDBM Database Manager library package [9].

Search Engine

The search engine employs the so called TFxIDF search and ranking algorithm which assigns rele-

vance scores to documents (the term *documents* here refers to text files in general, which also applies to WWW pages) using the vector space model [12]. The scores indicate the similarities between a given query, represented by a query vector, and the documents, represented by document vectors. In the vector space model, the similarities are measured by the cosine of the angle between the query vector and each of the document vectors. Each component of such a vector corresponds to the weight of a word or term in a query or a document. The weight of a term in a document is a function of the term's term frequency (TF) and the term's inverse document frequency (IDF). Generally speaking, the relevance score of a document is the sum of the weights of the query terms appearing in the document. More formally, the relevance score of *document(i)* with respect to query Q is defined as in Equation 1 below:

$$\left(R_{i,Q} = \sum_{term_j \varepsilon Q} \left(0.5 + 0.5 \frac{TF_{i,j}}{TF_{imax}} \right) IDF_j \right) \delta$$

where *TF(i,j)* is the term frequency of *term(j)* in *document(i)*, *TF(i,max)* is the maximum term frequency of a keyword in *document(i)*, and *IDF(j)* is the inverse document frequency of *term(j)*, which is defined in Equation 2 below:

$$IDF_j = \log N / DF_j$$

where *N* is the number of documents in the collection, and *DF(j)* is the number of documents containing *term(j)*.

This term-weighting function gives higher weights to terms which occur frequently in a small set of the documents. As shown in Equation 1, the term weight is normalized for document length, so that short documents have retrieval chances equal to those of longer documents. In our earlier work [15], it was shown that

---

[*] *http://web.nexor.co.uk/users/mak/doc/robots/norobots.html*

vector length normalization [13] does not work well for the WWW environment.

Given a query, the search engine computes the scores of WWW pages in the index, and returns at most the top H pages, where H is the *maximum number of hits*. By default H is set to 40, although the user can set it to a different value if so desired. Since the index database contains all of the information needed for ranking, the ranking process does not have to access any WWW pages physically.

The search engine supports Boolean constructs which make use of **&** (logical AND), **|** (logical OR), and *brackets* (scope marker) notations. To accommodate users who are not familiar with Boolean constructs, the engine allows the keywords to be separated by white spaces, which are treated as logical AND operators. Hyphens may also be used as keyword separators to specify phrases for keyword-order specific searching.

User Interface

The user interface to the search engine is an HTML form which can be invoked by standard WWW client programs such as Mosaic and Netscape. The form allows the user to type in a query, execute a search, set the maximum number of hits, access documentation pages about our server, access/run sample queries or saved queries, and invoke other HTML forms for registering a URL or writing comments to us. Figure 2 shows a screen dump of the user interface's home page. The version of the user interface shown in Figure 2 has an algorithm selection option which allows the user to use a different algorithm other than the default TFxIDF. The modular design of the search engine makes it easy for us to plug in and out new algorithms for experimentation. In our earlier work, we have implemented and evaluated four different algorithms [15]. The user interface mechanism is implemented using the standard Common Gateway Interface (CGI) and is run by NCSA HTTPD version 1.3 WWW Server program.

After the user types in the keywords, the query can be sent to the search engine by clicking on the *Search the Web* submit button. Upon receiving the result from the search engine, the user interface displays a list of URLs and their respective titles ordered in descending relevance scores. The user can physically access these URLs by clicking on the titles. In addition to the above-ordered list, the result page also shows other information and buttons for various functionalities, which are described in the following paragraphs.

Hierarchical page map

In order to help the user identify the content of the hit pages without having to physically access them, the hit pages, represented by their titles, are displayed in a hierarchical organization. This organization, shown by the use of line indentations, depicts the parent-child or referrer-referee hyperlink relationships among the pages (see Figure 3).

Accompanying each of the page titles is an icon is shown that indicates the page's data format (image file, sound file, video file, etc.) or one of two special icons representing an expandable item (closed suitcase) and a shrinkable item (open suitcase) respectively. Figure 4 shows the page icons and their meanings.

When the user clicks on a closed suitcase icon, a new result page is then displayed with the WWW pages referenced by the page whose icon was clicked on, shown as a list of titles with line indentations under the title of the referencing page. At this point the referencing page is shown with an open suitcase icon. Clicking on this open suitcase icon will revert the result page to its original state, i.e., shrinking the result by removing child pages under the referencing page whose icon was clicked on. This expand/shrink operation is performed by the user interface using the hyperlink data available from the index database. Figure 5 shows an example of the result page after a page expansion operation.

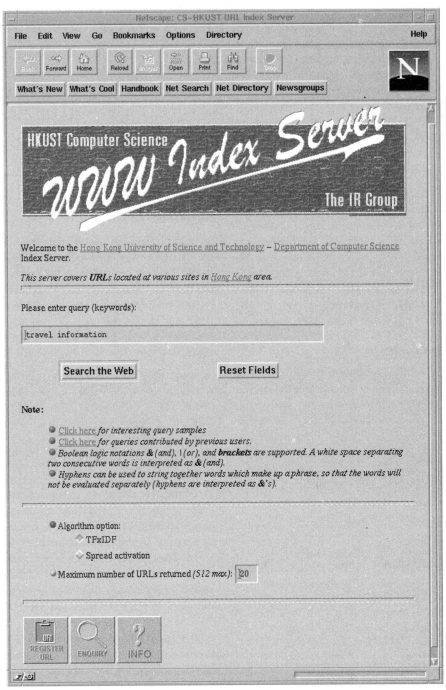

Figure 2:   The home page of the WWW Resource Discovery System's user interface

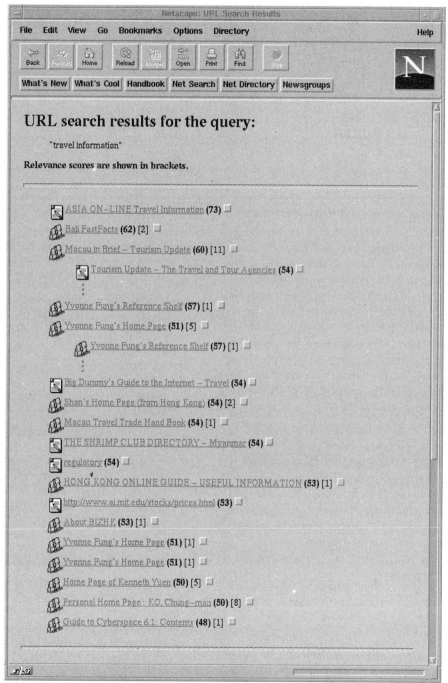

Figure 3: The result page displaying a list of hit pages (represented by their titles) ordered in descending relevance scores; line indentation is used to depict hierarchical dependence relationships among the pages

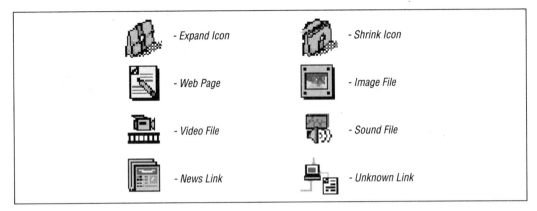

Figure 4: The page icons and their meanings

In Figure 5, the page entitled "Home Page of Kenneth Yuen" is expanded into a group with five child pages. In addition to the page icons, the number of pages referenced by each hit page, referred to here as child pages, is shown in square brackets. Because the use of the hierarchical organization, where hit pages are shown in groups with their child pages, the ordering of the hit pages on the list is based on the maximum relevance score within each group (see Figure 3).

The user can physically access any of the pages displayed on the result page by clicking on its title. Finally, the system keeps track of the user's session state by assigning a unique page-ID to every result page it generates. Every request issued by the user's clicking on a click-able item on a result page is tagged with the page's ID. The system maintains the information associated with every page-ID for a period of time.

Relevance feedback

The remaining part of the result page is an HTML form used for the relevance feedback mechanism (see Figure 6).

First, the user is asked to mark WWW pages judged as relevant to his/her query by clicking on a check box button next to each of the pages' titles. Next, the user can select the query expansion algorithm to use, if so desired, by clicking on one of the radio buttons under the algorithm option. The algorithms supported are as follows:

High

This algorithm a number of the most frequently occuring keywords from the feedback pages, and appends them to the original query. This is the default algorithm.

Low

Similar to High, but this algorithm selects the least frequently occurring keywords from the feedback pages.

Hits

A hit is when a word in the original query appears in a feedback page. This algorithm selects a number of keywords surrounding the hit word in the feedback pages, and appends them to the query.

The keywords, their occurrence frequencies, and their positions in the feedback pages are obtained from the forward index described previously in the section on indexer robot. The user is allowed to specify the number of words to select from each of the feedback pages; otherwise, the default value of 5 is used. These three algorithms are designed to refine a query by capturing the context in which the original query words appear in the feedback pages. A thorough study on these algorithms can be found in [8] where High

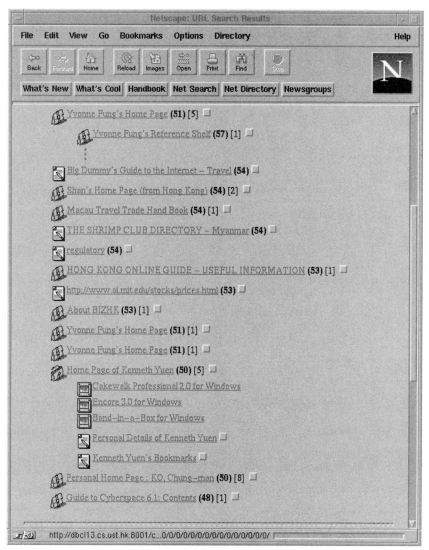

Figure 5: The resulting page after a page expansion operation by the user's clicking on the icon of the page entitled "Home Page of Kenneth Yuen"

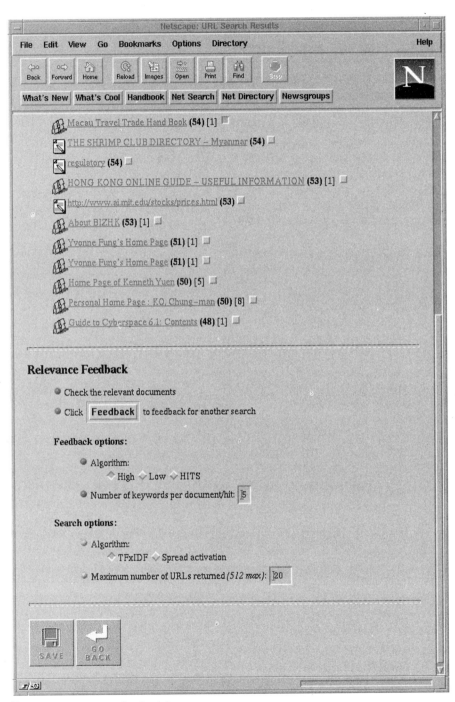

Figure 6:   The relevance feedback form

and Hits algorithms are shown to be the most effective ones.

As in the home page, search options for selecting the search/ranking algorithm and specifying the maximum number of hits are also provided. Finally, the relevance feedback parameters are submitted to the system for processing when the user clicks on the *Feedback* button, and another result page is then shown. We are aware of the fact that providing the user with so many options can cause some confusion. In the prototype version described in this paper, all parameter setting options are made available to the user for the purpose of experimentation.

The user-interface component consists of two separate modules, one for handling page expansion/shrinking operations and the other for handling the relevance-feedback mechanism. These modules are written in the C language and run as CGI scripts.

Query sharing

At the bottom of the result page, a clickable icon is provided for the user to save the query (see Figure 6), so that others who find it interesting can readily reuse it. Clicking on the icon will invoke an HTML form which allows the user to supply the title of the query, if so desired, and submit the query to the system. Saved queries are stored in a list of clickable query statements. By clicking on one of these statements, a user can resubmit the query to the search engine.

Lessons Learned

Although most of our system's components are still in prototype stage where developments and evaluations are still underway, the system is fully operational. The following discussion is based on data we collected from our test users and from the system's access log since May 1995.

Retrieval Effectiveness

Evaluating an information retrieval system for the WWW environment is a difficult task. The difficulty stems from the unavailability of standard test data and also the highly subjective nature of the notion of relevance of WWW pages retrieved with respect to the user's information need. In our previous work we empirically demonstrated the effectiveness of TFxIDF ranking algorithm using a traditional recall-precision measurement with an actual WWW collection obtained from an academic site in Hong Kong. The reader is referred to our report [15] for the full detail of the study.

Usability

Another aspect on which the system's effectiveness should be judged is its usability. We have not conducted a formal usability study on our system. However, from our access log file, we learned that the average query length is 1.3 words; in other words, most queries have only one word. While there is nothing wrong with single-word queries, as users often just want to browse around without any specific information need in mind, such a query often results in more pages than the maximum number of hits allows, particularly when the word is a common one. In such case, the user may not aware of the existence of pages which may be of his/her interest but were cut off by the maximum number of hits.

We also learned from the access log that most users did not attempt to refine their queries, e.g., by adding or dropping keywords, to narrow down or broaden up the scope of their searches when we expected them to do so. However, we cannot tell what happened without any verbal protocol data. It may be that the user lost interest in the search, or the user already found what he/she was looking for, or our system was too clumsy to interact with, or the user was not familiar enough with the keyword searching process to be able to fine-tune the query. The latter pessimistic view may also be the reason why, as the log file showed, not many users try to use our relevance feedback mechanism. This observation is not something new to those who work with systems which employ advanced information retrieval techniques. Even constructing a boolean query with logical notations is not something that an average user can be expected to do.

Another possible explanation for such under utilization is that the users are overwhelmed by the number of parameter setting options presented to them. One of the solutions to this problem is to hide as many parameter setting options as possible in separate pages or pull-down/pop-up menus. Other usability techniques, such as single-line help technique which shows a single-line description of the item pointed by the cursor, can also help. However, implementing these techniques on the server's side, as opposed to on the client's side, is not practical. Ideally, functionalites such as hypertext mapping and relevance-feedback mechanism should be implemented on the client's side, where the client downloads the necessary data from the server and performs the computation locally. This scheme will also make better display techniques, such as graphical hypertext maps with fish-eye view [14] or zooming capabilities, possible.

Hypertext Mapping

One of the critical issues in hypertext navigation is the user disorientation which may be experienced as the user traverses a densely entangled network of hyperlinks. One of the commonly proposed solutions is the use of graphical maps which display the information as networks with documents as the nodes and hyperlinks as the edges. We consider our hierarchical page maps as one step toward realizing such an approach.

The main design objective of our hierarchical page maps is to provide efficient means for the user to identify a WWW page by showing its context, represented by links to the neighboring pages, and the data format of the page, without having to physically access the page and its neighboring pages. This approach can help preserve the network's bandwidth and save the user

time to load the pages, especially on slow networks or from busy servers.

Our hierarchical page maps use page titles, for lack of better representation, to represent the contents of WWW pages. The problem with this scheme is that some page titles do not reflect the contents of the pages they represent. Also, it is not uncommon to find a group of pages, usually within the same directory path, to have the same title. Still some other pages do not have titles for various reasons. Obviously, a better page representation scheme is needed to make this approach effective. One possible alternative is to use keywords. Another related design issue is how to make the representation concise yet meaningful enough to be displayed, possibly in graphical format, as network nodes in a hypertext map.

Scalability

Another important issue that needs to be addressed if a resource discovery system is to be useful is the scalability. With the current rate of growth of the WWW, indexing a large number of WWW sites will be no longer practical. As of this writing, the overall size of our index database, which covers almost all sites in Hong Kong, is still manageable at about 10 MBytes. Ideally, a WWW resource discovery system should cover all sites around the world, which is what other WWW index servers such as WebCrawler, WWWW, Lycos, etc., do. However, maintaining the validity and updating such a large database is not practical and will put too much burden on the physical network. The problem becomes worse when such a maintenance is performed by many index servers with overlapping coverages.

For the above reason, we strongly advocate a system of distributed index servers with minimal overlapping coverages (e.g., by regional division). We are currently working on a mechanism that facilitates interchange of meta information among autonomous distributed index servers so that each of these servers can redirect a query to another server that could potentially give a better result. This approach is similar to that of other server-indexing methods such as GLOSS [6] and the directory of servers in WAIS [7]. Upon receiving a query, an index server checks whether it should process the query or redirect it to other index servers which can potentially give better results. A simple communication protocol is used by the servers to exchange server keywords with each other.

Other Work

There are many robot-based WWW index and search services on the Internet today (a list of WWW robots compiled by M. Koster can be found at *http://web.nexor.co.uk/mak/doc/robots/active.html*. However, among the well known robots, only a few employ full-text indexing, e.g., WebCrawler [11], the Repository Based Software Engineering (RBSE [5]), and Lycos(1). Other services index only page titles and first-level headings (e.g., JumpStation*) or titles, headings and anchor hypertexts (e.g., World Wide Web Worm - WWWW†). Our indexer robot takes other HTML tokens such as words in bold-face or italics, the first sentence of every list item (in addition to titles), headings of all levels, and anchor hypertexts. Our scheme is a balance between full-text and title-only schemes, and takes advantage of HTML meta-information as much as possible. On a WWW page containing mostly lists such as an index page, our scheme extracts nearly as much words as a full-text scheme.

Not many index servers use sophisticated information retrieval models beyond a simple Boolean model or pattern matching based on UNIX *egrep* (e.g., WWWW), with exception of the RBSE, the WebCrawler, and Lycos. The RBSE uses WAIS search engine which ranks WWW pages based on the occurrence frequencies or term frequency (TF) of the query words [10]. The WebCrawler and Lycos, as with our search engine, rank the pages based on term frequency and inverse-document frequency (TFxIDF).

As the WWW grows at an increasing rate, efforts to make the technology more manageable are highly in demand. Applying advanced information retrieval techniques is one approach to such efforts. Despite the potential benefit of these techniques in reducing user information overload and improving the effectiveness of access to online information, little research has been done on applying them to the WWW environment. The work presented in this paper is but an early stage of such research. We believe that there is still room for improvements and many strategies yet to be explored. For instance, search strategies which take advantage of WWW-specific meta information such as the semantic of hyperlinks may offer a better retrieval performance. Finally, the other important issue that may have been hindering the application of advanced information retrieval techniques to the WWW environment, or any other online information environment for that matter, is usability. Better user-interface designs can make these techniques more intuitive for average users. ∎

References

1. Berners-Lee, T., *Uniform Resource Locators, Internet Working Draft*, January 1994.

2. Berners-Lee, T., *Hypertext Transfer Protocol, Internet Working Draft*, November 1993.

3. Berners-Lee, T., and Connolly, D., *Hypertext Markup Language, Internet Working Draft*, July 1993.

4. Berners-Lee, T., Cailliau, R., Groff, J., and Pollermann, B., *World Wide Web: The Information Universe, Electronic Networking: Research, Applications and Policy*, v.1, no.2, 1992.

5. Eichmann, D., *The RBSE Spider—Balancing Effective Search against Web Load*, in *Proceedings of the First International Conference on the World Wide Web*, Geneva, May 1994

6. Gravano, L., Tomasic, A., and Garcia-Molina, H. , *The Efficacy of GLOSS for the Text Database Dis-*

---

* *http://www.stir.ac.uk/jsbin/js*
† *http://www.cs.colorado.edu/home/mcbryan/WWWW.html*

covery Problem, Technical Report STAN-CS-TR-93-2, Stanford University, October 1993.

7. Kahle, B., and Medlar, A., *An Information System for Corporate Users: Wide Area Information Servers, Technical Report TMC-199*, Thinking Machines, Inc., April 1991.

8. Lee, D. L., and Chuang, A. H., *Performance of Document Ranking and Relevance Feedback*, (submitted for publication).

9. Nelson, P., *GDBM—The GNU Database Manager*, online manual pages, Version 1.7.3, 1990.

10. Pfeifer, U., Fuhr, N., and Huynh, T., *Searching Structured Documents with the Enhanced Retrieval Functionality of freeWais-sf and SFgate, Computer Networks and ISDN Systems*, v.27, no.7, 1995, p1027-1036.

11. Pinkerton, B., *Finding What People Want: Experiences with the WebCrawler*, in *Proceedings of the First International Conference on the World Wide Web*, Geneva, May 1994.

12. Salton, G., *Automatic Text Processing: The Transformation, Analysis, and Retrieval of Information by Computer*, Addison-Wesley, 1989.

13. Salton, G., and Buckley, C., *Term-Weighting Approaches in Automatic Text Retrieval, Information Processing & Management*, v.24, no.5, 1988, p513-523.

14. Sarkar, M., and Brown, M., *Graphical Fish-Eye Views of Graphs*, in *Proceeding of CHI '92: Human Factors in Computing Systems*, ACM Press, 1992, p83-92.

15. Yuwono, B., and Lee, D. L., *Search and Ranking Algorithms for Locating Resources on the World Wide Web* (to appear).

About the Authors

Budi Yuwono is a Ph.D. candidate at the Department of Computer and Information Science, the Ohio State University, Columbus, OH, and a research associate at the Department of Computer Science, Hong Kong University of Science and Technology, Clear Water Bay, Hong Kong.

Savio L. Y. Lam is a master of philosophy (MPhil) student at the Department of Computer Science, Hong Kong University of Science and Technology, Clear Water Bay, Hong Kong.

Jerry H. Ying is a master of philosophy (MPhil) student at the Department of Computer Science, the Hong Kong University of Science and Technology, Clear Water Bay, Hong Kong.

Dik L. Lee is an associate professor at the Department of Computer Science, the Hong Kong University of Science and Technology, Clear Water Bay, Hong Kong.

This research is supported by grants from the Sino Software Research Center (SSRC), project number: SSRC94/95.EG01; and the Hong Kong Research Grant Council (RGC), project number: HKUST670/95E.

THE KRAKATOA CHRONICLE

AN INTERACTIVE PERSONALIZED NEWSPAPER ON THE WEB

Tomonari Kamba, Krishna Bharat, Michael C. Albers

Abstract

*This paper describes The Krakatoa Chronicle, a highly interactive, personalized newspaper on the World Wide Web (WWW). It is intended for Java-savvy WWW browsers such as HotJava, and is architecturally quite different from conventional Web-based newspapers. Its high interactivity and powerful personalization are the result of sending an interactive agent along with the text of the newspaper to operate within the user's Web-browser. The agent keeps a network connection open to the WWW server site to fetch resources dynamically, and for updating the user's personal profile as it garners relevance feedback. Users are provided a variety of article browsing options such as scrolling, maximizing, resizing, and the ability to "peek." These operations not only enhance the reading experience in ways conventional newspapers cannot, but also transparently provide information to our agent about the user's locus of interest. Ours is the first Web newspaper to attempt a realistic rendering of a newspaper, with a multicolumn format and embedded custom widgets for easy browsing. We provide dynamic layout control mechanisms that let the user specify how personal and community interests should be interpreted by the agent in designing the layout. **Keywords:** Online newspaper, personalization, information retrieval, interactive agent, active documents, automatic layout*

Introduction

Although noncommercial usage has dominated the Internet for a long time, some commercial applications have been emerging recently at a rate which is increasing. According to Outing [1], "more than 230 supplemental online services are operated or under development by newspapers worldwide, an increase of about 130% since the end of 1994." Of these, online newspapers are particularly well suited for the WWW, since the Web readily facilitates information retrieval, presentation, and to some extent, layout. However, there are a lot of challenges to be met before they become as pervasive as their hard-copy counterparts. Some of the issues are social and some are technical. While printed hard-copy newspapers tend to be more portable and easier to manipulate, online newspapers have a powerful argument in their favor—personalization.

Bogart notes that personalization has a strong appeal to newspaper readers [2]. Practical considerations have prevented them from being real-ized under the conventional hard-copy publishing setup. Web newspapers are not subject to the constraints of printed matter. Their reach is equally large and electronic dissemination allows newsfeed to be custom-tailored for individual users. The presentation can be personalized in terms of contents, layout, media (text, graphics, video, etc.), advertisement, and so on. Newspapers have two important social functions to perform: education and entertainment. Personalization may seem to enhance the latter at the expense of the former. Hence we would need a mechanism to mix in news items with either great popular appeal or high intrinsic value (in the editor's opinion) into the set of articles that match the user's interests. To allow multiple perspectives into the same newsfeed, the user should have the ability to dynamically affect the way in which the two kinds of articles are combined. This functionality would allow the newspaper to keep pace with changes in reading style as time passes. For instance, a user may want headlines and matters of public interest in the morning, and gradually move to a newspaper composed of articles with personal appeal by evening.

In this paper, we describe an experimental system which implements an interactive, personalized newspaper on the WWW. Some of the parameters for personalization are computed at the server end, based on user profiles and the composition of the newsfeed. Personalized layout happens at the client end, based on other parameters under user control. There are already many online newspapers on the Web, such as those accessible from the list of "Dailies"[3]; some of which provide personalization (e.g., CRAYON [4], Fishwrap [5]). However, these have been subject to the limitations of HTML [6]. The precise formatting and multicolumn layout one is accustomed to in printed newspapers is hard to support. Interactivity is restricted to point-and-click style interaction, and changes take a long time to occur, due to the high, client-server, round-trip latency and the restrictive update model in standard HTTP [7]. Since HTML is not dynamically extensible and tends to evolve slowly, it is unlikely that the custom widgets needed to program a newspaper will ever be supported. Hence we turned to a new paradigm, the embedded Java application (or "applet") feature available in Java-compliant browsers such as HotJava [8] and (future versions of) NetScape [9].

Java [8] is an object-oriented programming language which can be compiled to architecture-neutral, byte-code for safe execution within a Java virtual machine. A Java applet is a Java program designed specifically to be embedded in HTML documents. Java applets can implement arbitrary user interfaces, and can communicate with other entities over the network. A Java-aware browser is a WWW browser that embeds Java virtual machine and can handle applet tags. Since the downloaded code runs on the client locally, fairly involved computation and interactive, custom-designed user interfaces can be supported. In addition, Java has a library for handling TCP/IP protocols and can access remote objects via URLs [10] easily, which allows us to have continuous bidirectional communication between server and client.

The Krakatoa Chronicle provides some interactive features that other online newspapers do not:

- *Flexible Layout Control.* Users can change the syntactic/semantic layout strategy of the newspaper while browsing. For example, they can change the number of articles on the screen with immediate re-layout. They can also change how their personal interests and other people's interests are combined to decide the layout; personal interests are represented as a *user profile*, which is a mapping from a set of keywords to weights.

- *Implicit and Immediate Reflection of User Interests.* A user's profile is modified by the explicit feedback provided by the user on the relevance of various articles, and when this is unavailable, from implicit feedback derived from observations made by the embedded Java agent. The agent observes the manner in which the user interacts with the articles in the document, and based on the time spent, the interaction techniques used (e.g., scrolling, peeking at, maximizing, resizing), it tries to estimate the user's interest and modifies the user's profile suitably. Users can provide explicit feedback about an article employing that article's attached score bar. They can implement part of their profile explicitly by managing a set of keywords.

In the following sections, we will describe our system architecture and implementation, and also how the personalization strategy adopted in *The Krakatoa Chronicle* can be applied to other interactive applications on the WWW.

System Architecture

Figure 1 shows the system architecture of *The Krakatoa Chronicle*. The system consists of two parts: the server end and the client end.

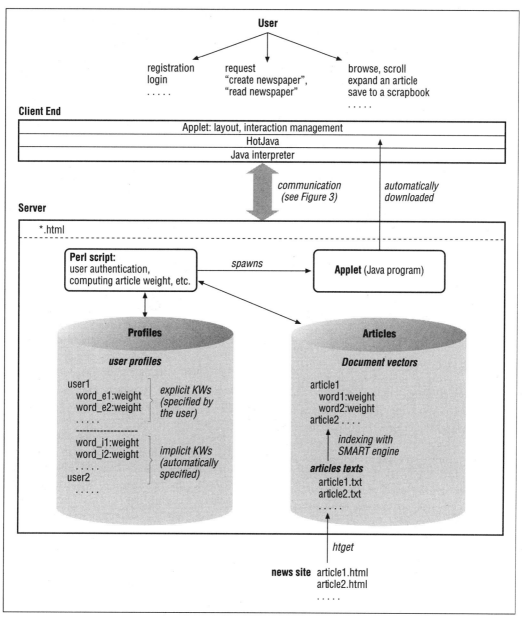

Figure 1: System architecture of *The Krakatoa Chronicle*

The Server End

The server-side software does user authentication, manages user-profiles, collects and processes the articles from the news source, builds index databases, and computes some of the parameters needed to do the layout of the newspaper at the client end.

- *Management of everyday articles.* First, articles are to be collected from several news sites daily, and changed into plain text for content-analysis and reformatting. Currently we get articles from a single site, the *News and Observer* [11], with their permission. Then, a document vector is computed for each article. Since our research focus is not on indexing, we used a well-known indexing engine, SMART [12] to convert articles into document vectors. Articles are converted into representative term-vectors, via the TFIDF (term frequency times inverse document frequency) metric. A term-vector is a set of keywords and associated weights. The weight of a term shows how well it represents the article within the current set.

- *Management of profiles.* The server end maintains user profiles. Each user profile has almost the same format as a document vector. The weight of each keyword represents the system's reckoning of the user's interest in the keyword. It is computed when feedback is given. Feedback provides a score for the whole article, which is then used to compute scores for individual keywords in its document-vector. Then it is integrated into the user's profile. If a keyword receives both positive and negative feedback it will cease to be a good indicator of the user's interest after a period of time, as its cumulative score will go to zero by a process of averaging. Instead if it continuously receives either a positive or negative score, it will become a good indicator by virtue of the significant cumulative score it receives. For computing a community score for each article, the scores of individual users are averaged over the community. A community is a group of users with similar interests who would like to benefit from each other's preferences [13, 14, 15], but in the simplest case it could include all the users of the system. As interaction proceeds, the user's browser

provides relevance feedback to the server end, and the user profile is modified.

- *Computing each article's weight.* The server computes each article's weight for a specific user based on how well the article's document vector and the user's profile match. Once the document set has been indexed, we use the personal profile as a query to the SMART engine to compute the weight.

It is worth mentioning that there is no live process at the server end save the HTTP daemon, which spawns cgi-scripts [16] written in Perl when necessary. Indexing is done offline and in batch mode whenever articles are added.

The Client End

The client end manages user interaction and newspaper layout within the browser. The code needed to drive the presentation and interaction is downloaded when the user accesses the newspaper's Web page. Subsequently, the code runs locally and may periodically contact the server site to fetch documents or provide feedback. Since the layout is computed at the client on the fly, the user can change its strategy flexibly. The user can scroll, peek, maximize, resize, or save an article to a scrapbook. When the user performs these operations, it is taken to be an indication of the user's interest in the article and gets reflected in the user profile. The user can also explicitly specify his/her personal interest in each article selecting the score on a feedback bar. Details of layout control and interaction will be described later.

Creating/Reading a Newspaper

Figure 2 shows the user's view of a session with the personalized newspaper, and Figure 3 shows the communication that occurs between the server and the client during this process.

First, the user types in their user ID and password within a login form. After authentication by the cgi-script on the server, the user can select

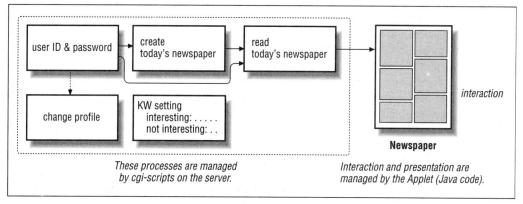

Figure 2: Reading a newspaper (user's view)

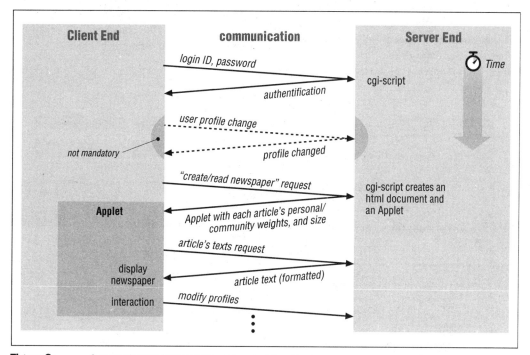

Figure 3: Communication between the server and the client

either "Change Profiles," "Create Today's Newspaper," or "Read Today's Newspaper." The "Read Today's Newspaper" option is available only if at least one version of the day's newspaper is present (having been created earlier).

Selecting the "Change Profiles" button is not mandatory, but with this, the user can bootstrap his/her profile before the first newspaper is created. This allows users to maintain a part of their profile explicitly, by specifying topics of interest/ disinterest using keywords. These "explicitly specified" keywords differ from "implicitly extracted" (inferred) keywords in that they have either the maximum or minimum possible weight and are not subject to automatic change over time. The weights for explicitly specified keywords are not modified by implicit feedback. Even if the user doesn't provide feedback explicitly, the system can automatically create and modify personal profiles during the user's reading process by observing the user's actions.

When the user chooses the "Create Today's Newspaper" button, each article's personal and community weights are computed, and a java newspaper applet is composed by the cgi-script and sent to the client. The applet computes the layout using each article's weight and other factors, and displays the composite newspaper after getting formatted pieces of text from the server. When the user chooses the "Read Today's Newspaper" button, the last newspaper viewed by the user is sent over. This allows users to return to the same newspaper even though their profiles have changed.

Layout Control

Figure 4 shows a typical screen of *The Krakatoa Chronicle*. It is the first Web newspaper to attempt a realistic rendering of a newspaper with a multicolumn format to resemble actual newspapers, and utilize embedded widgets for convenient browsing. The newspaper is divided into a set of pages, with articles of greater importance appearing earlier in the sequence. A page-scrollbar is available for browsing at the page level. Each page is divided into a set of article widgets, separated by "bars" which can be dragged. An article widget holds the contents of an article and supports various browsing techniques.

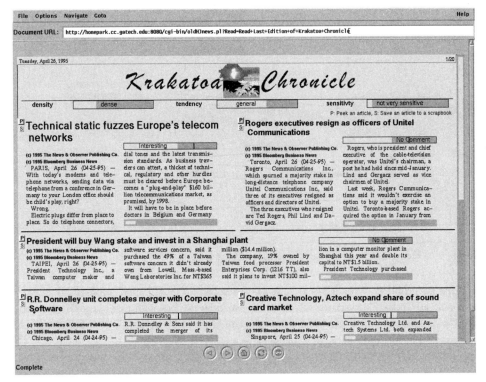

Figure 4:   Example of the *Krakatoa Chronicle* screen

We will not discuss the layout process in detail. We make use of the following criteria:

- Articles should be laid out in their entirety whenever possible.

- The title should be placed in a single line preferably. The size of the title is a factor in deciding how many columns to allocate a given article.

- Rectangular tesselations of the page are adequate.

- Pictures may need to be scaled down to fit in the space available and linked to the original.

- Single-column articles should be scrolled vertically, and multicolumn articles should be scrolled horizontally.

An important feature that differentiate *The Krakatoa Chronicle* from other WWW-based newspapers is its flexible layout control. Layout is a function of several parameters: the score that each article receives based on the user's profile (the user score), the average score received by each article over the community of users (the community score), and also the size and composition of each article (e.g. title length, the number of pictures). Since there are many ways in which these parameters may be combined to decide the final layout, we give users a set of controls which they can manipulate to dynamically change the significance of various layout parameters. Specifically, the following parameters can be controlled (see Figure 5):

- *User score vs. community score*. This decides the ratio in which the scores are combined in deciding the layout. The order of articles (left-top is the most important and right-bottom is the least) for a user is decided by each article's score, and the score is a function of the user's score and the community score:

```
final_score = personal_score   r
+ community_score   (1-r)
wherein 0 <;= r <= 1
```

This factor is important from a social point of view as no two people will want the same mix of personal and community content, and a given user may want a different mix at different times.

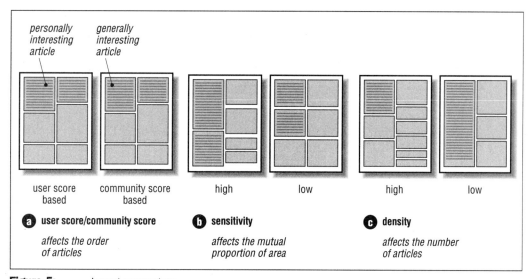

a user score/community score	**b** sensitivity	**c** density
affects the order of articles	*affects the mutual proportion of area*	*affects the number of articles*

Figure 5:   Layout parameters

- *Sensitivity factor.* This decides how significant the scores are in deciding the space allocated to each article. If this variable is large, important articles will have much more space than articles of lesser importance, but if this variable is small, article will enjoy approximately equal portions of screen real estate, although an article's importance will still affect its position.

- *Density of articles per page.* This decides how many articles will be shown on the page. If this variable is large, all the articles will be shrunk while keeping to the inter-article ratios dictated by the sensitivity factor.

We hope to let users arrive at a comfortable setting for these controls over the course of the experiment, and probably learn something in the process. The ability to change layout settings flexibly will allow users to obtain multiple views of the newspaper. We believe these multiple views show users what the community is interested in while allowing for custom views based on (previous) user feedback.

In *The Krakatoa Chronicle*, this flexible layout control was implemented by having the applet code on the client fetch articles from the server side (see Figure 6). A client-side cache allows for pre-fetching and significantly reduces the cost of browsing and re-layout. Whenever the user changes the setting of layout parameters (via the sliders), a new layout is computed. Article files are cached, and the agent fetches new articles from the server end only if needed.

Interaction

The Krakatoa Chronicle provides interaction techniques to support browsing in ways a hard-copy newspaper cannot.

- *Scroll/Automatic scroll.* This slides the article vertically if it is single column, or horizontally if it is multicolumn to prevent discontinuities in the flow of text.

- *Peek.* This displays the article over the entire screen as long as the mouse is held down over the peek button in the top left corner.

- *Maximize/Revert.* This is like "Peek" but requires double-clicking on the body of the article to switch states.

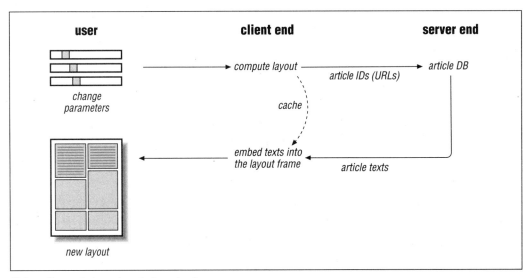

Figure 6:   Layout control mechanism

- *Resize*. The user resizes the article by dragging a bounding box, and permanently affects layout.

- *Save to a scrapbook*. This saves the article to a scrapbook, which is a page with links to all the articles that the user saved.

From the system's point of view, all these interactions give feedback about the relevance of the article to various degrees (see Figure 7). When the user scrolls, peeks at, maximizes, resizes, or saves an article to a scrapbook, *The Krakatoa Chronicle* increments the user's interest in the article by a corresponding amount, and subsequently changes the personal profile. There is a score bar beside each article which shows both personal score and community score at the same time, and the user can see changes in the score immediately. The score bar ranges from "Not Relevant" to "Very Relevant" through "No Comment. " Initially, this score shows the user's predicted interest, estimated from the user profile and the article's document vector.

Once explicit feedback is given by dragging the attached score bar, no further implicit feedback is given for the article. The user's feedback is taken to be the final word. The community score is the average of all the users of the group that the user belongs to, and it cannot be controlled directly by the user. This score shows which articles other people are interested in, and will help the user to understand "generally important articles." This score is important in the absence of human editors to assign intrinsic scores to articles.

Discussion and Future Work

A set of server end programs fetch each day's articles, translate them into plain text, index them using SMART, and help users register and log on. This is implemented using cgi-scripts written in Perl. Code size of the script to maintain the database and create newspaper is about 500 lines, and the one to handle the login sequence, create new accounts, and interact with the user is about 2000 lines. A set of client end programs manage the layout of the newspaper and user interaction. They are written in Java Release 1.0 Alpha3. Code size is about 3000 lines.

We get about 100 articles a day, and the size of each article ranges from 10-200 Kbytes without images. The batch process to index all the articles takes about half an hour and requires the system to be shut down, and is done at a time when demand is low. On a Sun SPARCstation 10 on our Ethernet LAN environment, it takes about eight seconds to compute each article's score, and

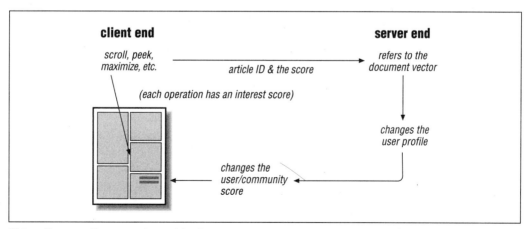

Figure 7:   User operation and feedback

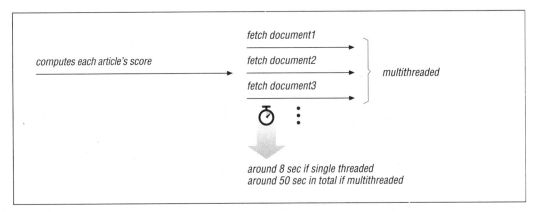

computes each article's score

fetch document1

fetch document2

fetch document3

multithreaded

around 8 sec if single threaded
around 50 sec in total if multithreaded

Figure 8:   Time to show a newspaper

approximately eight seconds to retrieve an article from the server to the client as a single-threaded process. On an initial visit to a newspaper page with six articles, about fifty seconds are required to compute the newspaper, bring it over, and display the entire page's contents (see Figure 8).

We have also implemented a version of our personalized online newspaper, to be shown on conventional (non Java-compliant) browsers such as Mosaic. Its architecture is similar to other personalizable newspapers on the WWW like Fishwrap [5]. The indexing and user profile/document vector management functions are handled by the same system that implements *The Krakatoa Chronicle*'s backend. However, instead of sending over an applet, it follows the traditional strategy of generating HTML pages for each view into the newspaper, with links to other views. There is no way to dynamically change the layout or get implicit feedback. The newspaper has a listing of articles ordered and font-size coded by relevance, with links to individual articles. The user can show explicit interest in individual articles, by clicking on a color-coded score bar, attached to the article which modifies the user profile.

Of the many ways to build a user profile, the most common and simplest way is to ask the user to type in keywords that he/she is interested in [17]. With this approach, it is difficult to track changes in a user's interest over time and topics of interest they are not conscious of. An indirect way is to ask the user to provide a score for articles he/she reads, and to compute the weights of keywords from the score [18, 19]. This method also requires the user's conscious involvement, which is often annoying. A more subtle way is to consider the time that the user spends on each article, as in prior work on USENET News [20], where it seems to have worked fairly well. Unfortunately they insisted that subjects devote their entire concentration to the task of reading the article and not take breaks, which is not a very realistic solution. In *The Krakatoa Chronicle*, we included some of these methods, namely, typing explicit keywords and/or adding a score to each article. However, the system works even without explicit user involvement. Since anticipated interest values are explicitly represented on the score bars the user will notice that the profile has indicated an erroneous value and will then proceed to give explicit feedback which will correct the profile.

We plan to have about thirty subjects reading *The Krakatoa Chronicle* newspaper daily. After the experiment runs for several weeks, we will reassess the manner in which user actions affect user profiles. Currently, the importance of operations such as "Peek at an Article" is arbitrarily decided. We are also planning to to get statistics on the way people will browse the newspaper, given the choice of interaction techniques they have. In future work, we plan to include dynamic components into a newspaper framework. These would include billboards, live maps, crossword puzzles, shared whiteboards, animated comic strips, etc. These are easily implemented and can use a similar scoring/personalization mechanism.

Conclusion

We have developed a highly interactive, personalized newspaper on the WWW. It is implemented as an active agent that runs within the Web-browser as the newspaper is being displayed. Its main features are realistic render-ing, dynamic layout control, interactivity, and implicit feedback leading to personalization without conscious user involvement. Information personalization is very important on the WWW, especially for commercial services seeking to provide a value-added service for a set of registered users. Our approach to personalization has applicability to other multimedia services on the Web as well.

Acknowledgment

We wish to thank the *News and Observer* for permitting us to use their news articles for our experiment.

Note

The Krakatoa Chronicle is named after the active volcano, Krakatoa, in the Java Sea, which is literally a piece of "Hot Java." ∎

References

1. *MediaInfo Interactive e-newspapers main menu, MediaInfo Interactive*, 1995. URL: *http://www. mediainfo.com/edpub/e-papers.home.page.html*

2. Leo Bogart, *Press and Public: who reads what, when, where, and why in American newspapers*, Lawrence Erlbaum Associates Publishers, 1989.

3. *Dailies: U.S.Newspaper Services on the Internet* URL: *http://marketplace.com/e-papers.list.www/e-papers.us.dailies.html*

4. *CRAYON*, URL: *http://sun.bucknell.edu/~boulter/crayon/*

5. *Fishwrap*, URL: *http://fishwrap.mit.edu/*

6. *HyperText Markup Language (HTML): Working and Background Materials*, URL: *http//www.w3. org/hypertext/WWW/MarkUp/*

7. *Overview of HTTP*, URL: *http://www.w3.org/hypertext/WWW/Protocols/Overview.html*

8. *HotJava Home Page*, URL: *http://java.sun.com*

9. *Introducing Netscape Navigator 2.0 and Netscape Navigator Gold 2.0*, URL: *http://home.mcom.com/comprod/products/navigator/version_2.0/index. html*

10. *A Beginner's Guide to URLs*, URL: *http://www.ncsa. uiuc.edu/demoweb/url-primer.html*

11. *The NandO Times,URL: http://www.nando.net/newsroom/nt/nando.html*

12. *SMART*, URL: *ftp://ftp.cs.cornell.edu/pub/smart*

13. *Community-Based Navigation*, URL: *http://www. ncsa.uiuc.edu/SDG/IT94/Proceedings/HCI/hill/home-page.html*

14. *The Webhound WWW Document Filtering System*, URL: *http://webhound.www.media.mit.edu/projects/webhound/doc/*

15. Upendra Shardanand and Patti Maes, *Social Information Filtering: Algorithms for Automating "Word of Mouth,"* Proceedings of CHI'95, 1995. URL: *http://agents.www.media.mit.edu/groups/agents/papers/ringo/chi-95-paper.ps*

16. *Overview of CGI*, URL: *http://www.w3.org/hypertext/WWW/CGI/Overview.html*

17. Tak W. Yan and Hector Garcia-Molina, *SIFT - A Tool for Wide-Area Information Dissemination*, USENIX Technical Conference, 1995, pp. 177-186. URL: *ftp://db.stanford.edu/pub/sift/sift.ps*

18. Ken Lang, *NewsWeeder: Learning to Filter Netnews*, ML95, URL: *http://anther.learning.cs.cmu.edu/ml95.ps*

19. Kenrick J. Mock and V. Rao Vemuri, *Adaptive User Models for Intelligent Information Filtering*, URL: *http://www.glue.umd.edu/enee/medlab/filter/gwic.ps*

20. Masahiro Morita and Yoichi Shinoda, *Information Filtering Based on User Behavior Analysis and Best Match Text Retrieval*, SIGIR'94, 1994.

About the Authors

Tomonari Kamba

Graphics, Visualization, & Usability Center
College of Computing
Georgia Institute of Technology
Atlanta, GA 30332-0280
tomo@cc.gatech.edu

Tomonari Kamba received his B.E. and M.E. in Electronics from the University of Tokyo in 1984 and 1986 respectively, and joined NEC corporation. Currently, he is a visiting scientist at the Graphics, Visualization & Usability Center at the College of Computing, Georgia Institute of Technology. His research interests include multimedia user interfaces, mobile computing, and online information services.

Krishna Bharat

Graphics, Visualization, & Usability Center
College of Computing
Georgia Institute of Technology
Atlanta, GA 30332-0280
kb@cc.gatech.edu

Krishna Bharat received his B.Tech. in Computer Science from Indian Institute of Technology, Madras, in 1991, and M.S. from Georgia Institute of Technology in 1993. He is currently pursuing his doctoral research in distributed user interfaces at the College of Computing, Georgia Institute of Technology.

Michael C. Albers

School of Industrial & Systems Engineering
Center for Human-Machine Systems Research
Georgia Institute of Technology
Atlanta, GA 30332-0205
malber@isye.gatech.edu

Michael C. Albers is a Master's student at the School of Industrial & Systems Engineering, Center for Human-Machine Systems Research, Georgia Institute of Technology.

WebMap
Concept Mapping on the Web

Brian R. Gaines, Mildred L. G. Shaw

Abstract

Concept maps have long provided visual languages widely used in many different disciplines and application domains. This article reports experience in taking an existing open architecture concept mapping tool and making it available on the Web in a number of ways: as a client helper downloading and uploading concept maps; as an active controller of the browser, indexing multimedia material through URLs embedded in concept maps; as a concept map creator controlled by the browser, generating concept maps through the browsing process; and as an auxiliary HTTP server making concept maps available as clickable maps for users who do not have the client helper or want to use active concept maps embedded in documents. **Keywords**: *Concept maps, semantic networks, active documents, client helpers, clickable map servers.*

Introduction

This article describes the integration of concept mapping tools with World Wide Web browsers and servers, as client helpers on the one hand and gatewayed, clickable image servers on the other. Abstractly, concept maps are sorted graphs visually represented as nodes having a type, name, and content, some of which are linked by arcs. Each type of node has associated visual attributes, such as shape and color scheme, and the arcs may be nondirectional, directional, or bidirectional. Links between nodes may also be labeled and typed by constructing them from a pair of arcs with an intervening node whose name is the link name and whose type is the link type. Figure 1 shows a typical concept map from a knowledge-based system that solves a room allocation problem [1].

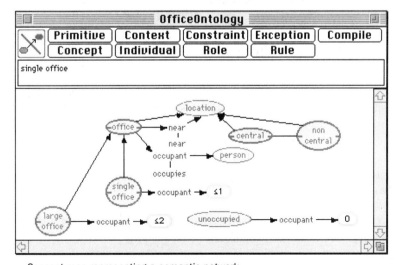

Figure 1: Concept map representing a semantic network

The map in Figure 1 is a *semantic network* [2] with a formal logical interpretation that allows it to be automatically compiled for a KL-ONE inference engine [3]. This is typical of artificial intelligence, engineering, and mathematical applications of concept maps. In these disciplines various forms of concept map are used as formal knowledge representation systems, for example, bond graphs in mechanical and electrical engineering [4], Petri nets in communications [5], and category graphs in mathematics [6]. More generally, concept maps have been used in education [7, 8], policy studies [9, 10], and the philosophy of science [11, 12] to provide a visual representation of knowledge structures and argument forms. They provide *visual languages* as complementary alternatives to natural languages as a means of communicating knowledge.

Concept maps have been used for a wide range of purposes, and it would be useful to make such usage available over the World Wide Web. This article reports on the development of WebMap, a system for integrating concept maps with existing Web media and technologies. WebMap is based on an existing open architecture concept mapping tool, KMap, developed for the Apple Macintosh platform. The next section gives an overview of KMap, and subsequent sections illustrate its application as a client helper to Web browsers and as an auxiliary server to Web servers.

KMap: A Concept Mapping Tool

KMap is a concept mapping tool written for Apple Macintosh computers. It is open architecture, first in allowing different forms of concept map to be defined and second in supporting integration with other applications through the Apple Object Event protocol and AppleScript. KMap has been used in a wide variety of situations ranging from concept mapping in education [13], through multimedia indexing [14] and semantic nets for knowledge-based systems [1, 15], to workflow support for scientific communities on the Internet [16-18].

Entering a Concept Map in KMap

Figure 2 shows a concept map from an application in which KMap was used to index a multimedia CD-ROM [19] of materials comprising the final report of the GNOSIS project [20], part of the international Intelligent Manufacturing Systems (IMS) research program [21]. The user creates a new node by selecting its type on the popup menu at the top left (currently showing type "ConMap" which is used to reference another concept map), typing its label into the text box below (currently showing "GNOSIS Final Reports"), and clicking on the popup menu text "ConMap." KMap then inserts a new node as shown, wrapping the text to create a horizontal rectangle.

The new node can be dragged anywhere in the window. The arrows to and from the new node are drawn by a simple process. The corners of the node are sensitive, and the cursor changes to an arrow symbol when over the lower right corner. Clicking on the mouse creates a "rubber-band" line. Dragging this over another node highlights the node. Releasing the move over the highlighted node draws an arrow from the original node to the highlighted one.

Selecting Node Types in KMap

There are many different nodes types with differing appearances in the concept map of Figure 2. The selection of the node type is made through a popup menu. When the cursor browses over the node type at the top left it assumes a button shape, as shown in Figure 2, to indicate that clicking will create a new node. However, as the user moves to the right of the node type name, the cursor becomes a popup menu and mousing down produces the menu shown in Figure 3 which lists the available node types for selection. KMap also supports an alternative interface through buttons as shown at the top of Figure 1 where the node types are each listed on a separate button.

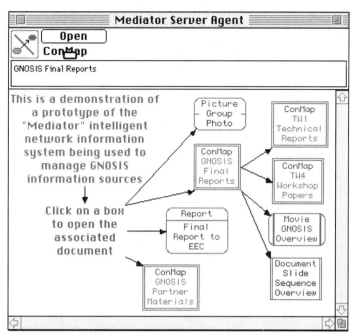

Figure 2:   Concept map indexing a CD-ROM

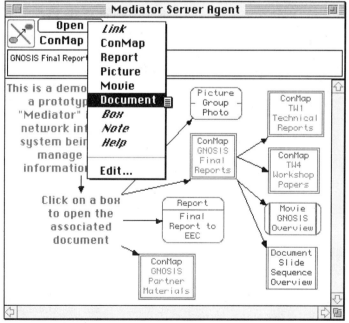

Figure 3:   Popup menu for node types

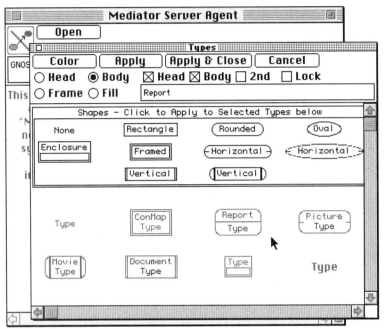

Figure 4:   Node type editing and creation

Creating and Editing Node Types in KMap

At the bottom of the popup menu in Figure 3 there is an "Edit..." option. Selecting this opens a floating dialog as shown in Figure 4 which enables the user to edit existing node types and create new ones. The user creates a new node type by typing its name in the text box at the top, selecting a shape in the palette below, defining the colors of the surround, fill, heading text and body text, texts sizes and styles, and whether the head and/or body text should be shown.

Programming KMap

So far KMap has been shown as a flexible concept mapping or diagramming tool. However, it is also programmable so that user actions can communicate with other applications. Each node in a map has not only a label but also a hidden content, which is an arbitrary text string. The hidden content may be accessed and edited by holding down the "Option" key when double-clicking

on a node. This brings up the content, rather than the label, in the text box for editing.

User actions in the concept map send messages to a script attached to the map which has access to all the map data, including the hidden content. This script is created and edited in a script editor activated by "Open Script" in the "File" menu as shown in Figure 5. The script receives messages when a concept map is open or closed, when it is edited in any way, when the user clicks in a node, a button, a popup menu, and so on. A full record of the map affected, the node within it, the menu selection, and so on, is passed as a parameter to the routine in the script. This enables concept maps to be used as active documents providing user interfaces to any functionality on the Macintosh, including control of other applications either locally or through a network. In particular, multiple versions of the same concept map open on different machines may be kept mutually updated as users edit them.

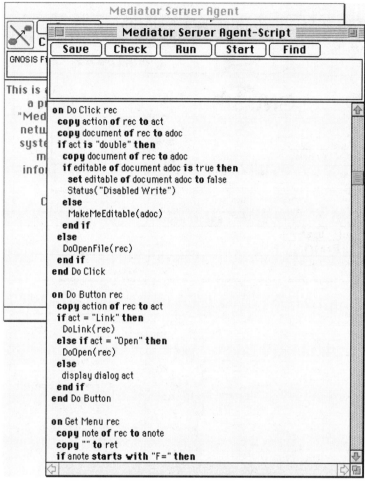

Figure 5:   Scripting a concept map

Integrating KMap with Other Applications

KMap scripting has been used to create a wide range of computer-supported cooperative work applications in multimedia environments. The semantic network shown in Figure 1 can be sent to a compiler which converts it to the text form of KL-ONE definitions and loads these into the KRS [22] knowledge representation system for execution as part of the solution of a room allocation problem. The script for the concept map of Figure 2 provides multimedia indexing capa-

bilities by interpreting a click on a node as a request to load the file specified by a URL stored in the node content. The file loaded can be another concept map, providing multi-level indexing, or it can be any file openable by another application. For example, the GNOSIS final report CD-ROM contains digitized photographs, digital movies, expert system knowledge bases, engineering drawings, reports in Word, Replica, and so on.

For example, in Figure 6 the node "GNOSIS Final Reports" has been clicked in the "Mediator Server

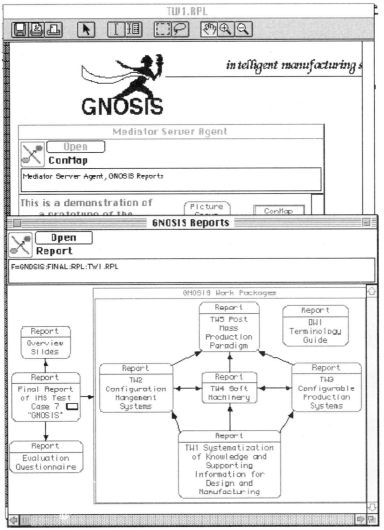

Figure 6: Multimedia indexing through concept maps

Agent" window of Figure 2. This has opened a concept map of the GNOSIS final reports as shown overlaying it in the lower part of the figure. Clicking on the node "Final Report of IMS Test Case 7 GNOSIS" at the middle left of this concept map has opened the Farallon Replica document shown in the window behind the two concept maps.

It should be noted that the only script operating is that in the "Mediator Server Agent" concept map. If it opens another concept map it links it to itself so that the script responds to actions in the new concept map, essentially acting as an active agent for otherwise passive documents. This is important to applications that fetch concept maps across the Internet since one does not want to accept arbitrary script functionality that can have detrimental effects on the local machine.

Using Concept Maps Across the World Wide Web

KMap is written in a C++ class library [23] that provides a wide range of application functionality including TCP/IP communications and protocols, typographic documents with active embedded components [24], knowledge processing, and so on. Hence, it has been simple to support collaborative groupware systems operating across local and wide area networks and providing end users with interfaces through concept maps and through active documents with embedded maps. However, much of the functionality required in these applications is now available with high quality at low cost in the form of World Wide Web browsers such as Mosaic and Netscape. These browsers support inter-application protocols allowing them to be integrated as components in a system involving other applications. They are also available on all major platforms making it possible to support a heterogeneous environment with minimal constraints on end users.

Hence, it is attractive to investigate the integration of the concept mapping techniques and tools already described with World Wide Web tools with a view to extending Web functionality to support collaborative activities with user interfaces largely through visual languages. In particular, the Mediator system illustrated above has been reimplemented to operate with HTTP servers and browsers, with KMap operating as a client helper tightly coupled to Netscape, and also with KMap operating as an auxiliary server either through its own HTTP support or through a common gateway interface (CGI) to WebStar. The following subsections illustrate some of the features of these implementations.

KMap as a Client Helper to Netscape

It was simple to reimplement the type of multimedia indexing functionality described above and illustrated in Figure 5. KMap was registered as a client helper with Netscape for the MIME type application/x-kss (which is the generic file type for all our knowledge support systems), and this MIME type was registered with our NCSA and WebStar servers and with Netscape as corresponding to the file suffix *.kss*. This is sufficient to allow concept maps to be fetched over the Web and opened in KMap. To allow the concept maps to be used as active documents to fetch other documents across the Web, a script was written for a concept map to act as a "Netscape Agent" similar to the "Mediator Server Agent" shown in Figure 4 but passing the appropriate part of the hidden content of nodes to Netscape using the "OpenURL" Apple event.

Figure 7 shows KMap acting as a client helper to Netscape to index the GNOSIS reports. The concept map of Figure 6 has been fetched as *GNOSISReports.kss*; clicking on the node "Final Report of IMS Test Case 7 GNOSIS" at the middle left has sent a message to Netscape requesting it open the URL *http://ksi.cpsc.ucalgary.ca/IMS/GNOSIS/TC7Final.kss*. This is another concept map shown at the bottom right which provides an overview of the structure of the GNOSIS final report. Clicking on the node "Project Objectives, Activities and Organization" has sent a message to Netscape requesting that it open the URL *http://ksi.cpsc.ucalgary.ca/IMS/GNOSIS/TC7FF2.kss*. This is an HTML document that Netscape opens in its own window as shown at the back. Clicking on other nodes in the concept map at the front will cause Netscape to index through the sections of the report.

Since the HTTP protocols support fetching documents in different formats for different applications, for example, fetching an AutoCAD dataset and opening it in AutoCAD, many of the design objectives of Mediator can be satisfied through this integration of KMap, Netscape, and the World Wide Web HTTP/HTML protocols. Mediator on the Web, coupled with various agent technologies, can provide a system supporting the manufacturing life cycle across a virtual enterprise distributed internationally [18].

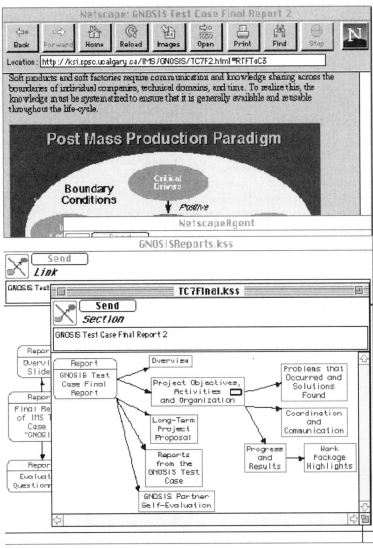

Figure 7:   KMap as a client helper to Netscape

Generating Concept Maps by Browsing in Netscape

Netscape allows an external application to register itself to receive a range of information about user interaction with Netscape. This enables a KMap agent to receive a trace of user interactions with the World Wide Web, build a concept map of linked documents, and use this to provide access to those documents—a graphic "hotlist." Figure 8 shows such a hotlist being developed and used. The "NetscapeAgent" in KMap has sent a "Register URL Message" to Netscape requesting that it be informed when Netscape shows a document. Each time that Netscape does so it sends KMap a message giving the URL of the document, the URL of the referring document if there was one, and the window in which the document is being shown.

The "NetscapeAgent" script stores the URLs and displays the name of the window in the text box near the top of its window. If the user clicks on the popup menu button, the script creates a new node of the type specified in the popup menu. It stores the name of the window in the visible content of the node because this name is the <TITLE> field of the HTML document. It stores the URL of the document in the invisible content of the node so that clicking on the node may be used to request Netscape to fetch the document. If there is already a node for the referring document, then the script links it with an arrow to the new node. The overall effect is to create a hotlist of locations visited that can be used to access these locations again.

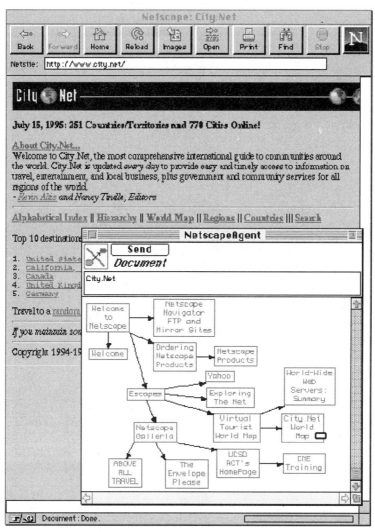

Figure 8:   Concept maps being generated by Netscape

KMap as a Clickable Map Server to WebStar

KMap is currently implemented only for the Apple Macintosh and hence can act as a client helper only on Macintosh computers. Ports to Windows and Motif are being developed which will make KMap helpers available on all major platforms. However, there will always be users who do not have, or want to use, the helpers, but where it is appropriate to provide non-editable concept maps as *clickable maps* in HTML documents. Hence KMap has also been interfaced as an HTTP server to allow the same concept maps to be used as clickable maps.

Clicking on the "Send" button at the top left of the "NetscapeAgent" concept map in Figure 8 uploads the concept map data to the server using Netscape's capability to accept an "Open URL"

event with POST parameters. The map data is automatically stored under the same concept map name in an upload directory named "X" using an auxiliary HTTP server written in the same class library as KMap operating through a common gateway interface to WebStar.

KMap itself is also accessible through the CGI for two functions: first, to download concept maps as clickable maps in GIF format; and, second, to receive clicks on these maps and take the same action as if the concept map had been clicked locally in a KMap helper. Figure 9 shows the uploaded flow-chart concept map of Figure 8 being fetched using the URL *http://tiger.cpsc. ucalgary.ca/WMClick/:X:NetscapeAgent.k* which is recognized as an action to be passed to KMap by WebStar.

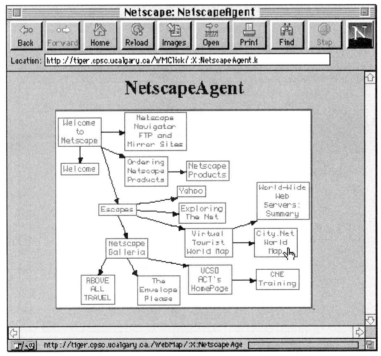

Figure 9:   KMap acting as an HTTP server for clickable maps

KMap returns the HTML shown below with the name of the concept map as a title and an embedded call for an image of the concept map. The image URL is again interpreted as an action passed to KMap which, since there are no search arguments, loads the concept map, converts its image to a GIF, and returns it as an HTTP message. Clicking on the node "City.Net World Map" sends the coordinates of the point clicked back to KMap on the server as search arguments, and KMap then takes the same action as if the map had been clicked locally in a helper, in this case to redirect Netscape to the URL for City.Net World Map.

```
<HTML>
 <HEAD>
  <TITLE>NetscapeAgent</TITLE>
 </HEAD>
<BODY>
  <H1 ALIGN="CENTER">NetscapeAgent</H1>
  <P ALIGN="CENTER">
  <A HREF="http://tiger.cpsc.ucalgary.
   ca./WebMap/:X:NetscapeAgent.k">
   <IMG SRC="http://tiger.cpsc.ucalgary.
   ca./WebMap/:X:NetscapeAgent.k"
   ISMAP>
  </A>
 </BODY>
</HTML>
```

Thus KMap supports the use of concept maps on World Wide Web through client helpers and through servers in an integrated way. Concept maps created in KMap for use in conjunction with Netscape as a local helper can be automatically uploaded and used in the same way as clickable maps through KMap as an auxiliary server. In particular, this allows concept maps to be used by browsers running on platforms other than the Macintosh.

It can be seen from the HTML that any number of concept maps may be embedded as clickable maps in an HTML document. This enables much of the functionality of our active document tool, KWrite [24], to be recreated on World Wide Web. For example, knowledge bases may be embedded in documents as semantic networks and used as part of expert systems [15]. The only

capability missing is for the user to be able to edit the knowledge base within the document. In the near future it should be possible to implement this also by rewriting the concept-mapping tools in a Web code tool such as Java [25].

Conclusion

Concept maps have long provided visual languages widely used in many different disciplines and application domains. Abstractly, they are sorted graphs visually represented as nodes having a type, name and content, some of which are linked by arcs. Concretely, they are structured diagrams having discipline- and domain-specific interpretations for their user communities and, sometimes, formally defining computer data structures. Concept maps have been used for a wide range of purposes, and it would be useful to make such usage available over the World Wide Web.

This article has reported experience in taking an existing open architecture concept mapping tool and making it available on the Web in a number of ways: as a client helper downloading and uploading concept maps through an open architecture browser such as Netscape; as an active controller of the browser, indexing multimedia material through URLs embedded in concept maps; as a concept map creator controlled by the browser, generating concept maps through the browsing process; and as an auxiliary HTTP server making concept maps available as clickable maps for users who do not have the client helper or want to use active concept maps embedded in documents. All of these various usages have been shown to complement one another effectively to support the simple and natural integration of concept maps with other World Wide Web media and technologies.

As the development of Web functionality proceeds it will become possible to embed concept mapping tools even more effectively as active components of HTML documents. Meanwhile the current development of WebMap shows that much can be achieved within the existing Web capabilities. ∎

Acknowledgments

This work was funded in part by the Natural Sciences and Engineering Research Council of Canada.

References

1. Gaines, B.R., *A situated classification solution of a resource allocation task represented in a visual language. International Journal Human-Computer Studies* 40(2), 1994, pp. 243-271.

2. Sowa, J.F., ed. *Principles of Semantic Networks: Explorations in the Representation of Knowledge.* San Mateo, California: Morgan-Kaufman, 1991.

3. Gaines, B.R., *An interactive visual language for term subsumption visual languages,* in *IJCAI'91: Proceedings of the Twelfth International Joint Conference on Artificial Intelligence.* San Mateo, California: Morgan-Kaufman, 1991, pp. 817-823.

4. Karnopp, D., R.C. Rosenberg, and J.J. van Dixhorn, *Bond Graph Techniques for Dynamic Systems in Engineering and Biology. Journal Franklin Institute* 308(3), 1989.

5. Reisig, W., *Petri Nets: An Introduction.* Berlin: Springer, 1985.

6. Mac Lane, S., *Categories for the Working Mathematician.* New York: Springer-Verlag, 1971.

7. Lambiotte, J.G., et al., *Multirelational semantic maps.* Educational Psychology Review 1(4), pp. 331-367, 1989.

8. Novak, J.D., and D.B. Gowin, *Learning How To Learn,* New York: Cambridge University Press, 1984.

9. Axelrod, R., *Structure of Decision,* Princeton, New Jersey: Princeton University Press, 1976.

10. Eden, C., S. Jones, and D. Sims, *Thinking in Organizations,* London: Macmillan, 1979.

11. Toulmin, S., *The Uses of Argument,* Cambridge, UK: Cambridge University Press, 1958.

12. Thadgard, P., *Conceptual Revolutions,* Princeton, New Jersey: Princeton University Press, 1992.

13. Gaines, B.R., and M.L.G. Shaw, *Supporting the creativity cycle through visual languages,* in *AAAI Spring Symposium: AI and Creativity,* Menlo Park, California: AAAI, 1993, pp. 155-162.

14. Gaines, B.R., and M.L.G. Shaw, *Concept maps indexing multimedia knowledge bases,* in *AAAI-94 Workshop: Indexing and Reuse in Multimedia Systems,* Menlo Park, California: AAAI, 1994, pp. 36-45.

15. Gaines, B.R., and M.L.G. Shaw, *Documents as expert systems,* in *Research and Development in Expert Systems IX. Proceedings of British Computer Society Expert Systems Conference,* M.A. Bramer and R.W. Milne, Editors, Cambridge, UK: Cambridge University Press, 1992, pp. 331-349.

16. Gaines, B.R., and M.L.G. Shaw, *Using knowledge acquisition and representation tools to support scientific communities,* in *AAAI'94: Proceedings of the Twelfth National Conference on Artificial Intelligence,* Menlo Park, California: AAAI Press/MIT Press, 1994, pp. 707-714.

17. Gaines, B.R., and D.H. Norrie, *Mediator: information and knowledge management for the virtual factory,* in *SIGMAN AAAI-94 Workshop: Reasoning about the Shop Floor,* Menlo Park, California: AAAI, 1994, pp. 30-39.

18. Gaines, B.R., D.H. Norrie, and A.Z. Lapsley, *Mediator: an Intelligent Information System Supporting the Virtual Manufacturing Enterprise,* in *Proceedings of 1995 IEEE International Conference on Systems, Man and Cybernetics,* New York: IEEE, 1995.

19. *GNOSIS: Intelligent Manufacturing Systems: IMS Test Case 7: Hybrid-CD, Macintosh (native), PC, Unix (ISO 9660).* CD-GNOSIS-May 94, Calgary, Canada: Knowledge Science Institute and Division of Manufacturing Engineering, University of Calgary, 1994.

20. *Knowledge Systematization: Configuration Systems for Design and Manufacturing: Final Report of the Test Case. http://ksi.cpsc.ucalgary.ca/IMS/GNOSIS,* Calgary, Canada: Knowledge Science Institute, University of Calgary, 1994.

21. Gaines, B.R., and D.H. Norrie, *Knowledge systematization in the international IMS research program,* in *Proceedings of 1995 IEEE International Conference on Systems, Man and Cybernetics,* New York: IEEE, 1995.

22. Gaines, B.R., *Empirical investigations of knowledge representation servers: Design issues and applications experience with KRS. ACM SIGART Bulletin* 2(3), 1991, pp. 45-56.

23. Gaines, B.R., *Class library implementation of an open architecture knowledge support system. International Journal Human-Computer Studies,* 41(1/2), 1994, pp. 59-107.

24. Gaines, B.R., and M.L.G. Shaw, *Open architecture multimedia documents,* in *Proceedings of ACM Multimedia 93,* 1993, pp. 137-146.

25. Sun, *HotJava Home Page. http://java.sun.com,* Sun Microsystems, 1995.

About the Authors

Brian R. Gaines

[*http://ksi.cpsc.ucalgary.ca/KSI*]
Knowledge Science Institute
University of Calgary, Alberta, Canada T2N 1N4
gaines@cpsc.ucalgary.ca

Dr. Brian R. Gaines is Killam Memorial Research Professor and Director of the Knowledge Science Institute at the University of Calgary. His previous positions include Professor of Industrial Engineering at the University of Toronto, Technical Director and Deputy Chairman of the Monotype Corporation, and Chairman of the Department of Electrical Engineering Science at the University of Essex. He received his BA, MA, and PhD from Trinity College, Cambridge, and is a Chartered Engineer, Chartered Psychologist, and a Fellow of the Institution of Electrical Engineers, the British Computer Society and the British Psychological Society. He is editor of the *International Journal of Human-Computer Studies* and *Knowledge Acquisition,* and of the *Computers and People* and *Knowledge-Based Systems* book series. He has authored over 400 papers and authored or edited 10 books on a wide variety of aspects of computer and human systems. His research interests include the socio-economic dynamics of science and technology; the nature, acquisition and transfer of knowledge; software engineering for heterogeneous systems; knowledge-based system applications in manufacturing, the professions, sciences and humanities; and the systematic acceleration of scientific research through computer-mediated collaboration.

Mildred L. G. Shaw

[*http://ksi.cpsc.ucalgary.ca/KSI*]
Knowledge Science Institute
University of Calgary, Alberta, Canada T2N 1N4
mildred@cpsc.ucalgary.ca

Dr. Mildred L. G. Shaw is Professor of Computer Science at the University of Calgary. She received her BSc and MSc from the University of London, and her PhD from Brunel University, and is a Chartered Mathematician and Chartered Psychologist. She is a Fellow of the Institute of Mathematics and its Applications and the British Computer Society and an Associate Fellow of the British Psychological Society. Dr. Shaw is a member of the editorial boards of the *International Journal of Human-Computer Studies* and *Applied Intelligence.* She has authored over 150 papers and authored or edited 5 books on a wide variety of aspects of computer and human systems. Her research interests include human-computer interaction; the acquisition and transfer of knowledge; software engineering; and knowledge-based system applications.

SWOOP

AN APPLICATION GENERATOR FOR
ORACLE/WWW SYSTEMS

Andrew Hunter, Ian Ferguson, Steven Hedges

Abstract

The development of a software package named Swoop is described. Swoop is designed to support the generation and maintenance of WWW information systems which store information in ORACLE databases: a so-called hyperbase program. The biggest problem with hyperbases is that they require a sophisticated program to interpret Forms, query appropriate databases, and merge information into hypertext. There is a clear need for application-generator tools which allow hyperbase programs to be constructed with minimal expertise on the part of the designer. It is this problem which Swoop addresses. **Keywords:** *ORACLE, interface, hyperbase*

Introduction

Swoop is a software package designed to support the generation and maintenance of WWW information systems which store information in an ORACLE database. In these hybrid systems (which we refer to as *hyperbases*), information from a relational database is merged into hypertext documents for presentation.

The World Wide Web has facilities which make the provision of hyperbases possible. The basic capability of WWW is to download text files via hypertext links. Dynamic documents [1] are programs which can be invoked in place of a document download, and generate the text as output; a suitable program can hence extract information from a database and present it as HTML. The Forms interface, available using CGI [2], allows Web pages to be built which include user-interface elements such as fields, buttons, and checkboxes; this can be used to provide user-input to dynamic-document pages.

Hyperbase programs may be presented to the user in two ways. First, the user may browse what appear to be normal Web pages, with no Forms interface, although the pages are actually being dynamically constructed from the database. Second, the user may be presented with Forms,

which generate input, for example, to specify keywords to be used in searches. Forms could also be used to present output, although this is rarely done; most hyperbase programs present the results of searches as simple hypertext.

The biggest problem with hyperbases is that they require a sophisticated program to interpret Forms, query appropriate databases, and merge information into hypertext. There is a clear need for application-generator tools which allow hyperbase programs to be constructed with minimal expertise on the part of the designer.

What Is Swoop?

A number of tools have been developed which go some way towards merging WWW and ORACLE [4]. WOW [5] allows hyperbase programs to be written in PL/SQL and stored in an ORACLE database; it requires appropriate ORACLE programming skills. WOW programs may output a mixture of raw HTML and database information. DECOUX [6] supports an augmented form of HTML which includes some embedded SQL statements. This is interpreted by a forms-based interface, and is somewhat low-level in syntax. Nevertheless, it requires less programming skill than WOW and provides a simple method of describing a hyperbase page. WORA [7] dynamically constructs HTML forms as an interface to ORACLE tables; it provides sophisticated query facilities, but the information cannot be merged into a hypertext presentation.

Swoop supports the construction of hyperbases using an ORACLE database as a back-end. Information is presented to the user as simple hypertext pages; these pages are specified using a simple augmented HTML syntax. It also has facilities to aid in maintenance and specification of the database. Swoop provides a single, integrated solution to the generation of hyperbase systems.

Swoop has the following major components:

Swoopgen. This is an application generator which produces dynamic page programs from special augmented HTML files called *swoop-files*. Swoop-files can include embedded pieces of SQL, the standard language for accessing Relational Databases [3]. The SQL inserts in swoop-files corresponds to points where information extracted from the database should be merged into the page. A tool called *swoopgen* translates these special swoop-files into PRO*C programs (PRO*C is ORACLE's precompiler to support embedded

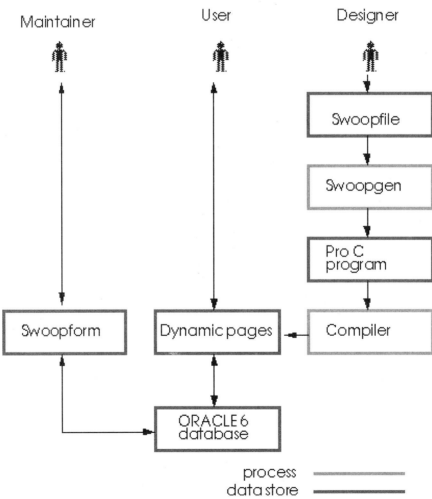

Figure 1:   Major Swoop system components

SQL statements within the C programming language), which when compiled act as dynamic page programs which will extract information from the database and present it merged into hypertext, as specified by the swoop-file. Thus, the system-designer using Swoop needs only a rudimentary knowledge of ORACLE and HTML.

Swoopform. Whereas *swoopgen* tool provides the facility needed to support browsing of the merged HTML/ORACLE pages, *swoopform* supports database maintenance. It provides a Forms-based interface which allows information to be Queried, Added, Updated, and Deleted from tables in the Swoop database. It is provided primarily for the use of the system-maintainer, rather than system users, although in practice it has also been found useful for supporting limited user-input. *Swoopform* can automatically produce a form for any Swoop table.

Using swoopgen to Build Dynamic Pages

One of the major components of Swoop is *swoopgen*, an application-generation program. Swoopgen takes as input swoop-files, which contain HTML and embedded *swoop statements.* Swoop statements may include pieces of SQL.

Swoopgen produces the source code for dynamic page programs, in PRO*C. This source is then compiled to produce the executable dynamic page programs. When invoked from the Web, these produce HTML on standard output, which is displayed by the user's Web browser. This HTML has inserted in it information extracted from the ORACLE database. The information inserted is determined by the embedded swoop statements.

This section discusses the format of swoop-files, and how they can be used to produce interlinked sets of Web pages.

To illustrate the discussion, a simple case study will be used: a system to track members of staff at an academic institution. It includes:

- A home page for each member of staff

- A telephone list of all staff in the institution, with links to home pages

- A list of departments

- A home page for each department, including a list of staff in the department with links to their home pages

The database for this system is defined in Tables 1 and 2.

Table 1: Staff

Code	Name	Department	Telephone	Additional
GK	Khan	CIS	0225	Not to be argued with
AH	Hunter	CIS	2778	Likes writing *software*
SG	Garrick	ENG	3425	Hands-on worker
CP	Porter	ART	2345	

Table 2: Department

Code	Name	Head
CIS	Computing	GK
ENG	Engineering	ATH

Note that the database has been left deliberately incomplete: the head of department for Engineering (ATH) hasn't been listed in the staff table, and the ART department has been omitted from the departments table; CP has provided no additional information for his Home page; Swoop will support this incomplete information to the best of its ability.

Stage 1: Producing a Simple Swoop-file

The first page required is a telephone list for all staff. The HTML for a simple version of this with no hypertext links is presented here:

```
<title>Telephone Listing</title>
<h1>Telephone Listing</title><hr>
Hunter, 2778<p>
Garrick, 3425<p>
Khan, 0225<p>
Porter, 2345<p>
```

The above HTML can be produced by a dynamic page program called *tellist*, which has been automatically generated by Swoop from the swoop-file illustrated here:

```
$sql staff order by name$
<h1>Telephone Listing</title><hr>
$repeat$
$name:0$, $telno:0$<p>
$endrepeat$
```

Swoop-files contains HTML, augmented by swoop statements. Swoop statements are enclosed in dollar "$" characters (the dollar character itself is available by using $$). Swoop supports the following types of statements:

- SQL statements

- SQL variable statements

- Repetition statements

Embedded SQL is divided into two parts within swoop-files. *$sql...$* statements contain the tail end of SQL select statements, from the table name(s) onwards. They may be placed anywhere in the file, although it is most convenient to place them together at the top. *Sql variable statements* are embedded within the HTML text; they con-

tain the name of a table column, a separating colon, and a number identifying a corresponding *$sql...$* statement. *swoopgen* constructs appropriate SQL SELECT statements by matching the variables and sql statements together. The advantage of this dual representation is that a single SQL statement can be used to fetch information needed in a number of places.

In the example above, the *name* and *telno* columns are required, so *swoopgen* will construct the following SQL statement: `select name, telno from staff order by name;`

The values retrieved from the database by the program will be inserted in place of the sql variables at run time.

$repeat$ ... $endrepeat$ statements can be used to produce repeated sections of HTML if the SELECT statement is expected to return more than a single row of information (as is the case here). If an sql variable is encountered outside *$repeat$ ... $endrepeat$* statements, then it is assumed that only a single value will be returned, and only the first value returned is shown.

Stage 2: Producing Interlinked Pages Using Swoop-files

The *tellist* program is particularly simple because it produces a general list. However, many pages need to provide different output depending on some qualifying information. For example, the staff home pages can be supported by a single dynamic page program (called *homepage*), provided that we tell it *which* member of staff is required. We can do this by passing an appropriate piece of information (the staff code) to *homepage* as a parameter. The *homepage* swoop-file is shown below. It uses a special specifier (*arg-0*) within an SQL statement to qualify the search, using the first (i.e., zeroth) argument passed to the page; this argument should be the code of the staff member whose home page is required. A *$arg-n$* tag may also be used anywhere within a file, if you want to output an argument rather than use it to select further information.

There is the Swoop file for *homepage*:

```
$sql staff where code = arg-0 $
$sql staff s, dept d where s.code = arg-
    0 and s.dept = d.code$
<title>Home Page for $name:0$</title>
<h1>Home page for $name:0$</h1>
<hr>
<i>Code number:</i> $code:0$<p>
<i>Department:</i> <a href="dept?$d.
    code$">$d.name:1$<p>
<hr>
<h2>Additional information</h2>
$additional:0$
<hr>
```

Sample HTML output by *homepage*:

```
<title>Home Page for Hunter</title>
<h1>Home page for Hunter</h1>
<hr>
<i>Code number:</i> AH<p>
<i>Department:</i> <a
    href="CIS">Computing<p>
<hr>
<h2>Additional information</h2>
Likes writing <i>software</i>!
<hr>
```

To access the individual home pages from the telephone list, we can modify *tellist* to include URLs which invoke *homepage*, passing the staff code as a parameter. The code below shows an updated version of the *tellist* swoop-file, and resulting HTML output, which contains links to each home page.

Swoop-file:

```
$sql staff order by name$
<h1>Telephone Listing</title><hr>
$repeat$
<a href="homepage?$code:0$">$name:0$</
    a>, $telno:0$<p>
$endrepeat$
```

HTML generated:

```
<title>Telephone Listing</title>
<h1>Telephone Listing</title><hr>
<a href="homepage?AH">Hunter</a>,
    2778<p>
<a href="homepage?SG">Garrick</a>,
    3425<p>
<a href="homepage?GK">Khan</a>, 0225<p>
<a href="homepage?CP">Porter</a>,
    2345<p>
```

The second select statement in the *homepage* swoop-file, shown in the code below, is used to get information about the user's department (specifically, its name rather than its code) from the department table, using a JOIN condition to ensure that the department corresponding to this particular person is located. In the case of Porter, this statement will not find any information, since Porter's department (ART) is missing. Swoop will simply leave the department blank in this case. The department is also further hyperlinked to the *dept* page, which is listed in the sample HTML output.

Swoop-file for *dept* dynamic page:

```
$sql dept where code = arg-0 $
$sql staff s, dept d where d.code = arg-
    0 and s.dept = d.code and
s.code = d.head $
$sql staff where dept = arg-0 order by
    name$
<title>Department: $name:0$</title>
<h1>Department: $name:1$ ($arg-0$)</h1>
<hr>
<i>Head of department:</i> $s.
    name:1$<hr>
<h2>Staff</h2>
$repeat$
<a href="homepage?$code:2$">$name:2$<p>
$endrepeat$
<hr>
```

Sample HTML output:

```
<title>Department: Computing</title>
<h1>Department: Computing (CIS)</h1>
<hr>
<i>Head of department:</i> Khan<hr>
<h2>Staff</h2>
<a href="homepage?AH">Hunter<p>
<a href="homepage?GK">Khan<p>
<hr>
```

The interlinking of pages in this fashion is typical of Swoop, which can thus implement interfaces to quite complex database structures with minimal effort. Many hyperbase programs tend to concentrate on a particular, simple approach to structuring the search space, in order to reduce programming complexity. Swoop reduces that complexity to a level no worse than that encountered in any database system design problem.

Linking Swoop-files and Other HTML Files

As a final part in this section, it is worth noting that swoop-files can be intermixed quite freely with separate HTML files The information which is stored in the database is itself in HTML format (it is inserted directly into the merged page when displayed), which means that particular pages can include links to other information. For example, the *additional* information section in the homepages above could contain links to further user-specific information. It is also possible to link to information stored, for convenience, outside the database. For example, by adding a link such as `<img src="$code:0$.gif"><p>` to the home page, a picture of each member of staff can be included, where these are assumed to be stored in files *AH.gif*, *GK.gif*, etc.

Using Swoopform for Database Maintenance

The *swoopgen* tool produces dynamic page programs which are invoked through hypertext links to produce information on-screen; the user thus sees only hypertext, and need not even be aware that a database is being used at all. However, somebody must provide the information in the database in the first place. Although tables for use in Swoop must be created using special tools (since Swoop maintains some auxiliary information about tables in its own special tables), once a table has been created, it may be maintained using whatever database facilities are available. The maintainer might prefer to provide an sql-forms-based interface, or to upload from an Access database, for example.

Swoop also provides a facility to support table maintenance via WWW: *swoopform*. Swoopform is a program which generates a CGI Form containing fields for each column in a table. The form may be used to create new rows, to update or delete existing ones, and to search for existing rows using a query. The table to be queried is passed as a parameter when *swoopform* is invoked. Since all the tables known to Swoop are themselves described in a special table, it is a trivial matter to produce a swoop-file for *swoopgen* which generates a list of all tables, with hypertext links to *swoopform* for each—such a swoop-file is provided with the Swoop system. Thus, the maintainer automatically has access to Forms-based facilities to maintain all Swoop tables. The downside of this powerful automatic facility, is that *swoopform* is not configurable—it always presents a Form in the same fashion, which can be used solely to update a single table.

Swoopform has the following features:

- There is a Submit button at the bottom, together with a set of radio buttons for the three options: Query, Insert, and Delete. The action of the Submit button is determined by which radio button is pressed.

- A Query will retrieve the first row of the table matching the information in the fields; the match must be exact. This is used to retrieve table entries for update.

- Insert will update existing information or create new entries. Swoop tables have their Primary Key identified upon creation (and Primary Key fields have italicized prompts in *swoopform*, so that they stand out). Upon Insert, if the Primary Key matches an existing row in the table, then it is updated; if the Primary Key doesn't match, a new row is created. To avoid accidentally overwriting existing entries, the maintainer should fill in the Primary Key first and execute a Query to check that nothing is retrieved.

- Delete will remove the first row of the table matching the information in the fields; multiple deletions are not supported to avoid accidental damage to the database (these can always be done using the native database facilities).

- Fields are automatically sized to match the column width.

- Fields can contain HTML source, and *swoopform* will correctly store it in the database and merge it into pages upon display.

- A small amount of additional information can be included for use by *swoopform* when tables are created; this allows links to additional pages to be added.

- A link to table-specific help is automatically provided, although the database designer needs to provide the HTML file which it attempts to access!

- A link to a general *swoopform* help page is automatically provided.

- Swoop tables can be marked as secure or insecure; if a table is marked as secure then *swoopform* includes a password field, and will not allow access to the table unless the password is entered. Insecure tables can be freely accessed; this allows *swoopform* to be used to gather information from users. For example, we have used a simple *swoopgen* program to generate an Electronic Student Notice Board, which includes a link to *swoopform* to maintain it. Thus, students can both read the notice board and add messages to it. Messages can be assigned priority ratings and post/remove time stamps, all of which are handled very simply through SQL in the swoop-file (the notice board source is provided as an example with the Swoop source pack).

Swoop Maintenance Utilities

Swoop provides tools at a number of levels; *swoopgen* is used by the system designer to generate dynamic page programs; *swoopform* is used by database maintainers (sometimes solely the system designer; sometimes a wider group) to add and update information. It also provides a small number of additional facilities to aid the system designer.

Although ORACLE maintains a great deal of information about individual tables, not all of it is easily retrieved, and there are some additional pieces of information (for example, the prompts used for fields on *swoopform*) which ORACLE doesn't support. Swoop therefore maintains two auxiliary tables in the database: SWOOPTABLES and SWOOPCOLUMNS. The information in these two tables must correspond to the profile of the tables accessed by Swoop. To make this correspondence simple to maintain, the Swoop distribution includes two scripts which create and delete Swoop tables. The *createhtmltable* script takes as an argument a file name; the file may include a number of Swoop Create statements, which are essentially augmented SQL Create statements. The *deletehtmltable* script takes as an argument a table name, and deletes both the table and any references to it in the Swoop auxiliary tables.

Further details on the Swoop maintenance utilities can be found in the Swoop source distribution.

Future Work

The purpose of Swoop is to make the generation of ORACLE hyperbase programs on WWW simple. In this it has succeeded; producing a Swoop-based database system is no harder than producing a conventional database system on any platform (actually, often easier since there is no need to generate any Forms-based interface). However, there are a number of enhancements which could be made:

SQL syntax. The approach taken to embedding SQL in swoop-files is effective, but untidy. Currently, the $sql ...$ statement contains only the tail end of the SELECT statement, which is constructed by assembling the variable tags associated with it to form the prefix. This has several consequences:

- It is sometimes difficult, on first reading, to tell the exact purpose of an SQL statement (because it is effectively scattered through the swoop file).

- If complex compound variables are to be fetched (e.g., SUBSTR(NAME,0,1) to extract an initial from a forename) then these must be included as variable tags, and are difficult to read.

- The DISTINCT clause, which comes at the beginning of the SQL statement, necessitates an additional tag *$sql_distinct ...$*.

The approach taken was adopted because it precludes any need to parse the SQL statement: the construction of a prefix is relatively easy. A better approach would be to augment the SQL SELECT statement with tag names and to remove these using a parser if necessary:

```
$sql select distinct d.name, substr(s.
    name,0,1) into dept, init from dept
    d, staff s where d.code = s.dept$
```

is translated into the SELECT statement:

```
select distinct d.name, substr(s.
    name,0,1) from dept d, staff s
    where d.code = s.dept;
```

and the tag variables *$dept:0$* and *$init:0$* refer to the first and second columns fetched respectively.

Interpretative Swoop. swoopgen generates dynamic page programs, in PRO*C, which are compiled and run. This is the most time-efficient approach when actually using the dynamic page programs. However, PRO*C programs are extremely large, and take some time to compile. An interpretative version, which read a swoop-file and dynamically constructed pages from it would be useful, particularly during the developmental phase.

Integration into Web servers. The requirement to integrate Web pages with SQL-based databases is extremely common. It would be convenient if embedded SQL was supported within an extended version of HTML, with sophisticated

Web servers able to interpret such statements. Obviously, the syntax of embedded SQL statements would be adjusted to fit into HTML standard, specifically, by replacing the $ tag delimiters with standard HTML <> delimiters. Swoop uses $ tag delimiters specifically to highlight the different interpretation that is placed upon them. A suggested standard is:

```
<sql select="<select statement>">
<sql repeat>
<sql endrepeat>
<sql variable="<variable name>">
```

Replacement for Swoop

A replacement package, which uses an intrepretive approach and has a far simpler syntax, together with an improved *forms* interface, is currently under development and will be available in the near future.

Availability

Swoop is available solely via WWW at: *http://osiris.sund.ac.uk/abu/swoop/home.html*.

If you need anonymous FTP to download it, you have no use for it anyway! ∎

References

1. Ford, A., *Spinning the Web*, International Thompson, p.143.

2. McCool, *http://booboo.ncsa.uiuc.edu/cgi/index.html*

3. Sturner, G., *ORACLE 7: A User and Developers Guide*, Van Nostrand Reinhold.

4. OWWWIK. *The Oracle World Wide Web Interface Kit, http://dozer.us.oracle.com:8080/index.html*

5. WOW. *The WOW Gateway, http://dozer.us.oracle.com:8080/sdk10/wow/*

6. Decoux, *The Decoux Gateway, http://dozer.us.oracle.com:8080/sdk10/decoux/*

7. Ocrainets, *The WORA Gateway http://dozer.us.oracle.com:8080/sdk10/wora/*

About the Authors

Dr. **Andrew Hunter**
[*http://osiris.sunderland.ac.uk/ahu/home.html*]
Department of Computing and Information Systems, University of Sunderland, England.
cs0ahu@sunderland.ac.uk

Andrew Hunter is a Senior Lecturer, with interests in Genetic Algorithms, Neural Networks, and Interactive Software. He produces the Sugal public-domain Genetic Algorithms package.

Mr. **Ian Ferguson**
[*http://osiris.sunderland.ac.uk/rif/welcome.html*]
Department of Computing and Information Systems, University of Sunderland, England.
cs0rif@sunderland.ac.uk

Ian Ferguson is a Senior Lecturer with interests in Object Oriented software and the Internet.

Mr. **Steven Hedges**
[*http://www.iisl.co.uk/*]
Internet Information Services, Ltd, 498 Dereham Road, Norwich, NR5 8TU, England.
steve@maxx.co.uk

Steven Hedges runs IISL, a WWW training and consultancy service.

MULTI-ENGINE SEARCH AND COMPARISON USING THE METACRAWLER

Erik Selberg, Oren Etzioni

Abstract

*Standard Web search services, though useful, are far from ideal. There are over a dozen different search services currently in existence, each with a unique interface and a database covering a different portion of the Web. As a result, users are forced to repeatedly try and retry their queries across different services. Furthermore, the services return many responses that are irrelevant, outdated, or unavailable, forcing the user to manually sift through the responses searching for useful information. This paper presents the MetaCrawler, a fielded Web service that represents the next level up in the information "food chain." The MetaCrawler provides a single, central interface for Web document searching. Upon receiving a query, the MetaCrawler posts the query to multiple search services in parallel, collates the returned references, and loads those references to verify their existence and to ensure that they contain relevant information. The MetaCrawler is sufficiently lightweight to reside on a user's machine, which facilitates customization, privacy, sophisticated filtering of references, and more. The MetaCrawler also serves as a tool for comparison of diverse search services. Using the MetaCrawler's data, we present a "Consumer Reports" evaluation of six Web search services: Galaxy [5], InfoSeek [1], Lycos [15], Open Text [20], WebCrawler [22], and Yahoo [9]. In addition, we also report on the most commonly submitted queries to the MetaCrawler. **Keywords:** MetaCrawler, WWW, World Wide Web, search, multiservice, multithreaded, parallel, comparison*

Introduction

Web search services such as Lycos and WebCrawler have proven both useful and popular. As the Web grows, the number and variety of search services is increasing as well. Examples include: the Yahoo "net directory"; the Harvest home page search service [7]; the Query By Image Content service [12]; the Virtual Tourist [24], a directory organized by geographic regions; and more. Since each service provides an incomplete snapshot of the Web, users are forced to try and retry their queries across different indices until they find appropriate responses. The process of querying multiple services is quite tedious. Each service has its own idiosyncratic interface which the user is forced to learn. Furthermore, the services return many responses that are irrelevant, outdated, or unavailable, forcing the user to manu-ally sift through the responses searching for useful information.

This paper presents the MetaCrawler, a search service that attempts to address the problems outlined above. The premises underlying the MetaCrawler are the following:

- No single search service is sufficient. Table 2 shows that no single service is able to return more than 45% of the references followed by users.

- Many references returned by services are irrelevant and can be removed if the user is better able to express the query. Table 3 shows that up to 75% of the references returned can be removed if the user supplies a more expressive query.

- Low-quality references can be detected and removed fairly quickly. Table 4 shows that an average of about 100 references can be verified in well under 2.5 minutes, while simple collation and ranking takes under 30 seconds.

- These features will be used by the Web's population. The MetaCrawler is receiving over 7000 queries per week, and that number is growing, as shown in Figure 1.

- The MetaCrawler log facilitates an objective evaluation and comparison of the underlying search services. Tables 5 through 8 detail trade-offs between the services. For example, Lycos returns over 5% more followed references than any other service, yet WebCrawler is the fastest, taking an average of 9.64 seconds to return answers to queries.

The MetaCrawler logs also reveal that people search for a wide variety of information, from "A. H. Robins" to "zyx music." While the most common queries are related to sex and pornography, these only account for under 4% of the total queries submitted to the Metacrawler as shown in Table 1. Nearly half of all queries submitted are unique.

The remainder of this paper includes discussions of the design and implementation of the MetaCrawler, experiments to validate the above premises, a discussion of related work, and our ideas for future work and potential impact. We end with our conclusions.

The MetaCrawler

The MetaCrawler is a free search service used for locating information available on the World Wide Web. The MetaCrawler has an interface similar to WebCrawler and Open Text in that it allows users to enter a search string, or *query*, and returns a page with clickable references or *hits* to pages available on the Web. However, the internal architecture of the MetaCrawler is radically different from the other search services.

Standard Web searching consists of three activities:

- *Indexing* the Web for new and updated pages, a process that demands substantial CPU and network resources.

- *Storage* of the Web pages retrieved into an index, which typically requires a large amount of disk space.

- *Retrieval* of pages matching user queries. For most services, this amounts to returning a ranked list of page references from the stored index.

Standard search services create and store an index of the Web as well as retrieve information from that index. Unlike these services, the MetaCrawler is a *meta-service* which uses no internal database of its own; instead, it relies on other external search services to provide the information necessary to fulfill user queries. The insight here is that by separating the retrieval of pages from indexing and storing them, a lightweight application such as the MetaCrawler can access multiple databases and thus provide a larger number of potentially higher quality references than any search service tied to a single database.

Another advantage of the MetaCrawler is that it does not depend upon the implementation or existence of any one search service. Some indexing mechanism is necessary for the Web. Typically, this is done using automated robots or spiders, which may not necessarily be the best choice[13]. However, the underlying architecture of the search services used by the MetaCrawler is unimportant. As long as there is no central complete search service and several partial search services exist, the MetaCrawler can provide the benefit of accessing them simultaneously and collating the results.

The MetaCrawler prototype has been publicly accessible since July 7, 1995. It has been steadily growing in popularity, logging upwards of 7000 queries per week and increasing. The MetaCrawler currently accesses six services: Galaxy, Info-

Seek, Lycos, Open Text, WebCrawler, and Yahoo. It works as follows: given a query, the MetaCrawler will submit that query to every search service it knows in parallel. These services then return a list of references to WWW pages, or hits. Upon receiving the hits from every service, the MetaCrawler *collates* the results by merging all hits returned. Duplicate hits are listed only once, but each service that returned a hit is acknowledged. Expert user-supplied sorting options are applied at this time. Optionally, the MetaCrawler will *verify* the information's existence by loading the reference. When the Meta-Crawler has loaded a reference, it is then able to rescore the page using supplementary query syntax supplied by the user.

When the MetaCrawler has finished processing all of the hits, the user is presented with a page consisting of a sorted list of references. Each reference contains a clickable hypertext link to the reference, followed by local page context (if available), a confidence score, verified keywords, and the actual URL of the reference. Each word in the search query is automatically boldfaced. So that we may determine which references are followed, each clickable link returned to the user points not to the reference, but to a script which logs that the reference was followed and then refers the user's browser to the correct URL.

Querying many services and simply collating results will return more results than any one service, but at the cost of presenting the user with more irrelevant references. The MetaCrawler is designed to increase *both* the number of hits and relevance of hits returned. The MetaCrawler yields a higher proportion of *relevant* hits by using both a powerful query syntax as well as expert options so that users can more easily instruct the MetaCrawler how to determine the quality of the returned references. The query syntax used specifies required and non-desired words, as well as words that should appear as a phrase. The expert options allow users to rank hits by physical location, such as the user's country, as well as logical locality, such as their Internet domain.

User Interface

Although giving the user a Web form with added expressive power was easy, presenting the user with a form that would facilitate actually using the novel features of the MetaCrawler proved to be a challenge. We strove for a balance between a simple search form and an expressive one, keeping in mind interface issues mentioned by service providers [23].

In our early designs, we focused on syntax for queries with several additional options for improving the result. This syntax was similar to InfoSeek's query syntax: parentheses were used to define phrases, a plus sign designated a required word, and a minus designated a non-desired word. For example, to search for "John Cleese," naturally requiring that both "John" and "Cleese" appear together, the syntax required was the unwieldy (+John +Cleese). Not surprisingly, we discovered that while most users attempted to use the syntax, they often introduced subtle syntactical errors causing the resulting search to produce an entirely irrelevant set of hits.

In our current design, we have reduced the need for extra syntax, and instead ask the user to select the type of search. The three options are:

- *Searching for words as a phrase.* Treat the query text as a single phrase, and attempt to match the phrase in pages retrieved, e.g., "Four score and seven years ago."

- *Searching for all words.* Attempt to find each word of the query text somewhere in the retrieved pages. This is the equivalent of logical "and."

- *Searching for any words.* Attempt to find any word of the query text in the retrieved pages. This is the equivalent of logical "or."

The older syntax is still supported, although it is not advertised prominently on the main search page, save for the minus sign, which was the most widely used element of the query syntax. Since we changed the search page to this new design, the number of malformed requests has dropped significantly.

In addition to the query entry box, we maintain various expert options which can be activated via menus. The MetaCrawler currently uses two menus to provide extra expressiveness. The first describes a coarse grain Locality, with options for the user's continent, country, and Internet domain, as well as options to select a specific continent. The second menu describes the sundry Internet domain types, e.g., .edu, .com, etc. These options allow users to better describe what they are looking for in terms of where they believe the relevant information will be.

Client-Server Design

Current search services amortize the cost of indexing and storing pages over hundreds of thousands of retrievals per day. In order to field the maximal number of retrievals, services devote minimal effort to responding to each individual query. Increases in server capacity are quickly gobbled up by increases in pages indexed and queries per day. As a result, there is little time for more sophisticated analysis, filtering, and post-processing of responses to queries.

By decoupling the retrieval of pages from indexing and storage, the MetaCrawler is able to spend time performing sophisticated analysis on pages returned. The MetaCrawler just retrieves data, spending no time indexing or storing it. Thus, the MetaCrawler is relatively lightweight. The prototype, written in C++, comes to only 3985 lines of code including comments. It does not need the massive disk storage to maintain an index nor does it need the massive CPU and network resources that other services require. Consequently, a MetaCrawler client could reside comfortably on an individual user's machine.

An individualized MetaCrawler *client* that accesses multiple Web search services has a number of advantages. First, the user's machine bears the load of the post-processing and analysis of the returned references. Given extra time, post-processing can be quite sophisticated. For example, the MetaCrawler could divide references into clusters based on their similarity to each other, or it could engage in *secondary search* by following references to related pages to determine potential interest. Second, the processing can be customized to the user's taste and needs. For example, the user may choose to filter advertisements or parents may try to block X-rated pages. Third, the MetaCrawler could support scheduled queries (e.g., what's new today with the Seattle Mariners?). By storing the results of previous queries on the user's machine, the MetaCrawler can focus its output on new or updated pages. Finally, for pay-per-query services, the MetaCrawler can be programmed with selective query policies (e.g., "go to the cheapest service first" or even "compute the optimal service querying sequence").

Organizations can choose to have an institutional MetaCrawler with enhanced caching capabilities, on the presumption that people within an organization will want to examine many of the same pages. The cache could also facilitate local annotations, creating a collaborative filtering and information exchange environment of the sort described elsewhere [17].

Finally, while our prototype MetaCrawler depends on the good will of the underlying services, a MetaCrawler client would not. In the future, an underlying service may choose to block MetaCrawler requests, which are easily identified. However, it would be nearly impossible to distinguish queries issued by a MetaCrawler client versus queries made directly by a person.

Common Usage

One of the frequently asked questions regarding search on the Internet is "What are people searching for?" Table 1 summarizes the top ten repeated queries out of a total of 50,878 queries

Table 1:   Top Ten Queries Issued to the MetaCrawler

No.	Query	Times Issued
1	sex	533
2	erotica	219
3	nude	217
4	porn	158
5	penthouse	127
6	pornography	112
7	erotic	105
8	porno	89
9	adult	89
10	playboy	67

"Times Issued" lists the number of times the corresponding query was issued from July 7 through Sept. 30, 1995. Note that while each query is sexually related, the combined total amounts to less than 4% of the total queries processed by the MetaCrawler. Also, 46% of the queries issued were unique.

made from July 7 through September 30. Each query in the top ten is related to sex. However, the combined top ten queries amount only to 1716 queries out of 50,878 total queries, or 3. 37%. Furthermore, 24,253 queries, or 46.67%, were not repeated.

Evaluation

The MetaCrawler was released publicly on July 7, 1995. Averages and percentages presented in this paper are based on the 50,878 completed queries, starting on July 7 and ending September 30, except those in reference to Open Text, which are based on 19,951 completed queries starting September 8, when Open Text was added to the MetaCrawler's repertoire. The log results from seven days were omitted due to a service changing its output format, causing that service to return no references to the MetaCrawler even though the service was available. The Meta-

Crawler is currently running on a DEC Alpha 3000/400 under OSF 3.2.

The first hypothesis we confirmed after we deployed the MetaCrawler was that sending queries in parallel and collating the results were useful. To confirm this, we used the metric that references followed from the page of hits returned by the MetaCrawler contained relevant information. We calculated the percentage of references followed by users for each of the search services. Table 2 demonstrates the need for using multiple services; while Lycos did return the plurality of the hits that were followed, with a 35.43% share (42.17% in the last month recorded), slightly under 65% of the followed references came from the other five services. Skeptical readers may argue that service providers could invest in more resources and provide more comprehensive indices to the web. However, recent studies indicate the rate of Web expansion and change makes a complete index virtually impossible [16].

Table 2:   Market Shares of Followed References

	% followed Jul. 7 - Sept. 30	% followed Sept. 8 - 30
Lycos	35.43	42.17
WebCrawler	30.76	25.74
InfoSeek	18.55	15.70

Table 2: Market Shares of Followed References (Continued)

	% followed Jul. 7 - Sept. 30	% followed Sept. 8 - 30
Galaxy	17.10	15.60
Open Text	n/a	14.70
Yahoo	10.67	6.59

This table shows the percentage each service has of the total followed references. References returned by two or more services are included under each service, which is why the columns sum to over 100%. The table demonstrates that a user who restricts his or her queries to a single service will miss most of the relevant references.

We then analyzed the data to determine which, if any, of the added features of the MetaCrawler were helping users. The metric we used was the number of references pruned. Table 3 shows the average number of references removed for each advanced option.

Using syntax for required or non-desired words typically reduces the number of returned results by 40%. Detecting dead pages allowed the removal of another 15%. Finally, the expert options were very successful in removing unwanted references. When all of these features are used in conjunction, up to 75% of the returned references can be removed.

MetaCrawler Benchmarks

We have shown that the MetaCrawler improves the quality of results returned to the user. But what is the performance cost? Table 4 shows the average times per query, differentiating between having the MetaCrawler simply collate the results or verify them as well.

Table 4 shows that the MetaCrawler finished relatively quickly. The average time to return collated results is a little over 5 seconds longer than the slowest service as shown by Table 8. This result is to be expected given the percentage of the time a service times out, which causes the MetaCrawler to wait for a full minute before returning all the results. We are pleased with the times reported for verification. Our initial prototype typically took five minutes to perform verification. We recently began caching retrieved pages for three hours, and have found that caching reduces the average verification time by nearly one-half. We are confident that this time can be further reduced by more aggressive caching as well as improvements in the thread management used by the MetaCrawler.

Since the MetaCrawler was publicly announced, the daily access count has been growing at a linear rate. We are also pleased with an increased use of the user options. Figure 1 plots the data points for the weeks beginning July 7 until September 30. "Feature Use by Week" shows the number of queries where any of the MetaCrawler's advanced features, such as verification, were used.

Table 3: Effect of Features in Removing Irrelevant Hits

Feature	% of Hits Removed
Syntax	39.79
Dead	14.88
Expert	21.49

This table shows the percentage of hits removed when a particular feature was used. "Syntax" refers to queries that were removed due to sophisticated query syntax (e.g., minus for undesired words), "Dead" refers to unavailable or inaccessible pages, and "Expert" refers to hits removed due to restriction on the references' origins.

Table 4:   Average Time for MetaCrawler Return Results

	Wall Clock Time	User Time	System Time	Lag Time
Collated	25.70	0.32	1.87	23.51
Verified	139.30	22.72	4.50	112.08

All times are measured in seconds. "Wall Clock Time" is the total time taken for an average query, and is broken down into User, System, and Lag Time. "User Time" is the time taken by the MetaCrawler program, "System Time" the time taken by the operating system, and "Lag Time" the time taken for pages to be downloaded off the network.

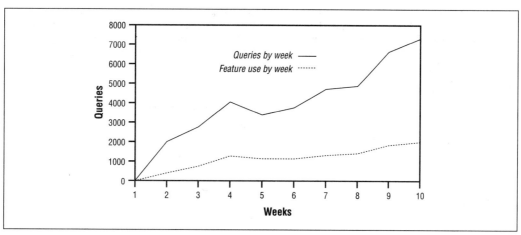

Figure 1:   Queries per week from July 7 - Sept. 30

Search Service Comparison

In addition to validating our claims, the MetaCrawler's logs also allow us to present a "Consumer Reports" style comparison of the search services. We evaluate each service using three metrics:

- *Coverage.* How many hits will be returned on average?

- *Relevance.* Are hits returned actually followed by users?

- *Performance.* How long does each service take, and how often does it time out?

Coverage

Given a preset maximum on the number of hits returned by each service, we measured both the percentage of references returned as well as references unique to the service that returned them.

Thus, 75% returned with 70% unique shows that on average a service returns 75% of its maximum allowed, with 70% of those hits being unique.

Tables 5 and 6 detail our findings in terms of raw content. They show that with default parameters, Open Text returns 80% of the maximum hits allowed, with nearly 89% of those hits being unique. Lycos and WebCrawler follow, also returning over 70%, with slightly over 90% of those hits being unique. Yahoo has particularly poor performance on the total hits metric, but this was not surprising to us. We included Yahoo on the hypothesis that people search for subjects, such as "Mariners Baseball," at which Yahoo excels. However, this hypothesis was proven incorrect, as people tended to use the MetaCrawler to search for nuggets of information, such as "Ken Griffey hand injury." Yahoo does not index this type of information, and thus

Table 5:   Returned References by Service

	% of Max Hits Returned	Ave. Hits Returned/Maximum Allowed
Open Text	80.0	8.0 / 10
Lycos	76.3	19.1 / 25
WebCrawler	70.2	17.6 / 25
Galaxy	56.9	28.4 / 50
InfoSeek	43.5	4.4 / 10
Yahoo	11.1	11.1 / 100

The first column shows the percentage of the maximum hits allowed that each service returned. Each percentage was calculated by dividing the average hits returned by the maximum allowed for that service, as shown in the second column. This percentage is a measure of how many hits a service will provide given a pre-set maximum. The MetaCrawler used different maximum values for services, as some had internal maximum values, and others would either accept only certain maximums or none at all.

Table 6:   Unique References by Service

	% of Unique Hits Returned
Galaxy	99.6
Yahoo	92.8
Lycos	90.6
WebCrawler	90.3
Open Text	88.8
InfoSeek	79.5

This table shows the percentage of references each service returned that were unique to that service.

shows poor content. Presumably, most topic searches go to Yahoo directly.

Although each service returns mostly unique references, it is not clear whether those references are useful. Furthermore, unique references are not necessarily unique to a service's database, as another service could return that reference given a different query string.

Relevance

To measure relevance, two metrics are used. The first is which service is returning the most references that people follow. This is shown by Table 2. The second metric is what percent of references returned by each service are people following. Table 7 summarizes these calculations, showing that nearly 6% of all references returned

by InfoSeek were followed. Lycos, Open Text, and WebCrawler follow, each having about 2.5% of its hits followed.

This data has two caveats. The first is that the relevant information for people may be the list of references itself. For example, people who wish to see how many links there are to their home page may search on their own name just to calculate this number. The second caveat is that these numbers may be skewed by the number of hits returned by each service. Thus, while InfoSeek has nearly 6% of its results followed, only a total of 13,045 references returned by InfoSeek were followed, compared with the 24913 references followed that were contributed by Lycos, which on average had only 2.5% of its 19 hits examined.

Table 7:   Relevance of Returned Hits by Service

	% of Hits Returned that are Followed	Total Hits Followed
InfoSeek	5.89	13,045
Lycos	2.56	24,913
Open Text	2.51	4,025
WebCrawler	2.42	21,631
Yahoo	1.33	7,503
Galaxy	0.83	12,022

This table shows the percentage of followed hits for each service. References returned by multiple services are counted multiple times. Column 2 shows the actual number of references followed for each service. These numbers are out of 50,878 queries, except Open Text which is out of 19,951 queries.

Performance

Finally, we measure each service's response time. Table 8 summarizes our findings. Although not surprised, we were disappointed to find that average times vary from just under 10 seconds to just under 20. The percent of time the services timed out is under 5% for all services except Open Text, which is the newest and presumably still going through some growing pains. One explanation for the length of times taken by these services is that the majority of requests are during peak hours. Thus, results are naturally skewed towards the times when the services are most loaded. Times during non-peak hours are much lower.

Related Work

Unifying several databases under one interface is far from novel. Many companies, such as PLS [21], Lexis-Nexis [14], and Verity [30] have invested several years and substantial capital creating systems that can handle and integrate heterogeneous databases. Likewise, with the emergence of many Internet search services, there have been many different efforts to create single interfaces to the sundry databases. Perhaps the most widely distributed is CUSI [18], the Configurable Unified Search Index, which is a large form which allows users to select one service at a time and query that service. There are also several other services much like CUSI, such as the All-in-One Search Page [2], or W3 Search Engine list [19]. Unfortunately, while the user has many services on these lists from which to choose, there is no parallelism or collation. The user must submit queries to each service individually, although this task is made easier by having form interfaces to the various services on one page.

Table 8:   Performance of Services

	Ave. Time (sec)	% Timed Out
WebCrawler	9.64	2.30
InfoSeek	12.30	3.01
Open Text	16.26	14.13
Yahoo	18.32	2.28
Lycos	18.99	4.87
Galaxy	19.52	3.10

This table shows the average time in seconds taken by each service to fulfill a query. The second column gives the percent of time that the service would time out, or fail to return any hits under one minute.

The Harvest system [6] has many similarities to the MetaCrawler; however, rather than using existing databases as they are and post-processing the information returned, Harvest uses "Gatherers" to index information and "Brokers" to provide different interfaces to extract this information. However, while Harvest may have many different interfaces to many different internal services, it is still a search service like Lycos and WebCrawler, instead of a meta-service like MetaCrawler.

There are also other parallel Web search services. Sun Microsystems supports a very primitive service [27], and IBM has recently announced infoMarket [11] which, rather than integrating similar services with different coverage, integrates quite different services, such as DejaNews [26], a USENET news search service, McKinley [29], a clone of Yahoo with some editorial ratings on various pages, in addition to Open Text and Yahoo.

The closest work to the MetaCrawler is SavvySearch [3], an independently created multithreaded search service released in May 1995. SavvySearch has a larger repertoire of search services, although some are not WWW resource services, such as Roget's Thesaurus. SavvySearch's main focus is categorizing users' queries, and sending them to the most appropriate subset of its known services [4].

Like the MetaCrawler, the Internet Softbot [8] is a meta-service that leverages existing services and collates their results. The Softbot enables a human user to state what he or she wants accomplished. The Softbot attempts to disambiguate the request and to dynamically determine how and where to satisfy it, using a wide range of Internet services. Unlike the MetaCrawler, which focuses on indices and keyword queries, the Softbot accesses structured services such as Netfind and databases such as Inspec. The Softbot explicitly represents the semantics of the services, enabling it to chain together multiple services in response to a user request. The Softbot uses automatic planning technology to dynamically generate the appropriate sequence of service accesses. While the MetaCrawler and the Softbot rely on radically different technologies, the vision driving both systems is the same. Both seek to provide an expressive and integrated interface to Internet services.

Future Work

We are investigating how the MetaCrawler will scale to use new services. Of particular importance is how to collate results returned from different types of Internet indices, such as USENET news and Web pages. Also important is determining useful methods for interacting with specialized databases, such as the Internet Movie Database [28]. If the information requested is obviously located on some special purpose databases, than it does not make sense to query each and every service. We are investigating methods that will enable the MetaCrawler to determine which services will return relevant data based solely on the query text and other data provided by the user.

Future Design

The existing MetaCrawler prototype can cause a substantial network load when it attempts to verify a large number of pages. While one query by itself is no problem, multiple queries occurring at the same time can cause the system and network to bog down. However, with the emergence of universally portable Internet-friendly languages, such as Java [10] or Magic Cap [25], load problems can be lessened by having users' machines take on the workload needed to perform their individual query, as discussed in Section 2.2. The JavaCrawler, a prototype next generation MetaCrawler written in Java, supports most of the features already present in the MetaCrawler. However, instead of users running queries on one central service, each user has a local copy of the JavaCrawler and uses that copy to directly send queries to services. The load caused by verification will be taken by the user's machine, rather than the central server. This has the added benefit of inserting downloaded pages into the local cache, making retrieval of those pages nearly instantaneous. The JavaCrawler is loaded automatically from the MetaCrawler home page when visited with a Java-compatible browser.

Impact on Search Service Providers

We anticipate that a wide range of meta-services like the MetaCrawler will emerge over the next few years. However, it is uncertain what the relationship between these meta-services and search service providers will be. We envision that this relationship will hinge on what form the "information economy" used by service providers takes. The following sections discuss two different models.

Charge-per-access

In the charge-per-access model, service providers benefit from any access to their database. Info-Seek has already taken this model with their commercial service. InfoSeek is financially rewarded regardless of who or what sends a query to their commercial database. Many other databases, both on and off the Web, also use this model.

The MetaCrawler fits in well with this model. Since service providers benefit from any access, the added exposure generated by the Meta-Crawler is to their advantage. Furthermore, this model creates an implicit sanity check on the claims this paper makes on the use of its features. In order for the MetaCrawler, or any meta-service, to survive in such an economy, it must charge more per transaction than the underlying services, as the MetaCrawler will in turn have to pay each service for its information. Thus, users must be willing to pay the premium for the service. By voting with their pocketbook, they can determine if those features are truly desirable.

Advertising

In the advertising model, service providers benefit from sponsors who in turn gain benefit from exposure provided by the service. Nearly all major search services that do not charge users directly have adopted this model, as have many other unrelated services which are heavily accessed.

Under this model, the providers' relationship with the MetaCrawler can become problematic as the MetaCrawler filters away superfluous information such as advertisements. One promising method to ensure profitable co-existence is to use provider-created interfaces. Providers could create an interface for the MetaCrawler to access their service which, in addition to returning relevant hits, also returns the appropriate advertisement. Another solution involves the MetaCrawler accepting advertisements, and forming a profit-sharing relationship with the service providers. We are currently investigating these and other methods of mutually beneficial co-existence with service providers.

Conclusion

In this paper we have presented the MetaCrawler, a meta-service for Web searching with additional features designed to return more references of higher quality than standard search services. We demonstrated that users follow references reported by a variety of different search services, confirming that a single service is not sufficient (Table 2). Furthermore, due to the expressive power of the MetaCrawler's interface, the MetaCrawler was able to automatically determine that up to 75% of the hits returned can be discarded. Finally, the performance benchmarks and usage logs also show that the features provided by the MetaCrawler are both reasonably fast and actually used in practice.

The MetaCrawler provides a "Consumer Reports" of sorts for Web searchers. The individual service data extracted from the MetaCrawler's logs is compelling evidence concerning the quality of each service. By comparing services using the same query text and recording what links users follow, we are able to evaluate the services from a user's point of view. As far as we know, we are the first to quantitatively compare the search services used by MetaCrawler on a large sample of authentic user queries.

While it is possible that some MetaCrawler features could be integrated into the search services, others are intrinsic to meta-services. By definition, only a meta-service can provide the coverage gained by using multiple services. Also, as argued earlier, client-side meta-services can offer user and site customizations, and absorb the load caused by post-processing of search results. Finally, there are some features that do not belong under control of search services for purely pragmatic reasons. For example, as more commercial search services become available, tools will emerge that select which services to use on the basis of cost. An impartial meta-service such as the MetaCrawler avoids the conflict of interest that would arise if such a tool were offered by one of the commercial services.

New Web services are constantly being created. As the number and variety of services grows, it is natural to group existing services under one umbrella. The MetaCrawler goes further than merely organizing services by creating an integrated *meta-service* that moves the interface (and the associated computational load) closer to the user. We believe that this trend of moving up the information "food chain" will continue. The MetaCrawler is one of the first popular meta-services, but many more will follow. ∎

Acknowledgments

The research presented in this paper could not have been accomplished without the help of many individuals. We would like to thank Mary Kaye Rodgers, for editing assistance and for putting up with late nights. Ruth Etzioni and Ellen Spertus provided comments on an earlier draft. Dan Weld, Rich Segal, Keith Golden, George Forman, and Donald Chinn were very vocal and active in testing the early prototypes of the MetaCrawler, and Craig Horman and Nancy Johnson Burr were extremely helpful and patient in dealing with it when it ran amok. Lara Lewis was very helpful in finding references upon demand. The Internet Softbot group provided early insight into desirable features of the MetaCrawler, and Brian Bershad and Hank Levy contributed ideas relating to the impact the MetaCrawler could have on the Web. Ken Waln aided in early development for his form patches to the WWW C library, and Lou Montulli helped in later development by unlocking the secrets of nph scripts and Netscape caching. MetaCrawler development was supported by gifts from US West and Rockwell International Palo Alto Research. Etzioni's Softbot research is supported by Office of Naval Research grant 92-J-1946 and by National Science Foundation grant IRI-9357772.

References

1. InfoSeek Corporation. InfoSeek Home Page.
   http://www.infoseek.com

2. William Cross. All-In-One Internet Search Page.
   http://www.albany.net/~wcross/all1srch.html

3. Daniel Dreilinger. Savvy Search Home Page.
   http://www.cs.colostate.edu/~dreiling/smart-form.html

4. Daniel Dreilinger. Integrating Heterogeneous WWW Search Engines, May 1995.
   ftp://132.239.54.5/savvy/report.ps.gz

5. EINet. Galaxy Home Page.
   http://galaxy.einet.net/galaxy.html

6. C. Mic Bowman et al., "Harvest: A Scalable, Customizable Discovery and Access System." *Technical Report CU-CS-732-94*, Department of Computer Science, University of Colorado, Boulder, Colorado, March 1995.
   http://harvest.cs.colorado.edu/harvest/papers.html

7. Michael Schwartz et al., WWW Home Pages Harvest Broker.
   http://town.hall.org/Harvest/brokers/www-home-pages/

8. O. Etzioni and D. Weld, "A Softbot-Based Interface to the Internet." *CACM*, 37(7):72-76, July 1994.
   http://www.cs.washington.edu/research/softbots

9. David Filo and Jerry Yang, Yahoo Home Page.
   http://www.yahoo.com

10. James Gosling and Henry McGilton, "The Java Language Environment: A White Paper."
    http://java.sun.com/whitePaper/javawhitepaper_1.html

11. IBM, Inc. infoMarket Search Home Page.
    http://www.infomkt.ibm.com

12. IBM, Inc. Query By Image Content Home Page.
    http://wwwqbic.almaden.ibm.com/~qbic/qbic.html

13. Martijn Koster, "Robots in the Web: Threat or Treat?" *ConneXions*, 9(4), April 1995.

14. LEXIS-NEXIS. LEXIS-NEXIS Communication Center.
    http://www.lexis-nexis.com

15. Michael Mauldin. Lycos Home Page.
    http://lycos.cs.cmu.edu

16. Michael L. Mauldin and John R. R. Leavitt, "Web Agent Related Research at the Center for Machine Translation," *Proceedings of SIGNIDR V*, McLean, Virginia, August 1994.

17. Max Metral, *Helpful Online Music Recommendation Service*
    http://rg.media.mit.edu/ringo/ringo.html

18. Nexor. CUSI (Configurable Universal Search Interface).
    http://pubweb.nexor.co.uk/public/cusi/cusi.html

19. University of Geneva. W3 Search Engines.
    http://cuiwww.unige.ch/meta-index.html

20. Open Text, Inc. Open Text Web Index Home Page.
    http://www.opentext.com:8080/omw/f-omw.html

21. Personal Library Software, Inc. Personal Library Software Home Page.
    http://www.pls.com

22. Brian Pinkerton. WebCrawler Home Page.
    http://webcrawler.com

23. Brian Pinkerton, "Finding What People Want: Experiences with the WebCrawler," *Proceedings of the Second World Wide Web Conference '94: Mosaic and the Web*, Chicago IL USA, October 1993.

24. Brandon Plewe, The Virtual Tourist Home Page.
    http://wings.buffalo.edu/world

25. Daniel Sears, Guide to CodeWarrior Magic/MPW. Development Release 1
    http://www.genmagic.com/MagicCapDocs/CodeWarriorMagic/introduction.html, May 1995.

26. DejaNews Research Service, DejaNews Home Page.
    http://www.dejanews.com

27. Sun Microsystems, Inc. Multithreaded Query Page,
    http://www.sun.com/cgi-bin/show?search/mtquery/index.body

28. The Internet Movie Database Team, The Internet Movie Database.
    http://www.msstate.edu

29. The McKinley Group, Inc. Magellan: McKinley's Internet Directory.
    http://www.mckinley.com

30. Verity, Inc. Verity Home Page.
    http://www.verity.com

About the Authors

Erik Selberg

[*http://www.cs.washington.edu/homes/selberg*]
Department of Computer Science and
Engineering
Box 352350
University of Washington
Seattle, WA 98195
selberg@cs.washington.edu

Erik Selberg is pursuing his Ph.D. in computer science at the University of Washington. His primary research area involves World Wide Web search, although he also has interests regarding system performance and security as well as multi-agent coordination and planning. In April, 1995 he created the MetaCrawler, a parallel Web search meta-service. He graduated from Carnegie Mellon University in 1993 with a double major in computer science and logic, and received the first Allen Newell Award for Excellence in Undergraduate Research.

Oren Etzioni

[*http://www.cs.washington.edu/homes/etzioni*]
Department of Computer Science and
Engineering
Box 352350
University of Washington
Seattle, WA 98195
etzioni@cs.washington.edu

Oren Etzioni received his bachelor's degree in computer science from Harvard University in June 1986, and his Ph.D. from Carnegie Mellon University in January 1991. He joined the University of Washington as assistant professor of computer science and engineering in February 1991. In the fall of 1991, he launched the Internet Softbots project. In 1993, Etzioni received an NSF Young Investigator Award. In 1995, Etzioni was chosen as one of 5 finalists in the Discover Awards for Technological Innovation in Computer Software for his work on Internet Softbots.

His research interests include: software agents, machine learning, and human-computer interaction.

About This Document

Multiservice Search and Comparison Using the MetaCrawler

This document was generated using the **LaTeX2HTML** translator Version 95.1 (Fri Jan 20 1995). Copyright © 1993, 1994, Nikos Drakos, Computer Based Learning Unit, University of Leeds.

The command-line arguments were:

`latex2html -split 0 www4-final.tex`.

The translation was initiated by Erik Selberg on Mon Oct 9 17:24:12 PDT 1995.

DB

Browsing Object-Oriented Databases over the Web

C. Varela, D. Nekhayev, P. Chandrasekharan, C. Krishnan,
V. Govindan, D. Modgil, S. Siddiqui, D. Lebedenko, M. Winslett

Abstract

In this paper, we present critical issues that arise when users browse object-oriented databases over the World Wide Web, and performance results for the Database Browser (DB) implementation. Initially, given the statelessness of HTTP, we introduced a dispatcher-script architecture. In this architecture, a CGI script communicates with an intermediate data server connected to the database application, which keeps the database open for faster future transactions. Second, we used ODL, a standard object-definition language, and defined a simple intermediate data format for moving database objects across the network. Lastly, we defined generic hypertext interfaces for five distinct purposes: a database schema, a class definition, a class query form, a class extent, and a set of class instances. Our implementation used ObjectStore and two database applications: university registration and electronic mailboxes. The DB architecture provided dramatic improvements in performance. **Keywords:** *World Wide Web, object-oriented databases, dispatcher scripts, ObjectStore, Object Definition Language, Common Gateway Interface*

Introduction

Six years after its conception in 1989, the World Wide Web is arguably the most popular and powerful networked information system to date. Its growth in the past years has been exponential and it has started an information revolution that will probably continue to take place until the beginning of the next century. The database world with barely 25 years as a basic science research field [18] is by no means less interesting. Needless to say, the combination of networked information systems and database worlds provide new opportunities for creating advanced information-management applications.

In this paper, we present critical issues that arise when users browse object-oriented databases over the Web. In particular, we present the following topics:

- A dispatcher-script architecture that answers traditional Web requests in a stateless fashion, and improves performance by keeping the database application running across several transactions

- A simple intermediate data-exchange format

- Generic hypertext interfaces to object-oriented databases

We implemented two exemplary applications: a university course registration system and an electronic mailbox manager. On the WWW server side, we used C/Lex/Yacc for the dispatcher script and NCSA HTTPd [11], a high-performance HTTP server. On the database server side, we used C++ and ObjectStore [9], an object-oriented database-management system, with a page-server architecture. A remarkable result was the performance improvement gained by incorporating the dispatcher script architecture, as opposed to opening and closing the database server in every transaction.

The structure of this paper is as follows: in the second section, "Background and Related Work," we give some background information and introduce related work. In the third section, we describe our Database Browser (DB) architecture. The fourth section, "ObjectStore Examples and Performance Evaluation," shows two object-oriented Web database applications in action and presents some performance results. This paper concludes with result highlights and discussion of further research issues.

Background and Related Work

The World Wide Web

The World Wide Web [3, 4], offers easy access to a universe of information by providing links to documents stored on a worldwide network of computers in a very simple and understandable fashion. Much of the Web's success is due to the simplicity with which it allows users to provide, use, and reference information distributed geographically around the globe.

Another important feature is the Web's compatibility with other existing protocols, such as gopher, ftp, netnews and telnet. Furthermore, it provides users with the ability to browse multimedia documents independently of the computer hardware being used.

The World Wide Web consists of a network of computers which can act in two roles: as servers providing information; or as clients requesting information. Examples of server software are NCSA HTTPd [11] and Netscape Communication Server [13], while examples of client software are NCSA Mosaic [12] and Netscape Navigator [14].

The World Wide Web is based on the HyperText Transfer Protocol (HTTP), the HyperText Markup Language (HTML,) and Universal Resource Locators (URLs.)

- **The Hypertext Transfer Protocol**

  The HyperText Transfer Protocol defines how servers and clients communicate. HTTP is a generic object-oriented stateless protocol for transmitting information between servers and clients [1].

- **The Hypertext Markup Language**

  The HyperText Markup Language defines what is generally transmitted between nodes

in the network. HTML is a simple, yet powerful, platform-independent document language [2].

- **Universal Resource Locators**

  Universal Resource Locators provide a unique definition of where documents can be found. URLs compose the address space of documents in the Web.

Databases in the Web

When the documents to be published are dynamic, such as those resulting from queries to databases, the hypertext needs to be generated by the servers. For such instances, there are scripts, which are programs that perform conversions from different data formats into HTML on-the-fly. These programs also need to understand the queries performed by clients through HTML forms and the results generated by the applications owning the data (for example, a DataBase Manager System.)

- **Common Gateway Interface**

  The Common Gateway Interface [10] defines how these scripts communicate with the HTTP servers. By using the interface, we can reuse CGI-compliant scripts without regard to the server software providing information.

- **WAIS indexes and relational DBMS**

  A traditional searching mechanism in the Web is performed by WAIS [8] gateways. These are text-based indexes that allow keyword-based searches.

  Several attempts at integrating relational database management systems have been made, including GSQL [15], MORE [7], and Zelig [20, 21].

- **Object-Oriented DBMS and stateful transactions**

  A more interesting, but less explored, field is that of interacting with object-oriented data-

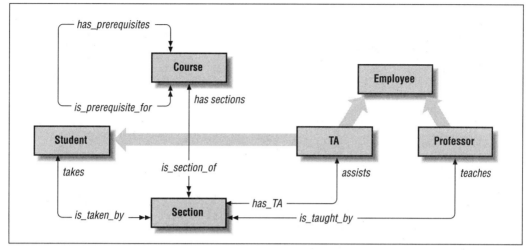

Figure 1:   University database schema

base management systems. [19] describes a front-end to LINCKS.

One desired feature is being able to use a stateful connection with the database for performance. But since HTTP is stateless, there is a need for an intermediate dispatcher script, or translation server. Some authors ([16, 17], have described their work on interacting stateful information services with the WWW.

Object Definition Language

For defining the database schemas, we used the Object Definition Language (ODL) developed by the Object Database Management Group (ODMG) and specified in [6]. The ODL specification conforms to the Object Data model, characterized by the following basic features:

- An object is the basic model constructional unit.

- Objects with the same structure can belong to one type.

- An object is characterized by its set of properties (attributes and relationships to other objects).

- An object can have a set of operations which is analogous to member functions in object-oriented languages.

- The ODL Object model supports multiple inheritance.

As an example, the Professor class in Figure 1 would be represented in ODL as follows:

```
interface Professor: Employee {
    extent professors;
    keys name, id;

    attribute string name;
    attribute int id;
    attribute string rank;

    relationship Set<Section> teaches
    inverse Section::is_taught_by;
    grant_tenure() raises (ineligible_
    for_tenure);
}
```

We refer the interested reader to the complete University schema with all classes as defined in Cattell's book. We have also annexed our ODL specification for the Electronic Mailbox schema.

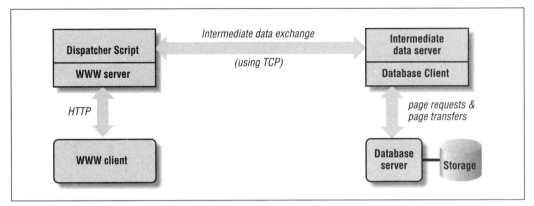

Figure 2:   Database Browser architecture

Database Browser Architecture

In the first version of our hypertext interface to the object databases, the database was accessed through CGI scripts which would, at each instance, open the database, process the request, and close the database. We found that this sequence of operations was extremely time-consuming and produced very slow responses.

We reasoned that this slow response was due to the fact that ObjectStore has a page-fault model with prefetch. Thus, every time the database is opened, the pages containing the data are brought into memory and the pointers are swizzled. Under regular circumstances, this paging activity would only be a one-time startup overhead and the subsequent database operations would be very fast. But, since the CGI scripts are stateless (in the sense that they cease to exist after the operation is performed), this overhead was being incurred on every database request. Each request entailed a separate "open database, perform operation, close database" sequence. We were consequently losing the performance gains of the paging model adopted by ObjectStore.

In our next and current version, we adopted the database browser architecture as illustrated in Figure 2. The main components of this architecture are the dispatcher script, the intermediate data server, and the simple intermediate

exchange format. Each component is discussed separately in the following subsections.

Dispatcher Script

The dispatcher program is a CGI script which provides a user-friendly interface to query the intermediate data server and returns the database schema, extent, and object data to the WWW browser. Separating this dispatcher from the intermediate data server is beneficial for several reasons. First, the separation allows us to keep the intermediate data server active even when the transaction is over, thereby increasing transaction performance increases significantly. Second, this architecture provides more flexibility for customizing the whole application. The database side can be changed without causing any interference with the user interface. On the other hand, the interface itself can be customized without affecting the database server.

The dispatcher script consists of the following modules:

Request manager
> Determines the type of the query and references the appropriate routine.

Parser for the ODL schema
> Parses the ODL schema [6] into a generic structure, suitable for handling any ODL

schema. This part was implemented using lex and yacc.

Formatter of the query string

Constructs the query string in the intermediate query format for the database server.

Data parser

Parses server data from the intermediate data format into a generic data structure. Hashing shortens the response to searches of each appropriate field of the structure.

Data and extent display

Provides representation of the object contents in HTML form. This part not only displays data, but also creates hyperlinks to related objects, superclasses, etc., in the same format as in the actual queries.

Schema display

Handles the display of the schema of a particular class or shows all the classes with links to extent, query, or schema page.

Query page

Handles the display of the page containing the query form for each particular class.

Client routine

Makes a connection with the database server, sends the query, and accepts the result stream from the server for utilization by other routines.

An Intermediate Data Server

The main characteristic of the intermediate data server is that it remains alive across multiple requests and thereby eliminates the earlier problem of the script ceasing to exist after every operation.

The data server was designed to use the standard BSD sockets and to listen on a predetermined port for requests. Whenever the dispatcher script gets a request, it connects to the data server which is listening for requests and sends the request in the simple intermediate data-exchange format described in the following section. The

server performs the database operation and sends back the results using the same connection to the dispatcher script. The dispatcher script in turn parses the results and converts them to HTML. They are then forwarded by the Web server to the browser.

Thus, the high startup overhead occurs only on the first database operation (which we term as cold time). Subsequent operations are relatively very fast (termed as warm time).

The server also keeps a queue of requests and, therefore, multiple simultaneous requests are handled serially by the server. The same server can also be used to handle operations on multiple databases. This ability is achieved through the liberal use of lookup tables to perform name-to-object and name-to-function translations.

A Simple Intermediate Data Exchange Format

The intermediate object-exchange format is used for communication between the CGI dispatcher script and the intermediate data server. The format has two parts: query format and data format.

Query format

- **Open-close request**

  open database:

      `database_name;DBOPEN`

  close database:

      `database_name;DBCLOSE`

  The database server opens the database in response to any data request.

- **Schema request**

  This is used to get the schema from the server.

      `database_name;SCHEMA`

  The ODL schema for the database is in a separate file; the server does not open the database in response to this request.

- **Extent request**

      `database_name;EXTENT`

- **Instance request**

  This request is based on key values:

  ```
  database_
  name;INSTANCE;class=class_
  name(&key_name=value_name)+
  ```

  If the key is a composite key, there is a sequence of strings of the form &key_name=value_name.

- **Query request**

  This request is based on attribute or relationship values:

  ```
  database_
  name;QUERY;class=class_
  name(&property_
  name=property_value)*
  ```

  Here again, (member)* designates zero or more strings of type member.

Data format

For many of the object-oriented databases, the data format described here is sufficient. This format is based on attribute-value pairs. In principle, the format can be augmented to fit multimedia data. However, we have only used data in text or numerical format. In such cases, attribute-value pairs are a natural intermediate representation.

As a response to a query, the database server can return several objects. In our format we use the line

```
%#%
```

as a delimiter between successive objects. The format for an object looks as follows:

```
attribute_1_name: attribute_1_value
attribute_2_name: attribute_2_value
.

.

attribute_n_name: attribute_n_value
relationship_1_traversal_path: target_
    instance_1_keys
target_instance_2_keys
.

.

target_instance_n_keys
```

```
relationship_2_traversal_path: target_
    instance_1_keys
.

.
```

As shown, attributes are given colon-separated name-value pairs. Attribute values can be complex text with newlines, special symbols, etc. Ambiguities may occur when the text of the attribute value at the beginning of a line coincides with the following attribute name. The intermediate data server resolves this special case by inserting a space immediately after the newline.

We assume that the key value is a simple string or number which cannot have colons, commas, spaces or newlines. The value part of a relationship-value pair is a newline-separated list of keys of all target instances. Each element of this list is a comma-separated list of all the keys of a particular target instance.

In case of EXTENT queries, the intermediate data server returns the data in a brief format containing only the keys to instances.

Generic Hypertext Interfaces to OODBs

The dispatcher script has five different presentation screens to represent database schemas, query forms and actual data. A description of each appears below.

Introduction format

The main purpose of the introduction format is to show the names of all the classes in the database schema. Each class name is a hyperlink to the schema format for that particular class. Additionally, there are three buttons for each class: SCHEMA, which does the same job as the above-mentioned hyperlink; EXTENT, which is a request button for all instances of this class (presents only if extent is in the class definition); and QUERY, which invokes the query form for the class. The CLOSEDB button at the bottom serves to close the database explicitly.

Class schema

This format represents the schema of a particular class, and has the following fields:

- Superclasses—List of all immediate parents of the class. All names are hyperlinks to corresponding superclass.
- Subclasses—List of all immediate children of the class. All names are hyperlinks to the corresponding derived classes.
- Keys—List of all keys. As we noted before, keys can be inherited.
- Attributes—List of class attributes. No inherited attributes are shown.
- Relationships—List of traversal path names.
- Operations—List of operation names.

Additionally, this page contains the EXTENT and QUERY buttons at the top.

Query form

The query form consists of two main parts: a set of attribute entry fields and the result filtering specification. By default, the result returns all attributes and relationships of any particular class. The user can filter the information by marking the corresponding checkbox.

Data-browsing format

This page contains all user-specified fields of matching objects of a given class. We present a list of keys of each target object with a hyperlink to the object itself. This format does not show inherited properties if they are not keys. The hyperlink with superclass name allows us to browse the superclass.

Extent format

This has a compact representation for displaying the extent of a class in which instances are indicated by a comma-separated list of object keys. These keys have hyperlinks to request the complete instance.

ObjectStore Examples and Performance Evaluation

University Course Registration System

This database was built using the example ODL schema given in the ODMG-93 book. This example demonstrates how an object database specified in ODL can be browsed in a generic manner and how one could build a hypertext interface to navigate through the database. The university database exemplifies many of the concepts specific to object-oriented databases like inheritance, operation functions, inverse relationships, exceptions, multiple inheritance, etc.

The database objects are the typical entities in a university as illustrated in the schema diagram and ODL specifications given in the subsection on ODL. To run this example, please proceed to the University Schema presentation page.

Electronic Mailbox Manager

This database was created to hold regular email, with particular emphasis on huge mailboxes. The database mainly consists of two basic objects: the message object and the folder object. One can associate multiple messages to one folder, and one a message to multiple folders. A parser was written to parse a regular mail folder and put it into the database. This database was created to evaluate the performance of the browser with huge databases and to provide a hypertext interface to a real-world application. To run this example, please proceed to the Mailbox Schema presentation page.

Performance Evaluation

We instrumented the server to obtain the time spent on the various operations. We measured the performance by recording the time required to perform various operations in different scenarios, as described below:

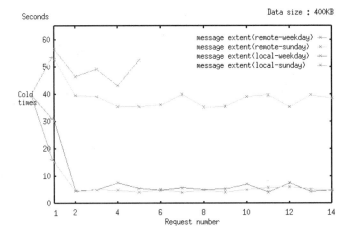

Figure 3:   Message extent in the mailbox database: (Large database, large results)

Cold versus Warm time

Cold time is the time taken for the first request. The first request causes the database to be opened, the data to be paged in, and the pointers to be swizzled. Warm time is the time taken to perform subsequent requests. In subsequent cases, the data is already in memory. We performed this scenario to measure the savings obtained by having the data server (which keeps the database open across multiple requests).

Remote versus Local request

By remote, we mean a physically distant machine. We obtained the time taken for queries made from a local machine (within the university campus) and a machine in Japan connected to the Internet through a 64 Kbps link. We performed this scenario to observe the effect of the network on the times.

Large versus Small database

This scenario was performed to observe the effect of the size of the database on performance. A large database occupies many more pages than a small one, and can greatly affect paging, swizzling etc.

Large versus Small result

This scenario was performed to observe the effect of the size of the query result on the times.

Sunday versus Weekday

We performed this to observe the effect of network traffic and machine load on the timings.

All the times were taken for a single user performing queries. We did not measure the performance with multiple, simultaneous requests.

The results of the performance measurements are summarized in the following three figures.

In this scenario, the size of the result (about 400 KB) causes quite a big difference in the times, especially in the remote case. We feel that the network overhead (congestion, packetizing, etc.) contributes to a major part of the time taken. The slow speed of the link (64 Kbps) in the remote case could also be a major cause for the delay, so a user over a phone line would get an even slower response.

We thus conclude that network delays are certainly a factor to be considered, especially for large query results.

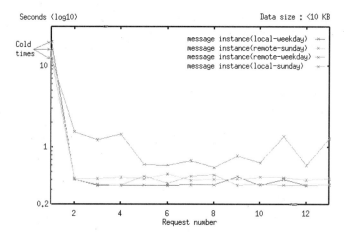

Figure 4: Message instance in the mailbox database: (Large database, small results)

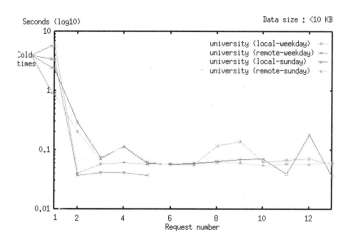

Figure 5: University database: (Small database, small results)

In this scenario, the network did not seem to play any significant role as in the earlier case. This could be attributed to the small size of the query results (< 10 KB). The cold times are still significant as the database itself is large and, therefore, a lot of pages need to be brought into memory at startup.

In this case, the time taken is really small as the query results are very small. Even the cold time is quite small since the database itself is very small

and hence, very few data pages would need to be paged in.

We also observed that closing the database does not actually result in a subsequent request taking a "cold time." This result, we concluded, was because ObjectStore has a page server model which means that even when the database is closed, the data pages are still in memory and are not reclaimed unless the data of some other application is paged into the same place.

Conclusion

In this paper, we presented an architecture for browsing object-oriented databases over the World Wide Web. This architecture consists mainly of a CGI dispatcher script, an intermediate data server, a simple intermediate data format for communicating between these two modules, and generic hypertext interfaces for browsing different database elements. We found remarkable performance improvements by using this Database Browser architecture.

- The main reasoning behind our architecture is that opening an object-oriented database is a time-consuming process that we didn't want to repeat in every database transaction. Furthermore, HTTP is a stateless protocol. As a consequence, we needed to introduce new modules that answer database requests in a stateless fashion, yet guarantee that the database stays open for future requests. These modules are the CGI dispatcher script in the WWW side and the intermediate data server in the database side. We believe that future information-providing servers will pass requests to specialized servers such as video servers, annotation servers, database servers, link servers, etc.

- Furthermore, we defined a simple intermediate data format for exchanging information in a generic manner between the dispatcher script and the intermediate data server. We found five basic object-oriented database components: a database schema, a class definition, a class query form, a class extent, and a set of class instances. Then, based on these fundamental components, we defined a format with which the CGI script could query the server for each of these elements, as well as a format with which the data server could return these elements to the script. Finally, we composed five generic hypertext interfaces to these database elements, to present them to the clients.

- We implemented two database applications using ObjectStore: a university registration system and an electronic mailbox manager. These systems served as a testbed for our experiments.

There is a need for further work on additional query options, since ObjectStore doesn't currently support OQL, the ODMG standard for OODB queries. We would also like to investigate further presentation issues for huge databases, as well as multimedia object handling.

We didn't consider security issues that would be crucial in extending our database operations. Currently, we only concentrated in browsing databases. There is a lot of research that needs to be done in authentication and authorization for databases operating in an open environment. [8] is a good study of some of these security issues. They present a role wrapper-based framework, that assigns roles to clients and controls their database access according to these roles.

We believe that there is a need for more research and development in advancing the state-of-the-art in performance and security for connecting databases to the World Wide Web. There are many applications that could benefit from this research including bibliographic databases, financial management systems, intelligent agents, data-mining applications, and countless others. ■

Acknowledgments

We would like to thank Dan Laliberte at NCSA for setting up our HyperNews project page; Mike Jerger for letting us use bunny, the database answering machine; Simon Kaplan for allowing us to use ObjectStore; International Systems Research, Tokyo and UMDS, Kobe for providing partial support to the first author; and last but not least, the WWW Organizing Committee for granting us a small extension to submit this paper.

References

1. Berners-Lee T. The Hypertext Transfer Protocol. World Wide Web Consortium. Work in progress. Available at *http://www.w3.org/hypertext/WWW/Protocols/Overview.html*

2. Berners-Lee T., and Connolly D. The Hypertext Markup Language. World Wide Web Consortium. Work in progress. Available at *http://www.w3.org/hypertext/WWW/MarkUp/MarkUp.html*

3. Berners-Lee T., Cailliau R., Groff J., Pollermann B. World Wide Web: The Information Universe. Electronic Networking: Research, Applications and Policy, 2(1), pp. 52-58, Meckler Publications, Westport CT, Spring 1992. Available in PostScript at *ftp://info.cern.ch/pub/www/doc/ENRAP_9202.ps*

4. Berners-Lee, T. Cailliau, R., Luotonen, A., Nielsen, H. F., Secret, A. The World Wide Web. Communication of the ACM. Volume 37, Number 8, August 1994.

5. Bina E., Jones V., McCool R., and Winslett M. Secure Access to Data Over the Internet. Proceedings of the Third ACM/IEEE International Conference on Parallel and Distributed Information Systems, Austin, Texas, September 1994. Available in PostScript at *http://bunny.cs.uiuc.edu/CADR/pubs/SecureDBAccess.ps*

6. Cattell, R.G.G., ed. The Object Database standard: ODMG-93, Release 1.1. San Mateo, CA: Morgan Kaufmann,1994. Information available at OMDG Welcome Page.

7. Eichmann, D., McGregor, T., Danley, D. Integrating Structured Databases into the Web: The MORE system. The First International Conference on the World Wide Web, May 25-27, 1994, CERN, Geneva. Available in PostScript at *http://www1.cern.ch/PapersWWW94/more.ps*

8. Kahle B., and Medlar A. An Information System for Corporate Users: Wide Area Information Servers. ConneXions—The Interoperability Report, 5(11), pp 2-9, Interop, Inc., Nov. 1991. Available at *http://www.w3.org/hypertext/Products/WAIS/Overview.html*

9. Lamb C., Landis G., Orenstein J., and Weinreb D. The ObjectStore Database System. Communication of the ACM. Volume 34, Number 10, October 1991, pp 50-63.

10. Rob McCool. National Center for Supercomputing Applications, University of Illinois at Urbana-Champaign. Common Gateway Interface Overview. Work in progress. Available at *http://hoohoo.ncsa.uiuc.edu/cgi/overview.html*

11. National Center for Supercomputing Applications, University of Illinois at Urbana-Champaign. NCSA HTTPd. A WWW Server. Work in progress. Available at *http://hoohoo.ncsa.uiuc.edu/docs/Overview.html*

12. National Center for Supercomputing Applications, University of Illinois at Urbana-Champaign. NCSA Mosaic. A WWW Browser. Work in progress. Available at *http://www.ncsa.uiuc.edu/SDG/Software/Mosaic/Docs/help-about.html*

13. Netscape Communications Corporation. Netscape Communications Server. A WWW Server. Work in progress. Available at *http://www.netscape.com/comprod/netscape_commun.html*

14. Netscape Communications Corporation. Netscape Navigator. A WWW Browser. Work in progress. Available at *http://www.netscape.com/comprod/netscape_nav.html*

15. J. Ng. GSQL: A Mosaic-SQL Gateway. National Center for Supercomputing Applications. University of Illinois at Urbana-Champaign. Work in progress. Available at *http://www.ncsa.uiuc.edu/SDG/People/jason/pub/gsql/back/starthere.html*

16. Perrochon, L. and Fischer R. IDLE: Unified W3-Access to Interactive Information Servers. The Third International Conference on the World Wide Web, April 10-14, 1995, Darmstadt, Germany. Available at *http://www.igd.fhg.de/www/www95/proceedings/papers/58/www95.html*

17. Putz, S. Interactive information services using World Wide Web hypertext. The First International Conference on the World Wide Web (WWW'95), May 25-27, 1994, CERN, Geneva. Available at *http://pubweb.parc.xerox.com/hypertext/www94/iisuwwwh.html*

18. Silberschatz A., Stonebraker M., Ullman J., eds. Database Systems: Achievements and Opportunities. Communication of the ACM. Volume 34, Number 10, October 1991, pp 110-120.

19. Sjolin M. A WWW Front End to an OODBMS. The Second International Conference on the World Wide Web, Oct 17-21, 1994, Chicago, Illinois, U.S.A. Available at *http://www.ncsa.uiuc.edu/SDG/IT94/Proceedings/Databases/sjolin/sjolin.html*

20. Varela C., and Hayes C. Zelig: Schema-based Generation of Soft WWW Database Applications. The First International Conference on the World Wide Web, May 25-27, 1994, CERN, Geneva, Switzerland. Available at *http://fiaker.ncsa.uiuc.edu:8080/WWW94.html* and in PostScript at *http://www1.cern.ch/PapersWWW94/cvarel.ps*

21. Varela C., and Hayes C. Providing Data on the Web: From Examples to Programs. The Second International Conference on the World Wide Web, Oct 17-21, 1994, Chicago, Illinois, U.S.A. Available at *http://www.ncsa.uiuc.edu/SDG/IT94/Proceedings/DDay/varela/paper.html*

About the Authors

C. Varela, D. Nekhayev, P. Chandrasekharan, C. Krishnan, V. Govindan, D. Modgil, S. Siddiqui, D. Lebedenko, M. Winslett

Department of Computer Science
1304 W. Springfield Ave
University of Illinois
Urbana, IL 61801. U.S.A.

{cvarela, d-nekha, p-chand, charuki, govindan, modgil, siddiqui, dlebeden, winslett}@uiuc.edu

TOWARD A NEW EDUCATIONAL ENVIRONMENT

Ming-Chih Lai, Bih-Horng Chen, Shyan-Ming Yuan

Abstract

There are two major problems when we first try to construct a campus wide educational environment on top WWW. First, interactions between teachers and students are basically one-way. Teachers put materials into the information store and students retrieve them. Secondly students often get lost when navigating in hypermedia documents. In order to improve the interaction between teachers and students, we make use of the existing communication facilities in Internet like electronic mail, text talk, and our newly designed communication facility, Notebook. In order to prevent students getting lost in hyperspace, we add two new navigation facilities to the current WWW system: Overview map and Guider. **Keywords:** *Notebook, overview map, guider*

Introduction

On our campus, using computer networks has become part of students' life. Students in our school can easily connect to the Internet with their personal computers by adding a simple network interface card. Every day students log in to obtain new information, to do their homework, or just to talk with others. With the growth of computer networks in our school, "How to use computer networks to make educational environment more efficient and better" becomes a new challenge we need to conquer. In order to find a new educational environment based on current computer network, we have started a new project called *Albatross*. In this project we want to derive a new educational environment in which:

- Teachers can easily edit their teaching materials and spread them quickly.

- Students can get teaching materials at any time and any place.

- Students can easily read through all the teaching materials.

- The interaction between teachers and students can be improved.

- Cooperative learning and cooperative teaching can be provided.

On the way to construct this new educational environment, we find that two primitives are necessary.

1. A good data model is needed to ease teachers' authoring and students' reading.

2. Proper communication facilities are needed to improve the interaction between teachers and students.

In our first design, we use WWW as our basic data model. WWW provides us with a very good hypermedia data model which can help teachers to organize their teaching materials and students to read through the whole documents. Because of the simplicity of HTML, teachers don't need any special skills to edit their teaching materials. Rich texts, graphics, movies, and animations can be used. As to communication facilities, we use electronic mail as an asynchronous communication way to connect people who are not online and use text-talk and chatroom as a synchronous communication way to connect people who are online.

However, there are some problems in our first design. We find that students are often lost in the hyperspace. The only navigation tool provided by WWW is a history-based mechanism. It seems not enough. In addition, many documents are missed by our students, because students don't know they exist. In order to solve these two problems, we design two new navigation tools: Overview map and Guider.

The communication facilities we adapt in our first design are electronic mail and text talk. They are all private and one-to-one. Teachers find that students always have the same problems about the same topic so that they have to answer the same questions frequently. We want our students to be able to share their experiences with others, so a communication facility, Notebook, is added.

In order to give students a friendly user interface, we redesign the interface of the original WWW client. Our new interface can reduce the operations that students need to make if they want to use our new facilities. In the following sections of this paper, we first give an overview of our new environment and an introduction of our new client. Then the three new facilities, Overview Map, Guider, and Notebook, are discussed in detail. Some concluding remarks then follow.

Overview of Our Educational Environment

Our educational environment is shown in Figure 1. In this new environment, students can make their own learning schedules. The role of a student changes from a passive listener to an active participant. Any time students want to learn, they can turn on their computer and execute our newly-designed client. Through our new client, they can get the learning materials provided by their teachers in the hypermedia form from the network server. Our new client also provides many new services. Overview map provides users a complete view of the whole course. Through the Overview Map, students can know the position of their current-reading document in the whole course. Students can directly access the document they want to read by just double-clicking the topic of the document in the Over-

view map. Another navigation facility is Guider. The main function of Guider is to help students read through all hypermedia documents smoothly. When students read the wrong documents, the Guider will give them the right documents they should read first. The knowledge about which documents should be pre-read is specified by the teachers.

In this environment, if students have any question about any topic, they can mail to their teachers or someone who has already read the topic via electronic mail systems. If students want to discuss some topic with some people, they can create a new chatroom or directly talk to someone who is online. If they have any conclusion or idea, they can post to our new facility, Notebook. Notebook is like a bulletin board on which everyone can post experiences for sharing. Students are encouraged to use Notebook, if they have any questions or ideas.

Guider, Overview Map, and Notebook are all implemented by CGI (Common Gateway Interface). Using CGI, we can easily add our new services. But we don't use the Fill-out Form to access our new services. We design new interface for our new services to save many wasted operations. The interface of our new client can be divided into three main panes: the right pane is WWW pane, the up-left pane is Overview Map pane, and the left-bottom pane is Notebook pane. Students can select any titles in the Overview Map pane or subjects in Notebook pane and show the data in the WWW pane. The size of these three panes is not fixed. Users can adjust the size of every pane by dragging the line-bar between panes. Since the computer monitor is too small to hold all information, the design enabled users to utilize the maximal monitor size to contain the information they are interested in.

Overview Map

The Overview Map is shown in Figure 2. The purpose of Overview Map is to give students a complete view of courses and to provide another way for students to access the documents in the

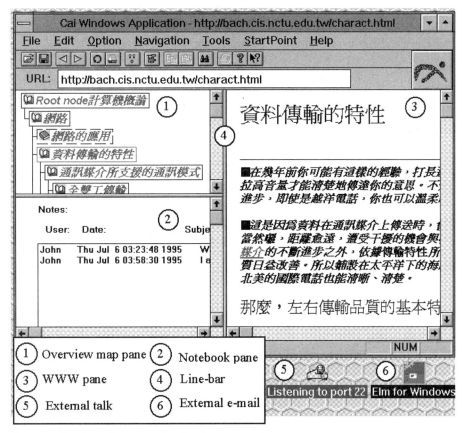

Figure 1: Overview of our new educational environment

site. In order to organize the whole documents of a course into a complete view, we provide another special link that is different from the WWW anchor. We call this kind of link an organization link. After connecting all relationships specified by organization links, a tree-link graph will appear. Organization link is like "the trunk of a tree." Teachers can use this link to construct the skeleton of their teaching materials. Because the graphic-architecture is too difficult to show in the current window system, our Overview Map is based on tree architecture instead of graph architecture.

The organization link is specified by two new HTML tags. The syntaxes of these two tags are:

- <PARENT HREF="URL"> is put in the child document to point out the parent document.

- <CHILD HREF="URL"> is put in the parent document to point out the child document.

When teachers edit their teaching materials, they can put these two special tags into the head of the HTML files. The Overview map will generate a tree structure by analyzing all tags of documents. The communication steps of Overview Map are as follows:

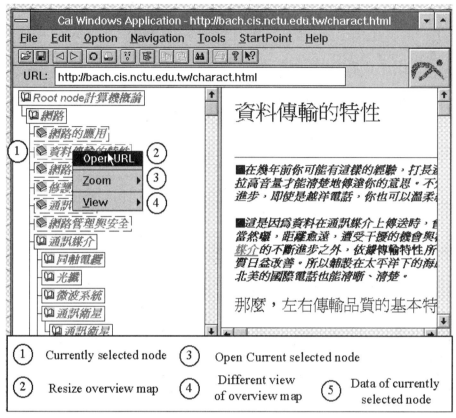

Figure 2:   Overview map

1. When users want to get the Overview Map of a course, the client invokes the Overview Map CGI program in the server.

2. The Overview Map CGI program analyzes every document that belongs to this course *on the fly* to construct the tree architecture.

3. The Overview Map CGI program translates the tree into the HTML unordered list and returns to the client.

4. The client analyzes the returned HTML to reconstruct the tree hierarchy.

In Step 3, we translate the tree architecture into the HTML unordered list to let other WWW browsers, like Mosaic and Netscape, use our Overview Map service. The Overview Map in Netscape is shown in Figure 3. The Overview Map by Netscape will disappear when users access other documents because Netscape has only one pane.

Guider

Guider is another navigation facility for preventing students from getting lost in hyperspace. Unlike other path control mechanisms of hypermedia, Guider doesn't directly influence the students' learning paths. It only works when students go to the wrong road. When a student turn on the Guider, the Guider will monitor learning path of the student. When students access the wrong documents, Guider will respond with some advice.

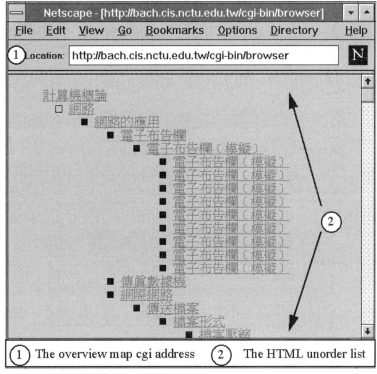

Figure 3:   Overview Map in Netscape

Figure 4 shows the basic idea about how Guider knows whether a student accesses the wrong documents or not. In the Guider, teachers can specify the pre-read documents of each document. If students want to read a particular document, all pre-read documents of the document must be accessed first. The pre-read link is another special link that is different from the original WWW anchor. The diagram constructed by all pre-read links must be acyclic. It is not natural to have a cyclic pre-read relationship. For example, if node A has a pre-read node B and node B has a pre-read node A, which one should we read first?

Because different students should have different learning schedules, Guider can let teachers design different learning schedules. For example, teachers can design three levels of learning schedules: novice, intermediate, and expert. The

three different levels are for different students according to their characteristics. Novices must read all the documents one by one; experts can skip many unnecessary documents.

Similarly, we provide another HTML tag for teachers to specify the pre-read relationship. The syntax of this tag is :

<PREREAD HREF="URL of pre-read document" LEVEL="level">

The HREF field is used to point out the address of pre-read documents. The LEVEL field is used to point out the level that should be applied.

Guider is implemented by CGI. The Guider CGI has two responsibilities. First, the CGI should keep records of the documents that the students have read. Second, if any request for a document comes in, the Guider CGI should check the pre-read documents of the requested document. If all

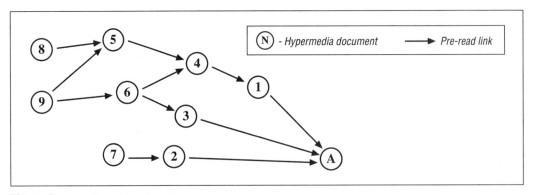

Figure 4:   Basic idea of Guider

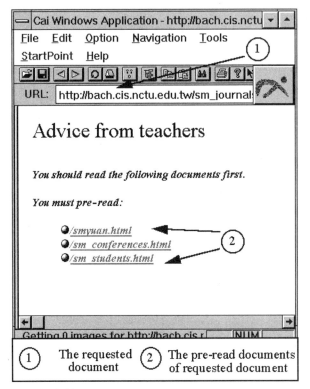

Figure 5:   Advice from the Guider

the pre-read documents on the level of the student who is requesting the document are read by the student, the Guider CGI returns the requested documents. Otherwise the Guider CGI returns a list of the pre-read documents that are not read by the students. Figure 5 give us a glance of the returned HTML when a student does not have the right to access his requested document.

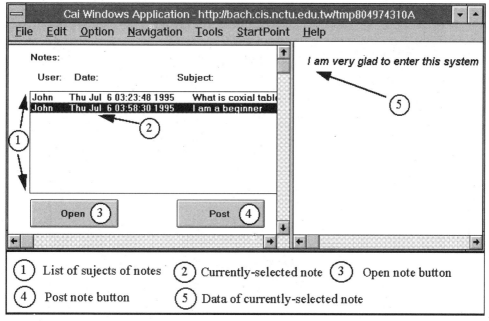

Figure 6: Notebook

Another advantage of Guider is that a teacher can design various learning schedules for different students. When designing a good path control mechanism in hypermedia, a designer often finds a conflict between the freedom of hypermedia and the strictness of his control mechanism. The freedom of hypermedia improves the organization ability of the students but can also get them lost in the hyperspace. By using the Guider, the freedom of hypermedia can be adjusted; teachers can design a very strict path to let students read documents one by one or can remove any limitation on the hyperspace.

Notebook

The purpose of Notebook is to let students share their experiences with others. Students can ask for help in the Notebook, and their seniors or teachers can answer the question. One or more teachers can answer questions in the Notebook. It is different from the traditional education environment. In traditional education, it is not easy to see two teachers teaching the same course at the same time in the classroom. In our environment, teachers can share their teaching experiences. Different answers will give students different views of the same problems. The interface of Notebook is shown in Figure 6.

The main idea of Notebook is from the Internet service, News. The Notebook is like a bulletin board on which everyone can record his opinion. But our Notebook is a little different. Our Notebook has a new kind of post we called private notes. Private notes are like annotations used to help students memorize their private ideas or summaries. Private notes cannot be read by other people.

We take care of all the behaviors of our users by two CGI programs in Notebook. Instead of doing all things in one program, we divided the behaviors of the students into two classes, posting and reading. Each class has its own program.

When students want to post, they can pop up the post dialog in which they can fill out their name, their password, the subject of their post, the post

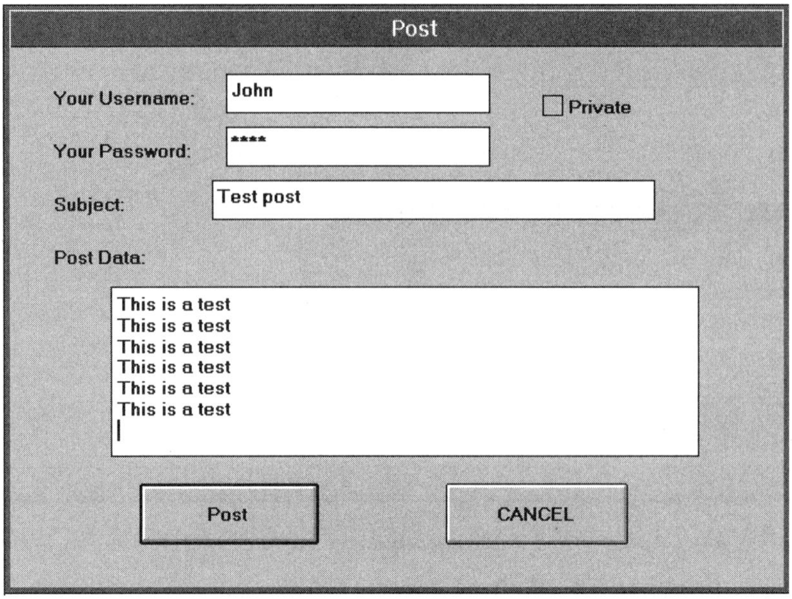

Figure 7: Post dialog of Notebook

data, and whether this post is private or not. The post dialog is shown in Figure 7. Our client will send the data in the post dialog with the filename of the currently-reading document to the Notebook CGI program. The Notebook CGI check the identification of the student. If the student is legal, the program will record the post data. Otherwise an error message will return.

In the reading session, users can retrieve a list of subjects of notes according to their requirements. They can request a list of subjects that relate to the currently-reading document or a list of subjects of his private note. A get note dialog is shown in Figure 8. After getting a list of subjects, students can choose one of the subjects they like and show it in the WWW pane.

All data saved by Notebook is in HTML format. The subjects of all post notes are stored in an HTML unordered list. Teachers can directly manage the posts of students. If they feel that some posts are useless, they can delete them just like deleting some elements in the HTML file.

Miscellaneous

In order to integrate our client with some external communication facilities, we provide another special service for our students. Our client and server will record all the learning history of students. When a student has a problem, he or she can query, "Who has already read this document?" A list of names of people who have already read this document with their email address will return. Students can then contact people according to the email address information. The learning history of students can also be used for studying learning behavior of students.

Conclusion

Currently, we have set up a fundamental network course for our freshmen. The homepage address of this course is *http://bach.cis.nctu.edu.tw/*. All our newly-designed facilities have already been applied in this course. An experiment that tries to find the difference between learning with and without our new facilities is in progress.

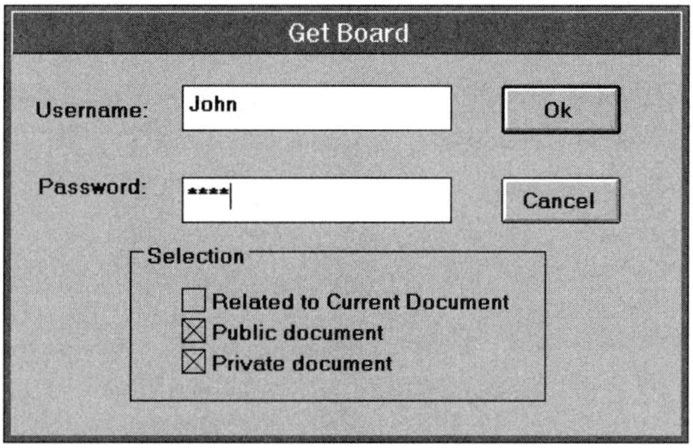

Figure 8: Get note dialog of Notebook

In this project we want to construct a new educational environment based on current computer technology. We adapt the WWW hypermedia model and many existing communication facilities. Moreover, we design some new facilities to make the process of teaching and learning more efficient and eliminate the uneasiness of teachers and students caused by facing new computer technology. In this new environment, learning and teaching are very different from the traditional face-to-face education environment. Teachers and students do not need to get together at particular times. The roles of teachers and students are also changed. Teachers are changed from speakers to assistants. Students are changed from listeners to active participants.

The educational outcome of this new environment seems good. With the advance of computer technology, everything seems to be getting better and better. On the way towards a new educational environment, we try our best to find a suitable method of education in current computer-mediated communication environments. With the responses of teachers and students, we can further enhance our environment in the future. ∎

Acknowledgments

This work is partially supported by the National Science Council of R.O.C., under the contract number: NSC84-2511-S009-004 CL.

References

1. Eleonora Bilotta, Mariano Fiorito, Dario Iovane, and Pietro Pantano, *An Educational Environment Using WWW*, Third WWW Conference 1995.

2. Sougata Mukherjea and James D. Foley, *Visualizing the World-Wide Web with the Navigational View Builder*, Third WWW Conference 1995.

3. David Nicol, Calum Smeaton, and Alan Falconer Slater, *Footsteps: Trail-blazing the Web*, Third WWW Conference, 1995.

4. Daniel LaLiberte and Alan Braverman, *A Protocol for Scalable Group and Public Annotations*, Third WWW Conference, 1995.

5. Martin Rercheisen, Christian Mogensen, and Terry Winograd, *Beyond Browsing: Shared Comments, SOAPs, Trails, and On-line Communities*, Third WWW Conference, 1995.

About the Authors

Ming-Chih Lai
[*http://cissun51.cis.nctu.edu.tw/~gis83502*]
Institute of Computer & Information Science
National Chiao Tung University
Hsinchu, Taiwan, R.O.C. 30050
gis83502@cis.nctu.edu.tw

Bih-Horng Chen
[*http://cissun51.cis.nctu.edu.tw/~gis84509*]
Institute of Computer & Information Science
National Chiao Tung University
Hsinchu, Taiwan, R.O.C. 30050
gis84509@cis.nctu.edu.tw

Shyan-Ming Yuan
[*http:tiger.cis.nctu.edu.tw:8080/smyuan.html*]
Institute of Computer & Information Science
National Chiao Tung University
Hsinchu, Taiwan, R.O.C. 30050
smyuan@cis.nctu.edu.tw 9

CyberProf
An Intelligent Human-Computer Interface for Asynchronous Wide Area Training and Teaching

Alfred Hubler, Andrew M. Assad

Abstract

*We introduce CyberProf, a robust software package which utilizes the full capabilities of a World Wide Web server as an intelligent human-computer interface for grading, creating, and presenting educational course materials. Students can solve course problems presented with text, graphics, animations, and sound on the Web and can receive instant feedback from a sophisticated grading package which makes use of the latest complex systems data analysis tools to handle ambiguous input in an intelligent manner. Fully integrated lecture notes and help files are hyperlinked to assist the student in solving an exercise. Instructors can make use of built-in problem set and lecture notes editors to create an entire online course customized for their needs. Early results of the system are promising. In the first university course in which CyberProf was used, class attendance rates were significantly higher, dropout rates were lower, and grade distributions were higher when compared to figures from the same course in previous semesters. **Keywords:** CyberProf, educational complex systems, online course grading*

Introduction

The Center for Complex Systems Research at the Beckman Institute of the University of Illinois at Urbana-Champaign has devoted much of its research efforts over the past seven years to developing tools for the analysis of complex data using diverse methodologies such as simulated annealing, neural networks, fuzzy logic, and those found in the relatively new field of complexity [1, 2, 3]. Now, with the emergence of the Internet as a primary medium of electronic communication and, in particular, the World Wide Web as a globally recognized standard for the rapid transfer of textual, graphical, and audio information, a unique opportunity is afforded software developers: the ability to combine the latest in complex systems modeling with a distributed computing interface to create truly multimedia educational software capable of handling ambiguous human input and providing access to the vast resources of the Web. CyberProf was specifically designed to take full advantage of this opportunity.

CyberProf is an intelligent human-computer interface for asynchronous wide area training and teaching which is being developed at the Department of Physics and the Center for Complex Systems Research at the Beckman Institute of the University of Illinois at Urbana-Champaign. Interested persons are always welcome to visit the CyberProf page on the World Wide Web at the following URL:

> *http://www.ccsr.uiuc.edu/cyberprof-docs/ general/*

The next section of this paper discusses the motivation behind the development of CyberProf. This is followed by a detailed description of the features of the system with particular emphasis placed on the grading module of the package. The following entails a brief description of the implementation details of the system, followed by a discussion of preliminary results of CyberProf in terms of its impact on student performance in the first classes to use it extensively. Finally, future enhancements to the system are proposed.

Motivation

Previous online networked educational systems developed at the University of Illinois such as PLATO [4] and NovaNET [5] were partially successful, but somewhat limited by the technologies and methods of their time. Students could perform exercises online, receive instant feedback on their solutions, and have their grades automatically recorded. However, these systems were not capable of particularly sophisticated handling of student input nor were they able to take advantage of the enormous amount of information available on the Web. Furthermore, it was difficult to integrate lecture notes, labs, and homework into a cohesive package.

Cyberprof was conceived with the notion of addressing these shortcomings by synthesizing all of the functionalities of the above systems with the new technologies of the World Wide Web and a much more robust student/computer interface engine based on modeling the human-computer interaction as a complex system. In recent years several key paradigms have been developed in complex systems research, such as adaptation to the edge of chaos, the principle of the dynamical key, the principle of least resistance,

neural nets, associative memories, etc. In the fall of 1994, A. Hubler proposed to employ and test these paradigms with the objective to make the learning process more efficient; i.e., create an intelligent learning environment for the student.

Features of CyberProf

Essentially, CyberProf acts as a Web interface between four agents: the student, the instructor, the World Wide Web, and an intelligent grading engine based on complex systems methods. Figure 1, below, illustrates this paradigm.

Along the student/system interface, students can:

- Submit solutions to online homework and quiz problems

- Receive immediate grading and obtain detailed information on how or why their solutions are incorrect from the complex systems engine

- Obtain appropriate hyperlinked references to resources on the Web

- Communicate with the instructor via a Web bulletin board

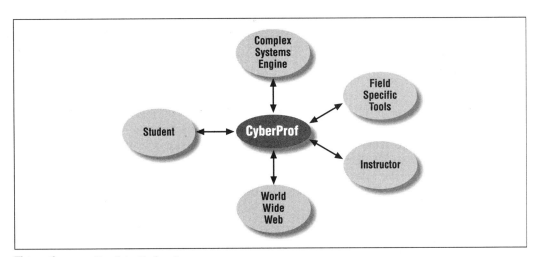

Figure 1:   The CyberProf system

- Access a Web gradebook to monitor their progress

Along the instructor/system interface, an instructor can:

- Create problem sets with a Web problem set editor

- Utilize field specific tools for creating problems specific to his/her field

- Create online lecture notes

- Communicate with students via a Web bulletin board

The following three sections list some of the important general features, problem-set generation capabilities, and features of the grading package of the system, respectively.

General Features

- Students and instructors have fast and easy access to the system using platform-independent Web browsers available at no cost.

- CyberProf, itself, is free.

- Students are encouraged to make use of the most recent technologies available on the Web.

- Integrated conferencing software helps the student to communicate with network teaching assistants and the instructor.

- Integrated Web tools allow for interactive drawing of pictures and creation of animations.

Problem Set Generation Features

- Extensive use can be made of graphical information and movies instead of text to describe complex situations. Instead of unrealistic oversimplifications, we encourage the instructor to use realistic, possibly quite complicated situations in problem sets and computer lessons. The complexity of the situation is communicated by images, movies,

and sound. Written text is kept at a minimum.

- The instructor can match the educational and social background of each individual student with appropriate language and presentation in the problem sets and computer lessons.

- Problem sets can take full advantage of (i) sound and other multimedia features of PowerMacs and other PC level computers and (ii) high data-transfer rates on the Internet.

- Problem sets, help files for problem sets, and lecture notes can be hyperlinked to form a coherent package.

- The source code of the problem sets is very simple and can be generated by a lay person. Complicated equations are typed in LATEX notation and displayed on the Web page.

- Integrated conferencing software helps the student to communicate with network teaching assistants and the lecturer.

Features of the Grading Software

- Careful analysis of student answers based on the most recent complex systems data-analysis techniques (e.g., physical number theory, fuzzy logic, associative memory) gives partial credit when appropriate.

- Careful study of the student answers: checks for sign errors, unit errors, and numerical errors are made. Specific hyperlinked help is offered, based on the error analysis.

- The time which the student takes to solve a problem is monitored and displayed on the student's Web page and can be compared with the "expected" time a student should need to solve that type of problem on an exam.

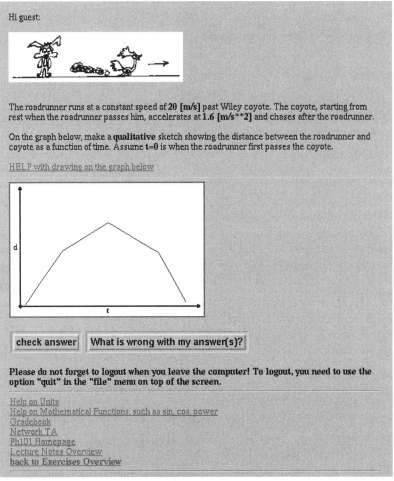

Hi guest:

The roadrunner runs at a constant speed of **20 [m/s]** past Wiley coyote. The coyote, starting from rest when the roadrunner passes him, accelerates at **1.6 [m/s**2]** and chases after the roadrunner.

On the graph below, make a **qualitative** sketch showing the distance between the roadrunner and coyote as a function of time. Assume **t=0** is when the roadrunner first passes the coyote.

HELP with drawing on the graph below

check answer   What is wrong with my answer(s)?

Please do not forget to logout when you leave the computer! To logout, you need to use the option "quit" in the "file" menu on top of the screen.

Help on Units
Help on Mathematical Functions, such as sin, cos, power
Gradebook
Network TA
Ph101 Homepage
Lecture Notes Overview
back to Exercises Overview

Figure 2:   An example CyberProf problem form

- Every student gets a different set of numbers, which are chosen by a personalized random-number generator.

- Every student gets a different set of problems, which are selected fom a large pool with a personalized random-number generator.

- Upon request by the student, a problem can be explained in detail in audio. Often a problem can be faster and more easily understood if it is explained with different words from a second perspective. The audio feature makes it possible to give more detailed explanations which would be time-consuming and cumbersome to read as text.

- The grading program can check symbolic expressions, numerical equations, and differential equations with symbolic expressions.

- Students can use an interactive drawing tool to draw graphs of functions on an XY plot which are instantly graded by comparing them to a theoretical curve generated by an instructor-specified function.

- The grading program keeps track of the progress of every student and saves the information instantly in a grade book. Students will not lose credit in case of network errors, power failures, or other interruptions of service.

Implementation

Cyberprof is implemented as a package of Perl scripts and C routines which handle student and instructor input via HTML forms submitted to a Web server running httpd. A typical problem HTML form is depicted in Figure 2.

This form illustrates most of the key features of the interface to the grading software. The student is presented at the top of the form with text and/ or images describing a situation and asking a question. On this particular form, the student is expected to draw a curve on the graph presented as an "image" type HTML input to the form utilizing CyberProf's interactive drawing capabilities. In general, depending upon the type of problem, a student might input text or numbers in a "text" HTML input on the form, or might be asked to choose an answer from a "select" type HTML input.

Once the student has entered an answer, he can press the "check answer" button to submit the form. The grading software is then invoked by the Web server to grade the student's answer. This software responds to the student by generating another HTML form which again presents the problem as described above, informs the student if his answer was correct or not, and provides specific hypertext references to locations in the online lecture notes which might assist the student in the event of an incorrect answer.

For some problems, the student might also be able obtain more detailed information on why his answer is incorrect by clicking on the "What's wrong with my answer?" button. Additionally, standard "help" and "hint" buttons which produce instructor-specified assistance to the student can be included in a problem.

Hyperlinks to references and other aspects of the system such as the gradebook, course bulletin board, and lecture notes are available at the bottom of the form.

Results

An early prototype of CyberProf, called PHYS-ICA, was first used in an actual course, Physics 101, at the University of Illinois at Urbana-Champaign during the spring semester of 1995. This section presents data taken from that class regarding student enrollment, attendance, and exam performance, comparing it to data from the same course offered in previous semesters.

Table 1 compares enrollment figures and dropout rates for Physics 101 courses since the spring semester of 1993.

As can be seen in Table 1, the dropout rate for the course for the semester in which CyberProf was introduced (Spring 1995) was 3.5%, almost three times lower than the average dropout rate, 10.0%, for the same course over the previous four semesters.

Figures 3 and 4 depict final exam score distributions for the Spring 1994 Physics 101 course and the Spring 1995 Physics 101 course, respectively.

Table 1: Enrollment Figures for Physics 101

	Spring 95	*Fall 94*	*Spring 94*	*Fall 93*	*Spring 93*
Initial Number Enrolled	317	407	306	434	351
Final Number Enrolled	306	362	285	384	314
Dropout Rate	3.5%	11.1%	6.9%	11.5%	10.5%

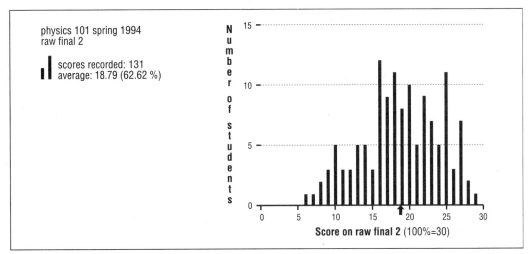

physics 101 spring 1994
raw final 2

scores recorded: 131
average: 18.79 (62.62 %)

Figure 3:   Score distribution for final exam, Spring 1994

The major discernible difference between these distributions would appear to be the lack of the lower tail in the final exam score distribution for the Spring 1995 semester (Figure 4), when Cyber-Prof was integrated into the course, compared to the score distribution for the Spring 1994 course which did not use CyberProf. In fact, this difference appeared fairly consistently when comparing the grade distributions for the three midterm exams given during the Spring 1994 and 1995 semesters as well.

In addition to the enrollment numbers and exam score distributions mentioned above, the instructor who taught the Spring 1995 course with CyberProf noticed a significant increase in lecture attendance, perhaps as much as 10 to 20 percent, compared to previous semesters when he taught the same course. Although the results of one course don't provide conclusive evidence that CyberProf was directly responsible for these perceived improvements in student performance, they seem to indicate, along with the generally enthusiastic response to the system from the students in that class, that CyberProf has a struck a resonant chord with the students. Enthusiasm for the system has spread rapidly within the university across many disciplines. CyberProf is cur-

rently being used to develop online Web courses at the University of Illinois in several different departments such as Physics, Agriculture, Economics, Electrical Engineering, Chemistry, Bioengineering, and Theoretical and Applied Mechanics. A full listing of hyperlinks to these courses is available on the Web at:

> *http://www.ccsr.uiuc.edu/cyberprof-docs/
> general/courses.html*

Future Work

The CyberProf team continues to enhance the software package to improve the existing interface and to add enhancements which address the needs of an expanding user base. Our main efforts for the immediate future are listed below:

- Improving and expanding the ability of the grading module to intelligently analyze a student's solution and answer questions about why a solution was incorrect

- Expanding Web communication tools to allow for easier online communication between the student and instructor

- Improving the user interface to allow for greater flexibility in inputting graphical infor-

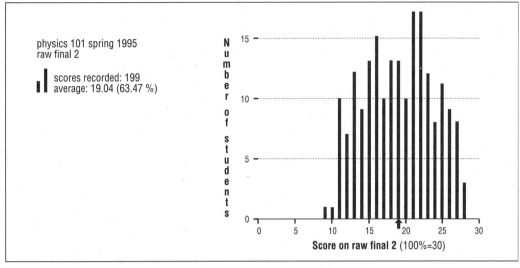

Figure 4:   Score distribution for final exam, Spring 1995

mation, whether it be in creating or answering an exercise

- Development of a fully featured Web drawing program which is comparable to a commercial drawing package AND is fully integrated with CyberProf's grading package and problem set editor

- Improving the interface for instructors to create problem sets and lecture notes ∎

Acknowledgments

The development of CyberProf(TM) is carried out at the Center for Complex Systems Research at the Beckman Institute of the University of Illinois at Urbana-Champaign. It is supported by a grant from the Department of Physics.

The Sloan Center for Asynchronous Learning Environments at the UIUC supports the development of CyberProf courseware with problem sets and lecture notes in Electrical Engineering, Economics, and Agriculture.

Of course, CyberProf would not be where it is today without the dedicated efforts of the Cyber-Prof development team: Lance Arsenault, Brian Rogers, Ed Chang, Brian White, Uli Kruse, Thao Tran, Denny Kane, Karl Schmidt, Navin Kiribamune, Ari Trachten, Laura Brandon, Renee Brockman, and Kaveh Ghaboussi.

Thanks are also due to several UIUC staff members, in particular, Lorella Jones, Bruce Hunter, J. Mochel, B.Oakley II, R.Borelli, and, J. Shannon for discussions and suggestions.

A large number of students of the Spring 1995 Physics 101 class have been contributing to this development with ideas, problems sets, and software.

References

1. Cowan, G., D. Pines, and D. Meltzer, editors, *Complexity: Metaphors, Models, and Reality*, Reading, MA, 1994. Addison-Wesley.

2. Forrest, S., editor, *Emergent Computation*, Cambridge, MA, 1991. MIT Press.

3. Lam, L. and V. Naroditsky, editors, *Modeling Complex Phenomena*, New York, NY, 1992. Springer-Verlag.

4. Sherwood, B. and Stifle, J., *The PLATO IV communications system*, Urbana, IL, 1975. University of Illinois Computer-based Education Research Laboratory.

5. Silver, D., *NovaNET : basic skills lessons for middle school, high school, and adult basic education students*, Urbana, IL, 1988. University of Illinois Computer-based Education Research Laboratory.

About the Authors

Alfred W. Hubler
Beckman Institute—Center for Complex Systems Research and the Physics Department
University of Illinois at Urbana-Champaign
405 North Mathews Avenue
Urbana, IL 61801, USA
alfred@ccsr.uiuc.edu

Andrew M. Assad
Department of Electrical and Computer Engineering
University of Illinois at Urbana-Champaign
1406 West Green Street
Urbana, IL 61801, USA
assad@eceuil.ece.uiuc.edu

A Modular Training System for Education in the WWW Environment

U. Schroeder, B. Tritsch, A. Knierriem-Jasnoch

Abstract

*This paper presents the architecture and WWW-independent implementation of a Modular Training System for networked workstations and personal computers. The emphasis of this system is on telecommunication-centred interactive multimedia technology, extending training beyond individual classrooms. The media representation in a client/server environment, the person-to-person communication needs of such a system, and the dynamic flow control of educational courses are addressed. This training system is compared to the existing WWW environment and its extensions for educational uses, giving hints for new functionality to be incorporated into the individual WWW components. **Keywords:** Computer-based training, modular training system, training and education on the Web*

Introduction

The increasing need to improve training and retraining in modern society is widely recognized. Using appropriate systems based on existing telecommunication services and information technology, this need can already be fulfilled in a certain degree of quality. Before the appearance of the *World Wide Web*, large production costs allowed only large companies to afford to develop adequate computer-based learning systems to train their technical staff. But the need for small- and medium-size enterprises to upgrade the knowledge of their employees is becoming more and more vital in order to meet a rapidly moving market. Moreover, many people need individual educational systems they can use from their homes, because education becomes an important factor in the work market. Responsibility for education is shifting from the employer towards the individual. This enhances the need for educational systems, which can also be used during spare time from the home PC.

Consequently, the WWW seems to be the adequate training platform for learning activities and many projects exploit its functionality for educational uses (see: Yahoo: Online Teaching and Learning, The World Lecture Hall, and Education within The Virtual Library). Despite the integration of the hypermedia and wide-area network functionality, the WWW itself does not provide a sufficient educational framework to meet the requirements derived from the statements above. Therefore, the HyperScript project adds methods for systematic courseware development based on integration of learning objectives and their evaluation [7], and uses existing WWW technology like CGI scripts and CCI control to integrate sophisticated and specialized tools for programming education [6]. With this, we set up a learning environment incorporated into a practical software engineering course [1], where student groups also utilize the WWW for software documentation and document management. Moreover it is used to support their group communication. Other requirements include easy-to-use and robust training systems that allow the users to be trained at the right time, with the adequate learning material being accessible via network, with potential help of a human tutor, and within their sometimes limited hardware and software environment. The courseware must be designed according to a network-based system architecture and being adaptable to different user groups and

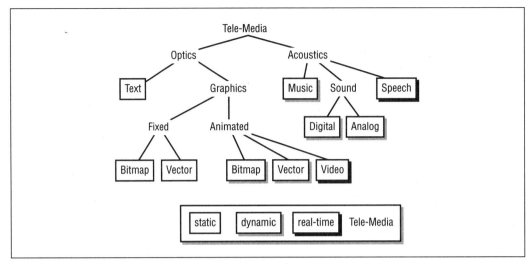

Figure 1:   The Tele-Media objects

pedagogical aspects. Even before the WWW became popular, these reasons lead to the design and the implementation of the *Modular Training System* (MTS). Its major modules are a cross-platform learning front-end, a pedagogical back-end, a dedicated networking module to connect front-end and back-end over LAN or WAN, and a human communication component.

On the first glance, the goals of the WWW and the MTS differ: while the WWW is an information system also allowing distance learning to some extent, the MTS is an education and training system also allowing information access to some extent. For this reason, we want to look at some details of the MTS architecture and its components. This leads to a better understanding of the current state of the WWW with respect to teaching environments. Moreover we state how MTS features can be mapped onto the Web technology in order to better suite educational needs.

The Architecture of the Modular Training System

Educational software in a distributed, wide area environment requires a new architecture of the computer-based training system. This architecture is component-oriented and is strictly following a client/server approach. It is derived from a reference model describing Tele-Communicating Multimedia Objects (*Tele-Media*) and their relations to transmission, synchronization, and real-time issues [9]. The Tele-Media model provides the mechanisms for the delivery and the presentation of the used multimedia objects. These Tele-Media objects represent learning material circulating through the different components of the distributed Modular Training System (see Figure 1).

In the following paragraphs, the individual components of the MTS architecture are introduced briefly. The *Generic Learning Support* (GLS) is a client application which creates the learning front-end. It presents the multimedia learning courses and allows the user to interact with the learning system. The *Course Domain* and the *Course Operating System* represent the pedagogical back-end. The course domain provides modular- and platform-independent course material of three levels. A dedicated server application, the *Course Interpreter* (CI), is the main component of the Course Operating System and supports course configuration and course execution.

The *Tele-Media Network Module* provides a network protocol and API functionalities, and enables the GLS to communicate with the CI. Finally, the *Human Communication Component* provides online audio and video tools for person-to-person communication on heterogeneous networks and platforms supporting active student-teacher communication.

We believe that a strict separation between these components is the key to courseware systems. Within the course domain, virtual components and methods can be used within the design of courses. This virtual material is mapped onto libraries of real learning materials residing in the course domain. Finally, within the Generic Learning Support, the real learning material is loaded and mapped onto the physical platform available to the student. Interfaces to standard tools for data access, transfer, presentation, and interaction are supported by the Tele-Media Network Module, enabling inter-operability between the platforms. Thus all higher-level development and education can be performed in parallel, increasing the portability of both learning tools and courses.

The Modular Training System was designed to run on heterogeneous multimedia platforms (Sun Sparc, Silicon Graphics Indigo, IBM-compatible PCs). To convey complex facts, the learner's understanding of the course material must be reinforced as much as possible and embedded multimedia is seen as the appropriate enabling technology to allow this reinforcement [2]. Therefore, device independence of the learning material data, interoperability between the different platforms, and portability of course controls were essential.

The Modular Training System was partially developed and evaluated at the House of Computer Graphics in Darmstadt, Germany within different projects on a European-wide scale. The results showed that the MTS allows sophisticated learning and teaching scenarios on distributed computer systems [10]. The MTS user front-end (the GLS) is based on the presentation of embedded

multimedia objects rather than using external viewers. This allows authors or designers to set up the layout of a course and to present formatted multimedia materials in a way that goes beyond the capabilities of a current WWW front-end.

The MTS Components

In the following sections, all MTS components are introduced in more detail. This information will later be used to discuss the functionalities of the corresponding WWW components.

The Generic Learning Support

The learning front-end GLS (see Figure 2) is implemented platform dependent, supporting different graphical user interfaces such as OSF/ Motif or MS-Windows. This implementation provides an optimized presentation performance for multimedia data and a "native look and feel." The GLS functionality covers both learning-dependent and learning-independent features such as formatted text (ASCII, RTF), raster images (TIFF, GIF, PCX, BMP, PPM), audio/video/animation objects (WAVE, AVI, MPEG, FLI), vector primitives (line, polyline, rectangle, arc, ellipse), menus, child windows, hot zones for hyperlinks, timers and a number of dialog objects (e.g., buttons, multiple choice tests, single- and multiple-line text inputs, sliders, selection boxes, different button boxes, browsing, and navigation tools).

All visible objects can be placed at any location within the main window or a child window of the course setup defined by its author. Clipping and scaling functionalities allow precise placement and size adjustment down to the scale of a pixel. By referencing RTF files, embedded formulas and tables may be handled. By using transparent text backgrounds, all ASCII and RTF strings may be placed on top of other visible object without completely hiding their graphical contents behind the strings. Since the GLS allows the exact placement of all visible objects it also supports individual manipulations and incremen-

Raytracing allows the user to calculate some natural effects like reflection and refraction by tracing the rays recursivly from the camera back to the lightsources. It is the most time-consuming rendering process.

Adv. Rendering ⟨⟨∥ ⟨- -⟩ ∥⟩⟩ Seite 6/7 leave Chap.

Figure 2: A screenshot during an MTS learning session using a book metaphor

tal redraws of these objects during their entire lifetime.

The Course Domain

The traditional meaning of the term *course* has been extended for the MTS course model. While in most traditional CBT courses, fixed sequences or at most conditional branching to predetermined sequences exist, the new MTS course model allows one to traverse through a domain of course material. The course material is dynamically selected with respect to the learner's profile, the equipment of the learning environment, and the learning progress. The course domain provides modular course material of three levels, covering curriculum control, interaction specification and basic multimedia learning material.

There are course modules (course nodes) being responsible for the goal-oriented specification of the course contents and for controlling the course structure. Each course node handles the representation of the subject on the client side. For this purpose, different mechanisms are used: appropriate knowledge presentation, user interaction (e.g., by means of simulators), and profiling of the learner's progress. Therefore, a Course Node refers at least to the three corresponding function units. Additionally, a course node may be composed of course (sub-) nodes in order to represent the functional hierarchy of learning material.

Function units operate event driven and refer to Material Objects representing either basic learning contents (Learning Material Objects or LMOs) or user-interface items like buttons, menus, etc. (Intrinsic Material Objects). A course domain is composed of the sum of course modules, while a specific "course" is a goal-oriented and learner-dynamic view of the domain.

Links between course modules may be either direct or virtual. The latter are specifications of demands and allowances to the desired module (computational hyperlinks). Virtual referencing is a mechanism for the computation of target-material alternatives and for presentation preferences during run-time: an audio file and a video sequence is chosen if the technical equipment is sufficient. Otherwise, text is used instead of audio and an image sequence instead of video.

LMOs describe the characteristics of the module (contents and requirements) and reference to the file(s) containing the basic multimedia learning material. Standard formats for the latter are: for text, ASCII and RTF; for images, TIFF, GIF, PCX, BMP, and PPM; for audio/video/animation, WAVE, AVI, MPEG, and FLI.

Course nodes and Function Units are represented by scripts in the *Course Description Language* (CDL). Each script consists of three sections: the *Characteristic Section* holds information on the modules' capabilities (e.g., the subject it treats) and its requirements (e.g., learner's experience, GLS support, etc.); the *Declaration Section* includes either direct or virtual references. In the second case, a mapping process is responsible for the selection of modules with the capabilities/ requirements matching best with the demands/ allowances specified in the references; the *Body Section* describes the presentation sequence of the referenced modules and their behavior on incoming events (e.g., user interaction).

The *Course Interpreter* is a server process translating CDL scripts by resolving all virtual references and launching the presentation of the material objects on a GLS platform. Moreover, the interpreter is responsible for the handling of the GLS responses generated by user interactions, timers, errors, or system-specific events. In combination with the course domain, the Course Interpreter is the "brain" of the Modular Training System.

Within the course domain, archiving of and access to the multimedia course modules are pro-vided by an underlying distributed database mechanism. Conceptually, this mechanism can either be realized by a standard network-file system or by using a distributed multimedia database system. The first solution is feasable for in-house training activities on a LAN; the second solution is rather adequate for learning scenarios in a WAN environment.

The Tele-Media Network Module

The Tele-Media Network Module, connecting client (GLS) and server (CI), provides the tele-control of multimedia objects over networks. It introduces a platform-independent and object-oriented network protocol addressed by an Application Programmer Interface (API). The API intends to hide the communication protocol between client and server. Therefore, it offers the application programmer a transparent way of sending and receiving the protocol messages by just using API function calls (see Figure 3). These API functions cover the complete spectrum of the MTS functionality as described above including the feedback from active interaction objects such as buttons, menus, dialogs, sliders, hot zones, etc. The advantage of separating the networking from the application and only allowing their communication over a common API is evident: Portability is made easy! If the Modular Training System is installed within environments using different kinds of networks, portability is only a matter of exchanging the Tele-Media Network Module.

The complete protocol-based communication between client and server is event oriented. This means that it is highly asynchronous and may create and process interrupts (events) at any time, also in parallel to a user. Therefore, the GLS is controlled by two instances simultaneously: the *user*, interacting with the user interface. This may create protocol messages that are transmitted to the server immediately and cause a reaction of the server; the *server*, sending protocol messages asynchronously to the GLS in order to control the course flow, can synchronize the presentation of

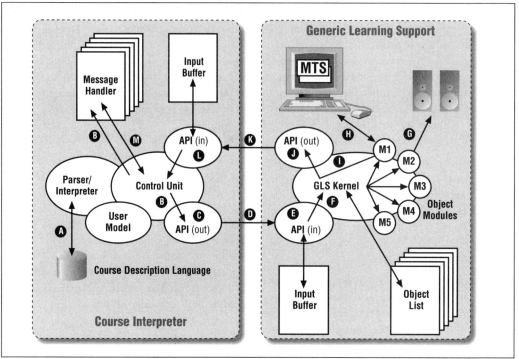

Figure 3: The message mechanism of the MTS: Interpretation of a course script (A); initialization of an object both on CI and GLS side (B to F); presentation of the object (G to H); handling of user interaction (H to L); decision of the system reaction on user input (M), which may start the message sequence again.

time-dependent multimedia objects and react on user input.

Human Communication Components

A particularly challenging feature of the Modular Training System was that of the integration of real-time video and audio, focusing on the communication aspects during learning sessions. This can be communication between two students facing the same problems during their course, or teacher-to-student(s) communication, where the teacher (or course author, tutor) has access to the Course Interpreter. The latter allows the teacher to modify the presentation logic at students' requests, or to adapt to a new situation.

Different multimedia platforms provide different types of audio devices and services. Nevertheless, all of them offer a common set of functionalities, such as record, store and playback. Online audio exchange for communication purposes was realized based upon these basic functionalities. In order to provide cross-platform usability, a common, intermediate exchange format was defined and a number of online bi-directional converters supporting different platform-dependent audio formats were implemented (see Figure 4).

Video communication for learning environments requires a fast codec algorithm that can be performed in real-time on either low-end hardware or by software. Because the real-time issues for video as a communication channel were more

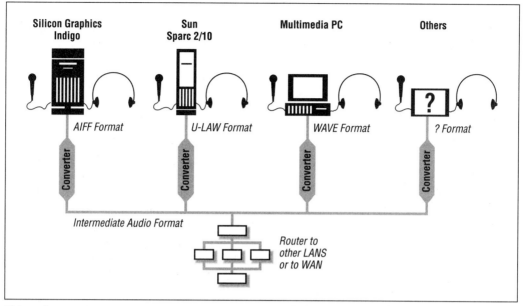

Figure 4: The audio communication mechanism using online converters for cross-platform usability

important than high-quality pixel and color resolution, we decided to use the JPEG (Joint Photographic Expert Group) codec standard for our video sequences, referred to as M-JPEG (Motion-JPEG) [5]. Within the MTS, a multipoint audio/video communication environment allows real-time discussions between groups of up to six teachers and students. MTS control elements are embedded in the GLS application.

Within the WWW, online communication is supported by using the M-Bone technology which is driven by the same idea of having people communicate in a more natural way. A big difference between M-Bone and the MTS Human Communication Component is that the first is used to broadcast real-time audio and video sequences to a big audience. In contrast, the latter connects small groups of teachers and students to allow vivid and more private discussions between the group members. Because this component of the MTS is not described here in more detail, we refer to [8] for further information.

From MTS to WWW: A Comparison

How can the described Modular Training System be compared to existing WWW technology tailored for educational uses? Most of the MTS components can be mapped directly to programs in the common WWW environment. However, some of the MTS funtionalities show shortcomings of the WWW when MTS is used as a learning platform. In order to support the extended pedagogical or technical aspects and requirements described in the chapters above, the WWW needs additional sophisticated tools. In the following sections, we first compare MTS and WWW components and then discuss differences in the underlying concepts.

WWW Clients

The GLS directly maps to a WWW browser like NCSA Mosaic, which is also implemented on all major platforms and would be used as learning front-end in an educational set up. Mosaic is an excellent WWW viewer and has been the driving force in the success of WWW. We have used it in the HyperScript approach without major drawbacks. Compared to GLS, one constraint regarding the formats accepted for inline images (GIF) and text formats (HTML, ASCII), along with an absence of inlined audio and video or animation. For these types of images, external viewers are launched. The disadvantages of this approach is the loss of uniformity in user interfaces and the fact that hypertext functionality is lost for these images. With GLS, one can define hotzones on graphics and other intrinsics. With HTML, you can do the same with clickable images. The disadvantage is that the URL to which the link points is not displayed in the browser's status bar as opposed to normal anchors within text areas.

The GLS intrinsics for menus, buttons, and text input correspond to menus, buttons and text area in interactive forms. Additionally, the GLS allows inlined images with different formats to be either clipped or scaled, while WWW clients can only clip inlined images or preformatted text areas. For formatted text with user-defined font type, size and color, the GLS supports clipping and panning operations which preserve the size of the selected fonts.

Additional visual elements like scrollbars, learning-specific dialogs, and browsing tools enable MTS course authors to produce advanced educational and highly interactive course frameworks. Moreover, a set of vector elements provides the graphical functionality for layout improvements that go far beyond the simple line primitives of the WWW browsers. Timers on both the GLS and CI sides allow exact timing and synchronization tasks for all multimedia objects. An example for an interactive course scenario using some of the features described above is that a learner can be asked to solve a problem by placing graphical objects within a given time, before a solution dependent on the learner's progress is presented automatically.

Most of the "intelligence" for repaint operations and the handling of object and element states is embedded within the GLS. Therefore, the processing and supervision of these operations is kept away from the network and server as much as possible. This makes the MTS fast and reduces the semantical network overhead of the communication between client and server component.

Course Domain

There is no specific course domain in WWW. The only structuring mechanism for sets of documents is the facility to incorporate direct links to other documents, implementing menus of hierarchical components. The MTS allows for a didactic concept by providing three layered module types: course nodes for course flow control, Function Units for interaction specification, and basic learning material for knowledge presentation. The WWW only provides the basic learning material.

In addition, the MTS distinguishes between three pedagogical types of Function Units:

- *Presentation*: Conveying knowledge

- *Exploration*: Making use of simulation programs allowing explorative learning by experiments

- *Test units*: Integrating evaluation forms to compute the learner's success and thus influencing the sequence of the course

Using WWW technology, the second and third types are implemented through the CGI interface: *external simulation* programs can be launched on the server machine again loosing hypertext functionality. One possibility of integration with the presented course material can be achieved by NCSA Mosaic's CCI "remote control," when the simulation program is used to control the WWW viewer.

Test units are one important feature of online courses as suggested by HyperScript [7]: interactive forms, representing evaluation forms, are linked to course nodes. The learner can always take an evaluation to find out about his/her success or failure of reaching the unit's learning objective. Upon submission, the forms start separate evaluation programs through CGI.

Within the MTS, test results are used to update the user profile, thus directly influencing the context and subject of the corresponding module. In WWW, user profiling, evaluation of technical requirements, and other characteristics must be implemented separately on top of the system. In the HyperScript project, user profiling uses the server's log data and results of evaluation forms and answers given directly by the learner, who can also readjust evaluation results. It is planned to incorporate specifications of module requirements, which ought to be met before loading a module. In a later phase, general indexing should be used so that modules can be computed using WAIS and other Internet searching techniques.

Furthermore, within the MTS the course structure, the interaction and the evaluation all are expressed in CDL. While the MTS offers an integrated, monolithic approach, the WWW is more flexible and offers a general programming interface (cgi scripts in Perl, Bourne Shell, C).

To implement computational hyperlinks (MTS technique for late module binding) one would create a set of tools at server side, which are activated through the CGI interface and compute the document to be presented on the fly. This technique is used in many educational projects [3]. One major difference between the compared systems is that the MTS has predefined attributes (module characteristics) which can be evaluated while mapping virtual references to a document to be presented.

Protocols

For educational purposes, the WWW's uni-directional and stateless HTTP protocol is one of the often-mentioned shortcomings. For this reason, extensions to WWW [4] start a seperate process on the server machine to log the user's action and compute the result of links followed by the user. Within MTS, this approach is easily imple-

mented by conditional hyperlinks (virtual references) and the bi-directional protocol. Moreover, the protocol may transport object and element states from client to server and commands to change these states from server to client.

While the network protocol between back-end and front-end of the WWW is based on the exchange of files containing either HTML commands or multimedia data, the MTS uses a learning-specific, bi-directional, and asynchronous communication protocol between client and server component. Each platform and network-independent message defined in this protocol may be addressed by a dedicated API function. This structure implements an easy-to-use interface to the communication processes between the different MTS components.

The API functions allow access to all course material objects including their initialization, activation, deactivation, destruction, and state manipulation (like position, size, color, etc.) at any time. Moreover all user interactions are handled by specific API functions, which send them asynchronously to the server.

The Underlying Concepts

The first obvious difference between MTS and WWW is the concept of layout and formatting: While the WWW is based on a mark up language (HTML), leaving the final layout to be computed by the used WWW browser, the MTS presentation can be defined exactly by the course author. This includes positions, sizes, colors, adjustment, and scaling of objects through CDL statements. The advantage of the MTS approach is the possibility of incremental redrawing, for instance when only a few attributes of learning objects are changed due to user interaction or timer events. With WWW, the complete document would have to be transmitted and redrawn by the browser. Because of the absolute formatting, MTS offers two modes of presentation for inlined graphics, video, and text areas: graphics can be either clipped (as in WWW) or scaled, while text can be clipped or panned (as opposed to WWWs line wrapping).

For educational purposes, incremental updating of presentation attributes of single objects can be used in many ways:

- activation or deactivation of hotzones and menu items or buttons, depending on the user's profile or learning context (notion of HyperScript views)

- change of background colors or bitmaps for buttons or anchors representing sub-modules, which have been visited and evaluated.

The latter allows an easy implementation of the HyperScript proposal of visualization of learning success which needs sophisticated tools on top of WWW (graphical presentation of the document structures with node coloring representing untouched, visited, successfully evaluated, and failed evaluations). The prize of the MTS approach of absolute formatting is the description effort every author has, when producing CBT material. In WWW, only few markup tags are needed, presentation being on the WWW clients responsibility.

The other major difference in concepts consists of a general higher-level education functionality of MTS. Pedagogical useful elements are predefined, which need to be constructed using HTML's basic features. For instance, there are units of radio buttons allowing 1-of-n, or m-of-n choices, or predefined dialog forms with answers (yes, no, undecided). Additional elements are sliders, which are best used for a learner's self-assessment, which is proposed in the HyperScript method.

Conclusion

The multimedia desktop workstation is the communication and learning center of the future. Towards the end of this century, information and training material must be accessible in many forms. Personal and co-operative multimedia on heterogeneous, networked PCs and workstations

provides interactive learning sessions among distributed users. We are now at the beginning of a new era of information management and distribution which could well change our society as dramatically as telephone technology only a few decades ago; the center of this new technology is not only the man-machine interface, but also the human-human interface.

The Modular Training System (MTS) gives valuable hints for the usage of the WWW for distance education. By implementing and evaluating the MTS during the last four years in Finland, France, Germany, Greece, and Portugal, an adequate environment for teaching and training on digital networks has been developed. This experience may be easily mapped onto the development and implementation of features for CBT on the WWW. Therefore, educational WWW projects should take advantage of the results achieved by the MTS. This can be a simple consideration on what can be adopted from the MTS when building tools on top of the WWW or may give some new directions for future extensions to the WWW.

From our point of view, the major implications for CBT on the WWW derived from the experiences with the MTS are the following:

- Add layout information, learning-specific elements, additional pedagogical mechanisms, and maintainance features for the provided learning material to the browser component (the front-end)

- Extend the protocol in a way that it can handle asynchronous and bi-directional messages containing object states

- Allow the server to react on user interactions in a flexible way by providing the adequate server components

Courses designed following the MTS concept are inherently adaptable to available environments, user groups, and pedagogic aspects. The modularity of the course material opens a wide range of flexibility and reusability in different courses and on different platforms, and supports different tasks and responsibilities within the Modular Training environment. In particular, the integration of tests and the facility to control the course flow dynamically and in relation to the test results offer a new dimension of computer-based training. In the future, CBT on the WWW should also be able to take advantage of all these features by adopting the extended MTS mechanisms described in this paper. ∎

References

1. M. Brunner, B. Kühnapfel, U. Schroeder, *New Media in Software Engineering Education*, Technical Report No. PI-R 3/95, Software Engineering Group, Department of Computer Science, Technical University of Darmstadt, 1995.

2. J.L. Encarnação, B. Tritsch, Ch. Hornung, *DEDICATED - Learning on Networked Multimedia Platforms*, Visualization in Scientific Computing: Uses in University Education, Elsevier Science Publisher B.V., 1993.

3. B. Ibrahim, *World-Wide Algorithm Animation*, Computer Networks and ISDN Systems, Vol 27, No. 2, Nov. 1994, pp. 255 - 265.

4. B. Ibrahim, S.D. Franklin, *Advanced educational uses of the World Wide Web*, Computer Networks and ISDN Systems, Vol 27, No. 6, April 1995, pp. 871 - 879.

5. Joint Photographic Expert Group ISO/IEC, *JPEG Technical Specification*, JTCI/SC2/WG8, CCITT SGVIII, 1989.

6. U. Schroeder, M. Brunner, *Utilizing WWW and Mosaic for Computer Science Education*, Proceedings of the First International Workshop on Training and Teaching on the Web, First WWW conference, CERN, May 1994.

7. U. Schroeder, *HyperScript - Innovative educational use of WWW*, Workshop proceedings at 3rd International WWW conference, Darmstadt, 1995.

8. B. Tritsch, A.S. Vieira, Ch. Hornung, *Video and Audio Communication over LAN*, Local Area Network Applications: Leveraging the LAN, Elsevier Science Publisher B.V., 1993, pp. 183-196.

9. B. Tritsch, *The Tele-Media Learning Architecture - A Distributed Multimedia Teaching Environment for Heterogeneous Computer Platforms in Digital Networks*, Dissertation in preparation.

10. B. Tritsch, A. Knierriem-Jasnoch, *A Modular Training System for Distributed Platforms in SMEs*,

Proceedings of the ED-Media 95 Conference, Graz, Austria, 1995.

About the Authors

Ulrik Schroeder

[*http://www.informatik.th-darmstadt.de/~uli/*]
University of Darmstadt
Ulrik Schroeder has worked as assistant professor for software engineering at the University of Darmstadt since 1995. He received his diploma in computer science in 1986 and a PhD degree in 1994, both at the University of Darmstadt, Germany. His major work areas and research interests include software engineering, object-oriented design methods, consistency control, and computer-based training and education.

Bernhard Tritsch

[*http://www.igd.fhg.de/~tritsch/*]
Fraunhofer Institute for Computer Graphics
Bernhard Tritsch received his diploma in physics at the University of Freiburg, Germany. Before joining the Fraunhofer Institute for Computer Graphics in Darmstadt in 1991, he worked at the Royal Nepal Academy for Science and Technology (RONAST) in Kathmandu, Nepal, the European Research Center for High-Energy Physics (CERN) in Geneva, Switzerland, and the Fraunhofer Institute for Solar Energy Systems in Freiburg, Germany. His major work areas and research interests include multimedia systems, cross-platform multimedia applications, and computer-supported communication.

Anette Knierriem-Jasnoch

[*http://www.igd.fhg.de/~anette/*]
Fraunhofer Institute for Computer Graphics
Anette Knierriem-Jasnoch received her diploma in mathematics at the University of Darmstadt, Germany in 1989. Before joining the Fraunhofer Institute for Computer Graphics in Darmstadt in 1994, she worked at the Interactive Graphics Systems Group in Darmstadt, Germany. Her major work areas and research interests include computer-based training and education, and open and distributed learning environments.

A WWW Learning Environment for Mathematics

Kostadin Antchev, Markku Luhtalahti, Jari Multisilta,
Seppo Pohjolainen, Kari Suomela

Abstract

*This paper discusses the components and implementation of a hypermedia-based educational system for the mathematical sciences. Existing (RTF, LaTeX) lecture notes are converted into HTML documents, and hypertext links are generated automatically into them. The hypertext courses contain hypertext, problems and examples with hints, and interactive exercises. A computer algebra system is used to generate and randomize exercises and to check the students' answers. Email, bulletin boards, and videoconferencing software are available on the system to enhance interaction between the teacher and the distance learners. **Keywords:** Hypermedia, learning environment, mathematics, conversion, automatic link generation*

Introduction

In this paper the design and implementation of a hypermedia-based learning environment on the World Wide Web (WWW) for the mathematical sciences will be discussed. This paper is an outcome of a national scale project lead by the Hypermedia Laboratory at Tampere University of Technology (TUT), supported by the Academy of Finland and the Finnish Ministry of Education. One of the purposes of the project is to produce mathematical hyperbooks on the WWW, to be used nationwide at schools, institutes, and universities, where the Internet is available. As such, Internet provides an inexpensive medium to transfer the material to different sites, and with WWW browsers the courses can be studied in different environments (UNIX, PC, and Macintosh).

The pilot material consists of two courses: a basic mathematics course for students starting their studies at university level and a course on matrix algebra. The purpose of the first course is to revise school mathematics and to provide help and support for mathematical problems that students will be facing. The structure of both of the courses consists of text, mathematical dictionary or database of definitions, exercises, examples,

and computer-aided interactive exercises. The mathematical concepts in the lecture notes are linked to the corresponding definitions in the mathematical dictionary or the definition database to provide online help for understanding them. Exercises, with two hint levels and examples, are given as a part of the lecture notes. The symbolic algebra package, Mathematica, is used for interactive exercises; it generates different numerical and symbolic exercises, and checks the answers given by students.

The structure of the hypermedia courses is based on the experiences that the authors have got from constructing a standalone hypermedia learning environment for Macintosh [7, 8]. Positive classroom experiences encouraged us to extend the basic design ideas for this WWW version.

Communication between distant learners and teachers will be supported by bulletin boards, email and videoconferencing software. The data transfer speeds at the university vary from modem speeds of 14,4 Kb/s up to 155 Mb/s using ATM-network.

The presented hypermedia courses will be used in an experimental way to support distance learning through the Internet. A special group for distance learners will be formed in fall 1995 and experience on distance education with the proposed system will be collected and analysed.

Converting Lecture Notes into HTML documents

The WWW courses can be based on existing textbooks or lecture notes. In our department quite a lot of lecture notes have been written with Microsoft Word (RTF) or LaTeX. In both cases the raw text can easily be converted with existing public domain (PD) converters. The quality of the converted text is rather good, but major problems were encountered due to the specific features of the mathematical notation, such as subscripts, superscripts, Greek alphabet, and other mathematical notation not supported by HTML 2. 0. In the future, when the browsers support HTML 3.0, it will be possible to use super- and subscripts in a much more elegant way. However, mathematical formulas have still to be converted from RTF or LaTeX to HTML 3.0. The quality of the final output depends on the WWW browser and the size of the selected font. Changing the font size in the browser does not scale the pictures, which is a bit annoying.

From LaTeX to HTML

There are several PD converters that convert LaTeX to HTML. Our choice was LaTeX2HTML by Nicos Drakos from the University of Leeds [4]. As pointed out by Drakos this conversion is inherently difficult. This difficulty stems mainly from the fact that LaTeX is programmable.

A mathematical dictionary was written with LaTeX, and it contains many postscript figures and mathematical formulas. Mathematical formulas were converted into GIF format by LaTeX2HTML. This results in quite a lot of small picture files for each page. Due to the difficulty mentioned above we have implemented some LaTeX macros in the dictionary as Perl scripts. These macros are used mainly for including pictures in HTML documents.

From RTF to HTML

An RTF file contains text, formatting commands, pictures, and formulas, and is used to transfer documents between different word processors or between Macintosh and PC. Many word processors can read and write RTF.

In the Macintosh environment RTF files can be converted to HTML documents using a PD converter called RTFtoHTML [5]. However, it does not convert super- and superscript or Greek letters to GIF pictures. This is why a preprocessor was programmed to read the RTF files, to search for super- and subscripts and to write them as RTF representations of pictures into the corresponding places in the RTF file.

RTFtoHTML converts pictures and formulas to Macintosh pictures (PICT). They have to be converted to GIF format using another converter. Most of the WWW browsers read GIF files that are binary compatible, so that GIF files can be created in Macintosh and then transformed to UNIX, where many WWW servers exist. Graphics files should be saved in transparent mode, so that they will be displayed well even if the background color in the WWW browser is not white.

In order to handle Greek letters the RTFtoHTML converter was customized by modifying certain configuration files. In our case the Greek letters are displayed as GIF pictures. Every time the converter encounters a Greek letter it places the corresponding HTML tag in the HTML file.

Creating Links Automatically to HTML Documents

Our WWW courses contain several hundred HTML files. Thus it was necessary to create hypertext links automatically. The material was divided into files so that a subchapter corresponds to a file. In addition, the definition of each mathematical concept was saved to a file. This file structure made it possible for us to implement a powerful tool for automatic linking, called Linktool.

Purpose and Usage

Linktool was written in C and it runs on a UNIX platform. The purpose of the program is to add links to HTML documents. The program is fairly easy to use. The user just has to write the hot words into the so-called link file.

The format of the link file is simple. A line in the link file contains just one hot word or phrase, which is the anchor of a link, and the corresponding target. The target of link a is a path to an HTML file or any URL. In order to handle phrases with several words, such as "Normal Matrix," they must be written into the link file before single hot words, such as "Matrix."

Technical Aspects

In the Finnish language there are many inflected forms of a word. Other European languages sharing this feature are for example Estonian, Hungarian, and Bulgarian. Because of inflected words, it is difficult to identify all the occurrences of the hot words in the text.

Linktool solves this problem in the following way. First it tries to find out the stem of the word. When the stem is found, the program adds nearly all the possible endings to the word. The program uses regular expressions as search terms, in special GNU regexp package and strsed function, written by Terry Jones. Both of these are public domain software available for example from [10]. The next example shows how the program adds some Finnish word endings using regexp engine. The regexp, given below, matches with the basic form of a word "matriisi" (matrix) and the inflected forms of "matriisit" (matrices), "matriisina" and "matriisin."

```
matrii[bcdfghjklmnpqrstvw][bcdfghjklmnpq
    rstvw]?([aeiouy]|&auml;
    |&ouml;)([aeiouy]|&auml;|&ouml;)?t?(n
    a)?\(ta)
    ?(n)?(en)?(jen)?(in)?(ssa)?(lla)?(ll
    e)?/
```

Interactive Exercises

A computer based learning environment should provide feedback for the students. Interactive online exercises form such an activity.

Overview

In a typical interactive exercise the computer will pose a problem and ask the student to fill in an online form. In some cases the user may be asked to answer the problem. The answer will be assessed, and a message will be returned describing whether the answer is correct or what went wrong. In some cases the form may serve as an aid for solving the actual problem. By submitting such a form the students may get a plot and/or results of calculations intended to help them, as it is for "Conic Sections"—an example described in the next section.

Often we would like to randomize a part of the problem's data, so that the students can work out several problems of the same type, successively. They may explicitly ask for "new values" to be generated by pressing a designated button, or they may simply arrive several times at the same node. From the authors' perspective, the users' inputs and the browsing history are valuable sources of information that are needed to improve the quality of the hypermedia materials.

Using Mathematica on WWW

The existing client- and server-side standards on the WWW support the development of distributed interactive applications using standard HTTP clients and servers. Our interactive exercises are such applications. For mathematics the ability of the server side to perform nontrivial numerical computations and symbolic manipulations is essential. Therefore, the idea of incorporating an advanced computer algebra system as part of the server-side software is natural. Mathematicareg. is such a system with powerful numerical, symbolic, and graphical capabilities [13]. It was chosen, because of its excellent communication protocol, namely MathLink [14], which allows other programs to use the whole power of Mathematica.

As front-ends for the exercises we use WWW browsers that support forms as defined in HTML 2. Certain text formatting capabilities are also necessary. In particular, to present mathematical formulas in the exercises we use a two dimensional form, made up of several preformatted lines of characters, which we surround by <PRE> and </PRE> tags (abbreviation from preformatted). In fact, this looks just like normal Mathematica syntax. Plots, which are created using Mathematica and then converted to GIF format, are best to present inlined in HTML documents along with explanatory text and other information.

Mathematica's programming language, a high level interpreted language with a vast amount of built-in functions and a sophisticated pattern matching mechanism, has been used to code the algorithms for generating the problems' data, processing of the forms' contents, and creating aesthetically pleasing plots. The availability of various Mathematica packages further simplifies many programming tasks, especially in mathematics. We have also written our own packages—one per interactive exercise—to encapsulate the code for each exercise and for ease of its maintenance.

Implementation of Exercise Server

The server side of interactive exercises (or more generally interactive documents) is implemented as an extension of a standard HTTP server. CGI is the standard for running such extension programs under HTTP servers [9]. Consequently, these programs are referred to as CGI-handlers (gateways and CGI-scripts are also in use). In UNIX, the HTTP server spawns the handler which is referred to by the URL of an incoming information request. The handler being invoked should return the appropriate HTML or other type of document, or it should generate such a document on the fly. Our CGI-handlers fall into the second category—an HTML document is generated and returned to the HTTP-server.

For the reasons outlined above, our CGI-handlers also use Mathematica by acting as clients of another server which incorporates it. It is worth mentioning that it is not desirable for each CGI-handler to launch a new copy of Mathematica whenever it is being invoked. First, it is largely time-consuming because of the initialization performed by Mathematica at startup—it may take up to 20 seconds on a well-loaded DEC Alpha station. Second, it may cause license violations if the number of Mathematica processes exceeds a certain limit. The solution was to implement a server which incorporates a single Mathematica process. This server is referred to as Exercise Server (ES) and, like the standard HTTP server, is running as a daemon process under UNIX. ES makes it possible for the CGI-handlers to redirect the incoming HTTP requests to Mathematica. It is Mathematica, appropriately programmed, which actually generates our interactive exercises and processes the forms' contents. To clarify this, an overall block diagram of the server side is given in Figure 1.

In most of the exercises there might be several requests which form a session. This entails that for each session certain state information has to be maintained and special care should be taken to support more than one session at a time. In this respect the HTTP protocol is stateless. Connections to the HTTP server are made only at the user's request, and between connections the HTTP server is not maintaining any information for or about individual users. Therefore there is no direct support, at the HTTP level, for interactive sessions which consist of several HTTP requests. It is the application's own responsibility to preserve such information. There is, however, a mechanism for accomplishing this in HTML 2. State information can be passed in special "hidden" fields to the clients which will resubmit it later along with the subsequent request [6]. In some applications the entire state information, that is, all the internal data structures which must persist, is flattened out and either written to a file or passed to the client as one or more hidden

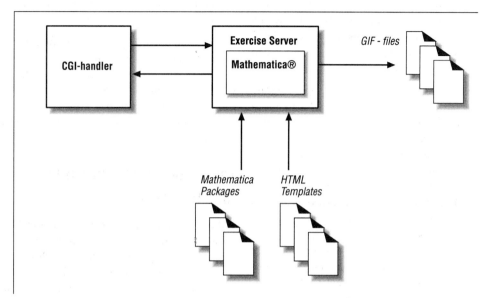

Figure 1:   The server side of interactive exercises

fields [2]. However, in our case, the use of Exercise Server simplifies the task of maintaining the state information. It is no longer necessary to encode/decode data structures to/from flat representation at each HTTP request because it can be kept throughout the entire session in Exercise Server's main memory. Consequently, only an identifier of the session is necessary to be passed in a hidden field. A convenient built-in structure to keep the state information is the context tree [13]. Contexts in Mathematica facilitate distinguishing different uses of a particular name and, as such, are used by our interactive exercises to store the state information of concurrent sessions.

Upon the client's request, the HTTP server spawns the corresponding CGI-handler and passes the encoded form's content to it (assuming the request is using the POST method; see Figure 1). The latter decodes the form's content and connects to ES. The communication between the CGI-handlers and ES is based on Berkeley Sockets API [11] and allows ES to be run either on the same computer, where the HTTP server and CGI-handlers are running, or on a remote

one over a TCP/IP network. An equivalent of the original request is forwarded first to ES and then via MathLink to Mathematica. It is either of the following commands:

```
DoOpenDocument["docname"]

DoSubmitForm["formname","con-
text",{"input1", ...,"inputn"}] ,
```

which directly comply with Mathematica's syntax. The first command explicitly refers to the exercise to be opened. It is an equivalent of the initial GET request. In response, inside Mathematica's environment, a session is initiated and a new context is devoted to it. Inside this context, the state of the session can be conveniently stored as values of symbols, safely isolated from other concurrent sessions. The name of the context is returned in a hidden field, which is part of each form which the generated document may contain. The second command corresponds to a POST request and always refers to a particular session by the name of its context. Formname is the name of the form being submitted. Input1 to inputn are the information entered by the user in the form. There is no explicit command used to terminate a session. Instead, periodically ES examines all opened sessions and closes (deleting their context) those which haven't been active during a certain time interval.

ES replies to any request by generating an HTML-document. It is based on an HTML-template which holds the static parts of the document—those which do not depend on the interaction between the user and the server. The HTML-templates are ordinary HTML files which are normally created with an HTML-editor or any text editor. The places where interactive elements (formulas, plots, text responses, etc.) should appear are marked with designated strings. These strings are then replaced by ES with relevant HTML-elements in order to produce the final HTML-documents, which are sent to the clients. All the plots created at runtime are converted to GIF files using UNIX utility programs and their URLs are embedded in the documents. These GIF-files are best kept in the UNIX system's temporary directory so that they are automatically destroyed on a regular basis.

Example on Conic Sections

"Conic Sections" is an interactive exercise in the course of basic mathematics. It consists of several HTML pages which can be viewed with standard WWW browsers. The example seen in Figure 2 can be studied on our WWW server [1]. The example runs as follows.

Page 1. A second order equation describing a quadratic curve in the xy-plane is generated by Mathematica, and the student is asked to determine the type of the curve.

Page 2. The second page is displayed after the question on Page 1 has been answered correctly. The new problem, related to the same curve, is to bring the curve into its canonical form using coordinate transformations. The computations are carried out by Mathematica. Students are asked to enter the parameters of the coordinate

transformations. To help them identify these parameters, the curve is plotted.

Page 3. The curve is presented in the new coordinate system both as an algebraic equation and as a plot. Students can see the effect of the coordinate transforms and compare their plots with the correct one. They may return to Page 2 to correct their transforms until the desired form is achieved.

Interaction Between Students and Teachers

Although the designed courses are suitable for distance learning and self-study, interaction between students and teachers is still desirable. The distant students should enroll in the courses, and they should know the order and the timetable in which the courses are being taught. They might have problems with the lectures and the exercises and would like to ask for advise or help. The final examination needs to be organized, and the results should be sent to the students. The designed hypermedia environment supports student-teacher interaction on several levels. For each hypermedia course a bulletin board will be set up. The bulletin board is in fact a Usenet newsgroup, and it is visible to every student. In the front page of the WWW course they find a button to open the bulletin board. The students may also put their messages on this board, if they like.

Students may also contact the teacher in a more personal way. At the designated places on the hypernotes they find buttons to send email to the teacher. This feature will be used to give the students personal assistance, to receive their solutions to given problems, and to give them personal feedback. The possibility of attaching documents with email is especially useful, since it allows the sender to point out details on the WWW material.

In addition to email connections and bulletin boards the students and their teacher can also

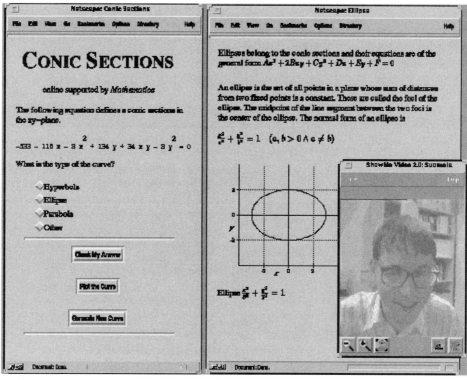

Figure 2: Learning environment with interactive exercise and video connection to the teacher

use videoconferencing software for their meetings and discussions. With ShowMe on Sun [12] and CU-SeeMe [3] on Macintosh and PC, it is possible to establish real-time videolinks. Generally, it is not possible to open a videolink from HTML document to a specific address automatically. Instead, the videolinks have to be opened manually by launching the videoconferencing software and entering the information needed to establish a connection to the teacher. However, the developers of CU-SeeMe videoconferencing software are planning to create a standard (i.e., URL specification) to open a videolink using HTML.

ShowMe includes audio, shared applications, video and whiteboard applications. It uses TCP/IP-protocol and supports Ethernet and ATM. With the Ethernet maximal speed of 10 Mbit/s picture refresh rate may be low and voice may be cropped. The available ATM-connections allow

speeds of up to 155 Mb/s, so that the quality of video and audio is better.

Audio provides 8-bit 8 KHz at 64 Kbps. Audio traffic can be multi- or one-way. Shared Application works with X11-compliant applications. A user can start applications that the other users can see and use. Applications run in the local computer and only send display to other participants screens. Video lets the users see all the participants and take images from participants' video-windows. The quality of the video is not yet sufficiently good to show teaching with, e.g., chalk and blackboard. Text and pictures can also be shown using special shared application called Whiteboard. Participants can see the Whiteboard and write or draw messages on it.

Conclusion

In this paper a hypermedia-based learning environment which supports self-studying and distance learning on the WWW has been presented. Apart from the text and graphics conversions, the main components of the environment are automatically linked hypertext, a database of definitions, exercises and examples with hints, and interactive exercises where an online computer algebra system is used to generate and randomize the problems and to check the answers. Interaction between the teacher and the distant learners will be supported by bulletin boards, email, and finally with videoconferencing software. An experimental group of distance learners will be set up this autumn to test the proposed learning environment both from the technical and the educational point of view. ■

References

1. Antchev K., Luhtalahti M., Suomela K., Pohjolainen S., Conic Sections, Available at *http://matwww.ee.tut.fi/cgi-bin/ConicSections*

2. Paul Burchard (1995), W3Kit 2.2, An Object-Oriented Toolkit for Interactive WWW Applications, The Geometry Center, University of Minnesota, Online document available at *http://www.geom.umn.edu/docs/W3Kit/W3Kit.html*

3. The CU-SeeMe Project (1995), Available at *http://CU-SeeMe.cornell.edu/*

4. Drakos N. From Text to Hypertext: A Post-Hoc Rationalisation of LaTeX2HTML. *First International Conference of the World Wide Web*, 1994 at CERN, Geneva. Available at *http://cbl.leeds.ac.uk/nikos/doc/www94/www94.html*

5. Hector Chris (1995) RTFtoHTML 2.7.5 Converter for Macintosh, Available at *ftp://ftp.ncsa.uiuc.edu/Mosaic/Mac/Related/rtf-to-html-converter-275.hqx*

6. Internet Engineering Task Force (1995), HTTP: A protocol for networked information, Internet draft available at *http://www.w3.org/hypertext/WWW/Protocols/HTTP/HTTP2.html*

7. Multisilta J., and Pohjolainen S. Using Hypermedia in Teaching Linear Algebra. In John G. Lewis (ed.): *Proceedings of the Fifth SIAM Conference on Applied Linear Algebra*, Philadelphia 1994.

8. Multisilta J., and Pohjolainen S. Implementation of Authoring Tools for Hypermedia Based Learning Environments in Mathematics. *Proceedings of CALISCE '94*, 31.8-2.9. Paris, France, 1994. Available at *http://matwww.ee.tut.fi/Docs/paris/paris.html*

9. NCSA httpd Development Team, The Common Gateway Interface, Online document available at *http://hoohoo.ncsa.uiuc.edu/cgi/overview.html*

10. Source Code Cdrom (1994), Walnut Creek CDROM, 1547 Palos Verdes Mall, Suite 260, Walnut Creek, CA 94596 USA, email: *info@cdrom.com*

11. Richard, Stevens W., UNIX Network Programming, Prentice Hall, Englewood, New Jersey, 1990.

12. Sun Microsystems (1995) ShowMe Product Overview. Available at *http://www.sun.com/cgi-bin/show?products-n-solutions/sw/ShowMe/index.html*

13. Wolfram S., Mathematica(TM) A System for Doing Mathematics by Computer, Addison-Wesley, Reading, MA, 1988.

14. Wolfram Research, MathLink Reference Guide, Technical Report, Wolfram Research Inc., 1992. Available at *http://www.wri.com/mathsource/*

About the Authors

Antchev Kostadin
Researcher, M.Sc.
kostadin@butler.cc.tut.fi

Luhtalahti Markku
Researcher, M.Sc.
luhtalah@butler.cc.tut.fi

Multisilta Jari
Researcher, M.Sc.
multisil@butler.cc.tut.fi

Pohjolainen Seppo
Ass. Prof.
pohjola1@butler.cc.tut.fi

Suomela Kari
Researcher, M.Sc.
suomela@harppu.ee.tut.fi

Tampere University of Technology (TUT)
Hypermedia Laboratory
PO BOX 692, FIN-33101, Tampere, FINLAND
http://matwww.ee.tut.fi/

WWW Meets Linda
Linda for Global WWW-Based Transaction Processing Systems

Werner J. Schoenfeldinger

Abstract

World Wide Web (W3) is a fast-growing tool for providing information globally. To cope with HTML it makes applications independent from the operating system and provides them a standard interface. Because there are limitations in the application structure of CGI scripts, we introduce Linda: a language that coordinates the cooperation of several processes. Including Linda in W3-based applications allows a separation of input/output processing and data processing. This new application structure creates the possiblility of W3-based front-ends for stateful transaction systems, distributed applications, and different programming languages. To demonstrate how easily Linda can be included in W3-based applications, we show code samples in Perl and two example applications that have already been inplemented with Linda and W3. **Keywords:** *World Wide Web (W3), user interfaces, Linda, CGI programming, Perl*

Introduction

Using WWW (W3) as a front-end for applications has recently become quite popular. Starting with simple interfaces for retrieval tools such as WAIS or Archie, programmers have decided to teach their programs HTML. The reason for this trend is that a W3-based application has a wide range of advantages for programmers and users alike:

- A W3-based interface makes applications globally accessible.

- With W3, one can develop applications with a system-independent, standardized graphical user interface.

- Text, graphics, sound, and forms can be easily displayed or accessed.

- The Common Gateway Interface (CGI) allows one to add functionality in the form of CGI scripts and/or programs.

- Data can be passed from the browser to the CGI program via the FORM tag.

- The results can be sent to the printer without any further processing.

- Often-used output elements are available in libraries for certain programing languages such as C++ [18], Perl [6], and others.

These advantages make W3 particularly attractive as a front-end for multiuser, transaction processing applications and mass-information systems. However, two severe problems limit the applicability of W3 for these kinds of systems:

- The problem of secure data transmission on the network

- The problem of integrating transaction processing with the W3-based front-end

In this paper, we suggest a uniform and general solution to the second problem by integrating the coordination language Linda [9] with the W3 front-end. Two simple applications are provided to illustrate the power of this approach.

WWW as a Front-end

This section provides a brief overview with W3-based front-ends for user applications. Starting with a short definition of the Common Gateway Interface, we describe the main parts of CGI scripts and try to point out problems with the use of W3 as a front-end via ordinary CGI scripts.

The clear and uncomplicated structure of the gateway allows great flexibility and makes it easy to implement applications with a W3-based front-end. But due to the flexible structure of the gateway we have to deal with two major problems, namely the security problem and the consistency of transaction problems which we will discuss at the end of this section.

Common Gateway Interface

The Common Gateway Interface, or CGI, is a standard for external gateway programs to interface with information servers such as HTTP servers [5].

CGI provides the functionality for passing data between World Wide Web pages and programs. For the data transfer, CGI uses for the actual data transfer both standard input and environment variables of the called process. The processing of passed data is left to the called program. The standard output of the program is returned to the HTTP server and is immediately sent to the browser for display. When we use CGI scripts to process the output of HTML forms, we can distinguish two major methods of passing data to the CGI script [11]:

- *The GET method.* If the form has METHOD="GET" in its FORM tag, the CGI script will receive the encoded form input in the environment variable QUERY_STRING.

- *The POST method.* If the form has METHOD="POST" in its FORM tag, the CGI script will receive the encoded form input on STDIN. The server will not send an EOF at the end of the data. The number of characters that should be read from STDIN is stored in the environment variable CONTENT_LENGTH.

The data is passed in a CGI-specific format [15]. In several programming languages, we can already find routines to handle and translate passed data in a suitable format for further computation.

CGI Scripts/Programs

CGI scripts are written to perform a certain user-defined task. The task can range from simple output-only scripts to sophisticated programs. Generally, we can identify three major parts in CGI scripts:

- Reading the data passed via the CGI and converting it into data structures suitable for further processing

- Processing the data and computing the results. For example, database access or simple computations. This is the main task of the program.

- Formatting the results of the program to HTML and sending the results to standard output

In most languages encoding or decoding from HTML is implemented in specific library routines such as cgi-lib.pl [6] for Perl or ReadParse [18] for C++. CGI scripts can receive data from a W3 page in several ways [19]:

- Via the PATH_INFO variable
  <A HREF="/CGI/myscript/this_ var=15"> testlink</A>

  In this case, data is passed in the PATH_ INFO variable. In the example, this variable contains "/this_var=15".

- Via the QUERY_STRING
  <A HREF="/CGI/myscript?this_ var=15"> testlink</A>

  This method works in the same way as the GET method with an HTML form. The data is passed in the variable QUERY_STRING. Note that the transfer requires a specific format.

- Via a FORM that can support both GET and POST

The programmer must decide how data is passed. If you use a method other than POST, the disadvantage is that the data string is displayed in the "Location" line of most browsers.

Output is given to the server by writing to STD-OUT. The first output line determines the type of the output. The second line should be left blank. From the third line on, additional output can follow.

The first line must be either:

- A reference to another document

  `Location: /path/to/some_doc.html`

  The reference will be interpreted by the server and the stated document will be browsed. This mechanism is used with ISMAP-structures.

- A full document of a specific type

  `Content-type: text/html`

  In this case the whole document is an output of the CGI script. The script has to give some hints to the server about the document's type. This is performed by stating type and subtype of the document. In our case, the type is HTML.

Under UNIX, the CGI program is invoked by the HTTP server under a specific user ID and group ID. Both IDs are set in the HTTP server configuration file. This gives the script the same access permissions and possiblities on the system as the invoking user.

Problems and Limitations of the CGI

As documented in [17], the HTTP server is a stateless server and, therefore, cannot keep any state information for running scripts. If applications require state information, the state has to be maintainted by the script. Two common ways to deal with this problem are:

- Storing the state information as hidden attributes in the W3 pages (Figure 1)

- Storing the state information on the host on which the server is running (Figure 2)

Both methods, however, have serious disadvantages. In using hidden attributes to store the state information, everyone can read the state information in the HTML source. For some applications disclosure of the internal system state is a severe security problem.

In multiuser environments, we have the problem of state consistency. This problem arises when the state of one client depends on the state of other clients. In such situations it is possible that a client can crash, the state information can get lost, and a deadlock in the whole application can result. We find these problems in many types of applications: computer games, credit card validation and credit approval, computer based exams, etc.

Using the file system of the HTTP server's host as a storage medium requires two things. First, the user ID, under which the HTTP server runs, must have access to an area in the file system. On

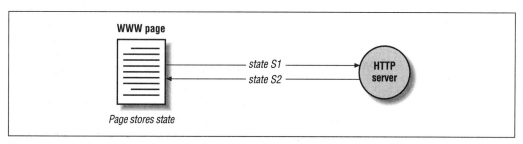

Figure 1:   State information stored in pages

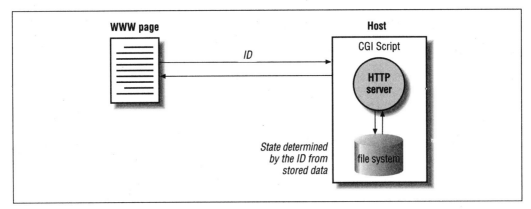

Figure 2:   State information stored at the host

UNIX systems, this could be */usr/tmp*. Second, this storage method implies that all necessary processes for the application have to run on the same host.

With NFS, we overcome this limitation by sharing the relevant data amongst hosts on which it is needed. In such a solution, the data has to be placed in a directory, accessible by all participating hosts.

For building large multiuser transaction systems, W3 is an attractive front-end. Unfortunately, however, transaction processing is a major problem for W3-based applications. Today, transaction processing, process communication and synchronization, data locking, etc. are not supported by the existing CGI toolbox that is available for most HTTP servers. The application programmer must ensure that no conflicts and deadlocks can occur when several users invoke CGI scripts at the same time. Because the file system is the only shared media between the different CGI processes, stability for multiuser transactions can only be achieved through lock files and access delays.

Linda

In this section we describe *Linda*, a language that coordinates the cooperation of several processes.

After a short introduction and a historical review, we focus on the Perl Linda server and the Perl Linda client [20], which we will use later for building applications.

Introduction

Linda was originally developed by D. Gelernter [9] and has already proved its usefulness for writing parallel programs [1, 3, 7, 21]. There are several programming languages that have been extended by Linda, such as APL [12], C [3], C++ [2], Lisp, ML [21], Prolog, and Perl [20].

The core of Linda is a small set of functions that can be added to a base language to yield a parallel dialect of that language. The core consists mainly of a shared data collection called *Tuplespace* and a set of functions to access and modify the data stored in the Tuplespace. The unit of communication is a *tuple*, a list of typed fields that can be either *actual* or *formal*. Actual fields have a specific value whereas formal fields are placeholders for values. Tuples stored in the Tuplespace can only have actual values. Apart from the limitations of the programming language, there are no limitations for number of fields in a tuple or the fieldlength. No empty fields can exist in tuples. How tuples are represented in the Tuplespace is highly dependent on the implementation. In the Perl Linda implementation, they are stored in encoded ASCII text. Some tuple examples are shown below:

- (this,is,an,example,for,a,tuple)

- (x,y,135,436)

In addition to storing and retrieving tuples, the Linda functions provide process synchronization. The basic functions for accessing and modifying the contents of the Tuplespace [3] are:

- out (*tuple*)

  The function out() puts a tuple into the Tuplespace. The tuple can be retrieved by all other processes with the help of other Linda functions. With out(), you can only put data tuples into the Tuplespace. Out never blocks.

- in (*pattern-tuple*)

  For retrieving tuples from the Tuplespace, we use the function in(). This function removes all tuples that match a given template from the Tuplespace and returns them. A template is a tuple with formal fields, to which actual values can be assigned during the matching process. However, no match exists in the Tuplespace in() blocks until at least one matching tuple appears in this space.

- rd (*pattern-tuple*)

  Read is quite similar to in(). The difference is that rd() does not remove the matching tuples from the Tuplespace.

- eval (*function-tuple*)

  Eval creates an active tuple, in fact a task descriptor for which, in Perl Linda, the Linda server is responsible for computation. The active tuple may consist of ordinary elements and functions that need evaluation. The results are stored as a passive tuple in the Tuplespace. Because the command is highly language-dependent, it is not yet implemented in the Perl-Linda implementation. We will not need eval() for our examples.

To prevent deadlocks, Perl Linda has two additional commands. They are nonblocking versions of the rd() and in() commands that have been implemented in the many versions of Linda [3, 1]. They are called nbin() (nonblocking in) and nbrd() (nonblocking read), and return an empty list if no matching tuple is found. The formal fields in templates, supplied with in(), nbin(), rd() and nbrd() functions, can have wildcards, which are symbolized in Linda by the character ?. A wildcard can be matched to any other field in a tuple of the Tuplespace.

Let us illustrate how a typical Linda transaction between two processes takes place. Consider the example of two communicating processes shown in Table 1.

In step 1, the clients put the tuples (x,b,2) and (a,c,4) in the Tuplespace. Client 2 tries to retrieve all three-element tuples with b as the second element using in(). Because there are matching tuples, they are retrieved from the

Table 1:   Two Communicating Processes Under Linda

Step	Tuplespace (Contents)	Client 1	Client 2
1	(x,b,3,x), (a,b,c)	out(x,b,2)	out(a,c,4)
2	(x,b,3,x), (a,b,c), (x,b,2), (a,c,4)	-	a=in(?,b,?)
3	(x,b,3,x), (a,c,4)	-	value of a:(a,b,c), (x,b,z)
4	(x,b,3,x), (a,c,4)	b=in(x,?,?,y)	-
5	(x,b,3,x), (a,c,4)	blocking	out(x,b,3,y)
6	(x,b,3,x), (a,c,4)	value of b:(x,b,3,y)	out(x,b,4,y)
7	(x,b,3,x), (a,c,4), (x,b,4,y)	-	-

Tuplespace and handed to Client 2. In step 4, we have an example of the blocking mechanism of `in()`. Tuples matching the pattern of the `in()` statement given by Client 1 are not found in the Tuplespace; therefore Client 1 blocks. The tuple sent by Client 2 in step 5 matches the pending request from Client 1 and it is transferred to Client 1 in step 6. The following `out()` statement of Client 2 is not sent to Client 1 because it was matching the pattern. This comes because a blocking `in()` or `rd()` is satisfied with just one matching tuple.

The steps shown in the example are logical processing steps of the Tuplespace. There is no need for further coordination between the two clients since `in()` blocks processing automatically until a matching tuple arrives in the Tuplespace.

Perl Linda

Perl Linda is an extension of the language Perl [22]. We have chosen Perl for the implementation of Linda because of its flexible structure and extensibility. Further, Perl has the advantage of being available on many systems, because the source code is public domain. Linda was implemented in Perl as described below:

- The commands of Linda have been added to Perl. Apart from the original Linda commands, commands for fault-tolerant updates of tuples have been added.

- The Linda coordination model has been transferred to a client-server model that is running on a TCP/IP network. In the client-server architecture, Linda consists of a Linda server which represents the Tuplespace and handles the process synchronization, and Linda clients which connect to the server through a TCP/IP network. In this single-server implementation, scaling is achieved through distribution of long running tasks to several idle hosts on which they are processed by the Linda clients. We assume that the actual data transfer is considerably small compared to the runtime of the whole task.

This two-layered implementation of Linda allows clients of different programming languages running on different hosts to access the Linda server and exchange information. The coordination is achieved by using the Linda functions in the specific language. All Linda clients access the data from the server in the same encoded format [20], therefore no compatibility problems between the clients of different programming languages arise.

We have already used Perl Linda for the implementation of distributed ray tracing, distributed processing, and multiuser computer games. In these applications, we have learned that the Linda coordination language is a very powerful tool to coordinate several clients, and that the resulting client programs are considerably smaller than programs using a classical approach [8]. Distributed Tuplespaces among several servers on different hosts have already been developed [1, 7, 21, 23], but have not yet been implemented in Perl Linda.

The requirements for using the Perl Linda server are a UNIX platform, Perl 4.036, and a TCP/IP-based network. We have already tested the Linda server on several platforms such as AIX, HP-UX, LINUX, OSF1, and ULTRIX.

Linda Clients

Because the Linda server handles only the incoming requests from clients, and then stores or retrieves tuples from the Tuplespace, the processing of the tuples and transactions are left to the clients. We have developed clients for the following programming languages, each of which has a certain specialization:

- APL
- C
- C++
- Perl

These clients can use the interface to the Linda server to cooperate and solve a given task. No further coordination is necessary due to the intrinsic blocking mechanism of the `in()` and

Example 1:   Count Client in Perl Linda

```
#!/usr/local/bin/perl                       # Invoking Perl
require "linda-cli.pl";                      # Adding the Linda library
                                             #
&register_client("aig.wu-wien.ac.at", 7999); # Registration to the Linda server
                                             #
@tuple=&nbrd("COUNTBEGIN");                  # Client determines if he is
&out("COUNT",1), &out("COUNTBEGIN")          # the first client ?
if @tuple==();                               #
                                             #
while($var<10000)                            # The count routine
{                                            #
@tuple=&in("COUNT", "?");                    # Get the actual tuple (COUNT, value)
&printtuple(@tuple);                         # Print the whole tuple
$var=&element("last",2,@tuple);              # Extract the value of  COUNT
$var++;                                      # Increase the value by 1
&out("COUNT",$var);                          # Put it to the Tuplespace
}                                            #
&close_client();                             # Say good bye
```

the rd() commands, which are implemented by the Linda server. The clients do not need to run on the same host as the server because they can connect to the Linda server via the network.

Because data is represented in an encoded form in the Tuplespace, the application programmer generally does not need to care about data compatibility between Linda clients in different programming languages. Compatibility should have been achieved by the programmer of the Linda functions in the specific language. He is the one to ensure that all data is converted from the language-specific representation to a suitable format for the Linda server, and vice versa.

The basic structure of a Linda client looks more or less like this:

1. The client connects to the Linda server.

2. Data is transferred between the client and the server. Then data is processed and the results are returned to the server. This strongly depends on the purpose of the program. For some applications only a confirmation might be needed.

3. The client disconnects from the Linda server. Usually the client should disconnect by

sending a disconnect command. However, if the client dies, the server will notice this too.

To illustrate using a sample Perl Linda, we show a Linda client for distributed counting in Example 1. Several Linda clients count a variable from 1 to 10000 simultanesouly. Only one client is able to increase the variable at a time. The coordination is left to the clients. Although this task is not useful in itself, it represents a very good example for parallel programming and coordination.

Restrictions of Perl Linda in Transaction Processing

The flexible structure of Linda generally allows us to easily distribute applications between different hosts and share data and work through a Linda Tuplespace [4]. Because Linda does not provide the full functionality needed for transaction management, we have to keep certain server and client restrictions in mind.

Bakken [1] points out two major problems caused by a crash of the client:

- *Lost tuple problem.* Linda provides only single-operation atomicity, i.e., atomic execution of a single Tuplespace operation. The lost tuple problem arises when one of the clients intends to update a tuple, gets it, and then dies before the updated version can be put back to the Tuplespace. If this tuple is a key tuple, its loss can block the whole application.

- *Duplicated tuple problem.* Consider a situation where a single tuple (describing a task) needs to be replaced by final result and a series of tuples containing information for new tasks. The client dies after writing some new-task tuples but before the client can put the final result to the Tuplespace. In a situation where we already have solved the "lost tuple problem," the originally retrieved tuple gets recovered and another client tries to do the task. The new-task tuple gets duplicated due to a lack of identification.

Perl Linda can cope with the lost tuple problem using the functions `uin()` and `uout()`, which provide a recovery of the updated tuple in case of a crash of the client. A solution to the "duplicated tuple problem" has been implemented in another version of Linda [1]. This solution with *atomic guarded statements* can provide atomicity for a series of `out()` operations. Although this solution is feasible for Perl Linda too, implementation is left to future work.

The second area of problems, when using Linda for transactions systems, is a failure on the server side. To prevent data loss due to a crash on the server side, we have to solve two problems:

- Restart the Tuplespace and restore the data it contained

- Reconnect the clients to the Tuplespace and recover the status

A solution for both problems has already been implemented through replication and use of multiple Tuplespaces [1]. In Perl Linda, the application programmer must provide the application such a facility, and can do so via signal handling. The server side has a mechanism that dumps the contents of the Tuplespace to the local file system and recovers the Tuplespace from it after the restart [20].

Linda Working With WWW

The basic reason for supporting W3-based applications with Linda is that the transaction of input/output processing and data processing can be separate. With Linda, CGI scripts are only responsible for input/output processing. On the other hand, the responsibility for all data processing and transactions is shifted to background application processes, which communicate with the CGI scripts via a Linda Tuplespace (see Figure 4). This procedure results in the following advantages:

- Applications can use services on different hosts. The state of the application is accessible by clients of different hosts but does not need to be saved in the pages.

- The application can use the strengths of several programming languages through a general interface.

- The actual CGI script is only responsible for displaying the data.

- There is no need for coordination between the interface and the application.

- CGI scripts without Linda enforce the structure shown in Figure 3.

In this approach, we see the chance to support W3-based applications with an interface to distributed computing that is both easy to implement and easy to use. The inclusion of Linda in such applications provides bridges between the most popular CGI script language, Perl, and other languages in which Linda clients already exist. These languages have their strengths in different fields, and we can build heterogeneous applications using the different languages wisely. Linda also provides W3 with an interface that meets the Transaction Processing Standards [10], as described below:

- *Portability:* Running and porting programs to many different types of computer systems by writing programs in standard languages.

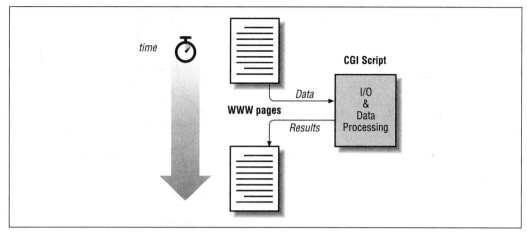

Figure 3:   CGI application without Linda

- *Interoperability:* Defining and implementing standard ways to exchange data.

Application Architecture

In a CGI script without Linda, the browser is being blocked until the CGI script is terminated. The structure of such an application is shown in Figure 3.

For many applications this structure is not sufficient for the following reasons:

- The user would have to wait too long for computation.

- Applications that collect data from several spacial distributed sources and display them in a compact form must not do the actual acquisition of data at the time of request. Facing many requests, this processing would lead to a large overhead and network traffic. One solution to this problem is to have the data updated in regular intervals. If there are many requests, using files to store and update the data is not a good idea.

- The request for information based on a CGI script would cause serious security troubles. The W3 user must have access permission to data. In this case, better protection can be

achieved by retrieving the data from a Tuplespace.

- The application does not depend on user data. W3 is just a front-end to view the current state of a system. All internal states reside in the Tuplespace.

Integrating Linda in W3-based applications results in changes in the application structure. The CGI script, in normal CGI programs responsible for the whole functionality, is only responsible for the data transfer to and from the Tuplespace. In addition to the transfer from the Tuplespace, the script has to convert the data into HTML format.

Figure 4 shows the typical structure of a W3 Linda application. The CGI script interacts between the front-end and the Tuplespace. The other clients that are connected to the Tuplespace can run on different hosts and, of course, in different languages.

Data is shared via the Tuplespace with the actual application. The CGI script waits with an `in()` statement until the application puts the data in the Tuplespace. Compared to the solution without Linda, more applications can use the data sent to the Tuplespace. This processing could, for example, result in a parallel search in several

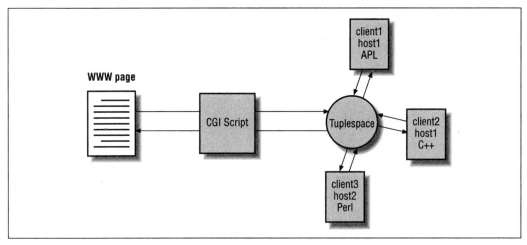

Figure 4:   W3 and Linda working together

databases. The structure of such an application is shown in Figure 5. In Figures 4 and 5, for matters of clarity, the interactions are only shown for one process; however, this application structure works for multiple requests as well. If the processing of a task is very time consuming, more worker clients can be added to the Tuplespace waiting for tasks.

By using Linda as an interconnector between front-end and application, we can develop a flex-

ible, termination-independent structure, as shown in Figure 6.

The application simply checks the Tuplespace for requests. If a request is found in the Tuplespace, the request is handled. Otherwise, the application sleeps for a certain amount of time in order to not exhaust the system resources. The user handles the situations in the same way. After sending the request, he receives a notification that his request is being processed. Meanwhile,

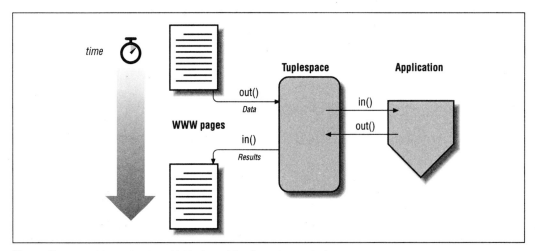

Figure 5:   CGI application with Linda, waiting for task completion

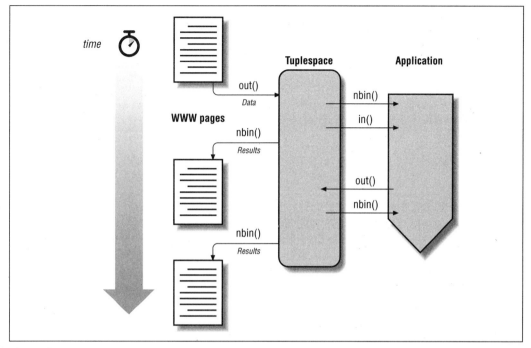

Figure 6:   Linda and W3, front-end is independent from application

he can do other things and then check if the results have arrived. This check can be completed either by automatically reloading the page or by a simple manual query.

Implementation

In this section, we show how the interaction between Linda and W3 is implemented. Our code examples will be in Perl because it is often used for programming CGI scripts. Another reason for using Perl is that the interaction between the front-end and the Tuplespace is not time critical. Therefore, for this class of applications, Perl represents a flexible and sufficient solution.

The only requirement for the Linda W3-based applications is that a Linda server is running on the chosen host and port. The server can be started by every user if the port number is above 1024. The default port number is 7999. The Linda Perl libraries have to be installed in the standard Perl include directory; otherwise, they cannot be found by the CGI script.

In Example 2, we show a very simple interaction between a form and the Tuplespace. No data processing is done; only the data transfer is implemented.

From this example we can see that very little code is needed to implement such a communication. This benefit is, to a great extent, due to the functionality embedded in the "required" libraries.

Example 3 deals with the data transfer in the other direction. Let us consider, as an example, a printer accounting system in which the spooler stores the information about the printed pages in a Tuplespace. The format for this is:

```
(PACC,<userid>,<number_of_pages_
    today>,<number_of_pages_total>)
e.g: (PACC,schoenf,23,542)
```

Example 2:   Data Transfer from Form to Tuplespace

```
#!/usr/local/bin/perl                               # Invoking Perl
require "linda-cli.pl";                             # Adding the Linda Library
require "cgi-lib.pl";                               # Adding the CGI-library [cgi-lib.pl]
&ReadParse;                                         # Reading Information passed by Form
&register_client("aig.wu-wien.ac.at", 7999);       # Registration to Linda Tuplespace
                                                    #
for( sort keys(%in))                                # Transfering data to Tuplespace
{ &out($_, $in{$_}); }                              #   in format (Name, Value)
&close_client();                                    #
                                                    #
print &PrintHeader;                                 # HTTP server needs
print "
```

The printer accounting system consists of two components. First, the spoolers responsible for the printers call a tiny feeder program for the user data in the Tuplespace. The first item, "PACC," is only necessary if the Tuplespace is used by several applications. The second component is the printer accounting statistic shown in Example 3.

The examples show that one can easily separate the acquisition of information from the actual input/output processing. Furthermore, updating information does not depend on user requests. However, a user-dependent update of information can be implemented by the application structure shown in Figure 5.

Example 3:   Source of Printer Highscore

```
#!/usr/local/bin/perl                               # Invoking Perl
require "linda-cli.pl";                             # Adding the Linda library
require "cgi-lib.pl";                               # Adding the CGI-library [cgi-lib.pl]
                                                    #
&register_client("aig.wu-wien.ac.at", 7999);       # Registration to Linda Tuplespace
@tuplelist=&nbrd(PACC,"?","?","?");                 # Transfering data from the
                                                    #     Tuplespace
&close_client();                                    # Closing the connection to the
                                                    #     Tuplespace
for(@tuplelist)                                     #
{                                                   #
($user,$day,$total) = &detrans(split(/,/, $_       # Extracting Data from the tuples
     ));
($usr{$total},$pday{$total})=($user,$day);         # Preparing data for sorted output
}                                                   #

print &PrintHeader;                                 # HTML-Output
print "
printf("%-15s %6s %6s
for( reverse (sort keys(%usr)))                     #
{                                                   #
printf("%-15s %6s %6s
}                                                   #
print "</pre>
```

Applications with Linda and WWW

In this section, we present W3-based applications which work with Linda. We present Disctool, an application which allows a system administrator to view the current usage of hard disks in a cluster, independent of his current working system. The second application, LVA-Express, is a program that implements continuous opinion polls with immediate statistical analysis of the results. This system is intended to improve the course-evaluation system at our university.

Disctool

In our department we now have a cluster of 23 UNIX workstations. Software and applications are distributed amongst the hard disks of these computers. The motivation for this application is that disk space is a scarce resource. Due to automatic processes (ftp mirrors, system logs, mail, backups), disk usage frequently approaches 100%. In this case, users on the network may not be able to save their work, and documents cannot be printed or received. Immediate intervention of a system administrator is required.

The current solution is that the system administrator tries to predict disk shortages in order to take counter measures. Because the task of manually checking 17 systems can be a very time consuming job, we decided to build a W3-based application.

To check the disk usage on a system, we use the UNIX commands *df* and *bdf*, depending on the UNIX version. These commands result in the output shown in Example 4.

Impementation based on Remote Procedure Calls (RPC) [8] implies access rights for the user nobody, which runs the HTTP server. For security reasons, this situation is unacceptable.

Our solution was to use Linda to overcome this problem. Tiny background scripts, running on every workstation, should feed the current disk usage to a Linda Tuplespace. The update intervals are variable and to be configured. A CGI script retrieves the information on request from the Tuplespace and converts it to HTML. The system administrators can check the status of the whole cluster at first glance. The structure of DiscTool is shown in Figure 7.

The information in the Tuplespace is updated by the clients every five to ten minutes. In the intervals between updates, the processes sleep in order to conserve CPU time. We have chosen a two-level interface for the output of disk usage. The first level shows an overview over the cluster, with each partition on the hard disk being represented by an icon. Figure 8 is a screenshot of this overview. If the administrator requires details about a specific partition, he clicks on the icon and further information is retrieved from the Tuplespace (see Figure 9).

Continuous Course Evaluation via W3

The second application we present in this paper is a transaction system, which allows continuous opinion polls. Course evaluations are completed at the Vienna University of Economics and Business Administration (WU-Wien) every year. This process is very time consuming. Much paperwork is involved; the evaluations are based on paper forms which the students complete to eval-

Example 4:   Output of UNIX commands *df* and *bdf*

Filesystem	1024-blocks	Used	Avail	Capacity	Mounted on
/dev/rz3a	41711	32553	4986	87%	/
/dev/rz3g	816425	693637	41145	94%	/usr
/dev/rz3d	51289	15818	30342	34%	/var
/dev/rz1c	1025374	921267	104107	90%	/disk2

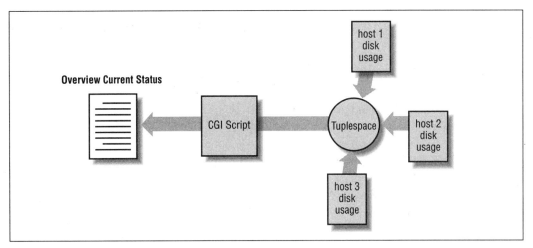

Figure 7: Structure of DiscTool

uate their courses. These questionnaires are entered in a spreadsheet, the output of which is a brochure, containing each lecturer and the corresponding evaluation. This output provides valuable information for new students seeking impressions of course quality.

Since editions of this brochure are usually released with large delays (six to nine months late), we decided to support course evaluation with a W3-based application. Requirements for this application are to provide configurable frontends for the polls that are available throughout the campus. Furthermore, a continuous evaluation, based on data entered, should be provided to give both the lecturers and students the opportunity to discuss course quality immediately at the end of each course.

With course evaluations, the implementation problem is that many students are evaluating the same course at the same time (e.g., after the course), and that each student needs exclusive access to the data file. Since the data has to be saved in files, the read/write access is only possible for one client at a time. A correct implementation of this client must use lock files and interprocess communication to ensure exclusive access to the data files. The second problem is

that a normal CGI script has to read, evaluate, and write all the data on every request.

Linda solves both problems. A Tuplespace is placed in between the evaluation process and the input/output process. The students fill out a questionnaire in an HTML form. The results of this questionnaire are sent to the Tuplespace, and each questionnaire is assigned a transaction number for identification. The CGI script gets the last used ID number from the Tuplespace and increases it by one. Then the number is stored in the Tuplespace again. After sending the data, the CGI script returns a confirmation to the frontend. The user can now decide what to do next. The evaluation process retrieves the stored data from the Tuplespace and evaluates it. This process is considerably faster, because the process keeps the evaluation data in memory and, therefore, does not need to read the data file. After the results are calculated, they are put into the Tuplespace, along with the URL of graph evaluation in gif format, which was specially created for the course. If the user decides to view the evaluation of the course, the information is retrieved from the Tuplespace and displayed. The user gets the newest updated version of the evaluation. The evaluation and update time depends on the number of simultaneous requests and the

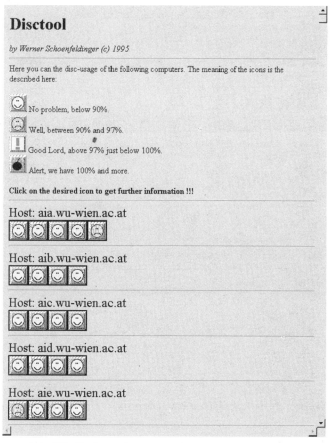

Figure 8: Screen shot of DiscTool overview

speed of the host. The structure of the application is very similar to the structure shown in Figure 6.

Conclusion

In this paper we presented the implementation of W3-based applications with Linda, a high-level set of functions for process coordination and parallel processing which have been added to several programing languages. The inclusion of Linda provides both a standardized interface to other systems and programming languages and the ability to overcome the limitations of conventional CGI scripts. These aspects are achieved by separating input/output processing and data processing. Linda is responsible for the coordination and synchronization of the application, whereas the CGI script is only responsible for input/output processing. Additionally, Linda allows interaction between distributed applications on different hosts connected with a TCP/IP network.

Combining Linda with W3 allows new types of applications such as multiuser interaction systems, cooperative games, and stateful server applications is to be used with a standard W3 front-end. These applications can be established on the input/output side with small Perl scripts. We showed two sample applications in which the W3 front-end proved to be easy to implement and easy to use.

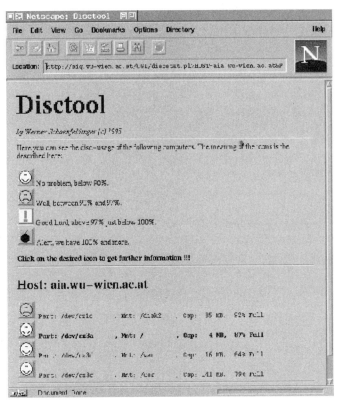

Figure 9:   Screen shot of DiscTool: detailed information

In future developments of Perl Linda, we intend to extend the current implementation with the feature of atomicity for multiple commands and usage of multiple workspaces with the possibility of replication. Future research in Linda WWW applications is planned in experimental economics. We intend to implement market simulations including interaction of human competitors with adaptive agents that interact via a Tuplespace. W3 is a very good front-end for this task, because it does not limit you to text mode and provides a system-independent interface to the prospective users. ∎

References

1. Bakken, D.E., and Schlichting, R.D., "Supporting Fault-Tolerant Parallel Programming in Linda," in *IEEE Transactions on Parallel and Distributed Systems,* Vol. 6, No. 3, March 1995.

2. Callsen, C.J., Cheng, I., and Hagen, P.L., "The AUC C++Linda System," in *Linda-Like Systems and Their Implementation*, Technical Report 91-13, Edinburgh Parallel Computing Center, Edinburgh 1991.

3. Carriero, N., and Gelernter, D., "How to write Parallel Programs: A Guide to the Perplexed," in *ACM Computing Surveys*, Vol.21, No.3, September 1989.

4. Carriero, N., Freeman, E., Gelernter, D., and Kaminsky, D., *Adaptive Parallelism with Piranha*, Technical Report 954, Yale University Department of Computer Science, Feb. 1993.
   http://www.yale.cs.edu/HTML/YALE/CS/Linda/ papers/workshop.ps

5. "The Common Gateway Interface," *http://hoohoo.ncsa.uiuc.edu/cgi/overview.html*

6. Steven E. Brenner, "CGI Form Handling in Perl," *http://www.bio.cam.ac.uk/web/form.html*

7. Ciancarini, P. "Distributed Programming with Logic Tuple Spaces," Technical Report UBLCS-93-

7, Laboratory for Computer Science, University of Bologna, 1993.

8. Comer, D.E., and Stevens, D.L., *Internetworking With TCP/IP, Vol III: Client-Server Programming And Applications*, Prentice Hall, Englewood Cliffs, New Jersey 1993.

9. Gelernter, D., "Generative Communication in Linda" in *ACM Transactions on Programming Languages and Systems*

10. Gray, J., and Reuter A., *Transaction Processing: Concepts and Techniques*, Morgan Kaufmann Publishers, San Mateo 1993.

11. "Supporting Forms with CGI," *http://boohoo.ncsa.uiuc.edu/cgi/forms.html*

12. Hietler, G., "The APL-Linda Client: A Technical Documentation," Technical Report, Janko-Hansen (Eds.) No.14, *Institut für Informationswirtschaft, WU-Wien, Augasse 2-6, A-1090 Wien/Austria*, Vienna September, 1995.

13. "The Hypertext Markup Language," *http://www.w3.org/hypertext/WWW/MarkUp/MarkUp.html*

14. "The Hypertext Transfer Protocol," *http://www.w3.org/hypertext/WWW/Protocols/HTTP/HTTP2.html*

15. Klute R., "Zweiter Gang," in *iX Multiuser Multitasking Magazine* 8/1994, p.140-146, Verlag Heinz Heisse GmbH & Co KG, Hannover 1994.

16. Martin J., and Loeben J., *TCP/IP Networking: Architecture, Administration and Programming*, Prentice Hall, Englewood Cliffs, 1994.

17. Perrochon L., and Fischer R., "IDLE: Unified W3 Access to Interactive Information Servers," in *Proceedings of the Third International WWW Conference*, Darmstadt 1995. *http://www.igd.fhg.de/www/www95/papers/58/www95.html*

18. "A C++-Class for processing the Output of HTML-Forms," */pub/WWW/tools/ReadParseCxx.tar.gz*

19. "The Common Gateway Interface," *http://boohoo.ncsa.uiuc.edu/cgi/primer.html*

20. Schoenfeldinger, W.J., "The Perl Linda Server: A Technical Documentation," Technical Report, Janko-Hansen (Eds.) No.12, *Institut für Informationswirtschaft, WU-Wien, Augasse 2-6, A-1090 Wien/Austria*, Vienna July, 1995.

21. Siegel, E.H., and Cooper E.C., *Implementing Distributed Linda in Standard ML*, Technical Report, CMU-CS-91-151, School of Computer Science, Carnegie Mellon University, Pittsburgh 1991.

22. Wall, L., and Schwartz, R. L., *Programming Perl*, O'Reilly & Associates, Sebastopol, CA, 1990.

23. Wilson, G., "Improving the Performance of Generative Cummunication Systems by Using Application-Specific Mapping Functions," in *Linda-Like Systems and Their Implementation*, Technical Report 91-13, Edinburgh Parallel Computing Center, Edinburgh 1991.

About the Author

Werner J. Schoenfeldinger

Department for Applied Computer Science
Vienna University of Economics and Business Administration
schoenf@aia.wu-wien.ac.at

INTERFACE-PARASITE GATEWAYS

Robert A. Barta, Manfred Hauswirth

Abstract

Apart from challenging new possibilities in resource discovery and retrieval, WWW gives the opportunity to provide legacy applications with a new look and feel and to add functionality without having to change the software itself. We describe problems and possible solutions in the area of connecting legacy software based on terminal sessions to WWW, especially focusing on the problems that arise from adapting stateful interactive services to the stateless HTTP. As a case study we present a WWW gateway to a stateful legacy application (Austrian national academic OPAC) by encapsulating it within a CGI conformant gateway. **Keywords:** *World Wide Web, gateways, legacy software, stateless and stateful, interactive sessions, online public access catalogs (OPAC)*

Introduction

Providing access to nonHTTP-based information systems through the World Wide Web [6] implies that two technical problems have to be tackled. First, WWW requests have to be transformed into queries for the information system—say a database—and, second, query results have to be converted into HTML [5]. There are numerous generic gateways (e.g., [15]) and programming language extensions (e.g., [20]) available for the skilled engineer with which prototypes or even complete applications can be built.

The trouble starts if no application programming interface (API) for the information or database system in question is available, or—similarly serious—no reliable documentation for the system exists. Applications of this kind are often euphemistically referred to as *legacy applications*. Most of them originated many years ago, providing access for querying and maintenance only through interactive, character-based terminal sessions (telnet, 3270) or dedicated user interfaces.

The standard way to "integrate" session-oriented resources into WWW is by providing a telnet URL [4]. A rich list of telnet-accessible resources can be found in [19]. Clicking onto such a link will start up a terminal emulation program at the client site. The user then has to navigate according to the application's interface philosophy which usually does not follow WWW's user interface paradigm. Even worse, most applications expect the terminal emulation to be perfectly configured, forcing the user to use special function keys or escape sequences.

A more seamless integration can be done by writing CGI [14] gateways which encapsulate these applications. Thus users just have to deal with the usual WWW point-and-click GUI paradigm. Carefully designed gateways will also result in a much simpler user interface compared to the original (e.g., [9]).

In the following sections we first describe interface-parasite gateways, an approach we successfully used for the integration of BIBOS, Austria's national academic OPAC. We then argue for a complete integration of gateways into existing information infrastructures. Next, we address the issue of statefulness, which is crucial in the design of WWW gateways, and present our WWW-BIBOS gateway as a case study. Finally, we describe how implementation of interface-parasite gateways can be supported by tools.

Interface Parasites

In the absence of an API interface to an existing system, the only reference is the user interface itself. Our approach is based on attaching to tex-

Figure 1:   Gateway as interface parasite

tual, character-stream-oriented user interfaces with (command) line or page logic.

Providing a seamless service integration into WWW means hiding the *terminal emulation feeling* from the user. This implies that a gateway has to run the terminal emulation on behalf of the client (Figure 1).

The gateway's task is to behave as a *virtual user*. It has to translate HTTP requests into (sequences of) keystrokes that are sent to the terminal emulation. When the application has reacted by showing a new *virtual screen*, the gateway has to analyze it and extract any relevant information. It does so by locally interpreting the data and control stream coming from the application. In the usual case of character-based terminal emulations this necessitates running a telnet or 3270 protocol automaton and interpreting terminal control sequences (e.g., that of VT100). Depending on the type of gateway, relevant information is hypertexted and forwarded to the client.

Detection of information is the key problem here. Any information on a user interface is first converted into an external representation (strings for textual interfaces). Usually semantical information is lost during this process. It is not possible to reverse this process in general. Often information is packed into a few lines because of space limitations on the display. This makes automated detection of information complicated or even impossible. One has to exploit position information which may give a clue to the meaning of a string or rely on heuristics.

Another problem concerns page-oriented interfaces. The end of a page has to be detected before the analysis process can start. In telnet-based services transmission of characters usually just stops at the end of the page. While this is obvious to the human client, it is not for an automated one. In order to avoid painful timeouts, the character stream must be analyzed to identify discriminating character sequences which give a clue to an end of the page. Sometimes heuristics have to be applied here, too.

From the above it is evident that interface-parasite gateways are vulnerable to any kind of layout modifications of the user interface. These, however, are by definition not likely for legacy applications.

Forward and Backward Integration

Providing gateways between WWW and other resources not only allows people to use this service without being bothered by its specialities. It also allows integration with other information systems (Figure 2).

Given a particular URL, the gateway will produce a document on the fly. *Backward integration* means that these virtual documents must have a systematically reproducible URL. Only then can another Web service make more use of the gateway than merely pointing to the gateway's start page. Examples of such gateways are those into X.500 or whois.

Forward integration conveys the approach where the gateway itself enriches its output by providing links to other relevant Web resources. A gateway to a staff database, for instance, could not only return the department and the telephone number of the sought-after staff member

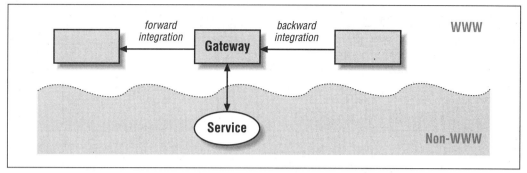

Figure 2:   Forward and backward integration

but could also generate a *mailto* link, say *commonName.surName@organization.country* supposing such an email address is valid.

The effort to maintain a small database of links to be included is often negligible in comparison to the gain of integration.

Stateful vs Stateless Gateways

WWW is based on the stateless HTTP protocol [23]. Using it as GUI for stateless (request-reply) applications, like many C/S applications, works perfectly well. For stateful (interactive) services state information has to be kept and maintained for a certain period of time. The decision what and where state information is stored is crucial for the design [16].

Stateful Gateways

Efficiency and security considerations may prevent the use of a simple stateless gateway approach as described below. In the OMNIS/ Myriad retrieval engine [8], for example, login/ logout is very resource-consuming, making it necessary to use a stateful WWW gateway with dedicated, permanently connected server processes.

Stateful gateways overcome such problems at the expense of having to maintain state information within the gateway. Followup HTTP requests are

related by gateway-maintained state information [16].

Usually a permanently running gateway process keeps up a connection to the server on one side (stateful) and serves successive requests on the HTTP client side. Every request is translated relatively to the gateway's state (Figure 3).

Translation servers [17] work according to this interaction pattern. Though flexible and fast, this approach suffers from a state bookkeeping problem. During a session the history of all requests has to be memorized to provide a stateful connection to the server. In the presence of client caches, which all state-of-the-art browsers use, this management of context information can be quite complicated; whenever the user decides to go back to a previous page, the client will not contact the gateway, but use the cached information instead. New requests issued from previous pages (i.e., previous client states) may confuse the gateway. It may even be forbidden in certain application states, even if no cache is used. Recovery procedures for the gateway will be complex, as some kind of request unification may have to be applied or even complete play-back of the whole session may be necessary.

A similar problem arises when the client interrupts an HTTP request. State may become inconsistent depending on the time the interrupt occurs and the gateway and service semantics. Recovery is hard or impossible in this case.

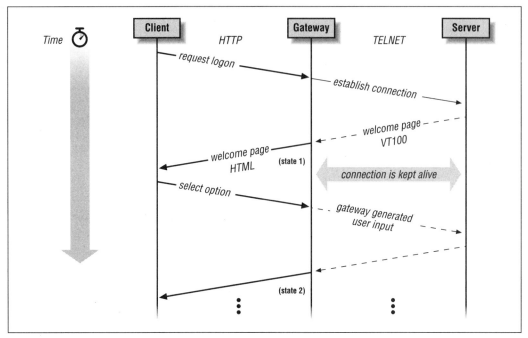

Figure 3:   Stateful gateways

The gateway has to take into account existing timeouts of the session-oriented service and coordinate these with its own (e.g., [17, 8]). This problem is further complicated by unstable client software (lost connections).

Many stateful services have restrictions for concurrent access, be it license agreements or performance problems to necessitate a user limit. Stateful gateways may deny access when the user limit is reached. This may lead to request starvation. In order to cope with this problem, services will try to prevent long inactive sessions. When a user waits too long for a followup HTTP request, the connection between gateway and server will time out. On issuing the next request the gateway either reacts with an error message or has to replay the whole session up to the last state, which might be rather time- and resource-consuming.

Stateless Gateways

Stateless gateways are the simpler type of gateway for stateful services. State information that is necessary to relate HTTP requests and replies is generated by the gateway and stored at the client either within URLs (see [18] for an example) or inside HTML code as hidden fields in forms. Thus stateless gateways make it possible to overcome the possible inconsistency problem of stateful gateways.

There are two extreme approaches:

The *bridge* mirrors the logical user interface structure on the server (e.g., the sequence of terminal pages a user has to navigate through) into WWW pages. User interaction is translated one by one into HTTP requests.

Since the communication pattern itself is stateless, a followup request causes the whole interaction to be replayed up to that context, which has already been built up between the client and the

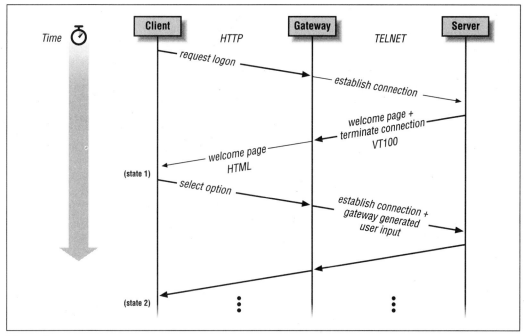

Figure 4: The bridge

service. This implies running through all previous states to build up this context before issuing the new request (Figure 4).

With a similar technique clients themselves work on FTP links. Here the client itself uses the link information to start an FTP session and navigate to the requested directory or file. Afterwards the FTP connection is closed and has to be reopened for followup FTP requests.

This type of gateway is mainly feasible for inherently stateful services like [18] or services that have some kind of "collect and submit" semantics; e.g., consider a shopping service where the user "collects" items and when finished submits a "buy" request. While collecting, the user can easily go back to any previous state (in case of mistakes), pause as long as wanted, and carry on later.

However, this solution also has some significant drawbacks: state information can quickly become rather large and due to replaying of sessions

computing resources are wasted. Additionally, since state information is visible to the user, there is no protection against modification of this information by the user.

One-shot gateways transform the application semantics itself and not only the syntactic server information. This is accomplished by a request/ reply interaction hiding intermediary states (pages) from the user.

This means that the user specifies the complete input information with a single HTML form [7]. After submitting it, the gateway runs a complete session on behalf of the user and returns the relevant information in hypertext representation (Figure 5). This frees the gateway from keeping connections open and provides a higher degree of scheduling freedom. As a byproduct this method offers inconsistency transparency [3], since no state information has to be kept between successive requests.

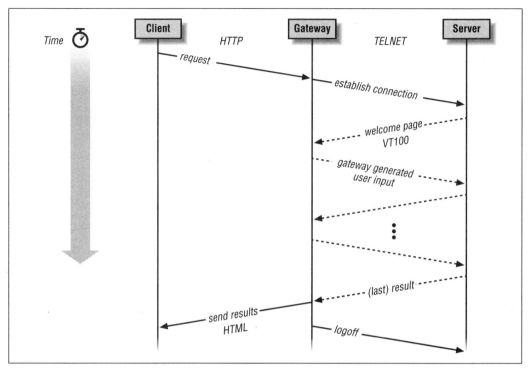

Figure 5:   One-shot gateways

This approach also facilitates a meaningful, seamless integration into WWW. Result information can be collected throughout the session and can be combined, converted, corrected, and enhanced at will and presented in a WWW conformant, hypertext way, not merely mirroring the legacy original.

This implies that the prevailing application has to be analyzed thoroughly. This approach also assumes that all necessary input is provided by the user with a form, redefining the service into a request/reply application. If this is not possible, more sophisticated gateways have to be used. Nevertheless, it seems that a considerably high percentage of applications can be transformed into one-shot applications.

Case Study: WWW-BIBOS Gateway

BIBOS is the Austrian national academic online public access catalog (OPAC) and encompasses almost all of Austria's academic libraries. It is a huge database running on a mainframe for several years now. Before the existence of the gateway, BIBOS only offered terminal emulation access [*telnet://opac.univie.ac.at*]. Some major drawbacks of this access method are:

- Users (especially students) are reluctant to learn how to search and navigate through BIBOS.

- Terminal emulations have to be configured well because the use of special function keys is mandatory.

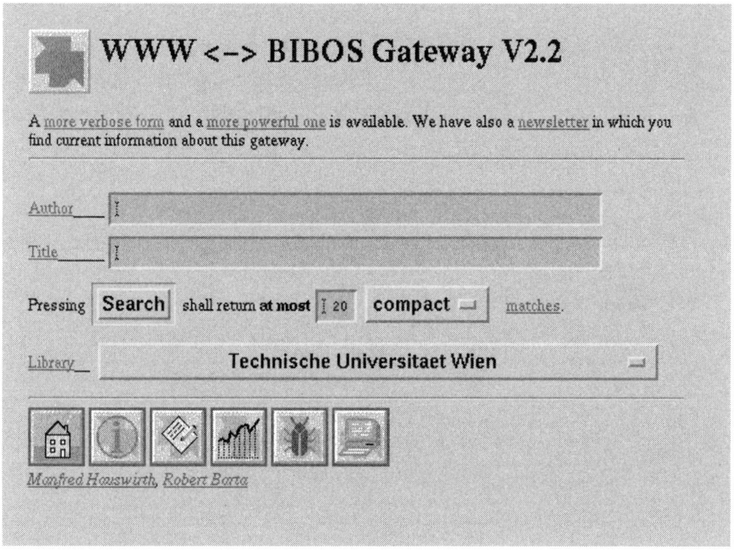

Figure 6:   Gateway query form

- Several pages have to be passed and filled out before the actual search form is reached. The same applies to logging out.

- Important functionalities are unnecessarily complicated to use; e.g., to get detailed information on books, users have to perform a query to get a list of matches first. Only then can one step through the search result and request detailed book information.

- BIBOS is full of acronyms and codes, only understandable to the professional librarian.

The database itself, however, offers exhaustive access to scientific publications. Since there was no BIBOS documentation available to us, we decided to prototype an interface-parasite gateway using the one-shot approach described earlier.

Initially the user is confronted with one out of three possible query forms: a form with all available input fields [*http://bibgate.univie.ac.at/*], the same form with descriptions for the fields [*http://bibgate.univie.ac.at/BIBOS-2/Search-verbose.html*], or a concise one [*http://bibgate.univie.ac.at/BIBOS-2e/Form.pl*] (Figure 6), only con-

taining the most important fields. All types of forms are linked to each other. Additional information (help, feedback, usage, deficiencies) is available via buttons at the bottom of each query page.

Having filled out the query specification, the user has to submit the form. On return, he/she will receive a list of matches. Every match is displayed in a compact or detailed way, depending on the user's selection in the query form. Figure 7 shows a compact query result.

Clicking on a specific match will repeat the query and will return a more detailed description. If the user wants detailed descriptions for all books there is a *gory details* link at the top of the result page.

To get in contact with our customers we offer a feedback form to them. Initially this was only a simple form where users could enter their freely formulated opinions. As we received only a few, mostly imprecise statements, we decided to offer an exhaustive questionnaire. We now receive lots of feedback with more meaningful bug descriptions and suggestions for improvements.

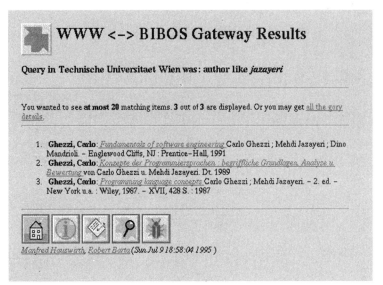

WWW <-> BIBOS Gateway Results

Query in Technische Universitaet Wien was: author like *jazayeri*

You wanted to see **at most 20** matching items. **3** out of **3** are displayed. Or you may get all the gory details.

1. **Ghezzi, Carlo**: *Fundamentals of software engineering* Carlo Ghezzi ; Mehdi Jazayeri ; Dino Mandrioli. - Englewood Cliffs, NJ : Prentice-Hall, 1991
2. **Ghezzi, Carlo**: *Konzepte der Programmiersprachen : begriffliche Grundlagen, Analyse u. Bewertung* von Carlo Ghezzi u. Mehdi Jazayeri. Dt. 1989
3. **Ghezzi, Carlo**: *Programming language concepts* Carlo Ghezzi ; Mehdi Jazayeri. - 2. ed. - New York u.a. : Wiley, 1987. - XVII, 428 S. : 1987

Manfred Hauswirth, Robert Barta (Sun Jul 9 18:58:04 1995)

Figure 7:   Query results

Extending the Functionality

The gateway offers a wealth of additional functionality to the user which was not present before.

- Detailed search results can now be requested directly. Also, the user may now restrict the maximum number of matches returned, to have better response times. Future gateway versions will provide a taggable list of compact results, where the user can select the match that will be displayed in detail.

- In order to support sporadic users we supply a simple context-sensitive help facility. By clicking on the label of a query field a verbose query form is displayed at corresponding page position (Figure 8). The user then can go back to the initial form (where parts of a query might already have been specified) or use the verbose form.

- Some entry fields in the original BIBOS interface require the user to enter special names and codes, e.g., library selection or the type of medium to look for. In the gate-

way these fields are offered through selection lists.

- We tried to integrate the existing information infrastructure into the gateway (forward integration). If, for instance, a particular book is located in a department and not in a library, we refer into an information system about departments and their staff (currently works only for our university). Otherwise we link to the library information service.

- While BIBOS allows a keyword search, the list of valid keywords is stored separately. The gateway provides access to that list via a link.

- Additionally, we analyze shelf codes and enhance these alpha-numerical codes with a more meaningful, user-friendly text and hyperlinks, if an appropriate information system exists (currently works only for our university).

- For backward integration the gateway now allows URLs to point to BIBOS references. These BIBOS links can easily be embedded into other HTML documents. Some Austrian

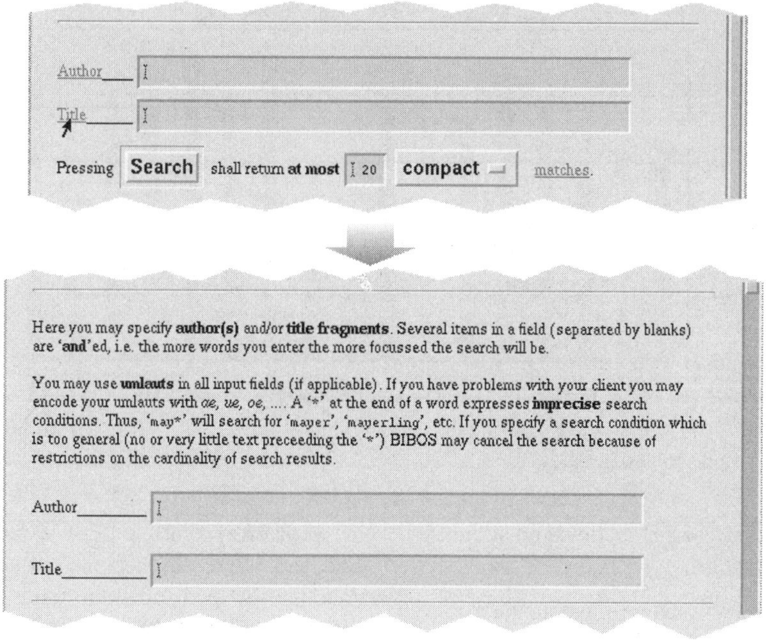

Figure 8: Context-sensitive help

universities have already included publication lists of their staff into their information systems by adding hyperlinks into the WWW-BIBOS gateway. Instead of having to fill out forms and submitting them, corresponding hyperlinks are generated automatically with appropriate parameters and link activations result in a query to BIBOS.

Other improvements simply result from using state-of-the-art WWW browser. Users now can go back to any previous page at any time using client caches. This is not possible in the page logic of BIBOS itself.

Due to BIBOS' terminal interface only a limited number of items can be displayed per output page. The user has to jump back and forth. Query results cannot be printed from inside BIBOS. The gateway, however, delivers all matches in a single HTML page which can also be printed readily.

Implementation Problems

In addition to the general issues of stateless interface-parasite gateways we had to cope with other problems when implementing the gateway.

The most serious and basic problems we encountered were the lack of an API and any documentation of the interface. We initially had to analyze BIBOS' output behavior which we did in a long and painful trial-and-error process.

Since we did not want to implement a full 3270 protocol automaton, we decided to use tn3270, which offers a telnet-based 3270 emulation. Our gateway then analyzes VT100 control sequences to keep a local virtual screen.

The virtual screen is necessary because the BIBOS interface returns data whose semantics derive from its position on the screen. Additionally, there exists no standard format for the reference information returned by BIBOS. The gateway has to guess which parts of a reference

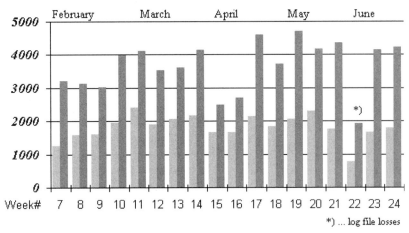

Figure 9:   BIBOS gateway usage

denote author, title, bibliographic and administrative information.

There are several situations when the gateway cannot precisely detect whether a page has been transferred completely or not. This end-of-page detection problem could only be solved by using appropriate heuristics.

Finally we had to cope with a couple of special cases the existing BIBOS interface exhibits. So, for instance, a query process works slightly different when searching in all libraries at once rather than in a single one. Also BIBOS returns detailed information instead of compact references when only one match is found for a query. These nonorthogonalities do not make sense in a WWW context, so the gateway hides them from the user.

Performance Considerations

Introducing such a gateway clearly simplifies the handling for the end user. Still, one should also consider the effects on the involved hosts and the traffic produced by such a service, especially when it gains widespread popularity. Figure 9 depicts access statistics of our gateway. The smaller bars represent the number of query-form fetches; the taller ones are actual search requests.

In pregateway times people were using telnet and, less often, 3270 emulations. The former is quite costly in bandwidth terms, since every typed character results in two packets on the network. Result pages may be fragmented, adding to the network cost. This problem is less serious with 3270 since it transmits on a page-by-page basis.

Our gateway, in turn, receives HTTP requests, uses 3270 as terminal emulation protocol, and ships back HTTP packets. This—especially over long distances—is cheaper than having a VT100-based telnet session.

This traffic reduction is attained at the cost of additional processing load on the gateway and on the database host. Currently, for every request a new 3270 connection has to be established. Since the gateway is stateless, the database host may be forced to repeat queries already performed. Nevertheless, it does not have to keep open long-lived sessions, thus giving it more scheduling freedom.

Planned Improvements

The gateway has left its prototype phase and is about to be institutionalized. This necessitates several procurements, such as providing a better online documentation and adding search demos.

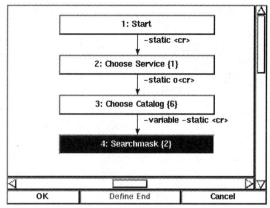

Figure 10:   Interface logic

Also, more sophisticated management tools have to be considered.

The most important goal, however, is an increase in performance. As already mentioned, the connection establishment is responsible for a good deal of the delay. To overcome this, we will run permanent terminal-emulation sessions. Particular search requests will be assigned by a global scheduler to one of these sessions. This will also lead to a more modular gateway architecture.

Concerning the functionality, we have to set up a more manageable, i.e., scalable scheme to integrate existing information systems. The idea is to include pointers to information systems that belong to the organization which hosts a book, or, if available, to link to an electronic version of the document. Furthermore comprehensive analysis of classification and shelf codes will be performed (currently this analysis is done only for our local university library). Their syntax and meaning depends on the sublibrary, making necessary an incremental process depending on the support we receive from the librarians.

Spin-off Projects

Our experiences with the gateway have encouraged us to benchmark the approach with other services. This resulted in prototypes for the Aus-

trian electronic telephone book (not publicly available) and for the Austrian stock exchange (service is cancelled due to licensing problems).

In general, during a session with an interactive service a user is confronted with a couple of pages. Each single page requires the user to input some commands or fill out a form. All possible pages build a network with the pages as nodes and commands as edges. Currently we are working on a tool which will support the designer when analyzing such a network.

Interface Logic

With the help of the tool the designer navigates through the pages. The tool memorizes pages already encountered and unifies those pages—with the help of the designer—which have to be regarded to be the same. During this process the tool learns about the significant and nonsignificant parts of a page.

In the same way the commands (edges) that link the individual pages are learned. In particular, the tool gains knowledge of which parts of a command are constant and which are variable (Figure 10).

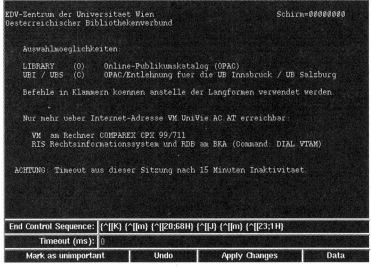

```
EDV-Zentrum der Universitaet Wien                          Schirm=00000000
Oesterreichischer Bibliothekenverbund


  Auswahlmoeglichkeiten:

  LIBRARY    (O)    Online-Publikumskatalog (OPAC)
  UBI / UBS  (C)    OPAC/Entlehnung fuer die UB Innsbruck / UB Salzburg

  Befehle in Klammern koennen anstelle der Langformen verwendet werden.


  Nur mehr ueber Internet-Adresse VM.UniVie.AC.AT erreichbar:

   VM  am Rechner COMPAREX CPX 99/711
   RIS Rechtsinformationssystem und RDB am BKA (Command: DIAL VTAM)


  ACHTUNG: Timeout aus dieser Sitzung nach 15 Minuten Inaktivitaet.
```

End Control Sequence:	{^[[K} {^[[m} {^[[20;68H} {^[[J} {^[[m} {^[[23;1H}
Timeout (ms):	0

| Mark as unimportant | Undo | Apply Changes | Data |

Figure 11:   Query session

Page Information

For every page the designer has to mark the positions on the screen where relevant information is expected. In this phase the tool learns about the semantics of a particular piece of information.

Query Session

Now the designer has to define a path through the network of pages. Along with that he has to specify how input parameters have to be mapped to the variable parts of commands (Figure 11).

Backend Generation

In this phase a code skeleton (we plan to use perl [22]) for running a query session is generated. Afterwards the designer has to supply code that defines how the collected information is presented to the client.

The tool will free the designer from digging into character codes and will help to adapt to small modifications in the interface logic.

Related Work

Considerable effort has been spent in many recent projects to integrate existing databases and legacy systems into WWW. Different application domains and requirements led to a high variety of solutions.

After a proof-of-concept gateway succeeded, the MORE [9] project team decided to completely redesign the underlying database. Switching from a stateful database environment to a stateless WWW interface environment transformed the original complex multifunction windows interface into a rather simplistic single function/single action interface.

Special attention to the user interface design area of gateways is paid in the OMNIWeb system [13]. Typical user sessions are analyzed to meet user requirements and a context-sensitive help facility is added.

Instead of using specialized gateways to access legacy data, the CUBAI project [2] promotes (bijective) conversion of such data into a common format, facilitating integration and interchange of heterogenous data. The benefit of needing only one WWW gateway to access the common data, however, is achieved at the expense of high conversion costs.

The OmniPort system [10] tries to integrate legacy data by bidirectionally translating the native search capabilities into a standard language. Thus consistent access to multiple information sources is offered regardless of particular access methods. It supplies new uniform search capabilities using WWW as front-end for easy and everywhere availability. A similar approach is used in Willow [21], which uses the architectural paradigm of database drivers to communicate to various databases in a uniform way. A driver for Z39.50 [1], a standard that defines a uniform procedure to query information resources, is supplied.

Other approaches try to cope with the problem of generating gateways by describing the original user interface and thus deriving an executable gateway. Expect [12] allows a definition of dialogs with interactive programs by programmatically characterizing interactions.

IDLE [17] is a description language for interactions with telnet-based, character-stream-oriented interfaces. IDLE programs are interpreted on the fly by a so-called translation server [16], thus providing the intended WWW-gateway functionality. Problems of gatewaying between stateless and stateful protocols are addressed in [16].

Conclusion

A considerable number of useful services is provided by so-called legacy systems. This does not necessarily mean bad software, but it indicates that its production standards make it difficult to modify it in respect to user interface techniques and/or functionality [11]. Especially code for the user interface is tightly embedded into the application's code and cannot be upgraded easily to modern user expectations.

Interface-parasite gateways are a cheap and—when carefully designed—an effective way to integrate an existing service into a global infor-

mation infrastructure like the World Wide Web. Their employment provides a new look and feel to an application and prolongs the application's lifetime. ∎

References

1. ANSI/NISO, *Information Retrieval (Z39.50): Application Service Definition and Protocol Specification, technical report Z39.50-1995*, May 1995. *ftp://ftp.loc.gov/pub/z3950/ftr/ftr[1-4].ps*

2. A. Balestra and M. Ferrucci, *Accessing libraries in a uniform way: the CUBAI project*, contribution to the workshop "Offering the same information via multiple services," First International Conference on the World Wide Web, Geneva, May 1994. *http://www.oat.ts.astro.it/www94/paper.html*

3. R. A. Barta, *Formal specification of distributed systems - A discrete space-time logic*, PhD thesis, Vienna University of Technology, 1995. *http://www.infosys.tuwien.ac.at/Staff/rbo/Dissertation/Dissertation.html*

4. T. Berners-Lee, *Uniform Resource Locators*, 1992. *http://www.w3.org/hypertext/WWW/Addressing/Addressing.html*

5. T. Berners-Lee, *HyperText Markup Language (HTML)*, 1993. *http://www.w3.org/hypertext/WWW/MarkUp/MarkUp.html*

6. T. Berners-Lee, R. Cailliau, A. Loutonen, H. F. Nielsen, and A. Secret. *The World Wide Web*, Communications of the ACM, 37(8), August 1994.

7. T. Berners-Lee and D. Connolly, *Hypertext Markup Language - 2.0*, World Wide Web Consortium, June 1995. *http://www.w3.org/hypertext/WWW/MarkUp/html-spec/html-spec_toc.html*

8. A. Clausnitzer, P. Vogel, and S. Wiesener, *A WWW interface to the OMNIS/Myriad literature retrieval engine*, Third International World Wide Web Conference (Darmstadt, Germany, 10-14 April 1995), *Computer Networks and ISDN Systems*, 27(6):1017-1026, Amsterdam, North-Holland, Elsevier, April 1995. *http://www.igd.fhg.de/www/www95/papers/65/omnis-www95/omnis-www.html*

9. D. Eichmann, T. McGregor, and D. Danley, *Integrating Structured Databases Into the Web: The MORE System*, First International Conference on the World Wide Web (Geneva, May 1994), *Computer Networks and ISDN Systems*, 27(2):281-288, 1994. *http://www1.cern.ch/PapersWWW94/more.ps*

10. S. G. Ford and R. C. Stern, *OmniPort: Integrating Legacy Data into the WWW*, Second International Conference on the World Wide Web (Chicago,

October 1994). *http://www.ncsa.uiuc.edu/SDG/IT94/Proceedings/CorInfSys/stern/stern-ford.html*

11. H. Gall, R. Klösch, and R. Mittermeier, *Architectural Transformation of Legacy Systems*, ICSE-17, Workshop on Program Transformation for Software Evolution (Seattle, USA, April 1995), April 1995.

12. D. Libes, *Expect - programmed dialogue with interactive programs*, National Institute of Standards and Technology, July 1994.

13. G. J. Mathews and S. S. Towheed, *NSSDC OMNIWeb: The First Space Physics WWW-Based Data Browsing and Retrieval System*, Third International Conference on the World Wide Web (Darmstadt, Germany, April 1995), *Computer Networks and ISDN Systems*, 27(6):801-808, Amsterdam, North-Holland, Elsevier, April 1995. *http://www.igd.fhg.de/www/www95/papers/68/omniweb_paper.html*

14. R. McCool, *The Common Gateway Interface*, 1994. *http://hoohoo.ncsa.uiuc.edu/docs/cgi/overview.html*

15. J. Ng, *GSQL - a Mosaic-SQL gateway*, NCSA, December 1993. *http://www.ncsa.uiuc.edu/SDG/People/jason/pub/gsql/starthere.html*

16. L. Perrochon, *Translation servers: gateways between stateless and stateful information systems*, Network Services Conference (London, November 1994), November 1994. *ftp://ftp.inf.ethz.ch/doc/papers/is/ea/nsc94.html*

17. L. Perrochon and R. Fischer, *IDLE: Unified W3-access to interactive information servers*, Third International Conference on the World Wide Web (Darmstadt, Germany, 10-14 April 1995), *Computer Networks and ISDN Systems*, 27(6):927-938, North-Holland, Amsterdam, Elsevier, April 1995. *ftp://ftp.inf.ethz.ch/doc/papers/is/ea/www95.html*

18. S. Putz, *Interactive Information Services Using World Wide Web Hypertext*, First International Conference on the World Wide Web (Geneva, May 1994), *Computer Networks and ISDN Systems*, 27(2):273-280, 1994. *http://www1.cern.ch/PapersWWW94/putz.ps*

19. P. Scott, *HYTELNET*, Northern Lights Internet Solutions, Saskatoon, Sask, Canada, 1995. *http://galaxy.einet.net/hytelnet/START.TXT.html*

20. K. Stock, *Oraperl*, 1992. *ftp://ftp.switch.ch/software/sources/perl/db/perl4/oraperl/*

21. University of Washington, *Washington Information Looker-upper Layered Over Windows (Willow)*, 1994. *http://www.washington.edu:1180/willow/home.html*

22. L. Wall and R. L. Schwartz, *Programming perl*, Cambridge, MA, O'Reilly & Associates, 1992.

23. World Wide Web Consortium, *Hypertext Transfer Protocol (HTTP)*, 1995. *http://www.w3.org/hypertext/WWW/Protocols/HTTP/HTTP2.html*

About the Authors

Robert A. Barta

[*http://www.infosys.tuwien.ac.at/Staff/rho/*]
EUnet Austria
Robert A. Barta is information manager at EUnet Austria [*http://www.eunet.co.at/*]. He received his M.Sc. in Computer Science in 1991 and a Ph.D. in Computer Science in 1995 from Vienna University of Technology. His current research interests include formal specification techniques, resource discovery, and distributed-information management. When this work was done Dr. Barta was at the Distributed Systems Department [*http://www.infosys.tuwien.ac.at/*], Information Systems Institute at the Vienna University of Technology. *rho@eunet.co.at*

Manfred Hauswirth

[*http://www.infosys.tuwien.ac.at/Staff/pooh/*]
Vienna University of Technology
Manfred Hauswirth is a Ph.D. student at the Distributed Systems Department [*http://www.infosys.tuwien.ac.at/*], Information Systems Institute at the Vienna University of Technology. He received his M.Sc. in Computer Science in 1994 from Vienna University of Technology. His research interests include distributed-information management, distributed multimedia systems, resource discovery, and user interfaces. *M.Hauswirth@infosys.tuwien.ac.at*

NOT JUST DECORATION
QUALITY GRAPHICS FOR THE WEB

Chris Lilley

Abstract

In some applications, high quality graphics are essential. This paper reviews factors affecting the display of accurate graphical information in a heterogenous networked environment, concentrating on the areas that must be addressed to implement Web user agents which offer good color fidelity. Image rendition strategies for a color-scarce environment are described and the color allocation strategies of several popular Web browsers are examined. Given current trends in provision of device independent color, projected future needs for Web user agents are described. Lastly, the implications of embedded image metadata are discussed. **Keywords:** *WWW web graphics, images, quality, portability, inline, CIE, color, color fidelity, gamma transparency, alpha, PNG*

Introduction

The means of providing and using high quality textual information on the Web has received a great deal of attention. Of course, there is still plenty of low-grade textual information out there. But the requirements are well understood and the infrastructure is in place for those who wish to generate or use quality text.

Much graphical material on the Web is also of poor quality, but in contrast the requirements for high quality graphics on the Web have received much less attention. Granted, many graphics are mere adornment, but some are not. Graphics can be valid information in their own right.

It would also be dangerous and limiting to assume that browsing constitutes the totality of present and future Web use. In some applications, the graphical component can be essential. Thus, it makes sense to evaluate the particular requirements for quality Web graphics.

Application Areas

A sample of existing and potential application areas dependent on high quality images:

- Inline graphics were first added to the Web because they were needed for a distributed, collaborative *scientific visualization* applica-

tion. Thus, NCSA Mosaic [1] was born. Scientific visualization remains an application where high quality graphics are an essential requirement and where graphics constitute the bulk of the information.

- Commercial applications such as *product design* and collaborative evaluation of prototypes clearly benefit from using the Web, and also require a high level of color fidelity in rendition of images.

- In the *medical* and *veterinary* fields, clear and portable images are essential if clinical decisions are to be made using them; there is also the need for tightly coupled image metadata for safety and liability reasons.

- Accurate, repeatable device-independent color representation is an emerging key requirement in *advertising*. Extreme care is currently taken with printed materials to ensure consistent colors for such things as brand identification and corporate identity, but the infrastructure is only slowly being put in place to assure a similar level of fidelity on the Web.

- Last but not least, computer graphics research has a clear need for the dissemination of accurate images for viewing and analysis by colleagues worldwide.

Scope

This paper will survey some major areas affecting two-dimensional, static, raster graphics quality. Vector graphics (such as CGM), three-dimensional graphics (such as VRML), animations, and movies are not considered.

It will focus on areas such as accurate color and tonal rendition which may as yet be unfamiliar to developers of Web user agents. Topics which are important for Web graphics in general, but do not strictly relate to graphics *quality*—such as compression efficiency—are also outside the scope of this paper.

Effect on Web User Agents

Computer Graphics can be seen as a somewhat specialized area—particularly where accurate rendition is required. Yet parts of it need to be understood to produce good graphics. Experience has shown that users can be harshly critical of browsers with poor image quality, even if these same browsers excel in other areas. The thrust of this paper is to pull together separate strands of computer graphics as they relate to Web user agents, to make it easier to provide the increasingly high levels of graphical quality that users are demanding.

A number of different quality requirements are discussed in this paper. Attempting to implement a single one of these in isolation can be difficult, as there are strong interactions between them. Partial implementation still requires an awareness of the other factors. This paper highlights known interdependencies to make the implementor's job easier and prevent nasty surprises.

Antialiasing—What Is It?

Aliasing is an artifact caused by inadequate sampling frequency.[*] The term is most commonly applied to spatial aliasing, which manifests as visible pixelation—a blocky or jagged effect—especially with near horizontal or near vertical lines of high contrast. It is thus particularly noticed with textual annotation of images. Figure 1 shows a sample image, converted from a PostScript file with one sample per pixel, that displays severe spatial aliasing.

How Is Aliasing Reduced?

Aliasing may be reduced by taking multiple samples of the underlying information. In the case of a computer graphics technique such as raytracing, this involves shooting multiple rays through different parts of each pixel. In the case of PostScript conversion to images, this is achieved by

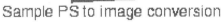

Figure 1:   A severely aliased image

---

* The standard reference is [12]. A shorter and more informal introduction is [13] by the present author.

Sample PS to image conversion

Figure 2:   An antialiased image

rasterizing at a higher resolution, then resampling down to the intended resolution. Figure 2 shows the same PostScript file rendered with 16 samples per pixel. Much less aliasing is seen. Careful examination of the edges of lettering and the colored blocks shows that the background and foreground colors have been blended together based on their subpixel coverage.

What is Transparency?

Image file formats that support transparency are able to make certain designated pixels wholly or partially transparent, so that the background color or texture shows through. In this way, non-rectangular images may be simulated regardless of the background color or texture of the user agent, as in seen in Figure 3.

The simplest type of transparency is binary—each pixel is either *on* or *off.* This may be specified by a binary transparency mask, or (particularly with palette-based formats) by nominating a particular color or group of colors to be transparent. The latter method is used by the GIF89a format [4] and is widely supported in current Web user agents.

The Problem

There is a **severe interaction** between antialiasing and binary transparency. Because the background color of the image is mixed in with the foreground colors, simply replacing a single background color with another is not enough to simulate transparency. There will be a whole host of shades which are *mixtures* of background and foreground colors, as Figure 4 shows. The effect in this case is a white halo around objects, because the original image was antialiased to a white background color.

The Solution

An improvement on binary transparency is variable transparency, also known as an alpha mask or alpha channel. Here each pixel can take any value between fully opaque and fully transparent, and this value is independent of the color of that pixel. Besides allowing smooth transitions between a graphic and the background, this permits a different type of antialiasing.

Foreground colors contributing to a particular pixel are mixed together according to their subpixel foreground coverage, *ignoring* contribution from the background. The alpha channel value is used to express the fractional contribution of the original background, irrespective of that back-

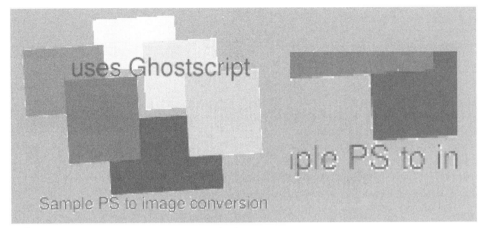

Figure 3:　　Halo effect caused by anti-aliased edges

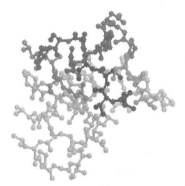

Figure 4:　　An image with binary transparency, on different backgrounds

ground's color. When rendered, this alpha channel specifies for each pixel what proportion of the existing background is to be mixed with the forground image data to produce the final color of each pixel. In this way, the antialiased image can be displayed on any background or texture, or indeed composited on top of another arbitrary image, without the artifacts seen with binary transparency.

Notes to Implementors

Interactions

There has been an increase in the number of antialiased images as people strive for better quality, and this brings to the fore a number of interactions. That between antialiasing and binary transparency has already been noted. Also, anti-aliased images contain a lot more colors than aliased ones, which puts pressure on the color allocation strategy.

Variable transparency is most easily implemented with a truecolor display, because if any image pixel may be mixed with the user agent's background color or texture in any proportion, the total number of colors in a displayed image can become quite large. It can be implemented in a color-scarce environment provided an off screen buffer is provided to composite the image before reducing it to the current palette.

Recommendations

Future Web user agents should permit as inline images formats that support variable transparency, to allow quality antialiased images that are independent of the background color or texture. Suitable formats include extended TIFF [5] and PNG [6]. This will encourage information providers to migrate away from formats that only support binary transparency, such as GIF89a.

This will also allow the OVERLAY attribute of the draft HTML 3.0 FIG element [7] to be deployed more effectively. Overlays are only of use if one can also see what is being overlaid.

Gamma Correction

When expressing a color in RGB, what we are trying to specify is the amount of light which will be emitted from each phosphor, as a fraction of full power. What we are *actually* specifying is, however, the voltage which will be applied to each electron gun.

The two are not linearly related, because the amount of light emitted is proportional to the beam power rather than the voltage. The beam power is the product of voltage and current, and current turns out to be roughly proportional to the grid voltage to the power 1.5. Thus, the light emitted is proportional to the voltage to the power 2.5 or so. The actual value of the exponent, called *gamma*, varies somewhat, and the power law is only an an approximate model of the real situation, albeit a good one. An additional optical effect caused by viewing images against a dim surround is that the effective gamma value is somewhat reduced, from a theoretical 2.5 to around 2.2

To deal with this nonlinearity, the inverse power function (1/2.2) is applied to the RGB data before display, compensating for the nonlinearities which will be introduced. Figure 5 shows a typical correction curve, which is a mirror image about the line Input = Output of the display nonlinearity. (In other words, the display nonlin-earity curves down from a straight line, and so the gamma correction curves up from that line [8].)

There are a number of places at which this correction could be applied, and this affects how Web user agents handle image data.

1. In the image data itself; in other words a correction has been applied at the server end.

2. In the user agent software; correction is being applied as the image is streamed in.

3. In the software of the underlying platform; the Apple Mac and SGI workstations are examples of systems which apply some correction at this stage, using corrections of 1/1.8 and 1/1.7 (by default) respectively.

4. In the hardware of the underlying platform, using variable attenuation or amplification; the Barco Calibrator is an example of a monitor which performs correction at this stage, using test signals and measured luminance values to correct itself.

The end result of all these potential corrections, plus the display nonlinearity, must equal a linear transformation for accurate tonal reproduction to be obtained. The Web user agent must therefore be aware of the amount of correction from step one (in the image file received from the server) and from steps two and three (provided by the underlying platform) so that the appropriate correction can be made.

Gamma: Avoiding Guesswork

With most image formats there is no way to determine if any correction has been applied at step one, and if so, what value was used. This results in considerable uncertainty among information providers as to how to proceed. The following quote is typical:

> We have no real stats on what people on the nets have and what looks best. Most Macs wash out the colors, while Windows 3.1 makes everything look

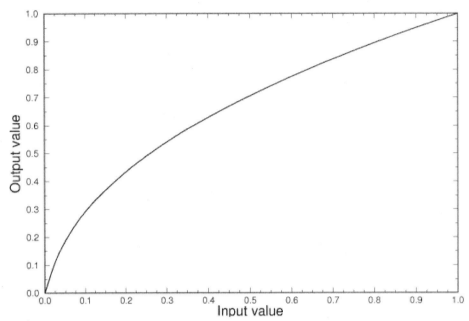

Figure 5: A typical gamma correction curve

dark. We need to know what is the best approach to providing free graphics. Please let us know what you want!

What is needed is for the image file to contain machine-readable details of the correction that has been applied. This facility has been part of the Utah RLE format [9] for several years. TIFF files [5] *can* contain very precise transfer curves although most in practice do not. PNG [6] also has the facility to record any gamma correction that has been applied. Kodak PhotoCD [10] uses a single standard transfer function. Clearly, such formats make the user agent implementor's job much easier.

Notes to Implementors

Interactions

If an image is under or over gamma corrected, this also affects the color balance. Over correction (in addition to making mid-tones too light) shifts colors towards neutral gray, while under

correction (in addition to making midtones too dark) shifts colors towards the display primaries.

Viewing on screen and printing on paper are two processes with very different transfer characteristics, so what is right for one is not right for the other. The extent of the mismatch depends on how much of the required correction has already been done to the image, how much is done in the viewing software, and how much (if any) is done by the software or hardware of the underlying platform.

Recommendations

User agents should provide some sort of gamma correction which does the right thing in as many cases as possible. This might be done by, in order of importance:

- Honoring explicit source gamma declarations in those image files that support them—currently TIFF, Utah RLE and PNG. Encouraging use of such formats to avoid guesswork.

- Providing well-chosen default settings, appropriate to the underlying platform.

- Using suitable heuristics based on the Internet Media type for image formats without explicit source gamma declarations. For example, GIF images typically have a source gamma of 0.45 (i.e., they are already corrected, for most displays) while JPEG JFIF [11] files often have a source gamma of 1.0 (i.e., they are uncorrected). Yes, this is a guess. It *will* sometimes be wrong. It is however an improvement on providing no gamma correction at all, or a blanket gamma correction on all types of images.

- Allowing setting of gamma in the preferences, for example, by providing a slider to adjust the screen gamma by eye until a user-agent-generated tone reproduction chart looks correct on screen, and saving this value for future use.

- Allowing customization by knowledgeable users or those with stringent requirements, for example by inputting measured transfer characteristics or providing an interface for external programs to be called to aid in accurate reproduction.

User agents which offer printing should be aware of the different gamma requirements for screen and print and might offer similar facilities (allowing customization, printing a test chart) to adjust gamma for printing.

Color Display

A quick spot of color theory before we can move on. The bare minimum, really!*

The Problem

The color of an object depends not only on the precise spectrum of light emitted or reflected from it but also on the observer—their species, what else they can see, even what they have recently looked at! Color is not an objective property of real-world objects; it is a subjective, biological sensation.

So What Is Color, Anyway?

Given the preceding description of color sensation, one might be forgiven for assuming that there is no way to cope with these vagaries. However, by treating the entire human eye/brain system as a black box and performing color matching experiments upon it, it has been possible to arrive at a surprisingly objective, measurable and repeatable *model* of color that corresponds in large measure with how we see color. This system, invented and standardized in the 1930s by the International Commission on Lighting (Commission Internationale de l'Eclairage, or CIE) [14] is called CIE XYZ [15] and is capable of representing all colors that can be seen by the human visual system. The XYZ value of a color can be measured by physical instruments or calculated from the spectrum of light given off by an object.

When we look at an image on a computer screen, what we see depends on the precise color and intensity of light emitted by each of the three phosphors in a computer monitor; this in turn depends on the make and the model, plus less tangible factors (such as the age—blue phosphors degrade faster than the other two). In the limit, each monitor is unique. This means that the same R,G,B values applied to two different monitors will give different colors; similarly, to produce exactly the same color on two different monitors, different R,G,B values must be applied.

Gamut

Provided the CIE XYZ measured colors of the red, green and blue phosphors are available for a particular monitor, any RGB color on that moni-

---

* One good introduction among many is Chaper 4 of [2]. A more detailed and mathematical treatment is Unit II of [3].

tor can be converted to CIE XYZ. Similarly, any measured CIE XYZ color can be reproduced on that monitor, provided it falls within the range of displayable colors—the *gamut*—bounded by the monitor primaries.

Figure 6 shows the triangular gamut of one particular monitor, drawn on a chromaticity diagram. This is a way of reducing the three dimensional CIE XYZ space to two dimensions by removing the brightness information (light orange and dark orange map the same chromaticities). Different monitors will have different gamuts.

Perceptual Color Space

CIE XYZ is the fundamental system for color *measurement*, but (like RGB space) it is not *perceptually uniform*. That is, the geometric distance apart of two colors does not relate to how different those colors appear. However, in 1976 the CIE came up with a transformation of CIE XYZ space that is (fairly) uniform. This is CIE LUV space, which will be used in the next section..

The L parameter stands for lightness. A gray scale with even numerical steps along the L axis will look even, and a mid gray will be at exactly the middle of the L axis. It is easier to think of the

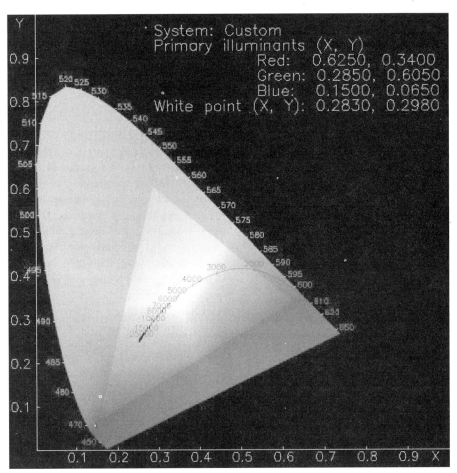

Figure 6:   The color gamut of a sample monitor (an HP A1097C)

other two axes in terms of polar coordinates. The further a color is from the central L axis, the more saturated it is. The angle round from the positive U axis relates to hue.

And, in summary, if we plot a series of colors in CIE LUV color space, we can tell how evenly spaced those colors are from each other.

Color Allocation Strategies

How Many Colors?

Graphical workstations and high-end personal computers are generally equiped with 24-bit *truecolor* displays—pixels can independently be set to any desired color. 8 bits (256 levels) of red, green, and blue are available giving 16.7 million displayable colors. This is enough to eliminate most banding except for large, slowly varying dark areas, or when gamma correction is done by lookup table. Higher quality systems use 10 or 12 bits per pixel, which is enough to eliminate visible banding from all areas of the RGB color space. Such systems are capable of displaying multiple high quality images.

16-bit displays are also typically used in a truecolor mode. This gives slightly worse results than *indexed* mode with single images containing 256 colors or less, but vastly better results with multiple images. A fine compromise between the somewhat inadequate 8-bit displays and the luxury of 24, 30, or 36 bit displays, they are now common on current PCs and Macs.

With an 8-bit indexed display, each pixel holds an index into a table of color cells. There can be at most 256 distinct colors on screen at once, although these colors are not fixed and can be set to any desired color. This system saves on expensive screen memory and is fine for non-graphics-intensive tasks such as displaying single images. It starts to struggle when multiple images are to be displayed concurrently, a common situation for a Web browser. 8-bit displays are common on current X terminals and on older computers.

The Problem

Systems with insufficient colors to display multiple arbitrary images have to *allocate* a small number of colors, which are then used to approximately represent the needed colors. This process is termed *quantization*. A number of strategies have been developed for this; each has its merits in certain situations, but none is universally suitable. *Dithering*, or trading spatial resolution for an increase in the apparent number of colors, can be used to mask the effect of the color shortage. A poor choice of dithering algorithm can cause objectionable graininess or spotting on an image.

First Come First Served

The simplest strategy is to start allocating colors with the first inline image and continue until you run out; then map all remaining colors to the nearest of those previously allocated. This works well when there is only a single inline image, or multiple images with few colors (such as hand-drawn icons), or when there are a number of images with similar colors such as several gray-scale images.

This strategy falls down when:

- There are several inline images which contain very dissimilar palettes.

- There are inline truecolor images.

- A multithreaded browser streams in several images concurrently.

Symptoms of this scheme breaking down are severe and objectionable color casts on those images which loaded last. Early versions of NCSA Mosaic for X [1] employed this approach. The latest versions appear to be using some sort of adaptive palette management, optimized for those inline images which are currently visible, although this has problems with rapid scrolling.

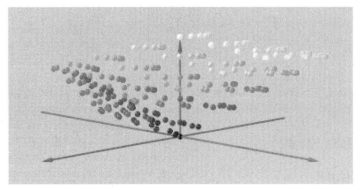

Figure 7:   A 6x6x6 Color Cube Without Gamma Correction

Color Cuboid, Without Gamma Correction

In an attempt to prevent the problems just described, this method allocates a *fixed* range of color cells in advance, and then maps all colors of all images to the nearest allocated color. The same color map is used for every HTML page.

In effect, it treats part of the 256-element lookup table as a truecolor display. With an even (in RGB space) allocation, colors from each inline images are speedily mapped to palette colors by multiplication and masking. The problem with this approach is that coverage of the device color space is necessarily sparse. Six levels each of red,

green, and blue (the maximum that can be used) requires 216 unallocated color cells.

Seen in CIE LUV color space, some clumping of the allocated colors is evident in Figure 7. The necessarily sparse sprinkling through the color gamut is clearly seen.

When other concurrent applications are also utilizing the color map, it frequently happens that 216 unallocated cells are not available. The cube must be contracted down to a 5x5x5 cube (125 colors) or even a sparse 4x4x4 (64 colors) cube shown in Figure 8. Huge gaps can clearly be seen. Dark greens, for example, will show severe specking as the nearest colors, dithered together to approximate the desired hue, will be very dissimilar.

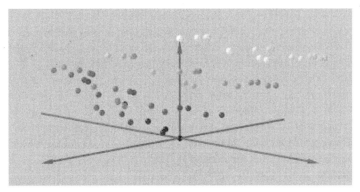

Figure 8:   A 4x4x4 color cube without gamma correction

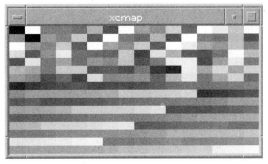

Figure 9: Sample color palette used by Netscape 1.1N for X

A color palette allocated by Netscape 1.1N for X [16] is shown in Figure 9. A 6x6x6 cube has been allocated in this instance. The cells used by Netscape start with the four greys at the end of the third row.

Color Cuboid, with Gamma Correction

There are two changes here. Firstly, the number of shades of green has been increased, to fill in the large perceptual range from black to green and from green to white; secondly the colors have been gamma corrected before being allocated (this assumes the underlying platform does not provide any hardware gamma correction, which is frequently the case). The effect, seen in Figure 10, is to move all the colors up the lightness axis. Compare this with Figure 7.

This plot shows a more even color distribution, although with a slight lack of the darker colors. In practice, ambient lighting, glare, electron scattering and similar factors increase the lightness of the darkest visible color, making this less noticeable.

Because of the different interval between adjacent green intensities (1/7th of the range) compared to red and blue (1/3rd the range), at no point within this cuboid is there a color with equal red, green and blue values (apart from black and white). Thus, there are no grays.

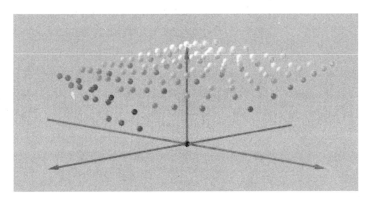

Figure 10: A 4x8x4 color cuboid with gamma correction

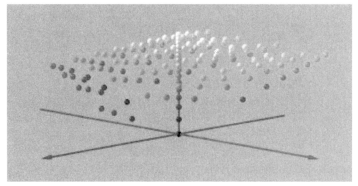

Figure 11:   A 4x8x4 color cuboid plus 16-element grey ramp, with gamma correction

The human eye is particularly sensitive to small changes in gray colors, steps in intensity, or deviations in hue from a pure gray. So, as it stands, the cuboid would give especially bad display of grayscale images. The addition of a 16-element grayscale ramp to the scheme in Figure 11 attends to this shortfall.

This sort of scheme is used by current versions of Arena [17] (0.96s and 0.97g) as the typical color-map in Figure 12 shows. The cells used by Arena start with the four grays at the end of the third row and finish at the end of the third last row. Notice that the gray ramp is allocated *first*. In conditions of severe color shortage, at least the grey ramp will have been allocated and Arena proceeds to convert all color inline images to

grayscale, preserving much of the graphical information and providing a pleasing appearance.

Improved Allocation Schemes

It would be possible to allocate a range of colors chosen to be evenly spaced in CIE LUV space, to minimize objectionable spotting when images are dithered. There would be no simple relationship between the image colors and the allocated colors (as there is with a cuboid scheme) so the image would have to be quantized to the new palette. Quantization is a slightly more time-consuming process than simple truncation or masking, and would make a browser feel slightly more sluggish.

Quantizing to a known fixed palette can be done as the image streams in. Image formats which

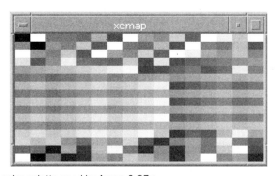

Figure 12:   Sample color palette used by Arena 0.97g

include popularity-sorted suggested palettes, such as PNG, can also be quantized as they stream in. If the palette is not fixed, and the image provides no hints, quantization cannot proceed until all the images have been loaded.

Another possible improvement would be to requantize all the inline images to an optimal adaptive palette, *after* they have all been loaded and displayed. This might be presented to the user as an `optimise this page` option, or a user agent might take advantage of idle CPU time while the user is reading and scrolling, to perform the quantization. The visual effect would be similar to the sharpening observed with interlaced GIF and PNG and progressive JPEG. This would require storage of the un-quantized images, which many user agents already do as a local caching optimization.

Some images with a limited number of colors, such as hand drawn icons with large areas of flat color, do not necessarily require good color fidelity. The speckling introduced by trying to simulate the desired color may be more objectionable than a change in hue. Smart user agents might detect such images—perhaps ones with 32 or fewer colors—and disable their dithering on a case by case basis.

Truecolor Displays

Moving from an 8-bit indexed scheme to a 16-bit true color scheme results in a marked improvement in color fidelity. Figure 13 shows a typical scheme with 5 bits for red and blue, 6 bits for green. (Note that this implies that a pure grey ramp is not produced, only an approximation, though the deviations are small.) The full range of the color gamut is densely occupied by the 65 thousand color points in this diagram, even though the size of each colored sphere has been reduced to a third of that used in the other diagrams.

Notes to Implementors

Interactions

User agents that use fixed color allocation and support binary transparency may have problems if their background color cannot be exactly represented.

Implementation of full transparency, or binary transparency with background textures, requires large numbers of colors even if the original image contains few colors.

Resampling (resizing) a limited color image by any method other than pixel replication will increase the number of colors needed for the resized image.

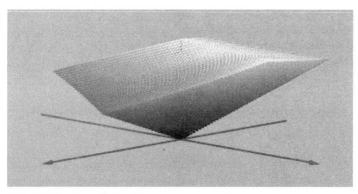

Figure 13:   A 32x64x32 color cuboid, without gamma correction

Recommendations

User agents forced to use displays with inadequate colors cannot really display arbitrary multiple graphics with any sort of fidelity, regardless of how evenly spaced the colors are. While some improvement can be made by allocating a perceptually even set of colors, this is counterbalanced by slower image display as all images are quantized. Thus, attempting to allocate a small fixed palette which is perceptually even is probably not worth the effort unless the underlying platform has a powerful CPU.

In conditions of profound color shortage, presenting all images to greyscale preserves the most detail and looks far better than attempting to quantize to 27 or fewer colors. Ensuring that grayscale data can be adequately represented at all times is also a sound policy.

The increasing availability of inexpensive truecolor displays should ease (and in time, eliminate) these problems. Truecolor displays are the prerequisite for further advances in accurate image reproduction.

Portable Color Graphics

The Problem

We have already seen that the same RGB image will display with different colors on two different monitors. To some extent this is unavoidable as some colors at the edges of one gamut are outside the other monitor's gamut, and vice versa.

Manufacturers currently take a great deal of care to ensure that certain colors, for example those associated with a particular brand or with a corporate logo, are reproduced precisely in printed media. It is only a matter of time before they demand a similar fidelity from online media.

In some cases, we *could* produce a more accurate color rendering, but we would need to know the CIE XYZ values of the monitor on which the *original* image was generated. In most cases, we do not know this.

By analogy with gamma, if this information was stored in the image file then a start could be made with increasing the color fidelity. There are currently three image formats that hold such information. One is Kodak PhotoCD [10], another is extended TIFF, and the third is PNG.

Accurate Color

Knowing the CIE XYZ values of the current system monitor and (from the image) of the originating monitor, a color transform for accurate display may be computed and applied to an image at minimal computational cost. In some cases, color management functions may be provided by the underlying platform.

Accurate Grey Scales

Knowing chromaticity data of the originating monitor it is trivial to compute the correct color to grayscale transformation. This gives *noticeably* superior results, even on an 8-bit indexed display, to the oft-quoted formula *Grey = 0.30R + 0.59G + 0.11B* which is only correct for the NTSC broadcast monitor, greatly atypical of modern computer monitors.

Better Color Printing

Whenever people acquire a color printer they are initially delighted, but typically soon become disillusioned as the quality of output falls far short of their expectations—a color magazine, for example. While accurate screen-to-print color matching is still not a fully automated process, advances have been made in recent years and modern printers with a Level 2 PostScript interpreter can take calibrated RGB data and do a better job of matching the on-screen colors than with raw RGB data.

But What of the Future?

More advanced methods of generating accurate portable color have been proposed, such as the International Color Consortium Profile [18]. A legitimate concern is whether these more complex methods will supersede the methods discussed in this paper. The answer is that they may well do, but as all such approaches are built upon the foundation, directly or indirectly, of the CIE XYZ color space, the simpler approaches are headed in the right direction and offer a smooth upgrade path.

Notes to Implementors

Interactions

Attempting to produce better colors for screen display or for printing assumes that simpler issues such as the gamma correction are being handled correctly and that a truecolor display is available.

Recommendations

Accurate device independent color reproduction has been spreading from high-end pre-press applications into the mainstream for the last five years or so. Web user agents which are able to make use of chromaticity information will be at an increasing market advantage in the years to come.

Embedded Metadata

The Problem

The topic of metadata has received some attention in connection with textual data. Graphics too can have important metadata, such as Copyright details, descriptions of the content of the image, legal disclaimers, or technical descriptions of the method of image synthesis employed. More application-specific metadata could include:

- The hospital number of a patient (for MRI or CT medical images)

- The accession number (for images of museum holdings)

- Dataset, algorithms used and parameter settings (for scientific visualization results)

- The artist name and the asking price (for a fine-art catalogue)

and so on. This information needs to be associated with the graphical information in some way. As images become used as more than mere adornment, the role of image metadata will grow. Quality graphics have associated metadata.

To Embed or Not to Embed

The traditional method of transmitting such information has been via a separate text file. There is however the risk that the two files will become separated. Metadata can also be supplied as an HTML file, with the image linked to or supplied inline, to make a stronger connection between the image and its metadata.

These methods have consistency problems—particularly in a caching proxy environment—when either the image or the metadata needs to be altered.

Rather than embedding the image in the metadata, several image formats allow text of various kinds to be contained within an image. The advantage of this is that the metadata cannot be inadvertently separated, and hence for example the copyright details of a graphic are unambiguous. Keeping the information in a single file also permits the use of message digests (as proposed in the draft HTML 3.0 specification [19]) on link anchors, to ensure that the currently linked-to graphic is exactly what the document author intended to link to with that URL.

The disadvantage of embedded metadata is that the Web user agent must extract the information and display it. The means of doing so are necessarily different for each Internet Media type. It is a tradeoff between inconvenience to the implementor and the convenience to the user of a single consistent user interface. This has to date been one of the Web's strengths, and a browser which presented embedded metadata by generating an HTML page would be highly suited to applications where image quality was considered important.

A third, compromise possibility would be to link to a multipart Internet Media type containing image data and an accompanying metadata file. There is as yet little experience, however, with the presentational aspects of multipart objects.

Notes to Implementors

Interactions

There are no known interactions between providing this facility and any other aspects of graphical excellence.

Recommendations

Providing the ability to directly view embedded metadata in graphics files for a small number of suitable Internet Media types associated with high quality graphics would be an interesting experiment. PNG is a relatively simple format which provides for text chunks with associated keywords, and the coded character set for these chunks is ISO Latin-1. There is a freely available C library for reading and writing PNG files, including extraction of text chunks. It would thus be a suitable candidate for trial implementation of this facility.

Conclusion

It is possible to provide high quality graphics on the Web if due consideration is given to the appropriate factors. This need not result in reduced interactive performance if care is taken. Inappropriate choices result in severely suboptimal graphics which users are quick to see and complain about; bad graphics are very visible. There is increasing demand for high quality graphics. User agents that take note of this trend will have a market advantage. ∎

References

1. Mosaic for X (the initial platform) is described at *http://www.ncsa.uiuc.edu/SDG/Software/XMosaic/help-about.html*

2. Watt, A. and Watt, M. *Advanced Animation and Rendering Techniques.* New York: Addison-Wesley, 1992.

3. Glassner, A.S. *Principles of Digital Image Synthesis.* San Francisco: Morgan Kaufmann Publishers, Inc., 1995.

4. The GIF 89a specification is widely replicated around the Internet. A sample URL is *ftp://ftp.ncsa.uiuc.edu/misc/file.formats/graphics.formats/gif89a.doc*

5. The Tagged Image File Format (TIFF) v.6 specification may be obtained from the site *ftp://ftp.sgi.com/graphics/tif/TIFF6.ps.Z*

6. The Portable Networked Graphics (PNG) specification is at *http://sunsite.unc.edu/boutell/png.html*

7. The FIG element of the HTML 3 draft specification is at the site *http://www.hpl.hp.co.uk/people/dsr/html/figures.html*

8. See for example Chapter 7 of Travis, D. *Effective Color Displays.* London: Academic Press, 1991.

9. The design of the Utah Raster Toolkit RLE format is described at the site *ftp://ftp.ncsa.uiuc.edu/misc/file.formats/graphics.formats/urt/rle.doc*

10. Some information about Kodak PhotoCD is at *http://www.kodak.com/productInfo/technicalInfo/technicalInfo.shtml*

11. JPEG compression is an International Standard ISO/IEC 10918-1. The FAQ for JPEG is at *http://www.cis.ohio-state.edu/hypertext/faq/usenet/jpeg-faq/faq.html*

12. Wyszecki, G. and Stiles, W.S. *Color Science—Concepts and Methods, Quantitative Data and Formulae.* New York: John Wiley & Sons, 1982.

13. The student notes from Lilley, C. Lin, F. Hewitt, W. T.H., and Howard, T.L.J.H. *Color in Computer Graphics.* Sheffield: CVCP/USDTU, 1993. *http://info.mcc.ac.uk/CGU/ITTI/Col/col-free.html*

14. The Commission Internationale de l'Eclairage Web page is at *http://www.hike.te.chiba-u.ac.jp/ikeda/CIE/*

15. Defined in Colorimetry, 2nd Edition, Publication CIE 15.2-1986. *http://www.hike.te.chiba-u.ac.jp/ikeda/CIE/publ/abst/15-2-86.html*

16. Netscape 1.1N for X is described at *http://home.netscape.com/eng/mozilla/1.1/relnotes/unix-1.1N.html*

17. Arena is described at *http://www.w3.org/hypertext/WWW/Arena/*

18. International Color Consortium Profile v3.0 is at *http://www.inforamp.net/~poynton/ICC_3.0a/icc-0.html*

19. The link model of the HTML 3.0 draft is described at the site *http://www.hpl.hp.co.uk/people/dsr/html/anchors.html*

Acknowledgments

Thanks to my colleague John Irwin for generating the Rayshade input files used to produce the CIE LUV scatter plots. Thanks also to Tom Lane of the Independent JPEG Group, Dave Martindale, Glenn Randers-Pehrson, and others on the PNG mailing list for helpful discussions on the requirements for a quality image format.

About the Author

Chris Lilley
[*http://info.mcc.ac.uk/CGU/staff/lilley/*]
Computer Graphics Unit
University of Manchester
In addition to various aspects of graphical quality, his interests include Web tools for collaborative working, Web standards, and the use of the Web for Education. He is an active participant in the IETF HTML Working Group and a contributor to the PNG working group. He is also the JISC representative to W3C.

BRINGING MUSIC TO THE WEB

Jacco van Ossenbruggen, Anton Eliëns

Abstract

To reduce the number of resources needed for high quality music on the WWW, we advocate the use of client-side sound synthesis techniques. This paper discusses techniques extending the functionality of Web browsers and describes the design of the hymne class library, which is used by the hush Web widget to synthesize the sound of musical scripts embedded in HTML pages. **Keywords:** *Music, software sound synthesis, client-side computation*

Introduction

Music can significantly enhance the perception of HTML pages, especially in a commercial or educational environment. At the moment, the Web allows hyperlinks to audio files, and most browsers simply delegate the playing of the samples to external viewers.

However, due to the relatively high costs of good quality audio, music is still a rare phenomenon on the Web. High bandwidth networks combined with new compression techniques may decrease the number of resources needed. Still, in the near future, audio on the Web will be associated with high costs and long network delays. So, at present, pages containing music are far less popular than they could be among both information providers and users.

The *DejaVu* project [2, 4] at the Vrije Universiteit takes a completely different approach in bringing music to the Web. We propose to transmit musical scores (instead of the raw samples) across the Internet and to add sound synthesis functionality to Web browsers.

Musical score files are usually a few orders of magnitude smaller than the raw samples, and the audio signal can be synthesized at the client side at any appropriate sample rate. Additionally, a high-level description of music provides the browser with far more information when compared to the raw samples. Future browsers, supporting dynamic documents, might need such information to provide high-level synchronization (e.g., "sync the start of the second scene of the video with the third measure of the intro tune"). Servers may use this information to answer specific queries (e.g., "select all tunes in 3/4 meter and key C-minor").

Developing a new MIME [1] type describing musical scores and requiring browsers to support the new type may not be feasible until standards for musical description languages become generally accepted.

Client-side Computation

The Web is currently moving its focus from server- to client-side computation. Browsers like Sun's HotJava and the hush Web widget [8] are able to execute program scripts and display the results within an HTML page. The functionality of such browsers can be easily extended with sound synthesis ability. The only requirement is that one can express commands to synthesize audio within the interpreted language. Thus, for the browsers mentioned above, the problem boils down to extending the language involved (Java and Tcl [5] respectively) with some kind of sound synthesis functionality.

Sound Synthesis and hush

Traditionally, sound synthesis is performed by dedicated hardware such as digital signal processors. Many modern personal computers can use such hardware to play MIDI encoded music, either through an external synthesizer or a sound card with a MIDI interface. As a result, extending browsers with MIDI support can be a relatively small effort. On UNIX platforms however, MIDI support is less common. Fortunately, today's workstations are fast enough to make real-time software sound synthesis (SWSS) possible. SWSS does not need special hardware except for a digital to analog converter (DAC), found on every modern workstation.

Hush (hyper utility shell) [3] is a C++ class library providing a convenient yet flexible access to the Tcl/Tk [6] toolkit. Every hush application is in fact a full-fledged Tcl/Tk interpreter, and the hush library can be used to add new commands and widgets to Tcl/Tk since hush provides a type-secure solution for connecting Tcl and C++ code.

Hymne [9] is a C++ API to Csound [10], a SWSS package developed at MIT's Media Lab in the tradition of the Music V system. We have used hymne and hush to extend Tcl/Tk with commands to make the functionality of Csound available from Tcl scripts. The notation used to describe the music is called Scot [10], and is translated to the notation used by Csound. The Scot translator comes with the standard Csound distribution.

The hush Web widget [7, 8] is another extension to Tcl/Tk, offering a graphical WWW browser as

an off-the-shelf component to hush programmers. The Web widget allows the execution of inline scripts by extending HTML with a new tag.

Since the hymne library provides sound synthesis commands from within these scripts, combining hymne with the Web widget enables you to use inline, real-time synthesized music in your HTML page. All other Tk widgets may be used as well. In Figure 1, we have used the scale widget to embed a tempo and volume scale inside an HTML page.

Score fragments may contain Tcl string variables, so one might change the tempo or even the key signature of a score by modifying the appropriate variables, and replay the modified tune without the need to retransmit the score. Note that window events (like mouse clicks) operating on the widgets generally do not result in a request to the remote server: they are handled by the widgets themselves.

In Example 1, the hush tag is used to execute a Tcl command playing some arbitrary notes. The optional text between the hush begin and end tags will be ignored by the Web widget. However, it will be displayed by widely available browsers, such as Netscape or Mosaic, that do not support hush's features. The hush tag can be used to provide alternative information or warning messages for users who are not using the hush Web widget.

Example 1:   An HTML Fragment

```
<h1>Inline Music on the WWW</h1>
<p>
Each time this page is displayed, some music will be
played as well.
</p>
<hush tcl="play 8acea(b,ec'b)<(4.a-8a-)">
This text will not be displayed by the hush Web widget.
Instead, it will play the notes above.
</hush>
```

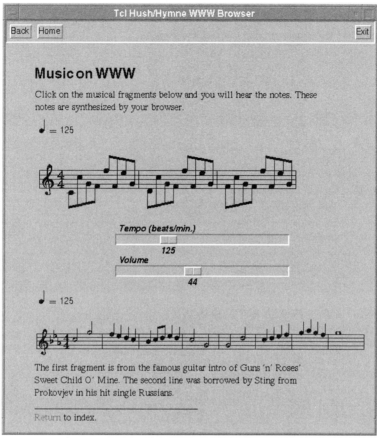

Figure 1:   Some musical fragments in an HTML page

Software Wrapping

The hush Web widget is just one of the many applications which may use the hymne library to synthesize music. However, the hymne library was designed to provide an application programmers interface (API) to Csound that is flexible enough to be used in a hypermedia environment.

The standard API of Csound is not flexible enough to satisfy the needs of a real hypermedia system. To provide the desired flexibility, we have developed a software wrapper (see Figure 2) with an object-oriented interface around Csound.

This wrapper allows the processing of musical events in the flexible manner required by a hypermedia system. The wrapper provides the necessary functionality to play arbitrary, real-time generated fragments of musical scripts. Additionally, this interface makes it possible to have access to information about the way playing proceeds: how many notes have been played, which notes are being played at the very moment, how long it will take to play the rest of the notes, etc.

For the implementation of this wrapper it is not, in principle, necessary to modify the Csound program. Instead, the interface runs Csound in a special mode that continuously reads the input for

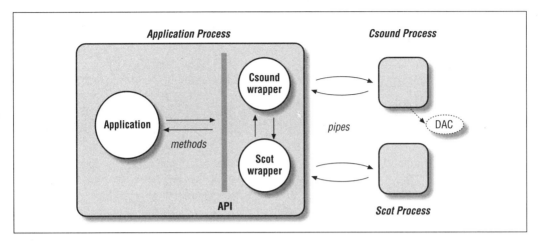

Figure 2:   Wrapper classes interfacing Csound and Scot

incoming events and continuously fills the audio buffer.

A C++ object executes Csound in another process and provides streams to write events to the Csound process, and to read its output. An arbitrary fragment of a Csound script can be played by writing it on the input stream. The wrapper object analyzes the produced output messages in order to provide the real-time information described above. Programmers can install their own handler object to use this information in application programs.

To be able to use the Scot language instead of the awkward note lists used by Csound, the Scot score translator is wrapped in the same way as the Csound program. Score fragments will be translated by the Scot translator and played by Csound. The Scot language is sufficiently powerful to denote most common note combinations (including chords, slurs, ties, triplets, etc.), but the plain Csound note lists may be used as well.

The set of instruments used to play the notes is described in the *orchestra file*. Csound provides many operators that can be combined to define new instruments. Most instruments make use of

stored wavetables to increase efficiency. In Example 2, a simple instrument is defined (with an arbitrary instrument and wavetable number). Hymne applications may use a set of default instruments or switch dynamically to other orchestra files.

Higher level classes, derived from that described above, provide primitives to (re)play fragments starting at an arbitrary moment in time and to perform other useful operations upon these fragments.

The details of this sound synthesis process are hidden behind the class interface of the top level objects of the hymne library. Application programmers can use these objects to use the hymne library in their C++ code. The hymne library can be used without the hush environment, to extend other browsers or arbitrary C++ applications with sound synthesis functionality.

Obviously, hymne has also been fully integrated with the hush library. As a result, application programmers may use the new Tcl commands and access the functionality of the library from Tcl scripts.

Example 2:   A Simple Instrument Definition

```
instr   7                                    ; Instrument # 7
ivolume = 5000                               ; Const volume
iftable = 5                                  ; use function table 5
asignal oscil   ivolume, cpspch, iftable     ; basic unit generator
out     asingal                              ; output signal
endin
```

Future Work

Currently, the hymne package employs pipes to communicate with the audio synthesis program. This part of the hymne library will be re-implemented using a client/server architecture. While this will hardly alter the programmer's interface, it will result in a better performance because it will be possible to run the Csound (server) process and the application (Web client) process on different hosts. Additionally, this implementation will make it possible to simultaneously run different applications that are all using the hymne library. This is not possible at the moment, because the digital to analog converter is regarded as an exclusive device. In the C/S implementation, there will simply be many clients communicating with one server process, that can have the exclusive access to the audio device while active.

We have planned to develop an experimental MIME document type to support musical documents in a less ad-hoc fashion. Because of the textual format of music description languages, it should be possible to employ anchoring and link facilities within musical documents as well.

At the moment, the technique of software wrapping, as described in this paper, is used to wrap (already available) video decoding software, in order to extend hush with a video widget. The video widget is used by the Web widget to allow for HTML pages with inline, interactive video as well.

Conclusion

Music can significantly enhance the perception of HTML pages. The main drawback of music on the Web is the large amount of (server) resources needed to store and transfer raw audio samples of good quality. By employing client-side sound synthesis, only the musical scores need to be stored and transmitted.

We have implemented a WWW browser capable of executing Tcl scripts and extended the Tcl language with a flexible interface to an existing sound synthesis package. This interface has been used in other, non-Tcl environments as well. The browser itself is implemented as a Tk widget and can be used as a GUI component like the other Tk widgets.

Using the new browser, we can enrich our HTML pages with music, which will be generated at the client side at any desired sample rate. ∎

Acknowledgments

Matthijs van Doorn designed and implemented the hush Web widget, and gave us some helpful comments on earlier versions of this paper.

References

1. N. Borenstein and N. Freed, *MIME (Multipurpose Internet Mail Extension) Part One*, September 1993, RFC-1521, obsoletes RFC-1341.

2. A. Eliëns, *DejaVu—A Distributed Hypermedia Application Framework*, available via FTP at URL *http://www.cs.vu.nl/~dejavu/papers/DejaVu.ps.gz*, December 1992.

3. A. Eliëns, *Hush: A C++ API for Tcl/Tk, The X Resource*, (14) April 1995, pages 111-155.

4. A. Eliëns, *Principles of Object-Oriented Software Development*, Addison-Wesley, 1995.

5. J.K. Ousterhout, *Tcl: An Embeddable Command Language, USENIX*, 1990.

6. J.K. Ousterhout, *An X11 Toolkit Based on the Tcl Language, USENIX*, 1991.

7. M.A.B. van Doorn and A. Eliëns, *Integrating WWW and Applications, ERCIM/W4G-International Workshop on WWW Design Issues*, Amsterdam, November 1994.

8. M.A.B. van Doorn and A. Eliëns, *Integrating Applications and the World Wide Web, in Computer Networks and ISDN Systems*, Proceedings of the Third International World Wide Web Conference, April 10-14, Darmstadt, Germany, April 1995, pages 1105-1110.

9. J.R. van Ossenbruggen and A. Eliëns, *Music in Time-based Hypermedia, ECHT'94*, The European Conference on Hypermedia Technology, September 1994, pages 224-270.

10. Barry Vercoe, *Csound, A Manual for the Audio Processing System and Supporting Programs with Tutorials*, 1993, available via *ftp://cecelia.media.mit.edu/pub/Csound/Csound.man.ps.Z*

About the Authors

Jacco van Ossenbruggen
[*http://www.cs.vu.nl/~jrvosse/*]

Faculty of Mathematics and Computer Science, Vrije Universiteit, de Boelelaan 1081a, 1081 HV Amsterdam, The Netherlands.

Jacco van Ossenbruggen is a Ph.D. student at the Vrije Universiteit. His research interests include open hypermedia sytems, SGML/HyTime, object orientation, and Pattern Languages.

Anton Eliëns
[*http://www.cs.vu.nl/~eliens/*]

Faculty of Mathematics and Computer Science, Vrije Universiteit, de Boelelaan 1081a, 1081 HV Amsterdam, The Netherlands.

Anton Eliëns is Associate Professor in the Computer Science department of the Vrije Universiteit, Amsterdam. He has recently written a book on the principles of object-oriented software development. His research interests include hypermedia, object orientation, and distributed logic programming.

POLYMAP

A Versatile Client-Side Image Map for the Web

Cheong S. Ang, M.S., Peter Brantley, M.A., Michael D. Doyle, PhD.

Abstract

*Image mapping techniques have been used to improve the interactivity of graphics-based content on the World Wide Web (WWW). However, the current WWW image-mapping technique requires a very cumbersome setup: a client-server architecture with the server acting as a point-in-polygon decoding engine to the inert client. While the advantages of having the server participate in the client/WWW browser users' activities are controversial, the need to move the decoding task to the browser is apparent, especially when better interactivity is desired. We propose a mechanism (Polymapping) that stores the hotspot information in an otherwise unessential part of the image file—the comment field of existing common image formats. Since adding data in the comment field does not violate most image format standards, this mechanism provides Polymap-enabled WWW browsers the information needed to achieve client-side hotspot decoding while allowing nonenabled clients to remain dependent on the servers. **Keywords:** Polymap, image map, ISMAP, GUI, user interface, anchor, hotspot*

Introduction

Image maps facilitate the interactivity of the WWW by simulating the hotspot mechanism in traditional multimedia applications. This feature allows WWW browser users to access URLs associated with objects within an inline image merely by clicking directly on the image. Much of the current popularity of the Web is related to the ease of use imparted by this functionality.

The currently popular image-mapping implementation (ISMAP) passes the work of decoding the image map to the HTTP server, which is usually already overloaded with requests for documents, and for gateway access to non-HTTP (HyperText Transfer Protocol) [1] servers. This situation interferes with the efficiency of hotspot decoding and doesn't allow realtime decoding of URLs, such as what users encounter when passing the mouse over text-based anchors. Seidman [8] and Doyle [4] both point out that the ISMAP standard also prevents the employment of image mapping on local file systems, which is necessary in order to distribute HTML-based applications on CDROM, where a WWW server is absent. The ISMAP implementation also imposes unnecessary net-

work overhead upon image-map decoding performance [8]. This degraded performance is the major reason for the lack of realtime interactive feedback for users, mentioned above.

Client-side image mapping is not a new concept. Ragget [7] introduced the FIG element in his HTML+ proposal. The FIG and SHAPE elements allow definition of shaped hypertext anchors in the associated image. Hotspot decoding may be performed locally because the polygon information is downloaded as part of the hypertext document. However, complete support for the complicated FIG and SHAPE elements is claimed to need significant additional processing [8]. Furthermore, both elements may not degrade gracefully in the browsers which don't support them.

Although Seidman addressed the issues of processing complexity and graceful degrading in his HTML [8] extension for client-side image mapping, his solution requires an entity definition which may become complex quickly as the complexity of the polygons grows. The polygon map and the associated image in this case are kept as two separate files. Embedding a polygon map of many complex objects in an ASCII HTML docu-

```
Polymap - Sun Microsystems' Home Page
</title>
<BODY>
<H1>Polymap as an Improvement to ISMAP</H1>
<IMG src="/home/cheong/www/tree/images/sunmap.gif">
<P>Hotspots on images are the major way designers of WWW home pag
distinguish themselves.  The latest and greatest home pages, such
at www.whitehouse.gov or www.sun.com, contain large ISMAPped imag
intent is that users will use these images as menus for browsing
```

Figure 1:   HTML source of the document in Figure 4

ment results in a very large file. Large document means increase in both transfer and parsing time.

Eòlas Technologies, Inc. [4] developed and implemented a client-side image map protocol based upon the MetaMAP® technology, which encodes object identifiers into image pixel data using a patented (U.S. patent 4,847,604) approach. This resulted in an extremely efficient method for encapsulating URL information with image data and for enabling realtime hotspot decoding. A disadvantage of this implementation, however, was that use of the resulting file format is constrained by the MetaMAP® patent. The Polymap work described in this paper was an attempt to allow advantages similar to those provided by the MetaMAP®-based file format, while allowing free use of the Polymap file format without concerns about patent issues relating to object encoding. Although the demonstrations of this technology we describe are based upon the GIF file format, and therefore commercial implementations may be subject to the Unisys LZW patent, the reader will note below that the Polymap approach is equally suitable for any of the

several public domain file formats that allow comment fields, such as PNG or JPEG.

The Solution

Our solution to the above problems is to include the polygon map data in the image. Many existing standard image data formats (e.g., GIF) have fields for application-specific data and/or comments, and adding data to those fields is legitimate. We utilize the comment field of the GIF 89 format to carry a compressed polygon map. With Polymap implementation, the HTML document does not differ in comparison to a simple inline image definition. Thus in addtion to client-side hotspot decoding and better visual feedbacks, the polymap mechanism provides WWW browsers with the versatility to either perform polygon decoding themselves, or use the conventional image mapping, the ISMAP [6] technique.

Creating a Polymap image map is actually far simpler than setting up an image for ISMAP. We have implemented a rudimentary version of the

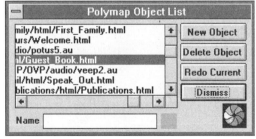

Figure 2:   Microsoft Windows version of the Polymapping toolkit (Object List)

Figure 3:   Microsoft Windows version of the Polymapping toolkit (Image Window), showing outlines around hotspots, as each would be displayed to the user during image-map decoding

Polymapping toolkit on the MS Windows platform (available soon) which allows polygon vertex specifications by point-and-click, or by freehand contour drawing. The polygon data is compressed using the same compression engine that encodes the image data when the mapped image is saved. Since the Polymap technique does not require a separate map file, this is all a WWW server administrator has to do.

In addition, Polymapping does not interfere with the setup of an ISMAP; the server administrator is free to prepare a mapping file on the server side for Polymap-ignorant browsers.

Implementation

The data in the GIF comment field is saved following a simple format, shown in Example 1.

Example 1:   GIF Data Format

```
GIF comment block indicator
7                            /* 7 bytes of flag.  7 is a 1-byte unsigned char */
PMAP1.0                      /* Polymap flag.  7 bytes of char */
N                            /* N bytes of encoded data. N is a 4-byte unsigned
                                integer
B                            /* The compression but size. B is a 1-byte unsigned
                                char */
GIF end of block indicator
```

The decoded data also has a straightforward format. The first unsigned short (2 bytes) designates the number of objects in the Polymap. Immediately following are null-terminated strings of the object names. In WWW Polymap applications, the object names are Universal Resource Locators (URLs) [3], but they may be any set of strings that is meaningful to a particular application. The name strings are followed by one or more blocks of the the following sequence:

0xFFFF
Object number
Polygon number
$(x_1,y_1), (x_2,y_2),..., (x_N,y_N)$

Enabling Polymap handling in WWW browsers merely requires extending the browsers' GIF reader comment handling routine to appropriately process the above format. There is no restriction on the implementation of the client-side decoding methods. Our browser, an enhanced version of NCSA Mosaic (download-

Figure 4:   Enhanced NCSA Mosaic with a Polymap HTML page

able from UCSF licensee's download page), deploys the windowing system's polygon and region functions to interactively highlight hotspots as the cursor passes over them. The browser responds to mouse clicks with the same routine the text-based hotspot respond function is using. Hence our browser reuses the hotspot handling codes efficiently, and gives its users a consistent look-and-feel.

Storage of Polymap vs ISMAP (in bytes)

Object	URL size	Num Pts
1	58	17
2	66	17
3	55	15
4	52	18
5	57	17
6	59	18
7	61	16
8	68	21
9	54	15
10	63	5
11	64	63

Number of Objects =	11
Total URL Size =	657
Total Num Pts =	222

Polymap

Header:

PMAP1.0	7	
N	4	
N bits	1	
Total		12
Per Object Overhead[1]:		66
Per Point Overhead:		0
Total URL Size:		657
Total Data Size:		888
Total Size:		1623

ISMAP

Header:	0
Per Object Overhead[2]:	66
Per Point Overhead[3]:	444
Total URL Size:	657
Total Data Size:	888
Total Size:	2055

Percentage of ISMAP larger than Polymap:	26.61

Original GIF file size:	52520
Polymap GIF file size:	53805
Compress Polymap data:	1285
Compression Ratio:	0.79

Percentage of ISMAP larger than compressed Polymap:	59.92

1. Each Polymap object has six bytes of the sequence (0xFFFF, object number, polygon number).

2. Each ISMAP polygon object specification is preceded by POLY url, thus six bytes, disregarding the size of variable, url, which has already been accounted for.

3. Each ISMAP polygon vertex needs a comma between its x-coordinate and y-coordinate, and a space to separate itself from the next point or an end-of-line character if it is the last point.

Table 1: Polymap and ISMAP Size Consideration for the White House Image in Figure 3

Storage of Polymap vs ISMAP (in bytes)

Object	URL size	Num Pts
1	64	17
2	64	21
3	46	20
4	59	18
5	53	13
6	50	14
7	18	5
8	47	14
9	50	14
10	53	149
11	60	9
12	59	5
13	52	5
14	54	5
15	55	5

Number of Objects =   15
Total URL Size =   784
Total Num Pts =   314

Polymap
Header:
    PMAP1.0   7
    N   4
    N bits   1
    Total   12
Per Object Overhead: 90
Per Point Overhead: 0
Total URL Size: 784
Total Data Size: 1256
Total Size: 2142

ISMAP
Header: 0
Per Object Overhead: 90
Per Point Overhead: 628
Total URL Size: .784
Total Data Size: 1256
Total Size: 2758

Percentage of ISMAP larger than Polymap: 28.75

Original GIF file size: 61931
Polymap GIF file size: 63621
Compress Polymap data: 1690
Compression Ratio: 0.78

Percentage of ISMAP larger than compressed Polymap: 63.19

Table 2:   Polymap and ISMAP Size Considerations for Sun Microsystem Home Page image in Figure 4

In the case of JPEG, another popular Internet image format, although the comment block is written as part of the file header, there are no restrictions on the format and processing of the comment block. However, the standard JPEG DCT (Discrete Cosine Transform) plus arithmetic-coded or Huffman encoding/decoding routines may not be reused because there will not be much sharable code between the lossless and lossy mode [5]. We may resort to several different solutions: (1) include the lossless spatial DPCM coding method, which will increase the size of the Polymapping program and the size of the Polymap-enabled WWW browsers; (2) leave the Polygon data uncompressed as if it is a regular

Fourth International World Wide Web Conference Proceedings

string of comment(s); or (3) a compromise between (1) and (2), use a smaller and simpler compressor.

A good way to realize (3) would be to use whichever image compression engine is accessible in-ternally by the WWW browser(s). Until another format becomes more prevalent, GIF's LZW encoding is a reasonable choice. The Polymap toolkit and the most common WWW browsers have GIF compression/decompression engines built-in, and the JPEG comment handling routine may invoke the engine when necessary. No extra code is needed.

Figures 2 and 3 show the Polymapping toolkit. New objects are created simply by adding their names through the Polymap Object List dialog box. The user may redo or delete the selected object by a button press. Double-clicking on an object in the object list will pop up a Name Change dialog, which allows the user to change the name of the object. The outline displayed for each object is also color-coded. The color icon beside the Name prompt reveals the color associated with the selected object. Clicking on the color icon will pop up a standard Microsoft Windows-style Color Choice dialog that enables changing the color for the selected object.

Figure 4 shows the Polymap-enabled NCSA Mosaic. Notice that the cursor is on a hotspot, a hot cup of coffee, which is highlighted with the hotspot outline. The URL indicator at the bottom of the image displays the location of the anchor.

Results

The results of the implementation are very encouraging. Our Polymapping implementation not only provides fast client-side decoding and realtime interactive feedback, but it also improves storage efficiency, setup speed, and network communication efficacy.

The hotspot polygon map of the image shown in Figure 3 would have consumed at least 2055 bytes of space if it had been stored in ASCII form (in an ISMAP file or HTML file as polygons[*]). Encapsulating the polygon data using the Polymap method yields an overhead of only 1285 bytes. The ISMAP file is 60% larger (Comparison in Table 1). Furthermore, Polymap storage effiency increases as the data size increases (sample comparison: Table 1 and Table 2).

Ongoing/Future Work

We are currently adopting the geometric primitive specification of ISMAP into Polymap. More efforts will be put into refining the Polymapping toolkit and improving the polygon decoding speed on slower machines. Although our decoding engine only performs a sequential search, the performance is acceptable on machines at as low as 486 PC level. Enhancing the decoding engine with object elimination based on bounding boxes, and possibly use of a hash table will likely speed up the process.

Since there is a striking resemblance between the recently proposed Portable Network Graphics [2] (PNG) format and GIF in terms of overall image structure and layout, the Internet and other online (e.g., CompuServe) communities are shifting their attention from GIF to PNG. We are also planning on supporting PNG in future implementations of the Polymap toolkit.

Conclusion

The Polymap protocol provides a solution to the major problems confronting the ISMAP method of hotspot interaction over the Web: redundant network access and dependence on the WWW server to decode local pointer events. Furthermore, because of the simplicity and efficiency of the implementation of this technique, we expect that Polymap will find wide acceptance on the

---

[*] Polymap, like ISMAP, may also contain predefined geometric shapes such as circles. To facilitate comparison, we used only polygons.

Web. Polymap technology clearly demonstrates the possibility of realizing a complete hyper-graphics multimedia system on the WWW based on the current electronic publishing infrastructure. ∎

References

1. Berners-Lee, Tim, *Hypertext Transfer Protocol*, Internet Draft.

2. Boutell, Thomas, *PNG (Portable Network Graphics) Specification, Tenth Draft*, URL: *http://sunsite.unc.edu/~boutell/png.html*

3. Connolly, Daniel W., *HTML 2.0 Specification Review Materials*, URL: *http://www.hal.com/users/connolly/html-spec*

4. Doyle, Michael D., *MetaMAP®*, URL: *http://www.eolas.com/metamap/metamap.html*

5. Independent JPEG Group, *JPEG System Architecture*, included in the publicly released JPEG "C" Library, February 18, 1993.

6. NCSA HTTPd Development Team, *NCSA Imagemap Tutorial*, URL: *http://hoohoo.ncsa.uiuc.edu/docs/setup/admin/Imagemap.html*

7. Ragget, Dave, *HTML+ Discussion Document*, URL: *http://info.cern.ch/hypertext/WWW/MarkUp/HTMLPlus/htmlplus_1.html*

8. Siedman, James L., *An HTML Extension to Support Client-Side Image Maps*, URL: *http://www.ncsa.uiuc.edu/SDG/IT94/Proceedings/DDay/seidman/seidman.html*

About the Authors

Cheong S. Ang, M.S.
[*http://wira.ckm.ucsf.edu/*]
University of California, San Francisco Library and Center for Knowledge Management
San Francisco, California 94143-0840

Peter Brantley, M.A.
[*http://www.ckm.ucsf.edu/*]
University of California, San Francisco Library and Center for Knowledge Management
San Francisco, California 94143-0840

Michael D. Doyle, PhD.
[*http://www.eolas.com/*]
Eòlas Technologies Incorporated
10 E. Ontario, Ste. 5106
Chicago, IL 60611

TRANSLATING ISO 12083 MATHEMATICAL MARKUP FOR ELECTRONIC DOCUMENTS

Keith Shafer, Roger Thompson

Abstract

In this paper, we describe a general translation tool that can transform tagged text into arbitrary output formats. Specifically, we describe how OCLC makes scientific documents containing mathematical markup available on the World Wide Web. The translation capabilities we developed to do this help realize the potential of the Standard Generalized Markup Language (SGML) to provide users with a single, non-proprietary document representation that can be translated on demand to other output formats. This enables publishers who target the WWW as a delivery medium to use the latest advances in HTML without constant revision of their document archives. **Keywords:** *Mathematical markup, translation, ISO 12083, entities.*

Introduction

The Hypertext Markup Language (HTML) is a specification language for describing the display characteristics of documents in a browser-independent manner [1]. Because of its small number of tags, simple structure, and declarative nature, HTML provides a relatively easy-to-use way of making documents available on the Internet. Another advantage of HTML is that it supports active documents. Authors can encode interface features into a document that allow readers to make selections, provide textual information, and, most significantly, jump to other related documents. Other document standards such as Postscript [2] and TeX [3] are print oriented and thus are passive. Readers cannot interact with a document encoded in these standards unless a special interface is used that supports interaction independent of the document.

While HTML provides a simple, convenient means to "publish" active World Wide Web (WWW) documents, it is not suitable for the construction of archival document databases that will be the core of online (scholarly or otherwise) publishing. There are several reasons for this. One is that HTML is undergoing constant revi-sion: its first major revision (V2.0) was just completed, and the second (V3.0) is under consideration. Furthermore, because HTML is so strongly output oriented, advances in output capabilities like those of Sun's HotJava WWW browser will cause further revisions of the markup [4]. As a result, authors of HTML documents typically will choose some combination of the features specified in the various versions of HTML to encode their documents. The choice is usually dependent on how well the author's browser of choice responds to particular HTML features.

Another reason for HTML's unsuitabilty for tagging archival documents is that it is primarily an output specification. Most tags are devoted to either describing various formatting features, linking the document to other documents, or providing various kinds of user interaction features. HTML contains only a few tags that outline a document's structure, and the minimal structure defined is there for the convenience of WWW browsers. A document's true structure is only hinted at by the different heading levels (tags H1 through H6), and it is left to the document's author to use these heading tags consistently. Because the structure is not directly specified and cannot be enforced by an SGML document parser, the temptation to use heading or other tags inconsistently to achieve desired visual effects is always present. A good example of this is the HTML markup required for documents accepted to the WWW '95 conference. The abstract and keywords were not specified by structurally oriented tags like or <keywords>. Instead, tags designed to format definition lists had to be used (<dl>, <dt>, and <dd>). All of these factors can lead to collections of documents in which the markup is inconsistent, potentially obsolete, oriented towards a particular software vendor's browser, and in need of constant maintenance.

A better way to store the information is to use markup that reflects abstract document structure using the Standard Generalized Markup Language (SGML) [5]. SGML is a meta-language for writing Document Type Definitions (DTD). A DTD describes how a conforming document should be marked up (i.e., the tags that may occur in the document, the ordering of the tags, and a host of other features). HTML is itself an SGML application with each of its three versions corresponding to a different DTD.

A single, well-crafted SGML DTD can explicitly and precisely specify the structure of a wide variety of documents. For example, a DTD can define tags for a very deep structural hierarchy with many section/subsection levels, and at the same time allow a document to be very shallow. DTDs can be difficult and time-consuming to create by hand, depending on how many features of SGML are used, but straightforward DTDs can be generated automatically [6]. Thus, the cost of developing them can be greatly reduced. With a DTD available, SGML parsers can be used to ensure that tagged text conforms to the structure defined by the DTD and is therefore consistently and correctly marked up.

After documents are in a consistent structurally-oriented markup, they can be translated into other formats on demand. For example, they can be transformed into files for loading into a relational database system, or they can be selectively indexed for building a text retrieval system, as well as be formatted for viewing. Several general translation tools are available, but most force users to use a predefined DTD (which may be difficult or impossible to do) or do not offer sufficient options to meet users' translation needs. For instance, while there is now an international standard for SGML mathematical markup, ISO 12083 Mathematics DTD [7], there are no systems that produce formatted documents from the complete standard.

At OCLC, we receive tagged text, including ISO 12083 mathematical markup, that must be translated to other formats to support OCLC's Electronic Journals Online (EJO) service [8]. This service provides online access to full-text scientific journals, so it must be able to handle all sorts of mathematics and other kinds of equations, such as those found in Chemistry or Physics literature. Guidon, OCLC's proprietary document viewer and retrieval interface, receives records from the database engine that have been translated to TeX's "DVI" format [9]. Guidon renders these records to produce the screen image, and, if desired, typeset-quality paper output.

To provide access to the EJO service via non-proprietary WWW browsers, these same source documents are also translated into HTML. One of the major difficulties in translating tagged text to HTML is that neither HTML version 1.0 nor 2.0 support the markup of mathematics. While HTML 3.0 has mathematical markup in it, it is not yet stable as a standard, and only one vendor's WWW browser currently handles it. To overcome this obstacle, we translate the mathematical markup to TeX which can then be rendered into GIF images. These GIF images are then used in the HTML versions of the documents. So for both Guidon and the WWW browsers we are required to translate mathematical markup to TeX. To handle these translation requirements, as well as others, we added translation capabilities to our Grammar-Builder Engine (*GB-Engine*) software.

The GB-Engine is a library of C++ objects that has been developed to support the *SGML Docu-*

ment Grammar Builder project [10]. This project is an ongoing research effort at OCLC studying the manipulation of tagged text. The GB-Engine can be used to automatically create reduced structural representations of tagged text (DTDs), translate tagged text, combine DTDs, automate database creation, and automate interface design—all from sample tagged text.

While the GB-Engine is embedded in a number of systems, *Fred* is the most popular. *Fred* is the GB-Engine embedded into the Tcl/Tk [11] environment. Tcl is a complete string-based interpreted programming language with variables, strings, lists, functions, etc.; Tk is an X-based graphical user interface toolkit. As a result, Fred is a complete interpreter/shell that has access to the GB-Engine objects and can be used easily to build X interfaces. We have also embedded the GB-engine into Perl [12] and Scheme [13], and ported the GB-Engine to Microsoft's NT operating system, so that it can be embedded into environments such as Microsoft's OLE.

In the remainder of this paper, we present requirements for mathematical markup translation, a discussion of the basic GB-Engine translation tool capabilities, an explanation about how those capabilities are used to include mathematical markup in HTML documents, and some translation examples.

Mathematical Markup Translation Requirements

In this section, we present the requirements for translating mathematical markup. Specifically, we look at the requirements for translating ISO 12083 to TeX, since this motivated the addition of translation capabilities to GB-Engine. While this would appear to be ISO 12083 or TeX-specific, we have found that these same requirements exist for many other kinds of translations. Thus, the reader need not be familiar with ISO 12083 or TeX to appreciate these general translation requirements. We merely use these requirements to make our discussion concrete.

One of our major observations is that the proper translation of tagged text is often *context dependent*. A system may have to determine where a particular tagged structure occurs within the structure of all the tagged text to know what to do with it. For example, one might have some text delimited by *author* tags. In the context of a title page the text would be handled one way, but in the context of a bibliography entry it would be handled in another.

The same can be said about translating mathematical markup. Some of the ISO 12083 structures have direct mappings to TeX control sequences. For instance, the tag *bold* maps directly to the TeX sequence *bf*. However, other ISO 12083 structures require that structure of the mathematical markup be examined in order to choose the appropriate TeX control sequence or combination of control sequences to produce correct formatting. There are three common contextual possibilities needed in the translation: *ancestor*, *descendant*, and *sibling*.

Text justification is a good example of the use of *ancestor* information. The justification of a *fraction* in the ISO 12083 mathematical standard can be specified in the *fraction* start tag as an attribute. In TeX, horizontal fill is generally used to manually justify text by placing space before or after the element to be justified. To translate the ISO 12083 *fraction*, horizontal fill must be generated in the TeX numerator or denominator sub-structures. To do this, the translation program must look "up" at the enclosing *fraction* structure for the value of its alignment attribute to know where to properly insert the horizontal fill. In some instances, the program may need to look even farther "up" into the enclosing mathematical markup to get the proper alignment, as it may be specified in a variety of places. (See the text justification example below for an example.)

Similarly, translation of the *radical* structure uses *descendant* information. TeX has two control sequences for radicals: one generates a simple square root and the other generates a general root with an explicit radix. To determine which control sequence to use, one must count the number (there are only two possible) of immediate sub-structures of the ISO 12083 *radical* structure. If there is one sub-structure, indicating that there is no radix, the simple square root control sequence is selected. If there are two, the general root sequence is selected. (See the radical example below for an example.)

The generation of TeX array cell separators requires that *sibling* knowledge be used. In ISO 12083, every array cell is marked with a start tag and, usually, the cell is completely delimited by an end tag. TeX, on the other hand, marks only the separation of cells. This means that the translation program must be able to determine whether or not a cell is last in a list of cells (i.e., the cell has no right siblings). If it is the last, the translation program does not generate a separator. (See the array separator example below for an example.)

Translation in all of the previous situations involved simple substitutions or insertions of text. Some translations are more complex in that they require the placement of text in locations other than those where the tags occur. An example of this is the placement of superscripts and subscripts before an element. The ISO 12083 mathematical standard specifies that all of the superscripts and subscripts for an element follow the element. For example, an N with a leading superscript i and a trailing superscript j is encoded as: <subform>N</subform>ⁱ^j. The assignment of the value *pre* to the attribute *loc* specifies that the superscript i is to appear before the subform N. TeX encodes this whole structure as '$\^iN\^j$', so the \^i that corresponds to 'ⁱ' must be moved in front of the target subform, N, when the text is translated. (See the leading superscript example below for an example.)

One problematic requirement is with regard to the translation of arrays. The ISO 12083 DTD allows arrays to be marked up as a sequence of columns as well as a sequence of rows. TeX only allows them to be specified as rows. This means

that the translation process must convert column order to row order, and at the same time preserve any justification information. Another problematic ISO 12083 structure is overlapping underlines and overlines. In ISO 12083 these are specified by reference *mark* tags that have an *id* attribute. These reference tags can be used by the *underline* and *overline* structures to determine where to start or finish. There is no corresponding TeX structure that directly encodes this.

The GB-Engine Translation Process

To meet these and related translation requirements at OCLC, we added translation capabilities to the GB-Engine. The GB-Engine translation capabilities provide a means for manipulation of tagged documents by translating, replacing, moving, or removing tags and their corresponding sub-structures. To accomplish this, GB-Engine translation requires three things:

- Tagged text to translate

- Translation script describing the desired transformation

- Optional entity translation table

We explain each of these parts in the following subsections. Examples will be presented in the Examples section below.

Tagged Text

The GB-Engine first processes the tagged text to construct a representation of its underlying structure. This is done by searching for start and end tags using traditional SGML syntax. These tags are matched to build a tree called a *tag structure* (or *document structure*). Once this structure is built, the translation capability can use it to determine the proper way to translate tags based on their context.

Translation Script

The GB-Engine translation is an interpreted process where the *translation script* is the user-supplied program of desired transformations. Every *translation script* is made up of *translation statements*. Each translation statement is composed of two parts, a *condition* and a block of *actions*:

```
if (condition)          { actions }
```

Translation *conditions* can be combined using the ' standard Boolean operators and can be parenthesized for grouping and readability. The conditions can test a tag in a variety of different ways, including whether it is a start or end tag, the presence or non-presence of attributes, the value of attributes, contextual location, as well as many of these same tests on ancestor, descendant, and sibling tags.

Translation *actions* can be nested and include sub-blocks of conditions and actions. Conditions are commonly enclosed in parentheses ()'s and action blocks are commonly enclosed in braces {}'s. Actions enable the translation to perform a wide variety of transformations ranging from simple textual substitution to reconfiguring the structure of a document. A more detailed description of the translation script syntax can be found in [14].

Given a well-tagged document structure and a translation script, the GB-Engine applies the *complete* translation script to each tag in the document structure in succession by performing a depth-first traversal of the document structure. (This tag traversal corresponds to the natural reading order of the document.) That is, *each tag* is checked against *each* statement condition in the translation script. If a statement condition evaluates to TRUE for a tag, the corresponding actions are applied to that tag. Thus, multiple translation statements may be applied to a single tag and a single translation statement may be applied to multiple tags.

The translation process has no effect on tags that have no conditions that evaluate to TRUE for

them in the translation script. They are simply passed through into the output of the translation. Accordingly, a null translation script will reproduce the original document—the only difference being that some non-tagged white space will be removed. (Many people add white space like carriage returns, tabs, and spaces to tagged documents to make them easier to read. In most cases, this white space is *not* part of the document structure because it is *not tagged*. Since the translation process allows for text movement, we do not attempt to retain non-tagged white space in the translated text. For that matter, we have no way of knowing where the non-tagged white space should go and arbitrary insertion of such non-tagged white space may produce invalid translation results.)

Entity Translation Table

The entity translation table is used after the translation script has been applied to all of the tagged text. The table contains simple mappings of SGML entity references to arbitrary text strings. The standard syntax for an SGML entity reference is an ampersand "&" followed by a sequence of alphanumeric characters, followed by a semicolon ";". For example, the entity representing the capital Greek delta, "&Dgr;", is replaced by the TeX delta, "\Delta". In the radical example below the use of the entity translation table is shown. Entities can be handled in this way because they are designed to be a representation of special characters that are not contained in a standard character set.

Putting the Mathematics in HTML

Given the understanding of how the GB-Engine translation works, we can now describe how the ISO 12083 mathematical markup is included in HTML documents (also see [15]). First, the document is processed to build the tree-structured representation. The structured representation is then used to extract and save the mathematical markup, which is delimited by *formula* tags for inline mathematics, or by *dformula* or *dformgrp* tags for display mathematics. These separate pieces are each passed through a Fred translation script for mathematical markup, resulting in a TeX translation for each piece. The TeX is then used to generate a DVI file, and the DVI file is rendered into a GIF image. Finally, a pointer to the GIF image is placed in the HTML document. When the document is loaded by a WWW browser, the image is brought along with it and displayed in the appropriate place.

Examples

Having presented the general GB-Engine translation process, we can now show how the GB-Engine handles the translation problems presented in the requirements section above. The sample tagged text, translation script, and resultant translation all appear immediately before the discussion of each example. Note that the line numbers in the examples are included for reference only and are not part of the actual syntax.

Example 1 shows how the GB-Engine can use ancestor information to generate proper text justification.

Example 1 shows how multiple conditions are met and applied to a tag during translation. The condition Start_Tag on line 1 of the script matches the *fraction* tag on line 1 of the sample text because the tag has the traditional SGML syntax for a start tag. In this case, the *fraction* start tag also has an attribute value assignment of "left" to "align". This assignment is not used in the translation of this tag, but is important later. The action "Literal" simply puts whatever is in its parentheses into the developing translation. If whitespace is desired, then the output must be enclosed in quotes. In this case, nothing is put into the translation, so the *fraction* start tag is "consumed." This will also be true for the *fraction* end tag as well. This is done by line 2 of the script.

Example 1:   Text Justification

SAMPLE TAGGED TEXT:
```
1   <fraction align=left>
2       <num>1</num>
3       <den>ax + b</den>
4   </fraction>
```

TRANSLATION SCRIPT:
```
1    if Start_Tag (fraction)                                  { Literal( )  }
2    if    End_Tag (fraction)                                 { Literal( )  }

3    if Start_Tag (num)                                       { Literal( { )  }
4    if Start_Tag (num) && Match_Parent (align,right)         { Literal ("\hfill ")  }

5    if    End_Tag (num) && Match_Parent (align,left)         { Literal (" \hfill")  }
6    if    End_Tag (num)                                      { Literal ("}\over")  }

7    if Start_Tag (den)                                       { Literal ( { )  }
8    if Start_Tag (den) && Match_Parent (align,right)         { Literal ("\hfill ")  }

9    if    End_Tag (den) && Match_Parent (align,left)         { Literal (" \hfill")  }
10   if    End_Tag (den)                                      { Literal ( } )  }
```

TRANSLATION OUTPUT:
```
{1 \hfill}\over {ax + b \hfill}
```

When the script is applied to the *num* start tag, the Start_Tag condition on line 3 of the script evaluates to true, and so the action "Literal" generates an opening brace to enclose the numerator. Line 4 succeeds on the Start_Tag condition, but fails on the "Match_Parent" condition. This condition checks attribute/value pair assignments for a node's immediate ancestor. In this case, *num*'s immediate ancestor is *fraction*, and has the value *left* and not *right* for its *align* attribute.

The next tag processed is the *num* end tag. This tag matches the conditions on both lines 5 and 6. End_Tag is true if a tag has the standard syntax of an SGML end tag. The result is that on line 5 the horizontal fill is generated and then, on line 6, the enclosing brace along with the TeX "over" control sequence is generated. The *den* start and end tags on line 3 of the sample tagged text are processed in the same way by line 7 through 10 of the script.

While the condition Match_Parent restricts the context search to a tag's immediate ancestor, there are a variety of other conditions for looking both up and down beyond the immediate context to find occurrences of specific tags, attributes, and attribute values.

Example 2 shows how a translation script can use descendant information. .

In the ISO 12083 Mathematics DTD the *radical* can have only one or two sub-structures, since the *radix* structure is optional and the *radicand* is required. If it has none or more than two, the markup is not valid. This constraint is encoded in the use of the "Child_Count" condition.

The first tag processed by this script is the *radical* start tag. Line 1 of the script checks to see if it is a start tag (true), and if it has only one immediate substructure (false). This line generates nothing since the whole condition part failed. Line 2 also checks to see if it is a start tag, and if the tag has two immediate substructures, which it does. The result of this line is that a TeX "\root" command is generated. The rest of the script is straight forward, processing the *radix* and *radi-*

Example 2:   Radical Example

```
SAMPLE TAGGED TEXT:
1    <radical>
2        <radix>3</radix>
3        <radicand>&Dgr;</radicand>
4    </radical>
```

```
TRANSLATION SCRIPT:
1    if Start_Tag (radical) && Child_Count (1)     { Literal (\sqrt) }
2    if Start_Tag (radical) && Child_Count (2)     { Literal (\root) }
3    if    End_Tag (radical)                       { Literal ( ) }

4    if Start_Tag (radix)                          { Literal ( { ) }
5    if    End_Tag (radix)                         { Literal ("}\of") }

6    if Start_Tag (radicand)                       { Literal ( {   ) }
7    if    End_Tag (radicand)                      { Literal ( }   ) }
```

ENTITY TRANSLATION TABLE:
"Dgr"   "\Delta "

TRANSLATION OUTPUT:
   \root{3}\of {\Delta }

Example 3:   Array Separator

SAMPLE TAGGED TEXT:
```
1   <array>
2     <arrayrow>
3       <arraycel> A </arraycel> <arraycel> B </arraycel>
4     </arrayrow>
5     <arrayrow>
6       <arraycel> C </arraycel> <arraycel> D </arraycel>
7     </arrayrow>
8   </array>
```

TRANSLATION SCRIPT:
```
1   if Start_Tag (array)                          { Literal ("\matrix{ ") }
2   if   End_Tag (array)                          { Literal ( } )   }

3   if Start_Tag (arrayrow)                        { Literal ( )   }
4   if   End_Tag (arrayrow)                        { Literal (" \cr ") }

5   if Start_Tag (arraycel)                        { Literal ( )   }
6   if   End_Tag (arraycel) &&  Right_Peer         { Literal (" & ")   }
7   if   End_Tag (arraycel) && !Right_Peer         { Literal ( )   }
```

TRANSLATION OUTPUT:
```
        \matrix{ A  &  B  \cr  C  &  D  \cr }
```

cand tags. This example also demonstrates entity sub-stitution.

Example 3 shows how a script can determine if a tag is the last in a sequence.

The sample tagged text encodes a simple 2x2 array. Lines 1 and 2 of the script handle the *array* start and end tags and generate respectively the TeX matrix control sequence, and an enclosing brace for it. Lines 3 and 4 handle the *arrayrow* tags. In this case the start tag is consumed and the end tag is translated to a row terminator. Line

5 consumes the *arraycel* start tag. Lines 6 and 7 check the *arraycel* end tag to see if it does or does not have a right peer in the document structure. If it does, a TeX array cell separator is put into the translation; if not, the tag is consumed.

The three previous examples have all shown translation occuring right where the tag occurs in the document text. Example 4 shows that, in some cases, proper translation requires text to be inserted in a place other than where the tag actually occurs.

Example 4:   Leading Superscript

SAMPLE TAGGED TEXT:
```
1   <subform> N </subform>
2   <sup loc=pre> i </sup>
3   <sup> j </sup>
```

TRANSLATION SCRIPT:
```
1   if Start_Tag (subform)                         { Literal ( { )   }
2   if   End_Tag (subform)                         { Literal ( } )   }

3   if Start_Tag (sup)                             { Literal (^{ )   }
```

Example 4:   Leading Superscript (Continued)

```
4   if Start_Tag (sup) && Match (loc,post)      { Literal ( )  }
5   if Start_Tag (sup) && Match (loc,pre)       { Move_Relative_Left }
6   if    End_Tag (sup)                         { Literal ( } )  }
```

TRANSLATION OUTPUT:

^{ i }{ N }^{ j }

Example 4 is the solution to the leading super-script problem presented in the requirements section above. Text "movement" actions do not alter the input text and its underlying structure. As translation is performed, an output structure is constructed that may be freely restructured by the translation script.

The *subform* start and end tags are handled by lines 1 and 2, and generate the enclosing braces. Next, the first *sup* start tag is translated by line 3, which generates a TeX superscript command and a brace to enclose any items that will be super-scripted. Lines 4 and 5 check the value of the *loc* attribute. Since *loc* has the value *pre*, the transla-tion of the superscript structure is moved to the left of the immediately preceding sibling tagged structure; the *subform* structure. The *sup* end tag is translated by line 6 of the script, and a closing brace is generated. Line 3 of the text is processed in the same manner except that it is not moved, since it has no *loc* attribute.

In summary, we have shown some specific examples of how the GB-Engine translation tool capability meets the requirements imposed by the task of translating ISO 12083 mathematical markup to TeX. These examples by no means show all the capabilities of the translation tool. There are nearly 40 conditions [18] to examine various properties of the tags and tree structure and nearly 70 processes to format and alter the structure of the output. In addition, function call-backs provide access to the outer programming environment enabling arbitrarily complex trans-formations. Translation to other formats is possi-ble by simply using different scripts.

Conclusion

In this paper, we have described how the GB-Engine translation capability provides a means whereby richly tagged documents can be trans-formed into other arbitrary formats. As a result, SGML is made more attractive as the underlying representation for archival document storage. This allows publishers who target the WWW as a delivery medium to take advantage of develop-ments in HTML without having to constantly revise their document archives. GB-Engine trans-lation also shows how some of the capabilities of advanced style sheet languages such as those suggested by Sperberg-McQueen [16] can be implemented.

It is interesting to note that this paper was itself written as tagged text using GB-Engine via Fred to simultaneously translate the single tagged source to ASCII, HTML, and TeX (PostScript). GB-Engine translation services are freely avail-able via a WWW Fred server [6]. ∎

References

1. T. Berners-Lee and D. Connolly, *Hypertext Markup Language—2.0*, 1995. Accessible at *http://www.w3.org/hypertext/WWW/MarkUp/html-spec/html-spec_toc.html*

2. Adobe Systems Incorporated, *PostScript Language Reference Manual*, Addison-Wesley Publishing Company, Reading, MA, 1985.

3. Donald E. Knuth, *The TeXbook*, Addison-Wesley Publishing Company, Reading, MA, 1984.

4. Sun Microsystems, *HotJava Home Page*, 1995. Accessible at *http://java.sun.com/*

5. *Information Processing—Text and Office Sys-tems—Standard Generalized Markup Language (SGML)*, International Organization for Standard-ization, Ref. No. ISO 8879:1986, 1986.

6. Keith Shafer, *Fred: The SGML Grammar Builder*, Fred's WWW home page, 1994. Accessible at *http://www.oclc.org/fred/*

7. *Electronic Manuscript Preparation and Markup*, ANSI/NISO/ISO 12083, 1994.

8. Andrea Keyhani, *The Online Journal of Current Clinical Trials: An Innovation in Electronic Journal Publishing, Database*, February 1993, pages 14-23.

9. Donald E. Knuth, *TeXWare*, Dept. of Computer Science, Stanford University Technical Report STAN-CS-89-1097, 1986.

10. Keith Shafer, *SGML Grammar Structure, Annual Review of OCLC Research July 1992-June 1993*, pages 39-40, 1994.

11. John K. Ousterhout, *Tcl and the Tk Toolkit*, Addison-Wesley Publishing Company, Reading, MA, 1994.

12. Larry Wall and Randal L. Schwartz, *Programming Perl*, O'Reilly & Associates, Inc., Sebastopol, CA, 1992.

13. Harold Abelson, Gerald Jay Sussman, and Julie Abelson, *Structure and Interpretation of Computer Programs*, The MIT Press, Cambridge, MA, 1985.

14. Keith Shafer and Roger Thompson, *Introduction to Translating Tagged Text via the SGML Document Grammar Builder Engine*, 1994. Accessible at *http://www.oclc.org:80/fred/docs/translations/intro.html*

15. Stuart Weibel, Eric Miller, Ralph LeVan, and Jean Godby, *An Architecture for Scholarly Publishing on the World Wide Web, Proceedings from the Second International WWW Conference: Mosaic and the Web*, 1994. Accessible at *http://www.oclc.org:5046/publications/weibel/web_pub_arch/*, pages 739-748.

16. C.M. Sperberg-McQueen and Robert F. Goldstein, "HTML to the Max: A Manifesto for adding SGML Intelligence to the World Wide Web," *World Wide Web Fall 1994 Papers*. Accessible at *http://www.ncsa.uiuc.edu/SDG/IT94/Proceedings/Autools/sperberg-mcqueen/sperberg.html*

17. Diane Vizine-Goetz, Jean Godby, and Mark Bendig, "Spectrum: A Web-Based Tool for Describing Electronic Resources," presented at the *Third International World Wide Web Conference*. Darmstadt, Germany, 1995.

18. Keith Shafer, *Quick Translation Reference for Fred*, 1994. Accessible at *http://www.oclc.org/fred/docs/help/quick.html*

19. Keith Shafer, *Fred Translation Information*, 1994. Fred's WWW translation home page. Accessible at *http://www.oclc.org/fred/docs/translations/*

20. Thomas B. Hickey and Terry Noreault, "The Development of a Graphical User Interface for The Online Journal of Current Clinical Trials," *The Public-Access Computer Systems Review*, 3(2):4-12, 1992.

21. Thomas B. Hickey, "Reference Client Software Design," *Annual Review of OCLC Research July 1992-June 1993*, pages 37-39, 1994.

About the Authors

Keith Shafer

[*http://www.oclc.org:5046/~shafer/*]

shafer@oclc.org

Roger Thompson

thompson@oclc.org

OCLC Online Computer Library Center, Inc.

6565 Frantz Road, Dublin, Ohio 43017-3395

FAX: (614) 764-6096

REAL-TIME VIDEO AND AUDIO IN THE WORLD WIDE WEB

Zhigang Chen, See-Mong Tan, Roy H. Campbell, Yongcheng Li

Abstract

*The architecture of World Wide Web (WWW) browsers and servers supports full-file transfer for document retrieval. TCP is used for data transfers by Web browsers and their associated Hypertext Transfer Protocol (HTTP) servers. Full-file transfer and TCP are unsuitable for continuous media, such as real-time audio and video. In order for the WWW to support continuous media, we require the transmission of video and audio on demand and in real time, as well as new protocols for real-time data. We extend the architecture of the WWW to encompass the dynamic, real-time information space of video and audio. Our WWW browser Vosaic, short for Video Mosaic, incorporates real-time video and audio into standard hypertext pages that are displayed in place. Video and audio transfers occur in real time; there is no file-retrieval latency. The video and audio result in compelling Web pages. Real-time video and audio data can be effectively served over the present day Internet with the proper transmission protocol. We have developed a real-time protocol called VDP that we specialized for handling real-time video over the WWW. VDP reduces inter-frame jitter and dynamically adapts to the client CPU load and network congestion. Our WWW server dynamically changes transfer protocols, adapting to the request stream and the metainformation in requested documents. Experiments show a 44-fold increase in received video-frame rate (0.2 frames-per-second (fps) to 9 fps) with the use of VDP in lieu of TCP, with a commensurate improvement in observed video quality. Our work enables a video-enhanced Web. **Keywords:** Video, audio, World Wide Web, real time, network protocols*

Introduction

Traditional information systems design for World Wide Web clients and servers has concentrated on document retrieval and the structuring of document-based information, for example, through hierarchical menu systems as is used in gopher, or links in hypertext as in the Hypertext Markup Language (HTML) [2]. The architecture of current information systems on the WWW has been driven by the *static* nature of document-based information. This idea is reflected in the use of the file transfer mode of document retrieval and the use of stream-based protocols, such as TCP [1]. Full-file transfer and TCP are unsuitable for continuous media, and we discuss the reasons below. In order to incorporate video and audio into the WWW, we have extended the architecture of the WWW to enable a *video-enhanced Web*.

The easy-to-use, point-and-click user interfaces of WWW browsers, first popularized by NCSA Mosaic, have been the key to the widespread adoption of HTML and the World Wide Web by the entire Internet community. Although traditional WWW browsers perform commendably in the static information spaces of HTML documents, they are ill-suited for handling continuous media, such as real-time audio and video. Research in our laboratory has resulted in *Vosaic*, short for *Video Mosaic*, a tool that extends the architecture of vanilla NCSA Mosaic to encompass the dynamic, real-time information space of video and audio. Vosaic incorporates real-time video and audio into standard Web pages and the video is displayed in place. Video and audio transfers occur in real time; thus, there is thus no retrieval latency. The user accesses real-time sessions with the familiar "follow-the-link" point-and-click method. Mosaic was chosen as the software platform for our work because it is a widely available tool for which the source code is available, and with which we have significant experience.

Vosaic is a vehicle for exploring the integration of video with hypertext documents, allowing one to embed video links in hypertext. In Vosaic, sessions on the Multicast Backbone (Mbone) [6] can be specified using a variant of the Universal Resource Locator (URL) syntax. For example, the URL *mbone://224.2.252.51:4739:127:nv* encodes an Mbone transmission with a *Time-To-Live* (TTL) factor of 127, a multicast address of 224.2.252.51, a port address of 4739, and an *nv* video-transmission format [12].

While our original intent was for Vosaic to support the navigation of the Mbone's information space, we have extended Vosaic to include real-time retrieval of data from arbitrary video servers. Vosaic now supports the streaming and display of real-time video, video icons, and audio within a WWW hypertext document display. The Vosaic client adapts to the received video rate by discarding frames that have missed their arrival deadline. Early frames are buffered, reducing playback jitter. Periodic resynchronization adjusts the playback to accommodate network congestion. The result is real-time playback of video data streams.

Present day httpd servers exclusively use the TCP protocol for transfers of all document types. Our experiments indicate that real-time video and audio data can be effectively served over the present day Internet with the proper choice of transmission protocols. The server uses an augmented Real Time Protocol (RTP) [13] called VDP (discussed later in this paper) with built-in fault tolerance for video transmission. Feedback within VDP from the client allows the server to control the video-frame rate in response to client CPU load or network congestion. The server also dynamically changes transfer protocols, adapting to the request stream and the metainformation in requested documents. Our initial experiments show a 44-fold increase in the received video-

frame rate (0.2 frames-per-second (fps) to 9 fps) with VDP in lieu of TCP, with a commensurate improvement in observed video quality. We describe the implementation and results of our experiments below.

In the next section, we enumerate the reasons why the current WWW architecture is highly unsuitable for continuous media. Next, we discuss how video and audio may be effectively incorporated into the current WWW, followed by a description of the architecture of our prototype WWW client Vosaic. Then we describe the extended HTTP server that we have constructed, our specialized video datagram protocol VDP, and experimental results. The last two sections are devoted to related work and conclusions.

Why WWW Is Unsuitable for Continuous Media

Full File Transfer as a Retrieval Paradigm

Multimedia browsers such as Mosaic are excellent vehicles for browsing information spaces on the Internet that are made up of *static* data sets. However, attempts at the inclusion of video and audio in the current generation of multimedia browsers are limited to pre-recorded and canned sequences that are *retrieved* as full files. While the file transfer paradigm is adequate in the arena of traditional information retrieval and navigation, it becomes cumbersome for real-time data. The transfer times for video and audio files can be very large. Video and audio files now on the Web take minutes to hours to retrieve, thus severely limiting the inclusion of video and audio in current Web pages, because the latency required before playback begins can be unacceptably long. The file transfer method of browsing also assumes a fairly static and unchanging data set for which a single uni-directional transfer is adequate for browsing some piece of information. Real-time sessions such as video conferences, on the other hand, are not static. Sessions happen in real time and come and go over the course of minutes to days.

TCP-Based Transfers

The Hypertext Transfer Protocol (HTTP) is the transfer protocol used between WWW clients and servers for hypertext document service. The HTTP uses TCP as the primary protocol for reliable document transfer. TCP is unsuitable for real-time audio and video for several reasons.

- TCP imposes its own flow control and windowing schemes on the data stream. These mechanisms effectively destroy the temporal relations shared between video frames and audio packets.

- Reliable message delivery is not required for video and audio. Video and audio streams tolerate frame losses. Losses are seldom fatal although detrimental to picture and sound quality. TCP retransmission causes further jitter and skew internally between frames and externally between associated video and audio streams.

How to Get Video and Audio in the WWW

The use of both full-file transfer and TCP as a transfer protocol is clearly unsuitable for supporting video and audio. We concluded that to truly support video and audio in the WWW, one requires:

- The transmission of video and audio *on-demand* and in *real time*

- *New protocols* for real-time data

On demand, real-time video and audio solves the problem of playback latency. In Vosaic, the video or audio is streamed across the network from the server to the client in response to a client request for a Web page containing embedded videos. The client plays the incoming multimedia stream in real time as the data is received in real time.

However, the real-time transfer of multimedia data streams introduces new problems of maintaining adequate playback quality in the face of network congestion and client load. As the WWW is based on the Internet, resource reservation to guarantee bandwidth, delay, or jitter is not currently possible (we discuss our work in relation to the RSVP [20] Internet resource reservation protocol in the "Related Work" section). The delivery of IP packets across the international Internet is typically best effort, and subject to network variability outside the control of any video server or client.

Our initial effort focuses on supporting real-time video in the Web. Inter-frame jitter greatly affects video-playback quality across the network (for our purposes, we take jitter as the variance in inter-arrival time between subsequent frames of a video stream). High jitter typically causes the video playback to appear "jerky." In addition, network congestion may cause frames delays or losses. Transient load at the client side may prevent it from handling the full-frame rate of the video. We created a specialized real-time transfer protocol for handling video across the Internet. Our experiments indicate that the protocol successfully handles real-time Internet video by reducing jitter and incorporating dynamic adaptation to the client CPU load and network congestion.

Vosaic

Vosaic's Roots

Vosaic is derived from NCSA Mosaic. Mosaic concentrates on HTML documents. While all media types are treated as documents, each media type is handled differently. Text and inlined images are displayed in place. Other media types, such as video and audio files, or special file formats (e. g., postscript) are handled externally by invoking other programs. In Mosaic, documents are not displayed until fully available (more modern browsers, such as Netscape [10], incrementally display a document as it is retrieved). The Mosaic client keeps the retrieved document in temporary storage until all of the document has been fetched. The sequential relationship between transferring and processing of documents makes the browsing of large video/audio documents and real-time video/audio sources problematic. Transferring such documents require long delay times and large client-side storage space. This makes real-time playback impossible.

There is one argument that the functions of Mosaic should be kept at a minimum while addi-

tional functionality is left up to specialized external viewers. Work along this line has led to the development of the Common Gateway Interface [18], a standard for harnessing external programs to view files according to their MIME [9,8] types. One key reason favoring the success of Mosaic is its incorporation of inlined images with text, resulting in a semantically rich environment. Leaving the display of audio and video to external viewers causes a loss of semantic content in a hypertext document that includes these media

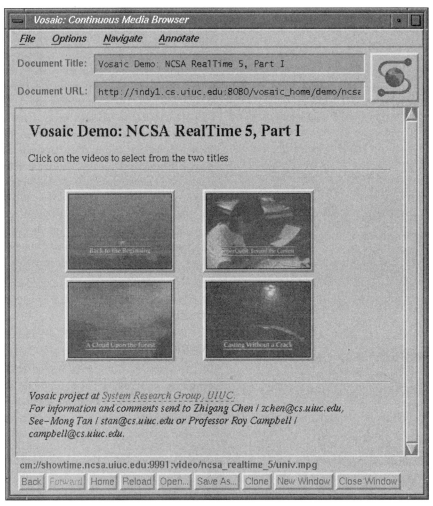

Figure 1:   A four-item video menu in Vosaic

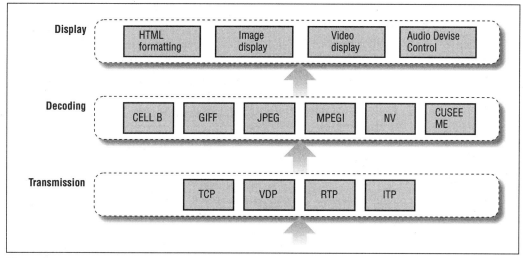

Figure 2:   Vosaic's internal structure

types. Real-time video and audio convey more information if directly incorporated into the display of a hypertext document. For example, we have implemented real time *video menus* and *video icons* as an extension of HTML in Vosaic. Figure 1 is a typical four-item video menu one may construct with Vosaic. Video menus present the user with several choices. Each choice is in the form of a moving video. One may, for example, click on a video menu item to follow the link, and watch the clip in full size. Video icons show a video in an small, unobtrusive icon-sized rectangle within the HTML document. Our experience indicates that embedded real-time video within WWW documents greatly enhances the look and feel of a Vosaic page. Video menu items convey more information about the choices available than simple textual descriptions or static images.

Vosaic's Internal Structure

HTML documents with video and audio integrated are characterized by a variety of data transmission protocols, data decoding formats, and device control mechanisms (e.g., graphical display, audio device control, and video board control). Vosaic has a layered structure to meet

these requirements. The layers are depicted in Figure 2. They are:

- Document transmission
- Document decoding
- Document display

A document data stream flows through these three layers by using different components from different layers. The composition of components along the data path of a retrieved document occurs at runtime according to document meta information returned by our extended HTTP server.

As discussed in the previous section, TCP is only suitable for static document transfers, such as text and image transfers. Real-time playback of video and audio requires other protocols. The current implementation in the Vosaic document transmission layer includes TCP, VDP, and RTP. Vosaic is configured to have TCP support for text and image transmission. Real-time playback of real-time video and audio uses VDP. RTP is the protocol used by most Mbone conferencing transmissions. A fourth protocol under consideration is for interactive communication (used for virtual reality, video games, and interactive distance learning) between the Web client and server.

The decoding formats currently implemented for images include:

- GIF
- JPEG

For video they include:

- MPEG1
- NV
- CUSEEME
- Sun CELLB

For audio they include:

- AIFF
- MPEG1

The display layer includes traditional HTML formatting and inline image display. We have extended the display to incorporate real-time video display and audio device control.

HTML and URL Extensions

Standard URL specifications include FTP, HTTP [3], WAIS [17], and others, covering most of the currently existing document-retrieval protocols. However, access protocols for video and audio conferences on the Mbone are not defined and not supported. We have extended the standard URL [4] specification and HTML to accommodate real-time continuous media transmission. The extended URL specification supports Mbone transmission protocols using the *mbone* keyword as a URL scheme and on-demand continuous media protocols using *cm* as the URL scheme. The format of the URL specifications for the Mbone and continuous real time are as follows:

- *mbone://address:port:ttl:format*
- *cm://address:port:format/filepath*

Examples are given below:

- *mbone://224.2.252.51:4739:127:nv*

- *cm://showtime.ncsa.uiuc. edu:8080:mpegvideo:puffer.mpg*

- cm://showtime.ncsa.uiuc. edu:8080:mpgaudio:puffer.mp2

The first URL encodes an Mbone transmission on the address 224.2.252.51, on port 4739, with a time-to-live factor of 127, using *nv* format video. The second and third URLs encode continuous media transmissions of MPEG video and audio respectively.

Incorporating inline video and audio in HTML necessitates the addition of two more constructs to the HTML syntax. The additions follow the syntax of inline images closely. Inlined video and audio segments are specified as follows:

- `<video    src="address:port/file-path option=cyclic|control">`
- `<audio    src="address:port/file-path option=cyclic|control">`

The syntax for both video and audio is made up of a *src* part and an *options* part. Src specifies the server information, including the address and port number, and options specifies how the media is to be displayed. There are two possible options, *control* or *cyclic*, which are described below:

- Control pops up a window with a control panel and the first frame of the video is displayed, with further playback controlled by the user.

- Cyclic displays the video or audio clip in a loop. The video stream may be cached in local storage to avoid further network traffic after the first round of display. This is feasible when the size of video or audio clip is small. If the segment is too large to be stored locally at the client end, the client may also request the source to repeatedly send the clip. Cyclic video clips are useful for constructing *video menus* and *video icons*.

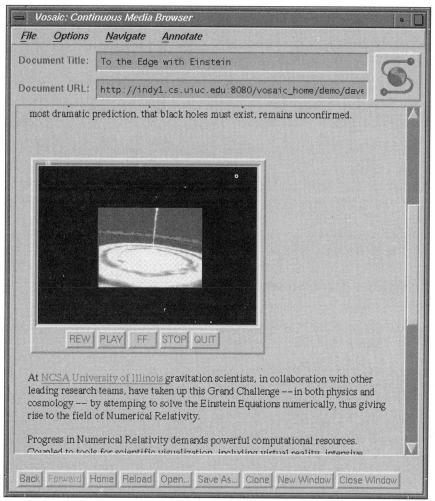

Figure 3: A video control panel in Vosaic

Control Interface

If the *control* keyword is given, a control panel is presented to the user, as shown in Figure 3.

The control interface allows users to browse and control video clips. We provide the following user-control buttons:

- *Play* starts to play the video.

- *Stop* ends the playing of the video.

- *Fast Forward* plays the video at a faster speed. We implement this by dropping frames at the server site.

- *Rewind* plays the video backwards at a fast speed.

- *Quit* terminates playback. When the user presses *Play* again, the video is restarted from the beginning.

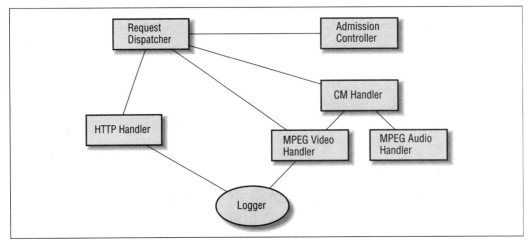

Figure 4: Server structure

Video Widgets and Client/Server Interaction

A new video widget is required in order to display the video. Video widget creation follows three steps:

1. Before widget creation, the client communicates with the server asking for the size information of the video stream.

2. On receipt of the size information, the browser creates the video widget.

3. After the widget creation, the browser forks a video player process. The player process receives and displays the video within the video widget.

Real-time video and audio use VDP as a transfer protocol. Control-information exchange uses a TCP connection between the client and server.

Server

Vosaic works in conjunction with an extended HTTP server. The server uses the same set of transmission protocols as does Vosaic.

It spawns a child to handle the transmission of each video stream. Video and audio are transmit-

ted with VDP. Frames are transmitted at the originally recorded frame rate of the video. The server uses a feed forward and feedback scheme to detect network congestion and automatically delete frames from the stream in response to congestion.

The main components of the server are shown in Figure 4. They are:

- Main request dispatcher

- Admission controller

- HTTP request handler

- Continuous media handlers

- Server logger

Admission Control

The main request dispatcher receives client requests. and passes the request to the admission controller. The admission controller then determines or estimates the requirements of the current request, which may include network bandwidth and CPU load. It then makes a decision on whether the current request should be served based on its knowledge of current conditions.

Traditional HTTP servers can do without admission control because document sizes are small, and request streams are bursty [16]. Requests are simply queued before service, and most documents can be handled quickly. In contrast, with continuous media transmissions in a video server, file sizes are large, and real-time data streams have stringent time constraints. The server must ensure that it has enough network bandwidth and processing power to maintain service qualities to current requests. The criteria used to evaluate requests may be based on the requested bandwidth, server available bandwidth, and system CPU load. Our current system simply limits the number of concurrent streams to a fixed number. However, the admission-control policy is flexible and can be made more sophisticated.

Request Handling

After the system grants the current request, the main request dispatcher hands the request to one of several specific request handlers. The server currently has handlers for the following:

- HTTP

- MPEG Video

- MPEG Audio

Each handler uses a different transmission protocol for handling requests. HTTP requests use TCP/IP. MPEG video and audio use VDP (described in the next section). We have striven to ensure that the server design is flexible enough to incorporate more protocols.

Logging

The *logger* is responsible for recording the request and transmission statistics. Reed, et al. [16], McGrath [11], and Mogul [7] have studied the access patterns of the current Web servers. We expect that the access patterns for a video-enhanced Web server will be substantially different from that of traditional WWW servers supporting mainly text and static images. The statis-

tics for the transmission of continuous media is recorded by the server logger in order that we can better understand the behavior of requests for continuous media. The statistics include the network usage and processor usage of each request, the quality of service data such as frame rate, frame drop rate, and jitter. The data will guide the design of future busy Internet video servers. These statistics are also important for analyzing the impact of continuous media on operating systems and the network.

VDP

VDP is an augmented real-time datagram protocol we developed to handle video and audio over the WWW. The design of VDP is based on making efficient use of the available network bandwidth and CPU capacity for video processing. It is different from RTP in that it takes advantage of the point-to-point connection between Web server and Web client. The server end of VDP receives feedback from the client and adapts to the network condition between client and server and the client CPU load. VDP uses an *adaptation algorithm* to find the optimal transfer bandwidth. A *demand resend algorithm* handles frame losses.

VDP Channels

VDP is an asymmetric protocol. A VDP connection has two distinguished endpoints belonging to a client and a video server. There are two channels associated with each VDP connection. The first is an unreliable data transmission channel used for transmitting data and uncritical feedback information. Another one is a reliable channel used to send control information from the client to the server. Control information includes playback control, such as *play, stop, fast forward, rewind*, as well as connection-management control, such as *connection termination*.

Transmission Mechanism

After the admission controller grants the request from the client, the server waits for the *play* command from the client. Upon receiving the *play* command, the server starts to send the video frames on the data channel using the *recorded frame rate*. The server end breaks large frames into smaller packets (currently 8 kilobytes), and the client end reassembles the packets into frames. Each frame is time-stamped by the server and buffered at the client side. The client controls the sending of frames by sending server control commands, like *stop* or *fast forward*, on the control channel.

Adaptation Algorithm

The adaptation algorithm dynamically adapts the video transmission rate to network conditions along the network span from the client to the server, as well as to the client end's processing capacity. The algorithm degrades or upgrades the server transmission rate depending on feed-forward and feedback messages exchanged on the control channel.

Protocols for the transmission of continuous media over the Internet must preserve network bandwidth as much as possible. If a client does not have enough processor capacity, it may not be fast enough to decode video and audio data. Network connections may also impose constraints on the frame rate at which video data can be sent. In such cases, the server must gracefully degrade the quality of service. The server learns of the status of the connection from client feedback. Feedback messages are of two types:

- *Frame drop rate.* The frame drop rate corresponds to frames received by the client but dropped because the client did not have enough CPU power to keep up with decoding the frames.

- *Packet drop rate.* The packet drop rate corresponds to frames lost in the network due to network congestion.

If the client-side protocol discovers that the client application is not reading received frames quickly enough, it updates the frame loss rate. If the loss rate is severe, it sends the information to the server. The server then adjusts its transmission speed accordingly. In our current implementation, the system degrades if the loss rate exceeds 15%, and upgrades if the loss rate is below 5%.

In response to a video request, the server begins by sending out frames using the recorded frame rate. The server inserts a special packet in the data stream indicating the number of packets sent out so far. On receiving the feed-forward message from the server, the client may then calculate the packet drop rate. The client returns the feedback message to the server on the control channel. In our implementation, feedback occurs every 30 frames. Our experiments indicate that adaptation occurs very quickly in practice--on the order of a few seconds.

Demand Resend Algorithm

The compression algorithms in some media formats use inter-frame dependent encoding. For example, a sequence of MPEG video frames has I, P, and B frames [5].

- I frames are intra-frame coded with JPEG compression

- P frames are predictive coded with respect to a past picture

B frames are bidirectionally predictive coded MPEG frames are arranged into groups with sequences that correspond to the pattern $I\ B\ B\ P$ $B\ B\ P\ B\ B$. The I frame is needed by all P and B frames in order to be decoded. The P frames are needed by all B frames. This encoding method makes some frames more important than the others. The display quality is strongly dependent on the receipt of important frames. Since data transmission is unreliable over the Internet, there is a possibility of frame loss. If, in a sequence group of MPEG video frames $I\ B\ B\ P\ B\ B\ P\ B\ B$ recorded at 9 frames/sec, the I frame is lost, the entire

Name	Frame Rate (fps)	Resolution	Number of Frames	Play Time (secs)
model.mpg	9	160 by 120	127	14
startrek.mpg	5	208 by 156	642	128
puffer.mpg	5	320 by 240	175	35
smalllogo.mpg	5	320 by 240	1622	324

sequence becomes undecodable. This produces a one-second gap in the video stream.

In VDP, the responsibility of determining which frames are resent is put on the client based on its knowledge of the encoding format used by the video stream. In an MPEG stream, it may thus choose to request retransmissions of only the *I* frames, or of both the *I* and *P* frames, or all frames. VDP employs a buffer queue at least as large as the number of frames required during one round trip time between the client and the server. The buffer is full before the protocol begins handing frames to the client from the queue head. New frames enter at the queue tail. A demand resend algorithm is used to generate resend requests to the server in the event a frame is missing from the queue tail. Since the buffer queue is large enough, resent frames will most likely be correctly inserted into the queue before the application requires it.

Experimental Results

We carried out several experiments over the Internet. Our test-data set consisted of four MPEG movies, digitized at rates ranging from 5 to 9 fps,

with pixel resolution ranging from 160 by 120 to 320 by 240. Table 1 tabulates the test videos.

The videos ranged from a short 14-second segment to one of several minutes duration.

In order to observe the playback video quality, we based the client side of all our tests in our laboratory in Urbana, Illinois, USA. In order to cover the widest possible range of configurations, we set up servers corresponding to local, regional, and international sites relative to our geographical location. We used a server at the National Center for Supercomputing Applications (NCSA) for the local case. NCSA is connected to the local campus network via Ethernet. For the regional case, we used a server at the University of Washington on the west coast of North America, in Washington state. Finally, a copy of our server was set up at the University of Oslo in Norway to cover the international case. Table 2 lists the names and IP addresses of the hosts used for our experiments.

Tables 3, 4, and 5 show the results for sample runs using the test videos by our Web client accessing the local, regional, and international servers respectively.

Table 2:   Hosts Used in Our Tests

Name	IP Address	Function
indy1.cs.uiuc.edu	128.174.240.90	local client
showtime.ncsa.uiuc.edu	141.142.3.37	local server
agni.wtc.washington.edu	128.95.73.229	regional server
gloin.ifi.uio.no	129.240.106.13	international server

Table 3:   Local Test

Name	% Dropped Frames	Jitter (ms)
model	0	8.5
startrek	0	5.9
puffer	7.5	43.6
smallogo	0.5	22.5

Table 4:   Regional Test

Name	% Dropped Frames	Jitter (ms)
model	0	46.3
startrek	0	57.1
puffer	0	34.3
smallogo	0.2	50.0

Table 5:   International Test

Name	% Dropped Frames	Jitter (ms)
model	0	20.1
startrek	0	22.0
puffer	19	121.4
smallogo	0.8	46.7

In the tables above, each test involved the Web client retrieving a single MPEG video clip. We used an unloaded SGI Indy as the client workstation. The numbers give the average frame-drop percentage and average application-level inter-frame jitter in milliseconds for 30 test runs. Frame-rate changes due to the adaptive algorithm was seen in only one run. That run used the *puffer.mpg* test video in the international configuration (Oslo, Norway to Urbana, USA). The frame rate dropped from 5 fps to 4 fps at frame number 100, then increased from 4 fps to 5 fps at frame number 126. The rate change indicated that transient network congestion caused the video to degrade for a 5.2 second period during the transmission.

The results indicate that the Internet can support a video-enhanced Web service. Inter-frame jitter in the local configuration is negligible, and below the threshold of human observability (usually 100 ms) in the regional case. Except for the *puffer. mpg* runs, the same holds true for the interna-

tional configuration. In that case, the adaptive algorithm was invoked because of dropped frames and the video quality was degraded for a 5.2-second interval. The VDP buffer queue efficiently reduces frame jitter at the application level.

Our last test exercised the adaptive algorithm more strongly. We used the local configuration and retrieved a version of *smalllogo.mpg* recorded at 30 fps at a pixel resolution of 320 by 240. This is a high-quality video clip at a medium size, requiring significant computing resources for playback. Figure 5 shows a graph of frame rate versus frame sequence number for the server transmitting the video.

The client-side buffer queue was set at 200 frames, corresponding to about 6.67 seconds of video. The buffer at the client side first fills up, and the first frame is handed to the application at frame number 200. The client workstation does not have enough processing capacity to decode the video stream at the full 30-fps rate. The cli-

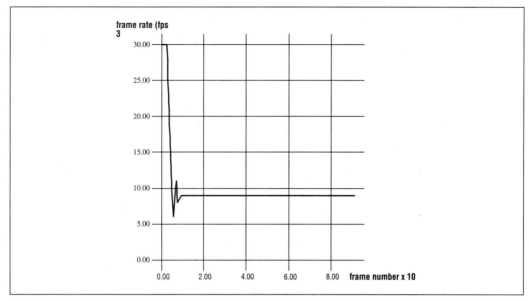

frame rate (fps

Figure 5:   Frame rate adaptation for smalllogo.mpg

ent-side protocol detects a frame-loss rate severe enough to report to the server at frame number 230. Our current criteria for degrading the transmission is when the frame loss rate exceeds 15%. The transmission is upgraded if the loss rate is below 5%.

The server begins degrading its transmission at frame number 268, that is, within 1.3 seconds from the client detecting that its CPU was unable to keep up. The optimal transmission level was reached in 7.8 seconds, corresponding to a 9 frame per second transmission rate. Stability was reached in a further 14.8 seconds. The deviation from optimal did not exceed 3 frames per second in either direction during that period. The results show a fundamental tension between large buffer queue sizes that reduce jitter and server response times.

The test with very high quality video at 30 fps with a frame size of 320 by 240 represents a pathological case. However, the results show that the adaptive algorithm is an attractive way to reach optimal frame transmission rates for video in the WWW. The test implementation changes

the video quality by one frame-per-second at each iteration. We are experimenting with other schemes based on more sophisticated policies, such as multiplicative decrease/additive increase.

Related Work

A major impediment to browsing Web documents which include video and audio clips is the long transfer latency for continuous media files. The commercial successors to Mosaic, like Netscape [10], attempt to reduce the transfer latency for large documents by incrementally displaying the document as it is retrieved. Although Netscape has the ability to stream data via external "helper applications," these employ TCP at the transport layer, and are not integrated into the browser proper.

Sun Microsystem's HotJava [15] product introduced a novel method for the inclusion of animated multimedia in a Web browser. HotJava allows the browser to download executable scripts written in the Java programming language. The execution of the script at the client end enables the animation of graphic widgets within a Web page. In contrast, we have concentrated on the streaming of real-time video and audio over the WWW.

Smith's CM Player [14] is a networked continuous media toolkit. It is used as part of an experimental video-on-demand (VOD) system at UC Berkeley. CM Player is a stand-alone system. In contrast, we have cast our work in a WWW context, incorporating continuous media into Web browsers and servers. CM Player employs Cyclic-UDP for the transport of video streams between the VOD server and the CM Player client. Frames are prioritized at the server, and clients request resends on detecting frame losses. Cyclic-UDP repeatedly resends high priority frames in order to give them a better chance of reaching the destination. VDP's demand-resend algorithm is similar to Cyclic-UDP, except that the client decides which frames get retransmitted. In an MPEG transmission, the client can decide to tolerate the loss of B frames but require the resend of all I frames.

The proposed RSVP [20] protocol will allow resource reservation in Internet routers and thus guarantee quality of service to the data flows of requesting applications. VDP, in contrast, is designed to preserve network bandwidth in response to both network congestion as well as client CPU load. VDP attempts to reach the best level of service possible under current conditions, thus minimum guaranteed bandwidths are neither necessary nor appropriate.

Since the completion of the initial draft of this paper and the release of the Vosaic browser, we have learned of the Distributed Real-Time MPEG Video Audio Player from Cen, Pu, Staehli, Cowan, and Walpole [19]. While their system is a stand alone distributed MPEG player like Berkeley's CM Player, we share many ideas in common regarding feedback in order to preserve network bandwidth. It is a pleasure to cite them in this paper.

Conclusion

In order to integrate real-time continuous media into the WWW, we extended the traditional full-file transfer paradigm of the WWW to include real-time transfer and browsing of video- and audio-enhanced HTML documents. The motivation behind Vosaic as a research tool is its integration of real-time multimedia information into an easy-to-use WWW client. The new video datagram protocol VDP is designed for video-data transfer over the Internet. Our experiments conclude that it is possible to transmit high quality video over the present day Internet with VDP.

Our work indicates that a *video-enhanced* World Wide Web is indeed possible.

As continuing work, we are implementing *annotations* in the browser and server. Annotations are a series of polygons that are added to a video stream with the aid of an annotation editor. The annotations accompany a video stream when it is transmitted. The system interpolates between polygons and users are thus able to click on parts of a moving video in order to follow hyperlinks.
∎

Acknowledgments

David Putzolu, now at Intel, together with See-Mong Tan, was one of the originators of the Vosaic idea. We thank Bruce Schatz for sparking our interest in information-systems design. We are grateful to our partners at NCSA for supporting our work on a video-enhanced Web. In particular, we thank Charlie Catlett and Jeff Terstriep at NCSA. Ellard Roush provided helpful comments at every stage. We thank our friends Jisheng Liang at the University of Washington and Dong Xie at the University of Oslo for their generous help with our experiments.

Software Release

The browser described in this paper is available at *http://choices.cs.uiuc.edu/research/Vosaic/vosaic2.html.*

References

1. D. Comer and D. Stevens, *Internetworking with TCP/IP*, Prentice Hall, Englewood Cliffs, NJ, 1991.

2. World Wide Web Consortium, Hypertext Markup Language, *http://www.w3.org/hypertext/WWW/MarkUp.*

3. World Wide Web Consortium, Hypertext Transfer Protocol, *http://www.w3.org/hypertext/WWW/Protocols*

4. World Wide Web Consortium, Uniform Resource Locators, *http://www.w3.org/hypertext/Addressing/URL*

5. D. Le Gall, "MPEG: A Video Compression Standard for Multimedia Applications," *Communications of the ACM*, 34(4):46--58, April 1991.

6. S. Deering and D. Cheriton, "Multicast Routing in Datagram Internetworks and Extended LANS," *ACM Transactions on Computer Systems*, pages 85--110, May 1990.

7. J.C. Mogul, "Operating Systems Support for Busy Internet Services," in *Fifth Workshop on Hot Topics in Operating Systems*, IEEE Computer Society, Orcas Island, WA, May 1995.

8. K. Moore, "MIME (Multipurpose Internet Mail Extensions) Part Two: Message Header Extensions for Non-ASCII Text," *Internet RFC* 1522, September 1993.

9. N. Borenstein and N. Freed, "MIME (Multipurpose Internet Mail Extensions) Part One: Mechanisms for Specifying and Describing the Format of Internet Message Bodies," *Internet RFC* 1521, September 1993.

10. Netscape Communications, Inc. Netscape. *http://www.w3.org/hypertext/Addressing/URL*

11. R. E. McGrath, "What We Do and Don't Know About the Load on the NCSA WWW Server," *http://www.ncsa.uiuc.edu/InformationServers/Colloquia/28.Sep.94/Begin.html*, September 1994.

12. Ron Frederick, "Experiences with software real-time video compression," Technical report, Xerox Palo Alto Research Center, July 1992. *ftp://parcftp.xerox.com/pub/net-research/nv-paper.ps*

13. H. Schulzrinne and S. Casner, "RTP: A Transport Protocol for Real time Applications," Internet Draft, October 1993.

14. Brian Smith, *Implementation Techniques for Continous Media System and Applications.* PhD thesis, University of California, Berkeley, 1993.

15. Sun Microsystems, Inc. Hot Java. *http://www.sun.com*

16. Thomas T Kwan, Robert E. McGrath, and Daniel A. Reed, "User Access Patterns to NCSA's World Wide Web Server," **Technical report**, University of Illinois at Urbana-Champaign, 1995. *http://www-pablo.cs.uiuc.edu/Projects/Mosaic/mosaic.html*

17. Trans-European Research and Education Networking Association, WAIS, *http://www.earn.net/gnrt/wais.html*

18. World Wide Web Consortium, Common Gateway Interface, *http://www.w3.org/htpertext/WWW/Overview.html*

19. Shanwei Cen, Calton Pu, Richard Staehli, Crispin Cowan, and Jonathon Walpole, "A Distributed Real-Time MPEG Video Audio Player," *Fifth International Workshop on Network and Operating System Support of Digital Audio and Video (NOSSDAV '95)*, April 18-21, Durham, NH, 1995.

20. L. Zhang, S. Deering, D. Estrin, and D. Zappala, "RSVP: A New Resource ReSerVation Protocol," IEEE Network, September 1993.

About the Authors

Zhigang Chen

[*http://www-sal.cs.uiuc.edu/~z-chen*]
zchen@cs.uiuc.edu

Zhigang Chen is a Ph.D. student with the Systems Research Group at the Department of Computer Science at the University of Illinois at Urbana, Champaign. He received his B.S. degree in 1991 from Tianjin University (Peiyang University) in China and his M.S. in 1993 from the University of Louisiana, both in Computer Science. He is interested in distributed continuous media applications, distributed systems, and high-speed networks.

See-Mong Tan

[*http://choices.cs.uiuc.edu/srg/stan/stan.html*]
stan@cs.uiuc.edu

See-Mong Tan is a Ph.D. candidate at the University of Illinois at Urbana, Champaign. He received a B.S. degree from the University of California at Berkeley in 1989 and a M.S. from the University of Illinois at Urbana, Champaign in 1991. He is a member of the Systems Research Group. His research interests include high-speed networks and multimedia operating systems.

Roy H. Campbell

[*http://www.cs.uiuc.edu/CS_INFO_SERVER/DEPT_INFO/CS_FACULTY/FAC_HTMLS/campbell.html*]
roy@cs.uiuc.edu

Roy H. Campbell is a professor at the University of Illinois at Urbana, Champaign and Director of the Systems Research Group in the Department of Computer Science. He received a B.S. degree in Mathematics and Physics from the University of Sussex in 1969, an M.S. and Ph.D. in Computing from the University of Newcastle upon Tyne in 1972 and 1976 respectively. The focus of Professor Campbell's research is complex systems software. He has been with the University of Illinois at Urbana, Champaign since 1976.

Yongcheng Li

[*http://choices.cs.uiuc.edu/srg/ycli/public_html/self.html*]
cli@cs.uiuc.edu

Yongcheng Li is a Ph.D. candidate at the University of Illinois at Urbana, Champaign. He received his B.S. degree and M.S. in Computer Science from Tsinghua University, in the People's Republic of China. He is a member of the Systems Research Group. His current research interests include operating systems, multimedia, and distributed systems.

LESSONS FOR THE WORLD WIDE WEB FROM THE TEXT ENCODING INITIATIVE

David T. Barnard, Lou Burnard, Steven J. DeRose, David G. Durand,
C.M. Sperberg-McQueen

Abstract

Although HTML is widely used, it suffers from a serious limitation: it does not clearly distinguish between structural and typographical information. In fact, it is impossible to have a single simple standard for document encoding that can effectively satisfy the needs of all users of the World Wide Web. Multiple views of data, and thus multiple DTDs, are needed.

The Text Encoding Initiative (TEI) has produced a complex and sophisticated DTD that makes contributions both in terms of the content that it allows to be encoded and in the way that the DTD is structured. In particular, the TEI DTD provides a mechanism for describing hypertextual links that balances power and simplicity; it also provides the means for including information that can be used in resource description and discovery. The TEI DTD is designed as a number of components that can be assembled using standard SGML techniques, giving an overall result that is modular and extensible. ***Keywords:*** *SGML, modular DTDs, extensible DTDs, linking mechanisms, header*

Introduction

The World Wide Web is growing with amazing rapidity, and with it, HTML (Hypertext Markup Language) document encoding. However, even in the presence of this success, there are problems which are evidenced by the frequent, and frequently bitter, divisions over HTML style and the conflicting approaches to extending HTML. These divisions are caused, to a great extent, by the fact that HTML has an underlying confusion of categories that leads to abuse and misuse of tags. Or, perhaps more correctly, to different uses and interpretations of HTML, based on different priorities. These conflicts reflect the fact that HTML is partly a markup scheme for structural markup, and partly a scheme for presentational markup; these two tendencies are at war both in the HTML specification and in the usage of document publishers and software developers.

Although at its inception this was not true, HTML is now defined as an application of SGML (Standard Generalized Markup Language). SGML is a metalanguage for defining document markup; it is defined by an international standard [8], and there is a handbook that interprets the standard [6]. Even more information about SGML can be found in the World Wide Web page maintained by Robin Cover [4]. SGML allows the definition of a markup language applicable to a set of documents by specifying the components that the documents will contain, the ways in which components can be combined together to make larger components and entire documents, and the ways in which the boundaries of components will be indicated in the document.

The information added to a document to delineate the components is called markup. The various parts of the formal specification of a document class are gathered together in a *document type definition* (DTD). For example, a simple DTD for office memoranda might include definitions for a *heading* and a *body*, with the heading including *to*, *from*, *date*, and *subject* components and the body containing *paragraph* components.

A component is (usually) delineated by preceding it with its name in angle brackets and following it with its name preceded by a slash in angle brackets, as in

```
<heading> ... <subject>Salary Pol-
icy</subject> ... </heading>
```

HTML is now formally defined as an application of SGML. This means that a DTD defines the components of HTML documents, and their possible hierarchical relationships [2]. Future versions of HTML promise to be tied to the formal SGML setting in increasingly explicit ways.

Although it makes concessions for the encoding of processing information—such as layout commands—SGML is designed to allow systems to focus on the structure of documents, to precisely describe what is present, rather than how it will be processed. In the document-processing model adopted by SGML, the description of document formatting (or any other processing) is consciously and explicitly separated from the description of document structure.

The same claim cannot be made for HTML. It contains structural concepts, such as the <P> tag to describe a paragraph. But the Web still bears visible traces of the first version of HTML, in which the paragraph was not, strictly speaking, a structural unit that was contained in some units and could contain others. Instead, as commonly implemented, the paragraph tag indicates a point at which specific processing is to occur. HTML also contains tags for such typographic features as images (with alignment constraints to control a formatting process), horizontal rules, and type styles. Perhaps the most extreme example of nonstructural encoding in some network documents is an HTML extension indicating that text is to blink when presented on the screen—a formatting indication that does not even have a meaning if the document is to be printed.

Of course, the most obvious, perhaps most frequent, and design-anticipated use of documents encoded in HTML is to display them on a screen with a network browser. And it is not surprising that this intended application should be—or, at least should still be—implicit in the document encoding. But this means that even users who would prefer to use a structural encoding cannot do so. Absent (at the moment) style sheets for mapping structural categories to display characteristics, users frequently resort to "tag abuse"— using existing tags for their typographical effects rather than for their structural significance, if any. In fact, "tag abuse" is possibly the most common style of markup on the Web, especially given the needs of the commercial users now flocking to the Internet.

The Text Encoding Initiative (TEI) is a large international project sponsored by the Association for Computers and the Humanities, the Association for Computational Linguistics, and the Association for Literary and Linguistic Computing. The project began at a planning meeting late in 1987, which was attended by researchers involved in encoding texts for research purposes (such as the production of critical editions and linguistic analysis) and in producing software to deal with encoded texts. There was agreement among the participants that the chaotic diversity of encoding techniques in use made it needlessly difficult to share texts, software, and research results among colleagues.

At the meeting, ACH, ACL, and ALLC agreed to sponsor a project to develop a common standard for encoding texts of interest to the communities they represented (humanistic researchers, linguists, and others involved in "language industries"). They supported the project by providing members for a Steering Committee and raising funds for the development work. Over the next several years, the U.S. National Endowment for the Humanities, Directorate General XIII of the Commission of the European Communities, the Andrew W. Mellon Foundation, and the Social Science and Humanities Research Council of Canada all provided funds.

The project's design goals were that the Guidelines should:

- Define a standard format for data interchange

- Provide guidance for encoding texts in this format

- Support the encoding of all kinds of features of all texts studied by researchers

- Remain application independent

These goals led to a number of important design decisions, such as:

- The choice of SGML

- The provision of a large predefined tag set

- A distinction between required, recommended, and optional encoding practices

- Encodings for different views of text

- Alternative encodings for the same features

- Mechanisms for user-defined extensions to the scheme

The work of the project was carried out by scholars at institutions in North America and in Europe. The main result of the project is a document entitled *Guidelines for Electronic Text Encoding and Interchange (TEI P3)*, edited by Sperberg-McQueen and Burnard [10]. This large document (almost 1300 pages) describes a collection of SGML tag sets that together make up a modular and extensible DTD, with which one may encode a wide range of documents.

The Guidelines can be found online in several places. The official project repository, containing the Guidelines and other project documents, is at *ftp://ftp-tei.uic.edu/pub/tei* (for users in North America) and its mirror sites *ftp://ftp.ifi.uio.no/ pub/SGML/TEI* (for users in Europe) and *ftp://TEI. IPC.Chiba-u.ac.jp/TEI/P3* (for users in Asia), or at *ftp://info.ex.ac.uk/pub/SGML/tei*. A searchable form is available via the World Wide Web at *http://etext.virginia.edu/T EI.html*; another Web form may be found at *http://www.ebt.com/usr-books/t eip3*.

The entire volume of *Computers and the Humanities* for 1995 is devoted to the TEI; the papers in that volume contain references to other TEI-related articles. In particular, the general papers in that volume are a good introduction to the project [7,11], and there is an introduction to SGML from the perspective of the project [3]. Although SGML has served the TEI well, we have identified some ways in which SGML could be improved [1].

The TEI is possibly the largest DTD created to date. And with world literature, dictionaries, and literary and linguistic analysis as its core concerns, it certainly covers the widest range of documents of any encoding standard. In the remainder of this paper we show how the creation of the TEI guidlines provides results that furnish key insights into the use of documents and document-encoding standards on the World Wide Web.

Using Multiple DTDs

It became clear early in the work of the TEI that a single comprehensive DTD that could encode every feature of interest to the communities contributing to the project would be so large as to be impossible to understand, and doubtless impossible to design. (Debates over HTML 3 suggest the same is true of a single DTD supporting all users of the Web.) Further, users of TEI documents are often interested in several views of a document at the same time, so that in effect multiple DTDs were required in any case.

As a result, the TEI DTD has been designed in a modular fashion. A particular document will use only those pieces of the DTD that apply to it. The selection of pieces to include is done using standard SGML mechanisms, so it can be specified to an SGML parser with minimal manual intervention and no additional software tools.

Further, the TEI DTD is extensible. Users can add other modules to it, again using standard SGML mechanisms. These extensions can be communicated to an SGML parser—and thus obviously to other users—in a formal manner, so that the extensions can be specified and documented as fully as the basic DTD. The need for extensibility is a direct consequence of the richness and open-endedness of the application areas for electronic documents. No language with a finite vocabulary can ever hope to suffice for electronic documents in the long run. In spite of the considerable amount of effort that has gone into designing the TEI DTD, there will inevitably be uses for which it is not well suited and forms of information that cannot be conveniently encoded using its structures. Our approach to dealing with this has been explicitly to provide an extension mechanism.

The modular structure of the TEI DTD groups SGML elements into the following categories:

Core tag sets
> Describe standard components of documents; they are included in all forms of the DTD. These include such things as paragraphs, lists, simple links and cross references, highlighting, and quotation, which are all familiar to users of HTML. The core tag set also includes tags for notes, indexes, bibliography entries, names, numbers and dates, and other commonly encountered textual phenomena.

Base tag sets
> Include the basic structures needed for describing a specific text type. Usually one of these is selected for a given document, although there are ways to use several of them together for complex documents. There are base tag sets for prose, for verse, for drama, for print dictionaries, for the transcription of spoken material, and for terminological databases.

Additional tag sets
> Define extra tags that are used for specific purposes. They are compatible with all the bases and with each other. Any combination of these tag sets can be used in a single document. At present, additional tag sets are defined for linking, segmentation, and align-

ment; encoding simple analytic mechanisms (linguistic segments); encoding critical apparatus associated with a text; handling graphics and tables; and several other purposes.

Documents explicitly indicate which extensions to the TEI DTD they use by identifying a base tag set and additional tag sets. The core tag sets are implicitly present, because they are included by the base. In a TEI document, a document parser is therefore able to check modifications to the DTD using standard SGML mechanisms, and the formal notation also serves the purpose of providing inline documentation of required changes to the defaults. The modifications are made possible by maintaining two versions of the DTD. There is a version for people to read, which is the version documented in the *Guidelines*. There is also a version for parsers to read; this version is derived programmatically from the first one by the introduction of SGML parameter entities for various purposes. Modifications to the DTD are made by changing the values of parameter entities, thus changing the DTD that is expanded in the parser.

The TEI DTD supports the following modifications:

- Deleting an element. An element defined in the TEI DTD can be suppressed so that it cannot be used in the document. An SGML parser will detect all uses of the tag as an error.

- Renaming an element. This can be used to rename the tags in a language other than English or to use local vocabulary within a project or collection of documents.

- Extending given classes. There are several predefined classes of tags in the TEI DTD. These classes typically share a set of attributes and thus can be treated in similar ways by applications. A particular document can specify that a tag is to be included in one of these classes.

- Specifying new content models. If the definition of what goes in an element is not sufficient for what needs to be expressed in a document, the element can be deleted and a new definition given. By introducing new names at this point, it is possible to extend the DTD with new tag sets for new applications.

It would be possible to use the parameter entity mechanism for other purposes as well, such as changing attribute names, redefining existing attributes, changing the inclusion and exclusion exceptions for an element, and so on. The set of modification possibilities given here was considered to be sufficient for most of the things that users claimed they needed to do.

The experience of the TEI in designing a complex DTD leads to several conclusions relevant to the World Wide Web community. First, a single fixed DTD, no matter how well it is designed, can never serve all users equally well. Users must have ways to specify structures not anticipated at DTD design time. Second, it is possible to design DTDs—or DTD families—that are modular and extensible. The TEI tagsets demonstrate one method of doing so. Third, a rich set of structures can already be described with the existing TEI DTD, and it can thus already be used for a rich variety of applications. We encourage readers to consider it for their applications.

We now turn to two specific content areas addressed by the TEI DTD that demonstrate helpful ways to use SGML for encoding information of value in World Wide Web applications. These are the specification of hypertext links and the description of documents and their contents.

Linking Mechanisms

The World Wide Web has grown because of its simplicity. In particular, the concept of a Uniform Resource Locator (URL) is a simple one: a text string provides an address of a location in a file on a machine on the network. However, the simplicity that contributes to rapid growth is limiting.

URLs cannot locate a portion of text or a substructure in a document, they cannot easily specify how links might be related in sets, and they cannot specify any semantics to be associated with a link.

Another approach for specifying hypertext links is to use the HyTime standard [9] (the book by DeRose and Durand contains a description of HyTime [5]). HyTime does not suffer from being too simple. It is, in fact, very powerful; it allows for very general cases of hypermedia links to be specified. Links can be separated from objects (documents), complex relationships can be specified, coordinate systems can be defined, and parts of documents selected based on those coordinate systems, and so on.

In our view, URLs as they stand are too simple to meaningfully encode many of the structures that are common in and among documents on the World Wide Web (though they are perhaps adequate to implement most of these). One the other hand, HyTime provides (and requires) a more powerful mechanism than many applications will need. The TEI linking mechanisms provide what seems to us a better balance between simplicity and power.

The TEI DTD provides linking mechanisms for several different kinds of structure. Simple links within a document are formed using the SGML "id" and "idref" mechanism. Links between documents, or links within a document to locations which bear no ID attribute, are provided through *extended pointers*. These latter exist in two different forms:

- The <xpTR> tag provides a pointer to another location, either in the current document or some other document.

- The <xref> tag allows the inclusion of textual commentary with the specification of the pointer.

While these extended pointers build on the SGML id and idref mechanism, they are specified by giving strings as the values of attributes of

SGML tags. Like HTML tags and URLs, these strings need to be interpreted by application software that understands their significance.

The TEI's extended pointers allow links to be specified in terms of:

- Hierarchical references to structures in a document (in much the same way that files can be named in a hierarchical file system)

- More general structural relationships (such as the identification of the "next" node with a given generic identifier, which is to be found by a simple, clearly specified rule about tree traversal)

- Locations that are defined relative to the node making the reference

- Patterns that are to be applied when the link is traversed or activated

- Queries that are related to HyQ, the HyTime query language

We will not give the details of extended pointers here. These can be found in the *Guidelines*. What is of interest here is the kinds of structures that can be easily encoded using the mechanisms provided by the TEI DTD. Here are some examples.

- A *segment* is a portion of a document. It can be used as the point of attachment of a link. Any arbitrary structure can be defined as a segment.

- An *anchor* is an arbitrary point in a document. It can be used as the point of attachment of a link. (This is similar to the definition of a name on an anchor in HTML.)

- A *correspondence* can be established between one span of content and another. For example, there might be a correspondence between a fragment of a document, and someone's comments on that fragment.

- An *alignment* shows how two documents (or fragments) are related. For example, there could be an alignment between a doc-

ument in one language and another document that is the translation into a second language. An alignment can be specified in a document outside the two documents (or fragments) that are to be aligned.

- A *synchronization* is a relationship that represents temporal rather than textual correspondence. For example, it is often necessary to synchronize overlapping text segments in a representation of speech where several speakers can be talking at the same time.

- An *aggregation* is a collection of fragments into a single logical whole. For example, the set of passages in a document relating to a specific topic, such as the set of paragraphs that discuss indexing in a paper on information retrieval, would be an aggregate.

- *Multiple hierarchies* occur, essentially, when more than one tree is to be considered as being built over the same textual frontier. For example, the logical structure of a document (chapters, sections, paragraphs) and its physical structure (pages, lines) are two different hierarchies over the same frontier. Although the SGML CONCUR feature can be used to specify structures of this sort, it has a number of associated problems: when a document is changed by the addition of a new view, it may be necessary to change existing markup (by the addition of a prefix indicating the view to which the existing tags correspond); the coding of tags becomes more verbose than otherwise, and many SGML applications at present do not implement the feature. There are tags provided to specify page and line boundaries, and thus in a rudimentary way to provide for this second commonly required hierarchy. The more general approach used is to mark boundaries of the elements in the multiple hicrarchies and to reconstitute the view, essentially by using aggregates.

These structures that have been identified by participants in the TEI as useful ones for encoding documents for research purposes seem to us to be useful in many other contexts in the World Wide Web as well. The TEI DTD provides mechanisms for encoding these structures in relatively straightforward ways. These mechanisms could be used without having to provide all of the processing power in Web application software that is required to process HyTime.

Resource Identification and Discovery

The World Wide Web contains many documents in many locations. One of the major challenges in a complex distributed environment like this is the identification and discovery of documents that are relevant to some task. In a traditional library, resources are identified by the preparation of catalog information in a restricted but rich and dynamic domain of categories. Identifying relevant resources often involves the expertise of the person who needs information, various programs that have access to catalogs for relatively simple searches, and experts in the domain of interest (subject librarians). While the search techniques applied to catalogs are relatively simple, the catalogs contain explicitly coded information about subject areas so that searches are usually able to identify a useful collection of materials.

Information retrieval in collections of electronic documents similarly involves the expertise of the person who needs information, sophisticated search programs, and sometimes experts in the domain (subject librarians). Information can be labeled with various category attributes, but larger amounts of text (abstracts, and perhaps complete documents) can be searched. Because there is little or no explicit encoding of the information in the text, sophisticated algorithms are often used to attempt judgements about relevance of a document based on the occurrences of patterns in the text.

Identifying relevant resources on the World Wide Web can take several forms. It can involve searching through structured subject indexes as in traditional library access, as well as searching through the text of documents as in traditional information retrieval.

But because the Web contains so many documents—orders of magnitude more than most databases used with traditional search strategies—identifying relevant resources can be difficult. It would seem attractive to allow documents to describe themselves so that a rich domain of categories can be used and so that judgments about relevance do not need to be restricted to algorithmic approximations.

Documents encoded according to the TEI DTD must include a *TEI header* that contains information about the electronic document. The information in the header can be used to facilitate the identification of resources and their discovery by search programs and by manual browsing.

The header has four major parts:

- A *file description* contains a full bibliographical description of the electronic document. A standard bibliographic citation can be derived from this information, so it could be used to make a standard library catalog record. This part of the header also includes information about the source of the electronic document (for example, the document may be appearing originally in electronic form, it may be transcribed from a printed form, and so on).

- An *encoding description* describes the relationship between the source and the electronic document. This part of the header can describe any normalizations applied to the text, the specific kinds of analytic encoding that have been used, and so on.

- A *text profile* contains information that classifies the text and establishes its context. This part of the header describes the subjects addressed, the situation in which the text was produced, those involved in producing it, and so on. This part can be used with a fixed vocabulary of subjects, for example, to catalog texts into some predefined subject structure. or it can be used more freely to allow a dynamic subject universe.

- A *revision history* allows the encoding of a history of changes made to the electronic document. This part of the header is useful for the identification and control of versions of a document.

Each part of the header is potentially complex, and can contain extensive amounts of information. Most parts of the header are optional, though, so exhaustive cataloging is not required. These fields need only be used when they are considered useful or necessary by document developers. A minimal header contains a file description including a title, publication statement, and source, together with a text profile identifying the language in which the document is written.

To take best advantage of the mass of information that is available on the Web, users must be able to find the documents that are relevant when they are looking for information. The best way to facilitate this is to have documents identify and describe themselves.

The TEI header is an example of how documents can be made to be self-identifying. Documents with a developer-created header can be indexed in the ways that are considered to be appropriate by their developers. The information that is provided can be used by readers of Web documents and by programs that search the Web to identify relevant resources for readers.

Conclusion

The World Wide Web is based on a set of simple tools and concepts, including HTML, that have made possible a phenomenal rate of acceptance and growth. These simple notions, though, will not be sufficient to support continued growth and a diversity of applications.

There are various ways in which full SGML can be provided on the Web, including server-side processing (such as mapping more complex structures to HTML for delivery to clients) and client-side processing (such as spawning applications that are capable of dealing with general SGML DTDs or a specific DTD).

The Text Encoding Initiative has developed a comprehensive specification for a DTD that provides a richer set of structures in a modular extensible framework. The DTD itself, together with its structuring principles and the specific contributions for hypertext links and for resource description, suggest fruitful approaches to developing and enhancing the World Wide Web. ■

References

1. Barnard, David T., Burnard, Lou, and Sperberg-McQueen, C.M., *Lessons Learned from Using SGML in the Text Encoding Initiative, Computer Standards and Interfaces* (accepted February 1995). Also appeared as Technical Report 95-375, Department of Computing and Information Science, Queen's University (1995).

2. Berners-Lee, T., and Connolly, D., *Hypertext Markup Language-2.0, <draft-ietf-html-spec-06. txt>*, Boston, HTML Working Group, September 1995.

3. Burnard, Lou, *What Is SGML and How Does It Help?, Computers and the Humanities 29,1*, 1995, 41-50.

4. Cover, Robin, *SGML Web Page, http://www.sil.org/ sgml/sgml ..html*, 1994.

5. DeRose, Steven J., and Durand, David G., *Making Hypermedia Work: A User's Guide to HyTime*, Boston/Dordrecht/London, Kluwer Academic Publishers, 1994.

6. Goldfarb, Charles, *The SGML Handbook*, Oxford, Oxford University Press, 1990. Contains the full annotated text of ISO 8879 (with amendments).

7. Ide, Nancy, and Sperberg-McQueen, C.M., *The Text Encoding Initiative: Its History, Goals, and Future Development, Computers and the Humanities 29,1*, 1995, 5-15.

8. ISO (International Organization for Standardization), *ISO 8879-1986 (E) Information Process-*

ing—*Text and Office Systems—Standard General-ized Markup Language (SGML)*, Geneva, International Organization for Standardization, 1986.

9. ISO (International Organization for Standardization) *ISO/IEC 10744:1992 Information Technology—Hypermedia/Time-based Structuring Language (HyTime)*, Geneva, International Organization for Standardization, 1992.

10. Sperberg-McQueen, C.M., and Burnard, Lou (eds.), *Guidelines For Electronic Text Encoding and Interchange (TEI P3)*, Chicago and Oxford, ACH-ACL-ALLC Text Encoding Initiative, May 1994, 1290 pages.

11. Sperberg-McQueen, C.M., and Burnard, Lou, *The Design of the TEI Encoding Scheme*, *Computers and the Humanities 29,1*, 1995, 17-39.

About the Authors

David T. Barnard

[*http://www.quc is.queensu.ca/home/barnard/info.html*]

Queen's University, Kingston, Canada

David T. Barnard joined the Department of Computing and Information at Queen's University in 1977, having studied at the University of Toronto. He is now Professor in that Department. His research applies formal language analysis to treating documents as members of a formal language, and to compiling programming languages with a focus on using parallel machines. He chaired one of the working committees of the Text Encoding Initiative, and is now a member of the Steering Committee of the project.

Lou Burnard

Oxford University Computing Services, Oxford University, England

Lou Burnard is Humanities Computing Manager at Oxford University Computing Services. His responsibilities include the Oxford Text Archive, which he founded in 1976, and the British National Corpus. He is also European editor of the Text Encoding Initiative, and coauthor of a report proposing the establishment of a networked UK Arts and Humanities Data service.

Steven J. DeRose

Senior Systems Architect, Electronic Book Technologies, Inc.

Steven J. DeRose is one of the founders of Electronic Book Technologies. He holds a Ph.D. in Computational Linguistics and has published and spoken widely on descriptive markup, hypermedia, natural language processing, information retrieval, artificial intelligence, and other topics. He has consulted on commercial projects in related fields since 1982, and is active in several standardization efforts through organizations including TEI, SGML Open, IETF, ANSI, and ISO.

David G. Durand

[*http://cs-www.bu.edu: 80/students/grads/dgd/*]

Computer Science Department, Boston University

David Durand is a doctoral candidate at Boston University, working on collaborative editing in hypertext systems. He served on the TEI committees on Metalanguage and Syntax and Committee on Hypertext. He is also a Senior Analyst at *Dynamic Diagrams* working on analysis of Web documents for visusalization and navigation, and the integration of the Web with SGML-based publication processes.

C.M. Sperberg-McQueen

[*http://www-tei.uic.edu/~cmsmcq/*]

University of Illinois at Chicago

C. M. Sperberg-McQueen is a senior research programmer at the computer center of the University of Illinois at Chicago. He currently works in the Network Information Services group. He was trained in Germanic philology in the U.S. and Germany, and is a member of the Association for Computers and the Humanities, the Association for Literary and Linguistic Computing, and the Association for Computational Linguistics. Since 1988 he has been editor in chief of the ACH/ACL/ALLC Text Encoding Initiative.

OMNIWARE
A UNIVERSAL SUBSTRATE FOR WEB PROGRAMMING

Steven Lucco, Oliver Sharp, Robert Wahbe

Abstract

This paper describes Omniware, a system for producing and executing mobile code. Next generation Web applications will use mobile code to specify dynamic behavior in Web pages, implement new Web protocols and data formats, and dynamically distribute computation between servers and browsers. Like all mobile code systems, Omniware provides portability and safety. The same compiled Omniware module can be executed transparently on different machines, and a module's access to host resources can be precisely controlled. In addition to portability and safety, Omniware has two unique features. First, Omniware is open. Omniware uses software fault isolation (SFI) to enforce safe execution of standard programming languages, enabling Web developers to leverage the vast store of existing software and programming expertise. For example, Omniware developers can use C++ to create programs for Web pages. Second, Omniware is fast. We evaluated Omniware under the Solaris 2.4 operating system on a SPARCstation 5 using eight C benchmark programs, including five programs from the C SPEC92 benchmark suite. We evaluated the performance of Omniware in two ways. First, we showed that Omniware modules can be represented compactly, reducing the space consumption compared to Sun-Pro cc shared object files by an average of 38%. Second, we showed that Omniware modules execute at near native speeds. Including the runtime overhead necessary to ensure that Omniware modules are both portable and safe, our benchmark programs ran within 6% of native performance.

Introduction

Mobile code is transforming next generation Web applications by adding interactivity to traditional Web content such as forms, text, graphics, audio, and video. Mobile code, like traditional software, is a sequence of executable instructions. Standalone programs such as Web browsers and servers dynamically incorporate mobile code to augment system capabilities or to enhance the presentation of a document.

Web developers are using mobile code to create a new class of dynamic Web applications. For example, Starwave plans to use mobile code to enhance their sports-related Web pages. These pages will feature a continuous ticker-tape of up-to-the-minute sports statistics. Web system developers can also use mobile code to simplify incorporation of evolving data formats and network protocols. For instance, as the Web community converges on a standard for electronic com-

merce, each revision of the standard billing protocol can be encapsulated as a set of mobile code modules and disseminated to Web browsers and servers. Browser users will no longer need to explicitly update their software to incorporate each new standard.

Finally, Web system developers can use mobile code to dynamically partition Web application functions between Web servers and browsers. Web systems can use dynamic application partitioning to increase an application's quality of service in the face of resource shortages, such as a lack of network bandwidth. When confronted with a slow modem connection, for example, an application can choose to regenerate graphics on the client machine rather than ship finished graphics from the server.

Consider the deployment of a 3D building walk-through service on the Web. A person relocating to a new city might use such an application to remotely tour prospective homes. Without mobile code, the application would require network messages to receive and respond to mouse and keyboard input. New screen images, perhaps in response to a moving joystick, would have to be calculated on the server and sent as data to the browser. Because all processing and data production take place at the server, each new user of the system imposes a burden on server processing resources and communication bandwidth. A Web developer can alleviate both of these scenario's difficulties—slow interactive response time and limited server resources—by using mobile code to provide application-specific caching, data prefetching, and interactive response.

Mobile Code Systems

To support our vision of next-generation Web systems, mobile code must be portable and safe. The same mobile code module will be retrieved and executed by Web tools running under different operating systems and on top of different hardware architectures. Given the striking heterogeneity of the Internet, mobile code must be operating system and hardware independent. Safety is also a key requirement; as users browse the Web, they will be downloading and executing hundreds of these executable code modules so the browser must be in complete control over each module's access to the host system.

In this paper, we introduce Omniware, a new mobile code system. Like all mobile code systems introduced so far, Omniware delivers both portability and safety. Portability is achieved by using a virtual machine called the OmniVM. For maximum performance and power, OmniVM is modeled after an enhanced RISC processor. When OmniVM loads a mobile-code module, it dynamically compiles the module into native machine code. Safety is ensured through the use of software fault-isolation technology [SFI93]. Software fault isolation (SFI) inserts specialized checking code into the module's native instruc-

tion stream so that a module's access to all resources can be controlled.

Omniware has two unique features:

First, Omniware is open. Because Omniware uses SFI to enforce safety, it can support *any* programming language. The current Omniware system provides a C and C++ development environment called OmniC++; work on a Visual Basic front-end is in progress. We began with C and C++ for two reasons. First, support for standard languages eliminates the time-consuming process of mastering a new language. Second, OmniC++ enables developers to incorporate legacy code into their Web applications. For example, a database front-end developer, using Omniware, can port the front end to a Web page without having to rewrite the bulk of the interface program or learn a new programming language.

More generally, Web applications, like traditional applications, will require functionality in the areas of data structures, data format conversions, security, network protocols, image processing, event handling, and text-search engines. This type of software infrastructure, and much of the world's software infrastructure, is held together by a vast base of C and C++ programs and libraries. Because of this, all high-level language systems, such as Visual Basic, Tcl, and PowerScript, provide the means for developers to specify complex or time-consuming tasks in C. Most of the major office tools, such as word processors, spreadsheets, and presentation systems, are written predominantly in C or C++.

Even applications developed with a rapid development language such as Visual Basic rely on third-party programs such as VBXs or OCXs, written in C and C++, to add power and professionalism to their interfaces. Typically, such applications have over 90% of their code written in a high-level language like Visual Basic, but spend over 90% of their processing cycles in small but crucial C++ modules. OmniC++ provides a means for Web developers to apply the existing C and

C++ programming infrastructure directly to Web pages.

Second, Omniware is fast. We evaluated Omniware under the Solaris 2.4 operating system on a SPARCstation 5 using eight C benchmark programs, including five programs from the C SPEC92 benchmark suite. The performance of the system was evaluated in two ways. First, we showed that Omniware modules can be represented compactly, reducing the space consumption compared to SunPro cc shared object files by an average of 38%. Second, we showed that Omniware modules execute at near native speeds. Each benchmark program was compiled into an Omniware module. We then ran these modules as mobile code within a simple browser shell. The average runtime overhead for safe and portable Omniware modules was 6% compared to fully optimized C code. These tests were performed with a beta version of Omniware and we expect that a tuned implementation will reduce these numbers even further.

Because Omniware supports standard languages such as C++ at near native performance, it is uniquely positioned to provide a universal substrate for programming the World Wide Web. Developers can use higher-level interpreted languages such as Visual Basic, Tcl, Lisp, and Perl, simply by incorporating their runtime interpreters as Omniware modules. For example, in the section called "Performance," we show that an Omniware version of the xlisp interpreter incurs only 5.1% execution overhead. Similarly, the standard Tcl interpreter run as an Omniware module incurs only 5.2% execution overhead. These interpreted languages can be mixed safely with C and C++ modules, as necessary. In short, Omniware enables Web programmers to apply to Web pages the same rapid-development techniques used in creating graphical desktop application programs.

This paper is organized as follows: we begin with an overview of the Omniware system, then describe, in some detail, the Omniware Runtime Environment. Then we presents our performance results, discuss related work, and provide a conclusion.

System Overview

The Omniware system enables Web browsers to manage compiled mobile-code modules called *Omniware modules*. The Omniware Runtime Environment (ORE) Plug-In enables any browser that supports Netscape's Plug-In API to run Omniware. Web system programmers can use the Netscape Plug-In API to add new facilities, such as Macromedia's Director, Sun's Java, and Colusa's Omniware to existing Web browsers and servers. Several browser companies have already announced support for Netscape's Plug-In API. As other plug-in APIs become accepted, Colusa will release compatible plug-in modules. The architecture for the system is shown in Figure 1.

An Omniware-enabled browser supports execution of mobile code embedded in Web pages, just as today's browsers support GIF and JPEG images. When a module is embedded into a page, the HTML command that refers to the module determines whether the module is executed automatically when the user loads the page (like an inlined image that displays immediately) or whether the module acts like an external reference so that execution does not start until the user clicks on the appropriate link in the browser.

The ORE plug-in controls the execution of a module and specifies the resources that are available to it. For example, the plug-in carefully restricts a module's access to memory. Modules can allocate and use a limited amount of memory but are prevented from accessing memory that is private to the browser.

Modules interact with the rest of the system and with the user through the Omni32 API. The Omni32 API includes routines to manage memory, threads, and I/O; it also includes a graphics and windowing library that is based on the abstractions used in the existing systems Tk

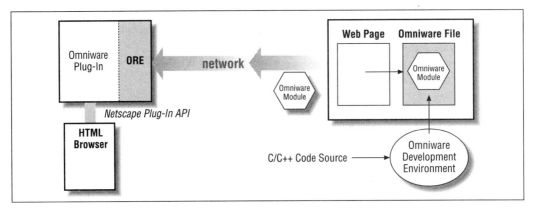

Figure 1:   Architecture for Omniware system

[Tcl94] and Java AWT [Java95] (both of which are discussed in the related work section).

The API functions check their arguments carefully, so that modules cannot use them as surrogates to violate protection safeguards. Omniware modules invoke the functions simply by calling them—there is no special linkage interface. When the module is loaded by the plug-in, the module identifies any references to exported functions and routes the calls appropriately.

Programmers build mobile code using the OmniC++ development environment, which compiles C and C++ programs into Omniware modules. OmniC++ is a full and unrestricted implementation of K&R C, ANSI C, and ANSI C++. OmniC++ also includes a graphical debugger that works with Omniware modules. Colusa plans to release a Visual Basic programming environment to support rapid development of Web applications.

Omniware Runtime Environment

This section describes the Omniware Runtime Environment (ORE). The ORE consists of two components: the Omniware Virtual Machine (OmniVM) and the Omni32 API. Compiled Omniware modules execute on top of OmniVM

just as conventional programs execute on standard hardware. The Omni32 API provides services typically handled by either conventional operating systems or standard system libraries.

One does not need to understand the system architecture of a conventional desktop computer in order to develop programs for it; similarly, one does not need to understand OmniVM to develop Omniware modules. The discussion of OmniVM that follows is provided for readers who are interested in the lowest-level details of the system. The discussion explains how OmniVM provides portability and near-native performance while maintaining strict control over the execution of Omniware modules. These details are invisible to programmers who write modules in high-level languages.

Omniware Virtual Machine

The design of OmniVM reflects four goals: safety, mobility, performance, and openness. To make Omniware an open system, we designed OmniVM to be a straightforward compilation target for a large variety of source languages. To achieve excellent performance, we used instruction mix and memory-system traces from existing RISC and CISC processors to determine the instruction set for OmniVM. To support mobility, we standardized OmniVM floating-point and integer-data formats and introduced OmniVM instructions that are compatible with the data formats of existing processors. Finally, to ensure safe execution of Omniware modules, we designed the OmniVM instruction set to support straightforward implementation of software fault isolation.

OmniVM instruction set architecture

OmniVM is a RISC processor enhanced in several respects with high-level (CISC-like) features. The high-level enhancements to OmniVM support portability and performance. For example, the OmniVM instruction set includes a memory-to-memory block-move instruction (`mov.b`) analogous to the `rep movsb` instruction on the Intel Pentium processor. This instruction gives the OmniVM translator the opportunity to generate optimal block-move code for the target machine. The Pentium OmniVM translator converts `mov.b` directly to `rep movsb`.

High-level instructions like `mov.b` give OmniVM translators the power to generate optimal code for the intended high-level operation. However, there are two reasons to avoid designing a virtual machine like OmniVM entirely around high-level instructions. First, the indiscriminate use of high-level instructions yields an unattractive compilation target. Because high-level instructions are specialized to a particular task, they require a compiler to identify and handle more distinct code generation cases. Similarly, the use of high-level instructions increases the complexity of each OmniVM translator.

But there is a more fundamental reason to prefer a simple, orthogonal design for the backbone of the OmniVM instruction set. A high-level language compiler cannot do a good job of OmniVM instruction selection because it has no information about the relative timing of OmniVM instructions. For example, the OmniVM is a load/store architecture. Suppose that we chose instead to provide memory addressed operands to instructions such as the add signed integer instruction (`add.iw`). Without instruction timing

information, a compiler might select to read an operand from memory, rather than use an extra instruction to regenerate that operand. On the Intel Pentium, this is sometimes a good decision. On most RISC architectures, regenerating an integer value with one or two register instructions will generally outperform reloading that value from memory.

To summarize, these were the design rules we followed for the OmniVM instruction set:

- If a high-level instruction can be synthesized from RISC instructions, choose the RISC instructions.

- If a high-level instruction (such as block move) can not be synthesized from simpler instructions, include the high-level instruction if instruction traces of representative applications on CISC machines (including the Motorola 68000 and Intel Pentium) include significant use of the high-level instruction.

- Choose a high-level instruction if it is necessary to standardize the handling of integer- and floating-point data formats.

The latter point is motivated by the central design goal for Omniware: if an Omniware module runs correctly on one processor architecture, it should run correctly on all other processor architectures without modification. This guarantee enormously simplifies the implementation of documents containing mobile code.

OmniVM protection architecture

To enforce protection constraints on Omniware modules, the OmniVM provides a simple protection architecture. The OmniVM protection architecture resembles in function the memory management unit (MMU) of a single computer. OmniVM supports a segmented virtual-address space—it divides addressable memory into segments, the size of which is fixed for a given instance of the OmniVM. The supervisor can use the OmniVM protection architecture to set the segment size and to define memory contexts called *protection domains*. Each protection domain has its own segment table that specifies its memory access permissions.

The ORE exports this functionality to trusted code such as browser software through the following interface:

```
int omni_get_segment_size()
OmniBoolean omni_mprotect(OmniPd *pd,
    void *addr,int size, OmniMemPerm
    mode)
```

The function `omni_mprotect` changes the access permissions on the mappings specified by the range `<addr, addr+size>` to be those specified by `mode`. `addr`. `size` must be multiples of the segment size as returned by the function `omni_get_segment_size()`. Read and write permission can be separately specified. Using this interface, a host program can specify precisely what data a protection domain is allowed to read and write.

When the ORE loads an Omniware module, ORE creates a new protection domain for the module. By default, a thread in the new protection domain can only access its stack and the code and data of the Omniware module associated with the protection domain. A host program such as a browser can direct the ORE to load multiple Omniware modules into a single protection domain; the modules would then share memory access permissions.

The ORE uses a technology called software fault isolation (SFI) to implement the semantics of the OmniVM protection architecture. This technology is described extensively elsewhere [14]. Three essential properties of software fault isolation are:

- It is based on the semantics of the underlying processor architecture and not the high-level source language.

- It uses a form of runtime checking that can be heavily optimized so that protection overhead is small (see performance measurements in [14] and the section called "Performance" of this paper).

- A software system can separate the *verification* of a fault-isolated module from its production. Verification is a simple, linear-time procedure.

Omni32 API

The Omniware Runtime Environment contains operating system independent libraries for graphics and windowing, memory management, file I/O, threads, synchronization and signals. Functions that may be called by an untrusted module verify the validity of their arguments. For example, the memory-management routine to deallocate memory, `free`, gracefully handles being passed an invalid pointer. The Omni32 API provides a comprehensive set of services for mobile-code applications.

Performance

Using eight standard benchmark programs, we evaluated the performance of Omniware under the Solaris 2.4 operating system on a SPARCstation 5 with 96 megabytes of memory. Each benchmark program was compiled, using OmniC, into an Omniware module. Each module was loaded into a browser shell and then executed as a mobile code module. The module was invoked simply by calling `main` with the appropriate arguments. Rather than modify the benchmark codes in any way, the browser shell provided a safe compatibility library for the various system calls needed by the modules. For example, when the module attempts to call the `open` system call, the Omniware Runtime Environment transparently redirects the call to `omniware_safe_open`, which then verifies its arguments.

We measured the performance of Omniware in two ways. First, we measured the size of each compiled Omniware module. Second, we measured its end-to-end execution time. For comparison, we performed these same measurements by compiling the benchmark programs into Solaris-

Table 1: Omniware performance results compared to using fully optimized native shared object files

Program	File Size (bytes)				Execution Time (seconds)			
	Source Lines	Shared Objects	Omniware	Overhead	Shared Objects	Omniware	Overhead
alvinn	1K	17K	12K	-42%	307.0	337.0	6.7%
ear	5K	208K	140K	-49%	1014.0	1067.0	5.2%
compress	2K	11K	7K	-57%	5.6	5.5	2.3%
lcc	25K	194K	163K	-19%	4.4	5.2	7.7%
gcc	325K	839K	687K	-22%	8.8	10.9	9.1%
tcl	27K	106K	97K	-9%	23.3	24.5	5.2%
tex	23K	161K	112K	-44%	4.1	4.3	4.9%
xlisp	8K	59K	37K	-59%	53.3	56.0	5.1%
Average				**-38%**			**5.8%**

shared object files. The programs were compiled using the Solaris ANSI SunPro cc compiler and linked with the standard Solaris dynamic linking facility. All modules were compiled with the highest level of optimization. The comparison of Omniware modules to standard shared object files is done only to illustrate Omniware's performance: unlike Omniware modules, shared object files are neither safe nor portable. The results are presented in Table 1.

We chose a diverse set of standard and well-known benchmark programs. The programs `alvinn`, `ear`, `compress`, `xlisp`, and `gcc`, are part of the C SPEC92 benchmark suite. The other benchmarks are well-known and widely used programs. This diverse set of benchmarks, which includes both floating-point and integer-intensive codes, should help readers predict how Omniware will perform in different contexts. For the SPEC92 benchmark programs, the input to each program was the standard input used in the SPEC92 benchmark. For Tcl, it was the test suite that comes with the standard distribution. For TeX, it was a 4 page document containing complicated mathematical equations. For `lcc`, it was the `lcc` file `x86.c`.

The average overhead for our benchmark programs was 5.8%. Two reasons exist for this overhead. First, because OmniC generates machine-independent code, the output cannot be perfectly tuned to any particular architecture. While the runtime environment's dynamic compiler can attempt to perform various machine-dependent optimizations, this two phase process inherently introduces some inefficiencies. The second source of overhead is the set of runtime checks needed to control a module's access to host resources.

Omniware's low execution overhead permits developers unparalleled flexibility. For example, a new Internet programming language could be widely introduced by simply providing the runtime environment as an Omniware module. When a Web tool retrieved a high-level mobile code module in an unknown language, it could simply download the appropriate runtime interpreter. Because the runtime environments for Tcl, xlisp, and Perl are written in C, an Omniware enabled tool would automatically support these popular languages. Further, Omniware's performance enables potentially computer-intensive data-conversion procedures, decompression algorithms, and other extensions to be dynamically distributed as Omniware modules. In general, because Omniware executes at near native speeds, the software techniques and practices that are viable for stand-alone applications will also be viable for next-generation Web applications.

Related Work

The question of how best to provide mobile code on the Internet is attracting a great deal of attention. A number of different strategies for providing mobile code have been proposed. All of the systems described in this section are *closed* in that they cannot effectively support multiple-source languages.

Sun Microsystem's Java system has three components: a new high-level object-oriented language called Java, a low-level virtual machine called the Java VM, and operating system independent libraries for file I/O, memory management, threads, synchronization, and graphic operations. Sun provides a browser, called HotJava, which supports Java programs embedded in Web pages. When a Java program is executed, it is compiled into Java VM instructions that are then loaded and interpreted by the Java VM. The Java VM lacks the necessary primitives to support standard programming languages.

Current implementations of the Java VM use a bytecode interpreter. No comprehensive performance numbers have been published, but current estimates are that Java programs run 1200% to 3000% percent slower than native code. At some point in the future the Java project plans to offer a virtual machine that employs dynamic compilation. Certain features of the virtual machine, such as array bounds checking, stack based operations, and garbage collection, will make efficient implementation difficult [1, 2, 3, 7].

Java and Omniware are similar in that both offer safety and portability. Java achieves these properties through restricting the programming language. Omniware uses software fault isolation to enforce safety, which enables Omniware to efficiently support standard programming languages.

Another approach to supporting mobile code is the Guile [4] project from Cygnus Support. Project implementation is still underway at the time this paper is being written, but the idea is to provide a library that includes an interpreter for a language based on Scheme [13]. The library provides a set of data structures and system services. Like Omniware, the Guile library is linked into a host application and allows the application to manage code modules. The host can declare functions that become new primitives in the Guile language and are thus available to the modules. No performance information has yet been published for Guile.

The Telescript [17] system from General Magic focuses on the development of *network agents*. These are autonomous programs that can move through a network, interacting with the hosts that execute them and with other agents that they encounter. Like Java, there are two levels of Telescript: High Telescript and Low Telescript. We have not been able to obtain detailed technical information or performance measurements for Telescript.

Safe-Python is a modified version of Python [11], an interpreted object-oriented scripting language that is popular for rapid development. Safe-Python is an altered version of the language that controls access to the operating system and provides additional primitives for building distributed applications. The intent is to merge the two versions of the language in the future so that Python can be used to build distributed applications and to support mobile code.

Safe-Tcl [12] is a modified version of the Tcl language [16]. Tcl was primarily designed to allow programmers to write graphical applications more quickly. Safe-Tcl is a restricted version of the full language that is safe to incorporate into a mail message. Safe-Tcl is intended to serve as an extension to the MIME mail message format that adds support for mobile code. When a message includes mobile code, MIME will send it to the safe-Tcl interpreter. Since an incoming mail message could be sent by anyone, the language needed to be carefully constrained to prevent mischief. Some of the normal Tcl language primitives are removed, some additional ones added to support integration with MIME, and a few commands are slightly altered.

Conclusion

A universal substrate for Web programming must be fast, safe, portable, and open. Speed is required so that no artificial restrictions are placed on mobile code and to allow sophisticated runtime systems, such as Visual Basic interpreters, to be implemented as mobile-code modules. Safety is important so that users and developers need only trust the mobile code substrate and not the myriad higher-level applications and libraries that might be employed. Given the striking heterogeneity of the Internet, portability is crucial. If a mobile-code module runs correctly on one processor architecture, it should run correctly on all other processor architectures without modification. Finally, a Web programming substrate should enable developers to apply to Web pages the vast existing base of desktop programming infrastructure.

This paper described a fast, safe, portable, and open system for Web development called Omniware. The Omniware virtual machine executes Omniware modules at native speeds. The average overhead among our eight benchmark programs was 6%. Through the use of software fault-isolation technology, the host application can precisely control a module's access to resources. The same compiled Omniware module can execute, without modification, across heterogeneous operating system and hardware architectures. Because Omniware does not rely on language semantics to enforce safety, it does not force Web programmers to remain within the confines of a single, non-standard programming language. Omniware frees programmers to choose the combination of high- and low-level programming language techniques most appropriate to a given development task, and delivers along with the ability to use standard programming techniques the performance that desktop developers expect.

■

References

1. J. L. Stefen, "Adding Run-Time Checking to the Portable C Compiler," *Software—Practice and Experience,* April 1992, vol.22, no.4, p. 305-16.

2. R. Brooks, "Trading Data Space for Reduced Time and Code Space in Real-Time Garbage Collection on Stock Hardware," *ACM Software Engineering Symposium on Practical Software Development Environments,* 1984, p. 256-262.

3. B. Zorn, "The Measured Cost of Conservative Garbage Collection," *Software—Practice and Experience,* vol. 23, no. 7, July 1993, p. 733-56.

4. T. Lord, "The Guile Architecture for Ubiquitous Computing," to appear in: *Usenix Tcl/Tk Workshop,* 1995.

5. I. S. Graham. *The HTML Sourcebook,* Wiley: New York, 1995.

6. *IEEE Standard 754-1985. IEEE Standard for Binary Floating-Point Arithmetic.* IEEE: New York, 1985.

7. J. P. Fitch and A. C. Norman, "Implementing LISP in a High-Level Language," *Software—Practice and Experience,* vol. 7, 1977, p. 713-725.

8. J. Gosling. "Java Intermediate Bytecodes," *ACM SIGPLAN Workshop on Intermediate Representations* (IR '95), San Francisco, CA, Jan. 1995.

9. *Pentium Processor User's Manual,* Intel Corporation: Mt. Prospect, IL, 1994.

10. L. Wall and R. L. Schwartz, *Programming Perl,* O'Reilly and Associates: Sebastopol, CA, 1992.

11. *http://minsky.med.virginia.edu/sdm7g/Projects/Python/SafePython.html*

12. N. S. Borenstein, "Email With a Mind of its Own: The Safe-Tcl Language for Enabled Mail," *IFIP International Conference,* Barcelona, Spain, June 1994.

13. J. Rees and W. Clinger, eds., "The Revised Report on the Algorithmic Language Scheme," *ACM Lisp Pointers,* vol. 4, no. 3, 1991.

14. R. Wahbe, S. Lucco, T. Anderson, and S. L. Graham. "Efficient Software-Based Fault Isolation," *14th ACM Symposium on Operating Systems Principles,* Ashville, NC, Dec. 1993.

15. *SPEC92 Release Notes.* Standard Performance Evaluation Corporation (SPEC): Fairfax, VA, 1992.

16. J. Ousterhout, *Tcl and the Tk Toolkit,* Addison-Wesley: Reading, Mass., 1994.

17. "Telescript Technology: The Foundation for the Electronic Marketplace," General Magic: Sunnyvale, CA, 1993.

18. T. Berners-Lee, R. Cailliau, A. Loutonen, H. F. Nielsen, and A. Secret. "The World-Wide Web," *Communications of the ACM,* vol. 37, no. 8, August 1994, p. 76-82.

About the Authors

Steven Lucco, **Oliver Sharp**, and **Robert Wahbe** are with Colusa Software in Berkeley, CA. They can be reached via the following e-mail addresses: *{steve.lucco, oliver.sharp, robert. wahbe}@colusa.com*. General inquires about Colusa and the Omniware system should be sent to: *info@colusa.com*.

LOW LEVEL SECURITY IN JAVA

Frank Yellin

Abstract

The Java(tm) language allows Java-compatible Web browsers to download code fragments dynamically and then execute those code fragments locally. However, users must be wary of executing any code that comes from untrusted sources or that passes through an insecure network. This paper presents the details of the lowest-levels of the Java security mechanism. Before any downloaded code is executed, it is scanned and verified to ensure that it conforms to the specifications of the virtual machine. **Keywords:** *WWW, Java, HotJava, security, remote execution*

Introduction to the Java Language

The Java(tm) language [1, 2] is a simple, object-oriented, portable, robust language developed at Sun Microsystems.

The language was created for developing programs in a heterogenous network-wide environment. Because one of the initial goals of the language was to employ it in embedded systems with a minimum amount of memory, the Java language is designed to be small and to use a small amount of hardware resources.

The Java compiler generates *class* files, which have an architecturally neutral, binary intermediate format. Embedded in the class file are *bytecodes*, which are implementations for each of the class's methods, written in the instruction set of a virtual machine. The class-file format has no dependencies on byte-ordering, pointer size, or underlying operating system.

The bytecodes are executed by means of a *runtime system*, or emulator for the virtual machine's instruction set. The same bytecodes can be run on any platform.

Security

Since Java language compiled code is designed to be transported in binary format across networks, security is extremely important. No one wants to bring across any piece of code if there is a possibility that executing the code could do any of the following:

- Damage hardware, software, or information on the host machine

- Pass unauthorized information to anyone

- Cause the host machine to become unusable through resource depletion

Because the Java bytecode is run on the host machine, there are special security concerns. Users who download Java class files from remote, possibly insecure (or hostile) sites must be satisfied that the downloaded code cannot subvert the Java bytecode interpreter to perform impermissible operations.

The lowest levels of the Java interpreter implement security in several ways as described in the following sections.

Security Through Being Published

The complete source code for both the Java interpreter and the Java compiler are available for inspection. We do not expect users to take our word for it that Java language is secure. Security audits of the Java source are currently being performed.

Security Through Being Well-defined

The Java language is strict in its definition of the language:

- All primitive types in the language are guaranteed to be a specific size.

- All operations are defined to be performed in a specified order.

Two correct Java compilers will never give different results for execution of a program. This ability differs greatly from that of C and C++, in which the sizes of the primitive types are machine- and compiler-dependent, and the order of execution is undefined except in certain specific cases.

Security Through Lack of Pointer Arithmetic

The Java language does not have pointer arithmetic, so Java programmers cannot forget a pointer to memory. All references to methods and instance variables in the class file are via symbolic names. The user cannot create code that has magic offsets in it that just happen to point to the "right place." Users cannot create code that bash's system variables or that accesses private information.

Security Through Garbage Collection

Garbage collection [3] makes Java programs both more secure and more robust. Two common bugs in C/C++ programs are:

- Failing to free memory once it is no longer needed

- Accidentally freeing the same piece of memory twice

Failing to free memory that is no longer accessible can cause a program to use increasing amounts of memory. Accidentally freeing the same piece of memory often causes subtle memory corruption bugs that are difficult to locate.

The Java language eliminates the need for programmers to be concerned with these issues.

Security Through Strict Compile-Time Checking

The Java compiler performs extensive, stringent, compile-time checking so that as many errors as possible can be detected by the compiler. The Java language is strongly typed; unlike C/C++, the type system has no loopholes:

- Objects cannot be cast to a subclass without an explicit runtime check.

- All references to methods and variables are checked to make sure that the objects are of the appropriate type. In addition, the compiler checks that "security barriers" (e.g., referencing a `private` variable or method from another class) are not violated.

- Integers cannot be converted into objects. Objects cannot be converted into integers.

The compiler also strictly ensures that a program does not access the value of an uninitialized local variable.

Class-File Verification

Even though the compiler performs thorough type checking, there is still the possibility of attack via the use of a "hostile" compiler. Applications such as the HotJava(tm) browser [4] do not download source code which they then compile; these applications download already-compiled class files. The HotJava browser has no way of determining whether the bytecodes were produced by a trustworthy Java compiler or by an adversary attempting to exploit the interpreter.

An additional problem with compile-time checking is version skew. A user may have successfully compiled a class, say `PurchaseStockOptions` to be a subclass of `TradingClass`. But the definition of `TradingClass` might have changed since the time the class was compiled: methods might have disappeared or changed arguments; variables might have changed types or changed from dynamic (per object) to static (per class). The visibility of a method or variable may have changed from `public` to `private`.

All class files brought in from "the outside" are subjected to a verifier. This verifier ensures that the class file has the correct format. The byte-codes are verified using a simple theorem prover which establishes a set of "structural constraints" on the bytecodes.

The bytecode verifier also enhances the performance of the interpreter. Runtime checks that would otherwise have to be performed for each interpreted instruction can be eliminated. Instead, the interpreter can assume that these checks have already been performed. Though each individual check may be inexpensive, several machine instructions for the execution of each bytecode instruction are eliminated.

For example, the interpreter already knows that the code will adhere to the following constraints:

- There are no stack overflows or underflows.

- All register accesses and stores are valid.

- The parameters to all bytecode instructions are correct.

- There is no illegal data conversion.

The verifier is independent of the Java compiler. Although it will certify all code generated by the current compiler, it should also certify code that the current compiler couldn't possibly generate. Any set of bytecodes that satisfy the structural criteria will be certified by the verifier.

The verifier is extremely conservative. It will refuse to certify some class files that a more sophisticated theorem prover might certify.

Other languages can be compiled into the class format. The bytecode verifier, by not being specifically tied to the Java language, allows users to import code from outside their firewall with confidence.

The Class-File Format

Each Java class file is downloaded across the network as a separate entity. The class file is simply a stream of 8-bit bytes. All 16- and 32-bit quantities are formed by reading in two or four 8-bit bytes, respectively, and joining them together in big-endian format.

The Basic Format

The following information is a brief sketch of the class-file format. Complete details can be found in [5].

A class file contains:

- A magic constant

- Major and minor version information

- The "constant pool"

- Information about this class (name, super-class, etc.)

- Information about each of the fields and methods in this class

- Debugging information

The *constant pool* is a heterogenous array of data. Each entry in the constant pool can be one of the following:

- A Unicode [6] string

- A class or interface name

- A reference to a field or method

- A numeric value

- A constant String value

No other part of the class file makes specific references to strings, classes, fields, or methods. All such references are through indices into the constant pool.

For each field and method in the class, the bytes in the class file indicate the field's or method's name and its type. The type of a field or method is indicated by a string called its *signature*. Fields may have an additional attribute giving the field's initial value. Methods may have an additional attribute giving the code for performing that method.

Methods may, in fact, have multiple code attributes. The attribute CODE indicates bytecode to be run through the interpreter. Methods might also have attributes such as SPARC-CODE or 386-CODE which are machine-code implementations of the method. The HotJava browser will ignore the machine-code implementation of any method from an untrustworthy source, because it cannot verify that machine code is structurally sound.

The current implementation of the HotJava browser believes that any class file that comes from the network is untrustworthy. The browser will only run machine code that has been loaded from local class files. However, the class format can allow authors to digitally sign class files. Future browsers may be more trusting of signed machine code coming from trusted sources.

Bytecodes and Virtual Machine

The CODE attribute supplies information for executing the method in the machine language of a virtual machine. The information for each method includes:

- The maximum stack space needed by the method

- The maximum number of registers used by the method

- The actual code for executing the method; these bytecodes are for the Java virtual machine

- A table of exception handlers. Each entry in the table gives a start and end offset into the bytecodes, an exception type, and the offset of a handler for the exception. The entry indicates that if an exception of the indicated type occurs within the code indicated by the starting and ending offset, a handler for the exception will be found at the given handler offset.

The Java virtual machine defines six primitive types:

- 32-bit integer (*integers*)

- 64-Iit integers (*longs* or *long integers*)

- 32-bit floating-point numbers (*single floats*)

- 64-bit floating-point numbers (*double floats*)

- pointers to objects and arrays (*handles*)

- pointers to the virtual machine code (*return addresses*)

The Java virtual machine also defines several array types: integers, longs, single floats, double floats, handles, booleans, bytes (8-bit integers), shorts (16-bit integers), and Unicode characters. Arrays of handles have an additional type field indicating the class of object the array can hold.

Each method activation has a separate expression-evaluation stack and set of local registers. Each register and each stack location must be able to hold an integer, a single float, a handle, or a return address. Longs and double floats must fit into two consecutive stack locations or two consecutive registers. The virtual-machine instructions (*opcodes*) will address longs and double floats in registers using the index of the lower-numbered register.

Objects on the stack and in registers are not (necessarily) tagged. The virtual-machine instruction set provides opcodes to operate on different primitive data types. For example, ineg, fneg, lneg, and dneg each negate the top item on the stack, but they assume that the top item on the stack is an integer, a single float, a long, or a double float, respectively.

The bytecode instructions can be divided into several categories:

- Pushing constants onto the stack

- Accessing and modifying the value of a register

- Accessing arrays

- Stack manipulation (e.g., `swap`, `dup`, `pop`)

- Arithmetic, logical, and conversion instructions

- Control transfer

- Function return

- Manipulating object fields

- Method invocation

- Object creation

- Type casting

Each bytecode consists of a one-byte opcode, followed by zero or more bytes of additional operand information. With the exception of two "table lookup" instructions, all instructions are a fixed length, based on the opcode.

The Verification Process

The Verifier operates in four passes.

Pass 1

The first pass is the simplest. It occurs when the class is first read into the interpreter.

This pass ensures that the class file has the format of a class file. The first several bytes must contain the right magic number. All recognized attributes need to be the proper length. The class file must not be truncated or have extra bytes at the end. The constant pool must not contain any unrecognized information.

Pass 2

In the second pass, the verifier delves a little bit more deeply into the class file format. It performs all verification that can be performed without looking at the bytecodes. The errors detected by Pass 2 include:

- Ensuring that `final` classes are not subclassed, and that `final` methods are not overridden

- Checking that every class (except `Object`) must have a superclass

- Ensuring that the constant pool satisfies certain constraints; e.g., class references in the constant pool must contain a field that points to a unicode string reference in the constant pool

- Checking that all field references and method references in the constant pool must have legal names, legal classes, and a legal type signature

Note that when looking at field and method references, this pass does not actually check to make sure that the given field or method really exists in the given class; nor does it check that the type signatures given refer to real classes. Rather, the signature must simply "look like" a legal signature. Further checking is delayed until passes 3 and 4.

Pass 3

This is the most complex pass of the class verification. The bytecodes of each method are verified. Data-flow analysis [7] is performed on each method. The verifier ensures that at any given point in the program, no matter what code path is taken to reach that point:

- The stack is always the same size and contains the same types of objects.

- No register is accessed unless it is known to contain a value of the appropriate type.

- Methods are called with the appropriate arguments.

- Fields are modified with values of the appropriate type.

- All opcodes have appropriate type arguments on the stack and in the registers.

For further information on this pass, see the section "Bytecode Verifier."

Pass 4

For efficiency reasons, certain tests that could be performed in Pass 3 are delayed until the code is actually run. Pass 3 of the verifier avoids loading class files unless it must do so.

For example, if a method contains a call to another method that returns an object of type foobarType, and that object is then immediately assigned to a field of the same type, the verifier doesn't bother to check if the type foobarType exists. However, if it is assigned to a field of the type anotherType, the definitions of both foobarType and anotherType must be loaded in to assure that foobarType is a subclass of anotherType.

The first time an instruction that references a class is executed, the verifier does the following:

- Loads in the definition of the class if it has not already been loaded

- Verifies that the currently executing class is allowed to reference the given class

The first time an instruction calls a method, or accesses or modifies a field, the verifier does the following:

- Ensures that the method or field exists in the given class

- Checks that the method or field has the indicated signature

- Checks that the currently executing method has access to the given method or field

This pass of the verifier does not have to check the type of the object on the stack. That check has already been done by Pass 3.

After the verification has been performed, the instruction in the bytecode stream is replaced with an alternative form of the instruction. For example, the opcode new is replaced with new_quick. This alternative instruction indicates that the verification needed by this instruction has taken place, and need not be performed again. It is illegal for these _quick instructions to appear in Pass 3.

Bytecode Verifier

As indicated above, Pass 3 of the verifier, the *bytecode verifier*, is the most complex pass of the class verification.

First, the bytes that make up the virtual instructions are broken up into a sequence of instructions, and the offset of the start of each instruction is kept in a bit table. The verifier then goes through the bytes a second time and parses the instructions. During this pass each instruction is converted into a structure. The arguments, if any, to each instruction are checked to make sure they are reasonable:

- All control-flow instructions go to the start of an instruction. Branches into the middle of an instruction are clearly not allowed. Similarly, branches to before the beginning of the code or to after the end of the code are not allowed.

- All register references are to a legal register. Code cannot access or modify any register greater than the number of registers that the method indicated it uses.

- All references to the constant pool must be to an entry of the appropriate type. For example, the opcode ldc1 can only be used for integers, floats, or String's. The opcode getfield must reference a field.

- The code does not end in the middle of an instruction.

- For each exception handler, the starting and ending point must point to the beginning of an instruction. The offset of the exception handler must be a valid instruction. The starting point must be before the ending point.

For each instruction, the verifier keeps track of the contents of the stack and the contents of the registers prior to the execution of that instruction.

For the stack, it needs to know the length of the stack and the type of each element on the stack. For each register, it needs to know either the type of the contents of that register or that the register contains an illegal value. The bytecode verifier does not need to distinguish between the various normal integer types (e.g., byte, short, char) when determining the value types on the stack.

(Some extra information is kept about each instruction in a finally clause. This information is discussed further in the section "Try/ Finally.")

Next, a data-flow analyzer is initialized. For the first instruction, the lower-numbered registers contain the types indicated by the method's type signature; the stack is empty. All other registers contain an illegal value. For all other instructions, indicate that this instruction has not yet been visited; there is yet no information on its stack or registers.

Finally, the data-flow analyzer is run. For each instruction, there is a "changed" bit indicating whether this instruction needs to be looked at. Initially, the "changed" bit is set only for the first instruction. The data-flow analyzer executes the following loop:

1. Find a virtual machine instruction whose "changed" bit is set. If no instruction remains whose changed bit is set, the method has successfully been verified. Turn off that changed bit.

2. Emulate the effect of this instruction on the stack and registers:
   - If the instruction uses values from the stack, ensure that there are sufficient elements on the stack and that the top element(s) of the stack are of the appropriate type. Otherwise, fail.
   - If the instruction uses a register, ensure that the specified register contains a value of the appropriate type. Otherwise, fail.
   - If the instruction pushes values onto the stack, add the indicated types to the top

of the stack. Ensure that there is sufficient room on the stack for the new element(s).
   - If the instruction modifies a register, indicate that the register now contains the new type.

3. Determine the virtual-machine instructions that can follow this one. Successor instructions can be one of the following:
   - The next instruction, if the current instruction isn't an unconditional goto, a return, or a throw. Fail if we can "fall off" the last instruction.
   - The target of a conditional or unconditional branch.
   - All exception handlers for this instruction.

4. Merge the state of the stack and registers at the end of the current instruction into each of the successor instructions. In the exception-handler case (2c), change the stack so that it contains a single object of the exception type indicated by the exception handler information.
   - If this is the first time the successor instruction has been visited, indicate that the stack and registers values calculated in Step 2 and Step 3 are the state of the stack and registers prior to executing the successor instruction; set the "changed" bit for the successor instruction.
   - If the instruction has been seen before, merge the stack and register values calculated in Step 2 and Step 3 into the values already there; set the "change" bit if there is any modification.

5. Go to Step 1.

To merge two stacks, the number of elements in each stack must be identical. A failure is indicated if this criteria isn't met. The stacks must be identical, except that differently typed handles may appear at corresponding places on the two stacks. In this case, the merged stack contains the common ancestor of the two handle types.

To merge two register states, compare each register. If the two types aren't identical, then unless both contain handles, indicate that the register contains an unknown (and unusable) value. For differing handle types, the merged state contains the common ancestor of the two types.

If the data-flow analyzer runs on the method without reporting any failures, then the method has been successfully verified by Pass 3 of the class-file verifier.

Certain instructions and data types complicate the data-flow analyzer. We now examine each of these.

Long Integers and Doubles

Long integers and double floats each take two consecutive words on the stack and in the registers.

Whenever a long or double is moved into a register, the following register is marked as containing the second half of a long or double. This special value indicates that all references to the long or double must be through the lower numbered register.

Whenever any value is moved to a register, the preceding register is examined to see if it contains the first word of a long or a double. If so, that preceding register is changed to indicate that it now contains an unknown value. Since half of the long or double has been eradicated, the other half can no longer be used.

Dealing with 64-bit quantities on the stack is simpler. The verifier treats them as single units on the stack. For example, the verification code for the dadd opcode (add two double floats) checks that the top two items on the stack are both double floats. When calculating stack length, longs and double floats on the stack have length two.

Stack manipulation opcodes must treat doubles and longs as atomic units. For example, the verifier reports a failure if the top element of the stack is a double float and it encounters the opcodes pop or dup. The opcodes pop2 or dup2 must be used instead.

Constructors and Newly Created Objects

Creating a usable object in the Java interpreter is a multi-step process. The bytecodes produced for the Java code:

```
new myClass(i, j, k);
```

are roughly the following:

```
new <myClass>          # allocate
    uninitialized space
dup                    # duplicate
    object on the stack
<push arguments>
invokenonvirtual myClass.<init>  #
    initialize
```

This code leaves the newly created and initialized object on top of the stack.

The myClass initialization method sees the new uninitialized object as its this argument in register 0. It must either call an alternative myClass initialization method or call the initialization method of a superclass on the this object before it is allowed to do anything else with this.

In normal instance methods (what C++ calls *virtual* methods), the verifier indicates that register 0 initially contains an object of "the current class"; for constructor methods, register 0 instead contains a special type indicating an uninitialized object. After an appropriate initialization method is called (from the current class or the current superclass) on this object, all occurrences of this special type on the stack and in the registers are replaced by the current class type. The verifier prevents code from using the new object before it has been initialized and from initializing the object twice.

Similarly, a special type is created and pushed on the stack as the result of the opcode new. The special type indicates the instruction in which the object was created and the type of the uninitialized object created. When an initialization method is called on that object, all occurrences of the special type are replaced by the appropriate type.

The instruction number needs to be stored as part of the special type since there may be multiple instances of a non-yet-initialized type in existence on the stack at one type. For example, the code created for the following:

```
new InputStream(new Handle(),new
    InputStream("foo"))
```

may have two uninitialized `InputStream`'s active at once.

Code may not have an uninitialized object on the stack or in a register during a backwards branch, or in a register in code protected by an exception handler or a finally. Otherwise, a devious piece of code could fool the verifier into thinking it had initialized an object when it had, in fact, initialized an object created in a previous pass through the loop.

Exception Handlers

Code produced from the current Java compiler always has properly nested exception handlers:

- The range of instructions protected by two different exception handlers will always either be completely disjoint or one will be a subrange of the other. There will never be a partial overlap.

- The handler for an exception will never be inside the code that is being protected.

- The only entry to an exception handler is through an exception. It is impossible to fall through or "goto" the exception handler.

These restrictions are not enforced by the verifier since they do not pose any threat to the integrity of the virtual-machine interpreter. As long as every nonexceptional path to the exception handler causes there to be a single object on the stack, and as long as all other criteria of the verifier are met, the verifier will pass the code.

Try/Finally

The Java language includes a feature called `finally`, which is like the similarly named feature of Modula-3 [8] or `unwind-protect` in Common Lisp [9]. Given the following code:

```
try {
  startFaucet();
  waterLawn();
} finally {
  stopFaucet();
}
```

The Java language guarantees that the faucet is turned off, even if an exception occurs while starting the faucet or watering the lawn. The code inside the brackets after the `try` is called the *protected code*. The code inside the brackets after the `finally` is the *cleanup code*. The cleanup code is guaranteed to be executed, even if the protected code does a "return" out of the function, or contains a `break` or `continue` to outside the `try`/ `finally`, or gets an exception.

To implement this construct, the Java compiler uses the exception handling facilities, together with two special instructions, `jsr` (jump to subroutine) and `ret` (return from subroutine). The cleanup code is compiled as a subroutine. When it is called, the top object on the stack will be the return address; this return address is saved in a register. At the end of the cleanup code, it performs a `ret` to return to whatever code called the cleanup.

To implement `try/finally`, a special exception handler is set up around the protected code which catches all exceptions. This exception handler:

1. Saves the exception in a register.

2. Executes a `jsr` to the cleanup code.

3. Upon return from the exception, re-`throw`'s the exception.

If the protected code has a `return`, it performs the following code:

1. Saves the return value (if any) in a register.

2. Executes a `jsr` to the cleanup code.

3. Upon return from the exception, returns the value saved in the register.

Breaks or continues inside the protected code that go to outside the protected code execute a `jsr` to the cleanup code before performing their `goto`. Likewise, at the end of the protected code is a `jsr` to the cleanup code.

The cleanup code presents a special problem to the verifier. Usually, if a particular instruction can be reached via multiple paths and a particular register contains incompatible values through those multiple paths, then the register becomes unusable. However, a particular piece of cleanup code might be called from several different places:

- The call from the exception handler will have a certain register containing an exception.

- The call to implement "return" will have some register containing the return value.

- The call from the bottom of the protected code may have trash in that same register.

The cleanup code may pass verification, but after updating all the successors of the `ret` instruction, the verifier will note that the register that the exception handler expects to hold an exception or that the return code expects to hold a return value now contains trash.

Verifying code that contains `finally`'s can be somewhat complicated. Fortunately, most code does not have `finally`'s. The basic idea is the following:

- Each instruction keeps track of the smallest number of `jsr` targets needed to reach that instruction. For most code, this field will be empty. For instructions inside cleanup code, the field will be of length one. For multiply-nested cleanup code (extremely rare!), it may be longer than one.

- For each instruction and each `jsr` needed to reach that instruction, a bit vector is maintained of all registers accessed or modified since the execution of the `jsr` instruction.

- When executing the `ret` from a subroutine, there must be only one possible subroutine target from which the instruction can be returning. Two different targets of `jsr` instructions cannot "merge" themselves into a single `ret` instruction.

- When performing the data-flow analysis on a `ret` instruction, modify the directions given above. Since the verifier knows the target of the `jsr` from which the instruction must be returning, it can find all the `jsr`'s to the target, and merge the state of the stack and registers at the time of the `ret` instruction into the stack and registers of the instructions following the `jsr` using a special set of values for the registers:

- If the bit vector (constructed above) indicates that the subroutine has accessed or modified, a register uses the type of the register at the time of the `ret`.

- For other registers, use the type of the register at the time of the preceding `jsr` instruction.

Conclusion

The Java language has generated much excitement with its ability to allow programmers to create and compile code that can be executed on multiple platforms. The HotJava browser, in particular, has shown that portable code can bring interactivity to the World Wide Web.

However, before users will consent to bring over executable code from untrustworthy sources (i.e. most of the network!), they want assurances that the code cannot damage them. The byte-code verifier is the lowest level of a many-tiered strategy [10]. ■

Acknowledgments

Thanks to James Gosling, Arthur van Hoff, Bill Joy, Tim Lindholm, Chuck McManis, Mark Showalter, and Richard Tuck for comments and suggestions. Special thanks to Mark Scott Johnson for encouraging me to write this paper.

References

1. *The Java Language Overview*. Available via *http://java.sun.com/1.0alpha3/doc/overview/java/index.html*

2. James Gosling and Henry McGilton. *The Java Language Overview: A White Paper*. Sun Microsystems Technical Report, May 1995. Available via *http://java.sun.com/whitePaper/javawhitepaper_1.html*

3. Donald E Knuth. *The Art of Computer Programming*, Volume 1: Fundamental Algorithms. Addison-Wesley, 1969.

4. *The HotJava Overview*. Available via *http://java.sun.com/1.0alpha3/doc/overview/hotjava/index.html*

5. *The Java Virtual Machine Specification*. Available via *http://java.sun.com/1.0alpha3/doc/vmspec/vmspec_1.html*

6. The Unicode Consortium. *The Unicode Standard: Worldwide Character Encoding*. Addison-Wesley, 1992. Available via *http://unicode.org/*

7. Alfred V. Aho, Ravi Sethi,, and Jeffrey D Ullman. *Compilers: Principles, Techniques, and Tools*. Addison-Wesley, 1988.

8. Samuel P. Harbison. *Modula-3*. Prentice-Hall, Inc. 1992.

9. Guy L. Steele Jr. *Common Lisp: The Language*, Second Edition. Digital Press, 1990. Available via *http://www.cs.cmu.edu/Web/Groups/AI/html/cltl/cltl2.html*

10. *HotJava(tm): The Security Story*. Available via *http://java.sun.com/1.0alpha3/doc/security/security.html*

About the Author

Frank Yellin
Sun Microsystems
Java Products Group
fy@eng.sun.com

Generated with CERN WebMaker

CCI-BASED WEB SECURITY
A DESIGN USING PGP

Judson D. Weeks, Adam Cain, Briand Sanderson

Abstract

We describe several ways of using the general-purpose Common Client Interface (CCI) for enhancing the security of communications on the World Wide Web (WWW). In this approach, the Web browser communicates with an external CCI application that handles the processing of digitally-signed and/or encrypted data. Our particular design uses the popular Pretty Good Privacy (PGP) software for all cryptographic operations. We define a PGP-CCI protocol which can be used to protect any HTTP message exchange, and we also describe a simpler scheme for PGP-protected form submissions (HTTP POSTs) which may be implemented without modifying web servers. Additionally, we point out the advantage of using a PGP-CCI application to handle pre-encrypted/signed Web documents in a user-friendly manner. Keywords: Security, Pretty Good Privacy (PGP), World Wide Web (WWW), Common Client Interface (CCI), cryptography

Introduction

The multifaceted issue of security is inexorably entangled in the World Wide Web. To make manageable the complex task of "securing the Web," we may (imperfectly) divide the issue into four interrelated components [17]:

System Security

Ensures that use of Web browsers or servers does not expose host computers to undesirable intrusions

Authentication

Verifies the identity of Web clients and servers on either end of a connection across an untrusted network

Authorization

Determines what operations are allowed for particular entities on the Web (e.g., server-side access control applied to Web documents)

Confidentiality/Integrity

Protects private information from capture or modification as it travels across the open network

While all of these security components are extremely important, most recent Web security development efforts have been aimed at improving the authentication and confidentiality aspects of communications on the Web. In fact, multiple solutions have been offered to address these needs. Secure-HTTP (S-HTTP) [16], as well as systems using Message Digest Authentication [10] and Kerberos-based approaches [4], provide application-layer solutions. Meanwhile, the Secure Socket Layer (SSL) [8], Private Communication Technology (PCT) [1], and DCE-Web [14] systems all address similar needs by providing security closer to the network layer. Despite the difference in approach, the main goals of all of these technologies are the same: to secure Web communications by authenticating Web clients and servers and to cryptographically protect the data exchanged between them.

How do we, both as developers and regular users, deal with this proliferation of Web security schemes? Having a diversity of security technologies is indeed desirable, as we would like to be able to quickly switch from one to another in case of, for instance, a new potentially catastrophic weakness discovered in a particular protocol, algorithm or implementation [11]. However, we would prefer to not have to install multiple browsers and servers for this purpose alone. And, from the developer's point of view, the dreaded "browser bloat" phenomenon will probably make supporting all desired security mechanisms infeasible.

A few systems have been proposed to allow for the peaceful coexistence of multiple Web security schemes. The Spyglass Security Plug-in Module (SPM) architecture [9] describes a new communication interface between a Web browser and multiple security "modules." The World Wide Web Consortium (W3C) is currently developing HTTP extensions to allow for more flexible negotiation of security parameters. Also, new "portable-code" languages, such as Sun's Java [12], have been suggested as technologies useful for easily adding browser support for various Web security schemes. Currently, none of these systems are in widespread use.

Using a General-Purpose Browser Interface for Web Security

As a novel approach to dealing with this dilemma, we look to the Common Client Interface (CCI) as a means to providing application-layer support for Web security features. By so doing, we hope to enable authenticated and/or signed Web communications in a way that is easily supported by any browser with a general-purpose interface similar to CCI. Additional advantages of this design include the graceful handling of documents which are themselves signed and/or encrypted, and the ability of browsers with no native capabilities for encryption to employ the design. This design will greatly ease the process of international distribution, as all security functionality is completely divorced from the Web browser.

Rather than implement all necessary security features needed by the CCI application from scratch, we make use of the popular Pretty Good Privacy (PGP) software [7] to handle data encryption, signature verification, key management, etc. In essence, the PGP-CCI application is a GUI-based

front end to PGP which communicates with the Web browser via CCI.

To demonstrate the feasibility of this scheme, we present the PGP-CCI protocol which can be used to allow the signing and/or encryption of HTTP messages. Similar to S-HTTP in design, this protocol uses HTTP extensions, new HTML anchor attributes, and advanced CCI features. The simpler "PGP-POST" scheme is also described, which uses the PGP-CCI application to encrypt and/or sign HTML FORM submissions and does not require modified web servers or advanced CCI functions.

Outline for the Remainder of This Document

Before jumping into the mechanics of the PGP-CCI and PGP-POST designs, we first clarify the utility of handling signed and or encrypted documents, as opposed to applying similar security enhancements to HTTP messages or communication channels. Next we review the relevant characteristics of CCI, PGP, and previous work combining PGP with the Web. The function and features of the PGP-CCI application are then described, followed by details of how to use this application to handle the viewing of PGP-enhanced documents. We then explain the PGP-CCI protocol and the PGP-POST system, giving example HTTP messages resulting from use of these schemes. Finally, we discuss the security protections offered by these new systems, as well as some security considerations for the use of CCI.

Assumptions About the Reader

Throughout this paper we assume that the reader has a working knowledge of the World Wide Web, HTML, the HTTP Protocol, and the basics of cryptography and digital signatures.

Where Do We Sign?

The distinctions between security of channels, messages, and documents are subtle but crucial.

Schemes such as SSL [8] and PCT [1] address the need for secure channels in the form of authenticated, encrypted socket connections which may be used by Web applications. S-HTTP [16] and the PGP-CCI protocol described below, allow for HTTP messages that are signed and/or encrypted. Both of these approaches to secure communications have their strengths and weaknesses, and each will probably have a place in the grand Web security context. However, thus far there has been minimal attention paid to the handling of documents which are security-enhanced. Such documents may be signed and/or encrypted using a variety of security applications in wide use today, such as PGP.

What's the difference? Consider the example of a Web site run by a government organization distributing documents which are important, but not secret.* Documents of this type may be digitally signed by the organization as a matter of course. In any case, a browser viewing such a document on the Web may wish to know that the document itself is authentic and has not been modified in transit. Furthermore, it may not matter at all from which Web server the document was retrieved or what encryption mechanisms were employed to secure the channel. All that matters is that the document was signed by the government organization in question.

Channel-oriented security schemes can only authenticate the parties on either end of the connection and provide an encrypted channel for the data. Using these systems alone, there is no possibility for signed messages or documents, and thus non-repudiation is not achievable. In other words, these schemes cannot, by themselves, provide signed data which can be stored and used later to prove that the signing party committed to a particular action. This is simply a consequence of putting the "security smarts" below the application layer.

With message-based security enhancements, we can obtain signed or encrypted HTTP messages. This achieves authentication of, and private communications between, the two message sources: the web server and the user of the web browser. Such messages could be stored (although this function is not usually implemented) and used to prove that a particular document was served by a particular web server. However, this is not the same as having a document signed by the information provider. To understand the difference, consider the case in which our governmental organization wishes to distribute an important document using many other organizations' web servers. We would like the document to bear the signature of the organization authoring it; the authentication of the particular web server used to serve the document may be of no interest at all.

Currently, Web applications do not deal well with signed/encrypted documents. A browser user certainly can fetch and view a digitally-signed text file, for example; but to verify the document's signature, the user would have to save the file locally and manually run PGP (or the user's preferred security program) with the local file as input. An improvement in usability is offered in [13] although a GUI-based scheme with tighter browser coupling would be preferable.

A New Approach: Security Using CCI, PGP

Given the relative strengths and weaknesses of sockets-layer security and application-layer security, we have adopted an application-layer security scheme that takes advantage of message-based security enhancements while making provisions for handling signed and/or encrypted documents as well. To this end, we exploit of the flexibility of the Common Client Interface com-

---

* The example would be equally valid for a standards body or a company with an online catalog.

bined with the power of the Pretty Good Privacy encryption package.

CCI

The Common Client Interface, or CCI* is a client-side API (Application Programmer Interface) that is designed to expand the functionality of browsers without having to alter the code of the browsers themselves. While there are many variations of CCIs (e.g. Spyglass' SDI [3]), they all provide a means for Web browsers to communicate with other applications that reside on the client, henceforth referred to as CCI applications.

The CCI is a two-way communication protocol with functions that drive the browser (such as `OpenURL()` [3], which tells the browser to load in a document at a specific URL, and Post() [17], which tells the browser to submit an HTTP Post of escaped data to a specific URL) and functions that re-route output from the browser to the CCI application (such as `SendOutput()` [17], which routes server responses with certain Content-types to the CCI application rather than having them viewed by the browser). These functions allow application developers to easily integrate a wide range of functionality with the features of a Web browser. For more information on CCIs, see [15], [3], and [18].

NOTE

While there is at least one CCI which enables communication between the browser and applications running elsewhere on the network, we assume that browsers supporting such CCIs are configured to communicate only with local applications. This is necessary in order to obtain a more secure link between the Web browser and the PGP-CCI application.

To explore the feasibility of CCI-based Web security features without building all necessary cryp-tographic tools from scratch, we chose to design a CCI application which would act as a frontend to the popular cryptographic software package known as "Pretty Good Privacy," or PGP.

PGP

PGP, originally designed by Phillip Zimmermann, is a sophisticated program to handle the bulk of security needs for documents and message-passing systems. PGP is a public-key cryptographic package that provides protection of documents and messages using symmetric or asymmetric encryption for confidentiality and digital signatures for authenticity and integrity. For further information on PGP see [7] and [19].

Besides providing the tools to secure Web documents and communication, PGP has several other advantages. First, it is freely available in various forms worldwide. Also, it is widely used on the net already, allowing for easy adoption. Next, it has a distinctive trust model in which each user decides how much they wish to trust the public keys of others. In essence, the user becomes his or her own certificate authority and is not forced to rely upon validation by some global authority. To accomplish this, each PGP user maintains his or her own *keyring*, which is a list of the public keys of others with an associated trust level for each key. As PGP encounters unrecognized public keys, PGP warns the user and asks whether he or she wants to add the key to his or her public keyring and if so, what trust level should be assigned to the key. Under this model, individuals sign the public keys of trusted entities and exchange these with other trusted entities, to build a "web of trust". This allows PGP to be used now, while the certification infrastructure is in its infancy, and then be integrated with the infrastructure as it develops.

Using these functions, we are able to construct a protocol that will allow clients and servers to authenticate each other, provide document

---

* It has recently been suggested that CCI be taken to stand for "Client Communications Interface" as this more aptly describes its functionality.

access control, keep messages and data confidential as they travels across unsecured networks, and even verify the integrity of documents stored on unprotected servers.

Related Work

While the use of a user-friendly CCI application as an interface between PGP and Web browsers is new, the idea of combining Web applications with external cryptography packages like PGP is not. In fact, simple external function calls, or hooks, were added to XMosaic and NCSA httpd to allow each to run PGP or PEM for handling encrypted, signed HTTP messages [2]. This was effectively a proof of concept implementation which lacked provisions for key management, secure passphrase handling, and other features essential for a valid Web security scheme.

Of special note is the fact that an early version of the Secure HyperText Transfer Protocol, S-HTTP [16], partially defined support for PGP-enhanced messages. The details of using PGP with S-HTTP were not fully specified, and an implementation of this mechanism was never created. In the current S-HTTP specification [16], the PGP-related definitions have been dropped altogether.

The PGP-CCI work described here builds on the previous PGP/PEM hooks, adding flexibility and user friendliness (via GUI-based CCI application), while avoiding the requirements that all keys be exchanged out of band and that cleartext passphrases be stored in scripts. This work follows a scheme similar to S-HTTP, although the protocol is considerably simpler than S-HTTP and may be implemented via CCI without native support for cryptography built into the browser.

PGP-CCI Application Description

The PGP-CCI application is essentially a link between the Web browser and the functions provided by PGP. The CCI application itself may be implemented as a GUI shell to a command-line interface for PGP, or as a complete application built using the PGP source code or even the upcoming PGP API. The PGP-CCI application also functions as a viewer for documents that have been encrypted or signed by PGP (see "Viewing PGP-Enhanced Documents via CCI" below). The security issues for the PGP-CCI application fall into two categories: those issues connected to the interactions between the PGP-CCI application, the browser and the server and those issues connected to the user interface of the application itself. The security issues with the interactions between the PGP-CCI application, the browser, and the server are detailed in the PGP-CCI protocol below. The user interface issues are as follows.

Given the potential for security breaches that automation can provide, the PGP-CCI application must display the following information to the user:

- Security status of the current message or document: plaintext, signed, encrypted, or signed and encrypted

- Encryption method used: symmetrical session key or the public key of the user

- If the message or document is signed, the PGP username, Key ID and date of signature on the message or document

- URL of the current message or document

All of these items are necessary to ensure that the user is properly informed about the security status of the messages or documents that are being handled. The third item is particularly important as neglecting to check this kind of certificate information can potentially allow certain types of spoofing attacks (although PGP's trust model makes such attacks less likely to succeed).

One of the cornerstones of PGP security is the importance attached to signing or decrypting a document. Each of these activities requires the use of the user's private key and therefore must be handled with great care. Accordingly, PGP defaults to prompting the user for a pass phrase on every such occasion. Given the frequency with which either of the activities will occur in a Web environment, the PGP-CCI application could optionally cache the user's pass-phrase after he or she enters it the first time; thereafter, the user is merely prompted whether he or she wishes to sign or decrypt. However, if this approach is used, it is very important that adequate measures be taken to insure that an unattended system cannot be abused (e.g. time-out features, periodic flushes of the pass-phrase to prevent recovery of the pass phrase from the cache or user-sloppiness).

Given the amount of HTTP messages and responses that normal web-surfing creates, running every HTTP request through the PGP-CCI application, as detailed in the PGP-CCI protocol below, can become quite a performance hindrance. For performance reasons, the PGP-CCI should be equipped with a feature to easily enable or disable the routing of HTTP requests to the CCI application from the browser. Note that even when the handling of HTTP requests is disabled, the PGP-CCI application should be able to handle the viewing of PGP-enhanced documents.

Viewing PGP-Enhanced Documents Using CCI

As outlined above (see "Where Do I Sign?"), viewing security-enhanced Web documents is a highly useful but often neglected function. However, using CCI makes the implementation trivial. No changes have to be made to the code of either the client or the server; all that is necessary is the addition of a new MIME type.

Storing PGP-Enhanced Documents on a Web Server

Documents signed and/or encrypted with PGP usually have filenames ending with *.pgp* or *.asc,* the latter extension signifying that the data is encoded in ASCII-armored (text) format. For transfer of PGP-enhanced documents, we propose the use of the following MIME type:

`Content-type: application/x-pgp`

Therefore, the only requirement of the Web daemon serving such documents is to map the appropriate file extensions to this new content type[*]. Usually this process involves adding a new line to the *mime.types* file on the Web server, such as the following:

`application/x-pgp  pgp  asc`

That's all there is to it for the server! Even Web daemons oblivious to PGP or any other sort of cryptography may serve PGP-enhanced documents by this method.

Viewing PGP-Enhanced Documents

On the client side, the PGP-CCI application registers as a viewer for the application/x-pgp type during its initialization. Thereafter, whenever the browser requests and receives a document of this type, the received data is sent to the PGP-CCI application, which passes the document on to PGP. By processing the output of PGP, the browser can obtain all the information it must display to the user. This includes taking appropriate action in the case of an invalid signature or a failed decryption. Also, if the document turns out to be encrypted using the client's public key, the CCI application should prompt the user before resubmitting the document to PGP along with the user's passphrase, as outlined above (see "PGP-CCI Application Description").

The elegance of this handling of PGP-enhanced documents is that after decrypting or verifying the document signature, the PGP-CCI application tells the browser to display the document. This should work equally well if the document is text, HTML, graphics, or any other media the browser can recognize.

---

[*] We need not distinguish between signed or encrypted content, since the type of PGP enhancements applied to any data is encoded in the data itself.

The PGP-CCI Protocol

Protocol Overview

In addition to handling all application/x-pgp Content-types, the PGP-CCI application registers with the browser to receive all requests for URLs with the http protocol and to handle all application/x-www-pgp-response Content-types. When doing this, the CCI application specifies that the browser give it the full HTTP messages involved in these actions, as well the anchor attributes for http URLs.

Hyperlinks pointing to documents to be retrieved using PGP-CCI contain special anchor attributes giving the server's public Key ID, as well as other optional information such as whether the HTTP request should be signed, encrypted, or both. Any requests for a HTTP hyperlinkthat do not contain these attributes will be passed from the CCI application to the browser, to be fetched normally.

A request for a hyperlink containing the PGP-CCI-related attributes proceeds as follows:

1. When the user clicks on such a link, the browser tells the CCI application that the http URL has been requested. The browser also passes to the CCI application the complete HTTP request it would normally send to the server, as well as the anchor attributes for the desired hyperlink.

2. The CCI application uses PGP to apply the proper enhancements to request, which usually involves encrypting the message using the web server's public key. If the client does not have this key on its keyring, the anchor attributes can be used to find it. Note that before signing or encrypting the request using PGP, the CCI application adds a Date header and also a header containing a ran-domly-generated session key. These lines allow the server to protect against replays of the enhanced request. The session key also allows the server to symmetrically encrypt a response for the client without having to deal with finding the client's public key. Note that any time the server's HTTP response is to be encrypted, the client's HTTP request must also be encrypted in order to securely transfer the session key. [*]

3. Once the request is processed by PGP, it is encapsulated within a generic HTTP request which is then given to the browser for retrieval on the network.

4. The server uses PGP to decrypt and/or verify the signature on the encapsulated request. PGP checks the configuration files to determine if the request is properly signed and/or encrypted for that URL, and whether or not the authenticated agent is authorized to access the requested document. It then prepares an HTTP response to be sent to the client. If the request was not properly authorized, the server sends a "401: Unauthorized" response with the HTML body containing a hyperlink for the requested document, complete with the anchor attributes needed to resubmit the request properly. Otherwise, the HTTP response is processed by PGP before it is returned to the client. This step may involve signing the message and/or encrypting it using the session key contained in the client's encrypted request. The Content-type for the response is "application/x-www-pgp-response."

5. If the server's response is a 401, the browser will display the server's HTML error message. The user may then click on the hyperlink (with the correct attributes) to resubmit the request. If, however, the server's response was a PGP-enhanced HTTP mes-

---

[*] Alternatively, the PGP-CCI application may include the public key of the client user with which the server may encrypt its response. Note that if this is done, the client's public key is not added to the key ring of the server (as that would imply that the server trusts the public key included in the client's request).

sage, its Content-type will cause the full HTTP response to be given to the PGP-CCI application.

6. The CCI application uses PGP to decrypt and/or verify the signature on the server's response. PGP then passes the plaintext of the encapsulated HTTP response to the browser by means of a temporary local file (which is deleted immediately after the browser has read it). The browser processes this response as it would handle any HTTP response, while the PGP-CCI application displays the relevant information to the user, including the server's PGP username and Key ID.

Below is a more detailed description of this protocol. Note that as this is an experimental scheme, the exact names and syntax are subject to change.

Hyperlink Attributes for PGP-CCI

In order to allow for pre-enhancement of HTTP requests, including encryption, there must be additional information in the hyperlink for the URL. For greater compatibility and flexibility, we use anchor attributes for this purpose, rather than defining an entirely new protocol ("pgp-http", for example). Note that the anchor attributes defined may be useful for other PGP-related schemes besides PGP-CCI.

PGPPUBKEYID (required)

This attribute identifies the public key of the server at the other end of the hyperlink. The CCI application verifies that all eight characters (32 bits) of the Key ID are present before it uses the Key ID to look up the key in its keyring.

Example: `PGPPUBKEYID="E9B2BB1D"`

PGPUSER (optional)

The full PGP username of the server is included here mainly for the purpose of providing additional information to the browser user (upon inspecting the HTML source

code). When the CCI application attempts to access the server's public key, it uses the Key ID (see above) to find it. If the CCI finds the public key, and the username does not match the value given in the PGPUSER attribute, the PGP-CCI application warns the user and asks for an "OK" before proceeding.

Example: `PGPUSER="Topsecret Web Server <www@topsecret.org>"`

PGPPUBKEYBLOCK (optional)

The server may include its public keyblock in the anchor. The CCI application will check first on its keyring for a public key matching the Key ID. If CCI doesn't find such a key, it will next look to see if the keyblock is provided in the anchor.

Example: `PGPKEYBLOCK="Version: 2.6.2 mQCNAy6sAAAEEAMrb2L1S8sPOwSbwAZg0psG OZrhgtGpjqd2RyC/H8Du 90yFpiANAVVuaZyEEgEtvA7ixX0CDJn1VyiL 3N agn5IVKN4ifupAAUR tCNKb24gTS4gRYW4gPGpkdWdhbkBuY3NhLnV pdWMuZWR1Pg== =CKpP"`

PGPPUBKEYSRC (optional)

If the CCI application doesn't find the public key on either its keyring or in a keyblock within the anchor, it will check for a pointer to the server's keyblock. The PGPPUBKEY-SRC attribute provides such an anchor. Naturally, the CCI PGP application checks to see that the public keyblock retrieved using this URL/URN has a Key ID which matches the value in the PGPPUBKEYID attribute.

Example: `PGPPUBKEYSRC="http://www. topsecret.org/pubkey.asc"`

PGPMODE (optional)

This attribute includes values indicating whether the HTTP request should be signed, encrypted or both. If this attribute is not found, "both" shall be assumed as the default.

Examples:

```
PGPMODE="request-signed,request-
encrypted"
PGPMODE="request-signed"
PGPMODE="body-only"
```

The latter example refers to the PGP-POST scheme described below, and it signifies that PGP-enhancements should be applied only to the data in the body of the HTTP request (the query string, in the case of a post).

Example hyperlink

A typical hyperlink might look like the one below. Note that the order of the attributes is not important.

```
<A HREF="http://www.topsecret.org/
    wherever/whatever.html"
PGPUSER="Topsecret Web Server
    <www@topsecret.org>"
PGPPUBKEYID="E9B2BB1D"
PGPPUBKEYSRC="http://www.topsecret.org/
    pubkey.asc"
PGPMODE="request-signed,request-
    encrypted"
> Click here for the secret formula </A
```

Relevant CCI Functions

While the function names and syntax differ across different implementations of CCI-like interfaces, most of the interfaces have commands which are semantically equivalent. Since many implementations are similar to Spyglass' Software Development Interface, we describe the commands used by PGP-CCI in terms of advanced functions based on the specification for Spyglass' SDI [3].

RegisterViewer (TO Browser)

To handle PGP-enhanced documents, the PGP-CCI application registers to view all documents with application/x-pgp MIME types. For the PGP-CCI protocol, the CCI application registers to handle application/x-www-pgp-response Content types, giving the additional "FullResponse" flag to signify that the browser should forward the entire server response to the CCI application.

RegisterProtocol (TO Browser)

The PGP-CCI application registers to handle all requests for URLs with protocol "http" in order to trap requests to be pre-processed using either the PGP-CCI or PGP-POST scheme. The additional flags, "ComposeRequest" and "LinkAttributes," are also included in the call, to tell the browser that it should give the CCI application the HTTP request it would normally send, as well as the anchor attributes for the requested hyperlink.

OpenURL (FROM Browser)

If a CCI application is registered to handle a requested URLs protocol, the browser uses this command to pass on the request to the CCI application. If the CCI application included the "ComposeRequest" flag during registration, the additional "Request" argument of OpenURL contains the HTTP request. If the CCI application asked for the anchor attributes during registration, they are included in the "Attributes" argument.

OpenURL (TO Browser)

This function is used by the CCI application to tell the browser to fetch a document specified by the URL argument. If the CCI application supplies the additional "Request" argument, the browser treats this as the full HTTP request to be put on the wire in order to resolve the URL. The PGP-CCI application also uses this command to tell the browser to view a local file (via the "file://" URL protocol) containing the plaintext of a PGP-protected document or HTTP message.

ViewDocData/File (FROM Browser)

If a CCI application has registered as a viewer for the Content-type of a received document, the browser uses these commands to pass the CCI application the data to be viewed. If the CCI application registered using the "FullResponse" flag, the browser sends the server's HTTP response to the CCI application.

Server Configuration

To use the PGP-CCI scheme, the server must have compiled support. The server's PGP-related information (such as its PGP username, the location of the PGP executable, keyrings, etc.) is specified in configuration files. When launching the server, the administrator enters the server's passphrase, which is stored in memory and then used for any decryption or signing operation (automatic means for specifying the pass-phrase are available, though not recommended).

Using .htaccess files, or equivalent means, the server may be configured to require PGP-CCI authentication/encryption for accessing certain Web documents. Particular entities, or groups of entities, may be specifically allowed access by referring to their PGP usernames. Furthermore, the necessary enhancements for the HTTP request and the corresponding response may be specified by "require" lines in these configuration files. An example ".htaccess" file for a document directory might look as follows:

```
AuthType PGP-CCI
AuthUserFile /etc/httpd/keyrings/
    pubring.pgp
AuthGroupFile /etc/httpd/.htgroup.pgp

require user "John Doe  <doe@foo.org>"
    "Ted Tedman <tt@bar.edu>"
require request-encrypted
require response-signed
```

Note that any "require user" lines imply that the HTTP request be signed. Also note that the appearance of a "response-encrypted" line implies that the request also be encrypted (in order to send the session key used to encrypt the response).

Unencapsulated HTTP Request

Assume that the browser user has clicked on a hyperlink like the example link given above (in "Hyperlink Attributes for PGP-CCI"). The PGP-CCI application adds a few lines to the HTTP request before signing/encrypting it with PGP. The resulting plaintext HTTP request might look like:

```
GET wherever/whatever.html HTTP/1.0
Date: Thu, 05 Oct 1995 16:57:05 GMT
Accept: */*
User-Agent: NCSA_Mosaic/2.7  libwww/2.
    12 modified
Extension: PGPMODE=response-
    signed,response-encrypted
Extension:
    PGPENCKEY=keyname1,mr18YmNIc+sU0tGpZ
    yE3
```

The PGP-CCI application adds the Date header, if not already present. The PGPENCKEY must be a 20-character radix-64 encoded string representing a 120-bit random number generated using a secure random number generator [6]. Note that PGP uses the hash of this string to create a 128-bit session key for use in performing the encryption.* The PGPMODE parameters are optional, and they are set according to user preferences on the PGP-CCI application. The web server should accommodate the client's requests for security enhancements specified in the PGPMODE, as long as they are not explicitly forbidden in the server's configuration file (via a "require response-unencrypted" line in the .htaccess file, for example).

HTTP Request After PGP Enhancements

After the request is processed by PGP, it is encapsulated within a generic HTTP request. The result might look as follows:

```
GET / HTTP/1.0
```

---

* If the user wishes the response to be encrypted using his or her PGP public key, the PGP-CCI application also includes a PGPPUBKEYBLOCK extension header containing the user's public key. This option consumes more bandwidth without providing much additional protection and is really only useful in the case that the PGP-CCI application does not have an adequate random number generator [6], [11].

```
Authorization: PGP-CCI
Content-type: application/x-www-pgp-
    request

-----BEGIN PGP MESSAGE-----
Version: 2.6.2

pwhjT53Ue2c2cv+mAAAIX+PUGxKzA4mRODtOPnRQ
    yqTwKOHmj81Q90aAuJX7
E8bNEU5OW+r413/
    ZwpEUiIlkCewco+61ufR7y5yvwoNn383eMM2
    AdcArGh28
HuYxPCSlxqRHlzFwOZNdhcfA2aPi8gduBBu2guPC
    7Vtbfg4n9K9PCmYXQPh6
=VSGG
-----END PGP MESSAGE-----
```

The Authorization line is set to "PGP-CCI" to indicate to the server that PGP-CCI scheme should be followed.

Server HTTP Response to Valid Request

If the enhancements on the client request match the server's requirements for the requested document, the request is considered valid. The server then prepares a HTTP response as it normally would and this response is encrypted and/or signed using PGP. The result is prepended with additional headers, and the result might look like:

```
HTTP/1.0 200 Document follows
Date: Mon, 11 Sep 1995 14:23:32 GMT
Server: NCSA/1.5
Extension: PGPENCKEY=keyname1
Content-type: application/x-www-pgp-
    response
Content-length: 874

-----BEGIN PGP MESSAGE-----
Version: 2.6.2

hGxuwKXyEBAwCkj3VdDLVnCDAqUy28gqK7R0GlVe
    j3L5b+x7C6FN4s4gdf
PUiZ4AkCewco+61ufR7y5D4ogWWtY6w3zI7BWfCe
    xxNHvHBRO9e+cQZhLg
i6cE8bNEU5OW+r413/
    ZwpEUiIlnzaJblq9xx4r12wEYlQlexjs1ThU
    TvXS
HzTCSlxqRHlzFwOZNdhcfA2aPi8gduBBu2guPC7V
    tbfg4n9K9PCmYXQPh6
```

```
=VSGG
-----END PGP MESSAGE-----
```

In this case, the encapsulated message has been encrypted using the session key named "keyname1"; the client supplied this name in the request and may use it to look up the value of the session key for decrypting the server's response. The server may also include its public keyblock in the body of the response, and PGP can use it for signature verification (in case the public key was not found already during the preparation of the HTTP request). Note that the Content-type application/x-www-pgp-response causes the data to be sent by the browser to the PGP-CCI application.

Server HTTP Response to Invalid Request

If the proper security enhancements were not applied to the request, as in the case where the user types in the URL by hand, the server sends back a 401 response. A hyperlink for the requested URL, including the relevant anchor attributes, is contained in the message body, so that a client may resubmit the request properly. The entire HTTP response might look as follows:

```
HTTP/1.0 401 Unauthorized
Date: Thu, 05 Oct 1995 03:09:19 GMT
Server: NCSA/1.5.1
Content-type: text/html
WWW-Authenticate: PGP-CCI

<HEAD>
<TITLE>Authorization Required</TITLE>
</HEAD>
<BODY>

<H1>Authorization Required</H1>

Browser not authentication-capable or
    authentication failed. <P>

This document requires that you enhance
    the request using PGP.
<H2> Try requesting this document
    again, using the link below, after
you have launched your PGP-CCI
    application </H2>
```

```
<A HREF="http://www.topsecret.org/
    wherever/whatever.html"
PGPUSER="Topsecret Web Server
    <www@topsecret.org>"
PGPPUBKEYID="E9B2BB1D"
PGPPUBKEYSRC="http://www.topsecret.org/
    pubkey.asc"
PGPMODE="request-signed,request-
    encrypted"
> Click here to resubmit your request </
    A>

</BODY>
```

PGP-POST Description

We now describe a simpler version of the PGP-CCI Protocol that, while limited, can be deployed without having to upgrade to a PGP-aware server. This method is used with HTTP POSTs only and is a variant of the general PGP-CCI protocol described above. Its purpose is simply to allow strong encryption and/or signing of form data.

The main difference between the PGP-POST and the standard PGP-CCI protocol is that in PGP-POST only the data in the query string, and not the whole HTTP message, gets signed and/or encrypted. In this mode, the PGP-CCI application has to make sure that the important data that would normally be in the signed/encrypted portion of the message headers gets escaped and prepended to the query string of the POST data. For example the Date field would be:

```
Date=Sat+07+Oct+1995+16:57:05+GMT
```

The fields that have to be handled this way are precisely the headers from the standard protocol that have to be encrypted, namely:

- PGPENCKEY

- Date

- PGPPUBKEYBLOCK (optional)

These fields are supplied by the PGP-CCI application.

Server Operation

On the server side, instead of having the PGP functionality built in to the server or communicating with the server through interprocess communication, PGP actually resides in (or is launched by) a CGI script. Under PGP-POST, the CGI script is responsible for checking the date stamp and optionally keeping track of the PGPENCKEY values to detect replay. While this processing increases the workload of the CGI programmer, it does provide added flexibility in implementation. As with the PGP-CCI protocol, the PGPENCKEY, if present, is used to encrypt the response, which should then have an application/x-pgp MIME-type.

Given the dangers inherent in CGI scripts, we must point out that if the CGI developer wishes to use the PGP-POST method, certain precautions must be taken. First, we recommend that the CGI script be written in a compiled rather than interpreted language with the pass phrase(s) either embedded in the script or in a file that only the CGI program can access. Second, note that the permissions on the CGI script are set so only root or other authorized users can access the script.

Client Operation

The primary differences of the PGP-POST method on the client side have to do with the way in which the document containing the form launches the HTTP POST in question. The author has an option of embedding the necessary information (such as PGPMODE, PGPPUBKEYID, et cetera—see above for further details) in the FORM attributes as was done for the PGP-CCI method described above. Alternatively, the author could embed this information in the name-value pairs of hidden fields within the form. The latter alternative is supplied mostly for compatibility with current browsers that might not have the advanced CCI features to trap attribute values. Either way, if the author intends to use the PGP-POST method of encryption, he or she must include an extra field in the PGP-

MODE attribute/name: "body-only". This field tells the PGP-CCI application that only the body of the HTTP POST, and not the entire HTTP message, is to be encrypted and/or signed. Before encryption, the query string would look something like:

```
query
    string="name=John+Doe&CC=Master+Card
    &...
&PGPPUBKEYID=E9B2BB1D
&PGPMODE=request-encrypted,request-
    signed, body-only"
&Date=Sat+07+Oct+1995+16:57:05+GMT
&PGPENCKEY=a4d83e1c80af9ce02e5d3f230dc5e
    63b
```

This example assumes that the user is embedding the PGP relevant fields as hidden data elements within the form.

Since the PGP-POST method can only function with HTTP POSTs, the PGP-CCI application could trap only the POSTs instead of all HTTP requests. This is assuming, of course, that the CCI that the application is using supports trapping HTTP POST requests from the browser.

Security Considerations

While a complete analysis of the security provisions and concerns for the PGP-CCI and PGP-POST schemes is outside the scope of this document, we do consider some of the more important threats and the protections offered against them. Potential attacks may be divided into two categories: network-based attacks relating to the security protocols, and attacks on the CCI communications between the browser and the PGP-CCI application.

Network/Protocol Security

Assume that the browser user starts with a trusted document containing hyperlinks for PGP-CCI-protected pages (if an attacker has fooled the user with a bogus starting page, all is already lost). Thus, the public Key ID's of the servers in the hyperlink attributes are also trusted. Now let's say the user clicks on a PGP-CCI hyperlink. At this point, any attacker who attempts to impersonate the desired Web server will either be detected before the request is sent or will be easily identified after the response is received. To decrypt an encrypted request, or to provide a signed or encrypted response, the attacker would have to posses the private key corresponding to the public Key ID in the hyperlink. If the attacker intercepts a request for the Web server's public keyblock (using the PGPPUBKEYSRC attribute) and interject the attacker's public key, the PGP-CCI application will immediately notice that the Key ID for the key received does not match the one in the anchor and will abort the exchange.

The main weakness of this scheme is probably the handling of "401—Unauthorized" server responses. An attacker could intercept a PGP-enhanced request and return a 401 message with the attacker's Key ID in the re-submission anchor. However, the fact that the entity issuing the responses is not the desired Web server should be obvious to the user. This aspect would be clear if the user noticed the different Key ID (and most likely the PGP username as well) displayed in either the 401 message's HTML source, or in the PGP-CCI application's display of the security information for the attacker's next response. A solution to this weakness could be to have the PGP-CCI application also register as a viewer for all text/html responses; it could then detect the 401 and respond appropriately (any other text/html responses would be sent back to the browser for viewing). This change would require a modified PGP-CCI protocol, and could have a significant performance impact. Another solution would involve changing the Common Client Interface to include routing of messages based on Authorization headers.

The main defense mechanism against these types of attacks is PGP's handling of public keys. If an attacker attempts to fool the client into using the attacker's public key which is not on the user's keyring, the PGP-CCI application demands that the user acknowledge that this is an untrusted key before continuing. Also, if an attacker's key already exists on the user's keyring, then the user is assumed to recognize the identity of the key-holder and thus immediately detects any attempted masquerades.

CCI Security

Since there is the communication link between the browser and the CCI application, either in the form of message passing, or in our case, storing data in temporary files, security is highly dependent upon the security of the operating system as a whole. These concerns are beyond the scope of this paper.

In developing these CCI-based security systems, it has become clear that current CCI implementations were not designed with security as a major priority. For instance, many of the schemes have undefined behaviors when more than one CCI application tries to register with the browser. The main threats of interest, however, involve attacks where the adversary attempts to force the PGP-CCI application to inadvertently sign or decrypt attacker-chosen data using the client's private key. To guard against this, the processes of signing or decrypting data with the user's private key should be explicitly performed by the user. Also, in CCI protocols where communication can take place across machines, it is essential that care is taken to only communicate with CCI applications on the same machine as the browser.

Future Work

An important aspect of this type of design is the set of performance tradeoffs involved, and these have yet to be tested and quantified. We also hope to consider schemes for handling multiple simultaneous security-oriented CCI applications; this might be possible using one "master" security CCI application which routes data between the browser and several other CCI applications. Additionally, it would be desirable to investigate the applicability of new mail object security proposals, such as MOSS (MIME Object Security Services) and Secure-MIME, to the CCI-based security approach.

Conclusion

The systems described in this document demonstrate the feasibility of using a security package like PGP with the general-purpose Common Client Interface in order to achieve strong authentication and encryption of Web communications. The PGP-CCI and PGP-POST schemes may be lacking in simplicity and elegance, due primarily to the constraints of CCI and HTTP. We hope that the new protocol extension features proposed for HTTP 1.2, along with next-generation browser interfaces combining elements of both CCI and the Spyglass SPM architecture, will help to rectify this situation.

Finally, we feel that the ability to handle document-level security enhancements, via CCI or otherwise, will be of increasing interest in the near future. As the World Wide Web grows to include commercial digital publishing, online electronic commerce, and wide-spread caching, we suspect that document security will become at least as important as the security of channels and messages. ■

NOTE

The current version of this spec can be found at *http://sdg.ncsa.uiuc.edu/ ~jweeks/www4/paper/current_rev*

References

1. Benaloh, J. et al. *Private Communication Technology Protocol*, September, 1995. *http://www.microsoft.com/windows/ie/pct.htm*

2. Bina, E, V. Jones, R. McCool, and M. Winslett. *Secure Access to Data Over the Internet*, Proceedings of the Third ACM/IEEE International Conference on Parallel and Distributed Information Systems, September, 1994. *http://bunny.cs.uiuc.edu/CADR/pubs/SecureDBAccess.ps*

3. Black, P. *Software Development Interface*, August, 1995. *http://www.spyglass.com/techspec/sdi_spec.html*

4. Cain, A. *Kerberizing the Web*, August, 1995. *http://snapple.ncsa.uiuc.edu/adam/khttp/intro.html*

5. Cain, A. and J. Weeks. *Web Support of PGP Via the Common Client Interface, A Protocol Specification,* October, 1995. *http://www.ncsa.uiuc.edu/InformationServers/WebSecurity/pgp-cci-spec.html*

6. Eastlake, D, S. Crocker, and J. Schiller. *RFC 1750: Randomness Recommendations for Security,* December, 1994. *ftp://ftp.internic.net/rfc/rfc1750.txt*

7. Garfinkel, S. *PGP: Pretty Good Privacy,* O'Reilly & Associates, 1994.

8. Hickman, K. and T. Elgamal. *The SSL Protocol,* June, 1995. *ftp://ietf.cnri.reston.va.us/internet-drafts/draft-hickman-netscape-ssl-01.txt*

9. Hostetler, J. *Spyglass Security Protocol Module API,* May, 1995. *http://www.spyglass.com/techspec/spm_spec.html*

10. Hostetler, J. et al. *A Proposed Extension to HTTP: Digest Access Authentication,* March, 1995. *ftp://ds.internic.net/internet-drafts/draft-ietf-http-digest-aa-01.txt*

11. Husum, D. ed. *Security Flaw Found in Netscape Navigator. Fix is in the Works, WEBextra,* September, 1995. *http://www.tgc.com/websec/20460.html*

12. *Java (tm) Language: A White Paper* , May, 1995. *http://www.javasoft.com/1.0alpha3/doc/overview/java/index.html*

13. Kolletzki, S. *Privacy Enhanced Mail for WWW, Proceedings of the Third International World Wide Web Conference,* April, 1995.

14. Lewontin, S. et al. *DCE-Web Home Page,* September, 1995. *http://www.osf.org/www/dceweb/index.html*

15. Magliery, T. *The Definitive CCI Refernce.* *http://sdg.ncsa.uiuc.edu/~mag/work/CCI.html* *http://www.osf.org/www/dceweb/index.html*

16. Rescorla, E. and A. Schiffman. *The Secure Hyper-Text Transfer Protocol* , July, 1995. *http://info.internet.isi.edu/in-drafts/files/draft-ietf-wts-shttp-00.txt*

17. Shaffer, S. and Simon A. *Network Security,* Cambridge, MA: Academic Press Professional, 1994.

18. Thompson, D., *Common Client Interface Protocol Specification,* April, 1995. *http://yahoo.ncsa.uiuc.edu/mosaic/cci.spec*

19. Zimmermann, P., *The Official PGP User's Guide,* Cambridge, MA: MIT Press, 1995.

About the Authors

Judson D. Weeks
[*http://sdg.ncsa.uiuc.edu/~jweeks/*]
jweeks@ncsa.uiuc.edu

Adam Cain
[*http://www.ncsa.uiuc.edu/People/acain*]
acain@ncsa.uiuc.edu

Briand Sanderson
[*http://sdg.ncsa.uiuc.edu/~briand/*]
briand@ncsa.uiuc.edu

Software Development Group
National Center for Supercomputing Applications
152 Computing Applications Building
605 E. Springfield Ave.
Champaign, IL 61820

SECURING THE WORLD WIDE WEB
SMART TOKENS AND THEIR IMPLEMENTATION

Michael F. Jones, Bruce Schneier

Abstract

This paper introduces Smart Tokens, discusses some of their basic properties, and outlines their general role in securing software applications on the World Wide Web. In addition, the completed hardware and software architecture of a current implementation is described. Finally, an electronic commerce application for Smart Tokens involving major U.S. financial institutions is discussed.

Introduction

Security concerns impose a severe constraint on a vast array of products and services that can be offered within the context of the World Wide Web. Electronic commerce on the Web will be enabled by emerging security protocols such as S-HTTP and SSL. Introducing additional choices such as Microsoft's recent release of STT and PCT may have the effect of causing confusion and, therefore, delaying implementations. However, it is clear that serious attention to security has now become mainstream. S-HTTP and SSL, which incorporate Public-Key cryptosystems, are just beginning to be implemented by WWW applications developers. Recent announcements by major software vendors indicate that widespread implementation of these standards is likely to occur [10].

Public-Key cryptosystems involve an authority issuing a pair of complimentary encryption keys to each user in the system. One of the keys is intended to be made public, analogous to an email address, and is called the Public-Key component. The other key in the pair must be available for use only by the "owner" of the key-pair and is called the Private-Key component. Application software making use of the key-pairs provides users with a rich set of security functions that essentially lifts the current constraints on electronic commerce in the WWW environment. For an introduction to Public-Key cryptography, please refer to [3].

Although Public-Key cryptosystems have many desirable characteristics in securing distributed systems, they typically rely upon the ability of the system to protect the beneficial use of the Private-Key component from all but the intended user. If the Private-Key component can be copied, or is made public, the authenticity of transactions using that Public-Key pair is called into question and therefore, cannot be trusted. In the commercial internetworked environment, software-only solutions for protecting the Private-Key component are inherently vulnerable to attack by viruses and other methods of compromise such as password guessing schemes.

Smart Tokens, the subject of this paper, are hardware devices with associated software that have the ability to perform Private-Key operations without the Private-Key ever being vulnerable to compromise. The WWW security community is in general agreement that Smart Tokens will play a major role in the future of electronic commerce on the Internet. This paper further describes a Smart Token implementation with characteristics that make it suitable for use with general purpose software applications such as word processors, email packages, and WWW browsers. Portability and isolation from the hardware layers are important architectural goals. Finally, a major electronic commerce application in which the Smart Token is used as the analog of traditional checkbook functionality is then discussed.

Smart Tokens

A "smart token" is an easily portable device that does special-purpose operations for its user, generally identifying the user to some larger computer system. A smart token can look like a PC Card, 3.5" diskette, credit card, pocket calculator, or many other things—the important feature is that it carries some secret information for you and that it does some internal calculations when you need them performed. A smart token is often designed to be tamper-resistant: It is difficult to take apart. It is protected with a user password, so that even if it is physically stolen, it will be difficult to impersonate its owner.

Just as most pocket calculators are used to do arithmetic, most smart tokens are used to identify their user to some remote computer. If the user's identification checks out, then she is allowed to do something: make a purchase on her credit card account, read her email from a public terminal, board a plane, or log in to a remote computer system, etc.

The Role of Smart Tokens

To see the value of this, consider making a purchase on the Internet. People used to type their credit card numbers directly into a computer, and then send those numbers to the merchant. This is insecure both because those credit card numbers can be easily collected by someone who monitors network traffic, and because the merchant has no way to confirm that the person who typed in the credit card number is the same person who owns the credit card.

Current solutions include encryption, which hides the buyer's personal information during transition, and digital signatures, which confirm the identity of the buyer. Financial models include digital checks, digital credit cards, and digital cash. These solutions protect against network monitoring, but do nothing to stop password guessing, password collection at the buyer terminal, or password compromise. The seller still has to trust that the person who signed the digital payment order has not accidentally disclosed his password or private signature key.

Tamper-resistant tokens are needed to compute the digital signatures for electronic commerce applications; they are the best way to prevent disclosure of the signer's private signature key. If the private signature key is disclosed, then anyone can use it to forge the signer's signature. If significant numbers of private keys are disclosed and are used to forge electronic checks, electronic credit cards, or electronic cash, then these forms of money will not be accepted. In a situation like purchases on the WWW, where other forms of identification can't be used, merchants must rely on the security of the signer's private signature key.

Enough tamper-resistance is needed to make it economically unattractive for attackers to steal signature cards, extract the private key, and pass bad "checks" with that key before the card is reported stolen and the account changed.

Smart tokens often require a password in order to function. This provides the token some certainty that the person using it is the person who is supposed to be using it. This isn't always necessary—for some applications, entering a password each time the token is used is more trouble than it's worth. In general, if a person can use the token to spend money or access sensitive data, it will have a password. The user enters the password on his keyboard, or directly into the token via a keypad. Even if the computer has been hacked to record passwords, that won't allow anyone to break the system; they still have to get possession of the smart token.

The most common application for a smart token is to convince some larger system of a user's identity, so that the larger system, perhaps with help from the token, will allow the user to do something. Protocols for proof of identity are a well-studied area of cryptography, and several techniques are discussed in [8]. For example, in order to allow a user to log in to a remote system, a computer might require the user to use a "one-time password" stored in the token. Since only the token and the remote computer know what the next password should be, only this token could have given the right password.

Once the user and token have identified themselves to the larger system, then the system and the token can work together to allow the user to do something. For example, a software metering token, after it has identified itself to the software being metered, can authorize another execution of the software and increment its internal counter by one.

Applications of Smart Tokens

Restricting access to remote computer systems

A physical "key" token can be used to restrict access a computer system accessible via Internet or modem. The computer system and the smart token can work through an interactive protocol that verifies each to the other, and can even agree on a session encryption key. This type of system allows a user to log in through an untrustworthy terminal without leaving access to his remote account with the terminal.

A physical "key" for digital signatures

Suppose a user has a private signature key that she uses to authorize contracts of up to $10 million. She may not feel comfortable trusting this key to her personal computer. Even if it's protected with a password, a really capable attacker might install some software to capture her password, and, later, her key. A million-dollar contract can't be signed without both smart token and personal computer being involved. The smart token can be kept physically locked up, and will be protected by a password in any event. Similarly, she could use a threshold signature scheme, which might require the agreement of (say) three of five high-level executives in order to sign a major contract. Each of these executives can be given a smart token, and can be required to enter their password to permit the contract to be signed. These protocols are described in [8].

WWW purchases

In place of a normal VISA card, a user has a smart token. When she wants to buy something, she puts her card in her computer and enters her password. The card then handles the transaction automatically. It should be impossible for anyone to capture enough information from the transaction to perform more transactions. It's even possible for the smart token to keep a transaction log. Other payments systems, called "digital cash" systems, keep the user's transactions anonymous unless she tries to defraud the payment system (i.e., by spending the same electronic dollar twice). These sorts of schemes are discussed in [8].

Software metering

Another nice application for smart tokens is in application software metering. Ideally, a user would be able to load up a single token (perhaps a PC Card) with the licensing information for all her software. Each time she or one of her employees opened an application, that application's meter would be incremented by one. The metering might measure hours or minutes of application time used, maximum number of users, or might even bill specific functions of some applications more heavily than others. This kind of token mimics the little meters that are used in some self-service photocopy shops, where a user is given a meter, which is required to run the copying machines and which counts the copies used. When the meter is returned, the user is charged for her copies. The physical security of the token is trusted to prevent the user from resetting the counters. The same metering token can also be used for other metering applications: interactive-TV set-top boxes, automobile tolls, and public transportation payments.

Single-copy documents

If a user has a document that needs to be readable, but not copyable, a smart token can act as that document. When someone reads the smart token, they first verify its identity, then read the contents of the token's document. This document may also be digitally signed by some kind of notary. So long as an attacker cannot recover the token's secret information, which it uses to identify itself, the token can't be copied. A single token can conceivably carry many such documents. Variations on this allow the token to "spend" the documents (perhaps they're rail or bus passes), deleting the special identifying information from each document as it is spent. This is discussed in [2]. Note that this doesn't prevent anyone from copying the document from the token--instead, it simply keeps them from claiming that their copy is the original.

Electronic subscriptions

If a user wishes to purchase a six-month subscription to an electronic newspaper or news service, he buys a newspaper token. When he gets to a terminal (maybe in a hotel room), his token can authorize him to access the latest news from this newspaper. Probably, additional services will be made available for extra charges, such as more extensive photo coverage or expanded coverage of specific areas of the news—these can also be known and authorized by the smart token.

Secure storage devices

Some smart tokens hold significant amounts of flash-RAM, which can be used to hold secret user data. The token also holds some physically secure memory, which keeps an encryption/decryption key. The user must enter the right password to gain access to the data. (Often, the password and the internally stored data must both be used to determine the encryption/decryption key.) It is possible to split the flash-RAM into many partitions, and encrypt each with different passwords and keys.

Secure tokens can also be used to implement protocols for electronic auctions, secure voting, anonymous transactions, and others.

How Smart Tokens Work

This section is meant as a brief introduction to the operations of smart tokens. To get a better understanding of the algorithms and protocols discussed here, see [2, 8].

Passwords

A token can deal with passwords in two basic ways. The simplest is to check the user's password against an internally stored value and authorize the user's request if the password matches that value. (The actual password isn't usually stored. Instead, some value based on the password is stored, so that the password isn't revealed even if an attacker manages to read the token's internal memory.) The second way, more complex but more secure, uses the password as a decryption key, to decrypt some internal set of values, which are then used to authorize the user's request. In this case, the token itself has no way to determine whether the password was correct—the larger system being connected to must do that. When secret data is stored in the token, it is common for it to be encrypted under a key derived from the password.

Identification protocols

A token can identify itself to another system in many different ways. The most common method is for the system and the token to share some secret data. The outside system sends a "challenge" (a random string of bits) to the token, and the token must calculate the proper "response," based on the secret data. Other systems allow a token to identify itself, using a public and private key. The token must hold the private key, the outside system must only know the public key. For a good introduction to this kind of system, see [8].

Digital signatures and message authentication codes

A token may authorize a transaction if the token digitally signs a timestamped request for the transaction to take place. This involves a secret key kept in the token, and a public key known by the system. See [2, 8] for discussions of this kind of algorithm and system. More generally, a digital signature may be used anytime a block of data needs to be verified as having come from this token, and the systems that will do the verification don't share any secret data with this token.

Cryptographic API Standards

In order to integrate cryptographic functionality with "off the shelf" commercial software, there have been many recent efforts to develop a modular Cryptographic Application Program Interface (CAPI). Of these, there are three proposals that are proving to be widely accepted. They are the GSS-API (Internet Engineering Task Force)[5], the GCS-API (X/Open)[9], and Cryptoki (RSA)[5].

Although it is beyond the scope of this section to describe these three CAPIs, it is important to note that they differ significantly in the degree of cryptographic knowledge required on the part of the application developer for implementation. The GSS-API requires the least knowledge of the underlying cryptography and Cryptoki requires the most understanding. In addition, Cryptoki is the only one of the three CAPIs that was written primarily for smart cards and tokens. It includes an abstract token interface that is intended to be the only layer in a software architecture that requires change in order to implement a wide variety of Smart Tokens. A useful analysis of CAPIs can be found in [7].

Since Cryptoki requires more knowledge of the underlying cryptography, it will be helpful to some application developers for an additional higher level API to be provided along with the Smart Token software development tools.

An Existing Smart Token Implementation

General Description

The currently implemented Smart Token combines high-density flash memory and data security functions in a ubiquitous PC Card Type I package. It is compatible with PC Card release 1.x and 2.x memory card specifications. The design provides the computer user with removable, secure nonvolatile memory plus data and communications security support in a single package.

This Smart Token implementation is available with storage capacities from 1 to 24 Megabytes. In normal operation, the Smart Token's memory is compatible with host computers having PC Card adapter slots for additional memory or removable media. The Smart Token uses flash memory with 64-Kbyte block erase capability and supports both word-wide and byte-wide transfer modes.

Security features provide memory access control as well as support for data security functions such as secure remote log in, Public-Key encryption, digital signatures, etc. The security feature is provided by the FIPS PUB 140-1 Level 3 compliant Cryptographic Support Processor (CSP) embedded in the card. The CSP is an integrated circuit based on ISO standard smart card technology which is recognized internationally as a secure vessel for key and password storage. The Smart Token's CSP provides secure computing functions such as random number generation, key encoding, and key comparisons, while the private key information never leaves the secure silicon. Multiple passwords can be stored on the chip.

Passwords stored in the CSP can be changed, but not read, by host resident software. The Smart Token is shipped with default memory passwords installed in the CSP. The operating environment and software resident in the CSP prevents access to the secure storage, but allows certain defined operations using the secure data. The CSP can detect physical security violation, attempts such as probing the chip, de-soldering the chip, and electronic probing involving single stepping the clock.

Access to the CSP is through host-resident software and Smart Token drivers described below. The electrical interface between the host and the Smart Token is compatible with PC Card memory-only release 1.x and 2.x. Data transfer between the host and the CSP interface is controlled by the card interface ASIC which supports the ISO 7816-3 standard. Host resident software supports the RSA Cryptoki standard.

The presence of the CSP allows host resident software to execute secure data interchange such as remote login, data communications, digital signatures, information "metering," and electronic funds transfer (EFT), using standards including DES, DSS, PKCS, and RSA. The Smart Token is all solid state, requires no batteries and is robust compared to storage media such as floppy disks.

Software Architecture

This section provides an overview of the software architecture of the PC Card Smart Token. Applications are presented in a Microsoft Windows 3.1 environment, with PC Card software support provided by SystemSoft card and socket services. Some of the architectures presented are considered to be building blocks for higher level functionality and are designed in a way which will promote future advanced application development. There are six major software components which interface with various levels of DOS, Windows, and PC Card architectures:

- Smart Token resident software for encryption and protection services provided by the CSP

- A DOS driver interface to the CSP, with block driver hooks to support transparent file encryption.

- A DOS card service vendor specific driver to support file system initialization.

- A Windows DLL which implements a CSP API protocol layer through DPMI services and the CSP driver.

- A Windows GUI user application for administration of card protection and encryption.

- A Cryptoki support library which implements the Cryptoki API with CSP services

The first component is Motorola 6805 instruction code, which is resident in the CSP memory space of the Smart Token card. The other components are loadable or installable drivers and applications that execute on the host machine. A configuration for these components is illustrated in Figure 1. In this scheme, the CSP and encryption support driver is a DOS TSR application which is loaded at boot time and executes in real or virtual 86 processor modes. The card and socket service components are contributed by SystemSoft and provide PC Card 2.1 compliant support for Smart Token card interfacing. A Smart Token specific DOS driver is provided which implements a card service vendor specific call to reinitialize file system components when required by Smart Token protocols. The flash translation layer (FTL) is a SystemSoft character driver which emulates a random access block device on a flash platform. In Windows, several components allow for high level application and end-user card management. The CSP protocol DLL implements an API for performing CSP operations through the CSP driver. The Cryptoki support library implements a similar interface packaged into a Cryptoki API set. Cryptoki applications may link with the library to receive Cryptoki support on the Smart Token platform. The Windows File Manager is the standard Windows 3.1 file system management application, and represents any number of high level file components running in

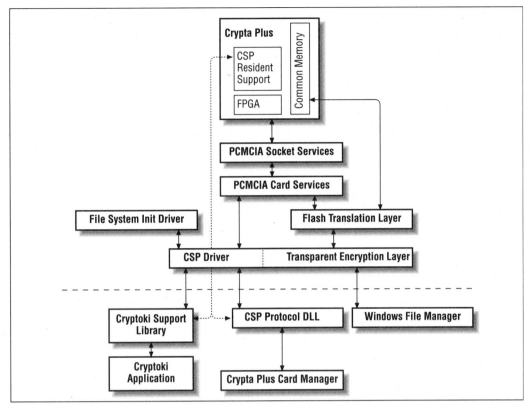

Figure 1: Software components of PC Card Smart token

Windows protected mode. Lastly, the Smart Token Card Manager is a Windows protected mode GUI administration utility.

Socket Services

Socket Services provides an interface between Card Services and the host socket hardware. It is intended to allow software layers above it to be independent of the socket hardware implementation, aiding software portability.

Card Services

Card Services coordinates access to cards, sockets, and system resources.

CSP access support

This driver contains an application service function for high level pass through commu-

nication to the Smart Token CSP. The driver acts as a PC Card, Card Services client, and registers for callbacks on card insertion and removal. When a Smart Token card is inserted, the driver handles the required CSP initialization functionality of requesting a memory window to the Smart Token card and mapping the window to the CSP control register space. It also resets the CSP controller and looks for the proper response sequence. The driver is implemented as a DOS TSR application, loaded prior to Windows.

FTL transparent encryption support

Support for transparent file encryption to the Smart Token flash is implemented on top of SystemSoft's flash translation layer (FTL).

The driver traps file system requests targeted to FTL and, if the request is directed to an unlocked Smart Token card, may automatically encrypt or decrypt the request data with the embedded Smart Token key. Encryption is implemented with DES cipher block chaining on a sector basis. Transparent encryption is enabled through high level applications by setting the Smart Token encryption state using the CSP resident API.

Card service vendor specific driver

A DOS character device driver is implemented to provide special vendor specific services required by the Smart Token card. Following a card lock or unlock, high level file system access to the Smart Token flash area changes. However, without notification of the change, the file system will not reinitialize itself to detect the new state. This driver monitors card service registrations for memory clients, and saves card service callback addresses. Following a lock or unlock of the card, a vendor specific card service API is provided which allows for issuing a card service REMOVE or INSERT callback to registered clients in order to force data structure reinitialization.

Cryptoki support

The Smart Token Cryptoki application library provides public entry points for Cryptoki defined functions. This library implements general Cryptoki layer support for token, session, and object management. The library makes use of the RSA BSAFE library for key generation and the support of Cryptoki defined cryptographic functionality. In the current implementation, the Smart Token card supports two predefined global objects which are created with the C_InitToken function. These objects are a public and private RSA key pair. All global objects (predefined or user defined) are stored in an encrypted format on the flash memory of the Smart Token card. Access to this memory is protected by the locking mechanism inherent to the Smart Token hardware design. When a Cryptoki session is started with an application, the Smart Token card must be unlocked, and the global objects loaded into memory. The software logic for unlocking the Smart Token card is implemented in the CSP driver and Smart Token CSP resident support. Once the card is unlocked, an application has access to global Cryptoki objects through the flash file system. Before objects can be loaded, they must be decrypted using a CSP resident secret key. When a Cryptoki session is closed, all global objects (including any new defined objects) are stored on the flash and encrypted with the CSP secret key. The Smart Token card is then relocked until another session is started.

WWW Implementation—FSTC Electronic Check Project

The Financial Services Technology Consortium (FSTC) is a collaboration of major banks, technology companies, and laboratories that was formed to address the critical need for viable means of conducting electronic commerce on public networks such as the Internet. Currently, over sixty organizations are members of the consortium. A secure payment system and deposit gathering mechanism for the banks is considered to be an essential enabling component in the commercialization of these networks.

The Electronic Check Project was developed by the FSTC to provide a secure, all electronic payment system modeled after the familiar paper check. It is an integration of a traditional form of payment within the existing financial services infrastructure and the rapidly growing electronic networks. A detailed description of the project, the functional flows and its objectives can be found in [4]. On September 21, 1995, a live demo of the Electronic Check Project took place at the Bank of America in San Francisco. Participants in the demo included Bank of America, Bank of

Boston, Bank of Montreal, Bank One, Chemical Bank, BBN, IBM, Sun Microsystems, Telequip, and Bellcore.

The demo was conducted over the Internet using the World Wide Web. It included the purchase and payment by electronic check of a "Teddy Bear" for the Vice President of the United States, Al Gore, from PC Gifts and Flowers. One of the more remarkable aspects of the demo was that the check actually cleared electronically through the Automated Clearing House of the US banking system. Telequip's PC Card Smart Token implemented as described in the preceding section, performed the role of the Electronic Checkbook, generating and signing the first electronic check through the U.S. banking system.

In the demo and subsequent pilot program, Electronic Check makes use of a PC Card Smart Token in the form of an Electronic Checkbook which can be used within the context of the World Wide Web. A Web browser in conjunction with an Electronic Check application has been integrated with the implementation described in the section called, "An Existing Smart Token Implementation." Two additional software layers are provided between the Electronic Check client application and the Cryptoki API in order to provide a higher level interface as discussed in the section called, "Cryptographic API Standards," and to fulfill specific functional requirements of the Electronic Check initiative. The overall goal of this architecture is to make maximum use of existing standards and lower the risks associated with lower level interfaces to cryptographic devices.

Functional Flows

Unlike some of the newer stored value proposals for electronic commerce such as Mondex, Electronic Check is based on the familiar paper check model. Email is substituted for paper delivery by the postal service and digital signatures on the Electronic Check message replace the hand written signatures on paper checks. Since the functional flows are essentially the same as in the paper check model, the system is easy to understand. It is anticipated that rapid adoption of the Electronic Check will take place due to ease of integration and significant cost savings. Support for payment instruments like certified checks, cashiers checks, credit card charge slips, and additional features such as future dating, limit checks, and multicurrency payments can be accommodated.

Several scenarios for functional flows are described below.

Figure 2 depicts the typical Electronic Check flow. The payer receives an invoice from payee, generates an Electronic Check, and sends it to the payee via email. The payee then emails the received payment to his bank and settles the transaction with payer's bank.

In Figure 3, the payer receives a bill/invoice from payee, issues an Electronic Check, and sends it to the payee. The payee presents it directly to the payer's bank to be paid to the payee's account at his bank.

In Figure 4, the Payer receives a bill/invoice from payee, issues an Electronic Check, and sends it to the payee's bank, either directly or via a lockbox. The Payee's Bank then sends accounts receivable information to the payee and clears the payment with the payer's bank. In this scenario, there may be no payee endorsement.

In Figure 5, the payer receives a bill/invoice from his bank (assuming electronic bill presentment allows for capture of the payee's bills by the payer's bank), issues an Electronic Check, and sends it to his bank. The payer's bank, in turn, transfers funds to the payee's account at the payee's bank.

Key Design Objectives

Parameterized electronic payments instrument

By specifying parameters in the Electronic Check message, the check can be transformed into various instruments such as a

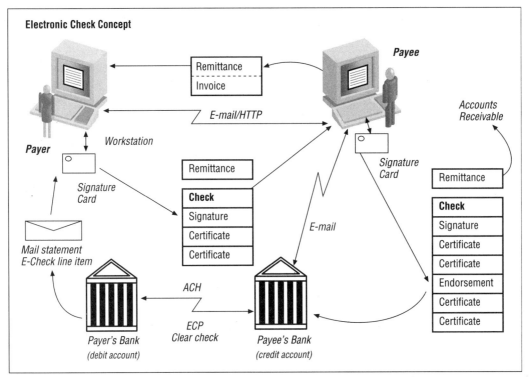

Figure 2:   Electronic Check flow

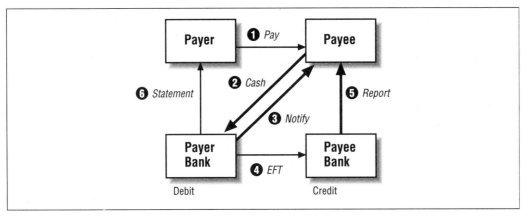

Figure 3:   The cash and transfer scenario

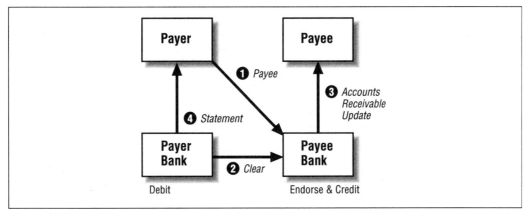

Figure 4:   The lockbox scenario

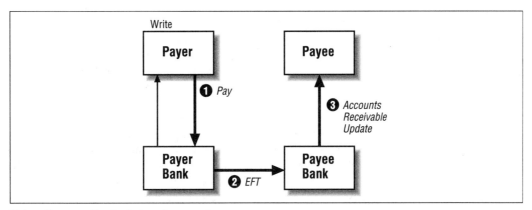

Figure 5:   The funds transfer scenario

traveler's check, credit card slip, cashier's check, etc.

Open integration with accounting systems
Commercial accounting systems will have the ability to interface with Electronic Check modules through standard API's.

Open integration with xxisting interbank payments mechanisms
Trusted gateways will allow connectivity between the public networks and the secured financial networks.

Authentication of electronic checks
Checks and checkbooks at any point in set-tlement cycle through the use of public key certificates.

Fraud prevention and confidentiality
Smart Token technology will help eliminate most of the losses due to forgery, alteration, duplication, and fraudulent deposits.

Project Plan

The demonstration phase of the project was completed in September of 1995. A limited commercial pilot is expected to commence in 1996 and be in place for approximately six months. After evaluation and subsequent modifications have been implemented, a more extensive pilot will be followed by a full production version of the system.

Conclusion

Smart Tokens have the potential to enable a revolutionary expansion in products and services that can be offered on internetworked systems. The essential elements needed to bring this expansion to fruition are just beginning to appear in the marketplace. APIs have now evolved to the point at which mainstream commercial software applications can be architected to include Smart Token capability as a standard feature. Implementations in conjunction with projects initiated by major financial institutions, such as the one described in this paper, offer a starting point and a glimpse of a whole new industry that will underpin the future of electronic commerce on the Web. ■

Acknowledgments

The authors would like to thank John Kelsey, who assisted with the theoretical sections on smart tokens, and Chris Carlisle, who assisted with the section on the current implementation

Glossary of Cryptography Terms

Digital Cash

An anonymous electronic payment system, where users withdraw electronic "coins" from their bank, and spend them with other users, without ever having to reveal their identity. Should the user try to spend the same "coin" more than once, his identity would be revealed.

Digital Signature

A digital signature is a way of marking a digital document (like a computer file), so that only a person who knew some private key value could have marked this document this way. There is a public key value that can be used to verify that this document was properly signed, which is published somehow. Digital signatures are commonly done using systems such as RSA, DSA, and El Gamal. A good introduction to this is [3].

Encryption/Decryption

Encryption scrambles a message so that it can't be read without a key which is known to the intended recipients of the message. Decryption unscrambles the scrambled message, so that it can again be read. Encryption is a generally good way to keep private data (such as a premium television channel) away from unauthorized users.

One-time password

Many computer systems require a password to allow a user to log in. Unfortunately, if a user is logging in over a modem or the Internet, her password can be seen by someone eavesdropping on the line. To defeat this, there are systems that use a different password each time a user wants to log in. The new passwords are generated by some cryptographic scheme, so that even when an eavesdropper catches a user's password, he can't use it to log in to the system. Generally, a token carried around by the user either generates the one-time passwords or stores them for the user.

Public/Private Key

A public key system has two keys—a private key, known only to an authorized user or system, and used to digitally sign or decrypt documents, and a public key, used to verify digital signatures or to encrypt messages to the owner of the public/private key pair.

Tamper Resistant

A tamper-resistant device is difficult for someone to take apart and change its operation, or recover secret information in it. It's probably not possible to design a computer device that's absolutely tamper resistant, just as it's probably not possible to design a safe that can't be drilled through. It is possible, however, to make tampering with a computer device (such as a smart token) so time-consuming, difficult, and expensive, that it's not worth the trouble to try.

Threshold Scheme

A method for splitting up a secret into n "shares," so that it takes k of those n shares to recover the secret. For example, a 2-of-5 threshold scheme creates five shares of a secret, and any two of the five shares together can recover the secret, but a single share can't recover it. See [3] for more information on this kind of scheme.

References

1. R.J. Anderson, "Why Cryptosystems Fail," *Communications of the ACM*, v. 37, n. 11, Nov 1994, pp. 32-40.

2. D.W. Davies and W.L. Price, *Security for Computer Networks*, John Wiley & Sons, 1989.

3. P. Fahn, "Answers to Frequently Asked Questions About Today's Cryptography," Version 2.0, RSA Laboratories, 1993.

4. FSTC, "Electronic Check Proposal: Public Document," Financial Services Technology Consortium, 1995.

5. B. Kaliski, PKCS #11, Cryptoki, RSA Laboratories, 1995.

6. J. Linn, "Generic Security Service Application Programming Interface," RFC 1508, Nov 1993.

7. National Security Agency, "Security Service API: Cryptographic API Recommendation," NSA Cross Organization CAPI Team, 12 Jun 1995.

8. B. Schneier, *Applied Cryptography*, Second Edition, John Wiley &amp Sons, 1996.

9. X/Open, "X/Open Preliminary Specification: Generic Cryptographic Service API," draft 3, Mar 1995.

10. M. Zurko, "WWW Security Standards Forecast: Partly Cloudy," IEEE Cipher #7, 1995.

About the Authors

Michael F. Jones
[*http://www.telequip.com*]
Telequip
20 Trafalgar Square
Nashua, NH 03063
mfjones@telequip.com

Bruce Schneier
Counterpane Systems
3841 Bloomington Ave
Minneapolis, MN 55407
schneier@chinet.chi.il.u.s.

Introducing CandleWeb and Å (awe), Bringing Animation Power to the World Wide Web

Kjell Øystein Arisland, Svein Johansen, Gunnar Rønning

Abstract

The World Wide Web has limited interactive capabilities, and does not support animated graphics well. To allow real-time interaction and animated graphics that are both pedagogically and commercially motivating, we must extend the Web. A new tool called CandleWeb is presented. CandleWeb works together with standard HTML browsers, and uses the hypertext transport protocol (HTTP). The tool has been implemented for X11, and interprets a language called Å (awe) which combines a simple C-like syntax with standardized graphics objects to provide a programming environment in which presentations including animation can be produced efficiently. An authoring tool called Å (awe) Composer allows programmers to save considerable time in implementing animated presentations, compared to text-based programming, using graphics libraries. The CandleWeb client for X11 V1.0beta and the Å (awe) language are openly available on the Internet at the site http://www.oslonett.no/~candle/. **Keywords:** *Advertising, animation, awe, authoring, browser, C, CandleWeb, client, commercial, composer, education, graphics, HTML, HTTP, interactive, interpretation, language, programming, real-time, tool, World Wide Web, Å*

Introduction

The World Wide Web is arguably the most useful thing that has happened to the Internet since TCP/IP. However, whenever something new and powerful comes along, there is a desire to make it even better and use it for more than it was intended for. This paper, which is our attempt to expand the power of the Web, discusses interactivity and animated graphics in a new tool called CandleWeb.

Educational Use of the Web

For many years now, the computer has been heralded as a tool that would some day pervade schools and homes and would become both helper and teacher. For an overview of literature in the field of computer applications to education, see [8]. Tools and courseware have been developed to take pedagogical advantage of often very limited hardware, and sometimes powerful hardware has been used for teaching

using limited pedagogy. Mostly, however, the hardware, its powers and its availability has been the limiting factor. Today, with multimedia workstations and wide-area networking, the hardware is becoming less and less of a problem, and the era of the computer teacher is about to begin. A naturally useful tool for teaching is the Internet, and more specifically the World Wide Web [2]. It is embraced as such at universities and other educational institutions across the globe.

However, during more than three decades of experience experimenting with computers and learning, many techniqes have been developed that speed up the process of using the Web efficiently for teaching. Therefore, those who wish to unleash the power of the Web on their students can do so without relying on trial and error.

As an example, in spite of many attempts, "electronic textbooks" have never been conclusively shown to be generally superior to a normal printed textbook as a tool for teaching. The so-called "Hawthorne effect" [5] may lead experimenters to believe that electronizing textbooks has intrinsic value, when in reality the process only yields a novelty effect.

Even hypermedia organization of documents may not be more than a passing fancy that does not add any real value in a teaching situation. In any case, hypermedia may or may not add value to instructional material, depending on how it is used [5].

However, there are at least two features of the Web and of computers in general that can improve on the learning environment when used well. These include:

- User/computer interactivity

- Moving graphics (animation)

These features will be discussed in greater detail below.

Commercial Advertising on the Web

The World Wide Web is also useful for commercial purposes, and the advertising industry is gradually becoming aware of its powers of influence and explosive growth. It is interesting to note how teaching and advertising have very much in common. Both fields require capturing the attention of the learner or potential customer (the user), increasing the user's interest in the subject at hand, and finally motivating the user to act either to buy something or to invest time in continued learning. For a thorough introduction to most of the aspects of advertising relevant to Web designers, see [3]. Because of the similarities, both educational and advertising use of the Web require basically the same types of mechanisms to be present in the Web. The two features that we concentrate on in this paper, interactivity and animation, are certainly just as important to commercial advertising as they are to educational use of the Web.

User/Computer Interactivity in the Web

Interactivity is a basic teaching tool that the computer naturally possesses. In comparison, the use of printed material offers very limited interactivity. Interactivity may take many forms depending on the time factor. For day-to-day interactivity, using the Web as a message center for general distributed communication is clearly useful. In a teaching environment, more short-term interactivity (real-time interactivity) may be even more useful. It is a basic tenet of pedagogy that the effect of learner action as opposed to just hearing or seeing is quite strong relative to human ability to retain and recall information. Therefore, an increased degree of interactivity in the Web would be beneficial from an educational as well as a commercial advertising point of view.

Such real-time interactivity is the basis of all action-type computer games, and thus clearly has appeal to the masses. Given the fact that children today spend more and more time playing computer games and less time watching television, one could conjecture that the real-time interactivity of the computer has even more appeal to the masses than the traditional story telling that is the basis of more conventional media like television and movies. This conjecture certainly remains to be proven, and only time can tell. However, at the moment, such interactivity is undoubtedly quite attractive to a large percentage of all potential Web users.

Unfortunately, the Web is somewhat limited in its support of short-term or real-time interactivity. This limitation is due to the fact that wide-area networking generally means overly long delays for real-time interactivity.

Still, many have had the desire to use the Web for applications that basically demand real-time interactivity, and have tried to implement different types of games. The Web's lack of support for such interactivity has so far limited most such attempts to just that, attempts. In order not to offend anyone, we offer no references, but there are many examples to be found on the Web.

One method of real-time interactivity found in the Web is that of forms. Forms offer real-time interactivity because the process of filling in the form is supported by the browser itself and the HTML document only provides code for specifying what the form should look like to the user, and what types of fields should be included in the form. The latter can be viewed as a specification of how the browser should allow the user to interact with the form. In this view the browser performs active interpretation of the HTML specification, as opposed to just presenting static information. Forms thus differ functionally from most of the rest of HTML.

Another HTML feature of real-time interactivity is that of maps. In maps, areas within a bit-mapped image can be specified as anchors, and a script in the server can interpret which URL to activate whenever the user presses a button at certain pointer (mouse) coordinates. The only real-time interactivity involved here, however, occurs in determining the mouse coordinates before they are transmitted over the WAN via HTTP. Since this local interactivity demands HTTP communication for each click of the mouse, the only gain in interactivity is in allowing mouse input relative to a graphic area, and not in the speed of the interactivity.

Relative to interactivity, SUN Microsystems' Hot Java [9] needs to be mentioned. The Java language, when used to implement Web browsers, has an advantage over most traditional languages in that it can be compiled to a code that is hardware independent and can be interpreted on different hardware platforms. This makes it possible to extend HTML in various directions to provide, among other things, stronger interactivity.

In conclusion, it is obvious that the need for and desire for real-time interactivity in the Web is considerable, but so far, good solutions have not been plentiful.

Moving Graphics (Animation) in the Web

Animation is one of the most powerful motivation tools available today both for pedagogical and commercial applications. Several generations of people in the industrial world have been raised on cartoons from Disney and Hollywood, and the so-called MTV generation literally demands fast-paced animated material; they simply may not notice commercial presentations that do not communicate in the same exaggerated way as Hollywood cartoons.

Video games and computer games are another reason why many people expect more from the Web in terms of animated graphics than what it is capable of delivering today. There is a world of difference in the liveliness of the graphics in the game Doom, compared to that of Mosaic or Netscape, and one may ask why. One answer is certainly the limited bandwidth on the net, but this is not the whole truth. Lack of standards both in hardware and operating systems is probably just as important.

The two types of graphics supported in the Web are basically bitmap images, either in GIF or JPEG format, and video clips in MPEG format. The process of using methods for storing images is quite wasteful in terms of storage space and bandwidth requirements. Both JPEG and MPEG are certainly state of the art in compression schemes for digitized natural images, however, reproducing natural images is not necessarily the best way to deliver educational or commercial messages.

Much thriftier methods, such as vector graphics and palette animation, are well known in the world of computing and are the basis for much of the mentioned games industry. When small bitmap images are moved around against vector graphics or textured backgrounds, quite powerful animation can be produced over relatively low bandwidth channels.

In conclusion, good reasons exist for enhancing the Web with more visually stimulating animations, and the means for doing so exist as well. There are two obvious questions that arise: Why does the Web not support animation already, and how can it be added?

There may not be a conclusive answer to the first question. However, HTML has its basis in document publishing, and this is most probably the reason. Information structuring as defined by markup is a far cry from animation, and adding so-called media types to a hypermedia document as one adds icing on a cake does not change the cake into steak. To make things difficult, animation is basically pixel and coordinate oriented, while HTML and SGML are strongly text string oriented.

The second question, concerning how animation can be added, is addressed in nearly half of the remaining sections, and one approach will be explained in some detail.

Authoring Systems, Multimedia, and the Web

In the field of Computer Assisted Learning, developing educational software has for several years been an industry in its own right. While educational software is produced for the masses by large companies, a large segment of this industry is comprised of corporations with in-house development of educational software for their own purposes. A consulting segment also exists in this field. Common to both segments is that they do, to some extent, use authoring tools for producing their software, and such authoring tools exist in many variations. Examples of tools holding large market shares are TenCore, Author-Ware, and MacroMedia Director.

Common to most authoring systems are implementors that produce educational software more efficiently than when general programming languages are used. Some tools also specialize in supporting simulation in various forms, including application-specific.

For the World Wide Web, authoring has been limited mostly to general text-based formatting

such as that in Microsoft's Word for Windows, and conversions of such texts to HTML. This type of authoring is quite primitive compared to the capabilities of multimedia authoring tools like Director; however, the Web does not support the kind of primitives needed to apply such tools today.

CandleWeb and Å (awe)

CandleWeb and Å were designed to increase the functionality of the Web with respect to real-time interactivity and animated graphics. This increase was achieved by:

1. Designing a language (called Å, pronounced "awe," an acronym for "another web extension") with dynamic vector graphics objects and code suited for interpretation

2. Designing and implementing a client application, called CandleWeb, for downloading a program using HTTP and then interpreting this program locally on the user's host computer

3. Designing and implementing a composer tool, called Å Composer, for efficiently implementing animation-based presentations using the new language

The Basic Architecture

Figure 1 illustrates the basic architecture of CandleWeb and Å (awe).

The CandleWeb client application is capable of interpreting .awe files; therefore ASCII-files with the extension .awe are downloaded using HTTP and your favorite Web browser. When they arrive at your host computer, an application client called CandleWeb is fired up and fed with the .awe file. CandleWeb interprets the .awe file interactively on your host computer, showing dynamic graphics locally and letting the user interact with the interpreted program through input-objects.

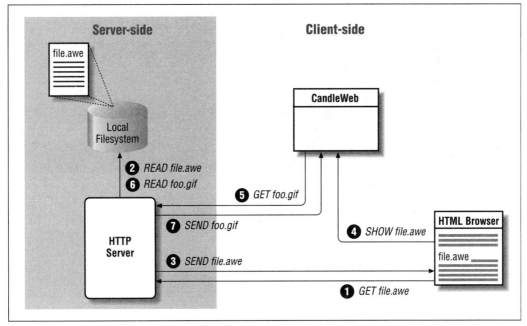

Figure 1:   Architecture of CandleWeb and Å (awe)

The Å Language

The following is just a short introduction to the Å language. A more detailed description is found in [7], and the language specification is found at [4].

"Å" is the last letter of the Norwegian alphabet. It is an A with a small ring placed right above it, and it is pronounced like the English word "awe. " This single letter was chosen for the language name in keeping with the "C" tradition.

Å was specified as a language in the Algol tradition [11], with a subset of the C programming language syntax [6] as the base, to avoid creating a whole new language. Many of the basic C language constructs are included in Å, with the notable exception of pointers and structures. These were left out mainly to simplify the demands put on the CandleWeb client which has the job of interpreting programs written in Å in a secure manner.

In addition to the traditional features of programming included in Å by means of the C language,

Å also includes so-called dynamic graphics objects. These are basically vector graphics objects like lines, boxes, and polygons, but may also be specialized objects like GIF or JPEG bitmaps, text objects, dynamic windows or input objects.

As an example, consider a line object. A line has start and end point coordinates, thickness, color and rendering. For all of these parameters, a fixed value may be specified, or the parameter may be given as the name of a variable, or as an expression involving a variable. In the latter cases, the object is said to be tied or bound to the variable, and the variable is said to influence the object. For all the graphics objects, any parameter may be tied to a variable. When the C code is interpreted, the interpreter keeps track of all objects with parameters bound to variables. Whenever a statement in the code changes a variable, all objects influenced by that variable are also changed. The interpreter executes the changes, and the programmer does not have to

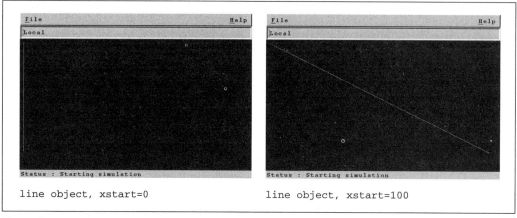

```
File                              Help      File                              Help
Local                                       Local

Status : Starting simulation                Status : Starting simulation
```

line object, xstart=0   line object, xstart=100

Figure 2:   Two line object examples

worry about them. Whenever the programmer wants the current changes to become visible on the screen, the statement "output;" is inserted in the code.

Line object examples are shown in Figure 2. In Figure 2a, the line is shown with variable xstart=0, and in Figure 2b, the same line is shown after variable xstart has changed to xstart=100.

```
Line object, xstart=0 Line object,
    xstart=100
Figure 2a        Figure 2b
```

More specialized objects like bitmaps in GIF or JPEG format may also have the same dynamic parameters. The image itself is fixed, but the coordinates may be bound to variables, thus making it possible to move the bitmaps around in the display window.

Two other types of objects deserve special mention. The first is the *window object.* These are not conventional windows with frames and backgrounds, in fact they are invisible to the user. The windows behave like normal windows in that they can contain other objects such as lines, boxes, bitmaps, and texts, and can perform a normal clipping function. However, as mentioned, the windows themselves are invisible, and serve mainly to group other objects. When the window coordinates are changed, the con-

tained objects are moved around on the screen; when a window's on/off variable is turned off, the entire contents of the window disappears. These features make windows very useful for producing animation in various forms.

As an example, consider a set of images, each of which is contained in its own window. Every window has its coordinate parameters bound to the same variables; thus moving them all requires a change to the two variables for x- and y-coordinates. By turning the windows on and off, one may easily switch between the various images to produce cell-based animation.

The second object that must be mentioned is the *input object.* Practically all user input is handled uniformly through the input objects. The input objects may also be bound to variables, but in this case, the tables are turned. Instead of the variables changing the graphics, the input objects change the variables. The objects themselves are invisible, and are made of virtual rectangles of the screen that react to mouse clicks, keyboard input, or a combination of the two. Whenever some input object is activated, the object's action may directly influence one or more variables. As with graphics output, it is practical to control the exact point in time at which input is allowed to change variables via "input;" statement.

When input objects are used to change variables that influence graphics objects, the user may do so without any code other than the "input;" and "output;" statements.

The CandleWeb Client

As illustrated in Figure 1, the CandleWeb client receives a file with extension *.awe* from the Web browser and interprets this file in its own window on the screen. The *.awe* file may contain references to GIFs, JPEGs or other *.awe* files, and the CandleWeb client will fetch these using HTTP whenever necessary.

Since the Web browser doesn't tell the CandleWeb client the source of the *.awe* file, that file must contain a reference to its place of origin so the CandleWeb client can find any other files that have local references. This referencing is done using a function in the Å subroutine library called setAnchor().

The fact that the Web browser did not include a way for the CandleWeb application to find the source of the *.awe* file is regarded as a deficiency in the current Web application protocols; hopefully, this will be remedied in the future.

As the CandleWeb client is a standalone application started from the Web browser, it is not much influenced by which Web browser is used. Similarly, it isn't influenced by developments in HTML, since it does not use HTML.

When unknown application programs are downloaded, using HTTP, from anywhere in the world, and are to be interpreted on one's own host computer, strict security measures should be taken by the interpreter. One must trust that the interpreter will not allow any malicious program to make changes to the file system. The CandleWeb application does currently not allow any file writes at all. Additionally, there are no functions for exporting information from the host computer; however, functions for importing information using HTTP exist.

The Å (awe) Composer Tool

The direct link between variables and graphics objects in the Å language is a very simple, yet very powerful construct which greatly reduces the amount of program code necessary to produce graphics applications. Typically, applications stay below a few hundred lines of code, and on the average only about a third of the code is program code, while the remaining two thirds consist of declarations of graphic objects.

When the predecessor to CandleWeb and Å, the Candle 1.0 system, was developed for MS-DOS in 1988-90, many recognized quite early that implementation efficiency could be increased considerably by implementing drawing tools for direct manipulation of graphics and automatic generation of the graphic objects code. Therefore, an authoring tool called Chandler was implemented. The authoring tool went through two generations of relatively different implementations and both implementations were used in several projects of developing educational software for apprentices in heavy industry in Norway [1].

One of the many observations noted was that implementing graphics-oriented educational software was three to five times more efficient with the authoring tool as opposed to specifying the graphics by text input. This is hardly unexpected, and quite well established in industries that rely heavily on educational software. Authoring tools like TenCore, AuthorWare, Director, and many others allow programmers, and to some extent nonprogrammers, to produce educational software far more efficiently than with general programming languages.

As a result of the success of the Chandler authoring tool, an Å Composer for X11 is currently being implemented as well. This tool allows direct graphic drawing and manipulation of the graphic objects, the window objects and the input objects in the Å language. The tool also provides specific support for accessing and manipulating the special relationship between variables in the program code and the graphic objects. The Å Composer tool is further described in the paper [10].

A Simple Example

For a simple example of what Å code looks like, the short file *logoflash.awe* is listed below. Note how relatively simple this program is. If possible, compare its simplicity to the magnetic effect it can have on a user at an X11 workstation using CandleWeb. The file can be found at *http://www.oslonett.no/~candle/demos/logoflash.awe* a-long with several other demonstration programs.

Example 1:   logoflash.awe

```
int main ()
{ // Simple program demonstrating the power of CandleWeb and    (awe)

// Variable declaration
int x, y;

// Background color
box points = ((0, 0), (800, 600)), fill = 1, color = 0x4444FF;

// Window containing image
window points = ((x,y), (x+130,y+150)), sb=0;
image points=((0, 0), (0, 0)), sb = 0, image = "candle.gif";
endwindow;

// Header text
textobj points=((20, 30)),
outtext="Computers and Learning AS' logo shown at randomly chosen points.",
color=0xFFFFFF, level = 1;

// Setting window size to 800 pixels horizontal and 600 vertical
resizeWindow (800, 600);

// Setting anchor location so the CandleWeb client will find image file
setAnchor("http://www.ifi.uio.no/~candlweb/demos/logoflash.awe");

while (1) {

// Draw random point
x = random( 4 , 660 );
y = random( 50 , 460 );

// Draw screen
output;

// Loop delay
wait( 50 );
}
}
```

Why CandleWeb and Å?

A basic assumption of this paper is that support for real-time interactivity and animation is needed in the Web, and that it will be used a lot when made available. The big question concerns how these capabilities will be provided. This paper presents a full-fledged proposal, including implementations.

The next question, then, is the following: Is this proposal good enough to become a standard in any way? Or phrased differently: Will it be used?

We cannot answer this question now, but we can present some of the reasons for the choices made in designing CandleWeb and Å.

Standards

Even though CandleWeb and Å seem to represent some fairly new and unusual thinking relative to the Web, designers stuck to defacto standards, changing as little as possible with something known to work well.

The Å language itself is such an example. It is based on the C programming language, borrowing most of its constructs from C. For a more detailed introduction to Å see [7] and [4]. The reason for choosing C is that it is one of the best known programming languages today, and a very efficient and uncluttered one. Because the object of designing Å was not to produce a new programming language, but rather to specify a language for a specific purpose, designers used a subset of a well known language and enhanced this subset with the necessary extensions. An added bonus is that a great number of programmers are already familiar with most of the new language, and need only learn which parts of C are not supported and what the extensions are.

The CandleWeb communications architecture is quite simple, and basically uses HTTP. In addition, Å code may include links to other Å files through function calls to links.

Since HTML is basically a markup language, and is not a pixel-oriented graphics language, designers decided that if HTML was to remain reasonably small and uncluttered, they should design a separate and fully graphics-oriented environment rather than extend HTML in a direction that would contradict some of its original intensions. The authors' opinion is that part of HTML's power will be lost if one tries to make it all things to all people. Therefore the CandleWeb/Å graphics environment is a pixel-oriented drawing canvas in a CandleWeb window, separate from the user's HTML browser. An added bonus from this choice is that CandleWeb does not have to compete with HTML browsers, and vice versa.

Interpretation and Security

Since Å is an interpreted language, it is a hardware- and OS-independent programming environment. This feature is very advantageous for producers of educational software. The demand for such software is much greater than what can be produced in a few years: the fact that much of what is produced quickly becomes technically obsolete because of changing hardware poses a problem. An interpreted language can survive several generations of hardware and many versions of the language itself. Currently a few system dependencies exist, noticeably regarding fonts, but the goal is maximum system independence.

Interpretation does present security problems. When code is downloaded and run on a local host, the hosts security relies to a great extent on the interpreter. The Å language has been kept very simple in order to make it easier to keep the interpreter safe. The omission of pointers and structures is one example; not allowing local file access is another.

Speed

Vector graphics can be extremely compact in terms of code needed to produce quite complex pictures. The graphics objects in the Å language are based on a combination of vector graphics and bitmaps. This combination increases the speed of following *.awe* links in two ways:

1. The code to be downloaded is very compact

2. The downloaded code utilizes hardware that is often optimized for vector graphics operations, such as line drawing, polygon fills, and the like.

Authoring

CandleWeb and Å are designed to take advantage of the Å Composer tool, which in turn is the result of several years of work in the field of graphics-oriented software authoring. It is time for Web designers to start using more of the results from related disciplines such as Human Computer Interaction and Computer Assisted Learning. Some of these results are quite general and need not be reinvented or rediscovered.

Current State and Future Plans

The CandleWeb client for X11, V1.0Beta has been released. A complete V1.0 will be released when the feedback on the beta release justifies it.

Å Composer for X11 is currently being implemented.

A CandleWeb client for Windows is planned for implementation and the work will be starting early in August 1995.

Å Composer for Windows is planned for implementation starting in 1995.

Both the CandleWeb client for X11 and the Å language specification have been released for public, academic, private, and commercial use (the latter only in unmodified form) at no charge. For details, see the license at *http://www.oslonett.no/~candle/license.html*.

Source code for CandleWeb client for X11 is available at no charge for academic use (research and education).

Conclusion

We have presented a new tool called CandleWeb that extends the capabilities of the World Wide Web on the Internet to include real-time interactivity and full-screen graphics animation. The tool works with standard HTML browsers, and uses HTTP. The tool has been implemented for X11, and is the successor of a similar tool, Candle, that has been used very successfully for several years implementing animations for MS-DOS-based hardware.

The tool also includes an interpreted language called Å, which combines a simple C-like syntax with standardized graphics objects to provide a programming environment in which presentations including animation can be produced efficiently.

Finally, the tool includes an authoring tool called Å Composer that allows programmers to save considerable time in implementing animated presentations, compared to text-based programming, using graphics libraries.

The CandleWeb client for X11 V1.0beta and the Å language are openly available on the Internet at *http://www.oslonett.no/~candle/* .

Acknowledgments

Kjell Øystein Arisland, Yngvar Berg and Arne Kinnebergbråten specified the original Candle architecture and language and implemented MS-DOS-based clients. Knut Tvedten implemented most of the Candle composer-tool called Chandler for MS-DOS.

The Federation of Norwegian Process and Manufacturing Industries funded several of the early development projects involving pedagogical software from which the Candle architecture and language got its start. The following people deserve special mention for their support: Bjørn Lassen, Svein Hyggen, Morten Allum, and Per Nørbech.

Svein Johansen and Gunnar Rønning have specified the Å language as a successor to the Candle

1.0 Language, and have implemented the current CandleWeb client V1.0beta for X11.

Tore Engvig, Bjørn Thirud, and Kent Vilhelmsen are currently implementing the Å Composer for X11. ∎

References

1. Arisland, K.Ø., "The Good, the Bad, and the Unusual in Computer Assisted Learning," Proceedings MULTICOMM'94, Vancouver, Nov 2-3, 1994.

2. Berners-Lee, T., *http://www.w3.org/hypertext/ WWW/Protocols/HTTP/HTTP2.html*

3. Faison, E.W.J., Advertising: A Behavioral Approach for Managers. John Wiley & Sons, 1980.

4. Johansen, S., and G. Rønning, "Å (awe) specification.", Web document at *http://www.ifi.uio.no/ ~candleweb/spec/spec.html*, 1995.

5. Hutchings, G.A., W. Hall, J. Briggs, N.V. Hammond, M.R. Kibby, C. McKnight, D. Riley, Authoring and Evaluation of Hypermedia for Education. Computers Educ. Vol 18, No. 1-3, 1992, 171-177.

6. Kernighan, B.W., and D.M. Ritchie, "The C Programming Language," Prentice-Hall, Inc, 1978.

7. Rønning, G., S. Johansen, and K.Ø. Arisland, "Å (awe), an interpreted animation language for the Web," Paper in preparation, 1995.

8. Rubincam, I., "A Taxonomy of Topics in Computer Applications to Education Based Upon Frequently Cited Books, Articles and Reports." Journal of Research on Computing in Education, 1987 - Winter, 165-187.

9. *http://java.sun.com*

10. Vilhelmsen, K., B. Thirud, T. Engvig, and K.Ø. Arisland, "Å (awe) Composer, graphics authoring for the animated Web," Paper in preparation, 1995.

11. Naur P., "Revised Report on the Algorithmic Language ALGOL 60.," Comm. ACM 6, 1963.

About the Authors

Kjell Øystein Arisland
Department of Informatics, University of Oslo
Norway
kjell@ifi.uio.no

Svein Johansen
Department of Informatics, University of Oslo
Norway
sveinj@ifi.uio.no

Gunnar Rønning
Department of informatics, University of Oslo
Norway
gunnarr@ifi.uio.no

LOCAL CONTROL OVER FILTERED WWW ACCESS

Brenda S. Baker, Eric Grosse

Abstract

This paper describes a software system called Signet that provides local control over restricting access to resources on the World Wide Web (WWW). The strategy is to make it easy for a parent or teacher to rate WWW resources and place the tables of ratings into a proxy server designed to restrict Internet access according to the access permissions of the users. Ratings can be made dynamically as the rater browses, so that the rater can insert new ratings into the ratings database at any time. Ratings can also be shared by different raters or organizations so that rating of WWW materials can proceed in a distributed fashion. **Keywords:** *World Wide Web, proxy, firewall, ratings, censorship, Exon amendment*

Introduction

Senator J. James Exon proposed an amendment to the United States Telecommunications Competition and Deregulation Act of 1995 that would make it unlawful to transmit indecent material over the Internet. This amendment was approved by the Senate with an overwhelming majority in June, 1995. Subsequently, the House of Representatives approved a bill calling for an evaluation of technical means of restricting distribution of unwanted material. As of October, 1995, these bills have been referred to a conference committee. Other countries are also considering the issue [1,8].

Many computer scientists have been opposed to the amendment on the grounds of freedom of speech, the projected adverse effects on the Internet if all resources and email must be censored, and the impossibility of restricting access to foreign sites containing prohibited material.

However, the political issue would be defused if Internet access to inappropriate materials could be restricted for children through technical means. This paper describes a flexible, dynamic method that could serve the needs of schools and parents without depriving adults of free speech rights and without imposing a uniform national standard.

The ability to limit Internet access could also be useful for reasons other than to protect children from pornography. A teacher may want to limit students to viewing resources in the day's lesson plan; otherwise, as described by a middle-school computer laboratory teacher [16], a teacher facing the backs of a room full of monitors cannot tell whether students have left the lesson content to browse among more entertaining topics. Some managers are concerned that employees are squandering work time on "surfing the Net" [6]; they might like to restrict employees to access only work-related resources. In these instances, it may be desirable to change access permissions dynamically, e.g., for the current class hour or for lunch-break browsing.

Some people express the opinion that it is unlikely that a person will come across inappropriate material accidentally. However, the authors know of incidents where adults or children have unexpectedly encountered "adult" images or subject matter without being able to predict from the preceding page what the link would lead to. In addition, what is inappropriate depends on the viewer; for example, two mature women have asked the authors for protection from encountering "adult" material.

Internet access can be direct or through a proxy server and a firewall. In the latter case, a client

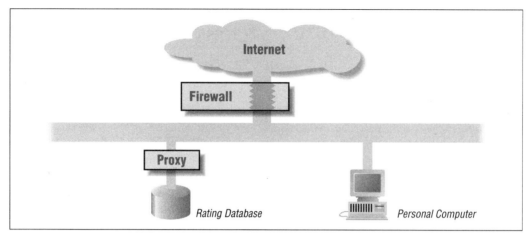

Figure 1:   The Signet model

sends requests for remote resources to a WWW proxy server which forwards them through a fire-wall to the remote server and forwards the responses from the remote server back to the client. The proxy server is a focal point at which access permissions can be checked for remote resources. If the firewall is configured to forward requests only from the proxy servers, client machines cannot bypass the permission checking, no matter what software is surreptitiously loaded onto them. Ordinary routers can act as such a firewall. The situation is illustrated in Figure 1.

This paper describes a system called Signet that operates in this manner to provide restricted access to the WWW under local dynamic control. Signet consists of a modified HTTP proxy server and a ratings server. The ratings server maintains a ratings database. The Signet proxy server has two modes, rating mode (which is also an unre-stricted browsing mode) and restricted browsing mode. By communicating with the rating daemon through HTTP, authorized people rate pages, directories, or sites while browsing and place access permissions dynamically into a database of permissions used by the proxy server. In restricted browsing mode, every attempt to access a remote resource causes the proxy server

to check access permissions. Consequently, a student cannot follow a link from an approved page to an unapproved page.

The focus of Signet is on allowing students access to approved sites while denying them access to unapproved or unrated sites. This approach can be viewed as a Seal of Approval (SOAP) approach. The name Signet was chosen because a signet is a seal used to mark approval on a document.

Signet could be used immediately by teachers planning class lessons using WWW resources or by parents who find particular resources they would like their children to access. As more ratings are created, sharing of ratings created by trusted individuals or organizations will make wider browsing feasible under restricted mode.

There are many thousands of pages on the WWW, and more are created daily. Consequently, no organization will be able to stay completely up-to-date in rating everything on the WWW. Using our system, parents and teachers can supplement ratings by organizations with their own.

An Internet service provider running Signet would provide an authentication mechanism for accessing rating mode and could make available ratings by individuals or organizations. However, decisions about inclusions of ratings and access permissions would be up to the authorized parent or teacher and would not be the responsibility of the Internet service provider.

Approaches Suggested Previously

Some schools ask students to abide by policy statements by which they agree to restrict their exploration of the WWW, such as by agreeing not to download obscene material. An example of such a policy is the California Department of Education Electronic Information Resources Acceptable Use Policy District Guidelines [2]. However, students trying to comply with such a policy are not protected from accidental downloading of resources that are not readily identifiable as inappropriate prior to downloading.

Quality Computers [12] offers to schools a service called LINQ that selects resources appropriate for school children and downloads them to schools. In addition, LINQ offers direct Internet access using a browser provided with a menu of links to resources whose links are believed not to lead indirectly to inappropriate material; the browser does not permit requesting an arbitrary URL. However, this does not permit inclusion of certain resources that are themselves suitable for kids, such as a very popular and well-designed kids' page from which six clicks led to very adult images as of March 30, 1995.

One approach has been software that runs on the client machine and blocks access to a list of sites considered inappropriate for children. SurfWatch [19], Microsystems Software's CyberPatrol [9], and Solid Oak Software's CYBERsitter [17] have taken this approach. These companies offer updates to their lists either monthly or on request. Unfortunately, sites undetected by these companies or new since the last update can still be accessed. New*View's NetGuardian [11] promises to offer a choice of blocking of explicitly forbidden resources and blocking of all resources not

explicitly approved; it requires software both on the client machine and at a central site. SurfWatch also blocks access to resources that contain certain words likely to be associated with inappropriate content. Net Nanny [20] and CYBERsitter [17] use a similar approach for monitoring chat groups and email. However, word filtering alone will not detect obscene pictures.

Some people have called for voluntary self-rating of sites by their creators. One such proposal [10] describes an encoding called KidCode that would encode in the URL whether material was appropriate for children. For example, *http://www.sizzle.com/KidCode.21.violence/*, would indicate that the directory contained material suitable only for people age 21 and over because of violence. However, there would be no guarantee that everyone would rate pages, have the same standard, or even be honest in the ratings.

Finally, standards committees are considering setting standards for protocols that would allow communication of content ratings, so that software could request a rating for a URL from a ratings organization and then filter access based on the rating. On September 11, 1995, the World Wide Web Consortium announced the development of a Platform for Internet Content Selection (PICS) [21]. The Internet Engineering Task Force (IETF) is exploring formation of a workgroup for Voluntary Access Control. An earlier group, the Information Highway Parental Empowerment Group (IHPEG) [7], formed by Microsoft, Netscape, and Progressive Networks, has merged with the PICS effort.

Services that provide ratings of content will be useful. However, no one rating scale will be satisfactory to everybody. It is well-known that different communities have different standards; what is acceptable in Berkeley, California, may not be acceptable in Little Rock, Arkansas. Furthermore, different groups will disagree on what content children should see. For example, some librarians have objected to SurfWatch's blocking access to gay and lesbian materials [4]. Finally, if a new resource is created, there may be a delay before an organization rates it and distributes the rating.

Therefore, it seems valuable to allow for flexible and dynamic rating schemes under local control. Our method can be used independently or can be used to supplement the ratings provided by other organizations. A parent or teacher hearing of a new resource can place a rating in the database immediately without waiting for an organization to get around to rating it.

(Brands or product names may be the trademarks, registered trademarks, or servicemarks of their respective holders.)

Description of Our Method

The key elements of Signet are the following:

- Access is controlled by a proxy server that enforces limits per machine or user, with a firewall to prevent bypass.

- Ratings are made using unmodified Web browsers, small modifications to a standard proxy server, and a rating daemon that maintains the ratings database.

- No cooperation from WWW servers is required.

- Any authorized person can rate materials and set access permissions in the proxy server, and raters can share rating lists.

- Permissions can be a combination of allowed and disallowed URLs and wild cards. Signet addresses the parts of the Internet that can be addressed via a URL, such as HTTP, WAIS, FTP, Gopher, and Usenet news. It does not address email or chat groups.

For concreteness, imagine a school full of PCs running Web browsers and an Internet connection with firewall and proxy server. (The latter could be in the school or part of the network service offering.) There are two classes of users in our system: users who are authorized to control

rating tables and those who are not. For convenience, we refer to the former as teachers and the latter as students.

Ratings

We assume a rating scale that would have levels in the same way that the movie industry uses G, PG, PG-13, and NC17. For the purposes of discussion, we will use a scale with three levels: "anyone," "13 and up," and "18 and up." There is also an orthogonal grouping into categories. A category could represent a subject such as history or even a day's lesson plan for a teacher. The rating scale applies within each category, so that each rating is a category-scale pair. In addition, the rater of each rating is recorded.

Ratings can be given either for individual URLs (Uniform Resource Locators) or for expressions consisting of a URL followed by a wild card * that matches any string. Thus, a rating can specify that every resource contained (recursively) within a particular directory is rated with the same category-scale pair.

A resource may match the expression for more than one rating in the same category. In this case, the most specific rating applies. Thus, a subdirectory rating or URL rating takes precedence over a directory rating. For example, it is possible to specify that a whole directory is rated as "13 and up" except for a particular subdirectory rated as "anyone." Obviously, use of wildcards requires some judgment as to when it is appropriate.

Resources on the WWW can be changed at any time. We store the MD5 checksum [14] and the "Last-Modified" date with the rating for a file and allow access permissions to specify that the student proxy server should refuse access if the checksum has changed; the proxy could also notify the rater that the page should be rechecked. Obviously, checksums can be used only for individual URLs and not for directory or site ratings. For sites that are trusted not to lie about dates but not trusted to restrict material, the proxy might save the cost of recomputing checksums by only checking for a changed date. Some resources such as WebWeather [5] change frequently, and for these, the rater will have to rely on judgment about the consistency and trustworthiness of the site rather than on checksums.

Use of directory or site ratings is risky in that it is not generally possible to obtain a list of all URLs within a directory or site and in any case, resources can be modified or added. However, a rater may choose, for example, to trust a government agency directory with the name K12 that appears to contain resources for children. Note that approving a directory or site does not imply approval of links leading to other directories or sites, respectively, so that if the rated site or directory is itself trustworthy, the "six clicks to pornography" example described above for the LINQ approach [12] is avoided.

Rating sites, directories, and pages separately can lessen the impact of Web page changes on permissions in a way that a single rating per URL cannot handle. For example, a rater can rate individual pages as "anyone/unchanged-checksum," but also rate all resources at the site as "13 and up." In this case, access to a changed resource at that site could be allowed to older children with permissions including "13 and up," but denied to young children authorized only to access "anyone" pages. If this approach is used by raters, teenagers could browse widely even among changing pages, while young children would be more restricted.

Access permissions for restricted browsing mode are specified as a list of category-scale-rater triples. For example, if Mr. Smith's ratings are trusted by a fellow history teacher Mrs. Jones, Mrs. Jones could specify

History/13 and up/Jones
History/13 and up/Smith

to set access permissions for a history class. This would result in allowing access to resources whose most specific rating is "13 and up" or "anyone" but not to resources that are unrated or whose most specific rating is "18 and up." Wild cards can be used as well, so that */13 and up/* would specify any materials rated as "13 and up" by any rater.

Rating Mode

In rating mode, the user can browse the WWW without restriction. When the user wants to rate a resource, the user requests a rating page.

Our method of requesting a rating page is to append a '!' to the current URL and submit this request to the proxy server. (The '!' should go before #anchors, if present, to avoid being truncated by the browser.) In rating mode, the proxy server detects the '!', and immediately returns the rating page, illustrated in Figure 2. This includes the current rating or ratings, possibly comments about why the rating was given (e.g., "includes sexual material"), and a form that allows submission of a new rating to the rating daemon. The form includes buttons for specifying the category-scale pair and for applying the rating to anything in a directory (including files and subdirectories) or to anything at the site. (We plan to extend the form to allow for creation of new categories as well.) This method of requesting rating pages fits within the current HTTP protocol without requiring that a special browser be used.

An HTML page may contain inline images that would not normally be viewed separately. The rating for an HTML page is also assigned to URLs for inline images on the page, so that they do not need to be rated separately. In case of conflict between ratings derived from separate pages, the least restrictive rating applies, on the assumption that whatever caused the more restrictive rating was somewhere else on the page.

Restricted Mode

The basic sequence in student mode is the following. The browser sends a request to the proxy, the proxy looks it up in the configuration tables for access permission, and if access is permitted, the proxy requests the resource from the remote server and forwards the response to the client browser. This mechanism is sufficient to

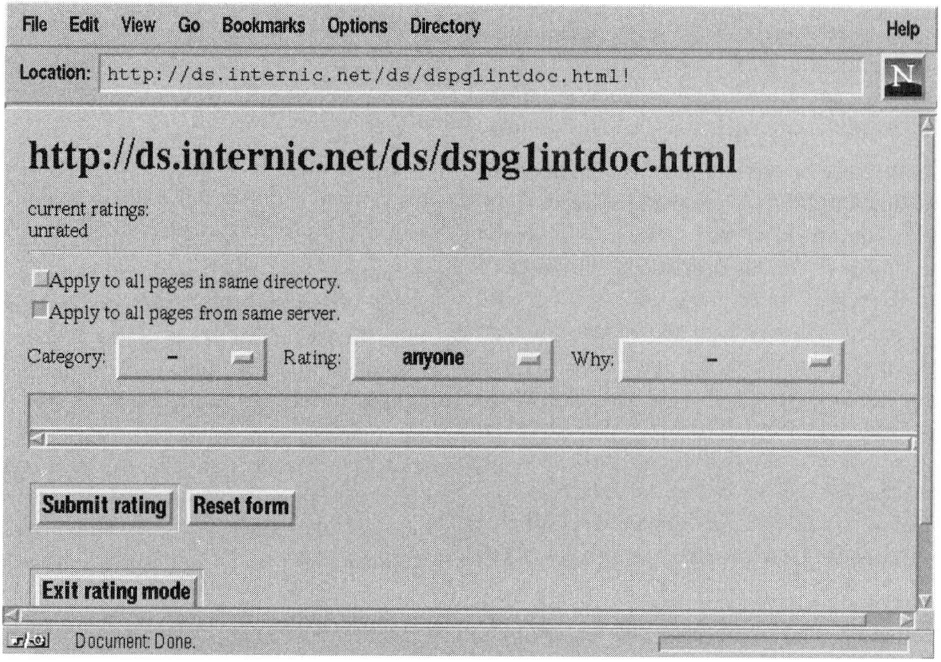

Figure 2:   A rating page

handle requests for many resources. A typical request would be for an HTML page, possibly with inline images, or perhaps a PostScript or image file.

There are several common situations in which a request for a URL may be met by a response containing or referring to a resource with a different URL. One is when the user clicks on an image map, and the resulting GET is for a URL containing a '?' and a query string encoding the mouse click position. A second is submission of a form. A third is a directory name request, which may be redirected to another URL. A fourth is the "random link" or other cgi-bin command.

Under our rating procedures, a resource is normally rated after being received by the browser so that the response URL is known at rating time and placed in the ratings database. Unfortunately, in restricted browsing mode, the response URL is not known to the proxy at request time for comparing with the access permissions.

However, all is not lost. The proxy's action depends on the response code.

Often the remote server returns a redirection status code 301 or 302 with another URL, and the browser is expected to send a separate request for the new URL. In this case, the proxy forwards the response to the client because the new URL will be checked in a separate request.

If the remote server returns the resource itself along with a new URL, the proxy can check the URL for access permission. The HTTP standard makes no guarantees that the URL is correct; however, if false URLs should be a problem, correctness could be verified by comparing the resource checksum with the URL checksum stored in the ratings database. Alternatively, a redirection could be sent to the client.

The checksum of a resource can also be useful as an index into the ratings database. One such situation is when a response URL is ephemeral even though the resource itself exists over an extended period of time, as when the server encodes "session identification" in a URL such as *http://www.pathfinder.com/@@7XmEsaFcpw IAQEU8/time/magazine/magazine.html*. A second such situation is when (under HTTP/0.9) a remote server returns a resource without a new URL.

With an HTML form, submission causes the browser to send a POST or GET that includes a query string with information typed into the form. Forms are difficult to deal with because both the POST sent on submission and the URL (if any) sent on response may be too varied to be stored in the database and checksums are also so varied as to be useless. The most reasonable way to handle forms may be the use of wild cards in ratings and permissions.

These problems illustrate a fundamental naming inconsistency in the WWW: a resource can have more than one name, the name relationship is not necessarily known to the proxy, and names can change over time. The proxy server handles some instances of multiple names by canonicalizing the URL through simplification. Mirror sites must currently be handled explicitly in the ratings. In the future, naming problems may be reduced by the use of Uniform Resource Names (URNs) [18].

Security

Security is a fundamental problem when trying to impose restrictions on a previously free environment. We assume that the proxy server resides on a machine other than the client browser and that this machine is inaccessible to the students being restricted.

For our prototype, we use IP addresses to control security. All IP addresses are in restricted mode except when specifically authorized to be in rating mode. A teacher desiring unrestricted access to the Internet for browsing or rating pages requests an authorization form. If desired, authentication could use a challenge-response password scheme to avoid sending the password in the clear across a network. An authorization program then places the IP address of the teacher in a file of rating-mode IP addresses on the proxy machine. When the teacher signals the end of the session, the IP address is removed from the rating-mode IP address file.

Note that rating must never be enabled on the proxy machine, since access by a student through the proxy would have the rating IP address and be inadvertently authorized.

In order to get unrestricted privileges, a student hacker would have to forge the IP address of a machine currently in use by a teacher for ratings. The duplication of IP addresses would be likely to be detected quickly, unless the teacher's machine was turned off. Leaving authenticated machines unattended and accessible to students should obviously be forbidden. To discourage such unsafe practices, in our implementation submission of a new rating does not immediately place it in the data base; it is held temporarily until the teacher does a "commit" and simultaneously exits rating mode.

Proxy caching proceeds as usual for nonrating requests in both rating and restricted modes. Rating pages are not cached but are constructed on the fly. Some browsers do local caching, however, and local caching of inappropriate materials during rating sessions could make them accessible to students if students have access to the machine later. The rater should in this case turn off local caching. If this degrades browsing performance unacceptably, the rating-mode proxy can be modified to place an immediate expiration date in the header, so that the local browser should not cache.

Access permissions for students may change from hour to hour if the teacher chooses to restrict students to accessing the lesson plan for the current class in a shared laboratory. There is no protection against students having the browser save material to a file for later viewing when the permissions have changed. But at least this material will be material that has been approved by some teacher for student use.

Implementation

We have implemented the prototype by modifying the publicly available source of the CERN httpd proxy server [3]. We have modified the source to allow for both a rating mode and a restricted mode as described above. Modifications involved touching about seven places in five files and adding about 600 lines of C and included checking authorization for rating mode, generating rating pages, and checking response codes. A separate HTTP server called the rating daemon, about 1200 lines of C, is invoked via HTML forms for rater authentication and ratings database transactions.

The original CERN server is a good base on which to implement restricted mode because its configuration file can specify rules including wild cards to determine which resources should be passed or failed. The CERN server applies the first rule it finds. Since our permission specification requires that more specific rules take priority over less specific rules, we generate the configuration rules in lexicographic order so that more specific rules precede less specific rules. The main change to the code to implement restricted mode was to allow for delaying authorization until a response code is received, as described above. However, further modifications will have to be made to implement checksums and to improve efficiency for large ratings databases.

Planned Extensions

We plan to extend our initial prototype implementation to improve efficiency as the number of ratings gets large. In addition, we plan auxiliary programs to facilitate the rating process.

Efficiency

Efficiency has not been of concern as yet with the prototype because it has been used only experimentally. For the moment, we use linear search on the ratings database and on access permissions. As demands on the server grow, we plan to hash individual URLs and use a trie data structure for the rating expressions with wild cards.

Eventually, garbage collection may be useful to shrink the ratings database by eliminating "dead" or redundant ratings.

Facilitating the Rating Process

Just as people can get "lost" while browsing on the WWW because it is hard to keep track in your head of where you are in a large graph, people will have trouble keeping track of what pages they have rated, when they feel it is necessary to rate each page separately. Our plan is to provide a rating-progress tool for the rater.

The simplest form of rating-progress display would show a list of the links in the HTML resource, with color-coded marks or icons to show which ones have already been rated. It would be straightforward to implement this within the proxy by parsing the HTML and looking up the URLs in the database. More generally, it would be desirable to show rating progress for pages reached indirectly through multiple links from a given page. To restrict the search space, the tool could show rating progress as a breadth-first search of bounded depth or could show rating progress for links remaining within the same directory or site.

A tool that extracts information from bookmark files and annotation databases [13] to guide the rating process would also be valuable. Such rating-progress and annotation tools might run as servers, in keeping with the strategy of letting raters use their favorite unmodified browser, or in the browser if a market niche opens for specialized rating browsers or applets.

Social Issues

A generic problem faced by all schemes based on filtering at the client machine is preventing bypass. This could involve merely running a different browser or, in the extreme case, booting a different operating system. Our proposal, using a proxy and firewall, is secure against such attack. However, one might be satisfied with administratively requiring that approved browsers be used and only monitoring firewall logs occasionally for violations.

The effectiveness of Signet will depend on the quality of the ratings versus the dynamic nature of the WWW. Restricting children to explicitly rated resources via checksums is safe but will prevent access to many resources that have changed but are still suitable for viewing by children. Conversely, use of directory or site ratings would speed up the ratings process and allow children access to changing pages, but will not protect against unexpected introduction of inappropriate content. Finally, creation of resources on request through cgi-bin commands makes it impossible for a rater to be sure what might appear at some later date.

Many companies, agencies, and organizations would undoubtedly be happy to cooperate in facilitating filtering of access for children by following conventions such as redirection responses to image map and cgi-bin requests when a fixed resource is returned, use of client-side image maps [15], and self-rating of pages and directories.

No technical system can be totally and eternally safe. Children may walk down the street to a home with a less restrictive browsing mode, servers may deliberately issue misleading ratings or masquerade as trusted server. Ultimately it is more satisfactory to raise children, or hire employees, who have the maturity not to abuse the resource. We think of Signet as playing the role of a sturdy guardrail at a scenic vista, not an eight-foot fence topped with barbed wire.

Conclusion

Our prototype proxy server provides a flexible, dynamic means of rating resources on the WWW and controlling access. We hope that the availability of such a method will satisfy Congress that it is possible for parents and teachers to control WWW access so that children will not encounter inappropriate material. Unlike existing proposals, our method places control of both standards and access in the hands of parents and teachers so that they can apply their own local standards. ■

References

1. Ang, Peng Hwa, "Censorship and the Internet: A Singapore Perspective," *Proceedings of INET '95*, *http://inet.nttam.com/HMP/PAPER/132/abst.html*, June 22, 1995.

2. California Department of Education, "Electronic Information Resources Acceptable Use Policy District Guidelines," *gopher://goldmine.cde.ca.gov:70/00/C_D_E_Info/Technology/Acceptable_Use/Policy*, December, 1994.

3. CERN, "CERN httpd," *http://www.w3.org/hypertext/WWW/Daemon/*, April, 1995.

4. Cisler, Steve, "Children on the Internet (Draft)," *ftp://ftp.apple.com/alug/rights/kids.internet*, Apple Computer Company, June 20, 1995.

5. Davenport, Ben, "WebWeather," *http://www.princeton.edu/Webweather/ww.html*, 1995.

6. Hayes, Mary, "Working Online, or Wasting Time?" *Information Week*, May 1, 1995, pp. 38-51.

7. Information Highway Parental Empowerment Group, "Leading Internet Software Companies Announce Plan to Enable Parents to 'Lock out' Access to Materials Inappropriate to Children," Netscape Press Releases, *http://home.netscape.com/newsref/pr/newsrelease29.html*, 1995.

8. Jackson, Colin, "Internet Policy in New Zealand," *Proceedings of INET '95*, *http://inet.nttam.com/HMP/PAPER/078/abst.html*, June 22, 1995.

9. Microsystems Software, "CyberPatrol," *http://www.microsys.com/cyber/default.htm*, August 18, 1995.

10. New, D., and N. Borenstein, "KidCode: Naming Conventions for Protecting Children on the World Wide Web and Elsewhere on the Internet Without Censorship," *ftp://ietf.cnri.reston.va.us/internet-drafts/draft-borenstein-kidcode-00.txt*, June 5, 1995.

11. New*View, Inc., "NetGuardian," *http://www.new-view.com/*, August 20, 1995.

12. Quality Computers, "The LINQ—Custom Internet Access for Education," 1995.

13. Röscheisen, M., C. Mogensen, and T. Winograd, "Beyond Browsing: Shared Comments, SOAPs, Trails, and On-line Communities," *Proceedings of the Third International World Wide Web Conference*, Darmstadt, Germany, April 1995, *http://www-pcd.stanford.edu/COMMENTOR/*.

14. Schneier, Bruce, *Applied Cryptography: Protocols, Algorithms, and Source Code in C*, New York, Wiley, 1994.

15. Seidman, James, "A Proposed Extension to HTML: Client-Side Image Maps," IETF Internet-Draft, *ftp://ietf.cnri.reston.va.us/internet-drafts/draft-ietf-html-clientsideimagemap-01.txt*, August 8, 1995.

16. Skarecki, Eileen, Columbia Middle School, Berkeley Heights, NJ, personal communication, June 19, 1995.

17. Solid Oak Software, "CYBERsitter," *http://www.solidoak.com/cybersit.htm*, 1995.

18. Sollins, K., and L. Masinter, "Functional Requirements for Uniform Resource Names," *Network Working Group*, Request for Comments: 1737, *http://ds.internic.net/rfc/rfc1737.txt*, December 1994.

19. SurfWatch Software, "SurfWatch," *http://www.surfwatch.com/*, 1995.

20. Trove Investment Corporation, "Net Nanny: the best way to protect your children and free speech on the Internet," *http://giant.mindlink.net/netnanny/home.html*, 1995.

21. World Wide Web Consortium, "W3C Content Selection: PICS," *http://www.w3.org/pub/WWW/PICS/*, September 11, 1995.

About the Authors

Brenda S. Baker
[*http://www.cs.att.com/csrc/baker.html*]
Eric Grosse
[*http://www.cs.att.com/csrc/grosse.html*]

AT & T Bell Laboratories
600 Mountain Avenue
Murray Hill, NJ 07974
bsb@research.att.com
ehg@research.att.com

MULTI-HEAD MULTI-TAIL MOSAIC

Brian C. Ladd, Michael V. Capps, P. David Stotts, Rick Furuta

Abstract

*The explosive growth of the World Wide Web is attributable, in large part, to the simplicity of the distributed graph model it uses for information storage and retrieval. The model is simple, general, and ubiquitous; the reader may choose almost any browsing path. Information providers, though, then use every trick at their disposal in an attempt to increase their power over how readers browse their pages. Two major shortcomings of current Web protocols are lack of support for concurrent browsing and synchronization of multiple browsing paths. This paper presents a computer-aided instruction scenario where the author (instructor) must overcome these weaknesses. In traditional hypermedia systems, a link relates a single source node to a single destination node. Projects such as Xanadu [3] and Trellis [6] previously generalized links to allow connection of multiple source nodes to multiple destination nodes. This generalization, which we term a **Multi-Head/Multi-Tail (MHMT)** link, allows an author to create concurrent browsing paths in a document, and to synchronize those concurrent paths if desired. This has applications to groupware as well as to documents browsed by single users. We describe our solution embodied in **MHTML** as a straightforward extension to HTML for defining multi-head/multi-tail links and an experimental browser called **MMM** that implements the extensions. **Keywords:** Automata, hypertext, hypermedia, World Wide Web, Petri nets*

Introduction

The explosive growth of the World Wide Web is attributable, in large part, to the simplicity of the distributed graph model it uses for information storage and retrieval. The model is simple, general, and ubiquitous; the reader may choose almost any browsing path. Information providers are using every trick at their disposal to control the presentation of their data on browsers around the world. Instructional material with linearly linked document structures enforces a given reading path; browsing-path encoding in URLs permits tracking of a reader's path; and documents written as a single page ensure that readers see information in a specified order.

These solutions are ad hoc and limited; what is missing is a unified method for authors to express the browsing semantics they want over the information they are presenting. Such control has proven useful in other hypertext information systems (such as Trellis [6]) in such fields as software engineering and computer-aided instruction.

The research presented here was prompted by two particular problems the current generation of Web protocols fails to handle: concurrent browsing streams and synchronization of browsing streams. Concurrent browsing streams are two or more paths of browsing, all of which are part of the same user's browsing session. Many current browsers permit the reader to follow a link in such a way that a new window is opened with the content at the end of the link; they do not, however, permit authors to include this behavior directly in their documents. Synchronization of multiple browsing streams is also important. Being able to advance only so far in one stream without advancing another or advancing multiple streams in lock step are examples of behaviors needing synchronization. Current Web browsers and protocols fail to address this (not surprising considering the lack of concurrent browsing ability).

Concurrency and synchronization allow authors to "program" the browsing path behaviors they want readers to follow, including:

- Multiple simultaneous pages

- Must-be-seen-before relationships

- Parallel browsing streams

The degenerate model of such multi-links is the standard single-in, single-out Web link type, which allows traditional unconstrained browsing semantics.

We have encapsulated this extended Web graph model in a novel browsing client, **Multi-head Multi-tail Mosaic (MMM)**. We have created **MHTML**, an extension of HTML with facilities for expressing multi-head/multi-tail links. The resulting graph semantics are equivalent in a formal context to those of a Parallel Finite Automaton (PFA) [5]. PFAs can be used in similar manner to Petri nets for specifying hyperdocument structure, as explored in the Trellis system [1, 7, 6]. Automata have been used to good effect in computer-aided instruction and other fields where control over the traversal of a graph is important. It is useful to note that neither the author nor the reader need be familiar with Petri nets to interface comfortably with MMM.

The remainder of this paper contains a CAI scenario which serves as the driving example, the design requirements for MMM, the language extensions for MHTML and the MMM browser, a comparison of HTML and MHTML solutions for our scenario, a look at our continuing and future research plans, and references.

Scenario

Authors of computer-aided instructional material have, traditionally, had great control over the order of presentation of their material. The power of hypermedia, though, is that readers can follow train-of-thought explorations in linked information structures. As CAI applications migrate to the Web, authors find HTML restricts

their ability to express orderings more complicated than a linear progression. Our methods allow authors to integrate some control of presentation order with this traditional browsing freedom. The generalizations of the link we have created allows a mixing of both capabilities.

As a concrete example, consider the following scenario: A pathology instructor is preparing a corpus of information to teach students how to read an autopsy report. For pedagogical reasons, the instructor has three goals: (1) Students should always be aware of the autopsy protocol (the summarizing cover sheet for the autopsy). (2) Students should refer to both the textual description and high-resolution photographs for most sections of the autopsy. (3) Due to the nature of the current case, students should not progress past the internal examination of the neck without having already seen the external evidence relating to the neck.

Looking at current Web protocols, there are two approaches to handling these goals: Adding information to the nodes (such as the autopsy protocol) so the node content is what the author wanted, or describing in the content of the nodes what the desired browsing behavior is and how to achieve it. For a more complete description of these approaches and comparison with the MHTML alternatives see the Comparison section.

Requirements

Current World Wide Web protocols use a general graph model consisting of nodes (pages) and links (embedded URLs) with all browsing semantics provided by the client browser. Links go from one page to one other page unless the reader uses a browser function to launch concurrent (unsynchronized) browsing streams. Note that it is possible, using a browser which can open new windows, for the reader to create the same browsing states as those specified with MMM; this would require the author describing the desired states to the reader (more discussion of this can be found in the Comparison section below).

Providing authors with explicit browsing controls with the power of parallel finite automata requires (at a minimum) the addition of multi-headed links and multi-tailed links. Multi-headed links are links pointing at multiple nodes all of which are opened (in separate browsing windows) when the link is followed; multi-tailed links are links which are only active when the browser has all the input nodes open and which close all the input nodes when followed.

The MMM project's original goal was to test the usefulness of PFA semantics in the World Wide Web setting. As such, rather than spending our time building a complex client-server infrastructure, we chose to build a working prototype as soon as possible. To ensure an appropriate sample population, it was necessary to make that prototype acceptable to current Web users.

From a high level the Web architecture is very simple: a reader's browser requests a page of HTML marked-up text from the author's Web server and then renders it for the reader. Early on we recognized that in order for authors to be able to define the reader's browsing semantics at the time they compose the hypertext, it was necessary to modify either the author's server or the markup language they write in; it was also likely that some modifications would be necessary to browsers to handle more complex browsing patterns.

The decision to extend HTML rather than modify server code was made for three reasons: to keep control of browsing semantics as close as possible to the author; it was easier to code; and to encourage wider acceptance of our changes. Since one of the goals of this work is to allow authors to define the browsing semantics they want their documents to have, it seemed right to keep control of those semantics in the author's document rather than in some server configuration file. Since we recognized that browser modifications would be necessary in any case, it was easier to limit our code changes to only one side of the client-server transaction if we could. Finally, modifying server code would mean that one version of one platform's server would be able to handle multi-head, multi-tail links. Unless we were willing to extend a large number of servers on a variety of platforms (and could somehow convince the world to switch to our new and improved servers), our changes would never be widespread. Another obstacle to widespread acceptance with server-side modifications would be the increased use of server resources to support multi-head, multi-tail links.

Mechanisms that fail to work across the range of browsers greatly limit the potential audience for Web pages that require those mechanisms. Fortunately for the designers of variant HTML syntaxes, the behavior of Web browsers is to silently ignore markup elements that are not understood. Thus the author who uses the Netscape <BLINK> environment can be assured that everyone will see the content of the passage, although its rendition may be static. It is worth emphasizing that the difference between a Web browser that shows blinking text and one that does not is presentational; the content shown is the same in both cases.

In adding semantics to the Web, we faced the similar problem of retaining accessibility to sites that did not choose to use the modified browsers supporting that semantics. As we considered the semantics of multi-headed, multi-tailed links, we realized that a sensible alternate semantics to concurrent and synchronized link access would be to permit sequential access to the links. We encode the new link specification as a new environment type (MHMT), place the parameters needed for presentation of the new environment into its beginning marker, and retain the normal markup specification for anchors (A). Thus a modified browser recognizes the added environment and understands the new semantics to be associated with its display. An unmodified browser ignores the environmental specifications and treats its contents as standard links.

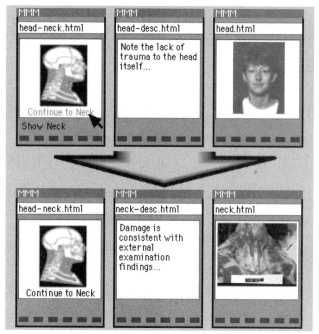

Figure 1: Following the "Continue to Neck" multi-link

MHTML: Extensions to HTML

Two considerations guided our extensions of HTML: Ease of use for authors and logic of presentation for unmodified browsers. Using existing constructs as much as possible forwarded both goals. The tendency of browsers to ignore unrecognized tags permitted us to accomplish the second goal fairly easily.

Example

A multi-headed/multi-tailed link is enclosed between a <MHMT> and </MHMT> pair of tags. Between these tags text, anchors, and our incoming reference (<IREF>) tag are all treated specially by our modified browser. An example link from the autopsy training scenario follows:

```
<MHMT text="Continue to Neck" display_
    text="Show Neck">
<A HREF="head-neck.html">X-Rays</A>,
<A HREF="neck.html">Neck Photos</A> and
<A HREF="neck-desc.html">Neck
    Description</A>.
```

```
<IREF HREF="http://www.cs.unc.edu/
    ~capps/mmm/head.html">
<IREF HREF="http://www.cs.unc.edu/
    ~capps/mmm/head-desc.html">
</MHMT>
```

This example has three incoming and three outgoing links. Incoming links are defined by the <IREF> tag, but remember that the file containing this MHMT definition is itself the head of one of the incoming links... so only two <IREF> definitions appear. Refer to Figure 1 to see how MMM displays and follows this multi-link.

The author's intention is that this link only be active if the current page (head-neck.html), the head photo page (head.html), and the head description page (head-desc.html) are all being displayed by the browser. Note that there are only two <IREF> tags; the current page is always implicitly in incoming link to any multi-link. As can be seen in the diagram, the multi-link is displayed in the browser window with the contents of the TEXT field in the MHMT tag. When the

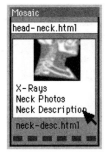

Figure 2:   A multi-link in an unmodified browser

mouse pointer is over the active multi-link, the DISPLAY_TEXT field's contents are shown in the browser's status line.

The author's second intention is that the head photo and head description pages should be advanced in parallel to the neck photo and neck description pages. In terms of the MHTML, the current page and any pages refered to in <IREF>s in the multi-link will be closed and any pages listed as anchor references in the multi-link will be opened in separate windows. Hence the three anchors in the MHMT construct above lead to the three pages in the bottom portion of the diagram above when the mouse is clicked on the multi-link. Note that the multi-link is no longer active (display color went from green to black) since the two pages in the <IREF>s are no longer displayed.

So, with the MHMT construct the author has control of what the user sees, where the user is told that he is going (as opposed to the bare URL displayed by most browsers), the pages the user must have already visited (synchronization), and the pages the user will see afterwards (concurrent browsing).

As seen in Figure 2, an unmodified browser displays the three outgoing links as regular anchors. This is because they appear in standard HTML anchor constructs within the MHMT region and the MHMT region is ignored by unmodified browsers. The <IREF> tag is also ignored. Users of unmodified browsers are able to use an MHTML document, though the author's concurrency and synchronization semantics are lost.

MHTML's Extended Syntax

```
Multi-link: <MHMT (tx | dtx | tx dtx |
    e)> body </MHMT>
tx: TEXT=text
dtx: DISPLAY_TEXT=text
text: any plain text string
body: (text | iref | anchor)*
iref: <IREF HREF=url>
anchor: <A HREF=url> text </A>
url: Universal Resource Locator
e: Empty string
```

The *tx* element is the text to display as the multi-link anchor text in the document and *dtx* is the display text to display in the status line when the cursor passes over the multi-link while it is active. If the *tx* element is omitted then the text within the MHMT block is rendered as normal HTML text; if it is present, then the text in the MHMT block is not rendered at all (somewhat like the description elements within an HTML 3.0 FIG block [4]). If the *dtx* is excluded the string "MHMT Anchor" is displayed in the status line when the anchor is active and passed over.

Prototype System

The Multi-Head, Multi-Tail Mosaic browser prototype is based on NCSA Mosaic 2.6 for X-Windows and compiles on multiple workstation platforms. Less than two thousand lines of code preprocess MHTML into HTML which the standard Mosaic renderer presents to the user. Hooks in the code

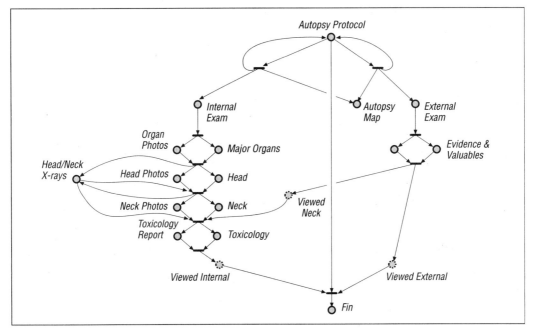

Figure 3:   Overview of the autopsy report

present the DISPLAY_TEXT field when a pointing device passes over an MHMT anchor, open and close appropriate windows when one is selected, and update the status of MHMT anchors when windows open or close.

Screen dumps from MMM showing more details of concurrency and synchronization can be found at URL *http://www.cs.unc.edu/~stotts/elon/mmm.html*

The prototype MMM binary can be downloaded for experimentation at URL *http://www.cs.unc.edu/~stotts/MMM/index.html*

Handling the Scenario: HTML vs MHTML

Recall our example: A pathology instructor with three goals: (1) Students should always be aware of the autopsy protocol (the summarizing cover sheet for the autopsy). (2) Students should refer to both the textual description and high-resolu-

tion photographs for most sections of the autopsy. (3) Due to the nature of the current case, students should not progress past the internal examination of the neck without having already seen the external evidence relating to the neck. A PFA presenting the entire autopsy report as it should be read for study appears in Figure 3.

There are two approaches to structuring the presentation in HTML: change page content or describe how to create the next desired browsing configuration in the document. The first presentation goal of keeping the autopsy protocol visible for the student's entire session with the autopsy can reasonably be handled in either way. Since the autopsy protocol is relatively short it could be prepended in its entirety to every page in the corpus (a task potentially simplified by server-side includes). Alternatively, the author could place a statement above the links to the internal and external examinations that they should be opened in another window, perhaps including instructions on how to do that with various browsers.

These approaches may well work in this case because the autopsy protocol is short (necessary for the first approach) and the desired browsing semantics are simple (necessary for the second approach). They would fail in the face of longer documents with arbitrarily complex browsing semantics. MHTML solves the first presentation goal with a minimum of hassle: each link to one of the examination pages is really a multi-tailed link specifying the autopsy protocol and the appropriate examination page as tail pages. The autopsy protocol does not participate in any other MHMT links so it remains up for the duration of the student's traversal of this material.

Either approach to HTML can be used with the second presentation goal that students see text and photos simultaneously for various sections. Modifying the appropriate sections to include the photographs inline takes advantage of one of the Web's most compelling features. In this case, however, the images are as tall as the Web browser's presentation area; scrolling up to see the picture and down to the descriptive text distracts the student. The instructor could include directives to the students to bring the images up in another window and to advance both the image and description pages as they move from section to section.

This second presentation goal is addressed directly by MHTML: links from section to section are multi-headed (including the description and image pages from the current section) and multi-tailed (including the description and image pages from the next section). For example, look at the link from Major Organs and the associated Organ Photos page to the Head, Head Photos and Head/Neck X-ray pages. (Note also that going from the Head and associated images to the Neck and associated images the Head/Neck X-ray page remains visible like the autopsy protocol above.)

The third presentation goal, synchronizing the browsing of two browsing paths, is much harder to handle in HTML. It would be possible to modify the Neck section of the internal examination to include the text and photos of the External Evidence Photos and Evidence and Valuables sections, though if the student had seen them before this would be redundant. Alternately, a pointer to the Evidence and Valuables section could be included with an admonition to make sure it is seen before proceeding (it would then be necessary to handle a photograph and description as in presentation goal two).

In MHTML, browsing state is kept through the use of "empty" or "invisible" pages, which are marked but not presented to the user. Invisible pages are indicated in the PFA diagram by dotted outlines. Viewed Neck is one such page which is marked in parallel with the Belt Photos and Evidence and Valuables sections and not unmarked until it is used to pass beyond the Neck section of the internal exam. Hence if the student has seen the evidence information at some time during this session, it is possible to pass beyond the Neck section as soon as it is entered. If not, the student can follow the multi-link to the evidence description and photos, activating the link past the Neck section.

It is possible to get close to the desired browsing semantics using HTML, but the presentation is not quite what is desired (in the case of inlining images or prepending the overview) or it requires the author to describe how the reader's browsing should proceed. It is our belief that authors should concentrate on what to show, not how to get it shown. The MHMT construct in MHTML permits the author to describe the desired browsing semantics in a clear, compact method, concentrating on the interrelations of the data, not the user interface of the readers' browsers.

Conclusion and Future Work

We simplified the original design and implementation process as much as possible to allow us to test the feasibility and usefulness of multi-links in

Web browsing. We feel that we have proven the practicality of the MHTML construct and interface, and have seen numerous direct applications of its functionality, including the scenario discussed earlier in this paper.

While the original modifications to the Mosaic package were simple, they were made keeping extendability and flexibility in mind; indeed, the groundwork for some logical enhancements to our original design is already included. First and foremost, with the increasingly frequent new Mosaic for X releases, we found it necessary to make our changes easily portable to new versions. As new releases become supported by NCSA, we will update our patch files accordingly. Now that the feasibility and usefulness of MHTML have been shown we expect to extend the HTML parser to parse MHTML directly, removing the current preprocessor.

Development on increasing support for Petri net (and other graph type) attributes is continuing as demanded by trial users. Multiple marking (plural tokens) and multiple marking modes (colored tokens) are two examples of this. In addition, we hope to allow the user to select a specific graph model, like And-Or, Petri net, or General, for interpreting MHTML. Related to this, and certain to make MMM much more attractive to authors, would be creating a graphical authoring environment for building MMM documents or sites.

Probably the single greatest hindrance in reaching the goals of the project was the requirement that MHTML be handled correctly by an unmodified Web browser. We feel that one of our best directions for new development will be to remove that restriction.

Colored tokens, as mentioned above, are most commonly used in Petri nets for multi-user concurrent browsing. An example of this is running a moderated meeting using a deterministic order such as Robert's Rules [2]. Any sort of multi-user stateful model requires inter-user communication, either by modifying the Web server or causing the Web clients to communicate among themselves, at which point we have altered the client-server model. Our original requirements called for no server modification, but we are investigating both of these methods. Future work includes implementation and experimentation with these new mechanisms. ∎

References

1. R. Furuta and P. D. Stotts, *"Interpreted Collaboration Protocols and their use in Groupware Prototyping,"* Proc. of the 1994 ACM Conference on Computer Supported Cooperative Work (CSCW '94), Research Triangle Park, NC, October 1994, pp. 121-131.

2. R. Furuta and P. D. Stotts, *A Hypermedia Basis for the Specification, Documentation, Verification, and Prototyping of Concurrent Protocols, Department of Computer Science Technical Report No. TAMU-HRL-94-003*, Texas A&M University, College Station, Texas, 1994.

3. Theodor Holm Nelson, *Computer Lib/Dream Machines*, Redmond: Microsoft Press, 1987.

4. D. Raggett, *HyperText Markup Language Specification Version 3.0*, IETF Draft, 28 March 1995.

5. P. D. Stotts and W. Pugh, *Parallel Finite Automata for Modeling Concurrent Software Systems, Journal of Systems and Software (Elsevier Science)*, vol. 27, 1994, pp. 27-43.

6. P. D. Stotts and R. Furuta, *Petri Net Based Hypertext: Document Structure with Browsing Semantics, ACM Trans. on Information Systems*, vol. 7, no. 1, January 1989, pp. 3-29.

7. P. D. Stotts, R. Furuta, and J. C. Ruiz, *Hyperdocuments as Automata: Verification of Trace-based Browsing Properties by Model Checking, ACM Trans. on Information Systems*, to appear 1996.

About the Authors

Brian C. Ladd
[*http://www.cs.unc.edu/~ladd*]
University of North Carolina at Chapel Hill

Michael V. Capps
[*http://www.cs.unc.edu/~capps*]
University of North Carolina at Chapel Hill

P. David Stotts
[*http://www.cs.unc.edu/~stotts*]
University of North Carolina at Chapel Hill

Rick Furuta
Texas A&M University

MOBILE GUI ON THE WEB

Daniel Dardailler

Abstract

This article presents an architecture allowing network graphical applications, such as X Window clients, to be activated and render themselves directly onto World Wide Web browser screens. The intention is both to offer Web information providers better and finer control over the exact presentation of their documents, and to provide the ability to demonstrate real applications or products over the Web. After presenting some rationales and requirements for this work, the paper explores the set of issues that need to be resolved to implement such a system. **Keywords:** *X Window System, embedding, remote execution, RX document type*

Introduction

One of the major characteristics of the World Wide Web (WWW) system as it operates today is that document providers have very little freedom over the final presentation of their documents. This happens because the large majority of documents presented to the end-user are expressed using a simple SGML-based markup language, the hypertext markup language (HTML), whose only function is to convey structural content information.

As an author of an HTML document, you may say: This is a section title, This is a table, and so on. With HTML Forms in place, you can even say: This is an active option menu or This is a text entry area. However, HTML alone doesn't let you draw simple objects like pie charts or line histograms, with text at a specific location and orientation, or run some animation directly in the browser window.

Putting the emphasis on the logical content and leaving the final presentation details (e.g., exact layout, font, color) to the browser and the user works just fine for certain classes of documents. However, this situation is not well-suited for a whole different set of materials. There is a lot of information out there for which the exact presentation, or "look," matters more than the words: advertisement pages, advanced live GUI, visual art, structured graphics, active multimedia, etc

(just look at the nature of the graphics found on CD-ROM versus your basic GUI environment).

Work has been going on for several years in the SGML community to provide authors with better control over the final presentation using Style Sheet [1] specifications. Such presentation languages attached to HTML would improve the information provider control over the document visuals, but still have intrinsic limitations due to their declarative approach.

Another path people have taken is to complete or replace HTML with a richer language, changing the once static Web documents into programs that get downloaded and executed at the user's site. This is usually refer to as the Mobile Code [2] paradigm. The problem with this solution is that existing applications have to be rewritten in the "applet" language, Java for instance, they have to be downloaded, and they might have to be installed/de-installed as well.

This paper presents an architecture that is somewhat similar to the Mobile Code approach, since a real program complements or replaces HTML, but in our case, the code doesn't move, only the graphical layer does. It can therefore be referred to as the *Mobile GUI* approach.

A low-level UI protocol, such as the X11 Protocol [3], effectively solves the presentation problem by offering providers of information the "pixel-level" functionality they sometimes desire. Of course, X also solves the "remote demo/try before you use" case, since it is already the natural vehicle of hundreds of graphical-networked applications. Since X operates at the same network Internet transport level as the HTTP protocol, TCP/IP, it is also a natural fit for this task.

Although X11 is the UI network protocol of choice in the industry today, others, based on Microsoft Windows, OS/2, and NeXT also exist, and one requirement of this design is to allow for their inclusion. That being said, the rest of the document focuses mainly on X and less on the other potential UI protocols.

Technical Issues

The main goal of this article is to break the overall problem into smaller pieces. If we identify the problem as how to let a remote application, such as an X client, render itself directly onto a Web browser screen, then we can break the problem into the following five subproblems:

- How to convey remote execution information in a Web document

- How to remotely activate an application

- How to deal with embedding inside a browser window

- How to allow the X connection to operate through a firewall

- How to deal with latency and bandwidth issues

As you can see, this is a very broad set of issues, having to deal with a number of areas, including existing Web protocols and formats, X security and X embedding techniques, and more generic network protocols for remote execution. The rest of this paper describes some of the available options for each of the issues listed above.

The Web

There are basically three different ways of expressing a new kind of datum on the Web:

- A new URL (Uniform Resource Locator) scheme

- A new HTML tag

- A new document content type

Let's look at all three in turn.

In HTML, the language in which most Web documents are written, URLs are usually used in anchors, as with the HREF parameter. From the user's perspective, clicking on the associated anchor text causes the browser to fetch the data to be displayed. One approach for describing a new remote execution paradigm would be to introduce a new URL scheme, RX (for Remote eXecution), that would look like this in an HTML document:

```
<A HREF = "rx://www.x.org/programs/pix">
Click here for a demo of the Pix
    editor</A>
```

This has the effect of starting *pix* remotely, with the display done locally in a separate top-level window on the user's screen. This scheme can also be supported in the embedded case, where the program runs directly in the browser's window, as follows:

```
<IMG SRC = "rx://www.x.org/nice_home"
ALIGN=top  ALT="X">
```

This code has the effect of starting the program referred to as *nice_home* remotely, with the display embedded in the local browser viewing window.

The problem with creating a new URL scheme is that it requires creating a new associated protocol and a new scheme registration, which is in our opinion changing too much of the current infrastructure. It is also not necessary. The same is true for extending the HTML syntax to support remote execution by supporting a new RX tag. For example:

```
<RX SRC="some_program" EMBEDDED=YES>
```

The third option, creating a new RX document type, seems to be the easiest to introduce, and the rest of this article will only concentrate on this approach.

The purpose of an RX document is to provide the Web browser with information on how to activate the remote program, issues like the UI protocol to choose, embedding support, and size hints.

In HTML, RX document pointers can be used in the same context as any type of image file (e.g., *.gif*, *.xbm*), namely with the ANCHOR and IMG tags. Using an RX document with ANCHOR results in the program being started in its own top-level window, while using it with IMG results in the program being embedded in the browser window if both the browser and the remote client support embedding. The following HTML code shows the nonembedded case:

```
<A HREF = "http://www.x.org/rx/pix.rx">
Click here for a demo of the Pix
    editor</A>
```

In this case, when the user clicks on the anchor, *pix* appears as a separate application. Here's the embedded case:

```
<IMG SRC = "http://www.x.org/rx/ico.rx"
    ALIGN=top  ALT = "ICO.RX">
```

If the remote client and the browser support embedding, the user should see an *ico* animation running in a browser sub-window. If embedding is not supported, the user sees an image/logo that represents *ico*; when the user clicks on this image, *ico* is activated in a separate top-level window.

In both cases, the RX document contains information about the type of remote activation supported by this server. The syntax we use contain simple FIELD_NAME/*value* lines.

The first line is mandatory and describes the location of the server side activation script, for instance a perl script activated thru the Common Gateway Interface (CGI). This line uses the ACTION field name:

```
ACTION URL
```

The ACTION field is followed by an optional logo line:

```
LOGO URL
```

pointing to an image file (*.gif*, *.xbm*) used to represent the remote program "inline" if embedding is not supported. A list of data lines for each display protocol supported by the application follows; the UI_PROTOCOL is required, while the GEOM_HINT and EMBEDDABLE fields are optional:

```
UI_PROTOCOL x11 | ica | news | etc.
GEOM_HINT   width x height
EMBEDDABLE no | yes
```

For example (*ica* is the name of the network protocol used by WinDD), the RX document shown in Figure 1 represents an application that can be activated using either the X11 Window Protocol or WinDD, and for which there is a default logo provided and some different size hints depending on the type of UI selected. Figure 1 also shows the general architecture of the system.

The sequence of actions shown in Figure 1 is initiated when a browser, such as Mosaic or Netscape, finds an RX reference in an HTML document. Essentially, the browser sees the RX document link in the HTML file, so it asks the http server for the document. The *httpd* daemon serves the document and the browser spawns the *rx* agent. The *rx* agent then asks the *httpd* daemon to process the action script. When the script is activated, it uses the information in the RX document to activate the remote client, which is rendered in the browser display window.

In Figure 1, the RX document itself (anim.rx) is represented as a separate entity from the RX script (anim.pl). In our current implementation, we usually carry only one CGI script on the server side, which generates either the RX syntax (if requested via HTTP GET without argument) or activate the remote program (when requested a second time with arguments for Display, Geometry, etc.). Storing the information about *what* UI_ PROTOCOL is supported and *how* to activate programs for each protocol in one single file is

Example 1:   "Duo" RX script (*http://x.org/cgi-bin/xclock.pl*)

```perl
#!/usr/local/bin/perl

if (!$ARGV[0]) {
    print"Content-type: application/x-rx

        ACTION http://x.org/cgi-bin/xclock.pl   # myself
        UI_PROTOCOL x11
        GEOM_HINTS 200x200
        EMBEDDABLE yes
        LOGO http://x.org/icons/xclock.xbm";
} else {
    system ('xclock -window '.$ARGV[2].' -g '.$ARGV[1].' -d '.$ARGV[0].' &');
}
```

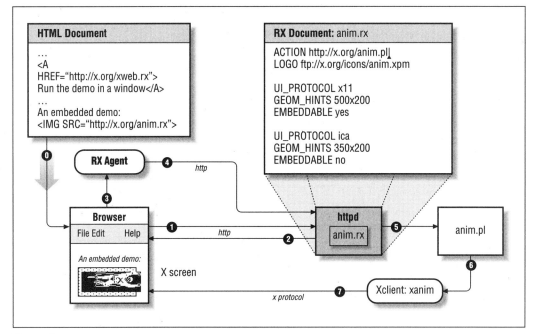

Figure 1:   General RX architecture

easier to maintain from an administrative point of view.

Embedding

The nonembedding case of handling RX documents, that is, activating the X client in a separate top level, can be implemented without any changes to the browser or the http server code. If separate RX documents are present on the *httpd* side (versus CGI scripts that generate RX Content-type on the fly—see previous section), one would need to extend the file suffix mapping (i.e., the .mime.types) to bind *.rx* file extensions to the MIME content type *application/rx* (or rather *application/x-rx* since it's not a registered IANA type yet). On the browser side, nonembedding support only requires you to add the following entry into the *.mailcap* file:

```
application/x-rx; rx %s
```

This binds the RX type to an external program, the *rx* agent. When the *.rx* document is passed to this program, it performs the remote activation in its own top-level window, as described in detail below.

For the embedding case, there is a clear need for support in a Web browser beyond the current case of remote execution. The problem is that this support just hasn't taken real shape yet. For instance, it would be appropriate to have MPEG animations rendered directly in the browser window, in the context of an `IMG` tag. This rendering would be handled by a separate process that is local to the browser, i.e., an external viewer, whose output would be redirected to the browser window instead of being displayed in a separate top-level window. If that mechanism were in place, then RX would become just another instance of an external-for-embedding viewer handling remote execution.

Recently, new mechanisms called "Plug-Ins" have appeared in popular browsers such as Netscape [5], allowing for embedding of arbitrary external applets via dynamic loading. The RX agent would just have to provide an external plug-in API to be integrated in such a Web browser.

The RX document also contains fields that provide information about embedding. The `EMBEDDABLE` field provides information to the browser about whether the remote client is capable of being embedded in one of the browser subwindows. For instance, it might tell the browser that the specified X client can be given a top-level window ID at startup time (as a *–window* ID command-line option). A browser can use this information (directly or indirectly thru the applet) and the file pointed to by `LOGO` to show a press-here-to-activate icon to replace a nonembeddable program in the `IMG` context. A browser can also elect to defer any activation of an embedded client until the user requests activation, in which case it can also use the `LOGO` icon by default.

`GEOM_HINT` gives information to the browser about the preferred geometry of the remote client. This is mostly useful in the case of an embedded program, where the browser needs to create an embedded window of the correct size up front. Note that GEOM_HINT is not required with HTML 3.0, where the IMG tag can include WIDTH and HEIGHT attributes. In any case, if the size information is not present, and embedding is still desired, the original size of the embedded window is browser-dependent. The browser can also deny any geometry changes thereafter, or it can allow for dynamic reconfiguration.

There are sundry technical issues related to designing general embedding in X, such as geometry negotiation, menu inclusion, and focus and session problems. In the Web browser case, though, one easy path would be to consider solving only a subset of the problems. Geometry negotiation, for instance, is not a necessity, given that browsers usually never resize their embedded graphics. The same principle could be enforced for more dynamic graphics, such as X applications. Menubar extension and command support could also be ignored for clients embedded in a Web browser.

Session management, however, is still a real issue that needs to be solved in this context. If you think about going back and forth between pages that provide "live" embedding, you need to consider what should happen to the active programs while you are surfing. This issue is true regardless of our Mobile GUI study: if embedding of MPEG is the goal (i.e., having *mpeg_play* displaying its output in a browser subwindow), then a way to stop the rendering and restart it in the same context later is clearly needed.

An embedded architecture is reminiscent of systems like OpenDoc and OLE, so we should not go into the details of solving this particular aspect of the larger problem without considering what is being done by these two systems.

Remote Execution

As mentioned in the previous section, the architecture presented here uses a program, *rx*, which runs on the browser side and handles all of the logic of activation and security. Depending on the browser, and if the result is embedded or not, this program could be activated through the .*mailcap* file, through a Plug-In API or some other mechanisms, but in all cases, the new RX MIME content-type will be used to do the binding.

The job of the *rx* agent, when resolving an RX link, is to remotely activate the specified program in the context of the current `GEOM_HINT` and `EMBEDDABLE` states. In order to do so, it uses the `ACTION` pointer and the `UI_PROTOCOL` information. `ACTION` is the activation script itself. It is either a valid URL or a local path, in which case the http server host is assumed. This activation script is common to all UI protocols; it is the sole entry point to the real execution of the remote program.

The *rx* agent, or applet, on the browser side, must send the necessary information to this CGI script for the remote execution to happen. It must first decide which UI protocol to use. This is simple and usually found in the environment (i.e. , the browser knows if it is an X browser or a Windows browser).

`UI_PROTOCOL` specifies the types of remote display protocols the program can speak. It's an indication for the browser side of what kind of information must be passed back in the remote execution protocol communication. If the browser determines that it cannot deal with any of the UI protocols specified, it needs to display an error message, or a specific image in case of embedding, as in the case when the `IMG` context specifies an incorrect image path.

In the case of an X11 `UI_PROTOCOL` connection, typical information to be sent back to the activation script includes:

- the UI protocol it has chosen

- The display/window IDs (or those of a firewall proxy)

- Any size information desired

- Authentication data

- Other information, such as optimization, language, time zone, or session information

It is the responsibility of the ACTION script to determine which program to activate, depending on the UI connection chosen by the browser. The flexibility in the architecture allows it to work with minimal modification of the existing software. In more advanced implementations, the *rx* agent work could be done by the browser, just as Mosaic and Netscape can treat GIF natively.

The *rx* agent also has to deal with security (see below). In the case of X, this may involve a firewall proxy server and/or use of the *xhost* program.

Security

Security here is only a concern for the browser side, not the http server side. It is up to the server host side, where the remote X client runs, to disallow things like a plain, unrestricted *emacs* or *xterm* to be started with access to the server's file system and display and control given to some rude netsurfer somewhere in cyberspace. In our case, we're only worried that a remote X client could "spy" on the user's keyboard and screen in some way, or somehow destroy the user's critical resources.

In the most trivial case, the browser X display can be accessed by the remote X client with no restriction. The browser side has only to authorize the connection for the remote host at large (e.g., xhost +hostname) and pass the X protocol information to the remote host so that it can execute the X client on the browser's display. This simple case probably covers a small part of today's Web usage—LAN internal connections or a company-wide network—but I think it is likely to grow in the future (note that there is still an issue with using xhost, related to the fact that the

X browser might not be run on the X Server host itself, but as a remote client already. Some sort of "transitive" X authentication might be needed in that case).

In the generic WAN case, direct X connectivity is not usually allowed between two given hosts and a firewall machine may be present. In this case, a firewall proxy X server is probably needed to guarantee a secure X connection between the remote X program and the browser session, where private information usually resides.

The X Consortium security working group is currently studying the X security proxy case. Several companies have already made experiments based on the *xscope* architecture, and new work in on its way in this area, so I won't elaborate further on that part. The basic idea is to look closely at the X protocol and determine which requests should be blocked, what interclient interchange can be allowed, etc.

Once such an infrastructure exists, the *rx* agent will just take advantage of it in the process of indicating to which X Display ID the remote program must connect.

Performance

One advantage of low-level UI protocols is that they give their users a lot of freedom over the presentation, the obvious price being greater network traffic. In order to address this bandwidth issue with X, one option is to use LBX (Low Bandwidth X), to minimize the flow of X requests and their size over slow connections. LBX could be used bundled with new X servers as a new proxy or together with the secure proxy architecture (i.e., have a single proxy X server that handles security and "decompression" of X requests at the same time). Although LBX was originally designed with serial line X connections in mind, it would also gracefully solve the performance problems that arise over today's Wide Area Network.

You'll note that the architecture presented doesn't preclude using a higher level UI protocol,

such as a UIMS. This is just a matter of having the correct UI server, such as a widget server, in place on the browser side, and specifying the correct UI protocol in the RX document.

Further Considerations

One important issue that needs to be considered is whether or not specialization of the remote X client is acceptable. For example, the client may need to be modified to speak the X proxy server protocol to handle security, or to deal with the embedding case. In other words, is it valid to require that existing X clients that want to be included in Web pages be relinked/recompiled/changed in some ways? Without extending the X server itself, that might be necessary at least to handle embedding (since the *–window* option is not supported by today's Xt or Motif libraries).

Last, and pragmatically, because they outnumber X Window browsers, we need to think about resolving issues surrounding non-X Window browsers (MS/Windows, Mac) so they may use this architecture with remote X Window clients (which in turn outnumber the non-X network-graphic applications).

The basic idea is to use PC-XServer as add-on applets for PC browsers.

For the nonembedding case, there are several PC-XServer software packages on the market that can provide X services integrated with native Windows service and therefore would easily solve the problem of creating top level X windows side by side with the PC browser window.

The embedding case is trickier, since the level of PC-XServer integration would have to move down to the subwindow level, and none or few of the existing systems currently allow for it. Another approach would be for the Windows or Mac Web browsers to understand the X protocol natively, and become *virtual X servers* for their own viewport window. Since the X server code for Intel and Mac is freely available from the X

Consortium, this might actually be a viable solution for the browser companies.

Conclusion

Network-based graphic applications should become an integral part of the Internet of tomorrow.

In this paper, we presented an architecture that utilizes the X Window System fundamental client-server nature in the context of the World Wide Web. To become truly operational, however, such a system requires the availability and the integration of several independent functionalities:

- Seamless embedding of external content-type viewer output in the Web browser window

- Embedding support in the X Window System and in hydrib X/PC environments

- X Protocol security

- X Protocol optimization for low bandwidth networks

The X Consortium is highly aware of the opportunity the growth of the Internet and the World Wide Web presents for the X community, and has recently announced a new major release of the X Window System, code name "Broadway,"

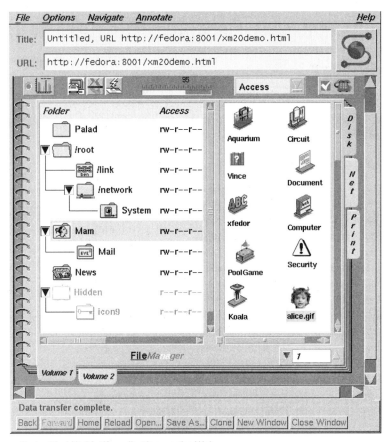

Figure 2:   Embedded Xt/Motif application on the Web

that will provide the necessary enhancements allowing for X to really fly over the Web! ■

Prototype

During the summer of 1995, a student intern joined the X Consortium team to work on a prototype of the RX system. Figure 2 shows the result of these experiments: an Xt/Motif application running on the http server side and displayed embedded inside a modified XMosaic browser window.

In this example, the Motif application is taking charge of the complete browser page content, so the source for the underlying HTML document is quite minimal:

```
<IMG ALIGN=MIDDLE SRC="xm20demo.pl"></A>
```

The associated *xm20demo.rx* httpserver-to-browser stream is listed below:

```
ACTION http://fedora:8001/cgi-bin/
    xm20demo.pl
UI_PROTOCOL x11
GEOM_HINTS 600x600
EMBEDDABLE yes
```

Acknowledgments

I'd like to thank Ellis Cohen, Bob Scheifler, Kaleb Keithley, Ian Jacobs, and Paula Ferguson for the feedback received. I'd also like to thank Helene Veslot, our graduate student working on the implementation prototype, for helping out in the making of this project.

This paper is available at *http://www.x.org/people/daniel/mobgui.html*

References

1. Web Consortium site, *Style Sheet for HTML*, *http://www.w3.org/hypertext/WWW/Style*

2. Web Consortium site, *Mobile Code model*, *http://www.w3.org/hypertext/WWW/MobileCode/*

3. Bob Scheifler, Jim Gettys, *The X Window System*, Digital Press, ISBN 1-55558-088-2. (Also *http://www.x.org*)

4. NCSA site, *Common Gateway Interface (CGI)*, *http://hoohoo.ncsa.uiuc.edu/cgi/overview.html*

5. Netscape site, *Netscape Client Plug-In API*, *http://www.netscape.com/comprod/development_partners/plugin_api*

About the Author

Daniel Dardailler

[*http://www.x.org/people/daniel*]

X Consortium

daniel@x.org

Daniel Dardailler holds a Ph.D. in CS from the University of Nice Sophia-Antipolis (France). He joined the X Consortium staff in 1994 to act as a software architect for the Common Desktop Environment project (CDE). Prior to that, he spent four years at the OSF as a principal software engineer in the area of the Motif widget set.

USING GRAPHIC HISTORY IN BROWSING THE WORLD WIDE WEB

Eric Z. Ayers, John T. Stasko

Abstract

Users of hypertext systems often find themselves eagerly following hypertext links deeper and deeper into a hypertext web, only to find themselves "lost" and unable find their way back to previously visited pages. As navigation aids to help users orient themselves in the Web, browsers often provide a list of the documents a user has visited, a way to move forward and backward along previously traversed links, and a quick way to return to a home document. Still, users often have trouble revisiting a page that was previously viewed in a session, especially after many invocations of the backtracking shortcuts.

*MosaicG is derivative work of NCSA Mosaic version 2.5 which enhances the history-keeping facility of the browser by providing a two-dimensional view of the documents a user has visited in a session. It is intended as an easy-to-use aid in navigating a collection of hypertext documents. By presenting titles, URLs, and thumbnail images of the documents a user has visited in a session, the Graphic History View allows a user to easily recognize a previously visited document and provides an easy way for the user to revisit that document and analyze the structure of a set of hypertext documents. **Keywords:** WWW, navigation, hypertext, Mosaic, history*

Introduction

The use of the Word Wide Web (WWW) has increased dramatically in just a few years. Its presence on the Internet has attracted the attention of researchers and the popular media alike. The availability of browsers for multiple computing platforms, many of them distributed for no cost, combined with new avenues for accessing the Internet allows even novice computer users with limited resources to make use of the wide range of services and information available on this global computer network. As electronic publishing on a large scale emerges, the advantages and drawbacks pertaining to hypertext systems have become familiar to a large user population.

To help users orient themselves in a hypertext web, browsers often provide a list of the documents a user has visited, a way to move forward and backward along previously traversed links, and a quick way to return to a home document. These navigation aids are essential in helping users manage the huge store of information available on the WWW. Hypertext links encourage users to explore related topics and references to other works from within a document. Although the backtracking aids and history list are helpful navigation tools, users often have trouble revisiting a page that was previously viewed in a session. This problem becomes acute after many invocations of the backtracking shortcuts. Users of hypertext systems often find themselves eagerly following hypertext links deeper and deeper into a hypertext web, only to find themselves "lost" in the sense that they are unable find their way back to previously visited pages. This difficulty in revisiting previously viewed pages may discourage users from engaging in such exploratory behavior. It is hoped that the addition of the graphic history view will encourage exploratory behavior and help users navigate the WWW more easily in general.

MosaicG is derivative work of the National Center for Supercomputing Applications' (NCSA) Mosaic Web browser, version 2.5. It enhances the history-keeping facility of the browser by providing a two-dimensional view of the documents a user has visited in a session, as shown in Figure 1. It is intended as an easy-to-use aid in navigating a collection of hypertext documents. By presenting titles, Uniform Resource Locators (URLs), and thumbnail images of the documents a user has visited in a session, the Graphic History View allows a user to easily recognize a previously visited document and provides an easy way for the user to revisit that document and analyze the structure of a set of hypertext documents.

Overview of the Graphic History View

For the purposes of this paper, a browsing session is defined to be the history of document accesses during a particular invocation of a browsing application. Opening a new browsing window delimits the beginning of a new browsing session. Closing a browsing window delimits the end of a browsing session. Within a browsing session, users often revisit documents. Traditional hypertext browsing applications have maintained a list of documents visited during a session in the order in which they were traversed. Another session-specific navigation aid that is often provided is a backtracking mechanism (i.e., the "forward" and "backward" buttons on the NCSA Mosaic Document View) to allow the user to return to the most recently visited documents in the list.

Although hypertext links can create a web-like structure of hypertext documents, many hypertext documents are arranged hierarchically. A user visits the document at the top level, traverses down the tree to read one subject in depth, and then backtracks up to the top node to find another subject. When the session history is viewed as a linear list of accesses, the top-level document may appear in the list many times. This represents the frequency of access to the document, but does little to convey the hierarchical organization of the document space. MosaicG attempts to create an easy-to-understand visual representation of these types of browsing patterns to match the user's mental model of the relationships between documents.

Other projects similar to MosaicG include WebMap and The Navigational View Builder. In these tools, the tool or an agent for the tool actively queries a set of documents and builds a representation of the relationships between these documents. This approach might be described as an "exploratory" approach. The structure of documents on a server or set of servers must be queried as a batch job to determine the structure of documents before the user attempts to browse the document space. This approach allows the user to visualize the space without having to visit any documents in the space, but comes at the price of many time-consuming and resource-intensive queries for the server or servers involved. These batch jobs must be rerun frequently to maintain an accurate representation of the document space because users are continually adding new documents to the server, and the contents of the documents themselves tend to be volatile.

In comparison, the approach of MosaicG might be described as a "reflective" approach, in that the representation is built passively as a user browses the document collection. The application makes no a priori assumptions of the structure of the space and builds the visualization only as new documents are encountered. Thus, the resulting visualization is customized to each session and is built to represent the way a user explores the hypertext.

In MosaicG, the history of the session is displayed as a two-dimensional tree built from left to right. Documents are represented as nodes in the tree, and links between documents are represented as arrows in the tree. A document at the source of an arrow contains the source anchor, and the document pointed to by the arrow contains the destination anchor. Since a document can be both the source and destination of many links, the visualization includes special arrows to indicate that a document is the destination of more than one hypertext link.

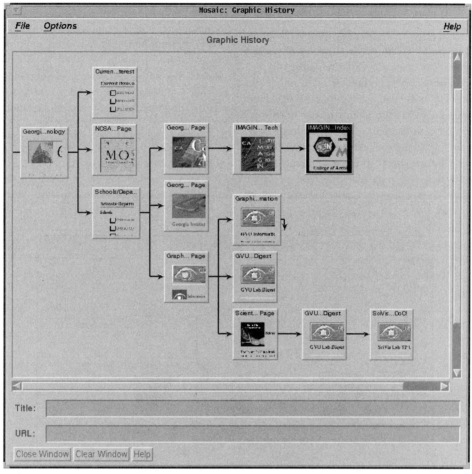

Figure 1: An overview of the Graphic History View

The visual quality of most WWW documents is such that most pages have a distinctive look and feel. MosaicG uses thumbnail images of the documents to allow the user of a browser to quickly recognize a page or set of pages in the tree. A quick glance at the thumbnail representation is often enough for a user to recognize a previously visited page. By building the structure to represent the history of browsing and by providing thumbnail images, the history browser attempts to lessen the burden on the user to recall titles of pages by facilitating quick recognition.

As a part of designing the Graphic History View, an informal survey was presented to a small sample of the WWW user population. One part of the survey asked users about their browsing habits. Almost all users said they frequently used the backtracking navigation buttons provided by the Mosaic Document View. This is important because it is this type of browsing that produces the branching layout of nodes in the Graphic History View. Several respondents noted the problem of navigating back to documents that had been previously visited in a session, but none of them reported having used the text-based history list to find a previously viewed document.

Another part of the survey also presented approximately 10 different options for displaying the tree of documents. Sample references to documents and a corresponding layout of nodes in a graph were presented with variations on layout direction (horizontal or vertical), ways to display nodes that are referenced as links from more than one page, and the use of color in the visualization. The responses to these different options varied widely. No particular layout or presentation strategy emerged as a clear favorite. Several of the respondents sketched novel schemes for creating such a visualization, while others wanted to see different types of information displayed. In preparing for a future release of the Graphic History software, it would be worth exploring this issue further and incorporating the option of displaying additional types of information, such as relative distance between servers, relationships between servers in the same DNS namespace, or the frequency in which a page was visited.

A primary consideration in the design of the browser was scalability. To eliminate visual clutter during a long browsing session, the view

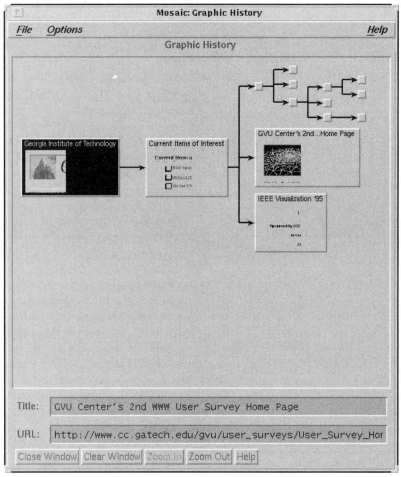

Figure 2: A portion of the tree is collapsed

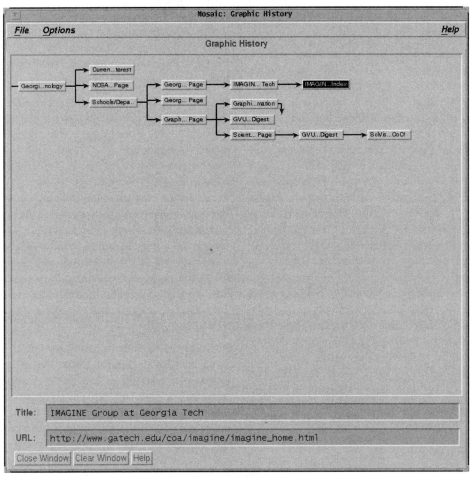

Figure 3:   Demonstrating the title-shortening algorithm

allows the user to condense branches of the tree which are no longer of interest to the user, as shown in Figure 2. This not only saves screen real estate, but it also allows the user to easily focus on a smaller part of the visualization. The user may also get an overview of the visited documents by zooming out for a smaller representation of all documents in the tree.

Features

The menu of the MosaicG Document View is identical to the distributed NCSA Mosaic browser, with the addition of one menu item in the "Navi-

gate" menu. The "Graphic History..." menu item opens another window that will display the sequence of documents visited by the associated Document View window. A separate Graphic History View is created for each Document View, each of which displays a different history. The Graphic History View allows the user to display different information as a part of the tree. The user can selectively display document titles, URLs, or a thumbnail image for each node. When the mouse is placed over a node in the tree, the title and URL of the document appear in the two text fields at the bottom of the Graphic History

View Window. A user can recall a document in the tree by double-clicking on a node in the Graphic History View window.

A daunting task for any visualization system is the management of screen real estate. In the graphic history view, horizontal screen space is the most critical resource, as the trees grow from left to right. This layout seems the most natural for English text strings, but we find that the tree quickly grows off of the right side of the page. To conserve horizontal screen space, the Graphic History View shortens the titles of the documents as the tree grows to the right as demonstrated in Figure 3. The amount of abbreviation can be manually controlled by a scale on the Graphic History View's "Preferences" dialog box. By default, the program will try to increase the amount of abbreviation as the tree grows. This behavior can be controlled by enabling or disabling the "auto resize" menu item. The title-shortening algorithm tries to preserve whole words in the title so the abbreviated title will make sense. It also tries to preserve whole words at either end of the title. It builds the abbreviated title back and forth from the beginning and end of the title, adding as many whole words as will fit at either end, and then adding characters to the title until the length of the title fills the width allotted for the node.

The Graphic History View allows the user to zoom out to get an overview of the structure of the documents that have been visited as shown in Figure 4. Each node is collapsed to a small square. When the user places the mouse pointer over a node in the tree, the title and URL of the document are displayed at the bottom of the window. The view also allows the user to collapse a portion of the tree into a smaller representation by clicking on an arrow head pointing to a node.

The way the tree is built depends on the way documents are accessed. Documents that are accessed by selecting anchors in a document are added as child nodes in the tree relative to the node that represents the document where the source anchor is found. Documents that are

opened by choosing a title from the hotlist or by entering a URL manually are added as the root of a new tree. Pressing the "forward" and "backward" buttons in the Document View changes the highlighted node in the Graphic History View but does not add new nodes to the tree.

One of the most difficult problems in visualizing the structure of documents on the Web arises from the N to N relationship between documents. A tree is meant to show hierarchical relationships, but hypertext documents are traditionally more complex. The challenge for MosaicG was to present a view that is simple enough to understand at a glance without cluttering the image with extra lines and arrows. When MosaicG encounters a document that is the destination of more than one link, a short arrow appears to the left of the node. By positioning the mouse over this arrowhead, the other nodes in the hypertext that contain links to this document are highlighted.

The user may save a browsing session as a file using the "Save" command. The history tree is saved in a text file of the user's choice. The thumbnail images are not preserved when the tree is saved, but will be updated if the node is revisited. Note that there are no guarantees that the structure of hypertext web as constructed at one time will correspond to the structure of the Web at any other time. Servers may become unavailable, documents may change location, or anchors in a document may change.

Implementation

The Graphic History View was added to the Mosaic 2.5 source in as unobtrusive a manner as possible. Although NCSA Mosaic allows communication between separate processes through a shared file, the browser view needed to be able to access the graphic output of the Document View and be able to track the difference between following a link, typing a URL, pressing the back or forward button, or selecting a URL from the hotlist. For these reasons it was decided to write

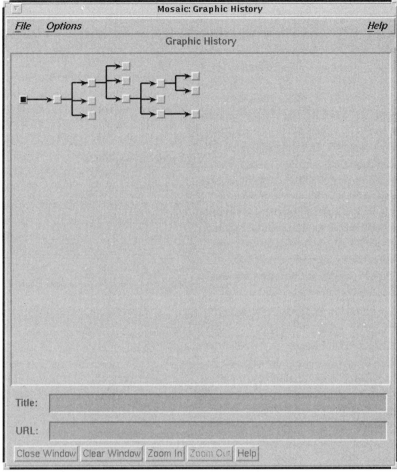

Figure 4:   The Zoom Out feature

the view to be compiled in with the source code and not implemented as a separate application. In spite of the integration of the Graphic History source code into the NCSA Mosaic source, reincorporating the browser code into a new release of Mosaic (from 2.4 to 2.5) took less than an hour.

History information is stored in a hash table and a tree structure that is separate from NCSA Mosaic's internal data structures. Care was taken to adhere to the same style of interface presented by Mosaic visually, while trying to keep the changes to the existing Mosaic source to a mini-

mum. The view does modify the existing code slightly to inform the graphic history view when certain actions take place in the Document View, and modifications were made to the HTML widget to allow the widget to generate a copy of the Document View. The Graphic History View also relies on Mosaic's "Xmx" wrapper for Motif.

When a document is visited, a hashing function is applied to the URL to assign the document a slot in the hash table. If an identical URL has already been cached, no new node is created, but an indication of a new link is added to the nodes at the source and destination of the link. The browser makes no attempt to determine if two different URLs reference the same document, so sometimes the same document can appear more than once in the Graphic History View.

The tree layout algorithm is from Sven Moen's Drawing Dynamic Trees. This algorithm draws ideas from other "tidy tree" drawing algorithms, optimizing them for drawing text. To describe the algorithm briefly, an outline is calculated for each node in the tree. The algorithm operates by recursively calculating an outline around each subtree from the leaves to the root of the tree. As the algorithm moves toward the root, it packs the nodes vertically by joining the outline of children to the outline of the parent. Children of sibling nodes are adjusted so that the outlines of subtrees do not cross. The end result is that the children of a node are packed in height and width, lining up the x coordinates of all children of a node, and centering the children of a node vertically about the node.

The thumbnail images are generated by slightly modifying the HTML widget that Mosaic uses in the Document View. This generation of a thumbnail image adds a constant amount of processing time whenever a new document is accessed. The user can specify through an X resource file the scaling factor to use for generating thumbnails, and the maximum width of a thumbnail image in pixels. After a document is retrieved, the widget performs a layout routine and renders an image of the document to the screen for the Document view. To generate the thumbnail, an off-screen pixmap is created and the widget redisplay routine is called, substituting the off-screen pixmap for the visible window as the target of all Xlib drawing routines. The image is then scaled down by simply copying every Kth pixel of the pixmap where K is the scaling factor to use in generating the thumbnail. Every Kth pixel in the horizontal direction is copied until the maximum thumbnail width is attained. Thus, the thumbnail image is a reduction of the top left corner of the original document which represents the first (K * max_width) by (K * max_height) pixels in the original

image. Note that no attempt is made to factor in the contribution of intermediate pixels to the thumbnails. This approach was taken to reduce problems with colormaps, although colormap problems are still not completely resolved. Using an antialiasing algorithm to sample groups of pixels would produce a smoother thumbnail image, but doesn't seem practical given the limitation of most workstations to 1-bit and 8-bit color.

Shortcomings

As mentioned earlier, the "exploratory" approach is expensive for both clients and servers. The "reflective" approach, on the other hand, has the disadvantage of only being able to show documents that have already been viewed. A happy medium between the exploratory and reflective approach could be achieved if some meta information about the structure of a server's document space were maintained by the server and made accessible via a single request. In this way, the server could quickly return the relationships between all documents on the server and the user could then cheaply browse the documents in the space without the expense of downloading all the text and images of each page.

Another shortcoming of the Graphic History View is related to the restriction of most color workstations to display only 256 colors at a time. This limitation imposes severe restrictions on the thumbnails. The images contained in this paper were captured from an X Server running with 24 planes of color. Although it is often possible to determine the content of an image whose colormap has been changed, it is not always easy and the image is usually not visually appealing. Any user that regularly uses a WWW Browser under the X Window System on a color workstation with 8-bit color has likely run across problems with the colormap when trying to run two or more applications or trying to view two documents simultaneously. As graphic information becomes more pervasive and more easily accessible via the Web, the need to display many images simultaneously will grow, as will the perceived inadequacy of 8-bit color displays. Hopefully, 24-bit color will be a standard offering for future generations of workstations as it is already becoming for personal computers. An intermediate solution to this problem might be to create a private colormap for each thumbnail and swap the colormaps as the cursor is dragged over each thumbnail, or creating a private colormap for the thumbnail images in general, and attempting to generalize that color palette to fit all thumbnails.

In some preliminary reviews of MosaicG, users have expressed interest in having more power to manipulate the documents and tree structure in general. It has been suggested that a user might want to reparent a node as the root of a tree, or erase branches of a tree completely. It has also been suggested that the Graphic History View concept serve as a model for a graphic hotlist, allowing node representations to be dragged and dropped between views and even applications. Such behaviors would be even more desirable in an object-based document environment, such as Microsoft Windows' OLE specification. A formal usability study of the Graphic History View is in progress as of the writing of this paper. ∎

References

1. Andreesen, Marc, NCSA Mosaic Technical Summary. Technical report, National Center for Supercomputing Applications, 1993.

2. Domel, Peter, "WebMap - A Graphical Hypertext Navigation tool," Second International Conference on the World Wide Web, 1994.

3. Moen, Sven. "Drawing Dynamic Trees," IEE Software, July 1990.

4. Mukherjea and Foley, "Visualizing the World-Wide Web with the Navigational View Builder," Computer Networks and ISDN System, Special Issue on the Third International Conference on the World Wide Web '95, April, 1995, Darmstadt, Germany.

About the Authors

Eric Z. Ayers
(*Eric.Ayers@compgen.com*)
John T. Stasko
(*stasko@cc.gatech.edu*)
Graphics, Visualization and Usability Center
College of Computing
Georgia Institute of Technology
Atlanta, GA 30332

AN HTTP-BASED INFRASTRUCTURE
FOR MOBILE AGENTS

Anselm Lingnau, Oswald Drobnik, Peter Dömel

Abstract

Mobile agents are an emerging technology attracting interest from the fields of distributed systems, information retrieval, electronic commerce, and artificial intelligence. We present an infrastructure for mobile agents based on the Hypertext Transfer Protocol (HTTP) which provides for agent mobility across heterogeneous networks as well as communications among agents. Our infrastructure supports the implementation and interoperation of agents written in various languages and takes advantage of current research in HTTP and the World Wide Web in general. **Keywords:** *Mobile agents, infrastructure, HTTP*

Introduction

Recent times have seen exciting new developments in computer networking. Applications like the World Wide Web have made computer networks such as the Internet available (and palatable) to users outside of computer science departments all over the world. Information servers offering all sorts of interesting data are cropping up, and, as researchers are trying to find ways of reliable electronic payment, the net will soon be important as a "virtual marketplace."

Yet the sheer amount of data available to users in such a network will be difficult to handle. How will they be able to locate the information they need? How are they going to find the best offer for some service they require? One possible solution brought forward to help in this situation consists of "mobile agents"—autonomous programs that move about the network on behalf of their owners while searching for information, negotiating with other agents, or even concluding business deals.

In this paper we propose an infrastructure for such agents. This infrastructure allows agents to move between hosts and communicate with other agents; it supports agents written using diverse languages and lets agent programmers implement a variety of interaction schemes based

on a general mechanism for agent communication. Our agent infrastructure uses the *Hypertext Transfer Protocol* (HTTP) [2] for agent transfer and communication, taking advantage of this widely accepted, platform-independent mechanism to make it as easy for providers to offer agent-based services as for users to access them. We also expect future advances in, for example, HTTP security and electronic payment, resulting from the World Wide Web research community to save considerable effort which would otherwise be necessary to implement such in some separate framework for mobile agents.

Mobile Agents

The term *agent* means many things to many people. This section defines a (mobile) agent for our purposes and gives a general overview of agent technology.

What Is an Agent?

According to our dictionary [22], an agent is "anyone who acts on behalf or in the interest of somebody else." Agent-based systems have recently gained considerable attention in computer science, although nobody has come up yet with a reasonably succinct definition of what an "agent" is actually supposed to be in this context. For the purposes of this paper, we assume that an *agent* is a computer program whose purpose is to help a user perform some task (or set of tasks). To do this, it contains persistent state and can communicate with its owner, other agents, and the environment in general. Agents can do routine work for users or assist them with complicated tasks; they can also mediate between incompatible programs and thus generate new, modular, and problem-oriented solutions, saving work.

Tasks that seem to be amenable to agents include electronic mail handling (an agent helps with prioritizing, forwarding, deleting, archiving, ...of mail messages [10]), scheduling of meetings (the people involved run agents that will negotiate a date and time, reserve a conference room etc.) or filtering an information source such as Usenet news for interesting bits according to various rules or heuristics.

Since agents consist of program *code* and the associated internal *state*, we can envision *mobile agents* which can move between computers in a network. An obvious application of this idea is in information retrieval, where it is easy to picture a mobile agent that gathers interesting data on some computer. If it has gone through all the available data, it moves somewhere else in order to find out even more tidbits before returning to its "owner" loaded with pertinent information. Of course the same information could be retrieved by the owner's computer itself using some suitable mechanism for remote access. The advantage of the agent-based approach is that complex queries can be performed by the agent at the remote side without having to transfer the raw data to the owner's computer first, which would likely waste considerable bandwidth. Other applications of mobile agents include active documents, electronic commerce (a hot topic in itself as far as the World Wide Web is concerned), network management, control of remote devices, and mobile computing.

It is important to emphasize that, even if an environment supports mobile agents, agents are not *required* to move about. There may be agents for which there is no point in mobility, or others which are just too big. However, if the environment allows agents to communicate, mobile and stationary agents can fruitfully work together on behalf of their owners.

Related Work

The interest in agents is fueled by the AI community as well as by researchers in the fields of distributed computing and communications. AI researchers tend to think of agents as entities that can observe and reason about the goings-on in their environment, while distributed computing scholars consider agents a new way of structuring distributed computer systems.

An overview of agents and, in particular, agent communication from the point of view of AI research is given by Genesereth and Ketchpel [12]. Kirn and Klöfer [21] discuss the applicability of organization theory to agent systems and examine their potential for "compound intelligence," while Kautz, Milewski, and Selman [20] take a look at how agents can assist and simplify person-to-person communication. As an example of concrete experiments with AI-based agents, Etzioni and Weld [10] present a stationary agent (*softbot*) which helps its owner access Internet resources. It is of course legitimate to ask whether mobile agents are worth the trouble at all; this question is discussed by Harrison, Chess and Kershenbaum [16]. Eichmann [9] examines the issue of ethics for agents (including stationary "Web crawlers" or "spiders") on the Web.

Requirements for an agent infrastructure (or *agent meeting point*) are considered by Chess et al. [7]. Goldszmidt and Yemini [13] extend the notion of an agent infrastructure to encompass real-time control and system management. A proprietary agent infrastructure is described by White [26,27]. Proposals abound for agent implementation languages: (Safe-)Tcl [6,23], Java [14,18], and Telescript [27,28] seem to be some of the more important contenders.

An Infrastructure for Mobile Agents

In this section we consider the requirements that mobile agents place on the systems they're running on, and vice-versa.

Why Do Agents Need an Infrastructure?

To be useful, an agent needs to interact with its host system and other agents—it must access information that the host offers or negotiate with other agents about the exchange of services. Agents must also be able to move within heterogeneous networks of computers. This is only possible if there is a common framework for agent operations across the whole network: a standardized *agent infrastructure*. This infrastructure must offer basic support for agent mobility and communications. It must also protect the host from unauthorized access by agents and safeguard the agents' integrity as well as possible.

An Architecture Model

The basis of our architecture model for an agent infrastructure is the notion of an *agent server*. This is a program (like a mail server, FTP server, ...) which runs on every computer that will be accessible to agents and is in charge of the agents running on that computer. Its tasks include accepting agents, creating the appropriate runtime environments, supervising the agents' execution (in the meantime answering queries about their status) and terminating them if so directed. The agent server must also organize agent transfer to other hosts, manage communications among agents as well as between agents and their owners and do authentication and access control for all agent operations. In a network of agent servers, each individual server may be expected to participate in management operations such as the gathering of usage statistics.

We assume that each agent server knows about other agent servers in its "neighborhood" and makes this information available to agents, who use it to pick a new destination when they decide to leave the host. Such "neighbors" do not have to be physically close to one another—for example, an agent server on a host which specializes in bibliographic databases could tell an agent about other servers that offer similar information. Thus no server (or agent) needs to know the topology of the whole network; if each server knows about its own vicinity, an agent will still be able to traverse an "interesting" subset of all servers. As a refinement, the list of neighbors presented to an agent can be customized according to the origin or purpose of the agent. That way, "firewall" schemes or domain boundaries can be realized.

For each agent running on a server, there is a dedicated *runtime environment*. The runtime environment interfaces between the agent and its host by making resources available to the agent in a controlled way.

The user interacts with the agent infrastructure through a *client*. The client will let the user submit an agent for execution, find out about its status, stop or recall it, and perform other operations as necessary. It is important to note that the client does not need a permanent connection to the rest of the agent infrastructure; it can, for example, reside on a mobile computer that communicates with the fixed infrastructure via a slow radio link.

The main design guideline for our agent infrastructure is to allow maximum flexibility concerning the implementation of agents, their access to the host system(s), and their communication. We do not want to prejudice our research by constraining, e.g., the language to be used for agent implementation. Furthermore, we are convinced that a general infrastructure for mobile agents must provide "mechanism, not policy" in order to gain wide acceptance.

Figure 1 shows an overview of the various components of our agent infrastructure.

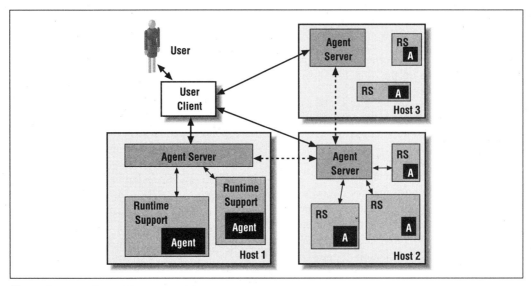

Figure 1:   The architecture model

A Mobile Agent Dissected

Before delving deeper into the details of agent support, we will examine the structure of a mobile agent more closely. A mobile agent contains:

- *Code.* The program (in a suitable language) that defines the agent's behavior

- *State.* The agent's internal variables, etc., which enable it to resume its activities after moving to another host

- *Attributes.* Information describing the agent, its origin and owner, its movement history, resource requirements, authentication keys, ...for use by the infrastructure. Part of this may be accessible to the agent itself, but the agent must not be able to modify the attributes. While some languages allow the representation of an agent's state as part of its code (e.g., by inclusion of appropriate assignment statements) we consider this not general enough.

Agent Communications

The model for agent communications in our infrastructure is based on an abstract *information space* which is maintained by each agent server on behalf of the agents in its charge. The information space contains triples consisting of an item's *key* (or name), an *access control list*, and the item's *value* (Figure 2).

Agents may write items to the information space and read them either destructively or nondestructively; all these operations are supposed to be atomic and serialized in order to avoid race conditions and inconsistency. The operations are enabled for specific agents, groups of agents, or all agents according to an item's access control list. More advanced interaction schemes such as RPC can be implemented easily on top of these primitives, or agents can simply publish "facts" in a declarative language (e.g., KIF [11]) for the perusal of others. The agent server uses the information space to volunteer data of general interest, e.g., a list of agents currently running under its control (so agents can get in touch with one another).

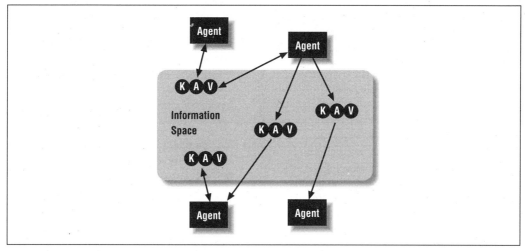

Figure 2:   The agent information space

While the information space mainly serves as a means of communication among agents, it can also be used for communication between agents and the host system. For example, in a security-conscious environment, a trusted stationary agent could be endowed with the higher privileges necessary to gather some data and hand out summaries to visiting agents via the information space.

An obvious generalization of this approach to communications would be to allow access to a server's information space from agents running on other servers. However, such a "global" information space cannot be arbitrarily scaled up without serious loss of efficiency. Furthermore, it is unclear whether a global information space would lead to a worthwhile increase in functionality when it is easy for agents to move between hosts.

Finally, there should be a way for agents to communicate with their owners. A simple approach is to let the agent send electronic mail back to its owner; this asynchronous method ties in nicely with the fact that the owner is probably not online all the time, e.g., in a mobile computing environment. Synchronous communication is not much more difficult in principle: An agent might want to check back with its owner about some aspect of its operation, so after attracting its owner's attention by sending a mail message it could—in an HTTP-based framework—provide a Web form to be filled out by the owner and suspend itself until a reply arrives.

Runtime Support

An agent server needs to provide runtime support to agents for various reasons: Firstly, agents must be able to take advantage of the agent server for communications and mobility services; therefore suitable primitives must be accessible from the agent implementation language. Secondly, agents are not supposed to misuse their access to the host system by, for example, collecting its password file for off-site cracking or by formatting the main hard disk. Potentially dangerous operations such as executing arbitrary operating system commands or opening files or network connections must be tightly controlled. A runtime environment can do this by either completely outlawing them or else by vetting their arguments and endorsing an operation only if it is "harmless." The most promising approach in this area is Safe-Tcl [5, 6], which distinguishes between a *trusted* and an *untrusted environment.*

The agent runs in the untrusted environment and may perform *safe calls* into the trusted environment. The trusted environment checks their validity and forwards them to the underlying system if they are acceptable.

It is important to note that the level of trust extended to an agent may vary considerably between agents. For instance, a locally developed agent is likely to be rather more trustworthy than some random piece of code coming in from the network. These different levels of trust can be accommodated by suitable selection of runtime environments, with a more highly trusted agent being allowed more freedom of access to the underlying system.

Using HTTP as a Basis of an Agent Infrastructure

An agent infrastructure needs protocols for agent mobility and communication. Here we explain why the Hypertext Transfer Protocol (HTTP) seems to be a sensible choice.

Why HTTP?

Using HTTP as the basis of an agent infrastructure offers several advantages:

- HTTP is a well-known, well-understood, and widely accepted protocol. Popularizing an agent infrastructure will be vastly easier if it is based upon HTTP rather than yet another home-brewed protocol.

- HTTP contains all the necessary primitives to support agent mobility. For example, the POST method can be used to submit an agent to a server for execution, and the GET method caters for status requests, etc. Also, the HTTP specification [2] leaves room for custom extensions, should those turn out to be needed.

- Existing Web browsers like Mosaic can be used for most of the user interface. This saves a lot of work and is convenient for

users, who don't have to learn how to use another incompatible tool.

- The Web's platform independence makes it easy to support mobile agents in a heterogeneous network. With Web access available even through lowly PDAs, instant agent-based computing is possible nearly everywhere.

- We can make use of ongoing Web research results on topics like secure transmission via HTTP and electronic commerce. Since one of the more important applications envisioned for mobile agents is to send them out shopping, integration with upcoming solutions for digital payment is essential for a viable agent system. Similar reasoning applies to security—it will be much easier to make use of whatever the Web community decides on than to convince everybody that some other approach is working equally well, or even to adapt a Web standard to a completely different environment.

- We will be able to integrate Web-based and agent-based services better if their technical basis is the same to begin with. Thus agent support becomes a "value-added" service that Web providers can offer in a clean and straightforward manner.

We have implemented a prototypical HTTP-based agent infrastructure which offers most of the features proposed in the section "An Infrastructure for Mobile Agents." It consists of a custom HTTP server written in Perl [25] and a set of language-dependent modules providing runtime services to agents. We will include some details of our implementation at appropriate places in the following sections; lack of space prevents us from a full discussion within the scope of this paper.

Encapsulation of Agents As MIME Contents

In HTTP, data (request/reply bodies) are transferred in a format based on MIME (Multipurpose

Internet Mail Extensions [4]). For the purposes of agent transport, we define an application-specific MIME-like content type, `application/agent`. This content type carries attributes describing, e.g., the programming language used and the agent *type* (say, library search agent). The agent server uses this information for choosing the right kind of runtime support or rejecting the agent if its requirements cannot be met.

The body of an `application/agent` part contains subparts that correspond to the agent's attributes, code, and state (using the content types `application/agent-attributes`, .../

`agent-code` and .../`agent-state`, respectively). The `agent-attributes` subpart gives agent attributes (see the section "A Mobile Agent Dissected") in a form similar to MIME headers (Example 1). The format of the latter subparts is not specified further; it is assumed that their contents will be defined in a manner appropriate to the programming language used for the agent. If necessary, a suitable content transfer encoding can be applied to any of the subparts, supporting, e.g., agents compiled to some form of byte code.

Example 1:   A MIME-encapsulated agent

```
From: lingnau@tm.informatik.uni-frankfurt.de
Date: Thu 13 Jul 1995 12:37:00 +0200
Content-Type: application/agent; boundary="AbCdEfG"; language="tcl";
   type="silly"; context="default"

--AbCdEfG
Content-Type: application/agent-attributes

Owner: lingnau@tm.informatik.uni-frankfurt.de
Agent-ID: <a123.950713123700@deneb.tm.informatik.uni-frankfurt.de>
Home-URL: http://deneb.tm.informatik.uni-frankfurt.de:5055/home/a123/
Start-Date: Thu 13 Jul 1995 12:34:56 +0200
Expires: Thu 20 Jul 1995 12:34:56 +0200
Log: deneb.tm.informatik.uni-frankfurt.de Thu 13 Jul 1995 12:34:56 +0200
   rigel.tm.informatik.uni-frankfurt.de Thu 13 Jul 1995 12:36:13 +0200
Authentication-Cookie: * fa389df25671e4a515ca87efda149852
--AbCdEfG
Content-Type: application/agent-code

puts "This is a useless agent"
sleep $sleep if [llength $visit_list} {
   set nextHost [lindex $visit_list 0]
   set visit_list [lreplace $visit_list 0 1]
   agent moveto $nextHost
} else {
   agent quit
}
--AbCdEfG
Content-Type: application/agent-state

set sleep 60
set visit_list {arktur algol}
--AbCdEfG--
```

Once an agent is encapsulated in a MIME-like message for transport, nothing precludes its being sent by email rather than HTTP. We have not explored this further to date, but there are obvious connections to research into *active mail* [5] which seem worth pursuing.

Agent Transport via HTTP

We have to distinguish two cases: a new agent being submitted to a server for the first time, and an agent moving from server to server of its own accord. In the first case, the server must be established as the *home server* for this agent, which will be keeping track of the agent's progress through the network. In the second case, the home server must be notified by the new server that the agent has moved to a new location.

Generally, an agent is moved by POSTing it to a special URL [3] managed by the agent server (*server*/create or *server*/move, respectively, in our implementation, where *server* is short for http://*host:port*). The agent server parses the agent, checks whether it is acceptable according to the server's policies and the agent's requirements as expressed by its attributes, and launches it in an appropriate runtime environment. In the case of a new agent, the client (owner) is returned a new URL identifying the agent for the purpose of status queries (the *home URL*—in our implementation it is of the form *server*/home/*id*, where *id* uniquely identifies the agent on this server); in the case of an agent moving between servers, the target server assigns a temporary *visitor URL* (*server*/visit/*id*) to the agent and POSTs this to the agent's home URL to notify the home server of the agent's new location.

Our agent server spawns a new process for each agent and its runtime environment. This separates the agent from its peers and the server, increasing security and the flexibility of the runtime suppor—this approach is instrumental in allowing agents implemented in arbitrary languages. It also makes it possible to take advantage of "resource limits" that the operating system can impose on processes to enforce limitations on the CPU time or memory used by agents.

Once an agent has been submitted to the infrastructure, its owner can query its status by accessing its home URL. Since the home server is kept up-to-date as to the whereabouts of the agent, it can issue an appropriate HTTP code 302 "moved temporarily" response specifying the current visitor URL of the agent. These will be handled transparently by most Web clients, giving the agent owner apparently instantaneous access to the agent. Such a status query returns an HTML document which not only advises the owner of the status of the agent, but also allows more detailed examination of attributes or part of the state (for example, a partial result) via links to special URLs. In our implementation, URLs like *visitorURL*/attributes or *visitorURL*/state are used for this purpose; again, these can be accessed via the home URL by redirection. More URLs are available for stopping or recalling the agent, e.g., *visitorURL*/recall.

Agent Communications via HTTP

HTTP lends itself not only to agent transport, but also to agent communications. The "information space" discussed in the section "Agent Communications" can be implemented as part of the agent server, accessible via a mechanism similar to other database queries. Information items can be added to the information space by POSTing them to a URL (*server*/info?*key*), with the access list information given in an Access: entity header. Suitable content transfer encoding allows values of arbitrary content and size (subject to space limitations on the server) to be entered as the message contents. The GET method is used to read information items, and a DGET method can be introduced into the HTTP protocol to enable atomic "destructive GET" for retrieving and removing an item in a single operation.

Another feature that would be nice to have is the ability of agents to be notified asynchronously of changes in the information space that are interesting to them. For example, an agent may want to be informed when a new agent turns up at the server or whenever a new piece of information has been put into the information space by its "opposite number" during negotiation. While an agent could find out about this by periodically polling the information space, asynchronous notification will be much more efficient. This is not currently implemented by our infrastructure, but work is underway to support this in the near future.

Security Considerations

Security is important in all operations related to the agent infrastructure. We have already discussed the need for protection of host systems from interference by agents and vice versa. In addition to this, an agent infrastructure must cater for encryption and authentication:

- Agents carry along their complete implementation, which may be of interest to malevolent people. While there seems to be little practical opportunity for protecting an agent's code while it is executing (an ingenious person could simply single-step the process or stop it and analyze its memory), agents can be protected in transit by encryption, for example, using suitable public-key schemes between servers. As far as looking at the code of a running agent is concerned, a simple solution may be the introduction of neutral "premises" where agents can meet to, e.g., hold an auction. The trust to be extended to such entities would be quite similar to the current situation with solicitors and other "disinterested" parties.

- It is important to be able to tell whether an agent has been changed (maliciously or through damage) during its transfer from one server to the next. Again, existing schemes for cryptographic hashing and digital signatures offer practical solutions.

- Operations on agents like status queries and agents' interactions with a server's information space must be authenticated. In the first case, we must make sure that only an agent's owner can find out important details about the agent, recall it, or kill it. Simple solutions include "magic cookies"—long random strings which are part of an agent's attributes and must be presented by a person in order to gain access to the agent—or digest authentication as proposed by Hostetler et al. [19].

In the second case, we want to restrict access to a server's information space to the agents running on this server. The server and an agent's runtime environment can agree on a magic cookie; since this will never be passed across the network it should be sufficient as a first approximation to provide the needed authentication.

Most of the issues to do with encryption and authentication depend on the security of HTTP transmission. This is a topic which is currently under research; various solutions [1,15,17,24] have been proposed. For the purposes of basic research simple authentication schemes are sufficient; we plan to accommodate whatever approach is eventually adopted by the Web community at large in order to avoid duplication of effort.

Summary and Further Work

Mobile agents have recently generated considerable interest from researchers in distributed systems, electronic commerce, information retrieval, the World Wide Web, and AI. To support experiments in this area, we have implemented a low-level infrastructure for mobile agents in an HTTP-based framework. The framework consists of a specialized HTTP server and language-specific modules that provide runtime support to agents written in various languages (we have until now concentrated on Tcl and Perl; others would be straightforward to integrate). Agents can employ various styles of interaction through a common information space as well as take advantage of customized runtime environments for specific tasks at different levels of trust. The framework also allows for stationary agents as a special case, making it possible to construct hybrid systems of agents.

Our aim is now to gain experience in the design, implementation, and use of mobile agents based on our infrastructure. Ongoing projects in our group include applications in scheduling meetings and filtering Usenet news; other areas under initial investigation are system monitoring and semantic routing.

Another set of open problems concerns encryption and authentication in our agent infrastructure (see the section "Security Considerations"). These matters have not yet attracted due attention in our implementation, but in order to promote consistency and avoid duplicate effort we are waiting for a standard for HTTP encryption and authentication to emerge from the World Wide Web community. In the meantime we plan to provide schemes which are sufficient to foil the efforts of "casual" crackers.

Agent navigation still poses a number of questions. How will an agent decide where to go next? Besides semantic routing, the use of hyperspace mapping tools like *WebMap* [8] may help in locating "interesting" places. This is also a topic for future research. ∎

References

1. Anderson, Scot, and Rick Garvin, "Sessioneer: flexible session level authentication with off the shelf servers and clients," *Computer Networks and ISDN Systems*, 27(6):1047-1053, April 1995.

2. Berners-Lee, T., R. T. Fielding, and H. Frystyk Nielsen, *Hypertext Transfer Protocol—HTTP/1.0*, Internet Draft draft-ietf-http-v10-spec-00, HTTP Working Group, March 1995, Work in progress.

3. Berners-Lee, T., L. Masinter, and M. McCahill, *Uniform Resource Locators (URL)*, RFC 1738, Network Working Group, December 1994.

4. Borenstein, N. and N. Freed, *MIME (Multipurpose Internet Mail Extensions) Part One: Mechanisms for Specifying and Describing the Format of Internet Message Bodies*, RFC 1521, Network Working Group, September 1993.

5. Borenstein, Nathaniel and Marshall T. Rose, *MIME Extensions for Mail-Enabled Applications: application/Safe-Tcl and multipart/enabled-mail*, Distributed as part of the Safe-Tcl 1.2 distribution available over the Internet, November 1993, Working Draft.

6. Borenstein, Nathaniel S., *EMail With A Mind of Its Own: The Safe-Tcl Language for Enabled Mail*, Distributed as part of the Safe-Tcl 1.2 distribution available over the Internet, 1994.

7. Chess, David, et al., *Itinerant Agents for Mobile Computing*, IBM Research Report RC 20010 (03/27/95), IBM Research Division, 1995.

8. Dömel, Peter, *WebMap—A Graphical Hypertext Navigation Tool*, In *Proceedings 2nd International WWW Conference*, Chicago, IL, December 1994.

9. Eichmann, David, *Ethical Web Agents*, In *Proceedings 2nd International WWW Conference*, December 1994.

10. Etzioni, Oren, and Daniel Weld, "A Softbot-Based Interface to the Internet," *Communications of the ACM*, 37(7):72-76, July 1994.

11. Genesereth, M. R., R. E. Fikes, et al., *Knowledge Interchange Format Version 3 Reference Manual*, Logic-92-1, Stanford University Logic Group, January 1992.

12. Genesereth, Michael R. and Steven P. Ketchpel, "Software Agents," *Communications of the ACM*, 37(7):48-53, 147, July 1994.

13. Goldszmidt, Germán and Yechiam Yemini, "Distributed Management by Delegation," In *Proceedings of the 15th International Conference on Distributed Computing Systems*, pages 333-340, Vancouver, Canada, May 1995. IEEE Computer Society, IEEE Computer Society Press.

14. Gosling, James and Henry McGilton, *The Java Language Environment: A White Paper*, Technical Report, Sun Microsystems, 1995.

15. Hallam-Baker, Phillip M., *Shen: A Security Scheme for the World Wide Web*.

16. Harrison, Colin G., David M. Chess, and Aaron Kershenbaum, *Mobile Agents: Are they a good idea?*, IBM Research Report, IBM Research Division, March 1995.

17. Hickman, Kipp E. B., *The SSL Protocol*, Draft Memo, Netscape Communications, February 1995.

18. Hohl, Fritz, *Konzeption eines einfachen Agentensystems und Implementation eines Prototyps*, Diplomarbeit, Universität Stuttgart, August 1995.

19. Hostetler, Jeffery L. et al., *A Proposed Extension to HTTP: Digest Access Authentication*, Internet Draft

draft-ietf-http-digest-aa-01, HTTP Working Group, March 1995, Work in progress (expires 9/1995).

20. Kautz, Henry, Al Milewski, and Bart Selman, *Agent Amplified Communication*, In *AAAI-95 Spring Symposium on Information Gathering from Heterogeneous, Distributed Environments*, Stanford, CA, March 1995.

21. Kirn, Stefan, and Andi Klöfer, *Verbundintelligenz kooperativer Softwaresysteme: or-gan-i-sa-tions-the-o-re-tische Grundlagen, Stand der Technik und Forschungsaspekte, KI*, 2:20-28, February 1995.

22. *Meyers Enzyklopädisches Lexikon*, Bibliographisches Institut, Mannheim, 1971.

23. Ousterhout, John K., *Tcl and the Tk Toolkit*, Addison-Wesley, Reading, MA, 1994.

24. Rescorla, E. and A. Schiffman, *The Secure Hyper-Text Transfer Protocol*, Internet Draft, Enterprise Integration Technologies, December 1994, Work in progress.

25. Wall, Larry and Randal L. Schwartz, *Programming Perl*, O'Reilly & Associates, Sebastopol, CA, 1990.

26. White, James E., "Mobile agents make a network an open platform for third-party developers," *Computer (IEEE Computer Society)*, 27(11):89-90, November 1994.

27. White, James E., *Telescript Technology: The Foundation for the Electronic Marketplace*, General Magic White Paper GM-M-TSWP1-1293-V1, General Magic, Inc., 2465 Latham Street, Mountain View, CA 94040, 1994.

28. White, James E., *Telescript Technology: An Introduction to the Language*, General Magic White Paper GM-M-TSWP3-0495-V1, General Magic, Inc., 420 North Mary Avenue, Sunnyvale, CA 94086, 1995.

About the Authors

Anselm Lingnau
[*http://www.tm.informatik.uni-frankfurt.de/~lingnau/*]
Johann Wolfgang Goethe-Universität
Frankfurt, Germany

Anselm Lingnau studied computer science at Johann Wolfgang Goethe-Universität and obtained his master's degree in 1993. He is currently working as a researcher in the computer science department's distributed systems/telematics group; his main focus is on database issues in mobile communications, but he is also interested in mobile agents, programming, and user environments, and the foundations and applications of the Internet.

Oswald Drobnik
Johann Wolfgang Goethe-Universität
Frankfurt, Germany

Oswald Drobnik received his doctorate degree in computer science from the University of Karlsruhe in 1977. After spending a year as a postdoctoral fellow at IBM Th. J. Watson Research Center, he joined the faculty of the University of Karlsruhe in 1981 as a professor for distributed computing systems. Since 1988 he has been Professor of Distributed Systems/Telematics at Johann Wolfgang Goethe-Universität, Frankfurt.

Peter Dömel
[*http://www.tm.informatik.uni-frankfurt.de/Mitarbeiter/doemel.html*]
Johann Wolfgang Goethe-Universität
Frankfurt, Germany/General Magic, Inc.

Peter Dömel graduated from Johann Wolfgang Goethe-Universität in 1993 with a master's degree in computer science. After doing research with the University's distributed systems/telematics group in application management, object mobility, Web charting tools, and mobile agents he left in 1995 to work for General Magic, Inc.

JASPER
COMMUNICATING INFORMATION AGENTS FOR WWW

John Davies, Richard Weeks, Mike Revett

Abstract

This paper discusses a distributed system of intelligent agents for performing information tasks over the Internet World Wide Web (W3) on behalf of a user or community of users. We describe how agents are used to store, retrieve, summarize and inform other agents about information found on W3. Most current W3 clients (Mosaic, Netscape, and so on) provide some means of storing pages of interest to the user. Typically, this is done by allowing the user to create a (possibly hierarchical) menu of names associated with particular uniform resource locators (URLs). While useful, this quickly becomes unwieldy when a reasonably large number of W3 pages are involved. The solution we adopt to this problem is to allow the user to access information by a much richer set of metainformation than simply names assigned to particular URLs. Given the vast amount of information available on W3, it is preferable to avoid the copying of information from its original location to a local server. The local storage of only relevant metainformation also addresses this issue. The metainformation used includes automatically extracted keywords and summary, as well as the document title, URL and date and time of access. This metainformation is then used to index on the actual information when a retrieval request is made. When an agent stores a page, it will also automatically inform other users who it considers will be interested in the page's discovery via an email message. Thus Jasper is a small step towards automating the original vision for W3 as a network which supports cooperative working and the sharing of information. In addition, Jasper agents will modify a user's profile as the type of information the user is accessing changes. Pages stored in Jasper can be posted to interest groups, creating shared information resources about specific topics. **Keywords:** *Information agent, information sharing, information filtering, user profiling, information management, text summarization*

Introduction

In 1982, the volume of scientific, corporate, and technical information was doubling every five years. By 1988, it was doubling every 2.2 years and by 1992 every 1.6 years. With the expansion of the Internet and other networks the rate of increase will continue to increase. Key to the viability of such networks will be the ability to manage the information and provide users with the information they want, when they want it.

This paper discusses a distributed system of intelligent agents for performing information tasks over the Internet World Wide Web (W3) on behalf of a user or community of users. Below we describe how agents are used to store, retrieve, summarize and inform other agents about information found on W3 in a system called Jasper (Joint Access to Stored Pages with Easy Retrieval). In certain circumstances, Jasper agents will also identify an opportunity for performance improvement and will seek user feedback in order to improve.

Our approach is not motivated by any perceived requirement for another tool for searching W3; there are already many of these [1, 2] and they are being added to frequently with ever increasing coverage of the Web and sophistication of search engines. Our motivation is different but related: having found useful information on W3, how can it be stored for easy retrieval and how can other users likely to be interested in the information be identified and informed?

Given the vast amount of information available on W3, it is preferable to avoid the copying of information from its original location to a local server. Indeed, it could be argued that approach is contrary to the whole ethos of the Web. Rather than copying information, therefore, Jasper agents store only relevant metainformation. As we will see below, this includes keywords, a summary, document title, universal resource locator (URL), and date and time of access. This metainformation is then used to index on the actual information when a retrieval request is made.

Jasper agents also have the capability to learn their user's interests by observing the user's behavior. As the user stores more pages, the user profile held by the Jasper agent is modified automatically to better reflect the topics of interest to the user, as evidenced by the pages they have stored.

Most current W3 clients (Mosaic, Netscape, and so on) provide some means of storing pages of interest to the user. Typically, this is done by allowing the user to create a hierarchical menu of names associated with particular URLs. While this menu facility is useful, it quickly becomes unwieldy when a reasonably large number of W3 pages are involved. Essentially, the representation provided is not rich enough to allow us to capture all we would like about the information stored; the user can only provide a string naming the page. As well as the fact that useful metainformation such as the date of access of the page is lost, a single phrase (the name) may not be enough to accurately index a page in all contexts. Consider, as a simple example, information about the use of knowledge-based systems (KBS) in information retrieval, of pharmacological data; in different contexts, it may be KBS, information retrieval or pharmacology which are of interest. Unless a name is carefully chosen to mention all three aspects, the information will be missed in one or more of its useful contexts. This problem is analogous to the problem of finding files containing desired information in a UNIX (or other)

file system [3], although in most filing systems one at least has the facility to sort files by creation date.

The solution we adopt to this problem is to allow the user to access information by a much richer set of meta-information. How Jasper agents achieve this and how the resulting meta-information is exploited is the subject of the next section.

Agent Architecture

In this section, we will discuss the facilities which Jasper agents offer the user in managing information. These can be grouped in two categories, storage and retrieval.

Storage

Figure 1 shows the actions taken when Jasper stores information in its intelligent page store (IPS). The user first finds a W3 page of sufficient interest to be stored by Jasper in his IPS and sends a "store" request to Jasper via a menu option on his favourite W3 client (Mosaic and Netscape versions are currently available on all platforms). Jasper then invites the user to supply an annotation to be stored with the form. Typically, this might be the reason the page was stored and can be very useful for other users in deciding which pages retrieved from IPS to visit. The user can also specify at this point one of a predefined set of *interest groups* to which to post the page being stored. We discuss information sharing and interest groups below.

Jasper next extracts the source text from the page in question, first stripping out HTML tags. Jasper then sends the text to ConText, a natural language processing system from Oracle Corporation (ORACLE and ORACLE ConText are trademarks of ORACLE Corporation).

ConText first parses a document to determine the syntactic structure of each sentence. Following sentence level parsing, ConText enters its "concept processing" phase. Among the facilities offered are:

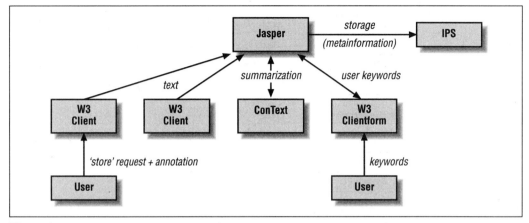

Figure 1:   Jasper's storage process

- *Information Extraction.* A master index of a document's contents is computed, indexing over concepts, facts, and definitions in the text.

- *Content Reduction.* Several levels of summarization are available, ranging from a list of the document's main themes to a précis of the entire document.

- *Discourse Tracking.* By tracking the discourse of a document, ConText can extract all the parts of a document which are particularly relevant to a certain concept.

ConText is used by Jasper in a client-server architecture; the server parses the documents and generates application-independent marked-up versions. API calls from Jasper can then interpret the markups. Using these API calls, metainformation is obtained from the source text. Jasper first extracts a summary of the text of the page. The size of the summary can be controlled by the parameters passed to ConText and Jasper ensures that a summary of 100-150 words is obtained. Using a further call to ConText, Jasper then derives a set of keywords from the source text. Following this, the user is presented with the opportunity to add further keywords of his own via an HTML form. In this way the user can provide keywords of particular relevance to himself, while Jasper supplies a set of keywords which may be of greater relevance to a wider community of users.

At the end of this process, Jasper has the following meta-information about the W3 page of interest:

- The ConText-supplied general keywords

- User-specific keywords

- The user's annotations

- A summary of the page's content

- The document title

- Universal Resource Locator (URL)

- Date and time of storage

Jasper then adds the page to the IPS. In the IPS, the keywords (of both types) are used to index files containing the other metainformation, as shown in Figure 2.

Retrieval

There are four modes in which information can be retrieved from IPS using Jasper. One is a standard keyword retrieval facility, while the other three are concerned with information sharing between a community of agents and their users.

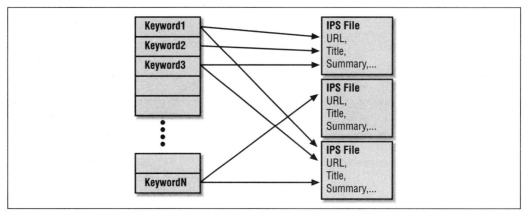

Figure 2:   IPS structure

We will describe each in turn in the sections following.

When a Jasper agent is installed on a user's machine, the user provides a personal profile: a set of keywords which describe information he is interested in obtaining via W3. This profile is held by the agent in order to determine which pages are potentially of interest to its user. The way this is done is described below.

Keyword retrieval

As is shown in Figure 3, for straightforward keyword retrieval, the user supplies a set of keywords to his Jasper agent via an HTML form provided by Jasper. The Jasper agent then retrieves the ten most closely matching pages held in IPS, using a simple keyword matching and scoring algorithm. Keywords supplied by the user when the page was stored (as opposed to those extracted automatically by ConText) are given extra weight in the matching process. The user can specify in advance a retrieval threshold below which pages will not be displayed. The agent then dynamically constructs an HTML page with a ranked list of links to the pages retrieved and their summaries. Any annotation made by the original user is also shown, along with the scores of each retrieved page. This page is then presented to the user on his W3 client.

"What's New?" facility

Any user can ask his Jasper agent "What's new?" The agent then interrogates the IPS and retrieves the most recently stored pages. It then determines which of these pages best match the user's profile based on the same keyword matching algorithm as that mentioned above. An HTML page is then presented to the user showing a ranked list of links to the recently stored pages which best match the user's profile and the other pages most recently stored in IPS, with annotations where provided. Thus the user is provided with a view both of the pages recently stored of most interest to himself and also of a more general selection of recently stored pages.

A user can update the profile which his Jasper agent holds at any time via an HTML form which allows him to add and/or delete keywords from the profile. In this way, the user can effectively select different *contexts* in which he wishes to work. A context is defined by a set of keywords (those making up the profile or, indeed, those specified in a retrieval query) and can be thought of as those types of information which a user is interested in at a given time.

The idea of applying human memory models to the filing of information was explored by Jones [3] in the context of computer filing systems.

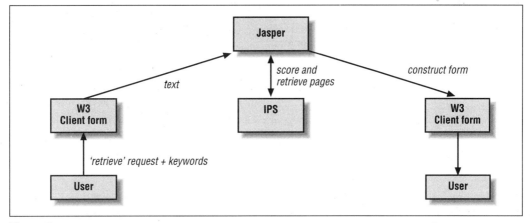

Figure 3: Jasper's keyword retrieval process

Building on his ideas, we can draw an analogy between a directory in a file system and a set of pages retrieved by a Jasper agent. The set of pages can be thought of as a dynamically constructed directory, defined by the context in which it was retrieved. This is a highly flexible notion of "directory" in two senses: first, pages which occur in this retrieval can of course occur in others, depending on the context, and second, there is no sharp boundary to the directory; pages are "in" the directory to a greater or lesser extent depending on their match to the current context. In our approach, the number of ways of partitioning the information on the pages is thus only limited by the diversity and richness of the information itself.

Communication with other interested agents

Jasper agents are currently being tested by a group of users. When a page is stored in IPS by a Jasper agent, the agent checks the profiles of other agents' users in its "local community" (here the agents in the trial, although this could be any predefined community). If the page matches a user's profile with a score above a certain threshold, an email message is automatically generated by the agent and sent to the user concerned, informing him of the discovery of the page.

The email header is in the format: Jasper KW: {keyword}*

This allows the user before reading the body of the message to identify it as being one from Jasper, and since a list of keywords is provided the user can assess the relative importance of the information to which the message refers. The keywords in the message header vary from user to user depending on the keywords from the page which match the keywords in their user profile, thus personalizing the message to each user's interests. The message body itself informs the user of the page title and URL, who stored the page, and any annotation to the page which the storer provided.

Other forms of automatic notification (e.g., via dynamically constructed W3 pages) are also being studied.

As we argue below, the ability to share relevant W3 information with other users quickly and easily is a key part of the original vision of W3. A Jasper agent can automate this information task for a user to some extent.

Jasper interest groups

As mentioned above, when a user stores a page in Jasper, he has an opportunity to specify one of a predefined set of interest groups to which to post the page. Interest groups are somewhat analogous to Usenet newsgroups and gather together pages of related information. Examples of interest groups which have been used are: Artificial Intelligence, ATM, Agents, Data Mining, Films, and Electronic Commerce.

Jasper users can visit interest group pages which are dynamically constructed from the pages which have been posted to them and consist of a list of links to the pages and their summaries, along with any annotation provided by the original storer of the page.

Interest groups are similar to the "list of links" pages found in many W3 locations, with the important extensions that multiple users can contribute to the list (automatically via the storage process) and that summaries of the information and annotations by the original poster of the link are available.

Interest groups can be thought of an alternative to Jasper's automatic emailing facility as a way of sharing information among Jasper users. It complements the email facility in that it is less immediate, email messages being generated by Jasper agents as soon as a page is stored, but more permanent. It is also a way of clustering the stored pages into related topic areas.

Learning from Feedback

In certain circumstances, Jasper agents will identify an opportunity for performance improvement and will seek user feedback in order to maximize the performance enhancement.

A Jasper agent can modify a user's profile if the agent identifies that the profile does not reflect the pages which the user is storing. When a page is stored, the agent compares the content of the page (as analyzed by ConText) with the user's profile. If the profile does not match the page

content above a given threshold, Jasper informs the user and invites the user to modify his profile by adding some keywords suggested by the agent based on the page's content.

The user can then select from the suggested keywords and/or provide some new keywords of his own to be added to the profile. In this way, the user profile should evolve over time to better reflect the user's interests or indeed evolve as those interests change.

Related Work

The services provided by existing Internet information retrieval tools can be divided into four main functions: search, storage, access, and organization.

There are many systems which offer some or all of these to the W3 user, including WAIS [10], Archie [11] and the Harvest system [9]. Harvest is one of the most sophisticated of these types of systems and we briefly describe Harvest and compare it with Jasper. All the systems mentioned above can be characterized as "offline" systems in the sense that their indexes and stores are not built incrementally as in Jasper but are rather constructed offline for later use. The key elements of the Harvest approach are *gatherers* and *brokers*. Gatherers collects indexing information from a given collection of information (http, FTP, and Gopher protocols are supported). Brokers provide query interfaces to the gathered information. Brokers can access more than one gatherer, as well as other brokers. Experiments indicate that Harvest reduces load on servers and networks. This is due to efficient gathering software and the sharing of information among indexes that need it, in contrast to other comparable information retrievers which use expensive object retrieval protocols and fail to coordinate information gathering among themselves.

Harvest queries on W3 brokers return references to relevant information sources, an indication of the degree of match to the query and a content summary. The summarization performed on text files is simply to extract the first 100 lines plus the first sentence of each remaining paragraph. Keywords seem to be an alphabetical list of this summary. It is possible in principle to write and plug in your own summarizer. Harvest also "summarizes" other formats of information, albeit in a fairly simple way. The summary of an audio file, for example, is the file name, while the summary of a perl script is the procedure names and comments therein.

Harvest and Jasper thus differ in several ways: firstly, Harvest is inherently "offline" as discussed above while Jasper is "incremental." Secondly, Harvest summaries are more simplistic than those attempted by Jasper (using ConText), although Harvest provides "summaries" of a wider range of information types.

More similar to Jasper than offline indexers of information is "Warmlist" [12], a tool for caching, searching and sharing W3 documents. Like Jasper, Warmlist extends the idea of the hotlist. W3 documents in the Warmlist are automatically cached on the local server, along with the original links to other information. This gives much quicker access to Warmlist pages. A useful feature of a Warmlist is the ability to include other Warmlists as part of one's own Warmlist. The Glimpse indexing and searching package [13] is used to search cached pages.

In Jasper, we take a different approach by not storing whole pages but rather storing meta-information about a page. As described above, this allows much enhanced, richer indexing on pages of interest without the necessity of copying remote information to local servers. It is possible that with many users on a W3 server using Warmlist, the server would rapidly fill up with cached pages. Also the concept of a page being copied and stored in many different places (i.e., on multiple Warmlists) seems somewhat against the ethos of the web. Given that Warmlist caches entire pages, it is unsurprising that it provides no facilities for information summarization.

W3 documents in a Warmlist can be organized in a hierarchical way with nested directories. As we have argued above, however, a more flexible way to access information is via a set of keywords describing the contents of the page. This removes the necessity to remember where documents have been stored (e.g., Did I store the letter to Smith about the Internet in letters/smith/Internet or Internet/letters or smith/letters or ...?)

We mentioned above the four main functions (search, storage, access, and organization) common to many Internet information tools. In the Jasper system, we have taken the first steps towards adding two further functions: firstly, automated information sharing, secondly, the ability of the agent to model the user's interests based on the user's interaction with the tool. This functionality is not provided by any other Internet tools of which we are aware.

Future Work

In this section, we describe several areas of ongoing or future work.

Retrieval

Jasper agents currently use a very simple keyword retrieval algorithm. No doubt the precision of retrievals could be improved by the adoption of more advanced retrieval techniques such as vector space or probabilistic models [5]. However, the main thrust of the work reported here is not the implementation of document retrieval algorithms but rather an investigation into novel ways of organizing W3 information. An improved retrieval algorithm will nevertheless be included in a future version of Jasper.

Another area of work is the improvement of retrieval capabilities in other directions. Currently, Jasper agents only index pages by ConText-generated and user-supplied keywords. In the introduction to this paper, we discussed the limitations of the filename oriented approach of standard operating systems. We elaborate on this below and suggest a solution to the problem currently being implemented in Jasper.

There are two main problems with the use of filenames to retrieve information: *recall* (remembering the name of a file containing particular information) and *recognition* (knowing the information contained in a given file). As discussed above, we have addressed this problem in Jasper by indexing the information stored on multiple terms (keywords). We now intend to extend this approach in two ways.

Firstly, we will allow indexing on meta-information other than keywords. Initially, the extra meta-information will be the date of storage of a page and the originating site of the page (which Jasper can extract from the URL). These extra indices will allow users (via an HTML form) to frame commands of the type:

Show me all pages I stored in 1994 from Cambridge University about artificial intelligence and information retrieval.

An initial version of this capability has been added to the system, allowing the user to specify the date range of the pages to be retrieved.

Secondly, a thesaurus will be used by Jasper to exploit keyword synonyms. This will reduce the importance of entering precisely the same keywords as were used when a page was stored. Indeed, it is intended to exploit the thesaurus in several other areas, including the personal profiles which an agent holds for its user. Detailed discussion of this idea is beyond the scope of the present paper. In addition, it is hoped that this profile enhancement process will help to improve the relevance of email messages sent by Jasper agents to users. In the current trial, it has been found that overgeneration of email messages can be a problem. This can lead to users preferring to use the What's New? and Interest Group retrieval mechanisms. In effect, there is currently a trade-off between accuracy on the one hand and timeliness and automation on the other; email messages are immediate and proactive but may sometimes be irrelevant, while the other retrieval mechanisms require more effort on the part of the user and are slower but typically yield a higher percentage of relevant information. Feedback from users indicates that the potential of the email approach is recognized and with improved accuracy would be the preferred mechanism.

Adaptive Agents

The use of user profiles by Jasper agents to determine information relevant to their users, though powerful, is currently somewhat clumsy. When the user wants to change context (perhaps refocusing from one task to another, or from work to leisure), he must respecify his profile by adding and/or deleting keywords. A better approach would be for the agent to change the user's profile as the interests of the user change over time, this change of context to occur in two ways. There could be a short-term switch of context from, for example, work to leisure. The agent should identify this from a list of current contexts it holds for a user and change into the new context. This change could be triggered, for example, when a new page of different information type is visited by the user. There will also be longer term changes in the contexts the agent holds based on evolving interests of the user. These changes can be inferred from observation of the user by the agent. Work has not yet begun in this area, but techniques under investigation for a learning agent include genetic algorithms, learning from feedback, and memory-based reasoning [3, 7].

Integration of Remote and Local Information

Finally, a possible further development of Jasper would be to integrate the user's own computer filing system with the IPS, so that information found on W3 and on the local machine would appear homogenous to the user at the top level. Files could then be accessed similarly to the way in which Jasper agents access W3 pages, freeing the user from the constraints of name-oriented filing systems and providing a contents-addressable interface to both local and remote information of all kinds.

Conclusion

In his seminal article, Bush [6] describes a tool to aid the human mind in dealing with information. He states that previous scientific advances have helped humans in their interactions with the physical world but have not assisted humans in dealing with large amounts of knowledge and information. Bush proposed a tool called a "memex" which could augment human memory through associative memory, where related pieces of information are linked. Trails through these links could then be stored and shared by others. W3 itself fulfils Bush's vision in some respects; Bush's associative memory can be seen in the hyperlinks of W3. What is lacking is a way of organizing this vast "memory" of W3 pages into coherent "trails" which can be saved and communicated to others. Currently, only relatively simplistic hotlists and menus are available.

Jasper goes some way to addressing these problems by providing agents which, as we have seen, can store meta-information about W3 pages which can then be used to retrieve relevant pages quickly and easily and share the information contained in those pages with other users with the same interests. Jasper leaves aside the issue of how best to search W3 for information (many other researchers are working on this) and is an attempt to address the complementary problem of how best to store information once it has been found and how to share information with others with the same interests. As we have discussed, Jasper agents also have the ability to proactively suggest improvements to users' profiles based on the behavior of the user.

As discussed above, much remains to be done; in particular, the exploitation of more of the metainformation obtained by Jasper agents, improving the ability of a Jasper agent to identify pages of interest to a user, and the provision of adaptive

agents which can infer context from users' actions will be useful enhancements to the current system. However, we believe Jasper is a small step along the road towards the original vision for W3 [8] as a network which supports cooperative working and the sharing of information. ■

Acknowledgments

Mike Knul of BT Laboratories contributed to the early discussions which led to the development of Jasper.

References

1. *http://lycos.cs.cmu.edu*

2. *http://www.stir.ac.uk/jsbin/jsii*

3. Jones, W.P., "On the applied use of human memory models: the memory extender personal filing system," *Int. J. Man-Machine Studies,* 25, 191-228, 1986.

4. Lahkari, Y., Metral, M., and Maes, P., "Collaborative Interface Agents," *MIT Internal Report,* 1994.

5. Salton, G., "Automatic Text Processing," Addison-Wesley, Reading, Mass., USA, 1989.

6. Bush, V., "As We May Think," *The Atlantic Monthly,* July 1945. Also available as *http://www.csi.uottawa.ca/~dduchier/misc/vbush/as-we-may-think.html*

7. Sheth, B. and Maes, P., "NEWT: A Learning Approach to Personalised Information Filtering," MIT Thesis, 1993.

8. Berners-Lee, T., *http://www10.w3.org/hypertext/W3/Summary.html*

9. Bowman, C.M., Danzig, P.B., Hardy, D., Manber, U., and Schwartz, M., "The Harvest Information Discovery and Access System," *Proceedings of the 2nd International WWW Conference,* Chicago Illinois, October 1994.

10. Brewster, K. and Medlar, A., "An Information System for Corporate Users: Wide Area Information Servers," *Connections—The Interoperability Report,* 5(11), November 1991. Also available from *ftp://think.com/wais/wais-corporate-paper.text*

11. Emtage, A. and Deutsch, P., "Archie: an electronic directory service for the Internet," *Proceedings of the Usenix Winter Conference,* January 1992.

12. Klark, P. and Manber, U., "Developing a Personal Internet Assistant," *http://glimpse.cs.arizona. edu:1994/~paul/warmlist/paper.html*

13. Manber, U. and Wu, S., "GLIMPSE: A Tool to Search through Entire File Systems," *Usenix Winter 1994 Technical Conference*, San Francisco, January 1994.

About the Authors

John Davies, Richard Weeks, and **Mike Revett**
Advanced Applications & Technology
BT Laboratories
Ipswich IP5 7RE UK
{*john.davies, richard.weeks, mike.revett*}*@bt-sys. bt.co.uk*

CONSTELLATION

A WEB-BASED DESIGN FRAMEWORK FOR
DEVELOPING NETWORK APPLICATIONS

Nino Vidovic, Dalibor F. Vrsalovic

Abstract

Constellation is a Web-based design framework for developing distributed applications which allows a single user or group of users to concurrently access and manipulate different aspects of a distributed application from a simple Mosaic-like front-end tool. Users can edit and build programs and documents, manage source code, debug and instrument running distributed programs, read manual pages and other documents, browse through source code and much, much more from a simple yet powerful front-end tool. Constellation is designed to work in a heterogeneous networked environment. It works with different host types and different OS environments, and supports different communication protocols. It is designed to work with hybrid client/server applications that consist of new as well as legacy code. Constellation is easily extensible to support new protocols, hosts, servers, services and back-end tools. **Keywords:** *Distributed applications, client/server applications, design framework, distributed debugging, group debugging, development environment*

Introduction

In response to societal demand, computer networks have been proliferating rapidly in recent years. Such networks include local area networks (LANS) and wide area networks (WANS) comprising a number of computers that may communicate with one another. Apart from sending messages, this communication between networked computers allows programs to be run on more than one computer in a network. For example, an airline reservation service may present a user interface on a client computer while data input to the interface is transmitted to a server computer where a reservation database is accessed. This type of program execution, known as distributed programming, may be much more complicated than the above example but is nonetheless extremely common and efficient.

Distributed programs, however, are often written, developed and tested on different computers with different tools which are tightly bound to the particular machine upon which they operate

and are integrated around language, computing platform, or type of application.

This problem is illustrated in Figure 1.

In the above example, the graphic user-interface portion may be developed on the client computer with a set of program tools for the Visual C++ programming language for PC Windows and a different set of tools for a graphic user-interface (GUI) builder. Similarly, the reservation database may be developed on the server with a set of program tools from the C++ Workshop programming language running under Unix. In Figure 1, those development environments are denoted as DE1, DE2 and DE3. Furthermore, a program initially developed with a tool set can frequently be redeveloped under a later version of the same tool set, and possibly from a different manufacturer.

Thus, distributed programs present substantial difficulties to programmers since they must learn to operate the tool set that was used to develop each distributed program segment. These tool sets are usually quite detailed and require days, weeks, and even months to master. Furthermore,

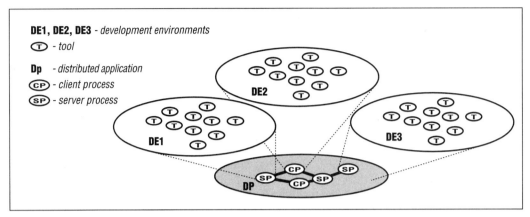

Figure 1: Designing network applications using traditional programming environments

to edit, view, or debug the distributed program currently requires performing these functions under one tool set for a particular program segment, exiting the tool set, locating the tool set for a different program segment, which may be on a different computer, and entering that tool set. This type of operation is extremely time consuming, especially where a program has a large number of segments, each developed with a different tool set.

By employing a particular protocol, the World Wide Web has met the challenge of allowing users, through a single front-end tool, to browse documents that reside on a large number of different platforms. The World Wide Web, however, which has been in existence for a number of years, does not provide for any other types of functions apart from browsing and the previously described problems presented by distributed programs remain.

So, there is a need for a system that provides the capability to develop distributed programs that operate on different computers, operating systems, and communication protocols, while requiring only one set of tools. Furthermore, there is a need for a system that allows such integration for programs that have already been partially developed or completely developed under a variety of tool environments and that require

modification. More broadly, there is a need for a system that allows a single front-end tool to perform operations on a plurality of files that reside on different platforms without requiring a user to separately access each separate platform-specific piece on that platform.

The Constellation framework answers these and many other needs.

Constellation

The Constellation framework provides methods and mechanisms for a front-end navigating tool (the "Navigator") that may access and manipulate files distributed across different platforms. Figure 2 depicts Constellation framework as a cone with the Navigator at the top and a distributed program in its base. The front-end navigating tool communicates with a multitude of server processes, resident on networked servers, to perform all types of file manipulations such as debugging and editing. The server processes communicate with gateway processes (resident on the same machine as the calling server process) that perform the desired function on any of a multitude of program segments that may be distributed across a network of computers.

Debugging is one example of a function that may involve distributed files. To service a debugging

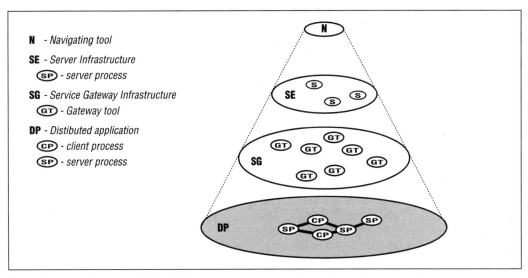

Figure 2: Cone model of a distributed programming environment

request, the navigator issues a request according to the URL protocol. Thus, a request is of the form: <server_type://<machine/<request, where server type is a protocol such as, for example, HTTP or process, machine is the actual server address, and request is the program or file that is requested. The appropriate machine and server process is then contacted by the navigator and provided with the name of the file, *file A*. The server process in turn selects the appropriate gateway process to perform the desired function. The gateway process attaches to the desired program, which is subsequently debugged. If the program calls a program on a different machine, the Constellation framework provides a variety of mechanisms, transparent to the user, for allowing debugging to continue on the called program. In a preferred embodiment, the gateway process provides the server process with the address of the called program, file B. The server process notifies the navigator which then automatically assembles a request to the server process on the different host. The request is sent and the server process selects the appropriate gateway process, which then attaches to the target program, *file B*. If *file B* returns to *file A*, then control is again

passed to the navigator which calls *file A* as before except that the gateway process has maintained the appropriate address of the instruction after the call instruction to *file B*. Debugging then continues on *file A*.

Browsing, editing, and any other function requests are similarly serviced through the front-end navigator. A URL link contacts an appropriate server process resident on a target machine and the server process in turn selects the proper gateway process, which performs the desired function on the target file. The target file may include hypertext links to other files, and functions can easily be performed on these files by clicking on the file names and then indicating a desired function. In this manner, users can efficiently access and manipulate distributed files through a single front-end tool.

System Architecture

Figure 3 is an overview of the architecture of the Constellation framework. The architecture comprises a front-end navigating tool (Navigator) that communicates with a multitude of server processes (PROCD, HTTPD and PROGD) to perform different functions such as debugging, source-

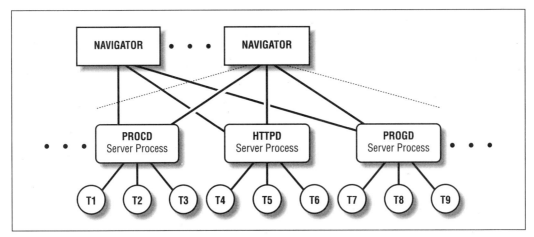

Figure 3:   Architecture of the Constellation design framework

code management, and source-code browsing and editing. The server processes PROCD, HTTPD, and PROGD communicate with gateway processes (tools) T1, T2, T3, T4, T5, T6, T7, T8, and T9 that perform a desired function on any of a multitude of program segments that may be distributed across a network of computers. As will be described more fully below, the navigating tool comprises a browser, editor, and interactive shell and allows users to perform a variety of functions on distributed program segments. For example, the server process HTTPD may comprise a document server that communicates with file, *man2html* and mail gateway processes T4, T5 and T6 to perform browsing functions. Similarly, the server process PROCD may comprise a process server that communicates with dbx, PC-debug, and gdb gateway processes T1, T2 and T3 to perform debugging functions. The architecture illustrated in Figure 3 may be easily extended to include many other server processes and gateway processes as indicated by the dashed lines. Furthermore, Constellation framework allows two navigators to simultaneously access the same server process, gateway tool, and file, Also, two Navigators can communicate with each other in a networked environment.

As will be described more fully below, each of the server processes PROCD, HTTPD and PROGD illustrated in Figure 3 may reside on a plurality of physical machines. The architecture of the Constellation framework provides for the integration of a variety of tools, including debugging, document-and source-code browsing and editing, source-code management, and program development and building. The implementation of these tools according to the architecture of the Constellation framework will be described in the following sections of this paper. The architecture of the Constellation framework as illustrated in Figure 3 may be applied to many other types of tools, including user-defined tools.

Navigating front-end tool

The Navigator is a browser and at the same time an editor and an interactive shell. Browser capabilities are similar to those of Web browsers such as Mosaic or HotJava. As an editor, the Navigator has basic text-editing functionality of point and click editors, such as Textedit with command bindings for Emacs and Vi. Editor's capabilities are augmented to support hyper-text (i.e., HTML) program annotations. Interactive shell capability allows users direct interactions with browser's interpreter engines as well as with interactive

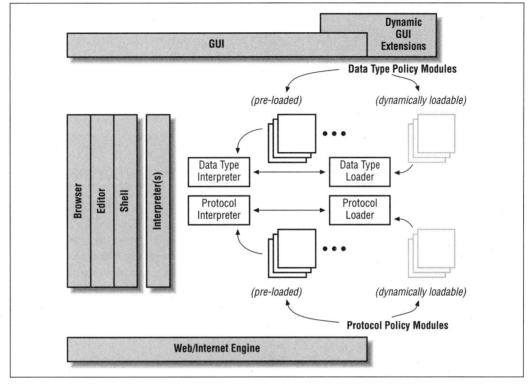

Figure 4:   An architecture of the Navigator front-end tool

programs with which the Navigator has established links (e.g., gateway debug engines such as dbx).

The architecture of the Navigator is shown in Figure 4.

The Navigator consists of the following basic components: Web/Internet engine, Browser, Editor, Interactive shell, Interpreters (e.g., Tcl or Java), Data-Types Processing Engine, Protocol-Processing Engine and GUI. The Web/Internet engine provides access to the Internet and Web. Browser provides basic Web client functionality. Editor allows pages in the Navigator to be edited. Interactive shell capability allows Navigator to hold interactive sessions. The Interpreters are mechanisms which allow dynamic extension of Web protocols and data types, as well as Navigators GUI. Data-Type Processing Engine allows

dynamic retrieval of policy modules (e.g., Tcl or Java programs) to process unknown data types. Protocol-Processing Engine allows the Navigator to process unknown protocol requests by dynamically loading protocol policy modules (e.g., Tcl or Java protocol driver programs).

The GUI module creates a control panel for the Navigator and maps the contents of users' searches into a graphic domain. The novel feature of the Navigator is its capability to dynamically reconfigure its control panel based on the type of the request and the domain in which browsing is performed. For example, when the user makes a request to debug a program, a debug server that services browsing requests in process domain will be contacted, and the appropriate protocol policy module in Navigator will be downloaded (if not already present) and activated. In a debugging example, this processing would result in a debugging menu being created and then attached to the Navigator's command panel. The debugging menu would stay attached for the duration of the debugging session. Upon completion of the debugging session, the debugging menu would be automatically removed from the Navigator's control panel.

The Navigator can operate in a stateless or statefull mode. Stateless mode is used in events such as directory browsing or information retrieval. Statefull mode is used during distributed debugging sessions. The statefull sessions are characterized by long-live connections into a browsing domain. The Navigator keeps track of all long-live connections for all active statefull sessions. The long-live connection represents a bi-directional communication channel into a browsing domain. The user can post a request to the server which is servicing given domain. Also, the server can generate events and send them back to the Navigator.

No limits exist on a number of the concurrent long-live connections. The Navigator allows all long-live connections to be active at the same time. Policy modules are responsible for coordinating events received from domain servers.

Constellation's service layer

The Constellation service layer consists of a collection of domain servers and gateway tools. Gateway tools are either interface, to service providers (e.g., database access) or service providers. The following list is a sample of domain servers and related gateway tools:

- Document Servers and Service Gateways
- http, file, ftp...
- *man2html, sccs2html, names2html*
- Process Servers and Service Gateways
- Debugging (Dynamic Services) server
- dbx, PC-debug, gdb, RTP, etc.
- Program Servers and Service Gateways

- Program (Static services) server
- cscope, c++class
- Teleconferencing Server and Service Gateways
- showme conference manager
- Audio, video, white board

Debugging

Figure 5 is a block diagram showing how the architecture of the Constellation framework communicates to service a debugging request.

First, the Navigator issues a request according to the Universal Resource Locator (URL) protocol. Thus, a request is of the form: <server_type:// <machine/<request, where server type is a protocol such as, for example, HTTP or process, machine is the actual server address, and request is the program or file that is requested. The appropriate server process PROCD resident on a host 1 is then contacted by the Navigator and provided with the name of the file of a running client process, file A. The server process PROCD in turn selects the appropriate gateway tool PC-debug to perform the desired function.

The gateway tool PC-debug attaches to the target program (application's client process), which is subsequently debugged. If the target program calls a program (application's server process) on a different machine, the Constellation framework provides a variety of mechanisms, transparent to the user, for allowing debugging to continue on the called program. In Figure 5, the gateway tool PC-debug provides the server process PROCD with the address of the called program, *file B*. The server process PROCD notifies the Navigator, which then automatically assembles a URL request to a server process PROCD on the different host. The request is sent and the server process PROCD selects the appropriate gateway process dbx which then attaches to the target program (application's server process), *file B*. If *file B* returns to *file A*, then control is again

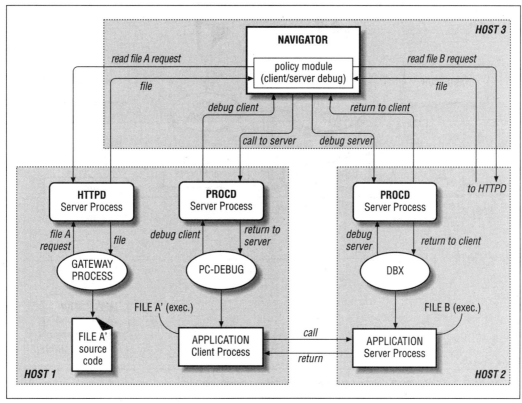

Figure 5:   Communication sequence when servicing a debugging request

passed to the navigator which calls *file A* as before except that the gateway process PC-debug has maintained the appropriate address of the instruction after the call instruction to *file B*. Debugging then continues on *file A*. In this manner, programs that are debugged by two different tools, for example dbx and PC-debug, may be debugged through a single front-end Navigator.

Constellation Framework supports groupware functions such as group debugging sessions and teleconferencing. Figure 6 is a block diagram showing how the architecture of the Constellation framework communicates to service a group debugging request.

First, the Navigator on host 1 issues a request according to the Universal Resource Locator (URL) protocol. Thus, a request is of the form:

process://<machine/pid=7lt;pid_number, where machine is the actual server address and pid number is the process-identification number of a running program. The appropriate server process PROCD resident on a host1 is then contacted by the Navigator and provided with the pid of a running server process. The server process PROCD in turn selects the appropriate gateway tool dbx to perform the desired function. The gateway tool dbx attaches to the target program which is subsequently debugged.

Request to clone The Navigator is then sent to host 1. After cloning navigator on host 2 is connected to the server process PROCD on host 1, a joint debugging session of the application server program is established. Furthermore, during the cloning process, navigator on host 1 issued a talk

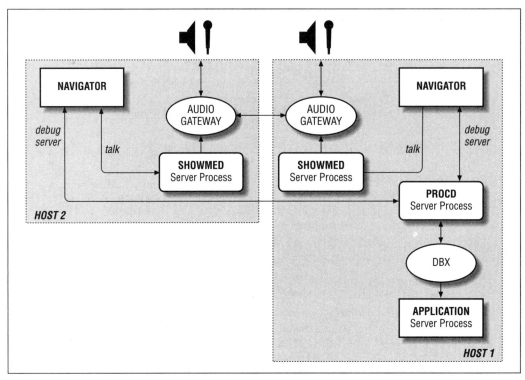

Figure 6:   Concurrent debugging session with teleconferencing

request to showmed conference manager. After the manager accepts talk request, audio gateway tools are launched on both hosts enabling navigators to concurrently have voice communications and group debugging session.

File browsing and editing

Figure 7 illustrates one possible block diagram for browsing and editing files, which may comprise source code or any other type of document. A user can browse and edit documents in an infinite number of ways and Figure 7 illustrates one possible browsing and editing session to illustrate the operation of a preferred embodiment of the Constellation framework. To read a file, *file A*, the Navigator issues a request according to the URL protocol, as previously described. The HTTPD server process on the appropriate machine is provided with the request, and the

appropriate gateway tool is contacted to retrieve the file. The file, *file A*, is then provided to the navigator for viewing and editing. Unlike World Wide Web browsing tools, the Constellation framework provides the ability to edit files and replace an old file with an edited file. Thus, the navigator allows the user to edit the file and the navigator then formulates the appropriate URL, indicating the file, *file B*, when the user desires to save the edited file. The appropriate server process and gateway process are contacted and the edited file is stored.

In addition to browsing, editing, and saving files, the Constellation framework dynamically generates information concerning the content of retrieved files. For example, a user may desire to analyze a program according to its data structures, function calls and other characteristics. To perform such an operation on a file, the naviga-

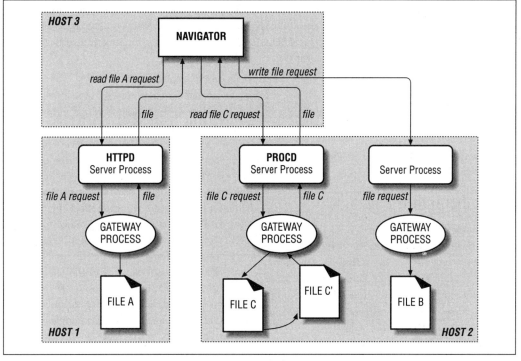

Figure 7:   Editing and source-code browsing functions of the Constellation framework

tor issues a request according to the URL proto-col, as previously described. An appropriate server process PROGD on the target machine is provided with the request and an appropriate gateway tool (e.g., cscope) analyzes the file and provides the results of the analysis to the naviga-tor.

Summary

The Constellation framework provides methods and mechanisms for a front-end navigating tool that may access and manipulate files distributed across different physical machines and platforms. The front-end navigating tool communicates with a multitude of server processes, resident on net-worked servers, to perform all types of file manipulations such as debugging, source-code management, and editing. The server processes communicate with gateway processes (resident on the same machine as the calling-server pro-cess) that perform the desired function on any of a multitude of program segments that may dis-tributed across a network of computers.

The Constellation framework supports many functions, such as debugging, source-code man-agement, source-code browsing, multi-platform builds, editing, and document browsing. The Constellation framework prototype has been developed mostly in Tcl7.4/Tk4.0 with approxi-mately one full-time and one part-time engineer in a 6-month period. It works on Solaris and Win-dows NT platforms. ∎

Acknowledgments

Thanks to John Ousterhout for early release of Tcl7.4/Tk4.0. Thanks to the DOE debugger team, Jon Masamitsu and Andrew Davidson, for bear-ing with me while installing DOE and integrating

DOE debugging support. Thanks to DevPro's Ivan Soleimanipour for volunteering to extend dbx's API with yet another call and Achut Reddy for sharing his experience and code for program browsing. Special thanks go to Steven Li for porting Constellation to the Windows environment.

References

1. "The World Wide Web, a global information initiative," *http://www.w3.org*

2. Ousterhout, J.K., *Tcl and the Tk Toolkit*, Addison-Wesley, 1994.

About the Authors *

Nino Vidovic

AT&T—Business Communication Services
Dr. Vidovic recently joined AT&T as Advanced Network Clients Technology Director in the BCS Operations group. His responsibilities include architecture development and implementation of next-generation network client systems. Prior to joining AT&T, Dr. Vidovic served as the Senior Staff Engineer in Advance Techology Group, Sun Microsystems, Inc. While at Sun Microsystems, he was responsible for identification of new technologies for development of network-enabled applications. He holds a doctorate in computer science from the University of Zagreb, Croatia, and an M.S. in computer engineering from Carnegie Mellon.

Dalibor F. Vrsalovic

AT&T—Business Communication Services
Dr. Vrsalovic recently joined AT&T as Advanced Technology Vice President in the BCS Operations group. His responsibilities include providing leadership to the architectural development effort for host platforms to be used in the next generation of network-based services as well as establishing AT&T's long-term leadership in global services and distributed computing. Prior to joining AT&T, Dr. Vrsalovic served as the Chief Scientist for Sun Microsystems, Inc. While at Sun Microsystems, he was responsible for the architecture development and implementation of software products. In addition to R&D, he has held leadership roles in bringing new technologies to general business use and product quality assurance. He holds a doctorate in computer science and an M.S. in computer engineering from the University of Zagreb, Croatia.

---

* This work was done while authors were working at SunSoft Inc.

Linking in a Global Information Architecture

Karen R. Sollins, Jeffrey R. Van Dyke

Abstract

*As network-based applications and knowledge-based systems become more prevalent and useful, it will become increasingly important to provide a common, long-lived model of the infrastructure on top of which such applications will exist. Not only does the longevity and evolvability of the infrastructure have a direct impact on the value of the information in it, but also the provisioning of a meta-level infrastructure capable of defining relationships among the pieces of information become increasingly important. In this paper, we first examine a general, flexible information architecture and then enhance it with an extensible, simple model of linking, recommended as a component of the substrate of network-based applications and knowledge-based systems of the future. **Keywords:** Information infrastructure, linking*

Introduction

A system of any sort has behind it a model or architecture that defines the components of the system and how they relate to each other. The architecture will determine the extent and limitations of the system, by providing a set of capabilities. Architectures can be more or less restrictive and more or less complex, making the capabilities of a system implementing the architecture more or less accessible to the client of the system. If the architecture is both restrictive and complex, it is likely that a system implementing it will be less understandable to a user of the system than simpler, less restrictive architectures.

As the Internet grows, we find ourselves in a world of evolving heterogeneity. There is a multiplicity of transport technologies, protocol suites, programming and runtime communications paradigms, and applications support services. In addition, there are the applications on top of all this. Many organizations find that although they want to be able to take advantage of new developments in technology in terms of speed, effective utilization of resources, and increased functionality, they also have at least some applications that are extremely stable; they do not want to revise or rewrite those applications as the technology evolves.

In addition, the information generated by the organizations often has a longer lifetime than we have traditionally expected, presenting us with two closely related issues. First, with time the computing universe is expanding. Second, this longer-lived information will often outlive the original application from or for which it was created. By being both more widely available and more independent of specific applications, the information becomes more valuable to society as a whole.

If we take a layered perspective, we have distributed and network-based applications supported by transport protocols between hosts. The discussion above motivates the provision of an information infrastructure, separating the applications from the supporting infrastructure. This is, in effect, moving the boundary of what is "in the network" yet further into the host machine and pushing to include not only references and access to information, but also information structure or relationships. The implication is that using a name to build, find, or access information or relationships among information objects will be comparable to accessing other resources provided by the network. We will need a global model with standard access models or protocols for learning about and accessing information resources.

Over a number of years the Internet community has developed various network-wide information architectures. One early such architecture is based on FTP [18], the file transfer protocol. The elements of FTP are file repositories and files themselves. The repositories or hosts are identified by the Domain Name System [13, 14] and communicate with each other by the FTP command set. Files are named by the repository on which they reside. FTP does not distinguish among sorts of files, although it does permit several transfer modes, such as ascii and binary, providing simplistic presentation models. With the growth of systems such as Gopher [1] and the widely used World Wide Web [2], the nature of Internet-based information architectures has taken another leap forward. At this point it is valuable to consider carefully the strengths of such an architecture and any future requirements for it, in order that it evolve effectively.

Setting aside any global architecture for information, distributed architectures have become popular for a variety of reasons. First, since much information and its management are by nature distributed, distributed capabilities better reflected the inherent nature of the information. Second, the parallelism of multiple machines provided higher throughput. And, third, distribution and replication provided improved resiliency to failures.

Within the general framework of global information architectures, we will focus most specifically on *linking*. One of the weaknesses of the FTP architecture was the inability to build a super-structure within it. For example, although a file name might be embedded in a file that was retrieved, the architecture and therefore the implementation had no way of recognizing the content of a retrieved object in order to discern any composite or structured relationship expressed within an object. In comparison, the hypertext model, as proposed, for example, in the Dexter model [7], reflecting a consensus among hypertext models, or instantiated in the World Wide Web, has as a central component of the model, the ability to build and recognize in the architecture arbitrary relationships among objects. Linking of this sort allows for a significantly increased value in the information system because there is an ability to store, manage, retrieve and manipulate not only the base information, but also the relationships among them or the infrastructure.

In the context of a general information infrastructure architecture, we will examine the issues surrounding linking, concluding with a system that supports general, flexible and extensible linking. First, we will explore the requirements for both a general information architecture and more specifically for linking within such an architecture. With this in mind we will consider the work of others, and in particular, other linking models. We will then lay out the information architecture of the Information Mesh, and with this general model in mind, address the architecture and design of links and related linking issues. The Information Mesh Project lays out a common, extremely general substrate that sits between network-based systems such as distributed programming or database environments and network transport protocols such as TCP or other bitstream protocols. The intention is to provide sharing and exchange of potentially long-lived information independently from the underlying transports protocols and related infrastructure. For a complete description of this work and its implementation see [23].

Requirements

We begin the discussion of requirements by considering those of an information architecture such as the Information Mesh in general terms. Within such an architecture, we then consider the specific requirements for linking. The general requirements lead to an object model by means which satisfies our requirements for linking.

Requirements for the General Information Architecture

As discussed above, allowing for heterogeneity while providing a stable architecture within which applications can exist is critically important. In addition, it is clear that, because network-based activities will occur across administrative and programming model boundaries, no single model, policy, or even set of policy mechanisms, nor, as a matter of fact, any single way of doing anything will suffice. As we will see in the Information Mesh architecture, implementations and realizations of it can be separated cleanly from the architecture, allowing for heterogeneity, multiplicity, and flexibility coincidentally with a common infrastructural model. In terms of layering, the Information Mesh architecture provides a minimal model below the level of any application, that will allow it to survive and permit new applications and applications paradigms to evolve unconstrained by the infrastructure.

The goals of the Information Mesh project are:

- *Ubiquity.* The Information Mesh should provide support for network-based applications accessing information that is distributed both physically throughout the net and administratively across regions of differing management policies.

- *Longevity.* Both information and identifiers for the information should be able to survive indefinitely; this means that, at some level of abstraction, the same object is considered to exist for all practical purposes 100 or more years.

- *Mobility.* Information should be able to move not only from one physical location to another, but also from one administrative region to another. An administrative region may range in scope from organizations claiming their own boundaries to individuals managing their own objects, or handing that control to someone else.

- *Homogeneity.* The Information Mesh should provide a single model for information identification, location, and access, as a substrate for distributed systems and applications. Such an abstraction barrier should allow for taking advantages of increased functionality only when desired. A stable substrate model is a requirement for a world in which applications and information have independent lives.

- *Heterogeneity.* The Information Mesh should be prepared for changes from both above and below. It should be flexible enough to encompass new network services as they evolve. It should also support a broad set of expectations from applications as well as administrative controls.

- *Resiliency.* In an extremely large network, unreliability is a fact of life. Hence, there may be situations in which it will be impossible to locate or access a particular piece of information. Both the Information Mesh and the applications using it should be resilient to such a lack of success.

- *Evolvability.* The Information Mesh should be prepared to evolve as application and administrative requirements evolve. This may mean supporting new sorts of information, as well as new sorts of relationships. Particular pieces of information may even evolve as new aspects of them are created or recognized. As mentioned above, the Mesh should also be prepared to take advantage of the evolution of lower-level support.

- *Minimality.* In order to succeed, the Information Mesh should be as simple as possible, placing a minimum of requirements and restrictions on its users. We must understand what is required of it to achieve the other goals identified here, and provide no more than that minimum.

In the section entitled "An Architecture: An Object Model," we will describe an architecture that meets these requirements.

Requirements for Linking

In addition to the requirements for the Information Mesh architecture, we can identify six additional requirements for linking and building relationships, as listed below. As we will see in the discussion in the section entitled, "A Linking Architecture," by making the features explicit, they can be managed and utilized in a consistent and clean manner.

- *Multiplicity.* One must be able to express relationships between two or more objects.

- *Link typing.* It is important to be able to express the nature of a link or relationship extensibly and with unlimited scope, in order to support evolution in the representation of knowledge.

- *Linking into the structure of objects.* In order to provide generality and flexibility in linking objects, it is necessary to be able to link components, aspects, views, or parts of objects to each other.

- *Linking to links.* There are situations in which the ideas being linked may be themselves links. We must be able to relate to links.

- *Composition of objects.* Relationships can be divided into those that are intrinsic or integral to an object and those that are not. If a relationship is intrinsic to an object, that composite object is unable to behave in the intended manner without its components. In contrast, other extrinsic relationships do not have a direct bearing on whether or not the related objects behave as expected. It is important to be able to express this distinction and support composite objects.

- *Support existing models of linking.* Existing systems define the minimum set of characteristics we must enable or support.

Of these issues, we will see later that composition will be provided by a separate mechanism, as a result of supporting the others with a single mechanism. Composition provides the ability to combine more than one object into a single composite object, expressing a "requires" relationship, a statement that a particular set of objects playing specified roles are required for the composite to behave in its intended manners. Composites will be discussed further in the section called "Composites." Within the context of the goals and requirements identified above, we will address related work.

Related Work

The related work that is addressed here falls into two categories. The first is work that relates to the Information Mesh in general. Here, the background is quite broad, so we will simply touch on a sampling, discussing both the naming and addressing issues, as well as typing. The second set of related works again are only a sampling, in this case to demonstrate the breadth of current thinking in linking models. One should understand the scope of linking models, because, if our proposal is to be general purpose, it must support existing systems as well as any requirements.

In terms of naming and addressing, the work that is most closely related to the Information Mesh is what is coming from the Internet Engineering Task Force, in particular the separation of location from long-lived naming, as found in URLs [9, 3] and URNs [20]. In this model, a URL specifies not only the location or address of an object, but also, at least traditionally, the access protocol as well. This is also current practice in the World Wide Web [4]. In contrast, URNs are intended to be long-lived, globally unique, and permanently assigned to a single network-based resource. There are older global naming schemes, such as the Domain Name System [13] and X.500 [17]. Although names in both of these systems are globally defined, there are no restrictions on reusing a name for different objects at different times. In contrast, in a system such as ANSA [21], naming [22] is not global, but rather a federation of more local naming contexts, with gateways among them to translate them. By this technique, within each context there is a single model of naming the whole universe. One can incorporate any legacy naming system at the cost of requiring both negotiation at the time of federation of legacy systems and that names always be recognizable as such at times of transmission, since translation is required. In addition, it is not clear whether cyclic naming can systematically be avoided.

The typing model has three major sources of references, those that provide functional abstraction, such as the CLU programming language [10] and CORBA interfaces [16], those that define a more structural abstraction, such as CLOS [8], and those that support polymorphism, in particular KRL [6] and Eiffel [12]. CLU provides the ability to define an extensible set of data abstractions. Representation and implementation are not part of the specification, but rather only the signatures of the procedures defined for each *cluster*. An object is created as an instance of a particular cluster and remains exactly that and no more throughout its existence. CORBA has a similar model for its *interfaces*, with the additional feature that an interface can inherit from one or more other interfaces, providing for an inheritance relationship among interfaces. CLOS defines classes which reflect the structure that an object of each class will have. Functionality is factored out in this model, but provided by a combination of *generic procedures* and the methods that implement them. A class does not specify which generic procedures are or should be provided for an object of a particular class. Eiffel and KRL both propose polymorphic typing models. In addition, KRL allows for an object to evolve in terms of the sort of knowledge it embodies as it becomes better defined. The Information Mesh *role* model takes aspects of all of these, in order to provide the functionality and structure that each object supports.

In terms of linking models, we will summarize the issues by considering various aspects of hypermedia modelling. In particular, the Dexter model [7], Xanadu [15], Aquanet [11], and the

World Wide Web [2, 5]. Rather than cataloguing all these systems, we will discuss them based on various features: scalability, typing, availability of substructures for linking, link endpoint capabilities, and characteristics of links themselves.

First is the question of ubiquity, and whether a system that supports or allows for it even exists. Neither Dexter nor Xanadu scales up; both require links and other system information be completely available at all times. The WWW does better, by providing URLs that are globally defined, but are location dependent, limiting one's ability to relocate or replicate documents in different places.

Second, the typing mechanisms for nodes and links in these systems vary widely. Xanadu provides no typing for nodes or links. The WWW provides a single "relation" name for links, allowing for a string, defined by the W3 Consortium. These are single valued strings with no formal definition behind them. Aquanet supports hierarchically extensible typing for nodes and links alike. These provide structural constraints based on the CLOS model, but no definition of functionality. Thus, Aquanet supports polymorphism, while the other models do not. The WWW and Dexter also provide an attribute-value mechanism for nodes and links. This allows for the association of characteristics with links and nodes, although this mechanism is, strictly speaking, not a typing mechanism as with the WWW single values for relations. It has a serious name conflict problem, because there is no model of global naming or attribute-name resolution in either system.

Each of these typing mechanisms has limitations. Single-value mechanisms limit the expressive capabilities of individual users. Hierarchical types limit type associations by requiring a single position in the hierarchy. Attribute-value pairs have naming conflicts which limit expressive capability. These limitations emphasize the need for an extensible typing mechanism.

Third, in general, the structure of objects being linked is not part of the link-typing facilities described above and therefore the question of exposure of the substructure of objects must be addressed separately. Aquanet provides no substructure exposure, allowing only linking to whole nodes. In contrast, Xanadu exposes complete documents, supporting linking to parts of documents by pattern matching against strings. Dexter and the WWW provide a middle ground in which arbitrary anchors can be defined on ranges within objects, at the instance level. There is no model that objects of one sort might all have the same names for some consistent set of anchors. HTML 3.0 [19] will provide naming and therefore linking to almost all syntactic structures. There will still be no model that there will be sorts, kinds or types of objects that will have consistently named substructures.

Fourth, link endpoint capabilities are generally loosely coupled to substructure exposure. For example, because Aquanet exposes no substructure, link endpoints can do no better than link to whole nodes. The WWW and Dexter base endpoints on anchors, linking from one object to another. One should note that in HTML, one can define either end of a link to be a whole object. By using the "link" feature of the header element, one can link from a whole object. One need not specify a remote anchor name, in which case the remote endpoint is the whole object. In HTML 2.0, the only elements of a object that can be the ends of a link are anchors. A third alternative is that found in Xanadu, of computed links. These are not related to exposed structure, but rather to the computations available on an object. A powerful link endpoint mechanism would use exposed substructure invariants, yet provide the capability to use computations on nodes.

Finally, there are a number of different sorts of characteristics that each of the systems considers important for links, each with its validity and utility. These are described below:

- *Dimensionality of links.* Xanadu, Aquanet, and Dexter can relate more than two enti-

ties. The WWW restricts links to being two-ended structures.

- *Directionality.* Xanadu expects a distinguishable FROM-SET and TO-SET. In contrast, Dexter marks individual endpoints as either TO, FROM, BIDIRECT, or NONE, although it is not explicit about the meaning of directionality. For example, Dexter might express evolution, transit, or one of a variety of other directional sorts of relationships. The WWW has implicit directionality from the markup in a document to the referent. HTML 3.0 will provide a REV flag to reverse the direction.

- *Presentations.* Dexter links provide a "presentation specifier" with both the link and each endpoint. Aquanet uses a graphical appearance specification associate with node and link types to designate the presentation of Aquanet objects. The WWW uses HTML as a markup language to describe presentations.

- *Link independence.* Aquanet and Dexter links are independent hypertext entities. The WWW and Xanadu require that links be embedded in a hypertext node.

- *Endpoint naming.* All Aquanet endpoints are named. Some WWW and Xanadu endpoints or anchors are named. Dexter does not name its link specifiers.

We will address these aspects of links again in relationship to our own proposal in the section entitled "A Linking Architecture."

An Architecture: An Object Model

Many of the requirements of the Information Mesh are also requirements of systems such as the World Wide Web, in particular ubiquity, support for heterogeneity and the need for homogeneity, as well as minimality. What makes the Information Mesh effort distinctive is the primary focus on longevity and the attendant requirements for mobility and evolution. If the system and the information in it is to survive and continue to be useful, it must be prepared for both mobility, information and clients of the information will move, and evolution, both the information itself and the applications may evolve with time. These are issues that will grow in importance with broader development and deployment of the WWW. As an example, we can consider a text document, which makes reference to a ten-second piece of a video and audio recording of a speech. In order for a client to "read" the text document, there must be available some mechanism for viewing and listening to the section of the speech. At a later date, the audio component is run through a speech recognition system, after which it can be enhanced to have a text component as well, with indications of the relationship between time in the audio and specific words in the text. If the client is prepared for such evolution, the next time the human wishes to read the document, one might be able to print it. Furthermore, at another time, a new, specially tuned video/audio storage service might come into existence. At that time the video/audio components may be moved to the new service for better access, while the whole object also remains at its original location.

In considering this simplistic example, two major issues are highlighted. First, we need to be able to name or identify the object independently of where it is located, or perhaps even of how one accesses it. Second, we need some model of the functionality that objects support, in order both to be able to understand them and also to allow them to evolve. We will consider these two aspects of the Information Mesh separately.

Names and Access

There are three functions that are often tightly coupled in naming. In this work we have separated them, in order to support longevity, mobility, and evolution more effectively. Names are often used for identification, in order to distinguish named objects from each other without direct access to the objects in question. Thus, for example, in many cases the ability to compare two names to determine whether or not they refer to the same object is useful. Depending on uniqueness, one can answer several different questions about the distinction among objects. If no name can be assigned to more than one object, then if two names are equal they refer to the same object. In contrast, only if each object can have no more than one name, can one be certain that if the names are not equal then the objects are not the same object. If a name can be reassigned to different objects, there is no way to use the names to test for equality or distinction among objects.

The second function often provided by names is access. This may take the form of an address with or without an access method, such as a transport protocol. For example, although this may not have been a requirement, URLs, as they are used in the WWW, generally define an address in an address space of a particular transport protocol. Furthermore, it is assumed that that protocol is the one that will be used for accessing the object. Thus, *http://www.w3.org* defines a location of a file. Another common practice is to assume that the machine providing that file expects HTTP to be used to access the file with that name.

The third function often ascribed to names is something descriptive in the name. This may be something that makes it easier for humans to remember the name, such as something about the nature or content of the object, or may be something of use to a program, such as identifying the programming language in which some piece of code is written. These are important functions to provide, although there is no single "best" way to capture them. For names that are intended to be human friendly, one probably does not want them to come from a global namespace. Furthermore, what is mnemonic for one person may not be for another, if for no other reason than that they have different interests in the named object. If we engineer a system in which applications expect to find information in a name, then that information had better remain correct for as long as the name will be used in that way. Many such characteristics cannot be guaranteed not to change. For humans, we are better off providing small, human friendly namespaces, with translations to globally unique names or identifiers, while for applications, we are better off providing some other way of learning about meta-information than embedding it in names.

The proposal for naming in the Information Mesh separates the provision of the three functions from each other. This is similar to the proposal in the IETF standards process. (See the work of the Uniform Resource Identifiers Working Group [9, 20, 3].) Each object or resource in the system has an *oid* (object identifier) or *URN* (Uniform Resource Name). These are globally unique, long-lived (in other words the intention is that they will never be reused), and are not required or expected to carry semantics. Thus an oid or URN will only ever be assigned to one object or resource, and that is its sole required semantics. It may have other semantics that the creator may choose to expose, but no one and nothing can depend on or expect there to be more. Beyond that, in the URI Working Group terminology, there will be Uniform Resource Locators (URL), and Uniform Resource Characteristics (URC). The URL indicates an access protocol and location. The URC is the source of meta-information about a resource. This may contain ownership, access constraints, URLs, and other information about an object. It is also a potential container for information about programming or natural languages, and any other information about an object or resource deemed useful. In the Information Mesh these two sorts of information are separated.

The Information Mesh has a need for a particular sort of meta-information, called *hints*. One assumes that there will be a number of services that are able to resolve URNs into location and protocol information. A collection of hints related to a particular URN will consist of a set of potential routes to accessing the object. The most

direct may be a previously known address. Slightly less direct would be the address of a previously successful resolution service, or a URN for such a service. There may be a variety of such services with varying access policies. Thus, for example, some may be limited to certain communities, or may require a fee, or provide fairly ubiquitous, but not very current information, while others may make an effort to be current, but may not be as readily available. The set of hints at one location may be different from those at another for a variety of reasons, such as varying access policies or previous successes and failures. When a resolution service receives a request, in addition to or in lieu of returning a resolution for a URN, it may return alternative hints, thus further increasing for methods of resolving the URN, and increasing the divergence of hint information for a URN at different locations.

The Information Mesh and the work of the URI group to some extent separate the provision of naming as described here from that needed for humans on an everyday basis. The URN requirements document [20] proposes that URNs should be "human transcribable," as distinct from "human friendly," implying that humans might easily remember and use them.

Thus we reach a position where objects have globally unique, human unfriendly, long-lived names or identifiers that are translated by some service into addresses, or the "names" used by the transport and access services. We have a model for a hint mechanism that supports that translation.

Typing: Roles

The Information Mesh provides a rather distinctive typing model for objects, allowing for more flexibility and evolution than is traditional. The Mesh also must operate in a universe in which, because of its federated nature enforcement of typing cannot be guaranteed. The mesh is composed of a set of cooperating components that can agree to behave correctly, but cannot be forced into correct behavior.

Object behavior in the Information Mesh is built around the concept of the *role*. A role has three aspects: *actions*, *parts*, and *makers*. In each case, some may be required and others optional. Only those that are required will necessarily be provided by all implementations. The actions of a role define the abstract functionality of that role. They are a specification of the actions, not implementations of them. Similarly, parts define the abstract structure of an object playing a particular role, but how the structure is represented in any particular situation is not part of the role specification. Finally, makers define the abstract functions used in creating objects playing a particular role. Again, realizations of makers are distinct from the specification.

Roles are arranged into an inheritance hierarchy such that if an object plays a particular role, it also plays all of that role's super roles. Inheritance is singly rooted in the *object-role* (see "The Basic Object-Role," in Appendix A), but beyond that multiple inheritance and, in fact full polymorphism, is provided. Not only can a role inherit from more than one super role, but also objects can play more than one role at any given time. Furthermore, the set of roles an object plays can evolve over time.

Finally, roles themselves are first class Mesh objects; a role is a Mesh object which describes the actions, parts and makers necessary for an object to play a particular role. Mesh objects which provide such services are said to be playing the *role-role*. Because roles are first class objects and the object-role requires the "roles-played" action, one can always determine the identities (oids) for those roles, and find the definitions of those roles, barring access limitations.

Implementations provide Mesh objects with the ability to "play" a role by describing a concrete representation of a particular role's actions, parts, and makers. Mesh objects may use multiple implementations. Implementations must actually

figure out how to implement new nature on old objects. Implementations are first class objects related to but not part of the roles they implement. There may be more than one implementation of any role.

Thus, the Information Mesh provides a single, extremely general object model. Everything is an object and an object is defined by having one or more oids and playing one or more roles.

Implications for Linking

With the object model supported by the Information Mesh, we provide a simple model in which to support linking that meets the requirement of longevity. There are two aspects to this. First, by separating naming from location, objects can move. Only if and when one needs to access an object identified in a link will resolution occur. Otherwise, if there is a guarantee that oids will not be reused, linking using oids can never cause unpredictable or surprising behavior by linking to a different object by using the original oid.

Second, the defined abstract parts of an object allow for implementation and representation independent linking into the structure of the object. Thus, one can link to a view, component or aspect of an object, with full knowledge that the existence of the part is independent of a particular implementation. It is not based simply on the syntax of a particular instance. Hence, when an object has evolved to a new representation either through time or because of a new location, by linking to parts as defined by a role, the link should remain valid, assuming the object has not mutated at the abstract level in the intervening time.

A Linking Architecture

The proposition of this paper is that the linking problem should be handled by two complementary architectural features. First, the link itself will be a first class Mesh object. Second, intrinsic relationships will be provided a "composite object" mechanism as an enhancement of the basic object-role. We will discuss these two separately.

Links as First Class Objects

In order to support links as objects, we will define a generic link-role. (See Appendix B.) Several other aspects of the object model will comprise the full link model. Each link will be a first class object with one or more oids assigned to it and playing one or more roles. At least one of these roles will be a link-role, either the generic link-role or a subrole of the generic link-role. In that capacity the link will be able to provide the answer to the "get-oids" action, enumerating the oids for all the objects linked by the link in question.

The parts of a generic link are simply an unordered, unnamed set of *endpoints*. Link endpoints, used to refer to an object and (optionally) object substructure, are implemented as *descriptors*. Note that we have not associated a type value with descriptors. A descriptor is a structure containing oid, role, part and selector information. There is no provision in the generic link-role for the selector to determine a set or range of parts. Each descriptor identifies exactly one endpoint. Subroles of the generic link-role can provide such capabilities, leaving the generic link-role as simple and general purpose as possible.

Capabilities to group or distinguish endpoints are not provided in the minimum link-role. Link-role endpoints can be listed in any order; there is no naming of endpoints in the base link-role. Endpoints do not contain an associated type or value, direction, or any other semantic description. The link-role contains two restrictive requirements. First, the number of link endpoints returned by "get-number-endpoints" is required to be a determinable value. Second, the link endpoints returned by "extract-endpoints" must be discrete and returnable. These minimum requirements are unlikely to restrict Mesh link capabilities significantly.

In terms of the sorts of issues addressed in considering other linking models, we can consider each separately. First, the linking model is general, flexible, and extensible enough to allow for whatever sort of link use might be required. None is dictated or proscribed by the model. Second, again because of the extensibility of the typing model, directionality can be expressed in any of the ways required by the pre-existing models. Mesh links are implicitly bidirectional, although this can be enhanced or restricted as needed. Third, links provide for multiplicity, although again any limit on the number of endpoints of a link can be provided by more restrictive link subroles. Fourth, because links are first class objects, they can support models such as Aquanet and Dexter. By being first class objects, links no longer can easily provide intrinsic relationships, but this topic will be addressed further below. Last, because links are relating abstractly structured objects with potentially named components, all the problems addressed in discussing endpoint capabilities and therefore linking into substructures are non-existent in a model such as this. One should note that the generic link-role does not provide for presentation information, but more refined subroles can do this. Mesh links can be defined to provide the more limited capabilities of each of the other systems.

It is important to remember that Mesh links can provide no guarantees about referenced objects; a link may be "dangling" because of object changes. In addition, the unavailability of complete entity information prevents the implementation of a mechanism to determine all links to a particular object. Thus, this feature cannot be provided for such systems as Dexter or Xanadu without further mechanism.

Mesh links can usually be viewed as passive data structures that relate but do not act on objects. We do not expect that the use of a particular link will result in many computations outside of the link object itself. However, there are a few special cases where a link should have the capacity to do more than simply refer to Mesh parts. For instance, Xanadu provides a mechanism for linking to nodes through the use of a computation involving character matching. Mesh links should be able to perform equivalent computations on Mesh objects.

Given the generic Mesh link-role, more interesting link subroles can be defined. For example, one might support endpoints named within the scope of a link, as in Aquanet. As detailed in Appendix C, the section entitled "The Named Link-Role", this will require additions to both the parts and actions of the link-role. As part of support the World Wide Web or Dexter links, one might need the binary-link subrole, requiring only a change or restriction in parts from the generic link-role, as demonstrated in Appendix C. In order to support models such as Dexter, the Web, Aquanet, or Xanadu, roles for their nodes need to be defined as well. For a full description of such roles, see [23]. A third interesting link subrole is the ordered link-role. Here the ordering of the endpoints of a link are important, as defined in Appendix C. Additional new subroles might be defined, inheriting from several of these such as a named binary link. Extensibility and inheritance are important features here.

Composites

There are several possible alternatives for expressing composition in Mesh objects. Security and availability considerations limit our realization options. The main issue is whether composites can be implemented using the basic Mesh capabilities or whether the model will need to be extended. We can identify five options:

- *Requires link.* In theory, all relationships among Mesh entities could be expressed using Mesh links. One could imagine creating a "requires" link to express that a particular Mesh object requires another set of Mesh objects. Unfortunately, independent links cannot describe intrinsic characteristics of Mesh objects because the independent link object could become "separated" in the Mesh. The reason for this is that there is no

implementable Mesh mechanism to determine if all possible link objects have been examined or determined. Thus, links cannot be used to create composite objects.

- *Composite role.* Under this implementation, composite objects play the *composite role*. When a Mesh object plays the composite role, it must answer "requires" questions for all other playable roles of the object. This means that the underlying representation of an object, whether it currently happens to be composed of several other objects, will determine which roles it does or does not play. This tight coupling between abstraction and implementation, and in particular this reverse dependency between them seems like a bad idea.

- *Monolithic object.* Monolithic objects bundle all required objects into a single object, wrapping objects via some as yet unspecified mechanism exposing the embedded objects through some interface. The advantage of this approach is that previously distinct objects are now accessed through a single, monolithic object. Unfortunately, security and practicality prevent use of such a mechanism on all objects. First, one may not have access permissions to all objects to be bound into the composite. Furthermore, one might desire a composite object without the requirement of moving all objects into one monolithic object. Finally, this mechanism does not work if an object is a component of more than one composite object.

- *Complete object awareness.* Another option is to require that every object maintain a list of all composite objects of which it is a member, contained or containing. This will ensure that every object is completely aware of the composite relationships of which it is a member. There are several problems with this approach. First, it would necessitate that all objects maintain a store describing all composites of which they are members. This would require that all objects be mutable and provide permission for modifying composite attributes. For public documents, this is untenable. Second, it would be necessary to synchronize all copies of an object to ensure linking to one object is exposed by all copies. Again, this is untenable.

- *Special "requires" action.* This approach pushes the notion of composites into the Mesh as a basic Mesh capability similar to "supports-action?" and "parts-supported." Thus, every role must support an action which returns the objects "required" by that role. This option is part of complete object awareness, in that an object is aware of its components, but not those object of which it is a component. The main problem with this approach is that it entails additional capability to the overall Mesh.

Our choice is the last of the options (See Appendix A), that of pushing the notion of "requires" into the core capabilities of the Mesh, by adding a new optional action to the object-role, "get-required-objects." Since "get-required-objects" is an optional action, it may either not be inherited in subroles, or not be implemented if inherited, since it is optional. In either case, an object playing such a role could not be a composite without an implementation of the action.

"Get-required-objects" does not produce the closure of required objects and roles, but only those objects and roles directly required by the specified object playing the specified role. The only exception occurs when three conditions are true simultaneously. First, the object must be playing multiple roles. Second, there must be an interaction among the roles. Finally, the object must have different notions of composition for the different roles. Under such conditions, the result of invoking 'get-require-objects' contains the required components of all the roles played by the object.

While a composite object conceptually "contains" other objects, the contained objects are not aware of their inclusion in a composite object. Thus, composites can specify any set of objects as being required without the need to notify the contained nodes. This provides privacy regarding objects contained in one's composite, and makes the determination of all composites containing a particular object impossible. Furthermore, composites can provide no guarantees about the "contained" objects; a "contained" object may change unexpectedly.

Thus, we have proposed incorporating the solutions to the linking problem fully into an object model such as that of the Information Mesh, in order to meet the requirements we set out initially. For the complete report on this work, including an implementation see [23].

Conclusion and Summary

Not only does the Information Mesh architecture meet the requirements originally set out for it, but also by making links first class Mesh objects and enhancing the object role with the ability to handle required components, we provide a simple self-consistent architecture that meets the requirements set out originally for linking. The general model of globally unique, long-lived oids with the attendant hint mechanism, and the role model, together meet the requirements of supporting ubiquity, longevity, mobility, homogeneity, heterogeneity, resiliency, evolvability, and minimality as they are defined in the "Requirements" section, earlier in the paper. In addition, for links we have provided support for multiplicity, link typing, linking into the structure of objects, linking to links, composite objects, and support of existing models, also as defined in the "Requirements" Section. There remain a number of open issues in this work. For further discussion see [23]. For example:

- Resource discovery with its implications for how to determine what should go into a link

- Generalized computations in endpoints with their implications for portable code and the role model

- Part naming in more detail) with the implications for the nature of selectors inside descriptors

There are a number of directions to pursue in making these ideas available in the World Wide Web. As several communities are considering as well, moving to an identifier rather than locator-based labelling scheme is important. In order to do this, either a single universal name resolution scheme will be needed or an architectural feature such as *hints* will be needed to allow for discovering and using a variety and evolving set of resolution services. *Roles* or a more generic and extensible typing scheme than is currently available is important. We are investigating a simple first step that requires no changes to the current infrastructure. Simple structural templates would be provided that would define commonly understood anchoring schemes for specific templates or "types." Another area where preliminary work is being done is in providing "link" web servers. These and other efforts are needed to move the World Wide Web to a more extensible, evolvable and long-lived infrastructure. ■

Acknowledgments

This work was supported by the Department of Defense Advanced Research Projects Agency, under contract number DABT63-92-C-0002.

We would like to acknowledge significant contributions to the Information Mesh Project as described above by: Bienvenido Velez-Rivera, for his work on roles, Alan Bawden, Timothy Chien, and Matthew Condell.

Note: Authors are listed alphabetically.

References

1. Anklesaria, F., et al., *The Internet Gopher Protocol (a distributed document search and retrieval protocol)*, Network Working Group RFC 1436, March, 1993. See also *ftp://ds.internic.net/rfc/rfc1436.txt*

2. Berners-Lee, T., et al., *The World Wide Web*, Communications of the ACM, 37 (8):76-82, August, 1994.

3. Berners-Lee, T., Masinter, L., McCahill, M., *Uniform Resource Locators (URL)*, Network Working Group RFC 1738, December, 1994. See also *ftp://ds.internic.net/rfc/rfc1738.txt*

4. Berners-Lee, T., *Universal Resource Identifiers in WWW*, Network Working Group RFC 1630, June 1994. See also *ftp://ds.internic.net/rfc/rfc1630.txt*

5. Berners-Lee, T. and Connelly, D., *Hypertext Markup Language - 2.0*, MIT/W3C. Sept. 1995. See also *http://www.w3.org/pub/WWW/MarkUp/html-spec/html-spec_toc.html*

6. Bobrow, D. and Winograd, T., *An overview of KRL, a knowledge representation language*, Cognitive Science, 1(1):3-46, January, 1977.

7. Halasz, F. and Schwartz, M., *The Dexter Hypertext Reference*, Communications of the ACM, 37(2):30-39, February, 1994.

8. Keene, S., Object-oriented programming in Common Lisp: A programmer's guide to CLOS, Addison Wesley, Reading, MA, 1988.

9. Kunze, J, *Functional Recommendations for Internet Resource Locators*, Network Working Group RFC 1736, February, 1995. See also *ftp://ds.internic.net/rfc/rfc1736.txt*

10. Liskov, B., et al., CLU Reference Manual, Springer-Verlag, New York, 1981.

11. Marshall, C. C., et al., *Aquanet: A hypertext tool to hold your knowledge in place*, **Proceedings Hypertext '91**, ACM New York, December, 1991, 261-275.

12. Meyer, B., Eiffel: The Language, Prentice Hall, New York, 1992.

13. Mockapetris, P., *Domain Names—Concepts and Facilities*, Network Working Group RFC 1034, November, 1987. See also *ftp://ds.internic.net/rfc/rfc1034.txt*

14. Mockapetris, P., *Domain Names—Implementation and Specification*, Network Working Group RFC 1035, November, 1987. See also *ftp://ds.internic.net/rfc/rfc1034.txt*

15. Nelson, T. H., Literary Machines, The Distributors, South Bend, IN, 1988.

16. Digital Equipment Corp, et al., The Common Object Request Broker Architecture and Specification, OMG Document Number 91.12.1, Rev. 1.1, Object Management Group, John Wiley & Sons, New York, 1991.

17. OSI, *ISO9594 and CCITT X.500 Directory Services*.

18. Postel, J. and Reynolds, J., *File Transfer Protocol (FTP)*, Network Working Group RFC 959, October, 1985.

19. Raggett, D., *HyperText Markup Language Specification Version 3.0*, Internet Draft, draft-ietf-html-specv3-00.txt, March, 1995. Note: This is a draft and expires in September, 1995. See also *ftp://ietf.cnri.reston.va.us/internet-drafts/draft-ietf-html-specv3-00.txt*

20. Sollins, K. and Masinter, L., *Functional Requirements for Uniform Resource Names*, Network Working Group RFC 1737, December 1994. See also *ftp://ds.internic.net/rfc/rfc1737.txt*

21. van der Linden, R., *An Overview of ANSA*, AR.000.00, Architecture Projects Management Ltd., May 1993. See also *ftp://ftp.ansa.co.uk/phase3-doc-root/ar/APM.1000.01.ps.gz*

22. van der Linden, R., *The ANSA Naming Model*, AR.003.01, Architecture Project Management Ltd., February, 1993. See also *ftp://ftp.ansa.co.uk/phase3-doc-root/ar/APM.1003.01.ps.gz*

23. Van Dyke, J. R., *Link Architecture for a Global Information Infrastructure*, MIT/LCS/TR-659, June, 1995. See also *http://ana-www.lcs.mit.edu/anaweb/pdf-papers/tr-659.pdf*

Appendix A: The Object-Role

The basic object-role

The object-role provides a starting point for all dialogs with Information Mesh objects. Since all Mesh objects must play the object-role, we are guaranteed that the required object-role actions are answerable by any Mesh object. Thus, the Object-Role describes the base set of actions and parts which all Mesh Objects must support.

Actions:

(**roles-played** *object*) Required
        Returns the list of roles that the
        object can play at this instant.

(**plays-role?** *object role*}) Required
        Returns true if the *object* plays
        role

(**play-role!** *object role implementation*)
        Required
        Makes the given object play the
        given role using the given
        implementation. Initially, all
        objects play the object-role.

(**is-role?** *object*) Required
        Returns true if the given object is
        a role. Objects which are roles can
        be used to describe the abstract
        behavior of other objects.
        Note that 'is-role?' is syntactic
        sugar for applying 'plays-role?' to
        an object and specifying the *role-role* for the role argument.

(**implementations-supported** *object role*)
        Required
        Returns the list of implementation
        objects for the given role
        that the object supports.

(**describe-yourself** *object*) Required
        Returns a description of the
        object. The nature of this
        documentation is out of the scope
        of this specification.

Parts:

whole Required
        The part containing the entire
        object.

documentation Required
        The documentation associated with a
        given object.

The "Composite" Additions

Our composite implementation is realized by pushing the notion of "requires" into the basic Mesh capabilities through the optional action, "get-required-objects." The absence of "get-required-objects" from a particular role implies that the object does not require any other objects when playing that role. Note that the actions for adding components to an object are specific to particular roles and do not appear in the general object-role. As with all actions, these will be invoked by any client of the object that is allowed to modify it, such as most likely its original owner.

Additional action:

(**get-required-objects** *object role*)
        Optional for all roles

Returns the set of oids necessary
for the object to play the
specified role. Associated with
each oid is the role or roles
required from that oid.

Appendix B: The Link-Role

Inherits from: object-role

Actions:

(**get-oids** *link role*) Required
Returns set of oids related by the
link

(**extract-endpoints** *link role*) Required
Returns set of endpoints which
describe the object and object
substructure related by the link.

(**get-number-endpoints** *link role*)
Required
Returns number of endpoints

(**set-endpoints!** *link role endpoint-
list*) Optional
Changes the link to relate the
specified endpoints and removes
any previous endpoints. Endpoints
provided as a set of
descriptors.

content extraction/manipulation:
We utilize the default part
manipulation mechanisms.

Parts:

(**endpoint**: *unordered-set-of descriptor*)
Required
Contains a descriptor pointing at
or into the exposed abstract
structure of an object.

Makers:

(**create** *oid implementation endpoint-
list*) Required
Create a link.

Appendix C: Sample Link Subroles

The Named Link-Role

Inherits from: link-role

Actions:

(**extract-named-endpoint** *named-link
endpoint-name*) Required
Returns endpoint described by
endpoint-name.

(**add-named-endpoint!** *named-link
endpoint-name endpoint-value*)
Optional
Deletes endpoint with endpoint-name.

(**remove-named-endpoint!** *named-link
endpoint-name*) Optional
Adds endpoint with endpoint-name.
Endpoint is a descriptor structure.

content extraction/manipulation:
We utilize the default part
manipulation mechanisms.

Parts:

(**named-endpoint**: *named-of descriptor*)
Required
Contains named-endpoints.

Makers:

(**create** *oid implementation named-
endpoint-list*) Required
Create a named-link. Named-
endpoint list is a list of names and
descriptor pairs.

The Binary Link-Role

Inherits from: link-role

Actions:

content extraction/manipulation:
We utilize the default part
manipulation mechanisms. Note that
the manipulation mechanisms must
maintain the two endpoint
characteristics.

Parts:

(**binary-endpoints**: *unordered-of descriptor*) Required
Contains two endpoints of a binary link.

Makers:

(**create** *oid implementation endpoint1 endpoint2*) Required
Create a binary-link.

The Ordered Link-Role

Inherits from: link-role

Actions:

(**get-ordered-endpoint-range** *ordered-link start end*) Required
Returns range of ordered endpoints.

(**extract-ordered-endpoint** *ordered-link position*) Required
Returns the endpoint at numbered position in ordering.

(**set-ordered-endpoint** *ordered-link ordered-endpoints*) Optional
Changes the ordered link to relate the specified endpoints.
Endpoints provided as an ordered set of descriptors.

content extraction/manipulation
We utilize the default part manipulation mechanisms.

Parts:

(**ordered-endpoint** : *ordered-of descriptor*) Required
Contains ordered-endpoints.

Makers:

(**create** *oid implementation endpoint-list*) Required
Create an ordered-link. Endpoint list is an ordered list of descriptor pairs.

About the Authors

Karen R. Sollins
[*http://ana-www.lcs.mit.edu/people/sollins*]
M.I.T. Laboratory for Computer Science
545 Technology Square
Cambridge, MA 02139
sollins@lcs.mit.edu

Jeffrey R. Van Dyke
[*http://ana-www.lcs.mit.edu/people/jvandyke*]
Trilogy Development Group
6034 W. Courtyard Dr.
Austin, TX 78730
jvandyke@trilogy.com

COMMERCIAL HYPERTEXT PUBLISHING
ELECTRONIC BOOKS USING TRAILS AND THE
AUTHOR-PUBLISHER-READER MODEL

Leslie D. Cuff

Abstract

Commercial hypertext publishing is presented with the author-publisher-reader model (APR). Two commercial products, ebooks and trails, are presented with mechanisms for their creation and delivery which support licensing and copy protection. Trails are used both in production and for overcoming reader disorientation during navigation. A hypertext composition system is described which translates Layman's Hypertext (LHT) into HTML file structures. LHT supports typed links, users, and context which are grafted into the World Wide Web hypertext model. **Keywords:** *Publishing, trail, hypertext, author, composer, language, commerce, navigation, disorientation, digression, theme, temporal fluidity, link, epage, ebook, edition*

Memex: The Original Model

In memex [1] three types of human knowledge exchange are developed to varying degrees. The user of the hypertext is initially developing a data resource for his own use; the user is both author and reader. The user replicates a portion of his memex for use by another researcher using a trail reproducer; the user is a publisher. Initially, many of the contents of the memex are purchased as books on tape; the owner is a consumer/reader who obtains data from a publisher.

The memex is a theoretical system. The memex model has no provision for respecting copy restrictions during reproduction. It assumes that the owner of the memex is the owner of all the data stored within it. There is no mechanism for enforcing the rights of originating hypertext composers and distributors. Memex was a model based on a unified, freely reproducible global data repository.

The model proposed in this paper captures the essence of user interaction in memex with three user classes: author, publisher, and reader. The APR model is an attempt to formally define the interface between the readers and the authors. APR is based on this author's experience working within a traditional print publishing company. The mechanisms which support the model have been the subject of research conducted in both academic circles and in a commercial online information setting.

The Author

For the purposes of the APR model, the author is the person or group of collaborators who compose a hypertext. Participants who wish to be involved in this process range from experienced nonlinear composers to artists who work with traditional media such as ink.

The strategic application of publisher resources should help eliminate the need for an author to have a wide hypertext experience or advanced computer knowledge. The traditional role of a publisher is to provide the author with a range of skills that the author himself may not possess.

Authors should write words. Visual artists produce images. The details of grammar, spelling, operating systems, communication links, servers, and network topologies can detract from the basic task at hand: composing art and imparting knowledge.

The only things that an author should have to know are how to submit information for review and where to pick up the check.

The Reader

The reader is the end-consumer of the public version of the hypertext (i.e., the published hypertext).

If a reader is expected to pay for the data he is consuming, the quality of the data should be fairly high. That is to say, the data must be consistent, timely, comprehensive, and relevant to the reader's desires.

Before a reader can purchase data, he must be able to locate and retrieve it. The reader should know (roughly) what he is getting, where he can get it, how he can use it, and how much it will cost him.

The Publisher

In the APR model, the publisher is the label applied to every intervening layer between the authors and the readers. The authors and readers interact with different portions of the publishing house. Authors and readers rarely interact directly. Authors interact with editorial staff while readers interact with a publisher's distribution network.

The publisher is responsible for these activities which are common to both print and electronic distribution media:

- Interfacing with the composers and authors

- Coordinating the in-house group work environment

- Maintaining production computer systems

- Polishing the product for delivery to consumers

- Promotion and market evaluation

- Delivering data to public distribution points

- Receiving compensation from the market

- Redistributing compensation to authors

- Protecting the rights of their authors

- Protecting the rights of other publishers

Publishers may also undertake the creation of search mechanisms, indices, and thematic groupings of related material. In the context of electronic publishing via the World Wide Web, they may also choose to maintain onsite Internet connections and servers.

A finer-grained breakdown of the interface between author and reader yields several subsets within the publishing network including: Internet service providers, bookstores, libraries, online services, ordering departments, warehouse and dispatch staff, editorial staff, proofreaders, layout, trailblazers, nonlinear integration specialists, advertising and promotions departments, legal advisors, management and accounts.

The Building Blocks—Epages and Links

Some terms employed in the hypertext field carry too much semantic baggage; people from different fields interpret them to mean different things. To overcome this confusion, this author will introduce some new terms for some traditional concepts.

The typical delineation in hypertext is to break the data component into two types: consumable content and content-relating associations.

For the purposes of this discussion, the basic unit of content for reader consumption is called an electronic page, or *epage*. An epage is, for an instant in time, a frozen atomic unit supplied for display to the consuming reader. It may be constructed from mixed media and from several independent subcomponents prior to delivery, but it must arrive as an integrated unit for display by the reader's information browser.

An epage is analogous to an HTML file after it has been pasted together for display by a browser. An epage has had many labels: an atomic base component [2], an item [3], a chunk [4], a node [5], and a frame [6].

The content-relating association are called *links* by most hypertext researchers. Links were considered to be the essential feature of the memex [1]. In the World Wide Web, the link is subordinate to the HTML file. The W3 browsers and the HTTP are only able to render, request, and deliver epages.

The Primary Product—Ebooks

Epages are the basic building blocks from which electronic books, or *ebooks*, are constructed.

An ebook can be an interactive, networked resource such as an HTML data set installed under a server. It could also be a standalone bundle for offline browsing like a CD. It may be a mixture of the two.

The epages themselves may contain embedded links in the spirit of HTML. Alternately, links may be applied to an epage from an external organizational layer.

Ebooks serve as one type of organizational layer to a set of epages. The organizational layer brings the ebook context to the epage. One ebook may closely associate two epages, while another may not connect them at all.

This ebook context has ramifications when an epage is retrieved by a reader. The epage must be constructed to fit the context of whatever ebook the reader is currently consuming.

That is not to imply, however, that every epage must be composed with all the contextual information built in. The context may be applied by the retrieving site and may contain components from different serving sites.

An epage, then, may be served differently on subsequent visits by the same reader during the same session. Network caches can affect the integrity of this type of transaction under the current URL resource identification system.

As it stands, the Web has no inherent ability to provide this level of flexibility, though servers can be forced to simulate this behavior [7]. A scalable solution involving proxies and browsers must be sought.

Another factor which affects the appearance of an epage is what resources the reader is authorized or licensed to access. If an epage contains components drawn from three different licensed resources, a reader with access to only one will not be able to access the other two (though he may be enticed to negotiate a license to access them). The author of that epage would receive a view different from that supplied to a reader with access to all three resources.

The Secondary Product—Trails

Trails formed an integral part of the memex [1]. A *trail* is a set of epages with a thematic relationship between them. The organizational layer must be separate from the epages.

In many respects a trail is analogous to an ebook; i.e., it is a set of epages with an organizational network. However, a trail may extend into many ebooks. These ebooks may not all be under the jurisdiction of the same publisher. In those circumstances, it is reasonable to consider the delivery of trails without the complete set of the epages they are built around.

Shrewd publishers may supply a set of trails along with every ebook they license. Consumers can then be made aware of other products which are available for purchase. The advertisements are built conceptually into the product at a point where they have the most relevance. A trail is advertised when a reader is on one of its thematically related epages.

The trail also provides an alternative mechanism for navigating within the ebook already purchased. It also provides a way for two complementary ebooks from the same publisher to have a utility greater than the sum of their parts. When the two books are co-located they contain the function of each independent ebook. They also have an additional organizational structure which capitalizes on their common themes.

Trails perform another useful purpose for publishers. By using a trail, a publisher can identify which epages from a data pool are to be distributed as a particular ebook. Thus when the publisher "sets his reproducer in action" on the trail [1], the result is an ebook ready for market.

Another advantage of trails is that they help achieve the memex goal of "anticipating the selective needs to be encountered later" [3]. The publisher anticipates a requirement for information relating to the theme of the trail.

The use of a trail is an example of where the epage must be served in context.

Navigating Using Trails

A user who is following a trail is taking a tour through a set of epages.

In [8], the authors conclude that "tours or path mechanisms... are hard to author and maintain." The link structures for trails suggested in this paper attempt to alleviate that problem. The trails are not embedded within the epages; rather they are applied as overlays on top of them. They can be manipulated using a special set of tools. This approach allows the epages to evolve separately from the trail.

It is possible to warn a user when he is following a link which will digress from the theme of the trail. In fact, it is possible to constrain the reader so that he cannot digress from the trail at all. This would be an attempt at overcoming the disorientation experienced by many hypertext users [4].

There is a more flexible, and possibly more useful mechanism for constraining the reader. Using the research into distance and metrics from [9] and the notion of depth from [8], we can set a numerical limit on the distance that a reader can digress called the trail *width*.

The width may be set by the composer of the trail (Bush called this person the *trailblazer*[1]), the trail publisher, or the trail reader. The publisher may set a maximum width for the trail. With sufficient software support, the reader may be able to reduce the trail width even further.

Self-constraint Using Trail Width

Consider the scenario where the reader wishes to familiarize himself with the entire contents of the epages related by a trail; the trail is a set of notes for a course.

The reader would first set the trail width to the minimum possible. The software would offer the set of epages (still possibly nonlinear) which were considered most fundamental by the trail's composer.

The reader would then increase the trail width and review the epages in order to increase his or her understanding of the information being presented. Eventually, the reader will operate with the maximum possible trail width, wandering freely within the nonlinear data structure that is closely associated with the theme of the trail.

This helps the reader build a mental map of the contents of the hypertext by modifying the view and providing a reduced frame of reference. The reader will come to view the links which connect the fundamental relationships differently from the ones which are tangential.

The reader may also be able to regain a sense of completeness which is otherwise difficult to achieve. If a student is to use a hypertext as a replacement for a printed text book, the student must have some way to gauge his or her progress through the course material.

Imposing Constraint to Support Commercial Data Licensing

The publisher may set a maximum digression limit for a given trail. That maximum width may be common throughout all the ebooks into which the trail is incident. However, it may also be desirable for a single trail to support different digression levels into different ebooks.

There are two reasons why this may be necessary: theme scope and commerce. The trail may overlap very superficially with one ebook while it may address the same core theme of another ebook. The trail publisher may have licensed two ebooks from different publishers; one publisher may permit liberal digression while the other may be more restrictive.

Control over maximum trail digression is in the hands of two publishers: the trail publisher and the ebook publisher.

There must be a mechanism to allow an ebook publisher to specify digression limits outside the trail which references it. A trail may be blazed by an uncooperative third-party publisher, and the ebook publisher may have no access to the distributed version of the trail.

Trail digression constraints become another impetus for consumers to license services from the publishers. Presumably, the trail forms an advertisement for the portions of the ebook which are not accessible by default. It becomes a subject of further negotiation between the consumer and the ebook publisher.

Trails in Support of Ebook Production

The trail width has one other application within the publishing process. The publisher can identify a set of in-house epages as belonging to a trail. This trail then forms the backbone of a new ebook. The publisher can then set a reproducer in action to retrieve the trail of a specified width from the body of works in progress.

These types of restrictions are necessary to provide a scalable hypertext creation model. If the author is writing a single ebook and is acting as her own publisher, then an all-or-nothing publication model may be feasible. If, however, the composition team is comprised of scores of authors working on dozens of conceptually distinct products, there must be some mechanism for controlling the reproduction of works for distribution via public access mechanisms.

In order to completely separate an ebook from a set of epages, it is useful to consider the trail boundary. The *boundary* of a trail of width w is the set of links which, if traversed, would retrieve epages which are farther than w units away from the trail. The set of boundary links require attention by the publisher prior to publishing the ebook.

The publisher has several alternatives for dealing with boundary links: replace them with vanilla text, replace the destination set with a class of link which supports followup contact, or let them dangle and hope for the best.

Time Changes Everything

The *fluidity* of an epage (ebook or trail) refers to the frequency and severity with which it changes over time.

Time plays an important part in some information resources while it plays less of a role in others. Complex temporal information sets stagnate if they are allowed to remain frozen for too long; they go stale.

When the author is the publisher, the fluidity of an epage is at the whim of a single individual. An advantage of the APR model in a collaborative working environment is that absent workers can be back-filled by other staff. This helps ensure that highly fluid data retains its relevance.

Editions

In the print world, a publisher will typically produce several editions of a popular book. The costs associated with print manufacturing and distribution act against the publisher's desire to provide frequent updates. Often, a consumer who has purchased the first edition will be reluctant to purchase a complete second edition which has significant overlap with a product they have already bought.

This restriction can be alleviated with ebooks. The reader can pay for just that portion of the ebook which has changed since the last edition he purchased. The publisher is able to supply the appropriate "patches."

The cost of manufacturing standalone errata is relatively low compared to an identical print volume. There is minimal extra cost associated with releasing both a new edition of an ebook and the self-contained errata in parallel. They are both products of the same production process.

This is not without its complications. Fluidity causes problems.

Suppose a reader has made significant extensions or, worse, modification to the original edition supplied by the publisher. If the errata are confined only to individual epages, update may be relatively straightforward, if interactive. If, however, the new edition involves restructuring the organizational layer, the update process becomes much more complex. This author can propose no solution that does not require significant human intervention.

Another complication with multiple editions relates to trails. Recall that trails could be combined with ebooks when they were bundled for market distribution. Eventually, the trail may come into contact with a later edition of an ebook known to contain relevant passages.

A solution for this would be for an ebook to carry with it a newer copy of the trail which could accommodate the older editions of known ebooks as well as any customizations applied by the reader after delivery of the original. This could easily cause an exponential growth in the amount of secondary information which must be bundled with each subsequent product.

Another approach would be for the trail to be extended into an arbitrary ebook. One mechanism for natural language processing which could be employed for this task was presented as a mechanism for automatically suggesting links in [10]. Another alternative is a concept-based retrieval system [11].

Layman's Hypertext—LHT

The hypertext scripting language developed, called the Layman's HyperText (LHT), is a simple ASCII scripting language for expressing hypertext content with separate or embedded organization layers [7].

The LHT source files are able to express entire ebooks, epages, links, and trails.

If an ebook is encoded along with all its epages in a single file, the linear ordering between adjacent epages is reflected in the resulting, compiled ebook. LHT shatters the mapping of an epage to a single file. An epage may be authored within several different source files.

An epage can identify not only the links which emanated from within its content, but it can also suggest epages and general themes (ebooks, trails) which might link to it. A link can be created which has a visible component on an epage other than the one within which it was composed. It may be composed within a source epage, within a destination epage, or outside both sets.

The language was implemented along with a set of translators which "compiled" the LHT source into a data structure for replay by a browser of the author's devising [12]. The prototype translator has been modified to produce HTML encoded ebooks. The compiler analogy equates HTML to machine code.

One of the abilities that LHT possesses that HTML lacks is the ability to embed codes in the source which, once compiled, produces epages which are served differently in different contexts. The composer of the LHT epage can specify sub-atomic components which are visible in one context and invisible in others.

A concept like this one was integrated with the Hypertext Abstract Machine (HAM) [5].

LHT can also express a link which should be dropped (parachuted) into another epage. These links may be created when an epage is retrieved, or at the point when the epage is compiled into the ebook. Parachute links are used to implement the organizational component of a trail. They are applied only when relevant to the context.

The Dexter model [2] formalizes the idea that a link is not subordinate to an epage; rather, the two are both specific cases of a component. The Dexter model can accommodate parachute links in the spirit of LHT. A Dexter link can have more than two end points [13]. It can also support a more flexible variety of directions [14]. In contrast, an HTML link is a one-way link routed within the source page.

LHT and the associated software can be used to provide a two-tiered approach to information delivery. The authors and editors control the essential content of the epages but the publisher can apply a standard stylistic look and feel to every epage that is produced. The publisher can also apply a standard organizational layer to every ebook produced.

Using LHT, it is possible for a publisher to develop the organizational layer within an ebook such as an encyclopedia in advance of receiving many of the authors' contributions. While the structural coordinator of such a project cannot anticipate every relationship that the researchers will uncover, high-level development can occur asynchronously with the supply of the contributions. Epages can be linked before they are composed.

The LHT server also provides a mechanism to enforce commerce. The first time a new reader retrieves any epage from an ebook he is funneled through a toll booth. Once license has been granted, the requested epage is supplied with prominent links to relevant background information about the ebook(s) and trail(s) which contain the epage.

The task of maintaining context is grafted as an extension of the server. The context could be easier to maintain as a shared record between the server, the browser software, and any intervening proxy/caches.

Conclusion

Fifty years after Vannevar Bush's memex [1] the World Wide Web is growing into a global information system which in some ways eclipses it. The task is not yet in hand.

Hypertext is traditionally based on author-reader interaction which doesn't scale to support commercial collaborative hypertext initiatives.

HTML is not a natural language within which to compose. The HTML pages are well-developed while the linkages are weak. Links must be accommodated as first class objects.

Trails with constrained digression can alleviate a significant disorientation problem that readers often experience. They can also help publishers prepare ebooks for distribution via a variety of protocols. Ebook editions complicate the matter of trails.

Trail following and trail blazing [3] both require formal attention by the W3O when it reviews the capabilities of the next generation of browsers. Digression and trail width must be supported by the browser or a proxy if a trail is to include epages from a mixed set of ebooks.

Research into a trail data construct which respects varying local widths is necessary.

LHT shatters the tight coupling of the organizational layer with the epage. This coupling pervades HTML. The separation of epages from the links permits an easy mechanism for building and maintaining trails. The tight coupling between the source epage and the one-way link will limit the ability to introduce trails to HTML.

Another significant enhancement to linking is its type. An HTML link can glean some type identifiers from the protocol for data retrieval and the mechanism for interpreting the returned epage. These types apply more to the epage being retrieved than to the link itself. A link has type of its own.

LHT supports link traversability by user class as an explicit link type. The work of Trigg [4] and other researchers (e.g., [15], [16], and [2] has extended the concept of links through types. There is a potential benefit afforded by link type which requires further investigation.

Epages must be displayed by the browser in context. A mechanism to serve the same epage differently depending on the context of the links is necessary. The context is built from variables at the server and the browser; it is a state shared between them. Contexts must be composed before they can be served.

The current implementation of the caching proxy is a hurdle to both commerce and context in the World Wide Web. Without context elements embedded in the URL, two users served from the same cache may experience epage crosstalk. If two users request the same licensed epage from the same caching proxy, the originating server may not license each user individually.

Trail width and constrained digression extends beyond the epages which form the backbone of the trail. The appearance of the epages served during trail following is a function of trail, ebook, server- and browser-side context. Without context, these types of trails cannot be accommodated using HTML.

The trail boundary may help control ebook production and selective replication. The boundary which consists of a set of links requires more

study. Trails and their boundaries might be used to define open and closed sets within the hypertext which, in turn, may lead to a meaningful definition of the topology of a hypertext.

Fluctuation and fluidity in hypertext is a serious problem. Delivery of editions of ebooks and trails illustrates some of the difficulties which can arise when data goes out of sync. More research into data fluidity and decay is warranted. ∎

References

1. Bush, V., "As We May Think," *Atlantic*, Vol 176, pp 101, 108. July 1945.

2. Halasz, F., and Schwartz, M., 1994, "The Dexter Hypertext Reference Model," *Communications of the ACM*, Vol 37(2), pp 30,39. February 1994.

3. Bush, V., "Memex Revisited," *Science Is Not Enough*, William Morrow & Company. New York, U.S.A., 1967.

4. Trigg, R., and Weiser, M., 1986, "TEXTNET: A Network-Based Approach to Text Handling," *ACM Transactions on Office Information Systems*, Vol 4(1), pp 1,23. January 1986.

5. Campbell, B., and Goodman, J., 1988, "HAM: A General Purpose Hypertext Abstract Machine," *Communications of the ACM*, Vol 31(7), pp 856,861. July 1988.

6. Akscyn, et al., 1988, "KMS: A Distributed Hypermedia System for Managing Knowledge in Organizations," *Communications of the ACM*, Vol 31(7), pp 820,835. July 1988.

7. Cuff, L., 1995, "Publishing Compiled Hypertext with LHT and the World-wide Web." Master's Thesis (in prep.--title in flux) Memorial University of Newfoundland, St. John's, Newfoundland, Canada.

8. Botafogo, R., et al., "Structural Analysis of Hypertexts: Identifying Hierarchies and Useful Metrics," *ACM Transactions Information Systems*, Vol 10(2), pp. 142-180. April 1992.

9. Rivlin, E., Botafogo, R., Schneiderman, B., "Navigating in Hyperspace: Designing a Structure-Based Toolbox," *Communications of the ACM*, Vol 37(2), pp 87,96. February 1994.

10. Bernstein, Mark, "An Apprentice That Discovers Hypertext Links," Cambridge University Press. pp 212,223.

11. Arents, H., and Bogaerts, W., "Concept-Based Retrieval of Hypermedia Information: From Term

Indexing to S Hyperindexing," Information Processing and Management, Vol 29(3), pp 373,386.

12. Cuff, L., "Trailblazer: a DOS browser for hypertext. " Report for Software Engineering masters course, Memorial University of Newfoundland, St. John's, Newfoundland, Canada.

13. Leggett, J., and Schnase, J., "View with Open Eyes," *Communications of the ACM*, Vol 37(2), pp 76,86. February 1994.

14. Grønbaek, K., and Trigg, R., "Design Issues for a Dexter-Based Hypermedia System," *Communications of the ACM*, Vol 37(2), pp 40,49. February 1994.

15. Garzotto, et al., "HDM—A Model-Based Approach to Hypertext Application Design," *ACM Transactions on Information Systems*, Vol 11(1), pp 1,26. January 1993.

16. Snaprud, M., Kaindl, H., "Types and Inheritance in Hypertext," *International Journal of Human-Computer Studies*, Vol 41, pp 223,241.

About the Author

Leslie D. Cuff

[*http://www.cs.mun.ca/~lez/home.html*]
The Enterprise Network, Inc.

Leslie Cuff is enrolled in the Master of Science program in the Department of Computer Science at Memorial University of Newfoundland where he has developed the LHT language and translator. In addition to time spent writing scientific software and working with The Enterprise Network, he was an image technician and photographer for the Encyclopedia of Newfoundland and Labrador, Volumes 4 and 5.

He resides in St. John's, Newfoundland and Labrador, Canada (a mere 10 kilometers from Cape Spear, the most easterly point in North America) with his wife and son. He is a birdwatcher and an all-season outdoors explorer. He attended WWW-2 at Chicago in October 1994. He participated in w3collab at Boston in September 1995. He is a member of the W3O working group for treating links as first-class objects.

He is involved in a project to commercialize the LHT multimedia processing kit with a consortium of Newfoundland-based media producers, information disseminators and telework agencies.

He can be contacted at *lez@cs.mun.ca* or *les_cuff@porthole.entnet.nf.ca* via email.

INGRID
A Self-Configuring Information Navigation Infrastructure

Paul Francis, Takashi Kambayashi, Shin-ya Sato, Susumu Shimizu

Abstract

This paper presents Ingrid, an architecture for a fully distributed, fully self-configuring information navigation infrastructure that is designed to scale to global proportions. Unlike current designs, Ingrid is not a hierarchy of large index servers. Rather, links are automatically placed between individual resources based on their topic similarity in such a way that clusters of term combinations are formed. The resulting topology can potentially be searched and browsed by a robot efficiently. This paper describes the fundamentals of Ingrid--the topology design and the algorithms for creating and searching the topology. It discusses the scaling characteristics of Ingrid, and gives the scaling results of a limited experiment. **Keywords:** *Information, retrieve, navigate, browse, distributed, self-configure, infrastructure, Ingrid*

Introduction

Current *browsing* on the Web consists of the traversal of (1) hypertext-style links between explicitly related documents, and (2) indexes and metaindexes, which are usually structured according to organization, sometimes by topic, and are in any event almost always incomplete in their coverage. What is missing is general and complete *topic-level* browsing—that is, where all resources are linked according to topic.

Current *searching* on the Web consists of querying single-database search engines. While this method is effective, single-database search engines are necessarily (and usually intentionally) incomplete in their coverage. This is likely to become more rather than less true as the Internet grows. What is missing is complete Internet-wide searching.

This paper describes Ingrid—a distributed, scalable, self-configuring information navigation infrastructure. The goal of Ingrid is to provide these two missing functions. In a nutshell, Ingrid works by automatically creating links between resources that are topically related. Resources are searched by "routing" (robot-style) from topic to

topic until the appropriate resources are found. Browsing is accomplished in a similar way, except that movement from topic to topic is directed by the user. Browsing is truly topic to topic (versus document to document) because the browsing robot can efficiently traverse multiple links and produce a topic summary for the user.

The following describes one of many typical usage scenarios for Ingrid. An Ingrid "resource publishing" background process is running in conjunction with a mail archive. When new mail arrives, the Ingrid publisher automatically generates a profile of the mail (author, title, high-weight terms), and sends the profile to the Ingrid forward information server associated with the mail archive. The Ingrid forward information server "inserts" the profile into the Ingrid infrastructure by searching for and attaching links to similar profiles.

Later, a user wishes to find resources related to the topic of the previously inserted mail. Using an Ingrid browser, the user inputs keywords related to the topic. The Ingrid browser launches a robot that, by querying various forward information servers, traverses links of the Ingrid infra-

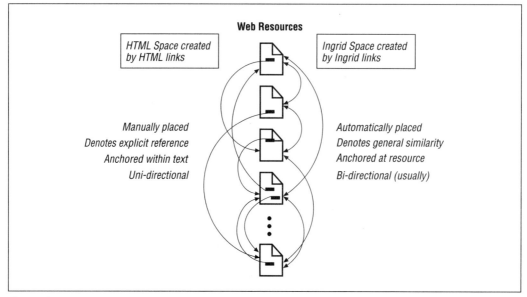

Web Resources

HTML Space created
by HTML links

Ingrid Space created
by Ingrid links

Manually placed
Denotes explicit reference
Anchored within text
Uni-directional

Automatically placed
Denotes general similarity
Anchored at resource
Bi-directional (usually)

Figure 1:   HTML space versus Ingrid space

structure in search of resource profiles with matching terms. Because of the organization of the links, the robot is able to efficiently find better and better matches. The Ingrid browser presents the best matching resource profiles to the user, along with a set of related terms. The user then expands and focuses his/her search using some of the related terms.

In the following sections, Ingrid is contrasted with current Web practices. These sections serve both to review existing techniques (admittedly incompletely) and to give an overview of Ingrid.

Ingrid as Compared to HTML

Ingrid can be viewed as a Web space parallel to (and complementary to) the Web space that exists by virtue of HTML links (see Figure 1). The two Web spaces are similar in that they are both composed of (URL-type) links between resources. The similarity, however, stops there.

HTML links are manually placed (by and large) and denote an explicit reference from one resource to another. Ingrid links are automatically placed and denote a general topical similar-

ity between two resources. HTML links individually have a strong local meaning, but collectively (index and metaindex documents notwithstanding) do not contribute well to the global organization of information. Ingrid links, on the other hand, have a somewhat weak local meaning, but collectively create a meaningful global organization of information.

Browsing in HTML space can be considered as having two forms. One is browsing through index documents, and the other browsing among leaf documents (see Figure 2). Navigation among leaves takes place at the "micro" level, and tends to be from individual document to individual document. Navigation through indexes is at the macro level, and seems to be most often oriented towards organizations. Sometimes it is oriented towards topic area, but to the extent that this is true, it is usually somewhat incomplete.

Navigation in Ingrid space is envisioned to take place almost entirely at the "macro" level, from topic area to topic area (where a topic area is composed of a group of documents, see Figure 3). In addition, the topic areas are intercon-

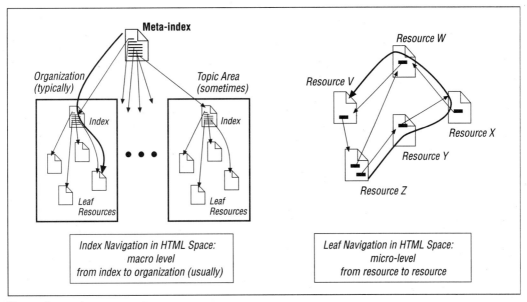

Figure 2:   Navigation with HTML

nected. Thus, one can browse among related topic areas. Because of these differences in the two Web (or information) spaces, they are highly complementary.

Ingrid as Compared to Single-Database Search Engines

Currently, the most effective way of searching the Web is through one of the growing number of available single-database search engines. These search engines can be categorized into two kinds:

1. Those that attempt to index the entire Web

2. Those that index a selected portion of the Web

WAIS and Harvest are just two of many examples of the latter category. As illustrated in Figure 4,

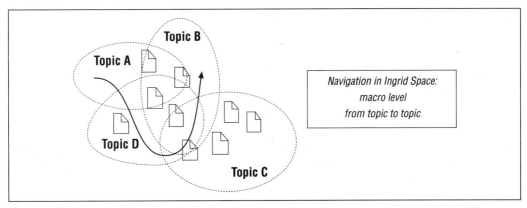

Figure 3:   Topic-level navigation

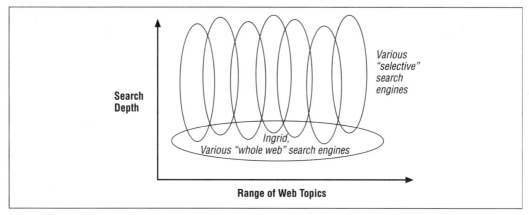

Figure 4:   Comparison of search techniques

the goal of Ingrid is to allow searching of the whole Web, but necessarily with less depth than can be achieved with a single-database search engine. Thus, the functionality of Ingrid is complementary with that of limited-coverage single-search engines.

Two examples of search engines that attempt to index all Web resources are Lycos and World Wide Web Worm (WWWW). As shown in Figure 4, these whole-web search engines and Ingrid are attempting to do roughly the same job, and are therefore essentially competing technologies. Thus, we wish to briefly justify the work of Ingrid in light of whole-web search engines.

The primary justification for work on Ingrid is scaling. It is not clear that the single-database approach will be able to keep pace with the growth of the Web. So far, Lycos has apparently been able to keep pace, as it seems to consistently be indexing approximately 75% of the estimated 4 million (as of July 1995) total URLs. On one hand, 4 million documents barely scratches the surface of the total number of documents that can be expected to be available over the Web in the future. On the other hand, Lycos has probably barely scratched the surface of what a "single" search engine can do, given massive parallelism, huge memory farms, and the like.

In short, the ability of a single-database search engine to be able the index the entire Web, and the associated costs, are unknown. Likewise, the ability of Ingrid to search the entire Web is also unknown. Thus, it seems prudent to experiment with both methods.

Ingrid as Compared to Other Distributed Searching Techniques

There are many different (actual or proposed) distributed searching techniques. These range in functionality and complexity from strict traversal of a naming tree (DNS [3]), to automatic dispersion of terms over a mesh of forward information servers (Centroids). In this section, we limit ourselves to examples of distributed searching techniques that are administratively distributed and fully automatic. In particular, we consider Centroids and Fish-Search.

Table 1 compares Centroids and Fish-search (along with Ingrid and single-database engine search techniques). Centroids proposes building a superstructure of index servers above the existing search engines. These metasearch engines are able to forward queries to the appropriate leaf-level search engines and to other metasearch engines. (Note that the primary purpose of Ingrid is not to find search databases—Ingrid directly searches for and finds individual resources. To

Table 1:   Characteristics of Various Search Techniques

	Required New Infrastructure	*Pre-Search Activity*	*Search-Time Activity*
Single-Database, Search Engines (Lycos, WWW, etc.)	None	Gather Web Resources (Robot-style), Build (single-database) Index	Search Single-Database Search Engine
Mesh of Super-Indexes (Centroids)	Mesh of Index Services	Summarize Databases, Build Index-Server Indexes	Route through Index Services, Search Search Engines
Mesh of HTML links (Fish-search)	None	None	Gather Web Resources (Robot-style) Search Resources
Mesh of Local Indexes (Ingrid)	Topic-based resource links, Global Single-Term Servers	Summarize Resources, Create Links and Global Single-Term Entries	Occasionally search Global Single-Term Server, Route through Ingrid Topology

the extent that the contents of a search database can be summarized in a single document, however, Ingrid could be used to find search databases.)

Fish-search, on the other hand, traverses current HTML links, robot-style, until matching resources are found or until specified limits (time, number of resources traversed) are exceeded. Navigation in Ingrid is similar to Fish-search in that the Ingrid Navigator follows links in search of the desired terms. The primary difference is that the Ingrid Navigator follows links specifically created for the purpose of term-navigation, while Fish-search searches HTML links--a rather more ad hoc process.

Scaling of Fish-Search and Centroids

As with the single-database search engines, a critical issue with the distributed search mechanisms is scaling.

Fish-search, in our opinion, has little hope of scaling well. Because the organization of HTML links is ad hoc, the resources that match any given fish-search query may be far apart in the HTML topology. Thus, Fish-search may require a very large number of link traverses to find all of the matching resources.

The scalability of any superstructure of index servers depends entirely on how the information in the index servers is organized. The idea with Centroids is that a search engine (or metasearch engine) automatically summarizes its contents by listing once each term that exists in any of its resources. (Note that these terms may include full-text or may be selected high-weight terms only.) These summaries are transmitted to metasearch engines, which may in turn summarize their contents and pass them on.

Search queries are sent to metasearch engines. These engines refer the searcher to those engines that contain all of the terms in the query. These engines are in turn queried, and so on.

In some cases, the referral may be false. For instance, consider a query with terms A, B, and C. Because Centroids lists each term once, and gives no information about how terms relate, a Centroids summary does not distinguish between one resource with terms A, B, and C, and three resources each with only one of the terms. The primary scaling issue, then, is that of how many false referrals (and subsequent fruitless queries) occur. (Note that memory size of the metasearch engines is not a scaling issue, precisely because information about how terms relate is suppressed. Thus, memory scales linearly with the size of the global vocabulary, which we believe to be manageable.)

This issue remains open, and we believe can't be answered without significant experience. Ingrid of course has its own scaling issues, and so again we believe that it is appropriate to experiment both with Ingrid and Centroids (and of course any other proposals that appear promising).

Basic Components of Ingrid Infrastructure

As shown in Figure 5, the basic component of the Ingrid Infrastructure is the so-called *Resource Profile*. The Resource Profile is essentially a (text) summary of the resource that it represents (though the resource itself can be anything—an audio/video file, a physical object, or a service). The two required elements of the Resource Profile are: (1) Terms (or rather, *term combinations*) that describe the resource and (2) a pointer

(URL) back to the resource. Other information may be available, such as resource title, authors, date, size, type, etc.

The term combinations in a given Resource Profile characterize the resource. These are the terms that will match up against the terms in a search query.

One or more Resource Profiles are installed in a Forward Information Server (*FIServer*). The FIServer adds the term combinations of the Resource Profile to its searchable database. The Resource Profile is also linked with a selected set of similar other Resource Profiles (possibly in other FIServers). Thus, the Resource Profile essentially becomes a node in a mesh network of Resource Profiles. This network is called the *Ingrid Topology*.

The practical effect of the link is that the Resource Profile's FIServer will add the terms of the neighbor Resource Profiles to its searchable database. Thus, the FIServer is able to answer

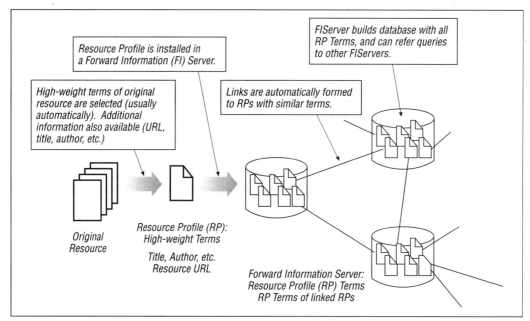

Figure 5:   Resource profile

queries in two ways: (1) By listing its own matching Resource Profiles and (2) by referring the querying system to other FIServers that have matching Resource Profiles.

This allows an *Ingrid Navigator* (searcher or browser) to "route" itself through the Ingrid Topology (or, more accurately, through the mesh of FIServers) and find relevant Resource Profiles. In this sense, Ingrid's FIServer is similar to the metasearch engines of Centroids discussed in the last section. One practical difference, however, is that the FIServer in Ingrid contains only terms for its own Resource Profiles and a very selected set of other (similar) Resource Profiles. Thus, every document server (FTP, gopher, WAIS, HTTP, etc.) can potentially become an FIServer. This can be contrasted with Centroids, where even the lowest-level metasearch engine indexes the entire databases of multiple search engines.

Ingrid will in general have a larger number of smaller FIServers than a scheme like Centroids. This has its advantages and disadvantages. The primary advantage is that we can leverage the enormous aggregate latent computing resources (CPU, memory, bandwidth) of every computer that holds a resource (or, more accurately, holds the Resource Profile, since they need not be on the same computer). In other words, if a computer is capable of storing and transmitting a network-retrievable resource, then for some extra (CPU, memory, bandwidth) cost, it can contribute to the overall navigation infrastructure. (What this extra cost is remains to be seen.)

The major disadvantage of distributing navigation across many small servers is that the overall control of the navigation infrastructure is diffused, thus making it difficult to control, for instance, performance or correctness. On the other hand, if this turns out to be an insurmountable problem, it is always possible to simply store all the Resource Profiles in a relatively small number of machines, thus effectively making those machines large, dedicated metasearch engines.

Finding the First FIServer

As described above, an Ingrid Navigator will "route" from FIServer to FIServer as it searches for the best matching resources. In some cases, however, an FIServer may not initially know of any FIServers that contain desired terms. Especially given the potentially large number of FIServers in Ingrid, we assume that it would be too expensive to randomly query successive FIServers in the hope of finding one with one or more desired terms.

To prevent this from happening, we require the existence of a special type of forward information server called a Global Single-Term Server (GSTServer) (see Figure 6). Each GSTServer contains one entry for every term in all of Ingrid space. Each entry points to a small number (perhaps three, for robustness) of FIServers that contain that term at least once. The GSTServer is only used to "bootstrap" an Ingrid Navigator's search. Once an Ingrid Navigator finds at least one FIServer with a given term, it can be referred to others without having to query the GSTServer again.

We expect the GSTServers to scale in terms of memory because the list size is that of the global vocabulary, which is bounded (at some millions of terms, but bounded nonetheless) and manageable. The GSTServers should scale in terms of number of queries because we expect most searches to already know of relevant FIServers from the start. This is because Ingrid Navigators cache the results of previous searches.

Description of Ingrid

Nothing said in this paper up to now is particularly novel. The functional components described above are little different from what has already been proposed, and are in fact only minor extensions to what already exists. Indeed, the primary reason for the above is simply to set the context for describing what is unique about Ingrid.

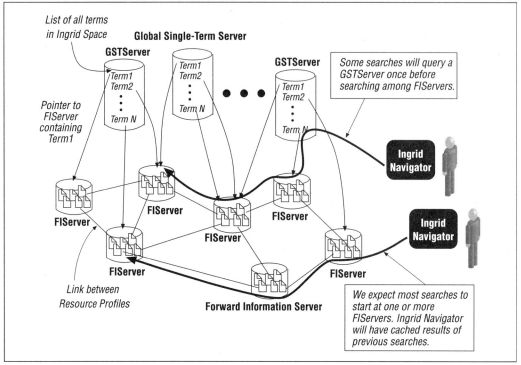

List of all terms in Ingrid Space

Global Single-Term Server

GSTServer

Term1
Term2
⋮
Term N

GSTServer

Term1
Term2
⋮
Term N

GSTServer

Term1
Term2
⋮
Term N

Pointer to FIServer containing Term1

Some searches will query a GSTServer once before searching among FIServers.

Ingrid Navigator

Ingrid Navigator

FIServer

FIServer

FIServer

FIServer

FIServer

FIServer

FIServer

Link between Resource Profiles

Forward Information Server

We expect most searches to start at one or more FIServers. Ingrid Navigator will have cached results of previous searches.

Figure 6: Global single-term servers

Two things make Ingrid unique and potentially feasible: (1) the logical organization of the Ingrid Topology (and how it leads to efficient navigation) and (2) the algorithm for automatically building the Ingrid Topology. They are described in the following sections.

The Ingrid Topology

The definition of the Ingrid Topology is actually quite simple. Assume a set of Resource Profiles, each with a term combination (set of terms). Each Resource Profile is a node in the Ingrid Topology. Define a *cluster* as a connected sub-topology. That is, there is a path between any two nodes in a cluster that contain only nodes in that cluster. The Ingrid Topology is a mesh topology whereby for every combination of terms, the Resource Profiles that contain those terms are connected so as to form a cluster.

For instance, Figure 7 shows 13 Resource Profiles connected in a mesh topology. Each of the Resource Profiles has one or more of terms A, B, and C. All Resource Profiles that have the same term or set of terms form a cluster. For instance, all Resource Profiles with term C (those numbered 7 through 13) form a connected cluster. Likewise those with both terms A and C (10 through 13) form a cluster, as do those with all three terms (11 through 13).

Within the limitations of the above definition, we try to keep the Ingrid Topology sparse. That is to say, we strive to minimize the number of links each Resource Profile has. (A fully connected graph—every node connected to every other—strictly speaking satisfies the above definition, but is obviously of little benefit.)

Keeping the topology sparse has two performance benefits. First, the amount of information

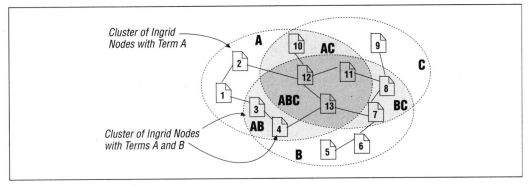

Cluster of Ingrid Nodes with Term A

Cluster of Ingrid Nodes with Terms A and B

Figure 7:   Example Ingrid topology

that must be stored by each FIServer is minimized. Second, the amount of information that must be searched by the FIServer when it is queried by an Ingrid Navigator is minimized.

A possible downside of a sparse topology is that the overall network diameter is bigger. In practice, however, we believe for a number of reasons that this will have little negative effect. One reason is that the node degree is expected to be rich enough that diameter will be small in any event. Another reason is that, in order to know when a search is exhausted, it is necessary to query all FIServers that contain Resource Profiles in the cluster. Thus, the cost of the search is dependent more on the number of FIServers in a cluster and less on the diameter.

Searching the Ingrid Topology

One of the major open questions about Ingrid is the efficiency of its search (how many queries are required, how long it takes, and so on).

Before discussing searching, it is worth reminding the reader that the search is directed by the Ingrid Navigator, not by the FIServers it queries. That is, the Ingrid Navigator queries FIServers, gets back some forward information about neighboring FIServers, and then decides itself which FIServers to query next. In this sense, searching in Ingrid is similar to current Web robots, particularly Fish-search, and different from network-

layer routing, where the intermediate nodes themselves manage the routing of the packet.

First some nomenclature. Assume three terms, A, B, and C. In what follows, we denote an FIServer that contains at least one Resource Profile that contains all three terms A, B, and C, as an *ABC FIServer*. We denote the set of all ABC FIServers as an *ABC Cluster*. If an Ingrid Navigator knows of at least one ABC FIServer, then it is said that the Ingrid Navigator is *in* the ABC Cluster. Note that the ABC Cluster is said to be a subcluster of the AB Cluster (because all FIServers in the ABC cluster are, by definition, also in the AB Cluster).

The basic idea behind searching the Ingrid Topology is to successively find a subcluster of the already found cluster until either (1) the desired cluster is found or (2) the search is exhausted. In this sense, searching the Ingrid Topology is hierarchical in nature.

For instance, assume that an Ingrid Navigator is searching for a resource with terms A, B, C, and D. Further, assume that an AB FIServer has already been found. The Ingrid Navigator queries the AB FIServer for any Resource Profiles with the terms A, B, C, or D. The answer will, at a minimum, list the neighbor AB FIServers. (Because of caching, the answer may contain other FIServers as well. This is further discussed later.)

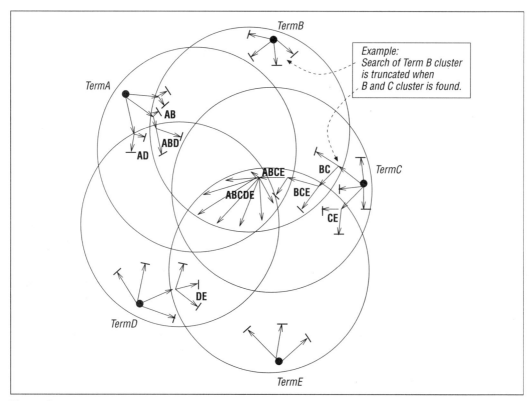

Figure 8:   Example of search procedure

The Ingrid Navigator then queries the neighbor AB FIServers, and so on. Eventually, either all AB FIServers will be queried, or one of the answers will contain an FIServer with additional matching terms (that is, an ABC, ABD, or ABCD FIServer). In the latter case, subsequent queries are limited to the FIServers with the additional matching terms. The search continues in this fashion until either (1) all useful FIServers have been queried, (2) some search limits, such as length of search or maximum number of queries, have been reached, or (3) a fully matching (ABCD) FIServer has been found. In the third case, all ABCD FIServers can then be queried to find all matching Resource Profiles.

This process is illustrated in Figure 8. This figure shows five clusters as five circles, for terms A, B, C, D, and E. The various subclusters are indicated by the overlap of the circles. Assume that the Ingrid Navigator knows of at least one FIServer for each single term (the solid small circles in the figure). This is always possible using the Global Single-Term Server (GSTServer), though in general the Ingrid Navigator should already have good starting points based on previous searches.

The Ingrid Navigator explores each of the one-term clusters until it finds one or more FIServers with two terms. This searching process is denoted by the arrows. In the case of Figure 8, we show the Ingrid Navigator finding AB, AD, BC, CE, and DE FIServers. At this point, any continued searching of one-term clusters is discontinued (as indicated by the line across the arrow tip). This is because searching a two-term cluster is, in most cases, more likely to yield good results than a one-term cluster. (The exception being, for instance, a one-term cluster with a very rare term versus a two-term cluster with two common terms.)

Figure 8 shows searching branching out within the two-term clusters until two three-term clusters are found, ABD and BCE. Any further two-term cluster searching is halted, and the three-term clusters are searched. Next we show that a four-term cluster ABCE is found. This cluster is explored until ABCDE Cluster is found. Finally, all of the FIServers in ABCDE Cluster are queried, thus finding all Resource Profiles with terms A, B, C, D, and E, and therefore all resources for which those five terms are considered high-weight terms.

Taking advantage of cached forward information

While the searching process as described above has the nice property of continuously narrowing the scope of the search, this in and of itself does not guarantee an adequately efficient search. A cluster for a common term (such as "computer") may include hundreds of FIServers and many thousands of Resource Profiles. Searching such a cluster for additional terms is likely to be unacceptably costly.

There are a number of techniques that might be used to increase the efficiency of the search. We are hoping that one in particular, simple caching of forward information, will prove adequate. The caching strategy we describe in what follows is, as of this writing, being implemented in the so-called alpha-version of the Ingrid prototype. (We hope that, as of this reading, it has already been implemented. :-)

Figure 9 shows two kinds of forward information, Persistent Forward Information and Cached Forward Information. Persistent Forward Information is that already discussed in the context of the Ingrid Topology—it is the forward information that gets installed as a result of inserting a Resource Profile into the Ingrid Topology. This forward information is persistent in that it remains as long as the Resource Profile stays valid (or, normally, as long as the resource itself stays valid).

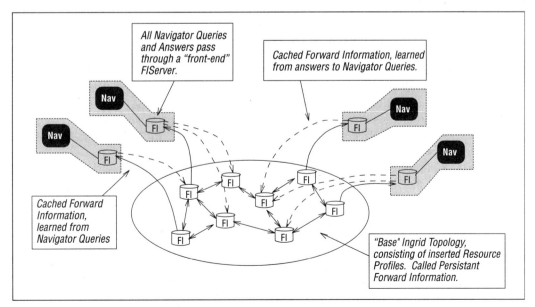

Figure 9:   Forward Information Caching architecture

The Persistent Forward Information can be thought of as forming a stable base topography over which terms can, with high probability, be successfully searched (even if, perhaps, inefficiently).

The Cached Forward Information, on the other hand, is derived from the results of previous searches. Since it is the Ingrid Navigators themselves that learn the results of searches, not the FIServers, one question is that of how to transfer the results of recent searches from the Ingrid Navigators to the FIServers.

Figure 9 shows that each Ingrid Navigator is behind a kind of "front-end" FIServer. All interactions with the Ingrid infrastructure pass through the FIServer. In particular, queries and query answers pass through the FIServer. These FIServers cache the query answers before passing them on to the Ingrid Navigators.

In addition, "regular" FIServers (we use quotes because in practice FIServers can serve both roles) cache received queries. This results in the following behavior. An Ingrid Navigator X conducts a search for some terms, using FIServer X as a front-end. In the process, a number of FIServers cache the queries from FIServer X. In addition, FIServer X caches the found Resource Profiles.

Later, another Ingrid Navigator Y conducts a search for some of the same terms. In the process of the search, Navigator Y queries one of the FIServers previously queried by Navigator X. The FIServer returns forward information about FIServer X. Navigator Y queries FIServer X, and learns of the Resource Profiles previously found by Navigator X. In other words, Navigator Y takes advantage of the work already carried out by Navigator X.

Note that, alternatively, we could have designed the caching scheme such that front-end FIServers are not required. Rather, after a search is completed, Ingrid Navigators explicitly inform the FIServers they previously queried about the Resource Profiles they found. Thus, all cached

forward information refers directly to Resource Profiles (rather than indirectly referring to Resource Profiles by first referring to Navigators).

Without getting into a long discussion about the pros and cons of the two schemes, we point out simply that the presence of front-end FIServers has other advantages, and so is likely to be an architectural component in any event. These advantages include:

- Acting as a proxy forward information cache service on behalf of the Navigators behind it,

- Managing certain Ingrid Topology maintenance (garbage collection) functions, thus simplifying Navigator implementation, and

- Acting as a firewall between internal Navigators and external Ingrid components.

There are many questions about the effectiveness and cost of this caching scheme and about searching efficiency in general. These questions can only be answered through real experience. Our expectation, however, is that typical operating parameters for forward information will be 10s of Persistent Forward Information "links" per Resource Profile, and 10s to 100s of Cached Forward Information links per Persistent Forward Information link.

Algorithm for Automatically Building the Ingrid Topology

This section discusses how to build the "base" Ingrid Topology—that is, how to install the Persistent Forward Information associated with each Resource Profile. In general, the term Ingrid Topology refers only to the Persistent Forward Information.

The basic principle behind installing Persistent Forward Information is simple: When a new Resource Profile needs to be installed, it searches for itself, and then connects to whatever it finds.

That having been said, let's discuss it a little further. Each Resource Profile is associated with a single FIServer. Each Resource Profile has a set of terms. From these terms, a (combinative) number of term combinations can be generated. For each such term combination, there may (or may not) exist a corresponding cluster. To fully join the Ingrid Topology, then, the Resource Profile must add a link to every existing such cluster.

A search of the Ingrid Topology will retrieve a set of Resource Profiles whose terms match as many of the term combinations in the joining Resource Profile as possible. By adding links to these Resource Profiles, the new Resource Profile effectively joins the appropriate clusters. The mechanism for creating a link is to add Persistent Forward Information both to the FIServer of the new Resource Profile, and to the FIServer of the neighbor Resource Profile.

In order to keep the topology sparse, the Resource Profile adds links to as small a number of other Resource Profiles as possible while still trying to join as many clusters as possible. So, for instance, if new Resource Profile ABCDE finds Resource Profiles ABCD and ABC, it will add a link to only Resource Profile ABCD, since a link to both would be redundant, and a link to Resource Profile ABC alone would result in fewer clusters being joined.

In many (most?) cases, a new Resource Profile may have to make a trade-off between the number of links created and the number of clusters joined. We don't know how this will play out, but one observation is that a Resource Profile only need join those clusters for which it "expects" to be searched. For instance, it may be possible for a Resource Profile to, over time, monitor how it has been searched, and to change clusters, or even change the weighting of its own terms, correspondingly.

Maintaining connected clusters

No system in Ingrid maintains any explicit state about clusters. This is because there are a combinative number of clusters, and Ingrid could not scale if it had to maintain any kind of per-cluster information. For instance, cluster boundaries are not labeled, and the only system that may ever explicitly know the full membership of a given cluster is a Navigator that recently fully explored a cluster. FIServers do not know the full membership of a cluster. They only know their neighbor Resource Profiles.

This raises the question of how it is known if a cluster is connected or partitioned. In fact, it is not known. When a Resource Profile X attaches to another Resource Profile Y, the assumption is that, for each term combination that can be generated from Y's terms, Y has successfully joined the corresponding cluster. There is no explicit information, however, that indicates whether or not this is true. Thus, clusters will on occasion be partitioned. How frequent this is in practice, what the practical consequences of it are, and what can be done about it if it is a problem remain to be seen.

One rule that is required to help maintain cluster connectivity is: A Resource Profile can only attach to Resource Profiles that are "older" than it. This is to prevent dependency loops. For instance, consider the case where, for a given term combination, Resource Profile Z attached to Resource Profile Y, which had attached to X, which had attached to W:

```
Z-->Y-->X-->W
```

Assume that later, Resource Profile X discovered that Resource Profile Z was a much better match, and that it could replace a number of links, including the one to W, by one link to Z. Z's path connectivity to W, however, depends on X. If X were to remove its link to W and attach to Z, a dependency loop would form (Z-Y-X-Z), and the cluster would become partitioned.

The mechanism for labeling the "age" of Resource Profiles is as follows. Every Resource Profile has a single Join Sequence Number. When a Resource Profile attaches to the Ingrid Topology, it sets its Join Sequence Number to be one higher than that of the neighbor with the highest Join Sequence Number. Subsequently, the Resource Profile cannot attach to another

Resource Profile with a higher Join Sequence Number (though Resource Profiles with higher Join Sequence Numbers can of course attach to it).

A note on the Global Single-Term Server (GSTServer)

A new Resource Profile may have term combinations that no other Resource Profile contains. When this happens, there is obviously no existing cluster with that term combination for the new Resource Profile to join. However, because of the new term combination, the corresponding new cluster is created by virtue of the new Resource Profile joining the Ingrid Topology (though the new cluster has only one member). The new Resource Profile has therefore created new points in Ingrid space (or, new locations in the Ingrid topography, however you like to think about it).

It also may happen that a new Resource Profile has an individual term that no other Resource Profile has. The new Resource Profile will know that it is a new term because the term will not be listed by the GSTServer. Because the new term will exist after the new Resource Profile joins the Ingrid Topology, the GSTServer must be updated with the new term. It is the responsibility of the FIServer that owns the new Resource Profile to insure that the GSTServer obtains the new term.

Essentially, the FIServer tells a GSTServer to add a Forward Information link for that term pointing back to it. The GSTServer will then update its neighbor GSTServers as to the new term, and they will update their neighbors, and so on until all GSTServers have the new Forward Information. (Note that the network of GSTServers will, according to current thinking on the topic, be manually configured as a sparse topology. This is similar to the scheme used by Harvest.)

Browsing the Ingrid Topology

It is well known that keyword-style searching is only a part of the overall searching process. "Rel-evance feedback" is an important part of any searching process, whether or not it is directly supported by the search mechanism. Relevance feedback is where the user indicates to the search system which (keyword) matching resources are in fact good matches. The system then finds resources strongly related to the good matches.

Another useful function of a typical searching system is to suggest alternative terms that the user may use in subsequent searches.

Because related resources are near each other in the Ingrid Topology, both of the above features can be efficiently provided.

For the case of relevance feedback, an Ingrid Navigator can efficiently traverse the links surrounding a selected Resource Profile, returning to the user those Resource Profiles that have the most terms in common with the selected Resource Profile.

For the case of suggesting alternative terms, an Ingrid Navigator can traverse the links in the clusters that match the user's search terms, and return to the user those terms that appear most often in the Resource Profiles found.

Note that in neither of the above cases is the user explicitly aware of the actual Ingrid links. The Ingrid Navigator automatically traverses nearby links on behalf of the user and returns the results. Actually, the first version of the Ingrid Navigator we developed early in 1995 allowed the user to follow Ingrid links (similar to the operation of HTML browsers). We quickly found, however, that this was of limited, and sometimes misleading, use. One reason is that it didn't allow the user to see the overall structure of information. Another reason is that, since Ingrid links are automatically placed, and since they are not anchored in the text of the resource, it is often not clear to the user why the link exists or if it should be followed. The second version of the Ingrid Navigator eliminated link-level browsing altogether.

The Ingrid Navigator under development for the alpha-release of Ingrid will have both of the above feedback features. When a search is executed using the Ingrid Navigator, it will display both (1) the set of matching resources (usually by title), in order of best match and (2) the set of related terms, in order of most related. The user will be able to tag resources and terms as being either particularly relevant or particularly irrelevant. This will result in an updated display, and may result in additional browsing (if the user so indicates). The user may of course modify the set of search terms and execute another search.

Scaling

The main scaling concern is the amount of Persistent Forward Information required to maintain a correct (or adequately correct, by some measure of adequate) Ingrid Topology.

For a fully correct Ingrid Topology, every Resource Profile must be connected to a cluster for each of its possible term combinations. From our (limited) experience in automatic term weighting, we found that from 10 to 15 terms were adequate to describe a medium-size document (around 10 pages). Assume a Resource Profile with 20 terms. In the theoretical worst case, it is possible to generate 184,756 different term combinations, none of which are subsets of any others (this is the case where each term combination has exactly 10 terms). Thus, in the worst case, such a Resource Profile would require 184,756 links.

For a lower bound, if there exists another Resource Profile with the same 20 terms, then the given Resource Profile can join all possible clusters with a single link. (Or, if no other Resource Profile exists with any of the 20 terms, no links are required.) Note that FIServers require no explicit labeling of cluster boundaries. FIServers know only what terms their own Resource Profiles have, and what terms their neighbor Resource Profiles have. Therefore, for the above case, even if the single link to another Resource Profile with the same 20 terms allows the Resource Profile to belong to roughly one million ($2^{**}20$) clusters, a simple list of the 20 terms is sufficient to effectively "label" all the clusters.

Somewhere between these two bounds—a single link and thousands of links—lies reality. The actual number of links cannot be predicted, because the number depends on what the collection of Resource Profiles is. There are, however, two positive characteristics that lead us to believe that the actual number of links will be manageable.

Consider a given Resource Profile X. All other Resource Profiles in the world can be put into one of two groups: (1) those that share no terms with Resource Profile X (the Zero Group) and (2) those that have terms in common with Resource Profile X (the Shared Group).

The first positive characteristic is that the total number of Resource Profiles in the Zero Group has absolutely no effect on the number of X's links. There is never a reason for Resource Profile X to attach to a Resource Profile with no shared terms. Practically speaking, this means that the large majority of resources in the world have no effect on a given resource (or, for that matter, on an Ingrid Navigator). They are as invisible.

The second positive characteristic is that, after a certain point, the more Resource Profiles there are in the Shared Group, the fewer links Resource Profile X requires. The graph of Figure 10 shows how increasing the total number of Resource Profiles effects the number of links per Resource Profile. As the number of Resource Profiles increases from zero, the number of links per Resource Profile increases. However, at some point, the number of links per Resource Profile begins to decrease with continued increase in the total number of Resource Profiles.

The reason for this can be seen from the line that plots the total number of different term combinations against increasing Resource Profiles. Because all of the Resource Profiles in the shared group can be said to come from the same "topic

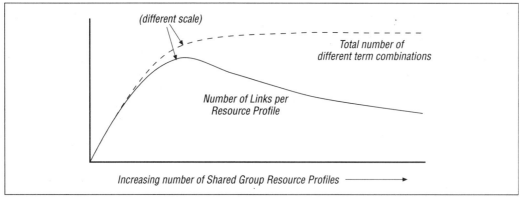

Figure 10:   Growth of links versus Resource Profiles

area," the total number of different terms is bounded. As a result, as the number of Resource Profiles grows, the total number of term combinations represented begins to saturate. New Resource Profiles start tending to have the same term combinations as existing Resource Profiles. Correspondingly, the increase in the total number of clusters also slows down. But, since the number of Resource Profiles continues to grow faster than the number of clusters, the task of maintaining connected clusters is spread across more and more Resource Profiles, with the result that each individual Resource Profile requires fewer links.

Even given this phenomenon, it is unknown where the peak of the curve lies. Therefore a scaling problem may still exist. This is one of the two main reasons that only high-weight terms are used to form the Ingrid Topology. By limiting the number of terms, we also limit the number of links required between Resource Profiles. The other reason is that the "quality" of the Ingrid Topology may be lowered if less than high-weight terms are used. The number of terms used for a Resource Profile is a trade-off between search quality and quantity. It is not clear whether the number of terms chosen will be limited by a desire for quality over quantity or limited by scaling.

Note also that it is not always necessary (or even possible, practically speaking) to maintain a fully

correct Ingrid Topology. An imperfect Ingrid Topology means simply that a search for a given set of terms will not yield every matching resource. It may be adequate for, say, 90% or 80% of the total number of Resource Profiles with a given term combination to actually be in the same cluster.

A reasonable strategy for inserting Resource Profiles into the Ingrid Topology is to have an upper bound on the average number of links per Resource Profile (within a given FIServer). An FIServer can add and delete links according to observed search patterns to maximize search quality.

Experimental Results

A small experimental Ingrid Topology was built in April of 1995. It consisted of roughly 4000 related documents (RFCs, IETF Internet Drafts and meeting reports, and the archives of a few IETF mailing lists). Terms were automatically weighted using term frequency by inverse document frequency style weighting [1]. The average number of terms selected per Resource Profile was approximately 12. The total set of selected terms resulted in around 5000 distinct terms.

The Ingrid Topology built was fully or near fully correct. We say near fully because, while the insertion software was designed to connect to all possible clusters, we did not in fact examine all clusters for full connectedness. Rather, we examined a small number of arbitrarily selected clusters, mainly for the purpose of checking correctness of the software.

The average number of links per Resource Profile was roughly 10. The Resource Profile with the most links had 50. The minimum was two links (which occurred when two versions of the same paper were inserted, with the result that one would find the other and attach only a single link).

While this experiment was way too small to be considered definitive, we were pleased by the results we did get. Ten links per Resource Profile is quite a low overhead. This is especially true when considering that the collection we chose is strongly related, as evidenced by the fact that 4000 resource produced only 5000 distinct terms. In other words, the collection truly represents a single topic area. The Resource Profiles of this collection would be strongly interconnected even in a "real" (large and diverse) Ingrid Topology. Therefore, these links may represent a significant proportion of the total number of links the Resource Profiles would have in a global Ingrid Topology.

Global Single-Term Servers

Another scaling concern is that of the GSTServers. In the current design, each GSTServer contains three entries for each term in all of Ingrid space. (We say "current" design, because if this proves excessive, it is always possible to create a hierarchy of GSTServers, at the cost of extra complexity.) This section provides some rough back-of-the-envelope calculations for GSTServer size.

Assume that each entry requires, on average, 200 bytes (one term plus three host names plus overhead). A good dictionary for any given language has on the order of 200,000 words (including proper names). As a worst-case estimate, assume that the most common 300 languages are fully represented. This requires 12 gigabytes of memory. Double this to (roughly) account for technical, scientific, and other specialized terms. Twenty-four gigabytes is still well within current technology.

To continue the worst-case assessment, assume that each entry requires updating once per week. (This implies that the average lifetime of a Resource Profile is one week—a conservative estimate.) According to the current protocol for updating an entry, three packets are required: (1) one to inform the GSTServer of the old and new entries, (2) one to request verification of the new entry, and (3) one to receive verification of the new entry.

This makes roughly 600 packets per second. Assuming that each packet is 200 bytes, we get around 100kbytes per second. Again, within current technology, though a system that can manage 200 updates per second of a 24 gigabyte database and still have processing leftover to handle queries is no small machine. On the other hand, it will be some time before 300 languages are fully represented.

Project Status and Goals

For an up-to-date project status, please consult our Ingrid project home page at *http://www.ntt.jp/ntt/soft-labs/ingrid/*.

We implemented a demo version of Ingrid in spring of 1995, and built a small Ingrid topology (4000 resources) spread over four machines, and a simple navigator (see the section "Experimental Results"). Nothing in that experiment led us to believe Ingrid would fail. However, we didn't build anywhere near big enough a topology to really test Ingrid.

Therefore, we are now working towards a medium-scale test of Ingrid. Our target is to start a limited alpha-test towards the end of 1995. By limited, we mean approximately 100 hosts and 100,000 resources. This should give us some preliminary estimates on the scaling and performance of Ingrid. Depending on how the alpha-test goes, we hope to release a beta-version sometime around mid 1996.

Last Comments

This paper describes the fundamental aspects of a scalable, fully distributed, fully self-configuring information navigation infrastructure. It compares it with both competing and complementary technologies, presents some arguments as to why it may scale, and gives some limited experimental results on scaling.

There are many issues that we have given considerable thought that are not discussed in this paper. These include (but are not limited to) implementation issues (our implementation is fully connectionless, running over UDP), topology maintenance issues (rather than do constant pinging, we discover and repair errors during normal use), coordination of distributed resource profiling (when different people profile and insert the same resource), quality control of resources, other applications (such as a resource referral service like the HOMR Music Recommendation Service), multilingual issues (the Ingrid Infrastructure uses only the Mule [2] MULtilingual Enhancement to GNU Emacs 19 character set), private Ingrid (firewalls and encryption), interaction with single-database search engines, and richer search semantics (boolean, partial matching).

We feel that we have reasonable answers for most of these issues. The two issues of greatest concern at this point (besides scaling) are (1) how not to be overwhelmed by irrelevant or garbage resources (understanding that one man's garbage is another man's gold) and (2) how to deal with the security problems created by the fact that, in the general case, any FIServer can request any other FIServer to add Persistent Forwarding Information.

In any event, implementation and experience will be required to better understand these issues. ∎

Acknowledgments

We would like to thank Jeff Smith for his review of this paper, and for many interesting and fruitful discussions of Ingrid. We would like to thank Shigeki Goto, Ryouichi Hosoya, Masaki Itoh, Katsunori Kon, Minoru Koyama, Kenichiro Murakami, Yutaka Ogawa, Hitoaki Sakamoto, Jeff Smith, and Kenji Takahashi (all of NTT) for their support of or contributions to the Ingrid project.

List of URLs

Centroids: *http://services.bunyip.com:8000/products/digger/digger-main.html*

Fish-Search: *http://www.win.tue.nl/win/cs/is/reinpost/www94/*

Harvest: *http://harvest.cs.colorado.edu/*

HOMR: *http://homr.www.media.mit.edu/projects/homr/*

Lycos: *http://query2.lycos.cs.cmu.edu/*

Robots: *http://web.nexor.co.uk/mak/doc/robots/robots.html*

WWWW: *http://www.cs.colorado.edu/home/mcbryan/WWWW.html*

References

1. Salton, G. *Introduction to Modern Information Retrieval*, McGraw-Hill, New York, 1983.

2. Mule, anonymous FTP at *ftp.iij.ad.jp:/pub/misc/mule*

3. Mockapetris, P. "Domain names—implementation and specification," RFC 1035, anonymous FTP at *ds.internic.net:/rfc/rfc1035.txt*

About the Authors

Paul Francis
[*http://www.ntt.jp/people/francis/*]
NTT Software Labs
francis@slab.ntt.jp

Takashi Kambayashi
[*http://www.ntt.jp/people/kam/*]

NTT Software Labs
kam@slab.ntt.jp

Shin-ya Sato
[*http://www.ntt.jp/people/sato/*]
NTT Network Service Systems Labs
sato@sphere.csl.ntt.jp

Susumu Shimizu
[*http://www.ntt.jp/people/shimizu/*]
NTT Software Labs
shimizu@slab.ntt.jp

(This document can be found at *http://www.ntt.jp/ntt/soft-labs/ingrid/*)

APPLICATION-SPECIFIC PROXY SERVERS AS HTTP STREAM TRANSDUCERS

Charles Brooks, Murray S. Mazer, Scott Meeks, Jim Miller

Abstract

If one wishes to execute specialized processing on the HTTP requests and responses that flow between WWW clients and servers, one can add the processing in the clients, in the servers, or between them. We describe a novel approach to the latter; we generalize the notion of proxy servers to construct application-specific proxies that act as transducers on the HTTP stream. We have built a sample set of transducers to demonstrate the idea and an initial toolkit to ease the task of constructing these transducers and attaching them to the HTTP stream. **Keywords:** *Proxy servers, stream transducers, HTTP*

Introduction

Typically, a WWW client (usually a browser) sends an HTTP request directly to the target WWW server, and that server returns the response directly to the client. WWW proxy servers [7] were designed to provide gateway access to the Web for people on closed subnets who could only access the Internet through a firewall machine. In the proxy technique, the WWW client sends the full URL (including protocol and server portions) to the designated proxy, which then connects to the desired server via the desired protocol, issues the request, and forwards the result back to the initial client. The key observation is that the client uses HTTP to communicate with the proxy, regardless of the protocol specified in the URL. An addition to proxy servers gave them the ability to cache retrieved documents to improve access latencies [7].

WWW clients and servers normally expect that the network will transport messages between them with the content unchanged; this is true whether a proxy is in the stream or not. That is, the correspondents expect the client's request to arrive at the server with exactly the content transmitted by the client, and they expect the server's response to reach the client intact. The underlying assumption is that the network is simply a mechanism for transporting messages between the communicating entities but is not a mechanism for applying application-specific processing to the message contents. A caching proxy, which may elect to serve the response itself instead of forwarding the request to the designated server, starts to challenge that assumption. Similarly, a load-balancing proxy, which might select a mirror site for a given request instead of the designated server, in order to reflect current network behavior, would further challenge that assumption. In both of these cases, the request may not reach the designated server but the response likely reaches the client intact.

We challenge this assumption even further: we suggest that, for some classes of client/server applications and their network transactions, substantial value may arise from inserting into the communication stream, application-specific transducers that may view and potentially alter the message contents. We are testing this hypothesis in the context of the World Wide Web by building a sample set of proxy-based transducers that are bound to the HTTP request/response stream. This approach extends the "standard" WWW architecture in a way we believe is both novel and useful.

The rest of this paper proceeds as follows. First, we describe the motivation for introducing transducers into the HTTP stream. Then we review our approach to building and using this enhanced architectural component. We describe some examples, followed by a discussion of our publicly available toolkit [8], its implementation, and its performance. Finally, we consider some future work.

Motivation

We are developing this technology in the context of a larger research program into approaches to building computerized *browsing assistants* [12] to aid the human user in accessing relevant information on the Web. We hypothesize that some of the browsing assistance is best achieved by monitoring and processing the HTTP stream between the user's browser and the Web. As an independent example, the idea of using an application-specific proxy was recently advocated for nonintrusive community content control [2]. Further, group-related assistance may arise from processing the stream between a workgroup's browsers and the Web; we are investigating a number of issues in this area.

We view the transducers as having four classes of functionality:

- Filtering individual HTTP requests and responses

- Characterizing sets of messages

- Transforming message contents

- Additional processing indicated by the messages

Here are some illustrative examples of each class in the WWW context:

Filtering
 Checks the validity of request headers (eliding improper ones or returning an error response to the sender); redirects requests according to dynamic models of current network behavior; and elides images from responses being sent to bandwidth-limited clients.

Characterizing
 Builds a dynamic model of current network behavior based on request/response latency; constructs a full-text index of all responses received by a workgroup (so that individuals may leverage the browsing behavior of the group).

Transforming
 Converts response formats into formats better suited for the client (e.g., downgrading video quality for a portable client); adds value to the content based on additional data sources (e.g., recognizing zip codes inside responses and converting them into anchors that link to census bureau data on the appropriate regions); and interprets location-specific references inside requests to determine the appropriate destination server.

Additional processing
 Prefetches links embedded in each response and applying appropriate transforms, such as constructing a tree showing all document titles lying within two links of the current document.

These transducers are essentially specialized processing modules, whose inputs include at least the HTTP stream. They may also take input from other sources, may communicate with other processing modules, and may create output of any kind appropriate to their function. For example, a full-text indexer could produce an index searchable via a Web form.

These transducers may serve at least four classes of users:

Individuals
 May support specific interests and preferences through selection of transducers.

Groups
 May effect group policy or provide benefit to individuals based on the actions of their peers.

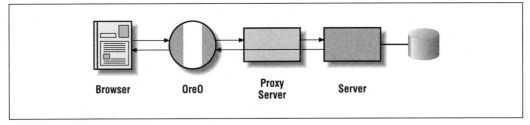

Figure 1: An OreO as part of the HTTP stream

Enterprises

Like groups, but on a larger scale.

Public

Innovators, information providers, and entrepreneurs may offer transducers to the public.

Approach

Our approach clearly derives from the proxy server model: as illustrated below in Figure 1 for WWW browsers and servers, one can use the mechanism to insert other kinds of processing entities into the stream.

We refer to our HTTP transducers as *OreOs* (with appropriate apologies to the cookie makers), because the transducer is structured with one "wafer" to handle browser-side communication, another "wafer" to handle server-side communication, and a functional "filling" in the middle. As illustrated below in Figure 2, the OreOs take advantage of the HTTP proxy mechanism, essentially appearing as a server to the client side and

as a client to the server side. Because the full URL is delivered intact to the OreO, the filling can use the scheme, server, server-relative URL, or request data in its processing.

In some cases, the OreO will forward the request to another proxy (using HTTP proxy, as illustrated above); in other cases, the OreO may forward the request directly to the designated WWW server.

Figure 3 shows various possible compositions of OreOs to serve the needs of individuals, groups, enterprises, and the public.

We advocate constructing highly specialized transducers that can be composed to produce more sophisticated aggregate behavior; this contrasts with building monolithic components that are hard to reuse. We propose that these composed functional chains may be configured dynamically as well as statically, on a granularity as fine as per-request or as coarse as per-session or across sessions. Currently, we have experience only with static configurations.

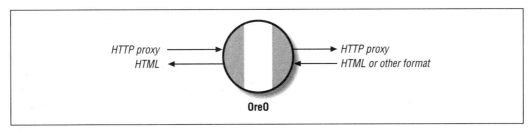

Figure 2: OreOs can use the HTTP proxy mechanism

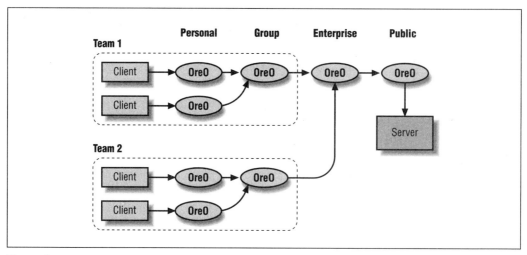

Figure 3:   Personal, group, enterprise, and public OreO servers

Our approach reflects the "stream model" of signal processing (later adopted and extended by the functional programming community [1]). Viewing the connection between the client and the server as a stream of data, one can build a standard box which accepts one or more such streams as input and produces one or more such streams as output. Each box can execute specialized processing on the stream(s). All of the boxes have the same basic interface (stream-in/stream-out), so they can be connected together, producing sophisticated processing from the composition of simple processing elements.

We expect that the selection of which transducers to use in which situations will in some cases be preconfigured, in others be under administrative control, in others be under user control, and in still others, be under OreO control. For applications which offer the user some direct control over the selection and invocation of network transactions, users will be able to select the functional modules to be used.

Examples

We have built several example HTTP transducers; these are meant to be evocative, rather than definitive. The first was constructed by deconstructing a CERN httpd and inserting the desired processing (written in C). The remainder were constructed in various languages using the toolkit discussed below. In addition, some of the functionality is enhanced by use of our internally developed experimental browser, Ariadne [9]. Here are some examples (others are under development):

- The first OreO performed several different functions:
    1. URL validation, to identify malformed URLs and report errors directly back to the browser, short-circuiting the request. In a sense, the OreO is "serving" part of the errorful URL space."
    2. Measuring data transfer rates from the various servers, and reporting these to the user via a TCP *backchannel* (a separate communication channel) to the Ariadne browser.
    3. Creating a *group history*, based on the HTTP requests of the set of browsers passing requests through the OreO and reporting the group history in one of two ways: (1) through a dynamic HTML document, created and updated by the

OreO, and accessed at a well-known URL, or (2) through the backchannel to Ariadne, and presented by Ariadne as a multicolored tree in a special window.

- A full-text indexing OreO, which creates a full-text index of all of the nontrivial terms appearing in the responses flowing through it. The OreO stores the index in a file system accessible by a CGI script sitting on a WWW server, and users may query the index via the usual forms interface. This OreO could serve an individual as well as a workgroup; the goal is to ease the problem of recalling the documents in which certain terms have appeared.

- A "protocol monitoring" OreO that is used to display the request/response traffic and to diagnose malfunctioning client/server interactions.

- A specialized "wafer" that acts as a gateway between unmodified browsers and WWW servers protected by DCE security mechanisms [10]. Communication between the wafer and the browser is via proxy HTTP, and communication between the wafer and the server is via DCE RPC [11].

- A "group annotation" OreO, that supports the Stanford annotation approach [14] but allows that functionality to be available to users of a variety of browsers, not just the Stanford one.

- A "rewriting" OreO that encapsulates each anchor inside the Netscape *Blink* extension, making anchors easier to spot on monochrome displays.

As becomes clear through these examples, an OreO will often create some sort of information space (e.g., full-text index or group history) that may be made available to the user through a variety of mechanisms, such as

- Query forms (e.g., the OreO writes data to a file that a CGI script can use to answer queries on the data)

- A well-known URL (e.g., the OreO writes an HTML page to a location that a server can access to respond to requests for the information)

- Interprocess communication (e.g., the OreO can send information updates or commands to a browser via a control channel to get the browser to display the relevant information to the user)

- URLs that the OreO serves itself (e.g., the OreO traps requests to a particular part of URL space and returns the corresponding HTML document, which it might create dynamically)

Toolkit

To ease the task of building these transducers, we have produced a toolkit [8] which allows the filling developer to focus on the application-specific aspects of the transducer. In the initial version of the toolkit, we provide a "shell" that implements the "wafers" between which the filling is placed. The developer may use any program development system to create the filling, which is simply executed by the shell after it performs appropriate setup functions. The shell ensures that the filling is connected into the request/response stream, so that the developer can simply operate on the contents and ignore the network-specific issues.

Processing Modes

The shell supports four processing approaches:

- At most one request/response pair extant at any time, each pair flowing through a newly instantiated filling

- At most one request/response pair extant at any time, flowing through a single, persistent filling

- Multiple outstanding request/response pairs flowing through a single, persistent filling

- Multiple outstanding request/response pairs, each one flowing through its own filling instantiation

Further, the filling developer may configure the shell so that the filling handles HTTP requests only, HTTP responses only, or both requests and responses; the shell handles the requests or responses (as a pass-through) if the filling does not.

Implementation

The OreO shell is implemented as a single UNIX process that runs as a UNIX daemon; this is due largely to the original example OreO's origin as the `main()` for the CERN (now W3C) HTTP daemon process (*httpd*). The shell accepts a series of command-line arguments that indicate the TCP/IP port on which it should accept connections, the program that it should execute to process the HTTP request and/or response, and whether the program should be executed in parallel or sequentially.

For each new connection, the shell can either open a connection to the downstream process (which can be specified either as an environment variable OREO_PROXY or via a command-line argument), or simply allow the filling code to determine the destination for the request. The latter mode allows filling code to support new protocol implementations (such as an RPC-based protocols).

A single, persistent filling

If a single, persistent filling has been specified, the shell `fork()`s and `exec()`s a copy of the filling: this filling is expected to meet the rules for the design of a *coprocess*: the process must retrieve a pair of UNIX file descriptors corresponding to the client and server sockets from a private IPC channel created between the shell and the coprocess. Once the process has retrieved these sockets, it must send an acknowledgement back to the shell (the above is encapsulated in an API provided as part of the toolkit).

At that point, the coprocess is responsible for the connections; it must read and write to the appropriate sockets, and close them as necessary.

The issue of multiple versus singular request/response pairs is thus the responsibility of the coprocess. Normally, the processing will be singular, since the coprocess will effectively execute the following loop:

```
do {
get a connection ;
process the connection ;
} while(1);
```

Newly instantiated fillings

If a single persistent filling has not been requested, then the shell determines what kind of processing has been specified. There are two options:

- Process the HTTP request, the HTTP response, or both (but provide a different filling for the request and response streams)

- Process both the request and response streams, but do so in a single filling.

In the first case, if the filling chooses not to handle the request or response, the shell simply reads and writes data from one socket to the other. Each filling is set up appropriately: a request filling has its standard input set to the client socket and its output set to the server socket; the process is reversed for a response filling. This model is useful if there is no need to maintain state in the filling between the HTTP request and response streams, and is most similar to the notion of UNIX filters (one way transforms).

In the second case outlined above, the shell sets the filling's standard input to the client socket and the standard output to the server socket; a supplied API hides this implementation detail from the filling writer. This mode allows the filling writer to maintain internal state across the HTTP requests and responses.

Future versions of the toolkit should add new levels of abstraction for the developer; for example, we have specified a higher-level API that can present the requests and responses as preparsed HTML entities, so that the developer does not have to replicate that effort. Further, a toolkit might provide appropriate interfaces to the underlying WWW protocol support.

Performance

To gauge the effects of OreOs on HTTP request/response latency, we measured the additional delay introduced to a series of HTTP transactions by a PERL-based pass-through OreO (one that merely forwards requests and responses without change). Our results are encouraging: the delay experienced was between 3% and 6%, depending on the mode of the OreO. We also performed simple tests to determine whether humans could perceive the additional delay. Four identical browsers were configured to point through various configurations of OreOs and proxies (the "worst" being a chain of four pass-throughs), and test subjects were asked to identify each of the four configurations; the subjects could only identify the browser proxied through four pass-throughs. This suggests that users are already conditioned to the variability experienced in network transactions, and the addition of a small extra delay does not stand out. The OreO shell appears to add no perceptible delay—the filling, however, can be arbitrarily complex and therefore add arbitrary delay.

Futures

We have already begun thinking about extensions to our basic model. These extensions fall into three general categories: implementing the OreO toolkit on multiple platforms, extending the notion of filtering agents themselves, and increased browser/OreO interactions.

Other Platforms

At present, the OreO shell has been compiled and tested under HP-UX and under OSF/1 running on Intel platforms. Time and resources allowing, we plan to reimplement the OreO shell

under Microsoft Windows/NT. This will require minor modifications to the networking code (vanilla BSD UNIX to WinSock compliant code), as well as modification to the process creation and process execution model. The latter should not prove difficult, as the details of this mechanism have been encapsulated in a single routine. Other possibilities including reimplementing the OreO shell to run as a Windows/NT service.

Extensions

We have several ideas on how to extend the notion of filtering agents, as illustrated by the OreO. These ideas break down into three categories:

- Improvements to the OreO shell
- Improvements to the OreO/Browser interaction model
- Improvements to the actual processing of content

Improvements to the OreO shell

We believe that the notion of the OreO shell is a good one: a layer of code that isolates the actual filling from the details of obtaining and processing network connections. The inspiration for this model is the standard input and output model for the UNIX operating system [6]: programs can read from the standard input unit and write to the standard output unit without regard for whether these are files, terminals, network connections, etc.

Our initial thought was that the filling developer would encapsulate the invocation of the OreO shell and the appropriate filling code inside a shell script. While this has been true, we have imagined other models that would provide enhanced functionality in packaging and exporting transducing services to a user community. At present, if one wished to support several long-running OreOs, one would have to arrange explicitly for each script to be run when the machine is initially started. The following suggestions offer improvements to this situation.

OreO shell as inetd

In this model, the OreO shell is implemented similarly to the standard UNIX *inetd*. Transducer fillings are configured similarly to the specification in the *inetd.conf* (perhaps specifying service name, protocol, port, program to run, etc.). As in the current *inetd*, the Oreo shell would accept connections on the various TCP/IP ports listed in its configuration file. New connections would result in a new process being created to run the filling code. Stdin, stdout, and stderr for the filling would be connected to the upstream (client) program by the shell; the filling would be responsible for connecting to the downstream (proxy) server by either reading a command line argument or an environment variable.

OreO shell as portmapper

In this model (inspired by the RPC daemons of both ONC and DCE [11]), the OreO shell functions as a registrar for the above transducers. Transducers register their services with the shell, at which time the shell listens on the port specified by the transducer. Clients connect to that port, and the shell redirects the connection to the appropriate IPC channel established between the transducer and the shell. Such a technique would permit dynamic registration of transducer code: the interface for clients would remain the same (proxy HTTP), whereas the interface between the shell and the transducer code would become more complex.

OreO shell as request broker

In this model, the OreO shell functions as a location-independent agent registrar, incorporating aspects of both the DCE *rpcd* and the DCE CDS (Cell Directory Services) servers. In addition to the functionality represented by the *portmapper* approach above, the shell would also be responsible for updating and maintaining a distributed database of agent functionality, such that an individual shell would be able to redirect a request for service to an appropriate location.

Generalized agent factory

In this model, the OreO shell becomes a "generalized agent factory" similar to the Softbot [13] or Sodabot [3] environments. Individual transforms are coded as functions that transform the HTTP stream as it is passed from transform to transform. The user may choose to implement these transforms in a programming language of some kind that provides its own specific GUI and other functionality.

OreO/Browser Interaction

We also intend to explore transducer/browser interaction. At present, our *Ariadne* browser sends an additional HTTP header (X-BackChannel:) that indicates a host, protocol, and port number on which the browser is willing to accept connections. This header is recognized by our OreO agents; servers simply ignore them. One can imagine extensions to this mechanism that are similar to the current `Accept:` headers, except that these headers indicate languages that the browser is willing to process: Safe-TCL, Python, Java, etc.

Finally, provided that browser's network point-of-presence is known (host, protocol, port), one can imagine using the NCSA Common Client Interface (CCI), the Spyglass Software Development Interface (SDI), or the NetScape API to communicate between a browser and an OreO. At this time, however, the mechanisms for establishing that point-of-presence are loosely specified, so it is not clear how well the above interfaces will work when the transducer would be running on a separate machine.

Improvements to processing information content

At present, the OreO shell presents a byte-stream interface to its client "fillings." While this is a very general and flexible model, it is too low-level to provide the kind of productivity improvements that we had initially hoped for when designing the OreO shell. Achieving the next level of productivity will require a higher level of abstraction; we have been evaluating the W3C's Library of Common Code (libWWW) [5] as a basis for that higher level of abstraction. We believe that, at a minimum, the next level will provide an abstraction of an HTTP request/response object: a series of HTTP headers optionally followed by an opaque content body. Parsing of the input byte stream, then, becomes part of the process of constructing this object; destructing this object might include converting it to a byte-stream and directing it to the downstream sink. This functionality would be provide by the API and not directly by the filling code itself.

Once the request/response object has been constructed, we then need to determine how to transfer this object between various OreO transducers. At present, this process is quite inefficient, in that each transducer must construct the request/response object, transform it, and then reconvert it to a byte-stream representation in order to pass it on the (potentially) next transducer. Transducers may desire to see only the HTTP headers or the content body, or both. Modifications to content may require modifications to the headers (e.g., conversion of GIF images to JPEG would require modification to the Content-Type header). The above model then leads to a view of transducers as functions in a programming language, or as "functors" (functions as instantiable objects) [4]: the HTTP protocol object is passed from one such functor to another based upon some user-specified sequence.

Finally, we may wish to expand on the notion of the transducer as HTTP server. As suggested in the introduction, the CERN HTTP proxy server with caching [7] enabled is one kind of transducer. Another kind of transducer is an OreO that manages its own virtual Web-based namespace that has no mapping to an underlying file store. In this model, the OreO simply caches various information in memory: browsers send proxy requests to *service.machine.org* which ful-

fills these request from memory. The CGI interface to this OreO would be to invoke internal functions with the appropriate arguments: each function returns an object of type HTML.

We are beginning to work on how OreOs might communicate with each other for control purposes, and to share information. At this time, we are pursuing the notion of implementing a network blackboard via HTTP (the blackboard server would be implemented as a stand-alone OreO) using the techniques described above (OreO manages its own internal namespace, etc.).

Conclusion

We have presented a novel approach to introducing specialized processing on the HTTP requests and responses that flow between WWW clients and servers. We generalized the notion of WWW proxy servers to that of application-specific proxies that act as transducers on the HTTP stream. Our prototype OreOs demonstrate the utility of the concept, and our toolkit aims to ease the task of building such OreOs, without adding undue performance penalties. We encourage experimentation to determine the kinds of application settings to which such an architectural component is especially suited and ways in which to extend the WWW architecture further.

Availability of Software

FTPable source and binaries for HP-UX (and possibly other platforms) are available by anonymous ftp from *riftp.osf.org* in */pub/web/OreO*. Please read the copyright notice. ∎

References

1. Abelson, H. et al., *Structure and Interpretation of Computer Programs*, MIT Press, Cambridge, MA 1986.

2. Behlendorf, B., *A Proposal for Non-Intrusive Community Content Control Using Proxy Servers*, *http://www.organic.com/Staff/brian/community-filters.html*

3. Cohen, M., *The SodaBot Home Page, http://www.ai.mit.edu/people/sodabot/sodabot.html*

4. Coplien, J., *Advanced C++: Programming Styles and Idioms*, Addison-Wesley, Reading, MA, 1992.

5. Frystyk, H., *Library of Common Code, http://www.w3.org/hypertext/WWW/Library/*

6. Kernighan, B., and Pike, M., *The Unix Programming Environment*, Prentice-Hall, Englewood Cliffs, NJ, 1984, "Filters," pp. 101-132.

7. Luotonen, A., and Altis, K., *World-Wide Web Proxies*, at site *http://www.w3.org/hypertext/WWW/Proxies/*

8. *OSF RI World-Wide Web Agent Toolkit (OreO), http://www.osf.org/ri/announcements/OreO_Datasheet.html*

9. *Ariadne*, at site *http://www.osf.org/ri/announcements/Ariadne_Datasheet.html*

10. *DCE-Web Home Page, http://www.osf.org:8001/www/dceweb/DCE-Web-Home-Page.html*

11. *OSF Distributed Computing Environment, http://www.osf.org:8001/dce/index.html*

12. *Wide-Area Browsing Assistance for the World Wide Web, http://www.osf.org/www/waiba/*

13. Perkowitz, M., *Internet Softbot, http://www.cs.washington.edu/research/projects/softbots/www/softbots.html*

14. Roscheisen, M. and Mogensen, C., *ComMentor: Scalable Architecture for Shared WWW Annotations as a Platform for Value-Added Providers, http://www-pcd.stanford.edu/COMMENTOR*

Acknowlegments

This research was supported in part by the Advanced Research Projects Agency (ARPA) under contract number F30602-94-C-020. The views and conclusions contained in this document are those of the authors and should not be interpreted as representing the official policies, either expressed or implied, of the Advanced Research Projects Agency of the U.S. Government.

About the Authors

Charles Brooks
OSF Research Institute
11 Cambridge Center
Cambridge, MA 02142
cbrooks@osf.org

Murray S. Mazer
OSF Research Institute
11 Cambridge Center
Cambridge, MA 02142
mazer@osf.org

Scott Meeks
OSF Research Institute
11 Cambridge Center
Cambridge, MA 02142
meeks@osf.org

Jim Miller
World Wide Web Consortium
Massachusetts Institute of Technology
Laboratory for Computer Science
545 Technology Square Cambridge, MA 02142
jmiller@mit.edu

DynaWeb
Integrating Large SGML Repositories and the WWW

Gavin Thomas Nicol

Abstract

Many companies are now establishing a presence on the World Wide Web, and are facing the problem of how to make their data available in an efficient, cost effective, and presentable manner. For large documents in non-HTML formats, the traditional approach has been to convert the data to a large number of small HTML pages. These pages are then made available on the WWW; however, this process results in lost information fidelity, and increased costs due to double-handling. DynaWeb is an HTTP 1.0 compatible server and CGI script that performs the conversion and the fragmentation at runtime, and uses the very same data used for publishing in other media. The rationale for this is that it dramatically simplifies the information management process, and thereby reduces the costs of publishing on the Internet. This paper discusses the design of DynaWeb, and the concepts behind it.

Introduction

The World Wide Web has enjoyed explosive growth over the last few years. There are many reasons for the success, among which the very low cost of entry plays a role. Browsers are free, or free for noncommercial use, free servers are available, and installation is not overly difficult for anyone with reasonable computing skills. HTML, the lingua franca of the World Wide Web, is likewise simple to learn (partly due to its own simplicity). As such, almost anyone with a reasonable level of computing know-how, can either publish or provide data within the World Wide Web. In addition, modern browsers lower the cost of entry for those not familiar with the traditional text-based Internet tools (FTP, Telnet, etc.); users can just point and click to get what they want (if they can find it). The above is a remarkable accomplishment: individual users have never had an easier way to create, distribute, and consume information, but at the same time, the very simplicity is an Achilles' heel. The World Wide Web is very much biased toward small-scale publishing using HTTP and HTML.

The Implicit Assumptions

While the initial vision of the World Wide Web was far grander, the current World Wide Web is largely a producer-consumer architecture. As part of the general mentality, there are a number of implicit assumptions made:

- *The URL will point to either a file, or a CGI script.* To date, in most cases where the URL did not point to a file, it did point to a CGI script, possibly a gateway to another program. It can be argued that CGI is a double-edged sword, because, despite its convenience, it can be inefficient, among other problems.

- *The browser will access files, and files will be small.* For most individual publishing efforts, the volume of data will generally not be large, and HTML pages suffice. However maintaining large amounts of data as myriad small files with hyperlinks between them is a nightmare. Many publishers have multi-megabyte books they would like to put online, but hesitate to do so using HTML.

- *The file will be in a data format the browser understands.* This is obviously false for a great deal of legacy data, which could be in any one of a huge number of formats. In addition, partly due to the simplicity of HTML, and also for ease of maintenance, data is generally left in its legacy format, and converted to HTML, if it is ever published on the WWW.

It is widely recognized that until better tools for the creation and maintenance of HTML arrive (and possibly not even then), that it seldom makes sense to work in native HTML for large amounts of data. Rather, most sites use whatever editing or desktop publishing environment they have installed, and then rely on tools to convert the data to HTML for publishing on the WWW. Verifying the output of such programs can be both time-consuming and error-prone, despite the best efforts of tool writers. In such cases, where the actual information management is taking place in a format other than HTML, WWW publishing becomes an additional step in an already complex process.

As data sizes increase, the costs associated with maintenance increase, especially if the data is frequently updated. This is a hidden and often overlooked cost associated with Web publishing. Indeed, the combination of software and data maintenance could easily be more costly in the short term, and will almost certainly be more costly in the long term, than actually setting up the initial WWW server (including costs for hardware). It is becoming common for a company to have fulltime staff working solely on the care and feeding of the company Web site (to which the situation's vacant areas bear adequate testimony). The thought *"There must be an easier way"* is probably at the fore of many people's minds.

DynaWeb is designed with a set of assumptions and goals, almost completely different from those found in other WWW servers:

- The URLs in DynaWeb may, or may not point to files or CGI scripts.

- The files may be small, though in general, the size of the text data will be at least 1MB, and often *much* larger.

- The file format may be HTML of whatever, but DynaWeb is also designed to handle large SGML documents in an intelligient manner.

- DynaWeb was designed to simplify the publishing process, and reduce maintenance, as much as possible.

- DynaWeb was designed to minimize effort required for publishing on multiple media (WWW and CDROM). Indeed, exactly the same data is used for both (DynaText books).

DynaWeb Goals

EBT is widely recognized as one of the leading suppliers of SGML-based online publishing tools. The DynaText product has been used in a number of industries to publish large SGML documents electronically. Some of DynaText's desirable features are:

- Native SGML support

- Almost unlimited data sizes

- Runtime formatting decided by stylesheets, thereby allowing mutliple views of a single dataset

- Automatically generated TOCs, also controlled by stylesheets

- Extensive stylesheet-controlled hyperlinking behavior

- Good search performance, with support for SGML-aware queries, as well as proximity, boolean, and regular expression searches

- Query form engine

With the advent of the WWW, it seemed desirable to provide EBT's customers with the tools required for publishing on the WWW, in addition to disk based publishing, and to bring these desirable features along in the process. The target set was to allow publishers to publish using the same techniques, and to bring as much DynaText functionality to the WWW as possible. This led to some smaller individual goals:

- Use current Dynatext books with minimum effort

- Perform SGML to HTML conversion at runtime

- Allow multiple stylesheets to be specified

- Solve the "large file" problem by fragmenting documents on the fly as needed

- Automatically generate TOCs and navigational aids

- Automatically generate hyperlinks for graphics, etc.

- Translate DynaText query forms to HTML forms at runtime

- Give full access to DynaText's search engine

- Make DynaWeb compatible to the NCSA HTTPD server

- Provide reasonable levels of performance

Basic Architecture

The basic architecture of the current DynaWeb server is the common *fork and exec* architecture, in which the server proper accepts connections, forks, and then executes an engine for processing requests. This architecture was selected primarily for its simplicity, and flexibility during the development cycle. In addition, from early in the project, there was thought of having a CGI script version of DynaWeb, and this architecture maximizes code sharing between the two different versions, though at some expense in raw performance. DynaWeb is largely HTTPD compatible, so it can quite obviously handle arbitrary data types in the same way that HTTPD does (via MIME-type mapping) in addition to allowing access to DynaText books. Like most other HTTP servers, the exact processing performed is largely decided by the HTTP method invoked and the URL. This architecture is shown in Figure 1.

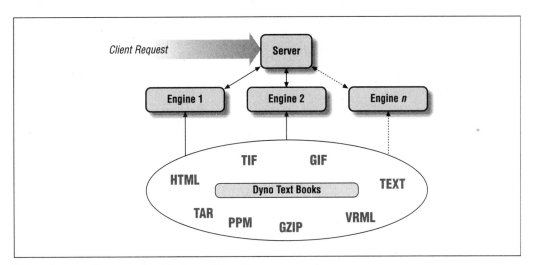

Figure 1:   The general architecture of DynaWeb

DynaWeb URLs

For a server like DynaWeb, a certain amount of state is required, but HTTP is a stateless protocol. So for this and other reasons, the commonly understood semantics attached to parts of a URL have been expanded.

Subdocument Addressing

DynaWeb needs to address *parts* of a document in order to be able to break it into fragments. The WWW defines no standard way to do this, so DynaWeb uses the addresses of the elements in a document. The resulting URLs look, for the most part, like normal filenames, making it easier for people accustomed to filenames to understand, but harder for the server, because some overlap of namespaces occurs. Such addresses can only occur in the context of DynaText book accesses, so this is generally not a problem. The URL syntaxes DynaWeb understands are:

File Access
http://www.ebt.com/path
This is the same as the normal file access URLs seen elsewhere.

CGI Script Access
http://www.ebt.com/keyword/path
When the server sees *keyword* it executes a CGI script, as found in other HTTP browsers.

Sub-document addressing
http://www.ebt.com/collection/book/eid
This is used to access parts of DynaText books. The *collection* part of the path could be considered a library, and a *book* a book within it. The *eid* is an address for an SGML element.

Early versions of DynaWeb also supported two other syntaxes taken from the TEI guidelines:

Child Number Path
http://www.ebt.com/n/n/n/n...
With this naming scheme, an element is addressed by descending from the root of the SGML document and taking the *nth* child as the new parent until the path has ben completely traversed. The resulting parent is the target element.

Child Type and Occurrence Path
http://www.ebt.com/gi[=x]/gi[=x]...
This is similar to the above method, except that it goes by child type, represented by *gi* in the above, which is possibly qualified by an occurrence indicator (i.e., specifying which child of that type). Again traversal starts at the root of the SGML document.

However, these were found to be unneccessary as the algorithms for generating navigational aids improved. They are still valuable as a standard means of accessing hierarchically structured data, however.

Forms Data as an Environment

The current method of sending data from forms to a server is to append the (possibly encoded) *name+value* pairs after the end of the URL, following a question mark. This area is also overloaded by being where keywords for searches are specified, and where data from ISMAP images is transferred. This area can also be used to manage state.

DynaWeb looks at the *name+value* pairs in much the same way many applications look at environment variables. User-specified options, and server-generated state are transferred from the server to the client in the links generated by the last request. When the client activates one of the links, the environment data will be sent to the server, starting the cycle once more. An example of how this is used can be found in DynaWeb's named-stylesheet support: the stylesheet name is passed back and forth betwen client and server. Apart from these semantics, and the URL extensions, DynaWeb should appear to clients exactly like any other typical HTTP server.

The DynaWeb Publishing Process

As mentioned earlier, one of the stated goals for DynaWeb was to make it as simple as possible for EBT's customers to publish to the WWW. To a very large degree this has been accomplished.

In order to produce a DynaText book, one first runs an indexer/compiler upon validated SGML source, which produces data files containing indexes, and associated data. Once this is accomplished, one then uses either the WYSIWYG stylesheet editor, or a text editor, to create sets of stylesheets controlling the display of text, TOCs, the behavior of hyperlinks, and other such things. The process for DynaWeb *is exactly the same* and more importantly, the data files produced in the DynaText publishing process can also be used for DynaWeb publishing. The only thing one needs to do to put a DynaText book into DynaWeb is to create new stylesheets.

One thing worth emphasizing is that the size of the DynaText books is irrelevant: DynaWeb will fragment them at runtime. Also, hyperlinks are not coded by hand, but rather generated at runtime by DynaWeb, based on entries in stylesheets. As such, no individual link validation is required by the document maintenance people; rather, they simply make sure their stylesheets are correct, and from then on, any books conforming to the same DTD will be able to make use of the same stylesheets. For example, if a publisher uses the Docbook DTD exclusively, then they need only write the stylesheets *once*, and update them as needed. Once the stylesheets for CDROM and WWW publishing have been created, the publisher can then produce DynaText books, and, to a large degree, not think about the distribution media at all.

The Conversion Process

SGML documents are inherently hierarchical; they consist of a tree of elements, which may, or may not have attributes associated with them.

Before looking at the actual conversion process, let's look at what is meant by *document structure*, and compare some typical structural markup defined using SGML and HTML (also defined using SGML). Here is a small sample document using structural markup:

```
<DOCUMENT>
 <TITLE>DynaWeb: Interfacing large
    SGML...</>
 <ABSTRACT>Many companies are now ...</>
 <CHAPTER>
  <TITLE>Introduction</>
  <PARA>The World Wide Web has enjoyed..
    .</>
  <SECTION>
   <TITLE>The Implicit Assumptions</>
   <PARA>While the initial vision...
    <TERM.LIST>
     <TERM>The URL will point to either.
    ..</>
     <EXPLANATION>To date, in most
    cases where...</>
     <TERM>The file will be in a format.
    ..</>
     <EXPLANATION>This is obviously
    false for...</>
    </TERM.LIST>
   </PARA>
  </SECTION>
  <SECTION>
   <TITLE>DynaWeb URLs</>
   <PARA>For a server like DynaWeb...</>
   <SUBSECTION>
    <TITLE>Sub-document Addressing</
    TITLE>
    <PARA>DynaWeb needs to address...</>
   </SUBSECTION>
  </SECTION>
 </CHAPTER>
</DOCUMENT>
```

Figure 2 shows the hierarchical nature of the document, by showing each element as a node in a tree. Note the special #DATA element. This represents a *psuedo-element*, or one which exists by *implication*.

In order for HTML-based browsers to display the document in a pleasing manner, the above document needs to be translated into a corresponding HTML document, such as the following one.

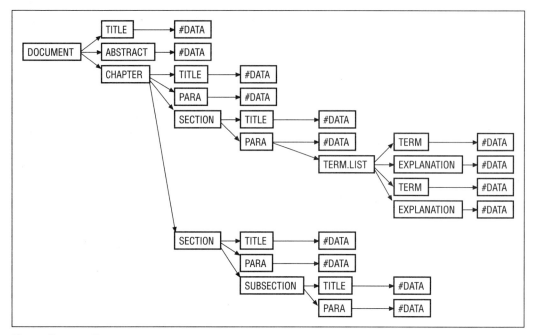

Figure 2: The tree structure of the sample SGML document

```
<HTML>
<H1>DynaWeb: Interfacing large SGML...</
   H1>
<H2>Abstract</H2>
<BLOCKQUOTE>Many companies are now ...</
   BLOCKQUOTE>
<H2>Introduction</H2>
<P>The World Wide Web has enjoyed...</P>
<H3>The Implicit Assumptions</H3>
<P>While the initial vision...</P>
<DL>
<DT>The URL will point to either...</DT>
<DD>To date, in most cases where...</DD>
<DT>The file will be in a format...</DT>
<DD>This is obviously false for...</DD>
</DL>
</P>
<H3>DynaWeb URLs</H3>
<P>For a server like DynaWeb...</P>
<H4>Sub-document Addressing</H4>
<P>DynaWeb needs to address...</P>
</HTML>
```

The above HTML file, when treated as SGML (as it should be), would have the tree structure shown in Figure 3.

It is immediately obvious that the HTML representation has far less structural depth than the native SGML representation. This is one reason why many people in the SGML field dislike the HTML DTD; they are used to far more structure (others abhor it).

The job of converting SGML to HTML is primarily that of converting one tree into another. Arbitrary SGML to SGML conversion is possible, in the same way that arbitrary conversion between programming languages is possible. However, like programming language conversion, there are some cases which cannot be handled elegantly, simply due to the grammars being too different. The HTML DTD has less structural depth, and is overall much simpler than most other SGML DTDs. This simplifies the conversion task a great deal, just as translating C into assembler represents a far simpler task than translating C into Ada. It should be noted that typesetting SGML can also be regarded as a translation process (SGML to Postscript).

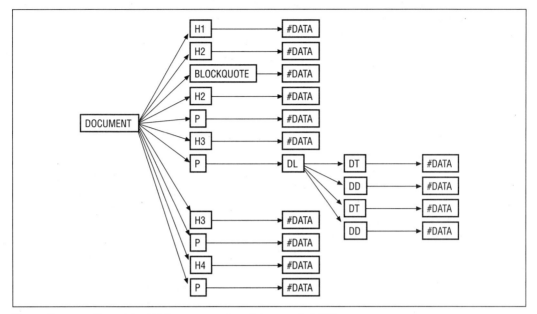

Figure 3:   Tree of the HTML representation of the sample SGML

There are many ways to perform the actual translation; some systems are driven by the events generated by the SGML parser, while other manipulate trees directly. Most use some form of scripting language to associate processing with elements, or in other words *stylesheets*. Hardcoded formatting is generally frowned upon in SGML applications.

DynaText books can be regarded as a static object oriented database of sorts; in them, the structure of the SGML as well as the text is stored. It is trivial to traverse the tree and regenerate a valid SGML representation of the original SGML data (though some things, like entity references, will be lost in some cases). In addition, the DynaText system already uses stylesheets extensively for online formatting, for printing, for TOC creation, and for hyperlink behavior. The stylesheets in DynaText define a set of properties to be associated with each node, which may be set by evaluating scripts written in the internal DynaText scripting language at runtime As such, the DynaText stylesheet language is quite well-suited to the SGML to HTML conversion task. While it is quite possible to simply use a tag mapping table (i.e., When *this* tag is seen, generate *that* tag.), the DynaText stylesheet mechanism brings an extra level of sophistication to the job at hand.

SGML to HTML conversion is accomplished by using the **#TEXT-BEFORE** and **#TEXT-AFTER** properties in the DynaText stylesheet language. These allow the stylesheet writer to add text *before* and *after* the element they are associated with, respectively. By setting these to the HTML start and end tags desired, conversion can be accomplished. Indeed, with the WYSIWYG stylesheet editor, it is possible to actually *see* the tags as you define them. This is made even simpler by the support for *stylesheet groups*, which makes formatting an element as simple as adding it to a group. EBT provides definitions for some groups to be used in HTML conversion.

One important capability of DynaWeb is the ability to use multiple named stylesheets. As HTML and browsers are evolving very rapidly, the problem of supporting multiple versions of one's document raises its head. In most normal servers, this requires multiple versions of files to be managed (one supporting HTML 2.0 without tables, another HTML 2.0 with tables, and another for HTML 3.0). In DynaWeb, one's data remains unchanged, and instead, one uses multiple *stylesheet* versions, representing a much more manageable task.

Of course, the DynaText stylesheet language was not designed for this application, so there are some limitations. In particular, converting between widely disparate table models can require quite complex scripts to be written, but as HTML matures, conversion of such things should become easier (i.e., the set of common features in the grammar for HTML, and other SGML DTDs will become larger).

Navigational Aids

This section discusses the navigational aids found within DynaWeb. The most important thing to remember is that these aids are generated *automatically* from the combination of SGML structure and stylesheets. This represents a significant advance over most current WWW publishing systems.

Autogenerated TOCs

One of the early requirements for DynaWeb was that it should, as far as possible, offer a similar level of functionality and a similar interface to DynaText. DynaText has automatically generated, expandable and collapsible TOCs, which also provide feedback on search results. In DynaText, the TOC is normally displayed along with the fulltext view, which scrolls to the position associated with a TOC entry being selected. However, almost all WWW browsers are restricted to single windows, and do not allow communication between windows. As such, the TOC feature had to be implemented as a standalone WWW page. Like DynaText, the contents,

and to a certain degree the look, of TOCs, is controlled by stylesheets.

The automatically generated TOCs have plus or minus buttons to the left of the title for the TOC entry. When a user clicks on a button, a request is sent to the server, telling it to regenerate the TOC with that section expanded or collapsed. Once no more TOC expansion can occur, selecting the TOC entry will bring up a page containing actual text data.

TOCs provide an excellent interface to the runtime chunking that DynaWeb perfoms, but a very difficult design decision is *when* they should be generated. If DynaWeb sees a URL, which accesses a DynaText book, and if that URL ends with a ".to" extension, it will generate a TOC. If the URL does *not* end with such an extension, then the size of the data *below* the target element is used to decide whether to generate a TOC. One of the configuration parameters specifies a desired limit on data sent to clients. If the size of the data below the target element exceeds that size, and then if a TOC *can* be generated, one will be; otherwise the data is sent to the client (possibly after prompting the user, or broken into pageable chunks).

Next and Previous Buttons

DynaWeb attaches navigational hints to text "pages" as well. At the top and bottom, buttons are attached that allow the user to enter into *page flipping* mode. Selecting the forward button causes the next page to be retrieved, and selecting the back arrow selects the previous page. A button in the center causes a TOC to be generated. This fragmentation occurs automatically, with boundaries being decided by SGML document structure, and TOC stylesheets. The meaning of *page* is equivalent to the meaning "logical block of data."

Autogenerated Links to Other Data

In addition to these automatically generated aids, the standard DynaText hyperlinking facilities work as well. In the stylesheets, one can specify links to graphics, links to other books, query links, and more. For example, if your SGML source has a <FIGURE> element:

```
<FIGURE NAME="widget.gif" TITLE="The
   Widget">
```

then one would use the following style definition:

```
<style name="ART.RASTER">
 <script>        ebt-raster
   filename=@(name) title="@(title)" </
   >
 <icon-type>     raster </>
</style>
```

causing *all* <FIGURE> elements to be displayed as an icon, which when selected would result in the image named by the **NAME** attribute to be retrieved. However, if one wanted inline images, one would write:

```
<style name="ART.RASTER">
 <inline>       raster filename=@(name)
   title="@(title)" </>
</style>
```

causing all <FIGURE> elements to generate the code required to display graphics inline. Specifying both `script` and `inline` properties allows one to create *hot images*. Other kinds of behavior are specified similarly.

The important thing to understand is that, again, after having defined such behavior *once*, the stylesheets can be used for any book conforming to the same DTD, and links will be generated automatically.

Searching

Another of the great benefits of leaving the data in structured SGML can be found in DynaWeb's searching capabilities. Not only does DynaWeb support proximity, boolean, and other such queries, but it also support SGML-aware queries. For example, one can do the following:

```
asimov inside <author>
<author> containing asimov
```

to perform a search limited to text found within an <AUTHOR> tag (text within an author tag or its children). DynaWeb also supports searches on attribute values and other such things as well.

DynaText has its own format for defining search forms, and these are translated to HTML forms at runtime, again providing for smooth interoperability between CDROM and WWW publishing. Search hits are reported via the TOCs, which display the number of hits per TOC entry, and also by highlighting within the actual text. It should be noted that searching is not limited only to books; queries can be made at almost any level within a DynaWeb server, allowing *exploratory querying* of DynaWeb sites.

Discussion

To date, DynaWeb has been deployed at some major sites, including EBT's home page, and for the manuals area of Novell's WWW site. Initial feedback from customers proves that we have met all of our initial goals. Large scale publishing with DynaWeb is a pleasure compared to the traditional methods, and the time involved in both publishing and maintenance is substantially reduced. For example, Novell published around 100,000 pages of documentation in a week, and another customer took a day to publish using DynaWeb, compared to the week spent previously in conversion to HTML. Performance of the current server is sufficient for most needs.

However, all was not smooth sailing. The fact that HTTP is a stateless protocol complicates the management of state in DynaWeb (including security) enormously. Also, the large behavioral differences in browsers presented a problem: the autogenerated HTML for things like the search sliver needed to be both legal *and* understood by all tested browsers. This proved difficult to achieve. Many other such problems were encountered.

The use of TEI locators proved to be very valuable initially, but as development progressed, they became less so. However, the author believes they still have great potential as a standard way of accessing hierarchically structured databases. For example, they could be used to address parts of a VRML file, or an object-oriented database, or even relational databases. They are certainly worth keeping in mind.

The author believes that systems such as DynaWeb represent the future of the WWW. HTML is unsuitable for large scale publishing, as is filesystem-based management of documents. Neither of these technologies scale when multiple megabytes of data are being manipulated, nor when multiple media types, and multiple file formats need to be supported.

The author also believes that as the WWW evolves, it will become steadily more object oriented, to a point in the future when instead of just documents and replication, we will also have objects that we can combine to create applications tied together via both replication and remote method invocation. Object location will steadily become something a user rarely need think about.

For DynaWeb, many enhancements are possible, even though the current product has delivered on its promises. Most of these enhancements are in the implementation rather than in the overall system design. For example, it seems natural that at some point in the future, the static object-oriented database be replaced by a true, large scale, SGML document repository, and for a multithreaded architecture to be used. ■

References

1. Charles Goldfarb, *The SGML Handbook,* Oxford University Press, 1990.

2. The Text Encoding Initiative Home Page, *http://etext.virginia.edu/TEI.html*

3. The Harvest Document Management System, *http://rd.cs.colorado.edu/harvest/*

4. Kenneth P. Brooks, "A Two-view Document Editor With User Definable Document Structure," Digital Systems Research Center report #33, *http://www.research.digital.com/SRC/home.html*

5. N. Borenstein and N. Freed, MIME (Multipurpose Internet Mail Extensions) Part 1, *http://ds.internic.net/rfc/rfc1521.ps*

6. K. Moore, MIME (Multipurpose Internet Mail Extensions) Part 2, *http://ds.internic.net/rfc/rfc1522.txt*

7. T. Berners-Lee, R. T. Fielding, H. Frystyk Nielsen, Hypertext Transfer Protocol—HTTP/1.0, *ftp://ds.internic.net/internet-drafts/draft-fielding-http-spec-01.txt*

About the Author

Gavin T. Nicol

[*http://www.ebt.com/*]

Electronic Book Technologies, Japan

1-29-9 Tsurumaki, Setagaya-ku,

Tokyo 154, Japan

Phone: +81-3-3230-3861

Fax: +81-3-3230-3863

gtn@ebt.com

Brought to you by the letters P, S, G, M and L, and S and P.

RMC

A Tool to Design WWW Applications

Alicia Díaz, Tomás Isakowitz, Vanesa Maiorana, Gabriel Gilabert

Abstract

We present the design of a computer-aided environment, RMCase, to support the design and construction of WWW applications. RMCase supports hypermedia design and development activities and produces HTML code. Support for cognitive design processes is achieved through three fundamental premises at the foundation of RMCase: (1) fluid feedback loops between the various methodological stages, (2) manipulation of objets at the instance level, and (3) lightweight prototyping. As a result, RMCase will support bottom-up, top-down, and middle-out software development styles.

Introduction

WWW application design and development is a complex task that involves a variety of activities at the storage, access, and presentation levels. As a consequence, the constituencies participating in hypermedia projects differ from those of traditional software development environments. Hypermedia projects involve content-authors, librarians, musicians, and graphic designers, as well as programmers, system analysts, software managers, and, of course, users. Moreover, aesthetic and cognitive aspects, so important for hypermedia applications, are foreign to existing software engineering environments. Thus, there is a need for special methodologies and tools to support the software development process of hypermedia applications.

In this paper we present the design of the Relationship Management Case Tool (*RMCase*), an environment to support the development of hypermedia WWW applications. This article represents a continuation of our efforts to construct a CASE tool for the development of hypermedia applications [1]. The Relational Management Design Methodology (*RMM*) [2] provides the methodological foundation for RMCase; its cognitive basis is drawn from work by Nanard and Nanard [3]. RMCase is, in principle, platform independent; it is capable of producing applications of systems running on the WWW [4], Tool-

book, Hypercard, or other hypermedia environments. In particular, RMCase is more than an HTML editor; it is a software development environment that produces, as one of its outcomes, HTML code. It also produces design specifications.

Requirements for a Hypermedia Design Environment

Nanard and Nanard [3] identify the following fundamental requirements for a hypermedia development environment, adopted in RMCase:

- Fast feedback loop spanning across methodological stages, to facilitate evaluation and redesign activities.

- Accessible and unconstrained cloning tools at the instance level, to facilitate the generation of material application instances that lend themselves to evaluation by designers, developers, and users.

- Abstraction and instantiation mechanisms that enable developers to alternate between bottom-up and top-down approaches.

This paper is organized as follows. *Relationship Management Methodology* briefly describes the RMM design methodology. The principal components of RMCase are presented in *Contexts in RMCASE*. Finally, *Conclusion* summarizes the contributions we make in this article.

Relationship Management Methodology (RMM)

The *Relationship Management Methodology (RMM)* [2] is a methodology for the design and construction of hypermedia applications. It consists of seven steps, some of which can be conducted in parallel. We will briefly explain the RMM's data model in what follows (for a more detailed elaboration, we refer the reader to [2]). Although RMM is, in principle, a linear methodology, our proposal in this paper results in an environment that supports feedback loops, cloning and prototyping to achieve a combination of top-down and bottom-up approaches.

The Relationship Management Data Model (RMDM)

A cornerstone of the RMM methodology is its data model, the *Relationship Management Data Model (RMDM)*, whose elements are shown in Figure 1. RMDM provides a language for describing information objects and navigation mechanisms in hypermedia applications. An application's design is specified with an RMD diagram, constructed from RMDM's elements (see Figure 2 further ahead). The RMDM model is based on the Entity-Relationship model [5] and on HDM [6]. ER relationships can be *one-one, one-many*, and *many-many,* representing associations between entities. As in database modeling, many-many relationships are factored into pairs of one-many relationships.

Because entities may have a large number of attributes of a different nature (e.g., salary information, biographical data, photograph), it may be impractical or undesirable to present all the attributes of an entity instance in one screen. Thus, attributes are grouped into *slices*. For example, a person entity with attributes *name, age, photograph*, and *biosketch* may have a *General* slice, containing *name, age*, and *photograph* and a *Biosketch* slice, with *name* and *biosketch*. The notation for slices is shown at the top of Figure 1 (supposed to resemble a pizza slice.).

Navigation is supported in RMDM by the six access primitives shown at the bottom of Figure 1. Uni- and bidirectional links are used to specify access between slices of an entity. The most significant access structures supported by RMDM are indices, guided tours, and groupings. An index acts as a table of contents to a list of information items, providing direct access to each listed item. A guided tour implements a linear path through a collection of items allowing the user to move either forwards or backwards on the path. Index Guided Tours combine the functionalities of indices and guided tours. These three access structures are augmented with logical conditions that act as select statements specifying the set of instances being accessed. For example, a condition rank="Associate" on an index into a faculty entity denotes an index to all associate professors. The grouping mechanism serves as an access point to other parts of the hypermedia document. For example, the initial screen of many applications contains a menu or set of buttons that provide access to different functions or classes of information.

A Sample Application

The ISWEB application ([9]) is a WWW site for the Information Systems Department at the Stern School of Business. The application contains information about faculty, courses, research, and other academic activities. Parts of this application are highly structured, so it lends itself to be modeled in RMDM. Figure 2 shows an RMD diagram for the ISWEB application. In contrast to an entity-relationship diagram that represents the design of a database, an RMDM diagram describes how users will navigate a hypermedia application. To avoid cluttering, slices are not included in Figure 2, and only *key* attributes of entities are shown. At the top of Figure 2 the grouping mechanism implements a "main menu." Access into the *Faculty* and *Courses* information is provided via guided tours; access into *Programs* by means of an index. On choosing the guided tour to the *Faculty* entity, the user can move back and forth among all faculty members

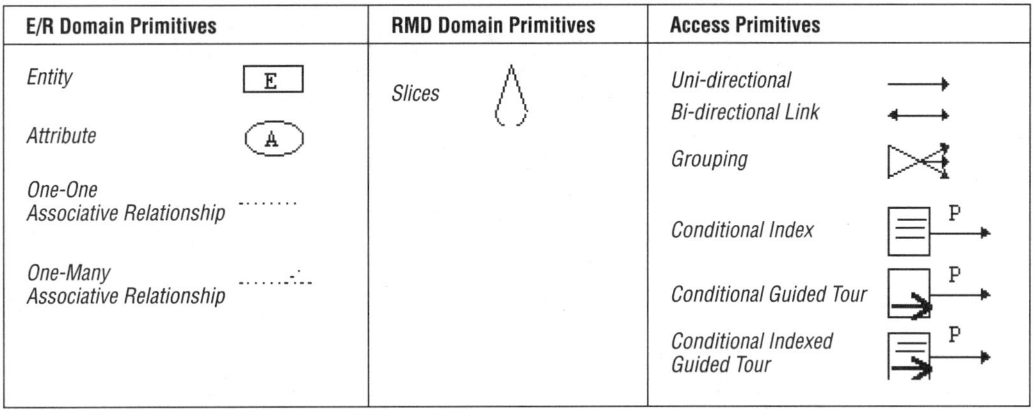

E/R Domain Primitives	RMD Domain Primitives	Access Primitives
Entity E Attribute A One-One Associative Relationship ········ One-Many Associative Relationship ······∴··	Slices	Uni-directional ⟶ Bi-directional Link ⟷ Grouping ⋈ Conditional Index P Conditional Guided Tour P Conditional Indexed Guided Tour P

Figure 1:   The elements of the RMM Data Model

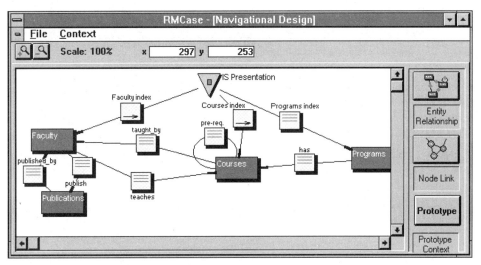

Figure 2:   The RMD diagram for the ISWEB application

(ordered alphabetically). There is a conditional index from the *Faculty* entity into *Courses* with predicate *teaches(F,C)*. The reciprocal index *taught_by(C,F)* can be accessed from *Courses*.

Contexts in RMCASE

RMCase supports the software life-cycle of an application through a set of contexts, one per stage, called *work contexts*. The concept of context is akin to that presented in [7] and to the *col-lections*, as defined in [8], in the sense that a context is a collections of nodes with associated browsing semantics. Rapid transitions between methodological stages are supported in RMCase via navigation among contexts. Since design objects are shared among different contexts, this kind of navigation enables developers to focus on one or more design objects while moving back and forth between the various stages in the methodology (one of the three fundamental

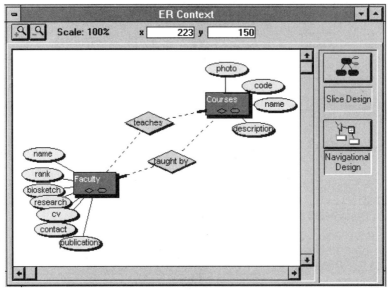

Figure 3:   The E-R context supports E-R design activities

requirements for a hypermedia software development environment).

The E-R Design Context

The E-R design context facilitates the construction of E-R diagrams, capturing the characteristics of the application domain. Three basic design objects are handled in this context: entities, attributes, and relationships.

- An *entity* is a conceptual element from the application domain, characterized by a set of attributes.

- An *attribute* represents a unit of information. Attributes have a name and type and are always associated with a unique entity or relationship.

- A *relationship* is a conceptual tie among two or more entities. A relationship's cardinality can be one-one, one-many or many-one. RMM splits many-many relationships into two one-many relationships. Relationships can also contain attributes.

The E-R design context, shown in Figure 3, has well-defined functionalities to manipulate entities, attributes, and relationships. The entities *Faculty* and *Courses*, and the relevant relationships are shown along with their attributes in Figure 3.

The Slice Design Context

The inner structure of an entity is designed in this context. The design objects are: attributes, slices, and links among slices. A *slice* is a set of attributes belonging to a given entity. An attribute can be part of number slices. Each entity has a distinguished slice, called the entity's *head*, that is to be used as a default entry point for incoming access constructs. The slice design context enables designers to "zoom" into each entity one at a time. Figure 4 shows a partial slice design for the *Faculty* entity as it appears in the slice design context

The Navigational Design Context

This context helps developers specify the navigational features of an application. Designers spec-

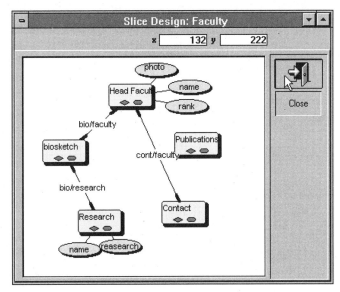

Figure 4: Slice design context

ify menu-like structures using groupings, indices, and guided tours. Designers also decide here what relationships will be navigable in the final application. In Figure 5, for example, the *teaches* and *taught_by* relationships are implemented via conditional indices. The designer also specifies the conditions that are part of the access structures (e.g., "teaches(Course)=last_name"). The diagram appearing in Figure 5 is an RMD diagram, which models access paths. *Presentation* is the opening screen, from which *Faculty* and *Courses* indices are reachable.

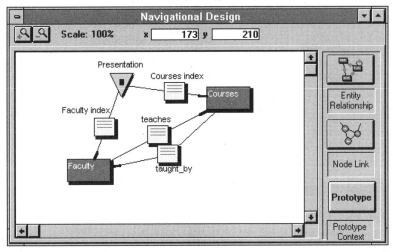

Figure 5: The Faculty-Course navigational design

Node-Link Conversion Context

The *node-link conversion* context contains several kinds of facilities to support the conversion of RMDM diagrams into node-link webs:

- Facilities to execute the conversion itself, a kind of "compiler." When activated, these facilities automatically generate a web of nodes and links.

- Facilities to manipulate the node-link web itself.

Each slice is mapped into a node, and each access structure into a web of links and nodes. Links between slices are passed along to the node-link web. In addition, anchors are defined for each outgoing link, including guided tours and indices. In an index, the anchor provides navigation into the item it denotes. In a guided tour, the first anchor selects the first element in the guided tour, the next anchor the second, and so on.

This context is conceived as a visualization tool; it has no other functionality.

User-interface Design Context

For many WWW applications it is importatnt to exhibit a common look and feel. This is importatnt, for example, for some large organizations who are interested on the Web ([10]). RMCase is specially well suited for these kinds of applications.

This context provides facilities to design and edit the user-interface. We conceive a set of screen-designing tools like those available in many commercial applications (e.g., Toolbook, Visual Basic, MS Access, etc.) to generate HTML templates.

We contemplate the following set of functionalities for the user-interface context:

- Associate to each node an HTML template

- Associate to each anchor an HTML anchor

In this context, the designer "draws" the interface, associating an HTML object to each node and access structure.

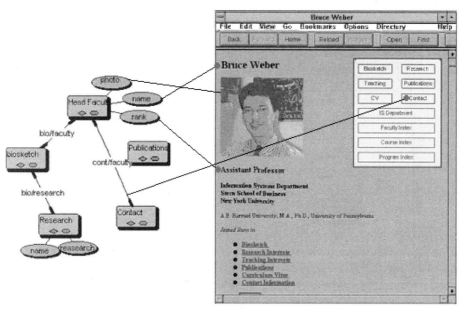

Figure 6: In User-interface context, the designer "draws" the interface

Figure 6 depicts the interface designed for *Faculty* head slice. For each attribute or link anchor there is an associated "slot" in the HTML template. Similarly, templates are created for all other components of the application design. In sum, the user-interface context assists developers in the generation of a set of HTML templates, that are to be populated with information in the *hyperbase population* context.

Hyperbase Population Context

This context supports the generation of an application by populating HTML templates with data. If the information resides within a database, there are at least two alternative approaches for hyperbase population.

- *Prepopulated applications.* The database information is "pumped" into a set of node instances at generation time. Thus, the data is hard-coded into the application. As a result, the data can only be updated either by regenerating it or, manually, with the assistance of software developers. This

approach is recommended for applications that are infrequently updated.

- *Dynamic applications.* The application obtains information "on demand" from the database by issuing queries. This approach is recommended for high volatility applications

By definition, this context is responsible for establishing a kind of bridge between the WWW application and information that is external to it. This rather complex task involves a special kind of system that is outside the scope of this paper.

The Prototyping Context

There is a specialized *prototyping* context that represents the instance level. The prototyping context is where software developers can test different aspects of the design of a hypermedia application, such as its information structure and navigation patterns.

The prototype context provides the following functionality:

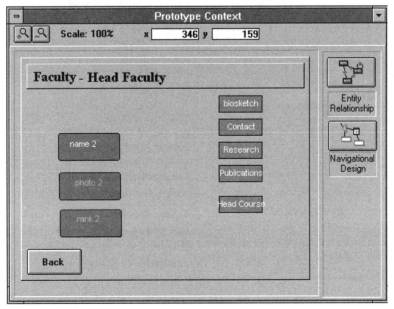

Figure 7: Prototyping context

- Testing capabilities that visualize data on the computer, navigate access structures, etc.

- Cloning capabilities that enable a designer to replicate parts of an application. The granularity of the cloning operation is adjustable. Hence a designer can also clone design artifacts, such as the RMDM-diagram along with an object at the prototype level.

Shown in Figure 7 is a skeleton of the *General* slice for *Faculty*. At left the boxes represent actual information. At right are buttons. These buttons represent links to other slices, and they are functional in the prototype context; clicking on them opens the appropriate slice.

Conclusion

We have presented the design of a computerized environment, RMCase, to support the design and development of WWW hypermedia applications. Not only does the environment follow a methodology (RMDM) but it takes into consideration cognitive aspects of hypermedia software development. RMCase is meant to support developers and designers in their evolutionary cycle of experimentation, building, and reshaping. The main benefits of our approach are that it will facilitate the work of designers and developers of hypermedia applications while simultaneously enhancing the quality of their products. ■

References

1. A. Díaz and T. Isakowitz, *RMCase: A Computer-Aided Support for Hypermedia Design and Development*, International Workshop on Hypermedia Design, Springer Verlag, 1995.

2. T. Isakowitz, E. A. Stohr, and P. Balasubramanian, "RMM: A Methodology for Structured Hypermedia Design," *Communications of the ACM*, August 1995.

3. J. Nanard and M. Nanard, "Hypertext Design Environments and Hypertext Design Process," *Communications of the ACM*, August 1995.

4. T. Berners-Lee, R. Cailliau, and J. Groff, *World Wide Web: The Information Universe*, Electron. Networking: Res. App. Policy 2, 1 (Spring 1992), 52-58.

5. R. Elmasri and S. Navate, *Fundamental of Database Systems*. The Benjamin/Cummings Publishing Company, second edition, 1990.

6. F. Garzotto, P. Paolini, and D. Schwabe, *HDM—A Model for the Design of Hypertext Applications*, ACM Trans. Info. Syst 11, 1 (Jan 1993) 1-26.

7. M. Casanova, L. Tucherman, J. L. Rangel Neto, N. Rodriguez, and L. Soares, *The Nested Context Model for Hyperdocuments*, Hypertext'91 Proceedings, ACM Press, 1991.

8. F. Garzotto, L. Mainetti, and P. Paolini, "Adding Multimedia Collections to Dexter Model," in *ECHT94 Proceedings*, ACM Press, 1994.

9. *http://is-2.stern.nyu.edu/isweb*

10. *http://eecns.stanford.edu/eecns/www/paper.html*

About the Authors

Alicia Díaz
Departamento de Informítica
Lifia—Universidad Nacional de La Plata
also CONICET
50 y 115, 1900 La Plata, Argentina
alicia@info.unlp.edu.ar

Tomás Isakowitz
[*http://is-2.stern.nyu.edu/~tisakowi*]
Information Systems Dept.
Stern School of Business
New York University
New York, NY 10012, USA
tomas@stern.nyu.edu

Vanesa Maiorana
Universidad de Belgrano
Buenos Aires—Argentina
vanesa@maiorana.satlink.net

Gabriel Gilabert
Nea Phronesis
Buenos Aires—Argentina
email:gabo@neap.satlink.net

PROGRAMMING THE WEB

AN APPLICATION-ORIENTED LANGUAGE FOR HYPERMEDIA
SERVICE PROGRAMMING

David A. Ladd, J. Christopher Ramming

Abstract

MAWL is an application language for programming interactive World Wide Web services. The language is small, because no construct was introduced without compelling justification; as with yacc [9], general-purpose computation is done in a host language. MAWL offers conveniences such as control abstraction, persistent state management, synchronization, and shared memory. In addition, the MAWL compiler performs static checking designed to prevent common Web programming errors. In this paper we discuss the design and engineering of MAWL in the context of our general language design philosophy. We also include an appendix of commentary on several short MAWL programs.
Keywords: *Programming languages, application-oriented languages, World Wide Web*

Introduction

The scope and diversity of the World Wide Web (the Web) are expanding daily. Much of the popularity of the Web is undoubtedly due to the simplicity and robustness of its underlying protocol, HTTP [3]. The source of this simplicity is the fact that HTTP is a stateless protocol: no HTTP transaction is defined in terms of the transactions that precede it. Because HTTP was originally designed for straightforward hypertext document publishing, the stateless nature of HTTP has been acceptable.

Now that Web browsers and servers are ubiquitous on the Internet, it is worthwhile to exploit the medium by using it to provide interactive services in addition to document serving. Although a stateless protocol is sufficient for serving stand-alone documents, it is an inconvenient basis for interactive services with an inherently sequential structure, such as banking transactions and ticket reservations.

In addition to obstacles posed by a stateless protocol, Web services must typically be constructed from the basic building blocks of modern programming practice. Lacking these building blocks, Web programmers must continually reimplement basic programming constructs. For example, memory, including some notion of a program counter, must be managed explicitly. Moreover, programmers must also address problems that are peculiar to Web service programming. For example, all Web programmers must guard against a user's failure to fill in required form fields. Also, because servers handle numerous requests concurrently, programmers are compelled to invent methods to protect resources such as shared files from conflicting simultaneous requests.

In order to provide quality services, Web programmers need appropriate reusable abstractions. Unfortunately, the languages that are commonly used to build Web services (Tcl [19], Perl [22], awk [1], and various shells [12]) offer little in the way of static analysis or guarantees. And general-purpose languages such as ML [16, 21], and Eiffel [17], which as a matter of policy guard against dynamically discovered errors, do not specifically address common Web-programming errors, such as dangling URLs and incorrect HTML. Therefore, it is worthwhile to explore systems which both make available reusable abstractions and detect Web-programming errors at compile time.

Web programmers encounter three major problems: First, a deficiency in the underlying protocol. Second, a lack of reusable solutions to common Web programming problems. And third, the need for a way to uncover Web-specific programming errors at compile time—independently of execution—rather than at run time. MAWL is a language designed to address these issues.

MAWL Services and Varieties of State

A Web site typically comprises a set of hypertext documents connected to each other and to the rest of the Web by hyperlinks. The most elementary Web programming is simply the design of Web pages using appropriate layout marks. Here the programmer's burden is essentially to produce correct HTML. But for interactive services, the real task is to specify complex interactions with multiple simultaneous users interacting over a network. Such services happen to use Web browsers and HTML as a convenient and universally available user interface.

A MAWL service consists of a MAWL program and documents written in an extension of HTML (MHTML). The MAWL compiler processes the MAWL program together with its MHTML documents. We draw a sharp distinction between MHTML markups and MAWL programs, and present separate syntaxes. Figure 1 describes how MHTML differs from HTML; the balance of the grammar rules given in the figure apply to MAWL program code. A MAWL program consists of one or more related *sessions,* which are similar to the procedures of other languages. Each session offers an entry point to the service.

We distinguish between a session and a service because many services are organized around resources that can be used in several ways. For instance, our department's Web-based book-ordering service is loosely organized around a database of book vendors and order records. The bookbot has several administrative functions as well as several user-related entry points. Each of these functions or entry points corresponds to a MAWL session, and collectively these sessions are referred to as a *service.*

MAWL services are distinguished by the fact that they are *stateful,* by which we mean that information is stored between HTTP transactions and used to affect subsequent transactions. In MAWL, *state* consists of a collection of variables with certain scoping and persistence attributes. This allows us to categorize MAWL services according to the kind of variables that they use. *Local variables* are variables that are visible only within a certain lexical region of a service description; *global variables* are variables that are available to any session in a service. Local variables are distinguished as being either *static* or *automatic.*

If a new copy of a local variable is associated with each interactive session then the variable is called *automatic.* For example, the *program counter* is a (hidden) variable that the system uses to implement sequencing. User-defined automatic variables can be used to hold intermediate results during the course of a session, and are an essential ingredient of *dialogues.*

A *session* is defined to be a sequence of MAWL statements, some of which involve presenting HTML forms and awaiting the replies. As in imperative computer programs, a program counter indicates the point within the session at which execution is taking place. Users cannot arbitrarily skip ahead or go back in a session. The most primitive application of a session is *sequencing;* that is, controlling the order in which HTML documents are presented. An advertiser-supported service may, for instance, insist that every fourth page be an advertisement. Without a notion of session there is no way to force users to step through the commercial messages.

Sequences in which the content depends on the history of a session are called *dialogues.* User authentication—for example, password-authentication on directories—is a particular kind of dialogue that has been provided for in HTTP.

Services with more complex dialogues—for example, the popular touchtone telephone service through which one can find out where and when specific films are showing, and then purchase tickets—are becoming increasingly common in the telephone network. Such services should be equally available on the Web. MAWL's sessions and user-defined local automatic variables form a basis for such services.

Although many services can be constructed using only variables that persist for the duration of a session (automatic variables), *static variables,* that is, variables that persist forever, are also useful. For instance, it is common practice to keep track of how many times a particular page has been served; in this case one would specify this quantity as a static local variable. Another application of static local variables is annotation, in which users of a particular service might add comments that will be visible to the next user.

In order to implement Web-based multiple-user services such as "chat" programs, through which people can communicate in real time, it is necessary for a server to mediate between two or more concurrent sessions. This is done using *global variables*—variables that are available to any session in a service. Global variables lead to a new class of collaborative Web services, such as shared editing and shared code inspection.

The design of an application language can be divided in two parts: the part meant to address general goals—goals that can be associated with any application—and the part that is special to the particular application domain. Our experience has resulted in several major design decisions of both kinds.

General Language Design Philosophy

A number of issues arise when designing application-specific languages. One question involves domain-specific errors and how to avoid them; this leads to choices about what should be implicit in all programs and what should be explicitly addressed by each programmer. Another question is how to handle general-purpose computing.

Error Avoidance

Programming is an inherently error-prone activity; therefore, we prefer languages that guard against common errors over those which do not. When feasible we make design choices that either eliminate the possibility of error or reduce it through effective compile-time analysis.

Sometimes entire classes of bugs can be eliminated by a method we call *implicit specification.* If a language does not offer constructs of a specific, troublesome kind, then errors associated with those constructs can never be blamed on the programmer. The language ML, for example, does not offer constructs for memory allocation and freeing; memory is managed without any explicit help from the programmer, and memory errors simply cannot occur.

On the other hand, the details of a programming problem often must be specified explicitly. Whenever an aspect of programming must be specified explicitly, errors can occur. The crucial issue is whether these errors will be detected statically or dynamically. Sometimes a language can be restricted in order to obtain compile-time safety, and other times it cannot.

For instance, in a language that had a single type, say "string," one would be forced to encode all values as strings. Such encodings cannot in general be analyzed at compile time, leading to dynamic errors and the need for careful testing.

For this reason, we prefer languages with expressive typing constructs. Such languages enable users to make distinctions that compilers can analyze, so that a wide class of errors can be uncovered at compile time.

In designing MAWL, we sought to handle certain programming problems implicitly. When that was impossible or undesirable, we strove to offer checks that would uncover bugs as early as possible in the software development cycle.

Approach to General-purpose Computing

An application programming language must address problems specific to a domain, but in most application domains, some measure of general-purpose computing is unavoidable. At issue is the way in which general-purpose computing is to be managed in application-oriented contexts.

We consider three general strategies:

- An existing general-purpose language can be extended with application-specific constructs.

- A specially constructed application language can include its own, idiosyncratic, general-purpose facilities.

- An application language can be designed with the capacity to interface with one or more existing general-purpose languages.

Three strategies

We have adopted the extension approach in earlier work [13], but the results have not been entirely satisfactory. One drawback is that there is no universally accepted language for general-purpose computing, so any choice will be the wrong one. Another pitfall is that the extended language is tied to (some particular implementation of) the base language, and any changes in the base language need to be reflected in the extended language.

Numerous application languages have been designed with their own general-purpose computing constructs (PostScript is a good example [8]). To learn a variety of syntaxes for similar language constructs is irritating, and subtle semantic variations can pose serious problems. Numerous application languages, each with its own general-purpose computing constructs, would be difficult to sustain.

Therefore we favor the third approach, which has been used to good effect by successful application languages such as yacc [9] and make [5]. On the principle of parsimony, we included no constructs in MAWL that were easily obtained from general-purpose computing languages. We strove for an application language in which each construct is clearly related to a design goal that could not be easily fulfilled by a general-purpose computing language. We have instead offered, in the spirit of yacc, an interface that should be easily adapted to the general-purpose-computing language of a user's choice.

Languages vs. libraries

Another approach to supporting application-specific programming is to eliminate the special-purpose language constructs entirely and write special-purpose application libraries in a general-purpose language.

It is commonly held that library design and language design are equivalent, or, stated in more general terms, that the abstraction facilities built into existing general-purpose languages are sufficient to achieve the effect of any application language [11,10]. To the contrary, we hold that application languages motivated only by functional abstraction, control abstraction, and/or data abstraction (possibly buried in syntactic sugar) are on shaky ground for precisely the reason that the same effect could be achieved with a good general-purpose language and an application library.

Instead, an application language should be justified on the grounds that it exploits the distinction between compile time and run time to effect useful analyses. Most general-purpose programming languages use this opportunity to detect flawed programs and perform optimizations. The most useful application languages perform domain-specific analysis at compile time. For instance, yacc users are offered some compile-time guarantee that their language can be implemented efficiently, as well as information about ambiguities. Users of make are informed of circular dependencies. A language called PRL5, for specifying database constraints, was designed at AT&T Bell Laboratories so that constraints expressed in the language could always be transformed into efficient transaction guards. [14,7]

Thus application-language design is primarily a problem of determining which compile-time analyses are useful in a particular domain, and then finding a way to express the necessary computation in ways that the analyses are nonetheless decidable. Since it is impossible to perform useful analyses on arbitrary programs in Turing-complete languages, the trick is often to balance restrictions against convenience. If a useful analysis can be performed on programs in the language, then the language has an advantage that cannot in general be matched by any approach involving libraries and general-purpose languages.

Application-driven Design Goals

Static analysis

From a software engineering perspective, a compelling justification for using a special application language is the kind of static analysis and computation that can be performed on programs in the language. Two of the most common benefits of compile-time analyses are optimizations and safety checks of various kinds. MAWL was designed primarily with safety checks in mind; the intent was to prevent common Web programming errors.

Static HTML analysis

One common problem with Web services is that their HTML documents can be syntactically incorrect. Syntax errors sometimes survive because no HTML parser has been invoked, but many errors are outside the realm of such parsers in any case because they occur in dynamically generated documents. For these documents the task is not HTML parsing: it is ensuring that scripts written in arbitrary languages will generate legal HTML—an undecidable problem. Ambitious Web services invariably generate HTML on the fly to reflect run-time conditions, and as a consequence have become notorious suppliers of fractured syntax.

The first requirement on MAWL was therefore that errors in the HTML used by MAWL services should be discoverable at compile time, independent of execution, whenever possible. MAWL achieves this (in conjunction with certain declarations) by extending HTML with the new marks described in Example 1. The purpose of these marks is to offer a way to place program variables in the document during execution. The complement, a way to collect values from a `<FORM...>` is provided by marks such as `INPUT...`, `TEXTAREA...`, and `SELECT...`. This scheme offers two advantages:

- It is possible to check the entire document at compile-time to determine that it is legal MHTML, and therefore can be transformed into legal HTML at runtime,

- It is possible to declare both the input and output type of a form, which leads to a new kind of consistency checking that further guards against errors.

The `MVAR` mark is for variable replacement; the *variable-name* is declared separately in the service logic, and is a variable of any scalar printable type. The `MITER` mark is used to iterate

Example 1:   New Marks Defined by MAWL-extended HTML (MHTML)

```
<MVAR NAME=variable-name>
<MITER NAME=variable-name MCURSOR=variable-name>...</MITER>
```

Example 2:   MHTML Declarations

```
declaration:
mhtml record-declaration : doc-name+ ;
| mhtml record-declaration -> record-declaration : doc-name+ ;

record-declaration:
{ field-decl-comma-list }

field-decl-comma-list:
field-decl
| field-decl-comma-list , field-decl

field-decl:
field-name : type
| field-name
```

over the list-typed variable specified by the NAME attribute; there is an iteration variable MCURSOR that is set to the value of each element, and the MHTML enclosed by the MITER marks is expanded once for each element. The MVAR mark is legal anywhere ordinary text is legal, and the MITER mark is legal only in places where zero or more of its enclosed MHTML are legal (this restriction guarantees that the resulting HTML document will conform to the standard HTML grammar).

In circumstances where, without MAWL, an entire document would have to be generated dynamically, users of MAWL-extended HTML are able to compose their documents statically, specifying portions that are run-time variabilities using variables with the MVAR syntax. In this way, the MHTML can be parsed at compile time and analyzed for correctness independent of execution; the scope of dynamically generated components is limited, as is the effect of any errors these fragments may contain.

Thus MHTML documents and forms used in Web services can be considered *typed*, particularly

with the introduction of variable substitutions. Variables that are expanded in an MHTML document may be considered the input parameters, and the values set by certain FORM marks— INPUT fields, TEXTAREA fields, and SELECT menus—can be considered the output parameters.

In order to eliminate certain HTML programming errors, all MHTML documents used in a MAWL program must be declared according to the syntax in Example 2.

The first part of an mhtml declaration declares the type of the form, giving the type (always a MAWL record) of the data passed from the program to the form, and optionally a type for the data coming back from the form. Following the type specification is a list of the form identifiers being declared to have the type. To display a particular form, it must be invoked with a record argument of the appropriate type according to the syntax of Example 3; the return value must also correspond to the declaration. Note that the MAWL expression for serving a document has the flavor of a remote procedure call.

Example 3:   MHTML Usage

```
expr:
mhtml.put [ doc-name, expr ]
```

With MHTML, MAWL users are able to statically specify much of what Web programmers are accustomed to generating with Tcl and Perl programs. In addition, when documents have input and output values, these values are declared and checked by the compiler. The net result is a dramatic reduction in certain common errors.

Compile-time optimizations

One advantage of programming languages is that they offer an opportunity to perform compile-time optimizations; application-specific languages therefore have an opportunity to perform application-specific optimizations. For MAWL, two interesting optimizations involve selecting its execution model and tuning the degree to which MHTML expansion is interpreted.

The choice of execution model has perhaps the greatest impact on service performance; we consider two models. In the first, a MAWL service executes under the control of a traditional Web server and communicates via the common gateway interface. In the second, the MAWL service is itself an HTTP server listening to a TCP port. The ML instantiation of MAWL (e.g., the version of MAWL which uses ML as its host language) can generate code for either execution model. In the case where the MAWL service assumes the role of HTTP server, each instance of a session corresponds to a Concurrent ML thread [20]. Thus, a form submission simply leads to the awakening of a lightweight thread with a new output file descriptor, not the `fork()`, `exec()`, and interpreter startup overhead of, for instance, a Tcl process.

Another factor in the execution efficiency of MAWL programs is the degree to which MHTML elaboration is interpreted. Many points along the spectrum from fully interpretive to fully compiled, inline code are possible. In the current instantiation of MAWL, MHTML documents are stored as text in the service's ML heap. An earlier prototype stored the documents as a vector of strings and variable substitution instructions.

Another plausible option is to encode each form as a function in the host language, consisting mainly of output of literal strings. Further options include storing the MHTML in the server file system and storing the MHTML in a compressed form. Once again, the fact that MAWL is a language rather than a library allows more flexibility in delivering Web services.

Abstractions

In addition to some constructs that were introduced to support static analysis, there are other constructs which are justified largely on the grounds of convenience.

Control flow abstraction

Traditionally, the Web has been a medium for publishing hypermedia documents; for such publishing, a stateless protocol is sufficient. However, more advanced Web services frequently need to present the user with certain documents in a certain order. Moreover, it is often necessary for a service to remember information over the life of a session with a user. These needs pose a significant obstacle for Web service programmers, who need to manage state and flow control explicitly. Web service programs often look as though they were produced by a compiler that was translating from an imperative language into a pure functional language. By this we mean that programmers must specify explicitly in each HTML form the instruction that should be executed next (the continuation), and in what environment. Such a programming style is tremendously inconvenient to humans, so MAWL offers facilities not only for declaring and checking HTML, but also for managing flow control and state for those who prefer to code imperatively.

In HTML documents the "next" activity is hard-coded into each form by offering its URL as the `ACTION` parameter of a `FORM` mark or providing an `HREF` which continues the interaction. Example 4 shows a user-registration form that asks for a user's name and email address. This informa-

Example 4:   CGI Form Example

```
<HEAD><TITLE>query form</TITLE></HEAD>
<BODY><FORM METHOD=post ACTION=/cgi-bin/registerUser>
What is your name? <INPUT VALUE=name>
What is your email address? <INPUT VALUE=email>
<INPUT TYPE=submit VALUE=execute>
</FORM></BODY>
```

tion is then passed to a program called `regis-terUser`, which presumably stores the information and then generates a new HTML document, which in turn must specify its next `ACTION`. But because the flow control is explicitly defined in the `ACTION` parameter of `FORM`, the forms cannot be rearranged or used in other contexts without modification. In addition, since the next state is specified explicitly, there is a possibility that programmers will introduce errors by incorrectly specifying a continuation.

By way of solution, MAWL{} supplies the form's `ACTION` and `METHOD` fields automatically. (In practice this is done by the same preprocessor that performs the variable substitutions described earlier.) A complete MAWL service therefore consists of a set of MHTML documents and a MAWL program that sequences the documents: it is this flow-of-control specification that forms the backbone of the MAWL language.

The purpose of a *session* is to describe the order in which MHTML forms should be served; the *compound-stmt* is the syntactic device for listing individual *stmt*s; it is this order that will specify the session's control flow. Because sequencing alone is often insufficient for describing real services, constructs are provided for conditional execution and looping.

By introducing flow-of-control syntax, it is possible to supply the `ACTION` field—heretofore specified explicitly by hapless programmers—automatically, thus reducing the possibility of error. At the same time, forms become more abstract and less tied to particular services or points in the execution of a program.

Memory management abstraction

Although some Web services can be constructed from sequenced HTML alone, it is often necessary to preserve values across the presentation of the HTML. As in most imperative programming languages, it is convenient to have some notion of state—a set of variables. Like control flow, implementing state is something of a trick for Web programmers, since HTTP is a stateless protocol.

Example 5:   Control-flow Specification Syntax

```
session: session session-name [arg-name = default-string-text] compound-stmt

stmt:
compound-stmt
| if expr   compound-stmt else compound-stmt
| for expr, expr, expr compound-stmt
| while expr compound-stmt
| break
| continue

compound-stmt: { stmt* }
```

Example 6:   CGI Form Example

```
<HEAD><TITLE>query form</TITLE></HEAD>
<BODY><FORM METHOD=post ACTION=/cgi-bin/search/email=benedikt@research>
What would you like to search for? <INPUT NAME=searchString>
<INPUT TYPE=submit VALUE=execute>
</FORM></BODY>
```

Example 6 illustrates a typical Web programming technique for maintaining state across form calls. The pathname of the ACTION part of the FORM mark has been extended with the state information of interest. (Here some variable "email" has the value "benedikt@research.") This information will be stripped out by the HTTP server and passed to the program in file /cgi-bin/ search, where it will be used. (There are a variety of mechanisms, for example *hidden fields,* that can be used to pass the context to the ACTION program, but all available methods suffer from the fact that they are nonetheless explicit.)

Explicit approaches to state management suffer from the fact that they are error-prone; nonportable constructs are often used, variable names are mistyped, and it is often necessary to effect encoding and decoding. When concurrency is introduced, additional complications arise because the atomicity of certain operations must be preserved. State management therefore becomes difficult to describe in a Web program, and this difficulty—a problem in its own right—is compounded because the resulting code can be hard to change as the service evolves.

Example 7:   Variable Declaration Syntax

```
declaration:
 auto datatype : varasgn-opt-list ;
 constant datatype : varasgn-list ;
 static datatype : varasgn-list ;

varasgn:
 var-name = expr

varasgn-opt:
 var-name
 | var-name = expr

varasgn-opt-list:
 varasgn-opt
 | varasgn-list, varasgn

varasgn-list:
 varasgn
 | varasgn-list, varasgn

datatype:
 integer
 | boolean
 | string
 | void
 | record-declaration
 | datatype list
```

Example 7:   Variable Declaration Syntax (Continued)

```
expr:
 var-name
 | varasgn

stmt:
declaration ;
```

MAWL addresses these problems by extending its statement sequencing with variable declarations, references, and assignments. Variables are either *automatic* or *static*. Each running session has its own private copy of the automatic variables. Static variables (which may be either local or global) are initialized when the service is started and maintained for the life of the service Static variables offer a way for different interactive sessions to communicate, and possibly to interfere, with each other. MAWL serializes access to each static variable, insuring that individual reads or writes are consistent. Longer periods of exclusive access, for example, a read-modify-write sequence, can be obtained using the *region* construct described below.

MAWL users need not be concerned with the details of variable implementation. Because the typing language is more expressive than that of common scripting languages, increased safety can be enjoyed by MAWL users, who no longer need to encode all values as strings. Through declarations and type-checking, many common errors are discovered independently of execution.

Concurrency

Concurrency is an issue that most Web service programmers must consider. Since HTTP servers handle requests that may execute in parallel, certain resources (often files) must be protected from conflicting simultaneous access. MAWL accordingly offers a construct that enables programmers to declare certain code segments to be critical regions; the system prevents multiple processes from executing code in the region. A process attempting to execute within an occupied region is blocked.

The *region* statement has two parts—the region name and a compound statement to be protected. There may be any number of regions throughout a service with the same name, because a given resource is often used in several places in a service. For instance, a file may be read by one session but written by another; in this case it is wise to surround both the reading and writing with regions of the same name.

General-purpose computing in MAWL

MAWL does not have any general-purpose computing constructs—not even primitive constant expressions such as strings and numbers. Instead, like yacc, MAWL defers to a host language that is capable of general computing. All MAWL programs, like yacc programs, are preceded up to the delimiter **%%** with declarations in the host language that may be referenced later in host-language fragments. Syntactically, these fragments are introduced with parentheses; nothing inside of parentheses is interpreted by the MAWL com-

Example 8:   Critical Region Syntax

```
stmt:
region region-name compound-stmt
```

Example 9:   General-purpose Programming Constructs

```
mawl-service-program:
host-lang-frag %% session *

expr:
( host-lang-frag )
```

piler; instead, everything inside is passed unchanged to the host language compiler.

The rules of MAWL type inference place type obligations on all such fragments; mistyped fragments are detected at compile-time, although typically by the host language's compiler rather than the MAWL compiler. MAWL variables can be referenced within these fragments, and the resulting value of the fragment is converted into MAWL terms so that the fragment can play its appropriate role in the service.

For the moment, MAWL uses Standard ML of New Jersey as its host language. Although ML has numerous advantages over other languages, it is not familiar to most Web programmers. MAWL is designed to allow any language that supports structured data types to serve as the host language.

An instantiation of MAWL with C as the host language is currently under development in our department.

Platform specialization

Web programmers must be aware that Web browsers have different and constantly evolving capabilities. Browsers typically support (a subset of) the HTTP and HTML standards, and many popular browsers include nonstandard but useful extensions to the protocols. The urge to take advantage of the latest features must be balanced against the increased complexity of one's code, and against the possibility that some browsers will be incapable of handling the special feature. Since there are no instructions that specify how MAWL accomplishes its intrinsic functions—such as storing state, managing flow control, blocking conflicting access to critical regions—these

implementation details are invisible to the programmer. Because all these details are concentrated in the hands of the presumably up-to-date compiler owner, MAWL services are more likely to take advantage of the latest browser features without incurring any penalty on application code or programmers.

Error handling

Like platform specialization, dealing with incorrect form submissions is implicit in MAWL.

Without MAWL, service developers must be careful to check that required fields of a form have been filled in; MAWL automatically returns users to incomplete forms after explaining what has been forgotten. Both careless users and misbehaving browsers are detected in this fashion.

Other Work

While several authors [2,18] have identified and addressed problems with current Web programming practice, the techniques needed for advanced Web programming have not been brought together in a single place. The state of the art still consists of monolithic, relatively inflexible daemons, ad-hoc CGI scripts, and interpretive languages for clients. The one notable exception to this rule is Mallery's Common Lisp HTTP server [15], which we will refer to as CL-HTTP.

CL-HTTP is a library for Common Lisp that allows Lisp applications to serve dynamic hypertext.

CL-HTTP and MAWL have differing orientations toward the programming problem. MAWL is geared toward specifying services, whereas CL-HTTP is geared toward permitting existing applications to use Web clients as user interfaces. Thus while MAWL can assume complete control over decisions such as how to store state between HTTP transactions and how users should be treated when a transaction is blocked, it seems as though CL-HTTP must force the user to make these decisions explicitly. Similarly, MAWL is able to offer mechanisms for controlling concurrency, whereas it seems that users of CL-HTTP perform such control at a low level.

CL-HTTP also differs from MAWL in many of the same ways that Common Lisp differs from Standard ML. While Lisp and CL-HTTP are highly dynamic, deferring many decisions and correctness checks until run time, ML and MAWL aim to verify correctness at compile time.

While part of this difference in error detection is due to the difference between ML and Lisp, some of this is due to the fundamental distinction between libraries and languages we raised in Section 3.2.2. Even if the combination of Lisp itself and the CL-HTTP library were to offer exactly the same functionality as MAWL, it would still not be possible in general to analyze the Lisp source itself to see if the library were used "correctly" (and in any case such analysis is not attempted). Therefore, whereas MAWL programmers do not need to test for certain errors (such as whether their HTML usage is in accordance with the needs of the service), users of the CL-HTTP server must work harder to achieve confidence in their programs.

Java vs MAWL

Like MAWL, the Java programming language [6] can be used to build sequential Web services. However, whereas Java applets can be used to create "active pages" that can offer network efficiency, these applets do not currently offer any solution for state management at the server side. A service that needs both active pages and server-side state could be constructed with a combination of MAWL and Java; the two are in some sense complementary. In addition, Java suggests some interesting MAWL optimization

strategies. Ideally, service programmers should enjoy distribution transparency just as the users of Web services do; service logic should not be cluttered with the details of where in the network it is executed. A clever MAWL compiler, using Java as its target language, might automatically find sequences that could be bundled into a single Java applet and executed at the client. Such an optimization scheme would offer both the simplicity of MAWL service programming and the efficiency of Java's client-side execution.

Conclusion

MAWL is an application-oriented language for World Wide Web services that encompasses server and client functions. MAWL simplifies service programming by allowing service providers to act as though clients interact with stateful services within sessions. Many details of Web programming—for instance, how to retain state and how to serialize access to server resources—are invisible to the application programmer. MAWL greatly simplifies the creation and maintenance of dynamic, interactive services on the World Wide Web. ∎

Acknowledgments

We are deeply indebted to Curt Tuckey, Michael Benedikt, David Atkins, and Ken Rehor for their suggestions and ideas.

Appendix: An Informal Introduction to MAWL

Mere words cannot replace the experience of programming—the only way to learn a new programming language is to program in it—but it is often helpful to look at examples. In this appendix we give several examples of simple MAWL services, but this is by no means intended as exhaustive documentation of the features and idioms of the language. (Further documentation, as well as details of installation and compilation, will be released with the software.)

Example 10:   Some Static HTML

```
<HTML>
<HEAD><TITLE>A Basic HTML Program</TITLE></HEAD>
<BODY>Hello, World</BODY>
</HTML>
```

"Hello, World" using basic HTML

"Web programming" is usually taken to mean specifying static document layout using HTML. We therefore begin our introduction to MAWL with an HTML program that displays the words "Hello, World"; the code is in Example 10.

Constructing this kind of document does not require MAWL. Doing it in MAWL is not more convenient, nor does it offer extra safety advantages, since any basic HTML parser would reveal syntactic errors.

Web programming in the MAWL sense is very different from mere document layout and presentation. MAWL services do not simply display static documents; they treat Web browsers as input devices that guide the execution of interactive concurrent programs.

"Time-of-Day" via the Common Gateway Interface

We first describe the typical way in which Web daemons are programmed to serve dynamic documents (i.e., documents which cannot be specified completely at composition time). This task is representative of the simplest Web services for which MAWL was designed; it is fundamentally different from ordinary Web programming (i.e.,

static document layout and presentation) because it must use the "common gateway interface" (CGI). The basic task of a Web server is to retrieve a file when presented with a URL. However, the common gateway interface involves a convention which interprets a URL as a program to run rather than as a document to retrieve. The programs, known as CGI programs, are supposed to produce legal MIME documents as their standard output.

Example 11 contains a shell script that could be used as the CGI program for a time-of-day service.

This simple example immediately brings to light an important class of problem; namely, that while one can imagine statically checking the shell program itself for correctness, there is no way (in general) to analyze the shell program to see whether it will always produce legal output. (In fact, since it can be a completely arbitrary program, there is no way to tell whether it will terminate, or interfere with the server itself, or any one of many other plausible disaster scenarios.) To obtain confidence that the CGI program is sensible, one must resort to testing—a notoriously expensive and inadequate method of finding bugs.

Example 11:   A Program That Generates HTML

```
#!/bin/sh
echo 'Content-type: text/html'
echo "
echo '<HTML>'
echo '<HEAD><TITLE>A Time-of-Day Page</TITLE></HEAD>'
echo "<BODY>The current time is '/bin/date'</BODY>"
echo '</HTML>'
```

Example 12:   MHTML Describing a Dynamic Document

```
<HTML>
<HEAD><TITLE>A Time-of-Day Page</TITLE></HEAD>
<BODY>The current time is <MVAR NAME=date> </BODY>
</HTML>
```

"Time-of-Day" via MAWL

Extended HTML. We now introduce the concept of *variable substitution*, so that most of an HTML document can be specified statically (and checked for correctness) while the variable part can be evaluated when the document is requested. Example 12 shows the MHTML (MAWL-extended HTML) version of Time-of-Day, which we will imagine sits in a file called TOD. mhtml.

Note that this is not a shell script, but rather something akin to ordinary HTML extended with a preprocessor-like variable substitution (where <MVAR NAME=date&gt means that the variable date should be substituted in the text). The advantage of MHTML is that it can be statically analyzed for correctness. It is important to note that if we were to use a general preprocessor for this task, our analysis goals would be foiled.

MAWL service logic. The MHTML code for the Time-of-Day example is only part of the solution; the variable date must be defined somewhere in order for that substitution to make sense. This is accomplished by what really constitutes the core of MAWL: its service logic component. Example 13 contains service logic for the Time-of-Day example.

The Time-of-Day service is approximately the simplest possible MAWL program; there is only one session, named timeOfDay, and the only

thing that service does is provide the single document that lives (by default) in file TOD.mhtml.

MAWL programs consist of a prelude and body separated by the delimiter %%. The prelude is where one places declarations written in the "host language" if they are necessary to the remainder of the program. In the current version of MAWL, the host language is Standard ML of New Jersey but could equally well be C, Java, or any other language that meets certain requirements. (Some other application languages have a notion of host language—for instance, most implementations of yacc use C as their host language; most versions of "make" use a UNIX shell as their host language.) In the Time-of-Day example, no host language declarations are necessary; so the prelude is empty.

The body of the MAWL program in Example 13 consists of a single session specification. Some MAWL services are organized around a common resource (usually persistent data), and in such cases the body might contain several session specifications. Sessions serve as entry points into a service. There is a convention by which these entry points are related to URLs so that the service can be accessed by a specific user input device—typically a Web browser).

A MAWL session. The session of Example 13 doesn't do very much; an MHTML document named TOD is declared, and the declaration asserts that TOD takes as its input parameter a

Example 13:   Service Logic for the Time-of-Day Example

```
%%
session timeOfDay {
mhtml { date }:  TOD;
mhtml.put [ TOD, ({ date=jcrlib.system "/bin/date" }) ];
}
```

record containing the field `date` (in this case there are no output parameters). Because `date` is not further qualified, its type defaults to `string`. The next line serves this document; `mhtml.put` is a primitive operation in MAWL, and its arguments are enclosed in square brackets. The first argument indicates which document to serve (it must have been declared previously), and the second argument must be an expression with the same type as the declared input parameter of the field—in this case, it must evaluate to a record with the single string field `date`.

Note that this second argument, which must be a record with the single field `date`, is a fragment of the host language. Host language fragments are easy to recognize because they are delimited with parentheses; the remainder of the MAWL language uses square brackets for grouping rather than parentheses. This particular host-language fragment computes a string containing the current date.

Some basic guarantees. In the Time-of-Day example, there are several important things to note:

- If the MHTML in file `TOD.mhtml` contains references to parameter fields other than `date`, or if it fails to contain a reference to `date`, then MAWL issues a complaint because the MHTML does not correspond to the declaration in the service logic.

- If the MHTML contains any HTML marks that imply retrieving information from the user (such as `INPUT`, `TEXTAREA`, or `SELECT`

marks), MAWL will complain because `TOD.mhtml` was not declared as having any output.

- If the expression that will be used as the input parameter for the `mhtml.put` of `TOD` is not of the correct type, then that error will be discovered at compile time. (In this case, the expression is an ML fragment, but MAWL's type inference puts certain obligations on that fragment; while the error will certainly be caught at compile time, it is possible that the error will be discovered by the host language compiler rather than the MAWL compiler).

By using MAWL in combination with MHTML, certain common Web errors can be avoided. However, the Time-of-Day service is relatively uninteresting, because it still involves generating only a single HTML document and presenting it. Although the MAWL features presented so far can be of tremendous value in complex examples of this same flavor, MAWL also provides features that apply primarily to more ambitious services.

A MAWL Program That Collects User Input

More ambitious Web services often request input from a user. When that happens, the HTML "forms extension" is used in combination with the CGI interface. Suppose one wished to collect a user's name before proceeding with some other activity. In HTML, one would first create a form like the one in Example 14.

Example 14:   An Interrogative HTML Form

```
<HTML>
<HEAD><TITLE>Login form</TITLE></HEAD>
<BODY>
<FORM METHOD=POST ACTION=http://somewhere.com/cgi-bin/time.sh>
Please fill in the fields below with the requested info:<P>
First name: <INPUT NAME=firstname><P>
Last name: <INPUT NAME=lastname><P>
```

```
<INPUT TYPE=SUBMIT NAME=Continue>
</FORM>
</BODY>
</HTML>
```

That form contains some information about the logical structure of the document and specifies two input fields for users to type their first and last names; these input fields are contained within the FORM marks; also, it describes a button labeled "continue" that the user is supposed to press when the two fields are filled in. The form's ACTION parameter identifies the recipient of the (encoded) input field information; it is a CGI program that must decode its input and produce a new HTML document as output. The CGI program that this HTML points to is necessarily much more complicated than the Time-of-Day example shown in Example 11.

There are numerous opportunities for error in the new script:

- The URL-decoding of firstname and lastname may be done incorrectly.

- time.sh may expect input other than what the interrogatory form produces; for instance, the shell script may mistakenly expect not just names but also rank and serial number.

- There may be an error in the additional error-handling code.

- The generated HTML may be a form that is syntactically incorrect.

- The generated HTML, if it is a form, may include an ACTION field that points to a continuation that does not exist or isn't what the user intended.

Even if the resulting system doesn't exhibit any of these problems, the solution is unsatisfactory in that each form (all but the first of which will be dynamically generated) points explicitly to its continuation; therefore, it is difficult to look at the system and understand its flow-of-control (not to mention that it would be difficult to change). A shell script that handles even this simple form correctly is already too complicated to present here, so in Example 15 we present instead the equivalent MAWL service logic.

The lines beginning with the keyword mhtml declare certain properties about MHTML documents that are found in other files. Note that the login document is declared with an arrow between two record descriptions: it requires an empty record as its input parameter and produces a record with two fields firstname and lastname as its output parameter. MHTML code for the login form is found in Example 16.

Example 15: Service Logic for a Personalized Greeting Service

```
%%
session fancyGreeting {
mhtml {} -> { firstname, lastname }:  login;
mhtml { firstname, lastname }:  greeting;
auto { firstname, lastname }: names;
names = mhtml.put [ login, ({}) ];
mhtml.put [ greeting, names ];
}
```

Example 16: A File Needed by the Greeting Service

```
<HTML>
<HEAD><TITLE>Login form</TITLE></HEAD>
<BODY>
Please fill in the fields below with the requested info:
<P>
First name: <INPUT NAME=firstname><P>
Last name: <INPUT NAME=lastname><P>
</BODY>
</HTML>
```

Note that neither the FORM mark nor the SUBMIT button appear; MAWL inserts these automatically when they are needed (MAWL will not allow the user to specify the ACTION parameter of a FORM mark). MHTML never contains explicit flow-of-control information, because that information is derived from the service logic; therefore, MHTML documents can be easily reordered.

The fancyGreeting session in Example 15 has another twist: a record variable (declared to be automatic as opposed to static) named names; this variable stores the results of the first login form and is subsequently passed to both the greeting form.

This example shows several advantages worth noting:

- MHTML forms are analyzed for occurrences of output fields (indicated by marks such as TEXTAREA, INPUT, and SELECT); such outputs are then compared against the form declaration, and type errors are noted.

- MAWL automatically collects and URL-decodes the output of a form; when user errors occur (for example, if the user neglects to fill out required forms), the user is notified and offered an opportunity to correct the error.

- All flow-of-control information is now present in the service logic, whereas in typical Web services it is distributed throughout various HTML forms.

MAWL includes not only sequencing, but also branching and looping constructs. Such control abstractions support services which the Web is poorly equipped to handle because of its reliance on a stateless protocol. MAWL is able to do this because it maintains a program counter during the execution of a session; that program counter is used to direct the execution of a session.

But a program counter is not the only interesting state that ought to persist over the life of a session: persistent user variables might also be required. If a value needs to persist beyond the immediate document presentation then the programmer must explicitly save and restore that value in whatever ad-hoc manner seems most suitable. Such ad-hoc activity introduces even more error possibilities:

Example 17: Another File Needed by the Greeting Service

```
<HTML>
<HEAD><TITLE>Greeting form</TITLE></HEAD>
<BODY>
Rather than "Hello, World", we now say:<P>
Hello, <MVAR NAME=firstname> <MVAR NAME=lastname>!
</BODY>
</HTML>
```

Example 18: Service Logic for a Fancier Personalized Greeting Service

```
%%
session fancierGreeting {
mhtml {} -> { firstname, lastname }:  login;
mhtml { firstname, lastname }:  howdy, sayonara;
auto { firstname, lastname }: names;

names = mhtml.put [ login, ({}) ];
mhtml.put [ howdy, names ];
mhtml.put [ sayonara, names ];
}
```

- One becomes prone to all of the usual programming errors one suffers in languages that do not require declarations for variables.

- The data, particularly if it is a complex data structure, often needs to be transformed as part of storage and retrieval.

- Ad-hoc storage mechanisms might be incorrectly maintained.

- Resources must be freed appropriately.

- Because Web servers execute requests concurrently, the ramifications for operations on resources such as files must be taken into account—persistent data associated with one session must not be confused with persistent data associated with other sessions, unless it is a shared variable in which case conflicting accesses must be avoided.

MAWL solves all of these problems (without loss of generality, since the ad-hoc solution could always be used if for some reason it were deemed important).

- Storage and retrieval of persistent variables are automated.

- Synchronization on shared variables is implicit (and care is taken to notify the user when blocked).

- MAWL frees session resources when the session terminates.

- MAWL's persistent variables are declared and typed, and all type errors are detected at compile time.

The `fancyGreeting` could therefore be easily extended so that the persistent information is used even later in the session, as in Example 18. This trivial change to the MAWL service logic would wreak havoc on an ordinary CGI program, because it would trigger the need for persistent management that might have been avoided if `firstname` and `lastname` were only needed to present the `aloha` document.

A Longer MAWL Program

It is now possible to look at a more complex MAWL program such as the one in Example 19. Such a service would be (relatively) unthinkable if written from scratch, but is easy to build with MAWL. The service is the old children's guessing game, where the system chooses a number between 1 and 100, and the player must figure out which number was chosen.

It is probably easy to figure out most of what this program is doing, but take special note of the static variables that keep track of how many people have played the game, and look at the interplay between the host-language fragments (anything in parentheses) and the rest of the language. Note how there are two entry points, one for playing the game and one to look up some statistics and who has achieved the quickest victory. Also note that MAWL variables can be used within the host-language fragments, and the return result of the host-language fragments is automatically translated into the appropriate MAWL representation (any type errors are caught at compile time).

Example 19:   Service Logic for a Guessing Game

```
fun number()=
let val s=Time.toSeconds(Time.now()) in 1 + (s mod 100) end
%%
static integer: numPlayed=(0), numWon=(0), minGuesses=(0);
static string:  bestPlayer=("");
session play {
mhtml { suggestion } -> { guess } : askUser;
mhtml {} -> { name, guess}: initQuestion;
auto integer : mynum=(number()), guesses=(0), guess=(0);
auto string : suggestion = ("");
auto { name, guess } : initresult;
auto { guess } : result;
auto string:  name;

numPlayed = (numPlayed + 1);
initresult = mhtml.put [
initQuestion,
({guessno=makestring guesses, suggestion=suggestion}) ];
guess = (jcrlib.atoi (#guess initresult));
while (mynum <> guess) {
suggestion = (if guess<mynum then "higher" else "lower");
result= mhtml.put [ askUser,
({ guessno=makestring guesses,
suggestion=suggestion}) ];
guess = (jcrlib.atoi (#guess result));
guesses = (guesses + 1);
}
numWon = (numWon + 1);
if (minGuesses < guesses andalso minGuesses <> 0) {
mhtml { best, gamelength } : youWin;
mhtml.put [ youWin,
({ best=bestPlayer,
gamelength=makestring guesses }) ];
} else {
mhtml {} : youBest;
bestPlayer = (#name initresult);
minGuesses = guesses;
mhtml.put [ youBest, ({}) ];
}
}

session admin {
mhtml { played, won, best }:  highScoresAndInfo;
mhtml.put [ highScoresAndInfo, ({
played=makestring numPlayed,
won=makestring numWon,
best=bestPlayer }) ];
}
```

References

1. A. V. Aho, B. W. Kernighan, and P. J. Weinberger. *The AWK Programming Language*. Addison-Wesley, 1986.

2. Scot Anderson and Rick Garvin. Sessioneer: Flexible session-level authentication with off-the-shelf servers and clients. In *Third International WWW Conference*, 1995.

3. T. Berners-Lee. Hypertext transfer protocol (HTTP). *Working Draft of the Internet Engineering Task Force*, 1993.

4. T. Berners-Lee and D. Connolly. Hypertext markup language (HTML). *Working Draft of the Internet Engineering Task Force*, 1993.

5. S. I. Feldman. Make: a program for maintaining computer programs. Technical report, Bell Telephone Laboratories, 1979.

6. James Gosling and Henry McGilton. The java language environment: A white paper. Technical report, Sun Microsystems Laboratories, 1995. Available at *http://java.sun.com/whitePaper/javawhitepaper_1.html*

7. T. G. Griffin and H. Trickey. Integrity maintenance in a telecommunications switch. *IEEE Data Engineering Bulletin*, June 1994.

8. Adobe Systems Inc. *PostScript Language Reference Manual*. Addison-Wesley, 1985.

9. S. C. Johnson. Yacc: Yet another compiler compiler. Technical report, Bell Telephone Laboratories, 1975.

10. Andrew R. Koenig. Language design is library design. *Journal of Object-Oriented Programming*, July 1991.

11. Andrew R. Koenig. Library design is language design. *Journal of Object-Oriented Programming*, June 1991.

12. D.G. Korn. Ksh—a shell programming language. Technical report, AT&T Bell Laboratories, 1986.

13. D. A. Ladd and J. C. Ramming. A*: A language for implementing language processors. In *IEEE International Conference on Computer Languages*, 1994.

14. D. A. Ladd and J. C. Ramming. Two application languages in software production. In *USENIX Symposium on Very High Level Languages*, 1994.

15. John C. Mallery. A common lisp hypermedia server. In *First International WWW Conference*, 1994.

16. D. B. McQueen and A. Appel. Standard ML of New Jersey. In *Proceedings of the 3rd International Symposium on Programming Language Implementation and Logic Programming*, pages 1–2. Springer-Verlag, 1991.

17. Bertrand Meyer. *Eiffel: the Language*. Prentice Hall, 1992.

18. David Nicol, Calum Smeaton, and Alan Falconer Slater. Footsteps: Trail-blazing the Web. In *Third International WWW Conference*, 1995.

19. John K. Ousterhout. *Tcl and the Tk Toolkit*. Addison-Wesley, 1994.

20. John H. Reppy. Concurrent ML: Design, application and semantics. In Peter E. Lauer, editor, *Functional Programming, Concurrency, Simulation and Automated Reasoning (LNCS 693)*, pages 165—198. Springer-Verlag, 1993.

21. B. Stroustrup. *The C++ Programming Language*. Addison-Wesley, 1986.

22. Larry Wall and Randal L. Schwartz. *Programming PERL*. O'Reilly & Associates, 1990.

About the Authors

David Ladd received the BS and MS degrees in Computer Science from the University of Illinois at Urbana-Champaign in 1987 and 1989. He joined AT&T in 1989, where he is currently a Member of Technical Staff in the Software Production Research Department. His current research interests are network services and application-oriented languages and environments.

Chris Ramming received degrees in Computer Science from Yale College (BA 1985) and the University of North Carolina at Chapel Hill (MS 1989). He joined AT&T Bell Laboratories in 1987 and is a Member of Technical Staff in the Innovative Services Research Department. His current interests include application languages and their use in software production.

Scalable, Secure Cash Payment for WWW Resources with the PayMe Protocol Set

Michael Peirce, Donal O'Mahony

Abstract

The use of the WWW as an electronic marketplace is increasing, and there is a need for a cash payment system that is scalable, anonymous, and secure. In this paper we examine two existing systems, Ecash and NetCash, discuss their strengths and weaknesses and propose a new system called the PayMe Transfer Protocol (PMTP). We show how it improves on existing systems and illustrate its use with an example based on purchase of goods across the WWW. ***Keywords:*** *Web payment, electronic cash, secure payment, scalable payment, Internet payment mechanisms, security*

Introduction

The World Wide Web has potential to become a highly efficient electronic marketplace for goods and services. When payments are effected electronically, there is always a risk that organizations may resort to gathering information relating individuals with the amounts that they have spent, locations involved, and types of good purchased. Misuse of such information can give rise to serious breaches of personal privacy [18]. If a payment system for the WWW is to receive widespread support, it must offer its users some form of protection against the gathering of such information. The most effective method of achieving this is to implement a form of electronic cash, where the coins being spent cannot be linked with their owner. This gives rise to a secondary problem in that since the coin is an electronic quality that is easily duplicated, such a payment system must guard against the coin being spent more than once. It should not be possible for an attacker to bypass the system or to falsely obtain monetary value from it.

At the time of writing, it has been estimated that there may be over 30 million users of the Internet spread across 96 different countries [12] using over 6.6 million host computers [15], and these figures are rising very rapidly. This means that an effective electronic payment system must be highly scalable. In practice, the system must support large numbers of buyers and sellers affiliated to many different banks. The problem of detection of double spending is particularly acute, and solutions must be found that allow for large numbers of payments to take place without requiring unreasonably large databases to be maintained. In the following section, we discuss related work on two systems for electronic payment and go on to propose a new set of protocols that surmounts some of their inherent problems.

Related Work

Recently, two electronic cash systems, requiring no additional hardware such as smart cards, which can be used to make payments for WWW resources have been published.

The first, Ecash, is a fully anonymous electronic cash system, using numbered bank accounts and blind signatures. The second, NetCash, uses identified electronic cash giving a more scalable but less anonymous system.

Electronic cash is the electronic equivalent of real paper cash, and can be implemented using public-key cryptography, digital signatures, and blind signatures. In an electronic cash system there is usually a bank, responsible for issuing currency, customers who have accounts at the bank and can withdraw and deposit currency, and merchants who will accept currency in exchange for goods or a service. Every customer, merchant, and bank has its own public/private key pair. The keys are used to encrypt, for security, and to digitally sign, for authentication, blocks of data that represent coins. A bank digitally signs coins using its private key. Customers and merchants verify the coins using the bank's widely available public key. Customers sign bank deposits and withdrawals with their private key, and the bank uses the customer's public key to verify the signature.

Ecash from DigiCash

Ecash [9, 10] is a fully anonymous electronic cash system, from a company called Digicash, whose managing director is David Chaum, the inventor of blind signatures and many electronic cash protocols[1, 2, 3, 4, 5, 6]. It is an online software solution that implements fully anonymous electronic cash using blind signature techniques.

The Ecash system consists of three main entities:

- Banks who mint coins, validate existing coins and exchange real money for Ecash

- Buyers who have accounts with a bank, from which they can withdraw and deposit Ecash coins

- Merchants who can accept Ecash coins in payment for information or hard goods. It is also possible for merchants to run a pay-out service where they can pay a client Ecash coins.

Ecash is implemented using RSA public-key cryptography. Every user in the system has their own public/private key pair. Special client and merchant software is required to use the Ecash system. The client software is called a "cyberwallet" and is responsible for withdrawing and depositing coins from a bank and paying or receiving coins from a merchant.

Withdrawing Ecash Coins

To make a withdrawal from the bank, the user's cyberwallet software calculates how many digital coins of what denominations are needed to withdraw the requested amount. The software then generates random serial numbers for these coins. The serial numbers are large enough so that there is very little chance that anyone else will ever generate the same serial numbers. Using a 100-digit serial number usually guarantees this. The serial numbers are then blinded using the blind signature technique [3]. This is done by multiplying the coins by a random factor. The blinded coins are then packaged into a message, digitally signed with the user's private key, encrypted with the bank's public key, and then sent to the bank. The message cannot be decrypted by anyone but the bank.

When the bank receives the message, it checks the signature. The withdrawal amount can then be debited from the signature owner's account. The bank signs the coins with a private key.

After signing the blind coins, the bank returns them to the user, encrypted with the user's public key. The user can then decrypt the message and unblind the coins by dividing out the blinding factor. Since the bank couldn't see the serial numbers on the coins it was signing there is no way to now trace these coins back to the user who withdrew them. In this way the cash is fully anonymous.

Spending Ecash

To spend Ecash coins, the user starts up their cyberwallet software and a normal Web client and then browses the Web until they find a merchant shop selling goods. The Ecash software can be used with any existing Web client and Web server software. A merchant shop is simply an HTML document with URLs representing the items for sale. To buy an item the user selects the URL representing that item. The following steps then occur as shown in Figure 1.

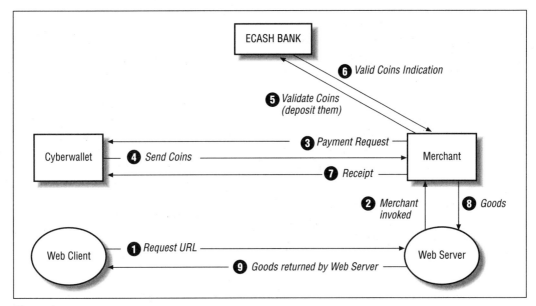

Figure 1:   Making a purchase with Ecash

The numbered items in Figure 1 are explained in more detail here:

1. The user's Web client sends an HTTP message requesting the URL to the Merchant's normal Web server. This URL will invoke a Common Gateway Interface (CGI) program [19].

2. The CGI program invoked will be the merchant Ecash software, and it will be passed details of the item selected encoded in the URL. The location of the buyer's host machine will also be passed in an environment variable from the server to the merchant Ecash software.

3. The merchant software now contacts the buyer's wallet using a TCP/IP connection, asking it for payment.

4. When the cyberwallet receives this request, it will prompt the user, asking them if they wish to make the payment. If they agree, the cyberwallet will gather together the exact amount of coins and send this as payment to

the merchant. The coins will be encrypted with the merchant's public key so that only the merchant can decrypt them:

{Coins}K[public,Merchant]

If they disagree or do not have the exact denominations necessary to make a correct payment, the merchant is sent a payment refusal message.

5. When the merchant receives the coins in payment, he must verify that they are valid coins, and have not been double spent. To do this he must contact the bank, as only the minting bank can tell whether coins have been spent before or not. Thus the merchant packages the coins, signs the message with his private key, encrypts the message with the bank's public key, and sends it to the bank.

{{Coins}K[private,Merchant]}K[public,Bank]

6. The bank validates the coins by checking the serial numbers with the large online database of all the serial numbers ever spent

and returned to the bank. If the numbers appear in the database then they are not valid, since they have been spent before. If the serial numbers don't appear in the database, and have the bank's signature on them, then they are valid. The value of the coins are credited to the merchant's account. The coins are destroyed, and the serial numbers added to the database of spent coins. Thus coins are good for one transaction only. The bank notifies the merchant of the successful deposit.

7. Since the deposit was successful, the merchant was paid, and a signed receipt is returned to the buyer's cyberwallet.

8. The purchased item, or an indication of successful purchase of hard goods, is then sent from the merchant Ecash software to the Web Server.

9. The Web server forwards this information to the buyer's Web client.

Ecash client and merchant software is available for many platforms. Currently no real money is used in the system, but an Ecash trial [11] with 10,000 participants, each being given 100 "cyberbucks" for free has been running since late 1994. There are many sample Web shops at which to spend cyberbucks.

Advantages and Failings

The strengths of Ecash are its full anonymity and security. The electronic cash used is untraceable, due to the blind signatures used when generating coins.

By employing secure protocols using RSA public-key cryptography, the Ecash system is safe from eavesdropping, and message tampering. Coins cannot be stolen while they are in transit. However, the protection of coins on the local machine could be strengthened by password protection and encryption.

The main problem with Ecash may be the size of the database of spent coins. If a large number of

people start using the system, the size of this database could become very large and unmanageable. Keeping a database of the serial number of every coin ever spent in the system is not a scalable solution. Digicash plans to use multiple banks each minting and managing their own currency with interbank clearing to handle the problems of scalability. It seems likely that the bank host machine has an internal scalable structure so that it can be set up not only for a 10,000 user bank, but also for a 1,000,000 user bank. Under the circumstances, the task of maintaining and querying a database of spent coins is probably beyond today's state-of-the-art database systems.

NetCash

NetCash [13, 14] is a framework for electronic cash developed at the Information Sciences Institute of the University of Southern California. Many of the ideas used in PayMe came from the NetCash proposal. It uses identified online electronic cash. Although the cash is identified there are mechanisms whereby coins can be exchanged to allow some anonymity. The system is based on distributed currency servers where electronic checks, such as NetCheque [16, 22] can be exchanged for electronic cash. The use of multiple currency servers allows the system to scale well.

The NetCash system consists of buyers, merchants, and currency servers. An organization wishing to set up and manage a currency server obtains insurance for the new currency from a central certification authority. The currency server generates a public/private key pair. The public key is then certified by being signed by the central authority. This certificate contains a certificate ID, name of the currency server, currency server's public key, issue date, and an expiry date, all signed by the central authority:

{Certif_id,CS_name,K[public,CS],issue_date,exp_date}K[private,Auth]

The currency server mints electronic coins, which consist of:

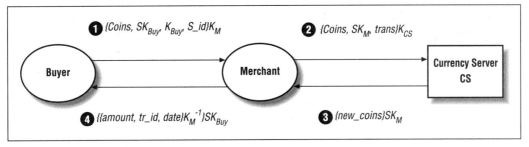

Figure 2:   Purchasing from a merchant using NetCash

- *Currency server name*. Identifies a currency server.

- *Currency server network address*. Where the currency server can be found; if this address is no longer in use, a name server can be queried to find the current address.

- *Expiry date*. Limits the state that must be maintained by each currency server.

- *Serial number*. Uniquely identifies the coin.

- *Coin value*. Amount coin is worth. The coin is signed with the currency server's private key:
  {CS_name,CS_addr,exp_date,serial_num,coin_val}K[private,CS]

The currency server keeps track of the serial numbers of all outstanding coins. In this way double spending can be prevented by checking a coin's serial number with the currency server at the time of purchase (or exchange). If the coin's serial number is in the database, it has not been spent already and is valid. When the coin is checked the serial number is then removed from the database. The coin is then replaced with a new coin (coin exchange).

An electronic check can be exchanged with a currency server for electronic coins. The currency server is trusted not to record to whom the coins are issued. To further aid anonymity a holder of coins can go to any currency server and exchange valid coins for new ones. The currency server does not know who is exchanging coins,

only the network address of where they are coming from. By performing the exchange and by choosing any currency server to do this with, it becomes difficult to track the path of the coins. If a currency server receives coins that were not minted by it, it will contact the minting currency server to validate those coins.

Figure 2 shows how a buyer uses NetCash coins to purchase an item from a merchant. In this transaction the buyer remains anonymous since the merchant will only know the network address of where the buyer is coming from. Net-Cash assumes that the buyer has or can obtain the public key of the merchant, and that the merchant has the public key of the currency server.

Implementation details of how the NetCash protocols might be linked with applications such as the Web are not available, but it could be done in a similar fashion to Ecash using an out-of-band communications channel. The transaction consists of the following four steps, starting from when the buyer attempts to pay the merchant:

1. The buyer sends the electronic coins in payment, the identifier of the purchased service(S_id), a freshly generated secret key (SK[Buyer]), and a public session key (K[public,Buyer]), all encrypted with the Merchant's public key, to the merchant.

   {Coins,SK[Buyer],K[public,Buyer],S_id}K[public,Merchant]

   The message can't be eavesdropped on or tampered with. The secret key is used by the merchant to establish a secure channel with the buyer later. The public session key is later used to verify that subsequent requests originate from the buyer who paid for the service.

2. The Merchant needs to check that the received coins are valid. To do this he sends them to the currency server to be exchanged for new coins or for a check. The merchant generates a new symmetric session key SK[Merchant] and sends this along with the coins and the chosen transaction type to the currency server. The whole message is encrypted with the server's public key so that only it can see the contents:

{Coins,SK[Merchant],transaction_type}K[public,CS]

3. The Currency server checks that the coins are valid by checking its database. A valid coin is one whose serial number appears in the database. The server will then return new coins or a check to the merchant, encrypted with the merchant's session key:

{New_coins}SK[Merchant]

4. Having received new coins (or a check) the merchant knows that he has been properly paid by the buyer. He now returns a receipt, signed with his private key and encrypted with the buyer's secret key:

{{Amount,transaction_id,date}K[private,Merchant]}SK[Buyer]

The buyer can then use the transaction identifier and the public session key to obtain the service purchased.

This is the basic purchase protocol used in Net-Cash. While it prevents double spending it does not protect the buyer from fraud. There is nothing to stop the merchant spending the buyer's coins without providing a receipt.

Extensions to the protocol are detailed in [14]. These are more complex and give protection against fraud for both the merchant and buyer.

There are also mechanisms to allow the merchant to, be fully anonymous to the buyer. Partially offline protocols where the bank does not need to be contacted during a purchase are also described. These, however, rely on the buyer contacting the currency server beforehand, and knowing who the merchant is at that time. They use a time window in which the coins are only valid for certain short lengths of time. Full technical details are given in [14].

The advantages of NetCash are that it is scalable and secure. It is scalable since multiple currency servers are present and security is provided by the cryptographic protocols used. Possible disadvantages of the system are that it uses many session keys and in particular public key session keys. To generate a public key of suitable length to be secure takes a very large amount of time compared with that involved in generating a symmetric session key. This could compromise the performance of the system as a whole.

NetCash is not fully anonymous, unlike Ecash. It is difficult but not impossible for a currency server to keep records of who it issues coins to and who it receives them back from. The ability to exchange coins and use any or multiple currency servers increases the anonymity of the system.

A NetCash system is currently being implemented, but no details are given as to how it will be linked with applications such as the Web. NetCheque will be used to provide checks that can be used to buy coins or that can be issued when coins are traded in.

Discussion

The two payment systems outlined each have their strengths and weaknesses. Ecash is a fully secure system that provides for very strong anonymity. The use of banks within the system reflects current practice in nonelectronic payment systems. Successful operation of the Ecash system depends on the maintenance of a central database of all coins ever issued within the system. If it were to become accepted as a global payment system, this would quickly become a major problem.

NetCash uses identified coins with multiple currency servers, and thus, while anonymity is maintained, there is only a requirement to keep track of all currency currently in circulation. This makes for a much more scalable solution to the payment problem. NetCash is also fully secure, and achieves this using protocols that are quite complex in nature.

The PayMe Protocol Set

In an attempt to combine the best features of the two systems described, a new payment system called the *PayMe Protocol Set* was devised. A major goal was to preserve as much of the anonymity provided by Ecash while adopting many of the features of NetCash that allow it to scale to large numbers of users with multiple banks. In the following sections, we will discuss the overall design of the protocol set and work through an example of a network payment. Since this paper concentrates on payment for WWW resources, detailed coverage will be given of both the cur-

rency representation and the protocol primitives used during a Web transaction.

The PayMe system and protocol set are now presented. Many of the design ideas are based on a close examination of systems such as NetCash, Ecash, and other related systems such as Magic Money [7] and Netbill [20, 21]. In this way PayMe is a collection of the successful parts from existing systems, minus the failings of those systems.

PayMe is an online electronic cash system. The entities involved are banks and users. Users can be either buyers or merchants, but each has the same functionality. They can make payments, accept payments, or deal with the bank. Each bank mints its own identified electronic cash with serial numbers. Double spending of coins is prevented by the bank maintaining a database of coins in circulation. This scales better than the blind signature electronic cash approach. Any user in the PayMe system can accept payments and make payments. Merchants can receive payments for selling Web goods but they can also make payments to the buyers. This can be used for making refunds or in pay-out services.

A simple model showing the basic functionality of the PayMe system can be seen in Figure 3.

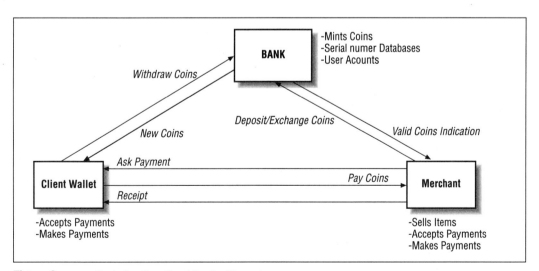

Figure 3:   Basic functionality of the PayMe system

Both symmetric and public-key cryptography are used. Each entity has its own public/private key pair. It is a standalone system that has been tailored for use with the Web.

The PayMe system uses its own secure communications protocol, the PayMe Transfer Protocol(PMTP), to communicate between entities. This provides security and a means of communicating out-of-band, that is, outside the Web's HTTP protocol. This approach was adopted to allow a full prototype to be developed that could eventually be used with any emerging Web security standard.

PayMe Currency

Coins are the pieces of data that represent monetary value within the system. The coins are digitally signed by the bank using public key cryptography to make them valid currency. Each coin has a serial number that is entered into the bank's database when the coin is minted. Coins have fields for the coin value, serial number, bank id, bank host name and port number, and expiry date.

When these five fields are put together and signed with the bank's private key, a valid coin is created. An example coin is of the form:

{10 MIK1234 BANK1 bank.cs.tcd.ie.8000 18-12-98}K[private,BANK1]

Here the coin is worth 10, its serial number is MIK1234, the userid of the bank's public key is BANK1, the bank is located at port 8000 on the machine bank.cs.tcd.ie, and the coin expires on 18th December 1998.

A bank within the PayMe system mints coins, maintains a database of the serial numbers of coins in current circulation to prevent double spending, and manages the accounts of merchants and buyers.

PayMe Transfer Protocol (PMTP)

PMTP is the set of secure messages designed to provide the communications necessary in the PayMe system. It uses both symmetric and public-key cryptography. PMTP consists of six request-response message types.[*] For each of the six message types there are three different possible message identifiers. There is one request message identifier and two different response message identifiers. These have been called request, response, and refusal respectively. A request is when the receiver is being asked to perform an action. A response message identifier indicates that the action has been performed, and the message body contains the results of that action. A refusal is when the receiver refused to perform the action, and the message body may contain a reason for this refusal.

The first three messages are used by a bank account owner to withdraw or deposit coins, or obtain a bank statement from the bank for that account.

- *Withdraw coins*. Requires an account identifier, matching account name, account password, and amount, digitally signed by the account owner.

- *Deposit coins*. Attempts to deposit coins into a bank account. The bank will check that the coins are valid before crediting the account. The account identifier, name, and digital signature are required to make a deposit. A deposit can be done with any bank with which the user has an account. If the coins are not minted by that bank then the minting bank will be contacted to validate the coins. Banks have accounts with other banks, and in this way records are kept of how much each bank owes another.

---

[*] A request/response message is where a client sends a request to a server and the server sends a reply message to that request.

Example 1:   Ask_payment Messages

Parms: amount (integer).
ask_payment_request:
[PAYMENT_REQ< *amount* >:$K_{Merchant}$:[< *nonce* >]$K^{-1}_{Merchant}$]
ask_payment_response:
Same as pay_coins_request. A successful response to a merchant's request for payment, is an attempt to pay that merchant.
ask_payment_refusal:
[PAYMENT_REFUSAL< *amount* >:< *nonce* >]$K_{Merchant}$

These accounts could then be settled using a real-world interbank clearing mechanism.

- *Request bank statement.* Returns a bank statement for an account; a digital signature is required to authenticate the account owner.

- *Exchange coins for new ones.* Any user who holds valid coins from a bank, can exchange the coins for new ones. The process for doing this is anonymous, but it is still secure. During the exchange the bank only knows the network address of where the coins are being sent from. If the coins it receives are valid it will return new ones in exchange. It is not necessary to have an account at a bank to exchange coins. For efficiency, an exchange must be done with the bank that minted the coins.

Either a buyer or merchant can use this mechanism to help hide their identity. When a user withdraws coins from a bank the bank could record the numbers on the coins and who it gave them to. Then when a merchant later deposits the coins the bank could check to whom it issued the coins. In this way the spending habits of a user could be recorded.

However, if during a purchase a merchant exchanges the coins rather than depositing them, then the bank does not know who has performed the exchange. Either the merchant or buyer, or even another trusted third party could perform this exchange to "launder" the money, making it more difficult to trace spending habits.

- *Ask for payment.* The last two messages are used between a user and another user such as a merchant. The ask_payment message is used to ask a buyer for a payment amount. During a purchase a buyer remains anonymous to the merchant. Ideally the buyer should have obtained the merchant's public key before the purchase. However, the merchant's public key is also sent within the payment request. There is some risk involved with this, since an attacker could replace the merchant's key with his own. The user is given the choice to accept a new merchant key in this way or not. If the user already holds the merchant's public key, then this is compared with the one received in the payment request as part of the procedure to authenticate the merchant. The ask_payment request and refusal messages are shown in Example 1.

- *Pay coins.* Attempt to pay coins to a merchant. The buyer remains anonymous to the merchant in this transaction. The merchant only knows the network address of the buyer. The specification of the pay_coins messages are shown in Example 2.[*]

The full specifications of all PMTP messages can be found in [17]. The parameters will often be generated automatically by the PayMe software.

---

[*] A Money_bag is an implement structure which holds coins.

Example 2:   Pay_coins Messages

Parms: Coins(Money_bag).
pay_coins_request:
[PAY_COINS_REQ< *Money_bag* >:< *symmetric_session_key* >:< *nonce* >]$K_{Merchant}$
pay_coins_response:
[PAY_COINS_RESPONSE< *Receipt* >:< *nonce* >]SK
pay_coins_refusal:
[PAY_COINS_REFUSAL< *reason* >:< *nonce* >]SK

The address of where to send the message also needs to be given.

PMTP Security

PMTP messages are secure from attacks using eavesdropping, message tampering, replay, and masquerading techniques.

Eavesdropping Prevention

An attacker cannot see the contents of a PMTP message because the message is either:

- Encrypted with the public key of the receiver; only the private key can decrypt the message.

- OR encrypted with a symmetric session key that has been distributed securely; the session key was distributed by sending it in a public-key encrypted message. The only exception to this is the ask_payment_request message. Since the buyer is to remain anonymous this message is transmitted in cleartext.

Message Tampering Prevention

Any encrypted message cannot be tampered with, since it will not be possible to decrypt it after it has been changed. By using message digests, a digitally signed message cannot be tampered with.

Replay Prevention

A nonce is used within each PMTP message to ensure that the message can be used for one occasion only and to prevent a replay of that message. It ensures that the message must come from a specific network address and within a small time window. If an attacker can forge the IP network address to be the same as that of the message sender, then he could possibly replay the message within the short time frame that it is valid. To help prevent this the software keeps track of all recently received nonces and will not accept two messages with the same nonce such as a replayed message would have.

Masquerading Prevention

Where possible all messages are authenticated with a digital signature. Bank withdrawals also require the password of the bank account. In the anonymous messages where a digital signature is not possible, knowledge of a symmetric session key is used. The network address within the nonce prevents an attacker at another site from masquerading as the message sender at the original network address.

Private Key Protection

The private key of a user is stored on file at the user's local site. It is encrypted with a secret passphrase. If the user's account is broken into, this prevents the attacker being able to access the private key. Without this private key any cash stored locally cannot be decrypted, and PMTP messages cannot be sent.

PayMe with the Web

PayMe was tailored for use with any Web client or server. To purchase an item a user starts up both their PayMe Wallet and any Web client.

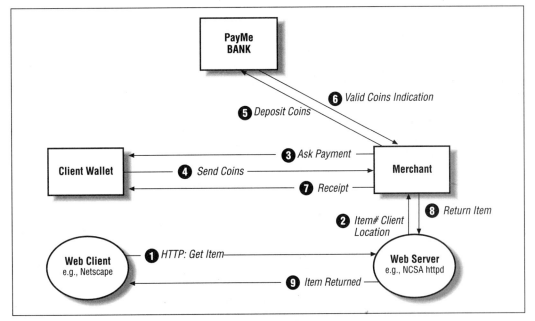

Figure 4:   Purchasing a Web service with PayMe

They browse the Web until they find a merchant shop, which will be presented by an HTML document. A combination of PMTP messages is used in a purchase transaction, as shown in Figure 4.

The numbered items in Figure 1 are explained in more detail here:

1. To purchase an item (information, hard goods, or pay-out service) a URL is selected representing that item. When selected the URL causes the Web server to automatically start up a merchant's Wallet software. This is done using the Common Gateway Interface(CGI)[19].

2. The Wallet is passed the item details and the network address of the requesting Web client. Additional information, such as a shipping address for hard goods, can be passed through a Web form if required.

3. The Wallet then looks up the cost of the item and contacts the buyer's Wallet soft-

ware asking for payment. This is a PMTP ask_payment_request.

4. The buyer will be notified of the request. He will then either refuse (ask_payment_ refusal) or accept (pay_coins_request) the payment request. If he accepts, the Wallet selects the coins needed to make the exact payment and sends them to the Merchant.

5. The Merchant validates the coins by either anonymously exchanging them for new coins or depositing them into a bank account. For efficiency, if an exchange is performed it must be done with the bank that minted the coins. A deposit can be done with any bank with which the merchant has an account. The minting bank checks the serial numbers of the coins with those in its database. If a serial number is not present in the database the coin is *not valid* and is rejected. If the serial numbers are present then the coins are valid.

Having performed the check the bank then removes the serial numbers from the database, thereby invalidating the coins. This must be done because otherwise the same coins could be presented many times and they would always be valid. The merchant is given new coins in replacement, or the amount can be credited to his bank account.

6. The merchant will receive an indication from the bank as to whether the coins were valid. A valid coin indication will be new coins in an exchange (exchange_coins_response), and a deposit acknowledgment (deposit_coins_response) with a deposit.

7. For a good payment, the merchant then issues a signed receipt to the buyer (pay_coins_response).

8. The purchased item is sent from the merchant to the Web server.

9. The Web server then forwards this to the buyer's Web client. Payments must be made with the exact amount. No change can be given since this could compromise anonymity if a merchant colluded with the minting bank.

Implementation

A prototype was implemented in a C++/UNIX environment on a Sun workstation cluster. An extended version of PgpTools[8], a set of C functions that provide low-level PGP[23,24] packet functionality in memory, was used to implement the cryptographic functions. It uses RSA to provide the public key cryptography, and IDEA for the symmetric key cryptography. Full technical details of the implementation can be found in [17]. Pgptools is subject to similar patent restrictions as PGP.

Coin backups and log files are maintained to increase the fault tolerance of the system. In this way the chance of losing coins, and hence monetary value, is kept to a minimum if any of the entities crash.

PayMe could be used for schemes other than just monetary payment. A coin within the system could be used to represent a unit of CPU time, or connection time to a limited resource, in order to provide resource sharing in an institution. Jobs that require units of CPU time could be submitted or initiated through the Web where the merchant would be the CPU host requesting the PayMe coins representing time on that CPU.

For applications where anonymity is important, the exchange coins mechanism can be used to anonymously exchange the coins with a bank, preventing the bank knowing who now holds the new coins. In an environment where anonymity is not necessary or desirable the banks involved can be configured to refuse any requests to exchange certain coins, such as those representing CPU time. In this way the bank can record to whom it issues the coins and who then deposits them, knowing for certain that no anonymous exchange has taken place. Thus the configuration of the bank can control the anonymity available to its users.

Discussion

Taking the best features of existing systems, a new payment mechanism using electronic cash for use with the Web has been designed and implemented. It offers the following desirable properties:

- *Security*. The system was designed to be secure from fraud. The possibility of an attacker being able to bypass the system or falsely obtain value in it was minimized. PMTP was designed to provide secure communication. Security steps were also taken to protect coins, the private cryptographic keys used, and the accounts at the bank.

- *Scalability and reliability*. Multiple banks can be used in the PayMe system, giving no central point of failure. The simple PMTP protocols can be used for interbank communication as well as with regular users. Electronic cash where only a database of the serial numbers in current circulation is used, much like in the NetCash system. In this way it is much more scalable than Ecash. The serial numbers of every coin ever spent need not be maintained. Secondly, the serial numbers can be short, unlike the long serial numbers of about 100 digits, necessary to prevent serial number collisions when using blind signatures.

- *Usable by all.* It is important that the system can be used by anyone provided they have the money to pay for the items they wish to buy. No credit card numbers are used, since not all Internet users, for whatever reasons, hold valid credit cards. In theory anyone who wants to can buy PayMe electronic coins and have an account at a PayMe online bank.

- *Usable with any Web client or server software.* PayMe can be used with any Web client or server software, and it is not limited to any specific product or HTTP version. As many new innovations and advances in Web technology are designed and released, it is important that a Web payment mechanism can be used with all of these. By using its own secure out-of-band protocol, PayMe can be used with both current and emerging Web technology and protocols.

- *Payment for information, hard goods, and pay-out services.* Web information of any type such as text, images, audio streams, or video can be purchased using PayMe. Hard goods can be paid for through the Web, using forms. The PayMe client software used by a buyer can also receive payments. In this way pay-out services can be used.

- *Hardware independent.* No special hardware, such as smart cards, is required to use PayMe. The system can be used right now using only software, and this is more suited to the global Internet where it would take time for users to obtain and begin to use new hardware.

- *Limited anonymity and privacy.* It is desirable to prevent a database being built with full details of every purchase made by an individual. Some anonymity can be provided by the system by anonymously exchanging coins with a bank, similar to NetCash's exchange mechanism[14]. A buyer will also remain anonymous to a merchant during a purchase transaction, as only the buyer's network address will be known. The system does not offer offline operation. It was not possible to fulfill all the above requirements and at the same time remove the need for a bank to be contacted during a purchase transaction. However, it is felt that with the trend towards faster and more reliable global networks, offline operation is not required. Secondly, on the Internet where it is easy to hide one's identity, it is not acceptable to use an offline electronic cash system where fraud will only be detected after it has occurred, as in [2].

The final implemented system provides a secure and scalable means of paying for all types of Web services. It would seem to be more scalable than the fully anonymous Ecash system, and more efficient than the complicated protocols and use of both symmetric and asymmetric session keys of NetCash.

Conclusion

We have examined two existing means of effecting anonymous electronic payment across networks and looked at their strengths and weaknesses. We then presented the design of PMTP, a hybrid of these two approaches that offers a fully secure, scalable anonymous payment system. We have shown how this can be combined with WWW client and server software, allowing payment to occur on an out-of-band link as users browse the Web. Only a payment system with these properties will allow the Web to be used as an electronic marketplace without compromising the privacy of its users. ■

References

1. J. Bos and D. Chaum, *Smart Cash: A Practical Electronic Payment System*, Technical Report, CWI-Report: CS-R9035, August 1990.

2. D. Chaum, A. Fiat, and M. Naor. "Untraceable Electronic Cash," *In Advances in Cryptology— Crypto '88 Proceedings*, Springer-Verlag, Berlin, 1990, pages 319-327.

3. D. Chaum, "Blind Signatures for Untraceable Payments," in *Advances in Cryptology—Crypto '82 Proceedings*, Plenum Press, 1983, pages 199-203.

4. D. Chaum, "Security without Identification: Transaction Systems to Make Big Brother Obsolete," *Communications of the ACM* v.28, n.10, October 1985, pages 1030-1044.

5. D. Chaum, "Online Cash Checks," in *Advances in Cryptology, EuroCrypt '89 Proceedings*, Springer-Verlag, Berlin, 1989, pages 288-293.

6. D. Chaum, A. Fiat, and M. Naor. Untraceable Electronic Cash. In Advances in Cryptology - Crypto '88 Proceedings, Springer-Verlag, Berlin, 1990, pages 319-327.

7. Product Cypher. Magic Money Digital Cash System, *ftp://ftp.csn.org*, 1994.

8. Product Cypher. The PGPTools Security Toolkit, *ftp://ftp.csn.org*, 1994.

9. DigiCash. Ecash, *http://www.digicash.com/*, 1994.

10. DigiCash Press Release. World's First Electronic Cash Payment over Computer Networks, May 27th 1994.

11. DigiCash Press Release, Ecash Trial is Now Worldwide, January 6 1995.

12. Larry Landweber. International Connectivity. Version 14 - June 15, 1995. *ftp://ftp.cs.wisc.edu/connectivity_table/Connectivity_table.ps*, Computer Sciences Department, University of Wisconsin--Madison, 1210 W. Dayton St., Madison, WI 53706, U.S.A.

13. Gennady Medvinsky and B.Clifford Neuman. Electronic Currency for the Internet. Electronic Markets Vol 3. No. 9/10, October 1993, pages 23-24.

14. Gennady Medvinsky and B. Clifford Neuman. NetCash: A design for practical electronic currency on the Internet. In Proceedings of the First ACM Conference on Computer and Communications Security, November 1993.

15. Network Wizards, Menlo Park, California, *http://www.nw.com/*. Internet Domain Survey, July 1995.

16. B. Clifford Neuman and Gennady Medvinsky. Requirements of Network Payment: The NetCheque Perspective. In Proceedings of IEEE Compcon'95, San Francisco, U.S.A., March 1995.

17. M. Peirce, PayMe: Secure Payment for World Wide Web Services, B.A. (Mod) Project Report, Computer Science Department, Trinity College Dublin, Dublin 2, Ireland. May 1995.

18. Jeffrey Rothfeder, Privacy for Sale, Simon & Schuster, 1992.

19. Tony Sanders, Ari Luotonen, George Philips, John Franks, and Rob McCool. The CGI Specification. *http://hoohoo.ncsa.uiuc.edu/cgi/interface.html*

20. Marvin Sirbu and J. Douglas Tygar. Netbill: An Electronic Commerce System Optimized for Network Delivered Information and Services. In Proceedings of IEEE Compcon '95, March 1995.

21. J. D. Tygar. NetBill: An Internet Commerce System Optimized for Network Delivered Services. Carnegie Mellon University, Pittsburgh, Pennsylvania 15213, 1995.

22. University of Southern California Chronicle. The Check is in the E-mail, usc-chronicle-941107, November 1994.

23. Phil Zimmermann. PGP User's Guide, Volume I: Essential Topics. Phil's Pretty Good Software, *ftp://ftp.pegasus.esprit.ec.org/pub/arne/pgpdoc1.ps.gz*. October 1994.

24. Phil Zimmermann. PGP User's Guide, Volume II: Special Topics. Phil's Pretty Good Software, *ftp://ftp.pegasus.esprit.ec.org/pub/arne/pgpdoc2.ps.gz*. October 1994.

About the Authors

Michael Peirce

[*http://www.cs.tcd.ie/www/mepeirce/mepeirce.html*]

Computer Science Department

Trinity College

Dublin 2, Ireland

Michael.Peirce@cs.tcd.ie

Michael Peirce graduated with a B.A.(Mod) in Computer Science from Trinity College Dublin, Ireland in June 1995. His final year dissertation concerned the design of a new scalable anonymous electronic payment mechanism for the purchase of goods and services on the WWW. He has acted as the maintainer of a highly popular

WWW page on Electronic Payment since December '94. He was senior technical reviewer for the popular "Internet: The Complete Reference," and chief researcher for "The Internet Yellow Pages" (1st and 2nd editions), both published by Osborne/McGraw-Hill. He has completed a summer internship with Hitachi Research Laboratory in Dublin. Currently he is pursuing a Masters degree, working in the area of mobility, with the Networks and Telecommunications Research Group (NTRG) at Trinity College, Dublin.

Donal O'Mahony
[*http://www.cs.tcd.ie/www/omahony/omahony. html*]
Computer Science Department
Trinity College
Dublin 2, Ireland
Donal.OMahony@cs.tcd.ie

Donal O'Mahony received B.A., B.A.I., and Ph.D. degrees from Trinity College Dublin, Ireland. After a brief career in industry at SORD Computer Systems in Tokyo and IBM in Dublin, he joined Trinity College as a lecturer in Computer Science in 1984. He is author of many papers and articles on networking and security and coauthor of *Local Area Networks and their Applications* published by Prentice-Hall. At Trinity, he coordinates a research group working in the areas of Networks and Telecommunications. Within this group, projects are ongoing in X.500, Electronic Data Interchange (EDI), Networked multimedia data streams, and Network Security. Dr. O'Mahony has acted as consultant to government and private industry organizations across Europe on a wide variety of projects involving strategic networking issues.

THE MILLICENT PROTOCOL FOR INEXPENSIVE ELECTRONIC COMMERCE

Steve Glassman, Mark Manasse, Martín Abadi, Paul Gauthier,
Patrick Sobalvarro

Abstract

Millicent is a lightweight and secure protocol for electronic commerce over the Internet. It is designed to support purchases costing less than a cent. It is based on decentralized validation of electronic cash at the vendor's server without any additional communication, expensive encryption, or offline processing. The key innovations of Millicent are its use of brokers and of scrip. Brokers take care of account management, billing, connection maintenance, and establishing accounts with vendors. Scrip is digital cash that is only valid for a specific vendor. The vendor locally validates the scrip to prevent customer fraud, such as double spending. **Keywords:** *Electronic commerce, electronic cash, scrip, broker, authentication*

Electronic Commerce Background

There are a number of existing and proposed protocols for electronic commerce, such as those from DigiCash [2], Open Market [14], CyberCash [1], First Virtual [3], and NetBill [12]. They are all appropriate for medium to large transactions, $5 or $10 and up, because the costs per transaction are typically several cents plus a percentage. When these costs are applied to inexpensive transactions, 50 cents and less, the transaction costs become a significant or even dominant component of the total purchase price, thereby effectively creating a minimum price for goods and services purchased using one of these protocols.

Forcing online charges to be above some threshold reduces the options for service providers. Online services providing newspapers, magazines, reference works, and stock prices all have individual items that could be inexpensive if sold separately. The ability to purchase inexpensive individual items would make these services more attractive to casual users on the Internet. In addition, secure low-priced transactions support grass-roots electronic publishing. A user who is not likely to open a ten-dollar account with an unknown publisher may be willing to spend a few cents to buy an interesting-looking article.

In this section, we look at four existing options for Internet commerce: accounts, aggregation, credit cards, and digital cash, and discuss why they are not appropriate for inexpensive electronic commerce. In the next section, we describe our model for reducing costs and making lightweight electronic commerce feasible.

Accounts

The simplest model for electronic commerce is for customers to establish accounts with vendors. When a customer wants to perform a transaction with the vendor, the customer identifies himself (securely) and the vendor adds the cost of the transaction to the customer's account. Vendors maintain the account information and bill the customers periodically.

With accounts, transaction costs and prices can be fairly low, but there is a fair amount of overhead. An account may need to be established ahead of time and maintained over an extended period. This makes sense only when assuming a relatively long-standing relationship between a customer and a vendor. There is often a minimum monthly charge associated with each account. The customer has separate accounts for each vendor, and the vendor needs to maintain accounts for every customer. All this overhead discourages casual users from making spur-of-the-moment purchases.

Aggregation

Aggregation amortizes billing charges over a sequence of less expensive transactions by accumulating transactions at the vendor until they exceed some threshold. Aggregation is another form of accounts and shares some of the problems of accounts. Although account setup is somewhat simplified, the vendor still has the problem of maintaining the accounts, accumulating enough transactions for a reasonable sized charge, and keeping transaction records for dispute resolution. Also, the customer must deal with separate charges from each vendor, minimum account charges, and the difficulty of contesting fraudulent charges.

Credit cards

Another simple model for electronic commerce is to use a credit card to pay for the purchase. Customers have credit cards; vendors register with credit card companies; customers give their credit card number to vendors; vendors contact their credit card companies for payment; the credit card companies handle the accounting and billing. There are established methods (like Netscape's SSL [13] based on RSA's public key encryption [16]) for ensuring secure transmission of the client's credit card number to the vendor.

Unfortunately, credit card transactions are (relatively) expensive since every purchase involves communication to a centralized credit card transaction service. In addition, credit card companies offer various features like individual item accounting, insurance, and fraud protection that add to the cost and aren't needed when purchasing inexpensive items.

Finally, customers may be unwilling to provide a credit card number to a vendor they don't know well. Although the credit card company insures the customer against any loss, there is still the inconvenience of clearing up any problems.

Digital cash

Digital cash is normally issued by a central trusted entity (like a bank). The integrity of digital cash is guaranteed by the digital signature of the issuer, so that counterfeiting digital cash is extremely hard. However, it is trivial to duplicate the bit pattern of the digital cash to produce and spend identical (and equally authentic) cash.

In an online digital cash scheme, when a vendor receives digital cash, he must contact the issuer to see if it is valid and not already spent. This extra communication makes the central site a bottleneck and adds cost to the transaction.

In an offline scheme (like one proposed by DigiCash [2]), the vendor authenticates the digital cash during the transaction and then later transmits it to the issuer to check for double spending. This scheme adds computational costs to the vendor for authenticating the digital cash, and adds messages and encryption to the protocol for pinpointing the source of the double spending.

Millicent

Our goal for Millicent is to allow for transactions that are inexpensive yet secure. We achieve this by using accounts based on scrip and brokers to sell scrip.

A piece of scrip represents an account the customer has established with a vendor. At any given time, a vendor has outstanding scrip (open accounts) with the recently active customers. The balance of the account is kept as the value of the scrip. When the customer makes a purchase with scrip, the cost of the purchase is deducted from the scrip's value and new scrip (with the new value/account balance) is returned as change. When the customer has completed a series of transactions, he can "cash in" the remaining value of the scrip (close the account).

Brokers serve as accounting intermediaries between customers and vendors. Customers enter into long-term relationships with brokers, in much the same way as they would enter into an agreement with a bank, credit card company, or Internet service provider. Brokers buy and sell vendor scrip as a service to customers and vendors. Broker scrip serves as a common currency for customers to use when buying vendor scrip, and for vendors to give as a refund for unspent scrip.

Millicent reduces the overhead of accounts in a number of ways:

- Communication costs are reduced by verifying the scrip locally at the vendor's site; there are almost no Millicent-specific communication costs during a normal transaction. There is also no need for a centralized server or an expensive transaction-processing protocol.

  In a centralized scheme, the central site is a bottleneck; the provider must have sufficient computing power to handle the peak transaction rate. In Millicent, there is no central server; there can be many brokers, a broker is only involved in a fraction of the transactions between a customer and a vendor, and the transactions involving a broker are lightweight.

- Cryptographic costs are reduced to keep them in line with the scale of transactions; we don't need strong or expensive cryptographic schemes because the value of the scrip is relatively low. We need only make the cost of breaking the protocol greater than the value of the scrip itself.

- Accounting costs are reduced by using brokers to handle accounts and billing. The customer establishes an account with a broker; the broker establishes its own accounts with the vendors. Using brokers allows us to split a customer-vendor account into two accounts: one between the customer and broker, and another between the broker and the vendor. This reduces the total number of accounts. Instead of many separate accounts for every customer-vendor combination, each customer has only one account with a broker (or, at most, a couple of brokers); and each vendor has long-standing accounts with just a few brokers.

In most account-based schemes, the vendor maintains the account balance. In Millicent, the customer maintains the account balance—it is encoded in the scrip held by the customer. There is no risk for the vendor because a digital signature prevents the customer from modifying the scrip's value. Since the scrip contains the account balance and a proof of correctness for that value, the vendor does not need to look up the customer's balance, saving disk activity.

- The minimum monthly charges are not as much of a problem because they are amortized over more activity. The single customer-broker account supports transactions with all vendors, and so it is likely to have enough activity to cover a minimum charge. By prepaying the broker, even the monthly accumulation of charges can be avoided.

Millicent is best suited for a series of inexpensive, casual transactions. We will rely on other protocols for initial account establishment between brokers and customers, and brokers and vendors. Other higher-value protocols are also used for the funds transfers that occur when accounts are periodically settled.

Security and Trust

The security model for Millicent is based on the assumption that scrip is used for small amounts. People and businesses treat coins differently than they treat bills, and treat small bills differently than large bills. In Millicent, we imagine people treating scrip as they would treat change in their pocket.

Since people don't need a receipt when buying candy from a vending machine, they don't need a receipt when buying an item using scrip. If they don't get what they paid for, they complain and get a refund. If they lose a coin every now and then, they aren't too upset.

We expect users to have a few dollars of scrip at a time. We don't expect them to have hundreds, or even tens, of dollars of scrip. As a result, scrip is not worth stealing unless you can steal lots of it; and if you steal lots, you will get caught.

Trust Model

Millicent assumes asymmetric trust relationships among the three entities—customers, brokers, and vendors. Brokers are assumed to be the most trustworthy, then vendors, and, finally, customers. The only time customers need to be trusted is when they complain about service problems.

We believe that brokers will tend to be large, well-known, and reputable financial institutions (like Visa, MasterCard, and banks) or major Internet or online service providers (like CompuServe, NETCOM, or AOL). We expect there to be many vendors covering a full spectrum of size and trustworthiness, as in the real world. Finally, there will be large numbers of customers who are as trustworthy as people are in general.

Three factors make broker fraud unprofitable. First, customer and vendor software can independently check the scrip and maintain account balances, so any fraud by the broker can be detected. Second, customers do not hold much scrip at any one time, so a broker would have to commit *many* fraudulent transactions to make

much of a gain, and this makes them likelier to be caught. Finally, the reputation of a broker is important for attracting customers and a broker would quickly lose its reputation if customers, have troubles with the broker. The repeat business of active customers is more valuable to a broker than the scrip that it could steal.

Vendor fraud consists of not providing goods for valid scrip. If this happens, customers will complain to their broker, and brokers will drop vendors who cause too many complaints. This acts as an effective policing mechanism, because vendors need a broker to easily conduct business in Millicent.

As a result, the Millicent protocol is skewed to prevent customer fraud (forgery and double spending) while providing indirect detection of broker and vendor fraud.

Security

The security of Millicent transactions comes from several aspects.

All transactions are protected

Every Millicent transaction requires that the customer knows the secret associated with the scrip. The protocol never sends the secret in the clear, so there is no risk due to eavesdropping. No piece of scrip can be reused, so a replay attack will fail. Each request is signed with the secret, so there is no way to intercept scrip and use the scrip to make a different request.

Inexpensive transactions limit the value of fraud

Inexpensive transactions can rely on inexpensive security: it's not worth using expensive computer resources to steal inexpensive scrip. In addition, it would take many illegal uses of scrip to acquire much money, and that raises the probability of getting caught.

Fraud is detectable and eventually traceable

Fraud is detected when the customer doesn't obtain the desired goods from the vendor, or when the balance returned to the customer doesn't match the balance due. If the customer is cheating, then the vendor's only loss is the cost of detecting the bad scrip and denying service. If the vendor is cheating, the customer will report a problem to the broker. When a broker notices a pattern of complaints from many customers against a vendor, it can pinpoint the fraud and cut off all dealings with the vendor. If a broker is cheating, the vendor will notice bad scrip coming from many customers, all originating from a single broker. The vendor can then publicize its complaint in an appropriate venue.

Scrip

The main properties of scrip are:

- It has value at a specific vendor.

- It can be spent only once.

- It is tamper resistant and hard to counterfeit.

- It can be spent only by its rightful owner.

- It can be efficiently produced and validated.

The next sections give more detail about scrip and its use, but the basic techniques to achieve these properties are outlined here:

- The text of the scrip gives its value and identifies the vendor.

- The scrip has a serial number to prevent double spending.

- There is a digital signature to prevent tampering and counterfeiting.

- The customer signs each use of scrip with a secret that is associated with the scrip.

- The signatures can be efficiently created and checked using a fast one-way hash function (like MD5 [15] or SHA [11]).

Scrip Structure

There are three secrets involved in producing, validating, and spending scrip. The customer is sent one secret, the `customer_secret`, to prove ownership of the scrip. The vendor uses one secret, the `master_customer_secret`, to derive the `customer_secret` from customer information in the scrip. The third secret, the `master_scrip_secret`, is used by the vendor to prevent tampering and counterfeiting.

The secrets are all used in a way that shows knowledge of the secret without revealing the secret. To attest to a message, the secret is appended to the message, and the result is hashed to produce a signature. The message (without the secret) and the signature prove—due to the one-way nature of the hash function—knowledge of the secret, because the correct signature can only be derived if you know the secret.

Scrip has the following fields (Figure 1):

- `Vendor` identifies the vendor for the scrip.

- `Value` gives the value of the scrip.

- `ID#` is the unique identifier of the scrip. Some portion of it is used to select the `master_scrip_secret` used for the certificate.

- `Cust_ID#` is used to produce the customer secret. A portion of `Cust_ID#` is used to select the `master_customer_secret` which is also used in producing the customer secret.

- `Expires` is the expiration time for the scrip.

- `Props` are extra data describing customer properties (age, state of residence, etc.) to the vendor.

- `Certificate` is the signature of the scrip.

Validation and Expiration

Scrip is validated in two steps. First (Figure 2), the certificate is recomputed and checked against

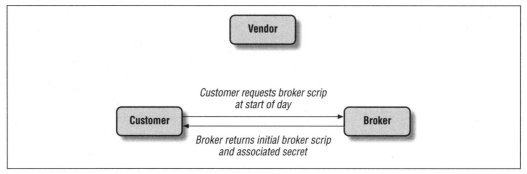

Figure 1: The certificate of a piece of scrip is generated by hashing the body of the scrip with a secret. The secret is selected using a portion of the scrip's ID#

the certificate sent with the scrip. If the scrip has been tampered with, then the two certificates will not match. Second, there is a unique identifier (ID#) included in the scrip body and the vendor can check for double spending by seeing if it has recorded that identifier as already spent. Generating and validating scrip each require a little text manipulation and one hash operation. Unless the secret is known, scrip cannot be counterfeited or altered.

The vendor records the unique identifier of every piece of scrip that is spent, so that it cannot be fraudulently respent. To save the vendor from maintaining this record forever, each piece of scrip is given an expiration time. Once the scrip expires, the vendor no longer has to worry about

its being respent and can erase its record of the scrip.

Customers are responsible for renewing or cashing in scrip before it expires. The old scrip is submitted to the vendor, who returns new scrip with a later expiration time (and a new serial number). Vendors may choose to charge a small fee for this service, discouraging users from obtaining more scrip than they will need in the near future.

Properties

Scrip also has fields for storing properties, which are inserted by the vendor or broker when the scrip is produced. The exact property fields and their values will depend on an agreement between the brokers and vendors. The brokers

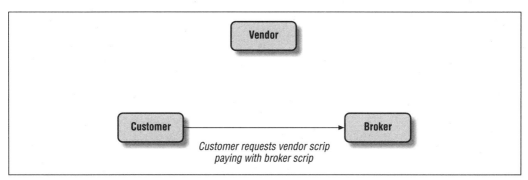

Figure 2: The received scrip is validated by regenerating the certificate and comparing it to the transmitted one. If they are identical, the scrip is valid

will get the information from customers when they create their account and enforce some set of rules when selling vendor scrip. Vendors, of course, are free to include whatever properties they desire in scrip they produce themselves.

Information such as the state of residence, or age of the consumer assists the vendor in making sales decisions. Adult material could only be bought if the scrip shows the customer is old enough. State sales tax charges can depend on a property included in the scrip.

Millicent Protocols

Scrip is the basis of a family of Millicent protocols. We will describe three of them and compare their simplicity, secrecy, and security. (A detailed description of the protocols is in the appendix.)

The first, "scrip in the clear," is the simplest and most efficient protocol. It is the basis for the other two protocols, but it may not be useful in practice because it is too insecure. The second, "private and secure," is secure and offers good privacy, but it is more expensive. The third, "secure without encryption," is also secure, but trades privacy for greater efficiency.

Scrip in the Clear

In the simplest possible Millicent protocol, the customer just sends an unspent piece of scrip in the clear (i.e., not encrypted or protected in any way) along with each request to the vendor. The vendor returns the desired result along with a new piece of scrip (also in the clear) as change.

This protocol offers almost no security; an eavesdropping third party can intercept the scrip being returned as change and use it himself. When the rightful owner later attempted to spend the scrip, the vendor would have a record of its being previously spent, and would refuse the request.

Private and Secure

To add security and privacy to the Millicent protocol, we establish a shared secret between the two parties and then use the secret to set up a secure communications channel using an efficient, symmetric encryption method (such as DES [10], RC4 [17], or IDEA [6]).

In Millicent, scrip can be used to establish this shared key. When a customer buys an initial piece of scrip for a vendor, a secret is generated based on the customer identifier, and returned securely with the scrip (Figure 3). This requires either that the transaction be performed using some secure non-Millicent protocol, or that the scrip be purchased using a secure Millicent transaction.

The vendor does not directly record the secret associated with the piece of scrip. Instead, the customer identifier (Cust_ID#) field of the scrip allows rapid recalculation of the secret. The customer identifier must be unique whenever scrip is transmitted to a new customer, but it need not have any connection to the identity of the customer.

When the vendor receives the request, he derives the customer secret from the customer identifier in the scrip, derives the message key from the customer secret, and uses the message key to decrypt the request. The change scrip can be returned in the clear, while the response and any new secrets are returned to the customer encrypted by the message key.

In this protocol the request and the response are kept totally private; unless an eavesdropper knows the customer secret, he can't decrypt the messages. In addition, an eavesdropper can't steal the scrip because it can't be spent without knowing the customer secret.

Secure without Encryption

The previous section describes how the secret shared by the customer and vendor can be exploited to achieve security and privacy. But a

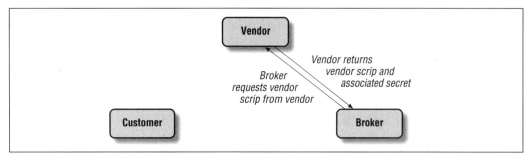

Figure 3: The customer secret is generated by hashing the customer identifier with a secret. The secret is selected using a portion of the customer identifier.

full-blown encrypted channel may be overkill for some Millicent applications. In this, our third variant of the protocol, we give up the privacy of the request and response to eliminate the use of encryption.

As in the previous protocol, the customer securely gets an initial piece of scrip and customer secret. To make a purchase, the customer sends the request, scrip, and a "signature" of the request to the vendor. The signature is produced in the same way that the certificate of the scrip is produced. The scrip and request are concatenated with the customer secret. The customer runs an efficient cryptographic one-way hash function over this string and sends the resulting hash as the signature.

When the vendor receives the request, he derives the customer secret from the scrip and regenerates the signature for the request. If the scrip or request have been tampered with in any way, the signature will not match (Figure 4).

The vendor now handles the request and returns a fresh piece of scrip as change. The change scrip shares the same customer identifier as the scrip submitted with the request, so that the original customer secret can be used to spend the change. There is no need to encrypt any of the response; an eavesdropper can't steal the scrip because the signature of the request can't be made without knowing the customer secret. The vendor may sign the response with the customer secret in order to prove authenticity to the customer.

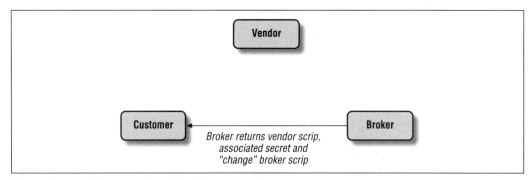

Figure 4: The request is validated by regenerating the request signature and comparing to the transmitted signature. If they match, the request is valid.

Thus, with only a few hashes, Millicent provides a lightweight and secure protocol.

Brokers

Brokers maintain the accounts of customers and vendors, and they handle all real-money transactions. The customer establishes an account with a broker by using some other method (like a credit card or a higher-security electronic commerce system) to buy some broker scrip. The customer then uses the broker scrip to buy vendor scrip.

The vendor and the broker have a long-term business relationship. The broker sells vendor scrip to customers and pays the vendor. There can be different business models for the way the broker gets vendor scrip, for example, pay in advance, consignment sale, or licensed production. In all models, the broker can make a profit selling scrip because he pays the vendor (at a discount) for scrip in bulk and sells individual pieces to customers.

When a customer wants to make a purchase, the customer contacts the broker to obtain the necessary vendor scrip. The customer uses his broker scrip to pay for the vendor scrip using the Millicent protocol. The broker returns the new vendor scrip along with change in broker scrip.

We will examine three ways in which the broker gets the vendor scrip. The "scrip warehouse" model assumes a casual relationship between the broker and vendor. The "licensed scrip producer" model assumes a substantial and long-lasting relationship between the broker and vendor. The "multiple broker" model assumes a relationship between brokers, but requires no relationship between the vendor and broker.

Scrip Warehouse

When the broker is acting as a scrip warehouse, the broker buys multiple pieces of scrip from a vendor. The broker stores the scrip and sells the pieces one at a time to customers (Figure 6-8).

This model assumes no special relationship between the vendor and broker. It works best when the broker's customers have a light to moderate demand for that vendor's scrip. The broker uses the Millicent protocol to buy the scrip from the vendor in the same way a customer would. Selling scrip in large blocks is more efficient for the vendor since the communication and financial transaction costs are amortized over all the pieces of scrip. We presume that the vendor offers some sort of volume discount to encourage brokers to buy large blocks of scrip. The broker makes a profit when it resells the scrip to customers at full price. The vendor depends on the broker to ensure any customer properties encoded in the scrip.

Licensed Scrip Production

If a broker's customers buy a lot of scrip for a specific vendor, it may be desirable for a vendor to "license" the broker to produce vendor scrip. This means that the broker generates scrip that the vendor can validate and accept. The vendor sells the broker the right to generate scrip using a given `master_scrip_secret`, series of scrip ID#'s, `master_customer_secret`, and series of customer identifiers. The vendor can validate the licensed scrip because the `master_scrip_secret` is known from the series of the scrip ID# and the `master_customer_secret` is known from the series of the customer identifier.

Brokers produce the scrip and collect money from customers; vendors record the total value of scrip originating from a particular broker. When all the scrip produced under a particular contract has expired, brokers and vendors can settle up. The broker presumably takes some commission for producing the scrip.

A license covers a specific series (unique range of identifiers—ID#'s) of scrip for a given period of time, and the secrets shared between the broker and vendor only apply to that series. A vendor can issue licenses to different brokers by giving out different series and secrets to each one.

Of course, a vendor can produce its own scrip using its own private series and secrets.

Licensing scrip production is more efficient for the vendor and broker than the scrip warehouse model. There is less communication because the license is smaller to transmit than a few pieces of scrip. The vendor does less computation since it does not have to generate the scrip itself. The broker does not have to store large blocks of scrip, since it can generate the scrip on demand. Additionally, it allows the broker to encode specific user properties into each piece of scrip it generates.

Multiple Brokers

In an environment where there are multiple brokers, a customer of one broker may want to make a purchase from a vendor associated with another broker. If the vendor only wants to have an account with its own broker (perhaps to simplify accounting), the customer will have to go through the vendor's broker to buy vendor scrip.

The entire transaction will go like this:

- The customer asks his broker for vendor scrip.

- The customer's broker tries to set up an account with the vendor.

- The vendor tells the customer's broker his broker's name.

- The customer's broker buys broker scrip from the vendor's broker.

- The customer's broker returns the vendor's broker's scrip to the customer.

- The customer buys vendor scrip from the vendor's broker.

- The customer uses the vendor scrip at the vendor.

The idea of licensed scrip production can be extended so that brokers can generate broker scrip for other brokers.

Customer, Broker, and Vendor Interactions

The following diagrams (Figures 5-10) present the steps for a complete Millicent session (including the broker buying scrip from the vendor). The initial step (Figure 5) happens only once per session. The second step (Figure 6) happens each time the customer has no stored scrip for a vendor. Step three (Figure 7) happens only if the broker must contact the vendor to buy the scrip. It is not needed for licensed scrip production. The fourth step (Figure 8) shows the broker returning the vendor scrip to the customer. The fifth step (Figure 9) shows the customer using the scrip to make a purchase from the vendor.

The last step (Figure 10) shows a typical Millicent transaction. The customer already has vendor scrip and uses it to make a purchase. There are no extra messages or interactions with the broker.

Status

We have produced an initial implementation of Millicent [9] consisting of a set of libraries, and a vendor and broker written using the libraries for Millicent transactions across a network using TCP/IP. Our measurements show that the Millicent protocol is efficient enough for sub-cent purchases. Our untuned vendor implementation can validate about 1000 Millicent requests per second (on a Digital AlphaStation 400 4/233) and, of that, most of the time goes into the TCP connection handling.

Using zero-cost transactions, Millicent scrip can be used as a distributed capability. Using this aspect of scrip, our first application of Millicent is in a Kerberos-like [5] authentication suite for our network firewall services. We have modified a SOCKs [7] based TCP relay, rlogin daemon, FTP daemon, and rlogin, telnet, and FTP clients to use Millicent scrip to convey authentication information. A user does one cryptokey (cryptographic challenge/response) authentication to get scrip

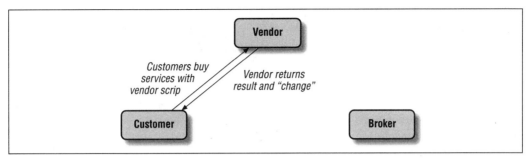

Figure 5:   The client makes a secure connection to the broker to get some broker scrip

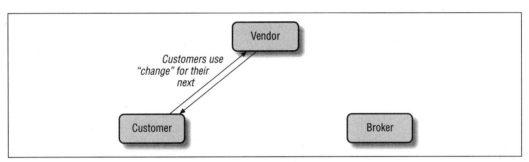

Figure 6:   If the client doesn't already have scrip for a particular vendor, he contacts the broker to buy some using his broker scrip

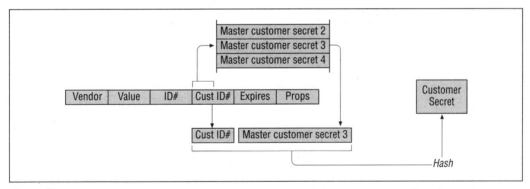

Figure 7:   If the broker doesn't already have scrip for that vendor, he buys some from the vendor

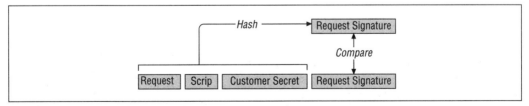

Figure 8:   The broker returns vendor scrip and change (in broker scrip) to the client

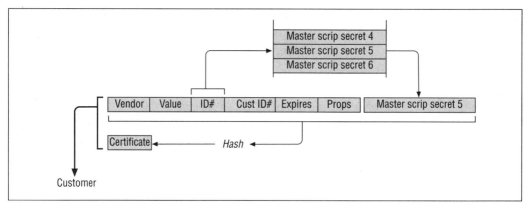

Figure 9: The customer uses the vendor scrip to make a purchase from the vendor. The vendor returns change (in vendor scrip) to the client

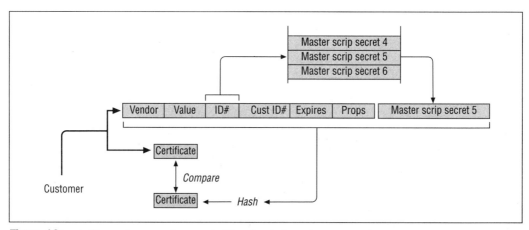

Figure 10: The customer continues using the change to make more purchases

from an authentication broker. Then, for the rest of the day, the user can use the authentication scrip to buy scrip for particular firewall services.

We are also working on Millicent-based World Wide Web (WWW) services. We have developed a local *pseudo-proxy* that intercepts all requests from the client's WWW browser and modifies the HTTP header to add scrip as necessary. The WWW server checks the HTTP request for sufficient scrip to buy the page and returns the page with change in the HTTP response. The pseudo-proxy extracts the change before forwarding the response to the browser. When Millicent

becomes popular, the functionality of the pseudo-proxy can be integrated in with the browser.

Future and Applications

The range of potential applications for Millicent is quite broad. With current technology, Millicent is appropriate for transactions from a few dollars to as little as one-tenth of a cent. The upper bound comes from the trust model for brokers and the availability of alternative protocols appropriate for transactions above a few dollars, while the lower bound comes from a conservative estimate based on the computational costs of a broker. This price range covers most print and information services that will be available in an online format—magazines, newspapers, encyclopedias, indices, newsletters, and databases.

MacKie-Mason and Varian [8] argue that as the Internet develops there will be increasing pressure for usage-based charges. Current free Internet services like email, file transfers, the Internet telephone, and teleconferencing will have to be paid for. At the lowest level, they estimate that the cost of transmitting one packet on the Internet backbone is one six-hundredth of a cent. We don't believe that Millicent is quite efficient enough for such packet-level charges; for these there are proposals like the noncryptographic *Digital Silk Road* [4]. We do believe that Millicent can be used for per-connection charges for these services.

Conclusion

We see growing opportunities for inexpensive Internet services. These services need an appropriate electronic commerce protocol. We believe that the Millicent protocol is a good candidate to be that protocol. ∎

Appendix

The following is a more precise description of the Millicent protocol for customer and vendor. The interaction between customer and broker relies on the same protocol, as explained in the main body of the paper.

We use the following notations:

X, Y, Z
> Represents the string encoding the tuple X, Y, Z

H(X)
> Is the result of hashing X with a cryptographic hash function, such as MD5

{X}Y
> Is the result of encrypting X with a cryptographic function, such as DES, under the key Y

A->B: X
> Means that A sends X to B

Before giving the protocol, we describe its fields. First, we list some of the ingredients of scrip; scrip includes the name of the vendor, some properties of the customer, a value, and an expiration time:

vendor_id:
> A unique identifier (or name) for the vendor

props:
> Any data describing customer properties (possibly including a name)

value:
> The value of the scrip

exp:
> The expiration time for the scrip

The customer and the vendor generate a request and a reply. Both of these are arbitrary strings.

request:
> The request from the customer

reply:
> The reply from the vendor. (We assume that, by its format, reply is distinguishable from request.)

In addition, the protocol relies on various secrets, and on corresponding identifiers for those secrets:

master_scrip_secret:
> A secret used for certifying scrip. The master_scrip_secret is known only to the vendor (when the vendor produces his own scrip) or only to the vendor and to the broker (when the broker may produce scrip).

id_series#:
> An identifier for master_scrip_secret.

The vendor can map `id_series#` to `master_scrip_secret`.

`id_sequence#`:

A unique identifier, such as a sequence number. The vendor accepts `id_sequence#` for at most one transaction in conjunction with `id_series#`.

`id# = id_series#, id_sequence#`

`master_customer_secret`:

A secret used for producing customer secrets. The `master_customer_secret` is known only to the vendor and to the broker.

`cust_id_series#`:

An identifier for `master_customer_secret`. The vendor can map `cust_id_series#` to `master_customer_secret`.

`cust_id_sequence#`:

A unique identifier, such as a sequence number. Together with `cust_id_series#`, it identifies the customer.

`cust_id# = cust_id_series#, cust_id_sequence#`

`customer_secret = H(cust_id#, master_customer_secret)`

A secret that the vendor or the broker sends to the customer. The customer gets this quantity along with cust_id# (but not master_customer_secret); the customer can map vendor_id and cust_id# to customer_secret. Both the vendor and the broker can generate customer_secret from cust_id# and master_customer_secret. No one else knows customer_secret.

Scrip is generated by combining all of the fields listed above, as follows:

```
id_material = vendor_id, id#, cust_id#
cert_material = props, value, exp
scrip_body = id_material, cert_material
```

`cert = H(scrip_body, master_scrip_secret)`

This is a certificate that proves the authentic-

ity of `scrip_body` for the customer associated with `cust_id#`.

`scrip = scrip_body, cert`

The vendor or the broker gives `scrip` to the customer; the customer presents it to the vendor along with a request.

For change returned from a transaction, the vendor issues new scrip, with a new certificate. The new quantities may differ from the previous ones in all their components except for `cust_id#` and `vendor_id`. If the broker initially knows `master_scrip_secret` and this quantity remains the same, then the broker is in principle capable of producing change instead of the vendor. This may not be desirable, since it implies unnecessary trust from the vendor to the broker; hence, when the vendor makes change, it is sensible for the vendor to use a new `master_scrip_secret` not known to the broker. In any case, the vendor should pick a new value for `id#` as a protection against replays. We write `scrip'` for the new scrip.

- In the clear (insecure)
  ```
  customer -> vendor: scrip, request
  vendor -> customer: scrip', reply
  ```

- Authentic and private
  ```
  customer -> vendor: vendor_id, cust_
      id#, {scrip, request} customer_
      secret
  vendor -> customer: vendor_id, cust_
      id#, {scrip', cert,
      reply}customer_secret
  ```

Most of the communication is under `customer_secret` for authenticity and privacy. It is possible to encrypt less, with a gain in efficiency. For example, some parts of `scrip'` are not sensitive and could be sent in the clear.

The response includes `cert` in order to allow the customer to check that the response received is in fact a response to the request.

Both messages include `vendor_id` and `cust_id#` in the clear in order to allow the recipient to generate `customer_secret`.

- Authentic but not private
```
customer->vendor: scrip, request,
    H(scrip, request, customer_
    secret)
vendor->customer: scrip', reply,
    H(scrip', cert, reply, customer_
    secret)
```

All messages are sent in the clear, but they are protected by the signatures (based on `customer_secret`).

No encryption is used and only five hashes are necessary at the server to handle a request. The hashes are: (1) for checking the old scrip, (2) for regenerating `customer_secret`, (3) for checking the customer's signature, (4) for generating the new scrip, and (5) for signing the response.

The response includes `cert` in order to allow the customer to check that the response received is in fact a response to the request.

Both messages include `vendor_id` and `cust_id#` in the clear (in `scrip` and `scrip'`) so the recipient can generate `customer_secret`.

References

1. CyberCash Inc., URL: *http://www.cybercash.com/*

2. DigiCash Inc., *http://www.digicash.com/*

3. First Virtual Holdings Inc., URL: *http://www.fv.com/*

4. Norman Hardy and Eric Dean Tribble, *The Digital Silk Road*, *ftp://ftp.netcom.com/pub/jo/joule/DSR/DSR1.txt.gz* or *http://web.gmu.edu:80/bcox/Bionomics/Extropians/HardyTribbleSilkRoad.html*

5. J. Kohl and C. Neuman, *The Kerberos Network Authentication Service (V5)*, IETF RFC 1510, *gopher://ds2.internic.net/00/rfc/rfc1510.txt*

6. Xuejia Lai, *On the Design and Security of Block Ciphers*, Institute for Signal and Information Processing, ETH-Zentrum, Zurich, Switzerland, 1992.

7. M. Leech, M. Ganis, Y. Lee, et al., *SOCKS Protocol Version 5*, draft-ietf-aft-socks-protocol-v5-04.txt, *http://src.doc.ic.ac.uk/computing/internet/internet-drafts/draft-ietf-aft-socks-protocol-v5-04.txt.Z*

8. Jeffrey K. MacKie-Mason, and Hal R. Varian. *Some FAQs about usage based pricing*. University of Michigan, September 1994, *ftp://gopher.econ.lsa.umich.edu/pub/Papers useFAQs.html*

9. Mark S. Manasse, *A Method for Low Priced Electronic Commerce*, Patent pending, *http://www.research.digital.com/SRC/personal/Mark_Manasse/uncommon/ucom.html*

10. National Institute for Standards and Technology (NIST), *Data Encryption Standard (DES), Federal Information Processing Standards Publication 46-2*, December 1993, *http://www.ncsl.nist.gov/fips/fips46-2.txt*

11. National Institute for Standards and Technology (NIST), *Secure Hash Standard, FIPS PUB 180-1: Secure Hash Standard*, April 1995, *http://csrc.ncsl.nist.gov/fips/fip180-1.txt*

12. NetBill, Carnegie Mellon University, *http://www.ini.cmu.edu/netbill/*

13. Netscape Inc., *SSL Protocol, http://home.netscape.com/newsref/std/SSL.html*

14. Open Market Inc., *http://www.openmarket.com/*

15. R. Rivest, *The MD5 Message-Digest Algorithm*, IETF RFC 1321, *gopher://ds2.internic.net/00/rfc/rfc1321.txt*

16. RSA Inc., *PKCS#1: RSA Encryption Standard, http://www.rsa.com/pub/pkcs/ps/pkcs-1.ps*

17. RSA Inc., *RSA's Frequently Asked Questions About Today's Cryptography, http://www.rsa.com/rsalabs/faq/faq_misc.html#misc.6*

About the Authors

Martín Abadi

[*http://www.research.digital.com/people/Martin_Abadi/bio.html*]

Systems Research Center, Digital Equipment Corporation

ma@pa.dec.com

Paul Gauthier

[*http://www.cs.berkeley.edu/~gauthier/*]

University of California Berkeley

gauthier@cs.berkeley.edu

Paul Gauthier is a Ph.D. student at the University of Califoria, Berkeley. He was a summer intern at SRC in Summer, 1995.

Steve Glassman
[*http://www.research.digital.com/people/Steve_
Glassman/bio.html*]
Systems Research Center, Digital Equipment Corporation
steveg@pa.dec.com

Mark S. Manasse
[*http://www.research.digital.com/people/Mark_
Manasse/bio.html*]
Systems Research Center, Digital Equipment Corporation
msm@pa.dec.com

Patrick Sobalvarro
[*http://www.psg.lcs.mit.edu:80/~pgs/*]
Massachusetts Institute of Technology
pgs@lcs.mit.edu
Patrick Sobalvarro is a Ph.D. student at the Massachusetts Institute of Technology. He was a
summer intern at SRC in Summer, 1995.

A Schema-Based Approach to HTML Authoring

Marcus Kesseler

Abstract

This paper presents a novel approach to high-productivity authoring of large, regularly structured hypertexts. By explicitly representing the objects in the hypertext and the relationships between them in a schema, it is possible to create, manipulate, and maintain large hyperdocuments with high efficiency. In the implementation, called the HSDL, all such schema operations are performed on a graphical user interface (GUI). Special attention has been given to the problem of schema evolution. In HSDL, the author can do nontrivial schema update operations even if classes have already been instantiated. The mapping from the schema to HTML, called compilation, is done by a series of programs in the programming language Scheme. These programs, called expanders, are integral parts of every schema. Although the default set of expanders will already provide fairly sophisticated HTML layout, users may easily adapt them to suit their special needs. A built-in, schema-aware HTML editor allows the integration of links defined in the schema into the HTML contents of a node. **Keywords:** *Authoring environments, information representation and modelling, consistency, integrity, authoring-in-the-large, schema evolution, hypertext linearization*

Introduction

Like Garzotto et al. [7], we would like to see the task of producing large hypertexts split into two intertwined but nevertheless clearly distinguishable activities: first, those that deal with the hypertext on a *per node* basis, which is called *Authoring-in-the-Small* (AIS), and second, those that deal with structuring decisions on a larger scale, possibly encompassing hundreds of nodes, accordingly called *Authoring-in-the-Large* (AIL). AIS usually involves dealing with layout oriented problems, or, in HTML, with local structuring decisions. The general idea of schema-based AIL is best conveyed by a four step procedure:

1. The author models the objects that exist in the target domain, i.e., the domain the document is about, and the relationships that exist between these objects. This model is called the *class schema*.

2. Using the classes in the class schema as templates, the author proceeds to create instances of the classes and instances of the

relationships in the *instance schema*. These operations are fairly intuitive when performed visually on the graphical user interface of the implementation.

3. The author then proceeds to fill the as-yet empty instances with content. This is where AIS in the conventional sense is done.

4. In a compilation step, the structural information in the schema is merged with the contents of the instances and gets translated into the target hypertext representation (HTML).

Of course, any approach that forces authors to proceed in such a strictly top-down manner is completely at odds with the way that authoring is actually done. Authoring, which is among the so called *complex design activities* [12], is an intrinsically opportunistic process. By this, we mean that authors seldom adhere to schematic procedures while creating large documents. Authors seem to randomly switch between contexts and levels (AIS, AIL). To develop this approach, a great deal of effort has been invested to reconcile

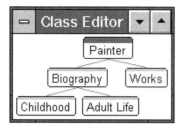

Figure 1: The painter class

the inflexibility inherent in schema-based approaches with the chaotic ways human authors usually go after their business.

The implementation, called HSDL (Hypertext Structure Description Language), evolved from initial experiments with a programming language into a full-blown visual hypertext authoring environment. The Structure Description Language as such, although now invisible to the user, lives on in HSDL as the base for the persistent schema storage mechanism.

The rest of this paper is structured as follows: We give a more detailed overview of the schema and the problems of schema evolution. We then proceed to show how a schema is compiled into HTML. After discussing related work in this area, we finish with our conclusions and future research directions.

The Schema

The schema consists of an intentional description, the *class schema*, and an extentional description, the *instance schema*.

The Class Schema

The class schema consists of *classes* and *link-classes* between them. A class is a tree-structured *composite object*. The objects in a class tree are called *components*. The top component is called the *root component*. Consider the class `Painter` in Figure 1.

`Painter` has a root component of the same name, which has the subcomponents `Biogra-`

phy and `Works`. `Biography` has two further subcomponents, called `Childhood` and `Adult Life` respectively. An arbitrary number of *link classes* may be defined between any two components or even from a component to itself (see below). Link classes are directed; we distinguish between the *source component* and the *target component* of a link class.

The Instance Schema

The instance schema consists of *instances* and *link instances*. All instances of a class are exactly alike; that is, classes are used as *templates* that are always instantiated as a whole. The nodes of an instance are called *instance-nodes* (or *i-nodes* for short).

Figure 2 shows an HSDL screen dump which contains the class and instance schemas of a gallery. The gallery consists of three painters and eight of their paintings. The paintings are also classified into four thematic collections. Note that the instances Picasso and van Gogh are not fully visible; the double frame around their root i-nodes indicates that they are *imploded*.

Link Instances Induce Ordered Collections

Large hypertexts are often organized as hierarchies. It is common practice to make the members of a set of nodes linked under a same anchor node (e.g., the sections of chapter, the paintings of Picasso) traversable by previous/next links. We refer to such a set of nodes connected by previous/next links as an *ordered col-*

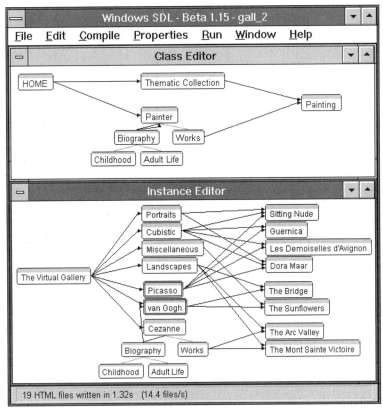

Figure 2: The class and instance schemas representing a gallery

lection, or simply a collection. The anchor node of the hierarchy is called the *owner* of the collection. In HSDL we generalize the idea of an ordered collection by specifying that the order within a collection is not a property of the i-nodes themselves, but rather of the link instances leading to them. A set of link instances of the same link class coming from a same source i-node is said to *induce* a collection of i-nodes. With this definition, it is possible to embed an i-node into an arbitrary number of collections. We move from hierarchies to true networks. Furthermore, a link instance induces a collection in *both* directions. The i-nodes that are the targets of a set of links from a same source are said to belong to a *target collection*. Likewise, the i-nodes that are the sources of a set of links to a same target are said to belong to a *source collection*.

Consider the very simple class schema in Figure 3: A set of authors and papers written by them are to be presented as a hypertext. In the instance schema we have three authors (A, B, C) and three papers (1, 2, 3).

The left screen dump of Figure 4 shows the target collection of Author A; i.e., A is author (or coauthor) of papers 1, 2, 3 (HSDL has a display mode in which only the links into or from a selected instance are visible). The right screen dump of Figure 4 shows the source collection of Paper 3, which was written by A and C. Therefore, the link instances of a single link class from `Author` to `Paper` naturally induce a collection of papers in the target direction ("Papers by this author") and a collection of authors in the source direction ("Authors of this paper").

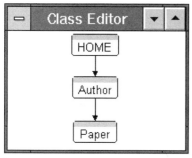 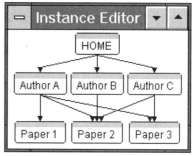

Figure 3:   The Authors & Papers class and instance schemas

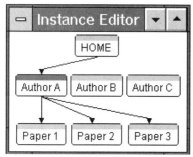

Figure 4:   A target and a source collection

Anchors from an owner to a collection usually form an *index*. By default, HSDL translates indices into the unordered list (<UL>) HTML environment. By manipulating the anchor expanders (see below) it is possible to create a wide variety of layouts for such indices. Changes to the order of a collection (i.e., sorting) is done by drag-and-drop in the HSDL GUI. Since collections are defined by link instances, reordering always occurs relative to a selected link instance and therefore affects only one of the many collections the instance may be part of.

Since authors may not want to include every possible hierarchy as an explicit index into an HTML node, their generation can easily be toggled in a link-class-properties pop-up menu. The same applies to the generation of previous/next links.

The anchors that aid navigation within the members of a target collection are organized into *previous/up/next-triplets* (or *previous/down/next-*

triplets for source collections). Consider Figure 5, which shows the compiled HTML result for the `Dora Maar` instance of Figure 2 in the NCSA Mosaic browser. `Dora Maar` is a member of three collections: it's a painting by `Picasso` and has been classified as a `Portrait` and a `Cubistic` painting. Such *crossing collections* are best visualized by color-coding the respective triplets according to their owners. In Figure 5 the *up* anchor of the first triplet, to `Picasso`, has been compiled into an up-arrow icon, while in the other two triplets, both to instances of `Thematic Collection`, have been compiled into the owner's name. For simple changes to triplets styles HSDL offers pop-up menus (e.g., Void, Arrow, Name, Name+Arrow, Color). For users wishing to go further, expander programming offers the necessary degrees of freedom.

It should be emphasized that Figure 5 has no edited contents whatsoever. All visible elements

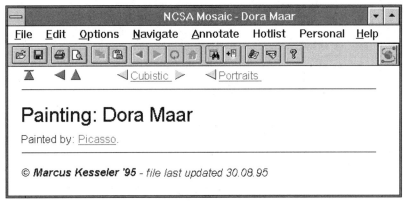

Figure 5: The Dora Maar instance in the NCSA Mosaic browser

are HSDL defaults. The "Painted by" label is entered by the user during link class definition and therefore produces this layout in *all* instances of `Painting`.

Nonhierarchical Links

Obviously, not all links in a hypertext will be hierarchical. One of the main characteristics of hypertext is the ability to explicitly represent associations between any two nodes in a network, completely disregarding any overall structure the nodes may be embedded into. With the slight restriction that every link is an instance of some link class, it is possible to create such links without introducing new concepts into HSDL. Suppose that Cezanne's biography mentions that he was influenced by van Gogh. Clearly, one would like to make the words "van Gogh" into a link to the node representing van Gogh. In Figure 2 the class `Painter` has a link class called `Influenced by` (link class names are not visible in the screen dump) from `Biography` to `Painter`. What at first looks like a puzzling link class from a class to itself works exactly how one would expect on the instance level; as shown in the instance schema of Figure 2, it is possible to link Cezanne's biography to van Gogh.

HTML anchors representing link instances are placed at default positions before or after the HTML contents of an i-node, depending on the current set of expanders. The built-in HSDL HTML-Editor provides the means to override such default placements and insert anchors anywhere into the HTML contents of an i-node. Link anchors can be *copied* or *grabbed*; a copied anchor will still have a duplicate at the default position; a grabbed anchor will be removed from it. Whole indices can also be copied or grabbed.

Note that some authors (e.g., Conklin [5] and Garzotto et al. [7]) make a clear distinction between *organizational links*, which span hierarchies, and *referential links*, which allow random linking of nodes.

In HSDL this distinction becomes somewhat blurred. At first sight, there really seems to be a great difference between the links from a chapter to its sections and a link expressing that van Gogh influenced Cezanne. On closer inspection, we find that the `Painted by` links from a painter to his or her paintings, which though seeming to carry much more meaning than an index of sections in a chapter, span a completely analogous structure. Now, if our gallery had, say, six painters that were influenced by van Gogh, even the instances of this link class, which seemed to carry a lot of semantics, would start looking like a collection (and hence hierarchy) of painters. Therefore, as seen from the HSDL formalism, there is no difference between referential and organizational links. Their seemingly different semantic weight is in the eye of the beholder.

Referential Integrity and Fast Prototyping

The HSDL implementation enforces strict referential integrity on the class and on the instance schemas. Therefore, it is *impossible* to create a dangling link or to make parts of the schema inaccessible (no orphans). Referential integrity is enforced by following three simple rules:

1. When a new class is created, a link class linking it into an existing class has to be created along with it.

2. When deleting a class, also delete all link classes leading into or out of it.

3. Class or link class deletions are not allowed if they make parts of the schema inaccessible.

The same rules apply to the instance schema. Deletions in the class schema are *cascaded* to the instance schema; that is, when a class schema object is deleted, all its instances are also deleted. If cascading a legal class schema deletion leads to an inconsistent instance schema, the class schema deletion is declared illegal and undone.

To efficiently enforce rules 2 and 3, the HSDL software architecture includes a *Change Manager*. Aided by an *undo-stack*, which records all schema changes that occur during an editing session, the Change Manager implements the *transaction concept* for schema update operations. Therefore, destructive operations that lead to a referentially inconsistent schema are simply *rolled back*. The pop operation on the undo-stack is also available to the user, thereby providing *full undo* capabilities within an editing session.

Given that referential integrity is ensured, it is possible to compile the schema into a working hypertext at any stage during development. This has great advantages for fast prototyping, since an author can generate *hypertext skeletons* very

fast. Such skeletons of HTML nodes, though devoid of edited content, contain default anchors generated by HSDL and are therefore fully navigable. They are of great help to check if the design and structuring decisions represented in a schema really mirror the author's intention on the hypertext level. Experienced HSDL users can create fully functional HTML skeletons consisting of hundreds of nodes and links in a couple of minutes.

Heterogeneous Collections, Guided Tours, and Multilink-Classes

As yet, there is one important feature missing in the expressiveness of HSDL: the ability to create heterogeneous collections, that is, collections composed of instances of different classes, which are needed in two main modelling situations:

Fine-grained modelling

Suppose we want to model the canonical "Article" hierarchy of sections and subsections. As such, it presents no problem. But suppose we want to go further and say that a subsection is composed of a random sequence of paragraphs, figures, or tables. With the HSDL indices presented so far, it is not possible to insert a link to a figure between two paragraphs. We would have an index of all paragraphs, followed by an index of all figures and an index of all tables. Although we could explicitly copy or grab the respective link instances into the i-node contents, thereby "welding" them to fixed locations, this unfortunately renders the link instances inaccessible to the reordering operators provided by the HSDL GUI.

Guided tours

These are sequential paths through random subsets of i-nodes of an instance schema.

To tackle this problem, we extend the definition of link classes as connecting a *set of source classes* to a *set of target classes*. A link class where the source or the target class set has a cardinality

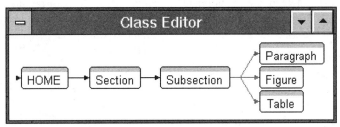

Figure 6:   The article schema with a multi-link-class

larger than one is called a *multilink-class*. A multilink-class defined from {*A, B*} to {*C, D, E*} allows for link instances from any instance of *A* or *B* to any instance of *C, D* or *E*.

Figure 6 shows the "Article" schema with a multilink-class from {Subsection} to {Paragraph, Figure, Table}.

Linearizing Hypertexts Along Link Classes

The fine-grained model of the "Article" hierarchy down to single paragraphs, as outlined above (Figure 5), raises a new problem; a single paragraph is usually too small an information unit to be presented as a hypertext node of its own. Ideally, one would like to lump many paragraphs together into a larger unit. Taking this idea one step further, it would be nice to **linearize the whole hypertext** into a single, large document, mainly to make it accessible in printed form.

To cater for this need, HSDL link classes and link instances have an *embedding* mode. When activated, the location of the anchor in the source i-node is replaced with the whole content of the target i-node. Setting the link classes of some "main" hierarchy of a schema into embedding mode, will linearize the whole hypertext. Note that other, nonembedding links remain fully functional within the single "super" node (at least in HTML). HSDL checks for and prevents attempts to create circular embeddings.

Schema Evolution

As mentioned above, authoring is an opportunistic process. Therefore, to be acceptable, a schema-based approach has to provide a wide range of operators that allow authors to revise schema design decisions. In the database field this problem is known as *schema evolution* [3]. In HSDL the following schema evolution operations are supported:

Add a component to a class
> All existing instances of the augmented class are extended by a corresponding node.

Reposition a component in a class
> All existing instances are restructured accordingly.

Delete a component
> The corresponding nodes are also removed from all instances. Links defined on the deleted component are moved up to the deleted component's parent.

Reclass an instance
> An instance can be made to change class. If the instance is source or target to link instances for which no equivalent link classes exist in the new class, corresponding new link classes will be inserted automatically.

Reanchor a link instance
> The source and/or target i-nodes of a link instance can be moved to new i-nodes. If no

link class exists between the components corresponding to the changed i-node, a new link class will be inserted automatically.

Transitive derivation of link classes

A pair of transitive link classes can be used to derive a new link class (e.g. A->B and B->C ==> A->C). On the instance schema new link instances corresponding to the inner product between the existing link instances are inserted.

Triangular derivation of link classes

From A->B and A->C derive B->C or C->B, depending on the user's choice. Again, on the instance schema new link instances corresponding to the inner product between the existing link instances are inserted.

Split a class into two new classes

Any component of a class, except the root, may be selected to become a class of its own. Any subcomponents of the selected component as well as any link classes into or from these components are also carried over to the new class. A link class between the new class and the source class is created automatically. All instances are also split accordingly.

Merge two classes into a new class

If, first, two classes have exactly the same number of instances and, second, there is a link class between the two classes, the link instances of which form a bijective (one-to-one) mapping between the instances, then it is possible to merge the two classes along this link class (target moves into source). If the target component is not a root component, the target class will continue existing but the target component will *migrate* over to the source class.

Compilation into HTML

The translation of a schema into HTML is controlled by a series of programs in the programming language Scheme *[1]*. These programs,

called *expanders*, can be attached to any object in an HSDL schema. As an example, consider the default expander that generates the visible title of an HTML node:

```
(define (title node)
    (emit "<H1 ALIGN=CENTER><B>"
        (name (class node)) ":(name
            (instance node))
        "</B></H1>"))
```

The *n*-ary function `emit` writes all its arguments into the HTML file corresponding to the node that is currently being compiled. The function `name` generally returns the name of an HSDL object as a string. The functions `instance` and `class` respectively return the instance the node belongs to and the class that the node is an instance of.

Applying the expander above to the root node of the instance `Picasso` of class `Painter` would generate the HTML title:

```
<H1 ALIGN=CENTER><B>Painter: Picasso</
    B></H1>
```

Expander Shadowing

Since expanders can be attached to any HSDL object, it is easily possible to customize the appearance of certain classes or even instances. If, for example, we attach the following (re)definition of the `title` expander to the class `Painting`

```
(define (title node)
    (emit "<H3>" (name (instance node))
        "</H3>"))
```

then this new expander will *shadow* the global one defined above, and the title of the painting `The Sunflowers` will be expanded into:

```
<H3>The Sunflowers</H3>
```

Instead of shadowing, we could also say that unless an expander is locally defined, it will be *inherited* from the higher schema levels.

To start translation into HTML the following function is called in turn for each node of the current schema:

```
(define (generate node)
  (heade(string-append "<H4>"
   (name (class (target link)))
   "</H4><OL><LI>"))r node)
  (body node)
  (footer node)
  (for-each generate (included-
   children node))
  (if (not included?) (signature)))
```

Compilation is incremental; that is, after an initial full compilation only changed instances are translated into HTML files. Note that expander programming is not necessary as long as the default expanders built into the system produce acceptable HTML structures (and hence layout). Only users wishing to adapt the structure to their own needs will have to deal with expander programming.

Mapping I-Node Trees to Files

Some hypertext systems support composite nodes; that is, nodes that have internal addresses which can be directly jumped to. Since HTML is also in this category, we are offered the possibility of mapping composite HSDL instances to a smaller number of HTML files than the instance has i-nodes. Consider the class **Painter** of Figure 1: in a hypertext system without composites, each component would be mapped into its own node (or file). In systems which do support composite nodes, we might insert all five components into a single node, separating them by appropriate visual cues (rulers, titles, etc).

To support this feature, HSDL components and i-nodes have an inclusion status, which may be set to *included* or *excluded*. If all i-nodes of a painter are included, HSDL will linearize the tree depth-first and generate a single composite HTML file. If they are all excluded, HSDL would generate five HTML files. Since inclusion is a property of each individual node, any mapping from a composite node to one or more HTML files is possible. In every case appropriate navigation is ensured by the insertion of the necessary link anchors. By default, the i-nodes of an instance inherit the inclusion status from the

respective components. Therefore, it is possible to change the mapping of all instances of a class by modifying the inclusion status on the class schema. On the other hand, the user can override the inherited status for individual i-nodes. HTML nodes are saved in a directory tree. The names of the directories and HTML files try to reflect the schema as much as possible. For example, the root i-node of the instance **van Gogh** of class **Painter** in the schema **Gallery** is written into the HTML file **gallery/painter/vangogh. htm**.

HTML Anchor Generation

During compilation links have to be translated into HTML anchors. To this end, the HTML string ultimately building the anchor is divided into seven parts:

1. The anchor prefix **html-prefix**, which, to generate the index of a collection, would be typically set to the string "**<LI>**" so that it will appear as a list item in a corresponding HTML environment. To create such an HTML environment we distinguish between the first **html-prefix** in an index and all the following ones. For example, to start an HTML enumeration with a header displaying the name of the link's target class in "**<H4>**" size, the first prefix is set to the string returned by the evaluation of

    ```
    (string-append "<H4>"
    (name (class (target link)))
    "</H4><OL><LI>"))
    ```

2. The HTML anchor start tag and attribute ("**<A HREF=\ "**").

3. The URL (generated by HSDL).

4. The SGML close tag ("**>**") .

5. The anchor label **html-label**, which in indices is set to the string returned by the evaluation of (**name (target link))**) so that the name of the corresponding node will be inserted. Of course, any legal HTML anchor label is permissible. The ubiquitous

previous/next links between members of collections or hierarchies will usually have iconic labels, often images of arrows. To do this in HSDL, the link label expander is simply set to something like "`<IMG SRC="images/arrow-lt.gif">`".

6. The HTML anchor end tag ("`</A>`").

7. The anchor trailer `html-trailer`, which will usually be used to set punctuation marks after labels. For example, setting the prefix to the empty string `""` and the trailer to `",  "` will produce a comma-separated list of anchors in an index. In analogy to the special first prefix in a collection, the last trailer in a collection is different from all preceding ones. It is therefore easily possible to close HTML environments. The last trailer in an enumerated list will then consist of the string "`</OL>`".

To compile a link into an HTML anchor the function `expand-anchor` is called with the link as parameter:

```
(define (expand-anchor link)
(emit (html-prefix link)    ;; 1 Anchor
    prefix
"<A HREF=""           ;; 2 HTML start tag
(html-href link)      ;; 3 Link target
    address
"">"                  ;; 4 SGML close tag
(html-label link)     ;; 5 Anchor label
"</A>"                ;; 6 HTML end tag
(html-trailer link)   ;; 7 Anchor trailer
))
```

Related Work

HDM

Garzotto et al. have shown the importance and the feasibility of using a schema-based approach to AIL in several applications of their Hypertext Document Model (HDM) [7]. The HDM schema, though, includes a much larger number of concepts than the HSDL schema. In HDM there often are *many ways* to model identical access structures. The lack of orthogonality can significantly

raise the complexity of the implementation, especially with regard to schema evolution problems. It is unclear if HDM has been implemented up to the GUI level and if users can adapt hypertext generation to their own needs. HDM is used to generate ToolBook (Asymetrix Corp.) applications [2]. To our knowledge HDM has not yet been ported to generate HTML.

MacWeb

MacWeb, by Nanard & Nanard [9, 10], also uses a class schema (called a *Web of Types*) and an instance schema (the *MainWeb*). It has a GUI (for MacOS) and a scripting language (*WebTalk*). MacWeb generates an internal hypertext format browsable with the MacWeb viewer. MacWeb aims to provide the means to capture knowledge about the target domain that will be used at run time to generate documents dynamically. Dynamic documents are adapted or even created at run time under the control of the author's WebTalk scripts. Such an approach could also be applied to HTML. Instead of WebTalk scripts one would have to generate programs for whatever is the scripting language of the respective WWW server. Portability would be strongly restricted, since it is not (yet) possible to intertwine HTML with code (although HotJava's Java language surely is an interesting possibility in this context). Notice that in such approaches the problems of hypertext authoring are augmented by the problems of programming (debugging, runtime errors, etc). Programming expanders in HSDL is on a completely different level, since they are used solely to generate HTML. After compilation, an HSDL-generated hypertext is a standard HTML application. Schema updates are much more complex if they are to transform the hypertext structure *and* the semantics of the attached scripts consistently. To our knowledge MacWeb has not yet been ported to generate HTML.

Text to HTML Translators

As yet, the only tools supporting AIL in the HTML world were *text to HTML* translators. Such systems exist for a variety of text formats. Two of the most popular are WebMaker [13] (originally from CERN, now available from Harlequin Inc.) and LaTeX2HTML [6] by Nikos Drakos. Text to HTML translators start from a linear document and translate the ubiquitous part/chapter/section hierarchy into a corresponding HTML hierarchy. Only anchors supporting navigation within this hierarchy are generated automatically (e.g., previous, next, up, contents). References within the text (e.g., citations) are also translated over to functional HTML anchors, but such links cannot be counted as automatically generated, they are merely translated. It is possible to embed HTML anchors into the text, but such links are created individually and the author has no global view onto the current net topology. Therefore, it is probably an arduous task to embed nodes into multiple hierarchies. One of the advantages of the text to HTML approach is that a high quality paper version of the same hypertext will by definition always be available. In HSDL we follow the reverse route to achieve the same effect: We start from a network of nodes and produce a linear paper version by specifying the *linearization hierarchy* afterwards. Complex schemas will often have a whole range of possible linearization hierarchies. The text to hypertext approach does offer this level of flexibility.

Conclusion and Future Work

We believe that the HSDL schema-based approach to HTML authoring of large hypertexts offers the following advantages:

- Easy creation and maintenance of complex access structures:
  - True networks (not just hierarchies)
  - Operations on whole sets of links
  - Inherent referential integrity
  - Fast prototyping
- Two level representation: class schema (intentional representation) and instance schema (extensional representation)

- Advanced schema evolution operators

- Classes work like coarse-grained templates, enforcing coherence over sets of nodes representing objects of the same kind

- Large parts of the layout and, more importantly, of the access pathways generated automatically from structural information

- The embedded extension language Scheme allowing for full customization of the generated HTML structure and hence layout

- Layout changes applicable to *whole sets of nodes* at a time

- Easy linearization of hypertexts

- Powerful Graphical User Interface

- Built-in schema-aware HTML editor

Several medium-scale projects employing HSDL are currently under way. Most of them are commercial applications revolving around technical documentation and business-to-business WWW marketing. We are looking forward to report on our and our users' experiences in the coming months.

Future work

The interfaces between the internal HSDL modules (formalism, GUI, persistent storage, compiler, etc) have been carefully crafted to provide a maximum of orthogonality. The multiple inheritance capability of the implementation language CLOS (see below) has been essential to achieve this goal. We see the current HSDL implementation as the *kernel* of a system extensible in various directions:

Support for CSCW (Computer Supported Cooperative Work):
    Obviously, the edition of large hypertexts will often be the task of a whole group of authors. Hence, we have to deal with the synchronization problems typical of CSCW. We believe that the easiest way to achieve

this is to use a database as the persistent storage and the database locking mechanisms to enforce consistency.

Versioning:

Effective version management for large bodies of information is *de rigueur* for any system claiming AIL capabilities. Like for CSCW, using a database as persistent storage should provide a firm foundation for the extension of HSDL with version management.

Improved Instance Schema Editor:

The current instance schema editor (see Figure 2) is not really well suited for AIL. A screen containing hundreds of interconnected items will always look clogged, no matter how cleverly they are arranged. In the short run we will be implementing an instance browser inspired on the class browsers usually found in object oriented programming environments (e.g. Smalltalk, CLOS).

As a medium term goal, we think that the article on *fisheye views* by Sarkar and Brown [11] offers some intriguing perspectives well worth exploring.

Appendix: Miscellaneous Implementation Details

Persistent Schema Storage

The schema is stored in an SGML file, tagged with a custom HSDL DTD.

Implementation Language/Platform

HSDL was implemented in CLOS, the Common Lisp Object System, in Allegro Common Lisp for Windows (ACL/W 2.0) by Franz Inc. HSDL has been tested under Windows 3.1, Windows95 and Windows NT.

Performance

In a typical application, the compiler will generate approximately 10 HTML files per second when running on a 90MHz Pentium processor (8MB RAM).

This paper has been produced with HSDL. A metahypertext describing the corresponding schema. Further HSDL features can be found at *http://faui80.informatik.uni-erlangen.de/IMMD8/staff/Kesseler/WWW4/www4meta.html.* ∎

References

1. Harold Abelson and G. J. Sussman. *Structure and Interpretation of Computer Programs.* MIT Press, Cambridge, 1985.

2. Andrea Caloini. "Matching Hypertext Models to Hypertext Systems: a Compilative Approach." In Lucarella et al. [8], pp. 91-101.

3. Jay Banerjee, Won Kim, Hyoung-Joo Kim, and Henry F. Korth. "Semantics and implementation of schema evolution in object-oriented databases." In *Proceedings of the ACM SIGMOD Conference,* 1987.

4. Emily Berk and Joseph Devlin, editors. *Hypertext/Hypermedia Handbook.* Software Engineering Series. MGraw-Hill Publishing Company, 1991.

5. J. Conklin. "Hypertext: An introduction and survey." *IEEE Computer,* 20(9):17-41, 1987.

6. Nikos Drakos. "From text to hypertext: A post-hoc rationalisation of LaTeX2HTML." 1994. (Available via WWW UCSTRI Computer Science Index: *http://www.cs.indiana.edu/ctr/search*).

7. Franca Garzotto, Paolo Paolini, Daniel Schwabe, and Mark Bernstein. *Tools for Designing Hyperdocuments,* pp. 179-207. In Berk and Devlin [4], 1991.

8. D. Lucarella, J. Nanard, M. Nanard, and P. Paolini, editors. *ACM Echt 92: Proceedings of the ACM Conference on Hypertext.* ACM Press, 1992.

9. Jocelyne Nanard and Marc Nanard. "Using Structured types to incorporate knowledge in hypertext." In *Proceedings of the Hypertext '91 Conference,* pp. 329-342, 1991.

10. Jocelyne Nanard and Marc Nanard. "Should anchors be typed too? An experiment with MacWeb." In *Proceedings of the Hypertext '93 Conference,* pages 51--62, 1993.

11. Manojit Sarkar and Marc H. Brown. "Graphical fisheye views." *Communications of the ACM,* 37(12):73--84, December 1994.

12. Norbert Streitz, Jörg Haake, Jörg Hannemann, Andreas Lemke, Wolfgang Schuler, Helge Schütt, and Manfred Thüring. "SEPIA: A Cooperative Hypermedia Authoring Environment." In Lucarella et al. [8], pages 11-22.

13. The Harlequin Group Limited. *WebMaker User's Manual*, 1995.

About the Author

Marcus Kesseler
[*http://faui80.informatik.uni-erlangen.de/ IMMD8/staff/Kesseler/kesseler.html*]

University of Erlangen-Nürnberg
IMMD VIII—Artificial Intelligence
Am Weichselgarten 9 / D-91058 Erlangen / Germany
kesseler@immd8.informatik.uni-erlangen.de

RULES FOR EXTENDING
A WWW CLIENT
THE SYMPOSIA API

Jean Paoli

Abstract

There is a great need for WWW clients to be extensible. The availability of the source code of some popular browsers (such as Mosaic) led many people to slice the original Mosaic or CERN code and to add diverse custom code for specific applications. In our view, a WWW authoring/viewing environment must be extensible enough to allow the building of interactive document authoring environments in which the user is able to access all relevant documentary information on the Web and incorporate it directly in to his/her document. Symposia (shipping since March 1995) is a joint INRIA/GRIF S.A. project for building a cooperative WYSIWYG authoring tool for the WWW. Symposia will soon be shipped with an API that we have developed that presents a set of solid principles for extending the user interface, document management, network extensibility, and interactive behavior of document fragments in a WWW client. In this paper we will discuss the advantages gained from basing the extensibility of a WWW client on a generic structured environment. We will present different ways proposed today to extend WWW clients: Forms/CGI and Java, and will compare them with the Symposia API.
Keywords: *Extensibility, authoring, symposia, structured documents, SGML, API, document oriented user interfaces*

Symposia

Symposia is a WYSIWYG authoring tool that enables you to create and modify HTML and SGML documents directly on the WWW. Symposia was developed by GRIF S.A. and INRIA as part of the European effort for the creation of more powerful tools for the World Wide Web.

Symposia is built on top of the Grif WYSIWYG SGML editor that allows files based on any DTD to be loaded, edited, and saved in native SGML format. Functions for handling each of the different HTML versions have been incorporated into the Grif software and the SGML parser used has been modified so as to accept HTML documents that are not strictly valid.

Thanks to the expandability of the Grif software, the CERN/W3C network library has been integrated with the SGML Editor, and OpenURL and SaveURL commands have been added by using the PUT element of the http protocol. This allows

documents to be created and saved directly on remote servers. Various cooperative strategies have been studied to allow collaborative authoring on the WWW and a simple strategy (lock/unlock file) has been developed [5].

Special user-friendly editing commands (click-and-point) for creating and modifying anchors have been written and links can be followed immediately after being created through the network. The tool accepts each of the HTML "dialects" and any other SGML DTD could be incorporated in the tool using the standard features of the Grif environment. This would allow the creation, editing, and remote saving of documents by multiple authors on the network in their original SGML format.

Further work is already underway in the field of collaborative authoring on the WWW, including the incorporation of annotated documents, handling large documents, support for different versions and the interactive incorporation of various fragments of data from different servers into one document.

A freeware version of Symposia can be downloaded from the INRIA WWW server at *http:// symposia.inria.fr* . A Pro version is commercialized by GRIF S.A.

Extensibility Criteria

The design of user interfaces to access or modify data on the WWW raises the need for WWW clients to support new data type handling, configurability, programmability, and open-endedness, as described in the following list:

- *Data type handling*: the support for new types of data (such as graphics or sound) or handling of new tags or attributes.

- *Configurability*: the adding, removing, disabling, or redefining of menus and editing functions.

- *Programmability*: the use of application-specific code to access internal data structures so as to modify, protect or generate parts of documents.

- *Open-endedness*: the possibility to access other applications or accept new or different network protocols for accessing data.

Extensibility is said to be dynamic if extensibility code can be loaded, installed and executed directly without rebuilding the software. It is said to be static if recompilation or rebinding of the software is needed to access the extended functions.

In WWW clients, extensibility could also more specifically address imaging or text processing, depending on the type of application needed.

We will examine in detail in the following section the characteristics of the extensibility features of Symposia. In the section called "Some Applications" we will give a few examples of applications which extend the functionalities of Symposia on the WWW, and in the section called "Related Methods for Extensibility" we will compare the extensibility methods of Symposia with the major ones proposed today for WWW clients. Finally, we will outline the conclusion the characteristics of the extensibility of Symposia with regard to the extensibility criteria presented here.

Extensibility in Symposia

Handling New Tags

Handling new tags in a WWW client raises the need to consider how to extend the client to parse, format and edit new tags.

Symposia is built on top of the Grif WYSIWYG SGML editor that handles generic structured documents [3].

Structured documents are documents that are internally organized according to their content. They follow Document Type Definitions that specify the logical elements that can be used in a document and how these elements may be arranged in a hierarchical way. New tags (represented syntactically by a start tag and an end tag) are manipulated as elements and can themselves contain other elements.

Incorporating new tags in Symposia involves adding the new tags to the HTML DTD supported by Symposia and compiling it using an external tool named Grif Application Builder. Grif Application Builder generates multiple parameterization files which enable Symposia to parse and edit the new tags.

- *Parsing the new tags*. The Symposia parser is an SGML parser that has been relaxed to support most of the common errors found in HTML documents created before the HTML 2.0 DTD became established as a standard [3]. The parser is still an SGML parser in the sense that automatic parsing rules are derived from the DTD by Grif Application Builder.

An interesting feature of this step is the possibility to define a different mapping of the structures defined in the HTML DTD and the structures that will be manipulated by Symposia.

- *Editing the new tags.* Structured editing is derived automatically from the DTD and valid contextual insertion menus are proposed to the user to create, modify or delete tags according to the DTD.

  HTML specific tailored commands could be added to the generic editing commands generated automatically by Grif Application Builder, using the Symposia API described in the sections called "Activity Trading" and "Data Tree Handling." For example, specific commands that manipulate the <A> anchor tag and its attributes have been added to facilitate the manipulation of anchors by automatically filling the URL HREF attribute when a new link to a document is created by the end user.

- *Formatting the new tags.* Document Type Definitions do not specify how the elements will be presented. In Symposia, a physical presentation on the screen or on paper can be associated with the logical organization of a document, as described in the DTD.

  A set of presentation rules, written in a separate file, is used by Symposia to associate presentation with structure in a declarative style sheet language named P. Multiple presentation files can be written for one DTD and two different presentation files have been written to present the HTML 2.0 DTD in a Mosaic/Netscape style, and in a presentation more suited for printing (by generating headers, footers, and page numbering).

  Formatting new tags in Symposia simply involves adding a few additional formatting rules in the P style sheet presentation file used for the HTML DTD.

In an approach that represents information and data as documents, we think that it is important to develop and make extensive use of SGML to formalize these documents [12]. Documentary

data are more clearly identified by semantic tags [9]. Semantic tags are used to precisely identify corporate or industry-specific information such as motors, product parts, transistors, or other objects that require a very precise description. This is one of the strong points of SGML and there is always a need for mission-critical data to be formalized and stored using such markup.

Because Symposia makes use of Grif SGML Editor's system for handling generic structured documents, incorporating new DTDs in Symposia is simply a matter of following the process previously described.

User Interface

Because the document concept plays such an important role in the WWW, it is only logical that extensibility rules for a WWW client consider carefully the extensibility of the user interface, not only around a document (for tailoring menus or dialog boxes), but essentially within the document itself.

In fact, a lot of the interaction between the end user and WWW servers is done through documents. For example, in Mosaic or Netscape:

- When an *error message* has to be displayed to a user (for example when a file can not be downloaded), an HTML error document is generated and displayed.

- Transparent areas defined by HTML tags on top of portions of images are tranformed into *active areas*: a user double-click can launch complex actions through CGI scripts.

- Data is typed within *forms* defined by HTML tags. If the user clicks on a specific tag, the form is validated and the data is collected and sent to a remote server.

In the above examples, the integration of multiple tools is done in a seamless way for the end user: data is generated within a document and sent from tool to tool, from server to server. The document is used as the natural vehicle between users and computers [6].

This kind of user interface is called Document Oriented user Interface (DOI): basic user operations on the document launch tools which operate distinctively on the selected portion of the document. We call this the document paradigm because complex applications could be disguised as document component behavior.

This user interface philosophy has been endorsed by major companies: Microsoft is increasingly committed to OLE and Apple; IBM, Novell, and others are creating and supporting OpenDoc. OLE and OpenDoc, although there are some differences between them, are both basically aimed at providing DOIs.

WWW clients must allow us to build, develop, and make extensive use of this user interface approach.

A WWW client can be likened to an interactive document environment in which the user has everything at hand to enable him to access relevant documentary information and to interact with other processes. The WWW client must constantly rearrange the data resulting from these interactions in such a way as to present the information intelligently to the user.

This environment is characterized by:

- Users who are constantly presented with on-screen documents

- A large volume of user interaction

- Many tools and processes that could be involved

- Many document fragments to be arranged dynamically

This environment reinforces the notion of content. Individual applications become relatively less important because many of them are used to build a single document.

- In the case of large documents edited by multiple authors on the network, the complete document could be browsed in a unique window. However, specific files or fragments could be locked by a user and edited—in place—in the same window.

- In an illustrated parts list catalog, keying the content of a part reference could automatically query a database for the part description while keying the same content in the title of the document would do nothing. A Database menu could also be available for the part reference to query the network and give the list of valid choices.

- When putting together a business offer, the action of keying in some text could turn on incorporation of pieces of documents available on a remote server such as a product description, bill of material, or contractual items.

An analysis of the key chararactistics of such environments shows that:

- The monolithic document concept disappears completely: We are in a world of fragments. Fragments are everywhere and the end user sees them. Fragments are assembled today in one document and tomorrow in another. The most important concept is no longer the document itself but the fragments that are used to construct the document.

- The user interface should be data oriented and no longer fixed uniformly throughout a complete document: the multiple fragments that a document might contain could each have their own behavior.

- Data exchange protocols must exist to be able to interchange fragments between tools from a server to a client in a transparent way (without asking the end user).

Two different but mutually complementary approaches could be considered:

- When building a document, you create or get frames and put them into a document window. When you select a frame, the appropriate tool to manipulate it becomes available. You see the document as a whole in the same window but a software mechanism distinguishes mouse clicks, menus, and similar features for each frame. This approach has been adopted by OLE, Open-Doc, and Java [7]. Each frame is managed by a different tool and is totally independant from the others.

- The second approach is to extend the notion of structured documents so that in the same document different structured elements can be managed by manipulating different tools or by using different programs. Semantic tags are used to identify more precisely corporate or industry specific information.

Because the system knows more about the semantic of this data, it can more easily identify what to launch and what to help. This is why semantic SGML tags constitute the ideal fragment of information that can be produced, manipulated, and exchanged over the network on the WWW by authoring tools wired to the network and based on a DOI.

Symposia implements the second approach.

Activity Tracking

Implementing activity tracking

Extensibility of a WWW client means that multiple tools become available together, even available in a single document. To be able to use structured documents (by scripting them) as user interfaces the issue of how to specify behavior (or "activity tracking") in a document becomes the key issue [11].

What is generally referred to as "writing scripts" is composed of three subjects:

- "Events," which are things such as a user click or a content modification

- "Naming," which allows the script to address and fetch data or collections of data (this fragment, this first character): addressed in Symposia by the implementation of a struc-

tured API (see the section called "Data Tree Handling")

- A "glue" language (procedural, object-oriented or declarative), which specifies how to deal with and to modify the data: addressed in Symposia using the C programming language.

We will address here more specifically the first subject.

Events must be clearly separated between user interface events and semantic events. User interface events pertain only to the state of the graphical user interface, not directly to its content. User interface events include mouse-clicks and keystrokes. For example, VisualBasic identifies Click, DblClick, DragOver, GetFocus, MouseDown, etc.

Semantic events pertain directly to the data content model. The list below contains just a few examples of semantic events:

- When a piece of data is constructed interactively by an end user or by another tool, an application must receive (or send) notifying events that indicate when elements or attributes are created, deleted, or modified.

- Two events for each basic structured operation are necessary: one before the operation occurs (PRE) and one after (POST). This is necessary to prepare an application to perform action before or after the modification of the data.

- Event notifications should also be received when the user decides to use a new entity (for example, by inserting a new image). The application must be able to recognize this in order to be able to generate an entity declaration.

- Events should also be generated when the value of a required attribute has been deleted by the end user (this is interactivity!): the application needs to know this to be able to ask the user (or the tool) to generate a new value for the required attribute.

- The application must know if the value of an attribute in an instance has been provided by default (by the DTD definition) or been assigned by the end user.

The definition of these events should contain the list of each event accompanied by their parameters: Applications should receive each individual edit separately and have access, in parameters, to the place and the context where the modification occurred.

Activity tracking in Symposia

In Symposia, our approach to activity tracking is an object-oriented approach for tailoring the behavior of SGML elements: SGML elements receive event messages reflecting the user interaction and in response they execute an appropriate action. Actions are written in C code (see the section called "Data Tree Handling").

Basic user interaction generates messages but the most important is that structure and content changes of the elements generate messages. The supported message list contains almost all of the SGML ESIS events related to the creation and modification of SGML elements and attributes. Content modification such as PCDATA text modification also generates messages to the appropriate element.

Associating messages to structured documents. The I (Interface) language was developed to allow the binding of messages to elements, to specify which actions should be called, and to define new messages and menu items. The syntax for specifying the parameterization of the behavior of SGML elements is [10, 9] :

```
ELEMENTNAME:
Message1: Action1;
Message2: Action2;
```

This indicates that Action1 has to be executed when the event message Message1 is sent to the element named ELEMENTNAME .

Messages can be associated with structured documents on an element basis.

Messages are bound to elements in an I file:

Each element records its interest in receiving a message in the RULES section.

An I file contains the following sections:

APPLICATION
  Defines which DTD the application is designed for, e.g., HTML2.0

DEFAULT
  Defines defaults actions bound to messages for all elements and attributes of the DTD

RULES
  Defines a set of messages and actions for each element

ATTRIBUTES
  Defines a set of messages and actions for each attribute

MENUS
  Defines all the menus and menu items presented in the menu bar, and a message for each item, on a DTD basis

By using one or multiple I files, a specific extension could be activated only on a certain type of element and on a specific type of user interaction (such as a double click on the element or the creation or the deletion of another element).

Standard messages available. This section gives a few examples of the standard messages that are provided in Symposia:

This list describes element messages. Here, messages are sent when a menu item is activated. Examples of this type of message include:

StdCut
  Indicates that the Cut item of the Edit menu has been activated

StdExit
  Indicates that the Exit item of the File menu has been activated

Messages are also sent following any user action other than activation of a menu item. Examples of this type of message include:

`StdSelect`

Indicates that an element in the document has just been selected

`StdTextModify`

Indicates that the modification of a text element (by inserting or deleting characters) has just been ended

`StdFollowLink`

Indicates that the user has double-clicked (or another standard interaction) and intends to follow a link starting from this element

`StdCreateNew`

Indicates that the element has just been created by the user using the standard Insert dialog box or by a carriage return

This list describes attribute messages. Here. messages are sent when an attribute is set on or removed from an element using the standard Attribute dialogbox. Examples of such messages include:

`StdAttrCreate`

Indicates that the attribute has just been set on the element using the Apply button in the Attribute dialog box.

`StdAttrModify`

Indicates that the value of the attribute has just been modified using the Apply button in the Attribute dialog box.

`StdAttrDelete`

Indicates that the attribute has just been removed from the element using the Remove button in the Attribute dialog box.

Replacing or refining standard edit functions. Each action attached to a message could replace, precede, or be executed after the corresponding standard Symposia edit function.

Thus, standard messages could be used as follows:

Message.Pre:TheAction

The action precedes the Symposia standard edit function

Message:TheAction

The action replaces the Symposia standard edit function

Message.Post:TheAction

The action follows the Symposia standard edit function

Using this syntax for a specific element, one could choose to override or to refine the standard Symposia editing command.

Other extensibility features. By using a set of API functions, it is possible to extend the user interface of Symposia by adding menus or dialog boxes. In this case, new messages are also defined for each new menu, and activity tracking is extended to these new elements of the user interface.

Other approaches to activity tracking

SGML

The SGML standard (ISO 8879) defines what is valid input to a parser and as such defines what an SGML parser must do. An SGML parser receives parsing events (ESIS) that are not sufficient to define activity tracking. This comes from the fact that parsing is commonly viewed as a batch operation and that what we are addressing here is interactivity: the way ESIS was defined is more compatible with the concept of batch parsing than with the interactive construction of SGML data.

HyTime

The base module of the HyTime standard [4] contains a section (Base module, 6.5.7) on activity tracking policy (attribute list form all-act). Six possible activities are described for an object: create, modify, link, access, unlink, delete. When considered together with the ESIS definition of low-level parser events that enable the parser to recognize markup constructs, we have here a framework that allows us to establish a good definition of activity tracking.

OpenDoc

In OpenDoc [2], scriptability is considered as a key issue and there is full support for the definition of semantic events, based on the content model of a Part. It would be interesting to investigate whether OSA could support the SGML content model.

Data Tree Handling

Symposia is built on top of the Grif WYSIWYG SGML editor that handles generic structured documents. Data are handled internally following the principles of structured editing and are represented as a set of in-memory tree constructs. These tree representations are updated incrementally when the user modifies the document.

Writing actions associated to messages

As we said in the section called "Activity Tracking in Symposia," to extend Symposia, actions are associated to messages in an I association file. These actions are executed in response to a user interaction and are implemented by the writer of the extension as C functions with the standard action function signature, as here:

```
void ExtensionAction(Element element)
{
/* Place user code here       */
/* Possibility to access      */
/* internal Sympiosia Structures */
/* using Symposia API         */
/* Could also call http/network */
/* functions and retrieve     */
/*          external data      */
}
```

The writer of the extension can call the Symposia API that enables him/her to access the HTML/SGML fragment, to read its content, to modify it, or to insert other fragments.

Services provided by the Symposia API

The Symposia API provides a programming interface to the HTML/SGML structure and content. The API supports element and attribute creation and manipulation, content modification, structural searches, and incorporation of fragments into the document.

Tree handling. The API includes functions that make it possible to create a new element, to modify its content, to create an element from a HTML/SGML fragment, to move through the tree structure, to search through the tree structure, or to define an element in the document as read only:

```
Element GtNewElement(document,
    elementType);
Element GtSetTextContent(element,
    content);
Element GtOpenBuffer(document, dtdname,
    buffer);
Element GtGetFirstChild(parent);
Element
    GtSearchTypedElement(searchedType,
    scope, element);
Element GtSetAccessRight(element,
    right);
```

Attribute handling. Other functions in the API make it possible to create a new attribute, to set its value, and to attach it to an element:

```
Attribute GtNewAttribute(attributeType);
void GtSetAttributeValue(attribute,
    value, element);
void GtAttachAttributeContent(element,
    attribute);
```

Listeners handling. The API includes functions that permit it to register a new source of input such as sockets or FIFO:

```
void GtRegisterListener(fd, callback);
```

View handling. The API includes functions to handle the multiple dynamic views defined by the Symposia style sheet mechanism, such as opening a view containing a list of all the anchors in a document.

```
View GtOpenView(document, viewName);
```

Network Handling

Symposia, as an authoring tool, is a WWW client and is wired on the network. Symposia has been designed to facilitate the creation and the maintenance of online data published directly on the Web. Symposia incoporates the CERN (now W3C) network library, and by using the Open URL and Save URL (using the PUT element of the http protocol) commands, one can directly follow a link or save a document on a remote server. For all these reasons, it was important to permit a great deal of flexibility of the network handling in Symposia.

The Symposia API uses a very short list of functions implemented on top of the network library:

The set of functions that call network services is:

- void GtLoadUrlIntoBuffer(char *url, char **pbuffer, in pNbCar);

- int GtSaveBufferToUrl(char *buffer, int nbCar, char *url);

- int GtPost(char *url, char *buffer, in nbCar, char **pbuffer, in *pNbCar);

The writer of an extension could call, in the C action code, these API functions to load over the network the content of a URL or to save remotely in a URL the content of a string buffer (which can contain, for example, HTML/SGML fragments of data).

The set of functions that has to be implemented in the network library to call Symposia for feedback is:

- HTStream *WWWPresent(HTRequest *req, void *param, HTFormat input_ format, HTFormat output_format, HTStream output_stream);

- void WWWAlert (const char *msg);

- void WWWProgress (const char *msg);

- WWWPromptUserNameAndPassword(const char *msg, char ** username, char **password);

The extensibilty of Symposia, with regard to network handling, is based on two characteristics:

- Access to documents over the network is entirely handled by the network library, and all protocols supported by the network library are automatically supported by Symposia (including ftp, gopher or others that might be added).

- Because Symposia relies on just a few of the network library API calls, it is very easy to use another network library by implementing the 7 function calls on top of the new one.

Some Applications

Online applications could be envisioned that make use of the extensibility features of Symposia for both the authoring or viewing process. These applications could be based on an HTML environment or on another SGML DTD.

For example, when creating manuals, an author often needs to gain access to information that has been created previously. This may involve taking fragments of data from various sources and integrating them into a single document.

The viewing process might require that the viewing tool provide the response to a user query regarding information stored on the network. In order to be accurate, the reply provided by the viewer should take account of certain constraints such as data contained in the document. The query could then be refined if such data was encoded within the document as SGML data.

The two applications that follow are examples of applications that have already been implemented using Symposia.

HTML 2.0 Forms

The HTML 2.0 support for Forms (editing and viewing) has been implemented in Symposia thanks to its extensibility:

```
<!-- The form HTML2.0 definition
     contains multiple inputs-->
<!-- Inputs attributes have been turned
     in memory-->
<!-- to elements to facilitate
     interactive editing-->
<!-- Inputs are read/written in their
     original form-->

<!ELEMENT form - -

  (Radio_Input,...
 >
<!ATTRIBUTE Radio_Input CHECKED
   (CHECKED) #IMPLIED)>
```

The description of the presentation of the radio element is expressed in the P presentation (style sheet) language of Symposia that can modify the presentation of an element The description of the behavior of the radio element is expressed in an I file as follows:

```
Radio_Input:
StdFollowLink: HTML2RadioAction;
```

The action HTML2RadioAction is executed when the message "StdFollowLink" (A Double click of the end user) is sent to the element Radio_Input:

```
HTML2RadioAction(Element element) {
/* This is written by calling the C
   structured API*/
/* Of Symposia on the HTML in memory
   instance */
For all elements Radio before or after
   element
{Search for attribute CHECKED
Remove the attribute CHECKED}
Create and Set the attribute CHECKED on
   element
}
```

Parts Lists

The previous example was built in the HTML environment. We give here another example using an SGML environment that models an illustrated parts list catalog. In an illustrated parts list catalog, keying the content of a part reference could automatically query a remote server for the part description, while keying the same content in the title of the document would do nothing. A Database menu could also be available for the part reference to give, through the network, the list of valid choices.

```
<!-- A Part List contains multiple
     block items-->
<!-- which describes parts and
     assemblies      -->
<!ELEMENT partlist (blockitem)*>
<!ATTRIBUTES partlist URL %URL>

<!ELEMENT blockitem - -

(supplier, supplierref, partref,
type, expire?, quantity)       >
```

The part list has an attribute that indicates the URL of a database (or a CGI script) that gives back the blockitem SGML fragment corresponding to a particular partref.

The description of the behavior of the partref element may be expressed as follows:

```
partref:
StdMsgTextModify: ApplicationTextModify;
```

The action ApplicationTextModify is executed when the message StdTextModify (text has been modified) is sent to the element partref.

```
ApplicationTextModify (Element element)
    {
Fetch The Value of PARTREF
Move up to the partlist element
Fetch its URL
Query through the network with the URL
    and the PARTREF
for receiving the corresponding
    BLOCKITEM
Move to the element SUPPLIER
Fill in this element from the Query
    Result
Move to the element SUPPLIERREF
Fill in this element from the Query
    Result
...
}
```

One has to understand that this action is executed (and a query is sent on the network) only when a user types in a partref number in a partref element.

Related Methods for Extensibility

CGI & Forms

The Common Gateway Interface (CGI) is a standard for interfacing external applications with information servers such as HTTP or Web servers [8]. A CGI program, written in any programming language such as C, or in interpreted languages like perl scripts, could be installed on a Web server and executed when a WWW client tries to access the program by its URL. The CGI program is then executed and its result is an HTML document that is sent to the WWW client.

Usually, CGI programs are executed through an HTML 2.0 Form tag [1]. HTML 2.0 Form tags are used as user interface objects in a WWW client to capture user preferences or user data and to execute on a remote server an attached CGI script with these data as parameters.

This method is very simple and works very well but has certain shortcomings:

- Every time the user makes use of the extended functionality, there is a need to contact the server and wait for the reply. For example, an online chess application would require a server request every time a move was made. In Symposia, the extended functionality could be installed locally, doing away with the need to contact the server after each event.

- New data retrieved from the network cannot be integrated into the current document, because feedback from the server is always received in the form of a separate document. In Symposia, API functions can be used to parse and integrate HTML/SGML fragments into the current document. In this way, CGI

scripts could be used together with Symposia to fetch fragments of documents rather then entire documents.

- Apart from the input fields contained in the HTML forms, there is no way to use data from the current document as the basis for a server query. In Symposia, activity tracking could define very precisely which elements are to be used as containers to be interfaced with server queries.

The method used by Symposia offers multiple advantages but requires a certain amount of programming in C and is therefore less simple to implement.

Java and HotJava

Java [7] is an object-oriented programming language used for the creation of distributed, executable applications. Java was defined by Sun Microsystems, which has also implemented HotJava, a WWW browser that can execute applets. An applet is a Java program that can be included in an HTML page, much like an image can be included.

Java applets are an excellent example of extensibility and have already been implemented in a wide range of useful applications, and which present the following advantages:

- HotJava automatically installs locally in the client the executable content (the Java applet) retrieved from a remote server. There is no need for recompilation. In Symposia, the C code needs to be compiled and linked in order to install the extension.

- Several applets can be installed within the same document in different frames and user interaction is redirected automatically to each applet.

However,

- Java has not been designed to let applets make use of document content, and document content cannot be used to activate or interact with a Java applet (there is no support for activity tracking on HTML/SGML structures). In Symposia, activity tracking is implemented and the extension has full access to elements of the document structure.

- Each applet handles its data too independently from other applets, or from document content. For example, the HTML 2.0 Forms could not be implemented as a Java applet that produces and checks interactively the HTML Form elements and attributes.

The greatest advantage of Java is undoubtedly the ease with which external applications are installed and accessed over the network. Symposia needs to evolve towards this kind of approach where the actions, currently defined in C, could be interpreted instead of compiled.

Conclusion

It is essential for WWW clients to be extensible if we are to be able to build integrated authoring environments on the WWW. These authoring environments must be adapted to the type of documents that we want to produce.

We have seen the advantages to be gained from basing the extensibility of a WWW client on a structured authoring environment such as that offered by Symposia, where data is clearly identified and where tools can access and work directly with these elements of data over the network.

By adopting a structured approach to information authoring and retrieval on the WWW, we can access and manipulate intelligently on both the client and the server sites the data which is semantically identified.

Such an approach enables us to build Document Oriented user Interfaces for the documentary data manipulated on the Web.

Symposia must evolve so that the installation and use of its extensions can be achieved with as much ease as is currently possible with the Java extensions. ■

Acknowledgments

We would like to thank V. Quint, I. Vatton from INRIA, L. Pedersen, B.V. Sydow and A. Slominski from the EUROMATH project, and P. Telegone from GRIF S.A. for the very interesting and fruitful discussions which have allowed the definition of needs for the extensibility of Symposia. We would also like to thank Stuart Culshaw at Grif S. A. for his help in reviewing this paper.

References

1. T. Berners-Lee and D. Connolly, "Hypertext Markup Language Specifications—2.0," Internet Draft, *http://www.w3.org/hypertext/WWW/MarkUp/html-spec/ html-spec_2.html*, May 1995.

2. The OpenDoc Design Team OpenDoc, "The Required Reading Packet," *http://www.info.apple.com/dev/du/intro_to_opendoc/iod0_index.html*, 1994.

3. V. Quint, C. Roisin, I. Vatton, "A structured authoring environment for the World-Wide Web," *Proceedings of the Third International World Wide Web Conference*, edited by Computer Networks and ISDN systems, pp. 831-840, April 1995.

4. S. DeRose, D. Durand, "Making Hypermedia Work, A User's Guide to HyTime," Kluwer Academic Publishers, 1994.

5. J.Paoli, "Cooperative work on the network: edit the WWW!," *Proceedings of the Third International World Wide Web Conference*, edited by Computer Networks and ISDN systems, pp. 841-847, April 1995.

6. E.Bier and A.Goodisman, "Documents as User Interfaces," EP 90, *Proceedings of the International Conference on Electronic Publishing, Document Manipulation & Typography*, R. Furuta ed., pp. 249-262, Cambridge University Press, September 1990.

7. SUN Microsystems, "The Java Programming Language," *http://java.sun.comp*, May 1995.

8. NCSA httpd Development Team, "The Common Gateway Interface," *http://hoohoo.ncsa.uiuc.edu/cgi*, May 1994

9. J.Paoli, "Creating SGML objects for End-Users—Establishing SGML in an interactive world," Pro-

ceedings of SGML & '94, GCA, ed., pp. 323-333, December 1994.

10. V. Quint, I. Vatton, "Making Structured Documents Active," *Electronic Publishing—Origination, Dissemination and Design*, vol. 7, num. 3, 1994.

11. D.B. Terry and D. G. Baker, "Active Tioga Documents: an Exploration of Two Paradigms," Electronic Publishing—Origination, Dissemination and Design, 105-122, May 1990 .

12. C. M. Sperberg-McQueen, Robert F. Goldstein, "HTML to the Max—A Manifesto for Adding SGML Intelligence to the World-Wide Web," *http://www. ncsa.uiuc.edu/SDG/IT94/Proceedings/Autools/ sperberg-mcqueen/sperberg.html*, October 1994.

About the Author

Jean Paoli is the Technical Director and a co-founder of GRIF S.A., a leader in the creation of SGML authoring tools. He supervizes the development and implementation of Grif's WYSIWYG SGML products, the latest being Grif SGML Editor for Macintosh and GATE, an interactive SGML API. Paoli manages GRIF S.A. application consulting groups as well as research and strategic planning toward the Grif technology.

He is currently driving a joint INRIA/GRIF S.A. project for the development of Symposia, a WWW editor which enables collaborative authoring on the network.

Paoli draws on more than 10 years of experience in the structured editing field. Before co-founding GRIF S.A., he worked on structured editors for programming languages with the leading French software house SEMA-GROUP and France's leading computing research institute, INRIA. Jean holds a specialization in software engineering and is graduated from the Ecole Nationale des Ponts et Chaussées.
Jean.Paoli@grit.fr

THE DISTRIBUTED LINK SERVICE
A TOOL FOR PUBLISHERS, AUTHORS, AND READERS

Leslie Carr, David De Roure, Wendy Hall, Gary Hill

Abstract

The World Wide Web is a distributed service for hypermedia document retrieval. Adding a complementary hypermedia link service, from which clients can make enquiries of distributed sets of link databases, provides extra functionality for users: readers gain more subject-specific content-based media-independent links, authors gain freedom and flexibility in creating, composing, and reusing their resources, and publishers can repurpose their information assets for different audiences. This paper describes a hypermedia link service that is based entirely on standard Web browsers and servers and is being used successfully in a spectrum of Web projects. **Keywords:** *Open hypermedia, links, republishing*

Distributed Link Service

The DLS is a new service which can be used to provide hypermedia links for users of information environments, in particular the World Wide Web. In the same way that a client connects to a remote Web server to access a document, DLS allows the client to connect to a link server to request a set of links to apply to the data in a document (as Figure 1 illustrates). From an abstract viewpoint it provides a hypermedia link service which can be used alongside, but separately from, the WWW's document data service: in practice the link service is mediated by the WWW (in HTTP messages), and implemented by CGI processes located on Web servers.

The provision of an independent link service is designed to allow any information environment to be augmented with hypermedia functionality, *whether or not it provides link-following facilities itself.* The WWW, of course, has a well-established method for expressing links as attributes of its native document format, and so the link service will provide a complementary set of links on top of those standard facilities. By contrast, a simple text editor (such as Window's Notepad) has no built-in hypertext links, and so the link service provides an otherwise non-existent service to such users. Without a link service, Web users can

follow links from HTML documents or "image-mapped" pictures into dead-end media such as spreadsheets, CAD documents or text; with the link service they can also follow links out of these media again [6].

Why a Link Service?

A link service can provide several practical benefits to information systems: it can act as an adjunct to provide hypermedia facilities for applications without requiring a rewrite of the applications themselves, and, by allowing links to be manipulated as independent objects, can aid in the document maintenance effort since a document no longer needs to be revised in order to change its links. In fact, a document does not even need to be revisable; links may be applied to legacy documents or data stored on read-only media, and the relationship of a document to the larger *docuverse* may evolve over time, even though the document itself remains static.

But how can a link service deal with disembodied links? A link is often considered to be similar to a GOTO instruction in a programming language, and since it is useless to examine a jump instruction extracted from its program context it would seem that a link extracted from its document would equally be an oddity. However, a

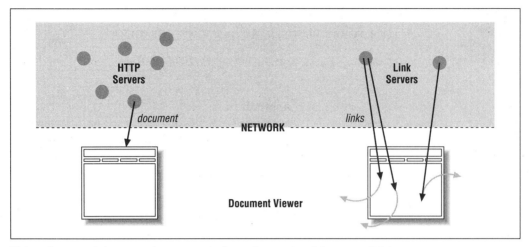

Figure 1: A document viewer requests first a document and then some links

link can instead be seen as a specification of a relationship between two data items (i.e., it is *declarative*); it expresses a relationship between its source and destination, and may even be expressed in a way to allow its source or destination to be parameterized. In this way the source may expand to one of several offsets in a particular set of documents, or the destination may resolve to any of a number of alternative documents. These flexible relationships can be expressed in a simple way, and stored together in database; the link service is effectively a database lookup service where the data items are interpreted as links between other data items.

The HyTime [8] standard for hypermedia links provides a comprehensive set of mechanisms for coding the relationship between objects using an SGML representation. It allows for both HTML-style links, where the link is coded *in situ* at one of its end points, and also for independent links, where the link is coded in a section or document separate from the data which it links together. Although the DLS does not yet use the HyTime standard coding, it uses the HyTime concepts of links as independent entities. The links themselves are distributed across a number of databases and the databases can be distributed across a number of servers. Further, the document

server may provide only a basic set of link databases, whereas the end user may have a private set of link databases and a third-party server may provide some sets of specialist links on a commercial basis.

Users of the DLS

Given the existence of this link service, there are a number of different ways that it can be used to achieve benefit for different groups of users.

Readers

Firstly, and perhaps most obviously, end-users (readers or browsers) may choose to subscribe to this service by running a small interface agent which communicates with both the link service and the document viewer (see the next section for precise details of the implementation). For an information consumer on the Web, the link service provides an additional means of navigation that can be tailored very precisely to his or her exact needs.

When the user wishes to investigate links for some information, they select the data of interest and choose the `Follow Link` menu item from the interface agent (Figure 2). The agent grabs the current selection, tries to determine the current document context (which document was that selection made in? what was its URL? where in the document was the selection located?), and parcels this information into a message which is sent to the link server. This process consists of creating an HTTP message with POST data and sending it to a Web server, since the link service is actually hosted by the Web.

The link server then responds with a set of links which are available from the specified selection in the specified document. These links are presented to the user in the form of a "clickable" list of destinations, displayed as a page of HTML by the Web viewer (Figure 3).

The user can select the Show Links menu item instead. This will send a similar message to the server which causes the selection to be analyzed word by word or phrase by phrase. All links which apply to any of the constituent words or phrases will be returned as if the user had selected Follow Link on each of them.

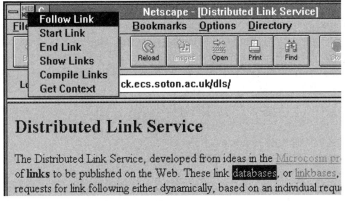

Figure 2:   A user requests a link from the link service

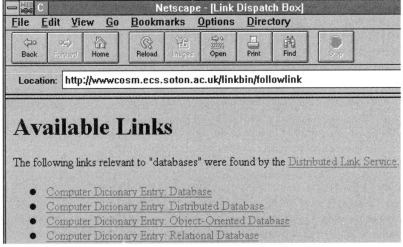

Figure 3:   The server responds with a page of available destinations

In some respects this process is similar to making an enquiry of a Virtual Library—certainly the same kind of database lookup is going on, and a similar-looking page of HTML is returned. On the other hand, this activity is both *document centered*, occurring while the user's focus is on the information content instead of the navigation superstructure, and *context specific*, parameterized by the location of the query data.

If this action is not totally like a database query, it is also not completely like a normal link-following operation. It is reader-driven rather than author-driven as it is the user who decides what is of interest for link following rather than the author's sole prerogative to determine what material can be followed up [7]. This has some positive benefits for some application environments (such as education) where an exploratory style is encouraged, but may be less useful for other areas where a more prescriptive style is appropriate.

The DLS is a particular kind of information service, and so bears some similarity to a WAIS server. In fact one kind of hypertext can be implemented using just such a text-retrieval service, where the links are all derived by a statistical analysis of the lexical data contained in the documents. This style of hypertext, known as a hyperbase, is characterised by the lack of internal structure as opposed to a hyperdocument in which the links are created by human authorship [10]. Services like WAIS and the Virtual Libraries provide some similar features to the DLS, but lack the capability to express human-authored links. The DLS on the other hand can implement a range of links, from the (expensive but highly relevant) human-authored variety through to the (cheaper and less specific) automatic keyword matching variety.

Another feature of the DLS is that it allows link following to be affected not just by the static document context of the link source, but also the reader's dynamic context: task-specific information that affects the kind of resources that they would like to follow up. A reader may choose to subscribe to a subset of many different linkbases, depending, for example, on whether they are to write an essay for an undergraduate or postgraduate course on Cell Motility, or whether they are interested in Computer Science in general or Parallel Computer Architectures in particular. This is achieved by the interface agent querying its link server about the link databases it supports; the list of named databases is offered to the user as a Context menu.

By selecting a different set of links using the Context menu, the user will see different responses to the `Follow Link` request: in effect they have the ability to reconfigure their hyperdocument, controlling their own view on the Web (a facility previously explored by users of the Intermedia system [11]). This can also be further achieved by choosing which link servers to connect to: a user may improve their Web connectivity by subscribing to a new commercial host which offers an enhanced sets of links across a greater set of Web sites.

Authors

As well as readers, authors may make use of the DLS by using the same interface agent. Since a part of the authoring process involves the author taking on the role of a reader, the author can benefit from the link service exactly as a reader can, but in addition an author can create links and edit link databases.

To create a link, the author highlights the link source, chooses `Start Link` from the interface agent, finds the link destination, highlights it, and chooses `End Link`. At this stage the interface agent packs the selections, static document context and dynamic user context information into a `Create Link` message and sends it to the link server via the Web. The newly created link may be added to the user's personal link database or to the current Context database; either of these may be subsequently edited by a forms-based interface in the Web browser.

This kind of functionality is fairly straightforward, but the real advantage for the author comes in the kinds of link definition that are allowed. Following the Microcosm model [1, 2], upon which much of this work is based, links may be declared to be more or less generic; i.e., having the location of the selected text constrained to appear more or less specifically within the static document context. A standard (or specific) link applies only at the exact place that the link source was selected, whereas a completely generic link will match the link source's selection at any place in any document. This facility allows the author to treat a link as a declaration which states "any place in such-and-such a document context that phrase 'X' is mentioned links to this data," and allows the author to create a set of documents along with a set of links that can be used to "come to" the documents from other places as well as a set of links which "go to" other documents from the current documents.

The "come-to" link type leads to a resource-based authoring style in which an author can publish a largely stand-alone suite of documents, together with some link databases which define the "routes" into, through, and out of the documents. Making use of the link service allows the author to "mix together" a number of these resources as the "into" links for each of them will act on the text of the others and bind them all together. In fact, the 'into' links can act to bind the resources not just to each other, but to the larger Web of documents outside the author's control—the readers' environment. One of the major benefits of this authoring style is the scope for information reuse: not only can the author vary the internal paths through the documents by changing the link databases, but also the documents themselves can be used and reused in many different situations by providing different sets of "into" and "out of" links.

Link databases use an SGML-based format, and so can be processed using standard tools like Perl, sed, or awk. In particular it is possible for an author to automatically create a simple link database from scratch by extracting sets of keywords from documents and turning them into generic links. Such a database would need a certain amount of author editing to become properly useful, but seeding a set of links in this way can provide a basic amount of hypertext functionality with minimal effort.

Publishers

Publishers, information providers, or information resellers may make indirect use of the link service by providing link databases for their customers to access in their roles as readers or authors. Publishers may, in fact, be ideally suited to act as link brokers, providing a more centralized service than hundreds of individual authors themselves. There is, however, an alternative role for the link service in the publishing environment as a tool for the management and generation of HTML resources.

As a variation to the standard use of the link service, a user can choose to send to the server not just a selection from a document but an entire document. The link service will then undertake to return that document with all the applicable links (from whichever context was chosen) hard-wired into the document in whichever native format the document was created. This option, available from the `Compile Links` menu item on the interface agent, currently handles HTML, RTF, PDF, and text document.

The effect of this facility is to place the links belonging to a document back into the document so that the new document can be used independently of the link service, especially if the document is to be distributed as part of a non-networked environment (on CD-ROM for example). This facility also allows publishers to work with a resource-based paradigm, creating a Web of information nodes for a specific niche market, and recreating a different Web over some of the same information for a different market.

The Open Journal Framework project (funded by HEFCE's Electronic Libraries programme in the

UK) is capitalizing on the link service's functionality from the publisher's points of view. The aim of the OJF is to enable electronic journals in a digital library to become cooperating assets in an information delivery environment rather than isolated, one-off resources. Based on a set of several hundred PDF files, which correspond to several volumes of the Company of Biologists journal *Development*, work is being done to establish link databases for those resources along with other network-accessible biology resources (gene sequence, biochemical, and research databases).

The OJF can easily be extended to provide guided or free searching through a prepared database to create a powerful learning environment. Installing expert system technology into the link server allows it to become an intelligent tutor to direct students through material available on the network. The Company of Biologists is at present negotiating with other publishers to allow the use of standard texts to complement the content of their journals for teaching purposes. The benefits of the project therefore extend beyond electronic libraries for research and into customized teaching and learning environments.

DLS Implementation

There are two aspects to the implementation of the Distributed Link Service: the client-side interface tool, and the server-side link database utilities. All communication between the client and server is provided using standard WWW protocols. The DLS client uses a standard WWW client to send linking requests encoded as URLs. These URLs allow the client to access a link server which operates via a WWW server.

Link Server

The server facilities of the DLS are implemented as CGI scripts, and are accessed using a standard WWW server. The main scripts are those that allow the creation, following, and editing of links which are stored in link databases.

Server interface

To carry out their functions, these scripts have access to a variety of different link databases, the exact selection depending on the end users configuration. There is a main link database for the server, which is always used, and additional link databases from which the user may choose. These additional databases allow the server to offer a range of different link sets, known as contexts. The end user is able to select a context from the whole set, thus allowing their linking activities to be tailored to their current requirements. For example, different contexts could be provided to cater for different levels of user knowledge. In addition, users are allocated a personal link database in which any links they wish to maintain for their own use may be stored. Databases are stored using an SGML-style markup, and record details of the source and destination of a link, the link type, time of creation, and the description of the link.

The various scripts determine the appropriate context from the information passed to them by the end user's WWW browser, and the user linkbase from the details of the user and host connecting to the server. The scripts then carry out their activities using the appropriate databases.

The script which handles requests to follow links simply checks in all appropriate databases for any applicable links and returns these to the user as a list of potential links in an automatically generated HTML document. The user may then go directly to the link destinations. The show links request is a special case of the follow link process; it takes a large selection and carries out several follow link requests on the words and phrases making up the selection.

The script which creates links accepts details of start and end points for a link, and inserts a link into either the database for the specified context, or the user's personal database if no context is given.

The edit link script offers a fill-in form which allows links to be entered directly into databases, deleted, or their details modified. In particular the user is able to update the description of the link, which by default is the name of the destination, or change the type of the link to make it more generally available. Links may be defined as one of two types: local, in which case it applies only in the document in which it was originally authored, or generic [5], in which case it applies whenever the source anchor selection is found, thus reducing authoring effort significantly.

Finally, a script is available to compile links held in these link databases into an HTML document, thus providing direct access to all applicable links without the need to make individual requests to the server. This can also provide a way in which material may be authored using the DLS and delivered as standard HTML.

Link databases

Link databases are the essential components of the Distributed Link Service. Each link in a link-base has the following format, and states the existence of a link from a source to a destination:

```
<link type=local>
 <src><doc>http://diana.ecs.soton.ac.uk/
    ~lac/cv.html
  <offset>
  <sel>Microcosm
<dest><doc>http://bedrock.ecs.soton.ac.
   uk/
  <offset>
  <sel>The Microcosm Home Page
<owner>Les@holly
<time-stamp>Fri Mar 31 13:32:34 GMT
   1995
<title>Hypermedia Research at the
   University of Southampton
```

Both the source and destination are described as a triple (document URL, offset within document, selected object within document) and allow the system to pinpoint the link anchors either by measuring from the beginning of a document (using the offset), or by matching a selection, or both.

A link is of type specific if its source anchor is constructed from a complete triple (i.e., a specific occurrence of a selected object in the named document), local if its anchor ignores the offset component of the triple (i.e., any occurrence of the selected object in the named document), or generic if only the selection is used (i.e., any occurrence of the selected object anywhere in any document).

In the Microcosm system (upon which this work is based) offsets are frequently used, but because of a lack of technical integration with the various viewing programs, the DLS usually ignores the offset. Hence only local and generic links can be created and manipulated by the various user interfaces, although it is possible to process specific links programmatically.

Note that the DLS provides flexibility in specifying the source anchor; this means that a single link to a destination may appear in many places at once, giving rise to a number of useful features for the hypertext author.

Linkbase processing

When a Web server hosting the DLS software receives a follow link request for a selection in a document D, the `followlink` script gathers together a number of link databases to try to satisfy the request. These are:

- *A document-specific linkbase.* Contains links which are pertinent only to that document itself. This linkbase is stored as a file in the document subdirectory of the DLS software.

- *A resource-specific linkbase.* Contains links which are pertinent to a group of files (probably a whole directory hierarchy). This link-base is also stored as a file in the document subdirectory of the DLS software.

- *A server-specific linkbase.* Contains links which may be relevant to any files provided by the server. This linkbase is stored in the file `server.links` at the top level of the links software installation.

- *A user-specific linkbase.* Contains links created by the user who issued the request. This linkbase is stored as the file `user@host` in the user subdirectory of the DLS software installation.

- *A context-specific linkbase.* Contains links customized for a specific task which the user interface allows the reader to choose at any time during a session.

This "chain" of linkbases is examined when the user asks to follow, show, or compile links. When a user makes a link, the link is either stored in their personal linkbase or, if they have a chosen a context, in the context database. Currently there is no way to create a link in the document, resource, or server-specific linkbases; these must be created in a dummy context and manually transferred at the server.

Client Interface

A client interface is available for PC, Mac, and UNIX platforms, and is a fairly simple utility whose task is to formulate requests for linking functions and to dispatch these requests to a DLS link server for processing.

The main task of the client utility is to react to a request from a user to carry out a particular linking function (e.g., start link, follow link) by extracting the details of the selection the user has made, and if possible, the details of the document in which the selection is. This information is encoded in an HTTP request reflecting the chosen function, and the selection details.

This request must then be delivered to the currently specified link server. This is done by communicating with the user's WWW browser, and requesting it to load the new URL. The results of the link request are returned as HTML, and displayed by the WWW browser. For example, in response to a request to follow a link from a particular selection, the response might indicate that no links were found, or list the links that were identified.

All versions of the client interface are currently designed to support the use of Netscape 1.1 for communication with DLS servers. The nature of the client interface, and the way in which it communicates depend on the particular platform being used. In the future, some or all of the functionality of the client interface may be achieved through programmable features in browsers.

Experience with the DLS

The first version of the Distributed Link Service was released in early June, 1995, initially to the ERCIM (*European Research Consortium for Informatics and Applied Mathematics*) WWW Working Group (W4G). It is being used in a spectrum of projects, reflecting the various groups of users discussed earlier in this paper.

One major project, described above, is the Open Journals Framework, which uses the software to support electronic publishing. Two other major projects involve a traditional Web server for large commercial organizations, and use the DLS in conjunction with our HTML "compilation" tool to ease the significant information maintenance and authoring task. Other projects include a Web-based distance learning course, which adopts a resource-based approach [4], and, in contrast to this manually authored service, the support of an information service for university administration: different users are provided with different views of the data according to their role, and the link service is used to automatically link new documents (such as committee minutes).

In each of these applications, the link databases are held on the same server as the documents (for access or for compilation). This is the simplest use of the DLS and is adequate for many applications. Meanwhile, the fully distributed version of the DLS is under development; this supports linkbases maintained on different servers, enabling the linkbases to scale and supporting localization of linkbases. Localization means that an individual user, or a group of users, can work with databases held as locally as possible (as in group annotation [9]). An early prototype of the fully distributed service used SMTP to provide a standard asynchronous messaging model for interserver communication, with MIME-encoded link resolution messages.

Experience has shown that taking a query-based approach (rather than precompiling into HTML) can cause a significant loss of performance where users make use of a proxy, since the results of the queries are not cached. This problem arises when there are remote users of a single DLS server, especially if those users are widely distributed (so the DLS server cannot be made local to all of them). There are various solutions: provision of a proxy with DLS extensions would allow require remote users to change their proxy; so the preferred solution is to modify the DLS server so that intermediate proxies cache appropriately.

Instructions for obtaining the Distributed Link software can be found at the site *http://www-cosm.ecs.soton.ac.uk/dls/dls.html.*

Conclusion

A hypermedia link service provides important functionality for the Web; it provides a powerful tool with which to address many of the restrictions often experienced with traditional Web services, including ease of information maintenance and enhanced authoring capability. We have shown that a simple link service can be implemented using standard Web browsers and servers.

We will continue to develop the Distributed Link Service following our open hypermedia philosophy, adopting new browser technology (e.g., we are currently using Java) and new server technology as it becomes available. We are also working with ANSA, investigating a CORBA-based approach to the distributed service [3]. Some of our existing applications will evolve to use the fully distributed implementations of the service, and we look forward to reporting on this work in due course. ∎

Acknowledgments

This work was partially supported by JISC grant ELP2/35 and a UK ROPA award.

References

1. H. Davis, W. Hall, I. Heath, G. Hill, R. Wilkins, "Towards an Integrated Information Environment with Open Hypermedia Systems," in *ECHT '92, Proceedings of the Fourth ACM Conference on Hypertext*, Milan, Italy, November 30-December 4, 1992, ACM Press, 181-190.

2. H. Davis, S. Knight, W. Hall, "Light Hypermedia Link Services: A Study of Third Party Application Integration," in *Proceedings of the Sixth ACM Conference on Hypertext,* Edinburgh, Scotland, September, 1994, ACM Press, 41-50.

3. D. DeRoure, G. Hill, W. Hall, L. Carr, "A Scalable, Distributed Multimedia Information Environment," *Proceedings of the International Conference on Multimedia Communications*, Society for Computer Simulation, 77-80, 1995.

4. D. DeRoure, L. Carr, W. Hall and G. Hill, "Enhancing Web support for Resource-based Learning," *Proceedings of Workshop H (Teaching and Training on the Web)*, WWW'95: Third International World Wide Web Conference.

5. A. Fountain, W. Hall, I. Heath, H. Davis, "Microcosm: an Open Model With Dynamic Linking," In *Hypertext: Concepts, Systems and Applications. Proceedings of the European Conference on Hypertext*, INRIA, France, November, 1990, 298-311.

6. W. Hall, L. Carr, H. Davis, R. Hollom, "The Microcosm Link Service and its Application to the World Wide Web," in *Proceedings of the First WWW Conference,* Geneva.

7. W. Hall, "Ending the Tyranny of the Button," *IEEE Multimedia* 1(1), 60-68, Spring 1994.

8. International Standards Organisation, Hypermedia/Time-based Structuring Language (HyTime), ISO/IEC Standard 10744, 1992

9. D. LaLiberte, A. Braverman, "A Protocol for Scalable Group and Public Annotations," *Proceedings of the Third International World-Wide Web Conference,* Computer Networks and ISDN Systems 27(6), 911-918, 1995.

10. P. Stotts, R. Furuta, *Hypertext 2000: Databases or Documents?* Electronic Publishing: Origination, Dissemination & Design, 4(2), 119-121, 1991.

11. N. Yankelovich, et al., "The Concept and Construction of a Seamless Information Environment," *IEEE Computer*, 81-96, January 1988.

About the Authors

Leslie Carr, **David De Roure**, **Wendy Hall**, and **Gary Hill**
Multimedia Research Group
Department of Electronics & Computer Science
University of Southampton.

STRUCTURED COOPERATIVE AUTHORING ON THE WORLD WIDE WEB

Dominique Decouchant, Vincent Quint, Manuel Romero Salcedo

Abstract

In this paper we present Alliance, a groupware application that allows several users located on different Web sites to cooperatively produce documents in a structured way. In addition to the local editing functions made available on each site by a structured editor, the application provides such basic functionalities as management of document storage and remote access to distributed documents. It offers services for handling user interaction and cooperation, for dynamically distributing roles to users, for showing documents through multiple views, for controlling the consistency of modifications, and for updating all copies of shared documents. **Keywords:** *Cooperative authoring, structured documents, group awareness, computer-supported cooperative work, World Wide Web, HTML*

Introduction

From its inception, the World Wide Web has been perceived as a system that allows people to cooperate and exchange information through a wide area network. This is achieved by several multimedia documents written by different users and made available to others on distributed servers. Each document contains links to some related documents, located on other sites.

In this paper, we take a slightly different approach to cooperation. We consider several persons involved in the task of writing a single document in a cooperative way. Each person has a specific role to play in the common task and should benefit from a software tool. The goal is to finally produce a large, well-structured document, rather than writing several pieces of information interconnected by various links. Since we consider some aspects of the problem to be very close to those considered in the World Wide Web, many solutions developed for the Web can be applied to cooperative editing. For studying the problems posed by cooperative editing, we have developed a distributed application, Alliance, which is a structured distributed cooperative editing tool built on top of the Grif editor [5].

Alliance has been designed to allow several users, distributed on a network, to work on shared structured documents. After the first version was developed for a local area network, it was recently adapted to the World Wide Web [3]. The aim of developing Alliance on the Web was to make this application more widely available, by using long-haul networks and allowing loosely coupled cooperation. For reaching this goal, evolutions of the Alliance cooperation services were needed to take into account most of the problems posed by the Internet and to obtain acceptable performances. From the implementation point of view, the document-management layer, initially based on NFS (Network File System), has been extended to the services provided by HTTP (HyperText Transfer Protocol) [1] on the Web.

The rest of this paper is divided into two main parts. The first part presents the basic principles on which the application is based. The application puts the emphasis on user roles, document fragmentation, and software architecture. The second part considers the specific problems posed by a wide area network for this kind of application and it shows how the Web technology has been used for solving these problems.

The Alliance Application

When developing Alliance, the goals were to study and better understand the specific problems of cooperative editing and to develop techniques that would allow complex structured documents to be handled more efficiently in a collaborative distributed environment.

The application has been developed for networked UNIX workstations. It controls several local instances of the Grif editor, running on different workstations, and allows their users to cooperate. In addition to the local editing functions inherited from Grif, it handles document storage and access to distributed documents; it offers high-level services for handling user interaction and cooperation, for defining shared document fragments, for distributing roles to users, for supporting group awareness, for updating copies of shared documents, and for controlling document consistency.

User Roles and Document Fragments

In the development of a large documentation project, the way in which people interact with each other is well defined: the work is organized, and each team member has a different role to play in the project. Therefore a notion of role has been introduced in Alliance. For each part of a document, a user may have one of the four available roles:

- As the purpose of the application is to edit documents, the first role that appears to be necessary is the *writer* role. A writer is a user who can modify (i.e. change the structure or the content) of (a part of) a document.

- The second role is the one of a *reader*. A reader is a user who can see and read a part of a document, but who cannot modify it. The writer role includes the reader role.

- A third role, called *null role*, has been introduced for preventing some users from even seeing some parts of a document that are

confidential for them. Obviously, a user with that role cannot modify the document either.

- The last role, called *manager*, is provided for people who give to other people the possibility of playing roles on documents. This manager role allows the manager to assign roles to new users, and to change the role of existing users. The operations allowed by this role include those allowed to a writer. Several users can play the manager role for a document or a part of a document.

The same user may have different roles on different parts of a document. He can then be authorized to modify some parts of the document, to only read some other parts, and to not even see the rest. These document parts for which user play different roles are called *fragments*.

As an example, Figure 1 shows the displays seen by two users (A and B) editing a shared document. This document is composed of four fragments. The first fragment contains the title, the author names, and affiliations. The second fragment contains the abstract. The third fragment includes the introduction and the heading of section 2. The fourth and last fragment contains all remaining parts. Fragments limits are represented in both views by various icons, which also indicate the current role played by the user on each fragment.

The content of the second fragment (the abstract) only appears in the view presented to user B who plays a writer role for that fragment. This fragment is accessed with the null role by user A (information is invisible). Conversely, the third fragment can only be seen by user A. The fourth fragment can be written by user B, who can also act as a manager, but the fragment can only be read by user A.

As a user may have different roles for different parts of a document, and as these roles can change, the user needs to be notified of the role he can really play on each part. This is achieved by using different colors and by inserting special

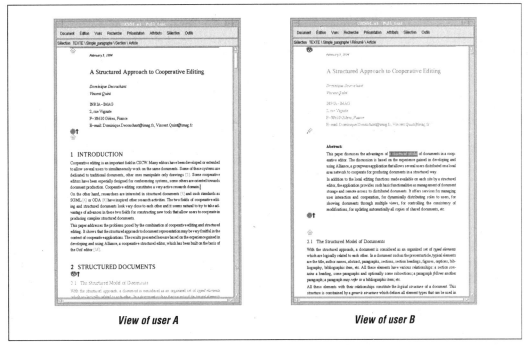

Figure 1: Two views of the same document

active icons at each fragment limit. When the user has a null role, the corresponding parts are not displayed, but the user may notice that they exist, as numbers (section numbers, figure numbers, etc.) take hidden parts into account. Parts where the user has the reader role are displayed with a specific color that each user can choose. Parts where the user has a writer or manager role are displayed with their normal color.

Roles allocated by a manager to other users are *potential* roles: users are allowed to play these roles, but they are not guaranteed to be able to play them at any time. When acting on a shared document, a user plays *effective* roles, which may be different from his/her potential roles. This is due to two different causes:

- For ensuring document consistency, only one user can play the writer or manager effective role at a time. Other users owning the writer potential role are then limited to a reader effective role. This policy is applied

by the application and cannot be bypassed by users.

- For improving cooperation, a user with the writer potential role may decide to play only the reader or null effective role on some fragments that he/she does not intend to modify for some time.

When a user changes his/her role, when a user leaves the session, or when a manager allocates new roles, the roles of other users are subject to changes. This is the reason why the icons marking fragment limits are useful and may change dynamically.

Alliance is an *asynchronous* application: all users do not see exactly the same state of the document at the same time. When a writer types a single character, this character is not displayed immediately on the screen of other users. Instead, each author must validate the changes he/she has made, in order to make them available to other users. The other users may decide whether they want these changes to be displayed automatically on their screen at validation time or later. In the second case, the icons indicate that a new version of the corresponding fragment is available and the user simply clicks the icon to get the latest version of that fragment.

The document is automatically divided into fragments by the application, according to the roles assigned by managers. This division is performed in such a way that the potential role of each user having a role for a given fragment does not change along the fragment. Changing potential roles of users can then lead to a different fragmentation of a document: fragments can be divided or merged by the application. Each fragment is stored in a separate file and these files can be located on different sites.

Document fragmentation is based on document structure. Being based on Grif, Alliance uses a structured model of documents. These documents can include a variety of components such as tables and equations, which can be shared in the same way as the rest of the document. The rich logical structure allows managers to handle document sharing efficiently. It also allows to dynamically change sharing granularity, thus permitting users to change role easily. As sharing is based on a well defined structure, document consistency can be guaranteed by simple ways.

Alliance Architecture

Basically, Alliance allows each user to edit locally an instance of a shared document and it allows all users sharing a document to communicate in order to be aware of the work performed by others. Therefore, two main functions can be identified in this application:

- *The editing function* allows users to process documents locally, in the core memory of their workstation,

- *The document-management function* provides support to the editing function for document naming, document storage, concur-

rency control, document replication, and group awareness.

The distributed application is constituted by several *instances*. An instance of Alliance is the piece of software that runs on a workstation for a single user. If several users share the same workstation, then several independent Alliance instances run on it.

In the LAN version of Alliance, an instance is a single process. As shown in Figure 2, it may be viewed as a main module that controls the functions performed by other modules.

The main module controls the editing module via the Grif API. It can update a fragment for which a new version has been sent from another instance; it can ask the editor to store a local fragment in a file; it can ask the editor to prevent the user from modifying some parts of the edited document; etc.

Editing events are transmitted via the ECF (External Call Facility) by the editing module, to inform the main module about some commands performed by the user. For instance, that is the way the main module knows what part of the document is currently selected, when the user playing the manager role changes the roles of other users for the selected part. More details about the API and the ECF mechanism provided by Grif are given in related documentation [6].

The main module also receives events (callbacks) from the user interface module (OSF/Motif) when the user issues commands that concern not editing, but cooperation, such as changing the role of other users.

Finally, the main module calls the document-management module when it needs to access the fragments stored in local or remote files.

Cooperative Editing on a Wide Area Network

In this section, we present the main issues that have been addressed when extending the LAN

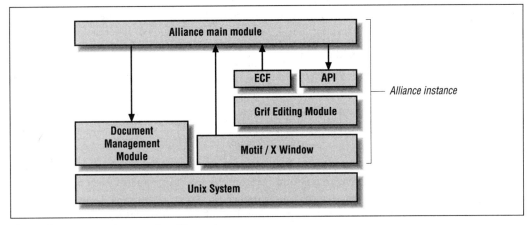

Figure 2: Architecture of an Alliance instance

version of Alliance to the Web. We focus first on the problems posed by the delays and failures that can occur in wide area networks and we discuss the impact of these problems on the architecture. Then, we discuss the issue of user identification and management in the the context of the Internet.

Finally, we describe the document storage mechanism that allows each user to work on shared documents when all sites can communicate and exchange information, but also when some users are isolated by network failures or simply because they are away.

From a LAN to the Internet

Porting Alliance to a wide area network would, one must think, allow users to benefit from the specific features of such networks. A WAN, such as the Internet, is composed of many sub-networks that communicate via gateways. This kind of network is inherently unreliable because of unpredictable communication delays, link failures, or computer crashes. In those cases, the network can be temporarily partitioned leading to disconnection of subnetworks. For an application such as Alliance, these failures make some remote-files unreachable and transmission delays unpredictable. All actions involving remote resources can cause long delays or even

locks, when these remote resources are treated as if they were local. Therefore the communication support of Alliance has been separated from the part that is in charge of user interface and local editing.

Another issue in a wide area network is remote-file access. We first considered a simple solution, which would avoid making changes to the way in which files are accessed. The same service as NFS is offered in WANs by other systems, such as the Andrew File System (AFS) for instance, which hide distribution and present remote files in the same way as local files. Although this solution would not change the architecture, it was rejected—we were looking for a file system that was widely available and used; one that would make the installation of Alliance on any site a simple task, even when used occasionally.

The World Wide Web satisfies these conditions. A number of servers run on the Web provide remote file access. A Web server can be easily installed on any computer and the software is widely available.

Web servers are based on the HTTP protocol [1]. HTTP allows on-line access to distant information using the client/server model. In the WAN version, Alliance fully exploits this model for allowing instances of the application to cooperate:

each instance acts as a client and each site acts as a server. Clients send requests to servers in order to:

- Obtain information about shared documents (list of users, effective role played by a user in a fragment, etc.)
- Get a new version of a fragment

On the server site, the work is carried out through the Common Gateway Interface, by executing scripts. Basically, a script is a program that can be executed for a HTTP client to perform some specific work on a server site. A script can receive information through input parameters and it can send results back to the calling client. Alliance uses a set of scripts that allow clients to get information about shared documents, or about fragments.

HTTP proposes three methods: Get, Post and Put. Get allows a client to request a document identified by its URL. Post is used to trigger execution of an existing script; a Post request is composed of the script URL and a list of input parameters to be provided to the script. Put is supposed to allow a client to write a file remotely, but very few servers implement this method, mainly for security reasons.

As the Put method is not widely available, a client must combine two methods for writing a file remotely (see Figure 3). It sends to the server a Post which starts a script sending back a Get message to the client. Then the client returns the file as the result of the Get message and the script that issued the Get message writes this file locally on the server. Due to the lack of the Put method, a HTTP server is also required on the client site.

The following example explains how a client can obtain the list of documents owned by a remote user. First, the client builds a request containing the URL of the script GetUserDocumentList, and the login name of the remote UNIX user as parameters. Then, it invokes the HTTP Post method and the script is executed on the server site. The script first checks that the user is registered on the server, then it loads the list of documents belonging to that user. Finally, the list is returned to the client through the standard output. On error, the script returns an appropriate diagnostic.

Executing scripts on a remote server poses several problems concerning message security and authentication of users and applications. These security issues are not addressed here, but they are considered for a future version of Alliance.

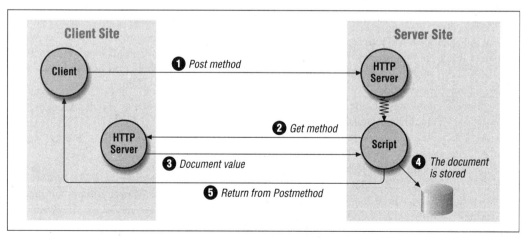

Figure 3:   Implementation of the Put method

In order to cope with the specific constraints of the Internet, each instance of Alliance is now divided into two processes (see Figure 4), the Editor and the Assistant:

- All editing functions for which the user is expecting an immediate feedback, and that do not depend on remote resources, are performed by the Editor.

- All functions that can cause transmission delays or locks are performed by the Assistant. These functions are almost the same as those performed by the document-management module in the LAN version. The Assistant takes care of all functions regarding the client side of remote access.

Each user on a site is served by an Editor process and an Assistant process. In addition to these processes, which are in charge of the local users, each Alliance site runs a daemon, even if no local user is active. This daemon process is a HTTP server that contains the Alliance scripts implementing all operations required by the remote Alliance Assistants. Each Alliance script is executed in response to an Alliance client request.

User Management

The notion of a user is fundamental in a groupware application. Some applications rely on the notion defined by the host operating system. These users are considered as persons who can login to make actions with well specified privileges on computer resources (disks, CPU, files, display, applications, drivers, etc.). Such a user definition is not adapted to the shared environment of distributed groupware applications, as it does not consider remote users, nor the specific resources of the application.

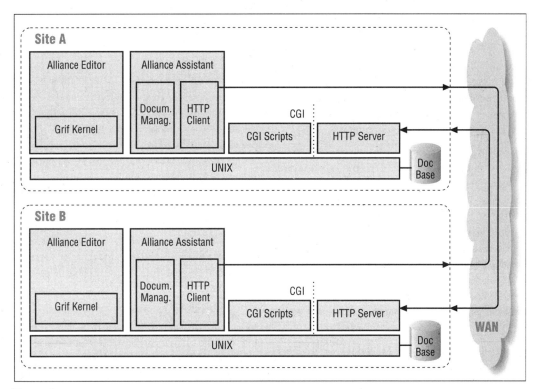

Figure 4:   Architecture for a wide area network

In Alliance, a user is simply a name (called "external name" below) that identifies a person. A list of users is associated with each document. This list is built by the document owner and is independent of the lists associated with other documents. The list indicates the users who are authorized to act on the document. The document owner can update this list at any time.

The document owner is the user who creates the document or makes it available in the Alliance environment. Initially, the owner plays the role of a manager for the whole document. He/she is free to assign various roles to other users.

A notion of group is also used in Alliance. A group is a name that represents several users playing the same role on documents. A user may be a member of several groups. A group can appear in the list associated with a document. It indicates that all users belonging to that group are allowed to act on the document.

All users of the list associated with a document can be involved in the commands for sharing documents. They will also be involved in future tools which are under development for negotiation, messaging or annotation. For instance, the document-sharing tool used by managers allocates roles to the users and groups according to the list associated with the document.

An Alliance user must be registered in the host system of one site involved in the application. This site contains the information needed for managing all documents belonging to that user. As the scope of a user is restricted to the host system where it is registered, users have not only an external name, but also an internal name that contains both the identification of their site and their login name on that site. The user list associated with each document contains both the external name and the internal name for each user.

When the document owner creates or updates the list of users, he provides the following data for each entry:

- The URL [2] (Universal Resource Locator) or the machine name (in a local area network) that identifies the site of that user

- The login name of the user on that site

- The directory where the document base is located on that site (user home directory by default)

After the list has been initialized, the owner sends a message to all users working with the document and gives them his/her URL, his/her login name and the local document name. Each remote user can then get a full copy of this document, and know the associated users and groups. Thus, all users are able to contact each other, even if they meet for the first time.

Document Distribution and Replication

In Alliance, a document is represented by a set of files which contain: document fragments, user roles for each fragment, the order of all fragments in the document, and the current state of each fragment.

In order to allow each user to work on a shared document, even in case of network failure, documents are copied on each site where they are needed. All document fragments and the corresponding management information are replicated among different sites (see Figure 5), where they are stored in local files. Each user can then work independently. In order to allow cooperation and group awareness, local copies must be updated when remote users have made modifications. But, as Alliance is based on an asynchronous model of cooperation, these updates do not need to be done in real time. Nevertheless, a mechanism is required for maintaining the consistency of all those copies.

Document consistency is based on a simple principle. In the whole system, there always exists one *master copy* for each fragment, which is the reference; there are as many *slave copies* as needed. On a given site where at least one user works on the document, all fragments of that document are available in local files and each fragment copy is either the master copy for that fragment or a slave copy. These two types of copies allow different effective roles to be played by a local user:

- The master copy (in grey in Figure 5) allows the user to act on it with any role, including the writer or manager role. As the master copy is unique, only one user can play these roles for a given fragment.

- A slave copy only allows the reader or null roles, even if a higher potential role is assigned to the user.

According to this principle, the set of all master copies constitutes the current document state. As a site usually does not own the master copies of all fragments of a given documents, each site, and then each user, may have a delayed perception of the document state. However, these different perceptions of the document are updated when a site owning the master copy of a fragment produces a new version of that fragment.

Master copies can migrate from one site to another. This operation is based on a transaction mechanism in order to avoid loss or duplication of the master copy that could be caused by communication failures. The possibility of moving the master copy of a fragment is evaluated each time a user tries to act on a fragment with the writer or manager role, in accordance with his potential role. The transaction fails if the master copy is unreachable or is already locked in reader or manager mode by its current owner. If no user is currently playing the writer or manager role on the site of the master copy, or if the user playing these roles accepts to change role, the master copy can move.

When a fragment is updated by a user acting as a writer, a copy of this fragment is not automatically sent to all sites working on the document. Only a short message is sent: it informs the remote sites that an updated version of the fragment is available. With the replication policy presented above, communication between sites is needed only to transmit these short messages, to transfer updated copies to the sites which ask for it, and to get remote user lists.

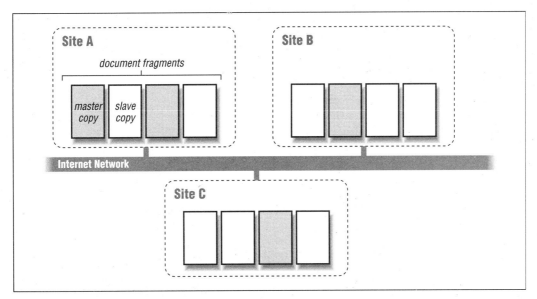

Figure 5:   Distribution of the fragment copies of a document

An advantage of document replication is that it allows disconnected cooperative work. We might think for instance of a user accessing the network and working in a collaborative way on a document. When he/she leaves his/her office, he/she disconnects his/her workstation and continues to work in disconnected mode, with the full editing environment. When the station is connected again to the network, Alliance automatically updates all document fragments. This kind of operation mode is the result of an intended disconnection. In case of any network failure, users can work on their documents in the same way. Obviously, disconnection should not last too long.

Conclusion and Perspectives

The current implementation of Alliance includes all functions presented in this paper. Additional services are under development for helping users to communicate with each other through an annotation mechanism and additional dialog options. Annotations will permit users to associate some comments with the document parts for which they have only the reader role. Private and shared annotations will be available.

The wide-area version of Alliance uses only one part of the services provided by the Web, the HTTP protocol, and servers. It does not take advantage of all the possibilities offered by the World Wide Web. For the moment, document fragments are stored in a specific format, not in HTML [4], which is the usual document format on the Web. The next version of Alliance will also integrate HTML. In fact, this work is in progress. The Grif editor has already been adapted to the Web and the result of this adaptation, Symposia, obviously handles HTML documents [7]. Alliance and Symposia are converging in order to provide Web users with a collaborative tool for producing HTML documents on the Web. ■

References

1. T. Berners-Lee, *Hypertext Transfer Protocol: A Stateless Search, Retrieve and Manipulation Protocol,* Internet draft, CERN, November 1993.

2. T. Berners-Lee, *Uniform Resource Locators—A unifying syntax for the expression of names and addresses of objects on the network,* Internet draft, CERN, January 1994.

3. T. Berners-Lee, R. Cailliau, A. Luotonen, H. Frystyk Nielsen and A. Secret, "The World Wide Web," *Communications of the ACM,* vol. 37, num. 8, pp. 76-82, August 1994.

4. T. Berners-Lee, *Hypertext Markup Language Specification—2.0,* Internet draft, CERN, November 1994.

5. V. Quint, I. Vatton, "Grif: an Interactive System for Structured Document Manipulation," *Text Processing and Document Manipulation, Proceedings of the International Conference,* J. C. van Vliet, ed., pp. 200-213, Cambridge University Press, 1986.

6. V. Quint, I. Vatton, "Making Structured Documents Active," *Electronic Publishing—Origination, Dissemination and Design,* vol. 7, num. 1, pp. 55-74, March 1994.

7. V. Quint, C. Roisin, I. Vatton, "A structured authoring environment for the World Wide Web," *Proceedings of the Third International World Wide Conference,* Computer Networks and ISDN systems, ed., pp. 831-840, The International Journal of Computer and Telecommunications Networking, vol. 27, April 1995.

About the Authors

Dominique Decouchant
CNRS-IMAG
Dominique.Decouchant@imag.fr

Vincent Quint
INRIA RhÔne-Alpes
Vincent.Quint@inria.fr

Manuel Romero Salcedo
INRIA RhÔne-Alpes / IMAG
Manuel.Romero@imag.fr

THE BOOMERANG WHITE PAPER
A PAGE AS YOU LIKE IT

Curtis E. Dyreson, Anthony M. Sloane

Abstract

*Boomerang is a dynamic HTML page reconfiguration system. A user accesses Boomerang via the Common Gateway Interface. The user supplies a page name and a template, Boomerang fetches the requested page and uses the template to reconfigure it. The template is a sequence of string manipulation rules. The rules are written in a simple regular expression-based pattern matching language. Boomerang also parses HTML variables in forms and query strings and makes those variables available in the template. By taking advantage of Boomerang's dynamic page reconfiguration features, users can easily add navigational links, suppress images, redefine HTML tags, and reshape a page as desired. Since Boomerang is reached through the Common Gateway Interface and understands HTML variables, Boomerang can also be used as a general form-handling script. Several examples are given to show the utility of Boomerang. Boomerang is compatible with existing browsers and servers and does not compromise their security. **Keywords:** HTML, document reconfiguration, structural regular expressions, parameterized documents, CGI*

Introduction

Hypertext document authors control how information on the World Wide Web is structured and presented. The authors write the raw text, include the appropriate HTML (HyperText Markup Language) tags, and insert all the links to other Web documents. In many cases, users are satisfied with the presentation because authors work hard to present that information in the best possible manner. But in some cases, there is a large gap between how the author has presented the information and how the user wants to view it.

An example is the lack of "return to point-of-entry" links in documents [2]. Suppose that the Web page authors at ACME On-line Shopping want to build an Internet mall. The mall will consist of a number of stores, each selling various items. It is reasonable to assume that each store is a unique hypertext document that is designed, developed, and maintained independently. Typically a store will be a sequence of forms that permit users to view items for sale, select items to purchase, enter payment information for those

items, etc. The mall itself will have a single "welcome" page. The welcome page is a list of store categories (e.g., shoe stores, clothing stores, etc.) so that the user can quickly find stores selling products that the user needs. Within a mall a shopper can enter a store under several different categories. For example, a sporting goods store could be listed under athletic equipment as well as shoes and clothing. Leaving the store should return the shopper to the list of stores in a category. That is, if the customer entered from shoes, the customer should return to the list of shoe stores. But since stores are independently written and maintained, one cannot assume that they will have "exit" buttons or links. Furthermore, even if an exit button is included in each store since a store may be entered from many different locations (e.g., a sporting goods store may sell shoes, clothing, and athletic equipment and can be entered from all three places), it is impossible to anticipate in advance to where the shopper should be returned.

In other situations, a user may simply prefer a presentation different than what is provided by the document author. A common example is the (over)use of images. Eye-popping colorful images are important for capturing the imagination of first-time document visitors, but in subsequent visits images tend to be of diminishing importance. In fact, they are often a source of irritation since images are large and slow browser response times. (Some browsers, such as Netscape, allow document navigation before images are fully retrieved, thus mitigating the problem of waiting for image retrieval.) Some authors maintain text-only and picture-only versions of documents, in part, to address this issue. (And in part to allow access by nonimage-supporting browsers such as Lynx.)

In both of these examples, supporting the desired functionality depends on the user's ability to dynamically reconfigure a document. An alternative to requiring document authors to maintain multiple versions of documents is to allow users to dynamically configure pages so that they can specify whether or not to include images [5]. In the absence of exit buttons, users should be allowed to enhance the document by adding such buttons.

This paper describes a system called Boomerang that supports dynamic reconfiguration of HTML documents. Boomerang allows users to control how information is presented. The two examples given above are only a tiny fraction of the power of reconfiguration. Users can (temporarily) add navigational buttons to pages, suppress images, combine information from multiple pages, redefine tags, and redesign poorly presented pages. But reconfiguration also helps document authors. It aids document reusability, allows individual users to be tracked, and creates a new class of hypertext documents, which we call *parameterized* documents.

This paper is organized as follows: The next section gives an overview of Boomerang and broadly discusses how Boomerang can reconfigure a page. That discussion is followed by a description of Boomerang's architecture. The heart of the architecture is a reconfiguration engine that can parse and rearrange a page. The engine is controlled by the user through a reconfiguration language, which is defined in the section "Boomerang Templates." The language borrows heavily from the sam editor [3]. Several examples are given in the section "Boomerang Examples" to demonstrate the utility of Boomerang. Finally, security issues, related work, and future work are presented.

Overview

In a typical browsing session, a user navigates from page to page. New pages are fetched through explicit user actions, e.g., a user activates a link, a submit button, or makes a "hotlist" jump.

Figure 1 shows the typical pattern of browser behavior. A user requests a page from a server, and the server returns the requested page.

Boomerang is an "intermediary" or "wrapper" script that sits between the browser and the server. When using Boomerang, a user has the same basic browsing behavior. However, when fetching new pages Boomerang serves as an intermediary agent between the user and a desired page as shown in Figure 2. Instead of directly requesting a new page, the user activates a link that starts Boomerang and instructs it to fetch the desired page. The user also tells Boomerang how to reconfigure the page. Boomerang "intercepts" the page fetch request, fetches the requested page, and reconfigures it according to user specification.

Architecture

Boomerang was initially designed to aid the construction and maintenance of a *forms document*. A forms document is a special kind of HTML document. Like an HTML document, a forms document contains a number of related *pages*. Each page is raw text interspersed with HTML tags. Unlike a standard HTML document, the pages in a forms document can also have one or more *forms*. A form consists of a number of data-entry widgets that are manipulated by the user and then submitted to a form-handling *script*.

A form has a number of *variables*. There is one variable for each data-entry widget in the form, plus any number of "hidden" variables. Hidden variables are added by the form's author to communicate values to the script (e.g., to pass state information through a sequence of forms). When a form is submitted, the variables are formatted as a list of name/value pairs and passed as a string to the script.

A user may also invoke a script via a hypertext link. In such situations, input to the script is passed in a "query string." The query string also consists of name/value pairs.

As described in the Overview, Boomerang is an "intermediary" agent which sits between the user and the server. Boomerang is a script. A browser invokes Boomerang when a user activates the appropriate hypertext link or submit button. The browser passes to Boomerang (either via a query string or hidden variables) a URL and a comma-separated list of *page templates*. The URL is either the name of a page to fetch or a script to execute. A page template specifies how to reconfigure the page. The user may give either the name of a file containing the template or might pass the template itself. The page is successively reconfigured by each template in the list. Examples are given in the "Boomerang Examples" section.

Boomerang has three basic components: an Input Variable Handler, a Page Fetcher, and a Reconfiguration Engine. The components are shown in Figure 3. Each component is discussed below.

The Input Variable Handler parses the input to Boomerang. It strips off the URL and template and passes those values to the Page Fetcher, along with any input variables or query string (since the page to be fetched might be produced by a script). The Input Variable Handler also maps all HTML variables in the input to Boomerang variables. (Boomerang variables are described in the next section.)

The Page Fetcher fetches the desired page(s). If a page to fetch is produced by a script, Boomerang passes the appropriate input to the script, executes the script, and collects the output. Otherwise, Boomerang simply reads the page. As regards fetching pages, the Page Fetcher duplicates some server functionality, since servers usually fetch pages. This duplication could be avoided by tightly integrating the server with Boomerang, but such integration would require substantial server modification.

The fetched pages, HTML input variables, and page templates are passed (as Boomerang variables) to the Reconfiguration Engine. The Reconfiguration Engine is the heart of Boomerang. It dynamically reconfigures the pages as directed by the page template producing a final page, which is displayed by the browser.

Boomerang Templates

The Boomerang Reconfiguration Engine uses *page templates* to describe how a page should be reconfigured. A template has two parts: a *prologue* and a *body*. The prologue specifies rules that are used to instantiate Boomerang *variables*. The body is essentially raw text with embedded HTML tags just like a regular page, so it can be readily produced by HTML authors. In addition, the body can contain variable references that are expanded by Boomerang using the results of executing the prologue rules.

The rest of this section describes the form of prologue rules and the semantics of variable substitution in bodies. More detailed examples are given in the following section.

Variables

Boomerang supports a single flat name space for variable bindings. The values bound to variables are (possibly empty) lists of strings. For example, a variable `meanings` might denote the possible definitions of the word "boomerang" with the following list of three strings:

```
Australian thin curved hardwood missile
```

```
Recoil on originator
A WWW page reconfiguration tool
```

(Separate strings are shown on separate lines.)

Inputs to the reconfiguration process are supplied via predefined Boomerang variables.

- *Original page contents.* The complete contents of the original page is bound to the variable `page`, while the header and body of the page are bound to `head` and `body`, respectively.

- *Input variables.* Each input variable (i.e., data-entry variable or hidden variable in a form) is passed as the value of a Boomerang variable with the same name. Since an input variable can have only a single value, the corresponding Boomerang variables initially denote a singleton list. Note that Boomerang is always invoked with a `url` and a `template` variable. The former identifies the page to fetch and the latter the reconfiguration desired.

- *Input variable names.* The Boomerang variable `args` is bound to a list of name/value pairs of the input variables (i.e., the HTML variables in a form).

Rules

The prologue of a Boomerang template is a list of rules. Instantiation of the template consists of evaluating the rules in the order given. The result is a set of bindings to Boomerang variables that are used to substitute variable references in the body of the template.

The general form of a Boomerang rule is:

`set var exp`

and has the effect of evaluating the expression *exp* and binding the result to the variable *var*. Since it is common to simply process the original page, a rule of the form:

`exp`

has the same meaning as:

`set page exp`

Expressions

The operation of Boomerang expressions is based on the editing model of the sam editor[3]. The main difference is that Boomerang allows any text stored in a variable to be edited and the result to be bound to a variable, whereas sam commands operate on file buffers.

Boomerang expressions have the following general form:

source cmd

Each Boomerang/sam command operates on a region of text called *dot*. Commands can operate on the contents of dot and update its value (i.e., the region to which it refers). In Boomerang, the form of the source for an expression determines how dot is set initially for that expression and the form of the result of the expression. There are two forms of sources:

- *var.* Dot is successively set to each string in the list of strings bound to *var* and the command is run on each of them. The result of the expression is the list of strings consisting of the result of each of the command applications.

- $ *var.* Dot is set to the single string formed by concatenating the strings in the list bound to *var* and the command is applied to it. The result of the expression is a list containing as elements the final value(s) of dot when the command finishes.

The value of the source variable is *not* modified by the evaluation of either type of expression, but it can be altered by naming the same variable as the target of an enclosing rule.

Table 1 (based on Table I in [3]) lists the Boomerang editing commands. The `a`, `c`, `d`, and `i` commands simply append to, change, delete, or insert after dot, respectively. The `<`, `>`, and `|` commands allow dot to be set by, passed to, or both passed to and set by a "safe" external script,

Table 1:   Boomerang Editing Commands[1]

`a/text/`	Append text after dot
`c/text/`	Change dot to *text*
`d`	Delete dot
`g/regexp/ cmd`	If dot contains a match with *regexp*, execute {em cmd/} on dot
`i/text/`	Insert *text* before dot
`m address`	Move text in dot to after *address*
`s/regexp/text/`	Substitute *text* for each match of *regexp* in dot
`t address`	Copy text in dot to after *address*
`v/regexp/ cmd`	If dot does not contain a match with *regexp*, execute *cmd* on dot
`x/regexp/ cmd`	Execute *cmd* with dot set to each match of *regexp* in dot
`y/regexp/ cmd`	Execute *cmd* with dot set to the strings between adjacent matches of *regexp* in dot
`< prog args...`	Replace dot with the standard output of the UNIX program *prog* run with the given arguments
`> prog args...`	Send dot to the standard input of *prog*
`| prog args...`	Replace dot with the standard output of *prog* when given dot as standard input
`! prog args`	Run *prog*, ignoring any output

[1] Text can be arbitrary text possibly including newlines; regexp stands for a standard UNIX regular expression

respectively (see the section called "Security" for a discussion of safe external scripts).

The `s` command performs a text substitution on dot, allowing the usual Unix regular expression notations.

Most of the power of sam (and hence Boomerang) derives from the `x`, `y`, `g` and `v` commands. An `x` command looks through dot for matches with its regular expression argument. The command argument is repeatedly executed with dot set to each of the matches. For example, the expression

```
meanings x/WWW/ c/World Wide Web/
```

returns a list of strings the same as that bound to the variable `meanings` except that all occurrences of "WWW" have been changed to "World Wide Web." In contrast, the expression

```
$meanings x/WWW/ c/World Wide Web/
```

returns a list of "World Wide Webs," one for each "WWW" in the value bound to `meanings`. More usefully, the expression

```
meanings x/^/ i/<LI>/
```

turns the list of dictionary definitions into a list of HTML list items (^ is a regular expression that matches the beginning of dot).

The `y` command is similar to `x` except that it executes the command argument on the strings *between* the matches. For example, the following rule deletes all text in the current page that is not an HTML tag.

```
y/<[^>]+>/ d
```

(The regular expression `[^>]+` matches any nonempty sequence of characters that does not contain a >.)

Similarly, the `g` and `v` constructs are conditional constructs. A `g` (`v`) command executes its command argument on dot if it matches (does not match) the regular expression. For example, the following expression adds boldface tags to every definition containing the word "WWW," not just to every word "WWW."

```
meanings g/WWW/ s/.*/<B></B>/
```

Table 2: Boomerang Addresses: in the + and - Forms, *a* Defaults to . and *b* Defaults to 1

•	Dot	a+b	Address b from the right end of a
n	Line n	a--b	Address b from the left end of a
/regexp/	First following match of `regexp`	a,b	Left end of a to the right end of b
-/regexp/	First previous match of `regexp`	a;b	Like a,b but sets dot after evaluating

(In an s command, & stands for the text matched by the regular expression.)

The definition of dot can be altered using *addresses* as supported by sam (summarized in Table 2 based on Table II of [3]). The most useful form of address is one that is relative to dot. For example, the address / *regexp/* finds the next match with *regexp* after dot. Similarly, –/ *regexp/* finds the first previous match before dot. (Addresses of this kind can be usefully used in conjunction with x commands.) If *regexp* is replaced by a number then these forms count by lines in the indicated direction. An address of the form *a,b* means from the beginning of the text denoted by *a* to the end of the text denoted by *b*.

Addresses enable complex editing tasks to be expressed concisely. For example, the following rule deletes the last item from each unnumbered list in the current page by finding the end of each list, searching backwards for the last item and deleting from there to the beginning of the line containing the end of the list.

```
x/<\/UL>/ -/<LI>/,-1 d
```

The m and t commands allow addresses to be used as targets for the text in dot to allow arbitrary text rearranging. For example, the following command copies all form submit buttons to the top of the form.

```
x/<INPUT TYPE="SUBMIT"/ .,/>/ t 0/
    <FORM>/
```

Template Bodies

Once all of the template rules have been executed, Boomerang instantiates the template body to produce the reconfigured page. The body can contain arbitrary text and will normally include HTML tags for markup. To enable variable values to be included in the final page, the body can

also include text of the form *$var*, where *var* is a Boomerang variable name. During instantiation, Boomerang replaces variable references with the concatenation of the strings bound to the variable. For example, below we show a body that might be used to produce a page for inclusion in an online dictionary.

```
<TITLE>Definition of $word</TITLE>
<BODY>
$word has the following meanings:<BR>
<P>
<UL>
$meanings
</UL>
</BODY>
```

Boomerang Examples

In this section we give several examples of templates to demonstrate the power and utility of Boomerang. Each example addresses a standard reconfiguration problem faced by a typical user or author.

Suppress Images

This template finds all `<IMG...>` tags in a page and replaces them with the string "`Image Replaced.`" (The lines starting with `%%` are comments.)

```
%% Prologue Suppress
x/<IMG[^>]*> c/Image Replaced/
%% Body
$page
```

Return to Point of Entry

The template given below adds a return to point of entry link to the bottom of a page. We assume that the link URL is passed to Boomerang in the `returnlink` variable (in a query string or as a hidden variable).

```
%% Prologue Return
%% Body
<HEAD>
$head
</HEAD>

<BODY>
$body
<P>
<A HREF="$returnlink"> Return to Point
    of Entry </A>
</BODY>
```

Access Counter

Access counters are popular page enhancements.
An access counter is a count of the number of
visitors to a page. In this example, we assume
that the access counter is maintained by the
script `access_count`, which updates and
returns the count for a given URL. In this example, the URL is passed to `access_count` on the
command line; alternatively, it could have been
passed in standard input.

```
%% Prologue Counter
set count < access_count $url
%% Body
<HEAD>
$head
</HEAD>

<BODY>
This page has been visited $count times.
<P>
$body
</BODY>
```

Keep Boomerang in Control

This template reconfigures a page so that all links
out of the page return control to Boomerang. We
assume that the `template` variable specifies the
template(s) to be executed on subsequent pages.
The URL location and replacement in this example have been simplified to assume absolute
links only.

```
%% Prologue Control
%% Find each link and make it a
%%   Boomerang call with the link
%%   passed in the
%%   url parameter
```

```
x/<A HREF="http:\/\/[^\/]+\// a/cgi-
   bin\/
   Boomerang?template=$template&url=/
%% Do the same for forms.  Find the
%%   action, skip the server, insert
%%   the call to Boomerang and hidden
%%   variables for the template and url
x/<FORM .* ACTION="http:\/\/[^\/]+\// a/
   cgi-bin\/Boomerang"> \
   <INPUT TYPE="hidden" NAME="template"
   VALUE="$template">\
<INPUT TYPE="hidden" NAME="url" VALUE="/
%% Body
$page
```

Track an Individual

Authors are sometimes interested in tracking individuals to determine browsing patterns for a set
of pages. Individuals can be tracked by reconfiguring a page to place a unique identifier on each
link and keeping Boomerang in control. When
the individual moves to a new page, Boomerang
is called instead and Boomerang calls the appropriate script to update the browsing database.

```
%% Prologue Track
%% Check to see if id exists, if not,
%%   then generate a new one
set id id g/^$/ < generate_unique_id
%% Update browser database to indicate
%%   where the individual is now
! update_browser_db $id $url
%% Transform the links out of the
%%   page to return control to Boomerang
%%   with tracking enabled
x/<A HREF="http:\/\/[^\/]+\// a/cgi-bin
   Boomerang?template=Track&url=/
%% and do the same for forms.
x/<FORM .* ACTION="http:\//[^\/]+\// a/
   cgi-bin\/Boomerang"> \
<INPUT TYPE="hidden" NAME="template"
   VALUE="Track">
<INPUT TYPE="hidden" NAME="url" VALUE="/
%% Find each link and add the id to the
%%   end of the query string
x/<A HREF="[^"]*/ a/&id=$id/
%% Do the same for forms, but add it as
%%   a hidden variable just before
%%   the end of the form
x/<\/FORM>/ i/<INPUT TYPE="hidden"
   NAME="id" VALUE="$id">/
%% Body
$page
```

Template Composition

Boomerang actions can be combined by specifying multiple templates. The templates are applied one at a time from the beginning to the ending of the list. The following link combines most of the previous reconfigurations; that is, it suppresses images, adds a return to point of entry link, displays an access counter: We give the link below.

```
<A HREF="http://server/cgi-bin/
    Boomerang?template=Control,
    Counter,Return,\ Suppress&url=base.
    html&returnlink=home.html">
```

Page Decompression and Decryption

In general, the fetched page does not have to even remotely resemble HTML; it could for instance be a LaTeX document. In this example, we assume that the page is encrypted and then compressed, with .Z or .gz compression. The decryption key must be passed to Boomerang in the key variable. We assume that uncompress and gunzip are in the list of safe commands as described in the section "Security."

```
%% Prologue
set page $url g/.gz/ < gunzip $url |
    decrypt $key
set page $url g/.Z/ < uncompress $url |
    decrypt $key
%% Body
$page
```

A Parameterized Page

A parameterized page is a page that mentions one or more variables. When the page is retrieved, the variables are replaced by their values (the values are passed in the query string or as HTML variables). Boomerang trivially supports parameterized pages. For example, the following "Welcome" page is parameterized by the **name** variable.

```
%% Prologue
%% Body
<HEAD>
<TITLE> Welcome </TITLE>
</HEAD>
```
```
<BODY>
Good morning $name
</BODY>
```

Additional Benefits

The previous examples illustrate some of Boomerang's power. Boomerang also eases the burden of writing a sequence of WWW forms and integrating that sequence with other such sequences. One problem faced by forms document authors is that the HTML is "hidden" in scripts. Most often, changes to forms documents are to the layout of a page, i.e., to the HTML rather than to the processing of a form. Such changes are quite simple to make in HTML, but become more involved if, as is commonly the case in a forms document, the page is dynamically generated during execution of a script. Even knowledgeable HTML authors cannot make simple changes to the page layout (such as the addition of a link) since they often do not understand the scripting language or script. Only authors that know HTML, the scripting language, and the structure of the script are able to make changes to a forms document. Moreover, hiding pages in scripts makes it difficult to integrate pages designed by WYSIWYG HTML editors.

In contrast, Boomerang favors HTML over a scripting language. Boomerang presents a standardized notation for processing WWW forms, so it can be used by expert programmers to better code and document their scripts. Moreover, by using Boomerang to describe the essential HTML interaction, commonalities between scripts in a variety of languages can be identified, supporting script reuse and the mix of form-handlers written in disparate languages.

Boomerang also can be used to easily integrate output from WYSIWYG editors with scripts.

Security

Security is an important concern on any server. In Boomerang, a user can create a template that executes scripts on the server. This is a powerful tool for users since it allows a limited form of CGI-bin programming without actually creating a script to reside in CGI-bin. Conceptually, this does not create a new security hole since servers should already ensure that each CGI-bin script, executed independently, is a "safe" script, regardless of the input it receives. However, since Boomerang makes it easier for users to execute scripts, it potentially permits outsiders to quickly probe for "unsafe" scripts. To patch this potential security hole, Boomerang can only execute scripts that are on a list of safe scripts. The list is created and maintained by the server administrators.

Related Work

Sato describes a LISP-based system for dynamically rewriting HTML [4]. In Sato's system, the author must first write a page (or simple text file, with tags of the author's choosing) and a LISP program that converts that file to HTML. When a client requests the document the server instead returns the LISP program. The LISP program is then executed on the client's machine and converts the text file (fetched from the server) into HTML. The rewriting is in cooperation with the author since the author supplies the LISP program. In contrast, Boomerang does not depend on author cooperation. Users reconfigure documents without involving the author at any stage. Boomerang also has a different implementation strategy. Sato uses MIME types and the Content meta resource in a page header to implement his system. Boomerang uses the Common Gateway Interface. Consequently, Boomerang has access to the variables in a form and supports parameterized documents. Boomerang shares the view espoused by Gleeson and Westaway [1], among others, that forms documents are important to the future of the WWW. Gleeson and Westaway lament the lack of tools to aid the design and maintenance of forms documents, Boomerang is one such tool. Sato also noted the security risk in downloading LISP code from a server to be immediately executed on a client's machine.

Boomerang does not suffer from this security problem.

Sperberg-McQueen and Goldstein advocate that full SGML intelligence be added to browsers. Such intelligence would allow browsers to incorporate "style files" to interpret SGML tags in a document. So, for example, a musician could add a "<HALF-NOTE C#>" tag to a document. The tag's translation to HTML would be loaded into a browser by a style file, and different style files might provide different translations. Boomerang differs from the SGML solution insofar as the style file approach still depends on the author to provide the appropriate tags. Also style files do not support parameterized documents or allow document rearrangement, such as the addition of "exit" buttons. In some sense the SGML solution is attacking a different problem, that of allowing authors to work in a special-purpose notation.

Conclusion

Currently HTML page presentation is a static process. Once a page is written, the presentation of that page is fixed. The presentation may vary among browsers (e.g., a page may look different on Netscape and Lynx), but a single browser will always display a page the same way. Static page display limits both users and authors. Boomerang makes page presentation a dynamic process.

Boomerang is a Common Gateway Interface script that "intercepts" a page fetch request, fetches the desired page, and reconfigures it. The user supplies a template (or a list of templates) that informs Boomerang how to reconfigure a page. Each template has a prologue and a body. The prologue is a sequence of rules written in a regular expression-based pattern matching language.

The language supports quick matching and replacement of patterns in a page. The body of a template is raw HTML mixed with Boomerang variables. Variables are used to temporarily hold the results of rules.

After the rules have been processed the body of the template is instantiated by substituting the value for each variable.

Boomerang helps users because users can reshape and enhance pages as desired. User reconfiguration demands no special preparations by page authors. But Boomerang also helps authors. It eliminates a need to support multiple versions of pages. Moreover, authors who are unable to program scripts can still write dynamically generated pages using parameterized pages.

Boomerang is currently being implemented. More information and release versions of Boomerang are available at *http://www.cs.jcu.edu.au/ ftp/pub/research/boomerang/welcome.html*. Future extensions include support for processing several pages simultaneously, transparent document migration, and parallel rule execution. ∎

References

1. M. Gleeson and T. Westaway. "Beyond Hypertext: Using the WWW for Interactive Applications," in *AusWeb95—The First Australian World Wide Web Conference*, Ballina, New South Wales, Australia, April 1995.

2. D. Nicol, C. Smeaton, and A. F. Slater, "Footsteps: Trail-blazing the Web," in *The Third International Conference on the World Wide Web*, Darmstadt, Germany, April 1995.

3. Rob Pike. "The text editor sam," *Software—Practice & Experience*, 17(11):813--845, 1987.

4. S. Sato. "Dynamic rewriting of HTML documents," in *The First International Conference on the World Wide Web*, Geneva, Switzerland, May 1994. CERN.

5. C. M. Sperberg-McQueen and R. F. Goldstein. "HTML to the Max: A Manifesto for Adding SGML Inetlligence to the World Wide Web," in *The Third International Conference on the World Wide Web*, Darmstadt, Germany, April 1995.

About the Authors

Curtis E. Dyreson
[*http://www.cs.jcu.edu.au/~curtis*]
Department of Computer Science
James Cook University
curtis@cs.jcu.edu.au

Anthony M. Sloane
[*http://www.cs.jcu.edu.au/~tony*]
Department of Computer Science
James Cook University
tony@cs.jcu.edu.au

A World Wide Web Telerobotic Remote Environment Browser

Eric Paulos, John Canny

Abstract

Robots provide us with a means to move around in, visualize, and interact with a remote physical world. We have exploited these physical properties coupled with the growing diversity of users on the World Wide Web (WWW) [1] to create a WWW-based active telerobotic remote environment browser. This browser, called Mechanical Gaze, allows multiple remote WWW users to actively control up to six degrees of freedom of a robot arm with an attached camera to explore a real remote environment. The initial environment is a collection of physical museum exhibits which WWW users can view at various positions, orientations, and levels of resolution. **Keywords:** *telerobotics, teleoperation, telepresence, robotics, museum*

Introduction

We have designed this teleoperated WWW server in order to allow users throughout the world to visit actual remote spaces and exhibits. It also serves as a useful scientific tool by promoting discussion about the physical specimens in the browser such as insects, live reptiles, rare museum collections, and recently discovered artifacts.

The use of an online controlled camera eliminates many of the resolution and depth perception problems of libraries of digitized images. The user has complete control over the viewpoint, and can experience the exhibit in its state at a particular moment in time, under the same conditions and lighting as a viewer who is in the actual space.

In addition, each exhibit has a hypertext page with links to texts describing the object, other WWW pages relevant to it, and to comments left by other users. These pages can be accessed by navigating the camera in a physical space, and centering on a particular object. The pages can be thought of as mark-ups of 3D objects in the spirit of VRML [2] [3] [4], but where the objects are actual physical entities in a remote space rather than simply models.

Exhibits can be added or removed in a matter of a few minutes, allowing for an extremely dynamic array of objects to be viewed over the course of only a few months. Users are encouraged not only to check back for upcoming exhibits, but to participate themselves. Users can leave commentary about an item on exhibit, creating dialogue about the piece, as well as feedback to the owner, artist, or curator of the object. Institutions, museums, curators, scientists, artists, and individual users are all invited to exhibit objects in the browser.

Goals and Motivation

Early in the summer of 1994, we realized that we had the equipment and resources to design an inexpensive publicly accessible tool for remote environment browsing. We were also inspired by the diversity and growth of the WWW as a medium for this tool. In addition we were driven to develop a useful application for interactive robots on the WWW.

The restrictions imposed by the HyperText Markup Language (HTML) made it difficult to design an intuitive user interface to a complex 6 axis robotic system. Certainly, we could have chosen to construct custom navigation software for users to download. While this would allow us more freedom in the design of the overall system, it would severely restrict the accessibility of the browser. Since we consider the quantity and diversity of users on the WWW as one of its most powerful aspects, we choose to constrain the development of our system within the accessibility of WWW users.

Background

One of the early goals of the project was to incorporate methods in which users could remotely examine and comment on actual museum exhibits. At first we were interested in how well such a tool would operate on insect exhibits. We developed a prototype telerobotic browser and presented it at the Biological Collections Information Providers Workshop in January of 1995. At this workshop we received feedback about the uses and implications of such an application to natural science research. Later, in April of 1995, we presented the browser at Wavelength, an art installation in San Francisco exploring the science and nature of movement. At these two arenas we were able to learn what elements of the browser were important, not only to scientists performing research, but also to novice users attempting to explore various remote spaces.

Goals

Before designing the system we set forth our goals for the project. Our primary goal is to provide a universal remote environment browsing tool that is useful for the arts, sciences, and in the development of education and distant learning. To meet this goal we agreed upon several elements that we felt were essential to any remote environment browser.

First, we wanted to ensure universal unrestricted access to the browser. This would allow access to artifacts and objects by a wider audience than previously available. Current access restrictions are usually the result of geographic, political, or monetary constraints preventing the individual from traveling to the object. Likewise, owners and curators of exhibits do not always have the

resources or the desire to tour the object throughout the world. We wanted to develop a tool that would attempt to solve many of these problems by bringing the people together with the objects at a minimum cost.

Rather than a fixed, static display, the browser must allow users true three-dimensional navigation around objects at varying positions, orientations, and levels of resolution. As David Gelernter suggests in his book *Mirror Worlds* [5], such systems that gaze into remote spaces should show each visitor exactly what they want to see. This requires the system to provide millions of different views from millions of different focuses on the same object. Certainly visitors will desire to zoom in, pan around, and roam through the remote environment as they choose. More importantly, they should be permitted to explore this space at whatever pace and level of detail they desire. Users should also be free to swivel and rotate the image, to get a better look at regions that might be obscured in the initial perspective.

The browser should provide to the exhibit owners, curators, and caretakers a forum to receive feedback and commentary about their exhibit. This same forum should also allow scientists to discuss details concerning classification of specimens such as insects or the origins of a recently discovered artifact. Essentially, some method for leaving comments and creating dialogue should be provided.

Finally, the system should allow exhibits to be added and removed with a minimum of effort, thus providing the possibility of exhibiting a wide variety of objects over the course of a few months. In addition, recently discovered/developed scientific objects should be able to be added for universal browsing within the order of a few minutes.

Why Use Live Images?

A common objection to our approach is why we simply do not use pre-stored digitized images for browsing objects and spaces. While we agree upon the importance of such pre-stored images, the remote environment browser offers several distinct advantages over conventional image database solutions.

For example, the standard approach to providing remote access to museum collections' visual data is to digitize and pre-store images of all artifacts or specimens. This solution requires considerable expense and time commitment to complete the capture, storage, and serving of digitized images. Our telerobotic approach allows remote users to interactively view museum artifacts and specimens on demand. This allows them to achieve much higher image resolution without the expensive digital storage requirements typically associated with large image databases. Our interactive viewing solution also relieves museums of the need to store digital images of entire collections over a variety of resolutions.

Our approach allows immediate visual access to any and all collection materials from the beginning of a project. Traditional image capturing can take several years for large research collections, with millions of specimens that require special handling. The remote environment browser solution eliminates the waiting period that usually occurs during serial indexing and image capture. Museums that utilize a remote browsing model are able to provide remote access to any and all of their collection materials at a moment's notice, as opposed to access to a serially increasing number of objects over time. The ability to view specimens is more valuable if all specimens are available, the fewer specimens in a collection that are digitized, the less research value accrues to the resource as a whole.

With a three-dimensional object there will always be arguments surrounding what view to capture. By allowing researchers to choose their own view and magnification of the specimen or artifact, arguments over which specific view or number of views a museum should provide to remote users are eliminated. Unless users can choose their own view of museum collections' materials, they will not be satisfied with using digital images for research. Even more importantly, some visually oriented research uses such as taxonomy and morphology cannot be supported in the digital environment without the provision of multiple views and magnifications. Useful statistics can be gathered by the browser as to which views are more popular among scientists and hence draw conclusions as to the relative importance of particular views and resolutions. This statistical information also provides useful data when later choosing a single static view to best represent the the object.

Certainly, dynamic exhibits such as live creatures, moving liquids, and mechanical systems must be viewed using live images. These live views are necessary to study the behavior of such systems.

Further discussions about the use of digital images in art and science, as well the implications of their use can be found in several sources [6] [7] [8] [9].

Previous and Related Work

The sensation of embodiment of an individual in a real-life distant location has provided more than enough impetus for people to develop remote telepresence systems.

Historical Telepresence Systems

Methods of achieving telepresence are not new. Early devices such as the *Camera Obscura* allowed viewers to be tricked into believing they were in another space. In the 1940s Joseph Cornell produced various boxes that created the illusion when peeped into of a miniature three-dimensional space. Later, in the 1960s, the picturephone, although never widely adopted, provided an early sensation of remote interaction.

One of the earliest mechanical teleoperational systems was developed by Goertz [10] in 1954. Many subsequent systems were aimed at safely exploring hostile remote environments such as battlefields, nuclear reactors [11], deep oceans [12], mining [13], and outer space [14]. Additional applications for teleoperated surgery [15] and manufacturing [16] have been explored by many researchers [17] [18] [19].

Most of these system are quite complex, requiring special purpose dedicated hardware to control and interact with the mechanism in the remote environment. As one of our goals states, we wanted to constrain development to a system that would be accessible to a wide audience without additional expensive or extraordinary hardware.

Telepresence on the WWW

The spontaneous growth of the WWW over the past several years has resulted in a plethora of remote-controlled mechanical devices that can be accessed via the WWW [20]. Some of these early systems employed fixed cameras in remote spaces where users could observe dynamic behavior such as the consumption and brewing of coffee in a coffee pot [21] or the activity of a favorite pet in its native habitat.

Systems evolved to allow users various levels of control via the WWW such as the LabCam [22] developed by Richard Wallace. His system allows remote users to aim a pan/tilt camera using an intuitive imagemap [23] interface.

Progression to intricate control of more degrees of freedom was realized by introducing robots to the WWW. Ken Goldberg et al. [24] developed a three-axis telerobotic system where users were able to explore a remote world with buried objects and, more interestingly, alter it by blowing bursts of compressed air into its sand-filled world. Mark Cox [25] developed a system for allowing users to request images from a remotely controlled telescope. Another remote robotic system, developed by Ken Taylor [26], allowed WWW users to remotely manipulate blocks using a robot with an attached gripper. More recently, Ken Goldberg et al. have developed a telerobotic system called the TeleGarden [27] in which WWW users are able to observe, plant, and nurture life within a living remote garden. As of this

writing, well over a hundred interesting mechanical devices are connected to the WWW with more spawning daily.

Currently, manipulation of three-dimensional virtual objects requires separate browsers such as WebSpace [28] for documents written in the Virtual Reality Modeling Language (VRML) [4] or browser extensions such as those for the Object Oriented Graphics Language [29]. Standardized systems for browsing *real* remote spaces have yet to come to maturity.

Overview

Our design choice for the user interface to the remote environment browser was to mimic much of the look and feel of a museum. We chose this approach, hoping that users would find it familiar to navigate, and thus more intuitive and inviting to use.

As a user enters Mechanical Gaze, she is presented with a chance to view some general information about the project, receive a brief introduction, obtain help in using the system, statically view previous and upcoming exhibits, or enter the actual exhibition gallery.

Users who enter the exhibition gallery are presented with an up-to-date listing of the exhibits currently available for browsing. These are the exhibits that are physically within the workspace of the robot and can be explored. The idea behind the exhibition gallery is to give only a brief introduction to each of the available exhibits. This typically consists of providing the name of each exhibit, the dates it will be available, the presenter(s), and perhaps a very brief description.

Users who wish to more closely examine an exhibit can simply select it from the listing. The user will then be presented with a more detailed description of the exhibit as well as a chance to either browse the exhibit using the robot or request to view the comments corresponding to that exhibit.

Hardware

The browser is composed of an Intelledex 605T robot, a 1970s era industrial robotic arm with six degrees of freedom. This robot's use as a research tool has diminished over the years, and it is now primarily used for laboratory instruction in an introductory robotics course. As a result, it is inactive for all but a few weeks a year. Through this project, we were able to place most of this equipment back into useful service.

Image capturing is performed using a camera and frame grabber hardware. Images are received from a modified RCA Pro843 8mm video camera mounted onto the last link of the robot. The auto-focus feature of the video camera allows users to view a variety of objects clearly, irregardless of the object's own height or the distance from which it is viewed. Typical exhibition spaces allow users to capture clear images anywhere from 1-30 cm from the surface of the object. Since we desired an easily reconfigurable exhibition space, a fixed focus camera would not be able to accommodate the wide variety of differently sized objects. Likewise, using a custom built mechanism that allowed users to adjust the focus manually, would unnecessarily complicate the hardware in the system and almost certainly the user interface. A manual or remote controlled focusing feature is more applicable in a teleoperated system with real-time image feedback such as that available through the multicast backbone (MBONE) [30] [31] of the Internet as discussed in the section called "Real-Time Audio and Video." Image digitization occurs on an SBUS-based VideoPix frame grabber card attached to a Sun IPC workstation. Eight bit 360x240 color images are captured in less than 50 ms. Further computation to convert the image into a compressed GIF or JPEG format for incorporation into HTML documents and save it to disk takes an additional 2-3 seconds. Overall, the time required to capture, convert, and save an image is on the order of 2-3 seconds.

The actual HyperText Transmission Protocol (HTTP) server containing the custom common gateway interface (CGI) scripts and state information for individual users operates from an HP 715/60 workstation. This machine provides the front-end interface to the system by receiving requests from users, employing the services of the other hardware in the system, and delivering the results back to the user in an HTML format. Figure 1 shows the delivery process used.

The browser has also used a four-axis Robot-World robot with an SGI-Based frame grabber. Our browser is designed to operate correctly on a variety of different physical robotic systems. In fact, plans to operate the browser simultaneously across several robots, transparent to the user, is in progress.

Robot Interface and Control

Control of the robot is through interpreted commands sent to the robot on a 9600 baud serial line connected to a Sun IPC workstation. In order to interface this to the WWW, two separate software tools were constructed. First, a daemon was set up to handle requests involving the robot and camera hardware. The interface from the WWW to this daemon is controlled by the second group of software.

Radius: The Robot Control Daemon

The Intelledex robot is connected via a serial line to a Sun Workstation where a robot daemon called **Radius** runs continuously. When first executed, this daemon initializes all of the hardware. This includes the serial line connection to the Intelledex, the VideoPix video digitizing board on this Sun workstation, and the Intelledex itself. It then listens for robot requests via a dedicated socket connection. All requests for any service that involves control of the robot or camera hardware are handled by **Radius**.

When a socket connection is made, **Radius** first checks for authentication using a known encod-

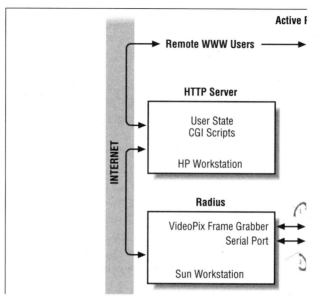

Active I

Remote WWW Users →

HTTP Server

User State
CGI Scripts

HP Workstation

Radius

VideoPix Frame Grabber
Serial Port

Sun Workstation

INTERNET

Figure 1:   System architecture

ing. This prevents unauthorized control of the robot hardware. This is particularly important as we move towards devices with the capacity of physical manifestations of energy in a remote environment. The damage resulting from an unauthorized access into such as system can cause not only irreparable damage to the robotic equipment and exhibits, but human injury as well. Therefore, measures to prevent at least the most naive attacks should be included in such systems.

Authorized connections to **Radius** include a 4-byte request type descriptor. The request encodes the type of request and a mask. The request type can be a position query, motion command, or image capture command. The robot can be queried or commanded using either direct commands to the robots joint motors or by providing a cartesian pose from which the inverse kinematics are calculated for the corresponding robot joint values. It's important to note that **Radius** keeps track of the robot's state so that no extra communication is necessary to the Intelledex to satisfy any robot position queries. In

addition the request mask determines which axis or joint values should be moved and the results, sent back to the client. This allows for movement of a single degree of freedom if desired.

Motion requests are converted by **Radius** into Intelledex native control commands and sent on the serial port to the robot hardware. **Radius** can also query the robot to determine when all motions have stopped, hence allowing an image to be captured.

Image capturing is also handled by **Radius**. When an image capture request is received, the VideoPix hardware digitizes an image, converts it to a Portable Pixmap (PPM) format internally and finally to a compressed GIF or JPEG file. The file is output into a temporary space and assigned a unique identification number. This number is passed back to the requesting process so that the correct image will be displayed in the HTML document passed back to the corresponding user.

This socket connection also provides the mutual exclusion necessary to insure the correct functionality of Mechanical Gaze even when handling multiple requests. Since our interface design is WWW based, requests are event driven. After a user has loaded an image, the robot is left idle until the user makes another request. Instead of allowing this exclusive access to the robot, leaving the robot idle while the user contemplates his or her next action, we service additional requests from other users. By multitasking, we provide increased access to the robot as well as a more efficient use of system resources. However, we must provide a method to guarantee that certain atomic operations are exclusive. For example, a request to move and grab an image, must be exclusive. This insures that no other motion occurs between the time we move the robot and capture the image. If we had failed to implement this, we would have no guarantee that the image delivered back to the user was actually taken from the location that they requested.

Remote Browser Page Construction

Requests to browse an exhibit are handled by a custom CGI script. Initially, the script is passed a unique identifying internal number corresponding to the exhibit to be browsed. The script reads in the current list of exhibits and extracts the relevant information for the exhibit of interest (see "Adding and Removing Exhibits"). One of these items is the physical location of the exhibit in the remote environment. Using this information, a socket connection is opened to **Radius**, the robot control daemon (see "Radius: The Robot Control Daemon"). Once the socket connection is established, a request is made to move the robot to the desired location and capture an image.

When the result of that request is received, the CGI script dynamically lays out the HTML page. First, it extracts information from the internal list of exhibits. This provides the name of the HTML file to place at the head of the browser page. Next, it inlines the captured and converted GIF or JPEG image, placing it within an imagemap with a unique user identification number. Then

the location of the robot relative to the boundaries of the exhibit provide a measure for composing the various status indicators. One of these indicators, shown in Figure 3, is a graphical representation of the location of the image displayed with respect to the boundaries of the exhibit volume. This indicator is image-mapped and can be used for navigation within the browser. The other indicators are also image-mapped and used for navigation. They reflect the current state of the zoom, roll, and pitch. All of the the status indicators are generated using GD, a graphics library for fast GIF creation developed by Thomas Boutell of the Quest Protein Database Center at Cold Spring Harbor Labs [32].

Additional navigation icons are attached to the page. These icons allow users to leave comments about the exhibit, move to the next or previous exhibit, returning to the list of exhibits, obtain help, or return home. Finally, the comments left by users viewing this exhibit are appended to the page, completing the delivery of the HTML file. The CGI script also writes out a unique internal user file. This file contains the state information concerning the page and accompanying image just delivered such as the position of the robot when the image was captured, the exhibit being viewed, etc. This allows for subsequent requests by this user to result in correct robot motions relative to a users current image. Remember that between requests from a particular user, any number of additional requests may have been handled by **Radius**, and there is no guarantee on the current location of the robot when the next request from that user is received. The final result of a remote environment navigation request is a page similar to the one depicted in Figure 2.

System Utilities

Our system is fairly distributed, employing several different pieces of hardware. To manage these systems as well as maintain the system in a functional state, several utilities were developed.

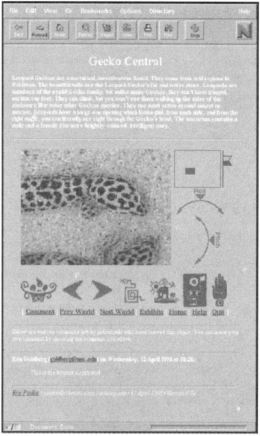

Figure 2:   An active browser navigation page

Dynamic HTML

Dynamic HTML (dHTML) is a superset of the HTML language. dHTML documents appear and behave similar to HTML except for a special escape sequence described by a series of double less-than signs (<<) , followed by a keyword, and terminated by corresponding greater-than signs (>>). Their main function is in describing relationships to other documents that may change dynamically. These dHTML documents are preprocessed by the dynamic HTML parser that converts the escaped keywords into "correct" HTML.

For example, in Mechanical Gaze we may desire that an anchor be set to link from the present exhibition document to the next exhibit. How-

ever, we don't know *a priori* the name of the HTML file for the next exhibit or if it even exists. Even if we did know, the removal of a single exhibit would require time consuming hand updating of many of the other active exhibit pages to maintain correct functionality of the system. Therefore, we exploit the property of dHTML documents to perform these tasks. We solve the above example and others like it by placing the escaped keyword sequence for "next exhibit" in the dHTML document in place of an HTML link to the next exhibit. When requested, this page passes through the dHTML pre-processor that knows information about all of the exhibits and the specific exhibit corresponding to the page it is processing. When it encounters the escaped keyword sequence, it substitutes the correct corresponding link dynamically.

Adding and Removing Exhibits

Since our system is dynamic by the very nature that it moves and delivers current images from a remote environment, we also wanted to allow the individual exhibits to be dynamic and change rapidly. The only limit on the number of exhibits available is the physical dimensions of the robot's workspace, which total approximately 8000 square cm.

Each exhibit contains an entry in the current exhibits file from which the CGI script extracts various information. Included in this file is the number of exhibits along with additional information about each exhibit such as the robot's location for entry into the exhibit and the physical bounding volume available for browsing this exhibit. The bounding volume is described by limits set on the length, width, and zoom for each object. There are also limitations on the amount of roll and pitch permitted. If while browsing an exhibit, a user makes a navigation request that would move the robot out of the legal boundary for that exhibit, an alert page is presented with a description of the illegal motion and help on how to continue browsing.

A unique directory name for each exhibit is also contained in the current exhibits file. This directory contains an introduction HTML file used to describe the exhibit when users request the list of current exhibits, a description HTML file containing additional information about the exhibit, a header HTML file to place at the beginning of each browser page, and a file containing the running dialogue and comments for the exhibit that is attached to the end of the browser page. Usage statistics corresponding to each exhibit are also located in this directory.

The result of this approach is that adding and removing exhibits is quick and easy. To add an exhibit, one places it into the robot workspace and provides the appropriate introduction,

description, and header files. The addition is immediately active by simply inserting the physical location of the exhibit and its boundaries into the list of current exhibits. Removing an exhibit is accomplished by the even easier task of taking its entry out of the current exhibits list. All modifications of the current exhibits list are effective immediately.

User Registration

One of our goals is to provide all WWW users unrestricted access to the browser. However, certain features of the system are more effective when reasonably accurate information is known about the user. For example, when leaving comments, it is helpful to append the message with the name of the user for identification, an email address that other users can use to correspond privately, and perhaps a pointer to a home page so viewers can familiarize themselves with that individual. Allowing users to enter all of this information manually for each comment is not only tedious but problematic. There's little preventing a user from assuming the identity of another user or anonymously dumping pages of garbage text into the commentary. Therefore, we developed a method for users to register themselves by providing a name, email address, and a home page pointer (optional). A password is mailed back to them to be used for registering themselves on subsequent visits. This request for information is not intended to be a violation of a user's privacy. Nor is it intended to be sold or given out. More importantly, this does not violate our goal of unrestricted access since *anyone* can become a member.

Registered users gain a few additional privileges. When navigating the robot, they are provided the roll and pitch control tools shown in Figure 6. These two tools permit full control of all robot axes. For non-registered users these tools are replaced with the simplified zoom in and zoom out buttons to guide the robot as shown in Figure 5. Also, only registered users are permitted to leave comments about the various exhibits.

Figure 3:   The location status indicator tool before and after scrolling

Navigational Tools

After receiving a remote environment browser page, a user may wish to modify the vantage point of the exhibit and obtain a new image. This modification takes place by employing one or more of the navigational tools presented to the user from the active browser navigation page shown in Figure 2. These tools are used often since they allow for motions that provide the user with the sensation of browsing or exploring a remote space.

Scrolling

The captured image is image-mapped and provides the interface to scroll the camera. Scrolling moves the camera in the direction relative to the center of the image and in the plane normal to its previous position. The distance from the center of an image also affects the magnitude of motion in that direction. For example, selections on the outer border of an image move the camera a predefined maximum step in that direction, while points closer to the center of the image result in smaller fractions of motion. This allows users to perform both coarse and fine motions. The maximum step is a function of the height of the camera from the exhibition floor. This provides the proper scaling of scroll motions when the camera is closely zoomed into an object. For most exhibits the result is that selections in the image are brought to the center of the image. However, this is difficult to guarantee since we have exhibits with a wide variety of heights and sizes.

Large macro-motions can be performed by selecting a new location within the exhibit space using the location status indicator tool shown in Figure 3. This indicator gives the location relative to the boundaries of the particular exhibit from which the image was taken. Selecting a new location within the indicator causes the next image to be delivered from that new vantage.

Zooming

Every exhibit allows a user to zoom closer to an object for more detailed inspection, as well as to zoom out to achieve a wide angle view. Zooming is accomplished through the zoom status indicator tool located on the right size of the image and shown in Figure 4. The camera mimics the motions of the thermometer indicator, raising and lowering itself from the exhibit. An imagemap on this tool allows transformation of user selections directly to zoom levels. Like the location status

Figure 4:   The zoom status indicator tool

Figure 5:   Simplified zoom control tool for non-registered users

indicator tool, this tool is re-scaled for each exhibit based on the zoom boundaries set for that exhibit.

Non-registered users are provided with two additional simplified zoom icons in place of the roll/pitch tools. These icons allow for easy control of image zoom and are shown in Figure 5. Selections anywhere within each of the two icons result in the obvious inward or outward zooming.

Rolling and Pitching

Rolling and pitching the camera are more complex actions and certainly a challenge to implement from within a two-dimensional HTML document. Therefore, these more advanced features are provided only to registered users (See the section called "User Registration"). Although this may sound contrary to our goal of providing unrestricted global access to all users, we remind the reader that *anyone* may become a registered user.

The roll and pitch tools are composed of semi-arcs with attached pointers. Choosing a point on an arc will cause the camera to roll or pitch depending upon the selection and deliver the resulting image. The current roll and pitch values are displayed within the tool itself by relocating the corresponding pointers as show in Figure 6.

When rolling or pitching, the focus is maintained on the surface in the center of the image. One can imagine this as walking along the surface of a semi-sphere with its center fixed.

Reloading

Often a user may be observing a dynamic event. To receive an updated image taken from the same position, the user selects the reload button provided within the document. The result is an updated image taken from the exact same camera pose. For example, a remote user observing a Leopard Gecko lizard consume a meal, may choose to reload during the sequence. A more applicable model for transmitting dynamic events is discussed in the next section.

Real-Time Audio and Video

Future remote browsing systems will allow for navigation of the remote spaces with real-time video and audio feedback. We wanted to begin preliminary research into this arena by allowing users to receive real-time video and audio from the remote browser without compromising our goal to provide real remote environment browsing without special equipment requirements. Multicasting, a form of intelligently routed real-time broadcasting is currently provided by utilizing protocols developed for the multicast backbone (MBONE) of the Internet [30] [31] [33] [34].

Essentially, the MBONE allows for broadcasting to multiple sites on the Internet providing a mechanism for real-time communications over wide areas, such as the world. This is possible because of the use of IP networks implementing a lightweight, highly threaded model of communication. The MBONE has only been developed

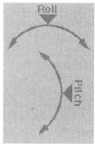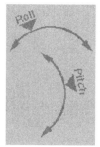

Figure 6:   Two different views of the roll and pitch tool

over the last few years but is poised to soon become the status quo of routing on the Internet.

Even more promising to the universal adoption of real-time audio and video tools is the CU-SeeMe [35] software developed for Macintosh and PC systems. Using this software, anyone with a personal computer and a Serial Line Internet Protocol (SLIP) or Point to Point Protocol (PPP) connection can connect to MBONE reflector sites and receive live video and audio feeds. Even home users, connected at 14.4 kb/s, can receive adequate 16-shade greyscale images at about a frame per second.

In our remote browser we have set up two Connectix QuickCam [36] cameras, transmitting 16-shade greyscale images to a reflector site at Berkeley and out onto the MBONE. Due to bandwidth limitation, these transmission are only made at specific announced times. One camera is mounted at the end of the last link of the robot, giving a view of the exhibits as they are browsed by the WWW browser. The second is fixed in the room and gives a view of the entire industrial robot and the exhibition table, including all of the exhibits. Plans are also in place to intermittently feed real-time audio so that users can listen to the sounds of the industrial robot or any creatures in the exhibit. All control is still carried out via the WWW interface.

Future Ideas and Discussion

There are many modifications, improvements, and additions that could be made to the present browser. We discuss a few of the more relevant ones here. Actual robot interaction with the exhibit should be possible. Currently, the risk of damaging the exhibits outweighs the benefits of implementing such a tool.

Mounting one or more additional cameras onto the robot, opens up several possibilities. 3D stereo vision images could be delivered to the user while scientists could benefit from additional high resolution cameras for research applications. The camera pair would be able to provide depth information to the user and aid in focusing. Besides extra cameras, a selection of colored lights for the user to select from when viewing would be a useful tool. Encoding unique views of objects as links would allow experts and individuals to design tours of collections of exhibits, pointing out features and details of interest.

The adoption of a new dynamic, extensible WWW browser called HotJava [37], will allow for even more levels of interaction between remote users and with mechanical devices. HotJava can run executable content in the form of applets— Java programs that can be included in an HTML page, much like images can be included. When you use the HotJava browser to view a page that contains an applet, the applet's code is transferred to your system and executed by the HotJava browser. This means that applets could be written to open a connection back to the machine controlling the actual mechanical device. Control signals to the devices can be generated and controlled directly by the applet. In addition the applet can execute a separate thread to handle receiving and updating of the continuously changing inline live image being fed back.

Using a similar interface, users could control other robotic systems, hopefully allowing browsing of much larger objects as well as microscopic ones. We are currently designing a helium blimp based mobile robotic environment browser for exploring larger spaces. Browsing and co-habitation of a smaller scale space filled with various reptiles is also in progress. ■

Acknowledgments

Many people were inspirational in helping with ideas, suggestions, comments, and feedback about Mechanical Gaze during its development: Ken Goldberg, Natalie K. Munn, Jim Beach, Jeff Wendlandt, Shankar Sastry, Ferenc Kovac, Robert Guralnick, Zane Vella, Mark Pauline, Christian Ristow, Mark Cox, David Pescovitz, and Tho Nguyen.

References

1. Tim Berners-Lee, et al, "World-wide web: The information universe," *Electronic Networking: Research, Applications and Policy*, 1(2), Westport CT, Spring 1992.

2. Tamara Munzner, Paul Burchard, and Ed Chi, "Visualization through the world wide web with geomview, cyberview, w3kit, and weboogl," in *WWW 2 Conference Proceedings*, 1994.

3. Sandy Ressler, "Approaches using virtual environments with mosaic," in *WWW 2 Conference Proceedings*, 1994.

4. *http://vrml.wired.com/*

5. David Gelernter, *Mirror Worlds*, Oxford University Press, 1992.

6. H. John Durrett, *Color and the computer*, Academic Press, 1987.

7. C.A. Lynch, "The technologies of electronic imaging," *Journal of the american society for informaion science*, pages 578-585, September 1991.

8. M. Ester, "Image quality and viewer perception," in *SIGGRAPH 1990 art show*, pages 51-63, August 1990.

9. J.L. Kirsch and R.A. Kirsch, "Storing art images in intelgent computers," in *Leonardo*, volume 23, pages 99-106, 1990.

10. Raymond Goertz and R. Thompson, "Electronically controlled manipulator," *Nucleonics*, 1954.

11. A.E.R. Greaves, "State of the art in nuclear telerobotic: focus on the man/machine connection," in *Transations of the American Nuclear Society*, 1994.

12. R. D. Ballard, "A last long look at titanic," *National Geographic*, December 1986.

13. C. Ntuen, E. Park, and S. Kimm, "A blackboard architecture for human-machine interface in mining teleoperation," in *Human Computer Interaction*, 1993.

14. C.R. Weisbin and D. Lavery, "Nasa rover and telerobotics technology program," in *IEEE Conference on Robotics and Automation Magazine*, 1994.

15. P.S. Green, J.W. Hill, J.F. Jensen, and A. Shah, "Telepresence surgery" in *IEEE Engineering in Medicine and Biology Magazine*, 1995.

16. J.V. Draper, "Teleoperators for advanced manufacturing: applications and human factors callenges" in *International Journal of Human Factors in Manufacturing*, 1995.

17. R. S. Mosher, "Industrial manipulators," *Scientific American*, 211(4), 1964.

18. R. Tomovic, "On man-machine control," *Automatica*, 5, 1969.

19. Hans Moravec, *"Mind Children. The Future of Robot and Human Intelligence."* Harvard University Press, 1988.

20. *http://www.yahoo.com/Computers_and_Internet/ Internet/Interesting_Devices_Connected_to_the_ Net/*

21. *http://www.cl.cam.ac.uk/coffee/coffee.html*

22. *http://found.cs.nyu.edu/cgi-bin/rsw/labcam1*

23. *http://booboo.ncsa.uiuc.edu/docs/setup/admin/ Imagemap.html*

24. K. Goldberg, M. Mascha, S. Gentner, N. Rothenberg, C. Sutter, and Jeff Wiegley, Robot teleoperation via www. In *International Conference on Robotics and Automation*. IEEE, May 1995.

25. *http://www.telescope.org/*

26. *http://telerobot.mech.uwa.edu.au/*

27. *http://www.usc.edu/dept/garden/*

28. *http://www.sgi.com/Products/WebFORCE/Web-Space/*

29. *http://www.geom.umn.edu/apps/cyberview3d/*

30. Steve Deering, "Mbone: The multicast backbone," in *CERFnet Seminar*, March 1993.

31. H. Schulzrinne and S. Casner, "RTP: A transport protocol for real-time applications," in *Internet Engineering Task Force*, October 1993.

32. *http://siva.cshl.org/gd/gd.html*

33. M. R. Macedonia and D. P. Brutzman, "Mbone provides audio and video across the internet," in *IEEE Computer*, volume 27, pages 30-36, April 1994.

34. S. Deering, D. Estrin, D. Farrinaci, V. Jacobson, C. Liu, and L. Wei, "Protocol independent multicasting (PIM): Protocol specification," in *IETF Network Working Draft*, 1995.

35. *http://www.jungle.com/msattler/sci-tech/comp/CU-SeeMe/*

36. *http://www.jungle.com/msattler/sci-tech/comp/hardware/quickcam.html*

37. *http://java.sun.com/*

About the Authors

Eric Paulos

[*http://www.cs.berkeley.edu/~paulos*]
Department of Electrical Engineering and Computer Science
University of California
Berkeley, CA 94720-1776
paulos@cs.berkeley.edu

John Canny

[*http://www.cs.berkeley.edu/~jfc*]
Department of Electrical Engineering and Computer Science
University of California
Berkeley, CA 94720-1776
jfc@cs.berkeley.edu

DATA TRANSPORT WITHIN THE DISTRIBUTED OCEANOGRAPHIC DATA SYSTEM

James Gallagher, George Milkowski

Abstract

The Distributed Oceanographic Data System (DODS) is a client-server system which enables existing data analysis programs to be transformed from software, which is limited to accessing local data, to clients, which can access data from any of a large number of data servers. This is done without requiring modification to the existing software's source code by reimplementing the data access API libraries used by those programs. Once a given API library is modified to read from a DODS data server, any program which uses that library as its sole means of accessing data can be relinked with the new implementation and can function as a client within DODS. Data servers which can be accessed by these clients are built using filter programs and one or more httpd Common Gateway Interface (CGI) programs. Data sets made available are thus accessible via URLs. While the data servers' principal function is to provide the client programs with values from the data sets, they also make available, as text, information about the variables in the data set and their data types. This information can be accessed by any WWW browser. **Keywords:** *Legacy software, science data, raw data, network access*

Introduction

It does not take long using the World Wide Web (WWW) to discover many hundreds of scientific datasets that are currently available online to researchers. For oceanographers the volume and diversity of data from national archives, special program offices, or other researchers that is of potential value to their research is overwhelming. However, while a large number of oceanographic datasets are online, from the research oceanographer's point of view there are significant impediments which often make acquiring and using these online data hard [7].

The storage format of data is often specific to a particular system, making it difficult to view or combine several datasets even though, as Pursch points out, combining data sets is often a key requirement of global-scale earth science [13]. Furthermore, most data archives have developed their own data management systems with specialized interfaces for navigating their data resources. Examples of such specialized systems include the

Global Land Information System (GLIS) [22] developed by the U.S. Geological Survey (USGS) and the NOAA/NASA Oceans Pathfinder Data System developed at the Jet Propulsion Laboratory (JPL) [10]. Virtually none of these data systems interoperate with each other, making it necessary for a user to visit many systems and "learn" multiple interfaces in order to acquire data. Finally, even after the data has been successfully transfered to the researcher's local system, in order to *use* the data a researcher must convert that data into the format that his or her data analysis application requires or alternatively modify the analysis application [13].

Many national data centers and university laboratories are now providing remote access to their scientific data holdings through the World Wide Web. Users are able to select, display, and transfer these data using WWW browsers such as Netscape and NCSA Mosaic. Examples of such systems are the NOAA/PMEL-Thermal Modeling and Analysis Project [12] and the University of Rhode Island Sea Surface Temperature Archive

[20]. However, current generation HTML browsers (Netscape 1.1, Mosaic 2.4) are limited and cumbersome when compared to other data access and display client-server systems such as the Global Land Information System (GLIS) developed by the USGS. While WWW browsers are very useful for pedagogical purposes they have limited capabilities in terms of data analysis or manipulation. In the era of Global Change researchers will need tools that provide both network access and data analysis functionality [13, 11].

Finally, while large data centers have a clearly defined data policy, and often a mandate to make data accessible to members of the research community [9], there is no infrastructure that enables individual scientists to make data accessible to others in a simple way. While many scientists in the earth-sciences community share data, and cite shared data as one of their most important resources, doing so is often cumbersome [2]. Systems like the World Wide Web make sharing research results vastly simpler, but do little to reduce the difficulty of sharing raw data.

To address these problems, researchers at the University of Rhode Island and the Massachusetts Institute of Technology are creating a network tool that, while taking advantage of WWW data resources, helps to resolve the issue of multiple data formats and different data systems interfaces. This network tool, called the Distributed Oceanographic Data System (DODS), enables oceanographers to interactively access distributed, online science data using the one interface that a researcher is already familiar with; existing data analysis application software (i.e., legacy systems) while at the same time providing a set of tools which can be used to build new application software specifically intended to work with distributed resources. The architecture and design of DODS make it possible for a researcher to open, read, subsample, and import directly into his or her data analysis applications scientific data resources using the WWW. The researcher will not need to know either what format is used

to store the data or how the data is actually accessed and served by the remote data system [2].

Extending Existing Data Access APIs

The Distributed Oceanographic Data System is a specification for directly accessing, representing, and transferring science data on a network. It is a *data access protocol*, which includes both a common functional interface to data systems and a data model for representing data on those systems. It is designed to be integrated with already existing user applications and resource management systems, not to replace them.

DODS models data analysis programs as some body of user written code linked with one or more API libraries. The API presents a specialized interface which the user program uses to read data. It is straightforward to split the user program at the program-library interface, and by adding suitable interprocess communication layers, create a classical client and server which can use peer-to-peer communications across a network. Figure 1 shows how this can be done using Sun's RPC technology [18]. However, any suitable network layer can accomplish this goal [16].

For the remainder of this paper a data access API that has been modified to satisfy each of its functions by communicating with a matching data server, as opposed to accessing a local file, will be referred to as a *client library*. The matching data server will be referred to as a *data server* or simply as a *server*.

Once a client library has been constructed for a given API, it is possible to relink many user programs written for the API with this new library. If the API hides the storage format of the data being accessed and the program uses the API correctly (i.e., without taking advantage of any undocumented features present in the original version but not present in the new client-library version),

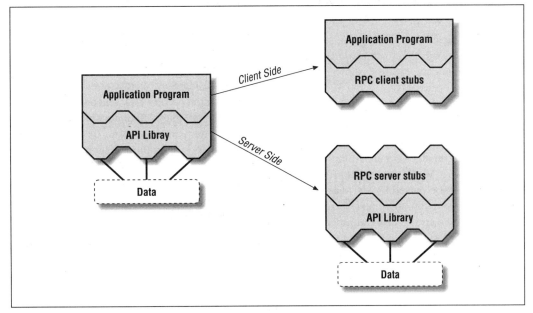

Figure 1:   Implementation of distributed application—API access using remote procedure calls

then the program will require no modification to work with the new implementation of the API. A program thus relinked can read data from any machine so long as that machine has installed a matching data server. Because the same API has been used by many programs, reimplementing it so that it reads information over the network facilitates the transformation of each program into a client capable of accessing data provided by any suitable server on the network.

Data Delivery Design

Several designs were considered for the data delivery mechanism of DODS. They were socket-based peer-to-peer communications, RPC-based peer-to-peer communications, virtual file systems, and HTTP/CGI-based client/server systems. The first three of these different designs are compared in: Report on the First Workshop for the Distributed Oceanographic Data System [2] and DODS-Data Delivery [6], which presents our rationale behind prototyping the RPC-based design for DODS. However, as a result of those prototypes

and the development of HTTP as a *de facto* data communications standard, we changed the data delivery design to an HTTP/CGI-based system.

By using HTTP as a transport protocol, we are able to tap into a large base of existing software which will likely evolve along with the Internet as a whole. Because the development of large-scale distributed systems is relatively new there are many problems which must still be addressed for these systems to be robust. These problems include naming resources independently of their physical location, choosing between two objects which appear to be the same but which differ in terms of quality. These are general problems which are hard to solve because they will be solved effectively only when the Internet community reaches a consensus on which of the available solutions are best. HTTP, because it is so widely accepted, provides a reasonable base for such solutions. This view is supported by the recent Internet Engineering Task Force (IETF) [3] work on extending the HTTP and HTML standards.

Client/server and Program/library Interfaces

The DODS client library and data server programs communicate information using URLs and MIME [1] documents. Figure 2 shows these two communication paths.

All information sent from the server programs to the client library is enclosed in a MIME document. Two of the three programs return information about the variables contained in the data set as `text/plain` MIME documents. These documents can then be parsed by software in the client library. In addition, these text documents can be read by any software that can process ASCII text. Thus, the responses made by the server are specifically suited to use by the DODS client libraries, they can also be used by many more general programs. For example, it is possible to use a general purpose World Wide Web browser to 'read' these documents.

The third data server program returns binary data encoded using Sun Microsystems External Data representation (XDR) [17] scheme. The data is enclosed in a binary MIME document. This document can be read by software that is part of the client library using the additional information contained in the two ASCII documents. This document can only be read by software that can interpret the datatype information sent by the server in the ASCII documents. Because of this, it is not possible for other general purpose WWW browsers to interpret this file (although most

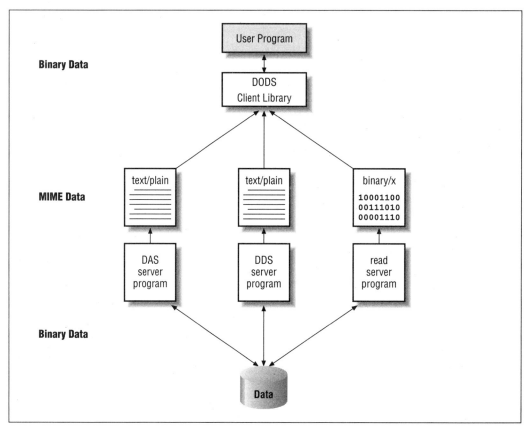

Figure 2:   MIME documents are used by the server programs to return information to the client processes

browsers can read and save to disk any arbitrary data).

In order to provide link-time compatibility with the original API libraries, the DODS client libraries must present *exactly* the same external interface as the original libraries. However, these new libraries perform very different operations on the data (although, for an API used to access a self-describing data format the operations are analogous). One difference between the two is that most data access APIs use file names to refer to data sets. In the simplest case these file names are given on the command line by the user and passed, without modification, to the API. The API uses the file name to open a file and returns an identifier of some type to the user program. Subsequent access to the data are made through this identifier.

In this simple scenario, it is possible to substitute a URL in place of a file name (in part because both are stored in string-type variables). This same user program can be invoked, on the command line, using a URL in place of the file name. The program will, in almost all cases, pass the URL to the API to open the data set. However, since the user program has been relinked with the DODS reimplementation of the API, the functions in the API will correctly interpret the URL as a remote reference. Clearly, one requirement that a user program must meet in order to be relinked with DODS is that it must not itself try to open or otherwise manipulate the "file name" which will be passed to the API.

Rewriting existing APIs is hard to implement; it would be much simpler to write our own data display and analysis program to read data from DODS data servers. However, it is important that as much legacy software as possible be able to read the data made accessible by DODS data servers. While this may sound like a trivial requirement, it is wrong to assume that existing data analysis software is simple or can be rewritten at little cost; the existing software in the sciences is no less expensive to rewrite than in any other field. Furthermore, some researchers tailor

there research efforts to the characteristics of particular data systems and see the costs of abandoning those systems as very high [2].

Data Servers

A DODS data server is a collection of three executable programs and/or CGIs which provide access to data using HTTP. Each of the program/CGI units is capable of satisfying one of the three requests which are defined in the dataset access protocol. The DAP defines two ways to access metadata which describes the contents of the data set (one for use by the DODS surrogate libraries and one for use by third-party software and users) and one way to access data. Data access is accomplished by reading the variables which comprise the data set. This access can be modified using a *constraint expression* so that only portions of the variable are actually read from the data set.

The ability to evaluate constraint expressions is an essential characteristic of a DODS data server. In many cases reading a single variable from a data set results in data which is of little or no interest to the user. Often users are interested in those values of a variable which meet some additional criteria (e.g., they fall within a certain time range). For a complete description of the data types supported by DODS and the constraint expression operators, see DODS-Data Access Protocol [21].

Basic Requirements for the Data Servers

The data servers must satisfy two requirements: they must provide access to data via the DAP and they must use online data without requiring its modification.

Providing access to data using the DAP is necessary because that is how the DODS architecture provides interoperability between different APIs. Because the data servers translate accesses to a data set from the DAP into either an API (e.g., netcdf if the data set is stored using that API) or a special format (e.g., GRIB), any (client) process that uses the DAP can access the data. The underlying access mechanism is hidden from the client by the API.

In the current design of DODS, meeting this requirement means that for each API or format in which data is stored, a new DODS data server must be built.

The other requirement which each server must satisfy is that data, however it is stored, should not require modification to be served by a DODS data server. This is important because many data sets are large and thus very expensive to modify. It is a poor practice to force data providers to modify their data to suit the needs of a system. Rather, DODS data servers must be able to translate access via the DAP into the local storage mechanism without changing that local storage mechanism.

This requirement limits DODS to those APIs and formats which are, to some extent, self-describing. Because the DAP bases access on reading a named variable, it must be possible, for each data set, to define the set of variables and to "read" those variables from the data set. However some data sets do not contain enough information to make remote access a reality. Instead, additional information, not in the data set itself, is needed. This information can be stored in ancillary data files which accompany the data set. Note that these files are separate from the data set, they are not added to the data set and do not require any modification of the data set.

The Data Access Protocol

The Data Access Protocol (DAP) is used as an intermediate representation for data which are nominally accessed using an established third-party Application Programmer Interface (API) (e. g., netCDF). Because, in addition to a method for data access, the DAP defines the content of ancillary information about data sets, it provides the means to access data sets through a single protocol using any of the DODS supported APIs.

Because the data access protocol serves as an intermediate representation for several different APIs, it can be used to translate between any two of those APIs [19]. Translation between various APIs was an important requirement for DODS because it was felt that any system which could not perform such translation would artificially limit the data accessible by any one client program [2].

The DODS DAP design contains three important parts: A data model which describes data types that can be supported by the protocol and how they are handled, the data set description and data set attribute structures which describe the structure of data sets and the data they contain, and a small set of messages that are used to access data. Each of these components are described in the following subsections.

The Data Model

Data models provide a way to organize scientific data sets so that useful relationships between individual datum are evident. Many data models have been specifically designed to make using the data in a computer program simpler [14, 8]. Examples of computationally oriented data models for scientific data are hierarchical, sequential, and gridded data models [19].

Data models are abstract, however, and to be used by a computer program they must first be implemented by a programmer. Often this implementation takes the form of an API—a library of functions which can read and write data using a data model or models as guidance [14, 8]. Thus every data access API can be viewed as implementing some data model, or in some cases several data models.

Because DODS needs to support several very different data models, it is important to design it around a core set of concepts that can be applied equally well to each of those data models. If that can be done, then translation between data represented in those different models may be possible [19].

Currently DODS supports two very different data access APIs: netCDF and JGOFS [4]. The netCDF API is designed for access to gridded data, but has some limited capabilities to access sequence data (although not with all of its supported programming language interfaces). The JGOFS API provides access to relational or sequence data. Both APIs support access in several programming languages (at least C and Fortran) and both provide extensive support for limiting the amount of data retrieved. For example a program accessing a gridded data set using netCDF can extract a subsampled portion or *hyperslab* of that data [14]. Likewise, the JGOFS API provides a powerful set of operators which can be used to specify which type of sequence elements to extract (e.g., only those corresponding to data captured between 1:00am and 2:00am) as well as masking certain parameters from the returned elements so that only those parameters needed by the program are returned.

The DODS DAP uses the concepts of variables and operators as the base for the data model. Within the data model, a data set consists of one or more variables where each variable is described formally by a number of attributes. Variables associate names with each component of a data set, and those names are used to refer to the components of the data set. In addition to their different attributes, it is possible to operate on individual variables or named collections of variables. The principal operation is *access*, although in a future version of DODS it will be possible to modify this in a number ways.

Base-type variables

Variables in the DODS DAP have two forms. They are either base types or type constructors. Base type variables are similar to predefined variables in procedural programming languages like C or Fortran (e.g., `int` or `integer*4`). While these certainly have an internal structure, it is not possible to access parts of that structure using the data access protocol. Instead the DAP is used to transfer the values of those variables from the server to the client and, once on the client side, access those values. These types of variables correspond to the simplest types of variables used in both common analysis software and data access APIs [19].

Type constructor variables

Type constructor variables describe the grouping of one or more variables within a data set. These classes are used to describe different types of relations between the variables that comprise the data set. This information can be useful to people who would like to understand more about the data set than can be conveyed with implicit relations. It is also designed to be useful to other programs/processes in the data access chain. There are six classes of type constructor variables defined by the DAP: lists, arrays, structures, sequences, functions, and grids. The type constructor classes besides structure provide information that is used in the translation of subsetting operations (hyperslabbing or selections and projections in netCDF or JGOFS parlance, respectively). They also provide a means to describe many different data types since each of the constructor types can contain each other (as well as instances of themselves). Thus, as is the case with programming languages such as C, DODS provides for an infinite variety of data types built using various combinations of the constructor and base types [15].

The External Representation of Variables

Each of the base-type and type constructor variables has an external representation defined by the data access protocol. This representation is used when an object of the given type is transferred from one computer to another. Defining a single external representation simplifies the translation of variables from one computer to another when those computers use different internal representations for those variable types. The data access protocol uses Sun Microsystems' XDR [17] protocol for the external representation of all of the base type variables. This representation was chosen so that values would be transparent across various machines without transforming them first to ASCII. For some types, ASCII is an acceptable "network" representation, but other types (e.g., floating point types) require significantly more storage when represented as ASCII. XDR was chosen because it defines binary representations for such types [17] and because of its widespread availability.

Dataset Descriptor Structure

In order to translate from the user program's API to the data set's API, the translator process must have some knowledge about the types of the variables, and their semantics, that comprise the data set. It must also know something about the relations of those variables—even those relations which are only implicit in the data set's own API. This knowledge about the data set's structure is contained in a text description of the data set called the *Dataset Description Structure.*

The data set description structure (DDS) does not describe how the information in the data set is physically stored, nor does it describe how the data set's API is used to access that data. Those pieces of information are contained in the data set's API and in the translating server, respec-

tively. The server uses the DDS to describe the logical structure of a particular data set—the DDS contains knowledge about the data set variables and the interrelations of those variables. In addition, the DDS can be used to satisfy some of the DODS supported APIs data set description calls. For example, netCDF has a function which returns the names of all the variables in a netCDF data file. The DDS can be used to get that information.

The DDS is a textual description of the variables and their classes that comprise the entire data set. The data set descriptor syntax is based on the variable declaration/definition syntax of C [5]. A variable that is a member of one of the base type classes is declared by by writing the class name followed by the variable name.

An example DDS entry is shown in Example 1. Suppose that three experimenters have each performed temperature measurements at different locations and at different times. This information could be held in a data set consisting of a sequence of the experimenter's name, the time and location of each measurement and the list of measurements themselves, and indicates that there is a relation between the experimenter, location, time, and temperature called temp_ measurement.

Example 1:   The Textual Representation of the Dataset Description Structure

```
data set {
int catalog_number;
function {
independent:
string experimenter;
int time;
structure {
float latitude;
float longitude;
} location;
dependent:
sequence {
float depth;
float temperature;
} temperature;
} temp_measurement;
} data;
```

Dataset Attribute Structure

The Dataset Attribute Structure (DAS) is used to store attributes for variables in the data set. We define an attribute as any piece of information about a variable that the creator of the data set wants to bind with that variable *excluding* the information contained in the DDS. This definition is essentially the one used by both netCDF [14] and HDF [8]. The characteristics described by the DDS are always defined for every variable; they are data type information about the variable. Attributes, on the other hand, are intended to store extra information about the data such as a paragraph describing how it was collected or processed. In principle, attributes are not processed by software other than to be displayed. However, many systems rely on attributes to store extra information that is necessary to perform certain manipulations on data. In effect, attributes are used to store information that is used "by convention" rather than "by design." DODS can effectively support these conventions by passing the attributes from data set to user program via the DAS. Of course, DODS cannot enforce conventions in data sets where they were not followed in the first place.

Every attribute of a variable is a triple: attribute name, type, and value. The attributes specified using the DAS are different from the information contained in the DDS. Each attribute is completely distinct from the name, type and value of its associated variable. The name of an attribute is an identifier, following the normal rules for an identifier in a programming language with the addition that the "/" character may be used. The type of an attribute may be one of: Byte, Int32, Float64, String, or URL. An attribute may be scalar or vector.

When the data access protocol is used to read the attributes of a variable and that variable contains other variables, only the attributes of the named variable are returned. In other words, while the DDS is a hierarchical structure, the DAS is *not*; it is similar to a flat-file database.

Conclusion

The Distributed Oceanographic Data System (DODS) is a client-server system which provides scientific researchers with a tool to access data from a wide variety of sources including other scientists as well as national data centers. Unlike most other distributed data systems, DODS uses existing analysis programs to access data by providing software developers and users with new implementations of existing data access APIs. These new implementations make use of remote data servers to satisfy the APIs function calls. Thus the user program needs no modification to read remote data and program authors, who may not be software development specialists, do not need to learn a new data access paradigm to use the remote data. By judiciously choosing which APIs to reimplement, a large body of software developed outside of the DODS project, with which users are already comfortable, is able to access remote data via DODS servers.

Data servers for DODS are built using the WWW server httpd from NCSA. A data server consists of three filter programs and a dispatch CGI. Each data set is referred to via a URL which contains the name of the CGI and some identifying keywords which vary from API to API. Two of the three programs which comprise a data server return textual descriptions of the contents of the data set and can be viewed by any WWW browser. However, the principal function of these two filter programs is to provide information to the client library which it will use to request and decode the information returned by the third filter program—the values of discrete variables within the data set.

Each data set is accessed using an intermediate representation that is independent of a particular machine representation or API. This enables the client library which replaces API X to access a data server which provides access to data stored on disk in files written using API Y given that a correct DODS data server for API Y and a correct client library for API X exist. Thus for the set of

APIs which DODS chooses to address, researchers are free to access data without concern for its native storage format.

Currently DODS supports two different data access APIs: netCDF and JGOFS. As of October 1995 a beta release of DODS is available (both C and C++ source code as well as precompiled binaries) from *ftp::/dods.gso.uri.edu/pub/dods.* Additional documentation on DODS may be found at *http://dods.gso.uri.edu/.* ∎

References

1. Borenstein, N., and Freed, N., *Mime (multipurpose internet mail extensions) part one: mechanisms for specifying and describing the format of internet message bodies*, DARPA RFC 1521, 1993.

2. Cornillon, P., Flierl, G., Gallagher, J., and Milkowski, G., *Report on the first workshop for the distributed oceanographic data system*, The University of Rhode Island, Graduate School of Oceanography, 1993.

3. Internet Engineering Task Force, *Home Page*, *http://www.ietf.cnri.reston.va.us/home.html*, 1995.

4. Joint Global Ocean Flux Study, *Home Page*, *http://www1.whoi.edu/jgofs.html*, 1995.

5. Kernigham, B. W., and Ritchie, D. M., *The C Programming Language*, Prentice-Hall, New Jersey, 1978.

6. Massachusetts Institute of Technology, *DODS—Data Delivery*, *http://lake.mit.edu/dods-dir/dods-dd.html*, 1994.

7. Muntz, R., Mesrobian, E., and Mechoso, C. R., *Integrating data analysis, visualization, and data management in a heterogeneous distributed environment*, *Information Systems Newsletter*, vol. 20(2), 7-13, 1995.

8. National Center for Supercomputing Applications, *Hierarchical data format, version 3.0*, University of Illinois at Urbana-Champaign, 1993.

9. National Oceanic and Atmospheric Administration, *Report to the Senate committee on commerce, science and transportation and the House of Representative committee on science, space and technology on a plan to modernize NOAA's environmental data and information systems based on the needs assessment for data management archival and distribution: NOAA's leadership role in environmental information services for the nation*, U. S. Department of Commerce, National Oceanic and Atmospheric Administration, Washington, DC. 1994.

10. National Oceanic and Atmospheric Administration, *NOAA/NASA Oceans Pathfinder Data System*, *http://podaac-www.jpl.nasa.gov/*, 1995.

11. National Science Foundation, *The U.S. global change data and information management program plan*, National Science Foundation, The Committee on Earth and Environmental Sciences, Interagency Working Group on Data Management of Global Change, 1992.

12. Pacific Marine Environmental Laboratory, *NOAA / PMEL-Thermal Modeling and Analysis Project*, *http://ferret.wrc.noaa.gov/ferret/main-menu.html*, 1995.

13. Pursch, A., Kahn, R., Haskins, R., and Granger-Gallegos, S., *New tools for working with spatially non-uniformly-sampled data from satellites*, The Earth Observer Vol.4(5), 19—26, 1992.

14. Rew, R. K., and Davis, D. P., *NetCDF: An interface for scientific data access*, IEEE Computer Graphics and Applications Vol.10(4), 76-82, 1990.

15. Ritchie, D. M., Johnson, S. C., Lesk, M. E., and Kernighan, B. W., *The C programming language*, in E. Horowitz, ed., *Programming Languages: A Grand Tour, 3ed.*, Computer Science Press, Rockville, MD., pp. 458-79, 1987.

16. Stevens, W. R., *UNIX Network Programming*, Prentice-Hall, New Jersey, 1990.

17. Sun Microsystems, Inc., *XDR: External data representation standard*, DARPA RFC 1014, 1987.

18. Sun Microsystems, Inc., *RPC: Remote procedure call protocol specification version 2*, DARPA RFC 1057, 1988.

19. Treinish, L., Kulkarni, R., Folk, M., Goucher, G., and Rew, R., *Data models, structure and access software for scientific visualization*, Proceedings of the Fourth IEEE Conference on Visualization, IEEE, pp. 355—60, 1993.

20. University of Rhode Island, *Sea Surface Temperature Archive*, *http://rs.gso.uri.edu/avhrr.html*, 1995.

21. University of Rhode Island, *DODS—Data Access Protocol*, *http://dods.gso.uri.edu/DODS/design/api/api.html*, 1994.

22. U.S. Geological Survey, *Global Land Information System*, *http://edcwww.cr.usgs.gov/glis/glis.html*, 1995.

About the Authors

James Gallagher
The University of Rhode Island
South Ferry Road
Narragansett, RI. 02881
U.S.A.
jimg@dcz.gso.uri.edu

George Milkowski
The University of Rhode Island
South Ferry Road
Narragansett, RI. 02881
U.S.A.
george@zeno.gso.uri.edu

Requirements for Taking Applications Beyond the Enterprise

Graeme Port, Clifford Heath, Phillip Merrick, Tim Segall

Abstract

*This paper presents the main facilities that are required or highly desirable for organizations using the Web to deploy their applications beyond the enterprise. Some of these facilities have not been getting sufficient attention from the Web community. We highlight a number of important issues in relation to these facilities. In many cases, these facilities are well understood by the User Interface Management System vendors who have developed specialized front-end systems for the development of internal corporate applications. We believe that these systems will play an important role in the deployment of Web applications. **Keywords:** WTW, UIMS, structured data interface, mobile code, transaction integrity*

Introduction

A recent report from Forrester Research [3] suggests that the World Wide Web (WWW) will evolve into something they dub the Worldwide Transaction Web (WTW). In addition to providing the largely non-interactive hyperlinked documents that constitute the current WWW, the WTW will permit corporations and government organizations to allow customers and suppliers access to selected internal applications. The WTW will also trigger the development of a large number of new customer-oriented service applications.

This paper presents what we see as the major facilities (in terms of service infrastructure and application development tools) that are required or highly desirable for the deployment of these applications.

The following facilities are required:

- *Full-function graphical user interface.* For usable complex applications to be deployed, the full range of graphic controls are required, running across all major GUI platforms.

- *Structured data interfaces.* Data provided by a server must be structured so that the client can extract the relevant information for presentation to the user.

- *Mobile code.* A programming language is required for client-side processing including dialog management, validation, and packing and unpacking data between the user interface and the structured data interface.

- *Security.* Security covers mechanisms for ensuring privacy, authentication, integrity, and implementation of trust policies. These areas are receiving considerable attention among Web developers.

- *Transaction integrity.* Submitted transactions will be processed as whole units of work, and server-side processing will always maintain consistency in the application database(s).

The following facilities are highly desirable:

- *Connection-oriented sessions.* Some applications use detailed context captured in the state of the server process. Servers like this must remain connected to the client for the duration of the session. Although stateless services are becoming more common, client/server computing is still widely used and remains mainly connection-oriented.

- *Same tool for internal and external development.* Corporate IT departments will want to use one tool for both internal and external applications.

- *Graphical application builder tool.* Application development is much easier with a function-rich graphical builder.

- *Application internationalization support.* Many global companies will deploy their applications in multiple languages. This list differs from the topics currently receiving most of the attention in the WWW community, but it does match quite closely with the main issues confronting the client/server cross-GUI User Interface Management Systems (UIMSs), such as OpenUI [6]. These systems are widely adopted in business for internal application development. It is our opinion that they will play an important role in the evolution of the WTW.

This paper presents in considerable depth the major issues related to the facilities listed above. But first we describe a real-world example to help highlight the particular concerns in the business community to the development of WTW applications.

A Real-World Example

A major telecommunications company offers a complex array of products and services. Their order entry application has extensive validation requirements for cross-checking the various items and options selected to ensure that each order has a valid configuration before it is submitted for processing. A single order could be up to 20 screens of data, and there are approximately 3,000 validation rules to be applied. All orders are currently entered by operators taking calls from customers, but the company wants to allow its customers to enter orders directly.

The architecture manager states the specific requirements as: "It needs to be as easy to access and use as the average Web page, but with all the GUI facilities, power and front-end validation possible in any installed stand-alone program. We'd also prefer to be able to develop just one version of the application to support both our own operators and our customers, even though they have different access and usability requirements." Consider the following scenario for meeting the architecture manager's requirements:

1. The user has been browsing the company's Web page and decides to place an order so they select Order Entry, which is a link to the order application viewer program.

2. The browser checks that the requisite support objects are already present to allow the application viewer to run, such as other mobile code objects or a generic application viewer. If not already present, these items are downloaded from a well-known FTP site and automatically configured.

3. The application viewer starts by making a network connection to an application server program running on the corporate Web server machine outside the corporate network.

4. The application server program makes an appropriate "pass through" network connection to an internal application server running on one of the internal corporate machines.

5. The application presents its main window and is now ready for the user to run.

This sequence of steps can be traced in Figure 1.

The application viewer itself might be:

- A machine-specific custom program

- A large module of mobile code supported by the Web browser

- A code module for a generic application viewer external to the browser

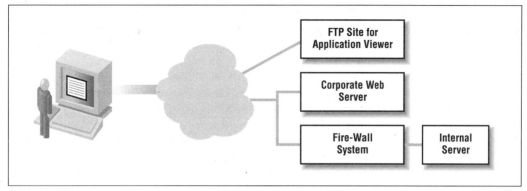

Figure 1:   Connecting to a corporate application

There will be situations where a custom application is appropriate, despite the requirement to support multiple versions for various hardware types and operating systems. For instance, a bank with hundreds of thousands of customers might be prepared to develop a custom home banking application for the use of its customers only. In particular market segments, independent software vendors might create custom applications for sale to a number of companies.

However, most application viewers (by number) will be modules of mobile code in one of the latter two classes. As we will see, some existing client/server cross-GUI UIMSs provide all the features required for client-side processing and can be used as the basis for generic application viewers.

Full-function GUI

Modern GUI tool kits provide an array of user interface controls (including buttons, edit texts, menus, combo-boxes and low-level graphics) allowing developers to build intuitive and productive interfaces. These controls can be arranged across multiple windows, and can be dynamically reconfigured to allow optimal presentation and direct manipulation of complex data.

In contrast, HTML Forms provide access to just a limited subset of these controls, and the only arrangements possible are static aggregations of the simplest kind. The basic model is along the lines of "fill out the form and press the submit key," a regression to the mainframe block-mode display terminal interfaces of old.

To be successful, WTW applications need to support the full range of user interface controls currently available in stand-alone applications.

One of the most important features required for a full-function GUI on the WTW is cross-GUI support. Users may have a variety of GUI environments, including Microsoft Windows, Apple Macintosh, OSF Motif, and OS/2 Presentation Manager. On each GUI platform, the application must look and feel like an application built specifically for that platform. The challenge here is to develop a framework for specifying user interfaces generically, while dealing with the differences between the GUI standards. A "lowest common denominator"—supporting only those facilities common to all GUI standards—can only be used to construct very simple user interfaces.

The frameworks of some existing cross-GUI UIMSs allow the presentation of GUI-independent user interfaces on a wide range of platforms.

Structured Data Interfaces

The rapid growth of the Web is testament to the simple elegance and power of HTML as a markup language and HTTP as a protocol for networked hypermedia documents. HTML, however, is a document markup language for describing documents to be read by humans. Writing software to extract data from HTML pages is comparatively difficult and easily broken by relatively minor changes to the content of pages.

WTW servers will need to present data in a manner that is easily parsed by the client software and relatively stable when changed. There are a number of ways this could be done with differing advantages and complexity. For example, the data could be presented:

- As a list of tag = value pairs, where each value could be a simple data type, an array of values, or a record of tag = value pairs. This format is easy to parse, and some changes can be accommodated by adding and deleting tags, or

- In binary form encoded according to an ASN.1-type specification.

The EDI format is in wide use in this type of application and could represent a suitable base from which to work.

For WTW applications to talk to a wide range of servers, a common structured data interface language and protocol must be adopted to play the equivalent role to HTML in the WWW. For the internal application server, it is much easier to communicate via a structured data interface than HTML. Many CGI programs are simply there to put an HTML wrapper around a few important data items contained in an HTML page. A WTW server will present the structured data directly.

The same structured data interface could be used by the client when it transfers data to the server, as is already done with the HTML Forms interface.

The database vendors are offering to provide HTML gateways to their databases in an attempt to increase the demand for database services. Unfortunately, giving end users direct access to flat, normalized tables in relational databases has not been a resounding success, as was amply demonstrated to the same vendors a decade ago. A much better approach is for the data from these databases to be presented through a structured data interface so that the WTW application can present the information in an appropriate way to the user.

Mobile Code

Mobile code executing on the client:

- Provides a convenient mechanism for carrying out localized UI processing such as complex data validation

- Can be used to manage the dialog between the user and the application

- Provides a framework for packing and unpacking data from the structured data interface

- Offloads this processing from the server machines

Without general-purpose programming language code running on the client machine, the dynamics of a full-function GUI cannot be maintained. Without this facility the WWW could not scale-up to the demands of the WTW; if HTTP servers and CGI programs were to do all data validation and dialog management, the Internet and the server machines would become completely overloaded.

The commonly understood form of mobile code is typified by the Java language [4], and is usually considered as integrated into the Web browser. A code module for a generic application viewer external to the Web browser is also a form of mobile code.

There are existing UIMSs that store their user interface definitions—including associated mobile code—in machine-independent format.

Downloading these definitions gives an effective mobile code deployment mechanism.

Security

Internal applications rely heavily on physical security for protection against eavesdropping, meddling, and fraudulent access, but the Internet does not offer such security. Security on the Internet must rely instead upon cryptosystems such as SSL [5], S-HTTP [7], and IPng. These cryptosystems have been discussed at length in the literature and there are trial implementations available today.

SSL provides protection of privacy, data integrity and server authentication, but until suitable tools for certificate management and the implementation of trust policies are standardized, client authentication is left without adequate support. Nonetheless, security is a problem receiving a lot of attention from the WWW community that will, in all likelihood, be progressively solved over the next twelve months.

Transaction Integrity

The basic principles of transaction integrity are described by the so-called ACID properties:

- *Atomicity.* Transactions are processed as a single, atomic unit of work, irrespective of the number of updates they comprise.

- *Consistency.* The effect of processing a transaction takes the application database(s) from one consistent state directly to another (different) consistent state.

- *Isolation.* Each transaction proceeds independently of other transactions.

- *Durability.* The effects of each transaction on the application database(s) are persistent. Even casual use of the Web demonstrates disturbing deficiencies in this area. Server hardware and software fail, or become hopelessly overloaded, communications links break, yet there are no mechanisms for ensuring the integrity of Web-based transactions.

The distributed computing community has already developed standards (for example, X/Open DTP Model and Standards, and CORBA2) and products (for example, Encina, Tuxedo, and Orbix) that address transaction integrity across internal corporate networks. It is unrealistic to expect every machine connected to the Internet to be equipped with the runtime libraries of all of these products. Instead what is needed is a lightweight and universal means of extending their protective umbrella out across the Internet.

UIMSs have shown their ability to integrate with these products and standards.

Highly Desirable Facilities

The issues related to the highly desirable facilities are presented somewhat more briefly.

Connection-Oriented Sessions

HTTP was designed as a light-weight protocol for transfer of documents. The browser opens a connection to a server, sends a single request, and waits for a response. The response arrives and the connection is closed. This is known as the request/response model.

There is a significant class of applications, however, for which the request/response model is unsuitable. These applications are connection-oriented, and often follow the client/server model. Most interactive applications fall into this category. For these applications it makes sense to keep a connection open for the duration of the session. An added benefit is the elimination of the overhead of setting up a connection and initializing the server process for each exchange of data.

A closely related issue concerns the limitations of HTTP and CGI to represent the state of an application. This has prompted the development of mechanisms like Persistent Client State HTTP Cookies [1]. These allow the server to store state information in a client, which then sends this state with each request to the server.

Storing state is one way of allowing a virtual connection to be maintained, even if several physical connections have to be opened and closed.

Same Tool for Internal and External Development

It is increasingly clear that the Internet represents the next frontier for application development. Given the limited resources available to many corporate IT departments, it is unreasonable to expect that they will use different technologies for developing internal and external applications. We can, therefore, anticipate a need for a single technology that meets the requirements for both internal and external application deployment.

The WTW requirements closely match those of a client/server cross-GUI UIMS tool, implying that such a tool may be the best candidate for unifying internal and external development. Such an approach is certain to find more acceptance than attempting to use a browser-embedded mobile code interface for internal applications.

Graphical Application-Builder Tool

Building the user interface of an application is much easier if it is visible on the screen so that the effect of each change can be seen immediately. It is important that the user interface is not mocked up, but is displayed exactly as it will appear in the running application, otherwise there may be differences and errors that are time-consuming to fix.

Application Internationalization Support

Many global companies will deploy their applications in multiple languages. The process of modifying an application to operate in a different human language or with different cultural conventions is called localization. This has increasing relevance in today's business environment.

A subtle problem with internationalization is that translated text is often different in length from the original. For example, German text is, on average, 30% longer than its English equivalent. If pixel-based geometry is used, the alignment of text and fields is ruined by the translation.

At least one UIMS has solved this problem by arranging the UI elements into a "logical grid," where UI objects manage their positioning in relation to one another by occupying cells in the grid. This gives a highly portable mechanism for geometry management.

Conclusion

This paper has presented what we see as the major facilities that are required or highly desirable for the evolution of the WTW to take place. The lists of required facilities includes full-function graphical user interface, structured data interfaces, mobile code, security, and transaction integrity. The list of highly desirable facilities includes connection-oriented sessions, same tool for internal and external development, graphical application builder tool, and application internationalization support.

A number of these facilities are well met by existing client/server cross-GUI UIMSs already being used for internal application development. We predict that these systems will play a major role in the development of the WTW and taking applications beyond the enterprise. ∎

References

1. Persistent Client State, HTTP Cookies, Netscape Communications Corp., 1995. *http://www. netscape.com/newsref/std/cookie_spec.html*

2. Richard Dratva, WWW-based Home Banking in Switzerland: A Case Study, Proceedings of the 2nd WWW Conference '94: Mosaic and the Web, October 1994. *http://www.ncsa.uiuc.edu/SDG/IT94/ Proceedings/ComEc/dratva/dratva.html*

3. The Forrester Report: CIO Meets Internet, May 1995, Forrester Research Inc., Cambridge MA.

4. The Java Project, Sun Microsystems, Inc., 1995. *http://java.sun.com/*

5. The SSL Protocol, Draft Specification, Netscape Communications Corp., February 1995. *http://www.netscape.com/newsref/std/SSL.html*

6. OpenUI Technical Overview, Open Software Associates, Ringwood, Australia, November 1993.

7. E. Riscorla and A. Schiffman, The Secure Hypertext Transfer Protocol, Internet Draft, December 1994. *http://www.eit.com/projects/s-http/shttp.txt*

About the Authors

Graeme Port
Open Software Associates
29 Ringwood Street
Ringwood 3134 Victoria
Australia
gsp@osa.com.au

Clifford Heath
Open Software Associates
29 Ringwood Street
Ringwood 3134 Victoria
Australia
cjh@osa.com.au

Phillip Merrick
Open Software Associates
29 Ringwood Street
Ringwood 3134 Victoria
Australia
phjm@osa.com.au

Tim Segall
Open Software Associates, Inc.
20 Trafalgar Square, Fifth floor
Nashua NH 03063
USA
tim@osa.com

CLASSIFYING INTERNET OBJECTS

F. Luís Neves, José N. Oliveira

Abstract

Navigation across the Internet may be an arduous task. Although bookmark and history mechanisms, available in browsers like Netscape and Mosaic, are a help, there is an absence of a classification scheme for the enormous amount of information available through billions of URLs. This paper presents a new approach for this problem based on the reuse methodology developed in the SOUR project. Internet links are seen as reusable objects, stored and maintained in a generalize/specialize structure based on a comparison-metrics algorithm. On the implementation side, SOUR is extended by making use of Netscape's OLE and Automation DDE interprocess communication mechanisms; these allow third party applications to remotely control the Netscape navigator client.

Introduction

Navigation across the Internet consists of jumping across a set of links interactively chosen by the user during a session with an Internet browser. This is arduous because of the absence of an effective classification scheme for the enormous amount of information available through billions of interlinked URLs. Altogether, this huge world-wide "information system" has the structure of an untyped *semantic network* [5]. The basic idea put forward in this paper is to use the SOUR software system as an Internet navigation assistant. SOUR is a system for comparing, classifying and retrieving information about large software systems. Figure 1 depicts the overall structure of the system [16, 15, 14, 18, 17, 19].

The unit of information in SOUR is the so-called *Abstract Object* (AO), a notion which combines the *enumerative* and *faceted* classification schemes [10, 11, 12] as an extension of the popular attributive view of objects in the context of a hierarchical semantic network information model.

A crucial decision to make is how to map Internet nodes onto the SOUR information model. A URL refers to the format used by World Wide Web (WWW) [21] documents to locate files on other servers. A URL gives the type of resource being accessed (e.g., gopher, WAIS), the address

of the server and the path of the file. The format is:

scheme://host.domain[:port]/path/filename

where *scheme* is one of:

file: a file on your local system, or a file on an anonymous ftp server
http: a resource on a World Wide Web server;
gopher: a resource on a Gopher server
WAIS: a resource on a WAIS server
news: a Usenet newsgroup
telnet: a connection to a telnet-based service

The above information scheme can be turned into a SOUR class scheme in a way that will be described in this paper. But a summary of the overall SOUR information model will be presented beforehand.

Introducing AOs

Information in the SOUR software system [19] is generically recorded in the form of so-called *Abstract Objects* (AOs) which are independent of their physical support (e.g., text file, POSTSCRIPT file) or location (e.g., pathname).

Abstract objects (AOs) are catalogued in the system's abstract archive according to an adopted standard of classification called *conceptualization*, which is factored in two layers:

- *Coarse level.* Hierarchical "is-a"-like enumerative classification, enabling conventional inherited attribute-based reasoning

- *Fine level.* Multifaceted classification schema based on fuzzy concept-network reasoning, which extends conventional keyword-oriented classification

The conceptualization approach is thus a combination of the enumerative and faceted classification schemes [12, 11], whereby a physical object like a piece of C-code "becomes" an AO. This is accomplished by attaching a *profile* to that object which consists of the following basic items:

- *Classname* (`code`). This item plugs the object into the system's standard "is-a" hierarchy.

- *Attributes* (`author`). These provide values for features or properties relevant about the objects, under a simple inheritance mechanism prescribed by the "is-a" hierarchy.

- *Links* (`implements`). These are AO-valued attributes which establish relevant relationships among AOs.

- *Facets* (`system=text-formatter`). These are fuzzy tuples of terms acting as "vague keywords" that index AOs.

- *Actions* (`compile`). These are "method-like" AO-attributes recording predefined procedures. AOs either are automatically submitted at standard instants of their life cycle or triggered by UI-events such as mouse double-clicking.

- *Members* (if an AO container). Collection of references to the subobjects contained in the object.

- *Relations* (if an AO cluster). Graph structure of links interrelating to the subobjects involved with the main object.

Every AO has a unique identity represented by its *Abstract Object IDentifier* (AOID). AOIDs are managed by the system and are transparent to the end user.

The Conceptualization Standard

It should be noted that two different physical objects may happen to be attached to the same conceptual profile. If this is the case, it leads to a notion of "conceptualization equivalence" among objects, which has to be managed by the system.

Classnames form a strict hierarchy representing the enumerative side of SOUR's classification scheme. From the user's perspective, the top of this hierarchy is *Abstract Object Generic attributes* (AOG), a class consisting of system controlled attributes such as the following:

name
AO name as defined by the user who created the object

pathname
Plugs Physical AOs (PAOs) into the underlying file system

inserted By
Username of creator

lastModifyDate
Date of last update

lastLookDate
Date of last browse

nModify
Number of updates so far

Facets are sextuples of terms, each term instantiating one of the predefined facet types shown in Figure 1.

Every term instantiating a facet must be present in a subsystem of SOUR called the Lexicon/Thesaurus Subsystem (LTS). Terms are related to each other by fuzzy concepts; they are supported by Context Thesaurus Subsystem (CTS), another component of the SOUR architecture [16, 15]. Facets may be regarded as "fuzzy" attributes. Reference [10] provides a formal discussion about the power of fuzzy classification in practice.

1. *function or action*

2. *object*   **Functionality**

3. *medium or data structure*

4. *system type*

5. *functional area*   **Environment**

6. *settings*

Figure 1:   SOUR Overall Architecture

Mapping URLs to AOs

The URL addressing format allows a user to specify any object in the Internet, along with sufficient information to retrieve it. The WWW server is responsible for mapping a supplied URL into an object or responding with an error message [4]. As a result, every Internet transaction is divided in two distinct phases: an *identification* phase, where the server validates the URL specification, and a *retrieval* phase, where the server delivers the corresponding data to the client.

If these two phases are successfully executed it is possible to access both the (now valid) URL and the data. Data access has a particular importance in the present study each time the URL identifies an HTML text file. In such cases, an analysis reveals that some parts of the text may be used for conceptualizing the URL.

The following sections will explain in detail how these two entities—the URL and the data which it identifies—provide the information that will be attached to an AO.

AO Identification

Assuming the previously (brief) description of an Abstract Object, it is possible to map the URL information scheme described earlier onto a SOUR object as shown below:

AO Name:
   scheme://host.domain[:port]/path/filename

AO Address:
   /path/filename

AO Type:
   filename extension (if any)

AO Class:
   scheme + filename extension (if any)

As expected, a URL alone provides the minimal information needed for a successful conceptualization [17]. However, if the URL is an HTML text file, then some extra information may be added according to its contents, otherwise no more information will be attached (see the following sections for more information).

AO Class

A specific class hierarchy must be created in order to accommodate the *host.domain* information which can be used to classify the AO at coarse level. The top of this hierarchy is a class named URL which must have (at least) the following attributes:

Domain_0 (*www, gopher, ftp, s700*)
Domain_1 (*ncsa, telepac, inescn,di*)
Domain_2 (*uiuc, inesc, uminho*)
     ...   (*...*)
Domain_n (*com, pt, org, edu*)

While the URL's subclasses reflect possible scheme values and filename extensions, if for a given URL the value *scheme + filename extension* is not the name of an existent (predefined) class, then only the *scheme* value is used. The following class hierarchy illustrates this idea and specifies some possible subclasses for the HTTP class.

URL
   FILE

HTTP	HTTPHTML	*Html documents*
	HTTPTXT	*Text documents*
	HTTPPS	*Postscript documents*
	HTTPDOC	*Word documents*
	HTTPTEX	*TeX documents*
	HTTPGIF	*Gif images*
	HTTPZIP	*Zipped files*
GOPHER	...	
	...	
WAIS	...	
	...	
NEWS	...	
	...	
TELNET	...	
	...	

Of course, other attributes may be added to the classes reflecting the specific information of their objects.

AO Facets

Faceted classification as proposed in this paper combines several text-scheme management tools such as full text indexing and retrieval, free-text scan, document clustering, unique word, and vector-space [3]. These approaches are discussed below.

The full text approach first generates a list of strings associated with a document. Then, at retrieval time, a string match will be tried between each string in the index and a string in the available thesaurus. This strategy is combined with the *unique-word* and the *vector-space* approaches in order to give more retrieval power to the strings that occur more often in the text.

Document clustering attempts to mimic the human thought process by grouping together documents with related ideas, concepts, and terminology [8]. This notion is managed by SOUR's COMPARATOR & MODIFIER subsystem [14] as described later in this paper (see the section entitled "AO Comparison").

Together, all these notions provide a default facet classification that will be tried by SOUR's *Attempt Automatic Conceptualization* (AAC) mechanism [17]. The AAC is applied to the HTML source text of the URL currently being accessed if, of course,

the URL identifies an HTML file. The quality of the available CTS/LTS pair is of crucial importance to obtain good results in faceted classification.

For the relevant information to be extracted from the HTML source text, we choose the words that are included in the following HTML structures [6]:

- *Title.* Words between the elements <TITLE> and </TITLE>

- *Headings.* Words between the elements <Hy> and </Hy> where y is a number between 1 and 6 specifying the level of the heading

Since we are interested in the classification of documents by their contents, these must be reflected in the lexical terms available in the LTS. If, for example, we have a special interest in documents talking about the WWW, then the LTS shall have terms like *Internet, Information, Web, Hypertext, Virtual, Browser, CERN, HTML,* and so on. This specialization of lexical terms, which can improve both the conceptualization and the query mechanism, is supported by SOUR's capability of working with several CTS/LTS repositories.

CTS provides the capability to cope with features of human reasoning such as *classifying by analogy* and *terminological vagueness* [10][16][15]. In particular, lexical terms can be connected by conceptual distances interrelating terms (words) according to their contextual meanings. These distances may be regarded as degrees of membership of arcs in a fuzzy graph.

Figure 2 shows a possible set of conceptual relations among the terms described above.

The *fuzzy logic* technique associated with this information structure provides a method to reduce the so-called *precision/recall* trade-off. This is one of the methods that has had some success in decreasing the chances of missing important information [3].

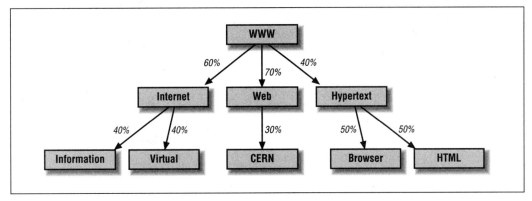

Figure 2: Example of conceptual relations

The 6-tuples of predefined terms presented earlier (see the previous section entitled "About the Conceptualization Standard") were designed by Prieto-Diáz for the specific task of software classification. How to extend or adapt them to generic information as accessed through the Internet is an open problem.

The pre-inserted values for each one of these facets will serve as guidelines for document classification. Possible matches among those values and the words extracted from the HTML text reflect part of the so-called AAC mechanism. The others will be described in the sections below.

AO Links

In this section, we show how the overall *semantic network* structure of the Internet matches with the internal AO-structure of SOUR.

The HTML source text of the URL currently being accessed can also be used to extract AO link information. Each hyperlink to an *external* file will be identified as an *inlink* of the AO that abstracts the current URL. Possible references include:

- *Hyperlink references*
  - e.g., <A HREF = "URL">...</A>

References of this kind will create links identified by the "Part Of" label.

- *Image references*
  - e.g., <IMG SRC = "URL">...</IMG>

References of this kind will create links identified by the "Image Of" label.

- *Embedded references*
  - e.g., <EMBED SRC = "URL">

References of this kind will create links identified by the "Embedded In" label.

Hyperlink, Image, and Embedded references become inlinks after the following procedures:

1. The references are mapped onto SOUR AOs following the way described earlier in this article.

2. The resulting AOs are conceptualized into the SOUR system.

3. The references are identified as links under the current conceptualization.

As an example, consider the access to the following address:

http://www.di.uminho.pt/cnw3.html

You can extract the following AO information directly from the URL:

AO Name: *http://www.di.uminho.pt/cnw3.html*

AO Address: */cnw3.html*

AO Type: *HTML*

AO Class: *HTTPHTML*

Domain0: *www*

Domain1: *di*

Domain2: *uminho*

Domain3: *pt*

Now consider that the HTML file identified by the previous URL is the following:

```
<HTML>

<HEAD> <TITLE> WWW National Conference
   </TITLE> </HEAD>

<BODY>

<H1>
<CENTER>
WWW National Conference <P>
<IMG ALIGN=MIDDLE SRC="/IMI/imi2-ing-
   interlace.gif"> <P>
Internet Multimedia Information
</CENTER>
</H1>

<H2>
<CENTER>
July 6-8, 1995 <P>
<A HREF="http://www.di.uminho.pt/
   english-um.html">Minho University</
   A> <P>
<A HREF="http://s700.uminho.pt/braga.
   html>Braga</A>,
<A HREF="http://s700.uminho.pt/homepage-
   pt.html>Portugal</A>
</CENTER>
</H2>

</BODY>

</HTML>
```

From the analysis of the HTML source text we obtain the following references:

1. <IMG ALIGN=MIDDLE SRC="/IMI/imi2-ing-interlace.gif">

2. <A HREF="http://www.di.uminho.pt/english-um.html">

3. <A HREF="http://s700.uminho.pt/braga.html>

4. <A HREF="http://s700.uminho.pt/home-page-pt.html>

References 1 and 2 will be analyzed in detail in the next section. References 3 and 4 will originate AOs as follows:

AO Namez: *http://s700.uminho.pt/braga.html*

AO Address: */braga.html*

AO Type: HTML

AO Class: HTTPHTML

Domain0: *s700*

Domain1: *uminho*

Domain2: *pt*

and:

AO Name: *http://s700.uminho.pt/homepage- pt.html*

AO Address: */homepage-pt.html*

AO Type: HTML

AO Class: HTTPHTML

Domain0: *s700*

Domain1: uminho

Domain2: *pt*

Finally, these two AOs will produce the inlinks:

- *http://s700.uminho.pt/braga.html*

  Part Of →

- *http://s700.uminho.pt/homepage-pt.html*

  Part Of →

which will become part of the conceptualization of the current URL.

Figure 3 shows the result of the conceptualization of the URL *http://www.di.uminho.pt/cnw3.html*. This figure displays both the links and the comparison relations among AOs.

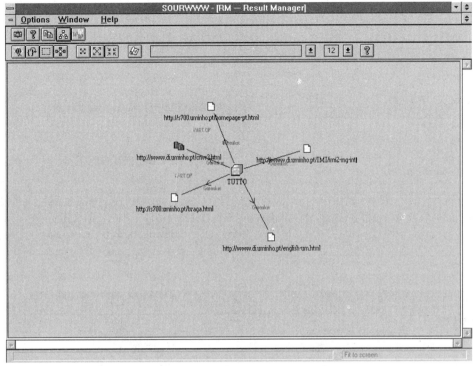

Figure 3: AO links

AO Members

The source text of the URL currently being accessed can also be used to extract AO member information. Each hyperlink to a *local* file will be identified as a member of the AO that maps the current URL. Possible references include:

- *Hyperlink references*
  - <A HREF = "FILE">...</A>

- *Image references*
  - <IMG SRC = "FILE">...</IMG>

- *Embedded references*
  - <EMBED SRC = "FILE">

All these references will create *member links* identified by the label "Member Of." In the running example above, references 1 and 2 from the previous section,

- <IMG ALIGN=MIDDLE SRC="/IMI/imi2-ing-interlace.gif">

- <A HREF="http://www.di.uminho.pt/english-um.html">

will produce the following AOs:

AO Name:
  http://www.di.uminho.pt/IMI/imi2-ing-interlace.gif

AO Address:
  /IMI/imi2-ing-interlace.gif

AO Type: *GIF*

AO Class: *HTTPGIF*

Domain2: *uminho*

Domain3: *pt*

and:

AO Name:

http://www.di.uminho.pt/english-um.html

AO Address:

/english-um.html

AO Type: *HTML*

AO Class: *HTTPHTML*

Domain0: *www*

Domain1: *di*

Domain2: *uminho*

Domain3: *pt*

Finally, these two AOs will produce the *member links*:

- *http://www.di.uminho.pt/IMI/imi2-ing-interlace.gif* Member Of

- *http://www.di.uminho.pt/english-um.html* Member Of

which will become part of the conceptualization profile of the current URL. Figure 4 shows the RM's **Zoom In** graphical functionality [19] operating on URL *http://www.di.uminho.pt/cnw3.html*.

The Query Mechanism

The Intelligent Query System is the SOUR subsystem intended for consulting SOUR's information [18]. It supports an assisted query mechanism for retrieving information based on standard attributes and "fuzzy" query templates. While the

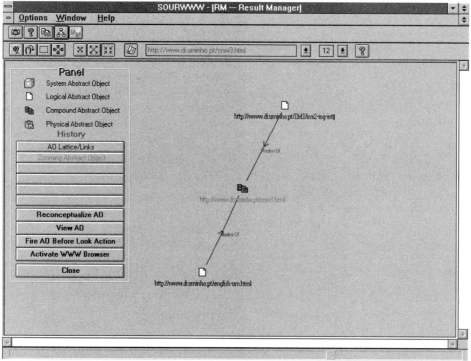

Figure 4:   AO members

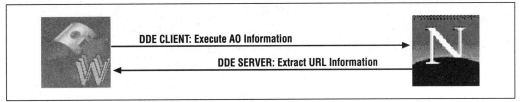

Figure 5: DDE protocol

former directly inspects the Internet Navigation hypertext structure, the latter looks deeper, allowing searches based on the contents of the target objects. In the running example of the previous sections, the following query:

Get all the URLs stored in Portuguese servers that use the HTTP protocol and that make references to the file http://s700.uminho.pt/homepage-pt.html0 (the Portuguese home page).

reflects the linked structure of the resulting URL (see Figure 3), while the following query is based on the contents of the referenced data:

Get all the the documents that talk about "WWW" with fuzziness level greater or equal to 60%.

This last query uses the *facet* values of each AO currently stored in the repository and the conceptual relations illustrated in Figure 2, in order to find the objects within the specified fuzziness level. The SOUR query mechanism combines both the expressive power of the SQL and *fuzzy-logic* searching techniques. The outcome is something we might call a "fuzzy SQL processor" with a highly assisted, interactive user interface [19].

AO Comparison

The notion of "proximity," which leads us to the idea of arrangement or grouping, is crucial for the classification problem in general and for document organization and retrieval in particular. As documents become more and more the center of computer activity, their identification, storage, tracking, retrieval, and presentation [13] will be of dramatic importance.

The COMPARATOR subsystem of SOUR[14] maintains an ordered structure of AOs that are grouped hierarchically according to a "proximity" order defined on the system's standard of conceptualization. It performs the crucial task of comparing Abstract Objects (AOs), while providing a meaningful decision procedure for AO-equivalence. The relevance of COMPARATOR cannot be underestimated—it amounts to the definition of AO-semantics itself, based upon the belief that document semantics can be effectively captured by the adopted *attributive* model.

The standard attribute-based comparison, at *coarse* level, is present as a preliminary, less discriminant decision procedure. But with such a procedure, the expressive power of the system does not go beyond the conventional, object-oriented information model.

The desired increase in expressive power is achieved at *fine* level, where object comparison is "fuzzy" and is decided according to a metrics or algebra of proximity that computes intersections of the proximity closures of facet values within their hierarchical conceptual graphs. For the technical aspects of this sophisticated tool, see [14] and [10].

Implementation Details

The Netscape Client APIs (NCAPIs) are provided as part of version 1.1N release of NETSCAPE. They are designed to allow third-party applications to remotely control the NETSCAPE Navigator client [9]. This mechanism includes both the Ole Automation and the DDE Protocol mechanisms.

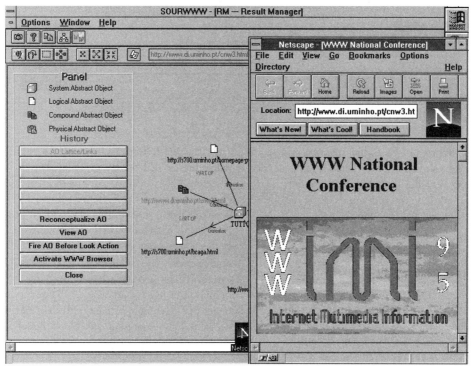

Figure 6:   Activating Netscape browser

Whenever interacting with these APIs, SOUR will regard its object repository as if it is stored in a dynamically "extended file system" across the Internet. For that, SOUR and NETSCAPE will cooperate based on the client/server technology supported by the DDE implementation of NETSCAPE version 1.1N [2]. In this way, SOUR will manipulate NETSCAPE to execute and/or extract the information of a given URL.

The first step is to gain access to Netscape's OLE Automation object (the Netscape.Network.1 Automation Object, to be more specific [1]). Using this object, SOUR will be able to access network data through the same mechanisms NETSCAPE uses. However, NETSCAPE's OLE AUTOMATION does not provide the functionality necessary to manipulate the NETSCAPE NAVIGATOR user interface. This is possible only by using the DDE protocol, which will make SOUR act simultaneously like a NETSCAPE client and

server, as illustrated in Figure 5. While acting as a NETSCAPE client, SOUR uses NETSCAPE to display the URLs that have been conceptualized. When it is working as a NETSCAPE server, SOUR is notified every time the loading of a URL occurs. After the notification, the URL is mapped to a SOUR AO (see the section entitled "Mapping URLs to AOs" while the HTML source text is saved for further analysis (see the descriptions earlier in this paper). After all these steps, the AO information is finally described in the *Conceptualization Batch Language* format [17] and saved into a text file. Whenever SOUR becomes the active application, it will verify and load all the files created by this process.

Once satisfactorily conceptualized, each URL will be classified in the system's repository as a conventional SOUR object. After that, it will be possible to use the SOUR software system both for access to its standard functionality (available in the release ß of the system [19]) or to launch a "batch" NETSCAPE navigation session, which is available through a specially developed capability of SOUR's RM (Result Manager) subsystem. RM is a generic SOUR service-tool for graphically displaying, consulting, and executing AO's related information which, in the present context, also becomes also a graphical environment for browsing the Internet linked structure (see Figures 3 and 4).

Figure 6 shows the result of activating the NETSCAPE NAVIGATOR to display a selected AO. This operation loads the correspondent URL (using the OLE AUTOMATION mechanism) into the current NETSCAPE window.

Conclusion and Future Work

This paper presents some modifications and extensions to the current SOUR prototype (running on Windows [19]) in order to make it a useful tool for the classification, storage, and retrieval of Internet information.

The key aspects of the SOUR information model reflect the way in which documents are regarded today: no longer as mere files, but rather as books of pointers to objects of several kinds [13]. On the one hand, SOUR can provide some important organizational mechanisms and, consequently, make Internet navigation simpler. On the other hand, as access to the information becomes easier and more powerful, SOUR can act like a personal tool for getting the information directly from the Web and, at the same time, storing and arranging it into a more human-based organization model in the personal workstation.

Among the topics discussed in the paper, probably the most complex is designing a general classification framework for arbitrary documents. However, the approach adopted by SOUR concerning software reuse in particular [11][12], as well as recent studies on fuzzy object-comparison [10] offer good perspectives for the future.

Future work includes the prospect of "globalizing" the adopted classification strategy. This means scaling up the approach from personal to world-wide classifiers. Some similarity between AOs and Universal Resource Citations (URCs) [22] suggests that the SOUR AO profile-based paradigm can be scaled up to a world-wide, Internet resource-based, "yellow-page"-like service of bibliographic metadata about WWW documents. Naturally, URCs would have to be extended with fuzzy attributes. Before that can happen, however, performance feasibility will have to be studied. ■

Acknowledgments

The authors wish to thank all the colleagues in the SOUR consortium (INESC, SYSTENA, SSS, and OIS RICERCA) who contributed to the many discussions along the project's lifetime. On the implementation side, comments by Garret Arch Blythe and Steve Caine are gratefully acknowledged.

References

1. Garret Arch Blythe. OLE Automation in Netscape. Technical report, Netscape Communications Corporation, March 1995.
   http://home.netscape.com/newsref/std/oleapi.html

2. Garret Arch Blythe's Implementation. Technical report, Netscape Communications Corporation, March 1995.
   http://home.netscape.com/newsref/std/ddeapi.html

3. Earlene Busch. Managing Infoglut: Search and Retrieval. In Dennis Allen, editor, *BYTE*. McGraw-Hill, 1992.

4. Bob Friesenhahn. Build Your Own WWW Server. In Raphael Needleman, editor, *BYTE*. McGraw-Hill, 1995.

5. Mark Handley and Jon Crowcroft. The World Wide Web—Beneath the Surf. Technical report, UCL Press, 1994.
   http://www.cs.ucl.ac.uk/staff/jon/book/book.html

6. A Beginner's Guide to HTML. Technical report, Nacional Center for Supercomputing Applications.
   http://www.ncsa.uiuc.edu/demoweb/html-primer.html

7. Donald E. Knuth. *The TeX Book*. Addison-Wesley, Reading, Massachusetts, 1984.

8. Thomas M. Koulopoulos. Managing Infoglut: Search and Retrieval. In Dennis Allen, editor, *BYTE*. McGraw-Hill, 1992. See the text box Document Clustering.

9. NETSCAPE Client APIs (NCAPIs) 2.0. Technical report, Netscape Communications Corporation, March 1995. News &References, Standards Documentation.
   http://home.netscape.com/newsrefs/

10. José Nuno Oliveira. Fuzzy Object Comparison and Its Application to a Self-Adaptable Query Mechanism. 1995. Invited paper, Sixth International Fuzzy Systems Association World Congress.

11. R. Prieto-Diáz. Implementing Faceted Classification for Software Reuse. *34(5):89-97, May 1991.*

12. R. Prieto-Diáz and P. Freeman. Classifying Software for Reusability. *IEEE Software*, 4(1):6-16, January 1987.

13. Andy Reinhardt. Managing the New Document. In Dennis Allen, editor, *BYTE*. McGraw-Hill, 1993.

14. Syntax Sistemi Software. Comparator and Modifer—Functional Specification and Architecture. Technical report, SOUR Project, 1993. Ver.1.4, © SSS, Via Fanelli 206-16, Bari, Italy.

15. Systena. Context Thesaurus Subsystem—Requirement Specification. Technical report, SOUR Project, September 1993. Ver.1.1, © Systena, Via Zanardelli 34, Rome, Italy.

16. Systena. Lexicon/Thesaurus Subsystem—Requirement Specification. Technical report, SOUR Project, July 1993. Ver.2.0, © Systena , Via Zanardelli 34, Rome, Italy.

17. Systena. Conceptualizer—Functional Specification and Architecture. Technical report, SOUR Project, 1994. Ver.2.1, © Systena, Via Zanardelli 34, Rome, Italy.

18. Systena. Intelligent Query System—Functional Specification and Architecture. Technical report, SOUR Project, 1994. Ver.2.1, © Systena, Via Zanardelli 34, Rome, Italy.

19. Systena and Syntax Sistemi Software. Integrated SOUR Software System—Demo Session Manual. Technical report, SOUR Project, 1994. Ver.1.2, © Systena &SSS, Via Zanardelli 34, Rome &Via Fanelli 206-16, Bari, Italy.

20. Haviland Wright. Managing Infoglut: SGML Frees Information. In Dennis Allen, editor, *BYTE*. McGraw-Hill, 1992.

21. The World Wide Web. Technical report, World Wide Web Consortium.
    http://www.w3.org/

22. WWW Names and Addresses, URIs, URLs, URNs. Technical report, World Wide Web Consortium. *http://www.w3.org/hypertext/WWW/Addressing/ Addressing.html*

F. Luís Neves and José N. Oliveira, "**Classifying Internet Objects**" in WWW National Conference '95, Minho University, Braga, Portugal

About the Authors

F. Luís Neves and **José N. Oliveira**
INESC Group 2361 and Dep. Informática
Universidade do Minho
4700 Braga, Portugal

A Generic Map Interface to Query Geographic Information Using the World Wide Web

David Crossley, Tony Boston

Abstract

Environmental information is intrinsically geographically-related. It pertains to a specific region of the earth. Users of such information require answers to questions that have a geographic basis. The Environmental Resources Information Network [8] Unit has developed a generic WWW map interface using a collection of simple map images and a standard lookup table to provide visual interactive access to geographically-related information. The map interface provides a generic mechanism to define a region of interest before selecting from various online forms interfaces to geographic information such as biological species distributions, a spatial data set directory, project information, bibliographies, and general textual indices of WWW documents. **Keywords:** *Spatial, Geographic Information Systems (GIS), geospatial, map, environmental, CGM, Scribble, ERIN, imagemap, vector, search*

Introduction

The Environmental Resources Information Network [8] is establishing a series of online information services that allow ready access to key information about the Australian environment through an easy-to-use interface. This information is maintained by various custodians over the network.

The World Wide Web (WWW) can be interfaced to other data sources such as relational databases, mapping and modelling tools, text indexing facilities, and geographic information systems to provide direct access to spatial information.

A high-quality interactive map interface can be achieved without the overhead (in both response time and running costs) of an online proprietary Geographic Information System (GIS). Other techniques such as pre-prepared static maps and dynamic map generation with graphics packages can do most mapping. Integrated WWW-GIS resources can then be directed at more complex spatial analysis without being bound up by simple map production.

The ERIN Unit has developed a generic map interface that allows the user to interactively define their region of interest. The interface uses static maps at various scales and the Imagemap facility to allow zooming and panning of the map images and selection of the region of interest.

Users can then select the type of information that they are interested in and retrieve this information using a combined geographic and keyword search.

The interface has been designed to be modular and expandable so that new map interfaces and new facilities to access geographic information can be easily configured.

Methods of Definition of a Geographic Region

A comprehensive spatial interface will require many different means of defining a geographic region of interest. Some are:

- Point locations (by single mouse click)

- Within a radius of a point (with mouse clicks or drag)

- A Minimum Bounding Rectangle (by mouse click/drag or entry fields)

- A bounding polygon (by multiple mouse clicks or text string)

- A complex polygon with exclusion regions

- Disjunct regions

- Mapsheets at various scales (using map images, or names, or numbers)

- Named regions (state, sea, terrestrial region (e.g. Cape York Peninsula))

- Catchment regions at various scales (using map images or names)

- Terrestrial biogeographic regions (using map images or names)

- Marine biogeographic regions (using map images or names)

- Local Government Area (using map images or names)

- Statistical Sub-division (using map images or names)

- A particular satellite pass (chosen from a map or a list)

- A locality description (using a natural language parser)

Various WWW facilities are currently available to build spatial interfaces to address some of these methods:

- HTML 2.0 forms allow presentation of list scrolling or drop-down lists of named regions.

- HTML 2.0 forms allow input fields to define a simple Minimum Bounding Rectangle of four geographic (latitude/longitude) coordinates.

- Simple imagemap which allows only a single mouse click.

- Some WWW spatial data services have been configured to interact with map generators such as the Xerox PARC map viewer [23].

- An integrated set of imagemaps

- A more complex interface can be configured by integrating the World Wide Web with Geographic Information Systems (GIS). Some service providors have been able to achieve this. The Canadian National Atlas Information Service is a good example [22].

The current WWW facilities are rather limited. The single click imagemap is obviously the most notable limitation. This prevents the definition of multiple regions, disjunct regions, and regions of complex shape (beyond a simple bounding rectangle).

Some future facilities, which will become available when WWW browsers support HTML 3.0, will assist with building comprehensive spatial interfaces. These developments are briefly discussed in the section "Future Directions," and include:

- The FIGure element

- A multiclick imagemap (scribble on image)

- Client-side applications

- Zoomable vector files

This paper will now go on to describe the online service that has been developed by the ERIN Unit to work around some of the present limitations.

Using Simple Imagemaps

The WWW facility, "Imagemap," provided by the Common Gateway Interface [2] allows a simple and effective spatial interface.

The imagemap facility comprises a raster image as the user interface, the Imagemap program [20], and a lookup file of image regions and related URLs. Imagemap transforms the image coordinates of a single click into effective URLs.

An imagemap of Australian World Heritage Areas [30] allows the user to gain access to documentation concerning Kakadu National Park by clicking on the relevant portion of the Northern Territory of Australia.

Here is the relevant line for "Kakadu" from the imagemap lookup table:

```
rect /portfolio/dest/wha/fossil.html
    168,100 247,135
rect /portfolio/dest/wha/kakadu.html
    111,29 251,77
rect /portfolio/dest/wha/wtropics.html
    247,93 305,126
```

Imagemap can also be used to pass parameters to another CGI script. This feature enables the provision of a host of spatial data services and is central to the ERIN Spatial Interface.

This line from one of the imagemaps of the "Mapsheet Information" service at ERIN shows how a parameter can be passed to a CGI script to generate a locality map for the "Jervis Bay 1:100,000 mapsheet."

```
rect /cgi-bin/mapsheet_lookup.pl?map_
    number=9027 502,331 520,344
```

ERIN Map Interface—the User View

When a client first accesses the spatial interface an initial page is generated and presented with the currently defined region as the extents of continental Australia.

The front page, shown in Figure 1, has two separate forms:

Define a different region

> Allows the interactive definition of a new region of interest using various methods

Discover information

> Generates various query forms as subject-specific interfaces to information that relates to the currently defined geographic region.

Define a Different Region

By default, the region of interest is set to the whole of continental Australia. The area of interest can be changed by choosing the "Define a different region" button.

Several different methods of defining the region of interest are available using map sheet series, geographic (latitude/longitude) coordinates as well as biogeographic regions, catchment regions, and lists of named regions that are under development.

Choosing the mapsheet index option presents a map of Australia and a choice of what type of region to define: state, 1:1,000,000 mapsheet, 1:250,000 mapsheet or 1:100,000 mapsheet.

After choosing a region type, a single mouse-click on the map will select the new region of interest. The initial page is returned with the newly defined region of interest.

If needed, the region of interest can be further refined by zooming-in to the State and 1:1,000,000 maps as showin Figure 2.

Discover Information

After the region of interest has been defined, a choice of various subject-specific interfaces provides access to information which relates to the currently defined geographic region.

At present the following interfaces are provided:

- A directory of spatial data sets that are held by various environmental agencies

- Project information for some projects that are funded by the Commonwealth Department of the Environment

- Biological species occurrence and distribution mapping, together with modelling and analysis

- Regional information that directly relates to the region of interest

An interface is then chosen from the above list. Pressing the "Discover Information" button will

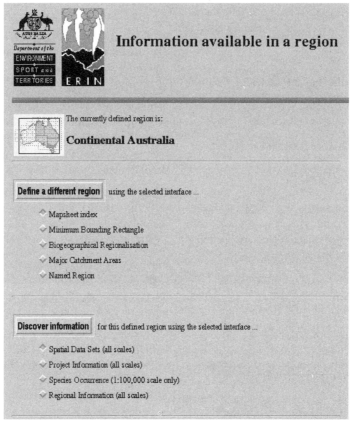

Figure 1: ERIN spatial interface at URL:http://www.erin.gov.au/cgi-bin/spatial_interface

present a subject-specific query form to allow the definition of other parameters to further refine the query. Submitting the form to the server will conduct the search and return the relevant document or list of hits.

Figure 3 shows part of the query interface for "Spatial Data Sets."

This would be a typical query to discover spatial data sets:

> Show a list of all MARINE data sets, documents, and associated information that pertain to the Jervis Bay region of south-eastern New South Wales and that mention the phrase "seagrass die-

back" together with the acronym CSIRO.

These subject interfaces can be easily added to, as other geographically related information services are made available.

Some probable future developments using the ERIN map interface are:

- Spatial text retrieval facilities
- Spatial bibliographies on various subjects
- Documentation entry facilities
- Integrated GIS services, such as online map production facilities, modelling and analysis

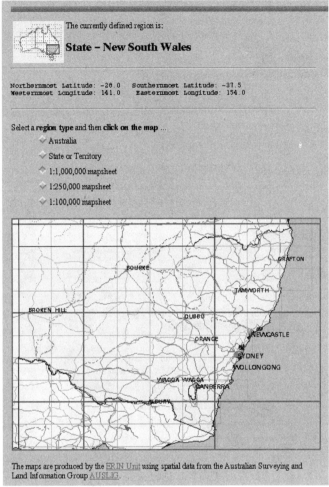

The currently defined region is:

State – New South Wales

Northernmost Latitude: -28.0   Southernmost Latitude: -37.5
Westernmost Longitude: 141.0   Easternmost Longitude: 154.0

Select a **region type** and then **click on the map** ...

- Australia
- State or Territory
- 1:1,000,000 mapsheet
- 1:250,000 mapsheet
- 1:100,000 mapsheet

The maps are produced by the ERIN Unit using spatial data from the Australian Surveying and Land Information Group AUSLIG.

Figure 2:   Defining a new region for the "Sydney 1:1,000,000 mapsheet" using the New South Wales (NSW) map

services, more sophisticated geographic query facilities

- Coordinated search facilities at various distributed agencies

ERIN Map Interface—the Technical Aspects

The interface uses an integrated collection of pre-prepared imagemaps at various scales (continental, state, regional, and 1:1,000,000 mapsheet). The imagemap is imbedded in an HTML form to allow the definition of other parameters in conjunction with the mouse click on the imagemap.

Behind the scenes, and underlying all maps, lies a logical and hierarchical mapsheet index as a lookup table. This simple file provides a means to geographically register all map images that comprise the interface. Any map or pick-list of named regions can be configured as an additional interface.

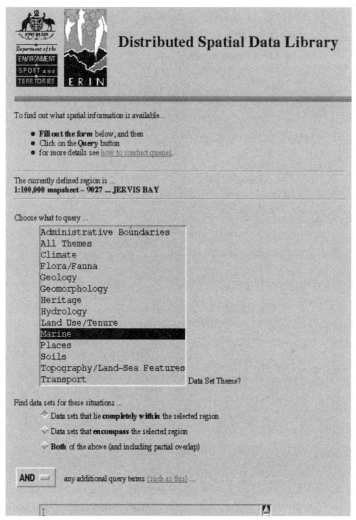

Figure 3: Query interface of the Distributed Spatial Data Library

The central aspects of the interface that allow the integration of various maps are:

- The Imagemap program passes a region identifier to another CGI script.

- A lookup table is consulted using the **region identifier** and the **region type** (the additional form parameter) as a key. This lookup table gives the details of the newly defined region.

Figure 4 indicates the interaction of the various components of the interface.

Pre-Prepared Maps as Raster Images

A collection of GIF images is pre-prepared to depict the various map interfaces (Australian, State, 1:1million, biogeographic regionalisation [IBRA], major catchments—this set comprises about 50 maps). Finer resolution maps could be

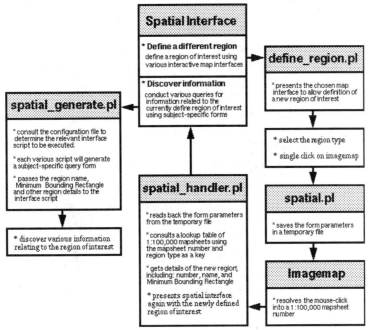

Figure 4: Program fuctions of the spatial interface

prepared. However, bearing in mind that each level of zoom means an order of magnitude of more maps, this is considered a good cutoff point where dynamic map generation should take over.

We use ARC/INFO GIS scripts to do this so that we can continually refine the maps.

Pre-Prepared Imagemaps

An imagemap is prepared for each of the various maps.

Some imagemaps have irregular polygons and are prepared by hand. It is possible that the GIS could be used to provide a very generalised polygon at map image resolution as a string of coordinates. This could be automatically mapped to image coordinates to build the imagemap lookup table.

Here is the relevant line for the Cape York Peninsula (CYP) region of northeastern Australia from

the "Biogeographic Regionalisation" imagemap shown in Figure 5:

```
poly /cgi-bin/spatial/spatial_handler.
   pl?CYP 441,13 430,69 433,102
   460,110 485,108 485,95 465,86 441,13
```

Some imagemaps, such as the Australian coastline mapsheet in Figure 6, have a regular index grid of 1:100,000 mapsheets and are automatically produced by an imagemap building script. This script simply consults a lookup table of region numbers and their Minimum Bounding Rectangles. It calculates the image coordinates for each mapsheet to build the imagemap table.

Here is the relevant line for the "Jervis Bay 1:100,000 mapsheet" from the "Sydney 1:1,000,000" imagemap:

```
rect /cgi-bin/spatial/spatial_handler.
   pl?9027 45,270 90,315
```

This whole set of files forms a static collection of various map interfaces. Other maps can be con-

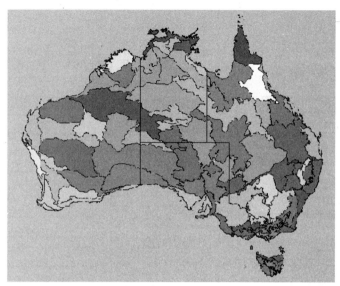

Figure 5: The Interim Biogeographic Regionalisation of Australia [19] (Australian Nature Conservation Agency (1995) "IBRA digital data set")

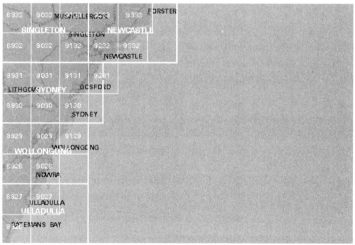

Figure 6: Imagemap of Australian coastline, showing image grid coordinates

figured at any time by adding entries to the table of region details.

Dynamically Generated Maps

The thumbnail images, which provide immediate graphical feedback about the currently defined region, are mostly dynamically generated. There are only 10 static images for Australia and each state, but there are about 3800 possible regions.

Thumbnail images are prepared using simple calls to a graphics package [14] by overlaying a pre-prepared thumbnail base map of Australia with a red filled rectangle to depict the minimum bounding rectangle of the currently defined region.

More sophisticated map preparation is possible using the scripting language provided by the utility package "GDInTerpreter" [15] which allows you to take a pre-prepared map image, overlay filled and coloured objects of any shape, add text, cut and paste sections from other library images, and even overlay an existing transparent image (such as roads and rivers) over the top. The prepared map can then be sent back to the client as an inline GIF image.

Maintaining State

Hidden form variables are used to maintain certain information about the state of the query. Knowing some information about the last query allows us to pass some crucial details about the region of interest to other CGI scripts.

Here are some of those hidden variables. You can always use "View Source..." on your browser to see hidden variables.

```
<INPUT TYPE="hidden" NAME="region"
    VALUE="100k">
<INPUT TYPE="hidden" NAME="map_name"
    VALUE="9027">
<INPUT TYPE="hidden" NAME="last_region"
    VALUE="million">
<INPUT TYPE="hidden" NAME="last_map"
    VALUE="SI56">
<INPUT TYPE="hidden" NAME="desc_region"
VALUE="1:100,000 mapsheet - 9027 ...
    JERVIS BAY">
<INPUT TYPE="hidden" NAME="mbr" VALUE="-
    35,151,-35.5,150.5">
```

Minimum Bounding Rectangles from Lookup Tables

There is a lookup table of region details for all of the various maps. Using the region identifier and region type as a key, the lookup table is consulted to determine the details of the new region to be defined. These comprise the simple details (name, number, minimum bounding coordinates)

and also the higher-level (smaller scale, coarser) regions of which this region is a member.

```
9027,JERVIS BAY,-35,151,-35.5,150.5,
    NSW,SI56-13,SI56,MAP-100
```

Integrated CGI Scripts

One script calls another by writing the variables to the QUERY_STRING CGI environment variable and "exec"ing the next script.

Another way is to issue a server directive to run another CGI script: **Location:/cgi-bin/ scriptname?name=value&name=value**

Zooming and Panning the Maps

A simple zoom and pan facility is enabled by embedding the imagemap in an HTML form. In this way additional parameters can be defined along with the imagemap click. For example, the user can select "Region Type = state" and click on the image. The imagemap program resolves the mouseclick into a 1:100,000 mapsheet. Then the CGI script consults the lookup table of region details to determine which state map covers that 1:100,000 mapsheet.

Interaction With Other Interfaces

Integration of the WWW and other systems such as Relational Database Management Systems (RDBMS), Geographic Information Systems (GIS), or Wide Area Information Servers (WAIS) has been possible using the ERIN map interface.

This is achieved by the combination of a region defined using the map interface with keyword parameters specified using HTML forms.

After the user has defined the region of interest, they can select the type of information they are interested in and generate a query form to access this information. The subject-specific forms interface may then access a relational database, GIS mapping or modelling packages, and document indices.

For example, the "Species occurrence" interface [26] enables users to find out what species occur in a particular region by accessing the ERIN ORACLE database. This is an integration of data held by various agencies and contains over 1.1 million records of the occurrence of Australian plants and animals.

How the Connection is Made

The spatial interface page has two separate forms: one for "Define a different region" and one for "Discover information." Each form contains hidden parameters defining the current region of interest.

The region of interest that was defined using the spatial interface can then be passed as a parameter to various other CGI scripts. This is achieved by consulting the simple interface configuration file to determine which CGI script to execute for the chosen query interface.

Each line of the configuration file has four fields which represent:

keyword, interface name, relevant scales, CGI script

```
sp_reg##Species Occurrence##100k##
    species_interface.pl
```

The ERIN Spatial Interface, together with supporting technical documentation, is available at URL: *http://www.erin.gov.au/cgi-bin/spatial_ interface*

Future Directions

The present interface has some limitations due to the support for only a single-click imagemap in HTML 2.0. Users can only indicate a limited area of interest using a single mouse click rather than being able to define their own complex areas of interest via multiple clicks, drags, or lines. Some of the developments with HTML 3.0 [18] will help to overcome these limitations.

FIGure Element

The specification for HTML 3.0, which is currently being developed, includes the figure <FIG> element to define in-line figures within HTML documents [12]. This new element provides many improvements over the present <IMG> element including defined captions, text flow around figures, alignment control, image overlays, and the ability to define hotzones in the image using HTML. The advantage of defining the hotzones using HTML is that the Web browser can interpret the HTML on the client side and make the appropriate request to the server based on where the user clicks.

This is much faster than the present method, which requires using the imagemap program on the server to resolve where the user has clicked.

Figures can also have transparent overlays. For example, a satellite image basemap can be overlain by a map of roads and rivers. Using overlays for small changes to images can make more effective use of image caching by Web browsers. The browser will cache the basemap because it has not changed and simply retrieve the new overlay from the WWW server.

Scribble on Image

HTML 3.0 provides some extensions to HTML forms [13] These include a new type of input field called SCRIBBLE [25]. The user is presented with an in-line image that they can click on multiple times using the mouse or by drawing with it. When the form is submitted to the server all of the mouse actions are passed. This provides a means for the user to define a more complex geographic area such as a bounding box or polygon.

Client-Side Applications

Zooming and panning of map images is faster if it is done on the user's workstation without having to access the server. Client-side programming languages like HotJava from Sun

Microsystems [17] or the Common Client Interface [1] used with NCSA Mosaic provide a means of interfacing Web browsers with other programs.

There is a good demonstration of "A Dynamic GIS Interface" using HotJava and the "Smalltalk" GIS engine. This was built by staff at the Argonne National Laboratory [27]. For those with no Hot-Java client, there is a slideshow accessible by normal WWW browsers [28].

There is also a current proposal for a client-side imagemap. This would use an HTML extension to allow clickable images to be processed without requiring server intervention [6].

Inline Vector Files

Electronic maps can basically be presented in two ways: as a bitmap (raster) image and as a vector file. A raster image is composed of colored cells or pixels. A vector file describes a drawing using lines, arcs, filled and shaded polygons, and other objects.

When a raster image is magnified or zoomed it effectively loses clarity because the pixels themselves become enlarged. However, when a vector file is zoomed the linework remains clear because it is simply redrawn at the new scale and the line thickness is maintained.

A vector file has many advantages that will prove useful for WWW spatial interfaces:

- A vector file can be delivered to the client, where the file can be zoomed and panned eliminating the need to expensively conduct every operation on a WWW server.

- A vector file is composed of layers that might represent roads, rivers, boundaries.

- The layers can be switched on or off.

- Some file formats allow a raster backdrop superimposed with layers of vectors.

- Hotzones can potentially be added to separate layers.

- A vector file allows a mechanism to limit the level of zoom so that spatial data is not pushed beyond its level of reliability.

- The size and efficiency of a simple vector file will help with network services and response times.

- Most GIS software can directly produce vector files.

- A vector file is really an interactive map.

It is envisaged that inline vector files would be embedded in the <FIG> element of HTML 3.0.

There are a number of candidate file formats for an inline vector file on the WWW:

- Simple Vector Format (SVF)
  - This new format was proposed at the Second International WWW Conference in Chicago in October, 1994 [5]
  - More information is at "SoftSource" [2]
  - Evidently, SoftSource is working with NCSA Mosaic to incorporate SVF. However, discussion and news seems very quiet

- Computer Graphics Metafile (CGM)
  - This is an existing and well established format that many people think will do the job
  - Various sites have more information on CGM, including example files and browser helper applications: [16, 3, 4]

Conclusion

The ERIN map interface provides a generic method of access to geographical information through the World Wide Web. The interface is modular and expandable so that new maps of geographic regions and new interfaces to information can easily be added.

About the Authors

David Crossley

Geographic Information Systems Manager
Environmental Resources Information Network
[ERIN]
Department of the Environment, Sport and Territories
GPO Box 787 Canberra ACT 2601 Australia
davidc@erin.gov.au

David Crossley completed the Bachelor of Surveying degree at the University of New South Wales in 1981. While working in private practice for five years he studied further to become a Registered Cadastral Surveyor in 1985. After a further five years in private practice he went on to the University of Canberra to complete a Graduate Diploma in Computing Studies in 1991.

In 1992 David joined the Environmental Resources Information Network (ERIN Unit) and worked on data set loading, data validation and quality control, and then as scientific computing support on the Cape York Peninsula Land Use Strategy [7].

Since 1994 he has been Geographic Information Systems Manager and involved with providing spatial information system facilities on the ERIN and developing the spatial and indexing aspects of the ERIN On-line Services.

Tony Boston

Database and On-line Systems Manager
Environmental Resources Information Network
[ERIN]
Department of the Environment, Sport and Territories
GPO Box 787 Canberra ACT 2601 Australia
tony@erin.gov.au

Tony Boston is the Database and On-line Systems Manager at the Environmental Resources Information Network (ERIN). ERIN is a unit within the Commonwealth Department of the Environment that is providing ready access to key information on the Australian environment. Since joining ERIN in 1990 Tony has managed the development of the ERIN database to store information such as records of the distribution of Australian plants and animals. In 1993 he set up the ERIN Gopher and World Wide Web servers to make ERIN's information more easily accessible and has developed several interfaces from the Web and Gopher to the ERIN database.

Tony graduated with a Bachelor of Science (Hons) degree majoring in Geology from the Australian National University in 1983. After working as a Petroleum Geologist in industry for several years, he moved into the computing field working at the Bureau of Mineral Resources and completed a Graduate Diploma in Computing Studies from the University of Canberra in 1992.

His main interests lie in the development and use of computer applications and tools to store, manipulate, analyze and display environmental information. ■

References

1. *NCSA Mosaic Common Client Interface (CCI)*, NCSA - National Center for Supercomputing Applications, *http://www.ncsa.uiuc.edu/SDG/Software/XMosaic/CCI/cci-spec.html*

2. *Common Gateway Interface (CGI)*, NCSA - National Center for Supercomputing Applications, *http://hoohoo.ncsa.uiuc.edu/cgi/overview.html*

3. *The Computer Graphics Metafile (CGM)*, Advisory Group on Computer Graphics (AGOCG), *http://www.agocg.ac.uk:8080/agocg/CGM.html*

4. *Spatial Interfaces with Computer Graphics Metafile (CGM)*, Environmental Resources Information Network (ERIN), *http://www.erin.gov.au/gis/develop/cgm/spatial_cgm.html*

5. *The Second International WWW Conference '94*, Chicago, USA (October, 1994), *http://www.ncsa.uiuc.edu/SDG/IT94/IT94Info.html*

6. *The Client-Side Image Map HTML Extension*, Seidman, James L. Spyglass, Inc. (January, 1994), *http://www.spyglass.com:4040/newtechnology/mapspec.htm*

7. *Cape York Peninsula Land Use Strategy (CYPLUS)*, *http://www.erin.gov.au/land/regions/cyplus/cyplus.html*

8. *Environmental Resources Information Network (ERIN)*, *http://www.erin.gov.au/*

9. *ERIN Spatial Interface*, Environmental Resources Information Network, *http://www.erin.gov.au/cgi-bin/spatial_interface*

10. *ERIN Technical Documentation*, Environmental Resources Information Network, *http://www.erin.gov.au/technical/contents.html*

11. *ERIN Technical References*, Environmental Resources Information Network, *http://www.erin.gov.au/technical/references/contents.html*

12. *HTML 3.0 - FIGure Element*, Internet Engineering Task Force (IETF) Draft, *http://www.hp.co.uk/people/dsr/html3/figures.html*

13. *HTML 3.0 - Fill-out Forms*, Internet Engineering Task Force (IETF) Draft, *http://www.hp.co.uk/people/dsr/html3/forms.html*

14. *GD*, Boutell, Thomas, *http://siva.cshl.org/gd/gd.html*

15. *GD InTerpreter*, Harvey-George, David (1994), *http://www.demon.co.uk/3Wiz/gdit/*

16. *Graphics Formats for WWW*, World Wide Web Consortium, *http://www.w3.org/hypertext/WWW/Graphics/Overview.html*

17. *HotJava*, SUN Microsystems, *http://java.sun.com/*

18. *HyperText Markup Language Specification Version 3.0*, Internet Engineering Task Force (IETF) Draft, *http://www.hp.co.uk/people/dsr/html3/CoverPage.html*

19. *Interim Biogeographic Regionalisation of Australia (IBRA)*, Australian Nature Conservation Agency (ANCA), *http://www.erin.gov.au/dsdl/data/ANCA/Regions:Biogeographic_IBRA_1.0.HTML*

20. *NCSA Imagemap Tutorial*, National Center for Supercomputing Applications (NCSA), *http://hoohoo.ncsa.uiuc.edu/docs/setup/admin/Imagemap.html*

21. *ERIN Technical Documentation: Image Mapping*, Environmental Resources Information Network (ERIN), *http://www.erin.gov.au/technical/CGI/image_mapping/image_mapping.html*

22. *Canadian National Atlas Information Service (NAIS)*, *http://ellesmere.ccm.emr.ca/naismap/naismap.html*

23. *Xerox PARC Map Viewer*, Xerox Palo Alto Research Center (PARC), *http://pubweb.parc.xerox.com/map*

24. *About the "perl" programming language*, Environmental Resources Information Network (ERIN), *http://www.erin.gov.au/gis/develop/perl_library/about_perl.html*

25. *HTML 3.0 - Forms: Input*, Internet Engineering Task Force (IETF) Draft, *http://www.hp.co.uk/people/dsr/html3/input.html*

26. *Interactive species distribution reporting, mapping and modelling using the World Wide Web*, Boston, Tony and Stockwell, David (1994), Second International WWW Conference. Chicago. USA. *http://www.erin.gov.au/database/WWW-Fall94/species_paper.html*

27. *A Dynamic GIS Interface*, Argonne National Laboratory, *http://www.dis.anl.gov:8001/GIS/stgis.html*

28. *Map-based access to Spatial Data using HotJava*, *http://h2o.er.usgs.gov:80/public/hjdemo/master.html*

29. *Simple Vector Format (SVF)*, SoftSource, *http://www.softsource.com/softsource/vector.html*

30. *Australian World Heritage Areas*, Australian Department of the Environment, Sport and Territories, *http://www.erin.gov.au/land/conservation/wha/auswha.html*

31. *ERIN TEchnical Documentation: WWW Graphics and Map Images*, Environmental Resources Information Network (ERIN), *http://www.erin.gov.au/technical/CGI/graphics/graphics.html*

How will you spend your time online?

A new and innovative online magazine that takes you to the world behind the Web. *Web Review* provides fresh insights into the people, places, technologies and issues of the World Wide Web. Through provocative features and in-depth reviews, *Web Review* delivers a real service by answering a real need: **how will you best spend your time online?**

Web Review *offers:*

Provocative Features

In-depth Reviews

Electronic Commerce

And Much, Much More

Check out Web Review and start making more of your time online

INTERNET

Books from O'Reilly & Associates, Inc.

FALL/WINTER 1995-96

The Whole Internet User's Guide & Catalog

By Ed Krol
2nd Edition April 1994
574 pages, ISBN 1-56592-063-5

Still the best book on the Internet! This is the second edition of our comprehensive—and bestselling—introduction to the Internet, the international network that includes virtually every major computer site in the world. In addition to email, file transfer, remote login, and network news, this book pays special attention to some new tools for helping you find information. Useful to beginners and veterans alike, this book will help you explore what's possible on the Net. Also includes a pull-out quick-reference card. For UNIX, PCs and the Macintosh.

"An ongoing classic."
—*Rochester Business Journal*

"The book against which all subsequent Internet guides are measured, Krol's work has emerged as an indispensable reference to beginners and seasoned travelers alike as they venture out on the data highway."
—*Microtimes*

"*The Whole Internet User's Guide & Catalog* will probably become the Internet user's bible because it provides comprehensive, easy instructions for those who want to get the most from this valuable electronic tool."
—David J. Buerger, Editor, *Communications Week*

The Whole Internet for Windows 95

By Ed Krol & Paula Ferguson
1st Edition October 1995
650 pages, ISBN 1-56592-155-0

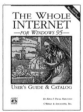

The best book on the Internet...now updated for Windows 95! *The Whole Internet for Windows 95* is the most comprehensive introduction to the Internet available today. For Windows users who in the past have struggled to take full advantage of the Internet's powerful utilities, Windows 95's built-in Internet support is a cause for celebration. And when you get online with Windows 95, this new edition of *The Whole Internet* will guide you every step of the way.

This book shows you how to use Microsoft Internet Explorer (the World Wide Web multimedia browser) and Microsoft Exchange (an email program). It also covers Netscape Navigator, the most popular Web browser on the market, and shows you how to use Usenet readers, file transfer tools, and database searching software.

But it does much more. You'll also want to take advantage of alternative popular free software programs that are downloadable from the Net. This book shows you where to find them and how to use them to save you time and money.

Bandits on the Information Superhighway

By Daniel J. Barrett
1st Edition January 1996 (est.)
288 pages (est.), ISBN 1-56592-156-9

Most people on the Internet behave honestly, but there are always some troublemakers. What risks might you encounter online? And what practical steps can you take to keep yourself safe and happy?

With first-person anecdotes, technical tips, and the advice of experts from diverse fields, *Bandits on the Information Superhighway* helps you identify and avoid risks online, so you can have a more productive and enjoyable time on the Internet.

This book discusses how much privacy you have on the Net and how you can get more; how to spot common Internet scams and where to look for help if you get ripped off; and the "Ten Commandments" of buying and selling personal items on the Net when you don't know the people involved. You'll learn what every parent should know about the Internet—including the simple truth behind popular "scare stories" about pornography and pedophiles—as well as the risks of meeting, trusting, or falling in love with people that you've never met.

MH & xmh: Email for Users & Programmers

By Jerry Peek
3rd Edition April 1995
782 pages, ISBN 1-56592-093-7

There are lots of mail programs in use these days, but MH is one of the most durable and flexible. Best of all, it's available on almost all UNIX systems. It has spawned a number of interfaces that many users prefer. This book covers three popular interfaces: *xmh* (for the X environment), *exmh* (written with tcl/tk), and *mh-e* (for GNU Emacs users).

The book contains: a quick tour through MH, *xmh*, *exmh*, and *mh-e* for new users; configuration and customization information; lots of tips and techniques for programmers—and plenty of practical examples for everyone; information beyond the manual pages, explaining how to make MH do things you never thought an email program could do; and quick-reference pages in the back of the book.

In addition, the third edition describes the Multipurpose Internet Mail Extensions (MIME) and describes how to use it with these mail programs. MIME is an extension that allows users to send graphics, sound, and other multimedia formats through mail between otherwise incompatible systems.

Using Email Effectively

By Linda Lamb & Jerry Peek
1st Edition April 1995
160 pages, ISBN 1-56592-103-8

When you're new to email, you're usually shown what keystrokes to use to read and send a message. After using email for a few years, you learn from your own mistakes and from reading other people's mail. You learn:

- How to organize saved mail so that you can find it again

- When to include a previous message, and how much to include, so that your reader can quickly make sense of what's being discussed

- When a network address "looks right," so that more of your messages get through the first time

- When a "bounced" message will never be delivered and when the bounce merely indicates temporary network difficulties

- How to successfully subscribe and unsubscribe to a mailing list

With first-person anecdotes, examples, and general observations, *Using Email Effectively* shortens the learning-from-experience curve for all mailers, so you can quickly be productive and send email that looks intelligent to others.

The USENET Handbook

By Mark Harrison
1st Edition May 1995
388 pages, ISBN 1-56592-101-1

USENET, also called Netnews, is the world's largest discussion forum, encompassing the worldwide Internet and many other sites that aren't formally connected to any network. USENET provides a forum for asking and answering technical questions, arguing politics, religion, and society, or discussing most scientific, artistic, or humanistic disciplines. It's also a forum for distributing free software, as well as digitized pictures and sound.

This book unlocks USENET for you. It includes tutorials on the most popular newsreaders for UNIX and Windows (*tin, nn, GNUS,* and *Trumpet*). It's also a guide to the culture of the Net, giving you an introduction to etiquette, the private language, and some of the history.

WebSite™ 1.1

By O'Reilly & Associates, Inc.
Documentation by Susan Peck
2nd Edition January 1996 (est.)
ISBN 1-56592-173-9
Includes three diskettes, 360-page book, and WebSite T-shirt

WebSite 1.1 now makes it easier than ever to start publishing on the Internet. WebSite is a 32-bit multi-threaded World Wide Web server that combines the power and flexibility of a UNIX server with the ease of use of a Windows application. Its intuitive graphical interface and easy install make it a natural for both Windows NT and Windows 95 users.

WebSite provides a tree-like display of all the documents and links on your server, with a simple solution for finding and fixing broken links. Using CGI, you can run a desktop application like Excel or Visual Basic from within a Web document on WebSite. Its access authentication lets you control which users have access to different parts of your Web server. WebSite is a product of O'Reilly & Associates, Inc. It is created in cooperation with Bob Denny and Enterprise Integration Technologies, Inc. (EIT).

New features of WebSite 1.1 include: HTML editor, multiple indexes, WebFind wizard, CGI with Visual Basic 4 framework and server push support, graphical interface for creating virtual servers, Windows 95 style install, logging reports for individual documents, HTML-2 and -3 support, external image map support, self-registration of users, and EMosaic 2.1 Web browser.

Marketing on the Internet

By Linda Lamb, Tim O'Reilly, Dale Dougherty & Brian Erwin
1st Edition May 1996 (est.)
170 pages (est.), ISBN 1-56592-105-4

Marketing on the Internet tells you what you need to know to successfully use this new communication and sales channel to put product and sales information online, build relationships with customers, send targeted announcements, and answer product support questions. In short, how to use the Internet as part of your overall marketing mix. Written from a marketing, not technical, perspective.

Internet In A Box,™ Version 2.0

Published by SPRY, Inc. (Product good only in U.S. and Canada)
2nd Edition June 1995
UPC 799364 012001
*Two diskettes & a 528-page version of **The Whole Internet Users Guide & Catalog** as documentation*

Now there are more ways to connect to the Internet—and you get to choose the most economical plan based on your dialing habits.

What will **Internet In A Box** *do for me?*

Internet In A Box is for PC users who want to connect to the Internet. Quite simply, it solves Internet access problems for individuals and small businesses without dedicated lines and/or UNIX machines. Internet In A Box provides instant connectivity, a multimedia Windows interface, and a full suite of applications. This product is so easy to use, you need to know only two things to get started: how to load software onto your PC and how to use a mouse.

New features of version 2.0 include:

- More connectivity options with the CompuServe Network.
- With Spry Mosaic and Progressive Image Rendering, browsing the Internet has never been easier.
- SPRY Mail provides MIME support and a built-in spell checker. Mail and News are now available within the Mosaic Toolbar.
- You'll enjoy safe and secure shopping online with Secure HTTP.
- SPRY News offers offline support for viewing and sending individual articles.
- A Network File Manager means there's an improved interface for dealing with various Internet hosts.

Internet Security

PGP: Pretty Good Privacy

By Simson Garfinkel
1st Edition December 1994
430 pages, ISBN 1-56592-098-8

PGP is a freely available encryption program that protects the privacy of files and electronic mail. It uses powerful public key cryptography and works on virtually every platform. This book is both a readable technical user's guide and a fascinating behind-the-scenes look at cryptography and privacy. It describes how to use PGP and provides background on cryptography, PGP's history, battles over public key cryptography patents and U.S. government export restrictions, and public debates about privacy and free speech.

"I even learned a few things about PGP from Simson's informative book."—Phil Zimmermann, Author of PGP

"Since the release of PGP 2.0 from Europe in the fall of 1992, PGP's popularity and usage has grown to make it the de-facto standard for email encyrption. Simson's book is an excellent overview of PGP and the history of cryptography in general. It should prove a useful addition to the resource library for any computer user, from the UNIX wizard to the PC novice."
—Derek Atkins, PGP Development Team, MIT

Building Internet Firewalls

By D. Brent Chapman & Elizabeth D. Zwicky
1st Edition September 1995
544 pages, ISBN 1-56592-124-0

Everyone is jumping on the Internet bandwagon, despite the fact that the security risks associated with connecting to the Net have never been greater. This book is a practical guide to building firewalls on the Internet. It describes a variety of firewall approaches and architectures and discusses how you can build packet filtering and proxying solutions at your site. It also contains a full discussion of how to configure Internet services (e.g., FTP, SMTP, Telnet) to work with a firewall, as well as a complete list of resources, including the location of many publicly available firewall construction tools.

Practical UNIX and Internet Security

By Simson Garfinkel & Gene Spafford
2nd Edition February 1996 (est.)
800 pages (est.), ISBN 1-56592-148-8

A complete revision of the first edition, this new guide spells out the threats, system vulnerabilities, and counter-measures you can adopt to protect your UNIX system, network, and Internet connection. It's complete—covering both host and network security—and doesn't require that you be a programmer or a UNIX guru to use it. This edition contains hundreds of pages of new information on Internet security, including new security tools and approaches. Covers many platforms, both System V and Berkeley-based (i.e. Sun, DEC, HP, IBM, SCO, NeXT, Linux, and other UNIX systems).

Computer Crime

By David Icove, Karl Seger & William VonStorch
1st Edition August 1995
464 pages, ISBN 1-56592-086-4

Computer crime is a growing threat. Attacks on computers, networks, and data range from terrorist threats to financial crimes to pranks. *Computer Crime: A Crimefighters Handbook* is aimed at those who need to understand, investigate, and prosecute computer crimes of all kinds.

This book discusses computer crimes, criminals, and laws, and profiles the computer criminal (using techniques developed for the FBI and other law enforcement agencies). It outlines the the risks to computer systems and personnel, operational, physical, and communications measures that can be taken to prevent computer crimes. It also discusses how to plan for, investigate, and prosecute computer crimes, ranging from the supplies needed for criminal investigation, to the detection and audit tools used in investigation, to the presentation of evidence to a jury.

Contains a compendium of computer-related federal statutes, all statutes of individual states, a resource summary, and detailed papers on computer crime.

Providing Web Content

CGI Programming on the World Wide Web

By Shishir Gundavaram
1st Edition February 1996 (est.)
375 pages (est.), ISBN 1-56592-168-2, Includes CD-ROM

As you traverse the vast frontier of the World Wide Web, you will come across certain documents that make you wonder, "How in the world did they create this?" These documents might consist of forms that ask for feedback or registration information, imagemaps that allow you to click on various parts of the image, counters that display the number of users that accessed the document, and search/index utilities. All of this magic can be achieved on the Web by using the Common Gateway Interface, commonly known as CGI.

This book offers a comprehensive explanation of CGI and related techniques for people who hold on to the dream of providing their own information servers on the Web. For most of the examples, the book uses the most common platform (UNIX) and the most popular language (Perl) used for CGI programming today. However, it also introduces the essentials of making CGI work with other platforms and languages. A diskette contains examples and other useful software written just for this book.

Using HTML

By Chuck Musciano & Bill Kennedy
1st Edition March 1996 (est.)
350 pages (est.), ISBN 1-56592-175-5

The *HTML Handbook* helps you become fluent in HTML, fully versed in the language's syntax, semantics, and elements of style. The book covers the most up-to-date version of the HTML standard, plus all the common extensions and, in particular, Netscape extensions. The authors cover each and every element of the currently accepted version of the language in detail, explaining how each element works and how it interacts with all the other elements. They've also included a style guide that helps you decide how to best use HTML to accomplish a variety of tasks, from simple online documentation to complex marketing and sales presentations.

Learning Perl

By Randal L. Schwartz, Foreword by Larry Wall
1st Edition November 1993
274 pages, ISBN 1-56592-042-2

Learning Perl is a step-by-step, hands-on tutorial designed to get you writing useful Perl scripts as quickly as possible. In addition to countless code examples, there are numerous programming exercises, with full answers. For a comprehensive and detailed guide to advanced programming with Perl, read O'Reilly's companion book, *Programming perl*.

Programming perl

By Larry Wall & Randal L. Schwartz
1st Edition January 1991
482 pages, ISBN 0-937175-64-1

An authoritative guide to the hottest new UNIX utility in years, coauthored by its creator, Larry Wall. Perl is a language for easily manipulating text, files, and processes. *Programming perl* Covers Perl syntax, functions, debugging, efficiency, the Perl library, and more.

Exploring Expect

By Don Libes
1st Edition December 1994
602 pages, ISBN 1-56592-090-2

Written by the author of Expect, this is the first book to explain how this new part of the UNIX toolbox can be used to automate Telnet, FTP, passwd, rlogin, and hundreds of other interactive applications. Based on Tcl (Tool Command Language), Expect lets you automate interactive applications that have previously been extremely difficult to handle with any scripting language.

Internet Administration

Getting Connected: The Internet at 56K and Up

By Kevin Dowd
1st Edition February 1996 (est.)
450 pages (est.), ISBN 1-56592-154-2

A complete guide for businesses, schools, and other organizations who want to connect their computers to the Internet. This book covers everything you need to know to make informed decisions, from helping you figure out which services you really need to providing down-to-earth explanations of telecommunication options, such as frame relay, ISDN, and leased lines. Once you're online, it shows you how to set up basic Internet services, such as a World Wide Web server. Tackles issues for the PC, Macintosh, and UNIX platforms.

DNS and BIND

By Paul Albitz & Cricket Liu
1st Edition October 1992
418 pages, ISBN 1-56592-010-4

DNS and BIND contains all you need to know about the Internet's Domain Name System (DNS) and the Berkeley Internet Name Domain (BIND), its UNIX implementation. The Domain Name System is the Internet's "phone book"; it's a database that tracks important information (in particular, names and addresses) for every computer on the Internet.
If you're a system administrator, this book will show you how to set up and maintain the DNS software on your network.

sendmail

By Bryan Costales, with Eric Allman & Neil Rickert
1st Edition November 1993
830 pages, ISBN 1-56592-056-2

This Nutshell Handbook® is far and away the most comprehensive book ever written on sendmail, the program that acts like a traffic cop in routing and delivering . mail on UNIX-based networks. Although sendmail is used on almost every UNIX system, it's one of the last great uncharted territories—and most difficult utilities to learn—in UNIX system administration.
This book provides a complete sendmail tutorial, plus extensive reference material on every aspect of the program. It covers IDA sendmail, the latest version (V8) from Berkeley, and the standard versions available on most systems.

Managing Internet Information Services

By Cricket Liu, Jerry Peek, Russ Jones, Bryan Buus & Adrian Nye
1st Edition December 1994
668 pages, ISBN 1-56592-062-7

This comprehensive guide describes how to set up information services and make them available over the Internet. It discusses why a company would want to offer Internet services, provides complete coverage of all popular services, and tells how to select which ones to provide. Most of the book describes how to set up Gopher, World Wide Web, FTP, and WAIS servers and email services.

Networking Personal Computers with TCP/IP

By Craig Hunt
1st Edition July 1995
408 pages, ISBN 1-56592-123-2

This book offers practical information as well as detailed instructions for attaching PCs to a TCP/IP network and its UNIX servers. It discusses the challenges you'll face and offers general advice on how to deal with them, provides basic TCP/IP configuration information for some of the popular PC operating systems, covers advanced configuration topics and configuration of specific applications such as email, and includes a chapter on NetWare, the most popular PC LAN system software.

TCP/IP Network Administration

By Craig Hunt
1st Edition August 1992
502 pages, ISBN 0-937175-82-X

A complete guide to setting up and running a TCP/IP network for practicing system administrators. *TCP/IP Network Administration* covers setting up your network, configuring important network applications including sendmail, and issues in troubleshooting and security. It covers both BSD and System V TCP/IP implementations.

At Your Fingertips—

A COMPLETE GUIDE TO O'REILLY'S ONLINE SERVICES

O'Reilly & Associates offers extensive product and customer service information online. We invite you to come and explore our little neck-of-the-woods.

For product information and insight into new technologies, visit the O'Reilly Online Center

Most comprehensive among our online offerings is the O'Reilly Online Center. You'll find detailed information on all O'Reilly products, including titles, prices, tables of contents, indexes, author bios, software contents, and reviews. You can also view images of all our products. In addition, watch for informative articles that provide perspective on the technologies we write about. Interviews, excerpts, and bibliographies are also included.

After browsing online, it's easy to order, too by sending email to **order@ora.com**. The O'Reilly Online Center shows you how. Here's how to visit us online:

☞ *Via the World Wide Web*

If you are connected to the Internet, point your Web browser (e.g., `mosaic`, `netscape`, or `lynx`) to:

`http://www.ora.com/`

For the plaintext version, `telnet` to:
`www.ora.com` (login: `oraweb`)

☞ *Via Gopher*

If you have a Gopher program, connect your `gopher` to:
`gopher.ora.com`
Or, point your Web browser to:
`gopher://gopher.ora.com/`

Or, you can `telnet` to: `gopher.ora.com`
(login: `gopher`)

A convenient way to stay informed: email mailing lists

An easy way to learn of the latest projects and products from O'Reilly & Associates is to subscribe to our mailing lists. We have email announcements and discussions on various topics. Subscribers receive email as soon as the information breaks.

☞ *To join a mailing list:*

Send email to:
listproc@online.ora.com

Leave the message "subject" empty if possible.

If you know the name of the mailing list you want to subscribe to, put the following information on the first line of your message: `subscribe` "listname" "your name" `of` "your company."

For example: `subscribe ora-news`
`Kris Webber of Fine Enterprises`

If you don't know the name of the mailing list, listproc will send you a listing of all the mailing lists. Put this word on the first line of the body: `lists`

To find out more about a particular list, send a message with this word as the first line of the body: `info` "listname"

For more information and help, send this message: `help`

For specific help, email to: **listmaster@online.ora.com**

The complete O'Reilly catalog is now available via email

You can now receive a text-only version of our complete catalog via email. It contains detailed information about all our products, so it's mighty big: over 200 kbytes, or 200,000 characters.

To get the whole catalog in one message, send an empty email message to: **catalog@online.ora.com**

If your email system can't handle large messages, you can get the catalog split into smaller messages. Send email to: **catalog-split@online.ora.com**

To receive a print catalog, send your snail mail address to: **catalog@ora.com**

Check out Web Review, our new publication on the Web

Web Review is our new magazine that offers fresh insights into the Web. The editorial mission of Web Review is to answer the question: How and where do you BEST spend your time online? Each issue contains reviews that look at the most interesting and creative sites on the Web. Visit us at **http://gnn.com/wr/**

Web Review is a product of the recently formed Songline Studios, a venture between O'Reilly and America Online.

Get the files you want with FTP

We have an archive of example files from our books, the covers of our books, and much more available by anonymous FTP.

ftp to:

ftp.ora.com (login: **anonymous** – use your email address as the password.)

Or, if you have a WWW browser, point it to:

ftp://ftp.ora.com/

FTPMAIL

The ftpmail service connects to O'Reilly's FTP server and sends the results (the files you want) by email. This service is for people who can't use FTP—but who can use email.

For help and examples, send an email message to:

ftpmail@online.ora.com

(In the message body, put the single word: **help**)

Helpful information is just an email message away

Many customer services are provided via email. Here are a few of the most popular and useful:

info@ora.com
> For general questions and information.

bookquestions@ora.com
> For technical questions, or corrections, concerning book contents.

order@ora.com
> To order books online and for ordering questions.

catalog@online.ora.com
> To receive an online copy of our catalog.

catalog@ora.com
> To receive a free copy of *ora.com*, our combination magazine and catalog. Please include your snail mail address.

international@ora.com
> Comments or questions about international ordering or distribution.

xresource@ora.com
> To order or inquire about *The X Resource* journal.

proposals@ora.com
> To submit book proposals.

O'Reilly & Associates, Inc.

103A Morris Street, Sebastopol, CA 95472
Inquiries: **707-829-0515, 800-998-9938**
Credit card orders: **800-889-8969** (Weekdays 6 A.M.- 5 P.M. PST)
FAX: **707-829-0104**

O'Reilly & Associates—
LISTING OF TITLES

INTERNET

CGI Programming on the World
    Wide Web (Winter '95-96 est.)
Getting Connected (Winter '95-96 est.)
Smileys
The USENET Handbook
The Whole Internet User's
    Guide & Catalog
The Whole Internet for Windows 95
Using HTML (Winter '95-96 est.)
Web Design for Designers
    (Winter '95-96 est.)
The World Wide Web Journal
    (Winter '95-96 est.)

SOFTWARE

Internet In A Box ™ Version 2.0
WebSite™ 1.1

WHAT YOU NEED TO KNOW SERIES

Bandits on the Information
Superhighway (Winter '95-96 est.)
Marketing on the Internet
    (Spring '96 est.)
When You Can't Find Your
    System Administrator
Using Email Effectively

HEALTH, CAREER & BUSINESS

Building a Successful Software Business
The Computer User's Survival Guide
Dictionary of Computer Terms
    (Winter '95-96 est.)
The Future Does Not Compute
Love Your Job!
TWI Day Calendar - 1996

USING UNIX

BASICS

Learning GNU Emacs
Learning the bash Shell
Learning the Korn Shell
Learning the UNIX Operating System
Learning the vi Editor
MH & xmh: Email for Users &
    Programmers
PGP: Pretty Good Privacy
SCO UNIX in a Nutshell
UNIX in a Nutshell: System V Edition
Using and Managing UUCP
    (Spring '96 est.)
Using csh and tcsh

ADVANCED

Exploring Expect
The Frame Handbook
Learning Perl
Making TeX Work
Programming perl
Running Linux
Running Linux Companion CD-ROM
    (Winter '95-96 est.)
sed & awk
UNIX Power Tools (with CD-ROM)

SYSTEM ADMINISTRATION

Building Internet Firewalls
Computer Crime:
    A Crimefighter's Handbook
Computer Security Basics
DNS and BIND
Essential System Administration
Linux Network Administrator's Guide
Managing Internet Information Services
Managing NFS and NIS
Managing UUCP and Usenet
Networking Personal Computers
    with TCP/IP
Practical UNIX and Internet Security
    (Winter '95-96 est.)
    sendmail
System Performance Tuning
TCP/IP Network Administration
termcap & terminfo
Volume 8 : X Window System
    Administrator's Guide
The X Companion CD for R6

PROGRAMMING

Applying RCS and SCCS
C++: The Core Language
Checking C Programs with lint
DCE Security Programming
Distributing Applications Across DCE
    and Windows NT
Encyclopedia of Graphics File Formats
Guide to Writing DCE Applications
High Performance Computing
lex & yacc
Managing Projects with make
Microsoft RPC Programming Guide
Migrating to Fortran 90
Multi-Platform Code Management
ORACLE Performance Tuning
ORACLE PL/SQL Programming
Porting UNIX Software
POSIX Programmer's Guide
POSIX.4: Programming for
    the Real World
Power Programming with RPC
Practical C Programming
Practical C++ Programming
Programming with GNU Software
    (Winter '95-96 est.)
Programming with Pthreads
    (Winter '95-96 est.)
Software Portability with imake
Understanding DCE
Understanding Japanese Information
    Processing
UNIX Systems Programming for SVR4
    (Winter '95-96 est.)

BERKELEY 4.4 SOFTWARE DISTRIBUTION

4.4BSD System Manager's Manual
4.4BSD User's Reference Manual
4.4BSD User's Supplementary Docs.
4.4BSD Programmer's Reference Man.
4.4BSD Programmer's Supp. Docs.
4.4BSD-Lite CD Companion
4.4BSD-Lite CD Companion: Int. Ver.

X WINDOW SYSTEM

Volume 0: X Protocol Reference Manual
Volume 1: Xlib Programming Manual
Volume 2: Xlib Reference Manual
Volume 3: X Window System
    User's Guide
Volume. 3M: X Window System
    User's Guide, Motif Ed.
Volume 4M: X Toolkit Intrinsics
    Programming Manual, Motif Ed.
Volume 5: X Toolkit Intrinsics
    Reference Manual
Volume 6A: Motif Programming Man.
Volume 6B: Motif Reference Manual
Volume 6C: Motif Tools
Volume 8 : X Window System
    Administrator's Guide
Volume 9: X Window Window
    Programming Extentions
    (Winter '95-96 est.)
Programmer's Supplement for Release 6
X User Tools (with CD-ROM)
The X Window System in a Nutshell

THE X RESOURCE

*A QUARTERLY WORKING JOURNAL
FOR X PROGRAMMERS*

The X Resource: Issues 0 through 16

TRAVEL

Travelers' Tales France
Travelers' Tales Hong Kong (1/96 est.)
Travelers' Tales India
Travelers' Tales Mexico
Travelers' Tales Spain
Travelers' Tales Thailand
Travelers' Tales: A Woman's World

O'Reilly & Associates—
INTERNATIONAL DISTRIBUTORS

Customers outside North America can now order O'Reilly & Associates books through the following distributors. They offer our international customers faster order processing, more bookstores, increased representation at tradeshows worldwide, and the high-quality, responsive service our customers have come to expect.

EUROPE, MIDDLE EAST, AND AFRICA
(except Germany, Switzerland, and Austria)

INQUIRIES
International Thomson Publishing Europe
Berkshire House
168-173 High Holborn
London WC1V 7AA, United Kingdom
Telephone: 44-71-497-1422
Fax: 44-71-497-1426
Email: itpint@itps.co.uk

ORDERS
International Thomson Publishing Services, Ltd.
Cheriton House, North Way
Andover, Hampshire SP10 5BE, United Kingdom
Telephone: 44-264-342-832 (UK orders)
Telephone: 44-264-342-806 (outside UK)
Fax: 44-264-364418 (UK orders)
Fax: 44-264-342761 (outside UK)

GERMANY, SWITZERLAND, AND AUSTRIA

International Thomson Publishing GmbH
O'Reilly-International Thomson Verlag
Königswinterer Straße 418
53227 Bonn, Germany
Telephone: 49-228-97024 0
Fax: 49-228-441342
Email: anfragen@ora.de

ASIA *(except Japan)*
INQUIRIES
International Thomson Publishing Asia
221 Henderson Road
#08-03 Henderson Industrial Park
Singapore 0315
Telephone: 65-272-6496
Fax: 65-272-6498

ORDERS
Telephone: 65-268-7867
Fax: 65-268-6727

JAPAN
O'Reilly & Associates, Inc.
103A Morris Street
Sebastopol, CA 95472 U.S.A.
Telephone: 707-829-0515
Telephone: 800-998-9938 (U.S. & Canada)
Fax: 707-829-0104
Email: order@ora.com

AUSTRALIA
WoodsLane Pty. Ltd.
7/5 Vuko Place, Warriewood NSW 2102
P.O. Box 935, Mona Vale NSW 2103
Australia
Telephone: 02-970-5111
Fax: 02-970-5002
Email: woods@tmx.mhs.oz.au

NEW ZEALAND
WoodsLane New Zealand Ltd.
21 Cooks Street (P.O. Box 575)
Wanganui, New Zealand
Telephone: 64-6-347-6543
Fax: 64-6-345-4840
Email: woods@tmx.mhs.oz.au

THE AMERICAS
O'Reilly & Associates, Inc.
103A Morris Street
Sebastopol, CA 95472 U.S.A.
Telephone: 707-829-0515
Telephone: 800-998-9938 (U.S. & Canada)
Fax: 707-829-0104
Email: order@ora.com